	k_{RF}	Rate of return on a riskless asset
	k_s	Cost of retained earnings
	k_{sL}	Cost of equity of a levered firm
	k_{sU}	Cost of equity of an unlevered firm
M/B		Market to book ratio
MCC		Marginal cost of capital
MIRR		Modified internal rate of return
n		(1) Number of periods or years
		(2) Number of shares outstanding
NPV		Net present value
NWC		Net working capital
P		(1) Price of a share of stock
		(2) Price per unit of output
		(3) Probability of occurrence
P/E		Price/earnings ratio
PI		Profitability index
PMT		Annuity payment
PV		Present value
Q		Unit sales
r		(1) Rate of return on new investment
		(2) IRR of a project
		(3) Correlation coefficient
ROA		Return on assets
ROE		Return on equity
RP		Risk premium
S		(1) Dollar sales
		(2) Total market value of equity
SML		Security Market Line
Σ		Summation sign (capital sigma)
σ		Standard deviation (lowercase sigma)
T		Tax rate
t		Time
TIE		Times-interest-earned ratio
V		(1) Value
		(2) Variable cost per unit
V_L		Total market value of a levered firm
V_U		Total market value of an unlevered firm
WACC		Weighted average cost of capital = k_a
YTM		Yield to maturity

FINANCIAL MANAGEMENT
THEORY AND PRACTICE
SIXTH EDITION

FINANCIAL MANAGEMENT
THEORY AND PRACTICE
SIXTH EDITION

EUGENE F. BRIGHAM
UNIVERSITY OF FLORIDA

LOUIS C. GAPENSKI
UNIVERSITY OF FLORIDA

THE DRYDEN PRESS
CHICAGO   FORT WORTH   SAN FRANCISCO   PHILADELPHIA
MONTREAL   TORONTO   LONDON   SYDNEY   TOKYO

Acquisitions Editor: Ann Heath
Developmental Editor: Judy Sarwark
Project Editor: Karen Hill
Design Manager: Alan Wendt
Production Manager: Barb Bahnsen
Director of Editing, Design, and Production: Jane Perkins

Text and Cover Designer: C. J. Petlick, Hunter Graphics
Copy Editor: Maureen Duffy
Compositor: The Clarinda Company
Text Type: 10/12 ITC Garamond Book Light

Library of Congress Cataloging-in-Publication Data

Brigham, Eugene F., 1930–
    Financial management: theory and practice/Eugene F. Brigham,
Louis C. Gapenski.—6th ed.
      p.   cm.
    Includes bibliographical references.
    ISBN 0-03-032672-9
    1. Corporations—Finance.   I. Gapenski, Louis C.   II. Title.
HG4026.B669   1991
658.15—dc20   90–2882

The paper used in this publication meets the minimum requirements of American
National Standard for Information Sciences—Permanence of Paper for Printed Library
Materials, ANSI Z39, 48–1984.

Printed in the United States of America
 12–039–98765432

Address orders:
The Dryden Press
Orlando, FL 32887

Address editorial correspondence:
The Dryden Press
908 N. Elm St.
Hinsdale, IL 60521

The Dryden Press
Holt, Rinehart and Winston
Saunders College Publishing

THE DRYDEN PRESS SERIES IN FINANCE

Berry and Young
Managing Investments: A Case Approach

Boyet
**Security Analysis for Investment
Decisions: Text and Software**

Brigham
Fundamentals of Financial Management
Fifth Edition

Brigham, Aberwald, and Ball
**Finance with Lotus 1-2-3®:
Text, Cases, and Models**

Brigham and Gapenski
Cases in Financial Management

Brigham and Gapenski
**Cases in Financial Management,
Module A**

Brigham and Gapenski
**Financial Management: Theory and
Practice**
Sixth Edition

Brigham and Gapenski
Intermediate Financial Management
Third Edition

Campsey and Brigham
Introduction to Financial Management
Third Edition

Chance
An Introduction to Options and Futures

Cooley
**Advances in Business Financial
Management: A Collection of Readings**

Cooley and Roden
Business Financial Management
Second Edition

Crum and Brigham
Cases in Managerial Finance
Sixth Edition with 1986 Tax Law Changes

Fama and Miller
The Theory of Finance

Gardner and Mills
**Managing Financial Institutions:
An Asset/Liability Approach**
Second Edition

Gitman and Joehnk
Personal Financial Planning
Fifth Edition

Goldstein Software, Inc.
Joe Spreadsheet Statistical

Harrington
**Case Studies in
Financial Decision Making**
Second Edition

Johnson
**Issues and Readings in
Managerial Finance**
Third Edition

Kidwell and Peterson
**Financial Institutions,
Markets, and Money**
Fourth Edition

Koch
Bank Management

Martin, Cox, and MacMinn
**The Theory of Finance:
Evidence and Applications**

Mayo
Finance: An Introduction
Third Edition

Mayo
Investments: An Introduction
Third Edition

Pettijohn
PROFIT+

Reilly
**Investment Analysis and
Portfolio Management**
Third Edition

Reilly
Investments
Third Edition

Seitz
Capital Budgeting and Long-Term Financing Decisions

Siegel and Siegel
Futures Markets

Smith and Spudeck
Interest Rates: Theory and Application

Smith and Weston
PC Self-Study Manual for Finance

Tallman and Neal
Financial Analysis and Planning Package

Turnbull
Option Valuation

Weston and Brigham
Essentials of Managerial Finance
Ninth Edition

Weston and Copeland
Managerial Finance
Eighth Edition with Tax Update

PREFACE

Our original goal in writing *Financial Management* was to create a text (1) that is current and complete enough to give students an operational knowledge of finance, (2) that combines theory and applications, and (3) that is sufficiently self-contained for use in follow-on case courses and, upon graduation, on the job. Furthermore, we wanted a text that students find "user friendly," meaning one that they enjoy reading and can learn from on their own. If students don't find a text interesting, useful, and understandable, they simply won't read it.

The book begins with basic concepts, focusing on securities markets and the valuation process, and it then shows how specific techniques and decision rules can be used to help maximize the value of the firm. This structure has three important advantages:

1. Explaining early in the book how financial markets operate, and how securities prices are determined within these markets, lays the groundwork for explaining how financial management can affect the value of the firm. Also, this organization gives students an early exposure to discounted cash flow techniques, to valuation concepts, and to methods of risk analysis, which in turn permits us to use and reinforce these key concepts throughout the book.

2. Structuring the book around markets and valuation concepts provides a unifying theme. Some texts develop a series of topics in modular form and then attempt to integrate them in later chapters. The organization of *Financial Management* gives students a better and more comprehensive understanding of how the topics interact with one another.

3. Students—even those who do not plan to major in finance—generally enjoy working with stock and bond valuation models, rates of return, and the like. Since a student's ability to learn a subject is a function of his or her interest and motivation, and since *Financial Management* begins with a discussion of securities markets and prices, the book's organization is sound from a pedagogic standpoint.

INTENDED MARKET AND USE

Financial Management is designed primarily for use as an introductory MBA text. However, it can be used as an undergraduate introductory text either with exceptionally good students or in schools where the introductory course is taught over two terms.

There is too much material in the text to cover everything thoroughly in one term, and it is certainly not possible to go over all the material in class. However, most students, especially MBA students, can read on their own and understand reasonably well all but the most technical sections, so classroom coverage of everything is not necessary. In our introductory MBA course, we have taken two somewhat different approaches. At times, we have covered only the material in Chapters 1 through 16 plus Chapters 22 and 23, or 18 chapters in total. At other times we have gone through the entire text. Obviously, we cover things in greater depth when we assign less material, but in both situations, we expect students to learn much of the assigned material by reading the book, and we concentrate on the more difficult concepts in our lectures.

We have made a special effort to make the text useful as a reference book, both in corporate finance case courses and for on-the-job applications after graduation. Based on reviewer comments, current casebook content, and our knowledge of current financial management practices, we have put into the book those materials that students are most likely to need to deal with most real-world financial decisions.

MAJOR CHANGES IN THE SIXTH EDITION

The financial management environment has changed significantly since 1987, when we last updated the book. Furthermore, academic researchers have been busy developing new theory, business practitioners have made increasing use of financial theory, and feedback from the real world has led to modifications and improvements in existing theory. We have made a concerted effort to incorporate these changes in the sixth edition, and this has led to new or expanded sections on such phenomena as leveraged buyouts, swaps, junk bonds, and futures hedging. Additionally, we received many comments from users who appreciated the depth of coverage in the fourth edition and who made a strong case for expanding the coverage of certain topics. After careful consideration, we concluded that the most important change in the sixth edition would be to *increase the depth of coverage* of selected topics. However, we also felt the need to deal with two significant changes that are currently taking place in financial management that cannot be handled by the addition of a few sections: *globalization* and *computerization*.

Expanded Coverage

The chapter on risk analysis in the fifth edition was relatively long, but even so, some important aspects of risk analysis were omitted. We have expanded the coverage of risk and return, mostly by the inclusion of sections on indifference curves, the efficient frontier, optimal portfolio selection, and the Capital Market Line. To accommodate the added material, we have expanded our risk and return coverage to two chapters. The first chapter covers risk analysis both in general and in a portfolio context, and the second chapter discusses asset pricing models, especially the Capital Asset Pricing Model (CAPM).

In addition to expanding our coverage of risk and return, we have added material on asymmetric information, signaling, effects of personal taxes on valuation, cost of capital estimation, project risk assessment, the IRR approach to lease analysis, and other topics too numerous to mention. The end result is a textbook with more depth across the board, and thus a book which is more suitable for a two-course sequence and for reference purposes. Throughout the process, however, we have not lost sight of our target audience, the introductory course MBA student. Thus, we have carefully written (and rewritten) the expansion material to ensure that *Financial Management* remains the "user friendly" book it has always been.

Globalization

Financial markets and institutions are becoming globalized. The largest commercial bank in the world is now Japanese, and Japanese and European commercial and investment bankers are aggressively moving into areas that were traditionally dominated by U.S. firms. The results are more competition in lending and underwriting and more access to and innovation in the financial markets. This means that financial managers must know more about foreign capital markets and securities.

In addition, successful firms are recognizing that it is becoming impossible to remain competitive in many industries without becoming a global player. Developing technologies have led to increasingly complex products, hence to higher development costs for autos, computers, aircraft, prescription drugs, and the like. High development costs require high sales volumes, which in turn is making it necessary for firms to sell globally. At the same time, improvements in air freight and other types of transportation, and in communications, are making it increasingly feasible to manufacture virtually anywhere, and strong competitive pressures from multinational companies make it imperative that companies manufacture wherever costs are lowest. Service companies, including banks, advertising agencies, and accounting firms, must follow their customers, so they too are "going global." Furthermore, even if one's own firm operates only domestically, international events influence domestic rates and economic activity, so no one is immune from global pressures. All of this means that financial managers must think globally about many decisions that formerly were considered on a domestic basis only.

Because of these trends, in the sixth edition we have incorporated a "think globally" theme. Throughout the text, we have weaved global threads in an effort to get students to recognize that success in today's world requires a multinational perspective. We are not attempting to make multinational finance experts out of introductory finance students, but we do want the students to leave the course with the understanding that successful firms must make decisions within a global context.

Computerization

In the third edition, published in 1982, we took the traditional approach to discounted cash flow analysis—we used tables. In the fourth edition (1985), we included footnotes to show how financial calculators could be used to solve most discounted cash flow problems. In the fifth edition (1988), the primary focus was on calculator solutions. Today, calculators are better than ever, but for many financial decisions they are being supplemented or even replaced by personal computers. Indeed, powerful new personal computers are now available to virtually all businesses, and new software such as *@RISK,* a *Lotus* add-in that performs Monte Carlo simulation, makes it easy to do things that simply were not feasible a few years ago.

Most important for our purposes, personal computers are changing the way financial managers think about structuring traditional types of financial analyses. Cash flows through time are thought of as cells across a row in a spreadsheet, and the cash flow determinants for a given year, such as sales price, unit sales, variable costs, and taxes, are thought of as cells down a spreadsheet column. Since analyses will be done using PCs, it is important that textbooks be structured to make the transition from the classroom to the real world as easy as possible. Students must recognize that computers are capable of providing answers to questions that were not even asked a few years ago, and problems must be structured so the power of computers can be brought to bear on the issues at hand.

With these thoughts in mind, we have restructured much of the book to reflect this important trend: Tables have been recast to reflect spreadsheet formats, and text discussions have been revised to enable students to visualize computer solutions.

Of course, students cannot use computers on exams, and, even if a particular type of analysis is to be set up on a spreadsheet, it will still be necessary to "go through the analysis by hand" to insure that the model is operating properly. Therefore, it is not at all necessary for students using the text to be proficient (or even literate) in computer usage, because students can still gain a feel for the power and usefulness of computers merely by reading the text discussion. However, for students who do have access to computers and *Lotus 1-2-3,* the book contains computer-oriented problems for most chapters, and a diskette containing the models is available to adopting instructors.

OTHER CHANGES

In addition to the major changes already discussed, we have made a number of other changes in the sixth edition. As always, we have updated and clarified the text, problems, and references. Particular emphasis has been placed on (1) including the latest tax laws, (2) updating the real world examples, and (3) including the latest changes in the financial environment and in financial theory. A sampling of these changes follows:

1. **Chapter Organization.** The fifth edition's organization was generally well received, but we have made two changes in chapter ordering.

    a. In the fifth edition, we covered discounted cash flow (DCF) analysis, then valuation models, and then risk and return. In this edition, we discuss risk and return, then DCF analysis, and finally valuation models. This new ordering permits us to explain how discount rates are developed before they are used in DCF analysis and security valuation. Also, the new sequence makes it easier for students to understand how risk, value, and the discounting process are related to one another.

b. We moved the chapter on cash and marketable securities ahead of the chapter on accounts receivable and inventory. People tend to think about short-term assets in the order in which they appear on a balance sheet, plus we wanted to discuss the cash budget as a planning tool early in the chapter sequence on short-term financial management.

2. **Self-Test Questions.** Within each chapter, at the end of each major section, we have added several short conceptual questions designed to provide students with immediate feedback on their understanding of the material in that section. If a student is unable to easily answer these questions, then he or she does not understand the main concepts presented, hence should reread the section before going on. Our students call these questions "waker-uppers," and they also like the idea of knowing what we think are the key concepts in the chapters.

3. **Mini Cases.** We have added to each chapter a long problem which covers the key elements of the chapter in an integrated, mini-case format.

Since we lecture on the mini cases, the *Instructor's Manual* solutions for them is much more detailed than for the normal end-of-chapter problems. Indeed, the mini-case solutions are structured in the form of lecture notes and are placed in a separate section of the manual. The mini cases can be (1) used as the basis for lectures, (2) assigned as homework, or (3) used by students as self-study problems. The format of the solutions makes it easy for instructors to make the answers available to students and for students to understand the material on their own.

We ask students to read the chapter and scan the mini case, and then we lecture on the chapter by going through the case. We encourage questions and discussion, and the mini-case format stimulates both. Generally, it takes about two hours to lecture on one of the mini cases, so we allocate that much time to them. Occasionally we finish up a few minutes early, in which case we move on to the next topic. More often, we don't quite finish, in which case we either finish up next period or file the solution in the library and move on to the next topic.

4. **Multinational Finance Sections.** We added several multinational finance sections, and we moved these sections from just after the summaries to just before them. The placement change makes students more likely to read the sections, which is important in view of the increasing significance of international markets and operations.

5. **Chapter Summaries.** In the last edition, the chapter summaries contained several paragraphs of text. In the sixth edition, we changed the format from text paragraphs to a listing of key points, making it easier for students to recall the key ideas of the chapter.

ANCILLARY MATERIALS

The following materials are available to adopters free of charge:

1. *Instructor's Manual.* The comprehensive, 500-page manual contains (1) a suggested course outline, (2) expanded solutions to the mini cases, and (3) answers to all end-of-chapter questions and problems.

2. *Transparencies.* A set of 150 transparency acetates, designed to accompany the mini cases for use as lecture illustrations, is available from The Dryden Press.

3. *Problem Diskette.* This diskette, which is available in both 3.5″ and 5.25″ sizes, contains *Lotus 1-2-3* models that accompany selected end-of-chapter problems.

4. *Test Bank.* A revised and enlarged test bank with more than 1,000 class-tested multiple-choice questions and problems is available both in book form and on diskettes. The diskettes may be obtained in either a self-contained computerized test bank format or in *WordPerfect.* The questions are arranged, within each chapter, by type (true/false, multiple-choice questions, and multiple-choice problems), by topic, and by degree of difficulty.

5. *Supplemental Problems.* In addition to the end-of-chapter problems, the mini cases, and the test bank problems, a set of supplemental problems, organized by topic and level of difficulty, is also available.

A number of additional items are available for purchase by students:

1. *Study Guide.* This supplement outlines the key sections of each chapter, provides students with self-test questions, and also provides them with a set of questions and solutions similar to those in the text and in the test bank.

2. *Casebook.* A new casebook, *Cases in Financial Management* by Eugene F. Brigham and Louis C. Gapenski, provides a set of 41 cases which illustrate applications of the concepts and methodologies developed in *Financial Management.* A brief version of the casebook, *Cases in Financial Management, Module A,* contains 12 cases and is a perfect supplement for adopters seeking a limited number of cases.

We usually assign a few cases in the introductory MBA finance course, but when we are using *Financial Management* in the second corporate finance course, we use about 12 cases. *Cases in Financial Management* provides a set of cases that are directly related to *Financial Management* and other modern texts and that require students to implement the types of analyses recommended in the texts. The new cases are also designed for use with *Lotus 1-2-3. Lotus* is not essential for working the cases, but it does reduce the amount of number crunching and thus leaves more time for students to consider conceptual issues.

3. *Readings Books.* A readings book, *Issues in Managerial Finance* (Dryden Press, 1987) edited by Ramon E. Johnson, provides an excellent mix of theoretical and practical articles which can be used to supplement the text. Another supplemental reader is *Advances in Business Financial Management: A Collection of Readings* (Dryden Press, 1989) edited by Philip L. Cooley, which provides a broader selection of articles from which to choose.

4. *Lotus Book.* A supplementary text, *Finance with Lotus 1-2-3: Text, Cases, and Models* (Dryden Press, 1988) by Eugene F. Brigham, Dana A. Aberwald, and Susan E. Ball, enables students to learn, on their own, how to use *Lotus 1-2-3,* and it further explains how many financial management decisions can be analyzed using spreadsheets.

ACKNOWLEDGMENTS

This book reflects the efforts of a great many people over a number of years. First, we extend our gratitude to Gershon Mandelker, University of Pittsburgh, who reviewed the manuscript and also worked through the end-of-chapter questions, problems, and mini cases to ensure their accuracy and clarity. Next, we would like to thank the following professors, who reviewed the book and provided many useful comments and suggestions:

Henry Arnold	Linda Hittle
G. Michael Boyd	J. Ronald Hoffmeister
John Crockett	Frederick Schadler
Theoharry Grammatikos	

In addition, the following reviewers completed a detailed survey paving the way for this new edition:

Syed Ahmad	Judy Maese
Dalton Bigbee	D. J. Masson
Gregg Dimkoff	Thomas McCue
Richard Edelman	Pietra Rivoli
Kendall Hill	John Settle
John Houston	Ernest Swift
Edward Lawrence	George Trivoli
Jules Levine	

We would also like to thank the following people, whose reviews and comments on prior editions and companion books have contributed to this edition: Mike Adler, Ed Altman, Bruce Anderson, Ron Anderson, Bob Angell, Vince Apilado, Bob Aubey, Gil Babcock, Peter Bacon, Kent Baker, Tom Bankston, Les Barenbaum, Charles Barngrover, Bill Beedles, Moshe Ben Horim, Bill Beranek, Tom Berry, Bill Bertin, Roger Bey, John Bildersee, Russ Boisjoly, Keith Boles, Geof Booth, Kenneth Boudreaux, Helen Bowers, Oswald Bowlin, Don Boyd, Pat Boyer, Joe Brandt, Elizabeth Brannigan, Greg Brauer, Mary Broske, Dave Brown, Kate Brown, Bill Brueggeman, Bill Campsey, Bob Carleson, Severin Carlson, David Cary, Steve Celec, Don Chance, Antony Chang, Susan Chaplinsky, Jay Choi, S. K. Choudhury, Lal Chugh, Maclyn Clouse, Margaret Considine, Phil Cooley, Joe Copeland, David Cordell, John Cotner, Charles Cox, David Crary, Roy Crum, Brent Dalrymple, Bill Damon, Joel Dauten, Steve Dawson, Sankar De, Miles Delano, Fred Dellva, Bernard Dill, Les Dlabay, Mark Dorfman, Gene Drycimski, Dean Dudley, David Durst, Ed Dyl, Charles Edwards, John Ellis, Dave Ewert, John Ezzell, Michael Ferri, Jim Filkins, John Finnerty, Susan Fischer, Steven Flint, Russ Fogler, Dan French, Michael Garlington, Jim Garvin, Adam Gehr, Jim Gentry, Philip Glasgo, Rudyard Goode, Walt Goulet, Bernie Grablowsky, Ed Grossnickle, John Groth, Alan Grunewald, Manak Gupta, Sam Hadaway, Don Hakala, Gerald Hamsmith, William Hardin, John Harris, Paul Hastings, Bob Haugen, Steve Hawke, Del Hawley, Robert Hehre, George Hettenhouse, Hans Heymann, Roger Hill, Tom Hindelang, Ralph Hocking, Jim Horrigan, John Howe, Keith Howe, Steve Isberg, Jim Jackson, Kose John, Craig Johnson, Keith Johnson, Ramon Johnson, Ray Jones,

Manuel Jose, Gus Kalogeras, Mike Keenan, Bill Kennedy, Joe Kiernan, Rick Kish, Don Knight, Dorothy Koehl, Jaroslaw Komarynsky, Duncan Kretovich, Harold Krogh, Charles Kroncke, Joan Lamm, P. Lange, Howard Lanser, Martin Laurence, Wayne Lee, Jim LePage, John Lewis, Chuck Linke, Bill Lloyd, Susan Long, Bob Magee, Ileen Malitz, Phil Malone, Terry Maness, Chris Manning, Terry Martell, John Mathys, John McAlhany, Andy McCollough, Bill McDaniel, Robin McLaughlin, Jamshid Mehran, Larry Merville, Rich Meyer, Jim Millar, Ed Miller, John Mitchell, Carol Moerdyk, Bob Moore, Barry Morris, Gene Morris, Fred Morrissey, Chris Muscarella, David Nachman, Tim Nantell, Don Nast, Bill Nelson, Bob Nelson, Bob Niendorf, Tom O'Brien, Dennis O'Connor, John O'Donnell, Jim Olsen, Robert Olsen, Jim Pappas, Stephen Parrish, Glenn Petry, Jim Pettijohn, Rich Pettit, Dick Pettway, Hugo Phillips, John Pinkerton, Gerald Pogue, R. Potter, Franklin Potts, R. Powell, Chris Prestopino, Jerry Prock, Howard Puckett, Herbert Quigley, George Racette, Bob Radcliffe, Bill Rentz, Ken Riener, Charles Rini, John Ritchie, Antonio Rodriguez, E. M. Roussakis, Dexter Rowell, Jim Sachlis, Abdul Sadik, Thomas Scampini, Kevin Scanlon, Mary Jane Scheuer, Carl Schweser, Alan Severn, Sol Shalit, Frederic Shipley, Dilip Shome, Ron Shrieves, Neil Sicherman, J. B. Silvers, Clay Singleton, Joe Sinkey, Stacy Sirmans, Jaye Smith, Steve Smith, Don Sorenson, David Speairs, Ken Stanly, Ed Stendardi, Alan Stephens, Don Stevens, Jerry Stevens, Glen Strasburg, Philip Swensen, Paul Swink, Gary Tallman, Dennis Tanner, Russ Taussig, Richard Teweles, Ted Teweles, Andrew Thompson, George Tsetsekos, Mel Tysseland, David Upton, Howard Van Auken, Pretorious Van den Dool, Pieter Vanderburg, Paul Vanderheiden, Jim Verbrugge, Patrick Vincent, Steve Vinson, Susan Visscher, John Wachowicz, Mike Walker, Sam Weaver, Kuo Chiang Wei, Bill Welch, Fred Weston, Norm Williams, Tony Wingler, Ed Wolfe, Don Woods, Michael Yonan, Dennis Zocco, and Kent Zumwalt.

Special thanks are due to Fred Weston, Myron Gordon, Merton Miller, and Franco Modigliani, who have done much to help develop the field of financial management and who provided us with instruction and inspiration; to Roy Crum, who coauthored the multinational finance sections; to Art Herrmann, who coauthored the bankruptcy appendix; to Dana Aberwald, Susan Ball, Mary Alice Hanebury, and Kay Mangan, who helped us develop the *Lotus 1-2-3* models; to Brian Butler, Brent Gibbs, and Andy Janssen, who helped on the ancillaries; and to Carol Stanton and Brenda Sapp who provided both word processing and editorial support.

Both our colleagues and our students at the University of Florida gave us many useful suggestions, and The Dryden Press staff—especially Barb Bahnsen, Maureen Duffy, Ann Heath, Karen Hill, Mary Jarvis, Jennifer Lloyd, Sue Nodine, Jane Perkins, Cate Rzasa, Judy Sarwark, Bill Schoof, Greg Teague, and Alan Wendt—helped greatly with all phases of the text development and production.

ERRORS IN THE TEXT

At this point in the preface, authors generally say something like this: "We appreciate all the help we received from the people listed above, but any remaining errors are, of course, our own responsibility." And in many books, there are plenty of remaining errors. Having experienced difficulties with errors ourselves, both as students and as instructors, we resolved to avoid this problem in *Financial Management*. As a result of our error-detection procedures, we are convinced that the book is relatively free of mistakes.

Partly because of our confidence that few errors remain, but primarily because we want very much to detect any errors that may have slipped by so we can correct them in subsequent printings, we decided to offer a reward of $10 per error (conceptual error, misspelled word, arithmetic mistake, and the like) to the first person who reports it to us. (Any error that has follow-through effects is counted as two errors only.) Two accounting students have set up a foolproof audit system to make sure we pay off. Accounting students tend to be skeptics!

CONCLUSION

Finance is, in a real sense, the cornerstone of the free enterprise system. Good financial management is therefore vitally important to the economic health of business firms, hence to the nation and the world. Because of its importance, financial management should be thoroughly understood, but this is easier said than done. The field is relatively complex, and it is undergoing constant change in response to shifts in economic conditions. All of this makes financial management stimulating and exciting, but also challenging and sometimes perplexing. We sincerely hope that the sixth edition of *Financial Management* will help you understand the financial problems faced by businesses today, as well as the best ways to solve those problems.

Eugene F. Brigham
College of Business Administration

Louis C. Gapenski
College of Business Administration
College of Health Related Professions

University of Florida
Gainesville, Florida 32611

August 1990

CONTENTS IN BRIEF

CONTENTS

PART V
Long-Term Financing Decisions   *565*

PART VI
Short-Term Financial Management   *729*

PART I

Foundations of Financial Management

CHAPTER 1

An Overview of Financial Management

It is often difficult to determine who is really in control of U.S. corporations. Management is being attacked from all sides. Takeover battles are both frequent and furious, and investors, especially the large pension and mutual funds, which own close to 40 percent of all traded stocks and account for about 80 percent of all trading, are removing managements who do not seem to be maximizing shareholder value. Outside directors (directors who are not full-time employees of the company) are asserting their independence and even getting sued if they do not. Labor leaders are seeking, and often getting, seats on boards of directors. Consumer boycotts have occurred with increasing frequency, and legislation has been proposed, and in some cases enacted, to change the rules by which corporate control is established. Everyone, it seems, wants to get in on the action.

This struggle for corporate control raises questions about the very nature of corporations. The conventional theory behind the corporate form of organization is that managers are hired by the firm's owners—the stockholders—for the express purpose of maximizing shareholder wealth. But is this theory really valid? Should, and do, managers focus exclusively on shareholders' interests, or should they have concerns about their firms' other stakeholders, including its bondholders, employees, customers, and suppliers?

Executives themselves are split on this issue. Some believe that managements' primary goal is shareholder wealth maximization, while others contend that a firm's managers must be responsive to the needs of all stakeholders and that only the managers can balance the diverse interests of the groups involved. Stockholders, on the other hand, argue that inept managers use "social responsibility" as an excuse for poor performance, in an effort to protect their jobs. Many investors are simply fed up with what they perceive as entrenched managers' inefficient use of corporate resources, and with their attempts to stop others from taking control and managing the resources more efficiently and hence increasing the value of the firm. Several organizations have been formed to actively promote shareholders' rights, including the United Shareholders Association, formed by T. Boone Pickens, a well-known corporate raider. Pickens and his group argue that if a competitive market for corporate control is fostered, then the best management teams will eventually run companies, overall efficiency will be improved, and all parties, including the general public, will benefit.

IN this chapter we explore the control issue in more depth. We also outline the changing role and increasing importance of financial management, and we introduce the major types of financial decisions. In the remainder of the book, we discuss how these decisions should be made.

What role does "finance" play within the firm? What specific tasks are assigned to the financial staff, and what tools and techniques are available for improving the firm's performance? On a broader scale, what is the role of finance in the U.S. economy, and how can financial management be used to further our national goals? As we shall see, proper financial management will help any business provide better products to its customers at lower prices, pay higher wages and salaries to its workers and managers, and still provide greater returns to the investors who put up the capital needed to form and operate the company. Since the economy consists of customers, employees, and investors, sound financial management contributes both to individual well-being and to the well-being of the general population.

CAREER OPPORTUNITIES IN FINANCE

Finance consists of three interrelated areas: (1) *money and capital markets,* or macro finance, which deals with many of the topics covered in macroeconomics; (2) *investments,* which focuses on the decisions of individuals and financial institutions as they choose securities for their investment portfolios; and (3) *financial management,* or "business finance," which involves the actual management of the firm. The career opportunities within each field are varied and numerous, but it should be noted that corporate financial managers must have a good knowledge of all three areas if they are to do their jobs well.

Money and Capital Markets

Many finance majors go to work for financial institutions, including banks, insurance companies, savings and loans, and credit unions. To be successful here, one needs a good knowledge of the money and capital markets, including the factors that cause interest rates to rise and fall, the regulations to which financial institutions are subject, and the types of instruments with which the markets deal (mortgages, auto loans, certificates of deposit, and so on). One also needs a good general knowledge of all aspects of business administration, because the management of a financial institution involves accounting, marketing, personnel, and computer systems, as well as financial management. An ability to communicate, both orally and in writing, is important, and "people skills," or the ability to get others to do their jobs, is critical.

The most common initial job in this area is that of a bank officer trainee, where you go into bank operations and learn about the business, from tellers' work, to deposit management, to personal and business lending, to managing trust accounts. You could expect to spend a year or so being rotated among these different areas, after which you would settle into a department, generally as an assistant manager in a branch. You might become a specialist in some area such as real estate lending, and be authorized to make loans going into the millions of dollars; you might become an expert on foreign currencies and import-export lending; or you might remain a generalist, skilled in general bank management. Similar career paths are available with insurance companies, credit unions, and consumer loan companies.

Investments

Finance graduates who go into investments generally work for a brokerage house such as Merrill Lynch, either in sales or as a security analyst; for a bank, a mutual fund, or an insurance company in the management of their investment portfolios; or for a financial consulting firm, advising individual investors or pension funds on how to invest their funds. The three main functions in the investments area are (1) sales, (2) the analysis of individual securities, and (3) the optimal mix of securities, or portfolio construction, for a given investor.

Financial Management

Financial management is the broadest of the three areas, and the one with the greatest number of job opportunities. Financial management is important in all types of businesses, including banks (which are just as interested in financial management as are industrial companies) and not-for-profit (charitable) organizations. Financial management is also important in governmental operations, from schools to highway departments to health systems. The types of jobs one encounters in financial management range from decisions as to whether to undertake major plant expansions to the choice of stock or bonds to finance expansions. Financial managers also have the responsibility for deciding the credit terms granted to customers, how much inventory to stock, how much cash the firm should carry, the specific types of securities to issue, whether to acquire other firms (merger analysis), and how much of the firm's earnings to retain versus to pay out as dividends.

Regardless of which area you go into, success requires a knowledge of the other areas. For example, a banker lending to businesses cannot do his or her job well without a good understanding of financial management, because he or she must be able to judge how well the businesses are operated. The same thing holds for one of Merrill Lynch's security analysts, and even stockbrokers must have an understanding of general financial principles if they are to give intelligent advice to their customers. At the same time, corporate financial managers need to know what their bankers are thinking about, and how security analysts are likely to judge their corporations' performances and thus influence stock prices. So, if you decide to make finance your career, you will need to know the basics of all three areas, regardless of which specific area you choose.

Self-Test Questions

What are the three main areas in which a finance major might seek a job?

If you have definite plans to go into one area, is it necessary that you know something about the other areas? Explain.

FINANCIAL MANAGEMENT IN THE 1990s

Financial management has undergone significant changes over the years. When it emerged as a separate field of study in the early 1900s, and through the boom of the 1920s, the emphasis was on the legal aspects of mergers, the formation of new firms, and the various types of securities issued to raise capital. During the Depression era of the 1930s, the emphasis shifted to bankruptcy and reorganization, to corporate liquidity, and to regulation of security markets. During the 1940s and early 1950s, finance continued to be taught as a descriptive, institutional subject, viewed more from the standpoint of an outsider rather than from that of management. However, a movement toward theoretical analysis with a managerial viewpoint developed during the late 1950s, and, in the 1960s and 1970s, financial management focused primarily on managerial decisions regarding the choice of assets and liabilities to maximize the value of the firm and the wealth of its stockholders. The focus on valuation continued during the 1980s, but the analysis was expanded to include these four factors: (1) inflation and its effects on business decisions, (2) deregulation of financial institutions and the resulting trend toward large, broadly diversified financial services companies, (3) the dramatic increase in both the use of computers for analysis and the electronic transfer of information, and (4) the increased importance of global financial markets and business operations. We predict that the two most important trends during the 1990s will be the continued globalization of business and the increased use of computer technology.

The Globalization of Business

Today, a California fruit grower can borrow from a Japanese bank to finance exports to France, while a New York manufacturer can issue securities through a Swiss investment banker to finance a plant in Singapore. This trend toward such worldwide linkages will continue at a fast pace in the 1990s. The European Community plans to create a barrier-free Europe by the end of 1992, resulting in a single European market. In that market, there will be free movement of capital; banks headquartered in one country will be allowed to operate in all the other European countries without further approval; and uniform standards for foodstuffs, electrical appliances, and industrial machines will be applied. The end result will be a highly integrated market with a population of over 300 million. Firms in the United States cannot afford to be frozen out of this market, so many are already establishing new operations and expanding old ones in Europe before the 1992 "deadline."

Three factors are making the trend toward globalization mandatory for many manufacturers: (1) Improvements in transportation and communications have lowered shipping costs and made international trade more feasible, and the political clout of consumers who desire low-cost, high-quality products has helped lower trade barriers designed to protect inefficient or high-cost domestic manufacturers. This has greatly increased competition. (2) As technology becomes more advanced, the costs of developing new products increase, and, as development costs rise, so must unit sales, if the firm is to be competitive. (3) In a world populated with multinational firms able to shift production to wherever costs are lowest, a firm whose manufacturing operations are restricted to one country cannot compete unless costs in its home country happen to be low, a condition that does not necessarily exist for U.S. corporations. As a result of these factors, survival requires that most manufacturers produce and sell globally.

Service companies, including banks, advertising agencies, and accounting firms, are also being forced to "go global," because such firms can better serve their multinational clients if they have worldwide operations. There will, of course, always be some purely domestic companies, but the most dynamic growth, and the best opportunities, will be with companies that operate worldwide.

Computer Technology

The 1990s will see incredible advances in computer technology, and this technology will revolutionize the way financial management decisions are made. Companies will have networks of personal computers that are linked to one another, to the firm's own mainframe computers, and to thousands of other computers worldwide. Thus, financial analysts will be able to share data and programs, and to have "face-to-face" meetings with distant colleagues through video conferencing. The accessibility of data on a real-time basis will also mean that quantitative analyses will be used routinely to "test out" alternative courses of action. As a result, financial managers of the future will need greater computer and quantitative skills than were required in the past.

Self-Test Questions

Outline the significant changes that financial management has undergone from the early 1900s through the 1980s.

What financial issues are likely to be prominent in the 1990s?

INCREASING IMPORTANCE OF FINANCIAL MANAGEMENT

The historical trends discussed in the previous section have greatly increased the importance of financial management. In earlier times the marketing manager would project sales, the engineering and production staffs would determine the assets necessary to meet those demands, and the financial manager simply had to raise the money needed to purchase the required plant, equipment, and inventories. This mode of operation is no longer prevalent; decisions are now made in a much more coordinated manner, and the financial manager generally has direct responsibility for the control process.

Two companies in the airline industry can be used to illustrate the importance of financial management and the effects of basic financial policy decisions. In the 1960s, Eastern Airlines' stock sold for more than $60 per share, while Delta's sold for $10. By 1990, Delta had become one of the strongest airlines, with its stock selling for more than $90 per share. Eastern, on the other hand, was forced into a shotgun merger with Texas Air in 1986, and it was operating under bankruptcy laws in 1990. Although many factors combined to produce these divergent results, financial decisions exerted a major influence. Because Eastern had traditionally used a great deal of debt, while Delta had not, Eastern's costs were increased significantly and its profits were lowered when interest rates rose dramatically; however, interest rates had only a minor effect on Delta. Further, when fuel price increases made it imperative for the airlines to buy new, fuel-efficient planes, Delta was able to do so, but Eastern was not. Finally, when the airlines were deregulated in the late 1970s, Delta was strong enough to expand into developing markets and to cut prices as necessary to attract business, but Eastern was not. This story and others like it are now well known, so most companies today are more concerned with financial planning, and this has greatly increased the importance of corporate financial staffs.

The value of financial management is reflected by the fact that more chief executive officers (CEOs) in the top 1,000 U.S. companies (based on market value) started their careers in finance than in any other functional area.[1] The next most prominent career path is marketing, followed by the engineering/technical field. Also, while corporate financial managers used to spend their days evaluating income statements and balance sheets, today's financial managers have moved far beyond accounting, into the realms of takeover defenses, overseas expansion, restructuring, and other strategic planning issues. In most firms, the chief financial officer (CFO)

---

[1]See the 1989 special bonus issue of *Business Week,* "The Corporate Elite," for an interesting discussion of the backgrounds, roles, and functions of both CEOs and CFOs.

now sits on the board of directors, ranks third in the company hierarchy (behind the chairman and the president), and is likely to move up to the top spot.

Further, it is becoming increasingly important for people in marketing, accounting, production, personnel, and other areas to understand finance in order to do a good job in their own fields. Marketing people, for instance, must understand how marketing decisions affect and are affected by funds availability, by inventory levels, by excess plant capacity, and so on. Similarly, accountants must understand how accounting data are used in corporate planning and are viewed by investors. The function of accounting is to provide quantitative financial information for use in making economic decisions, whereas the main functions of financial management are to plan for, acquire, and utilize funds in order to maximize the efficiency and value of the enterprise.[2]

Thus, there are financial implications in virtually all business decisions, and nonfinancial executives simply must know enough finance to work these implications into their own specialized analyses.[3] This point should make every student of business, regardless of major, concerned with finance.

Self-Test Questions

Explain why financial planning and controls are important to today's chief executives.

Why do marketing people need to know something about financial management?

THE FINANCIAL MANAGER'S RESPONSIBILITIES

The financial manager's primary task is to plan for the acquisition and use of funds so as to maximize the value of the firm. To put it another way, he or she makes decisions about alternative sources and uses of funds with the goal of maximizing the firm's value. Here are some specific activities which are involved:

1.   **Forecasting and planning**. The financial manager must interact with other executives as they jointly look ahead and lay the plans which will shape the firm's future position.

2.   **Major investment and financing decisions**. On the basis of long-run plans, the financial manager must raise the capital needed to support growth. A successful firm usually achieves a high rate of growth in sales, which requires increased investments in the plant, equipment, and current assets necessary to produce goods and services. The financial manager must help determine the optimal rate of sales growth, and he or she must help decide on the specific investments to be made as well as on the types of funds to be used to finance these investments. Decisions must be made

---

[2]American Institute of Certified Public Accountants, *AICPA Professional Standards*, Section 100 (New York, November 1987.)

[3]It is an interesting fact that the course "Financial Management for Nonfinancial Executives" has the highest enrollment in most executive development programs.

about the use of internal versus external funds, the use of debt versus equity, and the use of long-term versus short-term debt.

3.   **Coordination and control.** The financial manager must interact with executives in other parts of the business if the firm is to operate as efficiently as possible. All business decisions have financial implications, and all managers—financial and otherwise—need to take this into account. For example, marketing decisions affect sales growth, which in turn changes investment requirements. Thus, marketing decision makers must take account of how their actions affect (and are affected by) such factors as the availability of funds, inventory policies, and plant capacity utilization.

4.   **Interaction with capital markets.** The financial manager must deal with the money and capital markets. As we shall see in Chapter 3, each firm affects and is affected by the general financial markets where funds are raised, where the firm's securities are traded, and where its investors are either rewarded or penalized.

In sum, the central responsibilities of financial managers involve decisions regarding which investments their firms should make, how these projects should be financed, and how the firm can most effectively manage its existing resources. If these responsibilities are performed optimally, financial managers will help to maximize the values of their firms, and this will also maximize the long-run welfare of those who buy from or work for the firm.

Self-Test Questions

What is the financial manager's primary responsibility?

What are some of the specific actions involved in carrying out that responsibility?

ALTERNATIVE FORMS OF BUSINESS ORGANIZATION

There are three main forms of business organization: the sole proprietorship, the partnership, and the corporation. In terms of numbers, about 80 percent of business firms are operated as sole proprietorships, while the remainder are divided equally between partnerships and corporations. By dollar value of sales, however, about 80 percent of business is conducted by corporations, about 13 percent by sole proprietorships, and about 7 percent by partnerships. Because most business is conducted by corporations, we will concentrate on them in this book. However, it is important to understand the differences among the three forms, as well as their advantages and disadvantages.

Sole Proprietorship

A *sole proprietorship* is a business owned by one individual. Going into business as a single proprietor is easy—one merely begins business operations. However, most cities require even the smallest establishments to be licensed, and occasionally state licenses are required as well.

The proprietorship has two important advantages for small operations: (1) It is easily and inexpensively formed, and it is subject to few government regulations. (2) The business pays no corporate income taxes; as we shall see, however, this is not always a net advantage, as all earnings of the firm, whether they are reinvested in the business or withdrawn, are subject to personal income taxes at the owner's tax rate.

The proprietorship also has three important limitations: (1) it is difficult for a proprietorship to obtain large sums of capital; (2) the proprietor has unlimited personal liability for business debts, which can result in losses greater than the money invested in the company; and (3) the life of a business organized as a proprietorship is limited to the life of the individual who created it. For these three reasons, the individual proprietorship is restricted primarily to small business operations. However, businesses are frequently started as proprietorships and then converted to corporations if and when their growth causes the disadvantages of being a proprietorship to outweigh its advantages.

Partnership

A *partnership* exists whenever two or more persons associate to conduct a noncorporate business. Partnerships may operate under different degrees of formality, ranging from informal, oral understandings to formal agreements filed with the secretary of the state in which the partnership does business. The major advantage of a partnership is its low cost and ease of formation. The disadvantages are similar to those associated with proprietorships: (1) unlimited liability, (2) limited life of the organization, (3) difficulty of transferring ownership, and (4) difficulty of raising large amounts of capital. The tax treatment of a partnership is similar to that for proprietorships, and when compared to that of a corporation, this can be either an advantage or a disadvantage, depending on the situation. This point is illustrated in Chapter 2, where we discuss the federal tax system.

Regarding liability, the partners must risk all of their personal assets, even those assets not invested in the business, because under partnership law each partner is liable for the business's debts. This means that if any partner is unable to meet his or her pro rata claim in the event the partnership goes bankrupt, the remaining partners must take over the unsatisfied claims, drawing on their personal assets if necessary.[4]

The first three disadvantages—unlimited liability, impermanence of the organization, and difficulty of transferring ownership—lead to the fourth, the difficulty partnerships have in attracting substantial amounts of capital. This is no particular problem for a slow-growing business, but if a business's products really catch on, and if it needs to raise large amounts of capital to expand and thus capitalize on its opportunities, the difficulty in attracting capital becomes a real drawback. Thus,

---

[4]However, it is possible to limit the liabilities of some of the partners by establishing a *limited partnership,* wherein certain partners are designated *general partners* and others *limited partners.* Limited partnerships are quite common in the area of real estate investment, but they do not work well with most types of businesses because one partner is rarely willing to assume all of the business's risk.

growth companies such as Hewlett-Packard and Apple Computer generally begin life as a proprietorship or partnership, but at some point they find it necessary to convert to a corporation.

Corporation

A *corporation* is a legal entity created by a state. It is separate and distinct from its owners and managers. This separateness gives the corporation three major advantages: (1) *Unlimited life.* A corporation can continue after its original owners and managers are deceased. (2) *Easy transferability of ownership interest.* Ownership interests can be divided into shares of stock, which in turn can be transferred far more easily than can proprietorship or partnership interests. (3) *Limited liability.* To illustrate the concept of limited liability, suppose you invested $10,000 in a partnership which then went bankrupt owing $1 million. Because the owners are liable for the debts of a partnership, you could be assessed for a share of the company's debt, and you could be held liable for the entire $1 million if your partners could not pay their shares. Thus, an investor in a partnership is exposed to unlimited liability. On the other hand, if you invested $10,000 in the stock of a corporation which then went bankrupt, your potential loss on the investment would be limited to your $10,000 investment.[5] These three factors—unlimited life, easy transferability of ownership interest, and limited liability—make it much easier for corporations than for proprietorships or partnerships to raise money in the general capital markets.

The corporate form offers significant advantages over proprietorships and partnerships, but it does have two primary disadvantages: (1) Corporate earnings are subject to double taxation—the earnings of the corporation are taxed, and then any earnings paid out as dividends are taxed again as income to the stockholders. (2) Setting up a corporation, and filing required state and federal reports, is more complex and time-consuming than for a proprietorship or a partnership.

Although a proprietorship or a partnership can commence operations without much paperwork, setting up a corporation requires that the incorporators prepare a charter and a set of bylaws, or hire a lawyer to do it for them. The *charter* includes the following information: (1) name of the proposed corporation, (2) types of activities it will pursue, (3) amount of capital stock, (4) number of directors, and (5) names and addresses of directors. The charter is filed with the secretary of the state in which the firm will be incorporated, and, when it is approved, the corporation is officially in existence.[6] Then, after the corporation is in operation, quarterly and annual financial and tax reports must be filed with state and federal authorities.

The *bylaws* are a set of rules drawn up by the founders of the corporation to aid in governing the internal management of the company. Included are such points as (1) how directors are to be elected (all elected each year or, say, one-third each

---

[5]In the case of small corporations, the limited liability feature is often fictitious, since bankers and credit managers frequently require personal guarantees from the stockholders of small, weak businesses.

[6]Note that over 60 percent of U.S. corporations are chartered in Delaware, which has, over the years, provided a favorable legal environment for corporations. It is not necessary for a firm to be headquartered, or even to conduct operations, in its state of incorporation.

year for three-year terms); (2) whether the existing stockholders will have the first right to buy any new shares the firm issues; and (3) what procedures there are for changing the bylaws themselves, should conditions require it. Attorneys have standard forms for charters and bylaws in their word processors, and they can set up a corporation with very little effort.

The value of any business other than a very small one will probably be maximized if it is organized as a corporation. The reasons are as follows:

1. Limited liability reduces the risks borne by investors, and, other things held constant, *the lower the firm's risk, the higher its value*.

2. A firm's value is dependent on its *growth opportunities*, which in turn are dependent on the firm's ability to attract capital. Since corporations can attract capital more easily than can unincorporated businesses, they have superior growth opportunities.

3. The value of an asset also depends on its *liquidity,* which means the ease of selling the asset and converting it to cash. Since an investment in the stock of a corporation is much more liquid than a similar investment in a proprietorship or partnership, this too means that the corporate form of organization can enhance the value of a business.

4. Corporations are taxed differently than proprietorships and partnerships, and under certain conditions the tax laws favor corporations. This point is discussed in detail in Chapter 2.

As we will see later in the chapter, most firms are managed with value maximization in mind, and this, in turn, has caused most large businesses to be organized as corporations.

Self-Test Questions

What are the key differences among a sole proprietorship, a partnership, and a corporation?

Explain why the value of any business other than a very small one will probably be maximized if it is organized as a corporation.

FINANCE IN THE ORGANIZATIONAL STRUCTURE OF THE FIRM

Organizational structures vary from firm to firm, but Figure 1-1 presents a fairly typical picture of the role of finance within a corporation. The chief financial officer—who has the title of vice-president: finance—reports to the president. The financial vice-president's key subordinates are the treasurer and the controller. The treasurer has direct responsibility for managing the firm's cash and marketable securities, for planning its capital structure, for selling stocks and bonds to raise capital, and for overseeing the corporate pension fund. Also under the treasurer (but in some firms under the controller) are the credit manager, the inventory manager,

Figure 1-1   Place of Finance in a Typical Business Organization

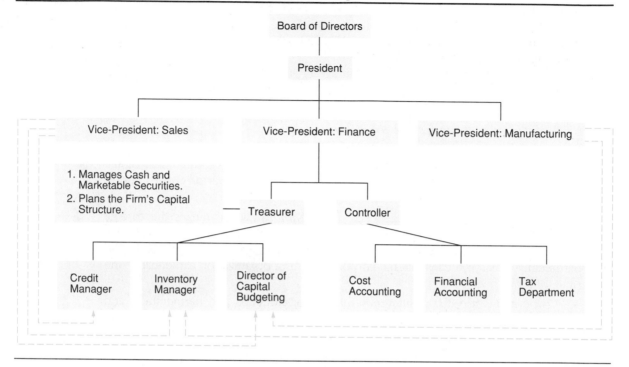

and the director of capital budgeting (who analyzes decisions related to investments in fixed assets). The controller is responsible for the activities of the accounting and tax departments.

Self-Test Question

Identify the two subordinates directly under a firm's chief financial officer and indicate the responsibilities of each.

THE GOALS OF THE CORPORATION

Decisions are not made in a vacuum but, rather, with some objective in mind. *Throughout this book we operate on the assumption that management's primary goal is* stockholder wealth maximization. As we shall see, this translates into *maximizing the price of the firm's common stock.* Firms do, of course, have other objectives; managers, who make the actual decisions, are interested in their own personal satisfaction, in their employees' welfare, and in the good of the community and of society at large. Still, for the reasons set forth in the sections that follow, *stock price maximization is the most important goal of most corporations,* and it is a reasonable operating objective on which to build decision rules.

Managerial Incentives to Maximize Shareholder Wealth

Stockholders own the firm and elect the management team. Management, in turn, is supposed to operate in the best interests of the stockholders. We know, however, that because the stock of most large firms is widely held, the managers of large corporations have a great deal of autonomy. This being the case, might not managers pursue goals other than stock price maximization? For example, some have argued that the managers of a large, well-entrenched corporation could work just enough to keep stockholder returns at a "reasonable" level and then devote the remainder of their efforts and resources to public service activities, to employee benefits, to higher executive salaries, or to golf.

Similarly, an established, self-satisfied, and well-compensated management might avoid risky ventures, even when the possible gains to stockholders were high enough to warrant taking the gamble. The theory behind this argument is that, since stockholders are generally well diversified in the sense that they hold portfolios of many different stocks, if a company takes a chance and loses, then the stockholders lose only a small part of their wealth. Managers, on the other hand, are not diversified, so setbacks affect them more seriously. Accordingly, some maintain that old-line corporate managers tend to "play it safe" rather than aggressively seeking to maximize the prices of their firms' stocks.

It is almost impossible to determine whether a particular management team is trying to maximize shareholder wealth or is merely attempting to keep stockholders satisfied while pursuing other goals. For example, how can we tell whether employee or community benefit programs are in the long-run best interests of the stockholders? Are relatively high executive salaries really necessary to attract and retain excellent managers, who in turn will keep the firm ahead of its competition, or just another example of managers' taking advantage of stockholders? When a risky venture is turned down, does this reflect management conservatism, or is it a correct judgment regarding the risks of the venture versus its potential rewards?

It is impossible to give definitive answers to these questions. However, we do know that the managers of a firm operating in a competitive market will be forced to undertake actions that are reasonably consistent with shareholder wealth maximization. If they depart from this goal, they run the risk of being removed from their jobs through a hostile takeover or a proxy fight.

A *hostile takeover* is the purchase by one company of the stock of another over the opposition of its management, whereas a *proxy fight* involves an attempt to gain control by getting stockholders to vote a new management group into place. Both actions are facilitated by low stock prices, so for the sake of self-preservation management will try to keep its stock value as high as possible. The dominant view is that takeovers rarely present a serious threat to a well-entrenched management team if that team has succeeded in maximizing the firm's value, for people attempt to take over undervalued, bargain companies, not fully valued ones. So, while it may be true that some managers are more interested in their own personal positions than in maximizing shareholder wealth per se, the threat of losing their jobs still motivates them to try to maximize stock prices. We will have more to say about the conflict between managers and shareholders later in the chapter.

Social Responsibility

Another issue that deserves consideration is *social responsibility:* Should businesses operate strictly in their stockholders' best interests, or are firms also partly responsible for the welfare of their employees, customers, and the communities in which they operate? Certainly firms have an ethical responsibility to provide a safe working environment for their employees, to ensure that their production processes are not endangering the environment, to engage in fair hiring practices, and to produce products that are safe for consumers. However, socially responsible actions such as these have costs, and it is questionable whether businesses would incur these costs voluntarily. It is clear, however, that if some firms do act in a socially responsible manner while other firms do not, then the socially responsible firms will be at a disadvantage in attracting capital. To see why this is so, consider first those firms whose profits and rates of return on investment are close to normal, that is, close to the average for all firms and just sufficient to attract capital. If one company attempts to exercise social responsibility, its product prices will have to be increased to cover the costs of these actions. If the other businesses in the industry do not follow suit, their costs and prices will remain constant. The socially responsible firm will not be able to compete, and it thus will be forced to abandon its efforts. Thus, any voluntary socially responsible acts that raise costs will be difficult, if not impossible, in industries that are subject to keen competition.

What about oligopolistic firms with profits above normal levels—cannot such firms devote resources to social projects? Undoubtedly they can, and many large, successful firms do engage in community projects, employee benefit programs, and the like, to a greater degree than would appear to be called for by pure profit or wealth maximization goals.[7] Still, publicly owned firms are constrained in such actions by capital market factors. To illustrate, suppose a saver who has funds to invest is considering two alternative firms. One firm devotes a substantial part of its resources to social actions, while the other concentrates on profits and stock prices. Most investors are likely to shun the socially oriented firm, thus putting it at a disadvantage in the capital market. After all, why should the stockholders of one corporation subsidize society to a greater extent than those of other businesses? For this reason, even highly profitable firms (unless they are closely held rather than publicly owned) are generally constrained against taking unilateral cost-increasing social actions.

Does all this mean that firms should not exercise social responsibility? Not at all, but it does mean that most significant cost-increasing actions will have to be put

---

[7]Even firms like these often find it necessary to justify such projects at stockholder meetings by stating that these programs will contribute to long-run profit maximization.

on a *mandatory* rather than a voluntary basis, at least initially, to insure that their burdens fall uniformly across all businesses. Thus, such social benefit programs as fair hiring practices, minority training, product safety, pollution abatement, and antitrust actions are most likely to be effective if realistic rules are established initially and then enforced by government agencies. Of course, it is critical that industry and government cooperate in establishing the rules of corporate behavior, that the costs as well as the benefits of such actions be accurately estimated and taken into account, and that firms follow the spirit as well as the letter of the law in their actions.

Stock Price Maximization and Social Welfare

If a firm attempts to maximize its stock price, is this good or bad for society? In general, it is good. Aside from such illegal actions as attempting to form monopolies, violating safety codes, and failing to meet pollution control requirements—all of which are constrained by the government—*the same actions that maximize stock prices also benefit society.* First, stock price maximization requires efficient, low-cost operations that produce the desired quality and quantity of output at the lowest possible cost. Second, stock price maximization requires the development of products that consumers want and need, so the profit motive leads to new technology, to new products, and to new jobs. Finally, stock price maximization necessitates efficient and courteous service, adequate stocks of merchandise, and well-located business establishments—these factors are all necessary to make sales, and sales are necessary for profits. Therefore, the types of actions that help a firm increase the price of its stock are also directly beneficial to society at large. This is why profit-motivated, free-enterprise economies have been so much more successful than socialistic and communistic economic systems. Since financial management plays a crucial role in the operation of successful firms, and since successful firms are absolutely necessary for a healthy, productive economy, it is easy to see why finance is important from a social standpoint.[8]

Self-Test Questions

What is management's primary goal?

What actions could be taken to remove the management of a firm operating in a competitive market if it departed from the goal of maximizing shareholder wealth?

---

[8]People sometimes argue that firms, in their efforts to raise profits and stock prices, increase product prices and gouge the public. In a reasonably competitive economy, which we have, prices are constrained by competition and consumer resistance. If a firm raises its prices beyond reasonable levels, it will simply lose its market share. Even giant firms like General Motors lose business to the Japanese and Germans, as well as to Ford and Chrysler, if they set prices over what will cover production costs plus a "normal" profit. Of course, firms *want* to earn more, and they constantly try to cut costs, to develop new products, and so on, and thereby to earn above-normal profits. Note, though, that if they are indeed successful and do earn above-normal profits, those very profits will attract competition and eventually drive prices down, so again the main long-term beneficiary is the consumer.

Explain the difference between a hostile takeover and a proxy fight. How does the firm's stock price influence those actions?

Explain what would happen if one competitive firm attempted to exercise social responsibility, while another competitive firm in the same industry did *not* exercise social responsibility.

Why must most significant cost-increasing, socially beneficial actions be put on a mandatory rather than a voluntary basis?

How does the goal of stock price maximization benefit society at large?

BUSINESS ETHICS

Ethics are defined in Webster's dictionary as "standards of conduct or moral behavior." Business ethics can be thought of as a company's attitude and conduct toward its employees, customers, community, and stockholders. High standards of ethical behavior demand that a firm treat each of these constituents in a fair and honest manner. A firm's commitment to business ethics can be measured by the tendency of the firm and its employees to adhere to laws and regulations relating to such factors as product safety and quality, fair employment practices, fair marketing and selling practices, the use of confidential information for personal gain, community involvement, bribery, and illegal payments to foreign governments to obtain business.

There are many instances of firms engaging in unethical behavior. For example, in 1988 employees of several prominent Wall Street investment banking houses were sentenced to prison terms for illegally using insider information on proposed mergers for their own personal gain, and E. F. Hutton, the stock brokerage firm, lost its independence through a forced merger after it was convicted of cheating its banks out of millions of dollars in a check kiting scheme. Also, Drexel Burnham Lambert recently agreed to a $650 million settlement, and its "junk bond king," Michael Milken, agreed to an additional $600 million in fines and penalties, for alleged securities-law violations. The Drexel settlement was a major factor in its 1990 bankruptcy and liquidation.

In spite of all this, the results of a recent Business Roundtable study indicate that the executives of most major firms in the United States believe that their firms should, and do, try to maintain high ethical standards in all of their business dealings.[9] In fact, most executives believe that there is a positive correlation between ethics and long-run profitability. For example, Chemical Bank suggested that ethical behavior has increased its profitability because such behavior (1) avoids fines and legal expenses, (2) builds public trust, (3) attracts business from customers who appreciate and support its policies, (4) attracts and keeps employees of the highest caliber, and (5) supports the economic viability of the communities in which it operates.

---

[9]The Business Roundtable, *Corporate Ethics: A Prime Business Asset* (New York, February 1988).

Most firms today have in place strong codes of ethical behavior, and they conduct training programs designed to ensure that all employees understand the correct behavior in different business situations. However, it is imperative that top management — the chairman, president, and vice-presidents — be openly committed to ethical behavior, and that they communicate this commitment through their own personal actions as well as through company policies, directives, and punishment/reward systems.

Self-Test Questions

How would you define "business ethics"?

How can a firm's commitment to business ethics be measured?

AGENCY RELATIONSHIPS

In a very important article, Michael Jensen and William Meckling defined an *agency relationship* as a contract under which one or more people (the principals) hire another person (the agent) to perform some service and then delegate decision-making authority to that agent.[10] Within the financial management framework, agency relationships exist (1) between stockholders and managers and (2) between stockholders and creditors (debtholders). These relationships are discussed in the following sections.

Stockholders versus Managers

A potential *agency problem* arises whenever the manager of a firm owns less than 100 percent of the firm's common stock. If a firm is a proprietorship managed by the owner, we can assume that the owner-manager will take every possible action to improve his or her own welfare, with welfare measured primarily in the form of increased personal wealth but also in more leisure or perquisites.[11] However, if the owner-manager relinquishes a portion of his or her ownership by incorporating and selling some of the firm's stock to outsiders, a potential conflict of interests immediately arises. For example, the owner-manager may now decide not to work as strenuously to maximize shareholder wealth, because less of this wealth will go to him or her, or to take a higher salary or consume more perquisites, because part of these costs will now fall on the outside stockholders. This potential conflict between two parties, the principals (outside shareholders) and the agent (manager), is one type of agency problem.

---

[10]See Michael C. Jensen and William H. Meckling, "Theory of the Firm: Managerial Behavior, Agency Costs, and Ownership Structure," *Journal of Financial Economics,* October 1976, 305–360. The discussion of agency theory which follows draws heavily from their work.

[11]*Perquisites* are executive fringe benefits such as luxurious offices, use of corporate planes and yachts, personal assistants, and so on.

Another potential conflict between management and stockholders arises in a *leveraged buyout,* a term used to describe the situation in which management itself (1) arranges a line of credit, (2) makes an offer, called a *tender offer,* to the stockholders to buy the stock not already owned by the management group, and (3) "takes the company private" after it has bought the outstanding shares. Dozens of such buyouts of New York Stock Exchange–listed companies have occurred recently, and a potential conflict clearly exists whenever one is contemplated. For example, RJR Nabisco's President, F. Ross Johnson, recently attempted to take the company private in an LBO. If he had been successful, Johnson and other RJR executives would have ended up owning about 20 percent of the company, worth several billion dollars. At the time, some stockholders believed that management paved the way for the LBO bid by (1) having the company repurchase 21 million shares of stock at $53.50 before their LBO bid of $75, (2) adopting a takeover defense designed to thwart any competing offers that were "not acceptable to management," and (3) conducting financial studies and analyses at stockholder expense concerning a possible restructuring of the company, and then using this information when deciding how much to bid.

RJR's management proclaimed that its bid was in all stockholders' interests, but many questioned that statement: If management itself was buying the stock, would it not be in management's own best interest to keep the price down until the deal was completed, and thus did not a clear conflict of interest exist? In general, if a conflict of interest did exist, what can be done to insure that management treats the outside stockholders fairly? As one response to the last question, the SEC now requires that management disclose all material information relating to a proposed deal, and that a committee of outside (i.e., nonofficer) directors be established to (1) seek other bids for the company, (2) evaluate and compare any other bids with that of management, and (3) then recommend the best bid to stockholders. Further, the outside directors' committee members cannot have any interest in the reorganized company; this requirement is designed to insure their independence, and lawsuits would quickly be filed if a conflict situation developed.

In RJR's case, the outside directors' committee received bids from several groups, including one from Kohlberg Kravis Roberts (KKR), an investment company that specializes in LBOs using pension funds as its primary source of equity capital. (KKR generally finances with about 10 percent equity and 90 percent debt, with the debt divided between short-term bank loans to be repaid out of funds generated by selling certain corporate assets and longer-term junk bonds.) A bidding war ensued, and in the end KKR beat out the management group with a bid of $109 per share, up from management's original $75 offer. Actually, the final management and KKR bids were similar, but the outside directors recommended KKR in part because of the widespread feeling that management had tried to "steal" the company. This whole episode is a good example of the fact that leveraged buyouts constitute an important type of agency problem arising between the stockholders and the managers of a firm.

To insure that its managers act in the best interests of the outside shareholders, the firm must incur *agency costs,* which may take several forms: (1) expenditures to monitor managerial actions, (2) expenditures to structure the organization so that the possibility of undesirable managerial behavior will be limited, and (3) opportunity costs associated with lost profit opportunities resulting from an organizational structure which does not permit managers to take actions on as timely a basis as would be possible if the managers were also the owners.

There are two extreme positions regarding how to deal with the agency problem. One extreme position calls for a firm's managers to be compensated only with shares of the firm's stock. Here, agency costs would be low because the managers would have less incentive to take excessive leisure, salary, or perquisites. However, it would be difficult to hire managers under these terms. The opposite position calls for the owners to closely monitor every managerial activity. However, this solution would be extremely costly and inefficient. Obviously, the optimal solution lies somewhere between the extremes, where executive compensation is tied to performance but some monitoring is also done. Several mechanisms which tend to force managers to act in the shareholders' best interests are discussed next. These include (1) the threat of firing, (2) the threat of takeover, and (3) the proper structuring of managerial incentives.

The Threat of Firing. Until recently, the probability of a large firm's management being ousted by its stockholders was so remote that it posed little threat. This situation existed because ownership of most firms was so widely distributed, and management's control over the proxy (voting) mechanism was so strong, that it was almost impossible for dissident stockholders to gain enough votes to overthrow the managers. However, today about 50 percent of the stock of an average large corporation is concentrated in the hands of large institutions rather than owned by individual investors, and the institutional money managers have the clout, if they choose to use it, to exercise considerable influence over a firm's operations. Examples of major corporations whose managements have either been ousted or been forced to change their operating philosophy include United Airlines, Disney, and Texaco.

The Threat of Takeover. *Hostile takeovers* (where management does not want the firm to be taken over) are most likely to occur when a firm's stock is undervalued relative to its potential because of poor managerial decisions. In a hostile takeover, the managers of the acquired firm are generally fired, and any who are able to stay on lose the autonomy they had prior to the acquisition. Thus, managers have a strong incentive to take actions which maximize stock prices. In the words of one company president, "If you want to keep control, don't let your company's stock sell at a bargain price."

Actions to increase the firm's stock price and to keep it from being a bargain are obviously good from the standpoint of the stockholders, but other tactics that managers can use to ward off a hostile takeover may not be. Two examples of questionable tactics are poison pills and greenmail. A *poison pill* is an action that a firm can take which practically kills it and thus makes it unattractive to potential suitors. Examples include Walt Disney's plan to sell large blocks of its stock at low prices to "friendly" parties, Scott Industries' decision to make all of its debt immediately payable if its management changed, and Carleton Corporation's decision to give huge retirement bonuses, which represented a large part of the company's wealth, to its managers if the firm was taken over (such payments are called *golden parachutes*). *Greenmail,* which is like blackmail, occurs when this sequence of events takes place: (1) A potential acquirer (firm or individual) buys a block of stock in a company, (2) the target company's management becomes frightened that the acquirer will make a tender offer and gain control of the company, and (3) to head off a possible takeover, management offers to pay greenmail, buying the stock of the potential raider at a price above the existing market price without offering the same deal to other stockholders. A good example of greenmail was Disney's buy-back of 11.1 percent of its stock from Saul Steinberg's Reliance Group, giving Steinberg a quick $60 million profit. A group of stockholders sued, and in 1989 Steinberg, the Disney directors, and others were forced to pay $45 million to Disney stockholders.

Structuring Managerial Incentives. More and more, firms are tying managers' compensation to the company's performance, and research suggests that this motivates managers to operate in a manner consistent with stock price maximization.[12]

Performance-based incentive plans have become an accepted management tool. In the 1950s and 1960s, most of these plans involved *executive stock options,* which allowed managers to purchase stock at some time in the future at a given price; the options would be valuable if the market price of the stock rose above the option purchase price. The firms which used these plans believed that allowing managers to purchase stock at a fixed price would provide an incentive for them to take actions which would maximize the stock's price. This type of managerial incentive lost favor in the 1970s, however, because the options generally did not pay off. The general stock market declined, and stock prices did not necessarily reflect companies' earnings growth. Incentive plans ought to be based on those factors over which managers have control, and since they cannot control the general stock market, stock option plans have proved to be weak incentive devices. Therefore, whereas 61 of the 100 largest U.S. firms used stock options as their sole incentive compensation in 1970, not even one of the largest 100 companies relied exclusively on such plans in 1990.

One important incentive plan now is *performance shares,* which are shares of stock given to executives on the basis of performance as measured by earnings per share, return on assets, return on equity, and so on. For example, Honeywell uses growth in earnings per share as its primary performance measure. The firm has two overlapping four-year performance periods, beginning two years apart. At the start of each period, the participating executives are allocated a certain number of performance shares, say, 10,000 shares for the president down to 1,000 shares for a lower-ranking manager. If the company achieves, say, a targeted 13 percent annual average growth in earnings per share, the managers will earn 100 percent of their shares. If the corporate performance is above the target, Honeywell's managers can earn even more shares, up to a maximum of 130 percent, which requires a 16

---

[12]See Wilbur G. Lewellen, "Management and Ownership in the Large Firm," *Journal of Finance,* May 1969, 299–322. Lewellen concluded that managers seem to make decisions that are largely oriented toward stock price maximization. Economic events since his study was published suggest that the incentives for stock price maximization are even stronger today than they were during the period his data covered.

percent growth rate. However, if growth is below 13 percent, they get less than 100 percent of the shares, and below a 9 percent growth rate, they get zero. Executives must remain with Honeywell through the performance period (four years) in order to receive the performance shares.

Performance shares have a value even if the company's stock price remains constant because of a poor general stock market, whereas, under similar conditions, stock options might have no value even though managers had been successful in boosting earnings. Of course, the *value* of the shares received is dependent on market price performance, because 1,000 shares of Honeywell stock are a lot more valuable if the stock sells for $200 than if it sells for only $100.

All incentive compensation plans—executive stock options, performance shares, profit-based bonuses, and so forth—are supposed to accomplish two things. First, they offer executives an incentive to act on those factors under their control in a manner that will contribute to stock price maximization. Second, the existence of such performance plans helps companies attract and retain top-level executives. Well-designed plans can accomplish both goals.[13]

Stockholders versus Creditors

The second agency problem involves potential conflicts between stockholders and creditors (debtholders). Creditors lend funds to the firm at rates that are based on (1) the riskiness of the firm's existing assets, (2) expectations concerning the riskiness of future asset additions, (3) the firm's existing capital structure (that is, the amount of debt financing it uses), and (4) expectations concerning future capital structure changes. These are the factors that determine the riskiness of the firm's cash flows and hence the safety of its debt, so creditors set their required rates of return, which represent the cost of debt to the firm, on expectations regarding these factors.

Now suppose the stockholders, acting through management, cause the firm to take on new projects that have greater risks than were anticipated by the creditors. This increased risk will cause the required rate of return on the firm's debt to increase, which in turn will cause the value of the outstanding debt to fall.[14] If the riskier capital investments turn out to be successful, all of the benefits will go to the stockholders, because the creditors get only a fixed return, but if things go sour, the bondholders will have to share the losses. What we would have, from the stockholders' point of view, is a game of "heads I win, tails you lose," which is obviously not a good game from the bondholders' standpoint. Similarly, if the firm increases

---

[13]One interesting aspect of incentive plans which involve stock rather than cash is their effects on reported corporate profits. To illustrate, suppose a company has operating income of $10 million before executive compensation. If it paid its executives $1 million in salary and cash bonuses, then it would report operating income of $9 million. However, if it gave them stock options worth $1 million, this would have no effect on reported profits, even though there is truly a cost to the company, because it will later have to sell the executives shares at a bargain price, which will reduce earnings available to the other stockholders. The Financial Accounting Standards Board is currently exploring ways to deal with this problem and thus to make reported profits more realistic and consistent across companies.

[14]In general, the higher the required rate of return on an existing debt issue, the lower its value. In Chapter 7 we will prove this point.

its level of debt in an effort to increase its return on equity, the value of the old debt will decrease, because the old debt's bankruptcy protection will be lessened by the issuance of the new debt. In both of these situations, stockholders would be gaining at the expense of the firm's creditors.

To illustrate the bondholder agency problem, consider what happened to RJR Nabisco's bondholders when RJR's CEO announced his plan to take the company private in an LBO. Stockholders saw their shares jump in value from $56 to over $90 in just a few days, but RJR's long-term bondholders suffered losses of approximately 20 percent. Investors immediately realized that the LBO would cause the amount of RJR's debt to rise dramatically, and thus its riskiness would soar. This, in turn, led to a higher required rate of return on RJR's outstanding bonds, so the prices declined.

In fact, the entire industrial bond market was shaken by the RJR announcement; bond investors realized that other large companies could become LBO targets. Indeed, the State of Ohio's pension fund administrator announced that he was liquidating the fund's entire industrial bond portfolio, and switching to Treasury bonds, because of the danger of LBOs. He announced that he would, however, continue to invest in bonds issued by utilities and banks; LBOs of companies in these industries are less likely because their regulated status limits the amount of leverage they can employ.

The bond market's disarray caught many experts by surprise. Even though bond investors have been stung many times in recent years by LBOs and restructurings, the gargantuan size of the RJR Nabisco deal made investors realize that no firm is too large to be a target. "Now, bond investors are going to have to pay much closer attention to the fine print in the credit agreements," said one analyst. He went on to say that "anybody that holds an industrial bond that is not protected against something like this is sitting on a credit toxic waste site."

The RJR merger gave rise to, or at least popularized, two new terms, event risk and poison puts. *Event risk* is the risk creditors face that some deliberate action, or event, will convert a high-grade bond into a junk bond overnight, and thus lead to a sharp decline in its value. Event risk is distinguished from credit risk, which generally involves a gradual deterioration in a company's creditworthiness due to poor operating conditions. A *put* is an option which gives the holder the right to sell something at a stipulated price, and a *poison put* is a provision in a bond indenture which permits the holder of the bond to sell it back to the issuer at par in the event of an LBO. We anticipate wide use of poison put provisions in the wake of the RJR deal.

Can and should stockholders, through their managers/agents, try to expropriate wealth from the firm's creditors? In general, the answer is no. First, because such attempts have been made in the past, creditors today protect themselves reasonably well against such stockholder actions through restrictions in credit agreements. Second, if potential creditors perceive that the firm will try to take advantage of them in unethical ways, they will either refuse to deal with the firm or else will require a much higher than normal rate of interest to compensate for the risks of such possible exploitation. Thus, firms which try to deal unfairly with creditors either lose access to the debt markets or are saddled with higher interest rates, which can lead to a decrease in the long-run value of the stock.

In view of these constraints, it follows that the goal of maximizing shareholder wealth requires fair play with creditors. Stockholder wealth depends on continued access to capital markets, and access depends on fair play and abiding by both the letter and the spirit of credit agreements. Therefore, the managers, as agents of both the creditors and the shareholders, must act in a manner which is fairly balanced between the interests of these two classes of security holders. Similarly, because of other constraints and sanctions, management actions which would expropriate wealth from any of the firm's *stakeholders* (employees, customers, suppliers, and so on) will ultimately be to the detriment of shareholders. We conclude that in our society the goal of shareholder wealth maximization requires the fair treatment of all stakeholders.

Self-Test Questions

What is an agency relationship, and, within the financial management framework, what two major agency relationships exist?

Identify some situations in which potential agency problems exist between stockholders and managers.

Explain what agency costs are and why they must be incurred by firms.

Briefly outline several mechanisms which tend to cause managers to act in the shareholders' best interests.

How might an agency problem arise between stockholders and creditors?

MANAGERIAL ACTIONS TO MAXIMIZE SHAREHOLDER WEALTH

To maximize the long-run value of a firm's stock, what types of actions should its management take? First, consider the question of stock prices versus profits: Will *profit maximization* also result in stock price maximization? In answering this question, we must analyze the matter of total corporate profits versus *earnings per share (EPS)*.

For example, suppose Motorola had 100 million shares outstanding and earned $400 million, or $4 per share, and you owned 100 shares of the stock, so your share of the total profits would be $400. Now suppose Motorola sold another 100 million shares and invested the funds received in assets which produced $100 million of income. Total income would rise to $500 million, but earnings per share would decline from $4 to $500/200 = $2.50. Now your share of the firm's earnings would be only $250, down from $400. You (and other current stockholders) would have suffered an earnings dilution, even though total corporate profits had risen. Therefore, other things held constant, *if management is interested in the well-being of its current stockholders, it should concentrate on earnings per share rather than on total corporate profits.*

Will maximization of expected earnings per share always maximize stockholder welfare, or should other factors be considered? Think about the *timing of the earn-*

ings. Suppose Motorola had one project that would cause earnings per share to rise by $0.20 per year for 5 years, or $1 in total, while another project would have no effect on earnings for 4 years but would increase earnings by $1.25 in the fifth year. Which project is better—in other words, is $0.20 per year for 5 years better or worse than $1.25 in Year 5? The answer depends on which project adds the most to the value of the stock, which in turn depends on the time value of money to investors. Thus, timing is an important reason to concentrate on wealth as measured by the price of the stock rather than on earnings alone.

Another issue relates to *risk.* Suppose one project is expected to increase earnings per share by $1, while another is expected to raise earnings by $1.20 per share. The first project is not very risky; if it is undertaken, earnings will almost certainly rise by about $1 per share. However, the other project is quite risky, so, although our best guess is that earnings will rise by $1.20 per share, we must recognize the possibility that there may be no increase whatsoever, or even a loss. Depending on how averse stockholders are to risk, the first project might be preferable to the second.

The riskiness inherent in projected earnings per share (EPS) also depends on *how the firm is financed.* As we shall see, many firms go bankrupt every year, and the greater the use of debt, the greater the threat of bankruptcy. *Consequently, while the use of debt financing may increase projected EPS, debt also increases the riskiness of projected future earnings.*

Yet another issue is the matter of paying dividends to stockholders versus retaining earnings and reinvesting them in the firm, thereby causing the earnings stream to grow over time. Stockholders like cash dividends, but they also like the growth in EPS that results from plowing earnings back into the business. The financial manager must decide exactly how much of the current earnings to pay out as dividends rather than to retain and to reinvest—this is called the *dividend policy decision.* The optimal dividend policy is the one that maximizes the firm's stock price.

We see, then, that the firm's stock price is dependent on the following factors:

1. Projected earnings per share
2. Timing of the earnings stream
3. Riskiness of these projected earnings
4. The firm's use of debt
5. Dividend policy

Every significant corporate decision should be analyzed in terms of its effect on these factors and hence on the price of the firm's stock. For example, suppose Occidental Petroleum's coal division is considering opening a new mine. If this is done, can it be expected to increase EPS? Is there a chance that costs will exceed estimates, that prices and output will fall below projections, and that EPS will be reduced because the new mine was opened? How long will it take for the new mine to start showing a profit? How should the capital required to open the mine be raised? If debt is used, how much will this increase Occidental's riskiness? Should Occidental reduce its current dividends and use the cash thus saved to finance the project, or should it maintain its dividends and finance the mine with external capital? Financial management is designed to help answer questions like these, plus many more.

Self-Test Questions

Will profit maximization also result in stock price maximization?

Identify five factors which affect the firm's stock price.

THE ECONOMIC ENVIRONMENT

Although managers can take actions which affect the values of their firms' stocks, there are additional factors which influence stock prices. Included among them are external constraints, the general level of economic activity, taxes, and conditions in the stock market. Figure 1-2 diagrams these general relationships. Working within the set of external constraints shown in the box at the extreme left, management makes a set of long-run strategic policy decisions which chart a future course for the firm. These policy decisions, along with the general level of economic activity and the level of corporate income taxes, influence the firm's expected profitability, the timing of its earnings and their eventual transfer to stockholders in the form of dividends, and the degree of uncertainty (or risk) inherent in projected earnings and dividends. Profitability, timing, and risk all affect the price of the firm's stock, but so does another factor, conditions in the stock market as a whole, because all stock prices tend to move up and down together to some extent.

Self-Test Question

Identify some factors beyond the firm's control which influence its stock price.

Figure 1-2   Summary of Major Factors Affecting Stock Prices

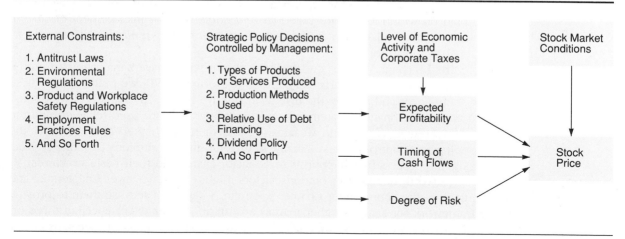

ORGANIZATION OF THE BOOK

Part I contains fundamental background materials and concepts upon which the book builds. Finance cannot be studied in a vacuum — financial decisions are profoundly influenced by the economic and social environment in which they are made. Our introduction to the economic/social side of this environment is contained in Chapters 1, 2, and 3.

Part II, consisting of Chapters 4 through 8, develops a set of valuation models which can be used to help see how different actions will affect the value of the firm's securities and the cost of its capital. The concepts and models developed here are used extensively throughout the remainder of the book.

Beginning with Part III, we move into the execution phase of the long-range strategic planning process, and in Chapters 9, 10, and 11 we consider the vital subject of long-term investment decisions, or capital budgeting. Since major capital expenditures take years to plan and execute, and since decisions in this area are generally not reversible and affect operations for many years, their impact on the value of the firm is profound.

Part IV, which contains Chapters 12, 13, and 14, sets forth the conceptual framework for an analysis of how the firm should raise the capital needed to finance its capital expenditures. Here we consider two fundamentally important issues — capital structure and dividend policy. Capital structure is, essentially, the firm's mix of debt and equity, while dividend policy relates to how much of its earnings the firm should retain and invest versus paying it out to the stockholders as dividends.

Part V, which includes Chapters 15 through 18, focuses on the specific types of long-term capital available to the firm, and it addresses these three questions: What are the principal sources and forms of long-term capital? How are the terms on each type of security established? And how should the financial manager choose among the various types of long-term capital?

Part VI consists of Chapters 19, 20, and 21, which examine current, ongoing operations as opposed to long-term strategic decisions. From accounting, we know that assets which are expected to be converted to cash within a year, such as inventories and accounts receivable, are called *current assets,* and liabilities which must be paid off within a year are called *current liabilities.* The management of current assets and current liabilities is known as *short-term financial management,* and Part VI deals with this topic.

Parts I through VI focus on specific decisions which have a major impact on the firm's value. In the final three chapters, which form Part VII, we pull together these separate pieces and analyze the firm as a cohesive whole. In Chapter 22 we discuss the analysis of financial statements and show how they are used to determine the firm's current strengths and weaknesses, and then in Chapter 23 we look at the planning and control process. Finally, in Chapter 24 we examine corporate restructuring, the process by which firms make major changes in their basic structures.

It is worth noting that some instructors might choose to cover Chapters 22 and 23 early in the course, after Chapter 3, or after Chapter 7, and use them to provide a framework for analysis rather than as a wrap-up. In our experience, all three orderings work well, so each instructor can choose the one that best meets his or her own situation.

MULTINATIONAL FINANCE
The International Environment

In theory, the concepts and procedures discussed in the text are valid for both domestic and multinational operations. However, several problems uniquely associated with the international environment increase the complexity of the manager's task in a multinational corporation, and often force managers to alter the way alternative courses of action are evaluated and compared. Five major factors complicate the situation and thus distinguish financial management as practiced by firms operating entirely in a single country versus those that operate in several different countries:

1. Cash flows in various parts of a multinational corporate system are denominated in different currencies. Hence, an analysis of exchange rates, and the effects of changing currency values, must be included in all types of financial analyses.

2. Each country in which the firm operates will have its own unique political and economic institutions. Institutional differences among countries can cause significant problems when the corporation tries to co-ordinate and control the worldwide operations of its subsidiaries. For example, differences in tax laws among countries can cause a given economic transaction to have strikingly dissimilar after-tax consequences, depending on where it occurred. Similarly, differences in the legal systems of host nations, such as the Common Law of Great Britain versus the French Civil Law, complicate many matters, from the simple recording of a business transaction to the role played by the judiciary in resolving conflicts. Such differences can restrict the flexibility of multinational corporations to deploy resources as they wish and can even make procedures illegal in one part of the company that are required in another part. These differences also make it difficult for executives trained in one country to operate effectively in another.

3. Even within geographic regions that have long been considered relatively homogeneous, different countries have unique cultural heritages which shape values and influence the role of business in the society. Multinational corporations find that such matters as defining the appropriate goals of the firm, attitudes toward risk-taking, dealings with employees, the ability to curtail unprofitable operations, and so on, can vary dramatically from one country to the next.

4. Most traditional models in finance assume the existence of a competitive marketplace, in which the terms of competition are determined by the participants. The government, through its power to establish basic ground rules, is involved in this process, but its participation is minimal. Thus, the market provides both the primary barometer of success and an indicator of the actions that must be taken to remain competitive. This view of the process is reasonably correct for the United States and the other major Western industrialized nations, but it does not accurately describe the situation in the majority of countries. Frequently, the terms under which companies compete, actions that must be taken or avoided, and the terms of trade on various transactions are determined not in the marketplace but by direct negotiation between the host government and the multinational corporation. This is essentially a political process, and it must be treated as such. Thus, our traditional financial models have to be recast to include political and other non-economic facets of the decision.

5. The distinguishing characteristic of a nation that differentiates it from other entities is that the nation exercises sovereignty over its people and property in its territory. Hence, a nation is free to place constraints on the transfer of corporate resources and even to expropriate without compensation the assets of the firm. This is a political risk, and it tends to be largely a given rather than a variable which can be changed by negotiation. Political risk varies from country to country, and it must be addressed explicitly in any financial analysis.

These five factors complicate financial management within the multinational firm. However, higher prospects for profit and the benefits of global diversification often make it well worthwhile, if not mandatory, for firms to operate in the international environment.

SUMMARY

This chapter has provided an overview of financial management. The key concepts covered are listed below.

- Finance consists of three interrelated areas: (1) *money and capital markets,* (2) *investments,* and (3) *financial management.*

- Financial management has undergone significant changes over the years, but four issues have received the most emphasis in recent years: (1) *inflation* and its effects on interest rates, (2) *deregulation of financial institutions,* (3) a dramatic increase in the *use of telecommunications for transmitting information and of computers* for analyzing financial decisions, and (4) the increased importance of *global financial markets and business operations.*

- *Financial managers* are responsible for *obtaining and using funds* in a way that will *maximize the value of the firm.*

- The three main forms of business organization are the *sole proprietorship,* the *partnership,* and the *corporation.*

- Although each form of organization offers some advantages and disadvantages, *most business is conducted by corporations because this organizational form maximizes most firms' values.*

- The primary goal of management should be to *maximize stockholders' wealth,* and this means *maximizing the price of the firm's stock.* Further, actions which maximize stock prices also increase social welfare.

- An *agency problem* is a potential conflict of interests that can arise between (1) the owners of the firm and its management or (2) the stockholders and the creditors (debtholders).

- There are a number of ways to *motivate managers to act in the best interests of stockholders,* including (1) the *threat of firing,* (2) the *threat of takeovers,* and (3) properly structured *managerial compensation packages.*

- The *price of the firm's stock* depends on the firm's *projected earnings per share,* the *timing of the earnings,* the *riskiness of the projected earnings,* the firm's *use of debt,* and its *dividend policy.*

- *International operations* are becoming increasingly important to individual firms and to the national economy. We shall discuss multinational finance throughout the text.

The book's organization reflects the stock price maximization goal. First, we discuss the economic and social environment, after which we develop valuation models that can be used to show how corporate actions will affect stock prices. Then, in the remainder of the book, we examine specific actions that financial managers can take to maximize stock prices.

Questions

1-1   Define each of the following terms:
   a.   Profit maximization; stockholder wealth maximization

b. Earnings per share; price per share
c. Social responsibility
d. Normal profits; normal rate of return
e. Dividend policy
f. Agency relationships; agency costs; performance shares
g. Proxy fight; hostile takeover; tender offer
h. Leveraged buyout
i. Poison pill; greenmail
j. Sole proprietorship; partnership; corporation

1-2 Would the "normal" rate of return on investment be the same in all industries? Would "normal" rates of return change over time? Explain.

1-3 Should stockholder wealth maximization be thought of as a long-term or a short-term goal? For example, if one action would probably increase the firm's stock price from a current level of $20 to $25 in 6 months and then to $30 in 5 years, but another action would probably keep the stock at $20 for several years and then increase it to $40 in 5 years, which action would be better? Can you think of actual examples which might have these general tendencies? How could such situations affect the attractiveness of leveraged buyouts (LBOs)?

1-4 Drawing on your background in accounting, can you think of any accounting procedure differences which might make it difficult to establish the relative performance of different firms? How would this affect the agency problem and managerial compensation schemes?

1-5 Would the management of a firm in an oligopolistic or in a competitive industry be more likely to engage in what might be called "socially conscious" practices? Explain your reasoning.

1-6 What is the difference between stock price maximization and profit maximization? Would profit maximization lead to stock price maximization?

1-7 If you were running a large, publicly owned corporation, would you make decisions to maximize stockholder's welfare or your own interests? What are some actions stockholders could take to insure that your interests and theirs coincided? What are some other factors that might influence your actions?

1-8 The president of Continental Manufacturing Corporation made this statement in the company's annual report: "Continental's primary goal is to increase the value of the common stockholders' equity over time." Later on in the report, the following announcements were made:
a. The company contributed $1 million to the symphony orchestra in the headquarters' city.
b. The company is spending $300 million to open a new plant in South America. No revenues will be produced by the plant for 3 years, so earnings will be depressed during this period versus what they would have been had the decision been made not to open the new plant.
c. The company is increasing its relative use of debt. Whereas assets were formerly financed with 40 percent debt and 60 percent equity, henceforth the financing mix will be 50–50.
d. The company has been paying out only 30 percent of its earnings as dividends, retaining and reinvesting the remainder in the business. Henceforth, management will pay out 70 percent and retain only 30 percent.
e. The company uses a great deal of electricity in its manufacturing operations, and it generates most of this power itself. Plans are to utilize nuclear fuel, rather than coal, to produce electricity in the future.
Discuss how each of these factors might affect Continental's stock price.

1-9 What are the three principal forms of business organization? What are the advantages and disadvantages of each?

Selected Additional References

For alternative views on firms' goals and objectives, see the following articles:

Cornell, Bradford, and Alan C. Shapiro, "Corporate Stakeholders and Corporate Finance," *Financial Management,* Spring 1987, 5–14.

Donaldson, Gordon, "Financial Goals: Management versus Stockholders," *Harvard Business Review,* May-June 1963, 116–129.

Meckling, William H., and Michael C. Jensen, "Reflections on the Corporation as a Social Invention," *Midland Corporate Finance Journal,* Fall 1983, 6–15.

Seitz, Neil, "Shareholder Goals, Firm Goals and Firm Financing Decisions," *Financial Management,* Autumn 1982, 20–26.

Treynor, Jack L., "The Financial Objective of the Widely Held Corporation," *Financial Analysts Journal,* March-April 1981, 68–71.

The following articles extend our discussion of agency relationships:

Barnea, Amir, Robert A. Haugen, and Lemma W. Senbet, "Market Imperfections, Agency Problems, and Capital Structure: A Review," *Financial Management,* Summer 1981, 7–22.

Hand, John H., William P. Lloyd, and Robert B. Rogow, "Agency Relationships in the Close Corporation," *Financial Management,* Spring 1982, 25–30.

For a general review of academic finance, together with an extensive bibliography of key research articles, see

Cooley, Philip L., and J. Louis Heck, "Significant Contributions to Finance Literature," *Financial Management,* Tenth Anniversary Issue, 1981, 23–33.

Weston, J. Fred, "Developments in Finance Theory," *Financial Management,* Tenth Anniversary Issue, 1981, 5–22.

For more information on managerial compensation, see

Cooley, Philip L., and Charles E. Edwards, "Ownership Effects on Managerial Salaries in Small Business," *Financial Management,* Winter 1982, 5–9.

Lambert, Richard A., and David F. Larcker, "Executive Compensation, Corporate Decision-Making, and Shareholder Wealth: A Review of the Evidence," *Midland Corporate Finance Journal,* Winter 1985, 6–22. The Winter 1985 issue of the *Midland Corporate Finance Journal* contains several other articles pertaining to executive compensation.

For more information on the role of corporate directors, see

"Corporate Governance: The Role of Boards of Directors in Takeover Bids and Defenses," *Journal of Applied Corporate Finance,* Summer 1989, 6–35.

For an overview of multinational finance, see

Shapiro, Alan C., *International Corporate Finance: A Survey and Synthesis* (Tampa: Financial Management Association, 1986).

CHAPTER 2

Financial Statements, Taxes, and Cash Flows

Congress is currently grappling with the problem of how to reduce the massive federal debt, which in 1990 totaled over $3 trillion. The United States began the 1980s as the largest creditor nation on earth, but it begins the decade of the '90s as the largest borrower. President Bush has vowed to veto any new taxes ("read my lips"), but many experts predict that Congress and the administration will have to devise some type of "revenue enhancement" (a euphemism for taxes) to increase revenues and hence decrease the annual deficit. Further, it is likely that corporations will be the hardest hit, possibly in the form of higher tax rates, but more likely in the form of increased limitations on deductions, including depreciation.

In 1989, the administration tried unsuccessfully to lower the capital gains tax rate. Under this proposal, capital gains, which are the profits earned from selling such assets as stock and real estate, would be taxed at a rate of 19.5 percent for two years, while other forms of income, including dividends, would be taxed at 28, or even 33 percent. This change, if it had been made, would probably have prompted some stockholders to sell and realize the large gains they had made in the bull market of the 1980s —they would have been willing to sell and pay taxes of about 20 percent on their gains, whereas they would have been unwilling to sell and pay a 28 or 33 percent rate. This greater-than-normal selling activity would have increased 1990 tax collections, but would have reduced tax collections in the long run. The Democrats generally opposed the capital gains cut, claiming that it favored the wealthy over the poor and middle classes.

While the administration was pushing for the ill-fated capital gains cut, Democrats were pushing to have the top rate increased to 33 percent on all income, rather than having it ultimately fall back to 28 percent as it does now. The rationale was that the dramatic tax-rate reductions that Ronald Reagan pushed through in 1986 gave too much of a break to the wealthy, so they are not currently bearing enough of the tax burden.

Tax changes, which occur virtually every year, with major changes occurring every 3 to 4 years, have a major impact on both firms' net incomes and on how shareholders are taxed on stock income, and thus on stock prices. Therefore, financial executives are busy trying to anticipate tax law changes, and then to see how these changes would affect their firms' profits, cash flows, and stock prices. To make matters more complicated, a long-term investment (say the construction of a new plant) may appear to be profitable when it is made, but if the tax laws are subsequently changed, Congress can turn a good investment into a bad one. Life for financial planners may or may not be fair, but it is certainly interesting!

IT is obvious from the preceding paragraphs that financial management cannot be studied in a vacuum; if the value of a firm is to be maximized, the financial manager simply must understand the legal environment in which financial decisions are made. This requires a consideration of the types of financial statements firms must provide to investors and the types of securities they may issue. Further, the value of any asset—be it a *financial asset* such as a stock or a bond, or a *real (physical) asset* such as land, buildings, equipment, or inventories—depends on the usable, or after-tax, cash flows the asset produces. Accordingly, this chapter presents some background information on financial statements, on the major types of securities used by businesses, and on the federal income tax system.[1]

FINANCIAL STATEMENTS AND SECURITIES

Any business must have *assets* if it is to operate, and in order to acquire assets, the firm must raise *capital*. Capital comes in two basic forms, *debt* and *equity*. There are many different types of debt—long-term and short-term, interest-bearing and non-interest-bearing, secured and unsecured, and so on. Similarly, there are different types of equity. For example, the equity of a proprietorship is called *proprietor's interest* or *proprietor's net worth,* whereas for a partnership, the word *partner* is inserted in lieu of *proprietor*. For a corporation, equity is represented by *preferred*

---

[1]This chapter contains essential information, but many business students will have been exposed to some or all of it in economics or accounting courses. Even if they have not, the material is both straightforward and descriptive. Therefore, some instructors may prefer to have students read Chapter 2 on their own rather than to cover it in class.

stock and *common stockholders' equity*. Common equity, in turn, includes both *paid-in capital* and *retained earnings*.

Table 2-1 shows a simplified balance sheet for Maynard Electronics Company, a large electronics components manufacturer, as of December 31, 1990. Maynard began life in 1957 as a proprietorship, then became a partnership, and finally converted to a corporation in 1965. Its 1990 sales were $802 million, and the $560 million of assets shown in Table 2-1 were necessary to support these sales. Maynard and other companies obtain the bulk of the funds used to buy assets (1) by buying on credit from their suppliers (accounts payable); (2) by borrowing from banks, insurance companies, pension funds, and other institutions (notes payable and long-term bonds); (3) by selling preferred and common stock to investors; and (4) by "saving money" (retaining earnings) as reflected in the retained earnings account. (Recall from your accounting courses that a corporation saves whenever the company pays dividends which are less than its net income, and the savings that have accumulated since the company began are reported as retained earnings on its balance sheet.) Also, because wages and taxes are not paid on a daily basis, Maynard obtains some "credit" from its labor force and from the government in the form of accrued wages and taxes.

The first claim against Maynard's income and assets is by its creditors—all those claims items listed on the right-hand side of the balance sheet above preferred stock. However, the creditors' claims are limited to fixed amounts. For example, most of the long-term debt bears interest at a rate of 9 percent per year, so the bondholders in total get interest of about $0.09 \times \$214$ million $= \$19.3$ million per year. If Maynard did extremely well and had profits of, say, $160 million, the bondholders would still get only $19.3 million. However, if Maynard lost money, the bondholders would still get their $19.3 million; assets would be sold, the cash raised would be used to pay the bond interest, and the value of the common equity would decline. Further, if the company's situation were so bad that it simply could not generate the cash needed to make the required payments to the bondholders and other creditors

Table 2-1   Maynard Electronics Company: Balance Sheet
as of December 31, 1990 (Millions of Dollars)

Assets		Liabilities and Equity	
Cash and marketable securities	$ 24.0	Accounts payable	$ 47.6
Accounts receivable	100.6	Notes payable to banks	60.0
Inventories	183.2	Accrued wages and taxes	5.2
Prepaid expenses and other current assets	3.2	Other current liabilities	10.0
Total current assets	$311.0	Total current liabilities	$122.8
		Long-term bonds	214.0
Gross fixed assets	299.4	Preferred stock (224,000 shares)	22.4
Less: depreciation	50.0	Common stockholders' equity:	
Net fixed assets	$249.4	Common stock (3,412,702 shares)	20.8
		Retained earnings	180.4
		Total common equity	$201.2
Total assets	$560.4	Total liabilities and equity	$560.4

(if this occurs, the firm is said to have *defaulted* on its debt), (1) the company would be forced into bankruptcy, (2) the assets would be sold off (generally at less than the values stated on the balance sheet), (3) the creditors (and perhaps the preferred stockholders) would receive the proceeds from the bankruptcy liquidation, and (4) the claims of the common stockholders would probably be wiped out.[2]

The preferred stockholders stand next in line, after the creditors, for the firm's income and assets. Maynard has 224,000 shares of preferred stock, each with a par value of $100. This preferred pays a dividend of $8.125 per year, or 8.125 percent on its $100 par value. The preferred dividends must be paid before any dividends can be paid on the common, and, in the event of bankruptcy, the preferred must be paid off in full before anything goes to the common stockholders.

After everyone else has been paid, the remaining income, also called the *residual income,* belongs to the common stockholders. This income may be retained and reinvested in the firm, or it may be paid out as dividends to the common stockholders. Firms like Maynard typically retain some earnings to support growth and then pay the rest out as dividends. Maynard has 3,412,702 shares of common stock outstanding. Investors actually paid the company about $6.09 on the average for these shares ($20,800,000/3,412,702 = $6.09), but the company has saved through retention of earnings $180,400,000/3,412,702 = $52.86 per share since it was incorporated in 1965.[3] Therefore, stockholders on the average have a total investment of $6.09 + $52.86 = $58.95 per share in the company; this is the stock's *book value.*

Maynard's debt and preferred stock are held primarily by its suppliers, by five banks, and by some institutions, such as life insurance companies and pension funds. The debt is rarely if ever traded, because this particular set of investors tends to hold debt until it matures. Maynard's common stock, on the other hand, is actively traded. Individuals own about 65 percent of the stock, with institutions owning the remaining 35 percent; these are typical percentages for a company Maynard's size. In the fall of 1990, the stock traded in the general range of $60 to $70 per share, and it has ranged from a high of $75 to a low of $10 during the past 10 years. The price rises and falls depending (1) on how the company is doing at a given point in time, (2) on what is happening to other stock prices, and (3) most important, on how investors expect the company to do in the future. The *market value* (or price) does not depend directly on, and is usually different from, the book value. Book value, or the firm's common equity per share, is determined by accountants as the sum of assets valued at their original costs minus accumulated depreciation, minus

---

[2]If anything were left from the proceeds of the asset sale after creditors had been paid off, this residual would go to the stockholders. The status of the different types of investors, and bankruptcy proceedings in general, are discussed in more detail in Appendix 16A. As a general rule, the order of priority of different claimants in the event of bankruptcy is: (1) secured creditors' claims from the proceeds from the sale of the specific assets securing their loans, such as a building which secures a mortgage; (2) employees for accrued wages; (3) federal and state governments for accrued taxes; (4) unfunded pension plan benefits; (5) unsecured creditors; (6) preferred stockholders; and (7), last in line, common stockholders. This priority system has a major effect on the riskiness and consequently on the required rates of return on different classes of securities.

[3]The $20.8 million shown in the common stock account indicates the actual dollars the company received for the 3,412,702 shares it has issued. As we discuss in Chapter 15, the common stock account is sometimes split into two accounts, one of which is called "par value" and the other called "paid-in capital," or the amount received in excess of par.

Table 2-2   Maynard Electronics Company: Income Statement for Year Ended December 31, 1990 (Millions of Dollars Except per Share Data)

Sales	$802.0
Cost of goods sold (excluding depreciation)	561.4
Other operating expenses	159.2
Depreciation	9.8
Total operating costs	$730.4
Earnings before interest and taxes (EBIT)	$ 71.6
Interest expense	25.2
Earnings before taxes	$ 46.4
Taxes (34%)	15.8
Net income before preferred dividends	$ 30.6
Preferred dividends	1.8
Net income available to common	$ 28.8
Common dividends	12.0
Additions to retained earnings	$ 16.8
Net cash flow (Net income + depreciation)	$ 38.6
Earnings per share (EPS)	$ 8.44
Dividends per share (DPS)	$ 3.52

all borrowed capital, minus preferred stockholders' claims, all divided by common shares outstanding. Market value, on the other hand, is a function of the cash expected to flow to stockholders in the future. It is easy to imagine a situation in which assets that were purchased years ago are worth far more today, hence it is easy to see why market values can be above (or below) book values.

Maynard's income statement for 1990 is shown in Table 2-2. We can see that Maynard had earnings available to common stockholders of $28.8 million, so the company earned $8.44 per share of stock outstanding. Of this amount, Maynard paid out $12 million, or $3.52 per share, in common dividends, and it retained $16.8 million.

Self-Test Questions

What are the two basic forms of capital?

List the priority of claims against a firm's income and assets.

Define a stock's book value and its market value. Why do the two generally differ?

ACCOUNTING INCOME VERSUS CASH FLOW

When you studied income statements in accounting, the emphasis was probably on determining the net income of the firm. In finance, however, we focus on *cash flows*. The value of an asset (or a whole firm) is determined by the cash flows it generates. The firm's net income is important, but cash flows are even more important, because dividends must be paid in cash, and cash is also necessary to purchase the assets required to continue operations.

As we discussed in Chapter 1, the goal of the firm should be to maximize the price of its stock. Since the value of any asset, including a share of stock, depends on the cash flows produced by the asset, managers should strive to maximize cash flows available to investors over the long run. A business's cash flows are generally equal to cash from sales, minus cash operating costs, minus interest charges, and minus taxes. Depreciation is an operating cost, so the greater the firm's depreciation charge, the lower its profits. However, depreciation is not a cash expenditure. Firms do not write checks to pay for depreciation, as they do for labor, materials, and taxes. Thus, a firm's cash flow in any year can be found by adding its depreciation expense to its net income. The greater the level of depreciation, other things held constant, the larger the firm's cash flows, because depreciation reduces taxable income, hence taxes.

To see more clearly how depreciation affects cash flows, consider the following simplified income statement (Column 1) and cash flow statement (Column 2). Here we assume that all sales revenues are received in cash during the year and that all costs except depreciation are paid in cash during the year. Cash flows are seen to equal net income plus depreciation:

	Income Statement (1)	Cash Flows (2)
Sales revenues	$1,500	$1,500
Costs except depreciation	1,050	1,050
Depreciation	150	—
Total costs	$1,200	$1,050 (Cash costs)
Taxable income	$ 300	$ 450 (Pretax cash flow)
Taxes (40%)	120	120 (From Column 1)
Net income	$ 180	
Add back depreciation	150	
Net cash flow	$ 330	$ 330

Now suppose Congress changes the tax laws and permits the company to depreciate its assets faster, which causes depreciation to rise from $150 to $300. Sales revenues and other costs remain unchanged. What effect will the change in depreciation have on net income and cash flows? The answer is worked out below:

	Income Statement (1)	Cash Flows (2)
Sales revenues	$1,500	$1,500
Costs except depreciation	1,050	1,050
Depreciation	300	—
Total costs	$1,350	$1,050 (Cash costs)
Taxable income	$ 150	$ 450 (Pretax cash flow)
Taxes (40%)	60	60 (From Column 1)
Net income	$ 90	
Add back depreciation	300	
Net cash flow	$ 390	$ 390

Thus, we see that the increase in depreciation caused the firm's net cash flow to increase from $330 to $390, or by $60.

The value of depreciation stems from the fact that it is tax deductible: One dollar in depreciation saves $1(Tax rate) in taxes. In this example, with a 40 percent tax rate, $150 of depreciation saves $150(0.40) = $60 in taxes, while $300 in depreciation saves $300(0.40) = $120 in taxes. Thus, an increase in depreciation from $150 to $300 increases the tax savings, hence the cash flow, by $120 − $60 = $60.

You might at this point notice that the increase in depreciation in the previous tables caused a decline in net income (from $180 to $90) and wonder if that is not bad. In other words, is the increase in depreciation good because it increases net cash flow or bad because it reduces net income? In this case, the assets are not wearing out any faster—all that has happened is that Congress has allowed the company to deduct larger depreciation charges before calculating its tax bill. The firm can, if it chooses, tell its accountants to calculate income for tax purposes as shown in the example, but to use a *different* (lower) amount of depreciation when they calculate the income they report to stockholders. Thus, because the increase in depreciation increases cash flow yet need not adversely affect net income as calculated by the accountants, the change in depreciation is unambiguously good.

As we shall see in Chapter 7, a stock's value is based on the *present value of the cash flows* which investors expect it to provide in the future. Although any individual investor could sell the stock and receive cash for it, the *cash flow* provided by the stock itself is the expected future dividend stream, and that expected dividend stream provides the fundamental basis for the stock's value.

Because dividends are paid in cash, a company's ability to pay dividends depends on its cash flows. Cash flows are generally related to *accounting profit,* which is simply net income as reported on the income statement. Companies with relatively high accounting profits generally have relatively high cash flows, but the relationship is not precise. Therefore, investors are concerned about cash flow projections as well as profit projections.

Firms can be thought of as having two separate but related bases of value: *existing assets,* which provide profits and cash flows, and *growth opportunities,* which represent opportunities to make new investments that will increase future profits and cash flows. The ability to take advantage of growth opportunities often depends on the availability of the cash needed to buy new assets, and the cash flows from existing assets are often the primary source for the funds used for profitable new investments. This is another reason for both investors and managers to be concerned with cash flows as well as profits.

For our purposes, it is useful to divide cash flows into two classes: (1) *operating cash flows* and (2) *other cash flows. Operating cash flows* are those that arise from normal operations, and they are, in essence, the difference between sales revenues and cash expenses, including taxes paid. Other cash flows arise from the issuance of stock, from borrowing, or from the sale of fixed assets, as illustrated by CBS's sale of The Dryden Press (the company that published this book) and its other textbook operations to Harcourt Brace Jovanovich for $550 million. Our focus here is on operating cash flows.

Operating cash flows can differ from accounting profits (or net income) for two primary reasons:

1. All the taxes reported on the income statement may not have to be paid during the current year, or, under certain circumstances, the actual cash payments for taxes may exceed the tax figure deducted from sales to calculate net income. The reasons for these tax cash flow differentials are discussed in detail in accounting courses, but we summarize them in Appendix 2A.

2. Sales may be on credit, hence not represent cash, and some of the expenses (or costs) deducted from sales to determine profits may not be cash costs. Most important, depreciation is not a cash cost.

Thus, operating cash flows could be larger or smaller than accounting profits during any given year. The effect of the major noncash expense, depreciation, was just discussed, and we consider the cash flow implications of sales on credit as opposed to sales for cash in a later chapter.

Self-Test Questions

Differentiate between operating cash flows and other cash flows.

List two reasons why operating cash flows can differ from net income.

In accounting, the emphasis is on the determination of net income. What is emphasized in finance, and why is that emphasis important?

Assuming that depreciation is the only non-cash cost, how can someone calculate a business's cash flow?

THE FEDERAL INCOME TAX SYSTEM

The value of any financial asset, such as a share of stock, a bond, or a mortgage, as well as the values of most real assets such as plants or even entire firms, depends on the stream of cash flows produced by the asset. Cash flows from an asset consist of *usable* income plus depreciation. Usable income means income *after taxes.* Proprietorship and partnership income must be reported by the owners, and it is taxed as their personal income. Most corporations, however, must first pay taxes on the corporation's own income, and then stockholders must pay additional taxes on all corporate after-tax income distributed as dividends. Therefore, both *personal* and *corporate* income taxes are important in the determination of the cash flows produced by financial assets.

Our tax laws can be changed by Congress, and in recent years changes have occurred almost every year. Indeed, a major change has occurred, on average, every 3 to 4 years since 1913, when our federal income tax system began. Further, certain parts of our tax system are tied to the rate of inflation, so changes automatically occur each year, depending on the rate of inflation during the previous year. Therefore, although this chapter will give you a good background on the basic nature of our tax system, you should consult current rate schedules and other data published by the Internal Revenue Service (and available in U.S. post offices) before you file your personal or business tax return!

Currently (1990), federal income tax rates for individuals go up to 33 percent, and when state and city income taxes are included, the marginal tax rate on an individual's income can exceed 40 percent. Business income is also taxed heavily. The income from partnerships and proprietorships is reported by the individual owners as personal income and, consequently, is taxed at rates going up to 40 percent or more. Corporate profits are subject to federal income tax rates of up to 39 percent, in addition to state income taxes. Because of the magnitude of the tax bite, taxes play an important role in many financial decisions.

Because the U.S. government is running a large fiscal deficit, many experts predict that tax rates will be raised in the not-too-distant future. Thus, by the time you read this chapter, rates may well be higher. Still, if you understand the chapter, you will be able to apply the new tax rates.

Taxes are so complicated that university law schools offer master's degrees in taxation to practicing lawyers, many of whom also have CPA certification. In a field complicated enough to warrant such detailed study, we can cover only the highlights. This is really enough, though, because business managers and investors should and do rely on tax specialists rather than trusting their own limited knowledge. Still, it is important to know the basic elements of the tax system as a starting point for discussions with tax experts.

Individual Income Taxes

Individuals pay taxes on wages and salaries, on investment income (dividends, interest, and profits from the sale of securities), and on the profits of proprietorships and partnerships. Our tax rates are *progressive* — that is, the higher one's income, the larger the percentage paid in taxes.[4] Table 2-3 gives the tax rates for single individuals and married couples filing joint returns under the rate schedules in effect in 1990.

1. *Taxable income* is defined as gross income less a set of exemptions and deductions which are spelled out in the instructions to the tax forms individuals must file. When filing a tax return in 1991 for the tax year 1990, each taxpayer will receive an exemption of $2,050 for each dependent, including the taxpayer, which reduces taxable income. However, this exemption is indexed to rise with inflation, and high-income taxpayers must pay a surtax, which takes away the value of personal exemp-

---

[4]Prior to the 1986 Tax Code revisions, individual rates were more steeply progressive, going from 11 percent to 50 percent, but higher-income taxpayers were able to use a variety of tax shelters that lowered effective tax rates substantially. Indeed, many people had cash income in the millions of dollars yet were able to completely avoid taxes. The 1986 changes eliminated most tax shelters. Also, the revisions increased dramatically the tax rate on capital gains, most of which are earned by wealthy individuals. Therefore, in reality, the new law did not lower the progressivity of our tax system.

Table 2-3   Individual Tax Rates for 1990

Single Individuals

If Your Taxable Income Is	You Pay This Amount on the Base of the Bracket	Plus This Percentage on the Excess over the Base	Average Tax Rate at Top of Bracket
Up to $19,450	$ 0	15%	15.0%
$19,450–$47,050	2,918	28	22.6
$47,050–$97,620	10,646	33	28.0
Over $97,620	27,334	28	28.0

Married Couples Filing Joint Returns

If Your Taxable Income Is	You Pay This Amount on the Base of the Bracket	Plus This Percentage on the Excess over the Base	Average Tax Rate at Top of Bracket
Up to $32,450	$ 0	15%	15.0%
$32,450–$78,400	4,868	28	22.6
$78,400–$162,770	17,734	33	28.0
Over $162,770	45,576	28	28.0

Notes:

a. The tax rates are for 1990 and beyond. However, the income ranges at which the 28 percent rate takes effect, as well as the ranges for the surtax discussed below, are scheduled to be indexed with inflation each year beyond 1990, so they will change from those shown in the table.

b. Technically, a surtax of 5 percent is imposed on income in the range $47,050 to $97,620 for single individuals and in the range $78,400 to $162,770 for married couples. This surtax is designed to eliminate the effects of the 15 percent rate on the first increments of income and to eliminate the benefits of the personal exemption. The surtax ceases when the personal exemption has been fully offset; thus, the dollar amount at which the marginal rate drops back to 28 percent depends on the number of exemptions claimed. The highest bracket amounts shown in this table assume one exemption for a single individual and two exemptions for a married couple. Different tables, similar to the one we present but with different numbers of exemptions, are available from the Internal Revenue Service.

tions. Also, certain expenses, such as mortgage interest paid, state and local income taxes paid, and charitable contributions, can be deducted and thus be used to reduce taxable income.

2.   The *marginal tax rate* is defined as the tax on the last unit of income. Marginal rates begin at 15 percent, rise to 28 and then to 33 percent, and finally fall back to 28 percent. The average tax rate on all taxable income rises from zero to 28 percent.

3.   One can calculate *average tax rates* from the data in Table 2-3. For example, if Jill Smith, a single individual, had taxable income of $35,000, her tax bill would be $2,918 + ($35,000 − $19,450)(0.28) = $2,918 + $4,354 = $7,272. Her *average tax rate* would be $7,272/$35,000 = 20.8% versus a *marginal rate* of 28 percent. If Jill received a raise of $1,000, bringing her income to $36,000, she would have to pay $280 of it as taxes, so her after-tax raise would be $720.

4.   As indicated in the notes to the table, current legislation provides for tax brackets to be indexed to inflation to avoid the *bracket creep* that occurred during the 1970s and that de facto raised tax rates substantially.[5]

Taxes on Dividend and Interest Income. Dividend and interest income received by individuals from corporate securities is added to other income and thus is taxed at rates going up to 33 percent. Since corporations pay dividends out of earnings that have already been taxed, there is *double taxation* of corporate income.

It should be noted that under U.S. tax laws, interest on most state and local government bonds, called *municipals* or *"munis,"* is not subject to federal income taxes. Thus, investors get to keep all of the interest received from most municipal bonds but only a fraction of the interest received from bonds issued by corporations or by the U.S. government. This means that a lower-yielding muni can provide the same after-tax return as a higher-yielding corporate bond. For example, a taxpayer in the 33 percent marginal tax bracket who could buy a muni that yielded 10 percent would have to receive a before-tax yield of 14.93 percent on a corporate or U.S. Treasury bond to have the same after-tax income:

$$\frac{\text{Equivalent pretax yield}}{\text{on taxable bond}} = \frac{\text{Yield on muni}}{1 - \text{Marginal tax rate}} = \frac{10\%}{1 - 0.33} = 14.93\%.$$

If we know the yield on the taxable bond, we can use the following equation to find the equivalent yield on a muni:

$$\text{Yield on muni} = \left(\begin{array}{c}\text{Pretax yield} \\ \text{on taxable} \\ \text{bond}\end{array}\right)(1 - \text{Marginal tax rate})$$

$$= 14.93\% \, (1 - 0.33) = 14.93\%(0.67) = 10.0\%.$$

The exemption from federal taxes stems from the separation of federal and state powers, and its primary effect is to help state and local governments borrow at lower rates than would otherwise be available to them.

Capital Gains versus Ordinary Income. Assets such as stocks, bonds, and real estate are defined as *capital assets*. If you buy a capital asset and later sell it for more than your purchase price, the profit is called a *capital gain;* if you suffer a loss, it is

---

[5]For example, if you were single and had a taxable income of $19,450, your tax bill would be $2,918. Now suppose inflation caused prices to double and your income, being tied to a cost-of-living index, rose to $38,900. Because our tax rates are progressive, if tax brackets were not indexed, your taxes would jump to $8,364. Your after-tax income would thus increase from $16,532 to $30,536, but, because prices have doubled, your real income would *decline* from $16,532 to $15,268 (calculated as one-half of $30,536). You would be in a higher tax bracket, so you would be paying a higher percentage of your real income in taxes. If this happened to everyone, and if Congress failed to change tax rates sufficiently, real disposable incomes would decline because the federal government would be taking a larger share of the national product. This is called the federal government's "inflation dividend." However, since tax brackets are now indexed, if your income doubled due to inflation, your tax bill would double, but your after-tax real income would remain constant at $16,532. Bracket creep was a real problem during the 1970s and early 1980s, but indexing—if it stays in the law—will put an end to it.

called a *capital loss.* An asset sold within one year of the time it was purchased produces a *short-term gain or loss,* whereas one held for more than one year produces a *long-term gain or loss.* Thus, if you buy 100 shares of Disney stock for $70 per share and sell it for $80 per share, you make a capital gain of 100 × $10, or $1,000. However, if you sell the stock for $60 per share, you will have a $1,000 capital loss. If you hold the stock for more than one year, the gain or loss is long-term; otherwise, it is short-term. If you sell the stock for exactly $70 per share, you make neither a gain nor a loss; you simply get your $7,000 back, and no tax is due.

From 1921 through 1986, long-term capital gains were taxed at substantially lower rates than ordinary income. For example, in 1986 long-term capital gains were taxed at only 40 percent of the tax rate on ordinary income. However, the tax law changes which took effect in 1987 eliminated this differential, and all capital gains income (both long-term and short-term) is now taxed as if it were ordinary income.

There was a great deal of controversy over the elimination of the preferential rate for capital gains. It was argued that lower tax rates on capital gains (1) stimulated the flow of venture capital to new, start-up businesses (which generally provide capital gains as opposed to dividend income) and (2) caused companies to retain and reinvest a high percentage of their earnings in order to provide their stockholders with capital gains as opposed to highly taxed dividend income. Thus, it was argued that elimination of the favorable rates on capital gains would retard investment and economic growth. The proponents of preferential capital gains tax rates lost the argument in 1986, but they did succeed in keeping in the law all the language dealing with capital gains, which would make it easy to reinstate the differential if economic conditions suggest that it is indeed needed to encourage growth. As we discussed in the opening section, the Bush administration tried to lower capital gains taxes in 1989, and there are strong indications that they will try again in 1990. Therefore, you should not be surprised if the capital gains differential is reinstated in the future.

When capital gains were taxed at lower rates, this had implications for dividend policy (it favored lower payouts and hence higher earnings retention). It also favored stock investments over bond investments, because part of the income from stock normally comes from capital gains. Thus, one can anticipate changes in corporate dividend and capital structure policy as a result of tax changes which affect capital gains tax rates.

Corporate Income Taxes

The corporate tax structure, shown in Table 2-4, is relatively simple. To illustrate, if a firm had $75,000 of taxable income, its tax bill would be:

$$\text{Taxes} = \$7,500 + 0.25(\$25,000)$$

$$= \$7,500 + \$6,250 = \$13,750,$$

and its average tax rate would be $13,750/$75,000 = 18.3%. Note that for all income over $335,000, one can disregard the surtax and simply calculate the corporate

Table 2-4   Corporate Tax Rates

If a Corporation's Taxable Income Is	It Pays This Amount on the Base of the Bracket	Plus This Percentage on the Excess over the Base	Average Tax Rate at Top of Bracket
Up to $50,000	$ 0	15%	15.0%
$50,000 to $75,000	7,500	25	18.3
$75,000 to $100,000	13,750	34	22.3
$100,000 to $335,000	22,250	39	34.0
Over $335,000	113,900	34	34.0

Notes:

a. The rates shown here are for 1990 and beyond.

b. For income in the range of $100,000 to $335,000, a surtax of 5% is added to the base rate of 34%. This surtax, which eliminates the effects of the lower rates on income below $75,000, results in a marginal tax rate of 39% for income in the $100,000 to $335,000 range.

tax as 34 percent of all taxable income. Thus, the corporate tax is progressive up to $335,000 of income, but it is constant thereafter.[6]

Interest and Dividend Income Received by a Corporation. Interest income received by a corporation is taxed as ordinary income at regular corporate tax rates. However, 70 percent of the dividends received by one corporation from another is excluded from taxable income, while the remaining 30 percent is taxed at the ordinary tax rate.[7] Thus, a corporation earning over $335,000 and paying a 34 percent marginal tax rate would pay only $(0.30)(0.34) = 0.102 = 10.2\%$ of its dividend

[6]Prior to 1987, many large, profitable corporations such as General Electric and Boeing paid no income taxes. The reasons for this were as follows: (1) expenses, especially depreciation, were defined differently for calculating taxable income than for reporting earnings to stockholders, so some companies reported positive profits to stockholders but losses—hence no taxes—to the Internal Revenue Service; and (2) some companies which did have tax liabilities used various tax credits, including the investment tax credit (discussed later in the chapter) to offset taxes that would otherwise have been payable. This situation was effectively eliminated in 1987.

The principal method used to eliminate this situation is the Alternative Minimum Tax (AMT). Under the AMT, both corporate and individual taxpayers must figure their taxes in two ways, the "regular" way and the AMT way, and then pay the higher of the two. The AMT is calculated as follows: (1) Figure your regular taxes. (2) Take your taxable income under the regular method and then add back certain items, especially income on certain municipal bonds, depreciation in excess of straight line depreciation, certain research and drilling costs, itemized or standard deductions (for individuals), and a number of other items. (3) The income determined in (2) is defined as AMT income, and it must then be multiplied by the AMT tax rate (21% in 1990) to determine the tax due under the AMT system. An individual or corporation must then pay the higher of the regular tax or the AMT tax.

[7]The size of the dividend exclusion actually depends on the degree of ownership. Corporations that own less than 20 percent of the stock of the dividend-paying company can exclude 70 percent of the dividends received; firms that own over 20 percent but less than 80 percent can exclude 80 percent of the dividends; and firms that own over 80 percent can exclude the entire dividend payment. Since most companies own less than 20 percent of other companies, we will, in general, assume a 70 percent dividend exclusion.

income as taxes, so its effective tax rate on intercorporate dividends would be 10.2 percent. If this firm had $10,000 in pretax dividend income, its after-tax dividend income would be $8,980:

$$\begin{aligned}
\frac{\text{After-tax}}{\text{income}} &= \text{Before-tax income} - \text{Taxes} \\
&= \text{Before-tax income} - (\text{Before-tax income})(\text{Effective tax rate}) \\
&= \text{Before-tax income}(1 - \text{Effective tax rate}) \\
&= \$10,000\,[1 - (0.30)(0.34)] \\
&= \$10,000(1 - 0.102) = \$10,000(0.898) = \$8,980.
\end{aligned}$$

If the corporation pays its own after-tax income out to its stockholders as dividends, the income is ultimately subjected to *triple taxation:* (1) The original corporation is first taxed, (2) the second corporation is then taxed on the dividends it received, and (3) the individuals who receive the final dividends are taxed again. This is the reason for the 70 percent exclusion on intercorporate dividends.

If a corporation has surplus funds that can be invested in marketable securities, the tax factor favors investment in stocks, which pay dividends, rather than in bonds, which pay interest. For example, suppose GE had $100,000 to invest, and it could buy either bonds that paid interest of $8,000 per year or preferred stock that paid dividends of $7,000. GE is in the 34 percent tax bracket; therefore, its tax on the interest, if it bought bonds, would be 0.34($8,000) = $2,720 and its after-tax income would be $5,280. If it bought preferred stock, its tax would be 0.34[(0.30)($7,000)] = $714 and its after-tax income would be $6,286. Other factors might lead GE to invest in bonds, but the tax factor certainly favors stock investments when the investor is a corporation.[8]

Interest and Dividends Paid by a Corporation. A firm's operations can be financed either with debt or equity capital. If it uses debt, it must pay interest on this debt, whereas if it uses equity, it must pay dividends to the equity investors (stockholders). The interest paid by a corporation is deducted from its operating income to obtain its taxable income, but dividends paid are not deductible. Therefore, a firm needs $1 of pretax income to pay $1 of interest, but if it is in the 40 percent federal-plus-state tax bracket, it needs

$$\frac{\$1}{1 - \text{Tax rate}} = \frac{\$1}{0.60} = \$1.67$$

of pretax income to pay $1 of dividends.

---

[8]This illustration demonstrates why corporations favor investing in lower-yielding preferred stocks over higher-yielding bonds. When tax consequences are considered, the yield on the preferred stock, $[1 - 0.34(0.30)](7.0\%) = 6.286\%$, is higher than the yield on the bond, $(1 - 0.34)(8.0\%) = 5.280\%$. Also note that corporations are restricted in their use of borrowed funds to purchase other firms' preferred or common stocks. Without such restrictions, firms could engage in *tax arbitrage,* whereby the interest on borrowed funds reduces taxable income on a dollar-for-dollar basis, but taxable income is increased by only $0.30 per dollar of dividend income. Thus, current tax laws reduce the 70 percent dividend exclusion in proportion to the amount of borrowed funds used to purchase the stock.

Table 2-5   Cash Flows to Investors under Bond and Stock Financing

	Use Bonds (1)	Use Stock (2)
Operating income before interest and taxes	$1,500,000	$1,500,000
Interest	1,500,000	0
Taxable income	$ 0	$1,500,000
Federal-plus-state taxes (40%)	0	600,000
After-tax income	$ 0	$ 900,000
Income to investors	$1,500,000	$ 900,000
Advantage to bonds	$ 600,000	

To illustrate, Table 2-5 shows the situation for a firm with $1.5 million of operating income before interest and taxes. As shown in Column 1, if the firm were financed entirely by bonds, and if it made interest payments of $1.5 million, its taxable income would be zero, taxes would be zero, and its investors would receive the entire $1.5 million. (The term *investors* includes both stockholders and bondholders.) As shown in Column 2, if the firm had no debt and was therefore financed only by stock, all of the $1.5 million of operating income would be taxable income to the corporation, the tax would be $1,500,000(0.40) = $600,000, and investors would receive only $0.9 million versus $1.5 million under debt financing.

Of course, it is generally not possible to finance exclusively with debt capital, and the risk of doing so would offset the benefits of the higher expected income. *Still, the fact that interest is a deductible expense has a profound effect on the way businesses are financed—our tax system favors debt financing over equity financing.* This point is discussed in more detail in Chapters 12 and 13.

Corporate Capital Gains.   Before 1987, corporate long-term capital gains were taxed at rates lower than ordinary income, just as with individuals. Under current law, however, corporations' capital gains are taxed at the same rates as their operating income. There is a chance, though, that a favorable capital gains tax rate will be reinstated in the future.

Corporate Loss Carry-Back and Carry-Forward.   Ordinary corporate operating losses can be carried back *(carry-back)* to each of the preceding 3 years and forward *(carry-forward)* for the next 15 years in the future to offset taxable income in those years. For example, an operating loss in 1991 could be carried back and used to reduce taxable income in 1988, 1989, and 1990, and forward, if necessary, and used in 1992, 1993, and so on, to the year 2006. The loss must be applied first to the earliest year, then to the next earliest year, and so on, until losses have been used up or the 15-year carry-forward limit has been reached.

To illustrate, suppose Apex Corporation had a $2 million *pretax* profit (taxable income) in 1988, 1989, and 1990, and then, in 1991, Apex lost $12 million as shown in Table 2-6. Also, assume that Apex's tax rate is 40 percent. The company would

Table 2-6   Apex Corporation: Calculation of Loss Carry-Back and Carry-Forward for 1988–1990 Using a $12 Million 1991 Loss

	1988	1989	1990
Original taxable income	$2,000,000	$2,000,000	$2,000,000
Carry-back credit	− 2,000,000	− 2,000,000	− 2,000,000
Adjusted profit	$ 0	$ 0	$ 0
Taxes previously paid (40%)	800,000	800,000	800,000
Difference = Tax refund	$ 800,000	$ 800,000	$ 800,000

Total refund check received in 1992: $800,000 + $800,000 + $800,000 = $2,400,000.
Amount of loss carry-forward available for use in 1992–2006:

1991 loss	$12,000,000
Carry-back losses used	6,000,000
Carry-forward losses still available	$ 6,000,000

use the carry-back feature to recompute its taxes for 1988, using $2 million of the 1991 operating losses to reduce the 1988 pretax profit to zero. This would permit it to recover the amount of taxes paid in 1988. Therefore, in 1992 Apex would receive a refund of its 1988 taxes because of the loss experienced in 1991. Because $10 million of the unrecovered losses would still be available, Apex would repeat this procedure for 1989 and 1990. Thus, in 1992 the company would pay zero taxes for 1991 and also would receive a refund for taxes paid from 1988 through 1990. Apex would still have $6 million of unrecovered losses to carry forward, subject to the 15-year limit, until the entire $12 million loss had been used to offset taxable income. The purpose of permitting this loss treatment is, of course, to avoid penalizing corporations whose incomes fluctuate substantially from year to year.

Improper Accumulation to Avoid Payment of Dividends.   Corporations could refrain from paying dividends to permit their stockholders to avoid personal income taxes on dividends. To prevent this, the Tax Code contains an *improper accumulation* provision which states that earnings accumulated by a corporation are subject to penalty rates *if the purpose of the accumulation is to enable stockholders to avoid personal income taxes.* A cumulative total of $250,000 (the balance sheet item "retained earnings") is by law exempted from the improper accumulation tax for most corporations. This is a benefit primarily to small corporations.

The improper accumulation penalty applies only if the retained earnings in excess of $250,000 are *shown to be unnecessary to meet the reasonable needs of the business.* A great many companies do indeed have legitimate reasons for retaining more than $250,000 of earnings. For example, earnings may be retained and used to pay off debt, to finance growth, or to provide the corporation with a cushion against possible cash drains caused by losses. How much a firm should properly accumulate for uncertain contingencies is a matter of judgment. We shall consider this matter again in Chapter 14, which deals with corporate dividend policy.

Consolidated Corporate Tax Returns. If a corporation owns 80 percent or more of another corporation's stock, it can aggregate income and file one consolidated tax return; thus, the losses of one company can be used to offset the profits of another. (Similarly, one division's losses can be used to offset another division's profits.) No business ever wants to incur losses (you can go broke losing $1 to save 34¢ in taxes), but tax offsets do make it more feasible for large, multidivisional corporations to undertake risky new ventures or ventures that will suffer losses during a developmental period.

Taxation of Small Businesses: S Corporations

The Internal Revenue Code provides that small businesses which meet certain restrictions as spelled out in the code may be set up as corporations and thus receive the benefits of the corporate form of organization—especially limited liability—yet still be taxed as proprietorships or partnerships rather than as corporations. These corporations are called *S corporations.*

Self-Test Questions

Explain what is meant by the statement: "Our tax rates are progressive."

Are tax rates progressive for all income ranges?

Explain the difference between marginal tax rates and average tax rates.

What is "bracket creep," and how did the government avoid it in the late 1980s?

What are capital gains and losses, and how are they differentiated from ordinary income?

How does the federal income tax system tax corporate dividends received by a corporation and those received by an individual? Why is this distinction made?

Briefly explain how tax loss carry-back and carry-forward procedures work.

DEPRECIATION

Suppose a firm buys a milling machine for $100,000 and uses it for 5 years, after which it is scrapped. The cost of the goods produced by the machine must include a charge for the machine, and this charge is called *depreciation.* Because depreciation reduces profits as calculated by the accountants, the higher a firm's depreciation charges, the lower its reported net income. However, depreciation is not a cash charge, so higher depreciation does not reduce cash flows. Indeed, higher depreciation *increases* cash flows, because the greater a firm's depreciation, the lower its tax bill.

Companies generally calculate depreciation one way when figuring taxes and another way when reporting income to investors: most use the *straight line* method for stockholder reporting (or "book" purposes), but they use the fastest rate permitted by law for tax purposes. Under the straight line method used for stockholder reporting, one normally takes the cost of the asset, subtracts its estimated salvage value, and divides the net amount by the asset's useful economic life. For an asset with a 5-year life, which costs $100,000 and has a $12,500 salvage value, the annual straight line depreciation charge is ($100,000 − $12,500)/5 = $17,500.

For tax purposes, Congress changes the permissible tax depreciation methods from time to time. Prior to 1954, the straight line method was required for tax purposes, but in 1954 *accelerated* methods (double declining balance and sum-of-years'-digits) were permitted. Then, in 1981, the old accelerated methods were replaced by a simpler procedure known as the Accelerated Cost Recovery System (ACRS). The ACRS system was changed again in 1986 as a part of the Tax Reform Act, and it is now known as the *Modified Accelerated Cost Recovery System (MACRS)*.

Tax Depreciation Life

For tax purposes, the cost of an asset is expensed over its depreciable life. Historically, an asset's depreciable life was determined by its estimated useful economic life; it was intended that an asset would be fully depreciated at approximately the same time that it reached the end of its useful economic life. However, MACRS totally abandons that practice and sets simple guidelines which create several classes of assets, each with a more-or-less arbitrarily prescribed life called a *recovery period* or *class life*. The MACRS class life bears only a rough relationship to the expected useful economic life.

A major effect of the MACRS system has been to shorten the depreciable lives of assets, thus giving businesses larger tax deductions and thereby increasing their cash flows available for reinvestment. Table 2-7 describes the types of property that fit into the different class life groups, and Table 2-8 sets forth the MACRS recovery allowances (depreciation rates) for selected classes of investment property.

Consider Table 2-7 first. The first column gives the MACRS class life, while the second column describes the types of assets which fall into each category. Property in the 27.5- and 31.5-year categories (real estate) must be depreciated by the straight line method, but 3-, 5-, 7-, and 10-year property (personal property) can be depreciated either by the accelerated method which uses the rates shown in Table 2-8 or by an alternate straight line method.[9]

As we saw earlier in the chapter, higher depreciation expenses result in lower taxes and hence higher cash flows. Therefore, since a firm has the choice of using the alternate straight line rates or the accelerated rates shown in Table 2-8, it should elect to use the accelerated rates. The yearly recovery allowance, or depreciation expense, is determined by multiplying each asset's *depreciable basis* by the applicable recovery percentage shown in Table 2-8. Calculations are discussed in the following sections.

---

[9]As a benefit to very small companies, the Tax Code also permits companies to *expense,* which is equivalent to depreciating over one year, up to $10,000 of equipment. Thus, if a small company bought one asset worth up to $10,000, it could write the asset off in the year it was acquired. This is called "Section 179 expensing." We shall disregard this provision throughout the book.

Table 2-7	Major Classes and Asset Lives for MACRS

Class	Type of Property
3-year	Computers and equipment used in research.
5-year	Automobiles, tractor units, light-duty trucks, computers, and certain special manufacturing tools.
7-year	Most industrial equipment, office furniture, and fixtures.
10-year	Certain longer-lived types of equipment.
27.5-year	Residential rental real property such as apartment buildings.
31.5-year	All nonresidential real property, including commercial and industrial buildings.

Table 2-8	Recovery Allowance Percentages for Personal Property

Ownership Year	Class of Investment			
	3-Year	5-Year	7-Year	10-Year
1	33%	20%	14%	10%
2	45	32	25	18
3	15	19	17	14
4	7	12	13	12
5		11	9	9
6		6	9	7
7			9	7
8			4	7
9				7
10				6
11				3
	100%	100%	100%	100%

Notes:

a. We developed these recovery allowance percentages based on the 200 percent declining balance method prescribed by MACRS, with a switch to straight line depreciation at some point in the asset's life. For example, consider the 5-year recovery allowance percentages. The straight line percentage would be 20 percent per year, so the 200 percent declining balance multiplier is 2.0(20%) = 40% = 0.4. However, because the half-year convention applies, the MACRS percentage for Year 1 is 20 percent. For Year 2, there is 80 percent of the depreciable basis remaining to be depreciated, so the recovery allowance percentage is 0.40(80%) = 32%. In Year 3, 20% + 32% = 52% of the depreciation has been taken, leaving 48%, so the percentage is 0.4(48%) ≈ 19%. In Year 4, the percentage is 0.4(29%) ≈ 12%. After 4 years, straight line depreciation exceeds the declining balance depreciaticn, so a switch is made to straight line (this is permitted under the law). However, the half-year convention must also be applied at the end of the class life, and the remaining 17 percent of depreciation must be taken (amortized) over 1.5 years. Thus, the percentage in Year 5 is 17%/1.5 ≈ 11%, and in Year 6, 17% − 11% = 6%. Although the tax tables carry the allowance percentages out to two decimal places, we have rounded to the nearest whole number for ease of illustration.

b. Residential rental property (apartments) is depreciated over a 27.5-year life, whereas commercial and industrial structures are depreciated over 31.5 years. In both cases, straight line depreciation must be used. The depreciation allowance for the first year is based, pro rata, on the month the asset was placed in service, with the remainder of the first year's depreciation being taken in the 28th or 32nd year.

Half-Year Convention. Under MACRS, the assumption is generally made that property is placed in service in the middle of the first year. Thus, for 3-year class life property, the recovery period begins in the middle of the year the asset is placed in service and ends 3 years later. The effect of the *half-year convention* is to extend the recovery period out one more year, so 3-year class life property is depreciated over 4 calendar years, 5-year property is depreciated over 6 calendar years, and so on. This convention is incorporated into Table 2-8's recovery allowance percentages.[10]

Depreciable Basis. The *depreciable basis* is a critical element of MACRS, because each year's allowance (depreciation expense) depends jointly on the asset's depreciable basis and its MACRS class life. The depreciable basis under MACRS is equal to the purchase price of the asset plus any shipping and installation costs. The basis is *not* adjusted for *salvage value* (which is the estimated market value of the asset at the end of its useful life) regardless of whether accelerated or the alternate straight line method is used.

Investment Tax Credit. An *investment tax credit (ITC)* provides for a direct reduction of taxes, and its purpose is to stimulate business investment. ITCs were first introduced during the Kennedy administration in 1961, and they have subsequently been put in and taken out of the tax system, depending on how Congress feels about the need to stimulate business investment versus the need for federal revenues. Immediately prior to the 1986 Tax Reform Act, ITCs applied to depreciable personal property with a life of 3 or more years, and the credit amounted to 6 percent for short-lived assets and 10 percent for longer-lived assets. The credit was determined by multiplying the cost of the asset by the applicable percentage. However, ITCs were eliminated by the 1986 tax revision. Nevertheless, you should be aware of what ITCs are, because they may be reinstated at some future date if Congress deems that they are needed to stimulate investment.

Sale of a Depreciable Asset. If a depreciable asset is sold, the sale price (actual salvage value) minus the then-existing undepreciated tax book value is added to operating income and taxed at the firm's marginal tax rate. For example, suppose a firm buys a 5-year class life asset for $100,000 and sells it at the end of the fourth year for $25,000. The asset's tax book value is equal to $100,000(0.11 + 0.06) = $100,000(0.17) = $17,000. Therefore, $25,000 − $17,000 = $8,000 is added to the firm's operating income and is taxed.

---

[10]The half-year convention also applies if the straight line alternative is used, with half of one year's depreciation taken in the first year, a full year's depreciation taken in each of the remaining years of the asset's class life, and the remaining half-year's depreciation taken in the year following the end of the class life. You should recognize that virtually all companies have computerized depreciation systems. Each asset's depreciation pattern is programmed into the system at the time of its acquisition, and the computer aggregates the depreciation allowances for all assets when the accountants close the books and prepare the financial statements and tax returns.

Depreciation Illustration. Assume that Apex Corporation buys a $150,000 computer, which falls into the MACRS 5-year class life, and places it into service on March 15, 1991. Apex must pay an additional $30,000 for delivery and installation. Salvage value is not considered, so the computer's depreciable basis is $180,000. (Delivery and installation charges are included in the depreciable basis rather than expensed in the year incurred.) Each year's recovery allowance (tax depreciation expense) is determined by multiplying the depreciable basis by the applicable recovery allowance percentage. Thus, the depreciation expense for 1991 is 0.20($180,000) = $36,000, and for 1992 it is 0.32($180,000) = $57,600. Similarly, the depreciation expense is $34,200 for 1993, $21,600 for 1994, $19,800 for 1995, and $10,800 for 1996. The total depreciation expense over the 6-year recovery period is $180,000, which is equal to the depreciable basis of the computer.

Self-Test Questions

What are the key differences between the straight line depreciation method used for reporting purposes and the MACRS accelerated method used for tax purposes?

What is the difference between the concept of useful economic life and the MACRS recovery period, or class life?

How do you determine the depreciable basis of an asset, and how does salvage value affect the depreciable basis of an asset?

How does one calculate an asset's MACRS depreciation expense?

What is the purpose of the ITC, and is it available under current tax laws?

How would you calculate the tax involved if a partially depreciated asset were sold?

SUMMARY

This chapter presented some background information on financial statements, business securities, income taxes, and cash flows. The key concepts covered are listed below.

- Firms need capital to acquire assets, and they raise this capital by issuing *debt* and *equity* securities, and by *retaining earnings*.

- *Debtholders,* or *creditors,* have first claim to the firm's earnings and assets, whereas the *common equity holders* (the firm's owners) are last in line to be paid. Stockholders' rewards can be high, but they can also be low.

- The value of any asset depends on the stream of *after-tax cash flows* it produces. Tax rates and other aspects of our tax system are changed by Congress every year or so.

- In the United States, income tax rates are *progressive* — the higher one's income, the larger the percentage paid in taxes, up to a point.

- Assets such as stocks, bonds, and real estate are defined as *capital assets.* If a capital asset is sold for more than the purchase price, the profit is called a *capital gain.* If the capital asset is sold for a loss, it is called a *capital loss.*

- Operating income paid out as dividends is subject to *double taxation,* because the income is first taxed at the corporate level, and then shareholders must pay personal taxes on their dividends.

- *Interest income* received by a corporation is taxed as *ordinary income;* however, 70 percent of the dividends received by one corporation from another are excluded from *taxable income.* The reason for this exclusion is that this income is ultimately subjected to *triple taxation.*

- Because interest paid by a corporation is a *deductible* expense, while dividends are not, our tax system favors debt financing over equity financing.

- Ordinary corporate operating losses can be carried back *(carry-back)* to each of the preceding 3 years and forward *(carry-forward)* for the next 15 years to offset taxable income in those years.

- Fixed assets are *depreciated* over time to reflect the decline in value of the assets. *Depreciation* is a tax-deductible, but noncash, expense. The higher the firm's depreciation, the lower its taxes and the higher its cash flows, other things held constant.

- Current tax laws permit fixed assets to be depreciated using the *Modified Accelerated Cost Recovery System (MACRS).* Tax depreciation rules have a major impact on the profitability of capital investments.

- Under MACRS, depreciation expense is calculated as the yearly *recovery allowance percentage* multiplied by the asset's depreciable basis. The asset's *depreciable basis* is equal to the purchase price of the asset plus any shipping and installation costs.

- If a depreciable asset is sold, the sale price minus the then-existing *undepreciated book value* is added to operating income and taxed at the firm's *marginal tax rate.*

- *Operating cash flows* differ from reported *accounting income.* Investors should be more interested in a firm's projected cash flows than in reported earnings, because it is cash, not paper profits, that is paid out as dividends and plowed back into the business to produce growth.

- *S corporations* are small businesses that enjoy the limited-liability benefits of the corporate form of organization, yet obtain the benefits of being taxed as a partnership or a proprietorship.

Questions

2-1   Define each of the following terms:
  a.   Retained earnings
  b.   Common equity
  c.   Progressive tax
  d.   Marginal and average tax rates
  e.   Bracket creep
  f.   Capital gain or loss
  g.   Tax loss carry-back and carry-forward
  h.   Improper accumulation

      i.   MACRS depreciation; half-year convention; depreciable basis
      j.   Investment tax credit (ITC)
      k.   S corporation
      l.   Cash flow; operating cash flow; accounting profit

2-2   Suppose you owned 100 shares of General Motors stock, and the company earned $6 per share during the last reporting period. Suppose further that GM could either pay all its earnings out as dividends (in which case you would receive $600) or retain the earnings in the business, buy more assets, and cause the price of the stock to go up by $6 per share (in which case the value of your stock would rise by $600).

      a.   How would the tax laws influence what you, as a typical stockholder, would want the company to do?

      b.   Would your choice be influenced by how much other income you had? Why might the desires of a 45-year-old doctor differ with respect to corporate dividend policy from those of a pension fund manager or a retiree living on a small income?

      c.   How might the corporation's decision with regard to dividend policy influence the price of its stock?

2-3   What does *double taxation of corporate income* mean?

2-4   If you were starting a business, what tax considerations might cause you to prefer to set it up as a proprietorship or a partnership rather than as a corporation?

2-5   Explain how the federal income tax structure affects the choice of financing (use of debt versus equity) of U.S. business firms.

2-6   How can the federal government influence the level of business investment by adjusting the investment tax credit (ITC)? By changing depreciation rules?

2-7   For someone planning to start a new business, is the average or the marginal tax rate more relevant?

Problems

(Note: By the time this book is published, Congress may have changed rates and/or other provisions of current tax law—as noted in the chapter, such changes occur fairly often. Work all problems on the assumption that the information in the chapter is still current.)

2-1   **(Corporate tax liability)** The Wingler Corporation had a 1990 taxable income of $140,000 from operations after all operating costs but before (1) interest charges of $10,000, (2) dividends received of $20,000, (3) dividends paid of $25,000, and (4) income taxes. What is the firm's income tax liability and after-tax income?

2-2   **(Corporate tax liability)** The Martell Corporation had $200,000 of taxable income from operations in 1990.

      a.   What is the company's federal income tax bill for the year?

      b.   Assume the firm receives an additional $20,000 of interest income from some bonds it owns. What is the tax on this interest income?

      c.   Now assume that Martell does not receive the interest income but does receive an additional $20,000 as dividends on some stock it owns. What is the tax on this dividend income?

2-3   **(Loss carry-back, carry-forward)** The Edwards Company has made $200,000 before taxes during each of the last 15 years, and it expects to make $200,000 a year before taxes in the future. However, this year (1991) the firm incurred a loss of $1,200,000. The firm will claim a tax credit at the time it files its 1991 income tax return, and it will receive a check from the

U.S. Treasury. Show how it calculates this credit, and then indicate the firm's tax liability for each of the next 5 years. Assume a 30 percent tax rate on *all* income to ease the calculations.

2-4   **(Loss carry-back, carry-forward)** The projected taxable income of the Potter Corporation, formed in 1991, is indicated next. (Losses are shown in parentheses.)

Year	Taxable Income
1991	($ 80,000)
1992	60,000
1993	50,000
1994	70,000
1995	(120,000)

What is the corporate tax liability for each year?

2-5   **(Form of organization)** Bernie Swift has operated his small repair shop as a sole proprietorship for several years, but projected changes in his business's income have led him to consider incorporating.

Swift is married and has two children. His family's only income, an annual salary of $40,000, is from operating the business. (The business actually earns more than $40,000, but Ernie reinvests the additional earnings in the business.) He itemizes deductions, and he is able to deduct $6,100. These deductions, combined with his four personal exemptions for 4 × $2,050 = $8,200, give him a taxable income of $40,000 − $6,100 − $8,200. (Assume the personal exemption remains at $2,050.) Of course, his actual taxable income, if he does not incorporate, would be higher by the amount of reinvested income. Swift estimates that his business earnings before salary and taxes for the period 1991 to 1993 will be:

Year	Earnings before Salary and Taxes
1991	$50,000
1992	70,000
1993	90,000

a.   What would his total taxes (corporate plus personal) be in each year under
      (1) A corporate form of organization? (1991 tax = $5,355.)
      (2) A proprietorship? (1991 tax = $5,778.)
b.   Should Swift incorporate? Discuss.
      (Do Parts c and d only if you are using the computerized diskette.)
c.   Suppose Swift decides to pay out (a) 50 percent or (b) 100 percent of the after-salary corporate income in each year as dividends. Would such dividend policy changes affect his decision about whether or not to incorporate?
d.   Suppose business improves, and actual earnings before salary and taxes in each year are twice the original estimate. However, Swift will continue to receive a salary of $40,000 and to reinvest additional earnings in the business. (No dividends would be paid.) Which form of business organization would allow him to pay the smallest amount of total income tax over the three years?

2-6   **(Personal taxes)** Karen Hill has this situation for the year 1990: salary of $60,000; dividend income of $10,000; interest on IBM bonds of $5,000; interest on State of Florida municipal bonds of $10,000; proceeds of $22,000 from the sale of IBM stock purchased in 1984 at a cost of $9,000; and proceeds of $22,000 from the November 1990 sale of IBM stock purchased in October 1990 at a cost of $21,000. Karen gets one exemption ($2,050), and she has allowable itemized deductions of $5,000; these amounts will be deducted from her gross income to determine her taxable income.
a.   What is Karen's tax liability for 1990?
b.   What are her marginal and average tax rates?

c.   If she had some money to invest and was offered a choice of either state of Florida bonds with a yield of 9 percent or more IBM bonds with a yield of 11 percent, which should she choose, and why?

d.   At what marginal tax rate would Karen be indifferent in her choice between the Florida and IBM bonds?

2-7   **(Depreciation)** The Pettit Corporation will commence operations on January 1, 1991. Here are some data on the company: Sales revenues in 1991 are projected at $1,000,000; labor and materials costs are $700,000; on January 1, the company will purchase $100,000 of equipment which will have a 5-year MACRS class life; the firm will receive $10,000 of dividends on some stock the company owns and $10,000 of interest on some bonds it owns. Also, on January 1 the company will issue $500,000 of long-term bonds which will carry an interest rate of 12 percent, and Pettit will pay its shareholders a dividend of $40,000 during 1991.

a.   What is the depreciation expense in each future year on the 5-year class life equipment?

b.   What is Pettit's 1991 tax liability?

c.   Suppose the firm had forecasted higher costs and lower revenues for the first few years of its operations, so when you developed the income statement, you found a loss and hence no taxes. Would this mean the company would lose the benefits of the loss? How would you recommend that it handle the situation? Assume for purposes of this question that losses were projected for 5 years, and after the 5-year start-up period, substantial profits were expected.

2-8   **(Depreciation and cash flows)** Broske Systems Incorporated (BSI) will commence operations on January 1, 1991. It expects to have sales of $200,000 in 1991, $250,000 in 1992, and $350,000 in 1993. Mary Broske, the founder, also forecasts that operating expenses will total 60 percent of sales in each year over this period and that BSI will have interest expenses of $10,000 in 1991, $12,500 in 1992, and $17,500 in 1993. BSI will make an investment of $100,000 on January 1, 1991, in fixed assets. Since they are used in research, the assets will be depreciated over a 3-year class life using MACRS.

a.   What is the depreciation expense in each future year on the 3-year class life equipment?

b.   What is BSI's tax liability in each year?

c.   What is BSI's cash flow in each year?

Mini Case

After graduating with a degree in computer science and spending several years with a large computer company, Joyce Reed has decided to go into business for herself. Initially, she will be the only employee of Reed's Security Service, and she plans to pay herself a salary of $30,000 per year. She must purchase $10,000 of equipment to get started, and although the equipment should last at least 7 years, assume that it will be depreciated over a 3-year MACRS class life. Reed estimates that her first-year revenues will be $60,000 and that her customer base, and hence her revenues, will grow by 10 percent a year thereafter. She also estimates that her operating expenses (for parts and so forth) will equal 30 percent of annual revenues. If her business grows as expected, she will hire additional employees after 3 years.

Reed believes that for liability reasons the business should be incorporated after 3 years, when she brings in additional employees, but she is not certain about whether she should incorporate it now. Consequently, she hired you to develop her projected income statements and to advise her on the form of organization that will minimize her taxes and maximize her cash flows over the first 3 years of operation. Reed is single, so her personal exemption is $2,050. In addition, she estimates that her itemized deductions will be $6,100 during each of the next 3 years. Since this is Reed's first experience running her own business, she has asked you to help her understand the reasons behind your recommendations. Consequently, you have developed the following list of questions which, when answered, will give Reed the information she needs to make her decision.

a. What is depreciation? How is depreciation calculated? Why must depreciation be included in the income statement? What effect does depreciation have on the firm's cash flows?

b. Calculate the depreciation expense for the first 3 years of operation. Will the tax savings resulting from depreciation be the same or different under a proprietorship versus a corporation?

c. If Reed incorporates, what will the corporation's tax bill, after-tax income, and cash flows be for each of the first 3 years? Assume that the company's only income is from security services, and that its only expenses are Reed's salary, the company's operating expenses, and depreciation.

d. Assume that Reed incorporates and pays herself a salary of $30,000 per year, that this is her only income, and that the personal exemption is $2,050 in each year. Also, assume that Reed can take deductions of $6,100 per year. Under these assumptions, what will her personal taxes be in each of the next 3 years?

e. What would Reed's total corporate and personal taxes be if she incorporates?

f. Now assume that Reed does not incorporate, and she operates the business as a sole proprietorship. What will her tax bill be in each of the next 3 years?

g. Strictly on the basis of minimizing taxes during Years 1 to 3, should Reed incorporate?

h. If she wanted to, could Reed organize her business as a corporation and still be taxed as if it were a proprietorship? Could she do the reverse? Under what conditions would it be desirable to elect one of these options?

i. Suppose Reed's business had an additional $30,000 of expenses in Year 2. What would this do to her taxes and her after-tax income in each of the next 3 years (1) if she incorporates and (2) if she operates as a proprietorship?

j. What does the term "progressive tax system" mean? Does such a system exist in the United States? Do the data in this problem illustrate such a system?

k. How would dividend income be treated by Reed as an individual? By the corporation? What about interest income?

l. Suppose Reed decided to incorporate, and the company was quite successful. Retained earnings in the amount of $600,000 were built up, and these funds were simply held as cash in the bank. How could Reed get the $600,000 for her personal use, and what would be the tax consequences of this action?

Selected Additional References

The following articles provide additional information on the effect of corporate taxes on business behavior:

Angell, Robert J., and Tony Wingler, "A Note on Expensing versus Depreciating under the Accelerated Cost Recovery System," *Financial Management,* Winter 1982, 34–35.

Comiskey, Eugene E., and James R. Hasselback, "Analyzing the Profit and Tax Relationship," *Financial Management,* Winter 1973, 57–62.

McCarty, Daniel E., and William R. McDaniel, "A Note on Expensing versus Depreciating under the Accelerated Cost Recovery System: Comment," *Financial Management,* Summer 1983, 37–39.

For a good reference guide to tax issues, see

Federal Tax Course (Englewood Cliffs, N. J.: Prentice-Hall, published annually).

Effects of Depreciation Methods on Taxes, Net Income, and Cash Flows

Managers and financial analysts are concerned primarily with the stream of cash flows firms generate from operations. As we saw in Chapter 2, net income and cash flows are rarely, if ever, the same. We also saw that a firm's cash flows are approximately equal to its net income plus depreciation. However, we noted that taxes paid can differ from reported taxes, and this too can affect cash flows. We explore all this in this appendix, and in the process we show how a firm's choice of reported depreciation affects both its reported cash flows and its accounting profits.

Depreciation for Tax Purposes versus Reporting Purposes

All firms are required to use either the Modified Accelerated Cost Recovery System (MACRS) accelerated method or the alternate straight line method when depreciating their assets for tax purposes. Most firms use the most rapid method, the MACRS accelerated method. The reason is that since depreciation is a tax-deductible expense, larger depreciation write-offs decrease current tax liabilities, and it is better to pay taxes later rather than sooner because the firm has the use of the money in the meantime. However, larger depreciation expenses can reduce firms' reported net incomes.

Generally accepted accounting principles, which specify the accounting methods a firm may use to determine its income as reported to its stockholders, state that a firm should depreciate its assets for reporting purposes using the method which most accurately reflects the decline in the value of the assets over time. For most firms, this method is straight line depreciation. A few firms use the MACRS accelerated method for both tax and reporting purposes, but it is far more common for firms to use the MACRS accelerated method for calculating taxes and straight line for reporting income to investors.

Effects on Taxes and Net Income. Table 2A-1 shows pretax income, taxes, and net income for a firm which has sales of $100 million a year, costs equal to 50 percent of sales, and a single asset whose cost was $100 million. This asset has a 10-year economic life, and it will have zero salvage value at the end of the 10 years. Section I of the table shows the calculation of actual taxes owed using the MACRS accelerated method; Section II shows the calculation of taxes and net income for reporting purposes using the straight line method; and Section III shows the income statements the company would report to investors if it used MACRS accelerated depreciation for both tax and reporting purposes.[1]

In Year 1, the firm reports to the Internal Revenue Service $20 million in depreciation and $30 million of taxable income, and it pays $10.2 million in taxes. If it uses the MACRS accelerated method for stockholder reporting, as shown in Section III, it reports net income of $19.8 million. However, if it uses straight line depreciation for stockholder reporting, as

---

[1]We do not show it, but if the straight line method had been used for both stockholder reporting and tax purposes, pretax income would have been $40 million each year (disregarding the half-year convention). Therefore, taxes would have been 0.34 × $40 = $13.6 million each year, or 10 × $13.6 = $136 million in total. This is exactly the same total as when the MACRS accelerated method is used for tax purposes, but the timing of the tax payments is quite different.

Table 2A-1	Effects of Depreciation on Taxes and Profits

1. The firm has a single asset which cost $100 million, has a 10-year economic life, and has a zero salvage value. Revenues are $100 million per year over the 10 years, and costs other than depreciation are $50 million per year. The firm's tax rate is 34 percent, and it has 10 million shares of stock outstanding.

2. Straight line depreciation charges are $100,000,000/10 = $10,000,000 per year. The asset has a 5-year tax life, so it can, under MACRS, be depreciated at the following rates (millions of dollars):

Year	MACRS Rate	Depreciation
1	0.20	$ 20.00
2	0.32	32.00
3	0.19	19.00
4	0.12	12.00
5	0.11	11.00
6	0.06	6.00
		$100.00

3. In the following sections of the table we show (1) how the tax liability is calculated and (2) how income is reported to investors (millions of dollars):

I. Tax Calculations

	Year						
	1	**2**	**3**	**4**	**5**	**6**	**7. . .10ª**
Sales	$100.00	$100.00	$100.00	$100.00	$100.00	$100.00	$100.00
Costs	50.00	50.00	50.00	50.00	50.00	50.00	50.00
Depreciation	20.00	32.00	19.00	12.00	11.00	6.00	0.00
Pretax income	$ 30.00	$ 18.00	$ 31.00	$ 38.00	$ 39.00	$ 44.00	$ 50.00
Taxes payable at 34%	10.20	6.12	10.54	12.92	13.26	14.96	17.00

shown in Section II, it reports $10 million in depreciation, $10.2 + $3.4 = $13.6 million in taxes, and net income after taxes of $26.40 million, even though the actual tax bill is only $10.2 million. The difference of $13.6 − $10.2 = $3.4 million in reported versus paid taxes is shown on the income statement as *deferred taxes*—that is, the firm has been able to defer paying these taxes until a later date by using an accelerated depreciation method for calculating taxable income.

Notice in Section III that net income using MACRS accelerated depreciation fluctuates for several years, then is stable at a level above net income as reported in Section II. Income reported to stockholders using straight line depreciation is stable during the entire period, and for this reason firms that use deferred tax accounting are said to be using a "normalization" procedure, where "normalize" means "stabilize." To the extent that investors (1) give weight to reported accounting profits and (2) prefer stable to fluctuating earnings, there is an advantage to using straight line depreciation for reporting purposes.

Effects on Cash Flows. The cash flows which accrue to the firm are calculated in Table 2A-2. Notice that cash flows, which are equal to net income plus depreciation plus

Table 2A-1	Effects of Depreciation on Taxes and Profits *(continued)*

II. Income Statements Reported to Stockholders: Straight Line Depreciation with Deferred Taxes

	Year						
	1	2	3	4	5	6	7 . . .10[a]
Sales	$100.00	$100.00	$100.00	$100.00	$100.00	$100.00	$100.00
Costs	50.00	50.00	50.00	50.00	50.00	50.00	50.00
Depreciation	10.00	10.00	10.00	10.00	10.00	10.00	10.00
Pretax income	$ 40.00	$ 40.00	$ 40.00	$ 40.00	$ 40.00	$ 40.00	$ 40.00
Taxes paid, 34% (from Section I)	10.20	6.12	10.54	12.92	13.26	14.96	17.00
Deferred taxes[b]	3.40	7.48	3.06	0.68	0.34	(1.36)	(3.40)
Net income after all taxes (NI)	$ 26.40	$ 26.40	$ 26.40	$ 26.40	$ 26.40	$ 26.40	$ 26.40
Earnings per share	$ 2.64	$ 2.64	$ 2.64	$ 2.64	$ 2.64	$ 2.64	$ 2.64

III. Income Statements Reported to Stockholders: MACRS Accelerated Depreciation

	Year						
	1	2	3	4	5	6	7 . . .10[a]
Sales	$100.00	$100.00	$100.00	$100.00	$100.00	$100.00	$100.00
Costs	50.00	50.00	50.00	50.00	50.00	50.00	50.00
Depreciation	20.00	32.00	19.00	12.00	11.00	6.00	0.00
Pretax income	$ 30.00	$ 18.00	$ 31.00	$ 38.00	$ 39.00	$ 44.00	$ 50.00
Taxes payable at 34%	10.20	6.12	10.54	12.92	13.26	14.96	17.00
Net income after taxes	$ 19.80	$ 11.88	$ 20.46	$ 25.08	$ 25.74	$ 29.04	$ 33.00
Earnings per share	$ 1.98	$ 1.19	$ 2.05	$ 2.51	$ 2.57	$ 2.90	$ 3.30

[a]The income statements do not change for Years 7 through 10.
[b]Deferred taxes = (Pretax income)(Tax rate) − Taxes paid from Part I = $40(0.34) − $10.2 = $3.4 in Year 1.

deferred taxes, are the same regardless of the depreciation method used for book purposes. Thus, we can see that the depreciation method used for reporting purposes has no effect on the cash flows which accrue to a firm from its assets—provided the firm uses MACRS accelerated depreciation for tax purposes. The important point is that both depreciation and deferred taxes must be added to net income to calculate cash flows.

Effects on the Balance Sheet. The cumulative deferred taxes for each year are reported on the right-hand side of the balance sheet under the account "Deferred taxes." Deferred taxes are regarded as a liability—in effect, a loan from the federal government. Our hypothetical company in Table 2A-1, Part II, would show deferred taxes on its end-of-Year 1 balance sheet of $3.40 million. The amount shown at the end of Year 2 would be $3.40 + $7.48 = $10.88 million, and the account would peak at $14.96 million at the end of Year 5. Then, in Year 6, the account would be reduced by $1.36 million, and in Years 7 through 10, the account would be reduced by $3.40 million per year. Finally, the account would show a zero balance at the end of Year 10.

Table 2A-2   Effects of Depreciation on Cash Flows

I. MACRS Accelerated Depreciation Used for Stockholder Reporting

	Year						
	1	**2**	**3**	**4**	**5**	**6**	**7 . . . 10^a**
Net income after taxes	$19.80	$11.88	$20.46	$25.08	$25.74	$29.04	$33.00
Depreciation	20.00	32.00	19.00	12.00	11.00	6.00	0
Deferred taxes	0	0	0	0	0	0	0
Cash flow^b	$39.80	$43.88	$39.46	$37.08	$36.74	$35.04	$33.00

II. Straight Line Depreciation Used for Stockholder Reporting

	Year						
	1	**2**	**3**	**4**	**5**	**6**	**7 . . . 10^a**
Net income after taxes	$26.40	$26.40	$26.40	$26.40	$26.40	$26.40	$26.40
Depreciation	10.00	10.00	10.00	10.00	10.00	10.00	10.00
Deferred taxes	3.40	7.48	3.06	0.68	0.34	(1.36)	(3.40)
Cash flow^b	$39.80	$43.88	$39.46	$37.08	$36.74	$35.04	$33.00

^{a}Cash flows do not change in Years 7 through 10.

^{b}Cash flow = Net income + Depreciation + Deferred taxes.

CHAPTER 3

Financial Markets, Institutions, and Interest Rates

The 1980s witnessed significant changes in financial markets and institutions, and one of the most dramatic was the trend towards the globalization of financial institutions. Going into the 1980s, the banks headquartered in each country did about all the banking business in that country, but that situation has changed. To illustrate, Japanese-owned banks now control about 25 percent of the commercial banking market in California, the most populous state. Indeed, more than 260 foreign banks were operating throughout the United States in 1990, and they represented more than 21 percent of the domestic banking market. The world's largest bank, Dai-Ichi Kangyo Bank, with $386 billion in total assets, is headquartered in Tokyo, while the largest U.S. bank, New York's Citicorp, has only $208 billion in assets.

The same trend toward globalization is occurring in investment banking. Although Merrill Lynch and Goldman Sachs are the top two global underwriters of debt and equity, Credit Swiss–First Boston holds third place, and Japan's Nomura Securities is fourth. In the underwriting of Eurosecurities, which are securities sold outside the issuer's home country, the top five underwriters are Japanese, and the sixth largest is West Germany's Deutsche Bank. In terms of capital, Nomura Securities is the largest investment banker in the world, and Japan has four banks in the top ten. As financial institutions and markets become more globalized, capital is transferred more freely between investors and borrowers, competition increases, and both parties benefit.

Merchant banking is another emerging trend in markets and institutions. The term is borrowed from Europe, where it describes banks which are relatively unfettered by regulation, and which can do everything from accepting deposits to buying and selling whole companies. On Wall Street, merchant banking means making an equity investment along with a loan, especially to finance a takeover or a leveraged buyout. In 1980, investment banks acted only as "middlemen" in takeover deals, but now they often commit some of their own funds, along with equity funds obtained from other sources. For example, Morgan Stanley has put up $225 million of its own funds and, along with capital supplied by pension funds, foreign institutions, and commercial banks, created a fund of $1.6 billion for the specific purpose of participating in buyouts. With added leverage (debt financing), plus the extra money that partners will put in later, the fund is large enough to buy $35 billion of assets. The fund's stated goal is to earn at least 40 percent on its investment. Obviously, the fund will have to accept a lot of risk to have a chance of meeting this goal, so entry into merchant banking activities is making some of our old line financial institutions riskier enterprises.

IT is critical that financial managers understand the environment and markets within which they operate. Therefore, in this chapter we examine the markets where capital is raised, securities are traded, and stock prices are established, as well as the institutions through which such transactions are conducted. In the process, we shall see how money costs are determined, and we shall explore the principal factors that determine the level of interest rates in the economy.

THE FINANCIAL MARKETS

Business firms, as well as individuals and government units, often need to raise capital. For example, suppose Carolina Power & Light (CP&L) forecasts an increase in the demand for electricity in North Carolina, and the company decides to build a new power plant. Because CP&L almost certainly will not have the $2 billion or so necessary to pay for the plant, the company will have to raise this capital in the financial markets. Or suppose Mr. Nohr, the proprietor of a Chicago hardware store, decides to expand into appliances. Where will he get the money to buy the initial inventory of TV sets, washers, and freezers? Similarly, if the Johnson family wants to buy a home that costs $100,000, but they have only $20,000 in savings, how can they raise the additional $80,000? If the City of Sacramento wants to borrow $20 million to finance a new sewer plant, or if the federal government needs $150 billion or so to cover its projected 1991 deficit, they too need access to the capital markets.

On the other hand, some individuals and firms have incomes which are greater than their current expenditures, so they have funds available to invest. For example,

Gary Powell has an income of $36,000, but his expenses are only $30,000, while Ford Motor Company has accumulated over $9 billion of excess cash, which it wants to invest.

People and organizations wanting to borrow money are brought together with those having surplus funds in the *financial markets*. Note that "markets" is plural— there are a great many different financial markets, each one consisting of many institutions, in a developed economy such as ours. Each market deals with a somewhat different type of instrument in terms of the instrument's maturity and the assets backing it. Also, different markets serve different sets of customers, or operate in different parts of the country. Here are some of the major types of markets:

1. *Physical asset markets* (also called "tangible" or "real" asset markets) are those for such products as wheat, autos, real estate, computers, and machinery. *Financial markets* deal with stocks, bonds, notes, mortgages, and other *claims on real assets*.

2. *Spot markets* and *futures markets* are terms that refer to whether the assets are being bought or sold for "on the spot" delivery (literally, within a few days) or for delivery at some future date, such as six months or a year into the future. The futures markets (which could include the *options markets*) are growing in importance, but we shall not discuss them until Chapter 18.

3. *Money markets* are the markets for debt securities with maturities of less than one year. The New York money market is the world's largest, and it is dominated by the major U.S., Japanese, and European banks. London, Tokyo, and Paris are other major money market centers. *Capital markets* are the markets for long-term debt and corporate stocks. The New York Stock Exchange, which handles the stocks of the largest U.S. corporations, is a prime example of a capital market.

4. *Mortgage markets* deal with loans on residential, commercial, and industrial real estate, and on farmland, while *consumer credit markets* involve loans on autos and appliances, as well as loans for education, vacations, and so on.

5. *World, national, regional,* and *local markets* also exist. Thus, depending on an organization's size and scope of operations, it may be able to borrow all around the world, or it may be confined to a strictly local, even neighborhood, market.

6. *Primary markets* are the markets in which corporations raise new capital, and in which newly issued securities are involved. If GE were to sell a new issue of common stock to raise capital, this would be a primary market transaction. The corporation selling the stock receives the proceeds from the sale in a primary market transaction. *Secondary markets* are markets in which existing, outstanding securities are traded among investors. Thus, if Edgar Rice decided to buy 1,000 shares of IBM stock, the purchase would (except for a new issue) occur in the secondary market. The New York Stock Exchange is a secondary market, since it deals in outstanding as opposed to newly issued stocks and bonds. Secondary markets also exist for mortgages, various other types of loans, and other financial assets. The corporation whose securities are being traded is not involved in a secondary market transaction and, thus, does not receive any funds from such a sale.

Other classifications could be made, but this breakdown is sufficient to show that there are many types of financial markets.

A healthy economy is dependent on efficient transfers of funds from people who are net savers to firms and individuals who need capital—that is, the economy depends on *operationally efficient financial markets.* Without efficient transfers, the economy simply could not function: Carolina Power & Light could not raise capital, so Raleigh's citizens would have no electricity; the Johnson family would not have adequate housing; Gary Powell would have no place to invest his savings; and so on. Obviously, the level of employment and productivity, hence our standard of living, would be much lower, so it is absolutely essential that our financial markets function efficiently—not only quickly, but also at a low cost.[1]

Self-Test Questions

Distinguish between physical asset markets and financial asset markets.

What is the difference between spot and futures markets?

Distinguish between money and capital markets.

What is the difference between primary and secondary markets?

FINANCIAL INSTITUTIONS

Transfers of capital between savers and those who need capital take place in the three different ways diagrammed in Figure 3-1:

1.   *Direct transfers* of money and securities, as shown in the top section, occur when a business sells its stocks or bonds directly to savers, without going through any type of intermediary. The business delivers its securities to savers, who in turn give the firm the money it needs.

2.   As shown in the middle section, transfers may also go through an *investment banking house* such as Morgan Stanley, which serves as a middleman and facilitates the issuance of securities. The company sells its stocks or bonds to the investment bank, which in turn sells these same securities to ultimate savers. The businesses' securities and the savers' money merely "pass through" the investment banking house. However, the investment bank does buy and hold the securities for a period of time, so it is taking a chance—it may not be able to resell them to savers for as much or more than it paid. Because the corporation receives money from the sale, this is a primary market transaction.

3.   Transfers can also be made through a *financial intermediary* such as a bank or mutual fund. Here the intermediary obtains funds from savers, issuing its own securities in exchange, and then it uses the money to purchase businesses' securities. For example, a saver might give dollars to a bank, receiving from it a certificate of

---

[1]When organizations like the United Nations design plans to aid developing nations, just as much attention must be paid to the establishment of cost-efficient financial markets as to electrical power, transportation, communications, and other infrastructure systems. Economic efficiency is simply impossible without a good system for allocating capital within the economy.

Figure 3-1	Diagram of the Capital Formation Process

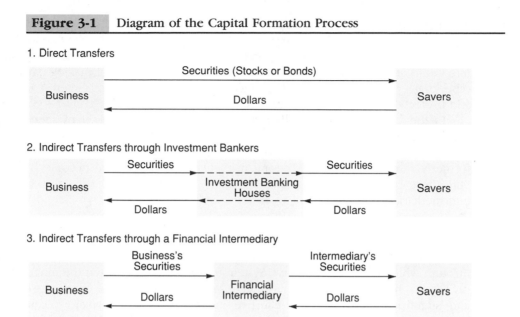

1. Direct Transfers

Business — Securities (Stocks or Bonds) → Savers
Business ← Dollars — Savers

2. Indirect Transfers through Investment Bankers

Business — Securities → Investment Banking Houses — Securities → Savers
Business ← Dollars — Investment Banking Houses ← Dollars — Savers

3. Indirect Transfers through a Financial Intermediary

Business — Business's Securities → Financial Intermediary — Intermediary's Securities → Savers
Business ← Dollars — Financial Intermediary ← Dollars — Savers

deposit, and then the bank might lend the money to a small business in the form of a mortgage loan. Thus, intermediaries literally create new forms of capital — in this case, certificates of deposit, which are more liquid than mortgages and hence are better securities for most savers to hold. The existence of intermediaries greatly increases money and capital market efficiency.

For simplicity, we assumed that the entity which needs capital is a business, and specifically a corporation, although it is easy to visualize the demander of capital as a potential home purchaser, a government unit, and so on.

Direct transfers of funds from savers to businesses are possible and do occur on occasion, but it is generally more efficient for a business to obtain the services of an *investment banking house*. Merrill Lynch, Salomon Brothers, Dean Witter, and Goldman Sachs are examples of financial service corporations which offer investment banking services. Such organizations (1) help corporations design securities with the features that will be most attractive to investors, (2) buy these securities from the corporation, and (3) then resell them to savers. Although the securities are sold twice, this process is really one primary market transaction, with the investment banker acting as a middleman in the process of transferring capital from savers to businesses.

As noted previously, the *financial intermediaries* shown in the third section of Figure 3-1 do more than simply transfer money and securities between firms and savers — they literally create new financial products. Since the intermediaries are generally large, they gain economies of scale in analyzing the creditworthiness of potential borrowers, in processing and collecting loans, and in pooling risks and thus helping individual savers diversify, which means "not putting all their financial eggs in one basket." Further, a system of specialized intermediaries can enable savings to do more than just draw interest. For example, individuals can put money into banks and get both interest income and a convenient way of making payments (checking), put money into life insurance companies and get both interest income and protection for their beneficiaries, and so on.

In the United States and other developed nations, a large set of specialized, highly efficient financial intermediaries has evolved. The situation is changing rapidly, however, and different types of institutions are performing services that were formerly reserved for others, causing institutional distinctions to become blurred. Still, there is a degree of institutional identity, and here are the major classes of intermediaries:

1. *Commercial banks,* which are the traditional financial "department stores," serve a wide variety of savers and those with needs for funds. Historically, the commercial banks were the major institutions for handling checking accounts and through which the Federal Reserve System expanded or contracted the money supply. Today, however, some of the other institutions also provide checking services and significantly influence the effective money supply. Conversely, commercial banks now provide an ever widening range of services, including stock brokerage services and insurance.

Note that commercial banks are quite different from investment banks. Commercial banks lend money, whereas investment banks help companies raise capital from other parties. Prior to 1933, commercial banks offered investment banking services, but the Glass-Steagall Act, which was passed in that year, prohibited commercial banks from engaging in investment banking. Thus, the Morgan Bank was broken up into two separate organizations, one of which is now the Morgan Guaranty Trust Company, a commercial bank, while the other is Morgan Stanley, a major investment banking house.

2. *Savings and loan associations (S&Ls),* which have traditionally served individual savers and residential and commercial mortgage borrowers, take the funds of many small savers and then lend this money to home buyers and other types of borrowers. Because the savers are provided a degree of liquidity that would be absent if they bought the mortgages or other securities directly, perhaps the most significant economic function of the S&Ls is to "create liquidity" which would otherwise be lacking. Also, the S&Ls have more expertise in analyzing credit, setting up loans, and making collections than individual savers could possibly have, so they reduce the cost and increase the availability of real estate loans. Finally, the S&Ls hold large, diversified portfolios of loans and other assets and thus spread risks in a manner that would be impossible if small savers were making mortgage loans directly. Because of these factors, savers benefit by being able to invest their savings in more liquid, better managed, and less risky accounts, whereas borrowers benefit by being able to obtain more capital, and at lower costs, than would otherwise be possible.

3. *Mutual savings banks,* which are similar to S&Ls, operate primarily in the northeastern states, accept savings primarily from individuals, and lend mainly on a long-term basis to home buyers and consumers.

4. *Credit unions* are cooperative associations whose members have a common bond, such as being employees of the same firm. Members' savings are loaned only to other members, generally for auto purchases, home improvements, and the like. Credit unions often are the cheapest source of funds available to the individual borrower.

5. *Pension funds* are retirement plans funded by corporations or government agencies for their workers and administered primarily by the trust departments of commercial banks or by life insurance companies. Pension funds invest primarily in bonds, stocks, mortgages, and real estate.

6. *Life insurance companies* take savings in the form of annual premiums, then invest these funds in stocks, bonds, real estate, and mortgages, and finally make payments to the beneficiaries of the insured parties. In recent years life insurance companies have also offered a variety of tax-deferred savings plans designed to provide benefits to the participants when they retire.

7. *Mutual funds* are corporations which accept money from savers and then use these funds to buy stocks, long-term bonds, or short-term debt instruments issued by businesses or government units. These organizations pool funds and thus reduce risks by diversification. They also gain economies of scale, which lower the costs of analyzing securities, managing portfolios, and buying and selling securities. Different funds are designed to meet the objectives of different types of savers. Hence, there are bond funds for those who desire safety, stock funds for savers who are willing to accept significant risks in the hope of higher returns, and still other funds that are used as interest-bearing checking accounts (the *money market funds*). There are literally hundreds of different mutual funds with dozens of different goals and purposes.

Financial institutions have historically been heavily regulated, with the primary purpose of this regulation being to insure the safety of the institutions and thus to protect depositors. However, these regulations—which have taken the form of prohibitions on nationwide branch banking, restrictions on the types of assets the institutions can buy, ceilings on the interest rates they can pay, and limitations on the types of services they can provide—have tended to impede the free flow of capital from surplus to deficit areas, and thus have hurt the efficiency of our capital markets. Recognizing this fact, Congress has authorized some major changes, and more will be forthcoming.

The end result of the ongoing regulatory changes is a blurring of the distinctions between the different types of institutions. Indeed, the trend in the United States today is toward huge *financial service corporations,* which own banks, S&Ls, investment banking houses, insurance companies, pension plan operations, and mutual funds, and which have branches across the country and even around the world. Sears, Roebuck is, interestingly, one of the largest financial service corporations. It owns Allstate Insurance, Dean Witter (a leading brokerage and investment banking firm), Coldwell Banker (the largest real estate brokerage firm), a huge credit card business, and a host of other related businesses. Other financial service corporations, most of which started in one area and have now diversified to cover the full financial spectrum, include Transamerica, Merrill Lynch, American Express, Citicorp, Fidelity, and Prudential.

Self-Test Questions

Identify the three different ways capital is transferred between savers and borrowers.

What is the difference between a commercial bank and an investment bank?

Distinguish between investment banking houses and financial intermediaries.

List the major classes of intermediaries and briefly describe each one's function.

THE STOCK MARKET

As noted earlier, secondary markets are those in which outstanding, previously issued securities are traded. By far the most active secondary market, and the most important one to financial managers, is the *stock market*. It is here that the prices of firms' stocks are established, and, since the primary goal of financial management is to maximize the firm's stock price, a knowledge of the market in which this price is established is essential for anyone involved in managing a business.

The Stock Exchanges

There are two basic types of stock markets — the *organized exchanges,* which include the New York Stock Exchange (NYSE), the American Stock Exchange (AMEX), and several regional exchanges, and the less formal *over-the-counter market.* Since the organized exchanges have actual physical market locations and are easier to describe and understand, we shall consider them first.

The *organized security exchanges* are tangible physical entities. Each of the larger ones occupies its own building, has specifically designated members, and has an elected governing body — its board of governors. Members are said to have "seats" on the exchange, although everybody stands up. These seats, which are bought and sold, give the holder the right to trade on the exchange. In 1979 seats on the NYSE sold for as little as $95,000, but in May 1987, they hit an all-time high price of $1.15 million. In April 1990, NYSE seats were selling for $351,000.

Most of the larger investment banking houses operate *brokerage departments,* which own seats on the exchanges and designate one or more of their officers as members. The exchanges are open on all normal working days, with the members meeting in a large room equipped with telephones and other electronic equipment that enable each member to communicate with his or her firm's offices throughout the country.

Like other markets, security exchanges facilitate communication between buyers and sellers. For example, Merrill Lynch (the largest brokerage firm) might receive an order in its Atlanta office from a customer who wants to buy 100 shares of IBM stock. Simultaneously, Dean Witter's Denver office might receive an order from a customer wishing to sell 100 shares of IBM. Each broker communicates by wire with the firm's representative on the NYSE. Other brokers throughout the country are also communicating with their own exchange members. The exchange members with *sell orders* offer the shares for sale, and they are bid for by the members with *buy orders*. Thus, the exchanges operate as *auction markets*.[2]

The Over-the-Counter Market

In contrast to the organized security exchanges, the *over-the-counter market* is a nebulous, intangible organization. An explanation of the term "over-the-counter" will help clarify exactly what this market is. The exchanges operate as auction markets; buy and sell orders come in more or less simultaneously, and exchange members match these orders. If a stock is traded less frequently, perhaps because it is the stock of a new or a small firm, few buy and sell orders come in, and matching them within a reasonable length of time would be difficult. To avoid this problem, some brokerage firms maintain an inventory of such stocks; they buy when individual investors want to sell and sell when investors want to buy. At one time the inventory of securities was kept in a safe, and the stocks, when bought and sold, were literally passed over the counter.

Today, the over-the-counter market is defined as all facilities that provide for any security transactions not conducted on the organized exchanges. These facilities consist of (1) the relatively few *dealers* who hold inventories of over-the-counter securities and who are said to "make a market" in these securities, (2) the thousands of brokers who act as *agents* in bringing these dealers together with investors, and (3) the computers, terminals, and electronic networks that provide a communications link between dealers and brokers. The dealers who make a market in a particular stock continuously post a price at which they are willing to buy the stock (the *bid price*) and a price at which they will sell shares (the *asked price*). These prices, which are adjusted as supply and demand conditions change, can be read off computer screens all across the country. The spread between bid and asked prices represents the dealer's markup, or profit.

---

[2]The NYSE is actually a modified auction market, wherein people (through their brokers) bid for stocks. Originally—a hundred or so years ago—brokers would literally shout, "I have 100 shares of Union Pacific for sale; how much am I offered?" and then sell to the highest bidder. If a broker had a buy order, he or she would shout, "I want to buy 100 shares of Union Pacific; who'll sell at the best price?" The same general situation still exists, although the exchanges now have members known as *specialists* who facilitate the trading process by keeping an inventory of shares of the stocks in which they specialize. If a buy order comes in at a time when no sell order arrives, the specialist will sell off some inventory. Similarly, if a sell order comes in, the specialist will buy and add to inventory. The specialist sets a *bid price* (the price the specialist will pay for the stock) and an *asked price* (the price at which shares will be sold out of inventory). The bid and asked prices are set at levels designed to keep the inventory in balance. If many buy orders start coming in because of favorable developments, or sell orders come in because of unfavorable events, the specialist will raise or lower prices to keep supply and demand in balance. Bid prices are somewhat lower than asked prices, with the difference, or *spread,* representing the specialist's profit margin.

   Special facilities are available to help institutional investors such as mutual funds or pension funds sell large blocks of stock without depressing their prices. In essence, brokerage houses which cater to institutional clients will purchase blocks (defined as 10,000 or more shares) and then resell the stock to other institutions or individuals. Also, when a firm has a major announcement which is likely to cause its stock price to change sharply, it will ask the exchanges to halt trading in its stock until the announcement has been made and digested by investors. Thus, when Texaco announced that it planned to acquire Getty Oil, trading was halted for one day in both Texaco and Getty stocks.

Brokers and dealers who make up the over-the-counter market are members of a self-regulating body known as the *National Association of Security Dealers (NASD),* which licenses brokers and oversees trading practices. The computerized trading network used by NASD is known as the NASD Automated Quotation System (NASDAQ), and *The Wall Street Journal* and other newspapers contain information on NASDAQ transactions.

In terms of numbers of issues, the majority of stocks are traded over the counter. However, because the stocks of larger companies are listed on the exchanges, about two-thirds of the dollar volume of stock trading takes place on the exchanges.

Some Trends in Security Trading Procedures

From the NYSE's inception in the 1800s until the 1970s, the vast majority of all stock trading occurred on the Exchange and was conducted by member firms. The NYSE established a set of minimum brokerage commission rates, and no member firm could charge a commission lower than the set rate. This was a monopoly, pure and simple. However, on May 1, 1975, the Securities and Exchange Commission (SEC), with strong prodding from the Antitrust Division of the Justice Department, forced the NYSE to abandon its fixed commissions. Commission rates declined dramatically, falling in some cases as much as 90 percent from former levels.

These changes were a boon to the investing public, but not to the brokerage industry. A number of "full service" brokerage houses went bankrupt, and others were forced to merge with stronger firms. Many Wall Street experts predict that once the dust settles, the number of brokerage houses will have declined from literally thousands in the 1960s to a much smaller number of large, strong, nationwide companies, all of which are units of diversified financial service corporations. Deregulation has also spawned a number of small "discount brokers," some of which are affiliated with commercial banks or savings and loans; several of these will be among the survivors.[3]

Self-Test Question

What are the two basic types of stock markets, and how do they differ?

THE COST OF MONEY

Capital in a free economy is allocated through the price system. *The interest rate is the price paid to borrow debt capital, whereas in the case of equity capital, investors' returns come in the form of dividends and capital gains.* The factors which affect the supply of and demand for investment capital, and hence the cost of money, are discussed in this section.

---

[3]Full service brokers give investors information on different stocks and make recommendations as to which stocks to buy. Discount brokers do not give advice—they merely execute orders. Some brokerage houses (institutional houses) cater primarily to institutional investors such as pension funds and insurance companies, while others cater to individual investors and are called retail houses. Large firms such as Merrill Lynch generally have both retail and institutional brokerage operations.

The four most fundamental factors affecting the cost of money are (1) *production opportunities,* (2) *time preferences for consumption,* (3) *risk,* and (4) *inflation.* To see how these factors operate, visualize an isolated island community where the people live on fish. They have a stock of fishing gear which permits them to survive reasonably well, but they would like to have more fish. Now suppose Mr. Crusoe had a bright idea for a new type of fishnet that would enable him to double his daily catch. However, it would take him a year to perfect his design, to build his net, and to learn how to use it efficiently, and Mr. Crusoe would probably starve before he could put his new net into operation. Therefore, he might suggest to Ms. Robinson, Mr. Friday, and several others that if they would give him one fish each day for a year, he would return two fish a day during all of the next year. If someone accepted the offer, then the fish which Ms. Robinson or one of the others gave to Mr. Crusoe would constitute *savings;* these savings would be *invested* in the fishnet; and the extra fish the net produced would constitute a *return on the investment.*

Obviously, the more productive Mr. Crusoe thought the new fishnet would be, the higher his expected return on the investment would be and the more he could offer to pay Ms. Robinson, Mr. Friday, or other potential investors for their savings. In this example we assume that Mr. Crusoe thought he would be able to pay, and thus he offered, a 100 percent rate of return—he offered to give back two fish for every one he received. He might have tried to attract savings for less; for example, he might have decided to offer only 1.5 fish next year for every one he received this year, which would represent a 50 percent rate of return to Ms. Robinson and the other potential savers.

How attractive Mr. Crusoe's offer would appear to potential savers would depend in large part on their *time preferences for consumption.* For example, Ms. Robinson might be thinking of retirement, and she might be willing to trade fish today for fish in the future on a one-for-one basis. On the other hand, Mr. Friday might have a wife and several young children and need his current fish, so he might be unwilling to "lend" a fish today for anything less than three fish next year. Mr. Friday would be said to have a high time preference for consumption and Ms. Robinson a low time preference. Note also that if the entire population were living right at the subsistence level, time preferences for current consumption would necessarily be high, aggregate savings would be low, interest rates would be high, and capital formation would be difficult.

The *risk* inherent in the fishnet project, and thus in Mr. Crusoe's ability to repay the loan, would also affect the return investors would require: The higher the perceived risk, the higher the required rate of return. Also, in a more complex society there are many businesses like Mr. Crusoe's, many goods other than fish, and many savers like Ms. Robinson and Mr. Friday. Further, people use money as a medium of exchange rather than barter with fish. When money is used, rather than fish, its value in the future, which is affected by *inflation,* comes into play: The higher the expected rate of inflation, the larger the required return.

Thus, we see that the interest rate paid to savers depends in a basic way (1) on the rate of return producers expect to earn on invested capital, (2) on consumers'/savers' time preferences for current versus future consumption, (3) on the riskiness of the loan, and (4) on the expected rate of inflation. Producers' expected returns on their business investments set an upper limit on how much they can pay for savings, while consumers' time preferences for consumption establish how much consumption they are willing to defer; hence how much they will save at different levels of interest offered by producers.[4] Higher risk and higher inflation also lead to higher interest rates.

Self-Test Questions

What is the price paid to borrow debt capital?

What is the "price" of equity capital?

What four fundamental factors affect the cost of money?

INTEREST RATE LEVELS

Capital is allocated among borrowers by interest rates: Firms with the most profitable investment opportunities are willing and able to pay the most for capital, so they tend to attract it away from inefficient firms or from those whose products are not in demand. Of course, our economy is not completely free in the sense of being influenced only by market forces. Thus, the federal government has agencies which help individuals or groups, as stipulated by Congress, to obtain credit on favorable terms. Among those eligible for this kind of assistance are small businesses, certain minorities, and firms willing to build plants in areas with high unemployment. Still, most capital in the U.S. economy is allocated through the price system.

Figure 3-2 shows how supply and demand interact to determine interest rates in two capital markets. Markets A and B represent two of the many capital markets in existence. The going interest rate, k, is initially 10 percent for the low-risk securities in Market A. Borrowers whose credit is strong enough to qualify for this market can obtain funds at a cost of 10 percent, and investors who want to put their money to work at low risk can obtain a 10 percent return. Riskier borrowers must obtain higher-cost funds in Market B. Investors who are more willing to take risks invest in Market B with the expectation of receiving a 12 percent return but also with the realization that they might receive much less.

If the demand for funds in a market declines, as it typically does during a business recession, the demand curves will shift to the left, as shown in Curve D_2 in Market A. The market-clearing, or equilibrium, interest rate in this example declines to 8 percent. Similarly, you should be able to visualize what would happen if the Federal Reserve tightened credit: The supply curve, S_1, would shift to the left, and this would raise interest rates and lower the level of borrowing in the economy.

Capital markets are interdependent. For example, if Markets A and B were in equilibrium before the demand shift to D_2 in Market A, then investors were willing to accept the higher risk in Market B in exchange for a *risk premium* of 12% —

---

[4]The term "producers" is really too narrow. A better word might be "borrowers," which would include corporations, home purchasers, people borrowing to go to college, or even people borrowing to buy autos or to pay for vacations. Also, the wealth of a society influences its people's ability to save and thus their time preferences for current versus future consumption.

Figure 3-2   Interest Rates as a Function of Supply and Demand for Funds

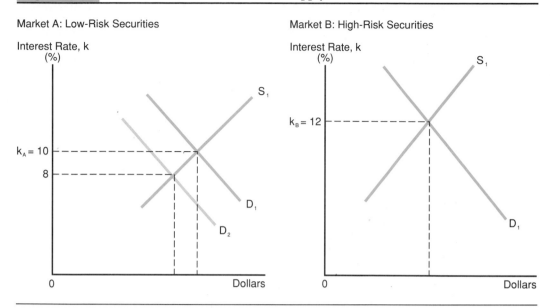

Market A: Low-Risk Securities

Market B: High-Risk Securities

10% = 2%. After the shift to D_2, the risk premium would initially increase to 12% − 8% = 4%. In all likelihood, this much larger premium would induce some of the lenders in Market A to shift to Market B; this, in turn, would cause the supply curve in Market A to shift to the left (or up) and that in Market B to shift to the right. This transfer of capital between markets would raise the interest rate in Market A and lower it in Market B, thus bringing the risk premium back closer to the original level, 2 percent.

There are many capital markets in the United States. U.S. firms also invest and raise capital throughout the world, and foreigners both borrow and lend capital in the United States. There are markets in the United States for home loans; farm loans; business loans; federal, state, and local government loans; and consumer loans. Within each category, there are regional markets as well as different types of sub-markets. For example, in real estate there are separate markets for first and second mortgages, and for loans on owner-occupied homes, apartments, office buildings, shopping centers, vacant land, and so on. Within the business sector, there are dozens of types of debt and also several sharply differentiated markets for common stocks.

There is a price for each type of capital, and these prices change over time as shifts occur in supply and demand conditions. Figure 3-3 shows how long- and short-term interest rates to business borrowers have varied since the 1950s. Notice that short-term interest rates are especially prone to rise during booms and then fall during recessions. (The shaded areas of the chart indicate recessions.) When the economy is expanding, firms need capital, and this demand for capital pushes rates up. Also, inflationary pressures are strongest during business booms, and that also

| **Figure 3-3** | Long- and Short-Term Interest Rates, 1953–1990 |

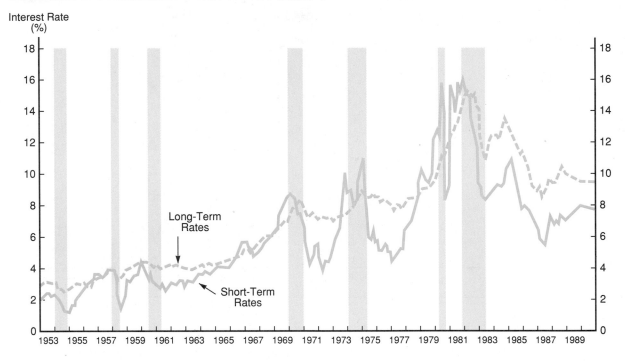

Notes:

a. The shaded areas designate business recessions.

b. Short-term rates are measured by four- to six-month loans to very large, strong corporations, and long-term rates are measured by AAA corporate bonds.

Source: *Federal Reserve Bulletin*.

exerts upward pressure on rates. Conditions are reversed during recessions—slack business reduces the demand for credit, the rate of inflation falls, and the result is a drop in interest rates.

These tendencies do not hold exactly—the period after 1984 is a case in point. The price of oil decreased dramatically in 1985 and 1986, reducing inflationary pressures on other prices and easing fears of serious long-term inflation. Earlier, these fears had pushed interest rates to record levels. The economy from 1984 to 1987 was fairly strong, but the declining fears about inflation more than offset the normal tendency of interest rates to rise during good economic times, and the net result was lower interest rates.[5]

---

[5]Short-term rates are responsive to current economic conditions, whereas long-term rates primarily reflect long-run expectations for inflation. As a result, short-term rates are sometimes above and sometimes below long-term rates. The relationship between long-term and short-term rates is called the *term structure of interest rates*. This topic is discussed later in the chapter.

The relationship between inflation and long-term interest rates is highlighted in Figure 3-4, which plots rates of inflation along with long-term interest rates. Prior to 1965, when the average rate of inflation was about 1.0 percent, interest rates on AAA-rated bonds generally ranged from 4 to 5 percent. As the war in Vietnam accelerated in the mid-1960s, the rate of inflation increased, and interest rates began to rise. The rate of inflation dropped after 1970, and so did long-term interest rates. However, the 1973 Arab oil embargo was followed by a quadrupling of oil prices in 1974, which caused a spurt in the price level, which in turn drove interest rates to new record highs in 1974 and 1975. Inflationary pressures eased in late 1975 and 1976 but then rose again after 1976. In 1980, inflation rates hit the highest level on record, and fears of continued double-digit inflation pushed interest rates up to historic highs. From 1981 through 1986, the inflation rate dropped steadily, and in 1986 inflation was only 1.1 percent, the lowest level in 25 years. Early in the period, investors' fears of a renewal of double-digit inflation kept long-term interest rates at relatively high levels, but as confidence built that inflation was under control, interest rates declined. Currently (1990), inflation is back up to about 5 percent, and interest rates have moved up accordingly.

Figure 3-4   Relationship between Annual Inflation Rates and
Long-Term Interest Rates, 1953–1990

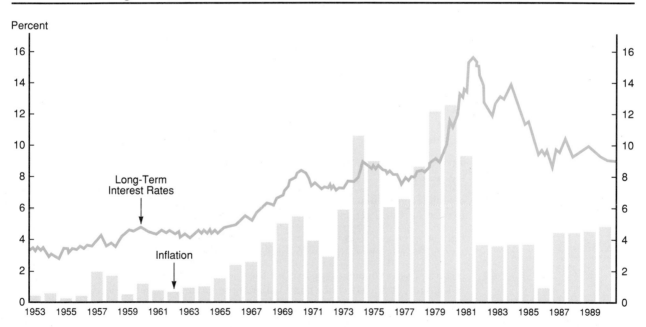

Notes:
a. Interest rates are those on AAA long-term corporate bonds.

b. Inflation is measured as the annual rate of change in the Consumer Price Index (CPI).

c. The 1990 figure is an estimate.

Source: *Federal Reserve Bulletin.*

Self-Test Questions

How are interest rates used to allocate capital among firms?

What happens to market-clearing, or equilibrium, interest rates in a capital market when the demand for funds declines? What happens when inflation increases or decreases?

Briefly explain why prices for capital change during booms and recessions.

THE DETERMINANTS OF MARKET INTEREST RATES

In general, the nominal (or stated) interest rate on a debt security, k, is composed of a real risk-free rate of interest, k^*, plus several premiums that reflect inflation, the riskiness of the security, and the security's marketability (or liquidity). This relationship can be expressed as follows:

$$\text{Market interest rate} = k = k^* + IP + DRP + LP + MRP, \qquad (3\text{-}1)$$

and if we combine $k^* + IP$ and let this sum equal k_{RF}, then we have this expression:

$$k = k_{RF} + DRP + LP + MRP. \qquad (3\text{-}2)$$

Here

k = the nominal, or stated, rate of interest on a given security.[6] There are many different securities, hence many different stated interest rates.

k^* = the real risk-free rate of interest; k^* is pronounced "k-star," and it is the rate that would exist on a riskless security if zero inflation were expected.

k_{RF} = the nominal risk-free rate of interest. This is the stated interest rate on a security such as a U.S. Treasury bill which is very liquid and free of most risks. Note that k_{RF} does include a premium for expected inflation, so $k_{RF} = k^* + IP$.

IP = inflation premium. IP is equal to the average expected inflation rate over the life of the security.

DRP = default risk premium. This premium reflects the possibility that the issuer will not pay interest or principal on a security at the stated time and in the stated amount.

LP = liquidity premium. This is a premium charged by lenders to reflect the fact that some securities cannot be converted to cash on short notice at a "reasonable" price.

MRP = maturity risk premium. As we explain later, longer-term bonds are exposed to a significant risk of price declines, and a maturity premium is charged by lenders to reflect this risk.

---

[6]The term *nominal* as it is used here means the *stated* rate as opposed to the *real* rate, which is adjusted to remove the effects of inflation. If you bought a 10-year Treasury bond in January 1990, the stated, or nominal, rate would be about 8 percent, but if inflation averages 5 percent over the next 10 years, the real rate would be about 8% − 5% = 3%. In Chapter 6 we will use the term nominal in yet another way: to distinguish between stated rates and effective annual rates when compounding occurs more frequently than once a year.

We discuss the components whose sum makes up the stated, or nominal, rate on a given security in the following sections.

The Real Risk-Free Rate of Interest, k*

The *real risk-free rate of interest, k*,* is defined as the interest rate that would exist on a riskless security if no inflation were expected, and it may be thought of as the rate of interest that would exist on short-term U.S. Treasury securities in an inflation-free world. The real risk-free rate is not static—it changes over time depending on economic conditions, especially (1) on the rate of return corporations and other borrowers can expect to earn on productive assets and (2) on people's time preferences for current versus future consumption. Borrowers' expected returns on real asset investments set an upper limit on how much they can afford to pay for borrowed funds, whereas savers' time preferences for consumption establish how much consumption they are willing to defer, and hence the amount of funds they will lend at different levels of interest. It is difficult to measure k* precisely, but most experts think that in the United States it has fluctuated in the range of 1 to 4 percent in recent years.

The Nominal Risk-Free Rate of Interest, k_{RF}

The *nominal risk-free rate, k_{RF},* is the real risk-free rate plus a premium for expected inflation: $k_{RF} = k* + IP$. To be strictly correct, the risk-free rate should mean the interest rate on a totally risk-free security—one that has no risk of default, no maturity risk, no liquidity risk, and no risk of loss if inflation increases. There is no such security, and hence there is no observable truly risk-free rate. However, there is one security that is free of most risks—a U.S. Treasury bill (T-bill), which is a short-term security issued by the U.S. government. Treasury bonds (T-bonds), which are longer-term government securities, are free of default and liquidity risks, but T-bonds are exposed to some risk due to changes in the general level of interest rates.

   If the term "risk-free rate" is used without either the modifier "real" or the modifier "nominal," people generally mean the nominal rate, and we will follow that convention in this book. Therefore, when we use the term risk-free rate, k_{RF}, we mean the nominal risk-free rate, which includes an inflation premium equal to the average expected inflation rate over the life of the security. In general, we use the T-bill rate to approximate the short-term risk-free rate, and the T-bond rate to approximate the long-term risk-free rate. So, whenever you see the term "risk-free rate," assume that we are referring either to the U.S. T-bill rate or to the T-bond rate.

Inflation Premium (IP)

Inflation has a major impact on interest rates because it erodes the purchasing power of the dollar and lowers the real rate of return on investments. To illustrate, suppose you save $1,000 and invest it in a Treasury bond that matures in 1 year and pays 5 percent interest. At the end of the year you will receive $1,050 — your original $1,000 plus $50 of interest. Now suppose the rate of inflation during the year is 10 percent, and it affects all items equally. If beer had cost $1 per bottle at the beginning of the year, it would cost $1.10 at the end of the year. Therefore, your $1,000 would have bought $1,000/$1 = 1,000 bottles at the beginning of the year but only $1,050/$1.10 = 955 bottles at the end. Thus, in *real terms,* you would be worse off — you would receive $50 of interest, but it would not be sufficient to offset inflation. You would thus be better off buying 1,000 bottles of beer (or some other storable asset such as land, timber, apartment buildings, wheat, or gold) than buying the Treasury bond.

Investors are well aware of all this, so when they lend money, they build in an *inflation premium (IP)* equal to the expected inflation rate over the life of the security. As discussed previously, for a short-term, default-free U.S. Treasury bill, the actual interest rate charged, $k_{T\text{-bill}}$, would be the real risk-free rate, k^*, plus the inflation premium (IP):

$$k_{T\text{-bill}} = k_{RF} = k^* + IP.$$

Therefore, if the real risk-free rate of interest were $k^* = 3\%$, and if inflation were expected to be 4 percent (and hence IP = 4%) during the next year, then the rate of interest on 1-year T-bills would be 7 percent. In January of 1990, the expected 1-year inflation rate was about 5 percent, and the yield on 1-year T-bills was about 8 percent. This implies that the real risk-free rate at that time was about 3 percent.

It is important to note that the rate of inflation built into interest rates is the *rate of inflation expected in the future,* not the rate experienced in the past. Thus, the latest reported figures might show an annual inflation rate of 3 percent, but that is for a past period. If people on the average expect a 6 percent inflation rate in the future, then 6 percent would be built into the current rate of interest. Note also that the inflation rate reflected in the interest rate on any security is the *average rate of inflation expected over the security's life.* Thus, the inflation rate built into a 1-year bond is the expected inflation rate for the next year, but the inflation rate built into a 30-year bond is the average rate of inflation expected over the next 30 years.[7]

Expectations for future inflation are closely related to, although not perfectly correlated with, rates experienced in the recent past. Therefore, if the inflation rate reported for last month increased, people would tend to raise their expectations for future inflation, and this change in expectations would cause an increase in interest rates.

---

[7]To be theoretically precise, we should use a *geometric average.* Also, since millions of investors are active in the market, it is impossible to determine exactly the consensus expected inflation rate. Survey data are available, however, which give us a reasonably good idea of what investors expect over the next few years. For example, in 1980 the University of Michigan's Survey Research Center reported that people expected inflation during the next year to be 11.9 percent and that the average rate of inflation expected over the next 5 to 10 years was 10.5 percent. Those expectations led to record high interest rates. However, the economy cooled in 1981 and 1982, and, as Figure 3-4 showed, actual inflation dropped sharply after 1980. This led to gradual reductions in the *expected future* inflation rate. In 1990, as we write this, the expected future inflation rate is about 5 percent. As inflationary expectations dropped, so did the market rate of interest.

Default Risk Premium (DRP)

The risk that a borrower will *default* on a loan, which means not to pay the interest or the principal, also affects the market interest rate on a security: the greater the default risk, the higher the interest rate lenders charge. Treasury securities have no default risk; thus, they carry the lowest interest rates on taxable securities in the United States. For corporate bonds, the higher the bond's rating, the lower its default risk, and, consequently, the lower its interest rate.[8] Here are some representative interest rates on long-term bonds during January 1990:

U.S. Treasury	8.0%
AAA	8.9
AA	9.1
A	9.4

The difference between the interest rate on a T-bond and that on a corporate bond with similar maturity, liquidity, and other features is the *default risk premium (DRP)*. Therefore, if the bonds listed above were otherwise similar, the default risk premium would be DRP = 8.9% − 8.0% = 0.9 percentage points for AAA corporate bonds, 9.1% − 8.0% = 1.1 percentage points for AA, and 9.4% − 8.0% = 1.4 percentage points for A corporate bonds. Default risk premiums vary somewhat over time, but the January 1990 figures are representative of levels in recent years.

Liquidity Premium (LP)

A highly *liquid* asset is one that can be sold at a predictable price and thus can be converted to a well-specified amount of spendable cash on short notice. Active markets, which provide liquidity, exist for government bonds and for the stocks and bonds of larger corporations. Also, claims on certain financial intermediaries such as bank time deposits are highly liquid because banks will redeem them for cash. Real estate, as well as securities issued by small companies that are not known by many investors, are *illiquid*—they can be sold to raise cash, but not quickly and not at a predictable price. If a security is *not* liquid, investors will add a *liquidity premium (LP)* when they establish the market rate on the security. It is very difficult to measure liquidity premiums with precision, but a differential of at least two and probably four or five percentage points is thought to exist between the least liquid and the most liquid financial assets of similar default risk and maturity.

Maturity Risk Premium (MRP)

U.S. Treasury securities are free of default risk in the sense that one can be virtually certain that the federal government will pay interest on its bonds and will also pay them off when they mature. Therefore, the default risk premium on Treasury secu-

---

[8]Bond ratings, and bonds' riskiness in general, will be discussed in detail in Chapter 16. For now, merely note that bonds rated AAA are judged to have less default risk than bonds rated AA, AA bonds are less risky than A bonds, and so on.

rities is essentially zero. Further, active markets exist for Treasury securities, so their liquidity premiums are also close to zero. Thus, as a first approximation, the rate of interest on a Treasury bond should be the risk-free rate, k_{RF}, which is equal to the real risk-free rate, k^*, plus an inflation premium, IP. However, an adjustment is needed for long-term Treasury bonds. The prices of long-term bonds decline sharply whenever interest rates rise, and since interest rates can and do occasionally rise, all long-term bonds, even Treasury bonds, have an element of risk called *interest rate risk*. As a general rule, the bonds of any organization, from the U.S. government to Eastern Airlines, have more interest rate risk the longer the maturity of the bond.[9] Therefore, a *maturity risk premium (MRP)*, which is higher the longer the years to maturity, must be included in the required interest rate.

The effect of maturity risk premiums is to raise interest rates on long-term bonds relative to those on short-term bonds. This premium, like the others, is extremely difficult to measure, but (1) it seems to vary over time, rising when interest rates are more volatile and uncertain and falling when they are more stable, and (2) in recent years, the maturity risk premium on 30-year T-bonds appears to have generally been in the range of one or two percentage points.[10]

We should mention that although long-term bonds are heavily exposed to interest rate risk, short-term bonds are heavily exposed to *reinvestment rate risk*. When short-term bonds mature and the funds are reinvested, or "rolled over," a decline in interest rates would result in reinvestment at a lower rate, and hence would lead to a decline in interest income. To illustrate, suppose you had $100,000 invested in 1-year T-bonds, and you lived on the income. In 1981, short-term rates were about 15 percent, so your income would have been about $15,000. However, your income would have declined to about $9,000 by 1983, and to just over $6,000 by 1988. Had you invested your money in long-term bonds, your income (but not the value of the principal) would have been stable.[11] Thus, although "investing short" preserves one's principal, the interest income provided by short-term bonds varies from year to year, depending on reinvestment rates.

---

[9]For example, if you bought a 30-year Treasury bond for $1,000 in 1972, when the long-term interest rate was 7 percent, and held it until 1981, when long-term T-bond rates were about 14.5 percent, the value of your bond would have declined to about $514. That would represent a loss of almost half your money, and it demonstrates that long-term bonds, even U.S. Treasury bonds, are not riskless. However, had you invested in short-term bills in 1972 and subsequently reinvested your principal each time the bills matured, you would still have had your $1,000. This point will be discussed in detail in Chapter 7.

[10]The MRP has averaged 1.2 percentage points over the last 64 years. See *Stocks, Bonds, Bills, and Inflation: 1990 Yearbook* (Chicago: Ibbotson Associates, 1990).

[11]Long-term bonds also have some reinvestment rate risk. To actually earn the stated rate on a long-term bond, the interest payments must be reinvested at the stated rate. However, if interest rates fall, the interest payments would be reinvested at a lower rate; thus, the realized return would be less than the stated rate. Note, though, that the reinvestment rate risk is lower on a long-term bond than on a short-term bond because only the interest payments (rather than interest plus principal) on the long-term bond are exposed to reinvestment rate risk. Only zero coupon bonds, discussed in Chapter 16, are completely free of reinvestment rate risk.

Self-Test Questions

Write out the two equations for the nominal interest rate on a debt security.

Distinguish between the *real* risk-free rate of interest, k*, and the *nominal* risk-free rate of interest, k_{RF}.

What inflation rate is built into the interest rate on a security?

Does the interest rate on a T-bond include a default risk premium? Explain.

Distinguish between liquid and illiquid assets, and identify some assets that are liquid and some that are illiquid.

Briefly explain the following statement: "Although long-term bonds are heavily exposed to interest rate risk, short-term bonds are heavily exposed to reinvestment rate risk."

THE TERM STRUCTURE OF INTEREST RATES

A study of Figure 3-3 reveals that at certain times, such as in 1990, short-term interest rates are lower than long-term rates, whereas at other times, such as in 1980 and 1981, short-term rates are higher than long-term rates. The relationship between long- and short-term rates, which is known as the *term structure of interest rates,* is important to corporate treasurers, who must decide whether to borrow by issuing long- or short-term debt, and to investors, who must decide whether to buy long- or short-term bonds. Thus, it is important to understand (1) how long- and short-term rates are related to each other and (2) what causes shifts in their relative positions.

To begin, we can look up in a source such as *The Wall Street Journal* or the *Federal Reserve Bulletin* the interest rates on bonds of various maturities at a given point in time. For example, the tabular section of Figure 3-5 presents interest rates for Treasury issues of different maturities on two dates. The set of data for a given date, when plotted on a graph such as that in the Figure 3-5 graph, is called the *yield curve* for that date. The yield curve changes both in position and in slope over time. In March of 1980, all rates were relatively high, and short-term rates were higher than long-term rates, so the yield curve on that date was *downward sloping.* However, in March of 1990, all rates had fallen, and short-term rates were lower than long-term rates, so the yield curve at that time was *upward sloping.* Had we drawn the yield curve during January of 1982, it would have been essentially horizontal, for long-term and short-term bonds on that date had about the same rate of interest. (See Figure 3-3.)

Figure 3-5 shows yield curves for U.S. Treasury securities, but we could have constructed them for corporate bonds; for example, we could have developed yield curves for IBM, General Motors, Eastern Airlines, or any other company that borrows money over a range of maturities. Had we constructed such curves and plotted them on Figure 3-5, the corporate yield curves would have been above those for Treasury securities on the same date because the corporate yields would include default risk

Figure 3-5   U.S. Treasury Bond Interest Rates on Different Dates

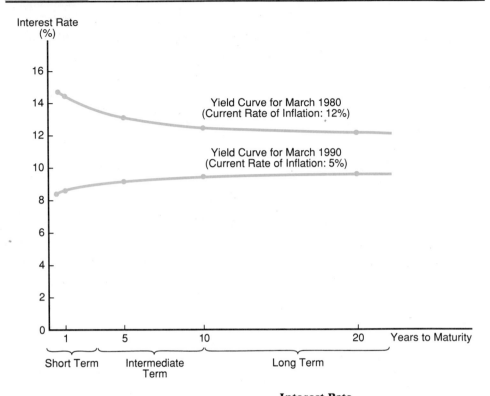

Term to Maturity	Interest Rate	
	March 1980	**March 1990**
6 months	15.0%	8.2%
1 year	14.0	8.3
5 years	13.5	8.6
10 years	12.8	8.7
20 years	12.5	8.8

premiums, but they would have had the same general shape as the Treasury curves. Also, the riskier the corporation, the higher its yield curve; thus, Eastern, which has declared bankruptcy and as of this writing is awaiting creditor approval of its business plan, would have had a yield curve substantially higher than that of IBM, which is an extremely strong company.

Historically, in most years long-term rates have been above short-term rates, so usually the yield curve has been upward sloping. For this reason, people often call an upward-sloping yield curve a *"normal" yield curve* and a yield curve which slopes downward an *inverted,* or *"abnormal," yield curve.* Thus, in Figure 3-5 the yield curve for March 1980 was inverted, but the one for March 1990 was normal. We explain in the next section why an upward slope is the normal situation, but, briefly, the reason is that short-term securities are less risky than longer-term securities, hence short-term rates are normally lower than long-term rates.

Term Structure Theories

Several theories have been used to explain the shape of the yield curve. The three major ones are (1) the market segmentation theory, (2) the liquidity preference theory, and (3) the expectations theory.

Market Segmentation Theory. Briefly, the *market segmentation theory* states that each lender and each borrower has a preferred maturity. For example, a person borrowing to buy a long-term asset like a house, or an electric utility company borrowing to build a power plant, would want a long-term loan. However, a retailer borrowing in September to build its inventories for Christmas would prefer a short-term loan. Similar differences exist among savers, and a person saving up to take a vacation next summer would want to lend in the short-term market, but someone saving for retirement 20 years hence would probably buy long-term securities.

The thrust of the market segmentation theory is that the slope of the yield curve depends on supply/demand conditions in the long-term and short-term markets. Thus, according to this theory, the yield curve could at any given time be either flat, upward sloping, or downward sloping. An upward-sloping yield curve would occur when there was a large supply of funds relative to demand in the short-term market but a relative shortage of funds in the long-term market. Similarly, a downward-sloping curve would indicate relatively strong demand in the short-term market compared to that in the long-term market, while a flat curve would indicate balanced demand in the two markets.

Liquidity Preference Theory. The *liquidity preference theory* states that long-term bonds normally yield more than short-term bonds for two reasons: (1) Investors generally prefer to hold short-term securities, because such securities are more liquid in the sense that they can be converted to cash with little danger of loss of principal. Investors will, therefore, accept lower yields on short-term securities. (2) At the same time, borrowers react in exactly the opposite way — borrowers generally prefer long-term debt, because short-term debt exposes them to the risk of having to repay the debt under adverse conditions. Accordingly, borrowers are willing to pay a higher rate, other things held constant, for long-term funds than for short-term funds. Taken together, these two sets of preferences — and hence the liquidity preference theory — imply that under normal conditions, a positive maturity risk premium (MRP) exists which increases with maturity; thus, the yield curve should be upward sloping.

Expectations Theory. The *expectations theory* states that the yield curve depends on expectations about future inflation rates. Specifically, k_t, the nominal interest rate on a U.S. Treasury bond that matures in t years, is found as follows:

$$k_t = k^* + IP_t.$$

Here k^* is the real risk-free interest rate, and IP_t is an inflation premium which is equal to the average expected rate of inflation over the t years before the bond matures. Under the expectations theory, the maturity risk premium (MRP) is assumed to be zero, and, for Treasury securities, the default risk premium (DRP) and liquidity premium (LP) are also zero.

To illustrate, suppose that in late December of 1990 the real risk-free rate of interest was $k^* = 3\%$ and expected inflation rates for the next 3 years were as follows:[12]

	Expected Annual (1-Year) Inflation Rate	Expected Average Inflation Rate from 1990 to Indicated Year
1991	4%	4%/1 = 4.0%
1992	6%	(4% + 6%)/2 = 5.0%
1993	8%	(4% + 6% + 8%)/3 = 6.0%

Given these expectations, the following pattern of interest rates should exist:

	Real Risk-free Rate (k^*)		Inflation Premium, Which is Equal to the Average Expected Inflation Rate (IP_t)		Treasury Bond Rate for Each Maturity $(k_{T\text{-bond}})$
1-year bond	3%	+	4.0%	=	7.0%
2-year bond	3%	+	5.0%	=	8.0%
3-year bond	3%	+	6.0%	=	9.0%

Had the pattern of expected inflation rates been reversed, with inflation expected to fall from 8 percent to 6 percent and then to 4 percent, the following situation would have existed:

	Real Risk-free Rate		Average Expected Inflation Rate		Treasury Bond Rate for Each Maturity
1-year bond	3%	+	8.0%	=	11.0%
2-year bond	3%	+	7.0%	=	10.0%
3-year bond	3%	+	6.0%	=	9.0%

These hypothetical data are plotted in Figure 3-6. According to the expectations theory, whenever the annual rate of inflation is expected to decline, the yield curve must be downward sloping, whereas it must be upward sloping if inflation is expected to increase.

---

[12]Technically, we should be using geometric averages rather than arithmetic averages, but the differences are not material in this example. For a discussion of this point, see Robert C. Radcliffe, *Investment: Concepts, Analysis, and Strategy,* 2nd ed. (Glenview, Ill.: Scott, Foresman, 1990), Chapter 6.

Figure 3-6   Hypothetical Example of the Term Structure of Interest Rates

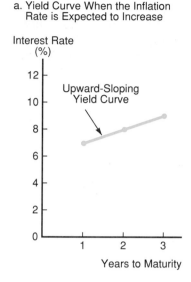

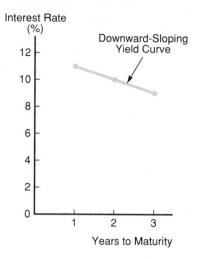

Various tests of the theories have been conducted, and these tests indicate that all three theories have some validity. Thus, the shape of the yield curve at any given time is affected (1) by supply-demand conditions in long- and short-term markets, (2) by liquidity preferences, and (3) by expectations about future inflation. One factor may dominate at one time, another at another time, but all three affect the term structure of interest rates.

Self-Test Questions

What is a yield curve, and what information would you need to draw this curve?

Distinguish among the following theories: (1) market segmentation theory, (2) liquidity preference theory, and (3) expectations theory.

Distinguish between the shapes of a "normal" yield curve and an "abnormal" yield curve and explain why each might exist.

OTHER FACTORS THAT INFLUENCE INTEREST RATE LEVELS

In addition to inflationary expectations, liquidity preferences, and the supply-demand situation, other factors also influence the general level of interest rates and the shape of the yield curve. The four most important ones are (1) Federal Reserve policy, (2) the level of the federal budget deficit, (3) the foreign trade balance, and (4) the level of business activity.

Federal Reserve Policy

As you probably learned in your studies of economics, (1) the money supply has a major effect on both the level of economic activity and the rate of inflation, and (2) in the United States the Federal Reserve System controls the money supply. If the Fed wants to stimulate the economy, it increases growth in the money supply. The initial effect of such an action is to cause interest rates to decline, but the action may also lead to an increase in the expected rate of inflation, which in turn could push interest rates up. The reverse holds if the Fed tightens the money supply.

To illustrate, in 1981 inflation was quite high, so the Fed tightened up the money supply. The Fed deals primarily in the short-term end of the market, so this tightening had the direct effect of pushing short-term interest rates up sharply. At the same time, the very fact that the Fed was taking strong action to reduce inflation led to a decline in expectations for long-run inflation, which led to a drop in long-term bond yields. Short-term rates decreased shortly thereafter.

During periods when the Fed is actively intervening in the markets, the yield curve will be distorted. Short-term rates will be temporarily "too high" if the Fed is tightening credit and "too low" if it is easing credit. Long-term rates are not affected as much by Fed intervention, except to the extent that such intervention affects expectations for long-term inflation.

Federal Deficits

If the federal government spends more than it takes in from tax revenues, it runs a deficit, and that deficit must be covered either by borrowing or by printing money. If the government borrows, this added demand for funds pushes up interest rates. If it prints money, this increases expectations for future inflation, which also drives up interest rates. Thus, the larger the federal deficit, other things held constant, the higher the level of interest rates. Whether long- or short-term rates are more affected depends on how the deficit is financed, so we cannot state, in general, how deficits will affect the slope of the yield curve.

Foreign Trade Balance

Businesses and individuals in the United States buy from and sell to people and firms in other countries. If we buy more than we sell (that is, import more than we export), we are said to run a *foreign trade deficit*. When trade deficits occur, they must be financed, with the main source of financing being debt. In other words, if we import $200 billion of goods but export only $100 billion, we run a trade deficit of $100 billion. We must borrow the $100 billion.[13] Therefore, the larger our trade

---

[13]The deficit could also be financed by selling assets, including gold, corporate stocks, entire companies, and real estate. The United States has financed its massive trade deficits by all of these means in recent years, but the primary method has been by borrowing.

deficit, the more we must borrow, and as we increase our borrowing, this drives up interest rates. Also, foreigners are willing to hold U.S. debt if and only if the interest rate on this debt is competitive with interest rates in other countries. Therefore, if the Federal Reserve attempts to lower interest rates in the United States, causing our rates to fall below rates abroad, then foreigners will sell U.S. bonds, those sales will depress bond prices, and the result will be higher U.S. rates.

The United States has been running annual trade deficits since the mid-1970s, and the cumulative effect of these deficits is that the United States is by far the largest debtor nation of all time. As a result, interest rates are very much influenced by the annual trade deficit situation (larger trade deficits lead to higher U.S. interest rates), and also by interest rate trends in other countries around the world (higher rates abroad lead to higher U.S. rates). Because of all this, U.S. corporate treasurers must keep up with developments in the world economy.

Business Activity

Figure 3-3, presented earlier, can be examined to see how business conditions influence interest rates. Here are the key points revealed by the graph:

1.   Because inflation had generally been increasing from 1953 to 1981, the general tendency during this period had been toward higher interest rates. Since 1981, the trend has generally been downward.

2.   Until 1966, short-term rates were almost always below long-term rates. Thus, in those years the yield curve was almost always "normal" in the sense that it was upward sloping.

3.   The shaded areas in the graph represent recessions, during which both the demand for money and the rate of inflation tend to fall, and, at the same time, the Federal Reserve tends to increase the money supply in an effort to stimulate the economy. As a result, there is a tendency for interest rates to decline during recessions.

4.   During recessions, short-term rates experience sharper declines than long-term rates. This occurs because (1) the Fed operates mainly in the short-term sector and hence its intervention has a major effect here, and (2) long-term rates reflect the average expected inflation rate over the next 20 to 30 years, and this expectation generally does not change much, even when the current rate of inflation is low because of a recession.

Self-Test Questions

Other than inflationary expectations, liquidity preferences, and normal supply-demand fluctuations, name four additional factors which influence interest rates, and explain their effects.

How does the Fed stimulate the economy, and what are the effects of this action on interest rates?

INTEREST RATE LEVELS AND STOCK PRICES

Interest rates have two effects on corporate profits: (1) Because interest is a cost, the higher the rate of interest, the lower a firm's profits, other things held constant; and (2) interest rates affect the level of economic activity, which affects corporate profits. Interest rates obviously affect stock prices because of their effects on profits, but, perhaps even more important, they have an effect due to competition in the marketplace between stocks and bonds. If interest rates rise sharply, investors can get higher returns in the bond market, which induces them to sell stocks and to transfer funds from the stock market to the bond market. Such transfers in response to rising interest rates obviously depress stock prices. Of course, the reverse occurs if interest rates decline. Indeed, the bull market of 1985–1987, when the Dow Jones Industrial Index rose from 1100 to over 2700, was caused almost entirely by the sharp drop in long-term interest rates.

The experience of Commonwealth Edison (CWE), the electric utility serving the Chicago area, can be used to illustrate the effects of interest rates on stock prices. In 1984 CWE's stock sold for $21 per share, and, since the company paid a $3 dividend, the dividend yield was $3/$21 = 14.3%. CWE's bonds at the time also yielded about 14.3 percent. Thus, if someone had $100,000 and invested it in either the stock or the bonds, his or her annual income would have been about $14,300. (The investor might also have expected the stock price to grow over time, providing some capital gains, but that point is not relevant for the example.)

By 1990, all interest rates were lower, and CWE's bonds were yielding only 9.7 percent. If the stock still yielded 14.3 percent, investors could switch $100,000 out of the bonds and into the stock and, in the process, increase their annual income from $9,700 to $14,300. Many people did exactly that—as interest rates dropped, orders poured in for the stock, and its price was bid up. In March 1990, CWE's stock sold for $33, up 57 percent over the 1984 level, and the dividend yield (8.8%) was close to CWE's bond yield (9.7%).

Self-Test Question

In what two ways do changes in interest rates affect stock prices?

INTEREST RATES AND BUSINESS DECISIONS

The yield curve for March 1990, shown earlier in Figure 3-5, indicates how much the U.S. government had to pay in 1990 to borrow money for 1 year, 5 years, 10 years, and so on. A business borrower would have had to pay somewhat more, but assume for the moment that we are back in 1990 and that the yield curve for that year also applies to your company. Now suppose your company has decided (1) to build a new plant with a 20-year life which will cost $1 million and (2) to raise the $1 million by selling an issue of debt (or borrowing) rather than by selling stock. If you borrowed in 1990 on a short-term basis—say for one year—your interest cost for that year would be only 8.3 percent, or $83,000, whereas if you used long-term (20-year) financing, your cost would be 8.8 percent, or $88,000. Therefore, at first glance, it would seem that you should use short-term debt.

However, this could prove to be a horrible mistake. If you use short-term debt, you will have to renew your loan every year, and the rate charged on each new loan will reflect the then-current short-term rate. Interest rates could return to their March 1980 levels, so by 1991 you could be paying 14 percent, or $140,000, per year. These high interest payments would cut into and perhaps eliminate your profits. Your reduced profitability could easily increase your firm's risk to the point where its bond rating would be lowered, causing lenders to increase the risk premium built into the interest rate they charge, which in turn would force you to pay even higher rates. These very high interest rates would further reduce your profitability, worrying lenders even more, and making them reluctant to renew your loan. If your lenders refused to renew the loan and demanded payment, as they have every right to do, you might have trouble raising the cash. If you had to make price cuts to convert physical assets to cash, you might incur heavy operating losses, or even bankruptcy.

On the other hand, if you used long-term financing in 1990, your interest costs would remain constant at $88,000 per year, so an increase in interest rates in the economy would not hurt you. You might even be able to buy up some of your bankrupt competitors at bargain prices — bankruptcies increase dramatically when interest rates rise, primarily because many firms do use short-term debt.

Does all this suggest that firms should always avoid short-term debt? Not necessarily. If inflation remains low in the next few years, so will interest rates. If you had borrowed on a long-term basis for 8.8 percent in March 1990, your company would be at a major disadvantage if its debt were locked in at 8.8 percent while its competitors (who used short-term debt in 1990 and thus rode interest rates down in subsequent years) had a borrowing cost of only 6 or 7 percent. On the other hand, large federal deficits might drive inflation and interest rates up to new record levels. In that case, you would wish you had borrowed on a long-term basis in 1990.

Financing decisions would be easy if we could develop accurate forecasts of future interest rates. Unfortunately, predicting future interest rates with consistent accuracy is somewhere between difficult and impossible — people who make a living by selling interest rate forecasts say it is difficult, but many others say it is impossible.

Even if it is difficult to predict future interest rate *levels,* it is easy to predict that interest rates will *fluctuate* — they always have, and they always will. This being the case, sound financial policy calls for using a mix of long- and short-term debt, as well as equity, in such a manner that the firm can survive in most interest rate environments. Further, the optimal financial policy depends in an important way on the nature of the firm's assets — the easier it is to sell off assets and thus to pay off debts, the more feasible it is to use large amounts of short-term debt. This makes it more feasible to finance current assets than fixed assets with short-term debt. We will return to this issue later in the book, when we discuss short-term financial planning.

Self-Test Questions

If short-term interest rates are lower than long-term rates, why might a firm still choose to finance with long-term debt?

Explain the following statement: "The optimal financial policy depends in an important way on the nature of the firm's assets."

MULTINATIONAL FINANCE
Eurocurrency Market

A *Eurodollar* is a U.S. dollar deposited in a bank outside the United States. (Although they are called Eurodollars because they originated in Europe, Eurodollars are really any dollars deposited outside the United States.) The bank in which the deposit is made may be a host country institution, such as Barclay's Bank in London, the foreign branch of a U.S. bank, such as Citibank's Paris branch, or even a foreign branch of a third-country bank, such as Barclay's Munich branch. Most Eurodollar deposits are for $500,000 or more, and they have maturities ranging from overnight to about 5 years.

The major difference between regular U.S. time deposits and Eurodollar deposits is their geographic locations. The deposits do not involve different currencies—in both cases, dollars are on deposit. However, Eurodollars are outside the direct control of the U.S. monetary authorities; therefore, U.S. banking regulations, such as fractional reserves and FDIC insurance premiums, do not apply. The absence of these costs means that the interest rate paid on Eurodollar deposits tends to be higher than domestic U.S. rates on equivalent instruments.

Interest rates on Eurodollar deposits (and loans) are tied to a standard rate known by the acronym *LIBOR,* which stands for *London Inter-Bank Offer Rate.* LIBOR is the rate of interest offered by the largest and strongest London banks on deposits of other large banks of the highest credit standing. In March 1990, LIBOR rates were approximately six-tenths of a percentage point above domestic U.S. bank rates on time deposits of the same maturity—7.9 percent for 3-month CDs versus 8.5 percent for LIBOR CDs.

Although the dollar is the leading international currency, German marks, Swiss francs, Japanese yen, and other currencies are also deposited outside their home countries; these *Eurocurrencies* are handled in exactly the same way as Eurodollars.

Eurodollars are borrowed by U.S. and foreign corporations and governments, which need dollars for various purposes, especially to pay for goods exported from the United States and to invest in the U.S. stock market. Also, U.S. dollars are used as an international currency, or international medium of exchange, and many Eurodollars are used for this purpose. It is interesting to note that Eurodollars were actually "invented" by the Russians in 1946. International merchants did not trust the Russians or their rubles, so the Russians bought some dollars (for gold), deposited them in a Paris bank, and then used them to buy goods in the world markets. Others soon found it convenient to use dollars this same way, and soon the Eurodollar market was in full swing.

SUMMARY

In this chapter we discussed the nature of financial markets, the types of institutions that operate in these markets, how interest rates are determined, and some of the ways in which interest rates affect business decisions. The key concepts covered are listed below.

- There are many different types of *financial markets*. Each market serves a different set of customers or deals with a different type of security.

- Transfers of capital between borrowers and savers take place (1) by *direct transfers* of money and securities, (2) by transfers through *investment banking houses,* which act as middlemen, and (3) by transfers through *financial intermediaries,* which create new securities.

- The *stock market* is an especially important market because this is where stock prices (which are used to "grade" managers' performances) are established.

- There are two basic types of stock markets—the *organized exchanges* and the *over-the-counter market.*

- Capital is allocated through the price system—a price is charged to "rent" money. Lenders charge *interest* on funds they lend, while equity investors receive dividends and capital gains in return for letting the firm use their money.

- Four fundamental factors affect the cost of money: (1) *production opportunities,* (2) *time preferences for consumption,* (3) *risk,* and (4) *inflation.*

- The *risk-free rate of interest, k_{RF},* is defined as the real risk-free rate, k^*, plus an inflation premium (IP): $k_{RF} = k^* + IP$.

- The *nominal interest rate* on a debt security, k, is composed of the real risk-free rate, k^*, plus premiums that reflect inflation (IP), default risk (DRP), liquidity (LP), and maturity risk (MRP): $k = k^* + IP + DRP + LP + MRP$.

- If the *real risk-free rate of interest and the various premiums were constant over time,* interest rates in the economy would be *stable.* However, the *premiums*— especially the premium for expected inflation—*do change over time, causing market interest rates to change.* Also, Federal Reserve intervention to increase or decrease the money supply, as well as international currency flows, lead to fluctuations in interest rates.

- The relationship between the yields on securities and the securities' maturities is known as the *term structure of interest rates,* and the *yield curve* is a graph of this relationship.

- The yield curve is normally *upward sloping*—this is called a *normal yield curve*—but the curve can slope downward (an *inverted yield curve*) if the demand for short-term funds is relatively strong, or if the rate of inflation is expected to decline.

- *Interest rate levels have a profound effect on stock prices.* Higher interest rates (1) depress the economy, (2) increase interest expenses and thus lower corporate profits, and (3) cause investors to sell stocks and transfer funds to the bond market. Each of these factors tends to depress stock prices.

- *Eurodollars* are U.S. dollars deposited in banks outside the United States. Interest rates on Eurodollars are tied to *LIBOR,* the *London Inter-Bank Offer Rate.*

Interest rate levels have a significant influence on corporate financial policy. Because interest rate levels are difficult if not impossible to predict, sound financial policy calls for using a mix of short- and long-term debt, and also for positioning the firm to survive in any future interest rate environment.

Questions

3-1   Define each of the following terms:
    a.   Money market; capital market
    b.   Primary market; secondary market
    c.   Investment banker; financial service corporation
    d.   Financial intermediary
    e.   Mutual fund; money market fund
    f.   Organized security exchanges; over-the-counter market
    g.   Production opportunities; time preferences for consumption
    h.   Real risk-free rate of interest, k^*; nominal risk-free rate of interest, k_{RF}
    i.   Inflation premium (IP)
    j.   Default risk premium (DRP)
    k.   Liquidity; liquid asset; liquidity premium (LP)
    l.   Interest rate risk; maturity risk premium (MRP)
    m.   Reinvestment rate risk
    n.   Term structure of interest rates; yield curve
    o.   "Normal" yield curve; inverted ("abnormal") yield curve
    p.   Market segmentation theory; liquidity preference theory
    q.   Expectations theory
    r.   Eurodollars; LIBOR

3-2   What are financial intermediaries, and what economic functions do they perform?

3-3   Suppose interest rates on residential mortgages of equal risk were 8 percent in California and 10 percent in New York. Could this differential persist? What forces might tend to equalize rates? Would differentials in borrowing costs for businesses of equal risk located in California and New York be more or less likely to exist than differentials in residential mortgage rates? Would differentials in the cost of money for New York and California firms be more likely to exist if the firms being compared were very large or if they were very small? What are the implications of all this for the pressure now being put on Congress to permit banks to engage in nationwide branching?

3-4   What would happen to the standard of living in the United States if people lost faith in the safety of our financial institutions? Why?

3-5   How does a cost-efficient capital market help to reduce the prices of goods and services?

3-6   Which fluctuate more, long-term or short-term interest rates? Why?

3-7   Suppose you feel that the economy is just entering a recession. Your firm must raise capital immediately, and debt will be used. Should you borrow on a long-term or a short-term basis?

3-8   Suppose the population of Area A is relatively young while that of Area B is relatively old, but everything else about the two areas is equal.
    a.   Would interest rates likely be the same or different in the two areas? Explain.
    b.   Would a trend toward nationwide branching by banks and savings and loans, and the development of nationwide diversified financial corporations, affect your answer to Part a?

3-9   Suppose a new process was developed which could be used to make oil out of seawater. The equipment required is quite expensive but it would, in time, lead to very low prices for gasoline, electricity, and other types of energy. What effect would this have on interest rates?

3-10   Suppose a new and much more liberal Congress and administration were elected, and their first order of business was to take away the independence of the Federal Reserve System and to force the Fed to greatly expand the money supply. What effect would this have

    a.   On the level and slope of the yield curve immediately after the announcement?

    b.   On the level and slope of the yield curve that would exist two or three years in the future?

3-11 It is a fact that the federal government (1) encouraged the development of the savings and loan industry; (2) virtually forced the industry to make long-term, fixed-interest-rate mortgages; and (3) forced the savings and loans to obtain most of their capital as deposits that were withdrawable on demand.

    a.   Would the savings and loans be better off in a world with a "normal" or an inverted yield curve?

    b.   Would the savings and loan industry be better off if the individual institutions sold their mortgages to federal agencies and then collected servicing fees or if the institutions held the mortgages that they originated?

3-12 Suppose interest rates on Treasury bonds rose from 8 to 15 percent. Other things held constant, what do you think would happen to the price of an average company's common stock?

Self-Test Problem (Solutions Appear in Appendix D)

ST-1 **(Inflation rates)** Assume that it is now January 1, 1991. The rate of inflation is expected to be 4 percent throughout 1991. However, increased government deficits and renewed vigor in the economy are then expected to push inflation rates higher. Investors expect the inflation rate to be 5 percent in 1992, 6 percent in 1993, and 7 percent in 1994. The real risk-free rate, k^*, is currently 3 percent. Assume that no maturity risk premiums are required on bonds with 5 years or less to maturity. The current interest rate on 5-year T-bonds is 9 percent.

    a.   What is the expected arithmetic average inflation rate over the next 4 years?

    b.   What should be the prevailing interest rate on 4-year T-bonds?

    c.   What is the implied expected inflation rate in 1995, or Year 5?

Problems

3-1 **(Yield curves)** Suppose you and most other investors expect the rate of inflation to be 8 percent next year, to fall to 6 percent during the following year, and then to run at a rate of 4 percent thereafter. Assume that the real risk-free rate, k^*, is 2 percent and that maturity risk premiums on Treasury securities rise from zero on very short-term bonds (those that mature in a few days) by 0.2 percentage points for each year to maturity, up to a limit of 1.0 percentage points on 5-year or longer-term T-bonds.

    a.   Calculate the interest rate on 1-, 2-, 3-, 4-, 5-, 10-, and 20-year Treasury securities, and plot the yield curve.

    b.   Now suppose IBM, an AAA-rated company, had bonds with the same maturities as the Treasury bonds. As an approximation, plot an IBM yield curve on the same graph with the Treasury bond yield curve. (Hint: Think about the default risk premium on IBM's long-term versus its short-term bonds.)

    c.   Now plot the approximate yield curve of a firm such as Eastern Airlines, which has serious financial problems, and is now in bankruptcy.

3-2   **(Yield curves)** The following yields on U.S. Treasury securities were taken from *The Wall Street Journal* of April 2, 1990:

Term	Rate
6 months	8.2%
1 year	8.4
2 years	8.6
3 years	8.6
4 years	8.7
5 years	8.7
10 years	8.8
20 years	8.8
30 years	8.8

Plot a yield curve based on these data. (Note: If you looked the data up in the *Journal*, you would find that some of the bonds—for example, the 3 percent issue which matures in February 1995—will show very low yields. These are "flower bonds," which are generally owned by older people and are associated with funerals because they can be turned in and used at par value to pay estate taxes. Thus, flower bonds always sell at close to par and have a yield which is close to the coupon yield, irrespective of the "going rate of interest." Also, the yields quoted in the *Journal* are not for the same point in time for all bonds, so random variations will appear. An interest rate series that is purged of flower bonds and random variations, and hence provides a better picture of the true yield curve, is known as the "constant maturity series"; this series can be obtained from the *Federal Reserve Bulletin.*)

3-3   **(Expected rate of interest)** Suppose the annual yield on a 2-year bond is 10.5 percent while that on a 1-year bond of comparable risk is 9 percent. Using the expectations theory, forecast the interest rate on a 1-year bond during the second year.

3-4   **(Expected rate of interest)** Assume that the real rate is 3 percent and that the maturity risk premium is zero. If the nominal rate of interest on 1-year bonds is 11 percent and that on 2-year bonds is 13 percent, what inflation rate is expected during Year 2? What is the 1-year interest rate that is expected for Year 2? Comment on why the average rate over the 2-year period differs from the 1-year rate expected for Year 2.

3-5   **(Inflation and interest rates)** In late 1980 the U.S. Commerce Department released new figures which showed that inflation was running at an annual rate of close to 15 percent. However, many investors expected the new Reagan administration to be more effective in controlling inflation than the Carter administration had been. At the time the prime rate of interest was 21 percent, a record high. However, many observers felt that the extremely high interest rates and generally tight credit, which were brought on by the Federal Reserve System's attempts to curb the inflation rate, would shortly bring about a recession, which in turn would lead to a decline in the inflation rate and also in the rate of interest. Assume that at the beginning of 1981 the expected rate of inflation for 1981 was 12 percent; for 1982, 10 percent; for 1983, 8 percent; and for 1984 and thereafter, 6 percent.

a.   What was the average expected inflation rate over the 5-year period 1981–1985?

b.   What average *nominal* interest rate would, over the 5-year period, be expected to produce a 2 percent real rate of return?

c.   Assuming a real risk-free rate of 2 percent and a maturity risk premium which starts at 0.1 percent and increases by 0.1 percent each year, estimate the interest rate in January 1981 on bonds that mature in 1, 2, 5, 10, and 20 years, and draw a yield curve based on these data.

d.   Describe the general economic conditions that could be expected to produce an upward-sloping yield curve.

e.   If the consensus among investors in early 1981 had been that the expected rate of inflation for every future year was 10 percent—that is, $I_t = I_{t+1} = 10\%$ for $t = 1$ to ∞—what do you think the yield curve would have looked like? Consider all the factors that are likely to affect the curve. Does your answer here make you question the yield curve you drew in Part c?

Mini Case

Assume that you recently graduated with a degree in finance and have just reported to work as an investment advisor at the firm of Lang & Puckett, Inc. Your first assignment is to explain the nature of the U.S. financial markets and institutions to Brigette Amberger, a professional tennis player who has just come to the United States from Germany. Amberger is a highly ranked tennis player who expects to invest substantial amounts of money through Lang & Puckett. She is also very bright, and, therefore, she would like to understand in general terms what will happen to her money. Your boss has developed the following questions, which you must answer to explain the U.S. financial system to Amberger.

a.   What is a financial market? How are financial markets differentiated from markets for physical assets?

b.   Differentiate between money markets and capital markets.

c.   Differentiate between a primary market and a secondary market. If Apple Computer decided to issue additional common stock, and Amberger purchased 100 shares of this stock from Merrill Lynch, the underwriter, would this transaction be a primary market transaction or a secondary market transaction? Would it make a difference if Amberger purchased previously outstanding Apple stock in the over-the-counter market?

d.   Describe the three primary ways in which capital is transferred between savers and borrowers.

e.   Securities can be traded on organized exchanges or in the over-the-counter market. Define each of these markets, and describe how stocks are traded in each of them.

f.   What do we call the price that a borrower must pay for debt capital? What is the price of equity capital? What are the four most fundamental factors that affect the cost of money, or the general level of interest rates, in the economy?

g.   What is the real risk-free rate of interest, k^*? The nominal risk-free rate, k_{RF}? How are these two rates measured?

h.   Define the terms inflation premium (IP), default risk premium (DRP), liquidity premium (LP), and maturity risk premium (MRP). Which of these premiums is included when determining the interest rate on (1) short-term U.S. Treasury securities, (2) long-term U.S. Treasury securities, (3) short-term corporate securities, and (4) long-term corporate securities? Explain how the premiums would vary over time and among the different securities listed above.

i.   What is the term structure of interest rates? What is a yield curve? At any given time, how would the yield curve facing a given company such as AT&T or Eastern Airlines (whose bonds are classified as "junk bonds") compare with the yield curve for U.S. Treasury securities?

j.   Several theories have been advanced to explain the shape of the yield curve. The three major ones are (1) the market segmentation theory, (2) the liquidity preference theory, and (3) the expectations theory. Briefly describe each of these theories. Which one do economists regard as being "true"?

k.   Suppose most investors expect the rate of inflation to be 5 percent next year, 6 percent the following year, 7 percent the third year, and 8 percent thereafter. The real risk-free rate is 3 percent, and the maturity premium is zero for bonds that mature in 1 year or less, 0.1 percent for 2-year bonds, and it increases by 0.1 percent per year thereafter for 20 years, after which it is stable. What is the interest rate on 1-year, 5-year, and 20-year Treasury bonds? Draw a yield curve with these data. Is your yield curve consistent with the three term structure theories?

Selected Additional References

Two of the most widely used textbooks on interest rates and financial markets are

Robinson, Ronald I., and Dwayne Wrightsman, *Financial Markets: The Accumulation and Allocation of Wealth* (New York: McGraw-Hill, 1980).

Van Horne, James C., *Financial Market Rates and Flows* (Englewood Cliffs, N. J.: Prentice-Hall, 1984).

For current empirical data and a forecast of monetary conditions, see the most recent edition of this annual publication:

Salomon Brothers, *Supply and Demand for Credit* (New York).

The classic works on term structure theories include the following:

Culbertson, John M., "The Term Structure of Interest Rates," *Quarterly Journal of Economics,* November 1957, 489–504.

Fisher, Irving, "Appreciation and Interest," *Publications of the American Economic Association,* August 1896, 23–29 and 91–92.

Hicks, J. R., *Value and Capital* (London: Oxford University Press, 1946).

Lutz, F. A., "The Structure of Interest Rates," *Quarterly Journal of Economics,* November 1940, 36–63.

Modigliani, Franco, and Richard Sutch, "Innovations in Interest Rate Policy," *American Economic Review,* May 1966, 178–197.

For additional information on financial institutions, see

Campbell, Tim S., *Financial Institutions, Markets, and Economic Activity* (New York: McGraw-Hill, 1982).

Gup, Benton E., *The Management of Financial Institutions* (Boston: Houghton Mifflin, 1984).

Kaufman, George G., *The U.S. Financial System: Money, Markets, and Institutions* (Englewood Cliffs, N. J.: Prentice-Hall, 1983).

Kidwell, David S., and Richard L. Peterson, *Financial Institutions, Markets, and Money* (Hinsdale, Ill.: Dryden Press, 1990).

Mishkin, Frederic S., *Money, Banking, and Financial Markets* (Boston: Little, Brown, 1986).

Wilcox, James A., *Current Readings on Money, Banking, and Financial Markets: 1989–1990 Edition* (Glenview, Ill.: Scott, Foresman/Little, Brown, 1989).

Williamson, J. Peter, *The Investment Banking Handbook* (New York: John Wiley & Sons, 1988).

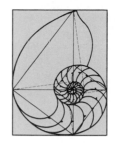

PART II

Valuation and the Cost of Capital

CHAPTER 4

Risk and Return: Part 1

On October 16, 1987, T. Boone Pickens, Chairman of Mesa Petroleum and one of the best-known financiers and corporate raiders in the United States, addressed the Financial Management Association's annual conference in Las Vegas. Pickens's talk was on the subject of whether the managements of most large corporations are more interested in their stockholders' welfare or in their own welfare. His position was that many, if not most, managers are primarily concerned about feathering their own nests, and that they are more interested in enhancing their own wealth than that of stockholders.

Early in his talk, someone handed Pickens a note, and he then announced to the 2,000-plus audience that the Dow Jones Industrial Average was down over 75 points so far that day. This so frightened a gentleman in the audience (who had borrowed heavily to invest in the market) that he rushed out to call his broker. When he returned a few minutes later, he told Pickens and the group that the Dow had fallen further, and it was then down over 100 points. Several other announcements were made during the talk, and by the time it was over, the Dow had lost 150 points. That was on a Friday, and the following Monday the decline became a panic, with the Dow losing over 500 more points, and an average stock losing almost 25 percent of its value on that one day. At the close on Monday, October 19, 1987, stocks in the United States and most other countries were down, on average, about 40 percent from the highs they had established a few weeks earlier. Of course, some stocks did much worse than the averages, but others did better, and some portfolio managers actually profited from the crash.

> Now, almost three years later, the average stock has regained all of its October 1987 losses, and the Dow has reached a new all-time high. So, on average, the October 1987 crash appears to have done no lasting harm. However, the averages obscure the damage done to many individual firms and investors—dozens of old-line securities firms, some of which had been in business a hundred years or more, were forced into bankruptcy; perhaps 50,000 people lost their jobs; and countless thousands who had been planning to take early retirement will now have to work indefinitely.

W E have no magic formula for avoiding crashes like the one of 1987, but there are ways one can judge the riskiness of individual securities, and there are ways of combining securities so that gains on some will serve to offset losses on others. Recall that in Chapter 3, when we examined the determinants of interest rates, we defined the real risk-free rate, k^*, to be the rate of interest on a risk-free security in the absence of inflation. The actual interest rate on a particular debt security was shown to be equal to the real risk-free rate plus several premiums which reflect both inflation and the riskiness of the security in question. In Chapters 4 and 5, we define more precisely the term *risk* as it relates to securities in general, we examine procedures managers use for measuring risk, and we discuss the relationship between risk and return. Then, in Chapters 6 and 7, we extend these relationships to show how security prices are determined in the financial markets. Financial managers should understand these concepts and use them as they plan the actions which will shape their firms' futures.

DEFINING AND MEASURING RISK

Risk is defined in *Webster's* as "a hazard; a peril; exposure to loss or injury." Thus, risk refers to the chance that some unfavorable event will occur. If you engage in skydiving, you are taking a chance with your life—skydiving is risky. If you bet on the horses, you are risking your money. If you invest in speculative stocks (or, really, *any* stock), you are taking a risk in the hope of making an appreciable return.

To illustrate the riskiness of financial assets, suppose an investor buys $100,000 of short-term government bonds with a yield to maturity of 10 percent. In this case, the rate of return on the investment, 10 percent, can be estimated quite precisely, and the investment is defined as being risk-free. However, if the $100,000 were invested in the stock of a company just being organized to prospect for oil in the mid-Atlantic, then the investment's return could not be estimated precisely. One might analyze the situation and conclude that the *expected* rate of return, in a statistical sense, is 20 percent, but it should also be recognized that the *actual* rate of return could range from, say, +1,000 percent to −100 percent, and, because there is a significant danger of actually earning a return considerably less than the expected return, the stock would be described as being relatively risky.

Investment risk, then, is related to the probability of earning a return less than the expected return — the greater the chance of low or negative returns, the riskier the investment. However, it is useful to define risk more precisely, and we will do so in later sections.

Self-Test Question

Explain the concept of investment risk.

PROBABILITY DISTRIBUTIONS AND EXPECTED RATES OF RETURN

Since risk refers to the probability of earning a return less than the expected return, probability distributions provide the foundation for risk measurement. To illustrate, suppose you are the financial manager of a firm which has $100,000 to invest for a period of one year. Four investment alternatives as shown in Table 4-1 are being considered:

1. One-year U.S. Treasury bills (T-bills) which offer an 8 percent rate of return. The T-bills would be bought at a discount and would return their par value at maturity.

Table 4-1   Return Estimates on Four Alternative Investments

State of the Economy	Probability of Occurrence	Investment's Rate of Return if State Occurs			
		T-Bills	Corporate Bonds	Project 1	Project 2
Deep recession	0.05	8.0%	12.0%	(3.0%)	(2.0%)
Mild recession	0.20	8.0	10.0	6.0	9.0
Average economy	0.50	8.0	9.0	11.0	12.0
Mild boom	0.20	8.0	8.5	14.0	15.0
Strong boom	0.05	8.0	8.0	19.0	26.0
	1.00				
Expected rate of return =		8.0%	9.2%	10.3%	12.0%

Notes:

a. Parentheses denote a negative return, or a loss.

b. The probabilities of occurrence must sum to 1.00 when all states are considered.

c. You should think of the returns under different states of the economy as being ranges, and the given returns as being points within those ranges. For example, think of the 10 percent return on corporate bonds during a mild recession as being the most likely return under that state of the economy, where a point value is used for convenience.

2.   Corporate bonds selling at par which have a 9 percent coupon (that is, which pay $9,000 in interest annually on a $100,000 investment) and a 10-year maturity. However, your firm will sell the bonds at the end of 1 year. Therefore, the rate of return realized on the bonds will depend on the interest rate level that prevails at the end of the year. This interest rate level, in turn, will depend on the state of the economy at the end of the year: A strong economy would probably lead to higher interest rates, which would decrease the market value of the bonds, while the opposite would be true if the economy were weak.

3.   Capital budgeting Project 1 which has a net cost of $100,000, zero cash flows during the year, and a payoff at the end of 1 year which depends on the state of the economy.

4.   An alternative capital project, Project 2, which also has a cost of $100,000 and a payoff at year-end, but its payoff distribution differs from that of Project 1.

A *probability distribution* is defined as a set of possible outcomes, with a probability of occurrence attached to each outcome. Thus, Table 4-1 contains four probability distributions, one for each of the four investment alternatives. The T-bills' rate of return is known with certainty—it is 8 percent irrespective of the state of the economy. Thus, T-bills have zero risk.[1] However, the actual, or realized, rates of return on the other three investments will not be known until the end of the holding period. Since their outcomes are not known with certainty, these three investments are defined as being *risky*.

Probability distributions may be either *discrete* or *continuous*.[2] A discrete probability distribution has a finite number of outcomes; thus, Table 4-1 contains discrete probability distributions. There is only one possible value, or outcome, for the T-bills' rate of return, although for the other three alternatives, there are five possible outcomes. Each outcome has a corresponding probability of occurrence. For example, the probability of the T-bills having an 8.0 percent rate of return is 1.00, and the probability of the corporate bonds having a 9.0 percent rate of return is 0.50.

If we multiply each possible outcome by its probability of occurrence and then sum these products, we have a weighted average of outcomes. The weights are the probabilities, and the weighted average is defined as the *expected value*. Since the outcomes are rates of return, the expected values are *expected rates of return*. The expected rate of return, $\hat{k}$, called "k-hat," is expressed in equation form as follows:

$$\text{Expected rate of return} = \hat{k} = \sum_{i=1}^{n} k_i P_i. \qquad \textbf{(4-1)}$$

---

[1]Note that the T-bill investment is riskless only in the sense that *nominal* returns are assured for one period. The *real* return on a T-bill is risky, as the real rate of return depends on the rate of inflation realized over the 1-year holding period. Further, T-bills can present a problem to an investor who relies upon his or her portfolio for continuing income: When the T-bills mature, they must be reinvested, and if interest rates have declined, the portfolio's income will drop. This risk, which is called *reinvestment rate risk*, is not a problem in our example since the firm's holding period matches the maturity of the bills. Finally, note that the relevant return on any investment is the return after taxes have been paid, so the rates used for decision purposes should be after-tax rates of return.

[2]We will concentrate on discrete distributions, because they are better for illustrating basic risk and return concepts. However, continuous distributions are also used extensively in financial analysis.

Here k_i is the ith possible outcome, P_i is the probability that the ith outcome will occur, and n is the number of possible outcomes.

Using Equation 4-1, we find Project 2's expected rate of return to be 12.0 percent:

$$\hat{k} = \sum_{i=1}^{5} k_i P_i$$

$$= k_1(P_1) + k_2(P_2) + k_3(P_3) + k_4(P_4) + k_5(P_5)$$

$$= -2.0\%(0.05) + 9.0\%(0.20) + 12.0\%(0.50) + 15.0\%(0.20) + 26.0\%(0.05)$$

$$= 12.0\%.$$

The expected rates of return on the other three investment alternatives were calculated similarly and are shown in Table 4-1.

Discrete probability distributions can be expressed in graphic as well as tabular form. Figure 4-1 shows bar graphs (or histograms) for Projects 1 and 2. The range of possible rates of return for Project 1 is from -3.0 to $+19.0$ percent, and the range for Project 2 is from -2.0 to $+26.0$ percent. Note that the height of each bar represents the probability of occurrence, and that the sum of the probabilities for each alternative equals 1.00. Also, note that the distribution of rates of return for Project 2 is symmetric, whereas the distribution for Project 1 is skewed to the left. Similar graphs for the T-bills and the corporate bonds would show the returns on the T-bills represented by a single spike, while the returns on the corporate bonds would have a graph that is skewed to the right.

Figure 4-1   Graphic Discrete Probability Distributions

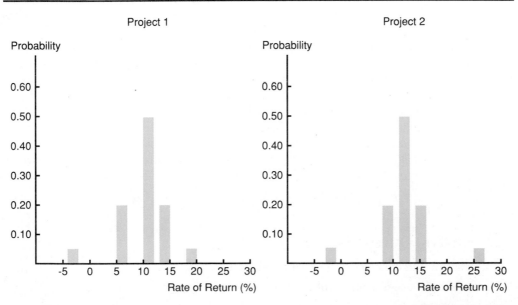

Self-Test Questions

What is a probability distribution?

Define the term "expected rate of return."

TOTAL RISK VERSUS MARKET RISK

The remainder of Chapter 4 and all of Chapter 5 are devoted to defining risk, measuring risk, and establishing relationships between risk and required rates of return. However, before we get into the details, it is useful to look forward to see where we are headed.

There are many ways that risk can be defined and measured; in Chapters 4 and 5 we concentrate on two types of risk: (1) *total risk*, which is the riskiness of an asset held in isolation, and (2) *market risk*, which is an asset's relevant, or effective, risk if it is held as one of a large number of assets in a portfolio. To illustrate total risk, suppose an investor holds a single risky asset, say a stock. In this case, the stock's risk is measured by the dispersion of returns about its expected return. The greater this dispersion, the higher the probability that the return will fall far below the expected return; thus, the greater the risk of the stock. However, when an investor holds a large number of stocks in a portfolio, say 40 or more, the important issue becomes the overall, or aggregate, risk of the portfolio of stocks because losses on one stock may be offset by gains on another stock. In this situation, the relevant risk of each stock is its market risk, which measures the stock's contribution to the overall riskiness of the portfolio, and thus accounts for diversification effects. The greater the impact of a stock on the overall riskiness of a portfolio (the more having it in the portfolio increases the portfolio's risk), the higher the market risk of the stock. As we will see in Chapter 5, a stock's market risk is affected by its total risk, but it is also influenced by the correlation of its returns with the returns on a portfolio of stocks.

Combining stocks into portfolios reduces risk, because those stocks that experience less-than-expected returns will be offset to some degree by stocks whose returns are greater than expected. Thus, rational investors will hold portfolios of stocks rather than single stocks. Further, since most investors are, presumably, rational, a stock's risk, and hence its price, will generally be based on its market risk and not on its total risk. The concepts of total and market risk are applicable to all risky assets: securities, such as stocks and bonds; real estate; precious metals; corporate capital investments; and so on. Our discussion here will focus on securities, but in Chapter 11 we will apply total and market risk concepts to corporate project analysis.

Self-Test Questions

Describe the concepts of total risk and market risk.

Are these concepts applicable only to securities? Explain.

TOTAL RISK ANALYSIS: ASSETS HELD IN ISOLATION

We can use the concepts of discrete probability distributions and expected values to help measure risk. We know that risk is present when the estimated distribution has more than one possible outcome, but how should risk be measured and quantified? To answer this question, we first focus our attention on *total risk,* which is the relevant risk for assets held in isolation.

Variance and Standard Deviation

Variance is a measure of the dispersion of a distribution around its expected value: The larger the variance, the greater the dispersion. To calculate the variance of a discrete distribution, we use the following formula:

$$\text{Variance} = \sigma^2 = \sum_{i=1}^{n} (k_i - \hat{k})^2 P_i. \tag{4-2}$$

Equation 4-2 shows that the variance is the sum of the squared deviations, weighted by each deviation's probability of occurrence.

To illustrate, we will calculate the variance of the rate of return on Project 2 from Table 4-1. We know that the project's expected rate of return, $\hat{k}$, is 12.0 percent. Thus, its variance is calculated by using Equation 4-2 plus data from Table 4-1 as follows:

$$\sigma^2 = \sum_{i=1}^{5} (k_i - \hat{k})^2 P_i$$

$$= (-2.0 - 12.0)^2(0.05) + (9.0 - 12.0)^2(0.20) + (12.0 - 12.0)^2(0.50)$$
$$+ (15.0 - 12.0)^2(0.20) + (26.0 - 12.0)^2(0.05)$$

$$= (-14.0)^2(0.05) + (-3.0)^2(0.20) + (0.0)^2(0.50)$$
$$+ (3.0)^2(0.20) + (14.0)^2(0.05)$$

$$= 9.8 + 1.8 + 0.0 + 1.8 + 9.8 = 23.2.$$

Variance is measured in the same units as the outcomes, in this case percentages, but squared.

Since it is difficult to attach meaning to a squared percentage, the standard deviation is often used as an alternative measure of dispersion about the mean. The *standard deviation* (*SD* or σ) is found by taking the square root of the variance:

$$\text{Standard deviation} = SD = \sigma = \sqrt{\sigma^2} = \sqrt{\sum_{i=1}^{n} (k_i - \hat{k})^2 P_i}. \tag{4-3}$$

Thus, the standard deviation of Project 2's rate of return can be found by using Equation 4-3 as follows:

$$\sigma = \sqrt{23.2} = 4.82\%.$$

Since the standard deviation is a measure of dispersion, we can draw some conclusions about the distribution of outcomes if the expected value and standard devia-

Table 4-2	Return and Risk Measures for the Table 4-1 Investment Alternatives			

Expected Rate of Return or Risk Measure	Investment Alternatives			
	T-Bills	**Corporate Bonds**	**Project 1**	**Project 2**
1. Expected return ($\hat{k}$)	8.00%	9.20%	10.30%	12.00%
2. Variance (Var or σ^2)	0.00	0.71	19.31	23.20
3. Standard deviation (SD or σ)	0.00%	0.84%	4.39%	4.82%
4. Coefficient of variation (CV)	0.00	0.09	0.43	0.40

tion are known. If the distribution is continuous and approximately normal, we can state that 68.3 percent of the outcomes will fall within one standard deviation of the expected value, that 95.5 percent will fall within two standard deviations, and that almost all outcomes (99.7 percent) will fall within three standard deviations.[3]

Table 4-2 contains the expected rates of return, variances, and standard deviations of all four investment alternatives, along with their coefficients of variation (CV), which we will discuss in the next section. We see that the T-bills have the smallest variance and standard deviation, while Project 2 has the largest.

On the basis of Table 4-2, one might be tempted to say that the T-bills are the least risky alternative and that Project 2 is the most risky. However, this may or may not be true; before reaching a definite conclusion, we must consider some other factors, including the magnitudes of the expected rates of return, the skewness of the distributions, our confidence in the probability distributions, and the relationship between each asset and other assets that might be held in the investment portfolio.[4]

Coefficient of Variation

As a general rule, investments with higher expected returns have larger standard deviations than investments with smaller expected returns. To illustrate, suppose some Project X has a 30 percent expected rate of return and a standard deviation of 10 percent, while some other Project Y has an expected rate of return of 10 percent

---

[3]Note that even if a distribution is not close to normal, we can evoke Tchebysheff's theorem and state that for *any* distribution, at least 89 percent of all outcomes will lie within three standard deviations of the expected value. See William Mendenhall, Richard L. Scheaffer, and Dennis D. Wackerly, *Mathematical Statistics with Applications* (Boston: Duxbury, 1981).

[4]It seems logical, in a risk analysis, to be more concerned about the probabilities of returns being less than expected rather than greater than expected. If the distribution is symmetric, the variance and standard deviation both provide true measures of the downside risk, which is simply half the total risk. However, if the distribution is skewed, the variance and standard deviation yield a distorted picture of the actual risk. If the distribution is skewed to the right, the variance and standard deviation overstate the downside risk, while if the distribution is skewed to the left, the opposite occurs. A statistic which eliminates this distortion is the *semivariance (SV)*, defined as follows:

$$\text{Semivariance} = SV = \sum_{i=1}^{m} (k_i - \hat{k})^2 P_i. \qquad \textbf{(4-2a)}$$

and a standard deviation of 5 percent. However, if the returns of Projects X and Y are approximately normal, then Project X would have a very small probability of a negative return in spite of its high σ, while Project Y, even with a standard deviation only half as large as that of Project X, would have a much higher probability of a loss. Therefore, to interpret properly the implications of standard deviations as measures of the *relative* risks of investments whose expected returns are different, we should standardize the standard deviation and calculate the risk per unit of return. This is accomplished by using the *coefficient of variation (CV)*, which is defined as the standard deviation divided by the expected value:

$$\text{Coefficient of variation} = CV = \frac{\sigma}{\hat{k}}. \tag{4-4}$$

$$\text{Project X: } CV_X = 10\%/30\% = 0.33.$$

$$\text{Project Y: } CV_Y = 5\%/10\% = 0.50.$$

Thus, we see that Project Y actually has more total risk per unit of expected return than Project X. Therefore, one could argue that Y is riskier than X in spite of the fact that X's standard deviation is larger.

Row 4 of Table 4-2 contains the coefficients of variation of the four original investment alternatives. We see that the rankings using the coefficient of variation as the risk measure are not the same as the rankings based on the standard deviation: Project 2 is riskier than Project 1 using the standard deviation, but the opposite is true when we correct for return differences and measure risk by the coefficient of variation.

Subjective versus Objective Probability Distributions

Thus far we have used subjectively estimated probability distributions in all of our examples of future, or *ex ante,* risk and return measures. We could apply the same techniques to historical, or *ex post,* data to obtain *objective* as opposed to *subjective* risk measures, provided historical data are available. For example, suppose investments similar to Project 2 have been made in each of the last 10 years. In this case, we would have 10 historical, or realized, rates of return ($\bar{k}$, pronounced "k-bar")

Here m is the set of outcomes that fall *below* the expected value. For example, look at the corporate bond alternative in Table 4-1. Remembering that its expected rate of return is 9.2 percent, the semivariance is calculated by using Equation 4-2a as follows:

$$SV = \sum_{i=1}^{3} (k_i - \hat{k})^2 P_i$$

$$= (8.0 - 9.2)^2(0.05) + (8.5 - 9.2)^2(0.20) + (9.0 - 9.2)^2(0.50) = 0.19.$$

The semivariances of all four alternatives listed in Table 4-1 are as follows: 0.00, 0.19, 12.54, and 11.60. In a symmetric distribution, we would find that the semivariance is one-half the variance. This occurs for Project 2. However, the semivariance of Project 1 is more than one-half the variance—because Project 1's returns are skewed to the left, its variance understates the downside risk. The corporate bond's semivariance is less than one-half the variance—because the bond's distribution is skewed right, its variance overstates its downside risk. Because financial data are generally not precise enough to warrant the use of highly refined analytical techniques, and because most of the distributions we deal with are relatively symmetrical, we concentrate on the variance and standard deviation as measures of dispersion.

available on these projects. We could use this set of data to determine Project 2's historical average, or *mean,* rate of return; its variance; and its standard deviation. We would have 10 sample points, and we could use the following procedures to evaluate them:

1. Average historical return $= k_{Avg} = \dfrac{\sum\limits_{t=1}^{n} \bar{k}_t}{n}$.

2. Variance $= \sigma^2 = \dfrac{\sum\limits_{t=1}^{n} (\bar{k}_t - \bar{k}_{Avg})^2}{n - 1}$.

3. Standard deviation $= \sigma = \sqrt{\dfrac{\sum\limits_{t=1}^{n} (\bar{k}_t - \bar{k}_{Avg})^2}{n - 1}}$.

These are the standard statistical procedures for handling sample data, and here we are treating the 10 years of data as if they were drawn from a larger universe of data. Of course, to use historical data to forecast future results, we must have reason to believe that conditions in the future will be similar to conditions in the past. If we do, then we could use the historical distribution as a proxy for the future, or ex ante, distribution, and the derived rate of return, variance, standard deviation, and coefficient of variation could be used to evaluate Project 2. Of course, this type of analysis is possible only for certain types of investments — if the project is an entirely new venture, then historical data will not be available, and we must rely on subjective probability estimates.

This discussion of subjective versus objective probability distributions illustrates an important point — in financial analysis, we generally face *two* sources of risk: (1) The risk associated with uncertain outcomes, given a known probability distribution, and (2) the additional risk that results from the fact that our assumed distribution may itself be incorrect. Historical data are often unavailable, and even where such data are available, the distribution itself may be changing over time. Therefore, the second source of risk is quite important. Risk analysis may appear to be quite precise, but a great deal of judgment always lies behind the analysis.

Self-Test Questions

What are some measures of total risk?

Is one of the risk measures better than the others?

What is the difference between subjective and objective probability distributions?

MARKET RISK ANALYSIS: ASSETS HELD IN PORTFOLIOS

Thus far, we have considered the riskiness of investment alternatives on the assumption that each is held in isolation. Now we analyze the riskiness of assets held in *portfolios,* or combinations of assets. As we shall see, an asset held as part of a portfolio is generally less risky than the same asset held in isolation. Indeed, an asset that would be relatively risky if held in isolation may not be risky at all if it is held in a well-diversified portfolio. Thus, considering risk in a portfolio context could completely change a decision based on an analysis of total risk.

Expected Return on a Portfolio

The expected rate of return on a portfolio is simply the weighted average of the expected returns of the individual securities in the portfolio:

$$\text{Expected return on a portfolio} = \hat{k}_p = \sum_{i=1}^{n} x_i \hat{k}_i. \qquad (4\text{--}5)$$

Here $\hat{k}_p$ is the expected rate of return on the portfolio; x_i is the fraction of the portfolio invested in the ith asset; $\hat{k}_i$ is the expected rate of return on the ith asset; and n is the number of assets in the portfolio. For example, suppose Stock A has an expected return of $\hat{k}_A = 10\%$, Stock B has $\hat{k}_B = 15\%$, and you plan to invest your money in A, in B, or in a combination of the two. If you put all your money in A, your one-stock portfolio will have an expected return of $\hat{k}_p = \hat{k}_A = 10\%$. If you invest only in B, your expected return will be $\hat{k}_p = \hat{k}_B = 15\%$. If you put half your money in each stock, then your expected portfolio return will be $\hat{k}_p = 0.5(10\%) + 0.5(15\%) = 12.5\%$, a weighted average of the two stocks' returns. Of course, after the fact and a year later, the realized rates of return on Stocks A and B, the $\bar{k}_i$ values, will probably be different from their expected values, so $\bar{k}_p$ will be somewhat different from $\hat{k}_p = 12.5\%$.[5]

Portfolio Risk

As we just saw, the expected return on a portfolio is simply a weighted average of the expected returns on the individual stocks in the portfolio, and each stock's contribution to the expected portfolio return is $x_i \hat{k}_i$. However, unlike the situation with returns, the standard deviation of a portfolio, σ_p, is generally *not* a weighted average of the standard deviations of the individual securities in the portfolio, and each stock's contribution to the portfolio's standard deviation is *not* $x_i \sigma_i$. Indeed, it is theoretically possible to combine two stocks which are, individually, quite risky as measured by their standard deviations, and to form from these risky assets a portfolio which is completely riskless, with $\sigma_p = 0\%$. To illustrate, consider the situation in Figure 4-2, where we present data on realized rates of return for Stocks W and M and for a portfolio invested 50 percent in each stock. (These stocks are called W and M because their returns graphs in Figure 4-2 resemble a W and an M.) Panel a plots realized returns in a time series format, while Panel b plots ex ante probability

---

[5]The realized rate of return on a portfolio, $\bar{k}_p$, is

$$\text{Realized return on a portfolio} = \bar{k}_p = \sum_{i=1}^{n} x_i \bar{k}_i,$$

where $\bar{k}_i$ is the realized rate of return on the ith asset.

Figure 4-2 Rate of Return Distributions for Two Perfectly Negatively
Correlated Stocks (r = −1.0) and for Portfolio WM

a. Rates of Return

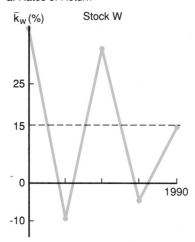 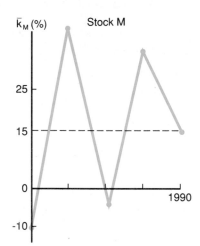 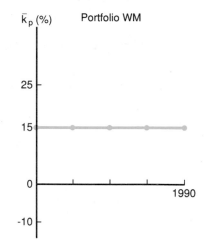

b. Probability Distribution of Returns

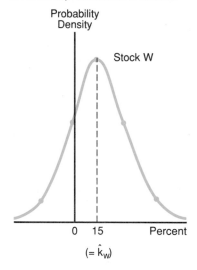 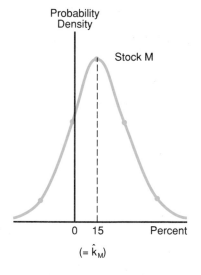 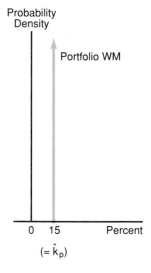

Year	Stock W $\bar{k}_W$	Stock M $\bar{k}_M$	Portfolio WM $\bar{k}_P$
1986	40%	(10%)	15%
1987	(10)	40	15
1988	35	(5)	15
1989	(5)	35	15
1990	15	15	15
Average return =	15%	15%	15%
Standard deviation =	22.6%	22.6%	0.0%

distributions of returns, assuming the distributions are approximately normal. The two stocks, each with $\sigma_i = 22.6\%$, would be quite risky if they were held in isolation, but when they are combined to form Portfolio WM, with $\sigma_p = 0.0\%$, they are not risky at all.

The reason Stocks W and M can be combined to form a riskless portfolio is that their returns move countercyclically to one another—when W's returns fall, those of M rise, and vice versa. In statistical terms, we say that the returns on Stocks W and M are *perfectly negatively correlated,* with r = correlation coefficient = -1.0.[6]

The opposite of perfect negative correlation, with r = -1.0, is perfect positive correlation, with r = $+1.0$. Returns on two perfectly positively correlated stocks would move up and down together, and a portfolio consisting of two such stocks would be just as risky as the individual stocks. This point is illustrated in Figure 4-3, where we combine Stocks M and M', which are perfectly positively correlated. We see that the portfolio's standard deviation is equal to that of the individual stocks, indicating that diversification does nothing to reduce risk if the portfolio consists of perfectly positively correlated stocks.

Figures 4-2 and 4-3 demonstrate that (1) when stocks are perfectly negatively correlated (r = -1.0), all risk can be diversified away, but (2) when stocks are perfectly positively correlated (r = $+1.0$), diversification does no good whatever in terms of reducing risk. In reality, most stocks are positively correlated, but not perfectly so. For New York Stock Exchange stocks, the correlation coefficient for the returns on two randomly selected stocks would be about $+0.6$, and for most pairs of stocks, r would lie in the range of $+0.5$ to $+0.7$. *Under such conditions, combining stocks into portfolios reduces risk but does not eliminate it completely.* Figure 4-4 illustrates this point with two stocks whose correlation coefficient is r = $+0.65$. The portfolio's average realized return is 15.0 percent, which is exactly the same as the average return for each of the two stocks, but the portfolio's standard deviation is 20.6 percent, which is less than the standard deviation of either stock. Thus, the portfolio's risk is *not* an average of the risks of its component stocks—diversification has reduced, but not eliminated, risk.[7]

From these examples, we see that in one extreme case (r = -1.0), risk can be completely eliminated, while in the other extreme case (r = $+1.0$), diversification does no good whatever. In between these extremes, combining two stocks into a portfolio reduces but does not eliminate the riskiness inherent in the individual stocks.[8]

---

[6]*Correlation* is defined as the tendency of two variables to move together. The *correlation coefficient, r,* measures this tendency, and it can range from $+1.0$, denoting that the two variables move up and down in perfect synchronization, to -1.0, denoting that the variables always move in exactly opposite directions. A correlation coefficient of zero suggests that the two variables are not related to one another; that is, changes in one variable are *independent* of changes in the other. We will discuss correlation in more detail in the next section.

[7]To be precise, a portfolio of two stocks will have less risk than the lower risk stock only if the correlation coefficient between the stocks is less than the ratio of the stocks' standard deviations, where the ratio is constructed with the lower standard deviation in the numerator. Thus, for Portfolio AB to have less risk than Stock A, $r_{AB} < \sigma_A/\sigma_B$.

[8]For ease of illustration, our examples in this section showed stocks which had the same average realized return and standard deviation. The implications would be the same if we had used stocks with differing returns and standard deviations.

Figure 4-3   Rate of Return Distributions for Two Perfectly Positively
Correlated Stocks (r = +1.0) and for Portfolio MM′

a. Rates of Return

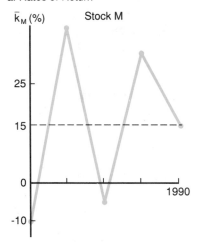

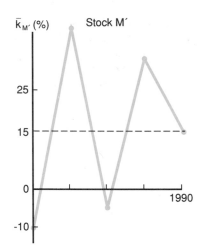

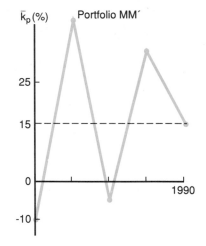

b. Probability Distribution of Returns

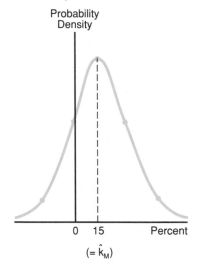

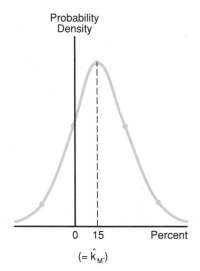

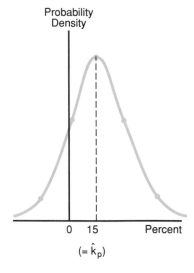

Year	Stock M $\bar{k}_M$	Stock M′ $\bar{k}_{M'}$	Portfolio MM′ $\bar{k}_P$
1986	(10%)	(10%)	(10%)
1987	40	40	40
1988	(5)	(5)	(5)
1989	35	35	35
1990	15	15	15
Average return =	15%	15%	15%
Standard deviation =	22.6%	22.6%	22.6%

Figure 4-4   Rate of Return Distributions for Two Partially Correlated
Stocks (r = +0.65) and for Portfolio WY

a. Rates of Return

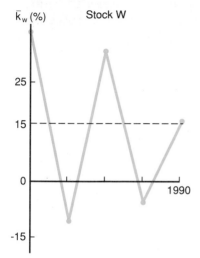
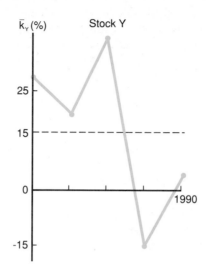
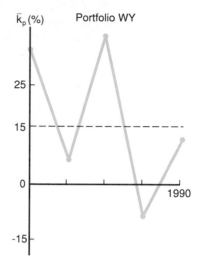

b. Probability Distribution of Returns

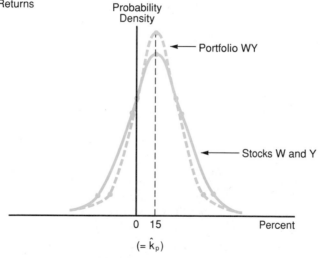

Year	Stock W $\bar{k}_W$	Stock Y $\bar{k}_Y$	Portfolio WY $\bar{k}_P$
1986	40%	28%	34%
1987	(10)	20	5
1988	35	41	38
1989	(5)	(17)	(11)
1990	15	3	9
Average return =	15%	15%	15%
Standard deviation =	22.6%	22.6%	20.6%

Measuring Portfolio Risk

In the preceding section, we examined portfolio risk at an intuitive level. With that base, we now describe how portfolio risk is actually measured and dealt with in practice. First, as noted previously, the riskiness of a portfolio is measured by the standard deviation of its return distribution.[9] Equation 4-6 is used to calculate the standard deviation of a portfolio containing n assets:

$$\text{Portfolio standard deviation} = \sigma_p = \sqrt{\sum_{i=1}^{n} (k_{pi} - \hat{k}_p)^2 P_i}. \qquad \textbf{(4-6)}$$

Here σ_p is the portfolio's standard deviation; k_{pi} is the return on the portfolio under the ith state of the economy; $\hat{k}_p$ is the expected rate of return on the portfolio; and P_i is the probability of occurrence of the ith state of the economy. This equation is exactly the same as Equation 4-3, for the standard deviation of a single asset, except that here the asset is a portfolio of assets (for example, a mutual fund share).

Covariance and the Correlation Coefficient. Two key concepts in portfolio analysis are (1) *covariance* and (2) the *correlation coefficient*. Covariance is a measure which reflects both the variance (or volatility) of a stock's returns and the tendency of those returns to move up or down at the same time other stocks move up or down. For example, the covariance between Stocks A and B tells us whether the returns of the two stocks tend to rise and fall together, and how large those movements tend to be. Equation 4-7 defines the covariance (Cov) between two variables such as Stocks A and B:

$$\text{Covariance} = \text{Cov(AB)} = \sum_{i=1}^{n} (k_{Ai} - \hat{k}_A)(k_{Bi} - \hat{k}_B) P_i. \qquad \textbf{(4-7)}$$

The first term in parentheses after the Σ is the deviation of Stock A's return from its expected value under the ith state of the economy; the second term is Stock B's deviation under the same state; and P_i is the probability of the ith state occurring. Before going through an example, note these points:

1.   If A and B tend to move together, the terms in parentheses will both be positive or both be negative for each state of the economy; that is, if k_{Ai} is above its expected value, $\hat{k}_A$, then k_{Bi} generally will be above $\hat{k}_B$, and vice versa. Therefore, if the assets move together, the terms in parentheses will both be positive or both be negative, hence the product $(k_{Ai} - \hat{k}_A)(k_{Bi} - \hat{k}_B)$ will be positive, while if the assets move counter to one another, the products will tend to be negative. However, if the two stocks' returns fluctuate randomly, then the products will sometimes be positive and sometimes be negative. Therefore, if Stocks A and B tend to move together, their covariance, Cov(AB), will be positive, while if they tend to move counter to one another, Cov(AB) will be negative. If they fluctuate randomly, Cov(AB) could be either positive or negative, but, in either event, it will be close to zero.

---

[9]Alternative risk measures, such as the coefficient of variation or semivariance, could also be used to measure the risk of a portfolio, but since portfolio returns (1) are approximately normally distributed and (2) have reasonably similar expected values, these refinements are generally not necessary and hence are not used.

2. If either A or B is highly uncertain, that is, if it has a high standard deviation, then its parentheses' terms will tend to be large, the products will tend to be large, and the absolute size of Cov(AB) also will tend to be large. However, the size of Cov(AB) will be small, even if σ_A and/or σ_B is large, if A and B move randomly, because the plus and minus terms will cancel out.

3. If either stock has a zero standard deviation, and hence is riskless, then all of its deviations $(k_i - \hat{k})$ will be zero, and Cov(AB) also will be zero. Similarly, if one asset is not completely riskless, but it does have a relatively low risk, then its deviations will tend to be small, and this will hold down the size of Cov(AB).

4. Therefore, Cov(AB) will be large and positive if two assets have large standard deviations and tend to move together; it will be large and negative for two high σ assets which move counter to one another; and it will be small if the two assets' returns move randomly, rather than up or down with one another, or if either of the assets has a small standard deviation.

To illustrate the calculation process, first look at Table 4-3, which presents the probability distributions of the rates of return on four stocks, and at Figure 4-5, which plots scatter diagrams between returns on several pairs of the stocks. We can use Equation 4-7 to calculate the covariance between Stocks F and G as follows:

$$\text{Cov(FG)} = \sum_{i=1}^{5} (k_{Fi} - \hat{k}_F)(k_{Gi} - \hat{k}_G)P_i$$

$$\begin{aligned}
&= (6 - 10)(14 - 10)(0.1) + (8 - 10)(12 - 10)(0.2) \\
&\quad + (10 - 10)(10 - 10)(0.4) + (12 - 10)(8 - 10)(0.2) \\
&\quad + (14 - 10)(6 - 10)(0.1)
\end{aligned}$$

$$= -4.8.$$

The negative sign indicates that the rates of return tend to move in opposite directions, which is consistent with the pattern shown in Panel b of Figure 4-5.

If we calculated the covariance between Stocks F and H, we would find Cov(FH) $= +10.8$, indicating that these assets tend to move together, as shown by the positive slope in Panel c. A zero covariance, as between Stocks E and F, indicates

---

Table 4-3   Probability Distributions of Stocks E, F, G, and H

Probability of Occurrence	Rate of Return Distribution			
	E	F	G	H
0.1	10.0%	6.0%	14.0%	2.0%
0.2	10.0	8.0	12.0	6.0
0.4	10.0	10.0	10.0	9.0
0.2	10.0	12.0	8.0	15.0
0.1	10.0	14.0	6.0	20.0
$\hat{k} =$	10.0%	10.0%	10.0%	10.0%
$\sigma =$	0.0%	2.2%	2.2%	5.0%

Figure 4-5   Scatter Diagrams

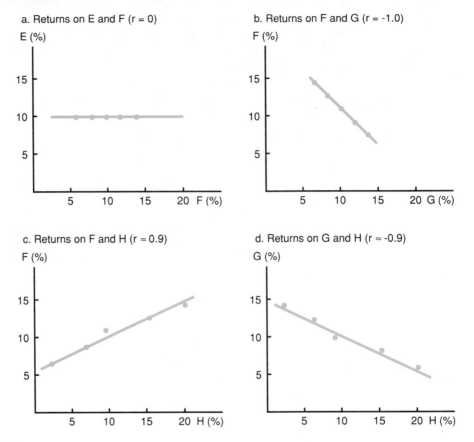

Notes:
a. The lines shown in each graph are called *regression lines;* they will be discussed in detail in Chapter 5.
b. These graphs are drawn as if each point had an equal probability of occurrence.

that there is no relationship between the variables; that is, the variables are independent. (E's return is always 10 percent; therefore, $\sigma_E = 0\%$, so the covariance of E with any other asset must be zero.)

It is difficult to interpret the magnitude of the covariance term. Therefore, a related statistic, the correlation coefficient, is often used to measure the degree of co-movement between two variables. The correlation coefficient standardizes the covariance by dividing by a product term; this facilitates comparisons by putting things on a similar scale. The correlation coefficient, r, is calculated as follows:

$$\text{Correlation coefficient} = r_{AB} = \frac{\text{Cov(AB)}}{\sigma_A \sigma_B}. \tag{4-8}$$

The sign of the correlation coefficient is the same as the sign of the covariance, so a positive sign means that the variables move together, a negative sign indicates that they move in opposite directions, and, if r is close to zero, they move independently of one another. Moreover, the standardization process confines the correlation coefficient to values between -1.0 and $+1.0$. Also, note that Equation 4-8 can be solved to find the covariance:

$$\text{Cov(AB)} = r_{AB}\sigma_A\sigma_B. \tag{4-8a}$$

Using Equation 4-8, we find the correlation coefficient between Stocks F and G to be -1.0 (except for a rounding error):

$$r_{FG} = \frac{-4.8}{(2.2)(2.2)} \approx -1.0.$$

These two stocks are said to be perfectly negatively correlated. As Panel b of Figure 4-5 shows, the regression line for these two assets' rates of return is negatively sloped, and all points lie exactly on the line. Wherever the points are all on the regression line, r must equal 1.0 if the line slopes up and -1.0 if the line slopes down.

The correlation coefficient between Stocks F and H is $+0.9$. Thus, there is a strong positive relationship—their regression line is upward sloping, but all points are not exactly on the line. Except in the case where one of the assets has zero variance, the closer the points are to the regression line, the higher the absolute value of the correlation coefficient.

The Two-Asset Case. Under the assumption that the distributions of returns on the individual securities are normal, a complicated looking but operationally simple equation can be used to determine the riskiness of a two-asset portfolio:[10]

$$\text{Portfolio SD} = \sigma_p = \sqrt{x^2\sigma_A^2 + (1-x)^2\sigma_B^2 + 2x(1-x)r_{AB}\sigma_A\sigma_B}. \tag{4-9}$$

Here x is the fraction of the portfolio invested in Security A, so $(1-x)$ is the fraction invested in Security B.

Self-Test Questions

What is a portfolio of assets?

How is the riskiness of a portfolio measured?

What does the correlation coefficient measure?

---

[10]Equation 4-9 is derived from Equation 4-6 in standard statistics books. Notice that if $x = 1$, all of the portfolio is invested in Security A, and Equation 4-9 reduces to σ_A:

$$\sigma_p = \sqrt{\sigma_A^2} = \sigma_A.$$

The portfolio contains but a single asset, so the risk of the portfolio and that of the asset are identical. Equation 4-9 could be expanded to include any number of assets by adding additional terms, but we shall not do so here.

EFFICIENT PORTFOLIOS

One important use of the statistical relationships we have discussed thus far is to select *efficient* portfolios—defined as those portfolios which provide the highest expected return for any degree of risk, or the lowest degree of risk for any expected return. To illustrate the concept, assume that two investment securities, A and B, are available, and that we have a specific amount of money to invest. We can allocate our funds between the securities in any proportion. Suppose Security A has an expected rate of return of $\hat{k}_A = 5\%$ and a standard deviation of returns $\sigma_A = 4\%$, while for Security B the expected return is $\hat{k}_B = 8\%$ and the standard deviation is $\sigma_B = 10\%$. Our first task is to determine the set of *attainable* portfolios, and then from this attainable set to select the *efficient* subset.

To construct the attainable set, we need data on the degree of correlation between the two securities' expected returns, r_{AB}. Let us work with three different assumed degrees of correlation, $r_{AB} = +1.0$, $r_{AB} = 0$, and $r_{AB} = -1.0$, and, using them, develop the portfolios' expected returns, $\hat{k}_p$, and standard deviations of returns, σ_p. (Of course, only one correlation can exist; our example simply shows three alternative situations that might exist.)

To calculate $\hat{k}_p$, we use Equation 4-5. First, substitute in the given values for $\hat{k}_A$ and $\hat{k}_B$, and then solve for $\hat{k}_p$ at different values of x. For example, when x equals 0.75, then $\hat{k}_p = 5.75\%$:

$$\hat{k}_p = x_A\hat{k}_A + x_B\hat{k}_B$$

$$= 0.75(5\%) + 0.25(8\%) = 5.75\%.$$

Other values of $\hat{k}_p$ were found similarly, and they are shown in Table 4-4.

Next, we use Equation 4-9 to find σ_p with different fractions of A and B in the portfolio. Substitute in the given values for σ_A, σ_B, and r_{AB}, and then solve Equation 4-9 for σ_p at different values of x. For example, in the case where $r_{AB} = 0$ and x = 0.75, then $\sigma_p = 3.9\%$:

$$\sigma_p = \sqrt{x^2\sigma_A^2 + (1 - x)^2\sigma_B^2 + 2x(1 - x)r_{AB}\sigma_A\sigma_B}$$

$$= \sqrt{(0.5625)(16) + (0.0625)(100) + 2(0.75)(0.25)(0)(4)(10)}$$

$$= \sqrt{9.00 + 6.25} = \sqrt{15.25} = 3.9\%.$$

The $\hat{k}_p$ and σ_p equations can be solved for other values of x, and for the three cases, $r_{AB} = +1.0$, 0, and -1.0. Table 4-4 gives the solution values for x = 1.00, 0.75, 0.50, 0.25, and 0.00, and Figure 4-6 gives plots of $\hat{k}_p$, σ_p, and the attainable set of portfolios, for each case. In both the table and the graphs, note the following points:

1.   The three graphs across the top row of Figure 4-6 designate Case I, where the two assets are perfectly positively correlated, that is, $r_{AB} = +1.0$. The three graphs in the middle row of Figure 4-6 are for the zero correlation case, and the three in the bottom row are for perfect negative correlation.

Table 4-4 $\hat{k}_p$ and σ_p under Various Assumptions

Proportion of Portfolio in Security A (Value of x)	Proportion of Portfolio in Security B (Value of 1 − x)	Case I ($r_{AB} = +1.0$)		Case II ($r_{AB} = 0$)		Case III ($r_{AB} = -1.0$)	
		$\hat{k}_p$	σ_p	$\hat{k}_p$	σ_p	$\hat{k}_p$	σ_p
1.00	0.00	5.00%	4.0%	5.00%	4.0%	5.00%	4.0%
0.75	0.25	5.75	5.5	5.75	3.9	5.75	0.5
0.50	0.50	6.50	7.0	6.50	5.4	6.50	3.0
0.25	0.75	7.25	8.5	7.25	7.6	7.25	6.5
0.00	1.00	8.00	10.0	8.00	10.0	8.00	10.0

Figure 4-6   Illustrations of Portfolio Returns, Risk, and the Attainable Set of Portfolios

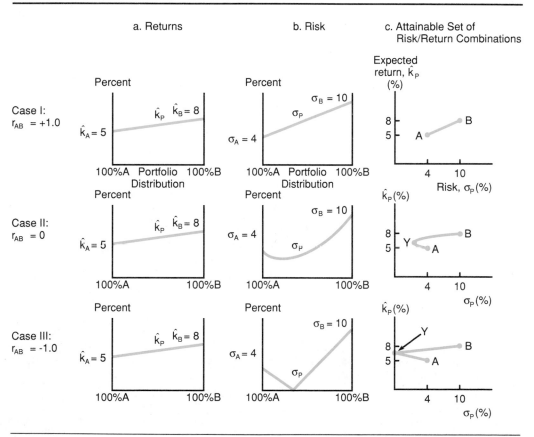

2.   All three cases are theoretical in the sense that we would rarely encounter $r_{AB} = -1.0$, 0.0, or $+1.0$. Generally, in the real world, r_{AB} would be in the range of $+0.5$ to $+0.7$ for most stocks. Case II (zero correlation) produces graphs which, pictorially, most closely resemble many real-world examples.

3.   The left column of graphs shows how the expected portfolio returns vary with different combinations of A and B; the middle column shows how risk is affected by the portfolio mix in the three cases; and the right column shows the attainable set of risk/return combinations.

4.   The graphs in the left column are identical in each of the three cases: The portfolio return, $\hat{k}_p$, is a linear function of x, and it does not depend on the correlation of the assets in the portfolio. This is also seen from the $\hat{k}_p$ data in Table 4-4.

5.   In the middle column of graphs, starting from the top, we see that portfolio risk, σ_p, is linear in Case I, where $r_{AB} = +1.0$; it is nonlinear in Case II; and Case III shows that risk can be completely diversified away if $r_{AB} = -1.0$. Thus, σ_p does depend on correlation, although $\hat{k}_p$ does not.

6.   The right column of graphs shows the *attainable,* or *feasible,* set of portfolios constructed with different mixes of Securities A and B. Each graph was plotted from pairs of $\hat{k}_p$ and σ_p as shown in Table 4-4. For example, Point A in the upper right graph is the point $\hat{k}_p = 5\%$, $\sigma_p = 4\%$ from the Case I data in Table 4-4. All other points on the curves were plotted similarly. With only two securities, the attainable set is a curve or line, and we can achieve each risk-return combination on the relevant curve by allocating our investment funds properly between Securities A and B.

7.   Are all portfolios on the attainable set equally good? The answer is no: only that part of the attainable set from Y to B in Cases II and III is defined to be *efficient,* while the part from A to Y is inefficient, because for any degree of risk on the line segment AY, a higher return can be found on segment YB. Thus, no rational investor would hold a portfolio that lay on segment AY. In Case I, however, the entire feasible set is also efficient — no combination of the securities can be ruled out in that case.

From these examples, we can see that in one extreme case ($r = -1.0$), risk can be completely eliminated, while in the other extreme case ($r = +1.0$), diversification does no good whatever. In between these extremes, combining two stocks into a portfolio reduces but does not eliminate the riskiness inherent in the individual stocks.[11]

---

[11]If we differentiate Equation 4-9, set the derivative equal to zero, and then solve for x, we obtain the fraction of the portfolio that should be invested in Security A if we wish to form the least-risky portfolio. Here is the equation:

$$\text{Minimum risk portfolio: } x = \frac{\sigma_B(\sigma_B - r_{AB}\sigma_A)}{\sigma_A^2 + \sigma_B^2 - 2r_{AB}\sigma_A\sigma_B}.$$

As a rule, we limit x to the range 0 to $+1.0$; that is, if the solution value is $x > 1.0$, set $x = 1.0$, and if x is negative, set $x = 0$. A negative x would imply short sales, and $x > 1.0$ would imply borrowing.

The Multi-Asset Case

What would happen if we added more and more stocks to the portfolio? In general, the riskiness of a portfolio will decline as the number of stocks held increases. If we added enough stocks, could we completely eliminate risk? In general, the answer is no, but the extent to which adding stocks to a portfolio reduces the portfolio's risk depends on the degree of correlation among the stocks: The smaller the correlation coefficient, the lower the remaining risk in a large portfolio. Indeed, if we could find enough stocks whose correlation coefficients were zero (or negative), all risk could be eliminated. However, in the typical case, where the correlations among the individual stocks are positive but less than $+1.0$, some but not all risk can be eliminated.

As noted previously, it is very difficult, if not impossible, to find stocks whose expected returns are negatively correlated — most stocks tend to do well when the national economy is strong and poorly when it is weak.[12] Thus, even very large portfolios end up with a certain degree of risk. Consider, for example, Figure 4-7, which shows how portfolio risk is affected by forming larger and larger portfolios of New York Stock Exchange (NYSE) stocks. Standard deviations are plotted for an average one-stock portfolio, an average two-stock portfolio, and so on, up to a portfolio consisting of all 1,500+ common stocks listed on the Exchange. The graph shows that the riskiness of a portfolio consisting of NYSE stocks tends to decline and to approach a limit asymptotically as the size of the portfolio increases.

According to data accumulated in recent years, σ_1, the standard deviation of an average one-stock portfolio (or an average stock), is approximately 28 percent, whereas a portfolio consisting of all stocks, which is called the *market portfolio,* would have a standard deviation of about 15.1 percent. The market portfolio's standard deviation is given the symbol σ_M, so $\sigma_M = 15.1\%$, as shown in Figure 4-7.

Since an average stock held in isolation would have a riskiness of $\sigma_i \approx 28\%$, and a very large portfolio would have $\sigma_M = 15.1\%$, almost half of the riskiness inherent in individual stocks can be eliminated by holding stocks in portfolios. Further, it is not necessary to hold all stocks — a portfolio consisting of about 40 randomly selected stocks will have σ_p close to σ_M. Some risk will always remain, however, even in the largest of portfolios, because it is virtually impossible to diversify away the effects of broad stock market declines that affect essentially all stocks.

Self-Test Questions

Define the term "efficient portfolio."

Explain what happens to the riskiness of a portfolio when more and more randomly selected stocks are added to an average, one-stock portfolio.

---

[12]It is not too hard to find a few stocks that happened to decline because of a particular set of circumstances in the past while most other stocks were advancing; it is much harder to find stocks that could logically be *expected* to decline in the future when other stocks are rising.

Figure 4-7   Effect of Portfolio Size on Portfolio Risk

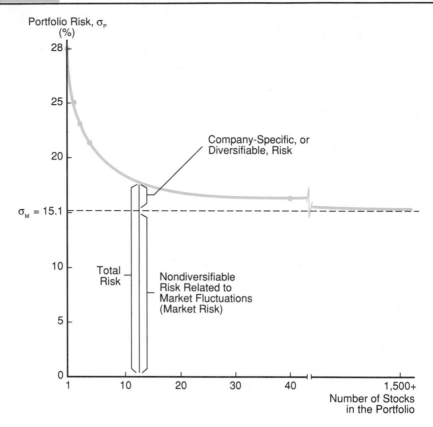

COMPONENTS OF A STOCK'S TOTAL RISK

That part of a stock's risk which can be eliminated is called *diversifiable, or company-specific, risk.* Diversifiable risk is caused by such company-specific events as lawsuits, strikes, successful and unsuccessful marketing programs, and winning and losing major contracts. Since occurrences that are unique to a particular firm (or to its industry) are essentially random, their effects on a portfolio can be eliminated by diversification—bad events in one firm will be offset by good events in another. *Nondiversifiable, or market, risk,* on the other hand, stems from such external events as war, inflation, recession, and high interest rates, which have an impact on all firms. Since all firms are affected simultaneously by these factors, market risk cannot be eliminated by diversification. Market risk is also known as *systematic risk,* because it shows the degree to which a stock moves systematically with other stocks, and diversifiable risk is sometimes called *unsystematic risk.*

Figure 4-8 The Efficient Set of Investments

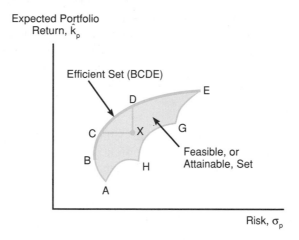

We know that investors demand a premium for bearing risk; that is, the higher the riskiness of a security, the higher its expected return must be to induce investors to buy (or hold) the security. However, if investors are primarily concerned with *portfolio risk* rather than the risk of the individual securities in the portfolio, how should the riskiness of the individual stocks be measured? The answer is this: *The relevant riskiness of an individual stock is its contribution to the riskiness of a well-diversified portfolio.* In other words, the riskiness of Stock X to a doctor who has a portfolio of 40 stocks, or to a trust officer managing a 150-stock portfolio, is the contribution that Stock X makes to the portfolio's riskiness. The stock might be quite risky if held in isolation, but if most of its risk can be eliminated by diversification, the stock's *relevant risk,* which is its contribution to the portfolio's risk, might be small.

With only two assets, the feasible set of portfolios is a line or curve as shown in the third column of graphs back in Figure 4-6. However, if we were to increase the number of assets, we would obtain an area such as the shaded area in Figure 4-8. The points A, H, G, and E represent single securities (or portfolios containing only one security). All the other points in the shaded area, including its boundaries, represent portfolios of two or more securities. The shaded area is called the *feasible, or attainable, region.* Each point in this area represents a particular portfolio with a risk of σ_p and an expected return of $\hat{k}_p$. For example, point X represents one such portfolio's risk and expected return, as do B, C, and D.

Self-Test Questions

Explain the difference between company-specific and market risk.

Which one is "relevant," and why?

CHOOSING THE OPTIMAL PORTFOLIO

Given the full set of potential portfolios that could be constructed from the available assets, which portfolio should actually be held? This choice involves two separate decisions: (1) determining the *efficient* set of portfolios and (2) choosing from the efficient set the single portfolio that is best for the individual investor.

The Efficient Frontier

In Figure 4-8, the boundary line BCDE defines the *efficient set* of portfolios, which is also called the *efficient frontier*.[13] Portfolios to the left of the efficient set are not possible because they lie outside the attainable set. Portfolios to the right of the boundary line (interior portfolios) are inefficient because some other portfolio would provide either a higher return with the same degree of risk or a lower risk for the same rate of return. For example, Portfolio X is dominated by Portfolios C and D.

Risk/Return Indifference Curves

Given the efficient set of portfolio combinations, which specific portfolio should an investor choose? To determine the optimal portfolio for a particular investor, we must know the investor's attitude toward risk as reflected in his or her risk/return tradeoff function, or *indifference curve*.

An investor's risk/return tradeoff function is based on the standard economic concepts of utility theory and indifference curves, which are illustrated in Figure 4-9. The curves labeled I_A and I_B represent the indifference curves of Individuals A and B. Ms. A is indifferent with regard to the riskless 5 percent portfolio, a portfolio with an expected return of 6 percent but with a risk of $\sigma_p = 1.4\%$, and so on. Mr. B is equally well satisfied with a riskless 5 percent return, an expected 6 percent return with risk of $\sigma_p = 3.3\%$, and so on.

Notice that Ms. A requires a higher expected rate of return to compensate for a given amount of risk than does Mr. B; thus, Ms. A is said to be more *risk averse* than Mr. B. Her higher risk aversion causes Ms. A to require a higher *risk premium* — defined here as the difference between the 5 percent riskless return and the expected return required to compensate for any specific amount of risk — than does Mr. B. Thus, Ms. A requires a risk premium (RP_A) of 2.5 percent to compensate for a risk of $\sigma_p = 3.3\%$, while Mr. B's risk premium for this degree of risk is only $RP_B = 1.0\%$. As a generalization, the steeper the slope of the indifference curve, the more risk averse the investor. Thus, Ms. A is more risk averse than Mr. B.

---

[13]A computational procedure for determining the efficient set of portfolios was developed by Harry Markowitz and first reported in his article, "Portfolio Selection," *Journal of Finance,* March 1952, 77–91. In this article, Markowitz developed the basic concepts of portfolio theory.

Figure 4-9   Indifference Curves for Risk and Expected Rate of Return

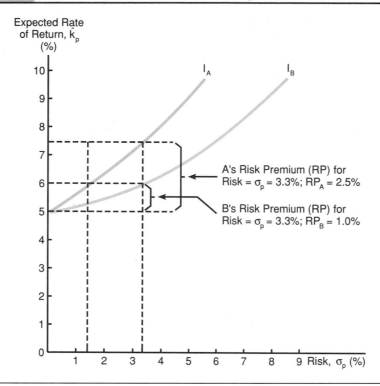

Each individual has a "map" of indifference curves; the indifference maps for Ms. A and Mr. B are shown in Figure 4-10. The higher curves denote a greater level of satisfaction (or utility). Thus, I_{B2} is better than I_{B1} because, for any level of risk, Mr. B has a higher expected return, hence greater utility. An infinite number of indifference curves could be drawn for each individual, and each individual has a unique set of curves.

The Optimal Portfolio for an Investor

Figure 4-10 also shows the feasible set of portfolios for the two-asset case, under the assumption that $r_{AB} = 0$, as it was developed in Figure 4-6. The optimal portfolio for each investor is found at the tangency point between the efficient set of portfolios and one of the investor's indifference curves. This tangency point marks the highest level of satisfaction the investor can attain. Ms. A, who is more risk averse than Mr. B, chooses a portfolio with a lower expected return (about 6 percent) but a riskiness of only $\sigma_p = 4.2\%$. Mr. B picks a portfolio that provides an expected

Figure 4-10   Selecting the Optimal Portfolio of Risky Assets

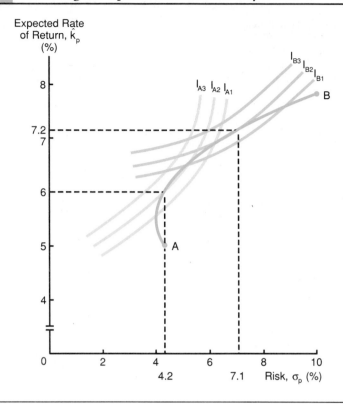

return of about 7.2 percent, but it has a risk of about σ_p = 7.1%. Ms. A's portfolio is more heavily weighted with the less risky security, while Mr. B's portfolio contains a larger proportion of the more risky security.[14]

Self-Test Questions

What is the efficient frontier?

What are indifference curves?

How does an investor choose his or her optimal portfolio?

---

[14]Ms. A's portfolio would contain 67 percent of Security A and 33 percent of Security B, whereas Mr. B's portfolio would consist of 27 percent of Security A and 73 percent of Security B. These percentages can be determined with Equation 4-5 by simply seeing what percentage of the two securities is consistent with $\hat{k}_p$ = 6.0% and 7.2%. For example, x(5%) + (1 − x)(8%) = 7.2%, and solving for x, we obtain x = 0.27 and (1 − x) = 0.73.

SUMMARY

The primary goals of this chapter were (1) to show how risk is measured for assets held in isolation, and (2) to explain how an asset's risk is affected when the asset is held as part of a portfolio of assets. The key concepts covered are listed below.

- In general, *risk* can be defined as the probability that some unfavorable event will occur.

- *Investment risk* is related to the probability of earning a return less than the expected return—the greater the chance of low or negative returns, the riskier the investment.

- The *expected return* on an investment is the expected value of the probability distribution of its possible returns.

- Rational investors hold *portfolios* of risky assets, and they are more concerned with the riskiness of the portfolio than with the riskiness of individual assets.

- *Total risk,* which is measured by the dispersion of returns about the mean, is relevant only for assets held in isolation.

- When assets are combined into portfolios, the relevant risk is an asset's *market risk,* which is the contribution of the asset to the riskiness of the portfolio.

- An asset's total risk can be measured by its *variance* of returns, σ^2, *standard deviation* of returns, σ, or *coefficient of variation* of returns, *CV*. For comparing assets' total risks, CV is generally the preferred measure.

- The *expected rate of return on a portfolio, $\hat{k}_p$,* is the weighted average return on the component assets, but the *standard deviation of a portfolio, σ_p,* is not the weighted average of the component assets' standard deviations.

- Since most assets are not perfectly positively *correlated,* combining assets into portfolios generally reduces risk.

- An asset's total risk consists of *company-specific risk,* which can be eliminated by diversification, and *market risk,* which cannot be eliminated by diversification.

- The *feasible set* of portfolios represents all portfolios that can be constructed from a given set of assets.

- An *efficient portfolio* is one that offers the most return for a given amount of risk or the least risk for a given amount of return.

- The *optimal portfolio* for an investor is defined by the tangency point between the *efficient set* of portfolios and the investor's highest *indifference curve.*

In the next chapter, we will continue the discussion of risk and return by (1) adding a risk-free asset and showing how it affects investors' choices, (2) defining a statistic which can be used to measure market risk (the "beta coefficient"), and (3) examining the relationship between risk and expected rates of return.

Questions

4-1   Define the following terms, using graphs or equations to illustrate your answers wherever possible:

   a.   Risk; probability distribution

   b.   Expected rate of return, $\hat{k}$

   c.   Standard deviation, σ; variance, σ^2; coefficient of variation (CV)

   d.   Total risk

   e.   Market risk

   f.   Portfolio

   g.   Expected return on a portfolio, $\hat{k}_p$

   h.   Correlation coefficient, r

   i.   Company-specific risk

   j.   Feasible set

   k.   Efficient portfolio

   l.   Efficient frontier

   m.   Indifference curve

   n.   Optimal portfolio

4-2   The continuous probability distribution of a less risky expected return is more peaked than that of a risky return. What shape would the continuous probability distribution have for (a) completely certain returns and (b) completely uncertain returns?

4-3   Suppose you owned a portfolio consisting of $500,000 worth of long-term U.S. government bonds.

   a.   Would your portfolio be riskless?

   b.   Now suppose you hold a portfolio consisting of $500,000 worth of 30-day Treasury bills. Every 30 days your bills mature and you reinvest the principal ($500,000) in a new batch of bills. Assume that you live on the investment income from your portfolio and that you want to maintain a constant standard of living. Is your portfolio truly riskless?

   c.   You should have concluded that both long-term and short-term portfolios of government securities have some element of risk. Can you think of any asset that would be completely riskless?

4-4   A life insurance policy is a financial asset. The premiums paid represent the investment's cost.

   a.   How would you calculate the expected return on a life insurance policy?

   b.   Suppose the owner of the life insurance policy has no other financial assets—the person's only other asset is "human capital," or lifetime earnings capacity. What is the correlation coefficient between returns on the insurance policy and returns on the policyholder's human capital?

   c.   Life insurance companies have to pay administrative costs and sales representatives' commissions; hence, the expected rate of return on insurance premiums is generally low or even negative. Use the portfolio concept to explain why people buy life insurance in spite of negative expected returns.

Self-Test Problem (Solutions Appear in Appendix D)

ST-1   **(Portfolio risk)** Stocks A and B have the following historical dividend and price data:

Year	Stock A Dividend	Stock A Year-End Price	Stock B Dividend	Stock B Year-End Price
1985	—	$12.25	—	$22.00
1986	$1.00	9.75	$2.40	18.50
1987	1.05	11.00	2.60	19.50
1988	1.15	13.75	2.85	25.25
1989	1.30	13.25	3.05	22.50
1990	1.50	15.50	3.25	24.00

a.   Calculate the realized rate of return (or holding period return) for each stock in each year. Then assume that someone had held a portfolio consisting of 50 percent of A and 50 percent of B. (The portfolio is rebalanced every year so as to maintain these percentages.) What would the realized rate of return on the portfolio have been in each year from 1986 through 1990? What would the average returns have been for each stock and for the portfolio? [Hint: The realized rate of return in any Period t is $\bar{k}_t = (D_t + P_t - P_{t-1})/P_{t-1}$.]

b.   Now calculate the standard deviation of returns for each stock and for the portfolio.

c.   On the basis of the extent to which the portfolio has a lower risk than the stocks held individually, would you guess that the correlation coefficient between returns on the two stocks is closer to 0.9 or to -0.9?

d.   If you added more stocks at random to the portfolio, what is the most accurate statement of what would happen to σ_p?

   (1) σ_p would remain constant.

   (2) σ_p would decline to somewhere in the vicinity of 15 percent.

   (3) σ_p would decline to zero if enough stocks were included.

Problems

4-1   **(Expected returns)** Stocks A and B have the following probability distributions of expected future returns:

Probability	A	B
0.1	(25%)	(40%)
0.2	5	0
0.4	15	16
0.2	30	40
0.1	45	66

a.   Calculate the expected rate of return, $\hat{k}$, for Stock B. ($\hat{k}_A = 15\%$.)

b.   Calculate the standard deviation and coefficient of variation of expected returns for Stock A. (Those for Stock B are 27.0 percent and 1.59.) Is it possible that most investors might regard Stock B as being *less* risky than Stock A? Explain.

4-2   **(Expected returns)** Suppose you were offered (1) $1 million or (2) a gamble where you would get $2 million if a head were flipped but zero if a tail came up.

a.   What is the expected value of the gamble?

b.   Would you take the sure $1 million or the gamble?

c.   If you choose the sure $1 million, are you a risk averter or a risk seeker?

d.   Suppose you actually take the sure $1 million. You can invest it in either a U.S. Treasury bond that will return $1,075,000 at the end of a year or a common stock that has a 50-50 chance of being either worthless or worth $2,300,000 at the end of the year.
   (1) What is the expected dollar profit on the stock investment? (The expected profit on the T-bond investment is $75,000.)
   (2) What is the expected rate of return on the stock investment? (The expected rate of return on the T-bond investment is 7.5 percent.)
   (3) Would you invest in the bond or the stock?
   (4) Just how large would the expected profit (or the expected rate of return) have to be on the stock investment to make *you* invest in the stock?
   (5) How might your decision be affected if, rather than buying one stock for $1 million, you could construct a portfolio consisting of 100 stocks with $10,000 in each? Each of these stocks has the same return characteristics as the one stock, that is, a 50-50 chance of being worth either zero or $23,000 at year-end. Would the correlation between returns on these stocks matter?

4-3   **(Total risk analysis)** The Berry Corporation is considering three possible capital projects for next year. Each project has a 1-year life, and project returns depend on next year's state of the economy. The estimated rates of return are shown in the table:

State of the Economy	Probability of Each State Occurring	Rates of Return if State Occurs		
		A	**B**	**C**
Recession	0.25	10%	9%	14%
Average	0.50	14	13	12
Boom	0.25	16	18	10

a.   Find each project's expected rate of return, variance, standard deviation, and coefficient of variation.
b.   Rank the alternatives on the basis of (1) expected return and (2) risk. Which alternative would you choose?

4-4   **(Portfolio effects and market risk analysis)** Refer to the three alternative projects contained in Problem 4-3. Assume that the Berry Corporation is going to invest one-third of its available funds in each project. That is, Berry will create a portfolio of three equally weighted projects.
a.   What is the expected rate of return on the portfolio?
b.   What are the variance and standard deviation of the portfolio?
c.   What are the covariance and correlation coefficient between Projects A and B? Between Projects A and C?

4-5   **(Realized rates of return)** Stocks A and B have the following historical dividend and price data:

Year	Stock A Dividend	Stock A Year-End Price	Stock B Dividend	Stock B Year-End Price
1985	—	$22.50	—	$43.75
1986	$2.00	16.00	$3.40	35.50
1987	2.20	17.00	3.65	38.75
1988	2.40	20.25	3.90	51.75
1989	2.60	17.25	4.05	44.50
1990	2.95	18.75	4.25	45.25

a.   Calculate the realized rate of return (or holding period return) for each stock in each year. Then assume that someone had held a portfolio consisting of 50 percent of A and 50 percent of B (the portfolio was rebalanced at the end of each year). What would the realized rate of return on the portfolio have been in each year from 1986 through 1990? What would the average returns have been for each stock and for the portfolio? [Hint: The realized rate of return in any Period t is $\bar{k}_t = (D_t + P_t - P_{t-1})/P_{t-1}$.]

b.   Now calculate the standard deviation of returns for each stock and for the portfolio.

(Do Parts c through e only if you are using the computerized diskette.)

c.   Add Stock C to the portfolio; C has the following historical dividend and price data:

	Stock C	
Year	**Dividend**	**Year-End Price**
1985	—	$23.40
1986	$1.85	23.90
1987	1.95	31.50
1988	2.05	27.20
1989	2.15	32.25
1990	2.25	26.00

Assume that the portfolio contains 33⅓ percent of A, 33⅓ percent of B, and 33⅓ percent of C. How does this affect the portfolio return and σ_p?

d.   Make some other changes in the portfolio percentages, making sure the percentages sum to 100 percent. For example, put 100 percent in A; 25 percent in A, 25 percent in B, and 50 percent in C; and so forth. Explain why k_p and σ_p change.

e.   Would you rather have a portfolio consisting of one-third of each stock or a portfolio with 50 percent A and 50 percent B? Explain.

Mini Case

Barbara Orban's first assignment at Southern Commerce Bank is to invest $1 million from an estate for which the bank is trustee. Because the estate is expected to be distributed to the heirs in about one year, Orban has been instructed to plan for a 1-year holding period. Further, her boss has restricted her to the following investment alternatives:

			Estimated Rate of Return			
State of the Economy	**Probability**	**T-Bills**	**Paragon**	**Luster**	**Apex**	**Market Portfolio**
Recession	0.05	8.0%	(22.0%)	28.0%	10.0%	(13.0%)
Below average	0.20	8.0	(2.0)	14.7	(10.0)	1.0
Average	0.50	8.0	20.0	0.0	7.0	15.0
Above average	0.20	8.0	35.0	(10.0)	45.0	29.0
Boom	0.05	8.0	50.0	(20.0)	30.0	43.0
	1.00					

The bank's economic and forecasting staff developed probability estimates for the state of the economy, and the trust department has a sophisticated computer program which estimated the rate of return on each alternative under each state of the economy. Paragon, Inc., is an electronics firm; Luster Corporation owns gold mines in the United States and Canada; and Apex Company manufactures tires and various other rubber and plastics products. The bank also maintains an "index fund" which owns a market-weighted fraction of all publicly traded stocks, and Orban can invest in that fund and thus obtain average stock market results. Place yourself in Orban's position, and answer the following questions:

a.   Define the term "investment risk."

b.   Why is the T-bill return independent of the state of the economy? Do T-bills promise a completely risk-free return? Why are Paragon's returns expected to move with the economy, whereas Luster's are expected to move counter to the economy?

c.   Calculate the expected rate of return on each alternative. Based solely on expected returns, which alternative should Orban choose?

d.   Briefly explain the concepts of total risk and market risk.

e.   Orban recognizes that basing a decision solely on expected returns is only appropriate for risk-neutral individuals. Since the trust's beneficiaries, like virtually everyone, are risk averse, the riskiness of each alternative is an important aspect of the decision. One possible measure of risk is the standard deviation of returns. Calculate this value for each alternative. What type of risk is measured by the standard deviation?

f.   Orban just remembered that the coefficient of variation (CV) is generally regarded as being a better measure of total risk than the standard deviation when the alternatives being considered have widely differing expected returns. Calculate the CVs for the different securities. Does the CV produce the same risk rankings as the standard deviation?

g.   Orban wondered what would happen if she created a two-stock portfolio by investing $500,000 in Paragon and $500,000 in Luster. What are the expected return and the standard deviation for this portfolio? How does the riskiness of the portfolio compare to the riskiness of the two individual stocks if they were held in isolation?

h.   What would happen to the riskiness of the portfolio if more and more randomly selected stocks were added to an average, one-stock portfolio?

i.   Should portfolio effects influence the way investors think about the riskiness of individual stocks? If you chose to hold a one-stock portfolio and consequently were exposed to more risk than diversified investors, could you expect to be compensated for all of your risk, that is, could you earn a risk premium on that part of your risk that could have been eliminated by diversifying?

j.   Construct a reasonable, but hypothetical, graph which shows risk, as measured by portfolio standard deviation, on the X-axis and expected rate of return on the Y-axis. Now add an illustrative feasible (or attainable) set of portfolios, and show what portion of the feasible set is efficient. What makes a particular portfolio efficient? Don't worry about specific values when constructing the graph—merely illustrate how things look with "reasonable" data.

k.   Now add a set of indifference curves to the graph created for Part j. What do these curves represent? What is the optimal portfolio for this investor? Finally, add a second set of indifference curves which leads to the selection of a different optimal portfolio. Why do the two investors choose different portfolios?

Selected Additional References and Cases

Probably the best sources of additional information on probability distributions and single-asset risk measures are statistics textbooks. For example, see

Kohler, Heinz, *Statistics for Business and Economics* (Glenview, Ill.: Scott Foresman, 1988).

Mendenhall, William, Richard L. Schaeffer, and Dennis D. Wackerly, *Mathematical Statistics with Applications* (Boston: Duxbury, 1981).

Probably the best place to find an extension of portfolio theory concepts is one of the investments textbooks. These are some good recent ones:

Francis, Jack C., *Investments: Analysis and Management* (New York: McGraw-Hill, 1980).

Radcliffe, Robert C., *Investment: Concepts, Analysis, and Strategy* (Glenview, Ill.: Scott, Foresman, 1990).

Reilly, Frank K., *Investment Analysis and Portfolio Management* (Hinsdale, Ill.: Dryden, 1989).

Sharpe, William F., *Investments* (Englewood Cliffs, N.J.: Prentice-Hall, 1985).

Those who want to start at the beginning in studying portfolio theory should see

Markowitz, Harry M., "Portfolio Selection," *Journal of Finance,* March 1952, 77–91.

The following case covers many of the concepts discussed in this chapter as well as concepts to be covered in Chapter 5:

Case 2, "Sun Coast Securities, Inc. (A)," in Brigham, Eugene F., and Louis C. Gapenski, *Cases in Financial Management* (Hinsdale, Ill.: Dryden, 1990).

CHAPTER 5

Risk and Return: Part 2

Common sense tells us that an investor's required rate of return increases as the investment's riskiness increases. However, as we discussed in Chapter 4, common sense does not tell us how to measure risk, and, indeed, the proper measurement of risk is rather subtle. To illustrate, consider these two examples:

1. Homestake Mining is the leading gold producer in the United States. In 1990, the firm produced about 800,000 ounces of gold from mines located in South Dakota, California, Nevada, and Australia. Gold prices are volatile, and since Homestake's profits vary with the price of gold, its earnings fluctuate widely from year to year. For example, Homestake's net income dropped from $102 million in 1980 to $29 million in 1981, and then to $17 million in 1982. By 1988, net income was back up to $66 million, but it then hit a low of $15 million in 1989. This seems to suggest that Homestake carries relatively high risks and that the required rate of return on its stock is higher than the returns required on stocks of most other companies. This, however, is not the case. Homestake's required rate of return has been, on average, well below the required rate of return on other firms. This indicates that investors regard Homestake as a low-risk company, in spite of its unstable profits.

2. General Electric (GE) is one of the largest and most diversified companies in the world. Its businesses fall into three broad categories: (1) technology, which includes jet engines, aerospace engineering, plastics, medical systems, and factory automation; (2) service, which includes financial services, broadcasting, and communications; and (3) core manufacturing, which includes major appliances, power systems, and electrical

137

equipment. The company has a leading position in all of its key markets, and its net income has grown at a relatively steady annual rate of 10 to 12 percent over the past 10 years. Further, GE has an A++ financial strength rating from *Value Line* (versus B+ for Homestake), so the company is in the top 1 percent in terms of its financial condition. All of this suggests that GE should be regarded as having a relatively low degree of risk vis-à-vis Homestake. This, however, is not the case. A careful analysis indicates that GE has a significantly higher required rate of return than Homestake. In fact, many large, relatively stable companies such as GE have higher required rates of return than a number of smaller, more volatile companies such as Homestake.

The reason behind this somewhat counterintuitive fact involves diversification and its effects on risk. Homestake's stock price tends to rise with inflationary expectations, whereas the price of GE and most other stocks tends to decline as inflation heats up. Therefore, holding Homestake as part of a portfolio of "normal" stocks tends to stabilize returns on the entire portfolio. Similarly, investors can reduce some of the risk inherent in small companies with volatile earnings by forming diversified portfolios of such stocks—investors can, to some extent, create their own "GEs" by constructing portfolios of small company stocks choosing from a number of different industries.

WE began our discussion of risk and return in Chapter 4. There, we saw that some of the total risk inherent in an asset can be eliminated by diversification; thus, investors should hold portfolios of assets. Further, each investor should choose between alternative efficient portfolios based on his or her degree of risk aversion as reflected by indifference curves. In this chapter, we continue the discussion of risk and return by adding a risk-free asset to the set of investment opportunities. As we will see, this leads all investors to hold a well-diversified portfolio of risky assets, and then to account for differing degrees of risk aversion by combining the risky portfolio in different proportions with the risk-free asset. However, this basic question remains to be answered: How much return is required to compensate for a given amount of risk? As we shall see, the Capital Asset Pricing Model (CAPM) provides one neat, precise answer. However, the CAPM has not been, and indeed cannot be, confirmed empirically—it may or may not represent the way investors actually behave. Thus, other risk/return models have been proposed, and we close this chapter with a discussion of the CAPM's most prominent competitor, the Arbitrage Pricing Theory (APT).

THE CAPITAL ASSET PRICING MODEL

As we saw in the preceding chapter, the riskiness of a portfolio as measured by its standard deviation of returns is generally less than the average risk of the individual assets in the portfolio. This phenomenon, in turn, has important implications for the required rate of return on any given security. Investors should (and generally do) hold portfolios of securities, not just one security, so it is reasonable to consider the riskiness of any security in terms of its contribution to the riskiness of a portfolio rather than in terms of its riskiness if held in isolation. The *Capital Asset Pricing Model (CAPM)* specifies the relationship between risk and required rates of return on assets when they are held in well-diversified portfolios.

Basic Assumptions of the CAPM

As in all financial theories, a number of assumptions were made in the development of the CAPM; they are summarized in the following list:[1]

1.   All investors are single-period expected utility of terminal wealth maximizers who choose among alternative portfolios on the basis of each portfolio's expected return and standard deviation.

2.   All investors can borrow or lend an unlimited amount at a given risk-free rate of interest, k_{RF}, and there are no restrictions on short sales of any asset.[2]

3.   All investors have identical estimates of the expected values, variances, and co-variances of returns among all assets; that is, investors have homogeneous expectations.

4.   All assets are perfectly divisible and perfectly liquid (that is, marketable at the going price), and there are no transactions costs.

5.   There are no taxes.

6.   All investors are price takers (that is, all investors assume that their own buying and selling activity will not affect stock prices).

7.   The quantities of all assets are given and fixed.

Theoretical extensions in the literature have relaxed many of the basic CAPM assumptions, and in general these extensions have yielded results that are reasonably consistent with the basic theory. However, even the extensions contain assumptions which are both strong and unrealistic. Therefore, the validity of the model can only

---

[1]The CAPM was originated by William F. Sharpe in his article "Capital Asset Prices: A Theory of Market Equilibrium under Conditions of Risk," which appeared in the September 1964 issue of the *Journal of Finance.* The assumptions inherent in Sharpe's model were spelled out by Michael C. Jensen in "Capital Markets: Theory and Evidence," *Bell Journal of Economics and Management Science,* Autumn 1972, 357–398.

[2]In a short sale, one borrows a stock and then sells it, expecting to buy it back later (at a lower price) in order to repay the person from whom the stock was borrowed. If you sell short and the stock price rises, you lose; you gain if the stock price falls after you go short.

be established through empirical tests. More will be said later in this chapter about the empirical validity of the CAPM, but first we must discuss its basic properties and conclusions.

Self-Test Questions

What are the assumptions inherent in the CAPM?

In what sense are these assumptions unrealistic? Explain.

THE CAPITAL MARKET LINE

Figure 4-10 in Chapter 4 showed the set of portfolio opportunities for the two-asset case and illustrated how indifference curves can be used to select the optimal portfolio from the feasible set. In Figure 5-1, we have constructed a similar diagram for the multi-asset case, but here we also include a risk-free asset with a return k_{RF}. The riskless asset by definition has zero risk, and hence $\sigma = 0\%$, so it is plotted on the vertical axis.

Figure 5-1 shows both the feasible set of portfolios of risky assets (the shaded area) and a set of indifference curves (I_1, I_2, I_3), which represent the tradeoff be-

---

Figure 5-1   Investor Equilibrium: Combining the Risk-Free
Asset with the Market Portfolio

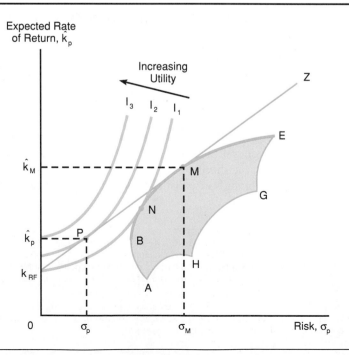

tween risk and expected return for a particular investor. Point N, where indifference curve I_1 is tangent to the efficient set, represents a possible portfolio choice; it is the point on the efficient set of risky portfolios where the investor obtains the highest possible return for a given amount of risk, σ_p, and the smallest degree of risk for a given expected return, $\hat{k}_p$.

However, the investor can do better than Portfolio N; he or she can reach a higher indifference curve. In addition to the feasible set of risky portfolios, we now have a risk-free asset that provides a certain return, k_{RF}. Given the possibility of investing in the risk-free asset, investors can create new portfolios that combine the risk-free asset with a portfolio of risky assets. This enables them to achieve any combination of risk and return that lies along the straight line connecting k_{RF} with M, the point of tangency between that straight line and the stock portfolio's efficient set curve.[3] All portfolios on the line $k_{RF}MZ$ are preferred to the other risky portfolio opportunities on the efficient frontier BNME, so the points on the line $k_{RF}MZ$ now represent the best attainable combinations of risk and return.

Given the new opportunity set $k_{RF}MZ$, our investor will move from Point N to Point P, which is on his or her highest attainable risk/return indifference curve. Note that line $k_{RF}MZ$ dominates the opportunities that could have been achieved solely from the efficient set of risky assets. In general, since investors can include both the risk-free security and a fraction of the risky portfolio, M, in a portfolio, it will be possible to move to a point such as P. In addition, if the investor can borrow as well as lend (lending is equivalent to buying risk-free debt securities) at the riskless rate, k_{RF}, it is possible to move out the line segment MZ, and one would do so if his or her indifference curve were tangent to $k_{RF}MZ$ to the right of Point M.[4]

---

[3]The risk/return combinations between a risk-free asset and a risky asset (a single stock or a portfolio of stocks) will always be linear. To see this, consider the equations presented in Chapter 4 for return, $\hat{k}_p$, and risk, σ_p, for any combination x and $(1 - x)$:

$$\hat{k}_p = xk_{RF} + (1 - x)\hat{k}_M, \tag{4-5a}$$

and

$$\sigma_p = \sqrt{x^2\sigma_{RF}^2 + (1 - x)^2\sigma_M^2 + 2x(1 - x)r_{RF/M}\sigma_{RF}\sigma_M}. \tag{4-9a}$$

Equation 4-5a is obviously linear. For Equation 4-9a, we know that k_{RF} is the risk-free asset, so $\sigma_{RF} = 0$; hence, σ_{RF}^2 is also zero. Using this information, we can simplify Equation 4-9a as follows.

$$\sigma_p = \sqrt{(1 - x)^2\sigma_M^2} = (1 - x)\sigma_M.$$

Thus, σ_p is also linear when a riskless asset is combined with a portfolio of risky assets.

If expected returns as measured by $\hat{k}_p$ and risk as measured by σ_p are both linear functions of x, then the relationship between $\hat{k}_p$ and σ_p when graphed as in Figure 5-1 must also be linear. For example, if 100 percent of the portfolio is invested in k_{RF} with a return of 8 percent, the portfolio return will be 8 percent and σ_p will be 0. If 100 percent is invested in M, with $\hat{k}_M = 12\%$ and $\sigma_M = 10\%$, then $\sigma_p = 1.0(10\%) = 10\%$, and $\hat{k}_p = 0(8\%) + 1.0(12\%) = 12\%$. If 50 percent of the portfolio is invested in M and 50 percent in the risk-free asset, then $\sigma_p = 0.5(10\%) = 5\%$, and $\hat{k}_p = 0.5(8\%) + 0.5(12\%) = 10\%$. Plotting these points will reveal the linear relationship given as $k_{RF}MZ$ in Figure 5-1.

[4]An investor who is highly averse to risk will have a steep indifference curve and will end up at a point such as P, holding some of the risky market portfolio and some of the riskless asset. An investor less averse to risk will have a relatively flat indifference curve, which will cause him or her to move out beyond M toward Z, borrowing to do so. The risk-prone investor might buy stocks on margin, which means borrowing and using the stocks as collateral. If individuals' borrowing rates are higher than k_{RF}, then the line $k_{RF}MZ$ will tilt down (that is, be less steep) beyond M. This condition would invalidate the basic CAPM, or at least require it to be modified. Therefore, the assumption of equal lending and borrowing rates is crucial to CAPM theory.

All investors should hold portfolios lying on the line $k_{RF}MZ$ under the conditions assumed in the CAPM. This implies that they would hold only efficient portfolios that are combinations of the risk-free security and the risky portfolio M. Thus, the addition of the risk-free asset totally changes the efficient set: The efficient set now lies along line $k_{RF}MZ$ rather than along the curve BNME. Also, note that if the capital market is to be in equilibrium, M must be a portfolio that contains every asset in exact proportion to that asset's fraction of the total market value of all assets; that is, if Security i is x percent of the total market value of all securities, x percent of the market portfolio M must consist of Security i. Thus, all investors should hold portfolios which lie on the line $k_{RF}MZ$, with the particular location of a given individual's portfolio being determined by the point at which his or her indifference curve is tangent to the line.

The line $k_{RF}MZ$ in Figure 5-1 is called the *Capital Market Line (CML)*. It has an intercept of k_{RF} and a slope of $(\hat{k}_M - k_{RF})/\sigma_M$.[5] Therefore, the equation for the Capital Market Line may be expressed as follows:

$$\text{CML:} \quad \hat{k}_p = k_{RF} + \left(\frac{\hat{k}_M - k_{RF}}{\sigma_M}\right)\sigma_p. \tag{5-1}$$

Equation 5-1 tells us that the expected rate of return on any efficient portfolio (that is, any portfolio on the CML) is equal to the riskless rate plus a risk premium, and the risk premium is equal to $(\hat{k}_M - k_{RF})/\sigma_M$ multiplied by the portfolio's standard deviation, σ_p. Thus, the CML specifies a linear relationship between expected return and risk, with the slope of the CML being equal to the expected return on the market portfolio of risky stocks, $\hat{k}_M$, minus the risk-free rate, k_{RF}, which is called the *market risk premium*, all divided by the standard deviation of returns on the market portfolio, σ_M:

$$(\hat{k}_M - k_{RF})/\sigma_M.$$

For example, suppose $k_{RF} = 10\%$, $\hat{k}_M = 15\%$, and $\sigma_M = 15\%$. Then, the slope of the CML would be $(15\% - 10\%)/15\% = 0.33$, and if a particular portfolio had $\sigma_p = 10\%$, then its $\hat{k}_p$ would be

$$\hat{k}_p = 10\% + 0.33(10\%) = 13.3\%.$$

A riskier portfolio with $\sigma_p = 20\%$ would have $\hat{k}_p = 10\% + 0.33(20\%) = 16.6\%$. Equation 5-1 states that the expected return on an efficient portfolio in equilibrium is equal to a risk-free return plus a risk premium which is equal to the slope of the CML multiplied by the standard deviation of the portfolio's returns. This relationship is graphed in Figure 5-2. The CML is drawn as a straight line with an intercept at k_{RF}, the risk-free return, and a slope equal to the market risk premium $(\hat{k}_M - k_{RF})$

---

[5]Recall that the slope of any line is measured as $\Delta Y/\Delta X$, or the change in height associated with a given change in horizontal distance. k_{RF} is at 0 on the horizontal axis, so $\Delta X = \sigma_M - 0 = \sigma_M$. The vertical axis difference associated with a change from k_{RF} to $\hat{k}_M$ is $\hat{k}_M - k_{RF}$. Therefore, slope $= \Delta Y/\Delta X = (\hat{k}_M - k_{RF})/\sigma_M$.

Figure 5-2   The Capital Market Line (CML)

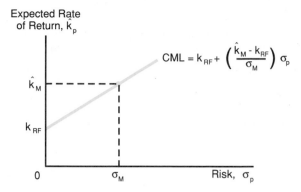

Note: We did not draw it in, but you can visualize the shaded space shown in Figure 5-1 in this graph, and the CML as the line formed by connecting k_{RF} with the tangent to the shaded space.

divided by σ_M. The slope of the CML reflects the aggregate attitude of investors toward risk.

Self-Test Questions

Draw the feasible set of risky assets, the efficient frontier, and the CML on one graph.

Write out the equation for the CML and explain its meaning.

THE SECURITY MARKET LINE

The next step in the development of the CAPM takes us from risk and returns on efficient portfolios to risk and returns on individual securities. Under the CAPM theory, the riskiness of a security is measured by its beta coefficient ("b," discussed in the next section), and the relationship between a security's risk and its return is known as the *Security Market Line (SML)*:

$$\text{SML: } k_i = k_{RF} + (k_M - k_{RF})b_i. \tag{5-2}$$

Here

k_i = the required rate of return on the ith stock. (We earlier defined $\hat{k}_i$ to be the expected rate of return. In equilibrium, $k_i = \hat{k}_i$.)

k_{RF} = the riskless rate of return, generally measured by the rate of return on U.S. Treasury securities.

k_M = the required rate of return on a portfolio consisting of all stocks, or the market portfolio. As we shall see, in equilibrium required returns must equal expected returns, so $k_M = \hat{k}_M$.

k_A = the required rate of return on an average stock in the market portfolio.[6] Thus, $k_A = k_M$.

$(k_M - k_{RF}) = RP_M$ = the market risk premium, or the price of risk for an average stock. It is the additional return over the riskless rate required to compensate investors for assuming an "average" amount of risk.

b_i = the beta coefficient of the ith stock. Betas are discussed in the next section.

$(k_M - k_{RF})b_i = RP_i$ = the risk premium on the ith stock. A stock's risk premium is less than, equal to, or greater than the premium on an average stock depending on whether its beta is less than, equal to, or greater than 1.0.

Thus, if $k_{RF} = 9\%$, $k_M = 13\%$, and $b_i = 0.5$, then by Equation 5-2, $k_i = 11\%$:

$$k_i = 9\% + (13\% - 9\%)0.5$$

$$= 9\% + (4\%)0.5$$

$$= 9\% + 2\% = 11\%.$$

Figure 5-3 shows the SML when $k_{RF} = 9\%$ and $k_M = 13\%$. Several features of the graph are worth noting:

1. Required rates of return are shown on the vertical axis, and risk as measured by beta is shown on the horizontal axis.

2. Riskless securities have $b_i = 0$; therefore, k_{RF} appears as the vertical axis intercept.

3. The slope of the SML [$\Delta Y/\Delta X = (k_M - k_{RF})/(1.0 - 0.0) = (k_M - k_{RF}) = 13\% - 9\% = 4$ percentage points in our example] reflects the degree of risk aversion in the economy—the greater the average investor's aversion to risk, then (1) the steeper the slope of the SML, (2) the greater the risk premium for any risky asset, and (3) the higher the required rate of return on risky assets in general. Note that beta is *not* the slope of the SML; the slope of the line in Figure 5-3 is the market risk premium, a constant 4 percentage points for each one unit increase in beta, while beta itself is calculated as described in a later section.

4. Required rates of return and risk premiums are shown for stocks with $b_i = 0.5$, $b_i = 1.0$, and $b_i = 2.0$.

As we can see from the SML, required rates of return depend not only on market risk as measured by beta, but also on the risk-free rate and the market risk premium. Since these variables change, the SML is not stable over time.

---

[6]The term "average stock" is a bit like "average U.S. family." The average family has 2.73 members, its head is 34.6 years old, its annual income is \$28,362, and so on. No one family actually conforms to average, but each family can be compared to the statistical average. Similarly, the "average stock" is a statistical concept measured in terms of its expected rate of return, standard deviation of returns, and covariance with other stocks.

Figure 5-3   The Security Market Line (SML)

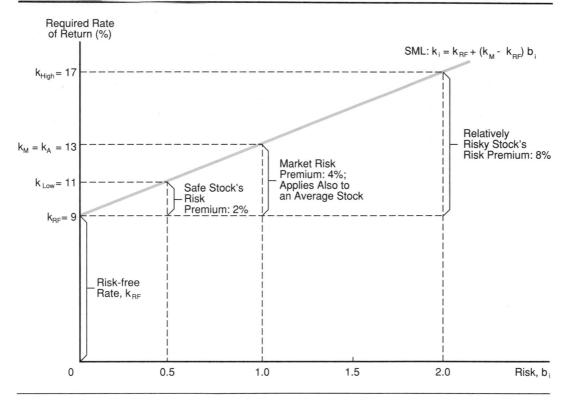

The Impact of Inflation

As we learned in Chapter 3, interest amounts to "rent" on borrowed money, or the price of money; thus, k_{RF} is the price of money to a riskless borrower. We also learned that the risk-free rate as measured by the rate on U.S. Treasury securities is called the *nominal rate,* and it consists of two elements: (1) a *real inflation-free rate of return, k*,* and (2) an *inflation premium, IP,* equal to the anticipated rate of inflation.[7] Thus, $k_{RF} = k^* + IP$. The real rate on long-term Treasury bonds has historically ranged from 2 to 4 percent, with a mean of about 3 percent. Therefore, if no inflation were expected, long-term Treasury bonds would yield about 3 percent. However, as the expected rate of inflation increases, a premium must be added to the real risk-free rate of return to compensate investors for the loss of purchasing power that results from inflation. Therefore, the 9 percent k_{RF} shown in Figure 5-3 might be thought of as consisting of a 3 percent real risk-free rate of return plus a 6 percent inflation premium: $k_{RF} = k^* + IP = 3\% + 6\% = 9\%$.

---

[7]Long-term Treasury bonds also contain a maturity risk premium, MRP. Here we include the MRP in k* to simplify the discussion.

Figure 5-4   Shift in the SML Caused by an Increase in Inflation

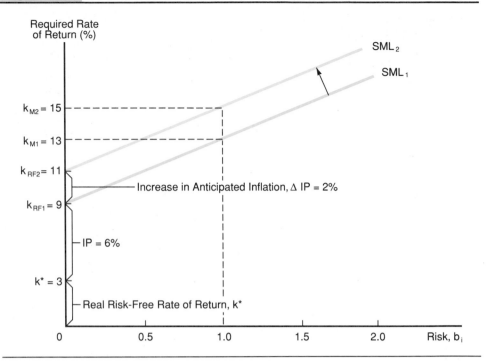

If the expected rate of inflation rose to 8 percent, this would cause k_{RF} to rise to 11 percent. Such a change is shown in Figure 5-4. Notice that under the CAPM, the increase in k_{RF} also causes an *equal* increase in the rate of return on all risky assets, because the inflation premium is built into the required rate of return of both riskless and risky assets.[8] For example, the rate of return on an average stock, k_M, increases from 13 to 15 percent. Other risky securities' returns also rise by 2 percentage points.

Changes in Risk Aversion

The slope of the Security Market Line reflects the extent to which investors are averse to risk — the steeper the slope of the line, the greater the marginal investor's risk aversion. If investors were indifferent to risk, and if k_{RF} were 9 percent, then

---

[8]Recall that the inflation premium for any asset is equal to the average expected rate of inflation over the life of the asset. Thus, in this analysis we must assume either that all securities plotted on the SML graph have the same life or else that the expected rate of future inflation is constant.

It should also be noted that k_{RF} in a CAPM analysis can be proxied by either a long-term rate (the T-bond rate) or a short-term rate (the T-bill rate). Traditionally, the T-bill rate was used, but in recent years there has been a movement toward use of the T-bond rate because there is a closer relationship between T-bond yields and stocks than between T-bill yields and stocks. We will discuss this in more detail in Chapter 8.

Figure 5-5 Shift in the SML Caused by Increased Risk Aversion

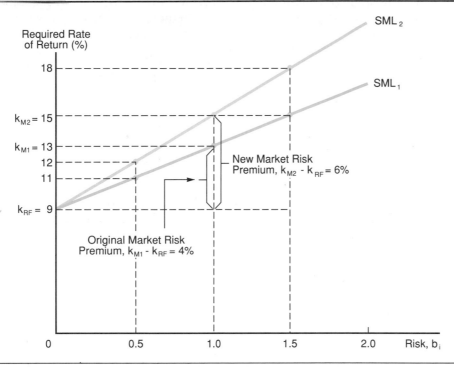

risky assets would also sell to provide an expected return of 9 percent: If there were no risk aversion, there would be no risk premium, so the SML would be horizontal. As risk aversion increases, so does the risk premium and, thus, the slope of the SML.

Figure 5-5 illustrates an increase in risk aversion. The market risk premium rises from 4 to 6 percent, and k_M rises from 13 to 15 percent. The returns on other risky assets also rise, and the effect of this shift in risk aversion is more pronounced on riskier securities. For example, the required return on a low-risk stock with $b_i = 0.5$ increases by only one percentage point, from 11 to 12 percent, whereas that on a high-risk stock with $b_i = 1.5$ increases by three percentage points, from 15 to 18 percent.

Changes in a Stock's Beta Coefficient

As we shall see later in the book, a firm can affect its market, or beta, risk through changes in the composition of its assets as well as through its use of debt financing. A company's beta can also change as a result of external factors, such as increased competition in its industry, the expiration of basic patents, and the like. When such changes occur, the required rate of return also changes, and, as we shall see in Chapter 7, this will affect the price of the firm's stock. For example, consider Smith

Electronics Corporation, with a beta equal to 1.0. Now suppose some action occurred that caused Smith Electronics's beta to increase from 1.0 to 1.5. If the conditions depicted in Figure 5-3 held, Smith's required rate of return would increase from

$$k_1 = k_{RF} + (k_M - k_{RF})b_i$$

$$= 9\% + (13\% - 9\%)1.0$$

$$= 13\%$$

to

$$k_2 = 9\% + (13\% - 9\%)1.5$$

$$= 15\%.$$

Any change which affects the required rate of return on a security, such as a change in its beta coefficient or in expected inflation, will have an impact on the price of the security. We will examine in detail the relationship between a security's required rate of return and its stock price in Chapter 7.

Self-Test Questions

Write out the equation for and graph the SML.

What happens to the SML graph (1) when inflation increases and (2) when inflation decreases?

What happens to the SML graph (1) when risk aversion increases and (2) when risk aversion decreases?

What is the difference between the CML and the SML?

PHYSICAL ASSETS VERSUS SECURITIES

In a book on the financial management of business firms, why do we spend so much time on the riskiness of security investments? Why not concentrate on the riskiness of such business assets as plant and equipment? *The reason is that, for a management whose goal is stock price maximization, the overriding consideration is the riskiness of the firm's stock, and the relevant risk of any physical asset must be measured in terms of its effect on the stock's risk.* For example, suppose Goodyear Tire Company is considering a major investment in a new product, recapped tires. Sales of recaps, hence the earnings on the new operation, are highly uncertain, so it would appear that the new venture is quite risky. However, suppose returns on the recap business are negatively correlated with Goodyear's regular operations — when times are good and people have plenty of money, they buy new tires, but when times are bad, they tend to buy more recaps. Therefore, returns would be high on regular operations and low on the recap division during good times, but the opposite situation would occur during recessions. The result might be a pattern like that shown in Figure 4-2 back in Chapter 4 for Stocks W and M. Thus, what appears to be a risky investment when viewed on a stand-alone basis might not be very risky when viewed within the context of the company as a whole.

This analysis can be extended to the corporation's owners, the stockholders. Because the stock of Goodyear and other companies is owned by stockholders, the real issue each time a company makes a major asset investment is this: How does this investment affect the risk of our stockholders? Again, the stand-alone risk of an individual project may look quite high, but viewed in the context of the project's effect on stockholders' risk, the project may not be very risky. We will address this subject again in Chapter 11.

Self-Test Question

Explain the following statement: "The stand-alone risk of an individual project may look quite high, but viewed in the context of a project's effect on stockholders' risk, the project may not be very risky."

THE CONCEPT OF BETA

An *average stock*, by definition, must move up and down in step with the general market as measured by some index such as the Dow Jones Industrial Average or the New York Stock Exchange Index. Such a stock will, by definition, have a beta of 1.0, which indicates that if the market moves up or down by 10 percentage points, the stock will also tend to move up or down by 10 percentage points. A portfolio of such b $=$ 1.0 stocks will move up and down in perfect synchronization with the broad market averages, and this portfolio will be just as risky as the averages. If a stock has b $=$ 0.5, the stock is only half as volatile as the market—it will rise and fall only half as much as the market—and a portfolio of such stocks is only half as risky as a portfolio of b $=$ 1.0 stocks. On the other hand, if b $=$ 2.0, the stock is twice as volatile as an average stock, so a portfolio of such stocks will be twice as risky as an average portfolio.

Betas are calculated and published by Merrill Lynch, Value Line, and numerous other organizations. The beta coefficients of some well-known companies, as calculated by Value Line, are shown in Table 5-1.[9] Most stocks have betas in the range of 0.75 to 1.50, and the average for all stocks is 1.0 by definition.

Portfolio Beta Coefficients

A portfolio consisting of low-beta securities will itself have a low beta, as the beta of any set of securities is the weighted average of the individual securities' betas:

$$\text{Portfolio beta} = b_p = \sum_{i=1}^{n} x_i b_i. \qquad \textbf{(5-3)}$$

---

[9]These betas are called "historical," or "ex post," betas because they are based strictly on historical, or past, data. Other types of betas, such as adjusted and fundamental betas, are also in wide use today. The different types of betas will be discussed in Chapter 8.

Table 5-1	Illustrative List of Beta Coefficients

Stock	Beta
Harley-Davidson	1.55
Seagate Technology	1.50
Winnebago	1.40
Dow Chemical	1.20
General Electric	1.10
Sara Lee	1.00
Chevron	1.00
Procter & Gamble	0.95
Pacific Gas & Electric	0.75
Homestake Mining	0.60

Source: Value Line, March 16, 1990.

Thus, if a high-beta stock (one whose beta is greater than 1.0) is added to an average risk portfolio ($b_p = 1.0$), then the beta and consequently the riskiness of the portfolio will increase. Conversely, if a low-beta stock (one whose beta is less than 1.0) is added to an average risk portfolio, the portfolio's beta and risk will decline. *Therefore, since a stock's beta measures its contribution to the riskiness of a portfolio, beta is the appropriate measure of the stock's riskiness.*

To illustrate, if you hold a $100,000 portfolio consisting of $10,000 invested in each of ten stocks, and if each stock has a beta of 0.8, then your portfolio will have $b_p = 0.8$, it will be less risky than the market, and it should experience relatively narrow price swings and hence have relatively small rate of return fluctuations.

Now suppose you sell one of the existing stocks and replace it with a stock with $b = 2.0$. This action will increase the riskiness of your portfolio from $b_{p1} = 0.8$ to $b_{p2} = 0.92$ as calculated using Equation 5-3:

$$b_{p2} = \sum_{i=1}^{n} x_i b_i = 0.9(0.8) + 0.1(2.0) = 0.92.$$

Had a stock with $b = 0.6$ been added, your portfolio's beta would have declined from 0.8 to 0.78.

Calculating Beta Coefficients: The Characteristic Line

When Professor Sharpe developed the CAPM, he noted that the market risk of a given stock can be measured by its tendency to move with the general market. His procedure for determining market risk is illustrated in Figure 5-6, which is explained in the following paragraphs.[10] First, however, familiarize yourself with the definitions of the terms used in Figure 5-6:

---

[10]It should be noted that beta analysis in practice is much more difficult than our discussion makes it sound. We will see this in Chapter 8.

$\bar{k}_J$ = historical (realized) rate of return on Stock J. (Recall that $\hat{k}_J$ and k_J are defined as Stock J's expected and required returns, respectively.)

$\bar{k}_M$ = historical (realized) rate of return on the market.

a_J = vertical axis intercept term for Stock J.

b_J = slope, or beta coefficient, for Stock J.

e_J = random error, reflecting the difference between the actual return on Stock J in a given year and the return predicted by the regression line.

Figure 5-6 Calculating Beta Coefficients

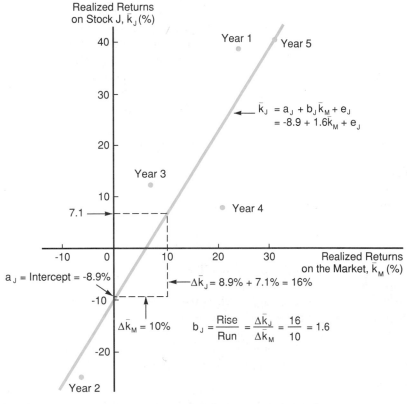

Year	Stock J($\bar{k}_J$)	Market ($\bar{k}_M$)
1	38.6%	23.8%
2	(24.7)	(7.2)
3	12.3	6.6
4	8.2	20.5
5	40.1	30.6
Average $\bar{k}$ =	14.9%	14.9%
$\sigma_{\bar{k}}$ =	26.5%	15.1%

The historical returns on Stock J are given in the lower section of Figure 5-6, along with historical returns on the market, $\bar{k}_M$. Notice that when returns on the market are high, returns on Stock J likewise tend to be high, and when the market is down, Stock J's returns are low. This general relationship is expressed more precisely in the regression line shown in Figure 5-6.

Recall what the term *regression line* or *regression equation* means: The equation $Y = a + bX + e$ is the standard form of a simple linear regression. It states that the dependent variable, Y, is equal to a constant, a, plus b times X, where X is the "independent" variable, plus a random error term. Thus, the rate of return on Stock J during a given time period depends on what happens to the general stock market, which is measured by $\bar{k}_M$, plus random events which affect Stock J but do not affect most other stocks.

The regression equation can be obtained by plotting the data points on graph paper and then drawing a line through the scatter of points "by eye." There is a mathematical line of best fit, the *least squares regression line,* but unless the data points all line up neatly, the "by eye" regression line will differ somewhat from the least squares line, and different students will draw in somewhat different lines.[11] In the 1964 article in which he developed the CAPM, Sharpe called the regression line the *characteristic line.* Thus, a stock's beta is the slope of its characteristic line.

Once the regression, or characteristic, line has been drawn, we can estimate its intercept and slope, the a and b values in $Y = a + bX$. The intercept, a, is simply the point where the line cuts the vertical axis. The slope coefficient, b, can be estimated by the "rise over run" method. This involves calculating the amount by which $\bar{k}_J$ increases for a given increase in $\bar{k}_M$. For example, we observe (in Figure 5-6) that $\bar{k}_J$ increases from -8.9 to $+7.1$ percent (the rise) when $\bar{k}_M$ increases from 0.0 to 10.0 percent (the run). Thus, b, the beta coefficient, can be measured as follows:

$$b_J = \frac{\text{Rise}}{\text{Run}} = \frac{\Delta Y}{\Delta X} = \frac{7.1\% - (-8.9\%)}{10.0\% - 0.0\%} = \frac{16.0\%}{10.0\%} = 1.6.$$

Note that rise over run is a ratio, and it would be the same if measured using any two arbitrarily selected points on the line.

Although the "by eye" approach is useful for visualizing what the beta concept is all about, an in-depth understanding as well as efficient applications of the concept require the use of statistics. Basic statistics courses demonstrate that the following procedure can be used to calculate the slope of any simple regression equation, and this formula is also programmed into the statistical functions on calculators and computers:

$$b_J = \frac{\text{Covariance between Stock J and the market}}{\text{Variance of market returns}} = \frac{\text{Cov}(\bar{k}_J, \bar{k}_M)}{\sigma_M^2}$$

$$= \frac{r_{JM}\sigma_J\sigma_M}{\sigma_M^2} = r_{JM}\left(\frac{\sigma_J}{\sigma_M}\right).$$

[11]In practical applications, the regression equation would always be fitted by the method of least squares, using either a hand-held calculator with statistical functions or a computer.

Thus, a stock's beta, hence its market risk, depends on (1) its correlation with the stock market as a whole, r_{JM}; (2) its own variability, σ_J; and (3) the variability of the market, σ_M. In the Figure 5-6 example, $r_{JM} = 0.91$, $\sigma_J = 26.5\%$, and $\sigma_M = 15.1\%$. Therefore, $b_J = 0.91(26.5\%/15.1\%) = 1.60$.

Some Observations about Betas

Now that we have plotted Stock J's historical rates of return and estimated its beta coefficient, we can note the following points:

1. The *predicted future* returns on Stock J are assumed to bear a linear relationship of the following form to those of the market:

$$\text{Predicted future rate of return} = \hat{k}_J = a_J + b_J\hat{k}_M + e_J \tag{5-4}$$

$$= -8.9\% + 1.6\hat{k}_M + e_J.$$

In other words, we assume that the historical relationship between Stock J and the market as a whole, as given by the characteristic line, will continue on into the future.[12]

2. In addition to general market movements, each firm also faces events that are unique to the firm and independent of the general economic climate. Such events cause the returns on any Firm J's stock to move somewhat independently of those for the market as a whole, and these random events are accounted for by the random error term, e_J. Before the fact, the expected value of the error term is zero; after the fact, it generally will be either positive or negative. This component of total risk is the stock's *diversifiable,* or *company-specific, risk,* and rational investors will eliminate its effects by holding diversified portfolios of stocks.

3. The regression coefficient, b (the beta coefficient), is a market sensitivity index; it measures the relative volatility of a given stock versus the average stock, or "the market." This tendency of an individual stock to move with the market constitutes a risk, because the market does fluctuate, and these fluctuations cannot be diversified away. This component of total risk is the stock's *market, or nondiversifiable, risk.* Even well-diversified portfolios are exposed to market risk.

4. The relationship between a stock's total risk, market risk, and diversifiable risk can be expressed as follows:

$$\text{Total risk} = \text{Variance} = \text{Market risk} + \text{Diversifiable risk}$$
$$\sigma_J^2 = b_J^2\sigma_M^2 + \sigma_{e_J}^2.$$

---

[12]The characteristic line equation is also called the *Market Model.* The market model asserts that the relationship between the returns on individual stocks and the returns on the market is linear and can be expressed by Equation 5-4. The Capital Asset Pricing Model (CAPM) states that, in equilibrium, returns on individual stocks can be expressed by the Security Market Line, Equation 5-2. The two models require different assumptions, thus, acceptance of one model does not necessarily imply acceptance of the other. We will use the market model, or characteristic line, only to estimate betas for use in the Security Market Line of the CAPM. For more information on the Market Model and the differences between the two models, see Sid Mittra and Chris Gassen, *Investment Analysis and Portfolio Management* (New York: Harcourt Brace Jovanovich, 1981).

Here σ_J^2 is the variance or total risk of Stock J, σ_M^2 is the variance of the market, b_J is Stock J's beta coefficient, and $\sigma_{e_J}^2$ is the variance of Stock J's regression error term.

5. If, in a graph such as Figure 5-6, all the points plotted exactly on the regression line, then the variance of the error term, $\sigma_{e_J}^2$, would be zero and all of the stock's total risk would be market risk. On the other hand, if the points were widely scattered about the regression line, much of the stock's total risk would be diversifiable. The shares of a large, well-diversified mutual fund would plot very close to the regression line, as would those of a broadly diversified conglomerate corporation such as GE.

6. If the stock market never fluctuated, then stocks would have no market risk. Of course, the market does fluctuate, so market risk is present; even if you hold an extremely well-diversified portfolio, you will still suffer losses if the market falls. In recent years, the standard deviation of market returns, σ_M, has generally run about 15 percent. However, on a single day, October 19, 1987, the Dow Jones Industrial Average, one measure of the market, lost 23 percent of its value.

7. Beta is a measure of market risk, but the actual market risk of Stock J is $b_J^2\sigma_M^2$. Market risk can also be expressed in standard deviation form, $b_J\sigma_M$, so Stock J's market risk is $b_J\sigma_M = 1.6(15.1\%) = 24.2\%$, while its total risk is $\sigma_J = 26.5\%$. For any given level of market volatility as measured by the market's standard deviation, σ_M, the higher a stock's beta, the higher its market risk. If beta were zero, the stock would have no market risk, while if beta were 1.0, the stock would be exactly as risky as the market—assuming the stock is held in a diversified portfolio—and the stock's market risk would be σ_M.

8. The diversifiable risk can and should be eliminated by diversification, so the *relevant* risk is not total risk, but market risk. If Stock J had b = 0.5, then the stock's relevant risk would be $b_J\sigma_M = 0.5(15.1\%) = 7.55\%$. A portfolio of such low-beta stocks would have a standard deviation of expected returns of $\sigma_p = 7.55\%$, or one-half the standard deviation of expected returns on a portfolio of average (b = 1.0) stocks. Had Stock J been a high-beta stock (b = 2.0), then its relevant risk would have been $b_J\sigma_M = 2.0(15.1\%) = 30.2\%$. A portfolio of b = 2.0 stocks would have $\sigma_p = 30.2\%$, so such a portfolio would be twice as risky as a portfolio of average stocks.

9. A stock's risk premium depends only on its market risk, not its total risk: $RP_J = (k_M - k_{RF})b_J$. Mr. S (for stupid) might have only one stock, hence be concerned with total risk and seek a return based on that risk. However, if other investors hold a well-diversified portfolio, they would face less risk from Stock J. Therefore, if Stock J offered a return high enough to satisfy Mr. S, it would represent a bargain for other investors, who would then buy it, pushing its price up and its yield down in the process. Since most financial assets are held by diversified investors, and since any given security can have only one price, hence only one rate of return, market action drives each stock's risk premium to the level specified by its relevant, or market, risk.

Self-Test Questions

Explain the meaning and significance of a stock's beta coefficient. Illustrate your explanation by drawing, on one graph, the characteristic lines for stocks with low, average, and high risk. (Hint: Let your three characteristic lines intersect at $\bar{k}_i = \bar{k}_M = 9\%$, the assumed risk-free rate.)

What is the relationship among total risk, market risk, and diversifiable risk?

EMPIRICAL TESTS OF THE CAPM

As noted earlier, the CAPM was developed on the basis of a set of unrealistic assumptions. If those assumptions were all true, then the CAPM would also have to be true. However, since the assumptions are not completely correct, the basic SML equation, $k_i = k_{RF} + (k_M - k_{RF})b_i$, might or might not represent an accurate description of how investors behave and how rates of return are established in the marketplace. For example, if many investors are not fully diversified, hence have not eliminated all diversifiable risk from their portfolios, then (1) beta would not be an adequate measure of risk and (2) the SML would not explain how required returns are set. Also, if the interest rate that investors must pay to borrow money is greater than the risk-free rate (that is, if the borrowing rate is greater than the lending rate), then the CML would not continue in a straight line beyond Point M as it does in Figure 5-1, and this too would invalidate the SML. And, of course, taxes and brokerage costs do exist, and their presence could distort the CAPM relationships.

For all these reasons, it is entirely possible that the CAPM is not completely valid, in which case the SML will not produce accurate estimates of k_i. Therefore, the CAPM must be tested empirically and validated before it can be used with any real confidence. The literature dealing with empirical tests of the CAPM is quite extensive, so we can give here only a synopsis of some of the key work.

Tests of the Stability of Beta Coefficients

According to the CAPM, the beta that should be used to estimate a stock's market risk reflects investors' estimates of the stock's *future* volatility in relation to that of the market. Obviously, we do not know now how a stock will be related to the market in the future, nor do we know how the average investor views this expected future relative volatility. All we have are data on past volatility, which we can use to plot the characteristic line and to calculate *historical betas*. If historical betas are stable over time, then there would seem to be reason for investors to use past betas as estimators of future volatility. For example, if Stock J's beta had been stable in the past, then its historical b_J would probably be a good proxy for its *ex ante,* or expected, b_J. By "stable," we mean that if b_J were calculated by using data from the period of, say, 1986 to 1990, then this same beta (approximately) should be found from 1991 to 1995.

Robert A. Levy, Marshall E. Blume, and others have studied the question of beta stability in depth.[13] Levy calculated betas for individual securities, as well as for portfolios of securities, over a range of time intervals. He concluded (1) that the betas of individual stocks are unstable, hence that past betas for *individual securities* are *not* good estimators of their future risk, but (2) that betas of portfolios of ten or more randomly selected stocks are reasonably stable, hence that past *portfolio* betas are good estimators of future portfolio volatility. In effect, the errors in the estimates of individual securities' betas tend to offset one another in a portfolio. The work of Blume and others supports Levy's position.

The conclusion that follows from the beta stability studies is that the CAPM is a better concept for structuring investment portfolios than it is for purposes of estimating the cost of capital for individual securities. We will address this issue in Chapter 8, when we discuss cost of capital estimation procedures.

Tests of the CAPM Based on the Slope of the SML

As we have seen, the CAPM states that a linear relationship exists between a security's required rate of return and its beta. Further, when the SML is graphed, the vertical axis intercept should be k_{RF}, and the required rate of return for a stock (or portfolio) with $b = 1.0$ should be k_M, the required rate of return on the market. Various researchers have attempted to test the validity of the model by calculating betas and realized rates of return, plotting these values in graphs such as that in Figure 5-7, and then observing whether or not (1) the intercept is equal to k_{RF}, (2) the regression line is linear, and (3) the line passes through the point $b = 1.0$, k_M. Monthly historical rates of return are generally used for stocks, and both 30-day Treasury bill rates and long-term Treasury bond rates have been used to estimate the value of k_{RF}. Also, most of the studies actually analyze portfolios rather than individual securities because security betas are so unstable.

Before discussing the results of the tests, it is critical to recognize that although the CAPM is an ex ante, or forward-looking model, the data used to test it are entirely historical. There is no reason to believe that *realized* rates of return over past holding periods are necessarily equal to *expected* rates of return with which the model should deal. Also, historical betas may or may not reflect either current or expected future risk. This lack of ex ante data makes it extremely difficult to test the true CAPM. Still, for what it is worth, here is a summary of the key results:

1.   The evidence generally shows a significant positive relationship between realized returns and systematic risk. However, the slope of the relationship is usually less than that predicted by the CAPM.

2.   The relationship between risk and return appears to be linear. Empirical studies give no evidence of significant curvature in the risk/return relationship.

---

[13]See Robert A. Levy, "On the Short-Term Stationarity of Beta Coefficients," *Financial Analysts Journal,* November-December 1971, 55–62, and Marshall E. Blume, "Betas and Their Regression Tendencies," *Journal of Finance,* June 1975, 785–796.

Figure 5-7   Tests of the CAPM

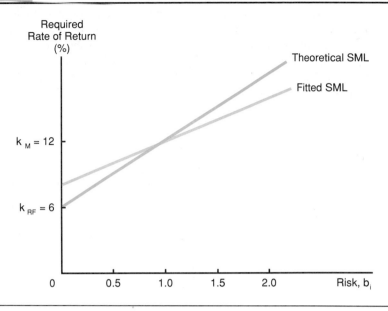

3.   Tests that attempt to assess the relative importance of market and company-specific risk do not yield definitive results. The CAPM theory implies that company-specific risk is not relevant, yet both kinds of risk appear to be positively related to security returns; that is, higher returns are required to compensate for diversifiable as well as market risk. However, it may be that the observed relationships are at least partly spurious; that is, they may reflect statistical problems rather than the true nature of capital markets.

4.   In an important paper, Richard Roll questioned whether it is even conceptually possible to test the CAPM.[14] Roll showed that the linear relationship which prior researchers had observed in graphs like that in Figure 5-7 resulted from the mathematical properties of the models being tested, hence that a finding of linearity proved nothing whatever about the validity of the CAPM. Roll's work did not disprove the CAPM theory, but he did show that it is virtually impossible to prove that investors behave in accordance with the theory.

5.   If the CAPM were completely valid, it should apply to all financial assets, including bonds. In fact, when bonds are introduced into the analysis, they *do not* plot on the SML. This is worrisome, to say the least.

---

[14]See Richard Roll, "A Critique of the Asset Pricing Theory's Tests," *Journal of Financial Economics,* March 1977, 129–176.

Current Status of the CAPM

The CAPM is extremely appealing at an intellectual level; it is logical and rational, and once someone works through and understands the mathematics, his or her reaction is usually to accept it without question. However, doubts begin to arise when one thinks about the assumptions upon which the model is based, and these doubts are as much reinforced as reduced by the empirical tests. Our own views as to the current status of the CAPM are as follows:

1.   The CAPM framework, with its focus on market as opposed to total risk, is clearly useful as a way of thinking about the riskiness of assets in general. Thus, as a conceptual model the CAPM is of truly fundamental importance.

2.   Although the CAPM appears to provide neat, precise answers to important questions about risk and required rates of return, the answers are really not clear. The simple truth is that we do not know precisely how to measure any of the inputs required to implement the CAPM. These inputs should all be ex ante, yet we only have ex post data available. Further, as we shall see in Chapter 8, historical data such as $\bar{k}_M$, k_{RF}, and betas vary greatly depending on the time period studied and the methods used to estimate them. Thus, although the CAPM may appear precise, its inputs cannot be estimated with any precision at all; thus, estimates of k_i found through use of the CAPM are subject to potentially large errors.

3.   Because the CAPM is logical, in the sense that it represents the way people who want to maximize returns while minimizing risk ought to behave, assuming they can get all the necessary data, the model is definitely here to stay. Attempts will, of course, be made to improve it and to make it more operational.

4.   It is appropriate to think about many financial problems in a CAPM framework. However, it is equally important to recognize the limitations of the CAPM when using it in practice. Again, this point will be made clear in Chapters 8 and 11.

Self-Test Questions

What are the two major types of tests that have been performed to test the validity of the CAPM?

Are there any reasons to question the validity of the CAPM? Explain.

ARBITRAGE PRICING THEORY

The CAPM is a single-factor model. That is, it specifies that risk is a function of only one factor, the relationship between a security's return and the market return, or, equivalently, the security's beta coefficient. Perhaps the risk/return relationship is more complex. If so, we might expect a stock's required return to be a function of more than one factor. For example, what if investors, because personal taxes on capital gains are deferred until the stock is sold, value capital gains income more highly than dividend income? Then, for two stocks with the same market risk, the stock paying the higher dividend would have a higher required rate of return. In that case, required returns would be a function of both market risk and dividend yield, or two factors.

Further, what if many factors were required to specify the equilibrium risk/return relationship rather than just one or two? Stephen Ross has proposed an approach called the *Arbitrage Pricing Theory (APT)*.[15] The APT can include any number of risk factors, so the required return could be a function of three, four, or even more factors. We should note at the outset that the APT is based on complex mathematical and statistical theory which goes far beyond the scope of this text. Although the APT model is widely discussed in the current academic literature, practical usage to date has been extremely limited. However, usage may increase, so students of finance should at least have an intuitive idea of what the APT is all about.

The CAPM states that each stock's required return is equal to the risk-free rate, plus the market risk premium times the stock's beta coefficient:

$$k_i = k_{RF} + (k_M - k_{RF})b_i. \tag{5-5}$$

The realized return, $\bar{k}_i$, will actually turn out to be

$$\bar{k}_i = \hat{k}_i + (\bar{k}_M - \hat{k}_M)b_i + e_i; \tag{5-6}$$

that is, the realized return, $\bar{k}_i$, will be equal to the expected return, $\hat{k}_i$, plus an increment or decrement, $(\bar{k}_M - \hat{k}_M)b_i$, whose magnitude depends jointly on the stock's sensitivity to market returns, b_i, and the realized excess or shortfall in the market return, plus a random error term, e_i.

The market return, $\bar{k}_M$, is actually determined by a number of factors, including economic activity as measured by gross national product (GNP), the strength of the world economy, the level of inflation, changes in tax laws, and so forth. Further, different groups of stocks are affected in different ways by these fundamental factors. Thus, rather than specifying a stock's returns as a function of one factor (returns on the market), one could specify required and realized returns of individual stocks to be a function of various fundamental economic factors. If this were done, we would transform Equation 5-6 into 5-7:

$$\bar{k}_i = \hat{k}_i + (\bar{F}_1 - \hat{F}_1)b_{i1} + \cdots + (\bar{F}_j - \hat{F}_j)b_{ij} + e_i, \tag{5-7}$$

where

$\bar{k}_i$ = realized rate of return on Stock i.

$\hat{k}_i$ = expected rate of return on Stock i.

$\bar{F}_j$ = realized value of economic Factor j.

$\hat{F}_j$ = expected value of Factor j.

b_{ij} = sensitivity of Stock i to economic Factor j.

e_i = effect of unique events on the realized return of Stock i.

---

[15]See Stephen A. Ross, "The Arbitrage Theory of Capital Asset Pricing," *Journal of Economic Theory,* December 1976, 341–360.

Equation 5-7 shows that the realized return on any stock is equal to the stock's expected return plus increments or decrements which depend on (1) changes in fundamental economic factors, (2) the sensitivity of the stock to these changes, plus (3) a random term which reflects changes in those factors unique to the firm or industry.

Certain stocks or groups of stocks are most sensitive to Factor 1, others to Factor 2, and so forth, and every portfolio's returns would depend on what happened to the different fundamental factors. Theoretically, one could construct a portfolio such that (1) the portfolio was riskless and (2) the net investment in it was zero (some stocks were sold short, with the proceeds from the short sales being used to buy the stocks held long). Such a zero investment portfolio must have a zero expected return, or else arbitrage operations would occur, which in turn would cause the prices of the underlying assets to change until the portfolio's expected return was zero. Using some complex mathematics and assumptions similar to those used to derive the CAPM relationships, plus the short sales assumption, the APT equivalent of the CAPM's Security Market Line can be developed from Equation 5-7:[16]

$$k_i = k_{RF} + (\lambda_1 - k_{RF})b_{i1} + \cdots + (\lambda_j - k_{RF})b_{ij} \qquad (5\text{-}8)$$

Here λ_j is the required rate of return on a portfolio with unit sensitivity to the jth economic factor ($b_j = 1.0$) and zero sensitivity to all other factors. Thus, for example, $(\lambda_2 - k_{RF})$ is the risk premium on a portfolio with $b_2 = 1.0$ and all other $b_j = 0.0$. Note that Equation 5-8 is identical in form to the SML, but it permits a stock's required return to be a function of multiple factors.

To illustrate the APT concept, assume that all stocks' returns depend on only three risk factors: inflation, industrial production, and the aggregate degree of risk aversion (the cost of bearing risk, which is reflected in the spread between the yields on Treasury and low-grade bonds). Further, suppose (1) the risk-free rate is 8.0 percent; (2) the required rate of return on a portfolio with unit sensitivity ($b = 1.0$) to inflation and zero sensitivities ($b = 0.0$) to industrial production and the degree of risk aversion is 13.0 percent; (3) the required return on a portfolio with unit sensitivity to industrial production and zero sensitivities to inflation and the degree of risk aversion is 10.0 percent; and (4) the required return on a portfolio (the risk bearing portfolio) with unit sensitivity to the degree of risk aversion and zero sensitivities to inflation and industrial production is 6.0 percent. Finally, assume that Stock i has factor sensitivities (betas) of 0.9 to the inflation portfolio, 1.2 to the industrial production portfolio, and -0.7 to the risk-bearing portfolio. Stock i's required rate of return, according to the APT, would be 16.3 percent:

$$k_i = 8\% + (13\% - 8\%)0.9 + (10\% - 8\%)1.2 + (6\% - 8\%)(-0.7) = 16.3\%.$$

Note that, if the required rate of return on the market was 15.0 percent and Stock i had a CAPM beta of 1.1, then its required rate of return, according to the CAPM, would be 15.7 percent:

$$k_i = 8\% + (15\% - 8\%)1.1 = 15.7\%.$$

[16]See Thomas E. Copeland and J. Fred Weston, *Financial Theory and Corporate Policy* (Reading, Mass.: Addison-Wesley, 1988).

The primary theoretical advantage of the APT is that it permits several economic factors to influence individual stock returns, whereas the CAPM assumes that the impact of all factors, except those unique to the firm, can be captured in a single measure, the volatility of the stock with respect to the market portfolio. However, the APT faces several major hurdles in implementation, of which the most severe is that the APT does not identify the relevant factors beforehand. Thus, APT does not tell us what factors influence returns, nor does it even indicate how many factors should appear in the model. However, there is some empirical evidence that only three or four factors are relevant; perhaps inflation, industrial production, the spread between low- and high-grade bonds, and the term structure of interest rates.

The APT's proponents note that it is not actually necessary to identify the relevant factors. Researchers use a complex statistical procedure called *factor analysis* to develop the APT parameters. Basically, they start with hundreds, or even thousands, of stocks and then create several different portfolios whose returns are not highly correlated. Thus, each portfolio is apparently more heavily affected by one of the unknown factors than are the other portfolios. Then, the required rate of return on each portfolio becomes the λ for that economic factor, and the sensitivities of each individual stock's returns to the returns on that portfolio are the factor sensitivities (betas). Unfortunately, the results of factor analysis are not easily interpreted; hence it does not provide significant insight into the underlying economic determinants of risk.

The APT is in an early stage of development, and there are still many unanswered questions. Nevertheless, the basic premise of the APT—that returns can be a function of several factors rather than just one—has considerable intuitive appeal. If the factors can be identified, and if the theory can be satisfactorily explained to practitioners, then there is a good chance that the APT will replace the CAPM as the primary model describing the relationship between risk and return.

Self-Test Questions

What is the primary difference between the APT and the CAPM?

What are some disadvantages to the APT?

MULTINATIONAL FINANCE
Risk and Return of International Investments

In this chapter, we have implicitly focused on the risk and return of *domestic investments.* Although the same concepts are involved when we move to the international scene, some important differences must also be observed. For example, someone who invests on a worldwide basis must be concerned with (1) sovereign risk and (2) exchange rate risk. *Sovereign risk* is the risk that the sovereign country in which the real assets backing an investment are located will take some action, such as nationalization without adequate compensation, that will decrease the value of the investment. Enron Corporation, a multibillion dollar U.S.-based energy company, experienced exactly this situation when Peru nationalized an Enron subsidiary in 1985, resulting in a sharp drop in Enron's stock price. Sovereign risk is diversifiable, but it is something that concerns both international investors and multinational corporations.

Figure 5-8   Portfolio Analysis with Global Diversification

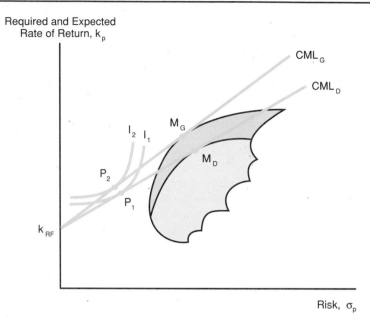

The second type of international risk, *exchange rate risk,* stems from the fact that different countries use different currencies, and the relative values of those currencies change over time. To illustrate, in 1985, the exchange rate between yen and dollars was 251:1, meaning that one dollar could buy 251 yen. By 1989, the exchange rate had dropped to 125:1. This decline in the value of the dollar had a major effect on both U.S. and Japanese firms and investors. First, suppose a U.S. investor bought 100 shares of Toyota stock at a price of 1,000 yen per share, or 100,000 yen in total. That investment would have a dollar cost of 100,000/251 = $398.41. If the yen price of Toyota's stock had remained constant at 1,000, the decline in the value of the dollar would have caused the dollar value of the stock to rise from $398.41 to 100,000/125 = $800, a 101 percent increase. Since the dollar also fell against most other major currencies, this same experience was repeated in other international capital markets, and, as a result, those U.S. investors who included foreign stocks in their portfolios did well from 1985 to 1989. Of course, the value of foreign stocks to U.S. investors will drop if the dollar rises in the future. (Indeed, by April of 1990 the dollar had strengthened back to 157 yen.)

One might think that because of the additional risks of international operations, U.S. firms that do business abroad would be viewed as being riskier than firms operating solely in the United States. If this were true, international firms would have higher betas, hence higher required rates of return, than purely domestic firms. However, a recent study of 84 multinational firms and 52 purely domestic firms showed that the betas of multinational firms are both lower and more stable than those of domestic firms.[17]

The results of this study indicate that international diversification reduces the degree of market risk for the firm, because market risk depends in large part on the economy of the country in which the firm operates. A multinational firm operates in many countries, and the economies of these countries are not perfectly correlated with each other, or with the firm's home country's economy. Thus, the effects of a poor economy in one country may be offset by strong economies in its other operating countries. As a result, a multinational firm is exposed to less market risk than a purely

---

[17]See Ali M. Fatemi, "Shareholder Benefits from Corporate International Diversification," *Journal of Finance,* December 1984, 1325–1344.

domestic firm. According to the CÁPM, only market risk must be compensated with higher expected rates of return. Since firms operating in international markets appear to have less market risk than domestic firms, international firms should have lower betas, lower required rates of return, and lower costs of capital than otherwise comparable domestic firms.

The addition of international investment opportunities can be viewed in a Capital Market Line (CML) framework. Consider Figure 5-8, where the lightly shaded area represents the feasible set of domestic risky assets; the heavily shaded area represents the addition to the feasible set when international assets are included; k_{RF} represents the rate of return on domestic riskless assets; M_D is the domestic market portfolio; and M_G is the *global market portfolio,* which contains

foreign as well as domestic securities. Note that there are no riskless foreign assets: even foreign treasury bills are risky because of exchange rate risk. Since returns on foreign securities are not perfectly correlated with those on domestic securities, the inclusion of foreign assets in the portfolio shifts the boundary (or feasible) set of portfolios upward and to the left. This has the effect of rotating the CML upward, from CML_D to CML_G. This, in turn, permits an investor to move from portfolio P_1, on indifference curve I_1, to portfolio P_2, on the higher indifference curve I_2. Portfolio P_2 contains a combination of domestic and foreign stocks, plus riskless domestic government securities, and it is better than P_1 in that it provides both a higher expected return and a lower level of risk.

SUMMARY

Chapter 5 completes our discussion of risk and return. The primary goals of this chapter were (1) to show how the addition of the risk-free asset affects individual investment decisions, and (2) to explain how risk affects rates of return. The key concepts covered are listed next.

- The *Capital Asset Pricing Model (CAPM)* is an equilibrium model which describes the relationship between market risk and required rates of return.

- The CAPM requires an extensive set of *assumptions.*

- The *Capital Market Line (CML)* describes the risk/return relationship for efficient portfolios.

- The *Security Market Line (SML)* describes the risk/return relationship for individual assets. The required rate of return for any Stock i is equal to the *risk-free rate* plus the *market risk premium* times the stock's *beta coefficient:* $k_i = k_{RF} + (k_M - k_{RF})b_i$.

- Stock i's *beta coefficient, b_i,* is a measure of the stock's *market risk.* Beta measures the *volatility* of returns on a security *relative to the market,* which is the portfolio of all risky assets.

- The beta coefficient is measured by the slope of the stock's *characteristic line,* which is found by regressing the historical returns on the stock versus the historical returns on the market.

- A *high-beta stock* is more volatile than an average stock, while a *low-beta stock* is less volatile than average. An *average-beta stock* has b = 1.0, by definition.

- The *beta of a portfolio* is a weighted average of the betas of the individual securities in the portfolio.

- Even though expected rates of return on stocks are generally equal to required returns, a number of things can happen to cause required rates of return to change: (1) the *risk-free rate* can change because of changes in anticipated inflation, (2) the *beta coefficient* can change, and (3) *investor's aversion to risk* can change.

- Although the CAPM provides a convenient framework for thinking about risk and return issues, it *cannot be proven empirically* and its parameters are very difficult to estimate. Thus, it should be used with caution in practice.

- Deficiencies in the CAPM have motivated theorists to seek other risk/return equilibrium models; the *Arbitrage Pricing Theory (APT)* is one important new model.

- *Foreign investments* are similar to domestic investments, but foreign investments contain *sovereign risk,* which is the risk that the foreign government will take some action that lowers the value of the investment, and *exchange rate risk,* which is the risk of losses caused by fluctuations in the value of the dollar. On the positive side, foreign investments *increase the slope of the Capital Market Line* by reducing the riskiness of the market portfolio.

In the next two chapters, we will see how a security's required rate of return affects its value. Then, in the remainder of the book, we will examine the ways in which a firm's management can influence a stock's riskiness and hence its price.

Questions

5-1 Define the following terms, using graphs or equations to illustrate your answers wherever feasible:
   a. Capital Asset Pricing Model (CAPM)
   b. Capital Market Line (CML)
   c. Market risk; company-specific risk; relevant risk
   d. Beta coefficient, b; average stock's beta, $b_A = b_M$
   e. Security Market Line (SML); SML equation
   f. Market risk premium
   g. Average stock
   h. Characteristic line
   i. Arbitrage Pricing Theory (APT)

5-2 Security A has an expected rate of return of 6 percent, a standard deviation of expected returns of 30 percent, a correlation coefficient with the market of -0.25, and a beta coefficient of -0.5. Security B has an expected return of 11 percent, a standard deviation of returns of 10 percent, a correlation with the market of 0.75, and a beta coefficient of 0.5. Which security is more risky? Why?

5-3 If investors' aversion to risk increased, would the risk premium on a high-beta stock increase more or less than that on a low-beta stock? Explain.

Self-Test Problem (Solutions Appear in Appendix D)

ST-1 **(SML)** Dalton Bigbee is a major department store chain. Its stock has a beta of 0.8, the risk-free rate is 8.0 percent, and the required rate of return on the market is 13.0 percent.
   a. What is the market risk premium?
   b. What is the required rate of return on Bigbee's stock?

c.   Graph the Security Market Line (SML) and indicate Bigbee's required rate of return on the graph.

d.   What would Bigbee's required rate of return be if inflation expectations increased by 2 percentage points? (Assume no change in risk aversion.)

e.   Return to the 8 percent risk-free rate. What would Bigbee's required rate of return be if investors' risk aversion increased, and the market risk premium rose to 7 percentage points?

f.   Return to the 5 percentage point market risk premium. What would the firm's required rate of return be if Bigbee's beta increased to 1.2?

Problems

5-1   **(Market risk analysis)** The Bowers Company has developed the following data regarding the rates of return available on a potential project and the market:

State of the Economy	Probability of Each State Occurring	Rates of Return if State Occurs	
		Market	Project
Deep recession	0.05	(20%)	(30%)
Mild recession	0.25	10	5
Average	0.35	15	20
Mild boom	0.20	20	25
Strong boom	0.15	25	30

Further, Bowers's financial analysts estimate the risk-free rate at 8 percent.
a.   What are the expected rates of return on the market and the project?
b.   What is the market's beta? The project's?
c.   What is the required rate of return on the project according to the CAPM?
d.   Should the project be accepted?

5-2   **(Market versus total risk)** Your eccentric uncle died and left you $100,000. However, the will stipulated that the entire amount must be invested in common stocks. Specifically, $50,000 must be invested in a single stock (one-stock portfolio) and the other $50,000 must be invested in a 100-stock portfolio. You are very risk averse, hence want to minimize the riskiness of each $50,000 investment.
a.   How would you choose your single-stock portfolio?
b.   How would you choose the stocks in your 100-stock portfolio?
c.   Should you view the riskiness of your one-stock portfolio in isolation, or should you consider the fact that you really own 101 stocks?

5-3   **(Security Market Line)** Suppose $k_{RF} = 10\%$, $k_M = 14\%$, and $b_A = 1.4$.
a.   What is k_A, the required rate of return on Stock A?
b.   Now suppose k_{RF} (1) increases to 11 percent or (2) decreases to 9 percent. The slope of the SML remains constant. How will this affect k_M and k_A?
c.   Now assume k_{RF} remains at 10 percent, but k_M (1) increases to 15 percent or (2) falls to 12 percent. The slope of the SML does *not* remain constant. How will this affect k_A?
d.   Now assume that k_{RF} remains at 10 percent and k_M at 14 percent, but beta (1) rises to 1.6 or (2) falls to 0.75. How will this affect k_A?

5-4   **(Portfolio beta and Security Market Line)** The Vantage Investment Fund has a total investment of $400 million in five stocks:

Stock	Investment	Stock's Beta Coefficient
A	$120 million	0.5
B	100 million	2.0
C	60 million	4.0
D	80 million	1.0
E	40 million	3.0

The beta coefficient for a fund such as this can be found as a weighted average of the betas of the fund's investments. The current risk-free rate is 7 percent, and the market return has the following estimated probability distribution for the next year:

Probability	Market Return
0.1	8%
0.2	10
0.4	12
0.2	14
0.1	16

a. What is the estimated equation for the Security Market Line (SML)?
b. Compute the required rate of return on the Vantage Investment Fund.
c. Suppose management receives a proposal to buy a new stock. The investment needed to take a position in the stock is $50 million; it will have an expected return of 16 percent; and its estimated beta coefficient is 2.5. Should the new stock be purchased? At what expected rate of return would management be indifferent to purchasing the stock?

5-5 **(Characteristic line and Security Market Line)** You are given the following set of data:

Year	Historical Rates of Return	
	NYSE	Stock X
1	(26.5%)	(14.0%)
2	37.2	23.0
3	23.8	17.5
4	(7.2)	2.0
5	6.6	8.1
6	20.5	19.4
7	30.6	18.2

a. Use a calculator with a linear regression function (or the computerized diskette) to determine Stock X's beta coefficient, or plot these data points on a scatter diagram, draw in the regression line, and then estimate the value of the beta coefficient.
b. Determine the arithmetic average rates of return for Stock X and the NYSE over the period given. Calculate the standard deviations of returns for both Stock X and the NYSE.
c. Assuming (1) that the situation during Years 1 to 7 is expected to hold true in the future (that is, $\hat{k}_X = \bar{k}_X$; $\hat{k}_M = \bar{k}_M$; and both σ_X and b_X in the future will equal their past values), and (2) that Stock X is in equilibrium (that is, it plots on the Security Market Line), what is the risk-free rate?
d. Plot the Security Market Line.
e. Suppose you hold a large, well-diversified portfolio and are considering adding to the portfolio either Stock X or another stock, Stock Y, that has the same beta as Stock X but a higher standard deviation of returns. Stocks X and Y have the same expected returns; that is, $\hat{k}_X = \hat{k}_Y = 10.6\%$. Which stock should you choose?

5-6   **(Characteristic line)** You are given the following set of data:

	Historical Rates of Return	
Year	**NYSE**	**Stock Y**
1	4.0%	3.0%
2	14.3	18.2
3	19.0	9.1
4	(14.7)	(6.0)
5	(26.5)	(15.3)
6	37.2	33.1
7	23.8	6.1
8	(7.2)	3.2
9	6.6	14.8
10	20.5	24.1
11	30.6	18.0
Mean =	9.8%	9.8%
σ =	19.6%	13.8%

a.   Construct a scatter diagram showing the relationship between returns on Stock Y and the market, and then draw a freehand approximation of the regression line. What is the approximate value of the beta coefficient? If you have a calculator with a linear regression function or the computerized diskette, check the approximate value of beta obtained from the graph.

b.   Give a verbal interpretation of what the regression line and the beta coefficient show about Stock Y's volatility and relative riskiness as compared to those of other stocks.

c.   Suppose the scatter of points had been more spread out, but the regression line was exactly where your present graph shows it. How would this affect (1) the firm's risk if the stock is held in a one-asset portfolio and (2) the actual risk premium on the stock if the CAPM holds exactly?

d.   Suppose the regression line had been downward-sloping and the beta coefficient had been negative. What would this imply about (1) Stock Y's relative riskiness, (2) its correlation with the market, and (3) its probable risk premium?

e.   Construct an illustrative probability distribution graph of returns on portfolios consisting of (1) only Stock Y, (2) 1 percent each of 100 stocks with beta coefficients similar to that of Stock Y, and (3) all stocks (that is, the distribution of returns on the market). Use as the expected rate of return the arithmetic mean as given previously for both Stock Y and the market and assume that the distributions are normal. Are the expected returns "reasonable"; that is, is it reasonable that $\hat{k}_Y = \hat{k}_M = 9.8\%$?

5-7   **(SML and CML comparison)** The beta coefficient of an asset can be expressed as a function of the asset's correlation with the market as follows:

$$b_i = \frac{r_{iM}\sigma_i}{\sigma_M}.$$

a.   Substitute this expression for beta into the Security Market Line (SML), Equation 5-2. This results in an alternative form of the SML.

b.   Compare your answer to Part a with the Capital Market Line (CML), Equation 5-1. What similarities are observed? What conclusions can be drawn?

Mini Case

In the Chapter 4 Mini Case, Barbara Orban, an analyst at Southern Commerce Bank, was instructed to evaluate some investment opportunities. The analysis was begun in Chapter 4, but not completed. Again place yourself in Orban's position, and complete the analysis by answering the following questions:

a.   What is the Capital Asset Pricing Model (CAPM)? What are the assumptions that underlie the model?

b.   Review your answers to Parts j and k of the Chapter 4 Mini Case. Then create a risk/return (σ, k) graph which shows the efficient frontier of portfolios. Now add the risk-free asset. What impact does this have on the efficient frontier?

c.   Write out the equation for the Capital Market Line (CML) and draw it on the graph. Interpret the CML. Now add a set of indifference curves, and illustrate how an investor's optimal portfolio is some combination of the risky portfolio and the risk-free asset. What is the composition of the risky portfolio?

d.   The expected rates of return and the beta coefficients of each alternative as supplied by the bank's computer program are as follows:

Security	Expected Return ($\hat{k}$)	Risk (Beta)
Paragon	18.0%	1.29
Market	15.0	1.00
Apex	12.5	0.68
T-bills	8.0	0.00
Luster	1.3	(0.86)

What is a beta coefficient, and what does it measure?

e.   Construct the Security Market Line (SML) and use it to calculate the required rate of return on each alternative. How do the expected rates of return compare with the required rates of return? Does the fact that Luster has a required rate of return that is less than the risk-free rate make any sense? What are the market risk and the required return of a 50-50 portfolio of Paragon and Luster? Of Paragon and Apex?

f.   Suppose investors raised their inflation expectations by 3 percentage points over current estimates as reflected in the 8 percent T-bill rate. What effect would this have on the SML and on the returns of high- and low-risk securities? Suppose instead that investors' risk aversion increased enough to cause the market risk premium to increase by 3 percentage points. What effect would this have on the SML and on returns of high- and low-risk securities?

g.   What is a characteristic line? How is this line used to estimate a stock's beta coefficient? Write out and explain the formula that relates total risk, market risk, and diversifiable risk.

h.   What are two potential tests that can be conducted to verify the CAPM? What are the results of such tests? What is Roll's critique of CAPM tests?

i.   Briefly explain the difference between the CAPM and the Arbitrage Pricing Theory (APT).

Selected Additional References and Cases

Probably the best place to find more information on CAPM and APT concepts is one of the investments textbooks. These are some good recent ones:

Francis, Jack C., *Investments: Analysis and Management* (New York: McGraw-Hill, 1980).

Radcliffe, Robert C., *Investment: Concepts, Analysis, and Strategy* (Glenview, Ill.: Scott, Foresman, 1990).

Reilly, Frank K., *Investment Analysis and Portfolio Management* (Hinsdale, Ill.: Dryden, 1989).

Sharpe, William F., *Investments* (Englewood Cliffs, N.J.: Prentice-Hall, 1985).

For a thorough discussion of beta stability, see

Kolb, Robert W., and Ricardo J. Rodriguez, "The Regression Tendencies of Betas: A Reappraisal," *The Financial Review,* May 1989, 319–334.

Those who want to start at the beginning in studying portfolio theory and the CAPM should see

Lintner, John, "Security Prices, Risk, and Maximal Gains from Diversification," *Journal of Finance,* December 1965, 587–616.

Markowitz, Harry M., "Portfolio Selection," *Journal of Finance,* March 1952, 77–91.

Mossin, Jan, "Security Pricing and Investment Criteria in Competitive Markets," *American Economic Review,* December 1969, 749–756.

Sharpe, William F., "Capital Asset Prices: A Theory of Market Equilibrium under Conditions of Risk," *Journal of Finance,* September 1964, 425–442.

Literally thousands of articles providing theoretical extensions and tests of the CAPM theory have appeared in finance journals. Some of the more important earlier papers are contained in a book compiled by Jensen:

Jensen, Michael C., ed., *Studies in the Theory of Capital Markets* (New York: Praeger, 1972).

For one challenge to the CAPM, see

Wallace, Anise, "Is Beta Dead?" *Institutional Investor,* July 1980, 23–30.

For additional discussion of Arbitrage Pricing Theory, see

Bower, Dorothy H., Richard S. Bower, and Dennis E. Logue, "A Primer on Arbitrage Pricing Theory," *Midland Corporate Finance Journal,* Fall 1984, 31–40.

Bubnys, Edward L., "Simulating and Forecasting Utility Stock Returns: Arbitrage Pricing Theory vs. Capital Asset Pricing Model," *The Financial Review,* February 1990, 1–23.

Additional references concerning the use of the CAPM are given in Chapters 8 and 11.

The following case covers many of the concepts discussed in this chapter:

Case 2, "Sun Coast Securities, Inc. (A)," in Brigham, Eugene F., and Louis C. Gapenski, *Cases in Financial Management* (Hinsdale, Ill.: Dryden, 1990).

CHAPTER 6

Discounted Cash Flow Analysis

The cover story in the July 31, 1989, issue of *Fortune* was called "Will You Be Able To Retire?" Although you will probably laugh when we say the article should be of interest to you, the fact is, it should be. First, the article cited some well-known statistics which indicate (1) that the savings rate in the United States is the lowest of any major industrial nation; (2) that the ratio of workers to retirees, which was 17 to 1 in 1950 and is currently down to 3.3 to 1, will decline to less than 2 to 1 after the Year 2000; and (3) that because of the above, the Social Security system is in trouble. The article then went on to present some figures on how much money the "Baby Boom" generation (people born in the post–World War II period of 1946 through 1968) will need when they retire, given projected trends in inflation, in how much members of that generation are saving, and in the rates of return savers are getting on their investments. The article concluded that even relatively affluent Baby Boomers (those with incomes of about $85,000) will have trouble maintaining a reasonable standard of living when they retire, and that the children of the Boomers will probably end up having to support their parents.

What does the retirement plight of the Baby Boomers (and their children) have to do with discounted cash flow analysis? Actually, a great deal. The techniques and procedures covered in this chapter are exactly the ones *Fortune* used to forecast the Boomers' retirement needs, their probable wealth at retirement, and the resulting shortfall. If you study this chapter carefully, perhaps you can avoid the trap into which many people seem to be falling.

Financial managers deal with discounted cash flow (DCF) concepts every day. For example, these concepts are used (1) by money managers in their decisions to invest in different securities, (2) by mortgage and commercial loan officers when establishing the terms of loans, and (3) by capital budgeting analysts when deciding which projects the firm should accept. These are only a few of the areas in which DCF concepts are used, but, as you can see, DCF analysis touches each of the three areas of finance discussed in Chapter 1: investments, money and capital markets, and financial management.

I N Chapter 1 we saw that the primary goal of the financial manager is to maximize the value of his or her firm's stock. We also saw that stock values depend in part on the timing of the cash flows investors expect to receive from an investment—a dollar expected soon is worth more than a dollar expected in the distant future. Therefore, it is essential that financial managers have a clear understanding of discounted cash flow analysis and its impact on the value of the firm. These concepts are discussed in this chapter, where we show how the timing of cash flows affects asset values and rates of return.

The principles of discounted cash flow analysis as developed here also have other applications, ranging from setting up schedules for paying off loans to deciding whether to acquire new equipment. *In fact, of all the techniques used in finance, none is more important than the concept of discounted cash flow analysis, often called time value of money analysis.* Since this concept is used throughout the remainder of the book, it is vital that you understand the material in this chapter thoroughly before going on to other topics.[1]

FUTURE VALUE

A dollar in hand today is worth more than a dollar to be received next year because, if you had it now, you could invest it, earn interest, and end up next year with more than one dollar. The process of going from present values to future values is called *compounding*. To illustrate compounding, let us suppose you had $100 which you

---

[1]This chapter, and indeed the entire book, is written on the assumption that students have financial calculators. As a result, procedures for obtaining financial calculator solutions are set forth in each of the major sections, along with procedures for obtaining solutions by using regular calculators or tables. It is highly desirable for each student to obtain a financial calculator and to learn how to use it, for calculators and computers—and not clumsy, rounded, and incomplete tables—are used exclusively in well-run, efficient businesses.

Even though financial calculators are efficient, they do pose a danger: People sometimes learn how to use them in a "cookbook" fashion without understanding the logical processes that underlie the calculations, and then, when confronted with a new type of problem, they cannot figure out how to set it up. Therefore, you are urged not only to get a good calculator and to learn how to use it but also to work through the illustrative problems "the long way" to insure that you understand the concepts involved.

deposited in a bank savings account that paid 5 percent interest compounded annually. How much would you have at the end of 1 year? Let us define terms as
follows:

PV = $100 = present value of your account, or the beginning amount.

k = 5% = interest rate the bank pays you per year. Expressed as a decimal, k = 0.05. On
financial calculators, the term i is frequently used rather than k.

I = dollars of interest you earn during the year = k(Beginning of year amount).

FV_n = future value, or ending amount, of your account at the end of n years. Whereas PV is
the value now, at the *present* time, FV_n is the value n years into the *future*, after compound interest has been earned. Note also that FV_0 is the future value *zero* years into
the future, which is the *present*, so FV_0 = PV.

n = number of periods, often years, involved in the transaction.

In our example, n = 1, so FV_n = FV_1 is calculated as follows:

$$FV_1 = PV + I$$

$$= PV + PV(k)$$

$$= PV(1 + k). \tag{6-1}$$

This means that the *future value, FV,* at the end of 1 period is the present value
times 1 plus the interest rate.

We can now use Equation 6-1 to find how much your $100 will be worth at the
end of 1 year at a 5 percent interest rate:

$$FV_1 = \$100(1 + 0.05) = \$100(1.05) = \$105.$$

Your account will earn $5 of interest [I = PV(k) = $100(0.05) = $5], so you will
have $105 at the end of the year.

Another way to view this problem is through a tool called the *time line.* On a
time line, Time 0 is today; Time 1 is 1 period from today, or the end of 1 period;
Time 2 is 2 periods from today, or the end of 2 periods; and so on. Thus, the values
on time lines represent end-of-period values. At Time 0 (today), when you open
your bank account, you have $100. The time line below shows $100 at Year 0. You
would like to know how much you will have at the end of the year, Year 1 on the
time line, if the account pays an interest rate of 5 percent. The interest rate of 5
percent is shown above the time line to indicate how much your deposit will increase. From Equation 6-1 we know that the account will grow to $105 at the end
of the year, so you could replace the first question mark with $105.

Now suppose you leave your funds on deposit for 5 years; how much will you
have at the end of the fifth year? The answer is $127.63; this value is worked out in
Table 6-1. Notice the following points: (1) You start with $100, earn $5 of interest

Table 6-1 Compound Interest Calculations

Year	Amount at Beginning of Year, PV	× (1 + k)	= Amount at End of Year, FV$_n$	Interest Earned, PV(k)
1	$100.00	1.05	$105.00	$ 5.00
2	105.00	1.05	110.25	5.25
3	110.25	1.05	115.76	5.51
4	115.76	1.05	121.55	5.79
5	121.55	1.05	127.63	6.08
				$27.63

during the first year, and end the year with $105 in your account. (2) You start the second year with $105, earn $5.25 on this now larger amount, and end the second year with $110.25. Your second-year earnings, $5.25, were higher because you earned interest on the first year's interest. (3) This process continues, and because in each year the beginning balance is higher, your interest income increases. (4) The total interest earned, $27.63, is reflected in the ending balance, $127.63, so you could replace the last question mark on the time line with $127.63.

Notice that the Table 6-1 value for FV$_2$, the value of the account at the end of Year 2, is equal to

$$FV_2 = FV_1(1 + k)$$

$$= PV(1 + k)(1 + k)$$

$$= PV(1 + k)^2$$

$$= \$100(1.05)^2$$

$$= \$110.25.$$

Continuing, we see that FV$_3$, the balance after Year 3, is

$$FV_3 = FV_2(1 + k)$$

$$= PV(1 + k)^3$$

$$= \$100(1.05)^3$$

$$= \$115.76.$$

In general, FV$_n$, the future value at the end of n years, is found as follows:

$$FV_n = PV(1 + k)^n. \tag{6-2}$$

Applying Equation 6-2 to our 5-year, 5 percent case, we obtain

$$FV_5 = \$100(1.05)^5$$

$$= \$100(1.2763)$$

$$= \$127.63,$$

which is the same as the value worked out in Table 6-1.

Table 6-2 Future Value of $1 at the End of n Periods:

$$FVIF_{k,n} = (1 + k)^n$$

Period (n)	1%	2%	3%	4%	5%	6%	7%	8%	9%	10%
1	1.0100	1.0200	1.0300	1.0400	1.0500	1.0600	1.0700	1.0800	1.0900	1.1000
2	1.0201	1.0404	1.0609	1.0816	1.1025	1.1236	1.1449	1.1664	1.1881	1.2100
3	1.0303	1.0612	1.0927	1.1249	1.1576	1.1910	1.2250	1.2597	1.2950	1.3310
4	1.0406	1.0824	1.1255	1.1699	1.2155	1.2625	1.3108	1.3605	1.4116	1.4641
5	1.0510	1.1041	1.1593	1.2167	1.2763	1.3382	1.4026	1.4693	1.5386	1.6105
6	1.0615	1.1262	1.1941	1.2653	1.3401	1.4185	1.5007	1.5869	1.6771	1.7716
7	1.0721	1.1487	1.2299	1.3159	1.4071	1.5036	1.6058	1.7138	1.8280	1.9487
8	1.0829	1.1717	1.2668	1.3686	1.4775	1.5938	1.7182	1.8509	1.9926	2.1436
9	1.0937	1.1951	1.3048	1.4233	1.5513	1.6895	1.8385	1.9990	2.1719	2.3579
10	1.1046	1.2190	1.3439	1.4802	1.6289	1.7908	1.9672	2.1589	2.3674	2.5937

We can solve future value problems in three ways:

1. **Use a regular calculator.** One can simply use a regular calculator, either by multiplying $(1 + k)$ by itself $n - 1$ times or by using the exponential function to raise $(1 + k)$ to the nth power. In our example, you would enter $1 + k = 1.05$ and multiply it by itself four times, or else enter 1.05, enter 5, and then press the y^x (or exponential) function key. In either case, you would get the factor $(1.05)^5 = 1.2763$, which you would then multiply by $100 to get the final answer, $127.63.

2. **Use compound interest tables.** The term *future value interest factor for k,n* $(FVIF_{k,n})$ is defined as being equal to $(1 + k)^n$, and tables have been constructed for values of $(1 + k)^n$ for a wide range of k and n values. Table 6-2 is illustrative, and a more complete table, with more years and more interest rates, is given in Table A-3 in Appendix A at the end of the book.[2]

Equation 6-2 can be written as $FV_n = PV(FVIF_{k,n})$. It is necessary only to go to an appropriate interest table (6-2 or A-3) to find the proper interest factor. For example, the correct interest factor for our 5-year, 5 percent illustration can be found in Table 6-2. We look down the first column to Period 5 and then across this row to the 5 percent column to find the interest factor, 1.2763. Then, using this interest factor, we find the value of $100 after 5 years to be $FV_5 = PV(FVIF_{5\%,5 \text{ years}}) = $100(1.2763) = 127.63, which is identical to the value obtained by the long method in Table 6-1.

3. **Use a financial calculator.** Financial calculators have been programmed to solve most discounted cash flow problems. In effect, the calculators first generate the $FVIF_{k,n}$ factors for a specified pair of k and n values, and then multiply the

---

[2]Notice that we have used the word *period* rather than *year* in Table 6-2. As we shall see later in the chapter, compounding can occur over periods of time other than one year. Thus, although interest is often compounded on an annual basis, it can be compounded quarterly, semiannually, monthly, or over any other period.

computed factor by the PV to produce the FV. In our illustrative problem, you would simply enter PV = 100, k = i = 5, and n = 5, then press the FV key, and the answer $127.63, rounded to two decimal places, will appear. The FV will appear with a minus sign on some calculators. The logic behind the negative value is that you put in the initial amount (the PV) and take out the ending amount (the FV), so one is an inflow and the other is an outflow. The negative sign reminds you of that. At this point, though, you can ignore the minus sign. Also, on some calculators you may need to press the Compute key before pressing the FV button. Finally, financial calculators permit you to specify the number of decimal places. We generally use two places for problems where the answer is in dollars or percentages and four if the answer is an interest rate in decimal form.

The most efficient way to solve most problems is to use a financial calculator. Therefore, you should get one and learn how to use it. However, you ought to understand how the tables are developed and used, and you should also understand the logic and the math that underlie all types of financial analyses. Otherwise, you simply will not understand stock and bond valuation, lease analysis, capital budgeting, and other critically important topics.

Graphic View of the Compounding Process: Growth

Figure 6-1 shows how $1 (or any other sum) grows over time at various rates of interest. The 5 and 10 percent curves are based on the values given in Table 6-2. The higher the rate of interest, the faster the rate of growth. The interest rate is, in fact, a growth rate. If a sum is deposited and earns 5 percent, then the funds on deposit grow at the rate of 5 percent per period. Note that these formulas can be applied to anything that is growing — sales, population, earnings per share, or whatever. If you ever need to figure the growth rate of anything, the formulas in this chapter can be used.

Self-Test Questions

Explain what is meant by the following statement: "A dollar in hand today is worth more than a dollar to be received next year."

What is compounding? What is "interest on interest"?

Explain the following equation: $FV_1 = PV + I$. (No calculations are necessary.)

Set up a time line that would show the following situation: (1) Your initial deposit is $100. (2) The account pays 5 percent interest annually. (3) You want to know how much money will be in your account at the end of 3 years.

PRESENT VALUE

Suppose you were offered the alternative of receiving either $127.63 at the end of 5 years or X dollars today. There is no question that the $127.63 will be paid in full (perhaps the payer is the U.S. government). Having no current need for the money,

Figure 6-1   Relationship between Future Value Interest
Factors, Interest Rates, and Time

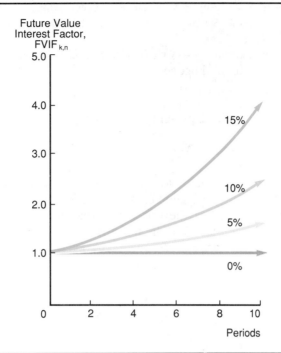

you would deposit the X dollars in a bank account that pays 5 percent interest. (This 5 percent is defined as your *opportunity cost,* or the rate of return you could earn on alternative investments of equal risk.) What value of X would make you indifferent in your choice between X dollars today and the promise of $127.63 after 5 years?

From Table 6-1 we saw that an initial amount of $100 growing at 5 percent a year would be worth $127.63 at the end of 5 years. Thus, you should be indifferent to the choice between $100 today and $127.63 at the end of 5 years. The $100 is defined as the *present value,* or *PV,* of $127.63 due in 5 years when the opportunity cost rate is 5 percent. Therefore, if X is anything less than $100, you should prefer the promise of $127.63 in 5 years to X dollars today; if X were greater than $100, you should prefer X.

The concept of present values can also be illustrated using a time line. The following one shows the future value amount of $127.63 at Year 5. A question mark appears at Year 0 — this is the value in which we are interested — and the interest rate of 5 percent appears above the time line, indicating your opportunity cost of money.

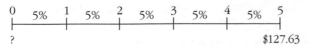

In general, the present value of a sum due n years in the future is the amount which, if it were on hand today, would grow to equal the future sum. Since $100 would grow to $127.63 in 5 years at a 5 percent interest rate, $100 is the present value of $127.63 due 5 years in the future when the appropriate interest rate is 5 percent.

Finding present values—or *discounting,* as it is commonly called—is simply the reverse of compounding, and Equation 6-2,

$$FV_n = PV(1 + k)^n, \tag{6-2}$$

can be transformed into a present value formula by solving for PV:

$$PV = \frac{FV_n}{(1 + k)^n} = FV_n(1 + k)^{-n} = FV_n\left(\frac{1}{1 + k}\right)^n. \tag{6-3}$$

Tables have been constructed for the last term in parentheses for various values of k and n; Table 6-3 is an example. (For a more complete table, see Table A-1 in Appendix A at the end of the book.) For our illustrative case, look down the 5 percent column in Table 6-3 to the fifth row. The figure shown there, 0.7835, is the *present value interest factor (PVIF$_{k,n}$)* used to determine the present value of $127.63 payable in 5 years, discounted at 5 percent:

$$PV = FV_5(PVIF_{5\%,5 \text{ years}})$$

$$= \$127.63(0.7835)$$

$$= \$100.$$

Again, you could use a financial calculator to find the PV of the $127.63. Just enter n = 5, k = i = 5, and FV = 127.63, and then press the PV button to find PV = $100. (Again, on some calculators, the PV will be given as −$100, and on some calculators you need to press the Compute key before pressing the PV button.)

Table 6-3   Present Value of $1 Due at the End of n Periods:

$$PVIF_{k,n} = \frac{1}{(1 + k)^n} = \left(\frac{1}{1 + k}\right)^n$$

Period (n)	1%	2%	3%	4%	5%	6%	7%	8%	9%	10%
1	.9901	.9804	.9709	.9615	.9524	.9434	.9346	.9259	.9174	.9091
2	.9803	.9612	.9426	.9246	.9070	.8900	.8734	.8573	.8417	.8264
3	.9706	.9423	.9151	.8890	.8638	.8396	.8163	.7938	.7722	.7513
4	.9610	.9238	.8885	.8548	.8227	.7921	.7629	.7350	.7084	.6830
5	.9515	.9057	.8626	.8219	.7835	.7473	.7130	.6806	.6499	.6209
6	.9420	.8880	.8375	.7903	.7462	.7050	.6663	.6302	.5963	.5645
7	.9327	.8706	.8131	.7599	.7107	.6651	.6227	.5835	.5470	.5132
8	.9235	.8535	.7894	.7307	.6768	.6274	.5820	.5403	.5019	.4665
9	.9143	.8368	.7664	.7026	.6446	.5919	.5439	.5002	.4604	.4241
10	.9053	.8203	.7441	.6756	.6139	.5584	.5083	.4632	.4224	.3855

Graphic View of the Discounting Process

Figure 6-2 shows how interest factors for discounting decrease as the discounting period increases. The curves in the figure, which were plotted with data taken from Table A-1, show (1) that the present value of a sum to be received at some future date decreases and approaches zero as the payment date is extended further into the future, and (2) that the rate of decrease is steeper as the interest (or discount) rate increases. If relatively high discount rates apply, funds due in the future are worth very little today, and even at relatively low discount rates, the present values of funds due in the distant future are quite small. For example, $1 due in 10 years is worth about 61 cents today if the discount rate is 5 percent, but it is worth only 25 cents at a 15 percent discount rate. Similarly, $1 due in 5 years at 10 percent is worth 62 cents today, but at the same discount rate $1 due in 10 years is worth only 39 cents today. At a 15 percent discount rate, $1 due in 100 years is worth only $0.00000085, or less than 1 millionth of $1, today.

Self-Test Questions

What is meant by the term "opportunity cost"?

What is discounting? How does it relate to compounding?

Briefly discuss how the present value of an amount to be received in the future changes as the time is extended and as the interest rate increases.

Figure 6-2   Relationship between Present Value Interest
Factors, Interest Rates, and Time

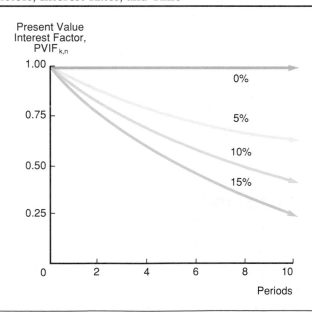

FUTURE VALUE VERSUS PRESENT VALUE

Equation 6-2, the basic equation for compounding, was developed from the logical sequence set forth in Table 6-1; the equation merely presents in mathematical form the steps outlined in the table. The present value interest factor ($PVIF_{k,n}$) in Equation 6-3, the basic equation for discounting or finding present values, was found as the *reciprocal* of the future value interest factor ($FVIF_{k,n}$) for the same k,n combination:

$$PVIF_{k,n} = \frac{1}{FVIF_{k,n}}.$$

Therefore, since the *future value* interest factor for 5 percent over 5 years is seen in Table 6-2 to be 1.2763, the *present value* interest factor for 5 percent over 5 years must be the reciprocal of 1.2763:

$$PVIF_{5\%,5\ years} = \frac{1}{1.2763} = 0.7835.$$

The $PVIF_{k,n}$ found in this manner does, of course, correspond with that shown in Table 6-3.

The reciprocal nature of the relationship between present values and future values permits us to find present values in two ways—by multiplying or by dividing. Thus, the present value of $1,000 due in 5 years when discounted at 5 percent may be found as

$$PV = FV_n(PVIF_{k,n}) = FV_5\left(\frac{1}{1+k}\right)^5 = \$1,000(0.7835) = \$783.50,$$

or as

$$PV = \frac{FV_n}{FVIF_{k,n}} = \frac{FV_5}{(1+k)^5} = \frac{\$1,000}{1.2763} = \$783.50.$$

To conclude this comparison of present and future values, compare Figures 6-1 and 6-2. Notice that the vertical intercept is at 1.0 in each case, but future value interest factors rise whereas present value interest factors decline.[3]

Self-Test Question

What is the relationship between $PVIF_{k,n}$ and $FVIF_{k,n}$?

SOLVING FOR TIME AND INTEREST RATES

At this point, you should recognize that we have been dealing with one equation, Equation 6-2, and its transformed version, Equation 6-3:

$$FV_n = PV(1+k)^n = PV(FVIF_{k,n}). \tag{6-2}$$

---

[3]Notice that Figure 6-2 is not a mirror image of Figure 6-1. The curves in Figure 6-1 approach ∞ as n increases; in Figure 6-2 the curves approach zero, not −∞.

$$PV = \frac{FV_n}{(1 + k)^n} = FV_n(PVIF_{k,n}).$$ (6-3)

Notice that there are four variables in the equations:

PV = present value = $100 in our examples.

FV = future value = $127.63 after 5 years at 5 percent.

k = interest (or discount) rate = 5% in our examples.

n = number of years = 5 in our examples.

If you know the values of three of the variables, you (or your financial calculator) can find the value of the fourth. Thus far we have always given you the interest rate, k, and the number of years, n, as well as either the PV or the FV. In many situations, though, you will need to solve for either k or n. Solution procedures for these values are discussed next.

Time

Suppose we were given the following information: PV = $100, FV = $127.63, and i = 5%. Could we determine the length of time, n, involved? The answer is yes. To do this, we would set up our problem as follows:

$$FV_n = PV(FVIF_{k,n})$$

$$\$127.63 = \$100(FVIF_{5\%,n})$$

$$FVIF_{5\%,n} = \$127.63/\$100$$

$$FVIF_{5\%,n} = 1.2763.$$

Because we are given the interest rate of 5 percent, and we are solving for the future value interest factor, all we need to do is to refer to Table A-3 in Appendix A. In Table A-3 we look down the 5% column until we reach the future value interest factor of 1.2763. We find that this interest factor is in Row 5; thus, the number of time periods it takes for $100 to accumulate to $127.63 is equal to 5.

We could also work the problem using Equation 6-3, solving for the length of time it takes $100 to grow to $127.63 at a 5 percent interest rate:

$$PV = FV_n(PVIF_{k,n})$$

$$\$100 = \$127.63(PVIF_{5\%,n})$$

$$PVIF_{5\%,n} = \$100/\$127.63$$

$$PVIF_{5\%,n} = 0.7835.$$

Because we are given the interest rate of 5 percent, and we are solving for the present value interest factor, all we need to do is to refer to Table A-1 in Appendix A. In Table A-1 we look down the 5% column until we reach the present value interest factor of 0.7835. We find that this interest factor is in Row 5; thus, the number of time periods it takes for $100 to accumulate to $127.63 is equal to 5.

Finally, the best way to solve the problem is by using a financial calculator. Just input k = i = 5, PV = 100, FV = 127.63 (or − 127.63), and then press the n button to find n = 5 years. (Note: In some problems, n will be a fraction, such as 5.2 years. Most calculators would display the fraction, 5.2, but some round up, and in this instance they would display 6.)

Interest Rate

Suppose we were given the following facts: PV = $100, FV = $127.63, and n = 5. We need to determine the interest rate at which $100 would grow to $127.63 over 5 periods. We could set up the equation as follows:

$$FV_5 = PV(FVIF_{k,5})$$

$$\$127.63 = \$100(FVIF_{k,5})$$

$$FVIF_{k,5} = 1.2763.$$

Because we are given the number of time periods, 5, and we are solving for the future value interest factor, all we need to do is refer to Table A-3 in Appendix A. We look across the Period 5 row until we reach the future value interest factor of 1.2763. We find that this interest factor is in the 5% column; thus, the interest rate at which $100 accumulates to $127.63 is equal to 5 percent.

Alternatively, we could set up this equation as follows:

$$PV = FV_5(PVIF_{k,5})$$

$$\$100 = \$127.63(PVIF_{k,5})$$

$$PVIF_{k,5} = 0.7835.$$

Because we are given the number of time periods, 5, and we are solving for the present value interest factor, all we need to do is refer to Table A-1 in Appendix A. We look across the Period 5 row until we find the present value interest factor of 0.7835. This interest factor is in the 5% column, so the interest rate at which $100 accumulates to $127.63 is equal to 5 percent.

By far the best way to solve the problem is with a financial calculator. Simply input PV = 100, FV = 127.63 (or − 127.63), and n = 5, and then press the k = i button to find k = i = 5%.

Self-Test Questions

Write out the two equations that can be used to determine the time period, assuming that you are given PV, FV, and the interest rate.

Write out the two equations that can be used to determine the interest rate, assuming that you are given PV, FV, and the time period.

FUTURE VALUE OF AN ANNUITY

An *annuity* is a series of equal payments at fixed intervals for a specified number of periods. Payments are given the symbol PMT, and if they occur at the end of each period, as they typically do, then we have an *ordinary annuity,* sometimes called a *deferred annuity.* If payments are made at the beginning of each period, then we have an *annuity due.* Since ordinary annuities are far more common in finance, when the word *annuity* is used in this book you may assume that payments are received at the end of each period unless otherwise indicated.

Ordinary Annuities

A promise to pay $1,000 a year for 3 years is a 3-year annuity, and if each payment is made at the end of the year, it is an *ordinary (or deferred) annuity.* If you were to receive such an annuity and then to deposit each annual payment in a savings account that paid 4 percent interest, how much would you have at the end of 3 years? The answer is shown graphically as a time line in Figure 6-3. The first payment is made at the end of Year 1, the second at the end of Year 2, and the third at the end of Year 3. Thus, the first payment is compounded over a 2-year period; the second payment is compounded for 1 year; and the last payment is not compounded at all. When the future values of each of the payments are summed, their total is the future value of the annuity. In the example, this total is $3,121.60.

Expressed algebraically, with FVA_n defined as the future value of the annuity over n periods, PMT as the periodic payment, t as the time period where 1 = Period 1 and n = the last period, and $FVIFA_{k,n}$ as the future value interest factor for the annuity, the formula is

$$FVA_n = PMT(1 + k)^{n-1} + PMT(1 + k)^{n-2} + \ldots + PMT(1 + k)^1 + PMT(1 + k)^0$$

$$= PMT[(1 + k)^{n-1} + (1 + k)^{n-2} + \ldots + (1 + k)^1 + (1 + k)^0]$$

$$= PMT\sum_{t=1}^{n}(1 + k)^{n-t} \tag{6-4}$$

$$= PMT(FVIFA_{k,n}) = \text{future value of an annuity.}$$

Figure 6-3   Time Line for an Ordinary Annuity:
Future Value with k = 4%

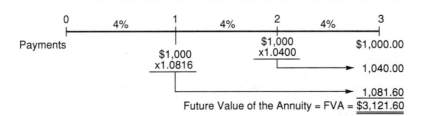

Future Value of the Annuity = FVA = $3,121.60

Note: $(1.04)^1 = 1.0400$ and $(1.04)^2 = 1.0816$.

Table 6-4   Future Value of an Annuity of $1 per Period for n Periods:

$$FVIFA_{k,n} = \sum_{t=1}^{n} (1 + k)^{n-t} = \frac{(1 + k)^n - 1}{k}$$

Number of Periods (n)	1%	2%	3%	4%	5%	6%	7%	8%	9%	10%
1	1.0000	1.0000	1.0000	1.0000	1.0000	1.0000	1.0000	1.0000	1.0000	1.0000
2	2.0100	2.0200	2.0300	2.0400	2.0500	2.0600	2.0700	2.0800	2.0900	2.1000
3	3.0301	3.0604	3.0909	3.1216	3.1525	3.1836	3.2149	3.2464	3.2781	3.3100
4	4.0604	4.1216	4.1836	4.2465	4.3101	4.3746	4.4399	4.5061	4.5731	4.6410
5	5.1010	5.2040	5.3091	5.4163	5.5256	5.6371	5.7507	5.8666	5.9847	6.1051
6	6.1520	6.3081	6.4684	6.6330	6.8019	6.9753	7.1533	7.3359	7.5233	7.7156
7	7.2135	7.4343	7.6625	7.8983	8.1420	8.3938	8.6540	8.9228	9.2004	9.4872
8	8.2857	8.5830	8.8923	9.2142	9.5491	9.8975	10.2598	10.6366	11.0285	11.4359
9	9.3685	9.7546	10.1591	10.5828	11.0266	11.4913	11.9780	12.4876	13.0210	13.5795
10	10.4622	10.9497	11.4639	12.0061	12.5779	13.1808	13.8164	14.4866	15.1929	15.9374

The expression in parentheses, $FVIFA_{k,n}$, has been calculated for various combinations of k and n. An illustrative set of these annuity interest factors is given in Table 6-4.[4] (A more complete set of annuity future value factors is given in Table A-4 of Appendix A.) To find the answer to the 3-year, $1,000 annuity problem, simply refer to Table 6-4, look down the 4% column to the row of the third period, and multiply the factor 3.1216 by $1,000. The answer is the same as the one derived by the long method illustrated in Figure 6-3:

$$FVA_n = PMT(FVIFA_{k,n})$$

$$FVA_3 = \$1,000(FVIFA_{4\%,3 \text{ years}})$$

$$= \$1,000(3.1216) = \$3,121.60.$$

Note also that Equation 6-4 is simply the summation of n values of Equation 6-2, that is, the FV of an annuity is the sum of n individual FVs.

We can also solve annuity problems using a financial calculator. To solve our illustrative problem, merely key in n = 3, k = i = 4, and PMT = 1,000, and then press the FV button to get the answer, $3,121.60.

---

[4]The equation given at the top of Table 6-4 recognizes that an FVIFA factor is the sum of a geometric progression. It is easy to use the equation to develop annuity factors; this is especially useful if you need the FVIFA for some interest rate not given in the tables—for example, 6.5 percent. The equation is also useful for finding factors for fractional periods—for example, 2.5 years—but one needs a calculator with an exponential function for this. Finally, this is the formula that is built into financial calculators, so, in effect, financial calculators can calculate the appropriate table value if you simply input PMT = 1, k, and n.

Annuity Due

Had the three $1,000 payments in the previous example been made at the beginning of each year, the annuity would have been an *annuity due*. In terms of Figure 6-3, each payment would have been shifted to the left, so there would have been a $1,000 under Period 0 and a zero under Period 3; thus, each payment would be compounded for one extra year.

We can modify Equation 6-4 to handle annuities due as follows:

$$FVA_n(\text{Annuity due}) = PMT(FVIFA_{k,n})(1 + k). \qquad \textbf{(6-4a)}$$

Each payment is compounded for one extra year, and multiplying the term $PMT(FVIFA_{k,n})$ by $(1 + k)$ takes care of this extra compounding. Applying Equation 6-4a to the previous example, we obtain

$$FVA_n(\text{Annuity due}) = \$1,000(3.1216)(1.04) = \$3,246.46$$

versus $3,121.60 for the ordinary annuity. Since its payments come in faster, the annuity due is more valuable.

Annuity due problems can also be solved with financial calculators, most of which have a switch or key marked "Due" or "Beg" that permits you to convert from ordinary annuities to annuities due. Be careful, though. People sometimes change the setting to work an annuity due problem, then forget to switch the calculator back and get wrong answers to subsequent ordinary annuity problems.

Self-Test Questions

What is the difference between an ordinary annuity and an annuity due?

How do you modify the equation for determining the value of an ordinary annuity to determine the value of an annuity due?

For all positive interest rates, is the $FVIFA_{k,n}$ larger, smaller, or equal to the number of periods of the annuity? Must this relationship always hold?

Which annuity has the greater future value: an ordinary annuity or an annuity due? Explain.

PRESENT VALUE OF AN ANNUITY

Suppose you were offered the following alternatives: (1) a 3-year annuity with payments of $1,000 at the end of each year or (2) a lump sum payment today. You have no need for the money during the next 3 years, so if you accept the annuity, you would simply deposit the payments in a savings account that pays 4 percent interest. Similarly, the lump sum payment would be deposited in an account paying 4 percent. How large must the lump sum payment be to make it equivalent to the annuity?

The time line shown in Figure 6-4 will help explain the problem. The present value of the first payment is $PMT[1/(1 + k)]$, the PV of the second is $PMT[1/(1 + k)]^2$, and so on. Defining PVA_n as the present value of an annuity of n

Figure 6-4   Time Line for an Ordinary Annuity: Present Value with k = 4%

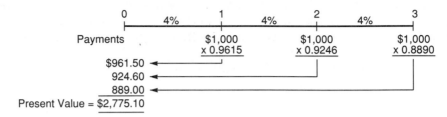

Note: $961.50 compounded for 1 year at 4 percent equals $1,000; $924.60 compounded for 2 years equals $1,000; and $889.00 compounded for 3 years equals $1,000. Also, note that $1/(1.04)^1 = 0.9615$, $1/(1.04)^2 = 0.9246$, and $1/(1.04)^3 = 0.8890$.

periods, and $PVIFA_{k,n}$ as the present value interest factor for the annuity, we may write the following equation in its several equivalent forms:

$$
\begin{aligned}
PVA_n &= PMT\left(\frac{1}{1+k}\right)^1 + PMT\left(\frac{1}{1+k}\right)^2 + \ldots + PMT\left(\frac{1}{1+k}\right)^n \\
&= PMT\left[\frac{1}{(1+k)^1} + \frac{1}{(1+k)^2} + \ldots + \frac{1}{(1+k)^n}\right] \\
&= PMT\sum_{t=1}^{n}\left(\frac{1}{1+k}\right)^t \\
&= PMT(PVIFA_{k,n}).
\end{aligned}
\tag{6-5}
$$

Again, tables have been worked out for $PVIFA_{k,n}$. Table 6-5 is illustrative, and a more complete listing is found in Table A-2 in Appendix A. From Table 6-5, the $PVIFA_{k,n}$ for a 3-year, 4 percent annuity is found to be 2.7751. Multiplying this factor by the $1,000 annual payment gives $2,775.10, the present value of the annuity:

$$
\begin{aligned}
PVA_n &= PMT(PVIFA_{k,n}) \\
PVA_3 &= \$1{,}000(PVIFA_{4\%,\,3\text{ years}}) \\
&= \$1{,}000(2.7751) = \$2{,}775.10.
\end{aligned}
$$

This value is identical to the long-method answer shown in Figure 6-4.

Notice that the entry for each value of n in Table 6-5 is equal to the sum of the entries in Table 6-3 up to and including Period n. For example, the PVIFA for 4 percent, 3 periods, as shown in Table 6-5, could have been calculated by summing values from Table 6-3:

$$0.9615 + 0.9246 + 0.8890 = 2.7751.$$

Table 6-5   Present Value of an Annuity of $1 per Period for n Periods:

$$\text{PVIFA}_{k,n} = \sum_{t=1}^{n} \frac{1}{(1 + k)^t} = \frac{1 - \dfrac{1}{(1 + k)^n}}{k} = \frac{1}{k} - \frac{1}{k(1 + k)^n}$$

Number of Periods (n)	1%	2%	3%	4%	5%	6%	7%	8%	9%	10%
1	0.9901	0.9804	0.9709	0.9615	0.9524	0.9434	0.9346	0.9259	0.9174	0.9091
2	1.9704	1.9416	1.9135	1.8861	1.8594	1.8334	1.8080	1.7833	1.7591	1.7355
3	2.9410	2.8839	2.8286	2.7751	2.7232	2.6730	2.6243	2.5771	2.5313	2.4869
4	3.9020	3.8077	3.7171	3.6299	3.5460	3.4651	3.3872	3.3121	3.2397	3.1699
5	4.8534	4.7135	4.5797	4.4518	4.3295	4.2124	4.1002	3.9927	3.8897	3.7908
6	5.7955	5.6014	5.4172	5.2421	5.0757	4.9173	4.7665	4.6229	4.4859	4.3553
7	6.7282	6.4720	6.2303	6.0021	5.7864	5.5824	5.3893	5.2064	5.0330	4.8684
8	7.6517	7.3255	7.0197	6.7327	6.4632	6.2098	5.9713	5.7466	5.5348	5.3349
9	8.5660	8.1622	7.7861	7.4353	7.1078	6.8017	6.5152	6.2469	5.9952	5.7590
10	9.4713	8.9826	8.5302	8.1109	7.7217	7.3601	7.0236	6.7101	6.4177	6.1446

This relationship can be seen from Figure 6-4. Notice that from the figure we have the following:

$$\text{PVA}_n = (\$1,000 \times 0.9615) + (\$1,000 \times 0.9246) + (\$1,000 \times 0.8890).$$

We can reduce this equation to

$$\text{PVA}_n = \$1,000 \times (0.9615 + 0.9246 + 0.8890)$$

$$= \$1,000 \times 2.7751$$

$$= \$2,775.10.$$

As you might expect, the easiest way to solve an annuity present value problem is with a financial calculator. For our illustrative problem, simply input n = 3, k = i = 4, and PMT = 1,000, and then press the PV button to find the answer, PV = $2,775.09. (Note the penny rounding difference. Calculators take numbers out to 10 significant digits versus 5 for our tables.)

Present Value of an Annuity Due

Had the payments in the preceding example occurred at the beginning of each year, the annuity would have been an *annuity due*. In terms of Figure 6-4, each payment would have been shifted to the left, so $1,000 would have appeared under Period 0 and a zero would have appeared under Period 3. Each payment occurs one period earlier, so it has a higher PV. To account for these shifts, we multiply Equation 6-5 by $(1 + k)$ to find the present value of an annuity due:

$$PVA_n(\text{Annuity due}) = PMT(PVIFA_{k,n})(1 + k). \tag{6-5a}$$

Our illustrative 4 percent, 3-year annuity, with payments made at the beginning of each year, thus has a present value of $2,886.10 versus a value of $2,775.10 on an ordinary annuity basis:

$$PVA_3 = \$1,000(2.7751)(1.04)$$

$$= \$2,775.10(1.04)$$

$$= \$2,886.10.$$

Since each payment comes earlier, an annuity due is worth more than an ordinary annuity.

Again, you can use a financial calculator to solve the problem. Simply set the switch to "Due" or "Beg" instead of "End" and proceed as before. When you finish, though, remember to switch back to "End."[5]

Self-Test Questions

For all positive interest rates, is the $PVIFA_{k,n}$ larger, smaller, or equal to the number of periods of the annuity? Why must this relationship hold true?

Which annuity has the greater present value: an ordinary annuity or an annuity due? Why?

PERPETUITIES

Most annuities call for payments to be made over some finite period of time—for example, $1,000 per year for 3 years. However, some annuities go on indefinitely; here the payments constitute an *infinite series*, and the series is defined as a *perpetuity*. The present value of a perpetuity is found by applying Equation 6-6:[6]

$$PV(\text{Perpetuity}) = \frac{\text{Payment}}{\text{Interest rate}} = \frac{PMT}{k}. \tag{6-6}$$

---

[5]There are occasions when it is necessary to find the present value or future value of an annuity whose payments are growing by some constant amount. For a discussion of this situation, along with solution formulas, see Richard Followill, "Present Value and Future Value of an Annuity Growing by a Constant Amount," *Journal of Financial Education,* Fall 1989, 15–18.

[6]Note that the present value of a perpetuity is given by

$$PV = \frac{PMT}{(1 + k)^1} + \frac{PMT}{(1 + k)^2} + \cdots + \frac{PMT}{(1 + k)^\infty}. \tag{6-6a}$$

Equation 6-6a may be rewritten as follows:

$$PV = PMT\left[\frac{1}{(1 + k)^1} + \frac{1}{(1 + k)^2} + \cdots + \frac{1}{(1 + k)^n}\right]. \tag{6-6b}$$

Perpetuities can be illustrated by some British securities issued after the Napoleonic Wars. In 1815, the British government sold a huge bond issue and used the proceeds to pay off many smaller issues that had been floated in prior years to pay for the wars. Since the purpose of the new bonds was to consolidate past debts, the bonds were called *consols*. Suppose each consol promised to pay $90 interest per year in perpetuity. (Actually, interest was stated in pounds.) What would each bond be worth if the going rate of interest, or the discount rate, were 8 percent? The answer is $1,125:

$$\text{Value} = \frac{\$90}{0.08} = \$1,125 \text{ if k is 8\%.}$$

Suppose interest rates rose to 12 percent; what would that do to the consol's value? The answer changes to $750:

$$\text{Value} = \frac{\$90}{0.12} = \$750 \text{ if k is 12\%.}$$

If k fell to 4 percent, the consol's value would rise to $2,250.

We see, then, that the value of a perpetuity changes dramatically when interest rates change. Perpetuities are discussed further in Chapter 7, where procedures for finding the values of various types of securities (stocks and bonds) are discussed.

Self-Test Question

What happens to the value of a perpetuity when interest rates increase? What happens when interest rates decrease? Explain why these changes occur.

PRESENT VALUE OF AN UNEVEN SERIES OF PAYMENTS

The definition of an annuity includes the words *constant amount*—in other words, annuities involve situations in which cash flows are *identical* in every period. Although many financial decisions do involve constant cash flows, some important decisions are concerned with *uneven* flows of cash; for example, common stocks are typically expected to pay an increasing series of dividends over time, and capital

---

Multiply both sides of Equation 6-6b by $(1 + k)$:

$$PV(1 + k) = PMT\left[1 + \frac{1}{(1 + k)^1} + \frac{1}{(1 + k)^2} + \cdots + \frac{1}{(1 + k)^{n-1}}\right]. \tag{6-6c}$$

Subtract Equation 6-6b from Equation 6-6c, obtaining

$$PV(1 + k - 1) = PMT\left[1 - \frac{1}{(1 + k)^n}\right]. \tag{6-6d}$$

As $n \to \infty$, $1/(1 + k)^n \to 0$, so Equation 6-6d approaches

$$PV(k) = PMT,$$

and thus we obtain Equation 6-6,

$$PV \text{ (Perpetuity)} = \frac{PMT}{k}.$$

Figure 6-5   Time Line for an Uneven Cash Flow Stream:
Present Value with k = 6%

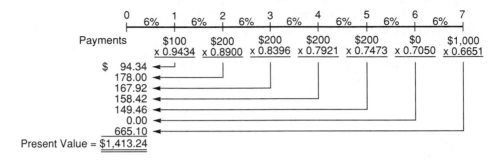

Year	Payment	×	PVIF$_{6\%,n}$	=	PV of Individual Payments
1	$ 100		0.9434		$ 94.34
2	200		0.8900		178.00
3	200		0.8396		167.92
4	200		0.7921		158.42
5	200		0.7473		149.46
6	0		0.7050		0
7	1,000		0.6651		665.10
				PV = Sum =	$1,413.24

Note: The PV of each cash flow (CF) can also be found as $CF_n/(1.06)^n$, where n = the year number.

budgeting projects do not normally provide constant cash flows. Consequently, it is necessary to expand our analysis to deal with *uneven payment streams.*

The PV of an uneven stream of future income is found as the sum of the PVs of the individual components of the stream.[7] For example, suppose we are trying to find the PV of the stream of payments shown in Figure 6-5, discounted at 6 percent. As shown in the tabular part of the figure, we multiply each payment by the appropriate PVIF$_{k,n}$ (taken from Appendix A, Table A-1), or we use a calculator to find the individual cash flow PVs, and then sum these values to obtain the PV of the stream, $1,413.24. The time line gives a pictorial view of the cash flow stream.

The PV of the payments shown in Figure 6-5 for Years 2 through 5 can also be found by using the annuity equation. This alternative solution process involves the following steps:

Step 1. Find the PV of $100 due in Year 1:

$$\$100(0.9434) = \$94.34.$$

---

[7]This general equation may be used to find the PV of an uneven series of payments:

$$PV = \sum_{t=1}^{n} PMT_t \left(\frac{1}{1 + k}\right)^t = \sum_{t=1}^{n} PMT_t(PVIF_{k,t}),$$

where PMT$_t$ is the payment in any Year t.

Step 2. Recognize that a $200 annuity will be received during Years 2 through 5. The value of the 4-year annuity at the end of Year 1 is

$$\$200(3.4651) = \$693.02.$$

The Year 0 value of the Year 1 $693.02 lump sum is

$$\$693.02(0.9434) = \$653.80.$$

Thus, the present value of the annuity component of the uneven stream is $653.80.

Step 3. Find the PV of the $1,000 due in Year 7:

$$\$1,000(0.6651) = \$665.10.$$

Step 4. Sum the components:

$$\$94.34 + \$653.80 + \$665.10 = \$1,413.24.$$

Either the Figure 6-5 method or the method utilizing the annuity formula can be used to solve problems of this type. However, the alternative annuity solution is much easier if the annuity component runs for many years. For example, the alternative solution would be clearly superior for finding the PV of a stream consisting of $100 in Year 1, $200 in Years 2 through 29, and $1,000 in Year 30.

The present value of a stream of future cash flows can always be found by summing the present values of each individual cash flow. However, cash flow regularities within the stream may allow the use of shortcuts, such as finding the present value of several cash flows that compose an annuity. Also, in some instances we may want to find the value of a stream of payments at some point other than the present (Year 0). In this situation, we proceed as before but compound and discount to some other point in time, say Year 2 rather than Year 0.

Problems involving unequal cash flows can be solved quite easily with most financial calculators. Most of these calculators permit you to input the separate cash flows plus the interest rate; then, when you press the PV (or NPV) button, you obtain the solution. Some of the newer financial calculators even allow you to specify annuities within the cash flow stream. For example, you could specify 1 payment of $100, 4 payments of $200, 1 payment of $0, and 1 payment of $1,000, along with an interest rate of 6 percent, to find the present value of the cash flow stream given in Figure 6-5.

The future value of a series of uneven payments, often called the *terminal value,* is found by compounding each payment and then summing the individual future values:

$$\text{Terminal value} = TV_n = \sum_{t=1}^{n} PMT_t(1 + k)^{n-t}.$$

We are generally more interested in the present value of a stream of payments from an asset than in the future (or terminal) value, because the PV is the value today, hence the market value of the asset. However, we will use the terminal value concept in Chapter 9, when we deal with capital budgeting.

Self-Test Questions

What are two examples of financial decisions that would typically involve uneven flows of cash?

What is meant by the term "terminal value"?

A FURTHER DISCUSSION ON DETERMINING INTEREST RATES

We can use the basic equations that were developed earlier in the chapter to determine the interest rates built into any financial contract.

Example 1. A bank offers to lend you $1,000 if you sign a note to pay $1,610.50 at the end of 5 years. What rate of interest would the bank be charging you?

1.   Recognize that $1,000 is the PV of $1,610.50 due in 5 years:

$$PV = \$1,000 = \$1,610.50 \left(\frac{1}{1 + k}\right)^n$$

$$\$1,000 = \$1,610.50(PVIF_{k,5 \text{ years}}).$$

2.   Solve for $PVIF_{k,5 \text{ years}}$:

$$PVIF_{k,5 \text{ years}} = \$1,000/\$1,610.50 = 0.6209.$$

3.   Now turn to Table 6-3 (or Table A-1). Look across the row for Period 5 until you find the value 0.6209. It is in the 10% column. Therefore, you would be paying a 10 percent rate of interest if you were to take out the loan.

4.   Financial calculators are especially useful for finding interest rates in problems like this. Enter PV = 1,000, n = 5, and FV = 1,610.50, and then press the k = i button to obtain the interest rate. The calculator blinks a few times, and 10.00 percent appears. Your calculator may require that either the PV or FV be entered as a negative in recognition of the fact that the PV is an inflow and the FV is an outflow. If you get an error message, try entering FV = $-1,610.50$.

Example 2. A bank offers to lend you $25,000 to buy a home. You must sign a mortgage loan agreement calling for payments of $2,545.16 at the end of each of the next 25 years. What interest rate is the bank offering you?

1.   Recognize that $25,000 is the PV of a 25-year, $2,545.16 ordinary annuity:

$$PV = \$25,000 = \sum_{t=1}^{25} \$2,545.16 \left(\frac{1}{1 + k}\right)^t$$

$$\$25,000 = \$2,545.16(PVIFA_{k,25 \text{ years}}).$$

2.   Solve for $PVIFA_{k,25 \text{ years}}$:

$$PVIFA_{k,25 \text{ years}} = \$25,000/\$2,545.16 = 9.8226.$$

3.   Turn to Table A-2. Looking across the row for 25 periods, you will find 9.8226 under the column for 9 percent. Therefore, the rate of interest on this mortgage loan is 9%.

4.   To solve this problem with a calculator, enter PV = 25,000, n = 25, and PMT = 2,545.16; then press the k = i button to determine that the interest rate the bank is charging is 9 percent. Note that this problem would be quite difficult to solve if you were using the Appendix A tables and the interest rate was not a whole percent. The approximate rate for the mortgage could be found by linear interpolation, which is discussed in algebra texts, but exact solutions can be found easily with calculators.

Although the tables can be used to find the interest rate implicit in single payments and annuities, it is more difficult to find the interest rate implicit in an uneven series of payments. One can use a trial-and-error procedure or a financial calculator with an IRR feature (IRRs are discussed in Chapter 9). We will defer further discussion of this problem for now, but we will take it up later in our discussion of bond values and again in the capital budgeting chapters.

Self-Test Question

How would one go about finding the interest rate implicit (1) in an annuity and (2) in an uneven series of payments?

SEMIANNUAL AND OTHER COMPOUNDING PERIODS

In all of our examples thus far, we have assumed that interest is compounded once a year, or annually. Suppose, however, that you put your $1,000 into a bank account which pays 6 percent annual interest, but compounded *semiannually*. How much will you have at the end of 1 year, 2 years, or some other period? Semiannual compounding means that interest is paid each 6 months. The procedures for semiannual compounding are illustrated in Section 2 of Table 6-6, and they are compared with annual compounding as set forth in Section 1. For semiannual compounding, the annual interest rate is divided by 2, but twice as many compounding periods are used because interest is paid twice a year. Comparing the amount in the account at the end of each year, we see that the $1,000 grows faster under semiannual compounding, so 6 percent interest compounded semiannually is better than a 6 percent annual rate from a saver's standpoint. This result occurs because under semiannual compounding you earn *interest on interest* more frequently.

Throughout the economy, different compounding periods are used for different types of investments. For example, bank accounts generally pay interest monthly or daily; most bonds pay interest semiannually; stocks pay dividends quarterly; and many loans pay interest annually.[8] Thus, if we are to compare securities with differ-

---

[8]Some banks and savings and loans even pay interest compounded continuously. Continuous compounding and discounting are discussed in a later section of this chapter.

Table 6-6	Future Value Calculations: Semiannual versus Annual Compounding

1. Annual Compounding at a 6% Rate

Year	Beginning Amount, PV	×	(1 + k)	=	Ending Amount, FV_n
1	$1,000.00		1.06		$1,060.00
2	1,060.00		1.06		1,123.60
3	1,123.60		1.06		1,191.02

Total interest earned over 3 years at 6%, annual compounding: $191.02

2. Semiannual Compounding at a 6% Nominal Rate

6-Month Period	Beginning Amount, PV	×	(1 + k/2)	=	Ending Amount, FV_n
1	$1,000.00		1.03		$1,030.00
2	1,030.00		1.03		1,060.90
3	1,060.90		1.03		1,092.73
4	1,092.73		1.03		1,125.51
5	1,125.51		1.03		1,159.27
6	1,159.27		1.03		1,194.05

Total interest earned over 3 years at 6%, semiannual compounding: $194.05

3. Annual Compounding at an Effective Annual Rate of 6.09%

Year	Beginning Amount, PV	×	(1 + k)	=	Ending Amount, FV_n
1	$1,000.00		1.0609		$1,060.90
2	1,060.90		1.0609		1,125.51
3	1,125.51		1.0609		1,194.05

Total interest earned over 3 years at 6.09%, annual compounding: $194.05

Notes:

a. Sections 1 and 2 demonstrate that if a given interest rate (6%) is paid each 6 months (semiannually), more interest is earned over time than if the same interest rate is paid annually.

b. Section 3 demonstrates that there is some annual interest rate, called the *effective annual rate,* which is equivalent to the *stated* (or *nominal*) semiannual rate. For a 6% nominal rate paid semiannually, the effective annual rate is 6.09%, found as follows:

$$\text{Effective annual rate} = \left(1 + \frac{k_{Nom}}{m}\right)^m - 1.0 = \left(1 + \frac{0.06}{2}\right)^2 - 1.0 = 0.0609 = 6.09\%.$$

Here m = number of compounding periods per year.

ent compounding periods, we need to put them on a common basis. This means that we must distinguish between the *nominal,* or *stated, interest rate* and the *effective annual rate (EAR).*[9]

---

[9]The term *nominal* as it is used here has a different meaning than the way it is used in Chapter 3. There, nominal interest rates meant market rates as opposed to real (without inflation adjustments) rates. In this chapter, the term *nominal rate* means the stated rate as opposed to the effective annual rate, which gives consideration to compounding more frequently than once a year.

The *nominal, or stated, interest rate* is the quoted rate; thus, in our example the nominal rate is 6 percent. The nominal interest rate is often called the *annual percentage rate (APR)* when it is reported by banks and other lending institutions.[10] The *effective annual rate* is the rate that would have produced the final compound value, $1,060.90, under annual rather than semiannual compounding. In this case, the effective annual rate is 6.09 percent, found by solving for k in the following equation:

$$\$1,000(1 + k) = \$1,060.90$$

$$k = \frac{\$1,060.90}{\$1,000} - 1 = 0.0609 = 6.09\%.$$

Thus, if one bank offered to pay 6 percent with semiannual compounding on its savings accounts, while another offered 6.09 percent with annual compounding, they would both be paying the same effective annual rate of interest. This point is demonstrated in Section 3 of Table 6-6.

In general, we can determine the effective annual rate, given the nominal rate, by solving Equation 6-7:

$$\text{Effective annual rate} = \left(1 + \frac{k_{\text{Nom}}}{m}\right)^m - 1.0. \qquad \textbf{(6-7)}$$

Here k_{Nom} is the nominal, or stated, interest rate, and m is the number of compounding periods per year. For example, to find the effective annual rate if the nominal rate is 6 percent and semiannual compounding is used, we make the following calculation:

$$\text{Effective annual rate} = \left(1 + \frac{0.06}{2}\right)^2 - 1.0$$

$$= (1.03)^2 - 1.0$$

$$= 1.0609 - 1.0$$

$$= 0.0609 = 6.09\%.$$

Semiannual compounding can be handled easily with a financial calculator. Simply set i = 3, n = 2, and PV = 1,000, and then press the FV button to get the solution, FV = $1,060.90. An alternative approach is to first calculate the effective annual rate, and then set i = 6.09, n = 1, and PV = 1,000. Again, the solution is FV = $1,060.90.

---

[10]The nominal interest rate, or the APR, is the rate typically reported by banks on loans. Although this meets the minimum requirements of the "truth in lending" laws, it is somewhat deceptive because the true effective annual rate, which ought to be reported to borrowers, always exceeds the nominal rate except where annual compounding is used. Banks are, however, quick to use the effective annual rate when advertising rates on savings accounts and certificates of deposit, because they want to make their published rates on savings accounts look high.

The points made about semiannual compounding can be generalized as follows. When compounding periods are more frequent than once a year, we use a modified version of Equation 6-2 to find the future value of a lump sum:

$$\text{Annual compounding: } FV_n = PV(1 + k)^n. \qquad \textbf{(6-2)}$$

$$\text{More frequent compounding: } FV_n = PV\left(1 + \frac{k_{Nom}}{m}\right)^{mn}. \qquad \textbf{(6-2a)}$$

Here m is the number of times per year compounding occurs, and n is the number of years. For example, when banks compute daily interest, the value of m is set at 365 and Equation 6-2a is applied.[11]

To illustrate further the effects of compounding more frequently than annually, consider the interest rate charged on credit cards. In January 1990, most interest rates had declined sharply from earlier levels. For example, the yield on 30-year Treasury bonds was 8.0 percent, down from 14.2 percent in December 1985. However, credit card rates (the rate of interest charged to credit card users who do not pay within the grace period) were generally unchanged from earlier levels. Most states set maximum rates for credit card loans, and most banks charge the allowed limit, which ranges from 12 to 21 percent, but averages 19 percent.

Certain members of Congress raised this question: Why haven't credit card rates dropped along with other rates? Is there some conspiracy among bankers to keep these rates up, thus helping bank profits but exploiting those consumers who borrow on credit cards? As expected, the bankers replied that both administrative costs and bad debt losses are high on credit card loans, and that the rates charged are completely justified. The interesting thing to note for our purposes, though, is that the rate the banks are actually charging is higher than the rate they say they are charging. For example, if a bank charges 1.5 percent per month, it will state that its annual percentage rate (APR) is 1.5 × 12 = 18%. Actually, though, the true rate is the effective annual rate of 19.6 percent:

$$\text{Effective annual rate} = (1.015)^{12} - 1.0 = 0.196 = 19.6\%.$$

If the bank states that it charges 21 percent, the true rate is 23.1 percent. Whether or not those rates are really justified is a moot question, but it surely pays to pay credit card bills within the grace period!

The interest tables can often be used when compounding occurs more than once a year. Simply divide the nominal, or stated, interest rate by the number of times compounding occurs, and multiply the years by the number of compounding periods per year. For example, to find the amount to which $1,000 will grow after 5 years if semiannual compounding is applied to a stated 8 percent interest rate, divide 8 percent by 2 and multiply the 5 years by 2. Then look in Table A-3 under the 4 percent column and in the row for Period 10. You will find an interest factor of 1.4802. Multiplying this by the initial $1,000 gives a value of $1,480.20, the amount

---

[11]To illustrate, the future value of $1 invested at 10 percent for 1 year under daily compounding is $1.1052:

$$FV_n = \$1\left(1 + \frac{0.10}{365}\right)^{365(1)} = \$1(1.105156) = \$1.1052.$$

to which $1,000 will grow in 5 years at 8 percent, compounded semiannually. This compares with $1,469.30 for annual compounding.

It should be clear that the tables in this book are not complete enough to handle much variability of interest rates. For example, to handle 9 percent, compounded quarterly, we would need a table for 2.25 percent; 10 percent quarterly would require a table for 2.5 percent; and so on. However, any compounding period can be handled easily with a financial calculator. To work our illustrative problem, simply enter i = k_{Nom}/m = 8/2 = 4, n = m × n = 2 × 5 = 10, and then proceed as before.

Semiannual and other compounding periods can also be used for discounting, for single payments, and for annuities. To illustrate semiannual discounting in finding the present value of an annuity, consider the case described in the section "Present Value of an Annuity": $1,000 a year for 3 years, discounted at 4 percent. With annual discounting, the interest factor is 2.7751 and the present value of the annuity is $2,775.10. If the annuity were actually $500 every 6 months, look under the 2 percent column and in the Period 6 row of Table 6-5 to find an interest factor of 5.6014. This is multiplied by the $500 received each 6 months to get the present value of the annuity, $2,800.70. The payments come a little more rapidly—the first $500 is paid after only 6 months (similarly with other payments)—so the annuity is a little more valuable if payments are received semiannually rather than annually. We should also note that an annuity with annual payments, but with semiannual compounding, is treated as an annual annuity. However, the interest rate applied should be the effective annual rate.

By letting m approach infinity, Equation 6-2a can be modified to the special case of *continuous compounding*. Continuous compounding is useful in theoretical finance, and it also has practical applications—for example, banks and savings associations sometimes pay interest on a continuous basis. Continuous compounding is discussed next.

Self-Test Questions

What changes would you make in your calculations to determine the future value of an amount that is being compounded semiannually versus being compounded annually at the same stated interest rate?

Why is semiannual compounding better than annual compounding from a saver's standpoint?

What is meant by the term "annual percentage rate"?

How does the term "nominal rate" used in this chapter differ from the term as it was used in Chapter 3?

CONTINUOUS COMPOUNDING AND DISCOUNTING

In this chapter, we have implicitly assumed that interest is added (growth occurs) at discrete intervals—annually, semiannually, and so forth. For some purposes, though, it is better to assume instantaneous, or *continuous,* growth. In this section, we discuss present value and future value calculations when the interest rate is compounded continuously.

Continuous Compounding

The relationship between discrete and continuous compounding is illustrated in Figure 6-6. Panel a shows the annual compounding case, in which interest is added once a year; in Panel b compounding occurs twice a year; and in Panel c, interest is earned continuously. As the graphs show, the more frequent the compounding period, the larger the final compounded amount, because interest is earned on interest more often.

Equation 6-2a was developed in the previous section to allow for any number of compounding periods per year:

$$FV_n = PV\left(1 + \frac{k_{Nom}}{m}\right)^{mn}. \tag{6-2a}$$

Here k_{Nom} = the stated interest rate, m = the number of compounding periods per year, and n = the number of years. To illustrate, let PV = \$100, k = 10%, and n = 5. At various compounding periods per year, we obtain the following future values at the end of 5 years:

$$\text{Annual: } FV_5 = \$100\left(1 + \frac{0.10}{1}\right)^{1(5)} = \$100(1.10)^5 = \$161.05.$$

$$\text{Semiannual: } FV_5 = \$100\left(1 + \frac{0.10}{2}\right)^{2(5)} = \$100(1.05)^{10} = \$162.89.$$

$$\text{Monthly: } FV_5 = \$100\left(1 + \frac{0.10}{12}\right)^{12(5)} = \$100(1.0083)^{60} = \$164.53.$$

$$\text{Daily: } FV_5 = \$100\left(1 + \frac{0.10}{365}\right)^{365(5)} = \$164.86.$$

We could keep going, compounding every hour, every minute, every second, and so on. At the limit, we could compound every instant, or *continuously*. The equation for continuous compounding is

$$FV_n = PV(e^{kn}), \tag{6-8}$$

where e is the value 2.7183 . . . .[12] If \$100 is invested for 5 years at 10 percent compounded continuously, then FV_5 is computed as follows:

$$\text{Continuous: } FV_5 = \$100[e^{0.10(5)}] = \$100(2.7183 . . .)^{0.5}$$

$$= \$164.872.$$

---

[12]Calculators with exponential functions can be used to evaluate Equation 6-8.

Figure 6-6   Annual, Semiannual, and Continuous
               Compounding: Future Value with k = 25%

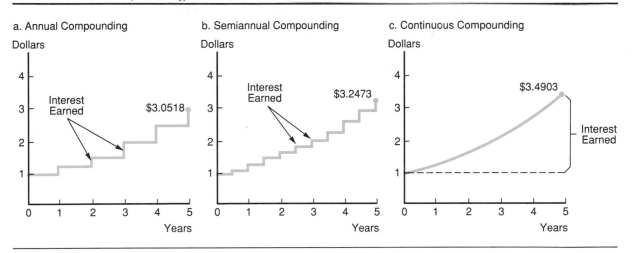

a. Annual Compounding

b. Semiannual Compounding

c. Continuous Compounding

Continuous Discounting

Equation 6-8 can be transformed into Equation 6-9 and used to determine present values under continuous discounting:

$$PV = \frac{FV_n}{e^{kn}} = FV_n(e^{-kn}). \qquad (6\text{-}9)$$

Thus, if $1,649 is due in 10 years, and if the appropriate *continuous* discount rate, k, is 5 percent, then the present value of this future payment is

$$PV = \$1,649 \left[\frac{1}{(2.7183\ldots)^{0.5}} \right] = \frac{\$1,649}{1.649} = \$1,000.$$

Self-Test Questions

What is the general equation that can be used to determine the future value for any number of compounding periods per year? Illustrate the equation for semiannual compounding and monthly compounding.

What is the equation for calculating the present value under continuous discounting?

FRACTIONAL TIME PERIODS

In all of the examples used thus far in the chapter, we have assumed that payments occur at the beginning or the end of periods, but not at some date *within* a period. However, we often encounter within-period situations. For example, you might deposit $100 in a bank that pays 10 percent interest, annual compounding, and leave it in the bank for 9 months, or 0.75 years. How much would be in your account?

Problems such as this can be handled very easily with a financial calculator — just input a fractional value for n. In our example, we would find the ending amount as follows:

$$FV_n = PV(1 + k)^n$$

$$= \$100(1.10)^{0.75} = \$100(1.0741) = \$107.41.$$

With a financial calculator, simply input PV = 100, k = i = 10, and n = .75, and then press the FV button to get the answer. Present values, annuities, and problems where you must find interest rates or number of periods can all be handled with ease. Note, though, that financial calculators are mandatory for most fractional year problems — the tables just won't do.

Self-Test Question

What is the best way to deal with fractional time periods?

AMORTIZED LOANS

One of the most important applications of compound interest involves loans that are to be paid off in installments over time. Included are automobile loans, home mortgage loans, and most business debt other than very short-term loans and long-term bonds. If a loan is to be repaid in equal periodic amounts (monthly, quarterly, or annually), it is said to be an *amortized loan*.[13]

To illustrate, suppose a firm borrows $1,000 to be repaid in 3 equal payments at the end of each of the next 3 years. The lender is to receive 6 percent interest on the loan balance that is outstanding at the beginning of each period. The first task is to determine the amount the firm must repay each year, or the annual payment. To find this amount, recognize that the $1,000 represents the present value of an annuity of PMT dollars per year for 3 years, discounted at 6 percent:

$$PV \text{ of annuity} = \frac{PMT}{(1 + k)^1} + \frac{PMT}{(1 + k)^2} + \frac{PMT}{(1 + k)^3}$$

$$\$1,000 = \frac{PMT}{(1.06)} + \frac{PMT}{(1.06)^2} + \frac{PMT}{(1.06)^3}$$

$$= PMT\left[\frac{1}{1.06} + \frac{1}{(1.06)^2} + \frac{1}{(1.06)^3}\right]$$

$$= PMT(PVIFA_{6\%, 3 \text{ years}}).$$

---

[13]The word *amortized* comes from the Latin *mors,* meaning "death," so an amortized loan is one that is "killed off" over time.

Table 6-7   Loan Amortization Schedule

Year	Beginning Amount (1)	Payment (2)	Interest[a] (3)	Repayment of Principal[b] (2) − (3) = (4)	Remaining Balance (1) − (4) = (5)
1	$1,000.00	$ 374.11	$ 60.00	$ 314.11	$685.89
2	685.89	374.11	41.15	332.96	352.93
3	352.93	374.11	21.18	352.93	0.00
		$1,122.33	$122.33	$1,000.00	

[a]Interest is calculated by multiplying the loan balance at the beginning of the year by the interest rate. Therefore, interest in Year 1 is $1,000(0.06) = $60; in Year 2 it is $685.89(0.06) = $41.15; and in Year 3 it is $352.93(0.06) = $21.18.

[b]Repayment of principal is equal to the payment of $374.11 minus the interest charge for each year.

The PVIFA is found in Table 6-5 to be 2.6730, so

$$\$1,000 = \text{PMT}(2.6730).$$

Solving for PMT, we obtain

$$\text{PMT} = \$1,000/2.6730 = \$374.11.$$

Therefore, if the firm pays the lender $374.11 at the end of each of the next 3 years, then the percentage cost to the borrower, and the rate of return to the lender, will be 6 percent.

To solve the problem with a financial calculator, simply enter n = 3, i = 6, and PV = 1,000, and then press PMT. The solution, PMT = $374.11 (or − $374.11) will appear.

Each payment consists partly of interest and partly of a repayment of principal. This breakdown is given in the *amortization schedule* shown in Table 6-7. The interest component is largest in the first year, and it declines as the outstanding balance of the loan goes down. For tax purposes, a business borrower reports as a deductible cost each year the interest payments in Column 3, while the lender reports these same amounts as taxable income.

Self-Test Question

In an amortization schedule, in general terms, how do you determine the amount of the periodic payments? How do you determine the portion of the payment that goes to interest and to principal?

SUMMARY

Financial decisions often involve situations in which someone pays money at one point in time and receives money at some later time. Dollars that are paid or received at two different points in time are different, and this difference is recognized

Figure 6-7   Illustration for Chapter Summary ($k = 4\%$)

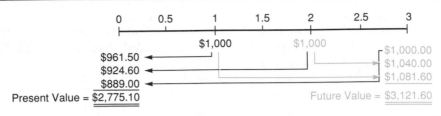

and accounted for by *discounted cash flow (DCF) analysis*. We summarize below the types of DCF analysis and the key concepts covered in this chapter, using the data shown in Figure 6-7 to illustrate the various points. Refer to the figure constantly, and find in it an example of the points covered, as you go through this section.

- *Compounding* is the process of determining the *future value* (FV) of a payment or a series of payments. The compounded amount, or future value, is equal to the beginning amount plus the interest earned.

- Future value: $FV_n = PV(1 + k)^n = PV(FVIF_{k,n})$.
  (single payment)

  Example: $961.50 compounded for 1 year at 4 percent.

  $$FV_1 = \$961.50(1.04)^1 = \$1,000.$$

- *Discounting* is the process of finding the *present value* (PV) of a future payment or a series of payments; discounting is the reciprocal of compounding.

- Present value: $PV = FV_n \left(\dfrac{1}{1 + k}\right)^n = FV_n(1 + k)^{-n} = FV_n(PVIF_{k,n})$.
  (single payment)

  Example: $1,000 discounted back for 2 years at 4 percent.

  $$PV = \$1,000\left(\dfrac{1}{1.04}\right)^2 = \$1,000(0.9246) = \$924.60.$$

- An *annuity* is defined as a series of equal, periodic payments (PMT) for a specified number of periods.

- Future value: $FVA_n = PMT(1 + k)^{n-1} + PMT(1 + k)^{n-2} + \ldots + PMT(1 + k)^0$
  (annuity)

  $$= PMT \sum_{t=1}^{n} (1 + k)^{n-t}$$

  $$= PMT\left[\dfrac{(1 + k)^n - 1}{k}\right] = PMT(FVIFA_{k,n}).$$

  Example: FVA of 3 payments of $1,000 when $k = 4\%$:

  $$FVA_3 = \$1,000(3.1216) = \$3,121.60.$$

- Present value:
  (annuity)

$$PVA_n = PMT \sum_{t=1}^{n} \left[\frac{1}{1+k} \right]^t$$

$$= PMT \left[\frac{1 - \frac{1}{(1+k)^n}}{k} \right] = PMT(PVIFA_{k,n}).$$

Example: PVA of 3 payments of $1,000 when k = 4%.

$$PVA = \$1,000(2.7751) = \$2,775.10.$$

- An annuity that has payments occurring at the *end* of each period is called an *ordinary annuity.* The formulas above are for ordinary annuities.

- If each payment occurs at the beginning of the period rather than at the end, then we have an *annuity due.* In Figure 6-7, the payments would be shown at Years 0, 1, and 2 rather than at 1, 2, and 3. The PV of each payment would be larger, because each payment would be discounted back one year less, and hence the PV of the annuity would also be larger. Similarly, the FV of the annuity due would also be larger, because each payment would be compounded for an extra year. These formulas can be used to convert the PV and FV of an ordinary annuity to an annuity due:

$$PVA(\text{annuity due}) = PVA \text{ of an ordinary annuity} \times (1+k).$$

$$FVA(\text{annuity due}) = FVA \text{ of an ordinary annuity} \times (1+k).$$

- If the payments in Figure 6-7 were unequal, we could not use the annuity formulas. To find the PV or FV of an uneven series, find the PV or FV of each individual payment and then sum them. However, if some of the payments constitute an annuity, then the annuity formula could be used to calculate the present value of that part of the payment stream.

- *Financial calculators* have built-in programs which perform all of the operations discussed in this chapter. It is essential that you buy such a calculator and learn how to use it. However, it is also essential that you understand the logical processes involved.

- If you know the payments and the PV (or FV) of a payment stream, you can *determine the interest rate.* For example, in the Figure 6-7 illustration, if you were given the information that a loan (or bond) called for 3 payments of $1,000 each, and that the loan (or bond) had a value today of PV = $2,775.10, then you could find the interest rate that caused the sum of the PVs of the payments to equal $2,775.10. Since we are dealing with an annuity, we could proceed as follows:

a. Recognize that $PVA_n = \$2,775.10 = \$1,000(PVIFA_{k,3})$.
b. Solve for $PVIFA_{k,3}$:

$$PVIFA_{k,3} = \$2,775.10/\$1,000 = 2.7751.$$

c. Look up 2.7751 in Table A-2, on the third row. It is in the 4% column, so the interest rate must be 4 percent. If the factor did not appear in the table, this would indicate that the interest rate was not a whole number. In this case, you could not use this procedure to find the exact rate. In practice, though, this is not a problem, because people use financial calculators to find interest rates.

- Thus far in the summary we have assumed that payments are made, and interest is earned, at the end of each year, or annually. However, many contracts call for more frequent payments; for example, mortgage and auto loans call for monthly payments, and most bonds pay interest semiannually. Similarly, most banks compute interest daily. When compounding occurs more frequently than once a year, this fact must be recognized. We can use the Figure 6-7 example to illustrate the procedures. First, the following formula is used to find an *effective annual rate:*

$$\text{Effective annual rate} = \left(1 + \frac{k_{Nom}}{m}\right)^m - 1.0.$$

For semiannual compounding, the effective annual rate is 4.04 percent:

$$\left(1 + \frac{0.04}{2}\right)^2 - 1.0 = (1.02)^2 - 1.0 = 1.0404 - 1.0 = 0.0404 = 4.04\%.$$

This rate could then be used (with a calculator but not with the tables) to find the PV or FV of each payment in Figure 6-7.

If the $1,000 per-year payments were actually payable as $500 each 6 months, you would simply redraw Figure 6-7 to show $500 each 6 months.

- The general equation for evaluating the future value for any number of compounding periods per year is:

$$FV_n = PV\left(1 + \frac{k_{Nom}}{m}\right)^{mn},$$

where

k_{Nom} = stated interest rate.

  m = number of compounding periods per year.

  n = number of years.

- The equation used to determine present values under continuous discounting is:

$$PV = \frac{FV_n}{e^{k,n}} = FV_n (e^{-k,n}),$$

where

e = the value 2.71828183.

- An *amortized loan* is one that is paid off in equal payments over a specified period. An *amortization schedule* shows how much of each payment constitutes interest, how much is used to reduce the principal, and the remaining balance of the loan at each point in time.

The concepts covered in this chapter will be used throughout the remainder of the book. In Chapter 7 we apply present value concepts to the process of valuing stocks and bonds; there we will see that the market prices of securities are established by determining the present values of the cash flows they are expected to provide. In later chapters, the same basic concepts are applied to corporate decisions involving both expenditures on capital assets and the types of capital that should be used to pay for assets.

Questions

6-1   Define each of the following terms:
a. PV; k; I; FV_n; n; PVA_n; FVA_n
b. $FVIF_{k,n}$; $PVIF_{k,n}$; $FVIFA_{k,n}$; $PVIFA_{k,n}$
c.   Opportunity cost
d.   Annuity; lump sum payment; uneven payment stream
e.   Ordinary (deferred) annuity; annuity due
f.   Perpetuity; consol
g.   Financial calculator versus "regular" calculator
h.   Compounding; discounting
i.   Annual, semiannual, quarterly, monthly, daily, and continuous compounding
j.   Effective annual rate; nominal (stated) interest rate; APR
k.   Amortization schedule; principal component versus interest component of a payment

6-2   Is it true that for all positive interest rates the following conditions hold: $FVIF_{k,n} \geq 1.0$; $PVIF_{k,n} \leq 1.0$; $FVIFA_{k,n} \geq$ number of periods the annuity lasts; and $PVIFA_{k,n} \leq$ number of periods the annuity lasts?

6-3   An *annuity* is defined as a series of payments of a fixed amount for a specific number of periods. Thus, $100 a year for 10 years is an annuity, but $100 in Year 1, $200 in Year 2, and $400 in Years 3 through 10 do *not* constitute an annuity. However, the second series *contains* an annuity. Is this statement true or false?

6-4   If a firm's earnings per share grew from $1 to $2 over a 10-year period, the *total growth* would be 100 percent but the *annual growth rate* would be *less than* 10 percent. Why is this so?

6-5   Would you rather have a savings account that pays 5 percent interest compounded semiannually or one that pays 5 percent interest compounded daily? Explain.

6-6   To find the present value of an uneven series of payments, you can use the $PVIF_{k,n}$ tables; the $PVIFA_{k,n}$ tables can never be of use, even if some of the payments constitute an annuity (for example, $100 each for Years 3, 4, 5, and 6), because the entire series is not an annuity. Is this statement true or false?

6-7   The present value of a perpetuity is equal to the payment on the perpetuity, PMT, divided by the discount rate, k: $PV = PMT/k$. What is the future value of a perpetuity of PMT dollars per year? (Hint: The answer is infinity, but explain why.)

Self-Test Problems (Solutions Appear in Appendix D)

ST-1 **(Future value)** Assume that it is now January 1, 1991. On January 1, 1992, you will deposit $1,000 into a savings account paying an 8 percent nominal interest rate.
  a.   If the bank compounds interest annually, how much will you have in your account on January 1, 1995?
  b.   What would your January 1, 1995, balance be if the bank used quarterly compounding rather than annual compounding?
  c.   Suppose you deposited the $1,000 in 4 payments of $250 each on January 1 of 1992, 1993, 1994, and 1995. How much would you have in your account on January 1, 1995, based on 8 percent annual compounding?
  d.   Suppose you deposited 4 equal payments in your account on January 1 of 1992, 1993, 1994, and 1995. How large would each of your payments have to be with annual compounding for you to obtain the same ending balance you calculated in Part a?

ST-2 **(Discounted cash flow analysis)** Assume that it is now January 1, 1991, and you will need $1,000 on January 1, 1995. Your bank compounds interest at an 8 percent rate annually.
  a.   How much must you deposit on January 1, 1992, to have a balance of $1,000 on January 1, 1995?
  b.   If you want to make equal payments on each January 1 from 1992 through 1995 to accumulate the $1,000, how large must each of the 4 payments be?
  c.   If your father were to offer either to make the payments calculated in Part b ($221.92) or to give you a lump sum of $750 on January 1, 1992, which would you choose?
  d.   If you deposit only $750 on January 1, 1992, what interest rate, compounded annually, would you have to earn to have the necessary $1,000 on January 1, 1995?
  e.   Suppose you can deposit only $186.29 each January 1 from 1992 through 1995, but you still need $1,000 on January 1, 1995. What interest rate, with annual compounding, must you seek out to achieve your goal?
  f.   To help you reach your $1,000 goal, your father offers to give you $400 on January 1, 1992. You will get a part-time job and make 6 additional payments of equal amounts each 6 months thereafter. If all of this money is deposited in a bank which pays 8 percent, compounded semiannually, how large must your payments be?
  g.   What is the effective annual rate being paid by the bank in Part f?
  h.   "Reinvestment rate risk" was defined in Chapter 3 to be the risk that maturing securities will have to be reinvested at a lower rate of interest than they were previously earning. Is there a reinvestment rate risk implied in the preceding analysis? If so, how might this risk be eliminated?

ST-3 **(Effective annual rates)** Bank A pays 8 percent interest, compounded quarterly, on its money market account. The managers of Bank B want its money market account to equal Bank A's effective annual rate, but interest is to be compounded on a monthly basis. What nominal, or stated, rate must Bank B set?

Problems

6-1 **(Present and future values for different periods)** Find the following values *without using tables,* and then work the problems with tables to check your answers. Then use a financial calculator as a further check on your answers. Disregard rounding errors.
  a.   An initial $300 compounded for 1 year at 8 percent.
  b.   An initial $300 compounded for 2 years at 8 percent.
  c.   The present value of $300 due in 1 year at a discount rate of 8 percent.
  d.   The present value of $300 due in 2 years at a discount rate of 8 percent.

6-2   **(Present and future values for different interest rates)** Use the tables to find the following values. Check your work with a financial calculator.
  a.   An initial $300 compounded for 10 years at 8 percent.
  b.   An initial $300 compounded for 10 years at 16 percent.
  c.   The present value of $300 due in 10 years at an 8 percent discount rate.
  d.   The present value of $1,323.42 due in 10 years at a 16 percent discount rate. Give a verbal definition of the term "present value," and illustrate it with data from this problem. As a part of your answer, explain why present values are dependent upon interest rates.

6-3   **(Time for a lump sum to double)** To the closest year, how long will it take $200 to double if it is deposited and earns the following rates? (Note: This problem cannot be solved with some financial calculators. For example, if you enter PV = -200, FV = 400, and k = i = 7 in a HP-12C, and then press the n key, you will get 11 years as the answer for Part a. The correct answer is 10.2448, which rounds to 10, but the calculator rounds up.)
  a.   7 percent.
  b.   9 percent.
  c.   12 percent.
  d.   100 percent.

6-4   **(Future value of an annuity)** Find the *future value* of the following annuities. The first payment in these annuities is made at the *end* of Year 1—that is, they are *ordinary* annuities.
  a. $200 per year for 10 years at 10 percent.
  b. $100 per year for 5 years at 5 percent.
  c. $200 per year for 5 years at 0 percent.
  d.   Now rework Parts a, b, and c assuming that payments are made at the *beginning* of each year, that is, they are *annuities due*.

6-5   **(Present value of an annuity)** Find the *present value* of the following *ordinary* annuities:
  a. $200 per year for 10 years at 10 percent.
  b. $100 per year for 5 years at 5 percent.
  c. $200 per year for 5 years at 0 percent.
  d.   Now rework Parts a, b, and c assuming that payments are made at the *beginning* of each year, that is, they are *annuities due*.

6-6   **(Uneven cash flow stream)**
  a.   Find the present (Year 0) values of the following cash flow streams. The appropriate discount rate is 10 percent.

Year	Cash Stream A	Cash Stream B
1	$100	$300
2	400	400
3	400	400
4	400	400
5	300	100

  b.   What is the value of each cash flow stream at a 0 percent discount rate?

6-7   **(Uneven cash flow stream)** Find the present value of the following cash flow stream, discounted at 5 percent: Year 1, $100; Year 2, $400; Years 3 through 20, $300.

6-8   **(Present value comparison)** Which amount is worth more at 10 percent: $1,000 in hand today or $2,000 due after 8 years?

6-9   **(Growth rates)** The Ezzell Company's 1990 sales were $6 million. Sales were $3 million 5 years earlier (in 1985).

a.   At what rate have sales been growing?

b.   Suppose someone calculated the sales growth in Part a as follows: "Sales doubled in 5 years. This represents a growth of 100 percent in 5 years, so, dividing 100 percent by 5, we find the growth rate to be 20 percent per year." Explain what is wrong with this calculation.

6-10   **(Rate of interest)**   Find the interest rates, or rates of return, on each of the following:

a.   You borrow $400 and promise to pay back $420 at the end of 1 year.

b.   You lend $400 and receive a promise of $420 at the end of 1 year.

c.   You borrow $40,000 and promise to pay back $65,156 at the end of 10 years.

d.   You borrow $4,000 and promise to make payments of $1,028.36 per year for 5 years.

6-11   **(Expected rate of return)**   The Hunt Company buys a machine for $20,000 and expects a return of $4,770.42 per year for the next 10 years. What is the expected rate of return on the machine? (Note: As we will see in Chapter 9, we are finding the internal rate of return [IRR] of the project.)

6-12   **(Expected rate of return)**   Taussig Forest Products invests $1 million to clear a tract of land and to set out some young pine trees. The trees will mature in 10 years, at which time the firm plans to sell the forest at an expected price of $3 million. What is the firm's expected rate of return?

6-13   **(Rate of interest)**   Your broker offers to sell you a note for $11,300 that will pay $2,000 per year for 10 years. If you buy the note, what rate of interest will you be earning?

6-14   **(Rate of interest)**   A mortgage company offers to lend you $50,000; the loan calls for payments of $5,477.36 per year for 20 years. What interest rate is the mortgage company charging you?

6-15   **(Required lump sum payment)**   In order to complete your last year in business school and then go through law school, you will need $8,000 per year for 4 years, starting next year (that is, you will need to withdraw the first $8,000 one year from today). Your rich uncle offers to put you through school, and he will deposit in a bank time deposit, paying 8 percent interest, a sum of money that is sufficient to provide the 4 payments of $8,000 each. His deposit will be made today.

a.   How large must the deposit be?

b.   How much will be in the account immediately after you make the first withdrawal? After the last withdrawal?

6-16   **(Repaying a loan)**   While Helen Burgess was a student at the University of North Carolina, she borrowed $5,000 in student loans at an annual interest rate of 9 percent. If Helen repays $900 a year, how long will it take her to repay the loan? (Note that some calculators automatically round up to the nearest whole period. For example, if the solution to a problem is 3.2 periods, the answer will be displayed as 4 periods. These calculators show the correct number of payments—you cannot make 3.2 payments—but fail to indicate that the final payment would be smaller than the previous payments. You should be aware of that potential discrepancy when working this problem.)

6-17   **(Reaching a financial goal)**   If you deposit $1,500 a year in an account which pays 12 percent interest compounded annually, how long will it take you to accumulate a balance of $10,000? (See the note in Question 6-16 above.)

6-18   **(Future value for various compounding periods)**   Find the amount to which $200 will grow under each of the following conditions:

a.   12 percent compounded annually for 5 years.

b.   12 percent compounded semiannually for 5 years.

    c.   12 percent compounded quarterly for 5 years.

    d.   12 percent compounded monthly for 1 year.

6-19 (Present value for various compounding periods) Find the present values of $200 due in the future under each of the following conditions:

    a.   12 percent nominal rate, semiannual compounding, discounted back 5 years.

    b.   12 percent nominal rate, quarterly compounding, discounted back 5 years.

    c.   12 percent nominal rate, monthly compounding, discounted back 1 year.

6-20 (Annuity value for various compounding periods) Find the indicated value of the following regular annuities:

    a.   FV of $200 each 6 months for 5 years at a nominal rate of 12 percent, compounded semiannually.

    b.   PV of $200 each 3 months for 5 years at a nominal rate of 12 percent, compounded quarterly.

6-21 (Effective versus nominal interest rates) The Denver National Bank pays 9 percent interest, compounded annually, on time deposits. The Boulder City Bank pays 8 percent interest, compounded quarterly.

    a.   In which bank would you prefer to deposit your money?

    b.   Could your choice of banks be influenced by the fact that you might want to withdraw your funds during the year as opposed to the end of the year? In answering this question, assume that funds must be left on deposit during the entire compounding period in order for you to receive any interest.

6-22 (Present value of a perpetuity) What is the present value of a perpetuity of $100 per year if the appropriate discount rate is 5 percent? If interest rates in general were to double, and the appropriate discount rate rose to 10 percent, what would happen to the present value of the perpetuity?

6-23 (Amortization schedule)

    a.   Set up an amortization schedule for a $20,000 loan to be repaid in equal installments at the end of each of the next 3 years. The interest rate is 10 percent.

    (Do Parts b through d only if you are using the computerized diskette.)

    b.   Set up an amortization schedule for a $40,000 loan to be repaid in equal installments at the end of each of the next 3 years. The interest rate is 10 percent.

    c.   Set up an amortization schedule for a $100,000 loan to be repaid in equal installments at the end of each of the next 3 years. The interest rate is 9 percent.

    d.   Rework Parts b and c using a 20-year amortization schedule.

6-24 (Effective rates of return) AT&T's pension fund managers recently had to choose between two investments. Their choices were (1) a bond which costs $680.58 today, pays nothing during its life, and then pays $1,000 after 5 years or (2) a bond which costs $1,000 today, pays $87.50 in interest at the end of each of the next 4 years, and pays $1,087.50 interest and principal at the end of Year 5.

    a.   Which alternative is expected to provide the higher rate of return?

    b.   Assume that the market interest rate dropped to 6 percent immediately after the bonds were purchased and that rates remained at that level for the next 5 years. (1) What would be the immediate gain or loss on the two bonds? (2) If AT&T holds the bonds until they mature, what annual rates of return would it realize on the two bond alternatives over the 5-year holding period?

6-25 (Required annuity payments) A father is planning a savings program to put his daughter through college. His daughter is now 13 years old. She plans to enroll at a university in 5 years, and it should take her 4 years to complete her education. Currently, the cost per year (for everything—food, clothing, tuition, books, transportation, and so forth) is $9,000, but a 10 percent inflation rate in these costs is forecasted. The daughter recently received $15,000 from her grandfather's estate; this money, which is invested in a bank account paying 8 percent interest compounded annually, will be used to help meet the costs of the daughter's education. The rest of the costs will be met by money the father will deposit in the savings account. He will make equal deposits to the account in each year from now until and including the year his daughter starts college. These deposits will also earn 8 percent interest.

a. If the first deposit is made today, how large must each deposit be in order to put the daughter through college?

(Do Parts b and c only if you are using the computerized diskette.)

b. How large must each deposit be if the interest rate is 6 percent?

c. How large must each deposit be if the interest rate is expected to remain at 8 percent for 2 years and then to fall to 6 percent?

6-26 **(Present value of an annuity)** Suppose that in January 1991, General Motors' engineers informed top management that they had just made a breakthrough which would permit them to produce an electric auto capable of operating at an energy cost of about 3 cents per mile versus an energy cost of about 5 cents for a comparable gasoline-powered car. If GM produces the electric car, it should be able to regain the market share it has lost to the Japanese. However, the investment required to complete development of the new batteries, to design the new car, and to tool up for production would amount to $5 billion per year for 5 years, starting immediately. Cash inflows from the $25 billion investment should amount to $3 billion per year for 15 years, or $45 billion total, starting 5 years from now, or 1 year after the final $5 billion investment payment. If the electric car project is not undertaken, GM will invest the $25 billion in investments which earn 10 percent, compounded annually.

a. Based on these cost and cash inflow estimates, should management give the go-ahead for full-scale electric car production?

(Do Part b only if you are using the computerized diskette.)

b. Suppose inflation is expected to average 5 percent per year over the 19-year forecast period. Therefore, all forecasted cash inflows and outflows will increase by 5 percent a year. Based on these cash flows, should GM produce the electric car?

Mini Case

Assume that you are nearing graduation and that you have applied for a job with a local bank. As part of the bank's evaluation process, you have been asked to take an examination which covers several financial analysis techniques. The first section of the test addresses discounted cash flow analysis. See how you would do by answering the following questions.

a. (1) Why are discounted cash flow (time value of money) concepts so important in financial analysis?

    (2) Draw time lines for a $100 lump sum cash flow at the end of Year 2, a regular annuity of $100 per year for 3 years, and an uneven cash flow stream of −$50, $100, $75, and $50 at the end of Years 0 through 3.

b. (1) What is the future value of $100 after 3 years if it is invested in an account paying 10 percent annual interest?

    (2) What is the present value of $100 to be received in 3 years if the appropriate interest rate is 10 percent?

c. What is the difference between an ordinary, or regular, annuity and an annuity due? What type of annuity is shown below? How would you change it to the other type of annuity?

d. (1) What is the future value of a 3-year ordinary annuity of $100 if the appropriate interest rate is 10 percent?

(2) What is the present value of the annuity?

(3) What would the future and present values be if the annuity were an annuity due?

e. What is the present value of the following cash flow stream? The appropriate interest rate is 10 percent.

Year	CF
0	$ 0
1	100
2	300
3	300
4	(50)

f. What annual interest rate will cause $100 to grow to $125.97 in 3 years?

g. (1) What happens if we compound more often than annually, for example, every 6 months, or semiannually?

(2) What is the difference between the stated, or nominal, rate and the effective annual rate?

(3) What is the effective annual rate for a nominal rate of 10 percent, compounded semiannually? Compounded quarterly? Compounded daily?

(4) What is the future value of $100 after 3 years under 10 percent semiannual compounding? Quarterly compounding?

h. (1) What is the value at the end of Year 3 of the following cash flow stream if the interest rate is 10 percent, compounded semiannually?

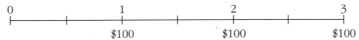

(2) What is the PV of the same stream?

(3) Is the stream an annuity?

i. (1) Construct an amortization schedule for a $1,000, 10 percent annual rate loan with 3 equal installments.

(2) What is the annual interest expense for the borrower, and the annual interest income for the lender?

Selected Additional References

For a more complete discussion of the mathematics of finance, see

Cissell, Robert, Helen Cissell, and David C. Flaspohler, *Mathematics of Finance* (Boston: Houghton Mifflin, 1978).

To learn more about using financial calculators, see the owner's handbook which came with your calculator. For example, see

Hewlett-Packard, *HP-17B Business Calculator Owner's Manual,* January 1988.

CHAPTER 7

Valuation Models

A recent *Wall Street Journal* article presented the results of its study, with Zacks Investment Research, of the major brokerage firms' performances, as measured by the average rate of return on the stocks they recommended during the preceding 12 months:

Smith Barney	26.7%
Paine Webber	23.8
Drexel Burnham	19.8
Dean Witter	18.5
Shearson	18.0
A.G. Edwards	18.0
Kidder Peabody	17.4
Prudential-Bache	12.6
Thomson McKinnon	10.7
Merrill Lynch	8.9
Average	17.4%

Yardsticks:

Dow Jones Industrial Average	20.0%
S&P 500 Index	18.1

How did the Smith Barney analysts do such a good job, and why did Merrill Lynch perform so badly? Was it luck or skill? And why did the major firms, on average, do less well than "the market" as measured by the Dow Jones or S&P indexes? Finally, what are the implications of these results for financial managers?

IN Chapter 1 we noted that financial managers should work to maximize the value of their firms. Then, in Chapters 4 and 5, we saw how investors determine the risk and hence rates of return they require on securities, and in Chapter 6 we examined discounted cash flow (DCF) analysis. Now, in this chapter, we use discounted cash flow techniques to explain how financial managers and investors go about establishing the values of stocks and bonds. The material covered in the chapter is obviously important to investors, and it is equally important to financial managers. *Indeed, since all important corporate decisions should be analyzed in terms of how they will affect the price of the firm's stock, it is essential that managers know how stock prices are determined.*

GENERAL VALUATION MODEL

Since the values of most assets stem from streams of expected cash flows, all such assets are valued in essentially the same way: (1) The cash flow stream must be estimated; this involves finding both the expected cash flow for each period and the riskiness of that cash flow. (2) The required rate of return for each cash flow is established on the basis of its riskiness and the returns available on other investments; these rates could be constant over time, or different rates might be required for each cash flow. (3) Each cash flow is discounted by its required rate of return. (4) Finally, these present values are summed to find the value of the asset. Equation 7-1 formalizes this process:[1]

$$V = \frac{CF_1}{(1 + k_1)^1} + \frac{CF_2}{(1 + k_2)^2} + \cdots + \frac{CF_t}{(1 + k_t)^t} + \cdots + \frac{CF_n}{(1 + k_n)^n}$$
$$= \sum_{t=1}^{n} \frac{CF_t}{(1 + k_t)^t}. \tag{7-1}$$

Here V is the current, or present, value of the asset; CF_t is the expected cash flow at Time t; k_t is the required rate of return for each period's cash flow; and n is the number of periods over which cash flows are expected to be generated. If the cash flow stream exhibits certain regularities, and if the required rate of return is constant, then Equation 7-1 can be reduced to a simpler form. We will examine several reduced forms in this chapter.

Note that the basic valuation model can be applied to physical assets as well as to securities. *Physical assets* are such properties as land, buildings, equipment, and even whole businesses. *Securities* are pieces of paper which represent claims against physical assets. Moreover, business securities are generally broken down into three primary classes: (1) *debt,* which is a contractual obligation calling for specific payments; (2) *preferred stock,* which is also contractual in nature but which has a claim to income and assets after the firm's debt; and (3) *common stock,* which represents

---

[1]Equation 7-1 is presented in *risk-adjusted discount rate* format. Later, in Chapter 11, we will see that assets can also be valued by the *certainty equivalent* method.

ownership and which has a residual claim to all income and assets after the claims of debtholders and preferred stockholders have been satisfied.

There are also variations within each of the primary types of business securities. For example, there is long-term and short-term debt, and some debt calls for periodic interest payments during its life and then a return of the principal in a lump sum at maturity, whereas other debt calls for amortization of the principal over the life of the debt. Some debt calls for fixed interest payments; other debt calls for variable interest payments, or even for payment in gold, silver, or oil rather than money. Some debt (and preferred stock) is convertible into common stock; some is backed by a mortgage on specific assets; and some is backed only by the firm's general credit strength.

Each of these variations calls for a somewhat different application of Equation 7-1. Indeed, since investment bankers have created an almost limitless variety of securities, with new ones being created every day, one could spend his or her career developing variations of the basic equation. However, at this point, we shall deal with models for the three basic securities — bonds, preferred stock, and common stock. Later in the book, we shall go on to physical asset valuation (capital budgeting) and also to such special cases as option securities, leases, and mergers.

Self-Test Questions

Why is valuation an important concept to financial managers?

Write out the formula for and then describe the general valuation model in words.

BOND VALUATION

Our first task in this chapter is to examine the valuation process for bonds, the principal type of long-term debt. A *bond* is a long-term promissory note issued by a business or governmental unit. For example, on January 2, 1991, the McCue Electronics Company borrowed $50 million by selling 50,000 individual bonds for $1,000 each. McCue received the $50 million, and it promised to pay the bondholders annual interest and to repay the $50 million on a specified date. The lenders were willing to give McCue $50 million, so the value of the bond issue was $50 million. But how did the investors decide that the issue was worth $50 million? As a first step in explaining how the values of this and other bonds are determined, we need to define some terms:

1. *Par value.* The *par value* is the stated face value of the bond; it is often set at $1,000, although multiples of $1,000 (for example, $5,000) are also used. The par value generally represents the amount of money the firm borrows and promises to repay at some future date.

2. *Maturity date.* Bonds generally have a specified *maturity date* on which the par value must be repaid. McCue's bonds, which were issued on January 2, 1991, will mature on January 1, 2006; thus, they had a 15-year maturity at the time they were issued. Most bonds have *original maturities* (the maturity at the time the bond is

issued) of from 10 to 40 years, but any maturity is legally permissible. Of course, the effective maturity of a bond declines each year after it has been issued. Thus, McCue's bonds had a 15-year original maturity, but in 1992 they will have a 14-year maturity, and so on.

3.   *Call provision.* Most bonds have a provision whereby the issuer may pay them off prior to maturity. This feature is known as a *call provision,* and it is discussed in detail in Chapter 16. If a bond is callable, and if interest rates in the economy decline, then the company can sell a new issue of low-interest-rate bonds and use the proceeds to retire the old high-interest-rate issue, just as a homeowner can refinance a home mortgage.

4.   *Coupon interest rate.* A bond requires the issuer to pay a specified number of dollars of interest each year (or, more typically, each six months). When this *coupon payment,* as it is called, is divided by the par value, the result is the *coupon interest rate.* For example, McCue Electronics' bonds have a $1,000 par value, and they pay $150 in interest each year. The bond's coupon interest is $150, so its coupon interest rate is $150/$1,000 = 15.0 percent. The $150 is the yearly "rent" on the $1,000 loan. This payment, which is fixed at the time the bond is issued, remains in force, by contract, during the life of the bond. Incidentally, some time ago, most bonds literally had a number of small (½-by-2-inch) dated coupons attached to them, and on the interest payment date, the owner would clip off the coupon for that date and either cash it at his or her bank or mail it to the company's paying agent, who then mailed back a check for the interest. A 30-year, semiannual bond would start with 60 coupons, whereas a 5-year annual payment bond would start with only 5 coupons. Today, however, most bonds are *registered*—no physical coupons are involved, and interest checks are mailed automatically to the registered owners of the bonds. Even so, we continue to use the terms "coupon" and "coupon interest rate," even for registered bonds.

5.   *New issues versus outstanding bonds.* As we shall see, a bond's market price is determined primarily by its coupon interest payments—the higher the coupon, other things held constant, the higher the market price of the bond. At the time a bond is issued, the coupon is generally set at a level that will cause the market price of the bond to equal its par value. If a lower coupon were set, investors simply would not be willing to pay $1,000 for the bond, while if a higher coupon were set, investors would clamor for the bond and bid its price up over $1,000. Investment bankers can judge quite precisely the coupon rate that will cause a bond to sell at its $1,000 par value.

A bond that has just been issued is known as a *new issue.* (*The Wall Street Journal* classifies a bond as a new issue for about one month after it has first been issued.) Once the bond has been on the market for a while, it is classified as an *outstanding bond,* also called a *seasoned issue.* Newly issued bonds generally sell very close to par, but the prices of outstanding bonds vary widely from par. Coupon interest payments are constant, so when economic conditions change, a bond with a $150 coupon that sold at par when it was issued will sell for more or less than $1,000 thereafter.

The Basic Bond Valuation Model

As we noted previously, bonds call for the payment of a specified amount of interest for a stated number of years, and for the repayment of the par value on the bond's maturity date. Thus, a bond represents an annuity plus a lump sum, and its value is found as the present value of this payment stream.

The following equation is used to find a bond's value:[2]

$$\text{Value} = V = \sum_{t=1}^{n} I\left(\frac{1}{1 + k_d}\right)^t + M\left(\frac{1}{1 + k_d}\right)^n$$

$$= I(\text{PVIFA}_{k_d,n}) + M(\text{PVIF}_{k_d,n}).$$

(7-2)

Here

I = dollars of interest paid each year = coupon interest rate × par value.

M = par value, or maturity value, which is often $1,000.

k_d = appropriate rate of interest (required rate of return) on the bond.[3]

n = number of years until the bond matures; n declines each year after the bond is issued, so a bond that had a maturity of 30 years when it was issued (original maturity = 30 years) becomes a 29-year bond a year later, then a 28-year bond, and so on.

We can use Equation 7-2 to find the value of McCue's bonds when they were issued. Simply substitute $150 for I, $1,000 for M, and the values of PVIFA and PVIF at 15 percent, 15 periods, as found in Tables A-2 and A-1 at the end of the book:

$$V = \$150(5.8474) + \$1,000(0.1229)$$

$$= \$877.11 + \$122.90$$

$$= \$1,000.01 \approx \$1,000 \text{ when } k_d = 15\%.$$

Figure 7-1 shows the same result in a time line graph.

You can also find the value of these bonds with most financial calculators. Enter n = 15, PMT = 150, FV = 1,000, and k_d − i = 15, and then press the PV key. The answer, $1,000 (or −$1,000), will appear.

---

[2]Actually, since most bonds pay interest semiannually, not annually, it is necessary for us to modify our valuation equation slightly. The modification is discussed later in the chapter. Also, we should note that some bonds issued in recent years either pay no interest during their lives (zero coupon bonds) or else pay very low coupon rates. Such bonds are sold at a discount below par, hence they are called *original issue discount bonds*. The "interest" earned on a zero coupon bond comes at the end, when the company pays off at par ($1,000) a bond which was purchased for, say, $321.97. The discount of $1,000 − $321.97 = $678.03 substitutes for interest. Original issue discount bonds are discussed at greater length in Chapter 16.

[3]The appropriate interest rate on debt securities was discussed in Chapter 3. The bond's riskiness, liquidity, and years to maturity, as well as supply and demand conditions in the capital markets, all have an influence.

Figure 7-1   Time Line for McCue Electronics Bonds

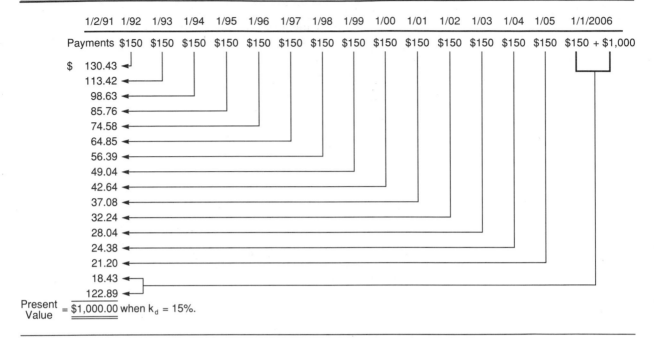

If k_d remained constant at 15 percent, what would the value of the bond be 1 year after it was issued? We can find this value using Equation 7-2, but now the term to maturity is only 14 years—that is, n = 14. We see that V remains at $1,000:

$$V = \$150(5.7245) + \$1,000(0.1413)$$

$$= \$999.98 \approx \$1,000.$$

With a financial calculator, just replace n = 15 with n = 14, press the PV button, and you will get the same answer. The value of the bond will remain at $1,000 as long as the appropriate interest rate for it remains constant at 15 percent.[4]

Now suppose interest rates in the economy fell after the McCue bonds were issued, and, as a result, k_d *decreased* from 15 to 10 percent. Both the coupon interest

---

[4]The bond prices quoted by brokers are calculated as described. However, if you bought a bond between interest payment dates, you would have to pay the basic price plus accrued interest. Thus, if you purchased a McCue Electronics bond 6 months after it was issued, your broker would send you an invoice stating that you must pay $1,000 as the basic price of the bond plus $75 interest, representing one-half the annual interest of $150. The seller of the bond would receive $1,075. If you bought the bond the day before its interest payment date, you would pay $1,000 + (364/365)($150) = $1,149.59. Of course, you would receive an interest payment of $150 at the end of the next day. Throughout the chapter we assume that the bond is being evaluated immediately after an interest payment date. The better financial calculators have a built-in calendar which permits the calculation of exact values between interest payment dates.

payments and the maturity value remain constant, but now 10 percent values for PVIF and PVIFA would have to be used in Equation 7-2. The value of the bond at the end of the first year would be $1,368.31:

$$V = \$150(\text{PVIFA}_{10\%,14 \text{ years}}) + \$1,000(\text{PVIF}_{10\%,14 \text{ years}})$$

$$= \$150(7.3667) + \$1,000(0.2633)$$

$$= \$1,105.01 + \$263.30 = \$1,368.31.$$

Thus, the bond would sell above par, or at a *premium*. (The calculator solution is V = $1,368.33.)

The arithmetic of the bond value increase should be clear, but what is the logic behind it? The fact that k_d has fallen to 10 percent means that if you had $1,000 to invest, you could buy new bonds like McCue's (every day some 10 to 12 companies sell new bonds), except that these new bonds would pay $100 of interest each year rather than $150. Naturally, you would prefer $150 to $100, so you would be willing to pay more than $1,000 for McCue's bonds to obtain its higher coupons. All investors would recognize these facts, and, as a result, the McCue bonds would be bid up in price to $1,368.31, at which point they would provide the same rate of return to a potential investor as the new bonds—10 percent.

Assuming that interest rates remain constant at 10 percent for the next 14 years, what would happen to the value of a McCue bond? It would fall gradually from $1,368.31 at present to $1,000 at maturity, when McCue Electronics will redeem each bond for $1,000. This point can be illustrated by calculating the value of the bond 1 year later, when it has 13 years remaining to maturity:

$$V = \$150(\text{PVIFA}_{10\%,13 \text{ years}}) + \$1,000(\text{PVIF}_{10\%,13 \text{ years}})$$

$$= \$150(7.1034) + \$1,000(0.2897) = \$1,355.21.$$

$$(\text{Calculator solution} = \$1,355.17.)$$

Thus, the value of the bond will have fallen from $1,368.31 to $1,355.21, or by $13.10. If you were to calculate the value of the bond at other future dates, the price would continue to fall as the maturity date approached.

Notice that if you purchased the bond at a price of $1,368.31 and then sold it 1 year later with k_d still at 10 percent, you would have a capital loss of $13.10, or a total return of $150.00 − $13.10 = $136.90. Your percentage rate of return would consist of an *interest yield* (also called a *current yield*) plus a *capital gains yield,* calculated as follows:

$$\text{Interest, or current, yield} = \quad \$150/\$1,368.31 = \quad 0.1096 = \quad 10.96\%$$

$$\text{Capital gains yield} = -\$13.10/\$1,368.31 = \quad -0.0096 = \quad \underline{-0.96\%}$$

$$\text{Total rate of return, or yield} = \$136.90/\$1,368.31 = \quad 0.1001 \approx \quad \underline{10.00\%}$$

Had interest rates risen from 15 to 20 percent during the first year after issue rather than fallen, the value of McCue's bonds would have declined to $769.49:

$$V = \$150(\text{PVIFA}_{20\%,14\text{ years}}) + \$1,000(\text{PVIF}_{20\%,14\text{ years}})$$

$$= \$150(4.6106) + \$1,000(0.0779)$$

$$= \$691.59 + \$77.90 = \$769.49.$$

$$(\text{Calculator solution} = \$769.47.)$$

In this case, the bond would sell at a *discount* of $230.51 below its par value:

$$\text{Discount} = \text{Price} - \text{Par value} = \$769.49 - \$1,000.00$$

$$= -\$230.51.$$

The total expected future yield on the bond would again consist of a current yield and a capital gains yield, but now the capital gains yield would be *positive*. The total yield would be 20 percent. To see this, let's calculate the price of the bond with 13 years left to maturity, assuming that interest rates remain at 20 percent. The price of the bond is calculated as follows:

$$V = \$150(\text{PVIFA}_{20\%,13\text{ years}}) + \$1,000(\text{PVIF}_{20\%,13\text{ years}})$$

$$= \$150(4.5327) + \$1,000(0.0935)$$

$$= \$679.91 + \$93.50 = \$773.41.$$

$$(\text{Calculator solution} = \$773.37.)$$

Notice that the capital gain for the year is the difference between the bond's value in Year 13 and the bond's value in Year 14, or $773.41 - $769.49 = $3.92. The interest yield, capital gains yield, and total yield are calculated as follows:

$$\text{Interest, or current yield} = \quad \$150/\$769.49 = 0.1949 = 19.49\%$$

$$\text{Capital gains yield} = \quad \$3.92/\$769.49 = 0.0051 = \underline{0.51\%}$$

$$\text{Total rate of return, or yield} = \$153.92/\$769.49 = 0.2000 = \underline{\underline{20.00\%}}$$

The discount or premium on a bond may also be calculated as follows:

$$\begin{array}{c}\text{Discount} \\ \text{or premium}\end{array} = \left[\begin{array}{c}\text{Interest payment} \\ \text{on the old bond}\end{array} - \begin{array}{c}\text{Interest payment} \\ \text{on the new bond}\end{array}\right](\text{PVIFA}_{k_d,n}),$$

where n = years to maturity on the old bond and k_d = current rate of interest on a new bond. For example, if interest rates had risen to 20 percent 1 year after the McCue bonds were issued, the discount on them would have been calculated as follows:

$$\text{Discount} = (\$150 - \$200)(4.6106) = -\$230.53.$$

(The minus sign indicates discount.) This value agrees, except for rounding, with the $-$230.51 value calculated previously. From these calculations, we see that the discount is equal to the present value of the interest payments you sacrifice when you buy a low-coupon old bond rather than a high-coupon new bond. The longer the bond has left to maturity, the greater the sacrifice, hence the greater the discount.

Figure 7-2 Time Path of the Value of a 15% Coupon, $1,000 Par Value Bond When Interest Rates Are 10%, 15%, and 20%

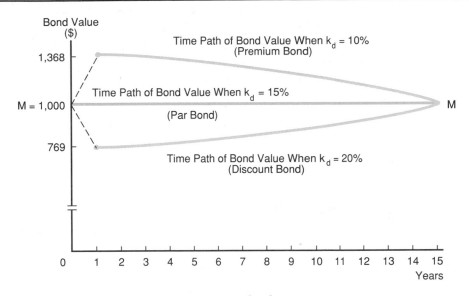

	Bond Value at:		
Year	$k_d = 10\%$	$k_d = 15\%$	$k_d = 20\%$
0	—	$1,000	—
1	$1,368.31	1,000	$ 769.49
.	.	.	.
.	.	.	.
.	.	.	.
15	1,000	1,000	1,000

Note: The curves for 10% and 20% have a slight bow.

Figure 7-2 graphs the values of the bond over time, assuming that interest rates in the economy (1) remain constant at 15 percent, (2) fall to 10 percent and then remain constant at that level, or (3) rise to 20 percent and remain constant at that level. Of course, if interest rates do *not* remain constant, then the price of the bond will fluctuate. However, regardless of what future interest rates do, the bond's price will approach $1,000 as it nears the maturity date (barring bankruptcy, in which case the bond's value might drop to zero).

Figure 7-2 illustrates the following key points:

1. Whenever the going rate of interest, k_d, is equal to the coupon rate, a bond will sell at its par value. Normally, the coupon rate is set at the going interest rate when a bond is issued, so it sells at par initially.

2.   Interest rates change over time, but the coupon rate remains fixed after the bond has been issued. Whenever the going rate of interest is *greater than* the coupon rate, a bond will sell *below* its par value. Such a bond is called a *discount bond.*

3.   Whenever the going rate of interest is *less than* the coupon rate, a bond will sell *above* its par value. Such a bond is called a *premium bond.*

4.   Thus, an *increase* in interest rates will cause the price of an outstanding bond to *fall,* whereas a *decrease* in rates will cause the price to *rise.*

5.   The market value of a bond will always approach its par value as its maturity date approaches, provided the firm does not go bankrupt.

These points are very important, for they show that bondholders may suffer capital losses or make capital gains, depending on whether interest rates rise or fall. And, as we saw in Chapter 3, interest rates do indeed change over time.

Finding the Interest Rate on a Bond: Yield to Maturity

Suppose you were offered a 14-year, 15 percent coupon, $1,000 par value bond at a price of $1,368.31. What approximate rate of interest would you earn on your investment if you bought the bond and held it to maturity? This rate is called the bond's *yield to maturity (YTM),* and it is the interest rate discussed by bond traders when they talk about rates of return.[5] To find the yield to maturity, you could solve Equation 7-2 for k_d:

$$V = \$1,368.31 = \frac{\$150}{(1 + k_d)^1} + \ldots + \frac{\$150}{(1 + k_d)^{14}} + \frac{\$1,000}{(1 + k_d)^{14}}$$

$$= \$150(\text{PVIFA}_{k_d,14}) + \$1,000(\text{PVIF}_{k_d,14}).$$

You can substitute values for PVIFA and PVIF until you find a pair that "works" and forces this equality:

$$\$1,368.31 = \$150(\text{PVIFA}_{k_d,14}) + \$1,000(\text{PVIF}_{k_d,14}).$$

What would be a good interest rate to use as a starting point? First, you know that because the bond is selling at a premium over its par value ($1,368.31 versus $1,000), the bond's yield to maturity must be *below* its 15 percent coupon rate. Therefore, you might try a rate of 12 percent. Substituting factors for 12 percent, you obtain

$$\$150(6.6282) + \$1,000(0.2046) = \$1,198.83 \neq \$1,368.31.$$

The calculated bond value, $1,198.83, is *below* the actual market price, so the YTM is *not* 12 percent. To raise the calculated value, you must *lower* the interest rate

---

[5]The yield to maturity is also the expected rate of return on a bond if (1) the probability of default is zero, and (2) interest rates are expected to remain at their current levels until maturity.

used in the process, because lower interest rates mean higher bond prices. Inserting interest factors for 10 percent, you obtain

$$V = \$150(7.3667) + \$1,000(0.2633)$$

$$= \$1,105.01 + \$263.30 = \$1,368.31.$$

This calculated value is equal to the market price of the bond; thus, 10 percent is the bond's yield to maturity: k_d = YTM = 10.0%.[6]

As you might guess, by far the easiest way to find a bond's YTM is with a financial calculator. In this example, enter n = 14, PMT = 150, FV = 1,000, and PV = 1,368.31 (−1,368.31 on some calculators). Now press the i button. The calculator will blink for several seconds, and then the answer, 10 percent, will appear.

The yield to maturity is identical to the total rate of return discussed in the preceding section. The YTM for a bond that sells at par consists entirely of an interest yield, but if the bond sells at a price other than its par value, the YTM consists of the interest yield plus a positive or negative capital gains yield. Note also that a bond's yield to maturity changes whenever interest rates in the economy change, and this occurs almost daily.

Yield to Call

If you purchased a bond that was callable, and the company called it, you would not have the option of holding it until it matured, so the yield to maturity would not be applicable. For example, if McCue Electronics's 15 percent coupon bonds were callable, and if interest rates fell from 15 percent to 10 percent, the company could call in the 15 percent bonds, replace them with 10 percent bonds, and save $150 − $100 = $50 interest per bond per year. This would be beneficial to the company, but not to its bondholders.

If current interest rates are well below an outstanding bond's coupon rate, then a callable bond is likely to be called, and investors should estimate the expected

---

[6]A few years ago, bond traders all had specialized tables called *bond tables* that gave yields on bonds of different maturities selling at different premiums and discounts. Because calculators are so much more efficient (and accurate), bond tables are rarely used any more.

R. J. Rodriguez recently developed a formula that can be used to find the *approximate* YTM on a bond:

$$\text{Approximate } k_d = \text{Approximate YTM} = \frac{I + (M - V)/n}{(M + 2V)/3}.$$

The numerator gives the average total return (coupon plus capital gain or loss) over the life of the bond, while the denominator is the average price of the bond. In our example, I = $150, M = $1,000, V = $1,368.31, and n = 14, so

$$\text{Approximate } k_d = \frac{\$150 + (\$1,000 - \$1,368.31)/14}{(\$1,000 + \$2,736.62)/3} = 0.0993 = 9.93\%.$$

The exact value is 10 percent, so Rodriguez's formula provides a close approximation.

rate of return on the bond as the *yield to call (YTC)* rather than as the yield to maturity. To calculate the YTC, solve this equation for k_d:

$$\text{Price of bond} = \sum_{t=1}^{N} \frac{I}{(1 + k_d)^t} + \frac{\text{Call price}}{(1 + k_d)^N}.$$

Here N is the number of years until the company can call the bond; call price is the price the company must pay in order to call the bond (it is often set equal to the par value plus one year's interest); and k_d is the YTC. In the balance of the chapter, we assume that bonds are not callable unless otherwise noted, but some of the end-of-chapter problems deal with yield to call.

To illustrate, if the $1,368.31 premium bond with $150 coupon payments could be called in 4 years at a call price of $1,150, its YTC would be only 7.39 percent:

$$\$1,368.31 = \sum_{t=1}^{4} \frac{\$150}{(1 + k_d)^t} + \frac{\$1,150}{(1 + k_d)^4}$$

$$= \$150 \, (\text{PVIFA}_{k_d,4}) + \$1,150 \, (\text{PVIF}_{k_d,4})$$

$$k_d = \text{YTC} = 7.39\%.$$

Call provisions can have a profound effect on a bond's value. Consider the following example. Several years ago, the Duval County (Florida) Housing Authority sold some 30-year zero coupon bonds (zeros) to yield 11.5 percent tax-exempt interest. The price of the bonds was $38.17—an investor would pay $38.17, and 30 years later he or she would get back $1,000. The money the housing authority received was made available to low-income home buyers; these home buyers were able to obtain mortgage money for 11.5 percent versus about 14.5 percent, which was the going conventional mortgage loan rate at the time.

A provision in the bond agreement stated that if the Housing Authority received cash from home buyers who were paying off their loans, then that cash could be used to call and pay off the zeros, with the call price being set at $38.17(1.115)^n$, with n being the number of years since the bonds were issued. However, because the rate home buyers were paying was so far below the going mortgage rate, few investors thought homeowners would want to pay off their mortgages, hence the call provision in the zeros was ignored.

Several years later, interest rates dropped sharply, and the rate on tax-exempt bonds fell from 11.5 to 8 percent. The Duval zeros' price shot up from $38.17 to $89.55, at which point they yielded 9 percent:

$$\$89.55 = \frac{\$1,000}{(1 + k_d)^{28}},$$

which solves to $k_d = 9\%$. (On a financial calculator, enter n = 28, PV = 89.55 or -89.55, and FV = 1,000, and then press the k = i key to obtain the yield, 8.999 ≈ 9 percent.) The 9 percent tax-exempt interest looked high in comparison to the 8 percent return on new municipal bonds with the same degree of default risk, so some University of Florida professors bought heavily. That turned out to be a big mistake. Because mortgage rates had dropped to 10 percent, homebuyers whose mortgages were at 11.5 percent started refunding (that is, paying off their old mortgages and replacing them with lower-interest ones). Duval County began receiving cash, so it started calling the bonds at a price of $38.17(1.115)^2 = $47.45. Thus, people who had bought a number of the bonds for $89.55 a few months earlier ended up with $47.45 per bond. They learned an expensive lesson about the implications of call provisions!

Bond Values with Semiannual Compounding

Although some bonds pay interest annually, most actually pay interest semiannually. To evaluate semiannual payment bonds, we must modify the bond valuation model (Equation 7-2) as follows:

1.   Divide the annual coupon interest payment by 2 to determine the amount of interest paid each 6 months.

2.   Multiply the years to maturity, n, by 2 to determine the number of semiannual periods.

3.   Divide the annual interest rate, k_d, by 2 to determine the semiannual interest rate.

By making these changes, we obtain the following equation for finding the value of a bond that pays interest semiannually:

$$V = \sum_{t=1}^{2n} \frac{I}{2} \left(\frac{1}{1 + k_d/2} \right)^t + M\left(\frac{1}{1 + k_d/2} \right)^{2n}$$

$$= \frac{I}{2}(PVIFA_{k_d/2,2n}) + M(PVIF_{k_d/2,2n}).$$

(7-2a)

To illustrate, assume now that McCue Electronics's bonds pay $75 interest each 6 months rather than $150 at the end of each year. Thus, each interest payment is only half as large, but there are twice as many of them. When the going rate of interest is 10 percent, the value of this 15-year bond is found as follows:

$$V = \$75(PVIFA_{5\%,30 \text{ periods}}) + \$1,000(PVIF_{5\%,30 \text{ periods}})$$

$$= \$75(15.3725) + \$1,000(0.2314)$$

$$= \$1,152.94 + \$231.40 = \$1,384.34.$$

With a financial calculator, you would enter n = 30, k = i = 5, PMT = 75, FV = 1,000, and then press the PV key to obtain the bond's value, $1,384.31. The value with semiannual interest payments is slightly larger than $1,380.32, the value when interest is paid annually. This higher value occurs because interest payments are received somewhat faster under semiannual compounding.[7]

---

[7]Note that we assumed a change in the effective annual interest rate, from 10 percent to 10.25 percent when we discounted the semiannual cash flows at a 5 percent rate:

$$(1.05)^2 - 1 = 1.1025 - 1.0 = 0.1025 = 10.25\%.$$

Most bonds pay interest semiannually, but the rates quoted are on a nominal basis, so effective annual rates are higher than quoted rates.

Students sometimes want to discount the maturity value at 10 percent over 15 years rather than at 5 percent over 30 periods of 6 months each. This is incorrect. Logically, all cash flows in a given contract must be discounted on the same basis, semiannually in this instance. For consistency, bond traders *must* apply semiannual compounding to the maturity value, and they do.

Interest Rate Risk on a Bond

As we saw in Chapter 3, interest rates go up and down over time, and as rates change, the values of outstanding bonds also fluctuate. Suppose you bought some 15 percent McCue bonds at a price of $1,000, and interest rates subsequently rose to 20 percent. As we saw before, the price of the bonds would fall to $769.49, so you would have a loss of $230.51 per bond.[8] Interest rates can and do rise, and rising rates cause a loss of value for bondholders. Thus, people or firms who invest in bonds are exposed to risk from changing interest rates, or *interest rate risk.* (This risk is also called *price risk.*)

One's exposure to interest rate risk is higher on bonds with long maturities than on those maturing in the near future. This point can be demonstrated by showing how the value of a 1-year bond with a 15 percent coupon fluctuates with changes in k_d and then comparing these changes with those on a 14-year bond as calculated previously. The 1-year bond's values at different interest rates are shown here:

Value at $k_d = 10\%$:

$$V = \$150(\text{PVIFA}_{10\%,1 \text{ year}}) + \$1,000(\text{PVIF}_{10\%,1 \text{ year}})$$

$$= \$150(0.9091) + \$1,000(0.9091)$$

$$= \$136.37 + \$909.10 = \$1,045.47.$$

Value at $k_d = 15\%$:

$$V = \$150(0.8696) + \$1,000(0.8696)$$

$$= \$130.44 + \$869.60 = \$1,000.04 \approx \$1,000.$$

Value at $k_d = 20\%$:

$$V = \$150(0.8333) + \$1,000(0.8333)$$

$$= \$125.00 + \$833.30 = \$958.30.$$

You could obtain the first value with a financial calculator by entering n = 1, PMT = 150, FV = 1,000, and i = 10, and then pressing PV to get $1,045.45. With everything still in your calculator, enter i = 15 to override the old i = 10, and press PV to find the bond's value at $k_d = i = 15$; it is $1,000. Then enter i = 20 and press the PV key to find the last bond value, $958.33.

---

[8]You would have an *accounting* (and tax) loss only if you sold the bond; if you held it to maturity, you would not have such a loss. However, even if you did not sell, you would still have suffered a *real economic loss in an opportunity cost sense,* because you would have lost the opportunity to invest at 20 percent and would be stuck with a 15 percent bond in a 20 percent market. In finance we regard "paper losses" as being just as bad as realized accounting losses.

Figure 7-3   Value of Long- and Short-Term 15%
Annual Coupon Rate Bonds at Different
Market Interest Rates

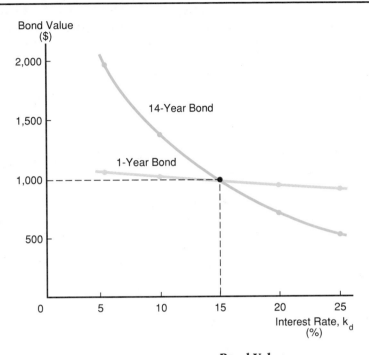

| | Bond Value | |
Current Market Interest Rate, k_d	1-Year Bond	14-Year Bond
5%	$1,095.24	$1,989.86
10	1,045.45	1,368.33
15	1,000.00	1,000.00
20	958.33	769.47
25	920.00	617.59

Note: Bond values were calculated using a financial calculator.

The values of the 1-year and 14-year bonds at several different market interest rates are summarized and plotted in Figure 7-3. Notice how much more sensitive the price of the long-term bond is to changes in interest rates. At a 15 percent interest rate, both the long- and the short-term bonds are valued at $1,000. When rates rise to 20 percent, the long-term bond falls to $769.47, but the short-term bond falls only to $958.33.

For bonds with similar coupons, this differential sensitivity to changes in interest rates always holds true — the longer the maturity of the bond, the greater its price changes in response to a given change in interest rates. Thus, even if the risk of default on two bonds is exactly the same, the one with the longer maturity is typically exposed to more risk from a rise in interest rates.

The logical explanation for this difference in interest rate risk is simple. Suppose you bought a 14-year bond that yielded 15 percent, or $150 a year. Now suppose interest rates on comparable-risk bonds rose to 20 percent. You would be stuck with only $150 of interest for the next 14 years. On the other hand, had you bought a 1-year bond, you would have a low return for only 1 year. At the end of the year, you would get your $1,000 back, and you could then reinvest it and receive 20 percent, or $200 per year, for the next 13 years. Thus, interest rate risk reflects the length of time one is committed to a given investment.[9]

Although a 1-year bond has less interest rate risk than a 14-year bond, the 1-year bond exposes the buyer to more *reinvestment rate risk*. Suppose you bought a 1-year bond that yielded 15 percent, and then interest rates on comparable-risk bonds fell to 10 percent. After 1 year, when you got your $1,000 back, you would have to invest it at only 10 percent, so you would lose $150 − $100 = $50 in annual interest. Had you bought the 14-year bond, you would have continued to receive $150 in annual interest payments even if rates fell. Of course, if you intended to spend the $1,000 after 1 year, investing in a 1-year bond would guarantee (ignoring bankruptcy) that you would get your $1,000 back, plus interest, after 1 year. The 14-year bond investment, on the other hand, if sold after 1 year, would return less than $1,000 if interest rates had risen.[10]

Bond Prices in Recent Years

We know from Chapter 3 that interest rates fluctuate, and we have just seen that the prices of outstanding bonds rise and fall inversely with changes in interest rates. Figure 7-4 shows what has happened to the price of a typical bond, Alabama Power's 8½ percent, 30-year bond which matures in 2001. When this bond was issued in 1971 it was worth $1,000, but at the 1981 interest rate peak, it sold for only $530. However, the ensuing drop in interest rates caused the price of the bond to rise, and by 1988 it was back over par, selling at a slight premium. In early 1989, interest rates rose again, and the bond's price fell back to $910, but by 1990 the price had risen to about $924. The graph also shows that if interest rates remain at the 1990 level, the price of the bond will gradually rise, and it will sell for $1,000 (plus accrued interest) just before it matures in 2001.

---

[9]If a 10-year bond were plotted in Figure 7-3, its curve would lie between those of the 14-year bond and the 1-year bond. The curve of a 1-month bond would be almost horizontal, but a perpetuity would have a very steep slope. Also note that, more precisely, a bond's interest rate risk is a function of its *duration*, which can be thought of as the "average date" on which the holder will receive cash flows, including both interest and principal repayment. A zero coupon bond, which has no interest payments, has a duration equal to its maturity. For a coupon bond, the duration is less than the bond's maturity. See any of the investments textbooks listed at the end of the chapter for more information on duration.

[10]A broader definition of reinvestment rate risk is "the risk that cash flows (interest plus principal) from a bond will have to be reinvested at a rate less than the YTM." Thus, even bonds with maturities that match investors' investment horizons have reinvestment rate risk associated with the coupon payments. A zero coupon bond, however, has no reinvestment rate risk if the investment horizon matches the maturity of the bond. This point is covered in detail in investments courses.

Figure 7-4 Alabama Power 8½ Percent, 30-Year Bond:
Market Value as Interest Rates Change

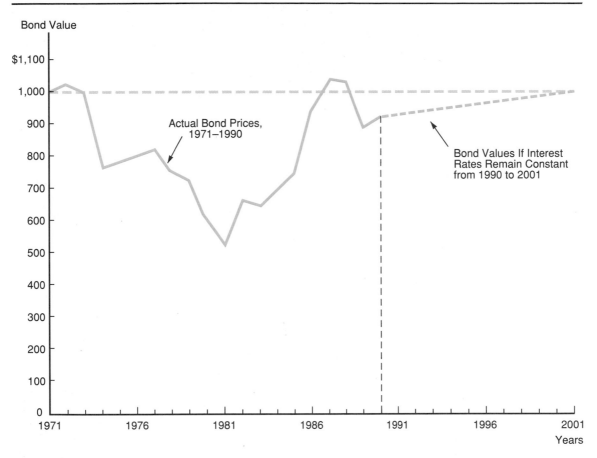

Note: The line from 1990 to 2001 appears linear, but it actually has a slight curve.

Bond Markets

Corporate bonds are traded primarily in the over-the-counter market. Most bonds are owned by and traded among the large financial institutions (for example, life insurance companies, mutual funds, and pension funds, all of which deal in very large blocks of securities), and it is relatively easy for the over-the-counter bond dealers to arrange the transfer of large blocks of bonds among the relatively few holders of the bonds. It would be much more difficult to conduct similar operations in the stock market among the literally millions of large and small stockholders, so most stock trades occur on the exchanges.

Information on bond trades in the over-the-counter market is not published, but a representative group of bonds is listed and traded on the bond division of the

Figure 7-5   NYSE Bond Market Transactions, March 14, 1990

CORPORATION BONDS
Volume, $41,200,000

Bonds	Cur Yld	Vol	Close	Net Chg.
AlaP 8½s01	9.2	12	92⅜	...
AlaP 7⅞s02	9.2	5	86 −	3
AlaP 8⅞s03	9.5	7	93⅞ −	⅜
AlaP 10⅞05	10.5	5	103⅝ −	⅛
AlaP 8¾07	9.4	57	92⅞ +	½
AlaP 9½08	9.9	10	96	...
AlaP 12⅝10	11.9	12	105¾ +	¾

Source: *The Wall Street Journal,* March 15, 1990.

NYSE. Figure 7-5 gives a section of the bond market page of *The Wall Street Journal* on trading for March 14, 1990. A total of 656 issues were traded on that date, but we show only the bonds of Alabama Power. Note that Alabama Power had 7 different bonds traded on March 14; the company actually had more than 20 bond issues outstanding, but many of them did not trade on that date.

The Alabama Power and other bonds can have various denominations, but most have a par value of $1,000—this is how much per bond the company borrowed and how much it must someday repay. However, since other denominations are possible, for example, $5,000, for trading and reporting purposes bonds are quoted as percentages of par. Looking at the first bond listed, which is the one we plotted in Figure 7-4, we see that there is an 8½ just after the company's name; this indicates that the bond is of the series which pays 8½ percent interest, or 0.0850($1,000) = $85.00 of interest per year. The 8½ percent is the bond's *coupon rate.* The 01 which comes next indicates that this bond matures and must be repaid in the year 2001; it is not shown in the figure, but this bond was issued in 1971, so it had a 30-year original maturity. The 9.2 in the second column is the bond's *current yield,* which is defined as the annual interest payment divided by the closing price of the bond: Current yield = $85/$923.75 = 9.2016%, rounded to 9.2 percent. The 12 in the third column indicates that 12 of these bonds were traded on March 14, 1990. Since the price shown in the fourth column is expressed as a percentage of par, the bond closed at 92.375 percent, which translates to $923.75, the same as the previous day's close.

Companies generally set their coupon rates at levels which reflect the "going rate of interest" on the day a bond is issued. If the rates were set lower, investors simply would not buy the bonds at the $1,000 par value, so the company could not borrow the money it needed. Thus, bonds generally sell at their par values on the day they are issued, but their prices fluctuate thereafter as interest rates change.

As you can see from Figure 7-5, Alabama Power's 8½ percent bonds maturing in 2001 were recently selling for $923.75, while the company's 10⅞ percent bonds maturing in 2005 were selling for $1,036.25. The difference in coupon rates reflects the fact that the going rate of interest in 1971, when the 8½'s were sold, was lower than in 1975, when the 10⅞'s were sold. The current (March 1990) interest rate is between 8½ and 10⅞ percent, so the 8½'s now sell at a discount while the 10⅞'s sell at a premium.

All of the bonds traded on a given day are listed in the newspaper (and hence in Figure 7-5) in alphabetical order by company and in the order of the dates on which they were originally issued, beginning with the earliest bond issued.

Self-Test Questions

What is meant by the terms "new issue" and "seasoned issue"?

Explain, verbally, the following equation:

$$V = I(PVIFA_{k_d,n}) + M(PVIF_{k_d,n}).$$

Explain what happens to the price of a bond if (1) interest rates rise above the bond's coupon rate or (2) interest rates fall below the bond's coupon rate.

How does the calculation of a bond's price differ between a bond that is callable and one that is not?

How is the general bond valuation formula changed to deal with bonds that have semiannual coupons versus annual coupons?

PREFERRED STOCK VALUATION

Preferred stock is a *hybrid* — it is similar to bonds in some respects and to common stock in other respects. Preferred dividends are similar to interest payments on bonds in that they generally are fixed in amount and generally must be paid before common stock dividends can be paid. However, like common dividends, preferred dividends can be omitted without bankrupting the firm. In addition, some preferred stock is similar to common stock in that it has no maturity date and is not callable; hence, such issues are perpetuities.

Most preferred stocks entitle their owners to regular fixed dividend payments. If the payments go on forever, the issue is a perpetuity whose value, V_p, is found as follows:

$$V_p = \frac{D_p}{k_p}. \tag{7-3}$$

V_p is the value of the preferred stock, D_p is the preferred dividend, and k_p is the required rate of return. McCue Electronics has perpetual preferred stock outstanding which pays a dividend of \$8.125 per year. If the required rate of return on this preferred stock is 10 percent, its value is \$81.25, found by solving Equation 7-3 as follows:

$$V_p = \frac{\$8.125}{0.10} = \$81.25.$$

If we know the current price of a perpetual preferred stock and its dividend, we can solve for the current rate being earned, as follows:

$$k_p = \frac{D_p}{V_p}. \tag{7-3a}$$

Most preferred stocks issued in recent years have *sinking funds,* in which a fixed percentage of the issue is retired each year until the entire issue is redeemed, or else have mandatory call provisions. Such issues are not perpetual, and thus must be valued using bond valuation techniques. Also, note that most preferred stocks pay quarterly dividends, so the effective annual rate of return is higher than the rate calculated by using Equation 7-3a.

Self-Test Questions

In what ways is preferred stock similar to bonds, and in what respects is it similar to common stock?

How are perpetual preferred stocks valued?

How are nonperpetual preferred stocks valued?

COMMON STOCK VALUATION

Common stock represents the ownership of a corporation, but to the typical investor, a share of common stock is simply a piece of paper distinguished by two features:

1. It entitles its owner to dividends, but only if the company has earnings out of which dividends can be paid and only if management chooses to pay dividends rather than to retain all the earnings. Whereas a bond contains a *promise* to pay interest, common stock provides no such promise (in a legal sense) to pay dividends—if you own a stock you may *expect* a dividend, but your expectations may not in fact be met. To illustrate, Long Island Lighting Company (Lilco) had paid dividends on its common stock for more than 50 years, and people expected these dividends to continue. However, when the company encountered severe problems a few years ago, it stopped paying dividends. Note, though, that Lilco continued to pay interest on its bonds; if it had not, then it would have been in default and declared bankrupt, and the bondholders would have taken over the company.

2. Stock can be sold at some future date, hopefully at a price greater than the purchase price. If the stock is actually sold at a price above its purchase price, the investor will receive a *capital gain.* Generally, at the time people buy common stocks, they expect to receive capital gains; otherwise, they would not buy the stocks. However, after the fact one can end up with capital losses rather than capital gains. For example, the stock price of Lomas Financial dropped from 12⅝ to 1 during 1989, so the *expected* capital gain on that stock turned out to be an *actual* 92 percent capital loss.

Definitions of Terms Used in the Stock Valuation Models

Common stocks provide an expected future cash flow stream, and a stock's value is found in the same manner as the values of other financial assets—namely, as the present value of that stream. The expected cash flows consist of two elements:

(1) the dividends expected in each year and (2) the price investors expect to receive when they sell the stock. The expected final stock price includes the return of the original investment plus a capital gain.

We saw in Chapter 1 that managers seek to maximize the values of their firms' stocks. Through their actions, managers affect both the stream of income to investors and the riskiness of that stream. Therefore, managers need to know how alternative actions will affect stock prices, so at this point we develop some models to help show how the value of a share of stock is determined. We begin by defining the following terms:

D_t = dividend the stockholder *expects* to receive at the end of Year t. D_0 is the most recent dividend, which has already been paid; D_1 is the first dividend expected, and it will be paid at the end of 1 year; D_2 is the dividend expected at the end of 2 years; and so forth. D_1 represents the first cash flow a new purchaser of the stock will receive. Note that D_0, the dividend which has just been paid, is known with certainty. However, all future dividends are expected values, so the estimate of D_t may differ among investors.[11]

P_0 = actual *market price* of the stock today.

$\hat{P}_t$ = (pronounced "P hat t") expected price of the stock at the end of each Year t. $\hat{P}_0$ is the *intrinsic,* or *theoretical, value* of the stock today; $\hat{P}_1$ is the price expected at the end of 1 year; and so on. Note that $\hat{P}_0$ is the intrinsic value of the stock today based on a particular investor's estimate of the stock's expected dividend stream and the riskiness of that stream. Hence, whereas P_0 is fixed and is identical for all investors, $\hat{P}_0$ could differ among investors depending on how optimistic they are regarding the company. The caret, or "hat," is used to indicate that $\hat{P}_t$ is an estimated value. $\hat{P}_0$, the investor's estimate of the intrinsic value today, could be above or below P_0, the current stock price, but an investor would buy the stock only if his or her estimate of $\hat{P}_0$ were equal to or greater than P_0.

    Since there are many investors in the market, there can be many values for $\hat{P}_0$. However, we can think of a "marginal" investor whose actions actually determine the market price. For this marginal investor, P_0 must equal $\hat{P}_0$; otherwise, a disequilibrium would exist, and buying and selling in the market would change P_0 until $P_0 = \hat{P}_0$ for the marginal investor.

g = expected *growth rate* in dividends. (If we assume that dividends are expected to grow at a constant rate, g is also equal to the expected rate of growth in the stock's price.) Different investors may use different g's to evaluate a firm's stock, but the market price, P_0, is set on the basis of the g estimated by the marginal investor.

k_s = minimum acceptable, or *required, rate of return* on the stock, considering both its riskiness and the returns available on other investments. Again, a stock's market price is set on the basis of the k_s estimated by the marginal investor. The determinants of k_s were discussed in detail in Chapters 4 and 5.

---

[11]Stocks generally pay dividends quarterly, so theoretically we should evaluate them on a quarterly basis. However, in stock valuation, most analysts work on an annual basis because the data generally are not precise enough to warrant the refinement of a quarterly model. For additional information on the quarterly model, see Charles M. Linke and J. Kenton Zumwalt, "Estimation Biases in Discounted Cash Flow Analysis of Equity Capital Cost in Rate Regulation," *Financial Management,* Autumn 1984, 15–21.

$\hat{k}_s$ = *expected rate of return* which an investor who buys the stock actually expects to receive. $\hat{k}_s$ (pronounced "k hat s") could be above or below k_s, but one would buy the stock only if $\hat{k}_s$ were equal to or greater than k_s. The expected rate of return is equal to the expected dividend yield plus the expected capital gains yield.

$\bar{k}_s$ = *actual,* or *realized, rate of return,* pronounced "k bar s." You may *expect* to obtain a return of $\hat{k}_s$ = 15 percent if you buy Exxon stock today, but if the market goes down, you may end up next year with an after the fact realized return that is much lower, perhaps even negative.

D_1/P_0 = expected *dividend yield* on the stock during the coming year. If the stock is expected to pay a dividend of \$1 during the next 12 months, and if its current price is \$10, then the expected dividend yield is \$1/\$10 = 0.10 = 10%.

$\dfrac{\hat{P}_1 - P_0}{P_0}$ = expected *capital gains yield* on the stock during the coming year. If the stock sells for \$10 today, and if it is expected to rise to \$10.50 at the end of 1 year, then the expected capital gain is $\hat{P}_1 - P_0$ = \$10.50 − \$10.00 = \$0.50, and the expected capital gains yield is \$0.50/\$10 = 0.05 = 5%.

Expected Dividends as the Basis for Stock Values

In our discussion of bonds, we found the value of a bond as the present value of interest payments over the life of the bond plus the present value of the bond's maturity (or par) value:

$$V = \frac{I}{(1 + k_d)^1} + \frac{I}{(1 + k_d)^2} + \dots + \frac{I}{(1 + k_d)^n} + \frac{M}{(1 + k_d)^n}.$$

Stock prices are likewise determined as the present value of a stream of cash flows, and the basic stock valuation equation is similar to the bond valuation equation. What are the cash flows that corporations provide to their stockholders? First, think of yourself as an investor who buys a stock with the intention of holding it (in your family) forever. In this case, all that you (and your heirs) will receive is a stream of dividends, and the value of the stock today is calculated as the present value of an infinite stream of dividends:

$$\text{Value of stock} = \hat{P}_0 = \text{PV of expected future dividends}$$

$$= \frac{D_1}{(1 + k_s)^1} + \frac{D_2}{(1 + k_s)^2} + \dots + \frac{D_\infty}{(1 + k_s)^\infty}$$

$$= \sum_{t=1}^{\infty} \frac{D_t}{(1 + k_s)^t}.$$

(7-4)

What about the more typical case, where you expect to hold the stock for a finite period and then sell it—what will be the value of $\hat{P}_0$ in this case? *The value of the stock is again determined by Equation 7-4.* To see this, recognize that for any individual investor, expected cash flows consist of expected dividends plus the expected sale price of the stock. However, the sale price the current investor receives will depend on the dividends some future investor expects. Therefore, for all present and future investors in total, expected cash flows must be based on expected future dividends. To put it another way, unless a firm is liquidated or sold to another concern, the cash flows it provides to its stockholders consist only of a stream of dividends; therefore, the value of a share of its stock must be established as the present value of that expected dividend stream.

The general validity of Equation 7-4 can also be confirmed by asking the following question: Suppose I buy a stock and expect to hold it for 1 year. I will receive dividends during the year plus the value $\hat{P}_1$ when I sell out at the end of the year, but what will determine the value of $\hat{P}_1$? The answer is that it will be determined as the present value of the dividends during Year 2 plus the stock price at the end of that year, which in turn will be determined as the present value of another set of future dividends and an even more distant stock price. This process can be continued ad infinitum, and the ultimate result is Equation 7-4.[12]

Equation 7-4 is a generalized stock valuation model in the sense that the time pattern of D_t can be anything: D_t can be rising, falling, or constant, or it can even fluctuate randomly, and Equation 7-4 will still hold. Often, however, the projected stream of dividends follows a systematic pattern, in which case we can develop a simplified version of the stock valuation model expressed in Equation 7-4. In the following sections we consider the cases of zero growth, constant growth, and non-constant growth.

Stock Values with Zero Growth

Suppose dividends are not expected to grow at all, but to remain constant. Here we have a *zero growth stock,* for which the dividends expected in future years are equal to some constant amount—that is, $D_1 = D_2 = D_3$ and so on. Therefore, we can drop the subscripts on D and rewrite Equation 7-4 as follows:

$$\hat{P}_0 = \frac{D}{(1 + k_s)^1} + \frac{D}{(1 + k_s)^2} + \ldots + \frac{D}{(1 + k_s)^n} + \ldots + \frac{D}{(1 + k_s)^\infty}. \quad \text{(7-4a)}$$

As we noted in Chapter 6 in connection with the British consol bond, and also in our discussion of preferred stocks, a security that is expected to pay a constant amount each year forever is a perpetuity. *Therefore, a zero growth stock is a perpetuity.*

Although a zero growth stock is expected to provide a constant stream of dividends into the indefinite future, each dividend has a smaller present value than the preceding one, and as n gets very large, the present value of the individual future

---

[12]We should note that investors periodically lose sight of the long-run nature of stocks as investments and forget that in order to sell a stock at a profit, one must find a buyer who will pay the higher price. If you analyzed a stock's value in accordance with Equation 7-4, concluded that the stock's market price exceeded a reasonable value, and then bought the stock anyway, then you would be following the "bigger fool" theory of investment—you think that you may be a fool to buy the stock at its excessive price, but you also think that when you get ready to sell it, you can find someone who is an even bigger fool. The bigger fool theory was widely followed in the summer of 1987, just before the stock market lost about one-quarter of its value.

Figure 7-6   Present Values of Dividends of a
Zero Growth Stock (Perpetuity)

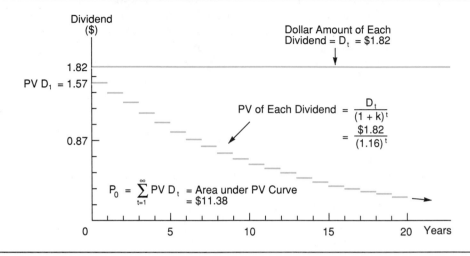

dividends approaches zero. To illustrate, suppose $D = \$1.82$ and $k_s = 16\%$. We can rewrite Equation 7-4a as follows:

$$\hat{P}_0 = \frac{\$1.82}{(1.16)^1} + \frac{\$1.82}{(1.16)^2} + \frac{\$1.82}{(1.16)^3} + \ldots + \frac{\$1.82}{(1.16)^{50}} + \ldots + \frac{\$1.82}{(1.16)^{100}} + \ldots$$

$$= \$1.57 + \$1.35 + \$1.17 + \ldots + \$0.001 + \ldots + \$0.000001 + \ldots.$$

We can also show the perpetuity in graph form, as in Figure 7-6. The horizontal line shows the constant dividend stream, $D_t = \$1.82$. The descending step function curve shows the present value of each future dividend. If we extended the analysis on out to infinity and then summed the present values of all the future dividends, the sum would be equal to the value of the stock.

As we saw in Chapter 6, the value of any perpetuity is simply the cash flow divided by the discount rate, so the value of a zero growth stock reduces to this formula:

$$\text{Value of a zero growth stock: } \hat{P}_0 = \frac{D}{k_s}. \qquad \textbf{(7-5)}$$

Therefore, in our example the value of this zero growth stock is $11.38:

$$\hat{P}_0 = \frac{\$1.82}{0.16} = \$11.38.$$

If you extended Figure 7-6 on out forever and then added up the present value of each individual dividend, you would end up with the intrinsic value of the stock,

$11.38.[13] The actual market value of the stock, P_0, could be greater than, less than, or equal to $11.38, depending on other investors' perceptions of the stock's dividend pattern and riskiness.

We could transpose the $\hat{P}_0$ and the k_s in Equation 7-5 and solve for k_s to produce Equation 7-5a:

$$\text{Expected return on a zero growth stock: } \hat{k}_s = \frac{D}{P_0}. \qquad \textbf{(7-5a)}$$

We could then look up the price of the stock and the latest dividend, P_0 and D, in the newspaper, and the value D/P_0 would be the rate of return we could expect to earn if we bought the stock. Since we are dealing with an *expected rate of return,* we put a "hat" on the k value. Thus, if we bought the stock at a price of $11.38 and expected to receive a constant dividend of $1.82, our expected rate of return would be

$$\hat{k}_s = \frac{\$1.82}{\$11.38} = 0.16 = 16\%.$$

Normal, or Constant, Growth

Although the zero growth model is applicable to some companies, the earnings and dividends of most companies are expected to increase each year. Expected growth rates vary from company to company, but dividend growth in general is expected to continue in the foreseeable future at about the same rate as that of the nominal gross national product (real GNP plus inflation). On this basis, it is expected that the dividend of an average, or "normal," company will grow at a rate of 6 to 8 percent a year. Thus, if a *normal,* or *constant, growth* company's last dividend, which has already been paid, was D_0, its dividend in any future Year t may be forecasted as $D_t = D_0(1 + g)^t$, where g is the constant expected rate of growth. For example, if McCue Electronics just paid a dividend of $1.82 (that is, D_0 = $1.82), and if investors expect a 10 percent growth rate, the estimated dividend 1 year hence will be D_1 = $1.82(1.10) = $2.00; D_2 will be $2.20; and the estimated dividend 5 years hence will be

$$D_5 = D_0(1 + g)^5 = \$1.82(1.10)^5 = \$2.93.$$

Using this method for estimating future dividends, we can determine the current stock value, $\hat{P}_0$, using Equation 7-4 as set forth previously—in other words, we can find the expected future cash flow stream (the dividends), calculate the present value of each dividend payment, and then sum these present values to find the value of the stock. Thus, the intrinsic value of the stock is equal to the present value of its expected future dividends.

---

[13]If you think that having a stock pay dividends forever is unrealistic, then think of it as lasting only for 50 years. Here you would have an annuity of $1.82 per year for 50 years. The PV of a 50-year annuity would be $1.82(6.2463) = $11.37, which would differ by only a penny from that of the perpetuity. Thus, the dividends from Year 51 to infinity contribute almost nothing to the value of the stock.

When g is constant, Equation 7-4 may be simplified as follows:[14]

$$\text{Value of a constant growth stock: } \hat{P}_0 = \frac{D_0(1 + g)}{k_s - g} = \frac{D_1}{k_s - g}. \qquad \textbf{(7-6)}$$

Inserting values into Equation 7-6, we find the value of our illustrative constant growth stock to be $33.33:

$$\hat{P}_0 = \frac{\$1.82(1.10)}{0.16 - 0.10} = \frac{\$2.00}{0.06} = \$33.33.$$

The *constant growth model* set forth in Equation 7-6 is often called the Gordon Model, after Myron J. Gordon, who did much to develop and popularize it.

Note that Equation 7-6 is sufficiently general to encompass the zero growth case described earlier: If growth is zero, this is simply a special case of constant growth, and Equation 7-6 is equal to Equation 7-5. Note also that a necessary condition for the derivation of Equation 7-6 is that k_s is greater than g. If the equation is used where k_s is not greater than g, the results will be meaningless.

The concept underlying the valuation process for a constant growth stock is graphed in Figure 7-7. Dividends are growing at the rate $g = 10\%$, but because $k_s > g$, the present value of each future dividend is declining. For example, the dividend in Year 1 is $D_1 = D_0(1 + g)^1 = \$1.82(1.10) = \$2.00$. However, the present value of this dividend, discounted at 16 percent, is $PV(D_1) = \$2.00/(1.16)^1 = \$1.72$.

---

[14]The proof of Equation 7-6 is as follows:
Rewrite Equation 7-4 as

$$\hat{P}_0 = \frac{D_0(1 + g)^1}{(1 + k_s)^1} + \frac{D_0(1 + g)^2}{(1 + k_s)^2} + \frac{D_0(1 + g)^3}{(1 + k_s)^3} + \cdots + \frac{D_0(1 + g)^n}{(1 + k_s)^n}$$

$$= D_0 \left[\frac{(1 + g)^1}{(1 + k_s)^1} + \frac{(1 + g)^2}{(1 + k_s)^2} + \frac{(1 + g)^3}{(1 + k_s)^3} + \cdots + \frac{(1 + g)^n}{(1 + k_s)^n} \right]. \qquad \textbf{(7-4b)}$$

Multiply both sides of Equation 7-4b by $(1 + k_s)/(1 + g)$:

$$\left[\frac{(1 + k_s)}{(1 + g)} \right] \hat{P}_0 = D_0 \left[1 + \frac{(1 + g)^1}{(1 + k_s)^1} + \frac{(1 + g)^2}{(1 + k_s)^2} + \cdots + \frac{(1 + g)^{n-1}}{(1 + k_s)^{n-1}} \right]. \qquad \textbf{(7-4c)}$$

Subtract Equation 7-4b from Equation 7-4c to obtain

$$\left[\frac{(1 + k_s)}{(1 + g)} - 1 \right] \hat{P}_0 = D_0 \left[1 - \frac{(1 + g)^n}{(1 + k_s)^n} \right]$$

$$\left[\frac{(1 + k_s) - (1 + g)}{(1 + g)} \right] \hat{P}_0 = D_0 \left[1 - \frac{(1 + g)^n}{(1 + k_s)^n} \right].$$

Assuming $k_s > g$, as $n \to \infty$ the term in brackets on the right-hand side of the equation $\to 1.0$, leaving

$$\left[\frac{(1 + k_s) - (1 + g)}{(1 + g)} \right] \hat{P}_0 = D_0,$$

which simplifies to Equation 7-6,

$$(k_s - g)\hat{P}_0 = D_0(1 + g) = D_1$$

$$\hat{P}_0 = \frac{D_1}{k_s - g}. \qquad \textbf{(7-6)}$$

Figure 7-7 Present Values of Dividends of a Constant Growth
Stock: $D_0 = \$1.82$, $g = 10\%$, $k_s = 16\%$

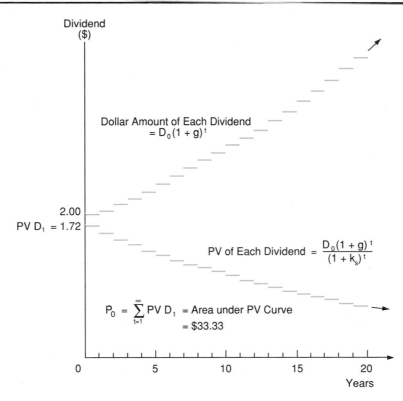

The dividend expected in Year 2 grows to $\$2.00(1.10) = \$2.20$, but the present value of this dividend falls to $\$1.64$. Continuing, $D_3 = \$2.42$ and $PV(D_3) = \$1.55$, and so on. Thus, the expected dividends are growing, but the *present value* of each successive dividend is declining.

If we summed the present values of each future dividend, this summation would be the value of the stock, $\hat{P}_0$. When g is a constant, this summation is equal to $D_1/(k_s - g)$, as shown in Equation 7-6. Therefore, if we extended the lower step function curve in Figure 7-7 on out to infinity and added up the present values of each future dividend, the summation would be identical to the value given by Equation 7-6, $\$33.33$.

Growth in dividends occurs primarily as a result of growth in *earnings per share (EPS)*. Earnings growth, in turn, results from a number of factors, including (1) inflation, (2) the amount of earnings the company reinvests, and (3) the rate of return the company earns on its equity (ROE). Regarding inflation, if output (in units) is stable, and if both sales prices and input costs rise at the inflation rate, then EPS also will grow at the inflation rate. In addition, EPS will normally grow as a result of the reinvestment, or plowback, of earnings. If the firm's earnings are not all paid out as dividends (that is, if some fraction of earnings is retained), the dollars of investment behind each share will rise over time, which should lead to growth in earnings and dividends.

Expected Rate of Return on a Constant Growth Stock

We can solve Equation 7-6 for k_s, again using the hat to denote that we are dealing with an expected rate of return:[15]

$$\begin{matrix} \text{Expected rate} \\ \text{of return} \end{matrix} = \begin{matrix} \text{Expected} \\ \text{dividend} \\ \text{yield} \end{matrix} + \begin{matrix} \text{Expected growth} \\ \text{rate (capital} \\ \text{gains yield)} \end{matrix}$$

$$\hat{k}_s \quad = \quad \frac{D_1}{P_0} \quad + \quad g. \qquad\qquad \textbf{(7-7)}$$

Thus, if you buy a stock for a price $P_0 = \$33.33$, and if you expect the stock to pay a dividend $D_1 = \$2.00$ one year from now and to grow at a constant rate $g = 10\%$ in the future, then your expected rate of return will be 16 percent:

$$\hat{k}_s = \frac{\$2.00}{\$33.33} + 10\% = 6\% + 10\% = 16\%.$$

In this form, we see that $\hat{k}_s$ is the *expected total return* and that it consists of an *expected dividend yield,* $D_1/P_0 = 6\%$, plus an *expected growth rate or capital gains yield,* $g = 10\%$.

Suppose this analysis had been conducted on January 1, 1991, so $P_0 = \$33.33$ is the January 1, 1991, stock price and $D_1 = \$2.00$ is the dividend expected at the end of 1991. What is the expected stock price at the end of 1991 (or the beginning of 1992)? We would again apply Equation 7-6, but this time we would use the 1992 dividend, $D_2 = D_1(1 + g) = \$2.00(1.10) = \$2.20$:

$$\hat{P}_{1/1/1992} = \frac{D_{1992}}{k_s - g} = \frac{\$2.20}{0.16 - 0.10} = \$36.67.$$

Now notice that $P_1 = \$36.67$ is 10 percent greater than P_0, the $33.33 price on January 1, 1991:

$$\$33.33(1.10) \approx \$36.67.$$

Thus, we would expect to make a capital gain of $36.67 - \$33.33 = \$3.34$ during the year, and a capital gains yield of 10 percent:

$$\text{Capital gains yield} = \frac{\text{Capital gain}}{\text{Beginning price}} = \frac{\$3.34}{\$33.33} = 0.10 = 10\%.$$

---

[15]The k_s value of Equation 7-6 is a *required* rate of return, but when we transform to obtain Equation 7-7, we are finding an *expected* rate of return. Obviously, the transformation requires that $k_s = \hat{k}_s$. This equality holds if the stock market is in equilibrium, a condition that will be discussed later in the chapter.

We could extend the analysis on out, and in each future year the expected capital gains yield would always equal g, the expected dividend growth rate.

Continuing, the dividend yield in 1992 could be estimated as follows:

$$\text{Dividend yield}_{1992} = \frac{D_{1992}}{\hat{P}_{1/1/92}} = \frac{\$2.20}{\$36.67} = 0.06 = 6\%.$$

The dividend yield for 1993 could also be calculated, and again it would be 6 percent. Thus, *for a constant growth stock,* the following conditions must hold:

1.   The dividend is expected to grow forever at a constant rate g.

2.   The stock price is expected to grow at this same rate.

3.   The expected dividend yield is a constant.

4.   The expected capital gains yield is also a constant, and it is equal to g.

5.   The expected total rate of return, $\hat{k}_s$, is equal to the expected dividend yield plus the expected growth rate: $\hat{k}_s$ = dividend yield + g.

The term *expected* should be clarified—it means expected in a probabilistic sense. That is, the expected growth rate is the expected value of some probability distribution of growth rates. Thus, if we say the growth rate is expected to remain constant at 10 percent, we mean that the best estimate in any future year is 10 percent, not that we literally expect the growth rate to be exactly equal to 10 percent in each future year. In this sense, the constant growth assumption is a reasonable one for many large, mature companies.

Nonconstant Growth

Firms typically go through *life cycles.* During the early part of their lives, their growth is much faster than that of the economy as a whole; then they match the economy's growth; and finally their growth is slower than that of the economy.[16] Automobile manufacturers in the 1920s and computer software firms such as Lotus in the 1980s are examples of firms in the early part of the cycle; these firms are called *supernormal growth* firms. Figure 7-8 illustrates supernormal growth and also compares it with normal growth, zero growth, and negative growth.[17]

---

[16]The concept of life cycles could be broadened to *product cycle,* which would include both small, start-up companies and large companies like IBM, which periodically introduce new products that typically give sales and earnings a boost. We should also mention *business cycles,* which alternately depress and boost sales and profits. The growth rate just after a major new product has been introduced, or just after a firm emerges from the depths of a recession, is likely to be much higher than the "long-run average growth rate," which is the proper number for a constant growth analysis.

[17]A negative growth rate indicates a declining company. A mining company whose profits are falling because of a declining ore body is an example. Someone buying such a company would expect its earnings, and consequently its dividends and stock price, to decline each year, and this would lead to capital losses rather than capital gains. Obviously, a declining company's stock price will be low, and its dividend yield must be high enough to offset the expected capital loss and still produce a competitive total return. Students sometimes argue that they would not be willing to buy a stock whose price was expected to decline. However, if the annual dividends are large enough to *more than offset* the falling stock price, the stock still could provide a good return.

Figure 7-8   Illustrative Dividend Growth Rates

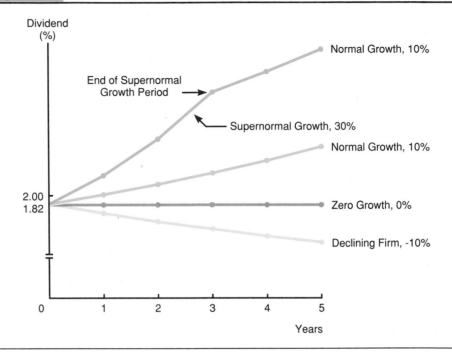

In the figure, the dividends of the supernormal growth firm are expected to grow at a 30 percent rate for 3 years, after which the growth rate is expected to fall to 10 percent, the assumed average for the economy. The value of this firm, like any other, is the present value of its expected future dividends as determined by Equation 7-4. In the case in which D_t is growing at a constant rate, we simplified Equation 7-4 to $\hat{P}_0 = D_1/(k_s - g)$. In the supernormal case, however, the expected growth rate is not a constant—it declines at the end of the period of supernormal growth. To find the value of such a stock, or any nonconstant growth stock when the growth rate will eventually stabilize, we proceed in three steps:

1.   Find the PV of the dividends during the period of nonconstant growth.

2.   Find the price of the stock at the end of the nonconstant growth period, at which point it has become a constant growth stock, and discount this price back to the present.

3.   Add these two components to find the intrinsic value of the stock, $\hat{P}_0$.

To illustrate the process for valuing nonconstant growth stocks, suppose the following facts exist for Solar Laser Technology (SLT):

k_s = stockholders' required rate of return = 16%.

N = years of supernormal growth = 3.

g_s = rate of growth in both earnings and dividends during the supernormal growth period
= 30%. (Note: The growth rate during the supernormal growth period could vary from
year to year. Also, there could be several different supernormal growth periods; e.g.,
30% for 3 years, then 20% for 3 years, and then a constant 10%.)

g_n = rate of constant growth after the supernormal period = 10%.

D_0 = last dividend the company paid = $1.82.

The valuation process is diagrammed in Figure 7-9, and it is explained in the steps
set forth below the time line. The value of SLT's stock is calculated to be $53.86.

Comparing Companies with Different Expected Growth Rates

It is useful to summarize our discussion of stock valuation models by comparing
companies with the four growth situations that were graphed in Figure 7-8. There
we had a zero growth company, one with a constant 10 percent expected growth
rate, one whose earnings are expected to decline at the rate of 10 percent a year,
and one whose growth rate is supernormal.

We can use the valuation equations developed previously to determine the stock
prices, dividend yields, capital gains yields, total expected returns, and price/earn-
ings (P/E) ratios for the four companies; these are shown in Table 7-1.[18] We assume
that each firm had earnings per share (EPS) of $3.41 during the preceding reporting
period (that is, EPS_0 = $3.41) and that each paid out 53.3 percent of its reported
earnings as dividends. Therefore, dividends per share last year, D_0, were $1.82 for
each company, but the values of D_1 differ among the firms.

The value of each stock equals its market price, and the expected and required
return is 16 percent on each; thus, $\hat{k}_s$ = k_s = 16%. For the declining firm, this
return consists of a high current dividend yield, 26 percent, combined with a capital
loss amounting to 10 percent a year. For the zero growth firm there is neither a
capital gain nor a capital loss expectation, so its 16 percent return has to be obtained
entirely from the dividend yield. The normal growth firm provides a 6 percent current dividend yield plus a 10 percent capital gains expectation. Finally, the supernormal growth firm has a low current dividend yield but a high capital gains expectation.

[18]Price/earnings (P/E) ratios relate a stock's price to its earnings per share (EPS). The higher the P/E ratio,
the more investors are willing to pay for a dollar of the firm's current earnings. Other things held
constant, investors will pay more per dollar of current earnings for a rapidly growing firm than for a slow
growth company; hence, rapid growth companies generally have high P/E ratios. This ratio is discussed in
more detail in Chapter 22. The relationships among the P/E ratios, shown in the last column of Table 7-1,
are similar to what one would intuitively expect—the higher the expected growth rate (all other things
the same), the higher the P/E ratio.

Differences in P/E ratios among firms can also arise from differences in the required rates of return,
k_s, which investors use in capitalizing the future dividend streams. If one company has a higher P/E ratio
than another, this could be caused by a higher g, a lower k_s, or a combination of these two factors.

Figure 7-9   Process for Finding the Value of a
Supernormal Growth Stock: Solar Laser Technology

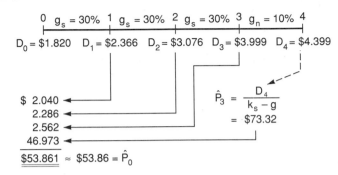

Step 1.   Find the dividends paid (D_t) at the end of Years 1 to 3, and then find the present values of these dividends (PV D_t), using the following procedure:

D_0	×	$(1 + g)^t$	=	D_t	×	$\left(\dfrac{1}{1 + k}\right)^t$	=	PV D_t
D_1: $1.82	×	1.3000	=	$2.366;	×	0.8621	=	$2.040
D_2: 1.82	×	1.6900	=	3.076;	×	0.7432	=	2.286
D_3: 1.82	×	2.1970	=	3.999;	×	0.6407	=	2.562
						Sum of PVs of supernormal period dividends	=	$6.888

Step 2.   The stock price at the end of Year 3 is the PV of the dividends expected from Year 4 to infinity. To find this, we first (a) find the expected value of the stock at the end of Year 3 and then (b) find the present value of the Year 3 stock price:

a.
$$\hat{P}_3 = \frac{D_4}{k_s - g_n} = \frac{D_0(1 + g_s)^3(1 + g_n)}{k_s - g_n} = \frac{D_3(1 + g_n)}{0.16 - 0.10}$$

$$= \frac{\$3.999(1.10)}{0.06} = \frac{\$4.399}{0.06} = \$73.32.$$

b.
$$PV \, \hat{P}_3 = \$73.32\left(\frac{1}{1.16}\right)^3 = \$73.32(0.6407) = \$46.97.$$

Step 3.   Find $\hat{P}_0$, the value of the stock today:

$$\hat{P}_0 = \$6.89 + \$46.97 = \$53.86.$$

What is expected to happen to the prices of the four illustrative firms' stocks over time? Three of the four cases are straightforward: The zero growth firm's price is expected to be constant; the declining firm is expected to have a falling stock price; and the constant growth firm's stock price is expected to grow at a constant rate, 10 percent. We do not prove it here, but the supernormal firm's stock price

Table 7-1 Stock Prices, Dividend Yields, and Price/Earnings Ratios for 16 Percent Returns under Different Growth Assumptions

	Price	Current Dividend Yield (D_1/P_0)	Growth: Capital Gains Yield in Year 1 $[(\hat{P}_1 - P_0)/P_0]$	Total Expected Return	P/E Ratio[a]
Declining constant growth (−10%)	$\hat{P}_0 = \dfrac{D_1}{k_s - g} = \dfrac{\$1.64}{0.16 - (-0.10)} = \$ 6.31$	26%	(10.0%)	16%	1.85
Zero growth (0%)	$\hat{P}_0 = \dfrac{D}{k_s} = \dfrac{\$1.82}{0.16} = 11.38$	16	0.0	16	3.34
Normal constant growth (10%)	$\hat{P}_0 = \dfrac{D_1}{k_s - g} = \dfrac{\$2.00}{0.16 - 0.10} = 33.33$	6	10.0	16	9.77
Supernormal growth	$\hat{P}_0 = $ (See Steps 1–3, Figure 7-9) $= 53.86$	4.4	11.6[b]	16	15.79

[a]It was assumed at the beginning of this example that each company is earning $3.41 initially. This $3.41, divided into the various prices, gives the indicated P/E ratios.

As the supernormal growth rate declines toward the normal rate (or as the time when this decline will occur becomes more imminent), the high P/E ratio must approach the normal P/E ratio—that is, the P/E of 15.79 will decline year by year and equal 9.77, that of the normal growth company, in the third year.

Note that D_1 differs for each firm. It is calculated as follows:

$$D_1 = EPS_0(1 + g)(\text{fraction of earnings paid out}) = \$3.41(1 + g)(0.533).$$

For the declining firm, $D_1 = \$3.41(0.90)(0.533) = \$1.64.$

[b]With $k = 16\%$ and $D_1/P_0 = 4.4\%$, the capital gains yield must be $16.0\% - 4.4\% = 11.6\%$. We could calculate the expected price of the stock at the end of the year, $\hat{P}_1$, using the supernormal growth procedures, to confirm that the capital gains yield in Year 1 is indeed 11.6 percent, but this is not necessary.

growth rate starts at 11.6 percent per year, then declines to 10 percent as the super-normal growth period ends.

Self-Test Questions

Explain the following statement: "Whereas a bond contains a promise to pay interest, common stock provides an expectation but no promise of dividends."

What are the two elements of a stock's expected returns?

How does the general stock valuation model (Equation 7-4) differ from the general bond valuation model (Equation 7-2)?

Write out and explain the valuation model for a zero growth stock.

Write out and explain the valuation model for a constant growth stock.

How does one calculate the capital gains yield and the dividend yield of a stock?

STOCK MARKET EQUILIBRIUM

Recall from Chapter 5 that the required return on Stock X, k_X, can be found using the Security Market Line (SML) equation as it was developed in our discussion of the Capital Asset Pricing Model (CAPM):

$$k_X = k_{RF} + (k_M - k_{RF}) b_X.$$

If the risk-free rate of return is 8 percent, the market risk premium is 4 percentage points, and Stock X has a beta of 2, all as estimated by the marginal investor, then he or she will require a return of 16 percent on Stock X:

$$k_X = 8\% + (12\% - 8\%) 2.0 = 16\%.$$

This 16 percent required return is shown as a point on the SML in Figure 7-10.

The marginal investor will want to buy Stock X if the expected rate of return is more than 16 percent, will want to sell it if the expected rate of return is less than 16 percent, and will be indifferent, hence will hold but not buy or sell, if the expected rate of return is exactly 16 percent. Now suppose the investor's port-folio contains Stock X, and he or she analyzes the stock's prospects and concludes that its earnings, dividends, and price can be expected to grow at a constant rate of 5 percent per year. The last dividend was $D_0 = \$2.8571$, so the next expected dividend is

$$D_1 = \$2.8571(1.05) = \$3.$$

Our marginal investor observes that the present price of the stock, P_0, is \$30. Should he or she buy more of Stock X, sell out, or maintain the present position?

The investor can calculate Stock X's *expected rate of return* as follows:

$$\hat{k}_X = \frac{D_1}{P_0} + g = \frac{\$3}{\$30} + 5\% = 15\%.$$

Figure 7-10 Expected and Required Returns on Stock X

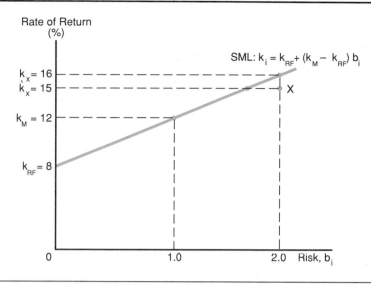

This value is plotted on Figure 7-10 as Point X, which is below the SML. Because the expected rate of return is less than the required return, this marginal investor will want to sell the stock, as will other holders. However, few people will want to buy at the $30 price, so the present owners will be unable to find buyers unless they cut the price of the stock. Thus, the price will decline, and this decline will continue until the stock's price reaches $27.27, at which point the market for this security will be in *equilibrium*, because the expected rate of return, 16 percent, will be equal to the required rate of return:

$$\hat{k}_X = \frac{\$3}{\$27.27} + 5\% = 11\% + 5\% = 16\% = k_X.$$

Had the stock initially sold for less than $27.27, say at $25, events would have been reversed. Investors would have wanted to buy the stock because its expected rate of return would have exceeded its required rate of return, and buy orders would have driven the stock's price up to $27.27.

To summarize, in equilibrium these two conditions must hold:

1. The expected rate of return as seen by the marginal investor must equal the required rate of return: $\hat{k}_i = k_i$.

2. The actual market price of the stock must equal its intrinsic value as estimated by the marginal investor: $P_0 = \hat{P}_0$.

Of course, some individual investors will believe that $\hat{k}_i > k$ and $\hat{P}_0 > P_0$, and hence they will invest most of their funds in the stock, while other investors will have an opposite view and will sell all of their shares. However, it is the marginal investor who establishes the actual market price, and for this investor, $\hat{k}_i = k_i$ and $P_0 = \hat{P}_0$. If these conditions do not hold, trading will occur until they do hold.

Changes in Equilibrium Stock Prices

Stock market prices are not constant—they undergo violent changes at times. For example, on October 19, 1987, the Dow Jones average dropped 508 points, and the average stock lost about 23 percent of its value in just one day. Some stocks lost over half of their value that day. To see how such changes can occur, let us assume that Stock X is in equilibrium, selling at a price of $27.27 per share. Its expected growth rate is 5 percent, so if all expectations were exactly met, during the next year the price would gradually rise to $28.63, or by 5 percent. However, many different events could occur to cause a change in the equilibrium price of the stock. To illustrate, consider again the set of inputs used to develop Stock X's price of $27.27, along with a new set of assumed input variables:

	Variable Value		Reason for Change
	Original	New	
Risk-free rate, k_{RF}	8%	7%	Reduced inflation
Market risk premium, $k_M - k_{RF}$	4%	3%	Lower risk aversion
Stock X's beta coefficient, b_X	2.0	1.0	Reduced risk product mix
Stock X's expected growth rate, g_X	5%	6%	Successful R&D program
D_0	$2.8571	$2.8571	
Price of Stock X	$27.27	?	

Now give yourself a test: How will the change in each variable, by itself, affect the price, and what is your guess as to the new stock price?

Every change, taken alone, would lead to an increase in the price. The first three variables influence k_X, which declines from 16 to 10 percent:

$$\text{Original } k_X = 8\% + 4\%(2.0) = 16\%.$$

$$\text{New } k_X = 7\% + 3\%(1.0) = 10\%.$$

Using these values, together with the new g value, we find that $\hat{P}_0$, and consequently P_0, rises from $27.27 to $75.71.[19]

$$\text{Original } \hat{P}_0 = \frac{\$2.8571(1.05)}{0.16 - 0.05} = \frac{\$3}{0.11} = \$27.27.$$

$$\text{New } \hat{P}_0 = \frac{\$2.8571(1.06)}{0.10 - 0.06} = \frac{\$3.0285}{0.04} = \$75.71.$$

---

[19]A price change of this magnitude is by no means rare. The prices of *many* stocks double or halve during a year. For example, during 1989 L.A. Gear increased in value by 199 percent; on the other hand, Integrated Resources suffered a 99 percent loss.

At the new price, the expected and required rates of return will be equal:[20]

$$\hat{k}_X = \frac{\$3.0285}{\$75.71} + 6\% = 10\% = k_X.$$

Evidence suggests that stocks, and especially those of large NYSE companies, adjust rapidly to disequilibrium situations. Consequently, equilibrium ordinarily exists for any given stock, and, in general, required and expected returns are equal. Stock prices certainly change, sometimes violently and rapidly, but this simply reflects changing conditions and expectations. There are, of course, times when a stock continues to react for several months to a favorable or unfavorable development, but this does not signify a long adjustment period; rather, it simply illustrates that as more new bits of information about the situation become available, the market adjusts to them. The ability of the market to adjust to new information is discussed in the next section.

The Efficient Markets Hypothesis

A body of theory called the *Efficient Markets Hypothesis (EMH)* holds (1) that stocks are always in equilibrium and (2) that it is impossible for an investor to consistently "beat the market." Essentially, those who believe in the EMH note that there are some 100,000 or so full-time, highly trained, professional analysts and traders operating in the market, while there are fewer than 3,000 major stocks. Therefore, if each analyst followed 30 stocks (which is about right, as analysts tend to specialize in the stocks in a specific industry), there would be 1,000 analysts following each stock. Further, these analysts work for organizations such as Citibank, Merrill Lynch, Prudential Insurance, Fidelity, and the like, which have billions of dollars available to invest in stocks. As a result of SEC disclosure requirements and electronic information networks, as new information about a stock becomes available, these 1,000 analysts all receive and evaluate it at approximately the same time. Therefore, the price of the stock adjusts almost instantly to any new developments.

Financial theorists generally define three forms, or levels, of market efficiency:

1.   The *weak-form* of the EMH states that all information contained in past price movements is fully reflected in current market prices. If this is true, then information about recent trends in a stock's price will be of no use in selecting stocks — the fact that a stock has risen for the past three days, for example, gives us no useful clues as to what it will do today or tomorrow. People who believe that weak-form efficiency exists also believe that "tape watchers" and "chartists" are wasting their time.[21]

---

[20]It should be obvious by now that actual realized rates of return are not necessarily equal to expected and required returns. Thus, an investor might have *expected* to receive a return of 15 percent if he or she had bought L.A. Gear or Integrated Resources stock in 1989, but after the fact, the realized return on L.A. Gear was far above 15 percent, whereas that on Integrated Resources was far below.

[21]Tape watchers are people who watch the NYSE tape, while chartists plot past patterns of stock price movements. Both are called "technicians," and both believe that they can see if something is happening to the stock that will cause its price to move up or down in the near future.

2.   The *semistrong-form* of the EMH states that current market prices reflect all *publicly available* information. If this is true, no abnormal returns can be gained by analyzing stocks.[22] Thus, if semistrong-form efficiency exists, it does no good to pore over annual reports or other published data, because market prices will have adjusted to any good or bad news contained in such reports as soon as it came out. However, insiders (say, the presidents or financial managers of companies), even under semistrong-form efficiency, might still be able to make abnormal returns on their own companies' stocks.

3.   The *strong-form* of the EMH states that current market prices reflect all pertinent information, whether publicly available or privately held. If this form holds, even insiders would find it impossible to earn abnormal returns in the stock market.[23]

Many empirical studies have been conducted to test for the three forms of market efficiency. Most of these studies suggest that the stock market is indeed highly efficient in the weak-form and reasonably efficient in the semistrong-form, at least for the larger and more widely followed stocks. However, the strong-form EMH does not hold, so abnormal profits can be made by those who possess inside information.

What bearing does the EMH have on investors' decisions? Since stock prices do reflect public information, most stocks do seem to be fairly valued. This does not mean that new developments could not cause a stock's price to soar or to plummet, but it does mean that stocks, in general, are neither overvalued nor undervalued—they are fairly priced and in equilibrium. However, there are cases in which managers do have information not known to outsiders.

If the EMH is correct, it is a waste of time for most of us to analyze stocks by looking for those that are undervalued. If stock prices already reflect all available information and hence are fairly priced, one can "beat the market" only by luck, and it is difficult, if not impossible, for anyone to consistently outperform the market averages. Empirical tests have shown that the EMH is, in its weak- and semistrong-forms, valid. However, people such as corporate officers who have insider information can do better than the averages, and individuals and organizations that are especially good at digging out information on small, new companies also seem to do consistently well. Also, some investors may be able to analyze and react more quickly than others to releases of new information, and these investors may have an advantage over others. However, the buy-sell actions of these investors quickly bring market prices into equilibrium. Therefore, it is generally best to assume that $\hat{k}_s = k_s$, that $\hat{P}_0 = P_0$, that stocks plot on the SML, and that returns on investments are just commensurate with the risks involved—no more and no less. Note that the EMH also applies to bond markets. Since bond prices and yields reflect all current public information, it is impossible to consistently forecast future interest rates—interest

---

[22]An abnormal return is one that exceeds the return justified by the riskiness of the investment—that is, a return that plots above the SML in a graph like Figure 7-10.

[23]Several cases of illegal insider trading have made the news headlines recently. These cases involved employees of several major investment banking houses, and even an employee of the SEC. In the most famous case, Ivan Boesky admitted to making $50 million by purchasing the stock of firms he knew were about to merge. He went to jail, and he had to pay a large fine, but he helped disprove the strong-form EMH.

rates change in response to new information, and this information could either lower or raise rates. Thus, bond investors should not make decisions on the basis of whether rates will be going down or up—nobody knows.

What bearing does the EMH have on financial management decisions? First, the EMH suggests that managers cannot affect the values of their firms by using accounting techniques to boost reported earnings: As long as sufficient public information is available to investors and analysts to estimate the true cash flows of the firm, changes in reported income caused solely by accounting changes which have no impact on cash flows will not affect a firm's stock price. Second, the EMH has implications for the issuance of securities by firms. Since security prices generally reflect all publicly held information, a firm's bond and stock prices should accurately reflect all information held by investors about the firm's future prospects, hence market prices should be "fair." To continue, if securities are fairly valued, it makes little sense for managers to try to "time" the issuance of securities to catch market highs or lows.

Note, however, that managers may have information about their own firms that is unknown to the general public. This condition is called *asymmetric information,* and its existence can have a profound effect on financial management decisions. For example, if the managers of an oil company know that the firm had made a major off-shore oil discovery, and if they do not want to announce it until they have bought up all the drilling rights in the area, then they might delay raising funds to develop the field until after announcing the discovery. Presumably, the markets will react to the new information positively, and new securities could be sold under more favorable terms at that time. This scenario does not mean that markets are inefficient, but, rather, that markets are not strong-form efficient. Managers can and should act on inside information for the benefit of the firm's shareholders, but inside information cannot legally be used for the managers' own benefit. We will discuss the impact of asymmetric information on financial management decisions throughout the book.

Actual Stock Prices and Returns

Our discussion thus far has focused on *expected* stock prices and *expected* rates of return. Anyone who has ever invested in the stock market knows that there can be and generally there are large differences between *expected* and *realized* prices and returns.

We can use IBM's experience during the 1980s to illustrate this point. On January 1, 1981, IBM's stock price was $67.875 per share. Its 1980 dividend, D_0, had been $3.44, and the consensus among security analysts was that IBM would experience a growth rate of about 11 percent in the future. Thus, an average investor who bought IBM at $67.875 would have expected to earn a return of about 16.6 percent:

$$\hat{k}_s = \begin{matrix} \text{Expected dividend} \\ \text{yield} \end{matrix} + \begin{matrix} \text{Expected growth rate, which is the} \\ \text{expected capital gains yield} \end{matrix}$$

$$= \frac{D_0(1 + g)}{P_0} + g = \frac{\$3.82}{\$67.875} + 11\% = 5.6\% + 11.0\% = 16.6\%.$$

IBM's bonds yielded about 13 percent at the time.

Figure 7-11   New York Stock Exchange Index, 1953–1989

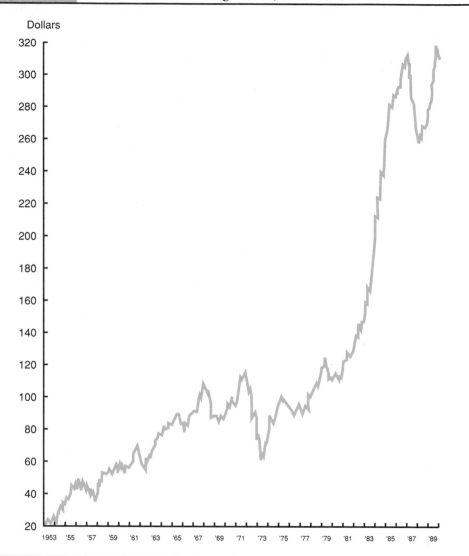

In fact, things did not work out as expected. The economy in 1981 was weaker than had been predicted, so IBM's earnings did not grow as fast as expected, and its dividend remained at $3.44. Further, interest rates soared during 1981, so the required rates of return on all stocks, including IBM, increased. As a result of these two events, IBM stock's price declined, and it closed on December 31, 1981, at $56.875, down $11 for the year. Thus, on a beginning-of-the-year investment of $67.875, the actual return on IBM for 1981 was −11.1 percent:

$$\bar{k}_s = \text{Actual dividend yield} + \text{Actual capital gains yield}$$

$$= \frac{\$3.44}{\$67.875} + \frac{-\$11}{\$67.875}$$

$$= 5.1\% - 16.2\% = -11.1\%.$$

Most other stocks performed similarly to IBM's in 1981.

The economy improved after 1981, however, and IBM's dividend and stock price improved apace. The total realized return on IBM in 1982 increased dramatically to 77 percent; in 1983 it was a strong 30 percent; it was only 5 percent in 1984; it was back up to 30 percent in 1985; and in 1986 the total return was a negative 19 percent, even though the market as a whole was strong. IBM's total return was −1 percent in 1987, 9 percent in 1988, and −12 percent in 1989, which was well below the market average. On average, the realized return on IBM stock during the 1980s was about 11 percent, somewhat below the rate of return investors expected at the beginning of the decade. However, in every single year, the realized return differed significantly from the expected return.

Figure 7-11 shows how the price of an average share of stock has varied in recent years, and Figure 7-12 shows how total realized returns have varied. The market trend has been strongly up, but it has gone up in some years and down in others, and the stocks of individual companies have likewise gone up and down. We know from theory that expected returns as estimated by a marginal investor are always positive, but in some years, as Figure 7-12 shows, negative returns have been realized. Of course, even in bad years some individual companies do well, so finan-

Figure 7-12   New York Stock Exchange, Total Returns: Dividend Yield + Capital Gain or Loss, 1953–1989

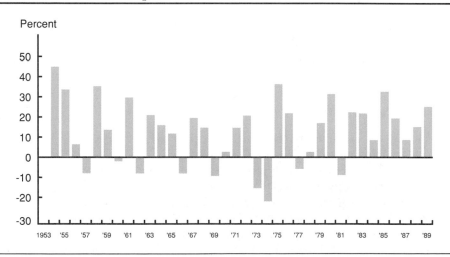

Figure 7-13 Stock Market Transactions, March 14, 1990

Quotations as of 4:30 p.m. Eastern Time
Wednesday, March 14, 1990

	52 Weeks Hi	Lo	Stock	Sym	Div	Yld %	PE	Vol 100s	Hi	Lo	Close	Net Chg
			-A-A-A-									
	37½	26	AAR	AIR	.48	1.7	17	370	28½	27⅞	28⅛	– ¼
n	9¾	8½	ACM OppFd	AOF	1.26	14.0	...	135	9¼	9	9	– ¼
	11⅝	10½	ACM Gvt Fd	ACG	1.26	11.6	...	620	11	10⅞	10⅞	– ⅛
n	9⅞	7⅞	ACM MgdIncFd	AMF	1.01	13.0	...	538	8	7⅝	7¾	– ⅛
	12⅛	11½	ACM MgdMultFd	MMF		...	...	280	11¾	11⅝	11⅝	...
	11½	10	ACM SecFd	GSF	1.26	11.5	...	891	11	10¾	11	+ ⅛
	9⅜	8⅛	ACM SpctmFd	SI	1.01	11.2	...	296	9	8¾	9	+ ⅛
	22¼	13	AL Labs A	BMD	.16	.7	20	277	21½	21⅜	21½	+ ⅛
	4⅛	3⅛	AMCA	AIL	.12e	3.6	42	207	3⅜	3¼	3⅜	+ ⅛
	6⅛	3¼	AM Int	AM		...	11	479	3⅜	3¼	3⅜	+ ⅛
	23½	16⅜	AM Int pf		2.00	11.9	...	14	16⅞	16¾	16⅞	...
	107¼	52½	AMR	AMR		...	9	6762	64⅝	63½	63¾	–1⅛
	27	25	ANR pf		2.67	10.6	...	2	25¼	25¼	25¼	– ½
	24⅞	23⅛	ANR pf		2.12	9.0	...	2	23½	23½	23½	– ¼
	5⅜	3⅛	ARX	ARX		...	...	118	4	3¾	3¾	– ⅛
	72¾	39	ASA	ASA	3.00a	5.7	...	1287	53⅞	52⅝	53	– ½
	70⅜	50⅜	AbbotLab	ABT	1.68	2.6	17	5144	63⅞	63	63⅝	+ ⅛
	17¼	11¼	Abitibi g	ABY	.50	...	...	86	13⅜	13⅜	13⅜	+ ⅛
	13	8⅞	AcmeCleve	AMT	.40	4.1	11	249	9⅞	9⅝	9⅞	+ ¼
	9¾	7	AcmeElec	ACE	.32	3.6	11	3	8⅞	8⅞	8⅞	– ⅛
	38½	27	Acuson	ACN		...	22	287	34⅞	34¾	34¾	– ⅛
	16½	12⅞	AdamsExp	ADX	2.06e	13.1	...	244	16⅛	15¾	15¾	– ¼
	15⅜	7¼	AdobeRes	ADB		...	...	34	13¼	13	13	– ¼
	20¼	16⅞	AdobeRes pf		1.84	9.7	...	28	19	18¾	19	+ ¼
	21⅝	19⅞	AdobeRes pf		2.40	11.2	...	173	21½	21⅜	21⅜	– ⅛
	10½	6⅞	AdvMicro	AMD		...	21	3658	9⅛	8⅞	9⅛	+ ¼
	35	28¼	AdvMicro pf		3.00	10.2	...	21	29½	29¼	29⅜	+ ⅛
	10⅛	5	Advest	ADV	.16	2.6	8	12	6¼	6⅛	6¼	...

Source: *The Wall Street Journal,* March 15, 1990.

cial managers attempt to take actions which will put their companies into the winners' column, but they do not always succeed. In subsequent chapters, we will examine the actions that managers can take to increase the odds of their firms doing relatively well in the marketplace.

Stock Market Reporting

Figure 7-13, taken from *The Wall Street Journal,* is a section of the stock market page on stocks listed on the NYSE. For each stock, the NYSE report provides specific data on the trading that took place the prior day. Similar information is available on stocks listed on the other exchanges, as well as on stocks traded over-the-counter.

Stocks are listed alphabetically, from AAR Industries to Zweig; the data in Figure 7-13 were taken from the top of the listing. We will examine the data for Abbott Laboratories, AbbotLab, shown about two-thirds of the way down the table. The two columns on the left show the highest and lowest prices at which the stocks have sold during the past year; Abbott Labs has traded in the range from $70⅜ to $50⅜ during the preceding 52 weeks. The figure just to the right of the company's ticker tape symbol is the dividend; Abbott Labs had a current indicated annual dividend rate of $1.68 per share and a dividend yield (which is the dividend divided by the closing stock price) of 2.6 percent. Next comes the ratio of the stock's price to its annual earnings (the P/E ratio), followed by the volume of trading for the day: 514,400 shares of Abbott Labs stock were traded on March 14, 1990. Following the volume come the high and low prices for the day, and then the closing price. On March 14, Abbott Labs traded as high as $63⅞ and as low as $63, while the last trade was at $63⅝. The last column gives the change from the closing price on the previous day. Abbott Labs was up ⅛, or $0.125, so the previous close must have been $63.625 − $0.125 = $63.50.

There are three other points to note in Figure 7-13. First, the "pf" following the stock name of the second AM Int listing tells us that it is a preferred stock rather than a common stock. Second, a "↑" preceding the column containing a stock's daily high indicates that the price hit a new 52-week high, whereas a "↓" preceding the column containing a stock's daily low indicates a new 52-week low. Thus, none of the stocks listed hit 52-week highs or lows. Third, an "n" to the left of the listing, such as that for ACM OppFd, indicates that the stock is a new listing (listed during the preceding 52 weeks). We discuss exchange listing in detail in Chapter 15.

Self-Test Questions

When a stock is in equilibrium, two conditions must hold. What are these two conditions?

What is the major conclusion of the Efficient Markets Hypothesis (EMH)?

What are the differences among the three forms of the EMH: (1) weak-form, (2) semistrong-form, and (3) strong-form?

What is meant by the term "asymmetric information"?

SUMMARY

Corporate decisions should be analyzed in terms of how alternative courses of action are likely to affect the value of a firm. However, it is necessary to know how bond and stock prices are established before attempting to measure how a given decision will affect a specific firm's value. Accordingly, this chapter showed how bond and stock values are determined, as well as how investors go about estimating the rates of return they expect to earn. The key concepts covered in this chapter are summarized next.

- The *value* of any security is merely the present value of the security's expected cash flows.

- A *bond* is a long-term promissory note issued by a business or governmental unit. The firm receives the selling price of the bond in exchange for a promise to make interest payments and to repay the principal on a specified future date.

- The *value of a bond* is found as the present value of an annuity (the *interest payments*) plus the present value of a lump sum (the *principal*). The bond is evaluated at the appropriate periodic interest rate over the number of periods for which interest payments are made.

- The equation used to find the value of an annual coupon bond is:

$$V = \sum_{t=1}^{n} \frac{I}{(1 + k_d)^t} + \frac{M}{(1 + k_d)^n}$$

$$= I(\text{PVIFA}_{k_d,n}) + M(\text{PVIF}_{k_d,n}).$$

  An adjustment to the formula must be made if the bond pays interest *semiannually*: divide I and k_d by 2, and multiply n by 2.

- The return earned on a bond held to maturity is defined as the bond's *yield to maturity (YTM)*. If the bond can be redeemed before maturity, it is *callable*, and the return investors will receive if it is called is defined as the *yield to call (YTC)*. The YTC is found as the present value of the interest payments received while the bond is outstanding plus the present value of the call price (the par value plus a call premium).

- The longer the maturity of a bond, the more its price will change in response to a given change in interest rates; this is called *interest rate risk*. Bonds with short maturities, however, expose the investor to high *reinvestment rate risk*, which is the risk that income will decline because funds received from maturing short-term investments will have to be reinvested at lower interest rates.

- Some preferred stocks are *perpetuities*, and the value of a share of perpetual preferred stock is found as the dividend divided by the required rate of return:

$$V_p = \frac{D_p}{k_p}.$$

- Preferred stocks with *finite maturities* are valued similarly to bonds.

- The *value of a share of stock* is calculated as the *present value of the stream of dividends* to be received in the future.

- The equation used to find the *value of a constant, or normal, growth stock* is:

$$\hat{P}_0 = D_1/(k_s - g).$$

- The *expected total rate of return* from a stock consists of an *expected dividend yield* plus an *expected capital gains yield*. For a constant growth stock, both the expected dividend yield and the expected capital gains yield are constant.

- The equation for $\hat{k}_s$, *the expected rate of return on a constant growth stock*, can be expressed as $\hat{k}_s = D_1/P_0 + g$, where g = expected constant growth rate = capital gains yield.

- A *zero growth stock* is one whose future dividends are not expected to grow at all, while a *supernormal growth stock* is one whose dividends are expected to grow much faster than average over some specified time period.

- To find the *present value of a nonconstant growth stock,* (1) find the PV of the dividends during the nonconstant growth period, (2) find the price of the stock at the end of the nonconstant growth period and discount this price back to the present, and (3) sum these two components.

- The *Efficient Markets Hypothesis (EMH)* holds (1) that stocks are always in equilibrium and (2) that it is impossible for an investor to consistently "beat the market." Therefore, according to the EMH, stocks are always fairly valued ($\hat{P}_0 = P_0$), the required return on a stock is equal to its expected return ($k_s = \hat{k}_s$), and all stocks' expected returns plot on the SML.

- In some situations, a company's managers may know more about the firm's future prospects than do well-informed investors. This situation is called *"asymmetric information."* Managers without superior information should view their companies' stocks and bonds as being "fairly" valued.

- Finally, in this chapter we saw that differences can and do exist between *expected* and *actual returns* in the stock and bond markets—only for short-term, risk-free assets are expected and actual (or realized) returns equal.

In Chapter 8, we will use the valuation concepts developed in this chapter to estimate a firm's cost of capital.

Questions

7-1   Define each of the following terms:
  a.   Bond
  b.   Par value; maturity date; call provision
  c.   Coupon payment; coupon interest rate
  d.   Premium bond; discount bond
  e.   Current yield (on a bond); yield to maturity (YTM); yield to call (YTC)
  f.   Interest rate risk; reinvestment rate risk
  g.   Intrinsic value, $\hat{P}_0$; market price, P_0
  h.   Required rate of return, k_s; expected rate of return, $\hat{k}_s$; realized rate of return, $\bar{k}_s$
  i.   Capital gains yield; dividend yield; expected total return
  j.   Perpetuity; zero growth stock
  k.   Normal, or constant, growth; nonconstant growth; supernormal growth
  l.   Efficient Markets Hypothesis (EMH)
  m.   Weak-form; semistrong-form; strong-form
  n.   Asymmetric information

7-2   Two investors are evaluating AT&T's stock for possible purchase. They agree on the expected value of D_1 and also on the expected future dividend growth rate. Further, they agree on the riskiness of the stock. However, one investor normally holds stocks for 2 years, while the other normally holds stocks for 10 years. Based on the type of analysis done in this chapter, they should both be willing to pay the same price for AT&T's stock. True or false? Explain.

7-3   A bond that pays interest forever and has no maturity date is a perpetual bond. In what respect is a perpetual bond similar to a no-growth common stock and to a share of perpetual preferred stock?

7-4   Is it true that the following equation can be used to find the value of an n-year bond that pays interest once a year?

$$\text{Value} = \sum_{t=1}^{n} \frac{\text{Annual interest}}{(1 + k_d)^t} + \frac{\text{Par value}}{(1 + k_d)^n}.$$

7-5   "The values of outstanding bonds change whenever the going rate of interest changes. In general, short-term interest rates are more volatile than long-term interest rates. Therefore, short-term bond prices are more sensitive to interest rate changes than are long-term bond prices." Is this statement true or false? Explain.

7-6   The rate of return you would get if you bought a bond and held it to its maturity date is defined as the bond's yield to maturity. If interest rates in the economy rise after a bond has been issued, what will happen to its price and to its YTM? Does the length of time to maturity affect the extent to which a given change in interest rates will affect the bond price?

7-7   If you buy a *callable* bond and interest rates decline, will the value of your bond rise by as much as it would have if the bond had not been callable?

7-8   If you bought a share of common stock, you would typically expect to receive dividends plus capital gains. Would you expect the distribution between dividend yield and capital gains to be influenced by the firm's decision to pay more dividends rather than to retain and reinvest more of its earnings?

7-9   The next expected dividend, D_1, divided by the current price of a share of stock, P_0, is defined as the stock's expected dividend yield. What is the relationship between the dividend yield, the total yield, and the remaining years of supernormal growth for a supernormal growth firm?

7-10 Is it true that the following expression can be used to find the value of a constant growth stock?

$$\hat{P}_0 = \frac{D_0}{k_s + g}.$$

Self-Test Problems (Solutions Appear in Appendix D)

ST-1 **(Bond valuation)** The Ferri Corporation issued a new series of bonds on January 1, 1967. The bonds were sold at par ($1,000), have a 12 percent coupon, and mature in 30 years, on December 31, 1996. Coupon payments are made semiannually (on June 30 and December 31).
   a.   What was the YTM on the bond on January 1, 1967?
   b.   What was the price of the bond on January 1, 1972, 5 years later, assuming that the level of interest rates had fallen to 10 percent?
   c.   Find the current yield and capital gains yield on the bond on January 1, 1972, given the price as determined in Part b.
   d.   On July 1, 1987, the bonds sold for $896.64. What was the YTM at that date?
   e.   What were the current yield and capital gains yield on July 1, 1987?
   f.   Now assume that you purchased one of the outstanding bonds on March 1, 1987, when the going rate of interest was 15.5 percent. How large a check must you have written to complete the transaction? This is a hard question!

ST-2 **(Constant growth stock valuation)** Sorenson Company's current stock price is $24, and its last dividend was $1.60. In view of the firm's strong financial position and its consequent low risk, its required rate of return is only 12 percent. If dividends are expected to grow at a constant rate, g, in the future, and if k_s is expected to remain at 12 percent, what is the firm's expected stock price 5 years from now?

ST-3   **(Nonconstant growth stock valuation)** Keenan Computer Chips, Inc., is experiencing a period of rapid growth. Earnings and dividends are expected to grow at a rate of 18 percent during the next 2 years, at 15 percent in the third year, and then at a constant rate of 6 percent thereafter. The firm's last dividend was $1.15, and the required rate of return on the stock is 12 percent.

   a.   Calculate the value of the stock today.
   b.   Calculate $\hat{P}_1$ and $\hat{P}_2$.
   c.   Calculate the dividend yield and capital gains yield for Years 1, 2, and 3.

Problems

7-1   **(Bond valuation)** The Teague Company has two bond issues outstanding. Both bonds pay $100 annual interest plus $1,000 at maturity. Bond L has a maturity of 15 years and Bond S a maturity of 1 year.

   a.   What will be the value of each of these bonds when the going rate of interest is (1) 6 percent, (2) 9 percent, and (3) 12 percent? Assume that there is only one more interest payment to be made on Bond S.
   b.   Why does the longer-term (15-year) bond fluctuate more when interest rates change than does the shorter-term bond (1-year)?

7-2   **(Yield to maturity)** The Nodine Company's bonds have 4 years remaining to maturity. Interest is paid annually; the bonds have a $1,000 par value; and the coupon interest rate is 8 percent.

   a.   What is the yield to maturity at a current market price of (1) $825 or (2) $1,107?
   b.   Would you pay $825 for one of these bonds if you thought that the appropriate rate of interest was 10 percent; that is, if $k_d = 10\%$? Explain your answer.

7-3   **(Semiannual bond valuation)** Suppose Exxon sold an issue of bonds with a 10-year maturity, a $1,000 par value, a 12 percent coupon rate, and semiannual interest payments.

   a.   Two years after the bonds were issued, the going rate of interest on bonds such as these fell to 8 percent. At what price would the bonds sell?
   b.   Suppose that 2 years after the initial offering, the going interest rate had risen to 14 percent. At what price would the bonds sell?
   c.   Suppose the conditions in Part a existed—that is, interest rates fell to 8 percent 2 years after the issue date. Suppose further that the interest rate remained at 8 percent for the next 8 years. What would happen to the price of the Exxon bonds over time?

7-4   **(Perpetual bond valuation)** The bonds of the Boyd Corporation are perpetuities with a 12 percent annual coupon and a par value of $1,000. Bonds of this type currently yield 10 percent.

   a.   What is the price of the Boyd bonds?
   b.   Suppose interest rate levels rise to the point where such bonds now yield 15 percent? What would be the price of the Boyd bonds?
   c.   At what price would the Boyd bonds sell if the yield on these bonds were 12 percent?
   d.   How would your answers to Parts a, b, and c change if the bonds were not perpetuities but had a maturity of 20 years?

7-5   **(Perpetual bond yield to maturity)** The yield to maturity (YTM) is, basically, the rate of return earned on a bond that is held to maturity. What will be the yield to maturity of a perpetual bond with a $1,000 par value, a 9 percent coupon rate, and a current market price of (a) $700, (b) $900, (c) $1,000, and (d) $1,300? Assume interest is paid annually.

7-6   **(Constant growth stock valuation)** Your broker offers to sell you some shares of Barn-grover Company common stock that paid a dividend of $2 *last year*. You expect the dividend to grow at the rate of 5 percent per year for the next 3 years, and if you buy the stock you plan to hold it for 3 years and then sell it.

   a.   Find the expected dividend for each of the next 3 years; that is, calculate D_1, D_2, and D_3. Note that $D_0 = \$2$.

   b.   Given that the appropriate discount rate is 12 percent and that the first of these dividend payments will occur 1 year from now, find the present value of the dividend stream; that is, calculate the PV of D_1, D_2, and D_3, and then sum these PVs.

   c.   You expect the price of the stock 3 years from now to be $34.73; that is, you expect $\hat{P}_3$ to equal $34.73. Discounted at a 12 percent rate, what is the present value of this expected future stock price? In other words, calculate the PV of $34.73.

   d.   If you plan to buy the stock, hold it for 3 years, and then sell it for $34.73, what is the most you should pay for it?

   e.   Use Equation 7-6 to calculate the present value of this stock. Assume that $g = 5\%$, and it is a constant.

   f.   Is the value of this stock dependent upon how long you plan to hold it? In other words, if your planned holding period were 2 years or 5 years rather than 3 years, would this affect the value of the stock today, $\hat{P}_0$?

7-7   **(Return on common stock)** You buy a share of the Johnson Corporation stock for $35.33. You expect it to pay dividends of $1.06, $1.1236, and $1.1910 in Years 1, 2, and 3, respectively, and you expect to sell it at a price of $42.08 at the end of 3 years.

   a.   Calculate the growth rate in dividends.

   b.   Calculate the current dividend yield.

   c.   Assuming that the calculated growth rate is expected to continue, you can add the dividend yield to the expected growth rate to get the expected total rate of return. What is this stock's expected total rate of return?

7-8   **(Constant growth stock valuation)** Investors require a 20 percent rate of return on Russell Company's stock ($k_s = 20\%$).

   a.   What will be the stock's value if the previous dividend was $D_0 = \$2$ and if investors expect dividends to grow at a constant annual rate of (1) -5 percent, (2) 0 percent, (3) 5 percent, or (4) 15 percent?

   b.   Using data from Part a, what is the Gordon (constant growth) model value for the firm's stock if the required rate of return is 20 percent and the expected growth rate is (1) 20 percent or (2) 25 percent? Are these reasonable results? Explain.

   c.   Is it reasonable to expect that a constant growth stock would have $g > k_s$?

7-9   **(Stock price reporting)** Look up the prices of IBM's stock and bonds in *The Wall Street Journal* (or some other newspaper which provides this information).

   a.   What was the stock's price range over the last year?

   b.   What is IBM's current dividend? What is its dividend yield?

   c.   What change occurred in IBM's stock price since the previous day's close?

   d.   If IBM were to sell a new issue of $1,000 par value long-term bonds, approximately what coupon interest rate would it have to set on the bonds if it wanted to bring them out at par?

   e.   If you had $10,000 and wanted to invest it in IBM, what return would you expect to get if you bought the bonds and what return if you bought IBM's stock? (Hint: Think about capital gains when you answer the latter part of this question.)

7-10   **(Discount bond valuation)** In February 1956 the Los Angeles Airport authority issued a series of 3.4 percent, 30-year bonds. Interest rates rose substantially in the years following the issue, and as they did, the price of the bonds declined. In February 1969, 13 years later, the price of the bonds had dropped from $1,000 to $650. In answering the following questions, assume that the bond has annual interest payments.

a. Each bond originally sold at its $1,000 par value. What was the yield to maturity of these bonds at their time of issue?

b. Calculate the yield to maturity in February 1969.

c. Assume that interest rates stabilized at the 1969 level and stayed there for the remainder of the life of the bonds. What would have been their price in February 1981, when they had 5 years remaining to maturity?

d. What would the price of the bonds have been the day before they matured in 1986? (Disregard the last interest payment.)

e. In 1969 the Los Angeles Airport bonds were classified as "discount bonds." What happens to the price of a discount bond as it approaches maturity? Is there a "built-in capital gain" on such bonds?

f. The coupon interest payment divided by the market price of a bond is called the bond's *current yield.* Assuming the conditions in Part c, what would have been the current yield of a Los Angeles Airport bond (1) in February 1969 and (2) in February 1981? What would have been its capital gains yields and total yields (total yield equals yield to maturity) on those same two dates?

7-11 (Declining growth stock valuation) Morrissey Mining Company's ore reserves are being depleted, so its sales are falling. Also, its pit is getting deeper each year, so its costs are rising. As a result, the company's earnings and dividends are declining at the constant rate of 10 percent per year. If $D_0 = \$6$ and $k_s = 15\%$, what is the value of Morrissey Mining's stock?

7-12 (Supernormal growth stock valuation) It is now January 1, 1991. O'Brien Electric, Inc., has just developed a solar panel capable of generating 200 percent more electricity than any solar panel currently on the market. As a result, the firm is expected to experience a 20 percent annual growth rate for the next 5 years. By the end of 5 years, other firms will have developed comparable technology, and O'Brien's growth rate will slow to 6 percent per year indefinitely. Stockholders require a return of 10 percent on O'Brien's stock. The most recent annual dividend, D_0, which was paid yesterday, was $1.50 per share.

a. Calculate the firm's expected dividends for 1991, 1992, 1993, 1994, and 1995.

b. Calculate the value of the stock today, $\hat{P}_0$. Proceed by finding the present value of the dividends expected at the end of 1991, 1992, 1993, 1994, and 1995 plus the present value of the stock price which should exist at the end of 1995. The year-end 1995 stock price can be found by using the constant growth model. Note that to find the December 31, 1995, price, you use the dividend expected in 1996, which is 6 percent greater than the 1995 dividend.

c. Calculate the current dividend yield, D_1/P_0, the capital gains yield expected in 1991, and the expected total return (dividend yield plus capital gains yield) for 1991. (Assume that $\hat{P}_0 = P_0$, and recognize that the capital gains yield is equal to the total return minus the dividend yield.) Also, calculate these same three yields for 1995.

d. How might an investor's tax situation affect his or her decision to purchase stocks of companies in the early stages of their lives, when they are growing rapidly, versus stocks of older, more mature firms? When does the firm's stock become "mature" in this example?

(Do Parts e and f only if you are using the computerized diskette.)

e. Suppose your boss tells you that she believes that the firm's annual growth rate will be only 15 percent over the next 5 years and that the firm's normal growth rate is only 5 percent. Calculate the expected dividends for the supernormal growth period and the value of the stock today under these assumptions.

f.   Suppose your boss also tells you that she regards the firm as being quite risky and that she believes the required rate of return is 13 percent, not 10 percent. Calculate the intrinsic value of the firm's stock. Also, do the calculations with k_s values of 15 percent and 20 percent to see how k_s affects the stock's value.

7-13   **(Supernormal growth stock valuation)** Jones Motor Corporation has been growing at a rate of 25 percent per year in recent years. This same growth rate is expected to last for another 2 years.

a.   If $D_0 = \$2$, $k_s = 14\%$, and $g_n = 6\%$, what is the firm's stock worth today? What are its current dividend yield and capital gains yield?

b.   Now assume that the period of supernormal growth is 5 years rather than 2 years. How does this affect the firm's price, dividend yield, and capital gains yield? Answer in words only.

c.   What will be the stock's dividend yield and capital gains yield the year after its period of supernormal growth ends? (Hint: These values will be the same regardless of whether you examine the case of 2 or 5 years of supernormal growth; the calculations are trivial.)

d.   Of what interest to investors is the changing relationship between dividend yield and capital gains yield over time?

(Do Parts e and f only if you are using the computerized diskette.)

e.   What will be the firm's stock price, dividend yield, and capital gains yield if the supernormal growth period is 5 years?

f.   What will be the price, dividend yield, and capital gains yield if the required rate of return is 16 percent and the supernormal growth period is 2 years?

7-14   **(Yield to call)** It is now January 1, 1991, and you are considering the purchase of an outstanding Pogue Corporation bond that was issued on January 1, 1989. The bond has a 10.5 percent annual coupon and a 30-year original maturity (it matures on January 1, 2019). There was originally a 5-year call protection (until December 31, 1993), after which time the bond can be called at 110 (that is, at 110 percent of par, or $1,100). Interest rates have declined since the bond was issued, and the bond is now selling at 115.174 percent of par, or $1,151.74. You want to determine both the yield to maturity and the yield to call for this bond. (Note: The yield to call considers the impact of a call provision on the bond's probable yield. In the calculation, we assume that the bond will be outstanding until the call date, at which time it will be called. Thus, the investor will have received interest payments for the call-protected period and then will receive the call price—in this case, $1,100—on the call date.)

a.   What is the yield to maturity in 1991 on the bond? What is its yield to call?

b.   If you bought this bond, which return do you think you would actually earn? Explain your reasoning.

c.   Suppose the bond had sold at a discount. Would the yield to maturity or the yield to call have been more relevant?

(Do Parts d and e only if you are using the computerized diskette.)

d.   Suppose the bond's price suddenly jumps to $1,250. What is the yield to maturity now, and what is the yield to call?

e.   Suppose the price suddenly falls to $800; now what would the YTM and YTC be?

Mini Case

Robert Balik and Carol Kiefer are senior vice-presidents of the Mutual of Chicago Insurance Company. They are co-directors of the company's pension fund management division, with Balik having responsibility for fixed income securities (primarily bonds), and Kiefer being responsible for equity investments. A major new client, the California League of Cities, has requested that the company present an investment seminar to the mayors of the represented cities, and Balik and Kiefer, who will make the actual presentation, have asked you to help them by answering the following questions.

Section I: Bond valuation

a. What are the key features of a bond?

b. How is the value of any asset whose value is based on expected future cash flows determined?

c. How is the value of a bond determined? What is the value of a 1-year, $1,000 par value bond with a 10 percent annual coupon if its required rate of return is 10 percent? What is the value of a similar 10-year bond?

d. (1) What would be the value of the bonds described in Part c if, just after they had been issued, the expected inflation rate rose by 3 percentage points, causing investors to require a 13 percent return?

 (2) What would happen to the bonds' value if inflation fell, and k declined to 7 percent?

 (3) What would happen to the value of the 10-year bond over time if the required rate of return remained at 13 percent, or remained at 7 percent?

e. (1) What is the yield to maturity on a 10-year, 9 percent annual coupon, $1,000 par value bond that sells for $887.00? That sells for $1,134.20?

 (2) What is the current yield and capital gains yield in each case?

f. What is interest rate risk? Which bond in Part c has more interest rate risk, the 1-year bond or the 10-year bond?

g. What is reinvestment rate risk? Which bond in Part c has more reinvestment rate risk, assuming a 10-year investment horizon?

h. Redo Parts c and d, assuming that the bonds have semiannual coupons.

i. What is the value of a perpetual bond with an annual coupon of $100 if its required rate of return is 10 percent? 13 percent? 7 percent? Assess the following statement: "Because perpetual bonds match an infinite investment horizon, they have little interest rate risk."

j. Suppose a 10-year, 10 percent, semiannual coupon bond having a par value of $1,000 is currently selling for $1,135.90, producing a yield to maturity of 8.0 percent. However, the bond can be called after 5 years for a price of $1,050.

 (1) What is the bond's yield to call?

 (2) If you bought this bond, do you think you would earn the YTM or the YTC?

Section II: Stock valuation
To illustrate the common stock valuation process, Balik and Kiefer have asked you to analyze the Bon Temps Company, an employment agency that supplies word processors and computer programmers to other businesses with temporarily heavy workloads. You are to answer the following questions.

a. (1) Write out a formula that can be used to value any stock, regardless of its dividend pattern.

 (2) What is a constant growth stock? How are constant growth stocks valued?

 (3) What happens if $g > k_s$? Will many stocks have $g > k_s$?

b. Assume that Bon Temps has a beta coefficient of 1.2, that the risk-free rate (yield on T-bonds) is 10 percent, and that the required rate of return on the market is 15 percent. What is the required rate of return on the firm's stock?

c. Assume that Bon Temps is a constant growth company whose last dividend (D_0, which was paid yesterday) was $2.00 and whose dividend is expected to grow indefinitely at a 6 percent rate.

 (1) What is the firm's expected dividend stream over the next 3 years?

 (2) What is the firm's current stock price?

(3) What is the stock's expected value in one year?

(4) What are the expected dividend yield, capital gains yield, and total return during the first year?

d. Now assume that the stock is currently selling at $21.20. What is the expected rate of return on the stock?

e. What would the stock be worth if its dividends were expected to have zero growth?

f. Now assume that Bon Temps is expected to experience supernormal growth of 30 percent for the next 3 years, then to return to its long-run constant growth rate of 6 percent. What is the stock's value under these conditions? What is its expected dividend yield and capital gains in Year 1? In Year 4?

g. Suppose Bon Temps is expected to experience zero growth during the first 3 years, and then to resume its steady-state growth of 6 percent in the 4th year. What is the stock's value now? What are its expected dividend yield and capital gains yield in Year 1? In Year 4?

h. Finally, assume that Bon Temps's earnings and dividends are expected to decline by 6 percent per year, that is, $g = -6\%$. Why would anyone be willing to buy such a stock, and at what price should it sell? What would be the dividend yield and capital gains yield in each year?

Selected Additional References and Cases

Many investments textbooks cover stock and bond valuation models in depth and detail. Here are some of the good recent ones:

Francis, Jack C., *Investments: Analysis and Management* (New York: McGraw-Hill, 1980).

Radcliffe, Robert C., *Investment: Concepts, Analysis, and Strategy* (Glenview, Ill.: Scott, Foresman, 1990).

Reilly, Frank K., *Investment Analysis and Portfolio Management* (Hinsdale, Ill.: Dryden, 1985).

Sharpe, William F., *Investments* (Englewood Cliffs, N.J.: Prentice-Hall, 1981).

The classic works on stock valuation models are:

Gordon, Myron J., and Eli Shapiro, "Capital Equipment Analysis: The Required Rate of Profit," *Management Science,* October 1956, 102–110.

Williams, John B., *The Theory of Investment Value* (Cambridge, Mass.: Harvard University Press, 1938).

The following classic article extends John B. Williams's works:

Durand, David, "Growth Stocks and the Petersburg Paradox," *Journal of Finance,* September 1957, 348–363.

For three more recent works on valuation, see

Bey, Roger P., and J. Markham Collins, "The Relationship between Before- and After-Tax Yields on Financial Assets," *The Financial Review,* August 1988, 313–343.

Hassell, John M., Robert H. Jennings, and Dennis J. Lasser, "Management Earnings Forecasts: Their Usefulness as a Source of Firm-Specific Information to Security Analysts," *Journal of Financial Research,* Winter 1988, 303–319.

Taylor, Richard W., "The Valuation of Semiannual Bonds between Interest Payment Dates," *The Financial Review,* August 1988, 365–368.

The following case in the Brigham-Gapenski casebook covers many of the valuation concepts contained in Chapter 7:

Case 3, "Sun Coast Securities, Inc. (B)."

APPENDIX 7A

Effects of Personal Taxes

All of the calculations in Chapter 7 were based on cash flows to the investor before personal taxes, CF. However, for investors who must pay taxes, the cash flows which they actually get to keep are the after-tax cash flows, ATCF:

$$\text{ATCF} = \text{CF} - \text{Tax} = \text{CF} - \text{CF(T)} = \text{CF}(1 - T).$$

Here T is the investor's effective tax rate applicable to the cash flow. It is these after-tax cash flows which constitute the *relevant* cash flows, and the relevant yield to maturity and expected rate of return are based on these flows. This distinction is quite important: Because different types of income are subject to different tax rates, it is often necessary to compare after-tax returns to make valid choices among alternative investment opportunities. This appendix presents the effects of personal taxes on bond and stock returns.

Bond Returns

To illustrate tax effects on bond returns, consider a 12 percent coupon, semiannual payment, 20-year bond. If the bond is not callable, then an investor in the 28 percent tax bracket who bought the bond at par would receive an after-tax return, k_{dAT}, found by solving this equation:

$$\$1,000 = \sum_{t=1}^{40} \frac{\$120}{2}(1 - 0.28)\left(\frac{1}{1 + k_{dAT}/2}\right)^t + \$1,000\left(\frac{1}{1 + k_{dAT}/2}\right)^{40}$$

$$= \sum_{t=1}^{40} \$43.20\left(\frac{1}{1 + k_{dAT}/2}\right)^t + \$1,000\left(\frac{1}{1 + k_{dAT}/2}\right)^{40}.$$

The after-tax yield to maturity is k_{dAT} = 8.64 percent, only $1 - T = 1 - 0.28 = 0.72 = 72$ percent of the before tax yield. Thus, the 12.0 percent before-tax return is reduced sharply by taxation.[1]

---

[1]Several points related to the taxation of bonds should be noted:

1. The interest on bonds issued by state and local governments (municipal bonds, or "munis") is normally exempt from federal taxes. However, munis issued to support revenue-producing activities may be subject to the alternative minimum tax (AMT).

2. If a bond was issued at a discount below its par value (an "original issue discount, or OID, bond"), the discount must be amortized over the bond's remaining life, and the annual amortization charge must be added to the coupon interest on an annual basis to determine taxable income.

3. If a bond is bought at a premium above its par value, the premium may be amortized over the bond's remaining life, and the annual amortization charge may be used to reduce the coupon interest, hence taxable income.

4. If you buy a security (other than an OID bond) at one price and sell it at another price, the difference is defined as a capital gain or a capital loss. Before 1987, long-term capital gains (gains on assets held for more than six months) were taxed at rates that were only 40 percent of the rates on ordinary income. That situation no longer exists.

Preferred Stock Returns

If interest rates are expected to remain constant, all of the yield expected on a share of perpetual preferred stock, or its total return, is a dividend yield.[2] For an individual investor, the dividend is taxed at the investor's marginal tax rate, so the after-tax yield is merely

$$\hat{k}_{pAT} = \hat{k}_p(1 - T). \qquad (7A\text{-}1)$$

Here $\hat{k}_{pAT}$ is the after-tax yield, $\hat{k}_p$ is the before-tax yield, and T is the investor's marginal personal tax rate.[3] If an investor in the 28 percent marginal tax bracket bought a preferred stock yielding 10 percent, his or her after-tax nominal rate of return would be 7.2 percent:

$$\hat{k}_{pAT} = 10\%(1 - 0.28) = 10\%(0.72) = 7.2\%.$$

If the owner of the preferred stock is a corporation, 70 percent of the dividend is exempt from income taxes. Thus, the after-tax yield to a corporate owner of preferred stock is found as follows:[4]

$$\hat{k}_{pAT(Corp)} = \hat{k}_p(1 - 0.30T).$$

Assuming the corporation is in the 40 percent federal-plus-state marginal tax bracket, a 10 percent pre-tax preferred would provide an after-tax yield of

$$\hat{k}_{pAT(Corp)} = 10\%[1 - (0.30)(0.40)] = 10\%(0.88) = 8.8\%.$$

This 8.8 percent for the corporate owner compares with a 7.2 percent after-tax yield for an individual in the 28 percent tax bracket. Thus, on an after-tax basis, preferred stocks offer higher returns to corporations than to individual investors when both are taxed at the top marginal tax rate. Thus, most nonconvertible preferred stocks in the United States are owned by corporations, not by individuals.

Common Stock Returns

As with bonds and preferred stocks, the relevant cash flow for a common stock investor who must pay personal taxes is the *after-tax cash flow,* and the relevant rate of return for decision purposes is the *after-tax rate of return.*

---

[2]Interest rates in the economy do change, causing a change in the value of the preferred stock and hence a capital gain or loss, but the *expected* gain or loss is usually zero because the expected future value of k_p is generally the current value, and the expected future price equals the current price.

[3]Note that Equation 7A-1, with k_d in place of $\hat{k}_p$, can also be used to find the after-tax yield to maturity on a bond which sells at par, because the entire yield is in the form of interest payments.

[4]The corporate owner of a share of preferred stock would receive this after-tax dividend from the stock:

$$\text{After-tax dividend} = D - 0.30(T)D = D(1 - 0.30T).$$

Divide by P_0 to put on a yield basis:

$$\hat{k}_{pAT(Corp)} = \frac{D}{P_0}(1 - 0.30T) = \hat{k}_p(1 - 0.30T).$$

Note, though, that if a corporation purchases preferred stock with debt, the exclusion is reduced by the interest deductions.

Constant Growth. Recall that a constant growth stock's expected total return, $\hat{k}_s$, consists of a constant expected dividend yield plus a constant expected capital gains yield. To find the expected total after-tax return, we must adjust both the dividend and the capital gains components for taxes. To illustrate, assume that an individual investor in the 28 percent marginal tax bracket is choosing between the stocks of these two constant growth companies: (1) High-Yield Corporation, with $P_0 = \$30$, $D_1 = \$3.60$, and $g = 3\%$ and (2) High-Growth Company, with $P_0 = \$30$, $D_1 = \$0.90$, and $g = 12\%$. The stock that is selected will be held for one year and then sold. What are the expected before-tax and after-tax rates of return on the two stocks?

Before-tax returns:

$$\text{High-Yield: } \hat{k}_s = \frac{D_1}{P_0} + g = \frac{\$3.60}{\$30} + 3\% = 12\% + 3\% = 15\%.$$

$$\text{High-Growth: } \hat{k}_s = \frac{D_1}{P_0} + g = \frac{\$0.90}{\$30} + 12\% = 3\% + 12\% = 15\%.$$

After-tax returns:

Prior to 1987, long-term capital gains were taxed at a lower rate than dividend income, and this made high-growth stocks much more attractive than those with high yields to stockholders in high tax brackets. Now that capital gains are taxed at the same rate as dividends, the tax advantage of capital gains has been significantly reduced, but not eliminated. The reason capital gains are still better than dividends from a tax standpoint is that the taxes on gains are deferred until the stock is sold, whereas taxes on dividends must be paid each year.

The advantage of the capital gains tax deferral depends upon the investor's time horizon, or the expected holding period. If an investor expects to sell within one year, there is no tax advantage, because taxes will be paid on the capital gains at the same time they are paid on the dividends. On the other hand, if the stock will be held forever (or, really, until the stockholder dies), then no capital gains taxes will ever be paid.[5]

For the High-Yield Corporation and the High-Growth Company, here are the expected after-tax yields for the two extreme holding periods for an investor in the 28 percent tax bracket:

1-Year Holding Period:

$$\text{High-Yield: } \hat{k}_{sAT} = \text{Dividend yield } (1 - T) + \text{Capital gains yield } (1 - T)$$

$$= 12\%(1 - 0.28) + 3\%(1 - 0.28)$$

$$= 8.64\% + 2.16\% = 10.80\%.$$

$$\text{High-Growth: } \hat{k}_{sAT} = 3\%(1 - 0.28) + 12\%(1 - 0.28) = 10.80\%.$$

---

[5]When a stockholder dies, his or her estate must pay estate taxes. However, if stock held by the deceased has risen in value, no capital gains tax liability is due, and the basis of the stock (or other asset) to the beneficiary is the stock's value at the time of death. Therefore, one can escape capital gains taxes by dying. Actually, it generally makes little sense for an elderly or seriously ill stockholder to sell stock that has appreciated greatly in price for precisely this reason.

Infinite Holding Period:

High-Yield: $\hat{k}_{sAT}$ = Dividend yield $(1 - T)$ + Capital gains yield

$$= 12\%(1 - 0.28) + 3\%$$

$$= 8.64\% + 3.00\% = 11.64\%.$$

High-Growth: $\hat{k}_{sAT}$ = $3\%(1 - 0.28) + 12\% = 14.16\%.$

For holding periods greater than one year but less than forever, it is necessary to solve this equation for $\hat{k}_{sAT}$:[6]

$$P_0 = \sum_{t=1}^{n} \frac{D_0(1 + g)^t(1 - T)}{(1 + \hat{k}_{sAT})^t} + \frac{[P_0(1 + g)^n - P_0](1 - T) + P_0}{(1 + \hat{k}_{sAT})^n}. \tag{7A-2}$$

Using *Lotus 1-2-3*, we evaluated Equation 7A-2 for several different holding periods. Here are the after-tax expected rates of return for 5- and 10-year holding periods:

	Expected Rate of Return	
Holding Period	**High-Yield**	**High-Growth**
5-year	10.96%	11.42%
10-year	11.13	12.04

Had the investor been in a zero tax bracket, as are pension funds, many foundations, and some students and retirees, the before- and after-tax returns would have been identical at 15 percent. But for tax-paying investors, more capital gains income than dividend income results in a higher after-tax rate of return.

Because of the deferral of capital gains taxes, stockholders might be expected to prefer corporations that retain earnings, plow them back into the business, and thus provide capital gains instead of paying out dividends. Before accepting this as gospel, however, we must consider many other factors which affect dividend policy. This will be done in Chapter 14. Nevertheless, from a tax standpoint, an investor with a long time horizon who is in a high tax bracket is better off if a high percentage of his or her total return comes as capital gains rather than as dividend income.

Nonconstant Growth. How do we calculate the after-tax expected rate of return on a nonconstant growth stock? Since the dividend yield and capital gains yield components are not constant, we cannot apply Equation 7A-2. Instead, we must revert to our general stock valuation model, and again, we must specify a holding period. We then proceed by (1) placing the expected before-tax cash flows on a time line consistent with the assumed holding period, (2) converting the cash flows to an after-tax stream, and (3) then calculating the expected rate of return on this stream, which is the expected after-tax rate of return.

To illustrate, we can determine the expected after-tax yield on the Solar Laser Technology (SLT) stock. SLT's last dividend (D_0) was $1.82, its growth rate is expected to be 30 percent for 3 years and 10 percent thereafter, and the required rate of return on its stock, k_s, is 16.0 percent. Assume that the investor in question has a marginal tax rate, T, of 28 percent and a holding period of five years, and that SLT's current market price is $53.86. Figure 7A-1 shows the time line solution; the expected after-tax rate of return is 12.12 percent.

---

[6]The after-tax expected rate of return to a corporation which holds another firm's stock is found in a similar manner, except only 30 percent of the dividends received are taxable.

Figure 7A-1   After-Tax Rate of Return: Solar Laser Technology

1. Before-Tax Cash Flows, End of Year:

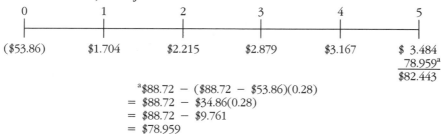

$$\hat{P}_5 = \frac{D_6}{k_s - g}$$

$$= \frac{\$5.323}{0.16 - 0.10}$$

$$= \$88.72$$

$D_0 = \$1.820$ $D_1 = \$2.366$ $D_2 = \$3.076$ $D_3 = \$3.999$ $D_4 = \$4.399$ $D_5 = \$4.839$ $D_6 = \$5.323$

$P_0 = \$53.86$

2. After-Tax Cash Flows, End of Year:

0	1	2	3	4	5
($53.86)	$1.704	$2.215	$2.879	$3.167	$ 3.484
					78.959[a]
					$82.443

[a]$88.72 − ($88.72 − $53.86)(0.28)
= $88.72 − $34.86(0.28)
= $88.72 − $9.761
= $78.959

3. Insert indicated after-tax cash flows into a financial calculator and solve for IRR:

$$IRR = \hat{k}_{sAT} = 12.12\%.$$

CHAPTER 8

The Cost of Capital

Electric utilities and telephone companies are, to a large extent, *natural monopolies,* which means that one firm can serve customers in a given area at a lower cost than could two or more firms. Therefore, utilities have been granted legal monopoly status in their service areas. While this improves operating efficiency, it also creates a problem—monopolists have the power to raise prices, to exploit their customers, and to earn unreasonably high rates of return on their invested capital. To obtain the efficiencies of single-firm operations yet prevent customers from being charged "unfair" prices, public utilities in the United States are regulated by public utility commissions.

What constitutes a fair price for a utility's services? There are many issues involved in this determination, but, to oversimplify a bit, the generally accepted answer is this: "The price that a utility is allowed to charge should be sufficient to cover all reasonable operating costs and to leave a profit which is just large enough to cover the cost of the capital investors have supplied to make it possible for the company to operate." Operationally, this means that a utility commission must examine each company under its jurisdiction to insure that its operating costs are reasonable, to ascertain how much capital investors have supplied, to determine the cost of that capital, to multiply the dollars of capital times the cost of capital to determine the company's target profit level, and then to set utility service rates that will produce that target profit level.

By far the most difficult part of this process is determining the cost of capital. That determination is made in rate cases, where utilities present evidence as to what their cost of capital is, and then other parties, especially people representing the utilities' customers, present their own counter-evidence. Invariably, the companies produce a relatively high estimate of the cost of capital (which would result in high profits), while consumer advocates produce low estimates (which would result in lower customer bills). The commissioners must sit as judge and jury, and must decide whose story to believe or how to reach a compromise. The decision is important, for if the cost of capital is underestimated, then the companies will not be allowed to earn their true cost of capital, the industry will not be able to attract sufficient capital in the long run, and, eventually, there will be power shortages and/or poor telephone service. On the other hand, if the estimated cost of capital is too high, utility customers will be charged too much, and there will be a transfer of wealth from utility customers to utility investors.

A firm's cost of capital is critically important for three reasons: (1) Maximizing the value of a firm requires that the costs of all inputs, including capital, be minimized, and to minimize the cost of capital we must be able to estimate it. (2) Capital budgeting decisions require an estimate of the cost of capital. (3) Many other types of decisions, including those related to public utility regulation, leasing, bond refunding, and short-term asset management, require estimates of the cost of capital.

At the 1989 Annual Meeting of the Financial Management Association, one session was devoted to a panel discussion on cost of capital. Here, financial managers from Hershey Foods, Du Pont, and Ameritech, among others, discussed procedures for estimating each corporation's cost of capital. All of the panelists agreed that while the task is difficult, it is essential to good decision making, especially in the key capital budgeting area. Further, they agreed that the overall corporate cost-of-capital estimate should be viewed only as the first step in the development of divisional and specific project costs of capital. In this chapter, we discuss the actual process of estimating a firm's overall, or weighted average, cost of capital. Then, in Chapter 11, we discuss the adjustment process used to estimate divisional and project costs of capital.

CAPITAL COMPONENTS AND COSTS

In developing the firm's overall cost of capital, we first identify and then determine the cost of each component, and then we combine the component costs to form the *weighted average cost of capital (WACC)*. Capital, as we use the term, represents the funds used to finance the firm's assets and operations. The sales which produce profits are not possible without the assets that are shown on the left side of the balance sheet, and those assets must be financed from the sources shown on the right side. Thus, capital constitutes the entire right-hand side of the balance sheet, including both short-term and long-term debt, preferred stock, and common equity.

Capital Components

Our first task is to decide which capital sources should be included when we estimate the WACC. Since the cost of capital is used primarily in the process of making long-term investment decisions, our discussion will focus on the development of the cost of capital for capital budgeting purposes. First, consider the firm's short-term, non-interest-bearing liabilities: accounts payable, accrued wages, and accrued taxes. All of these items arise from normal operations; if sales increase, then funds are spontaneously (automatically) generated from these sources. In capital budgeting analyses, the dollar amount of the spontaneously generated liabilities associated with a given project is subtracted from the amount that would otherwise be required to finance the project. To illustrate, assume that a potential project has a total cost of $2,000,000, consisting of $1,500,000 of fixed assets and $500,000 of required new current assets, say inventories. However, if payables and accruals will spontaneously increase by $200,000 if the project is undertaken, then these funds serve to offset the increase in current assets. Thus, the project's required net current assets (or net working capital) would be only $300,000, and the net funds required for the project would be only $1,800,000.

Increase in fixed assets		$1,500,000
Increase in current assets	$500,000	
Less: Increase in spontaneous liabilities	200,000	300,000
Net funds required for project		$1,800,000

It is the cost of this $1,800,000 that concerns us; will the return on the project be high enough to cover the cost of the $1,800,000 of nonspontaneous capital required to undertake it? Since we are concerned only with the cost of the nonspontaneous capital, spontaneously generated current liabilities are not included when the WACC is estimated.

We must also decide how to treat short-term notes payable, often bank loans, which are not generated spontaneously. The answer depends on whether the firm deliberately uses short-term debt to finance long-term investments. If short-term debt is only used as temporary financing to support cyclical or seasonal fluctuations in current assets, it should not be included in the firm's WACC. However, if the firm does use short-term debt as part of its permanent financing, then such debt should be included in the cost-of-capital estimate. As we will show in Chapter 19, the use of nonspontaneous short-term debt to finance long-term assets is highly risky, and it is not common among well-managed firms. Therefore, in this chapter, we shall assume that interest-bearing short-term debt is used to support cyclical or seasonal working capital, and since our primary focus is on developing a cost of capital for use in capital budgeting, we shall exclude short-term debt when we estimate the WACC unless otherwise noted. Long-term debt, preferred stock, and common equity (common stock plus retained earnings) are the primary sources of capital for capital expansion, so they are the components included in the WACC estimate.

In summary, the relevant capital components for cost of capital purposes include (1) that portion of short-term interest-bearing debt that is considered to be permanent financing; (2) all long-term debt; (3) all preferred stock; and (4) all common equity. Non-interest-bearing liabilities such as accounts payable and accruals are netted out in the capital budgeting process and are excluded from the cost of capital calculations.

Taxes

In developing the costs for the different capital components, the issue of taxes arises: Should we use a before- or an after-tax cost? In considering this question, remember that stockholders are concerned primarily with the cash flows that are available for their use, namely, those cash flows available to common shareholders after corporate taxes have been paid. Therefore, if management is to maximize stockholder well-being and thereby maximize the price of the stock, all cash flow/rate of return calculations must be done on an after-tax basis. *For this reason, the WACC must be developed on an after-tax basis, which means that we must consider corporate tax effects when we determine the cost of each relevant capital component.*

Historical versus New, or Marginal, Costs

Another issue is this: Is the historical, or embedded, cost of the capital that was raised in the past relevant, or should we focus on the cost of new, marginal funds? Embedded costs are important for some decisions. For example, the average cost of all the capital raised in the past and still outstanding is relevant to regulators who determine the allowed rate of return for a public utility. However, in financial management, the WACC is used primarily to make capital budgeting decisions, and these decisions hinge on the cost of new, or marginal, capital. *Thus, for our purposes in this chapter, the relevant costs are not historical costs but, rather, the marginal costs of new funds to be raised during the planning period.*

Self-Test Questions

What financing sources are typically included, and which ones excluded, when a firm estimates its WACC? Explain.

Should the component cost estimates be on a before-tax or after-tax basis? Why?

Should the component cost estimates reflect historical or marginal costs? Why?

COST OF DEBT

As discussed in the previous section, the relevant cost of debt is the after-tax cost of new debt. Although estimating this cost is conceptually straightforward, some problems arise in practice. First, as noted in an earlier section, it is necessary to decide whether or not short-term debt should be included in the WACC. Second, not all long-term debt has a fixed and known payment schedule: companies use both fixed and floating rate debt, straight and convertible debt, and debt both with and without sinking funds, and each form of debt generally has a somewhat different cost.

It is unlikely that the financial manager will know at the start of a planning period the exact types and amounts of debt that will be used during the planning period: the type of debt actually used will depend on the specific assets to be financed and on capital market conditions as they develop over time. Even so, the financial manager does know what types of debt are typical for his or her firm. For example, Nachman Computer Corporation (NCC), a full-line computer manufacturer, typically sells commercial paper to raise short-term money to finance cyclical working capital needs, and it uses 30-year bonds to raise long-term debt capital. Thus, for planning purposes, NCC's managers include only long-term debt in their WACC estimate, and they assume that this debt will consist of 30-year bonds.

Assume that it is January 1991, and NCC's financial managers are developing the firm's WACC estimate for the coming year. How should they determine the component cost of debt? Most financial managers would begin by discussing current and prospective interest rates with their firms' investment bankers. Assume that NCC's bankers stated that a new 30-year, noncallable, straight bond issue would require an 11 percent coupon rate with semiannual payments, and that it would be offered to the public at a $1,000 par value. Flotation costs are estimated to be 1 percent of the issue, or $10 for every $1,000 par value bond. Thus, the net proceeds from each bond would be $1,000 minus a $10 flotation cost, or $990. NCC's marginal federal-plus-state tax rate is 40 percent.

With this information, we would estimate the cost of debt in two steps:

1. Find the *before-tax flotation-adjusted cost to the company* using this equation:

$$\begin{array}{c}\text{Net proceeds} \\ \text{of bond}\end{array} = \sum_{t=1}^{2n} \frac{\begin{array}{c}\text{Semiannual} \\ \text{interest payment}\end{array}}{(1 + k_d/2)^t} + \frac{\text{Par value}}{(1 + k_d/2)^{2n}} \qquad \textbf{(8-1)}$$

$$\$990 = \sum_{t=1}^{60} \frac{\$55}{(1 + k_d/2)^t} + \frac{\$1,000}{(1 + k_d/2)^{60}}.$$

Using a financial calculator, we find $k_d/2 = 5.56\%$, hence the flotation-adjusted $k_d = 11.11\%$.

2. Adjust for taxes using this equation:

$$\text{After-tax cost of debt} = \text{Pre-tax cost}(1 - T)$$

$$= (\text{Flotation-adjusted } k_d)(1 - T) \qquad \textbf{(8-2)}$$

$$= 11.11\%(0.60) = 6.67\%.$$

Note that most public offerings of debt have flotation costs of less than one percentage point, and flotation costs are even lower on private placements. Thus, if flotation costs were simply ignored, and the component cost of debt were found as

$k_d(1 - T)$, the error would not be very large.[1] In our own example, $k_d(1 - T) =$ 11%(0.60) = 6.60%, hence the error would be only seven basis points.[2]

Before closing our discussion of the cost of debt, we should note one additional point regarding the tax adjustment. In our example, we used a marginal tax rate of 40 percent. Therefore, we were implicitly assuming that NCC's marginal tax rate over the next 30 years will remain at 40 percent. However, there are three potential problems with this assumption: (1) The value of the tax deduction depends on the taxable income for each year, and a change in taxable income might lead to a change in the marginal tax rate, hence to a change in the after-tax cost of debt. (2) Tax losses can only be carried back for three years; therefore, several years of consecutive losses would mean that the benefits of tax deductibility could not be realized in the year the interest is paid. Instead, this benefit would be delayed until the firm becomes profitable, and this would raise the after-tax cost of debt. (3) Congress could raise or lower the applicable tax rate, which would also have an effect on the after-tax cost of debt. For all these reasons, we should recognize that firms cannot be certain of the true effects of tax deductibility, so the true after-tax cost of debt could be higher or lower than the estimated cost.

Self-Test Questions

What impact do flotation costs have on the cost of debt? Are these costs generally material?

How is the before-tax cost of debt converted to an after-tax cost?

What could happen over time to cause the actual after-tax cost of debt to differ from the estimated cost?

COST OF PREFERRED STOCK

A number of firms, including Nachman Computer Corporation, use preferred stocks as part of their permanent financing mix. To determine this cost, we first note that preferred dividends, like common dividends, are not tax deductible. *Therefore, no*

---

[1]Several other points should be made. First, if the bond is callable, then we might want to analyze the yield to call. However, for newly issued bonds, the expected yield to call is equal to the yield to maturity. Second, it is sometimes suggested that the effective annual rate cost of debt should be used in the WACC. In our example, the flotation-adjusted effective annual rate is $(1.0556)^2 - 1.0 = 0.1143 = 11.43\%$. That position would be correct only if the cost of common stock were based on a quarterly compounding model and if, in capital budgeting, an attempt were made to determine exactly when, during the year, cash flows would come in rather than assuming end-of-year flows. In view of the uncertainties inherent in cost of equity estimation, and the even greater uncertainties about the cash flows of projects over their operating lives, we (and most people in industry) think it would be pointless to attempt to estimate effective rates and intra-year cash flows; it would even be misleading in that such calculations would imply greater accuracy than exists in the basic data. Further, it would be inconsistent to combine an effective bond yield with a nominal return on equity—the bond's cost would be inflated vis-à-vis that of the equity. Finally, note that the flotation cost can be amortized over the life of the bond ($10/30 = $0.33 per year, or $0.167 per semiannual period). This saves taxes in the amount of $0.167(T) = $0.167(0.40) = $0.067 per period. Theoretically, we should take this tax savings into account, but ignoring it does not introduce a material error.

[2]A basis point is 1/100 of a percentage point. Investment bankers in particular use this term.

tax adjustment is necessary when calculating the cost of preferred stocks. Second, although preferred used to be issued without a stated maturity date, almost all preferred issued in recent years does have a call feature and/or a sinking fund. Finally, although it is not mandatory that preferred stock dividends be paid, firms do generally have every intention of meeting their preferred dividend payments, because if they fail to do so (1) they cannot pay dividends on their common stock, (2) they will find it very difficult to raise additional funds in the capital markets, and (3) in some cases preferred stockholders have the right to assume control of the firm.

With these points in mind, assume that NCC's investment bankers indicated that the firm could sell perpetual preferred stock with a 10 percent yield. If the stock had a par value of $100, then the annual dividend would be $10. Additionally, the investment bankers stated that the flotation costs would amount to 2.5 percent of the par value. Thus, the firm would net $97.50 from each share sold, and it would have an obligation to pay $10 of dividends per share per year. Thus, we calculate the component cost of preferred stock as follows:

$$\text{Component cost of preferred stock} = k_p = \frac{D_p}{P_n}. \qquad \textbf{(8-3)}$$

Here D_p is the annual preferred dividend and P_n is the price the firm receives net of flotation costs. Applying Equation 8-3 to our example, we find NCC's cost of preferred stock to be 10.26 percent:[3]

$$k_p = \frac{D_p}{P_n} = \frac{\$10}{\$97.50} = 0.1026 = 10.26\%.$$

Self-Test Questions

Describe how the cost of preferred stocks is estimated.

Are any tax adjustments required when estimating the cost of preferred stocks? Explain.

COST OF RETAINED EARNINGS

A firm can raise common equity capital in two ways: (1) by retaining earnings and (2) by issuing new common stock. Thus, when we consider NCC's component cost of equity, we must consider the costs of two different types of equity. We first examine the cost of retained earnings.

---

[3]Most preferred stocks pay quarterly dividends, so we could calculate an effective return based on quarterly compounding. However, for the same reasons we discussed in Footnote 1 in connection with debt, it would be inappropriate (or at least not worthwhile) to do so. We should also note that firms have begun to issue variable, or floating rate, bonds and preferred stocks. Since future capital market rates are difficult, if not impossible, to predict, future interest payments and preferred dividends are normally estimated on the basis of current rates, hence the expected costs of floating rate securities are the same as for identical fixed rate securities. However, the realized cost of a floating rate issue can be higher or lower than expected, depending on the actual rates over the life of the security, whereas the realized cost of a fixed rate security is known with relative certainty. Finally, note that current tax laws do not permit either preferred or common stock flotation costs to be expensed against taxable income.

The costs of debt and preferred stock are based on the return that investors require on these securities, and the cost of equity obtained by retaining earnings can be defined similarly: *It is k_s, the rate of return stockholders require on the firm's common stock.* The reason why we must assign a cost of capital to retained earnings involves the *opportunity cost principle*. The firm's net income after taxes and after preferred dividends literally belongs to its common stockholders. Bondholders are compensated by interest payments; preferred stockholders are compensated by fixed dividend payments; and the firm's remaining income belongs to its common stockholders and serves to "pay the rent" on stockholders' capital.

Management may either pay out earnings in the form of dividends or retain earnings for reinvestment in the business. If part of the earnings is retained, an *opportunity cost* is incurred: stockholders could have received these earnings as dividends and then invested this money in stocks, bonds, real estate, and so on. *Thus, the firm should earn on its retained earnings at least as much as its stockholders themselves could earn on alternative investments of equivalent risk.*

What rate of return can stockholders expect to earn on other investments of equivalent risk? The answer is k_s, because they can earn this return in the market simply by buying the stock of the firm in question or the stock of a similar firm. Therefore, if our firm cannot invest retained earnings and earn at least k_s, then it should pay these earnings to its stockholders so that they can invest the money themselves in assets that do provide this return.

Whereas debt and preferred stocks are contractual obligations which have easily determined costs, it is not at all easy to estimate k_s. Three methods can be used: (1) the Capital Asset Pricing Model (CAPM), (2) the Discounted Cash Flow (DCF) model, and (3) the bond-yield-plus-risk-premium approach. These methods should not be regarded as mutually exclusive, for none of them dominates the others, and all are subject to error when used in practice. When faced with the task of estimating a company's cost of equity, we generally use all three methods and then choose among them on the basis of our confidence in the data used for each in the specific case at hand.

Self-Test Questions

What are the two types of common equity whose costs must be estimated?

Explain why there is a cost associated with retained earnings.

THE CAPM APPROACH

As we saw in Chapter 5, the Capital Asset Pricing Model is based on some unrealistic assumptions, and it cannot be empirically verified. Still, the model is often used in the cost of capital estimation process because of its logical appeal.

Under the CAPM we assume that the cost of equity is equal to the risk-free rate plus a risk premium that is based solely on the stock's beta coefficient and the market risk premium as set forth in the Security Market Line (SML) equation:

$$k_s = \text{Risk-free rate} + \text{Risk premium}$$

$$= k_{RF} + (k_M - k_{RF})b_i.$$

Given estimates of (1) the risk-free rate, k_{RF}; (2) the beta of the firm's stock, b_i; and (3) the required rate of return on the market, k_M, we can estimate the required rate of return on the firm's stock, k_s. This required return can then be used as an estimate of the cost of retained earnings.

Estimating the Risk-Free Rate

The starting point for the CAPM cost of equity estimate is k_{RF}, the risk-free rate. There is really no such thing in the U.S. economy as a riskless asset. Treasury securities are essentially free of default risk, but long-term T-bonds will suffer capital losses if interest rates rise, and a portfolio invested in short-term T-bills will provide a volatile earnings stream because the rate paid on T-bills varies over time.

Since we cannot in practice find a truly riskless rate upon which to base the CAPM, what rate should we use? Our preference — and this preference is shared by most practitioners — is to use the rate on long-term Treasury bonds. Our reasons follow:

1.   Capital market rates include a real, riskless rate (generally thought to vary from 2 to 4 percent) plus a premium for inflation which reflects the expected inflation rate over the life of the asset, be it 30 days or 30 years. The expected rate of inflation is likely to be relatively high during booms and low during recessions. Therefore, during booms T-bill rates tend to be high to reflect the high current inflation rate, whereas in recessions T-bill rates are generally low. T-bond rates, on the other hand, reflect expected inflation rates over a long period, so they are far less volatile than T-bill rates.

2.   Common stocks are long-term securities, and although a particular stockholder may not have a long investment horizon, the majority of stockholders does invest on a long-term basis. Therefore, it is reasonable to think that stock returns embody long-term inflation expectations similar to those embodied in bonds rather than the short-term inflation expectations embodied in bills. On this account, the cost of equity should be more highly correlated with T-bond rates than with T-bill rates.

3.   Treasury bill rates are subject to more random disturbances than are Treasury bond rates. For example, bills are used by the Federal Reserve System to control the money supply, and bills are also used by foreign governments, firms, and individuals as a temporary safe house for money. Thus, if the Fed decides to stimulate the economy, it drives down the bill rate, and the same thing happens if trouble erupts somewhere in the world and money flows into U.S. dollars seeking a temporary haven. T-bond rates are also influenced by Fed actions and by international money flows, but not to the same extent as T-bill rates. This is another reason why T-bill rates are more volatile than T-bond rates and, most experts agree, more volatile than k_s.

4.   T-bills are essentially free of interest rate risk, but they are exposed to a relatively high degree of reinvestment rate risk. Long-term investors such as pension

funds and life insurance companies are probably more concerned about reinvestment rate risk than interest rate risk. Therefore, most long-term investors would feel more exposed to risk if they held bills than if they held bonds.

5.   We have seen the CAPM used to estimate a particular firm's cost of equity over time. When T-bill rates were low, in 1977 and 1978, the CAPM cost of equity estimate was about 11 percent. When T-bill rates shot up in 1979 and 1980, the CAPM estimate more than doubled, to 23 percent. The company's bond yields, meanwhile, only rose from 9 to 14 percent. Neither we nor the company's management believed that the cost of equity rose by 12 full percentage points at a time when the cost of long-term debt was rising by only 5 percentage points. CAPM estimates based on T-bond yields produced much more reasonable results.[4]

In view of the preceding discussion, it is our view that common equity costs are more logically related to Treasury bond rates than to T-bill rates. This leads us to favor T-bonds as the base rate, or k_{RF}, in a CAPM cost of equity analysis. T-bond rates can be found in *The Wall Street Journal* or the *Federal Reserve Bulletin*. Generally, we use the yield on a 20-year T-bond as the proxy for the risk-free rate. Assuming that this rate was 8.0 percent in January 1991, we would use this as our estimate for k_{RF} in a January 1991 CAPM cost of equity estimate.

Estimating the Market Risk Premium

The market risk premium, $RP_M = k_M - k_{RF}$, can be estimated on the basis of (1) ex post, or historical, returns or (2) ex ante, or forward-looking, returns.

Ex Post Risk Premiums.   The most complete, accurate, and up-to-date ex post risk premium study is available annually from Ibbotson Associates, which examines market data over long periods of time to find the average annual rates of return on stocks, T-bills, T-bonds, and a set of high-grade corporate bonds.[5] For example, Table 8-1 summarizes some results from their 1990 study, which covers the period 1926–1989.

Note that common stocks provided the highest average return over the 64-year period, while Treasury bills gave the lowest. T-bills barely covered inflation over the

---

[4]All of this can be illustrated by a true but not-very-funny story. A particular state public utility commission hired a professor who used T-bill rates as the base rate in his CAPM analysis to estimate the cost of capital for the state's utilities. Each utility's cost of capital in turn was built into its electric, gas, or telephone rates. Therefore, the lower the cost of capital, the lower the utility service rates, and the lower the service rates, the less political heat the commission faced. This particular commission was very politically sensitive — so much so that one of its staff members admitted privately that the commission had selected its cost of capital expert on the basis of who could produce the lowest number.

The commission hired the professor in 1978, when T-bill rates were very low, as were his CAPM cost of equity estimates based on the T-bill rate. But the rate cases did not come up until 1979, and by then, the bill rate had gone through the roof. As a result, the professor's cost of equity estimates were even higher than the companies were asking permission to earn! At that point, the commission rejected the CAPM approach and sent the professor home.

[5]See *Stocks, Bonds, Bills and Inflation: 1990 Yearbook* (Chicago: Ibbotson Associates, 1990). Also, note that Ibbotson Associates now recommends using the T-bond rate as the proxy for the risk-free rate when using the CAPM. Before 1988, Ibbotson Associates recommended that T-bills be used.

Table 8-1   Selected Ibbotson Associates Data, 1926–1989

	Arithmetic Mean	Standard Deviation
Total Return Data		
Common stocks	12.4%	20.9%
Long-term corporate bonds	5.5	8.5
Long-term government bonds	4.9	8.6
Treasury bills	3.7	3.4
Inflation rate	3.2	4.8
Risk Premium Data		
Common stocks over T-bills	8.6%	20.8%
Common stocks over T-bonds	7.5	Not available
Common stocks over corporate bonds	6.9	Not available
T-bonds over T-bills	1.2	7.9

period, but common stocks provided a substantial real return. However, the superior returns on stock investments had its cost—stocks were by far the riskiest of the investments listed as judged by standard deviation, and they would also rank as riskiest within a market risk framework. To further illustrate the risk differentials, the range of annual returns on stocks was from −43.3 to 54.0 percent, while the range on T-bills was only 0.0 to 14.7 percent. The study provides strong empirical support for the basic premise that we discussed in earlier chapters—namely, that higher returns can be obtained only by bearing greater risk.

The study also reported the risk premiums, or differences, among the various securities. For example, Ibbotson Associates found the average risk premium of stocks over T-bonds to be 7.5 percentage points.[6] However, these premiums have large standard deviations, so one must use them with caution. Also, it should be noted that the choice of the beginning and ending periods can have a major impact on the calculated risk premiums. Ibbotson Associates used the longest period available to them, but had their data begun some years earlier or later, or ended earlier,

---

[6]It is worth noting that Ibbotson Associates calculated average returns on two bases: (1) by taking each of the 64 annual holding period returns and deriving the arithmetic average of these annual returns, and (2) by finding the compound annual rate of return over the whole period, which amounts to a geometric average. The stocks over T-bonds risk premium as measured by arithmetic averages is 1.8 percentage points higher than the geometric mean risk premium. This leads to the question of which average to use. The arithmetic average is most consistent with the standard CAPM; under the CAPM, investors are supposed to be concerned with returns during the next period (say one year) and to focus on the expected return and the standard deviation of this return.

It has also been argued that the 1926–1989 risk premiums overstate "true" risk premiums, because there was a long-term trend during that period toward more inflation, and the rising inflation rate raised long-term interest rates, lowered bond prices, and resulted in realized yields on long-term bonds that were below the ex ante expected yields. If realized bond yields were below expected yields, then the risk premium as measured by $\bar{k}_{Stocks} - \bar{k}_{Bonds} = RP_{Market}$ will overstate the "true" required risk premium. If this is correct, then the 7.5 percentage point market risk premium of stocks over T-bonds reported by Ibbotson Associates is too large for use in the CAPM.

their results would have been seriously affected. Indeed, over many periods their data would indicate *negative* risk premiums, which would lead to the conclusion that Treasury securities have a higher required return than common stocks, which in turn is contrary to both financial theory and common sense. All this suggests that historical risk premiums should be approached with caution. As one businessman muttered after listening to a professor give a lecture on the CAPM, "Beware of academicians bearing gifts!"

Ex Ante Risk Premiums. The ex post approach to risk premiums used by Ibbotson Associates assumes that investors expect future results, on average, to equal past results. However, as we noted, the estimated risk premium varies greatly depending on the period selected, and, in any event, investors today probably expect results in the future to be different from those achieved during the Great Depression of the 1930s, during the World War II years of the 1940s, and during the peaceful boom years of the 1950s, all of which are included (and given equal weight with more recent results) in the Ibbotson Associates data. The questionable assumption that future expectations are equal to past realizations, together with the sometimes non-sensical results obtained in historical risk premium studies, has led to a search for ex ante risk premiums.

The most common approach to ex ante premiums uses the Discounted Cash Flow (DCF) model to estimate the expected market rate of return, $\hat{k}_M = k_M$; then calculates RP_M as $k_M - k_{RF}$; and finally uses this estimate of RP_M in the CAPM model. This procedure recognizes that, if markets are in equilibrium, the expected rate of return on the market portfolio is also its required rate of return. Thus, if we can estimate $\hat{k}_M$, we also have an estimate of k_M:

$$\begin{array}{c}\text{Expected} \\ \text{rate of return}\end{array} = \hat{k}_M = \frac{D_1}{P_0} + g = k_{RF} + RP_M = k_M = \begin{array}{c}\text{Required} \\ \text{rate of return}\end{array}$$

Since D_1 for the market, say the S&P 500, can be predicted quite accurately, and since the current market value of the index (used for P_0) is also known, the major task is to estimate g, the average expected long-term growth rate for the market index. Even here, however, the estimation task is simplified, because one can more reasonably assume a constant long-term growth rate for a portfolio of stocks such as the S&P 500, than for any one stock.

Financial services companies such as Merrill Lynch publish, on a regular basis, a forecast based on DCF methodology for the expected rate of return on the market, $\hat{k}_M$. For example, Merrill Lynch puts out such a forecast in its bimonthly publication *Quantitative Analysis*. One can subtract the current T-bond rate from such a market forecast to obtain an estimate of the current market risk premium, RP_M. To illustrate, assume that Merrill Lynch's reported expected return on the market in January 1991 was 14.0 percent. The T-bond rate, as mentioned earlier, is assumed to be 8.0 percent. Thus, Merrill Lynch's implied market risk premium over T-bonds would be 6.0 percentage points.

Two potential problems arise when we attempt to use data from organizations such as Merrill Lynch. First, what we really want is *investors'* expectations, and not those of security analysts. However, this is probably not a major problem, since several studies have proved beyond much doubt that investors, on average, form their own expectations on the basis of professional analysts' forecasts. The second problem is that there are a number of securities firms besides Merrill Lynch, and, at any given time, their forecasts of future market returns are generally somewhat different. This suggests that it would be most appropriate to obtain a number of forecasts of $\hat{k}_M$, and then to use the average value to estimate RP_M for use in the CAPM. A service (Institutional Brokers Estimate System, or IBES) publishes data on the forecasts of essentially all widely followed analysts, so one can use the IBES aggregate growth rate forecast, along with an aggregate dividend yield, to develop a consensus RP_M forecast, and thus avoid potential bias from the use of only one organization's estimate. However, we have followed the forecasts of several of the larger organizations over a period of several years, and we have rarely found their $\hat{k}_M$ estimates to differ by more than ± 0.3 percentage points from one another. Therefore, for present purposes, the Merrill Lynch $\hat{k}_M = k_M = 14.0\%$ and $RP_M = 6.0$ percentage points may be considered to be a "reasonable" proxy for the expectations of the marginal investor. Note, though, that ex ante risk premiums are not stable: they vary over time. Therefore, when using the CAPM to estimate the cost of equity, it is essential to use current estimates of the ex ante RP_M.

Estimating Beta

The last parameter needed for a CAPM cost of equity estimate is the beta coefficient. Recall from Chapter 5 that a stock's beta is a measure of its volatility relative to that of an average stock, and that betas are generally estimated from the stock's characteristic line; that is, estimated by running a linear regression between past returns on the stock in question and past returns on some market index. We will define betas developed in this manner as *historical betas*.

Note, however, that historical betas show how risky a stock was *in the past,* whereas investors are interested in *future* risk. It may be that a given company appeared to be quite safe in the past, but that things have changed, and its future risk is judged to be higher than its past risk, or vice versa. AT&T is a good example. AT&T was among the bluest of the blue chips when it owned the regional telephone companies, but investors now recognize that AT&T as it exists today faces far more intense competition than it ever faced in the past. Chrysler, on the other hand, was practically bankrupt a few years ago, but it now appears to be quite healthy. Therefore, one would think that Chrysler's risk had declined while AT&T's had increased.

Now consider the use of beta as a measure of a company's risk. If we use a historical beta in a CAPM framework to measure the firm's cost of equity, we are implicitly assuming that its future risk is the same as its past risk. This would be a troublesome assumption for a company like Chrysler or AT&T today. But what about most companies in most years: As a general rule, is future risk sufficiently similar to past risk to warrant the use of historical betas in a CAPM framework? For individual firms, past risk is often *not* a good predictor of future risk, and historical betas of individual firms are often not very stable.

Since historical betas may not be good predictors of future risk, researchers have sought ways to improve them. This has led to the development of two different types of betas: (1) adjusted betas and (2) fundamental betas. *Adjusted betas* grew largely out of the work of Marshall E. Blume, who showed that true betas tend to move toward 1.0 over time.[7] Therefore, one can begin with a firm's pure historical statistical beta, make an adjustment for the expected future movement toward 1.0, and produce an adjusted beta which will, on average, be a better predictor of the future beta than would the unadjusted historical beta. The adjustment process involves some complex statistics, so we shall not cover it here.

Other researchers have extended the adjustment process to include such fundamental risk variables as financial leverage, sales volatility, and the like. The end product here is a *fundamental beta*.[8] These betas are constantly adjusted to reflect changes in a firm's operations and capital structure, whereas with historical betas (including adjusted ones) such changes might not be reflected until several years after the company's "true" beta had changed.

Adjusted betas are obviously heavily dependent on unadjusted historical betas, and so are fundamental betas as they are actually calculated. Therefore, the plain old historical beta, calculated as the slope of the characteristic line, is important even if one goes on to develop a more exotic version. With this in mind, it should be noted that several different sets of data can be used to calculate historical betas, and the different data sets produce different results. Here are some points to note:

1. Betas can be based on historical periods of different lengths. For example, data for the past one, two, three, and so on, years may be used. Most people who calculate betas today use five years of data, but this choice is arbitrary, and different lengths of time usually alter significantly the calculated beta for a given company.[9]

2. Returns may be calculated on holding periods of different lengths—a day, a week, a month, a quarter, a year, and so on. For example, if it has been decided to analyze data on NYSE stocks over a five-year period, then we might obtain $52(5) = 260$ weekly returns on each stock and on the market index. We could also use $12(5) = 60$ monthly returns, or $1(5) = 5$ annual returns. The set of returns on each stock, however large it turns out to be, would then be regressed on the corresponding market returns to obtain the stock's beta. In statistical analysis, it is generally better to have more rather than fewer observations, because using more observations generally leads to greater statistical confidence. This suggests the use of weekly returns, and, say, five years of data, for a sample size of 260, or even daily returns for a still larger sample size. However, the shorter the holding period, the more likely the data are to exhibit random "noise," and the greater the number of

---

[7]See Marshall E. Blume, "Betas and Their Regression Tendencies," *Journal of Finance,* June 1975, 785–796.

[8]See Barr Rosenberg and James Guy, "Beta and Investment Fundamentals," *Financial Analysts Journal,* May–June 1976, 60–72. Rosenberg, a professor at the University of California at Berkeley, later set up a company which calculates fundamental betas by a proprietary procedure and then sells them to institutional investors.

[9]A commercial provider of betas once told the authors that his firm, and others, did not know what the right period was to use, but they decided to use five years in order to reduce the apparent differences between various services' betas, because large differences reduced everyone's credibility!

Table 8-2   Beta Coefficients for Five Companies, April 1990

	Merrill Lynch	Value Line
Chrysler	1.46	1.40
Polaroid	1.29	1.25
IBM	0.84	0.90
Mobil	0.74	0.85
Southwestern Public Service	0.39	0.75

years of data, the more likely it is that the company's basic risk position will have changed (for example, see the preceding comments on Chrysler and AT&T). Thus, the choice of both the number of years of data and the length of the holding period for calculating rates of return involves tradeoffs between a desire to have many observations versus a desire to have recent and consequently more relevant data.

3.   The value used to represent "the market" is also an important consideration, and one that can have a significant effect on the calculated beta. Most beta calculators today use the New York Stock Exchange Composite Index (based on about 1,700 stocks, weighted by the value of each company), but others use the S&P 500 Index or some other group, including one (the Wilshire Index) with over 5,000 stocks. In theory, the broader the index, the better the beta: indeed, the index should really include returns on all stocks, bonds, leases, private businesses, real estate, and even "human capital." As a practical matter, however, we cannot get accurate returns data on most types of assets, so measurement problems largely restrict us to stock indices.

The bottom line of all this is that one can calculate betas in many different ways and, depending on the method used, different betas, hence different costs of capital, will result. To illustrate this point, consider Table 8-2 which contains the April 1990 beta coefficients for five well-known companies as reported by Merrill Lynch and Value Line. Merrill Lynch uses the S&P 500 as the market index, while Value Line uses the New York Stock Exchange Composite Index. Further, Value Line betas are adjusted, while the Merrill Lynch betas reported are pure historical betas. Merrill Lynch uses five years of monthly returns, or 60 observations; Value Line uses 260 weekly observations.

Where does this leave financial managers regarding the proper beta? They must "pay their money and take their choice." Some managers will calculate their own betas, using whichever procedure seems most appropriate under the circumstances. Others will use betas calculated by organizations such as Merrill Lynch or Value Line, perhaps using one service or perhaps averaging the betas of several services. The choice is a matter of judgment and data availability, for there is no "right" beta. With luck, the betas derived from different sources will, for a given company, be close together. If they are not, then our confidence in the CAPM cost of capital estimate will be diminished.

Illustration of the CAPM Approach

We are now in a position to estimate Nachman Computer's cost of equity from retained earnings by the CAPM method. We use as the risk-free rate the assumed T-bond rate in January 1991, which is 8.0 percent, and Merrill Lynch's assumed estimate of the expected return on the market, $\hat{k}_M = k_M = 14.0\%$. Thus, we can write the SML equation for January 1991 as follows:

$$k_s = k_{RF} + (k_M - k_{RF})b_i$$
$$= 8.0\% + (14.0\% - 8.0\%)b_i = 8.0\% + (6.0\%)b_i.$$

Therefore, if we know a company's beta, we can insert it into the SML equation and estimate the company's cost of retained earnings, k_s. For example, we have obtained two estimates of NCC's beta: One service reported an adjusted beta of 1.10, and the other estimated an unadjusted beta of 1.20. Using the adjusted beta, we obtain $k_{NCC} = 14.6\%$:

$$k_{NCC} = 8.0\% + (6.0\%)1.1 = 14.6\%.$$

Using the unadjusted beta, we obtain an estimate of 15.2 percent. Therefore, on the basis of this CAPM analysis, Nachman Computer Corporation's cost of retained earnings falls in the range of 14.6 to 15.2 percent.

Rather than picking single values, we could have developed high and low estimates for both the risk-free rate and the market risk premium. Then, by combining all of the low estimators and all of the high estimators, we could have estimated the extreme low and high values of NCC's cost of retained earnings. Obviously, this range would have been greater than 14.6 to 15.2 percent.

Self-Test Questions

What is the best proxy for the risk-free rate when using the CAPM? Why?

Explain the two methods used to estimate the market risk premium.

Name the three types of betas that can be used in the CAPM.

Should the CAPM estimate of k_s be thought of as a precise point estimate or as a range?

THE DCF APPROACH

The second major procedure for estimating the cost of retained earnings is the Discounted Cash Flow (DCF) approach. We know that the intrinsic value of a stock, $\hat{P}_0$, is the present value of its expected dividend stream:

$$\hat{P}_0 = \frac{D_1}{(1 + k_s)^1} + \frac{D_2}{(1 + k_s)^2} + \frac{D_3}{(1 + k_s)^3} + \cdots + \frac{D_\infty}{(1 + k_s)^\infty}.$$

Also, we know that we can recast this equation, given the market price of the stock, P_0, and solve for $\hat{k}_s$, the implied expected return:

$$P_0 = \frac{D_1}{(1 + \hat{k}_s)^1} + \frac{D_2}{(1 + \hat{k}_s)^2} + \frac{D_3}{(1 + \hat{k}_s)^3} + \cdots + \frac{D_\infty}{(1 + \hat{k}_s)^\infty}.$$

Finally, we know that in equilibrium, $\hat{k}_s = k_s$, so if a stock is in equilibrium, as it generally is, then an estimate of the expected rate of return also provides us with an estimate of the required rate of return.

If a stock is expected to grow at a constant rate, we can use the constant growth model to estimate $\hat{k}_s$:

$$\hat{k}_s = \frac{D_1}{P_0} + g.$$

Here P_0 is read from *The Wall Street Journal,* and next year's annual dividend, D_1, can be estimated relatively easily. It is not easy to estimate g, the growth rate expected by the marginal investor, but three approaches to the problem are discussed below.

Historical Growth Rates

First, if earnings and dividend growth rates have been relatively stable in the past, and if investors expect these trends to continue, then the past realized growth rate may be used as an estimate of the expected future growth rate. To illustrate, consider Figure 8-1, which gives EPS and DPS data from 1976 to 1990 for NCC, along with a plot of these data on a semilog scale. Note these points:

1.   **Time period.** We show 15 years of data in Figure 8-1, but we could have used 25 years, 5 years, or 10 years. There is no rule as to the appropriate number of years to analyze when calculating historical growth rates. However, the period chosen should reflect, to the extent possible, the conditions expected in the future.

2.   **Compound growth rate, point-to-point.** The easiest historical growth rate to calculate is the compound rate between two dates. For example, EPS grew at an annual rate of 7.5 percent from 1976 to 1990, and DPS grew at a 4.8 percent rate during this same period.[10] Note that the point-to-point growth rate could change radically if we used two other points. For example, if we calculated the 5-year EPS growth rate from 1984 to 1989, we would obtain 2.6 percent, but the 5-year rate one year later, from 1985 to 1990, is 11.0 percent. This radical change occurs because the point-to-point rate is extremely sensitive to the beginning and ending years chosen.

3.   **Compound growth rate, average-to-average.** To alleviate the problem of beginning and ending year sensitivity, some analysts use an average-to-average calculation.

---

[10]To obtain g_{EPS} using a financial calculator, enter 2.08 as PV, 5.73 as FV, 14 as n (because, with 15 data points, we have 14 growth periods), and then press i to obtain the growth rate, 7.5 percent.

Figure 8-1   Nachman Computer Corporation:
Semilog Plot of EPS and DPS, 1976–1990

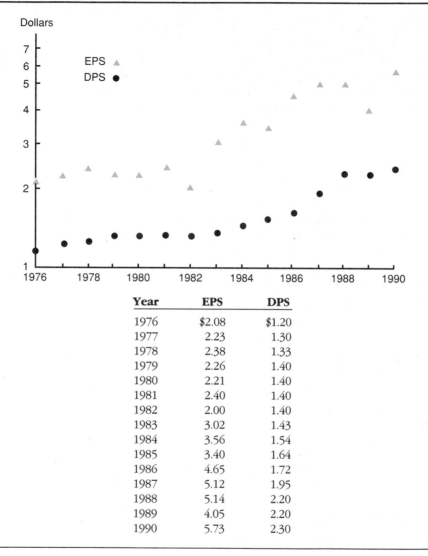

Year	EPS	DPS
1976	$2.08	$1.20
1977	2.23	1.30
1978	2.38	1.33
1979	2.26	1.40
1980	2.21	1.40
1981	2.40	1.40
1982	2.00	1.40
1983	3.02	1.43
1984	3.56	1.54
1985	3.40	1.64
1986	4.65	1.72
1987	5.12	1.95
1988	5.14	2.20
1989	4.05	2.20
1990	5.73	2.30

For example, to calculate NCC's EPS growth rate over the period 1984 to 1989, the Value Line analysts would (1) get the average EPS over the years 1983 to 1985 and use this value ($3.33) as the beginning year, (2) get the average EPS over the years 1988 to 1990 and use this value ($4.97) as the ending year, and (3) calculate a growth rate of 8.3 percent based on these data. This procedure is superior to the simple point-to-point calculation for purposes of estimating g.

Table 8-3   Nachman Computer Corporation: Historical Growth Rates

Method (Period)	EPS	DPS	Average
Point-to-point (1985–1990)	11.0%	7.0%	9.0%
Point-to-point (1976–1990)	7.5	4.8	6.2
Average-to-average (1984–1989)	8.3	7.7	8.0
Average-to-average (1977–1989)	6.9	4.7	5.8
Least squares regression (1985–1990)	6.6	7.6	7.1
Least squares regression (1976–1990)	7.9	4.6	6.3

4.   **Least squares regression**. A third way, and in our view the best way, to estimate historical growth rates is by log-linear least squares regression.[11] The regression method gives consideration to all data points in the series; thus, it is the least likely to be biased by a randomly high or low beginning or ending year. The only practical way to estimate a least squares growth rate is with a computer or a financial calculator.

5.   **Earnings versus dividends**. If earnings and dividends are growing at the same rate, there is no problem, but if these two growth rates are unequal, we do have a problem. First, the DCF model calls for the expected *dividend* growth rate. However, if EPS and DPS are growing at different rates, something is going to have to change: these two series cannot grow at two different rates indefinitely. There is no rule for handling differences in historical g_{EPS} and g_{DPS}, and where they differ, this simply demonstrates in yet another way the problems with using historical growth as a proxy for expected future growth. Like many aspects of finance, judgment is required when estimating growth rates.

Table 8-3 summarizes the historical growth rates we have just discussed. It is obvious that one can take a given set of historical data and, depending on the years and the calculation method used, obtain a large number of quite different growth rates. Now recall our purpose in making these calculations: We are seeking the future dividend growth rate that investors expect, and we reasoned that, if past growth rates have been stable, then investors might base future expectations on past trends. This is a reasonable proposition, but, unfortunately, one rarely finds much historical stability. Therefore, the use of historical growth rates in a DCF analysis must be applied with judgment, and also used (if at all) in conjunction with other growth estimation methods as discussed next.

---

[11]Log-linear regression is a standard time-series linear regression in which the data points are plotted as natural logarithms. The advantage of a log-linear regression is that the slope of the regression line is the average annual growth rate assuming continuous compounding. In a standard time-series linear regression of EPS or DPS, the slope of the regression line is the average annual dollar change. For a more complete discussion of log-linear regression, see Robert C. Radcliffe, *Investment: Concepts, Analysis, and Strategy* (Glenview, Ill.: Scott, Foresman, 1990).

Retention Growth

Another method for estimating the growth rate is to use Equation 8-4:

$$g = b(r). \tag{8-4}$$

Here r is the expected future return on equity, and b is the fraction of its earnings that a firm is expected to retain.[12] Equation 8-4 produces a constant growth rate, and when we use it we are, by implication, making four important assumptions: (1) we expect the payout rate, and thus the retention rate, $b = 1 -$ Payout, to remain constant; (2) we expect the return on equity on new investment, r, to equal the firm's current ROE, which implies that we expect the return on equity to remain constant; (3) the firm is not expected to issue new common stock, or, if it does, we expect this new stock to be sold at a price equal to its book value; and (4) future projects are expected to have the same degree of risk as the firm's existing assets.

NCC has had an average return on equity of about 15 percent over the past 15 years. The ROE has been relatively steady, but even so it has ranged from a low of 11.0 percent to a high of 17.6 percent during this period. In addition, NCC's dividend payout rate has averaged 0.52 over the past 15 years, so its retention rate, b, has averaged $1.0 - 0.52 = 0.48$. Using Equation 8-4, we estimate g to be 7.2 percent:

$$g = 0.48(15\%) = .7.2\%.$$

This figure, together with the historical EPS and DPS growth rates examined earlier, might lead us to conclude that Nachman Computer's expected growth rate is in the range of 6.5 to 7.5 percent. Therefore, if we forecasted NCC's next annual dividend to be $2.40, and if we determined that its current stock price is $32, then its dividend yield would be $D_1/P_0 = \$2.40/\$32 = 0.075$ or 7.5%, and its DCF cost of capital would be in the range of 14.0 to 15.0 percent:

$$\text{Lower end: } k_{NCC} = \hat{k}_{NCC} = 7.5\% + 6.5\% = 14.0\%.$$

$$\text{Upper end: } k_{NCC} = \hat{k}_{NCC} = 7.5\% + 7.5\% = 15.0\%.$$

This is reasonably close to the 14.6 to 15.2 percent range found by use of the CAPM method.

Analysts' Forecasts

A third growth rate estimating technique calls for using security analysts' forecasts. Analysts forecast and then publish growth rate estimates for most of the larger publicly owned companies. For example, Value Line provides such forecasts on about 1,700 companies, and all of the larger brokerage houses provide similar forecasts. Further, several companies compile analysts' forecasts on a regular basis and provide summary information such as the median and range of forecasts on widely followed

---

[12]Since there are more terms for which symbols are needed than there are letters in the alphabet, some letters are used to denote several different things. This is one of those instances, and b is standard notation for both the beta coefficient and the retention rate. Note also that the retention rate is the complement of the payout rate, that is, Retention rate = (1 − Payout rate).

companies. These growth rate summaries, such as the one compiled by Lynch, Jones & Ryan in its *Institutional Brokers Estimate System (IBES),* can be ordered for a fee and obtained either in hardcopy format or as on-line computer data.

However, these forecasts often assume nonconstant growth. For example, in January 1991, analysts were forecasting that NCC would have a 10.4 percent annual growth rate in earnings and dividends over the next 5 years, or from 1991 through 1995, and they were forecasting a steady-state growth rate beyond 1995 of 6.5 percent. On the basis of the current \$32 market price and a D_1 of \$2.40, we can use the nonconstant growth stock valuation approach developed in Chapter 7 to find the expected rate of return. However, obtaining the solution is no trivial matter—we used a *Lotus 1-2-3* model and found $\hat{k}_s = k_s$ to be 15.0 percent.

As an alternative, a nonconstant growth forecast can be used to develop a proxy constant growth rate. Computer simulations indicate that dividends beyond Year 50 contribute very little to the value of any stock—the present value of dividends beyond Year 50 is virtually zero, so for practical purposes, we can ignore anything beyond 50 years. If we consider only a 50-year horizon, we can develop a weighted average growth rate and use it as a constant growth rate for cost of capital purposes. In the NCC case, we assumed a growth rate of 10.4 percent for 5 years followed by a growth rate of 6.5 percent for 45 years, which produces an average growth rate of 0.10(10.4%) + 0.90(6.5%) = 6.9%. This constant growth proxy results in $k_s = \hat{k}_s = 14.4\%$:

$$k_s = \hat{k}_s = \frac{\$2.40}{\$32} + 6.9\%$$

$$= 7.5\% + 6.9\% = 14.4\%.$$

These nonconstant growth DCF calculations suggest a range for k_s of 14.4 to 15.0 percent.

Self-Test Questions

What are the three most commonly used methods for estimating the future dividend growth rate?

Briefly describe the retention growth method for estimating the dividend growth rate. Is it based on any underlying assumptions?

Can the DCF model be used to estimate k_s for a nonconstant growth stock? Explain.

BOND-YIELD-PLUS-RISK-PREMIUM APPROACH

A third method for estimating the required rate of return on retained earnings calls for adding an estimated risk premium to the company's own bond yield:

$$k_s = \text{Company's own bond yield} + \text{Risk premium}.$$

As discussed earlier, a corporate treasurer can easily estimate his or her own firm's bond yield to maturity if the bond is publicly traded, or ask an investment banker for k_d if the bonds are not traded. The real problem occurs when trying to estimate the appropriate risk premium for the firm.

As we saw in Table 8-1, the average historical risk premium of stocks over corporate bonds as reported by Ibbotson Associates is 6.9 percentage points. If risk premiums were stable over time, or if they fluctuated randomly about a stable mean, then the average historical premium could be used with confidence to estimate the current risk premium. However, risk premiums are not stable, so some analysts argue that more reliance should be placed on the current level of the risk premium than on its historical average. Studies suggest that risk premiums are reasonably stable during periods when interest rates are stable, but that they become volatile during periods in which interest rates are volatile.

There are two common methods of estimating current risk premiums: a survey approach and a DCF-based approach similar to the method we discussed earlier in connection with the market risk premium. One example of the survey approach is the work of Charles Benore, a security analyst with Paine Webber. Benore has for several years surveyed a large number of institutional investors, asking them what premium above the return on the company's bonds would make them indifferent between the stock and the bonds. In one survey, Benore found that most investors required a premium of from 2 to 4 percentage points on stock over the company's bond yield, with a mean value of 3.6 percentage points. This mean could be used as an estimate of the risk premium. Benore's survey analyzes only public utility companies, but the approach is applicable to any company or industry. Note, though, that in some years Benore has reported average risk premiums as high as 6 percent, but in other years he found values closer to 3 percent. The high premiums occurred during periods of low interest rates, and the low premiums in high rate periods. Thus, Benore's studies confirm that risk premiums are not stable, hence that using old survey data is questionable.

The second method for estimating risk premiums is based on the DCF model. To illustrate, we assumed earlier that in January 1991 Merrill Lynch, using the DCF approach, estimated that the required rate of return on the market, as measured by the S&P 500, was 14.0 percent. At the same time, assume that the *Federal Reserve Bulletin* reported that the yield on an average (A-rated) corporate long-term bond was 10.2 percent. Using these data, we would estimate the risk premium of an average stock over an average bond to be 14.0% − 10.2% = 3.8 percentage points, or 380 basis points. However, one should recognize that the figure of 3.8 percentage points is not precise; we would, ourselves, conclude that the risk premium of an average company's stock over its own bonds, in January 1991, was somewhere between 3.3 and 4.3 percentage points.

We can apply the DCF-based risk premium approach to estimate the required rate of return for NCC. The company has been experiencing some problems from lower-cost foreign producers, and its bonds are rated Baa. Therefore, whereas if the *Federal Reserve Bulletin* reported that an average corporate bond yielded 10.2 percent in January 1991, NCC's relatively risky bonds yielded 11.0 percent, ignoring flotation costs. (Our studies indicate that the average NYSE company's bonds are rated A; NCC's bonds are rated below A.) Assuming that every company's required equity return exceeds its own cost of debt by the same risk premium, we would determine the high and low values of NCC's cost of equity as follows:

$$\text{Low: } k_{NCC} = 11.0\% + 3.3\% = 14.3\%.$$

$$\text{High: } k_{NCC} = 11.0\% + 4.3\% = 15.3\%.$$

Had NCC had a higher bond rating, its cost of debt and consequently its estimated cost of equity would have been lower.[13]

Note again, however, that risk premiums have not been stable over time, so it may not be appropriate as a general rule to add 3.3 to 4.3 percentage points to a company's bond yield to indicate its cost of equity. In recent years, our work suggests that the over-own-debt risk premium has ranged from about 2 to about 5 percentage points. (The low premium occurred when interest rates were quite high and people were reluctant to invest in long-term bonds because of a fear of runaway inflation, further increases in interest rates, and losses on investments in bonds. The high premiums occurred in periods when interest rates were relatively low.) Therefore, we repeat our earlier warning: use a current risk premium when estimating equity capital costs by the bond-yield-plus-risk-premium method.

Self-Test Questions

Describe the concept underlying the bond-yield-plus-risk-premium approach.

How can the risk premium be estimated?

COMPARISON OF THE CAPM, DCF, AND RISK PREMIUM METHODS

We have discussed three methods for estimating the required rate of return on retained earnings — CAPM, DCF, and bond yield plus risk premium. Table 8-4 summarizes the results for Nachman Computer. We see that the estimates range from 14.0 to 15.3 percent, that the average highs and average lows produce a range of 14.3 to 15.1 percent, and that the overall average is 14.7 percent. In our view, there is sufficient consistency in the results to warrant the use of 14.7 percent as our estimate of the cost of retained earnings for Nachman Computer. If the methods produced widely varied estimates, then the financial manager would have to use his or her judgment as to the relative merits of each estimate, and then choose the estimate which seemed most reasonable under the circumstances. In general, this choice would be made on the basis of the financial manager's confidence in the input parameters of each approach.

---

[13]Note that if you know a company's bond rating, or can estimate from an analysis of its financial statements what rating it would have if its debt were rated, then you could find its approximate k_d in Moody's or Standard & Poor's bond yield publications. This procedure is useful for outsiders analyzing companies that have no publicly traded debt. The company's own treasurer would always know, or could quickly find out, the value of k_d from the firm's investment bankers.

Table 8-4   Estimated Required Rates of Return
for Nachman Computer Corporation

	Estimate	
Method	Low	High
CAPM	14.6%	15.2%
DCF (constant growth)	14.0	15.0
DCF (nonconstant growth)	14.4	15.0
Bond yield plus risk premium	14.3	15.3
Average	14.3%	15.1%
Overall average	14.7%	

Self-Test Question

How would you choose between widely different estimates of k_s?

COST OF NEWLY ISSUED COMMON EQUITY

The cost of retained earnings as estimated in the preceding section is appropriate when retained earnings are being used to finance expansion. However, if the firm is expanding so rapidly that its retained earnings have been exhausted, then it must raise equity by selling newly issued common stock, and common equity has a higher cost than retained earnings. Specifically, the sale of new common equity, as with the sale of preferred stock and debt, involves flotation costs. These costs lower the net usable dollars produced by new stock issues, and this in turn increases the cost of the funds. We took account of flotation costs in our estimates of the costs of debt and preferred stock, and the same general approach can be used with common equity.

When the firm sells new common stock, it nets $P_0(1 - F)$, where F is the percentage flotation cost expressed in decimal form. Note that F consists of issuance expenses such as printing costs and investment banker commissions, as well as price effects resulting from market pressure and information asymmetries, topics which are discussed in detail in Chapters 12 and 15. To begin, the constant growth DCF model, modified to include flotation costs, is used to estimate $\hat{k}_e$, the cost of equity raised by selling new common stock:

$$\text{Net proceeds} = P_0(1 - F) = \frac{D_1}{\hat{k}_e - g}. \tag{8-5}$$

Solving Equation 8-5 for $\hat{k}_e$ produces this expression:

$$\hat{k}_e = \frac{D_1}{P_0(1 - F)} + g. \tag{8-5a}$$

This procedure recognizes that the purchaser of a share of newly issued stock will expect the same dividend stream as the holder of an old share, but the company will, because of flotation expenses, receive less money from the sale of the new share, $P_0(1 - F)$, than the value of the old share, P_0. Therefore, the money raised from the sale of new stock will have to "work harder" to produce the earnings needed to provide the dividend stream. As a result, $k_e > k_s$.

Note also that we could rewrite Equation 8-5a as follows:

$$\hat{k}_e = \frac{D_1/P_0}{(1 - F)} + g = \frac{\text{Dividend yield}}{(1 - F)} + g. \qquad \textbf{(8-5b)}$$

Equations 8-5a and 8-5b are equivalent, and either can be used, depending on the form of the available data. Using Equation 8-5a, and a growth estimate of 6.5 percent, we obtain NCC's DCF cost of new common equity:

$$\hat{k}_e = \frac{\$2.40}{\$32(1 - 0.15)} + 6.5\%$$

$$= 8.8\% + 6.5\% = 15.3\%.$$

The DCF value for $\hat{k}_e$ is 15.3 percent versus the DCF $\hat{k}_s = 14.0\%$ for retained earnings that we estimated earlier, so the flotation cost adjustment is $+1.3$ percentage points, meaning that new outside equity costs about 1.3 percentage points more than retained earnings according to the DCF method:

$$\text{Flotation cost adjustment} = \text{DCF } \hat{k}_e - \text{DCF } \hat{k}_s$$

$$= 15.3\% - 14.0\%$$

$$= 1.3\%.$$

Notice that only one method (DCF) is commonly used to estimate the flotation cost adjustment, whereas three methods are used to estimate k_s. However, the DCF adjustment factor can also be added to the CAPM and risk premium estimates of the cost of retained earnings to find the cost of new stock as estimated by those methods. For Nachman Computer, our final estimate of the cost of retained earnings was 14.7 percent. Thus, NCC's cost of new equity is estimated to be 16.0 percent:

$$k_e = k_s + \text{Flotation cost adjustment}$$

$$= 14.7\% + 1.3\% = 16.0\%.$$

Self-Test Questions

Explain why the cost of new common stock is higher than the cost of retained earnings.

How is the flotation cost adjustment factor estimated?

WEIGHTED AVERAGE COST OF CAPITAL

Thus far, we have discussed how to estimate the costs of debt, preferred stock, retained earnings, and new common stock. Now we must combine these elements to form a weighted average cost of capital, WACC = k_a. Each firm has in mind a target capital structure, defined as that mix of debt, preferred, and common equity which causes its stock price to be maximized. Further, when the firm raises new capital, it generally tries to finance so as to keep the actual capital structure reasonably close to the target over time. Here is the general formula for the weighted average cost of capital:

$$\text{WACC} = k_a = w_d k_d (1 - T) + w_p k_p + w_s (k_s \text{ or } k_e). \qquad (8\text{-}6)$$

Here w_d, w_p, and w_s are the target weights for debt, preferred stock, and common equity, respectively. The cost of the debt component of the WACC would itself be an average of several items if the firm uses several types of debt for its permanent financing, while the common equity used in the calculation will be either the cost of retained earnings, k_s, or the cost of new common stock, k_e.

One point should be made immediately: *The WACC is the weighted average cost of each new dollar of capital raised at the margin* — it is not the average cost of all the dollars the firm has raised in the past, nor is it the average cost of all the dollars the firm will raise during the current year. We are primarily interested in obtaining a cost of capital for use in capital budgeting, and for such purposes a *marginal cost* is required.[14] That means, conceptually, that we must estimate the cost of each dollar the firm raises during the year. Each of those dollars will consist of some debt, some preferred, and some common equity, and the equity will be either retained earnings or new common stock.

To illustrate, suppose Nachman Computer has a target capital structure calling for 30 percent debt, 10 percent preferred stock, and 60 percent common equity. As we estimated earlier, the company's before-tax cost of debt, k_d, is 11.0 percent ignoring flotation costs; its cost of preferred stock, k_p, is 10.3 percent; its cost of common equity from retained earnings, k_s, is 14.7 percent; and its cost of equity from new common stock sales, k_e, is 16.0 percent. Further, the company's marginal tax rate is 40 percent.

Now suppose the firm needs to raise $100. In order to keep its capital structure on target, it must obtain $30 as debt, $10 as preferred, and $60 as common equity. (Common equity can come either from retained earnings or from the sale of new stock.) The weighted average cost of the $100, assuming the equity portion is from retained earnings, is calculated as follows, using Equation 8-6:

$$\text{WACC} = k_a = w_d k_d (1 - T) + w_p k_p + w_s k_s$$

$$= 0.3(11.0\%)(0.6) + 0.1(10.3\%) + 0.6(14.7\%) \approx 11.8\%.$$

---

[14]The only use we can think of for the average cost of all the capital a firm has raised, as opposed to the marginal cost of capital, is in public utility regulation, where utility commissions are supposed to set rates such that customers pay for all costs of service, including the cost of the capital that was used to buy the assets that are used to provide service.

Every dollar of new capital that NCC obtains consists of 30 cents of debt with an after-tax cost of 6.6 percent, 10 cents of preferred with a cost of 10.3 percent, and 60 cents of common equity with a cost of 14.7 percent. The average cost of each new dollar is 11.8 percent.

The weights could be based on the accounting values shown on the firm's balance sheet (book values), or on the market values of the different securities shown on the balance sheet, or on management's estimation of the firm's optimal capital structure, which becomes the firm's target market value weights. The correct weights are the firms' target weights, and the rationale for using the target weights is discussed in detail in Chapters 12 and 13.

The Marginal Cost of Capital (MCC) Schedule

NCC's optimal capital structure calls for 30 percent debt, 10 percent preferred, and 60 percent equity, so each new (or marginal) dollar will be raised as 30 cents of debt, 10 cents of preferred, and 60 cents of common equity. Otherwise, the capital structure would not stay on target. As long as the firm's debt has an after-tax cost of 6.6 percent, its preferred has a cost of 10.3 percent, and its common equity has a cost of 14.7 percent, then its weighted average cost of capital will be 11.8 percent. Thus, each new dollar will be raised as 30 cents of debt, 10 cents of preferred, and 60 cents of equity, and each new (or marginal) dollar will have a weighted average cost of 11.8 percent.

Breaks, or Jumps, in the MCC Schedule

Could NCC raise an unlimited amount of new capital at the 11.8 percent cost? The answer is *no*. As companies raise larger and larger sums during a given time period, the costs of both the debt and the equity components begin to rise, and as this occurs, the weighted average cost of new dollars also rises. Thus, just as corporations cannot hire unlimited numbers of workers at a constant wage, neither can they raise unlimited amounts of capital at a constant cost. At some point, the cost of each new dollar will increase above 11.8 percent.

Where will this point occur? As a first step to determining the point of increasing costs, recognize that all of NCC's existing capital was raised in the past, and all of it is invested in assets which are used in operations. Now suppose the capital budget calls for net expenditures of $100 million during 1991. This new (or marginal) capital will presumably be raised so as to maintain the 30/10/60 debt/preferred/common equity relationship. Therefore, the company will obtain $30 million of debt, $10 million of preferred, and $60 million of common equity.[15] The new common equity

---

[15]In reality, the company might raise the entire $100 million by issuing new debt, or perhaps by issuing new common equity. By issuing large blocks of securities, there are savings on flotation costs. However, over the long haul the firm will stick to its target capital structure. Thus, any financing deviation in one year will be offset by opposite financing deviations in future years, so the cost of capital remains a function of the target capital structure regardless of year-to-year financing decisions.

could come from two sources: (1) that part of this year's profits which management decides to retain in the business rather than use for dividends (but not from earnings retained in the past, because those dollars will have already been invested) or (2) the sale of new common stock.

The debt will have an interest rate of 11.0 percent, or an after-tax cost of 6.6 percent. The preferred stock will have a cost of 10.3 percent. The cost of common equity will be k_s if the equity is obtained by retained earnings, but it will be k_e if the company must sell new common stock. Consider first the case where the new equity comes from retained earnings. As we have seen, the company's cost of retained earnings is 14.7 percent, and its weighted average cost of capital when using retained earnings as the common equity component is 11.8 percent.

Now consider the case in which the company expands so rapidly that its retained earnings for the year are not sufficient to meet its needs for new equity, forcing it to sell new common stock. Since we previously estimated the cost of new equity, k_e, to be 16.0 percent, the WACC using new common stock is

$$WACC = k_a = w_dk_d(1 - T) + w_pk_p + w_sk_e$$

$$= 0.3(11.0\%)(0.6) + 0.1(10.3\%) + 0.6(16.0\%) \approx 12.6\%.$$

Thus, we see that the WACC is 11.8 percent so long as retained earnings are used, but it jumps to 12.6 percent as soon as the firm exhausts its retained earnings and is forced to sell new common stock.

How much new capital can NCC raise before it exhausts its retained earnings and is forced to sell new common stock? Assume that the company expects to have total earnings of $20 million for the year, and that it has a policy of paying out about 48 percent of its earnings as dividends. Thus, its *payout ratio,* which is the proportion of net income paid out as dividends, is 0.48. The *retention ratio,* which is the proportion of net income retained within the firm, is $1 - $ Payout ratio $= 1 - 0.48$ $= 0.52$. Therefore, the addition to retained earnings will be $0.52(\$20,000,000)$ $= \$10,400,000$ during the year. How much *total financing,* debt and preferred plus this $10.4 million of retained earnings, can be done before the retained earnings are exhausted and the firm is forced to sell new common stock? In effect, we are seeking some amount of capital, X, which is defined as a *break point* and which represents the total financing that can be done before NCC is forced to sell new common stock. We know that 60 percent of X will be the new retained earnings, while 40 percent will be debt plus preferred. We also know that retained earnings will amount to $10.4 million. Therefore,

$$0.6X = \text{Retained earnings} = \$10,400,000.$$

Solving for X, which is the *retained earnings break point,* we obtain

$$\text{Break point} = X = \frac{\text{Retained earnings}}{\text{Equity fraction}} = \frac{\$10,400,000}{0.6} = \$17,333,333.$$

Thus, the company can raise a total of $17,333,333, consisting of $10,400,000 of retained earnings and $17,333,333 - \$10,400,000 = \$6,933,333$ of new debt and preferred stock supported by these new retained earnings, without altering its capital structure:

New debt supported by retained earnings	$ 5,200,000	30%
Preferred stock supported by retained earnings	1,733,333	10
Retained earnings	10,400,000	60
Total expansion supported by retained earnings (that is, break point for retained earnings)	$17,333,333	100%

The left panel of Figure 8-2 graphs NCC's first approximation marginal cost of capital schedule. Each dollar has a weighted average cost of 11.8 percent until the company has raised a total of $17,333,333. However, if the firm raises $17,333,334 or more, each additional (or marginal) dollar will contain 60 cents of equity *obtained by selling new common equity at a cost of 16.0 percent,* so WACC = k_a rises from 11.8 to 12.6 percent.

The MCC Schedule Beyond the Retained Earnings Break Point

There is a jump, or break, in NCC's MCC schedule at $17,333,333 of new capital. Could there be other breaks in the schedule? Yes, there could be. The cost of capital could also rise due to increases in the cost of debt or the cost of preferred stock, or as a result of further increases in flotation costs as the firm issues more and more common stock. Some people have argued that the costs of capital components other than common stock should not rise. Their argument is that as long as the capital structure does not change, and presuming that the firm uses new capital to invest in profitable projects with the same degree of risk as its existing projects, investors should be willing to invest unlimited amounts of additional capital at the same rate. However, this argument assumes an infinitely elastic demand for a firm's securities. As we show in Chapter 15, the demand curve of investors for securities is downward sloping, so the more securities sold during a given period, the lower the price received for the securities, and the higher the required rate of return. In this situation, the more new financing required, the higher the firm's WACC.

As a result of all this, firms face increasing MCC schedules such as the one shown in Figure 8-3. Here we have identified a specific retained earnings break point, but because of estimation difficulties, we have not attempted to identify precisely any additional break points. However, we have (1) shown the MCC schedule to be upward sloping, reflecting a positive relationship between capital raised and capital costs, and (2) indicated our inability to measure these costs precisely by using a band of costs rather than a single line. Note that this band exists even at the first dollar of capital raised—our component costs are only estimates, these estimates become more uncertain as the firm requires more and more capital, and thus the band widens as new capital raised increases. In Chapter 11 we will use the MCC schedule to help determine a firm's optimal level of new investment.

Figure 8-2 Marginal Cost of Capital Schedules

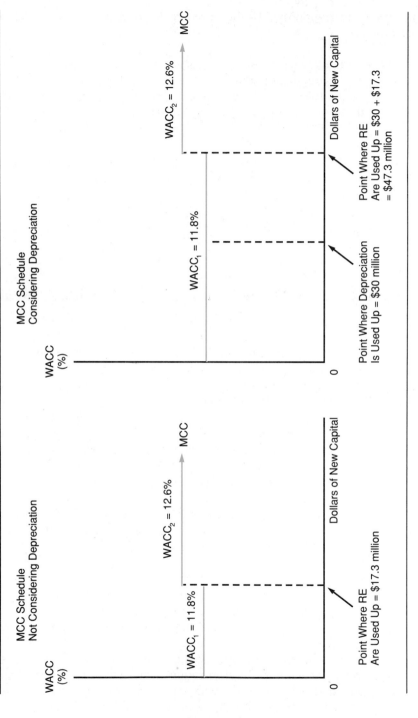

Figure 8-3   Marginal Cost of Capital Schedule Beyond
the Retained Earnings Break Point

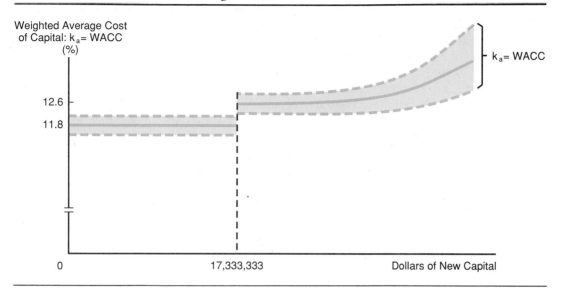

Self-Test Questions

What is the formula for a firm's WACC?

What weights should be used to estimate a firm's WACC? Why?

What is an MCC schedule?

What is the retained earnings break point?

What happens to the MCC schedule beyond the retained earnings break point?

OTHER ISSUES IN THE COST OF CAPITAL

Before concluding this chapter, we must discuss two items that affect the cost of capital. The purpose here is as much to raise questions as to answer them. Still, the material does have important practical implications, so anyone engaged in financial management should be aware of the issues and understand how they affect the practical, rule-of-thumb procedures that financial managers are necessarily forced to follow.

The Effects of Personal Taxes

We noted earlier that whenever a firm retains a portion of its net income rather than paying all earnings out in dividends, there is an *opportunity cost* to the stockholders. Nachman Computer has a required rate of return on equity (retained earnings) of 14.7 percent. This suggests that shareholders could invest retained earnings, if they were paid out in dividends, in the stock market in firms of similar risk and receive a 14.7 percent return. Therefore, NCC should retain and reinvest earnings only if the projects in which the retained earnings are invested yield 14.7 percent or more on the equity invested. The value $k_s = 14.7\%$ is defined as the opportunity cost of retained earnings.

Note that we have implicitly disregarded the facts that stockholders (1) pay income tax on dividends received and (2) incur brokerage costs when they reinvest dividends. When these costs are considered, it would seem that the opportunity cost of retained earnings should be lower than the required rate of return, k_s. However, publicly owned firms can repurchase their own stock in the marketplace and earn a return equal to k_s on the investment. Thus, publicly held firms should not invest equity capital to earn less than k_s, because they have the opportunity to earn k_s on stock repurchases. Still, personal tax effects are important for closely held firms, and such firms have a cost of retained earnings that is less than k_s.[16]

Cost of Depreciation-Generated Funds

Although we have ignored it thus far, the very first increment of internal funds used to finance any year's investments in new assets is depreciation-generated funds. Further, in their statements of cash flows, corporations generally show depreciation to be one of the most important, if not the most important, sources of funds. Of course, depreciation is an allowance for the annual reduction in value of a firm's fixed assets. Thus, for an ongoing firm, depreciation-generated funds would be used first to replace worn-out and obsolete assets, and then any remaining funds would be available to purchase new assets or to return to investors.

For capital budgeting purposes, should depreciation be considered "free" capital, should it be ignored completely, or should a charge be assessed against it? *The answer is that a charge should indeed be assessed against depreciation-generated funds, and the cost used should be the weighted average cost of capital before outside equity is used.* The reasoning here is that the firm could, if it so desired, distribute the depreciation-generated funds to its stockholders and creditors, the parties who financed the assets in the first place, so these funds definitely have an opportunity cost.

For example, suppose NCC has $30 million of depreciation-generated funds available. Suppose further that the firm has no projects available to it, not even projects which replace worn-out equipment, that return 11.8 percent or more. It obviously should not raise new capital, and it should not even retain any earnings for internal investment, because stockholders would be better off receiving the earnings as dividends and investing the funds themselves at $k_s = 14.7\%$ or having the

---

[16]For closely held firms, this expression can be used to estimate the cost of retained earnings, k_r:

$$k_r = k_s(1 - T_s)(1 - B).$$

Here k_s is the stockholders' required rate of return, T_s is the *stockholders'* marginal tax rate, and B is the percentage brokerage cost expressed in decimal form. To illustrate, if NCC were a closely held firm, and $T_s = 28\%$ and B = 5%, then its cost of retained earnings would be 10.1 percent:

$$k_r = 14.7\%(1 - 0.28)(1 - 0.05) \approx 10.1\%.$$

company repurchase its stock. Going on, NCC should not even invest its depreciation-generated $30 million. If it did keep and invest this money, it would receive a return of less than 11.8 percent. If it distributed the $30 million to its investors, with $18 million going to common stockholders, $3 million to preferred stockholders, and $9 million to bondholders so as to maintain its target capital structure, then the stockholders could buy the stock of companies with similar risk and earn 14.7 percent on their money, preferred stockholders could buy the preferred stocks of other companies and earn 10.3 percent, and bondholders could buy the bonds of companies with similar risk and earn 11.0 percent. (Such distributions would, under most conditions, be returns of capital, hence not taxable. If the equity distribution were taxable, then the company could repurchase its shares rather than make a direct distribution to stockholders.) *The conclusion from all this is that depreciation has a cost which is equal to the weighted average cost of capital before external equity is used.*

Since depreciation-generated funds have the same cost as the firm's WACC when retained earnings are used for the equity component, it is not necessary to consider them when estimating the WACC. However, depreciation does influence the point at which the WACC increases due to flotation costs on new stock sales. As shown in the right panel of Figure 8-2, presented earlier, depreciation-generated funds push the point where the WACC increases out to the right by the amount of depreciation, in this case $30 million. This topic will be discussed further in Chapter 11.[17]

Self-Test Questions

What impact does the personal tax have on the cost of retained earnings?

What are depreciation-generated funds?

Do depreciation-generated funds have a cost? If so, what is it?

How do depreciation-generated funds affect a firm's WACC and MCC schedule?

SUMMARY

This chapter showed how the firm's cost of capital is estimated. The key concepts covered are listed next.

- The cost of capital to be used in capital budgeting decisions is the *weighted average* of the various types of capital the firm uses, typically debt, preferred stock, and common equity.

- The *component cost of debt* is the *after-tax* cost of new debt. It is usually found by multiplying the cost of new debt by $(1 - T)$, where T is the firm's marginal tax rate: $k_d(1 - T)$.

---

[17]Like depreciation, deferred taxes on the income statement represent a noncash charge, and deferred taxes also constitute a source of funds in a cash flow sense. In constructing a firm's marginal cost of capital schedule, deferred taxes are treated the same way as depreciation cash flows: they are not included in the WACC calculation, but the retained earnings break point is extended to the right by the amount of deferred taxes for the year.

- The *component cost of perpetual preferred stock* is calculated as the preferred dividend divided by the net issuance price, where the net issuance price is the price the firm receives after deducting flotation costs: $k_p = D_p/P_n$.

- The *cost of common equity* is the cost of retained earnings as long as the firm has retained earnings, but the cost of equity becomes the cost of new common stock once the firm has exhausted its retained earnings.

- The *cost of retained earnings* is the rate of return investors require on the firm's common stock, and it can be estimated by three methods: (1) the *CAPM approach*, (2) the *DCF approach*, and (3) the *bond-yield-plus-risk-premium approach*.

- To use the *CAPM approach*, we (1) estimate the firm's beta, (2) multiply this beta by the market risk premium to determine the firm's risk premium, and (3) add the firm's risk premium to the risk-free rate to obtain the firm's cost of retained earnings: $k_s = k_{RF} + (k_M - k_{RF})b_i$.

- The best proxy for the *risk-free rate* is the yield on long-term T-bonds.

- There are three types of betas that can be used in the CAPM: (1) *historical*, (2) *adjusted*, and (3) *fundamental*.

- The market risk premium can be estimated either *historically (ex post)* or *prospectively (ex ante)*.

- To use the *DCF approach*, we solve for $\hat{k}_s$ in the stock valuation equation. Under constant growth, this is done by adding the firm's expected growth rate to its expected dividend yield: $k_s = \hat{k}_s = D_1/P_0 + g$.

- The growth rate can be estimated from historical data by using the *retention growth model*, $g = br$, or from securities analysts' forecasts.

- The *bond-yield-plus-risk-premium approach* requires one to add a risk premium to the firm's cost of debt: k_s = Company's own bond yield + RP.

- The *cost of new common equity* is higher than the cost of retained earnings because the firm must incur *flotation expenses* to sell stock. To find the cost of new common equity by the DCF method, the stock price is first reduced by the flotation expense, then the dividend yield is calculated on the basis of the price the firm will actually receive, and then the expected growth rate is added: $k_e = D_1/[P_0(1 - F)] + g$.

- Each firm has a *target capital structure*, and the target weights are used to estimate the firm's *weighted average cost of capital (WACC)*:

$$k_a = WACC = w_d k_d(1 - T) + w_p k_p + w_s(k_s \text{ or } k_e).$$

- The *marginal cost of capital (MCC)* is defined as the cost of the last dollar of new capital the firm raises. The MCC increases as the firm raises more and more capital during a given period. A graph of the MCC plotted against dollars raised is the *MCC schedule*.

The concepts developed in this chapter will be used extensively throughout the book, especially in capital budgeting decisions (Chapters 9, 10, and 11) and capital structure decisions (Chapters 12 and 13).

Questions

8-1   Define each of the following terms:
    a.   Weighted average cost of capital, WACC = k_a
    b.   After-tax cost of debt, $k_d(1 - T)$
    c.   Cost of preferred stock, k_p
    d.   Cost of retained earnings, k_s
    e.   Historical beta; adjusted beta; fundamental beta
    f.   Cost of new common equity, k_e
    g.   Flotation cost, F
    h.   Target capital structure
    i.   MCC schedule
    j.   Cost of depreciation-generated funds

8-2   In what sense is the WACC an average cost? A marginal cost?

8-3   How would each of the following affect a firm's cost of debt, $k_d(1 - T)$; its cost of equity, k_s; and its average cost of capital, WACC = k_a? Indicate by a plus (+), a minus (−), or a zero (0) if the factor would raise, lower, or have an indeterminate effect on the item in question. Assume other things are held constant. Be prepared to justify your answer, but recognize that several of the parts probably have no single correct answer; these questions are designed to stimulate thought and discussion.

	Effect on		
	$k_d(1 - T)$	k_s	WACC = k_a
a. The corporate tax rate is lowered.	_____	_____	_____
b. The Federal Reserve tightens credit.	_____	_____	_____
c. The firm uses more debt.	_____	_____	_____
d. The dividend payout ratio is increased.	_____	_____	_____
e. The firm doubles the amount of capital it raises during the year.	_____	_____	_____
f. The firm expands into a risky new area.	_____	_____	_____
g. The firm merges with another firm whose earnings are countercyclical to those of the first firm and to the stock market.	_____	_____	_____
h. The stock market falls drastically, and our firm's stock price falls along with the rest.	_____	_____	_____
i. Investors become more risk averse.	_____	_____	_____
j. The firm is an electric utility with a large investment in nuclear plants. Several states propose a ban on nuclear power generation.	_____	_____	_____

Self-Test Problem (Solutions Appear in Appendix D)

ST-1   (**MCC schedule**) Longstreet Communications, Inc. (LCI), has the following capital structure, which it considers to be optimal:

Debt	25%
Preferred stock	15
Common stock	60
Total capital	100%

LCI's net income expected this year is $17,142.86; its established dividend payout ratio is 30 percent; its tax rate is 40 percent; and investors expect earnings and dividends to grow at a constant rate of 9 percent in the futue. LCI paid a dividend of $3.60 per share last year (D_0), and its stock currently sells at a price of $60 per share. Treasury bonds yield 11 percent; an average stock has a 14 percent expected rate of return; and LCI's beta is 1.51. These terms would apply to new security offerings:

Common: New common stock would have a flotation cost of 10 percent.

Preferred: New preferred could be sold to the public at a price of $100 per share, with a dividend of $11. Flotation costs of $5 per share would be incurred.

Debt: Debt could be sold at an interest rate of 12 percent.

a.   Find the component costs of debt, preferred stock, retained earnings, and new common stock.

b.   How much new capital can be raised before LCI must sell new equity? (In other words, find the retained earnings break point.)

c.   What is the WACC when LCI meets its equity requirement with retained earnings? With new common stock?

d.   Construct a graph showing LCI's MCC schedule.

e.   Assume that LCI has forecasted $10,000 in depreciation expense for the planning period. What impact does this have on the MCC schedule?

Problems

8-1   (**Component cost of debt**) Calculate the after-tax cost of debt under each of the following conditions:
a.   Interest rate, 10 percent; tax rate, 0 percent.
b.   Interest rate, 10 percent; tax rate, 20 percent.
c.   Interest rate, 10 percent; tax rate, 40 percent.

8-2   (**Cost of retained earnings**) Krogh Company's last dividend per share was $1; that is, $D_0 = \$1$. The stock sells for $20 per share. The expected growth rate is a constant 5 percent. Calculate the firm's cost of retained earnings using the DCF method.

8-3   (**WACC estimation**) On January 1, the total market value of the Powell Company was $60 million. During the year, the company plans to raise and invest $30 million in new projects. The firm's present market value capital structure, shown below, is considered to be optimal. Assume that there is no short-term debt.

Debt	$30,000,000
Common equity	30,000,000
Total capital	$60,000,000

New bonds will have an 8 percent coupon rate, and they will be sold at par. Common stock, currently selling at $30 a share, can be sold to net the company $27 a share. Stockholders' required rate of return is estimated to be 12 percent, consisting of a dividend yield of 4 percent and an expected constant growth rate of 8 percent. (The next expected dividend is $1.20, so $1.20/$30 = 4%.) Retained earnings for the year are estimated to be $3 million. The marginal corporate tax rate is 40 percent. (Assume no depreciation cash flow.)

a.   To maintain the present capital structure, how much of the new investment must be financed by common equity?

b.   How much of the needed new common equity funds must be generated internally? Externally?

c.   Calculate the cost of each of the common equity components.

d.   At what level of capital expenditures will the firm's WACC increase?

e.   Calculate the firm's WACC using (1) the cost of retained earnings, and (2) the cost of new equity.

8-4   **(WACC estimation)** The following tabulation gives earnings per share figures for Hunt Manufacturing during the preceding 10 years. The firm's common stock, 140,000 shares outstanding, is now selling for $50 a share, and the expected dividend for the coming year (1991) is 50 percent of EPS for the year. Investors expect past trends to continue, so g may be based on the historical earnings growth rate.

Year	EPS
1981	$2.00
1982	2.16
1983	2.33
1984	2.52
1985	2.72
1986	2.94
1987	3.18
1988	3.43
1989	3.70
1990	4.00

The current interest rate on new debt is 8 percent. The firm's marginal federal-plus-state tax rate is 40 percent. The firm's market value capital structure, considered to be optimal, is as follows:

Debt	$ 3,000,000
Common equity	7,000,000
Total capital	$10,000,000

a.   Calculate the firm's after-tax cost of new debt and of common equity, assuming new equity comes only from retained earnings. Calculate the cost of equity assuming constant growth; that is, $\hat{k}_s = D_1/P_0 + g = k_s$.

b.   Find the firm's WACC, assuming no common stock is sold.

c.   How much can be spent for net new capital investments before external equity must be sold? (Assume no depreciation cash flow.)

d.   What is the WACC beyond the retained earnings break point if new common stock can be sold to the public at $50 a share to net the firm $45 a share?

8-5   **(Market value capital structure)** Suppose the Nelson Company has this *book value* balance sheet:

Current assets	$30,000,000	Current liabilities	$10,000,000
Fixed assets	50,000,000	Long-term debt	30,000,000
		Common equity:	
		Common stock	
		(1 million shares)	1,000,000
		Retained earnings	39,000,000
Total assets	$80,000,000	Total claims	$80,000,000

The current liabilities consist entirely of notes payable to banks, and the interest rate on this debt is 10 percent, the same as the rate on new bank loans. The long-term debt consists of 30,000 bonds, each of which has a par value of $1,000, carries a coupon interest rate of 6 percent, and matures in 20 years. The going rate of interest on new long-term debt, k_d, is 10 percent, and this is the present yield-to-maturity on the bonds. The common stock sells at a price of $60 per share. Calculate the firm's market value capital structure.

8-6   **(Cost of equity)** The Phillips Tractor Company's EPS in 1990 was $2.00. EPS in 1985 was $1.3612. The company pays out 40 percent of its earnings as dividends, and the stock currently sells for $21.60. The company expects earnings of $10 million in 1991. Its optimal market value debt/assets ratio is 60 percent, and the firm has no preferred stock outstanding.
a.   Calculate the firm's growth rate in earnings.
b.   Calculate the firm's dividend per share expected in 1991. Assume that the growth rate calculated in Part a will continue.
c.   What is the firm's cost of retained earnings, k_s?
d.   What amount of retained earnings is expected in 1991?
e.   At what amount of total financing will the firm's cost of equity increase? (Assume no depreciation cash flow.)
f.   The sale of new stock would net the company $18.36 per share. What is the firm's percentage flotation cost, F? What is the cost of new common stock, k_e?

8-7   **(Cost of equity estimation methods)** You have just estimated the cost of equity for Verbrugge Shipping Company using all three estimation techniques. The results are summarized in the following table:

Method	k_s Estimate
CAPM	12.1%
DCF	14.0
Bond yield plus risk premium	15.4

The inconsistency of the results are worrisome, but you must still develop your equity cost estimate. What factors might you consider as you attempt to place confidence in the above estimates?

8-8   **(WACC estimation)** A summary of the balance sheet of Travellers Inn, Inc. (TII), a company which was formed by merging a number of regional motel chains and which hopes to rival Holiday Inn on the national scene, is shown in the table:

Travellers Inn
December 31, 1990
(Millions of Dollars)

Cash	$ 10	Accounts payable	$ 10
Accounts receivable	20	Accruals	10
Inventories	20	Short-term debt	5
Current assets	$ 50	Current liabilities	$ 25
Net fixed assets	50	Long-term debt	30
		Preferred stock	5
		Common equity:	
		Common stock	$10
		Retained earnings	30
		Total common equity	40
Total assets	$100	Total claims	$100

These facts are also given for TII:

(1) Short-term debt consists of bank loans which currently cost 10 percent, with interest payable quarterly. These loans are used to finance receivables and inventories on a seasonal basis, so in the off-season, bank loans are zero.

(2) The long-term debt consists of 20-year, semiannual payment mortgage bonds with a coupon rate of 8 percent. Currently, these bonds provide a yield to investors of k_d = 12%. If new bonds were sold, they would yield investors 12 percent, but a flotation cost of 5 percent would be required to sell new bonds.

(3) TII's perpetual preferred stock has a $100 par value, pays a quarterly dividend of $2, and has a yield to investors of 11 percent. New perpetual preferred would have to provide the same yield to investors, and the company would incur a 5 percent flotation cost to sell it.

(4) The company has 4 million shares of common stock outstanding. P_0 = $20, but the stock has recently traded in a range of $17 to $23. D_0 = $1 and EPS_0 = $2. ROE based on average equity was 24 percent in 1990, but management expects to increase this return on equity to 30 percent; however, security analysts are not aware of management's optimism in this regard.

(5) Betas, as reported by security analysts, range from 1.3 to 1.7; the T-bond rate is 10 percent; and k_M is estimated by various brokerage houses to be in the range of 14.5 to 15.5 percent. Brokerage house reports forecast growth rates in the range of 10 to 15 percent over the foreseeable future. However, some analysts do not explicitly forecast growth rates, but they indicate to their clients that they expect TII's historical trends as shown in the table on the next page to continue.

(6) At a recent conference, TII's financial vice-president polled some pension fund investment managers on the minimum rate of return they would have to expect on TII's common to make them willing to buy the common rather than TII bonds, when the bonds yielded 12 percent. The responses suggested a risk premium over TII bonds of 4 to 6 percentage points.

(7) TII is in the 40 percent federal-plus-state tax bracket. Its dominant stockholders are in the 28 percent bracket.

(8) New common stock would have a 10 percent flotation cost.

(9) TII's principal investment banker, Henry, Kaufman & Company, predicts a decline in interest rates, with k_d falling to 10 percent and the T-bond rate to 8 percent,

although Henry, Kaufman & Company acknowledges that an increase in the expected inflation rate could lead to an increase rather than a decrease in rates.

(10) The firm expects depreciation expenses of $5 million for the coming year.

(11) Here is the historical record of EPS and DPS:

Year	EPS[a]	DPS[a]	Year	EPS[a]	DPS[a]
1976	$0.09	$0.00	1984	$0.78	$0.00
1977	−0.20	0.00	1985	0.80	0.00
1978	0.40	0.00	1986	1.20	0.20
1979	0.52	0.00	1987	0.95	0.40
1980	0.10	0.00	1988	1.30	0.60
1981	0.57	0.00	1989	1.60	0.80
1982	0.61	0.00	1990	2.00	1.00
1983	0.70	0.00			

[a]Adjusted for a 2:1 stock split in 1980, a 3:1 split in 1988, and 10 percent stock dividends in 1977 and 1985.

Assume that you are a recently hired financial analyst, and your boss, the treasurer, has asked you to estimate the company's WACC for both retained earnings and new common stock sales. Your cost of capital figures at each level should be appropriate for use in evaluating projects which are in the same risk class as the firm's average assets now on the books.

Mini Case

You have just been hired as a financial analyst by Harry Davis Industries, Inc. Your first assignment is to estimate the firm's cost of capital. To get you started, the CFO assembled the following information:

(1) The firm's federal-plus-state tax rate is 40 percent.

(2) The firm has outstanding an issue of 12 percent, semiannual coupon, noncallable bonds with 15 years remaining to maturity. They sell at a price of $1,153.72. The firm does not use short-term debt on a permanent basis.

(3) The current price of the firm's perpetual preferred stock (10 percent, $100 par value, quarterly payment) is $113.10. New perpetual preferred could be sold to the public at this price, but Davis would incur flotation costs of $2.00 per share.

(4) The firm's common stock is currently selling at $50 per share. Its last dividend (D_0) was $4.19, and investors expect the dividend to grow at a constant 5 percent rate into the foreseeable future. The firm's beta is 1.2; the current yield on T-bonds is 7 percent; and the market risk premium is estimated to be 6 percent. When using the firm's own bond-yield-plus-risk-premium approach, the managers assume a risk premium of 4 percentage points.

(5) New common stock would involve flotation costs, including market pressure, of 15 percent.

(6) The firm's target capital structure is 30 percent long-term debt, 10 percent preferred stock, and 60 percent common equity.

(7) The company forecasts retained earnings of $300,000 for the coming year.

(8) Depreciation expenses for the coming year are expected to be $500,000.

To structure the task a bit, the CFO asked you to answer the following questions:

a. (1) What sources of capital should be included in the estimate of Davis's WACC?
    (2) Should the component cost estimates be on a before-tax or an after-tax basis?
    (3) Should the cost estimates reflect historical (embedded) costs or new (marginal) costs?

b. (1) What is the firm's component cost of debt?
    (2) Should flotation costs be considered?
    (3) Should you use the nominal cost of debt or the effective annual cost?
    (4) Would a cost of debt estimate based on 15-year bonds be a valid estimate of k_d if the firm actually planned to issue 30-year bonds this year?

c. (1) What is the firm's cost of preferred stock?
    (2) Is the firm's preferred stock more or less risky to investors than its debt? Why is the yield to investors on the preferred lower than the yield to maturity on the debt?
    (3) Now suppose you discovered that the firm's preferred stock had a mandatory redemption provision which specified that the firm must redeem the issue in 5 years at a price of $110 per share. What would the firm's cost of preferred be in this situation?

d. (1) Why is there a cost associated with retained earnings?
    (2) What is the firm's estimated cost of retained earnings based on the CAPM approach?
    (3) Why is the T-bond rate a better estimate of the risk-free rate than is the T-bill rate?
    (4) What is the difference among historical betas, adjusted betas, and fundamental betas?
    (5) Describe two methods which can be used to estimate the market risk premium.

e. (1) What is the estimate of the firm's discounted cash flow (DCF) cost of retained earnings, k_s?
    (2) Suppose the firm has historically earned 15 percent on equity (ROE) and retained 35 percent of earnings, and investors expect this situation to continue in the future. How could you use this information to estimate the future dividend growth rate, and what growth rate would you get? Is this growth rate consistent with the 5 percent given earlier?
    (3) Could DCF methodology be applied if the growth rate was not constant? How?

f. What is the firm's cost of retained earnings based on the bond-yield-plus-risk-premium method?

g. What is your final estimate for k_s?

h. (1) What is the firm's cost of new common stock, k_e?
    (2) Explain in words why new common stock has a higher percentage cost than retained earnings.

i. (1) What is the firm's overall, or weighted average, cost of capital (WACC) when only retained earnings are used as the equity component?
    (2) When must new common stock be used?

j. (1) At what amount of new investment would the firm be forced to issue new common stock? (For now, ignore the depreciation cash flow.)
    (2) Construct the firm's MCC schedule. Is it reasonable to assume that the firm's MCC schedule would remain constant beyond the retained earnings break point regardless of the amount of capital required? Would what the company planned to do with the money it raised have any effect on the WACC?

k. We know that a firm's annual cash flows are equal to net income plus noncash expenses, typically net income plus depreciation, yet the analysis thus far has ignored the depreciation cash flow. What impact does depreciation have on Davis's MCC schedule? Would a consideration of depreciation affect the acceptability of proposed capital budgeting projects and the size of the total capital budget? Explain.

Selected Additional References and Cases

The following articles provide some valuable insights into the CAPM approach to estimating the cost of equity:

Beaver, William H., Paul Kettler, and Myron Scholes, "The Association between Market Determined and Accounting Determined Risk Measures," *Accounting Review,* October 1970, 654–682.

Bowman, Robert G., "The Theoretical Relationship between Systematic Risk and Financial (Accounting) Variables," *Journal of Finance,* June 1979, 617–630.

Cooley, Philip L., "A Review of the Use of Beta in Regulatory Proceedings," *Financial Management,* Winter 1981, 75–81.

Chen, Carl R., "Time-Series Analysis of Beta Stationarity and Its Determinants: A Case of Public Utilities," *Financial Management,* Autumn 1982, 64–70.

The weighted average cost of capital as described in this chapter is widely used in both industry and academic circles. It has been criticized on several counts, but to date it has withstood the challenges. See the following articles:

Arditti, Fred D., and Haim Levy, "The Weighted Average Cost of Capital as a Cutoff Rate: A Critical Examination of the Classical Textbook Weighted Average," *Financial Management,* Fall 1977, 24–34.

Beranek, William, "The Weighted Average Cost of Capital and Shareholder Wealth Maximization," *Journal of Financial and Quantitative Analysis,* March 1977, 17–32.

Boudreaux, Kenneth J., and Hugh W. Long; John R. Ezzell and R. Burr Porter; Moshe Ben Horim; and Alan C. Shapiro, "The Weighted Average Cost of Capital: A Discussion," *Financial Management,* Summer 1979, 7–23.

Reilly, Raymond R., and William E. Wacker, "On the Weighted Average Cost of Capital," *Journal of Financial and Quantitative Analysis,* January 1973, 123-126.

Some other works that are relevant include the following:

Alberts, W. W., and Stephen H. Archer, "Some Evidence on the Effect of Company Size on the Cost of Equity Capital," *Journal of Financial and Quantitative Analysis,* March 1973, 229–242.

Amihud, Yakov, and Haim Mendelson, "Liquidity and Cost of Capital: Implications for Corporate Management," *Journal of Applied Corporate Finance,* Fall 1989, 65–73.

Chen, Andrew, "Recent Developments in the Cost of Debt Capital," *Journal of Finance,* June 1978, 863–883.

Myers, Stewart C., "Interactions of Corporate Financing and Investments Decisions — Implications for Capital Budgeting," *Journal of Finance,* March 1974, 1–25.

Nantell, Timothy J., and C. Robert Carlson, "The Cost of Capital as a Weighted Average," *Journal of Finance,* December 1975, 1343–1355.

For some insights into the cost of capital techniques used by major firms, see

Gitman, Lawrence J., and Vincent A. Mercurio, "Cost of Capital Techniques Used by Major U.S. Firms: Survey and Analysis of Fortune's 1000," *Financial Management,* Winter 1982, 21–29.

Additional references on the cost of capital are cited in Chapters 5 and 9.

Case 4, "Beltway Technologies, Inc.," and Case 5, "Personal Assistance Corporation," in the Brigham-Gapenski casebook, focus on corporate cost of capital issues, while Case 6, "Wansley Manufacturing Company," illustrates divisional costs of capital.

PART III

Capital Budgeting

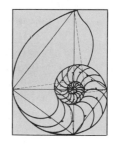

CHAPTER 9

The Basics of Capital Budgeting

Each year, businesses invest large amounts of capital in fixed assets. By their very nature, such investments affect a firm's fortunes for many years. A good decision can boost earnings sharply and increase the price of the firm's stock, but a bad decision can hurt earnings, lower the stock price, and even lead to bankruptcy.

One example of a bad capital budgeting decision which could have been avoided involved Lockheed's decision to produce the widebody L-1011 Tri-Star commercial airliner. When Lockheed made the final decision to produce the aircraft, it estimated a breakeven volume of about 200 airplanes. The company had orders for about 180 airplanes, and it was confident of getting at least 20 more orders. Consequently, it committed $1 billion to commence production.

However, Lockheed's analysis was flawed—it failed to account for the cost of the capital tied up in the project. Had the firm's managers properly appraised the project, they would have found that the breakeven point was far greater than 200 aircraft—so much greater, in fact, that the project was almost certainly doomed to be a financial failure. This mistake contributed to a decline in Lockheed's stock price from $73 to $3 per share.

In December 1989, Boeing announced plans for a new passenger airplane that is larger than its 767 but smaller than its 747 jumbo. Initial orders will probably be placed sometime in 1990 for the new 777, with first deliveries projected for 1995. Analysts considered the project to be favorable for the long term, in spite of the billions of dollars that it will take to create the new aircraft. Also, Boeing's timing may be perfect, because aging widebodies such as McDonnell Douglas's DC-10 and Lockheed's L-1011 will be increasingly withdrawn from service as the 1990s progress.

Boeing is currently riding high, but competition from McDonnell Douglas and Europe's Airbus Industries has made it increasingly difficult for Boeing to retain its position as industry leader. The 777 is intended to secure Boeing's dominant role in the industry, but at $100 million each, the aircraft will face stiff competition from McDonnell Douglas's MD-11 and Airbus's A-340.

Good capital investment decisions begin with sound numerical analyses. With the information in this chapter, you will be able to avoid the type of problem that Lockheed encountered, and you will better understand the types of tools that Boeing should apply when making new aircraft decisions.

IN the last chapter, we discussed the cost of capital. Now we turn to investment decisions involving fixed assets, or *capital budgeting*. Here the term *capital* refers to fixed assets used in production, while a *budget* is a plan which details projected inflows and outflows during some future period. Thus, the *capital budget* is an outline of planned expenditures on fixed assets, and *capital budgeting* is the whole process of analyzing projects and deciding whether they should be included in the capital budget.

Our treatment of capital budgeting is divided into three chapters. First, Chapter 9 gives an overview and explains the basic techniques used in capital budgeting analysis. Chapter 10 goes on to consider how cash flows are estimated. Finally, Chapter 11 discusses risk analysis in capital budgeting, and then it goes on to explain how the optimal capital budget is established.

IMPORTANCE OF CAPITAL BUDGETING

A number of factors combine to make capital budgeting decisions perhaps the most important ones financial managers must make. First and foremost, since the results of capital budgeting decisions continue over an extended period, the decision maker loses some of his or her flexibility. For example, the purchase of an asset with an economic life of 10 years more or less "locks in" the firm for a 10-year period. Further, because asset expansion is fundamentally related to expected future sales, a decision to buy a fixed asset that is expected to last 10 years involves an implicit 10-year sales forecast.

An erroneous forecast of asset requirements can have serious consequences. If the firm has invested too much in assets, it will incur unnecessarily heavy expenses. If it has not spent enough on fixed assets, two problems may arise. First, the firm's equipment may not be sufficiently modern to enable it to produce competitively. Second, if it has inadequate capacity, it may lose a portion of its market share to rival firms, and regaining lost customers typically requires heavy selling expenses, price reductions, and product improvements, all of which are costly.

Another aspect of capital budgeting is timing—capital assets must be ready to come "on line" at the time they are needed. Edward Ford, executive vice president of Western Design, a decorative tile company, gave the authors an illustration of the importance of capital budgeting. His firm tried to operate near capacity most of the time. During a four-year period, Western experienced intermittent spurts in the demand for its products, which forced it to turn away orders. After these sharp increases in demand, the firm would add capacity by renting an additional building, then purchasing and installing the appropriate equipment. It would take six to eight months to get the additional capacity ready, but frequently by that time Western found that there was no demand for its increased output—other firms had already expanded their operations and had taken an increased share of the market. If Western had properly forecasted demand and had planned its increase in capacity six months to a year in advance, it would have been able to maintain or perhaps even increase its market share.

Effective capital budgeting will improve both the timing of asset acquisitions and the quality of assets purchased. A firm which forecasts its needs for capital assets in advance will have the opportunity to purchase and install the assets before its sales are at capacity. In practice, though, most firms do not order capital goods until they approach full capacity, need to replace worn-out equipment, or add new product lines. If sales increase because of an increase in general market demand, all firms in the industry will tend to order capital goods at about the same time. This often results in backlogs, long waiting times for machinery, a deterioration in the quality of the capital goods, and an increase in their prices. The firm which foresees its needs and purchases capital assets early can avoid these problems. Note, though, that if a firm forecasts an increase in demand and expands capacity to meet the anticipated demand, and if sales then do not expand, it will be saddled with excess capacity and abnormally high costs. This can lead to losses or even bankruptcy. Thus, the sales forecast is critical.

Finally, capital budgeting is also important because asset expansion typically involves substantial expenditures, and before a firm spends a large amount of money, it must make the proper plans—large amounts of funds are not available automatically. A firm contemplating a major capital expenditure program may need to arrange its financing several years in advance to be sure of having the funds required for the expansion.

Self-Test Questions

Why are capital budgeting decisions so important to the success of a firm?

Why is the sales forecast the key element in a capital budgeting decision?

PROJECT CLASSIFICATIONS

Analyzing capital expenditure proposals is not a costless operation—benefits can be gained from a careful analysis, but such an investigation does have a cost. For certain types of projects, a relatively detailed analysis may be warranted; for others, cost/benefit studies suggest that simpler procedures should be used. Accordingly, firms generally classify projects into the following categories, and they analyze projects in each category somewhat differently:

1. **Replacement: maintenance of business.** Category 1 consists of expenditures necessary to replace worn-out or damaged equipment used to produce profitable products. These projects are necessary if the firm is to continue in its current businesses. The only issues here are (a) should we continue to produce these products or services, and (b) should we continue to use our existing plant and equipment? Usually, the answers are "yes," so maintenance decisions are normally made without going through an elaborate decision process.

2. **Replacement: cost reduction.** This category includes expenditures to replace serviceable but obsolete equipment. The purpose of these expenditures is to lower the costs of labor, materials, or other inputs such as electricity. These decisions are somewhat more discretionary, so a more detailed analysis is generally required to support the expenditure.

3. **Expansion of existing products or markets.** Expenditures to increase output of existing products, or to expand outlets or distribution facilities in markets now being served, are included here. These decisions are more complex, because they require an explicit consideration of future demand in the firm's product markets. Mistakes are more likely, so a still more detailed analysis is required, and the final decision is made at a higher level within the firm.

4. **Expansion into new products or markets.** These are expenditures necessary to produce a new product or to expand into a geographic area not currently being served. These projects involve strategic decisions that could change the fundamental nature of the business, and they normally require the expenditure of large sums of money over long periods. Invariably, a very detailed analysis is required, and final decisions on new products or markets are generally made by the board of directors as a part of the firm's strategic plan.

5. **Safety and/or environmental projects.** Expenditures necessary to comply with government orders, labor agreements, or insurance policy terms fall into this category. These expenditures are often called *mandatory investments,* or *non-revenue-producing projects.* How they are handled depends on their size, with small ones being treated much like the Category 1 projects described previously.

6. **Other.** This catch-all includes office buildings, parking lots, executive aircraft, and so on. How they are handled also depends on their size.

In general, relatively simple calculations and only a few supporting documents are required for replacement decisions, especially maintenance-type investments in profitable plants. More detailed analysis is required for cost-reduction replacements, for expansion of existing product lines, and especially for investments in new products or areas. Also, within each category, projects are broken down by their dollar costs: The larger the required investment, the more detailed the analysis, and the higher the level of the officer who must authorize the expenditure. Thus, although a plant manager may be authorized to approve maintenance expenditures up to $10,000 on the basis of a relatively unsophisticated analysis, the full board of directors may have to approve decisions which involve either amounts over $1 million or expansions into new products or markets. Statistical data are generally lacking for new product decisions, so here judgments, as opposed to detailed cost data, are a key element in the decision process.

Self-Test Question

Identify and briefly explain how capital project classification categories are used.

SIMILARITIES BETWEEN CAPITAL BUDGETING AND SECURITY VALUATION

Conceptually, capital budgeting involves exactly the same six steps that are used in security analysis:

1.   First, the cost of the project must be determined. This is similar to finding the price that must be paid for a stock or bond.

2.   Next, management estimates the expected cash flows from the project, including the value of the asset at a specified terminal date. This is similar to estimating the future dividend or interest payment stream on a stock or bond.

3.   Third, the riskiness of the projected cash flows must be estimated. To do this, management needs information about the probability distributions of the cash flows.

4.   Then, given the riskiness of the projected cash flows, management determines the appropriate cost of capital at which the project's cash flows are to be discounted.

5.   Next, the expected cash inflows are put on a present value basis to obtain an estimate of the asset's value to the firm. This is equivalent to finding the present value of expected future dividends.

6.   Finally, the present value of the expected cash inflows is compared with the required outlay, or cost, of the project; if the asset's value exceeds its cost, the project should be accepted. Otherwise, the project should be rejected. (Alternatively, the expected rate of return on the project can be calculated, and if this rate of return exceeds the project's required rate of return, the project is accepted.)

If an individual investor identifies and invests in a stock or bond whose market price is less than its true value, the value of the investor's portfolio will increase. Similarly, if a firm identifies (or creates) an investment opportunity with a present value greater than its cost, the value of the firm will increase. Thus, there is a very direct link between capital budgeting and stock values: The more effective the firm's capital budgeting procedures, the higher the price of its stock.

Table 9-1	Cash Flows for Projects S and L	
	Expected After-Tax Net Cash Flow, CF$_t$	
Year (t)	**Project S**	**Project L**
0	($1,000)[a]	($1,000)[a]
1	500	100
2	400	300
3	300	400
4	100	600

[a]Represents the net investment outlay, or initial cost. The parentheses indicate a negative number, or cash outflow.

Self-Test Question

List the six steps of the capital budgeting process, and relate them to security valuation.

CAPITAL BUDGETING DECISION RULES

Four primary methods are currently used to rank projects and to decide whether or not they should be accepted for inclusion in the capital budget: (1) payback, (2) net present value (NPV), (3) internal rate of return (IRR), and (4) profitability index (PI). We first explain how each ranking criterion is calculated, and then we evaluate how well each performs in terms of identifying those projects which will maximize the firm's stock price. Then, in a later section, we discuss a fifth method, the modified IRR (MIRR), which is a better indicator of relative profitability than the IRR.

We use the cash flow data shown in Table 9-1 for Projects S and L to illustrate each method, and throughout this chapter we assume that the projects are equally risky. Note that the cash flows, CF$_t$, are expected values, and that they are adjusted to reflect taxes, depreciation, and salvage values. Also, since many projects require an investment in both fixed assets and working capital, the investment outlays shown as CF$_0$ include any necessary changes in net working capital.[1] Finally, we assume that all cash flows occur at the end of the designated year. Incidentally, the S stands for *short* and the L for *long*: Project S is a short-term project in the sense that its cash inflows tend to come in sooner than L's.

---

[1]Perhaps the most difficult part of the capital budgeting process is the estimation of the relevant cash flows. For simplicity, the net cash flows are treated as a given in this chapter, which allows us to focus on our main area of concern, the capital budgeting decision rules. However, in Chapter 10 we will discuss cash flow estimation in detail. Also, note that *working capital* is defined as the firm's current assets, and that *net working capital* is current assets minus current liabilities.

Payback Period

The *payback period,* defined as the expected number of years required to recover the original investment, was the first formal method used to evaluate capital budgeting projects. When applied to Projects S and L, the payback period is $2\frac{1}{3}$ years for S and $3\frac{1}{3}$ years for L.[2]

$$\text{Payback}_S\colon 2\tfrac{1}{3} \text{ years.}$$
$$\text{Payback}_L\colon 3\tfrac{1}{3} \text{ years.}$$

If the firm required a payback of three years or less, Project S would be accepted, but Project L would be rejected. If the projects were *mutually exclusive,* S would be ranked over L because S has the shorter payback.[3]

Some firms use a variant of the regular payback, the *discounted payback period,* which is similar to the regular payback period except that the expected cash flows are discounted by the project's cost of capital.[4] Thus, the discounted payback period is defined as the number of years required to recover the investment from *discounted* net cash flows. Table 9-2 contains the discounted net cash flows for Projects S and L, assuming both projects have a cost of capital of 10 percent. To construct Table 9-2, each cash inflow in Table 9-1 is divided by $(1 + k)^t = (1.10)^t$, where t is the year in which the cash flow occurs and k is the project's cost of capital. After 3 years, Project S will have generated $1,011 in discounted cash inflows. Since the cost is $1,000, the discounted payback is just under 3 years, or, to be precise, 2 + ($214/$225) = 2.95 years. Project L's discounted payback is 3.88 years:

$$\text{Discounted payback}_S = 2.0 + \$214/\$225 = 2.95 \text{ years.}$$

$$\text{Discounted payback}_L = 3.0 + \$360/\$410 = 3.88 \text{ years.}$$

For Projects S and L, the rankings are the same regardless of which payback method is used; that is, Project S is preferred to Project L, and Project S would still be

---

[2]The easiest way to calculate the payback period is to accumulate the project's net cash flows and see when they sum to zero. For example, the annual and cumulative net cash flows of Project S are shown below:

Year	Cash Flow	Cumulative Cash Flow
0	($1,000)	($1,000)
1	500	(500)
2	400	(100)
3	300	200
4	100	300

Thus, the investment is recovered by the end of Year 3. If the cash flows actually occur evenly during the year, the recovery occurs one-third of the way into Year 3: $100 remains to be recovered at the end of Year 2, and since Year 3 produces $300 in net cash flow, the payback period for Project S is $2\frac{1}{3}$ years.

[3]*Mutually exclusive* means that if one project is taken on, the other must be rejected. For example, the installation of a conveyor-belt system in a warehouse and the purchase of a fleet of forklift trucks for the same warehouse would be mutually exclusive projects—accepting one implies rejection of the other. *Independent* projects are projects whose cash flows are independent of one another.

[4]A project's cost of capital reflects (1) the overall cost of capital to the firm and (2) the differential risk between the firm's existing projects and the project being evaluated. This concept will be discussed in detail in Chapter 11.

Table 9-2	Discounted Cash Flows for Projects S and L

	Discounted Net Cash Flow			
Year	**Project S**		**Project L**	
(t)	**Annual**	**Cumulative**	**Annual**	**Cumulative**
0	($1,000)	($1,000)	($1,000)	($1,000)
1	455	(545)	91	(909)
2	331	(214)	248	(661)
3	225	11	301	(360)
4	68	79	410	50

selected if the firm were to require a discounted payback of three years or less. Often, however, the regular and the discounted paybacks produce conflicting rankings.

Note that the payback is a type of "breakeven" calculation in the sense that if cash flows come in at the expected rate until the payback year, then the project will break even. However, the regular payback does not take account of the cost of capital—no cost for the debt or equity used to undertake the project is reflected in the cash flows or the calculation. The discounted payback does take account of capital costs—it shows the breakeven year after covering debt and equity costs. Still, as we shall see, both payback methods have some serious deficiencies, and other procedures are less likely to lead to errors in project selection. Therefore, we will not dwell on the finer points of payback analysis.[5]

Although the payback method has some serious faults as a project ranking criterion, it does provide information on how long funds will be tied up in a project. Thus, the shorter the payback period, other things held constant, the greater is the project's *liquidity*. Also, since cash flows expected in the distant future are generally regarded as being riskier than near-term cash flows, the payback is often used as a rough measure of a project's *riskiness*.

Net Present Value (NPV)

As the flaws in the payback and other early methods were recognized, people began to search for ways to improve the effectiveness of project evaluations. One such method is the *net present value (NPV)* method, which relies on *discounted cash flow* methodology. To implement this approach, we proceed as follows:

1.   Find the present value of each cash flow, including both inflows and outflows, discounted at the project's cost of capital.

---

[5]Another capital budgeting technique that was once used widely is the *accounting rate of return (ARR)*, which examines a project's contribution to the firm's net income. Since the ARR has no redeeming value, we will not discuss it in this text. See Eugene F. Brigham and Louis C. Gapenski, *Intermediate Financial Management,* 3rd Edition, Chapter 7.

2. Sum these discounted cash flows; this sum is defined as the project's NPV.

3. If the NPV is positive, the project should be accepted; if the NPV is negative, it should be rejected; and if two projects are mutually exclusive, the one with the higher positive NPV should be chosen.

The NPV can be expressed as follows:

$$NPV = \sum_{t=0}^{n} \frac{CF_t}{(1 + k)^t}.$$

(9-1)

Here CF_t is the expected net cash flow at Period t, and k is the project's periodic cost of capital.[6] Cash outflows (expenditures on the project, such as the cost of buying equipment or building factories) are treated as *negative* cash flows. In evaluating Projects S and L, only CF_0 is negative, but for many large projects such as the Alaska Pipeline, an electric generating plant, or IBM's new laptop computer project, outflows occur for several years before operations begin and cash flows turn positive. Also, note that Equation 9-1 is quite general, so inflows and outflows could occur on any basis, say quarterly or monthly, and t could represent quarters or months rather than years.[7]

At a 10 percent cost of capital, the NPV of Project S is $78.82:

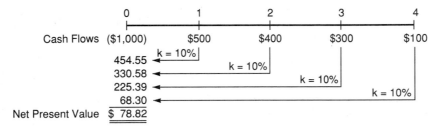

By a similar process, we find $NPV_L = \$49.18$. On this basis, both projects should be accepted if they are independent, but S should be the one chosen if they are mutually exclusive.

---

[6]In Equation 9-1, we assume that the project's cost of capital, k, is constant across all periods. Later in the chapter we discuss the situation in which k varies from period to period.

[7]If t represents any period other than years, then the cost of capital must be adjusted to reflect the periodic rate. For example, if the annual cost of capital were 10 percent, but we were evaluating a project on the basis of quarterly cash flows, the approximate periodic rate would be $10\%/4 = 2.5\%$, and the precise periodic rate, k/4 in the following equation, would be 2.41 percent:

$$(1 + k/4)^4 - 1.0 = 0.10$$
$$(1 + k/4)^4 = 1.10$$
$$(1 + k/4) = (1.10)^{1/4} = 1.0241$$
$$k/4 = 0.0241 = 2.41\%.$$

For most projects, calculation of the precise periodic rate is unwarranted because of the degree of uncertainty in the cash flows. However, there are projects—for example, the construction of a building for lease to the U.S. Postal Service on a long-term basis—for which the precise adjustment might be warranted.

When using a financial calculator, enter the cash flows, in order, into the financial registers, then enter k = i = 10, and finally push the NPV key (or compute NPV). When entering the cash flows, note that many calculators have a register labelled CF_0 for the initial cash flow, which is usually an outflow, and then registers labelled CF_j for the succeeding cash flows.

Rationale for the NPV Method

The rationale for the NPV method is straightforward. An NPV of zero signifies that the project's cash flows are just sufficient to (1) repay the invested capital and (2) provide the required rate of return on that capital. If a project has a positive NPV, then its cash flows are generating an excess return, and, since the return to bondholders is fixed, the excess return accrues solely to the firm's stockholders. Therefore, if a firm takes on a zero-NPV project, the position of the stockholders remains constant — the firm becomes larger, but the price of its stock remains unchanged. However, if the firm takes on a project with a positive NPV, the position of the stockholders is improved. In our example, shareholders' wealth would increase by $78.82 if the firm takes on Project S, but by only $49.18 if it takes on Project L. Viewed in this manner, it is easy to see why S is preferred to L, and it is also easy to see the logic of the NPV approach.[8]

Internal Rate of Return (IRR)

In Chapter 7, we presented procedures for finding the yield to maturity, or rate of return, on a bond—if you invest in the bond and hold it to maturity, you can roughly expect to earn the YTM on the money you invested. Exactly the same concepts are employed in capital budgeting when the IRR method is used. The IRR is defined as that discount rate, r, which equates the present value of a project's expected cash inflows to the present value of the project's expected costs:

$$PV(Inflows) = PV(Investment costs),$$

or, equivalently,

$$\sum_{t=0}^{n} \frac{CF_t}{(1 + r)^t} = 0. \tag{9-2}$$

---

[8]This description of the process is somewhat oversimplified. Both analysts and investors anticipate that firms will identify and accept positive NPV projects, and current stock prices reflect these expectations. Thus, stock prices react to announcements of new capital projects only to the extent that such projects were not already expected. In this sense, we may think of a firm's value as consisting of two parts: (1) the value of its existing assets and (2) the value of its "growth opportunities," or projects with positive NPVs. AT&T is a good example of this: the company has the world's largest long-distance network plus telephone manufacturing facilities, both of which provide current earnings and cash flows, and it has Bell Labs, which has the *potential* for coming up with new products in the computer/telecommunications area that could be extremely profitable. Security analysts (and investors) thus analyze AT&T as a company with a set of cash-producing assets plus a set of growth opportunities that will materialize if and only if it can come up with a number of positive NPV projects through its capital budgeting process.

For our Project S, here is the setup:

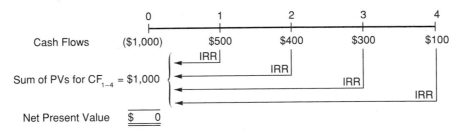

$$IRR_S = 14.5\% = \text{discount rate which forces the sum of the PVs of } CF_{1-4} \text{ to equal the project's cost, } \$1,000.$$

Internal rates of return can be calculated very easily with financial calculators and computers, and many firms have computerized their capital budgeting processes and automatically generate IRRs, NPVs, and paybacks for all projects. Thus, business firms have no difficulty whatever with the mechanical side of capital budgeting, and a serious business student should have a financial calculator capable of finding IRRs. All IRRs reported in this and the following chapters were obtained by using a financial calculator or a computer. By keying in the cash flows and then pressing the IRR button, we used a financial calculator to find that Project S has $IRR_S = 14.5\%$, while $IRR_L = 11.8\%$. If both projects have a cost of capital, or *hurdle rate*, of 10 percent, then the internal rate of return rule indicates that if the projects are independent, both should be accepted—they both are expected to earn more than the cost of the capital needed to finance them. If they are mutually exclusive, S ranks higher and should be accepted, while L should be rejected. If the cost of capital is more than 14.5 percent, both projects should be rejected.

Notice that the internal rate of return formula, Equation 9-2, is simply the NPV formula, Equation 9-1, solved for the particular discount rate that forces the NPV to equal zero. Thus, the same basic equation is used for both methods, but in the NPV method the discount rate, k, is specified and the NPV is found, whereas in the IRR method the NPV is specified to equal zero, and the value of $r = IRR$ that forces this equality is determined.

Rationale for the IRR Method

Why is the particular discount rate that equates a project's cost with the present value of its receipts (the IRR) so special? In effect, the IRR on a project is its expected rate of return. If the internal rate of return exceeds the cost of the funds used to finance the project, a surplus remains after paying for the capital, and this surplus accrues to the firm's stockholders. Therefore, taking on a project whose IRR exceeds its cost of capital increases shareholders' wealth. On the other hand, if the internal rate of return is less than the cost of capital, then taking on the project imposes a cost on current stockholders. It is this "breakeven" characteristic that makes the IRR useful in evaluating capital projects.

Profitability Index

Another method used to evaluate projects is the *profitability index (PI)*, or the *benefit/cost ratio*, as it is sometimes called:

$$PI = \frac{PV \text{ benefits}}{PV \text{ costs}} = \frac{\sum_{t=0}^{n} \frac{CIF_t}{(1 + k)^t}}{\sum_{t=0}^{n} \frac{COF_t}{(1 + k)^t}}. \tag{9-3}$$

Here CIF_t represents the expected cash inflows, or benefits, and COF_t represents the expected cash outflows, or costs. The PI shows the *relative* profitability of any project, or the present value of benefits per present value dollar of costs. The PI for Project S, based on a 10 percent cost of capital, is 1.079:

$$PI_S = \frac{\$1,078.82}{\$1,000} = 1.079.$$

Similarly, $PI_L = 1.049$. A project is acceptable if its PI is greater than 1.0, and the higher the PI, the higher the project's ranking. Therefore, both S and L would be accepted by the PI criterion if they were independent, and S would be ranked ahead of L if they were mutually exclusive.

Mathematically, the NPV, the IRR, and the PI methods must always lead to the same accept/reject decisions for independent projects: If a project's NPV is positive, its IRR must exceed k and its PI must be greater than 1.0. However, NPV, IRR, and PI can give conflicting rankings for mutually exclusive projects. This point will be discussed in more detail in later sections.

Self-Test Questions

What are the four capital budgeting ranking methods discussed in this section?

Briefly describe each method, and the rationale for its use.

What three methods always lead to the same accept/reject decision for independent projects?

What two pieces of information does the payback convey that are not conveyed by the other methods?

COMPARISON OF THE NPV AND IRR METHODS

Because, as we will demonstrate later, the NPV method is better than IRR and PI, we were tempted to explain NPV only, to state that it should be used as the acceptance criterion, and to go on to the next topic. However, the IRR and PI methods are familiar to many corporate executives, they are widely entrenched in industry, and they have some unique virtues. Therefore, it is important that finance students thoroughly understand the IRR and PI methods and be prepared to explain why, at times, a project with a lower IRR or PI may be preferable to one with a higher IRR or PI.

Figure 9-1   Net Present Value Profiles: NPVs of Projects
S and L at Different Costs of Capital

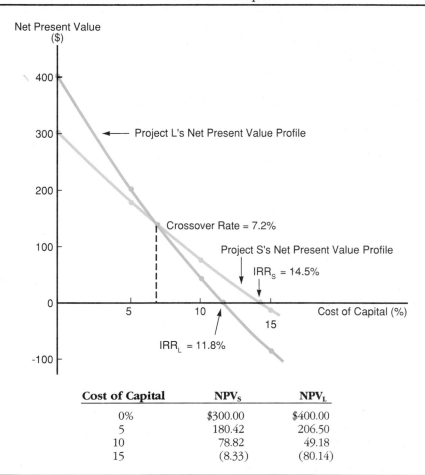

Cost of Capital	NPV$_S$	NPV$_L$
0%	$300.00	$400.00
5	180.42	206.50
10	78.82	49.18
15	(8.33)	(80.14)

NPV Profiles

A graph which relates a project's NPV to the discount rate used to calculate the NPV is defined as the project's *net present value profile;* profiles for Projects L and S are shown in Figure 9-1. To construct the profiles, we first note that at a zero discount rate, the NPV is simply the total of the undiscounted cash flows of the project; thus, at a zero discount rate NPV$_S$ = $300, and NPV$_L$ = $400. These values are plotted as the vertical axis intercepts in Figure 9-1. Next, we calculate the projects' NPVs at three discount rates, say 5, 10, and 15 percent, and plot these values. The four points plotted on our graph for each project are shown at the bottom of the figure.

Recall that the IRR is defined as the discount rate at which a project's NPV equals zero. Therefore, *the point where its net present value profile crosses the horizontal axis indicates a project's internal rate of return.* Since we calculated IRR$_S$ and IRR$_L$ in an earlier section, we have two other points which we can use in plotting the projects' NPV profiles.

When we connect the plot points, we have the net present value profiles.[9] NPV profiles can be very useful in project analysis, and we will use them often in the remainder of the chapter.

NPV Rankings' Dependence on the Discount Rate

We saw in Figure 9-1 that the NPV profiles of both Project L and Project S decline as the discount rate increases. But notice in the figure that Project L has the higher NPV at low discount rates, but NPV$_S$ exceeds NPV$_L$ if the discount rate is above 7.2 percent. Notice also that Project L's NPV is "more sensitive" to changes in the discount rate than is NPV$_S$; that is, Project L's net present value profile has the steeper slope, indicating that a change in k has a larger effect on NPV$_L$ than on NPV$_S$.

To see why L has the greater sensitivity, recall first that the cash flows from S are received faster than those from L—in a payback sense, S is a short-term project, while L is a long-term project. Next, recall the equation for the NPV:

$$NPV = \frac{CF_0}{(1 + k)^0} + \frac{CF_1}{(1 + k)^1} + \frac{CF_2}{(1 + k)^2} + \frac{CF_3}{(1 + k)^3} + \frac{CF_4}{(1 + k)^4}.$$

Now notice that the denominators of the terms in this equation increase as k and t increase, and the increase is exponential; that is, the effect of a higher k is more pronounced if t is larger. To understand this point more clearly, consider the following data:

PV of a $100 cash flow due in 1 year, discounted at 5%	$95.24
PV of a $100 cash flow due in 1 year, discounted at 10%	$90.91
Percentage decline in PV resulting from a 5 percentage point increase in k when t = 1	−4.5%
PV of a $100 cash flow due in 10 years, discounted at 5%	$61.39
PV of a $100 cash flow due in 10 years, discounted at 10%	$38.55
Percentage decline in PV resulting from a 5 percentage point increase in k when t = 10	−37.2%

A 5 percentage point increase in the discount rate causes only a 4.5 percent decline in the PV of a Year 1 cash flow, but the same discount rate increase causes the PV of a Year 10 cash flow to fall by 37.2 percent. Thus, if a project has most of its cash flows coming in the early years, its NPV will not be lowered very much by a discount rate increase, but a project whose cash flows come later will be severely penalized by high discount rates. Accordingly, Project L, which has its largest cash

---

[9] Notice that the NPV profiles are curved—they are *not* straight lines. Also, the NPVs approach the t = 0 cash flow (the cost of the project) as the discount rate increases without limit. The reason is that, at an infinitely high discount rate, the PV of the inflows would be zero, so NPV (k = ∞) = CF$_0$, which in our example is −$1,000. We should also note that under certain conditions the NPV profiles can cross the horizontal axis several times, or never cross it. This point is discussed later in the chapter.

flows in the later years, is hurt badly when the discount rate is high, while Project S, which has relatively rapid cash flows, is affected less by rising discount rates.

Independent Projects

If two projects are *independent,* then the NPV and IRR criteria always lead to the same accept/reject decision: if NPV says accept, IRR also says accept. To see why this is so, look back at Figure 9-1 and notice (1) that the IRR criterion for acceptance is that the project's cost of capital is less than (or to the left of) the IRR, and (2) that whenever the project's cost of capital is less than the IRR, its NPV is positive. Thus, for any cost of capital less than 11.8 percent, Project L is acceptable by both the NPV and the IRR criteria, while both methods reject the project if the cost of capital is greater than 11.8 percent. Project S—and all other independent projects under consideration—could be analyzed similarly, and it will always turn out that if IRR > k, then NPV > 0.

Mutually Exclusive Projects

Now assume that Projects S and L are *mutually exclusive,* rather than independent. That is, we can choose either Project S or Project L, or we can reject both, but we cannot accept both projects. Notice in Figure 9-1 that as long as the cost of capital is *greater than* the crossover rate of 7.2 percent, NPV_S is greater than NPV_L, and also that IRR_S is greater than IRR_L. Therefore, for k greater than the crossover rate of 7.2 percent, the two methods lead to the selection of the same project. However, if the cost of capital is *less than* the crossover rate, the NPV method ranks Project L higher, but the IRR method always indicates that Project S is better. Thus, a conflict exists. NPV says choose mutually exclusive L, while IRR says take S. Which answer is correct? Logic suggests that the NPV method is better, since it selects that project which adds the most to shareholder wealth.[10]

Conditions for Conflict. There are two basic conditions which are necessary for NPV profiles to cross, and thus which lead to potential conflicts between NPV and IRR: (1) when *project size (or scale) differences* exist, meaning that the cost of one project is larger than that of the other, or (2) when *timing differences* exist, meaning that the timing of cash flows from the two projects differs such that most of the cash flows from one project come in the early years and most of the cash flows from the other project come in the later years, as occurred with Projects L and S.[11]

---

[10]The crossover point is important, and it is easy to calculate. Simply go back to Table 9-1, where we set forth the two projects' cash flows, and calculate the difference in those flows in each year. The differences are $CF_S - CF_L = \$0, +\$400, +\$100, -\$100,$ and $-\$500$, respectively. Enter these values in the cash flow registers of a financial calculator, press the IRR button, and the crossover rate, $7.17 \approx 7.2$, appears.

[11]Of course, it is possible for mutually exclusive projects to differ with respect to both scale and timing. Also, if mutually exclusive projects have different lives (as opposed to different cash flow patterns over a common life), this introduces further complications, and for meaningful comparisons, some mutually exclusive projects must be evaluated over a common life. This point will be discussed in detail in the next chapter.

When either size or timing differences occur, the firm will have different amounts of funds to invest in the various years, depending on which of the two mutually exclusive projects it chooses. For example, if one project costs more than the other, then the firm will have more money at $t = 0$ to invest elsewhere if it selects the smaller project. Similarly, for projects of equal size, the one with the larger early cash inflows provides more funds for reinvestment in the early years. Given this situation, the assumed rate of return at which differential cash flows can be invested is an important consideration.

Causes of Conflict. The critical issue in resolving conflicts between mutually exclusive projects is this: What is the value of generating the cash flows earlier rather than later? The value of the cash flows depends on the opportunity rate at which we can reinvest differential early years' cash flows. *The use of the NPV method implicitly assumes that the opportunity rate at which cash flows can be reinvested is the cost of capital, whereas use of the IRR method implies that the firm has the opportunity to reinvest at the IRR.* These assumptions are inherent in the mathematics of the discounting process. Thus, the NPV method discounts cash flows at the cost of capital, while the IRR method discounts cash flows at the project's IRR. The cash flows may actually be withdrawn as dividends by the stockholders and spent on beer and pizza, but the assumption of a reinvestment opportunity is still implicit in the NPV and IRR calculations.

Resolution of Conflict. Which is the better assumption, reinvestment of each project's cash flows at the cost of capital or reinvestment at the project's IRR? We can answer the question as follows:

1.   Assume that the firm's cost of capital is 10 percent. Management can obtain all the funds it wants at this rate. This condition is expected to hold in the foreseeable future. Further, assume that all potential projects have the same risk as the firm's current projects.

2.   The capital budgeting process calls for all potential projects to be evaluated at $k = 10\%$. All projects with NPV > 0 are accepted. Plenty of capital is available to finance these projects, both now and in the future.

3.   As cash flows come in from past investments, what will be done with them? These cash flows can either (a) be paid out to the equity and debt investors who, on average, require a 10 percent rate of return, or (b) be used as a substitute for outside capital that costs 10 percent. Thus, since the cash flows are expected to save the firm 10 percent, this is their value to the firm, hence their opportunity cost reinvestment rate.

4.   The IRR method implicitly assumes reinvestment at the internal rate of return itself. Given (a) ready access to capital markets and (b) a constant expected future cost of capital, the appropriate reinvestment rate is the opportunity cost of capital, or 10 percent. Even if the firm takes on projects in the future whose IRRs average some high rate, say 30 percent, this is irrelevant—those projects could always be financed with new external capital costing 10 percent, so cash flows from past projects have an opportunity cost reinvestment rate which is only equal to the cost of capital.

Therefore, we come to the conclusion that *the correct reinvestment rate assumption is the cost of capital, which is implicit in the NPV method.* This, in turn, leads us to prefer the NPV method, at least for firms willing and able to obtain capital at a cost reasonably close to the current cost of capital. In Appendix 11A, when we discuss capital rationing, we will see that under certain conditions the NPV rule may be questionable, but for most firms at most times, NPV is conceptually better than IRR. .

We should reiterate that, when projects are independent, the NPV and IRR methods both make exactly the same accept/reject decision. However, *when evaluating mutually exclusive projects, especially those that differ in scale and/or timing, the NPV method should be used.*

Multiple IRRs

There is one other situation in which the IRR approach may not be usable—this is when nonnormal projects are involved. A *normal* capital project is one that has one or more cash outflows (costs) followed by a series of cash inflows. If, however, a project calls for a large cash outflow either sometime during or at the end of its life, then it is a *nonnormal* project. Nonnormal projects can present unique difficulties when evaluated by the IRR method. The most common problem encountered when evaluating nonnormal projects is multiple IRRs.

When one solves Equation 9-2 to find the IRR,

$$\sum_{t=0}^{n} \frac{CF_t}{(1 + r)^t} = 0, \tag{9-2}$$

it is possible to obtain more than one value of r, which means that multiple IRRs occur. Notice that Equation 9-2 is a polynomial of degree n, so it has n different roots, or solutions. All except one of the roots are imaginary numbers when investments are normal (one or more cash outflows followed by cash inflows), so in the normal case, only one value of r appears. However, the possibility of multiple real roots, hence multiple IRRs, arises when the project is nonnormal (negative net cash flows occur during some year after the project has been placed in operation).

To illustrate this problem, suppose a firm is considering the expenditure of $1.6 million to develop a strip mine (Project M). The mine will produce a cash flow of $10 million at the end of Year 1. Then, at the end of Year 2, $10 million must be expended to restore the land to its original condition. Therefore, the project's expected net cash flows are as follows (in millions of dollars):

	Expected Net Cash Flow	
Year 0	**End of Year 1**	**End of Year 2**
− $1.6	+ $10	− $10

These values can be substituted into Equation 9-2 to derive the IRR for the investment:

$$NPV = \frac{-\$1.6 \text{ million}}{(1 + r)^0} + \frac{\$10 \text{ million}}{(1 + r)^1} + \frac{-\$10 \text{ million}}{(1 + r)^2} = 0.$$

Figure 9-2 NPV Profile for Project M

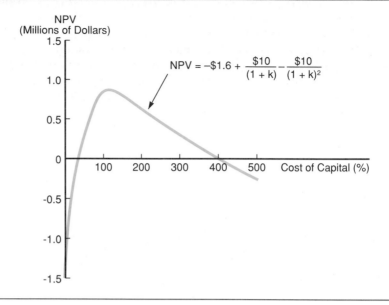

$$NPV = -\$1.6 + \frac{\$10}{(1 + k)} - \frac{\$10}{(1 + k)^2}$$

When solved, we find that NPV = 0 when r = 25% and also when r = 400%.[12] Therefore, the IRR of the investment is both 25 and 400 percent. This relationship is depicted graphically in Figure 9-2.[13] Note that no dilemma would arise if the NPV method were used; we would simply use Equation 9-1, find the NPV, and use this to evaluate the project. If Project M's cost of capital is 10 percent, then its NPV is − $0.77 million, and the project should be rejected. If k were between 25 and 400 percent, the NPV would be positive.

The authors encountered another example of multiple internal rates of return when a major California bank *borrowed* funds from an insurance company and then used these funds (plus an initial investment of its own) to buy a number of jet engines, which it then leased to a major airline. The bank expected to receive positive net cash flows (lease payments plus tax savings minus interest on the insurance

---

[12]If you attempted to find the IRR of Project M with many financial calculators, you would get an error message. This same message would be given for all projects with multiple IRRs. However, you can still find Project M's IRRs by first calculating NPVs using several different values for k and then plotting the NPV profile. The intersections with the X-axis give a rough idea of the IRR values. Finally, one can use trial and error to find the exact values of k which force NPV = 0.

[13]Does Figure 9-2 suggest that the firm should try to *raise* its cost of capital to about 100 percent in order to maximize the NPV of the project? Certainly not. The firm should seek to *minimize* its cost of capital; this will cause the price of its stock to be maximized. Actions taken to raise the cost of capital might make this particular project look good, but those actions would be terribly harmful to the firm's more numerous normal projects. Only if the firm's cost of capital is high, in spite of efforts to keep it down, will the illustrative project have a positive NPV.

company loan) for a number of years, then several large negative cash flows as it repaid the insurance company loan, and, finally, a large inflow from the sale of the engines when the lease expired.[14]

The bank discovered two IRRs and wondered which was correct. It could not ignore the IRR and use the NPV method, since the lease was already on the books, and the bank's senior loan committee, as well as Federal Reserve bank examiners, wanted to know the return on the lease. The bank's solution called for compounding the cash flows—both positive and negative—at an assumed reinvestment rate of 9 percent, its average return on loans, to arrive at a compounded terminal value for the operation. Then the interest rate that equated this terminal sum to the bank's initial cost was called the IRR, or the rate of return on the lease. This procedure satisfied both the loan committee and the bank examiners.

The examples just presented illustrate one problem, multiple IRRs, that can arise when the IRR criterion is used with a project that has nonnormal cash flows. Use of the IRR method on nonnormal cash flow projects could produce other problems such as no IRR or an IRR which leads to an incorrect accept/reject decision. In all such cases, the NPV criterion could be easily applied, and this method leads to conceptually correct capital budgeting decisions.

Self-Test Questions

Describe how NPV profiles are constructed.

What is a crossover point, and what impact does it have on mutually exclusive project selection?

What are the two basic conditions that can lead to conflicts between the NPV and IRR methods?

What is the underlying cause of conflicts between the NPV and IRR methods?

If a conflict exists, should the capital budgeting decision be made on the basis of the NPV or the IRR ranking? Why?

Explain the difference between normal and nonnormal projects.

What is the "multiple IRR problem," and what condition is necessary for its occurrence?

MODIFIED INTERNAL RATE OF RETURN (MIRR)

In spite of a strong academic preference for NPV, surveys indicate that business executives prefer IRR over NPV by a margin of 3 to 1. Apparently, managers find it intuitively more appealing to analyze investments in terms of percentage rates of return than dollars of NPV. Given this fact, can we devise a percentage evaluator that is better than the regular IRR? The answer is yes—we can modify the IRR and make

---

[14]The situation described here is a *leveraged lease*. See Chapter 17 for more on leveraged leases.

it a better indicator of relative profitability, hence better for use in capital budgeting. The new measure is called the *modified IRR, or MIRR,* and it is defined as follows:

$$\text{PV costs} = \text{PV terminal value}$$

$$\sum_{t=0}^{n} \frac{COF_t}{(1+k)^t} = \frac{\sum_{t=0}^{n} CIF_t(1+k)^{n-t}}{(1+MIRR)^n} \tag{9-2a}$$

$$\text{PV costs} = \frac{TV}{(1+MIRR)^n}.$$

Here COF refers to cash outflows, or the costs of the project, and CIF refers to cash inflows. The left term is simply the PV of the investment outlays when discounted at the cost of capital, and the numerator of the right term is the future value of the inflows, assuming that the cash inflows are reinvested at the cost of capital. The future value of the cash inflows is also called the *terminal value,* or *TV.* The discount rate that forces the PV of the TV to equal the PV of the costs is defined as the MIRR.[15]

If the investment costs are all incurred at t = 0, and if the first operating inflow occurs at t = 1, as is true for our illustrative Projects S and L which we first presented in Table 9-1, then this equation may be used:

$$\text{Cost} = \frac{TV}{(1+MIRR)^n} = \frac{\sum_{t=1}^{n} CIF_t(1+k)^{n-t}}{(1+MIRR)^n}. \tag{9-2b}$$

We can illustrate the calculation with Project S:

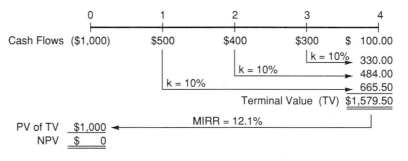

Using a financial calculator, enter PV = 1,000, FV = 1,579.5 (or −1,579.5), and n = 4, and press the i button to find MIRR$_S$ = 12.1%. Similarly, we find MIRR$_L$ = 11.3%.

The modified IRR has a significant advantage over the regular IRR. MIRR assumes that cash flows from all projects are reinvested at the cost of capital, while the regular IRR assumes that the cash flows from each project are reinvested at the project's

---

[15]There are several alternative definitions for the MIRR. The one we present here is effective and relatively simple to use. For a complete discussion, see William R. McDaniel, Daniel E. McCarty, and Kenneth A. Jessell, "Discounted Cash Flow with Explicit Reinvestment Rates: Tutorial and Extension," *The Financial Review,* August 1988, 369–385.

own IRR. Since reinvestment at k is generally more correct, the modified IRR is a better indicator of a project's true profitability. MIRR also solves the multiple IRR problem. To illustrate, with k = 10%, Project M (the strip mine project) has MIRR = 5.6%, and hence it should be rejected. This is consistent with the decision based on the NPV method, because NPV = − $0.77 million.

Is MIRR as good as NPV for selecting among competing (mutually exclusive) projects? If the two projects are of equal size and have the same life, then NPV and MIRR will always lead to the same project selection decision. Thus, for any projects like our Projects S and L, if $NPV_S > NPV_L$, then $MIRR_S > MIRR_L$ and the kinds of conflicts we encountered between NPV and the regular IRR will not occur. Also, if the projects are of equal size, but differ in lives, the MIRR will always lead to the same decision as the NPV when the MIRRs are both calculated on the basis of the longer project's life. (Just fill in zeros for the shorter project's missing cash flows.) However, if the projects differ in scale (or size), then conflicts can still occur — if we were comparing a large project with a small mutually exclusive one, then we might find $NPV_L > NPV_S$, but $MIRR_S > MIRR_L$.

Our conclusion is that the modified IRR is superior to the regular IRR as an indicator of a project's "true" rate of return, or "expected long-term rate of return," but the NPV method is still better for choosing among competing projects that differ in scale, because it provides a better indicator of how much the projects increase the value of the firm.[16]

Self-Test Questions

Briefly describe how the modified IRR (MIRR) is calculated.

What is the primary difference between the MIRR and the regular IRR?

What advantages does the MIRR have over the regular IRR in making capital budgeting decisions?

What condition is necessary for the MIRR and NPV methods to lead to different decisions?

COMPARISON OF THE NPV AND PI METHODS

The PI method, where PI = PV cash inflows/PV cash outflows, measures the present value of benefits per dollar of investment, whereas the NPV measures the total dollars of net present value. These two methods can lead to conflicts when used to evaluate mutually exclusive projects. To illustrate, suppose a firm is comparing Project L (for large), which requires a $5 million investment and returns $6 million after 1 year, with Project S (for small), which requires an outlay of $100,000 and re-

---

[16]Note that some financial calculators, for example the HP-17B, make it relatively easy to calculate MIRR. With the 17B, you enter two cash flow streams: (1) an outflow stream with zeros in place of inflows and (2) an inflow stream with zeros for costs. Then, the 17B calculates the terminal value of the inflow stream and the present value of the outflow stream. The final step is merely finding the MIRR.

turns $130,000 at the end of 1 year. Both projects have average risk and hence will be evaluated at the firm's 10 percent cost of capital. Here are the projects' NPVs and PIs:

$$NPV_L = -\$5,000,000 + \frac{\$6,000,000}{(1.10)^1} = \$454,545.$$

$$NPV_S = -\$100,000 + \frac{\$130,000}{(1.10)^1} = \$18,182.$$

$$PI_L = \frac{\dfrac{\$6,000,000}{(1.10)^1}}{\$5,000,000} = 1.09.$$

$$PI_S = \frac{\dfrac{\$130,000}{(1.10)^1}}{\$100,000} = 1.18.$$

Thus, the NPV method indicates that we should accept Project L because $NPV_L > NPV_S$, but the PI method indicates that Project S is preferable, because $PI_S > PI_L$.

Given this conflict, which project should be accepted? Remembering that shareholders' wealth increases by the NPV of a project, it is clear that Project L contributes more to shareholder wealth, so L should be selected over S. Thus, for a firm that seeks to maximize stockholders' wealth, the NPV method is better. Of course, if the projects were independent, both would be chosen, since both projects have positive NPVs and hence PIs greater than 1.0.

In general, the NPV method leads to better decisions than does the PI method. However, the PI may be useful when capital rationing exists. We explore this topic in Appendix 11A.

Self-Test Questions

What condition can lead to conflicts between the NPV and PI methods?

If a conflict exists, should the NPV or the PI method be used to make the decision? Explain.

PRESENT VALUE OF FUTURE COSTS

Firms often choose between mutually exclusive projects on the basis of the present value of future costs rather than on the basis of the projects' NPVs. For example, Moët & Chandon, a French champagne producer, recently evaluated several different methods for disposing of grape pulp at its California winery. The disposal system chosen would have no effect on either the prices or the quantity of sparkling wine produced by the plant—these would be set in the competitive marketplace. Therefore, the revenue stream would be the same regardless of which disposal process is used, so revenues are irrelevant to this capital budgeting decision.

Since the revenue stream will be the same, Moët & Chandon could make the decision on the basis of expected future costs alone, choosing the process that does the job for the lowest cost. Table 9-3 contains the expected net costs for the best

Table 9-3 Production Costs for Processes A and B

	Expected Net Cost	
Year	Process A	Process B
0	($50,000)	($100,000)
1	(22,000)	(10,000)
2	(22,000)	(10,000)
3	(22,000)	(10,000)
4	(22,000)	(10,000)
5	(22,000)	(10,000)
PV(12%)	($129,305)	($136,048)

two processes over their 5-year expected lives. Process A requires a lower expenditure on capital equipment than B, but A is more labor intensive. Therefore, A's Year 0 cost is relatively low, but its operating costs are relatively high.

The company's analysts judged the processes to both have the same risk as the company's average project, and thus they used the firm's overall cost of capital, 12 percent, to discount the flows of each project. As shown in Table 9-3, Process A has a lower present value of future costs, so it was chosen. We will have more to say about discounting costs (or outflows) in Chapter 11, where we discuss risk adjustments.

Self-Test Questions

Explain the procedure for evaluating two mutually exclusive projects on the basis of costs alone.

What condition is necessary to use the cost analysis approach? (Hint: Think about revenues, but explain.)

CHANGING CAPITAL COSTS

Up to this point, we have assumed that the firm expects its cost of capital to remain constant in the future. However, suppose the firm expects the cost of capital to change over time, either because it forecasts a general rise or fall in economy-wide capital costs or because it expects a change in its own situation. In this case, the NPV calculation should recognize that the project's cost of capital is not constant. To illustrate, suppose Project W has a cost of $10,000 and expected net cash inflows of $4,100 at the end of each of the next three years. If the project's cost of capital is expected to be a constant 10 percent, then $NPV_W = \$196$:

$$NPV_W = -\$10,000 + \frac{\$4,100}{(1.10)^1} + \frac{\$4,100}{(1.10)^2} + \frac{\$4,100}{(1.10)^3}$$

$$= -\$10,000 + \$10,196 = \$196.$$

However, what if the firm expects capital costs to increase over the next three years?[17] Assume that the first year's weighted average cost of capital, k_1, is 10 percent, but k_2 is expected to rise to 12 percent and k_3 to 14 percent. In this situation, the calculated NPV is $-\$26$:

$$NPV_W = -\$10,000 + \frac{\$4,100}{(1.10)} + \frac{\$4,100}{(1.12)(1.10)} + \frac{\$4,100}{(1.14)(1.12)(1.10)}$$

$$= -\$10,000 + \$3,727 + \$3,328 + \$2,919 = -\$26.$$

Thus, Project W would be accepted if capital costs were constant, but the project would be rejected if they were expected to increase.[18]

This simple example illustrates several points: (1) If capital costs are expected to change over time, and we can forecast these changes, then the NPV should be calculated using multiple costs of capital. (2) A project's acceptability can be reversed by changing capital costs. (3) Regardless of our assumption regarding capital costs, $IRR_W = 11.1\%$, so if capital costs are nonconstant, the rate to which the IRR must be compared to determine project acceptability is unclear. These points reinforce our preference for the NPV method over the IRR method.

Should firms attempt to predict future capital costs and then use them in the capital budgeting process? If they really think they can forecast these costs, then changes in capital costs should be considered. However, predicting future capital costs is a most difficult undertaking, so firms normally use today's capital costs as the best estimate of future capital costs, and this results in a constant cost of capital.

Self-Test Questions

How can the expectation of changing capital costs be incorporated into the capital budgeting decision?

In most situations, should firms use a constant or a changing project cost of capital? Explain.

---

[17] If the debt used to help finance the project has a maturity equal to the life of the project, then the cost of debt can be taken as a constant. However, the cost of equity would still change from year to year if the general level of interest rates moves up and down or the riskiness of the firm changes. Potential changes in equity costs due to inflation could, theoretically, be estimated from information contained in the term structure of interest rates.

[18] Another specification if capital costs are expected to change over time is

$$NPV = \sum_{t=0}^{n} \frac{CF_t}{(1 + k_t)^t}.$$

Note that here k is a constant when discounting a single cash flow, but that different cash flows can have different discount rates. The proper specification depends on the facts of the case. See Philip L. Cooley, It-Keong Chew, M. Chapman Findlay, III, Alan W. Frankle, and Rodney L. Roenfeldt, "Capital Budgeting Procedures under Inflation: Cooley, Roenfeldt and Chew vs. Findlay and Frankle," *Financial Management,* Autumn 1976, 83–90.

OUR VIEW OF THE CAPITAL BUDGETING DECISION METHODS

We have presented five potential capital budgeting decision methods in this chapter, and each has its own set of advantages and disadvantages. In the course of our discussion, we purposely compared the methods against one another to highlight their relative strengths and weaknesses, but in the process we probably created the impression that "sophisticated" firms would use only one method in the decision process, NPV. Today, virtually all capital budgeting decisions of importance are analyzed by computer, hence it is easy to calculate and list all the decision measures: (1) payback and discounted payback, (2) NPV, (3) IRR, (4) profitability index (PI), and (5) modified IRR (MIRR). In making the accept/reject decision, most large, sophisticated firms such as IBM, GE, or Royal Dutch Petroleum, calculate and consider all of the measures discussed, because each of the measures provides decision makers with a somewhat different piece of relevant information.

Payback and discounted payback provide an indication of both the risk and the liquidity of a project—a long payback means (1) that the investment dollars will be locked up for many years, hence the project is relatively illiquid, and (2) that the project's cash flows must be forecast far out into the future, hence the project is probably quite risky. A good analogy for this is the bond valuation process. You would never compare the yields to maturity on two corporate bonds without considering their terms to maturity (or durations), because a corporate bond's riskiness is significantly influenced by its maturity.

NPV is important because it gives a direct measure of the dollar benefit (on a present value basis) of the project to the firm's shareholders, so we regard it as the best single measure of *profitability*. IRR also measures profitability, but expressed as a percentage rate of return, which many decision makers, especially nonfinancial managers, seem to prefer. Further, IRR contains information concerning a project's "safety margin" which is not inherent in NPV. To illustrate, consider the following two projects: Project S (for small) which costs $10,000 at t = 0 and returns $16,500 at the end of 1 year, and Project L (for large) which costs $100,000 and has a payoff of $115,500 after 1 year. At a 10 percent cost of capital, both projects have an NPV of $5,000, and, if they were mutually exclusive, we would be indifferent between the two. However, Project S actually provides a much larger margin for error. The realized cash inflow could be almost 40 percent below the $16,500 forecast, and the firm would still recover its $10,000 investment. On the other hand, if the actual inflow fell by only 14 percent from the forecasted $115,500, the firm would fall short of recovering its Project L investment. Further, if no revenues were generated at all, the firm would lose only $10,000 with Project S compared to $100,000 with Project L. The NPV contains no information about either the "safety margin" inherent in a project's cash flow forecasts or the amount of capital at risk, but the IRR does provide "safety margin" information—Project S's IRR is a whopping 65.0 percent, while Project L's IRR is only 15.5 percent, so the realized return could fall substantially for Project S and it would still be a money maker.

The profitability index also provides a measure of a project's "safety margin," because it measures the profitability per dollar of investment, or the "bang for the buck." Project S's PI is 1.50 while Project L's PI is 1.05, and thus the PI, like the IRR, indicates that Project S has a greater tolerance for cash flow uncertainty than does Project L.[19] Finally, the modified IRR has all the virtues of the IRR, but it also incorporates the correct reinvestment rate assumption, and it avoids the problems that the IRR can have when applied to nonnormal projects.

In summary, the different measures provide different types of information to decision makers, and since it is so easy to generate the values for the measures, all should be considered in the decision process. For any specific decision, more weight might be given to one measure than another, but it would be foolish to ignore the information inherent in any of the methods.

Self-Test Questions

Describe the advantages and disadvantages of the five capital budgeting methods described in this chapter.

Should capital budgeting decisions be made solely on the basis of a project's NPV?

THE POST-AUDIT

An important aspect of the capital budgeting process is the *post-audit,* which involves (1) comparing actual results with those predicted by the project's sponsors and (2) explaining why any differences occurred. For example, many firms require that the operating divisions send a monthly report for the first six months after a project goes into operation, and a quarterly report thereafter, until the project's results are up to expectations. From then on, reports on the project are handled like those of other operations.

The post-audit has several purposes, including the following:

1. **Improve forecasts.** When decision makers are forced to compare their projections to actual outcomes, there is a tendency for estimates to improve. Conscious or unconscious biases are observed and eliminated; new forecasting methods are sought as the need for them becomes apparent; and people simply tend to do everything better, including forecasting, if they know that their actions are being monitored.

2. **Improve operations.** Businesses are run by people, and people can perform at higher or lower levels of efficiency. When a divisional team has made a forecast about an investment, its members are, in a sense, putting their reputations on the line. If costs are above predicted levels, sales below expectations, and so on, executives in production, sales, and other areas will strive to improve operations and to bring results into line with forecasts. In a discussion related to this point, an IBM

---

[19]For an interesting article which supports the use of the profitability index in capital budgeting decision making, see Edward M. Miller, "The Competitive Market Assumption and Capital Budgeting Criteria," *Financial Management,* Winter 1987, 22–28.

executive made this statement: "You academicians worry only about making good decisions. In business, we also worry about making decisions good."

The post-audit is not a simple process. There are a number of factors that can cause complications. First, we must recognize that each element of the cash flow forecast is subject to uncertainty, so a percentage of all projects undertaken by any reasonably venturesome firm will necessarily go awry. This fact must be considered when appraising the performances of the operating executives who submit capital expenditure requests. Second, projects sometimes fail to meet expectations for reasons beyond the control of the operating executives and for reasons that no one could realistically be expected to anticipate. For example, the decline in oil prices in the mid-1980s adversely affected many energy-related projects, as well as real estate projects in Texas and other oil-producing areas. Third, it is often difficult to separate the operating results of one investment from those of a larger system. Although some projects stand alone and permit ready identification of costs and revenues, the actual cost savings that result from a new computer system, for example, may be very hard to measure. Fourth, it is often hard to hand out blame or praise, because the executives who were actually responsible for a given decision may have moved on by the time the results of a long-term investment are known.

Because of these difficulties, some firms tend to play down the importance of the post-audit. However, observations of both businesses and governmental units suggest that the best-run and most successful organizations are the ones that put the greatest emphasis on post-audits. Accordingly, we regard the post-audit as being one of the most important elements in a good capital budgeting system.

Self-Test Questions

What is done in the post-audit?

Identify several purposes of the post-audit.

What factors can cause complications in the post-audit?

SUMMARY

This chapter discussed the capital budgeting process, and the key concepts covered are listed next.

- *Capital budgeting* is the process of analyzing potential expenditures on fixed assets and deciding whether the firm should undertake those investments. Capital budgeting decisions are probably the most important ones financial managers must make.

- The capital budgeting process requires the firm (1) to determine the *cost of the project,* (2) to estimate the *expected cash inflows* from the project and the riskiness of those cash flows, (3) to determine the appropriate *cost of capital* at which to discount the cash flows, and (4) to determine the *present values* of the expected cash flows and of the project.

- The *payback period* is defined as the expected number of years required to recover the original investment. The payback method ignores cash flows beyond the payback period, and it does not consider the time value of money. The payback does, however, provide an indication of a project's risk and liquidity, because it shows how long the original capital will be "at risk."

- The *discounted payback method* is similar to the regular payback method except that it discounts cash flows at the project's cost of capital. Like the regular payback method, it ignores cash flows beyond the discounted payback period.

- The *net present value (NPV) method* discounts all cash flows at the project's cost of capital and then sums those cash flows. The project is accepted if this sum, called the NPV, is positive.

- The *profitability index (PI)* is the ratio of the present value of cash inflows to the present value of cash outflows. The PI shows the profitability of a project per one dollar of investment.

- The *internal rate of return (IRR)* is defined as the discount rate which forces the present value of the future cash inflows of an investment to equal the present value of the project's cash outflows (costs). The project is accepted if the IRR is greater than the project's cost of capital.

- The NPV, PI, and IRR methods make the same accept/reject decisions for *independent projects,* but if projects are *mutually exclusive,* then ranking conflicts can arise. If conflicts arise, the NPV method should be used. The NPV, PI, and IRR methods are all superior to the payback, but NPV is the single best measure of a project's profitability.

- The NPV method assumes that cash flows will be reinvested at the firm's cost of capital, while the IRR method assumes reinvestment at the project's IRR. Because *reinvestment at the cost of capital is the better assumption,* the NPV is superior to the IRR.

- The *modified IRR (MIRR) method* corrects some of the problems with the regular IRR. MIRR involves finding the terminal value (TV) of the cash inflows compounded at the firm's cost of capital and then determining the rate (MIRR) which forces the present value of the TV to equal the present value of the outflows.

- Firms often choose among mutually exclusive projects on the basis of the *present value of future costs.*

- Sophisticated managers consider all of the project evaluation measures, because the different measures provide different elements of information.

- The *post-audit* is a key element of capital budgeting. By comparing actual results with predicted results, and then determining why differences occurred, decision makers can improve both their operations and their forecasts of projects' outcomes.

Although this chapter has presented the basic elements of the capital budgeting process, there are many other aspects of this crucial topic. Some of the more important ones are discussed in the following two chapters.

Questions

9-1   Define each of the following terms:
   a.   Capital budget
   b.   Regular payback; discounted payback
   c.   Mutually exclusive projects; independent projects
   d.   DCF techniques; net present value (NPV)
   e.   Internal rate of return (IRR)
   f.   Modified internal rate of return (MIRR)
   g.   Profitability index (PI)
   h.   NPV profile; crossover rate
   i.   Nonnormal projects; multiple IRRs
   j.   Project cost of capital, or discount rate
   k.   Post-audit
   l.   Reinvestment rate assumption

9-2   How is a project classification scheme (for example, replacement, expansion into new markets, and so forth) used in the capital budgeting process?

9-3   Explain why the NPV of a relatively long-term project, defined as one where a high percentage of its cash flows is expected in the distant future, is more sensitive to changes in the cost of capital than is the NPV of a short-term project.

9-4   Explain why, if two mutually exclusive projects are being compared, the short-term project might have the higher ranking under the NPV criterion if the cost of capital is high, but the long-term project might be deemed better if the cost of capital is low. Would changes in the cost of capital ever cause a change in the IRR ranking of two such projects?

9-5   For independent projects, is it true that if PI > 1.0, then NPV > 0 and IRR > k? Prove it.

9-6   In what sense is a reinvestment rate assumption embodied in the NPV, IRR, and MIRR methods? What is the implicitly assumed reinvestment rate of each method?

Self-Test Problem (Solutions Appear in Appendix D)

ST-1   **(Project analysis)** You are a financial analyst for the Hittle Company. The director of capital budgeting has asked you to analyze two proposed capital investments, Projects X and Y. Each project has a cost of $10,000, and the cost of capital for both projects is 12 percent. The projects' expected net cash flows are as follows:

	Expected Net Cash Flow	
Year	Project X	Project Y
0	($10,000)	($10,000)
1	6,500	3,500
2	3,000	3,500
3	3,000	3,500
4	1,000	3,500

   a.   Calculate each project's payback, net present value (NPV), internal rate of return (IRR), modified internal rate of return (MIRR), and profitability index (PI).
   b.   Which project, or projects, should be accepted if they are independent?
   c.   Which project should be accepted if they are mutually exclusive?

   d.   How might a change in the cost of capital produce a conflict between the NPV and IRR rankings of these two projects? At what values of k would this conflict exist? Plot the NPV profiles.

   e.   Why does the conflict exist?

Problems

9-1   **(Capital budgeting methods)** Project S has a cost of $10,000 and is expected to produce benefits (cash flows) of $3,000 per year for five years. Project L costs $25,000 and is expected to produce cash flows of $7,400 per year for five years. Calculate the two projects' NPVs, IRRs, MIRRs, and PIs, assuming a cost of capital of 12 percent. Which project would be selected, assuming they are mutually exclusive, using each ranking method? Which should actually be selected?

9-2   **(NPV and IRR analysis)** Southwest Products Company is considering two mutually exclusive investments. The projects' expected net cash flows are as follows:

	Expected Net Cash Flow	
Year	**Project A**	**Project B**
0	($300)	($405)
1	(387)	134
2	(193)	134
3	(100)	134
4	600	134
5	600	134
6	850	134
7	(180)	0

   a.   Construct NPV profiles for Projects A and B.

   b.   What is each project's IRR?

   c.   If you were told that each project's cost of capital is 10 percent, which project should be selected? If the cost of capital were 17 percent, what would the proper choice be?

   d.   What is each project's MIRR at a cost of capital of 10 percent? At k = 17%?

   e.   What is the crossover rate, and what is its significance?

   (Do Parts f and g only if you are using the computerized diskette.)

   f.   The firm's management is confident of the projects' cash flows in Years 0 to 6 but is uncertain as to what the Year 7 cash flows will be for the two projects. Under a worst case scenario, Project A's Year 7 cash flow will be − $300 and B's will be − $150, while under a best case scenario, the cash flows will be − $70 and + $120 for Projects A and B, respectively. Answer Parts b through d using these new cash flows. Which project should be selected under each scenario?

   g.   Put the Year 7 cash flows back to − $180 for A and zero for B. Now change the cost of capital and observe what happens to NPV at k = 0%, 5%, 20%, and 400% (input as 4.0).

9-3   **(Timing differences)** The Knight Exploration Company is considering two mutually exclusive plans for extracting oil on property for which it has mineral rights. Both plans call for the expenditure of $10,000,000 to drill development wells. Under Plan A, all the oil will be extracted in one year, producing a cash flow at t = 1 of $12,000,000, while under Plan B, cash flows will be $1,750,000 per year for 20 years.

   a.   What are the annual incremental cash flows that will be available to Knight Exploration if it undertakes Plan B rather than Plan A? (Hint: Subtract Plan A's flows from B's.)

b.   If the firm accepts Plan A, then invests the extra cash generated at the end of Year 1, what rate of return (reinvestment rate) would cause the cash flows from reinvestment to equal the cash flows from Plan B?

c.   Suppose a company has a cost of capital of 10 percent. Is it logical to assume that it would take on all available independent projects (of average risk) with returns greater than 10 percent? Further, if all available projects with returns greater than 10 percent have been taken, would this mean that cash flows from past investments would have an opportunity cost of only 10 percent, because all the firm could do with these cash flows would be to replace money that has a cost of 10 percent? Finally, does this imply that the cost of capital is the correct rate to assume for the reinvestment of a project's cash flows?

d.   Construct NPV profiles for Plans A and B, identify each project's IRR, and indicate the crossover rate of return.

9-4   **(Scale differences)** The Linke Publishing Company is considering two mutually exclusive expansion plans. Plan A calls for the expenditure of $50 million on a large-scale, integrated plant which will provide an expected cash flow stream of $8 million per year for 20 years. Plan B calls for the expenditure of $15 million to build a somewhat less efficient, more labor intensive plant which has an expected cash flow stream of $3.4 million per year for 20 years. The firm's cost of capital is 10 percent.

a.   Calculate each project's NPV and IRR.

b.   Set up a Project Δ by showing the cash flows that will exist if the firm goes with the large plant rather than the smaller plant. What are the NPV and the IRR for this Project Δ?

c.   Graph the NPV profiles for Plan A, Plan B, and Project Δ.

d.   Give a logical explanation, based on reinvestment rates and opportunity costs, as to why the NPV method is better than the IRR method when the firm's cost of capital is constant at some value such as 10 percent.

9-5   **(Multiple rates of return)** The Sachlis Uranium Company is deciding whether or not it should open a strip mine, the net cost of which is $4.4 million. Net cash inflows are expected to be $27.7 million, all coming at the end of Year 1. The land must be returned to its natural state at a cost of $25 million, payable at the end of Year 2.

a.   Plot the project's NPV profile.

b.   Should the project be accepted if k = 8%? If k = 14%? Explain your reasoning.

c.   Can you think of some other capital budgeting situations where negative cash flows during or at the end of the project's life might lead to multiple IRRs?

d.   What is the project's MIRR at k = 8%? At k = 14%? Does the MIRR method lead to the same accept/reject decision as the NPV method?

9-6   **(Multiple rates of return)** The Woods Development Company (WDC) has many excellent investment opportunities, but it has insufficient cash to undertake them all. Now WDC is offered the chance to borrow $2 million from the Pacific City Retirement Fund at 10 percent, the loan to be repaid at the end of one year. Also, a "consulting fee" of $700,000 will be paid to Pacific City's mayor at the end of one year for helping to arrange the credit. Of the $2 million received, $1 million will be used immediately to buy an old city-owned hotel and to convert it into a gambling casino. The other $1 million will be invested in other lucrative WDC projects that otherwise would have to be foregone because of a lack of capital. For two years, all cash generated by the casino will be plowed back into the casino project. At the end of the two years, the casino will be sold for $2 million.

Assuming that (1) the deal has been worked out in the sunshine and is completely legal and (2) cash from other WDC Company operations will be available to make the required payments at the end of Year 1, under what rate of return conditions should WDC accept the offer? Disregard taxes.

9-7 **(Present value of costs)** The Babcock Coffee Company is evaluating the within-plant distribution system for its new roasting, grinding, and packing plant. The two alternatives are (1) a conveyor system with a high initial cost, but low annual operating costs, and (2) several forklift trucks, which cost less, but have considerably higher operating costs. The decision to construct the plant has already been made, and the choice here will have no effect on the overall revenues of the project. The cost of capital for the plant is 8 percent, and the projects' expected net costs are listed in the table:

	Expected Net Cost	
Year	Conveyor	Forklift
0	($500,000)	($200,000)
1	(120,000)	(160,000)
2	(120,000)	(160,000)
3	(120,000)	(160,000)
4	(120,000)	(160,000)
5	(20,000)	(160,000)

a.   What is the IRR of each alternative?
b.   What is the present value of costs of each alternative? Which method should be chosen?

Mini Case

Your boss, the chief financial officer (CFO) for the Palmer Company, has just handed you the estimated cash flows for two proposed projects. Project L involves adding a new item to the firm's frozen foods line; it would take some time to build up the market for this product, so the cash inflows would increase over time. Project S involves an add-on to an existing line, and its cash flows would decrease over time. Both projects have 3-year lives, because Palmer is planning to introduce an entirely new frozen foods line at that time.

Here are the net cash flow estimates (in thousands of dollars):

	Expected Net Cash Flow	
Year	Project L	Project S
0	($100)	($100)
1	10	70
2	60	50
3	80	20

Depreciation, salvage values, net working capital requirements, and tax effects are all included in these flows.

The CFO also made subjective risk assessments of each project, and he concluded that the projects both have risk characteristics which are similar to the firm's average project. Palmer's overall cost of capital is 10.0 percent. You must now determine whether one or both of the projects should be accepted.

a.   What is capital budgeting? Are there any similarities between a firm's capital budgeting decisions and an individual's investment decisions?
b.   What is the difference between independent and mutually exclusive projects? Between normal and nonnormal projects?
c.   (1) What is the payback period? Find the paybacks for Projects L and S.
     (2) What is the rationale for the payback? According to the payback criterion, which project or projects should be accepted if the firm's maximum acceptable payback is 2 years, and Projects L and S were independent? Mutually exclusive?

(3) What is the difference between the regular payback and the discounted payback?

(4) What is the main disadvantage of discounted payback? Is the payback method of any real usefulness in capital budgeting decisions?

d. (1) Define the net present value (NPV). What is each project's NPV?

(2) What is the rationale behind the NPV method? According to NPV, which project or projects should be accepted if they are independent? Mutually exclusive?

(3) Would the NPVs change if the cost of capital changed?

e. (1) Define the internal rate of return (IRR). What is each project's IRR?

(2) How is the IRR on a project related to the YTM on a bond?

(3) What is the logic behind the IRR method? According to IRR, which projects should be accepted if they are independent? Mutually exclusive?

(4) Would the projects' IRRs change if the cost of capital changed?

f. (1) Define the profitability index (PI). What is each project's PI?

(2) What is the rationale behind the PI method? According to the PI, which project or projects should be accepted if they are independent? Mutually exclusive?

g. (1) Draw the NPV profiles for Projects L and S. At what discount rate do the profiles cross?

(2) Look at the NPV profile graph without referring to the actual NPVs and IRRs. Which project or projects should be accepted if they are independent? Mutually exclusive? Explain. Do your answers here apply for all discount rates less than 23.6 percent?

h. (1) What is the underlying cause of ranking conflicts between NPV and IRR?

(2) Under what conditions can conflicts occur?

(3) Which method is best? Why?

i. (1) Define the modified IRR (MIRR). Find the MIRR for Projects L and S.

(2) What are the MIRR's advantages and disadvantages vis-à-vis the regular IRR? What are the MIRR's advantages and disadvantages vis-à-vis the NPV?

j. As a separate project (Project P), the firm is considering sponsoring a pavilion at the upcoming World's Fair. The pavilion would cost $800,000, and it is expected to result in $5 million of incremental cash inflows during its one year of operation. However, it would then take another year, and $5 million of costs, to demolish the site and return it to its original condition. Thus, Project P's expected net cash flows look like this (in millions of dollars):

Year	Cash Flow
0	($0.8)
1	5
2	(5)

The project is estimated to be of average risk, so its cost of capital is 10.0 percent.

(1) What is Project P's NPV? What is its IRR? Its MIRR?

(2) Draw Project P's NPV profile. Does Project P have normal or nonnormal cash flows? Should this project be accepted?

Selected Additional References and Cases

For an in-depth treatment of capital budgeting techniques, see

Bierman, Harold, Jr., and Seymour Smidt, *The Capital Budgeting Decision* (New York: Macmillan, 1988).

Grant, Eugene L., William G. Ireson, and Richard S. Leavenworth, *Principles of Engineering Economy* (New York: Ronald, 1976).

Levy, Haim, and Marshall Sarnat, *Capital Investment and Financial Decisions* (Englewood Cliffs, N.J.: Prentice-Hall, 1982).

Osteryoung, Jerome S., *Capital Budgeting: Long-Term Asset Selection* (Columbus, Ohio: Grid, 1979).

Seitz, Niel E., *Capital Budgeting and Long-Term Financing Decisions* (Hinsdale, Ill.: Dryden, 1990).

For a discussion of strategic considerations in capital budgeting, see

Crum, Roy L., and Frans G. J. Derkinderen, eds., *Readings in Strategies for Corporate Investments* (New York: Pitman, 1981).

The following articles present interesting comparisons of four different approaches to finding NPV:

Brick, Ivan E., and Daniel G. Weaver, "A Comparison of Capital Budgeting Techniques in Identifying Profitable Investments," *Financial Management,* Winter 1984, 29–39.

Greenfield, Robert L., Maury R. Randall, and John C. Woods, "Financial Leverage and Use of the Net Present Value Investment Criterion," *Financial Management,* Autumn 1983, 40–44.

Four articles related directly to the topics in Chapter 9 are

Bacon, Peter W., "The Evaluation of Mutually Exclusive Investments," *Financial Management,* Summer 1977, 55–58.

Chaney, Paul K., "Moral Hazard and Capital Budgeting," *Journal of Financial Research,* Summer 1989, 113–128.

Lewellen, Wilbur G., Howard P. Lanser, and John J. McConnell, "Payback Substitutes for Discounted Cash Flow," *Financial Management,* Summer 1973, 17–23.

Miller, Edward M., "Safety Margins and Capital Budgeting Criteria," *Managerial Finance,* Number 2/3, 1988, 1–8.

For five recent articles which discuss the capital budgeting methods actually used in practice, see

Kim, Suk H., Trevor Krick, and Seung H. Kim, "Do Executives Practice what Academics Preach?" *Management Accounting,* November 1986, 49–52.

Mukherjee, Tarun K., "Capital Budgeting Surveys: The Past and the Future," *Review of Business and Economic Research,* Spring, 1987, 37–56.

Mukherjee, Tarun K., "The Capital Budgeting Process of Large U.S. Firms: An Analysis of Capital Budgeting Manuals," *Managerial Finance,* Number 2/3, 1988, 28–35.

Ross, Marc, "Capital Budgeting Practices of Twelve Large Manufacturers," *Financial Management,* Winter 1986, 15–22.

Weaver, Samuel C., Donald Peters, Roger Cason, and Joe Daleiden, "Capital Budgeting," *Financial Management*, Spring 1989, 10–17.

Additional capital budgeting references are provided in Chapters 10 and 11.

For a case which focuses on capital budgeting decision methods, see

Case 12, "Clifton Controls," in the Brigham-Gapenski casebook.

CHAPTER 10

Project Cash Flow Analysis

In 1989, RJR Nabisco announced the demise of its Premier smokeless cigarette. At the time, *The Wall Street Journal* called Premier "one of the most stunning new product disasters in recent history." The firm had spent over $300 million on the product and had test marketed Premier for 5 months prior to the announcement. RJR had built a pilot plant and had even broken ground for an addition to its main production plant to produce smokeless cigarettes in huge quantities.

The new cigarette had two fatal problems. First, it had to be lit with a high-quality butane lighter. If a match or another kind of lighter was used, impurities were created which contaminated the cigarette's filter and left a bad taste in smokers' mouths. Second, if the cigarette was not completely lit, the smoker would have to puff like crazy to get it going, and even then it might go out. This phenomenon was dubbed the "hernia effect."

Competitors and marketers were shocked that RJR's managers had allowed themselves to become so infatuated with their "new toy" that they assumed consumers would embrace the cigarette despite its obvious problems. Throughout Premier's development, the product rode a "wave of support" within the company—its backers thought (or hoped) it represented the next generation of cigarettes, and skeptics were afraid to voice their concerns out of fear of offending top managers. However, soon after the company underwent a $25 billion leveraged buyout in late 1988, the new management group voted to kill the Premier.

What led RJR's top managers to ignore Premier's fatal flaws and market the cigarette, at a cost of over $300 million? Did the developers conduct a proper capital budgeting analysis, or were they so overcome with enthusiasm that they biased their cash flow estimates? We may never know the

> answers to these questions, but we do know that good, unbiased cash flow estimates are essential to good capital budgeting decisions. In this chapter, we provide a framework for estimating and analyzing project cash flows.

THE basic capital budgeting decision methods were covered in Chapter 9. Now we examine some cash flow analysis issues, including (1) cash flow estimation, (2) replacement decisions, (3) cash flow estimation bias, (4) managerial options, (5) mutually exclusive projects with unequal lives, (6) abandonment value, and (7) effects of inflation on capital budgeting analysis.

CASH FLOW ESTIMATION

The most important, but also the most difficult, step in the analysis of a capital project is estimating its cash flows—both the investment outlays that will be required and the annual net cash inflows after the project goes into operation. Many variables are involved in cash flow forecasting, and many individuals and departments participate in the process. For example, the forecasts of unit sales and sales prices are normally made by the marketing department, based on its knowledge of price elasticity, advertising effects, the state of the economy, competitors' reactions, and trends in consumers' tastes. Similarly, the capital outlays associated with a new product are generally obtained from the engineering and product development staffs, while operating costs are estimated by cost accountants, production experts, personnel specialists, purchasing agents, and so forth.

It is difficult to make accurate forecasts of the costs and revenues associated with a large, complex project, so forecast errors can be quite large. For example, when several major oil companies decided to build the Alaska Pipeline, the original cost forecasts were in the neighborhood of $700 million, but the final cost was closer to $7 billion. Similar, or even worse, miscalculations are common in forecasts of product design costs, such as the costs to develop a new personal computer. Further, as difficult as plant and equipment costs are to estimate, sales revenues and operating costs over the life of the project are generally even more uncertain. The RJR smokeless cigarette is one example. Because of its financial strength, RJR was able to absorb losses on the project with no problem, but the venture could have forced a weaker firm into bankruptcy.

The financial staff's role in the forecasting process includes (1) coordinating the efforts of the other departments, such as engineering and marketing, (2) ensuring that everyone involved with the forecast uses a consistent set of economic assumptions, and (3) making sure that no biases are inherent in the forecasts. This last point is extremely important, because division managers often become emotionally involved with pet projects and/or develop empire-building complexes, leading to cash flow forecasting biases which make bad projects look good—on paper. The RJR smokeless cigarette is an example of this problem.

Note also that unbiased point estimates of the key variables are not sufficient — as we shall see in the next chapter, data on probability distributions or other indications of the likely range of variable values are also essential.

It is almost impossible to overstate the difficulties one can encounter in developing good cash flow forecasts. It is also difficult to overstate the importance of these forecasts. However, if the principles discussed in the next several sections are observed, forecast errors can be minimized.

Self-Test Questions

What is the most important step in the capital budgeting process?

Within a firm, what departments are involved in estimating a project's cash flows?

What is the financial staff's role in cash flow estimation?

IDENTIFYING THE RELEVANT CASH FLOWS

Cash flows for a project are defined as the differences in cash flows for each period if the project is undertaken versus if it is not undertaken:

$$\text{Project CF}_t = \frac{\text{CF}_t \text{ for corporation}}{\text{with project}} - \frac{\text{CF}_t \text{ for corporation}}{\text{without project}}. \qquad \textbf{(10-1)}$$

Defined this way, we see that project cash flows are *incremental cash flows*. In this section, we discuss how to measure the incremental cash flows attributable to a project.

Cash Flow versus Accounting Income

Accounting income statements are in some respects a mix of apples and oranges. For example, accountants deduct labor costs, which are cash outflows, from revenues, which may or may not be entirely cash (some sales may be on credit). At the same time, accountants do not deduct capital outlays, which are cash outflows, but they do deduct depreciation expenses, which are not cash outflows. In capital budgeting, it is critical that we base decisions strictly on cash flows, the actual dollars that flow into and out of the company during each time period.

As noted above, the relevant cash flows for capital budgeting purposes are the incremental cash flows attributable to a project. Theoretically, it is possible to construct a firm's pro forma cash flow statements with and without a project for each year of the project's life, and then to measure the annual project cash flows as the differences in cash flows between the two sets of statements. When this is done for operating flows, the following formula results:

$$\text{CF}_t = [(R_{1t} - R_{0t}) - (C_{1t} - C_{0t}) - (D_{1t} - D_{0t})](1 - T) + (D_{1t} - D_{0t}). \qquad \textbf{(10-2)}$$

Here CF_t is the project's net operating cash flow in Period t; R_1 is the corporation's cash revenue if the project is undertaken, while R_0 is the cash revenue if it is not accepted; C_1 and C_0 are the cash operating costs with and without the project; and D_1 and D_0 are the respective depreciation charges.[1]

To illustrate, suppose a firm is considering a new project that has a cost of $1,000 and a 10-year life. If the project is undertaken, the cash flow statement in the left column of the following table is expected to result, while if the project is not undertaken, the middle column is projected. The third column shows the changes resulting from the project, so the project's projected net operating cash flow is $298 per year for 10 years:

	With Project	**Without Project**	**Change**
Sales (R)	$1,600	$1,000	$600
Cash operating costs (C)	600	400	200
Depreciation (D)	200	100	100
Pre-tax income	$ 800	$ 500	$300
Taxes (34%)	272	170	102
Net operating income (NOI)	$ 528	$ 330	$198
CF = NOI + D	$ 728	$ 430	$298

Equation 10-2 would show exactly the same incremental cash flow, $298:[2]

$$CF_t = [(\$1,600 - \$1,000) - (\$600 - \$400) - (\$200 - \$100)] (1 - 0.34)$$

$$+ (\$200 - \$100)$$

$$= [\$600 - \$200 - \$100] \, 0.66 + \$100$$

$$= [\$300] \, 0.66 + \$100 = \$198 + \$100 = \$298.$$

---

[1]Note that we are concentrating solely on operating cash flows. Financing flows (interest expense) are not included in a project's cash flows because financing costs are incorporated in the firm's WACC. When we use the WACC as a discount rate to obtain a project's NPV, we are effectively reducing the values of the cash flows to account for capital costs, so we would be double counting if we reduced the cash flows directly by deducting interest expenses.

[2]There are times when a new project affects the sales and costs associated with the firm's original assets, and in such cases it is essential to think in terms of either Equation 10-2 or comparative cash flow statements as shown above. However, new projects often do not affect the firm's existing cash flows, and in such cases we can use a short-cut cash flow formula:

$$CF_t = [R_t - C_t - D_t](1 - T) + D_t. \qquad \textbf{(10-3)}$$

Here R, C, and D represent the cash sales, cash operating costs, and depreciation of the project itself, and T is the firm's marginal tax rate. To illustrate, suppose a project has a cost of $1,000, will increase sales by $600 per year for 10 years, will have operating costs of $200 per year, and will be depreciated by the straight line method toward a zero salvage value over 10 years. If the firm's marginal tax rate is 34 percent, then Equation 10-3 may be solved as follows:

$$CF_t = [\$600 - \$200 - \$100](0.66) + \$100 = \$298.$$

Going through some algebra, we can transform Equation 10-3 as follows:

$$CF_t = (R_t - C_t)(1 - T) + TD_t. \qquad \textbf{(10-3a)}$$

Equation 10-3a shows that the net operating cash flow, CF_t, consists of two terms: (1) cash revenues minus cash operating costs, reduced by taxes, and (2) a depreciation cash flow equal to the amount of depreciation taken during the period times the tax rate. In this form, we see that depreciation affects cash flows because it reduces taxes, and the higher the firm's tax rate, the greater the benefits from depreciation. Equations 10-3 and 10-3a are equivalent methods for calculating a project's net operating cash flows, and either can be used in capital budgeting analysis.

Cash Flow Timing

In financial analysis, we must be careful to account properly for the timing of cash flows. Accounting income statements are for periods such as years or months, so they do not reflect exactly when, during the period, cash revenues or expenses occur. Because of the time value of money, capital budgeting cash flows should in theory be analyzed exactly as they occur. Of course, there must be a compromise between accuracy and simplicity. A time line with daily cash flows would in theory provide the most accuracy, but daily cash flow estimates would be costly to construct, unwieldy to use, and probably no more accurate than annual cash flow estimates because we simply cannot forecast well enough to warrant this degree of detail. Therefore, in most cases, we simply assume that all cash flows occur at the end of every year. However, for some projects, it may be useful to assume that cash flows occur semiannually, or even to forecast quarterly or monthly cash flows.

Incremental Cash Flows

As noted previously, in capital budgeting our concern is with those cash flows that result directly from the project, or the project's *incremental cash flows.* Three special problems can occur when estimating incremental cash flows; they are discussed next.

Sunk Costs. Sunk costs are *not* incremental costs, so they should *not* be included in a capital budgeting analysis. A *sunk cost* refers to an outlay that has already occurred (or been committed), so it is an outlay that is not affected by the accept/reject decision under consideration. Suppose, for example, that in 1991 Southwest BankCorp was evaluating the establishment of a branch office in a newly developed section of Albuquerque. As a part of the analysis, Southwest had, back in 1990, hired a consulting firm to perform a site analysis at a cost of $100,000, and this $100,000 was expensed for tax purposes in 1990. Is this 1990 expenditure a relevant cost with respect to the 1991 capital budgeting decision? The answer is no. The $100,000 is a sunk cost; Southwest cannot recover it regardless of whether or not the new branch is built. It often turns out that a particular project looks bad (that is, has a negative NPV, or an IRR less than its cost of capital) when all the associated costs, including sunk costs, are considered. However, on an incremental basis, the project may be a good one, because the incremental cash flows may be large enough to produce a positive NPV on the incremental investment. Thus, the correct treatment of sunk costs is critical to a proper capital budgeting analysis.[3]

Opportunity Costs. The second potential problem relates to *opportunity costs:* All relevant opportunity costs must be included in a correct capital budgeting analysis. For example, suppose Southwest BankCorp already owns a piece of land that is

---

[3]For an old but still excellent example of the improper treatment of sunk costs by a major corporation, see U. E. Reinhardt, "Break-Even Analysis for Lockheed's TriStar: An Application of Financial Theory," *Journal of Finance,* September 1973, 821–838.

suitable for the branch location. When evaluating the prospective branch, should the cost of the land be disregarded because no additional cash outlay would be required? The answer is "no," because there is an opportunity cost inherent in the use of the property. For example, suppose the land could be sold to net $150,000 after commissions and taxes. Use of the site for the branch would require foregoing this inflow, so the $150,000 should be charged as an opportunity cost against the project. Note, though, that the proper land cost in this example would be the $150,000 market-determined value, net of any costs, irrespective of whether Southwest had paid $50,000, or $500,000 for the property when it was acquired.

Effects on Other Parts of the Firm (Externalities).   The third potential problem involves the effects of the project on other parts of the firm. For example, suppose some of the customers that Southwest predicts will use the new branch are already banking with Southwest's downtown office. The loans and deposits, hence profits, generated by these customers would not be new to the bank, but, rather, they would represent a transfer from the main office to the branch. Thus, the net revenues produced by these customers should not be treated as incremental income in the capital budgeting analysis. On the other hand, having a suburban branch might actually attract new customers to the downtown office, because some potential customers would like to be able to make transactions both from home and from work. In this case, the additional revenues projected to flow to the downtown office should be attributed to the new branch.

Although often difficult to determine, "externalities" such as these must be considered. They should, if possible, be quantified, or at least noted, so the final decision maker will be aware of their existence.

Self-Test Questions

Define the term "incremental cash flow."

Within the framework of capital budgeting cash flow estimation, briefly describe the meaning and treatment of (1) sunk costs, (2) opportunity costs, and (3) externalities.

OTHER CONSIDERATIONS

Taxes and net working capital changes can have major impacts on cash flows, and in many cases these effects can make or break a project. Therefore, it is critical that taxes and net working capital changes be dealt with correctly in capital budgeting decisions.

Taxes

Taxes affect project cash flow analyses in two ways. (1) They reduce project operating cash flows, and (2) tax laws prescribe the depreciation expense that can be taken in each year. Congress changes both tax rates and permissible tax depreciation methods from time to time. Prior to 1954 the straight line method was required for tax purposes, but in 1954 *accelerated* methods (double declining balance and sum-of-years' digits) were permitted. Then, in 1981, the old accelerated methods were replaced by a simpler procedure known as the *Accelerated Cost Recovery System* (*ACRS,* which is pronounced "acres"). The ACRS system was changed in 1986 as part of the Tax Reform Act, and it is now called the *Modified Accelerated Cost Recovery System (MACRS).* Since capital budgeting decisions focus on actual cash flows, tax depreciation rather than book depreciation is used in project cash flow analyses. Depreciation was discussed in detail in the corporate tax section of Chapter 2. If you need a review of depreciation concepts, take the time now to reread the relevant Chapter 2 material.

Changes in Net Working Capital

Normally, additional inventories are required to support a new operation, and new sales will often result in additional accounts receivable which must be financed. Thus, both inventories and receivables will usually increase as a result of capital budgeting decisions, so the "investment outlay" of a new project must include the associated current assets as well as the fixed assets involved. However, accounts payable and accruals will often increase spontaneously as a result of the expansion, and this will reduce the need to raise capital to finance the project. The difference between the projected increases in current assets and in current liabilities is defined as the *change in net working capital.* The change associated with a project is normally positive, so some additional investment, over and above the cost of the fixed assets, is required.[4] (In the unlikely event that the change in net working capital is negative, then the project would be generating an initial cash inflow from the change in net working capital.)

Net working capital changes may occur over several periods, so the increase (or decrease) could be reflected in cash flows for several periods. However, once the operation has stabilized, working capital will also stabilize at the new level, and beyond this time no changes will occur until the project is terminated. At the end of the project's life, the firm's net working capital requirements should revert to prior levels, so it will receive an end-of-project cash inflow equal to the net investment in working capital. This point is illustrated in the next section.

Self-Test Questions

Should tax or book depreciation be used in project cash flow analyses?

Briefly describe the mechanics of MACRS depreciation.

What is net working capital (NWC)?

How do changes in NWC affect estimates of a project's cash flows?

---

[4]Actually, the entire change in net working capital does not require additional investment, because some of the increase in receivables represents profits, hence does not require financing. However, profit margins are normally just a few percentage points, so ignoring this factor does not lead to serious errors. This topic is discussed further in Chapter 21.

CASH FLOW ANALYSIS EXAMPLE

Up to this point, we have discussed several important aspects of cash flow analysis, but we have not seen how they relate to one another and affect the capital budgeting decision. In this section, we illustrate all this by examining a capital budgeting decision that faces Robotics International Corporation (RIC), a San Francisco–based technology company. RIC's research and development department has been applying its expertise in microprocessor technology to develop a small computer specifically designed to control home appliances. Once programmed, the computer would automatically control the heating and air-conditioning systems, security system, water heater, and even small appliances such as coffee makers. By increasing the energy efficiency of a home, the device can save enough to pay for itself in a few years. This project has now reached the stage where a decision on whether to go forward with production must be made.

The marketing vice-president believes that annual sales would be 25,000 units if the appliance-control computers were priced at $2,200 each. The firm would need a new plant, which could be built and made ready for production in 2 years after the "go" decision is made. The plant would require a 25-acre site, and RIC currently has an option to purchase a suitable tract of land for $1.2 million; the option could be exercised in late 1991. Building construction would begin in early 1992 and would continue through 1993. The building, which would fall into the MACRS 31.5-year class, would cost an estimated $8 million; a $4 million payment would be made on December 31, 1992, and the remaining $4 million would be paid on December 31, 1993.

The necessary equipment would be installed late in 1993 and would be paid for on December 31, 1993. The equipment, which would fall into the MACRS 5-year class, would have a cost of $9.5 million, plus another $500,000 for installation.

The project would also require an initial investment in net working capital equal to 12 percent of the estimated sales in the first year. The initial working capital investment would be made on December 31, 1993, and on December 31 of each following year, net working capital would be increased by an amount equal to 12 percent of any sales increase expected during the coming year. The project's estimated economic life is 6 years. At that time, the land is expected to have a market value of $1.7 million, the building a value of $1.0 million, and the equipment a value of $2 million. The production department has estimated that variable manufacturing costs would total 65 percent of dollar sales, and that fixed overhead costs, excluding depreciation, would be $8 million for the first year of operations. Sales prices and fixed overhead costs, other than depreciation, are projected to increase with inflation, which is expected to average 6 percent per year over the 6-year life of the project.

RIC's marginal federal-plus-state tax rate is 40 percent; its weighted average cost of capital is 11.5 percent; and the company's policy, for capital budgeting purposes, is to assume that cash flows occur at the end of each year. Since the plant would begin operations on January 1, 1994, the first operating cash flows would thus occur on December 31, 1994.

Table 10-1 Investment Outlays, 1991–1993

	1991	1992	1993	Total Costs, 1991–1993	Depreciable Basis
Land	$1,200,000	$ 0	$ 0	$ 1,200,000	$ 0
Building	0	4,000,000	4,000,000	8,000,000	8,000,000
Equipment	0	0	10,000,000	10,000,000	10,000,000
Total fixed assets	$1,200,000	$4,000,000	$14,000,000	$19,200,000	
Net working capital[a]	0	0	6,600,000	6,600,000	
Total investment	$1,200,000	$4,000,000	$20,600,000	$25,800,000	

[a]12 percent of first year's sales, or 0.12($55,000,000) = $6,600,000.

As one of the company's financial analysts, you have been assigned the task of supervising the capital budgeting analysis. For now, you may assume that the project has the same risk as the firm's current average project, hence you may use the corporate WACC, 11.5 percent, for this project. Later on, we will examine additional information concerning the riskiness of the project, but at this point assume that the project is of average risk.

Analysis of the Cash Flows

The first step in the analysis is to summarize the investment outlays required for the project; this is done in Table 10-1. Note that the land cannot be depreciated, hence we show its depreciable basis to be $0. Also, since the project will require an increase in net working capital during 1993, this is shown as an investment outlay for that year.

Having estimated the capital requirements, we must now forecast the cash flows that will occur once production begins; these are set forth in Table 10-2. The operating cash flow estimates are based on information provided by RIC's various departments. Note that the sales price and fixed costs are projected to increase each year by the 6 percent inflation rate, and since variable costs are 65 percent of sales, they too will rise by 6 percent each year. The changes in net working capital (NWC) represent the additional investments required to support sales increases (12 percent of the next year's sales increase, which in this case results only from inflation) during 1994-1998, and the recovery of the cumulative net working capital investment in 1999. The depreciation amounts were obtained by multiplying each asset's depreciable basis by the MACRS recovery allowance rates set forth in Note c to Table 10-2.

The analysis also requires an estimation of the cash flows generated by salvage values; Table 10-3 summarizes this analysis. First, we compare the projected 1999 market values against the 1999 book values. The land cannot be depreciated, and it has an estimated 1999 salvage value greater than the initial purchase price. Thus, RIC would have to pay taxes on the profit. The building has an estimated salvage

Table 10-2   Net Cash Flows, 1994–1999

	1994	1995
Unit sales	25,000	25,000
Sale price[a]	$ 2,200	$ 2,332
Net sales[a]	$55,000,000	$58,300,000
Variable costs[b]	35,750,000	37,895,000
Fixed costs (overhead)[a]	8,000,000	8,480,000
Depreciation (building)[c]	120,000	240,000
Depreciation (equipment)[c]	2,000,000	3,200,000
Earnings before taxes	$ 9,130,000	$ 8,485,000
Taxes (40%)	3,652,000	3,394,000
Projected net operating income	$ 5,478,000	$ 5,091,000
Add back noncash expenses[d]	2,120,000	3,440,000
Cash flow from operations[e]	$ 7,598,000	$ 8,531,000
Investment in NWC[f]	(396,000)	(420,000)
Net salvage value[g]		
Total projected cash flow	$ 7,202,000	$ 8,111,000

[a]1994 estimate increased by the assumed 6 percent inflation rate.

[b]65 percent of net sales.

[c]MACRS depreciation rates are as follows:

Year	1	2	3	4	5	6
Building	1.5%	3%	3%	3%	3%	3%
Equipment	20	32	19	12	11	6

These percentages are multiplied by each asset's depreciable basis to get the depreciation expense for each year. Note that the allowances have been rounded for ease of computation.

value less than the book value—it will be sold at a loss for tax purposes. The loss will reduce the company's taxable income and thus generate a tax savings; in effect, the company has been depreciating the building too slowly, so it would write off the loss against ordinary income. On the other hand, the equipment will be sold for more than book value, so the company would have to pay ordinary taxes on the $2 million difference. In all cases, the book value is the depreciable basis less accumulated depreciation, and the total cash flow from salvage is merely the sum of the land, building, and equipment components.

Making the Decision

To summarize the data and get it ready for evaluation, it is useful to combine all of the net cash flows on a time line such as the one shown in Table 10-4. The table also shows the payback period, IRR, MIRR, and NPV (at the 11.5 percent cost of capital). The project appears to be acceptable using the NPV, IRR, or MIRR methods, and it would also be acceptable if RIC required a payback of six years or less. Note,

Table 10-2   *(continued)*

1996	1997	1998	1999
25,000	25,000	25,000	25,000
$ 2,472	$ 2,620	$ 2,777	$ 2,944
$61,800,000	$65,500,000	$69,425,000	$73,600,000
40,170,000	42,575,000	45,126,250	47,840,000
8,988,800	9,528,128	10,099,816	10,705,805
240,000	240,000	240,000	240,000
1,900,000	1,200,000	1,100,000	600,000
$10,501,200	$11,956,872	$12,858,934	$14,214,195
4,200,480	4,782,749	5,143,574	5,685,678
$ 6,300,720	$ 7,174,123	$ 7,715,360	$ 8,528,517
2,140,000	1,440,000	1,340,000	840,000
$ 8,440,720	$ 8,614,123	$ 9,055,360	$ 9,368,517
(444,000)	(471,000)	(501,000)	8,832,000
			5,972,000
$ 7,996,720	$ 8,143,123	$ 8,554,360	$24,172,517

[d]In this case, depreciation on building and equipment.

[e]Net operating income plus noncash expenses.

[f]12 percent of next year's increase in sales. For example, 1995 sales are $3.3 million over 1994 sales, so the addition to NWC in 1994 required to support 1995 sales is $(0.12)($3,300,000) = $396,000$. The cumulative working capital investment is recovered when the project ends in 1999.

[g]See Table 10-3 for the net salvage value calculation.

however, that the analysis thus far has been based on the assumption that the project has the same degree of risk as the company's average project. If the project is riskier than an average project, then it would be necessary to increase the cost of capital, which in turn might cause the NPV to become negative and the IRR and MIRR to fall below k. In Chapter 11, we will extend the evaluation of this project to include the necessary risk analysis.

Self-Test Questions

How does RIC account for inflation in the cash flow estimation process?

Why was it necessary to include changes in net working capital in the analysis?

Describe how depreciation tax effects were included in the Table 10-2 operating cash flows.

Explain the meaning of the negative taxes shown for the building in the net salvage value analysis in Table 10-3.

Table 10-3   After-Tax Salvage Values, 1999

	Land	Building	Equipment
Salvage (ending market) value	$1,700,000	$1,000,000	$ 2,000,000
Initial cost	1,200,000	8,000,000	10,000,000
Depreciable basis (1993)	0	8,000,000	10,000,000
Book value (1999)[a]	1,200,000	6,680,000	0
Capital gains income	$ 500,000	$ 0	$ 0
Ordinary income (loss)[b]	0	(5,680,000)	2,000,000
Taxes[c]	$ 200,000	($2,272,000)	$ 800,000
Net salvage value (Salvage value − Taxes)	$1,500,000	$3,272,000	$ 1,200,000

Net cash flow from salvage value = $1,500,000 + $3,272,000 + $1,200,000 = $5,972,000.

[a]Book value for the building in 1999 equals depreciable basis minus accumulated MACRS depreciation of $1,320,000. The accumulated depreciation on the equipment is $10,000,000. See Table 10-2.

[b]Building: $1,000,000 market value − $6,680,000 book value = $5,680,000 depreciation shortfall, which is treated as an operating expense in 1999.

Equipment: $2,000,000 market value − $0 book value = $2,000,000 depreciation recapture, which is treated as ordinary income in 1999.

[c]Since capital gains are now taxed at the ordinary income rate, all taxes are based on RIC's 40 percent marginal federal-plus-state rate. The table is set up to differentiate ordinary income from capital gains because Congress may reinstate differential tax rates on those two income sources.

REPLACEMENT ANALYSIS

RIC's appliance-control computer project was used to show how an expansion project is analyzed. All companies, including this one, also make *replacement decisions,* where cash flows from both the old asset and the new asset must be considered. Replacement analysis is illustrated with another RIC example, this time from the company's research and development (R&D) division.

A lathe for trimming molded plastics was purchased 10 years ago at a cost of $7,500. The machine had an expected life of 15 years at the time it was purchased,

Table 10-4   Time Line of Consolidated End-of-Year Net Cash Flows, 1991–1999

1991	1992	1993	1994	1995
($1,200,000)	($4,000,000)	($20,600,000)	$7,202,000	$8,111,000

Payback period: 5.3 years from first outflow.
IRR: 25.1% versus an 11.5% cost of capital.
MIRR: 17.9% versus an 11.5% cost of capital.
NPV: $12,075,384.

and management originally estimated, and still believes, that the salvage value will be zero at the end of the 15-year life. The machine is being depreciated on a straight line basis; therefore, its annual depreciation charge is $500, and its present book value is $2,500.[5]

The R&D manager reports that a new special-purpose machine can be purchased for $12,000 (including freight and installation) which, over its 5-year life, will reduce labor and raw materials usage sufficiently to cut operating costs from $7,000 to $4,000. This reduction in costs will cause before-tax profits to rise by $7,000 − $4,000 = $3,000 per year.

It is estimated that the new machine can be sold for $2,000 at the end of 5 years; this is its estimated salvage value. The old machine's actual current market value is $1,000, which is below its $2,500 book value. If the new machine were acquired, the old lathe would be sold to another company rather than exchanged for the new machine. The company's marginal federal-plus-state tax rate is 40 percent, and the replacement project is of average risk. Net working capital requirements will also increase by $1,000 at the time of replacement. By an IRS ruling, the new machine falls into the 3-year MACRS class, and the cost of capital is 11.5 percent. Should the replacement be made?

Table 10-5 shows the worksheet format the company uses to analyze replacement projects. A line-by-line description of the table follows.

Line 1.   The top section of the table, Lines 1 through 5, sets forth the cash flows which occur at (approximately) t = 0, the time the investment is made. Line 1 shows the purchase price of the new machine, including any installation and freight charges.

Line 2.   Here we show the price received from the sale of old equipment.

Line 3.   Since the old equipment would be sold at less than its book value, this creates a loss which reduces the firm's taxable income, hence its next quarterly income tax payment. The tax savings is equal to (Loss)(T) = ($1,500)(0.40) = $600, where T is the marginal corporate tax rate. The Tax Code defines this loss as

---

[5]This machine was purchased prior to the Economic Recovery Tax Act of 1981, so the Accelerated Cost Recovery System was not in place at the time. The company chose to depreciate the lathe on a straight line basis.

Table 10-4 *(continued)*

1996	1997	1998	1999
$7,996,720	$8,143,123	$8,554,360	$24,172,517

Table 10-5   Replacement Analysis Worksheet

I. Net Cash Flow at the Time the Investment Is Made

	t = 0
1. Cost of new equipment	($12,000)
2. Market value of old equipment	1,000
3. Tax savings due to loss on old equipment	600
4. Increase in net working capital	(1,000)
5. Total net investment	($11,400)

Year:	0	1	2	3	4	5
II. Operating Inflows over the Project's Life						
6. After-tax decrease in costs		$1,800	$1,800	$1,800	$1,800	$1,800
7. Depreciation on new machine		$3,960	$5,400	$1,800	$ 840	$ 0
8. Depreciation on old machine		500	500	500	500	500
9. Change in depreciation		$3,460	$4,900	$1,300	$ 340	($ 500)
10. Tax savings from depreciation		1,384	1,960	520	136	(200)
11. Net operating cash flow (6 + 10)		$3,184	$3,760	$2,320	$1,936	$1,600
III. Terminal Year Cash Flows						
12. Estimated salvage value of new machine						$2,000
13. Tax on salvage value						(800)
14. Recovery of net working capital						1,000
15. Total termination cash flow						$2,200
IV. Net Cash Flows						
16. Total net cash flow	($11,400)	$3,184	$3,760	$2,320	$1,936	$3,800

V. Results

Payback period: 4.1 years.
IRR: 10.1% versus an 11.5% cost of capital.
MIRR: 10.7% versus an 11.5% cost of capital.
NPV: − $388.77

---

an operating loss, because it reflects the fact that inadequate depreciation was taken on the old asset. If there had been a profit on the sale (that is, if the sales price had exceeded book value), Line 3 would have shown taxes *paid,* a cash outflow. In the actual case, the equipment would be sold at a loss, so no taxes would be paid, and the company would realize a tax savings of $600.[6]

---

[6] If the old asset were being exchanged for the new asset, rather than being sold to a third party, the tax consequences would be different. In an exchange of similar assets, no gain or loss is recognized. If the market value of the old asset is greater than its book value, the depreciable basis of the new asset is decreased by the excess amount. Conversely, if the market value of the old asset is less than its book value, the depreciable basis is increased by the shortfall.

Line 4.   The investment in additional net working capital (new current asset requirements less increases in accounts payable and accruals) is shown here. This investment will be recovered at the end of the project's life (see Line 14). No taxes are involved.

Line 5.   Here we show the total net cash outflow at the time the replacement is made. The company writes a check for $12,000 to pay for the machine, and another $1,000 is invested in net working capital. However, these outlays are partially offset by the sale of the old equipment.

Line 6.   Section II of the table shows the *incremental operating cash flows*, or benefits, that are expected if the replacement is made. The cash flows for each year are based on Equation 10-2 as set forth earlier in the chapter. The first of these benefits is the reduction in operating costs shown on Line 6, which (1) increases cash flows because operating costs are reduced by $3,000, but (2) reduced costs also mean higher taxable income, hence higher income taxes. Therefore, the after-tax benefit is $3,000(1 − T) = $3,000(1 − 0.40) = $3,000(0.60) = $1,800. Note that had the replacement resulted in an increase in sales in addition to the reduction in costs (if the new machine had been both larger and more efficient), then this amount would also be reported on Line 6 (or a separate line could be added). Finally, note that the $3,000 cost savings is constant over Years 1–5; had the annual savings been expected to change over time, this fact would have to be built into the analysis.

Line 7.   The depreciable basis of the new machine, $12,000, is multiplied by the appropriate MACRS recovery allowance for 3-year class property to obtain the depreciation figures shown on Line 7. Note that if you summed Line 7, the total would be $12,000, the depreciable basis.

Line 8.   Line 8 shows the $500 straight line depreciation on the old machine.

Line 9.   The depreciation expense on the old machine as shown on Line 8 can no longer be taken if the replacement is made, but the new machine's depreciation will be available. Therefore, the $500 depreciation on the old machine is subtracted from that on the new machine to show the incremental change in annual depreciation. The change is positive in Years 1–4, but negative in Year 5. The Year 5 negative net change in annual depreciation signifies that the purchase of the replacement machine results in a *decrease* in depreciation expense in that year.

Line 10.   The net change in depreciation results in a tax savings which is equal to the change in depreciation multiplied by the tax rate: Depreciation savings = T(Change in depreciation) = 0.40($3,460) = $1,384 for Year 1. Note that the relevant cash flow is the tax savings on the *net change* in depreciation, rather than on only the depreciation on the new equipment. Capital budgeting decisions are based on *incremental* cash flows, and since we lose $500 of depreciation if we replace the old machine, that fact must be taken into account.

Line 11.   Here we show the net operating cash flows over the project's 5-year life. These flows are found by adding the after-tax cost decrease to the depreciation tax savings, or Line 6 + Line 10.

Line 12.   Part III shows the cash flows associated with the termination of the project. To begin, Line 12 shows the estimated salvage value of the new machine at the end of its 5-year life, $2,000.[7]

Line 13.   Since the book value of the new machine at the end of Year 5 is zero, the company will have to pay taxes of $2,000(0.4) = $800.

Line 14.   An investment of $1,000 in net working capital was shown as an outflow at t = 0. This investment, like the new machine's salvage value, will be recovered when the project is terminated at the end of Year 5. Accounts receivable will be collected, inventories will be drawn down and not replaced, and the result is an inflow of $1,000 at t = 5.

Line 15.   Here we show the total cash flows resulting from terminating the project.

Line 16.   Part IV shows, on Line 16, the total net cash flows in a time line format suitable for capital budgeting evaluation.

Part V of the table, "Results," shows the replacement project's payback, IRR, MIRR, and NPV. The project is assumed to be of similar risk to the old project, and the old project is assumed to be about as risky as the company's average project. Therefore, an 11.5 percent project cost of capital is appropriate. At this cost of capital, the project is not acceptable, so the old lathe should not be replaced.

Self-Test Questions

What are the primary differences between the cash flow analyses for a new project and a replacement project?

Why is the depreciation tax savings negative in Year 5 in Table 10-5?

CASH FLOW ESTIMATION BIAS

As noted at the beginning of the chapter, cash flow estimation is the most critical, and the most difficult, part of the capital budgeting process. Cash flow components must be forecasted many years into the future, and estimation errors are bound to occur.[8] To illustrate, at the end of 1990, RIC's managers had to estimate unit sales and other cash flows for the appliance-control computer out to 1999. Clearly, large errors can and do occur. However, large firms evaluate and accept many projects every year, and as long as the cash flow estimates are unbiased and the errors are random, the estimation errors will tend to cancel each other out. That is, some projects will have NPV estimates that are too high and some will have estimates that

---

[7]In this analysis, the estimated salvage value of the old machine is zero. However, if the old machine could be sold at the end of five years, then replacing the old machine now would eliminate this cash flow. Thus, the after-tax salvage value of the old machine would represent an opportunity cost to the firm, and it would be included as a Year 5 cash outflow in the terminal cash flow section of the worksheet.

[8]For a discussion of the cash flow estimation practices of some large firms, as well as some estimates of the inaccuracies involved, see Randolph A. Pohlman, Emmanuel S. Santiago, and F. Lynn Markel, "Cash Flow Estimation Practices of Large Firms," *Financial Management,* Summer 1988, 71–79.

are too low, but the average realized NPV on all the projects accepted should be relatively close to the aggregate NPV estimate.

Unfortunately, several studies indicate that capital budgeting cash flow forecasts are not unbiased—rather, managers tend to be overly optimistic in their forecasts, and, as a result, revenues tend to be overstated and costs tend to be understated.[9] The end result is an upward bias in net operating cash flows and thus an upward bias in estimated NPVs. Often, this occurs because divisional managers are rewarded on the basis of the size of their divisions; thus, they are motivated to maximize the number of projects accepted rather than the profitability of the projects. Even when this is not the case, managers often become emotionally attached to their projects, and find themselves unable to objectively assess a project's potential negative factors. The RJR smokeless cigarette illustrates this point.

If this bias exists at a particular firm, then the acceptance of a project with a zero estimated NPV will likely result in a realized loss, hence in a decrease in shareholders' wealth. Recognizing that biases may exist, senior managers at many firms now develop data on the forecast accuracies of their divisional managers, and then consider this information in the capital budgeting decision process. Some companies lower the cash flow estimates of managers whose track records suggest that their forecasts are too rosy, while other companies increase the cost of capital, or hurdle rate, applied to such project submissions.

A first step in uncovering cash flow estimation bias, especially for projects that are estimated to be highly profitable, is to ask this question: What is the underlying cause of this project's profitability? If the firm has some inherent advantage, such as patent protection, unique manufacturing or marketing expertise, or even a well-known brand name, then projects which utilize such an advantage may truly be extraordinarily profitable. However, in the long run, above-normal profits will probably be eroded by competition until the returns on projects within an industry are close to the normal return, which is the cost of capital. If there is reason to believe that competition is indeed likely to increase, and if division managers cannot identify any unique factors which could support a project's continued high profitability, then senior management should be concerned about the possibility of estimation bias.

RIC's top management considered the possibility of estimation bias when they reviewed the appliance-control computer project. With an IRR of 25.1 percent and an MIRR of 17.9 percent versus a cost of capital of 11.5 percent, the project is clearly projected to earn above-normal profits. These high profits might attract other firms into the market, and new entry might cause the actual cash flows to fall far below those forecast in Table 10-2. However, RIC's top management concluded that competitors would not be able to develop and produce a competing product within the next several years. Further, they noted that the unit sales forecasts were held constant over the life of the project, which is probably very conservative. Finally, as we will see in Chapter 11, the project is actually quite risky, and the forecasted returns are not all that spectacular in view of the risks involved.

---

[9]For a discussion of cash flow estimation bias, see Stephen W. Pruitt and Lawrence J. Gitman, "Capital Budgeting Forecast Biases: Evidence from the *Fortune* 500," *Financial Management,* Spring 1987, 46–51.

Self-Test Questions

Why might cash flow estimation bias exist in the capital budgeting decision process? What can be done to counteract such a bias?

MANAGERIAL OPTIONS

In the previous section, we discussed the problem of cash flow estimation bias, which can result in overstating a project's profitability. Another problem that can arise in cash flow analysis is understating a project's true profitability by not recognizing the value that stems from *managerial options*. To illustrate, many investments have the potential to lead to a number of valuable opportunities (or options) that are beyond the scope of the original proposal. These options include (1) the opportunity to develop follow-up products, (2) the opportunity to expand product markets, (3) the opportunity to expand or retool manufacturing plants, (4) the opportunity to abandon a project, and so on. Note that some managerial options involve a company's strategic entry into new products or markets, and the value of such an option is often called *strategic value*. Since managerial options are many and diverse, and since they can be utilized at any time, it is usually not feasible to incorporate them directly into a project's cash flow estimates. Conceptually, the true NPV of a project can be thought of as the sum of the traditional DCF NPV and the values of inherent managerial options:

$$\text{True NPV} = \text{Traditional NPV} + \text{Values of managerial options.}$$

In some situations, it is possible to quantify the value of managerial options. To illustrate an explicit valuation, consider the situation recently faced by American Semiconductor Industries, a leading producer of computer chips. The firm was evaluating a project to build a new semiconductor fabrication plant, with a 10,000-chips-per-week capacity, that had a conventional NPV of $10 million. Additionally, American's managers were able to identify two inherent managerial options for the project: (1) The new plant created the option to close an older plant and consolidate its activities with the more up-to-date facility. (2) The new plant created the opportunity to easily expand production to 20,000 chips per week using technology now under development.

Here's how American handled the analysis. First, consider the option to consolidate manufacturing activities. American estimated that a consolidation would result in a $2 million value due to labor savings and a $3 million value due to increased equipment efficiency, for a total NPV of $5 million. Further, American estimated that there was an 80 percent chance that this option would be exercised. Thus, the expected value of the consolidation option is 0.8($5) = $4 million.

With the expansion option, American estimated that the probability of expanding the plant to a 20,000-chips-per-week capacity using new technology is 20 percent, and the value attributed to having the current project in place is $10 million, resulting in an expected NPV of 0.2($10) = $2 million.

Thus, after considering the value of the managerial options, American valued the new plant project at $16 million:

$$\text{True NPV} = \text{Traditional NPV} + \text{Values of managerial options}$$

$$= \$10 + \$4 + \$2 = \$16 \text{ million.}$$

Further, the range of potential NPVs runs from $10 million, assuming that no options are exercised, to $10 + $5 + $10 = $25 million, assuming that the consolidation and expansion both take place. In this situation, the value of managerial options was an added bonus to an already positive project, but in other situations the traditional NPV might be negative, thus, failure to recognize the value of managerial options could result in a project being rejected that would otherwise be accepted.

We should note that option pricing methods (which we discuss in Chapter 18) are now being used by financial managers in certain industries, such as mining, to value managerial options. In the future, we expect that more and more companies will be attempting to quantify the value inherent in managerial options.[10] For now, however, managers should recognize that some projects have true NPVs that exceed their DCF NPVs because of managerial options, and these values should, at a minimum, be subjectively considered when making capital budgeting decisions.

Self-Test Questions

What is meant by a project's managerial options?

How should projects with managerial options be valued?

EVALUATING PROJECTS WITH UNEQUAL LIVES

Note that a replacement decision involves two mutually exclusive projects: retaining the old asset versus buying a new one. To simplify matters, in our replacement example we assumed that the new machine had a life equal to the remaining life of the old machine. If, however, we were choosing between two mutually exclusive alternatives with significantly different lives, an adjustment would be necessary. We now discuss two procedures — (1) the replacement chain method and (2) the equivalent annual annuity method — to both illustrate the problem and show how to deal with it.

Suppose Robotics International Corporation is planning to modernize its production facilities, and as a part of the process, it is considering either a conveyor system (Project C) or forklift trucks (Project F) for moving materials from the parts department to the main assembly line. Table 10-6 shows both the expected net cash flows and the NPVs for these two mutually exclusive alternatives. We see that Project

---

[10]The spring 1987 edition of the *Midland Corporate Finance Journal* contains several articles related to the use of option concepts in capital budgeting analyses. For an overview, see Stewart C. Myers, "Finance Theory and Financial Strategy," 6–13.

Table 10-6   Expected Net Cash Flows for Projects C and F

Year	Project C	Project F
0	($40,000)	($20,000)
1	8,000	7,000
2	14,000	13,000
3	13,000	12,000
4	12,000	—
5	11,000	—
6	10,000	—
NPV at 11.5%	$7,165	$5,391

C, when discounted at an 11.5 percent cost of capital, has the higher NPV and thus appears to be the better project.

Replacement Chain (Common Life) Approach

Although the analysis in Table 10-6 suggests that Project C should be selected, this analysis is incomplete, and the decision to choose Project C is actually incorrect. If we choose Project F, we will have the opportunity to make a similar investment in 3 years, and if cost and revenue conditions continue at the Table 10-6 levels, this second investment will also be profitable. However, if we choose Project C, we will not have this second investment opportunity. Therefore, to make a proper comparison of Projects C and F, we could apply the *replacement chain (common life)* approach; that is, we could find the NPV of Project F over a 6-year period and then compare this extended NPV with the NPV of Project C over the same 6 years.

The NPV for Project C, as calculated in Table 10-6, is already over the 6-year common life. For Project F, however, we must take three additional steps: (1) determine the NPV of a second Project F three years hence, (2) discount this NPV back to the present, and (3) sum these two component NPVs:

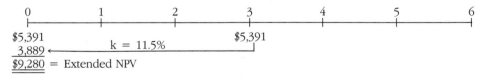

1.   If we make the assumption that Project F's cost and annual cash inflows will not change if the project is repeated in 3 years, and that RIC's cost of capital will remain at 11.5 percent, then Project F's second-stage NPV would remain the same as its first-stage NPV, $5,391. However, the second NPV would not accrue for 3 years, hence it would represent the project's value at t = 3.

2.   The present value (at t = 0) of the replicated Project F is determined by discounting the second NPV (at t = 3) back 3 years at 11.5 percent: $5,391/(1.115)^3 = $3,889.

3.   The extended NPV of Project F is $5,391 + $3,889 = $9,280. This is the value which should be compared with the NPV of Project C, $7,165. Since the "true" NPV of Project F is greater than the NPV of Project C, Project F should be selected.

Equivalent Annual Annuity Approach

Although the preceding example illustrates why an extended analysis is necessary if we are comparing mutually exclusive projects with different lives, the arithmetic is generally more complex in practice. For example, one project might have a 6-year life versus a 10-year life for the other. This would require a replacement chain analysis over 30 years, the least common multiple of the two lives. In such a situation, it is often simpler to use a second procedure, the *equivalent annual annuity (EAA)* method, which involves three steps:

1.   Find each project's NPV over its initial life. In Table 10-6, we found $NPV_C = $7,165$ and $NPV_F = $5,391$.

2.   Find the constant annuity cash flow (the equivalent annual annuity [EAA]) that has the same present value as each project's NPV. For Project F, here is the time line:

To find the value of EAA_F, enter 5,391 as the PV, $k = i = 11.5$, and $n = 3$ in your calculator and solve for PMT. The answer is $2,225. This cash flow stream, when discounted back 3 years at 11.5 percent, has a present value equal to Project F's original NPV, $5,391. The value $2,225 is called the project's "equivalent annual annuity (EAA)." The EAA for Project C was found similarly to be $1,718. Thus, Project C has an NPV which is equivalent to an annuity of $1,718 per year for 6 years, while Project F's NPV is equivalent to an annuity of $2,225 for 3 years.

3.   Assuming that continuous replacements can and will be made each time a project's life ends, these EAAs will continue on out to infinity; that is, they will constitute perpetuities. Recognizing that the value of a perpetuity is V = Annual receipt/k, we can find the net present values of the infinite EAAs of Projects C and F as follows:

$$\text{Infinite horizon } NPV_C = \$1,718/0.115 = \$14,939.$$

$$\text{Infinite horizon } NPV_F = \$2,225/0.115 = \$19,348.$$

In effect, the EAA method assumes that each project will, if taken on, be replaced each time it wears out, and will provide cash flows equivalent to the calculated annuity value. The PV of this infinite annuity is then the infinite horizon NPV for the project. Since the infinite horizon NPV of F exceeds that of C, Project F should be accepted. Therefore, the EAA method leads to the same decision rule as the replacement chain method—accept Project F.

The EAA method is generally easier to apply than the replacement chain method. However, the replacement chain method is often easier to explain to decision makers, and it does not require the assumption of an infinite time horizon. Still, the two methods always lead to the same decision if consistent assumptions are used. Also, note that Step 3 of the EAA method is not really necessary—we could have stopped after Step 2, because the project with the higher EAA will always have the higher NPV over any common life.

When should we worry about unequal life analysis? As a general rule, the unequal life issue (1) does not arise for independent projects, but (2) can arise if mutually exclusive projects with significantly different lives are being evaluated. However, even for mutually exclusive projects, it is not always appropriate to extend the analysis to a common life. This should only be done if there is a high probability that the projects will actually be replicated beyond their initial lives.

We should note several potentially serious weaknesses inherent in this type of unequal life analysis: (1) If inflation is expected, then replacement equipment will have a higher price, and both sales prices and operating costs will probably change, and thus the static conditions built into the analysis would be invalid. (2) Replacements that occur down the road would probably employ new technology, which in turn might change the cash flows. This factor is not built into either replacement chain analysis or the EAA approach. (3) It is difficult enough to estimate the lives of most projects, so estimating the lives of a series of projects is often just a speculation.

In view of these problems, no experienced financial analyst would be too concerned about comparing mutually exclusive projects with lives of, say, 8 years and 10 years. Given all the uncertainties in the estimation process, such projects could, for all practical purposes, be assumed to have the same life. Still, it is important for you to recognize that a problem does exist if mutually exclusive projects have substantially different lives. When we encounter such problems in practice, we build expected inflation and/or possible efficiency gains directly into the cash flow estimates, and then use the replacement chain approach (but not the equivalent annual annuity method). The cash flow estimation is more complicated, but the concepts involved are exactly the same as in our example.

Self-Test Questions

Is it always necessary to adjust project cash flow analyses for unequal lives? Explain.

Briefly describe the replacement chain (common life) approach.

Briefly describe the equivalent annual annuity (EAA) approach.

Under what circumstances do the two approaches lead to the same conclusions?

ABANDONMENT VALUE

Customarily, projects are analyzed as though the firm will definitely operate the project over its full physical life. However, this may not be the best course of action—it may be best to abandon a project prior to the end of its potential life,

Table 10-7   Investment, Operating, and Abandonment Cash Flows for Project A

Year (t)	Initial (Year 0) Investment and Operating Cash Flows	Net Abandonment Value at End of Year t
0	($4,800)	$4,800
1	2,000	3,000
2	1,875	1,900
3	1,750	0

and this possibility can materially affect the project's estimated profitability.[11] The situation in Table 10-7 can be used to illustrate the abandonment value concept and its effects on capital budgeting. The abandonment values are equivalent to net salvage values, except that they have been estimated for each year of Project A's life.

Using a 10 percent cost of capital, the expected NPV over the 3-year estimated life is − $117:

$$NPV = -\$4,800 + \$2,000/(1.10)^1 + \$1,875/(1.10)^2 + \$1,750/(1.10)^3$$

$$= -\$117.$$

Thus, Project A would not be accepted if we considered the single alternative of a 3-year life with a zero salvage (abandonment) value. However, what would its NPV be if the project were abandoned after 2 years? In this case, we would receive operating cash flows in Years 1 and 2, plus the abandonment value at the end of Year 2, and the project's NPV would be $138:

$$NPV = -\$4,800 + \$2,000/(1.10)^1 + \$1,875/(1.10)^2 + \$1,900/(1.10)^2$$

$$= \$138.$$

Thus, Project A becomes acceptable if we plan to operate it for 2 years and then dispose of it. To complete the analysis, we note that if the project were abandoned after 1 year, its NPV would be − $255. Thus, the optimal life for this project is 2 years.

As a general rule, any project should be abandoned when the net abandonment value is greater than the present value of all cash flows beyond the abandonment year, discounted to the abandonment decision point. For example, if we accept Project A and operate it for one year, then the abandonment value would be $3,000, but the present value at Year 1 of cash flows beyond Year 1 would be $1,875/(1.10)^1 + $1,750/(1.10)^2 = $3,151, assuming the project continues through Year 3; and $1,875/ (1.10)^1 + $1,900/(1.10)^1 = $3,432, assuming abandonment at the end of Year 2. Thus, the Year 1 abandonment value is less than the Year 1 present values of the expected future cash flows under either of the two alternative longer lives, so the project should not be abandoned at this point. However, a similar analysis at Year 2

---

[11]An old but still useful discussion can be found in Alexander A. Robichek and James C. Van Horne, "Abandonment Value and Capital Budgeting," *Journal of Finance,* December 1967, 577–589.

would show that the abandonment value of $1,900 is greater than the discounted value of future cash flows of $1,750/(1.10)^1 = $1,591$, so our decision rule would tell us to abandon the project in Year 2. This is, of course, the same conclusion that we reached from the NPV calculations.

Abandonment value should be considered in the capital budgeting process because, as our example illustrates, there are cases in which recognition of abandonment can make an otherwise unacceptable project acceptable. Indeed, this type of analysis is required to determine a project's economic life, which is defined as that project life which maximizes the project's NPV and thus maximizes shareholder wealth. For Project A, the *economic life* is actually two years, as opposed to the three-year *physical,* or *engineering, life.*

Two very different types of abandonment occur: (1) sale by the original user of a still-valuable asset to some other party who can obtain greater cash flows from the asset and (2) abandonment of an asset because the project is losing money. The first type of situation can be illustrated by Eastern Airlines' sale of its shuttle operation to Donald Trump. Trump had a better image than Eastern, and fewer labor problems. Thus, the shuttle was simply worth more to Trump than to Eastern.

The second type of abandonment—closing down money-losing operations—can cut losses and thus greatly reduce the riskiness of a project. This aspect of abandonment is illustrated by RJR's termination of its smokeless cigarette after it became apparent that the cigarette would never become the money-maker that the firm anticipated. We will have more to say about the impact of abandonment on project risk in Chapter 11. The main point for you to understand now is that the cash flows from a project can be materially different if it is abandoned (or sold off) at some point rather than operated to the end of its initially projected life, and if abandonment possibilities are not considered when in fact they exist, then the cash flows from the project may be badly misspecified.

Self-Test Questions

Define the economic life of a project (as opposed to its physical life).

Should projects be viewed as having only one life, or should alternative lives be considered in the capital budgeting process?

What are the two main situations where abandonment is desirable?

ADJUSTING FOR INFLATION

Inflation is a fact of life in the United States and most other nations, so it must be considered in any sound capital budgeting analysis.[12]

---

[12]For a formal discussion of this subject, see James C. Van Horne, "A Note on Biases in Capital Budgeting Introduced by Inflation," *Journal of Financial and Quantitative Analysis,* January 1971, 653–658; Philip L. Cooley, Rodney L. Roenfeldt, and It-Keong Chew, "Capital Budgeting Procedures under Inflation," *Financial Management,* Winter 1975, 18–27; and "Cooley, Roenfeldt, and Chew vs. Findlay and Frankle," *Financial Management,* Autumn 1976, 83–90.

Inflation Induced Bias

Note that *in the absence of inflation,* the real rate, k_r, and the nominal rate, k_n, are equal (as are the real and nominal expected net operating cash flows — RCF_t and NCF_t, respectively). In that situation, a project's NPV is calculated as follows:[13]

$$\text{NPV (no inflation)} = \sum_{t=0}^{n} \frac{RCF_t}{(1 + k_r)^t}. \qquad \textbf{(10-4)}$$

Now suppose the expected rate of inflation becomes positive, and we expect *all* of the project's cash flows — including depreciation — to rise at the rate i. Further, assume that this same inflation rate, i, will be built into the market cost of capital as an inflation premium, IP = i. In this event, the nominal net operating cash flow, NCF_t, will increase annually at the rate of i percent, producing this situation:

$$NCF_t = RCF_t(1 + i)^t.$$

For example, if we expected a net operating cash flow of $100 in Year 5 in the absence of inflation, then with a 5 percent annual rate of inflation, $NCF_5 = \$100(1.05)^5 = \$127.63$.

Now if net cash flows increase at the rate of i percent per year, and if this same inflation factor is built into the firm's cost of capital, then the NPV is calculated as follows:

$$\text{NPV (with inflation)} = \sum_{t=0}^{n} \frac{RCF_t (1 + i)^t}{(1 + k_r)^t (1 + i)^t} \qquad \textbf{(10-5)}$$

Since the $(1 + i)^t$ terms in the numerator and denominator cancel, we are left with Equation 10-4:

$$\text{NPV} = \sum_{t=0}^{n} \frac{RCF_t}{(1 + k_r)^t}.$$

Thus, if both costs and sales prices, hence annual cash flows, are expected to rise at the same inflation rate that investors have built into the cost of capital, then the inflation-adjusted NPV determined using Equation 10-5 is identical to the inflation-free NPV found using Equation 10-4.[14]

However, firms occasionally use base year, or constant (unadjusted), dollars throughout the analysis — say 1991 dollars if the analysis is done in 1991 — along with a cost of capital as determined in the marketplace as we described in Chapter 8. This is wrong: *If the cost of capital includes an inflation premium, as it typically does, but the cash flows are all stated in constant (unadjusted) dollars, then*

---

[13]Remember that the nominal rate of return includes an inflation premium that reflects investors' expectations about future inflation rates, while the real rate of return does not. If expected inflation is zero, then the inflation premium is also zero, and real and nominal rates are equal.

[14]For ease, we have simplified the situation somewhat. The precise nominal cost of capital is $k_n = w_d (k_{dr} + i)(1 - T) + w_s(k_{sr} + i)$ rather than $k_n = k_r + i$. Thus, we have ignored the impact of the tax deductibility of interest payments on the nominal cost of capital.

the calculated NPV will be downward biased. The denominator will reflect inflation, but the numerator will not, producing a downward bias in NPV.

Adjusting for Inflation

There are two ways to adjust for inflation. First, all project cash flows can be expressed as real (unadjusted) flows, with no consideration of inflation, and then the cost of capital can be adjusted to a real rate by removing the inflation premiums from the component costs. (See Footnote 14.) This approach is relatively simple, but to produce an unbiased NPV it requires (1) that all project cash flows, including depreciation, be affected identically by inflation, and (2) that this rate of increase equals the inflation rate built into investors' required returns. Since these assumptions generally do not hold in practice, this method is not as commonly used as the method we describe next.

The second method involves leaving the cost of capital in its nominal form, and then adjusting the individual cash flows to reflect the impact of inflation. This is what we did earlier in our RIC example as summarized in Table 10-2. There we assumed that sales prices, variable costs, and fixed overhead costs would all increase at a rate of 6 percent per year, but that depreciation charges would not be affected by inflation. Of course, we could have assumed different rates of inflation for sales prices, for variable costs, and for fixed overheads. For example, RIC might have long-term labor contracts which cause wage rates to rise with the Consumer Price Index (CPI), but its raw materials might be purchased under a fixed price contract, with the net result that variable costs are expected to rise by a smaller percentage than sales prices. In any event, one should build inflation into the cash flow analysis, with the specific adjustment reflecting as accurately as possible the most likely set of circumstances.

Our conclusions about inflation may be summarized as follows. First, inflation is critically important, for it can and does have major effects on businesses. Therefore, it must be recognized and dealt with. Second, the most effective way of dealing with inflation in capital budgeting analyses is to build inflation estimates into each cash flow element, using the best available information on how each element will be affected. Third, since we cannot estimate future inflation rates with precision, errors are bound to be made. Thus, inflation adds to the uncertainty, or riskiness, of capital budgeting as well as to its complexity. Fortunately, computers are available to help with inflation analysis, but an awareness of the nature of the problem is essential for good financial analysis.

Self-Test Questions

In what situation does inflation cause a downward bias in a project's estimated NPV? Explain.

What is the best way of handling inflation in a capital budgeting analysis, and how does this procedure eliminate the potential bias?

MULTINATIONAL FINANCE
Cash Flow Analysis of Foreign Investments

Cash flow analysis is much more complex when capital investments are being made in a foreign country. *The relevant cash flows from a foreign investment are the dollar equivalent cash flows that would be returned, or repatriated, to the parent company.* Since cash flows are earned in the currency of the foreign country, they must be converted to dollars, and thus they are subject to future exchange rate fluctuations.

International cash flow analysis can be illustrated by the Carlson Corporation's (CC) analysis of a proposed plant in Venezuela to assemble television sets for sale in South America. If the plant is built, a new CC subsidiary, wholly owned by the parent company, will be incorporated in Venezuela. CC has reached an agreement with the Venezuelan government allowing all of the subsidiary's earnings to be repatriated to the parent company. The investment, to be made in January 1991, will cost 50 million Venezuelan bolivars. CC has agreed to sell the subsidiary to Venezuelan investors at the end of 5 years at its expected book value of 25 million bolivars. Therefore, the firm's investment time horizon extends only to the end of 1995.

Table 10-8 summarizes the projected cash inflows from the investment. CC will evaluate the investment at a required rate of return of 15 percent. The subsidiary will have to pay income taxes of 20 percent to the Venezuelan government. In addition, CC will have to

pay U.S. income taxes on the earnings of the subsidiary, but it will receive credit for the Venezuelan taxes paid by the subsidiary. CC's marginal U.S. tax rate is 34 percent, and U.S. taxes are calculated as (Income before Venezuelan taxes)(U.S. tax rate − Venezuelan tax rate). Therefore, if the subsidiary has earnings of 20 million bolivars in 1991, it would pay Venezuelan taxes of 4 million bolivars, and then the parent company would pay (20 million bolivars)(0.34 − 0.20) = 2.8 million bolivars in U.S. taxes. Note that foreign governments sometimes limit the amount of funds that can be repatriated. When this occurs, the earnings repatriated will be less than the income generated by the subsidiary.

Table 10-9 converts the annual cash flows from bolivars to dollars and then calculates the present value of the dollar cash flows. Line 1 gives the annual cash flows in bolivars, while the estimated exchange rate, set equal to the current rate of 7.5 bolivars to the dollar, is shown on Line 2. Dividing the cash flows in bolivars by the exchange rate gives the expected cash flows in dollars as shown on Line 3. The present value of the expected dollar flows at a 15 percent required rate of return is $1.9 million.

Since the investment's NPV is positive, it appears to be acceptable. Note, however, that the actual value of the investment to CC will depend on the exchange

Table 10-8   Projected Cash Inflows, 1991−1995 (Millions of Venezuelan Bolivars)

	1991	1992	1993	1994	1995
Revenues	50.0	55.0	60.0	65.0	70.0
Total costs (60%)	30.0	33.0	36.0	39.0	42.0
Income before taxes	20.0	22.0	24.0	26.0	28.0
Venezuelan tax (20%)	4.0	4.4	4.8	5.2	5.6
Net income	16.0	17.6	19.2	20.8	22.4
Earnings repatriated	16.0	17.6	19.2	20.8	22.4
U.S. tax (34% − 20%)	2.8	3.1	3.4	3.6	3.9
Proceeds from sale	—	—	—	—	25.0
After-tax cash flows	13.2	14.5	15.8	17.2	43.5

Table 10-9   Cash Flows and NPV to Parent Company (Millions)

	1991	1992	1993	1994	1995
1. Cash flows (bolivars)	13.2	14.5	15.8	17.2	43.5
2. Exchange rate (bolivars per dollar)	7.5	7.5	7.5	7.5	7.5
3. Cash flows (dollars = bolivars/exchange rate)	$1.8	$1.9	$2.1	$2.3	$5.8
4. Present value of cash flows at 15%					$8.6
5. Less initial investment of 50 million bolivars at 7.5 bolivars per dollar, or $6.7 million					6.7
6. NPV of investment					$ 1.9

rate that exists when the earnings are repatriated. If U.S. exports increase relative to imports, then there will be an increase in the demand for dollars by foreigners to pay for the net U.S. exports. This would drive up the value of the dollar vis-à-vis currencies such as the bolivar. For example, the dollar might rise in value from 7.5 bolivars to $1 as shown on Line 2 to 10.0 bolivars to $1. That, in turn, would mean that the repatriated bolivars would purchase fewer dollars, so the dollar cash flows and hence the value of the investment would decline. For simplicity, we assumed in Table 10-9 that the exchange rate which existed when the project was undertaken would remain constant during the life of the investment. In reality, however, exchange rates change daily, and long-run trends associated with inflation and other fundamental factors occur, but not in a very predictable manner. Therefore, over a 5-year period, substantial changes could occur, but it is exceedingly difficult to predict what they will be. These exchange rate changes make international capital budgeting analysis quite complex, and they also increase the riskiness of foreign investments.[15]

---

[15]However, in a portfolio sense, foreign investments may be less risky than purely domestic investments, because the economies of different countries are not perfectly correlated. Thus, international diversification can lower the riskiness of investment portfolios.

SUMMARY

This chapter discussed several issues in project cash flow analysis. The key concepts covered are listed next.

- The most important, but also the most difficult, step in analyzing a capital budgeting project is *estimating the incremental after-tax cash flows* the project will produce.

- *Net operating cash flows* consist of (1) sales revenues minus cash operating costs, reduced by taxes, plus (2) a depreciation cash flow equal to the amount of depreciation taken during the period multiplied by the tax rate. In most situations, net operating cash flows are estimated by constructing cash flow statements.

- In determining incremental cash flows, *opportunity costs* (the cash flow foregone by using an asset) must be included, but *sunk costs* (cash outlays that have been made and that cannot be recouped) are not included. Any *externalities* (effects of a project on other parts of the firm) should also be included in the analysis.

- *Tax laws* affect project cash flow analyses in two ways: (1) They reduce project operating cash flows, and (2) tax laws prescribe the depreciation expense that can be taken in each year.

- Capital projects often require an additional investment in *net working capital (NWC)*. An increase in NWC must be included in the Year 0 initial cash outlay, and then shown as a cash inflow in the final year of the project.

- *Replacement analysis* is slightly different from that for *expansion projects* because the cash flows from the old asset must be considered in replacement decisions.

- Cash flow *estimation bias* can result if managers are overly optimistic in their forecasts.

- A project may have *managerial option* value that is not accounted for in a conventional discounted cash flow analysis.

- If mutually exclusive projects have *unequal lives,* it may be necessary to adjust the analysis to place the projects on an equal life basis. This can be done using either the *replacement chain* approach or the *equivalent annual annuity* approach.

- A project's value may be enhanced if it can be *abandoned* if things go poorly.

- *Inflation effects* must be considered in project analysis. The best procedure is to build inflation effects directly into the cash flow estimates.

- The cash flows from *international capital projects* are more difficult to analyze than purely domestic investments. The relevant cash flows in international capital budgeting are the dollar cash flows which can be turned over to the parent company.

We continue our discussion of capital budgeting analysis in Chapter 11, where we discuss risk analysis and the optimal capital budget.

Questions

10-1   Define each of the following terms:
    a.   Cash flow; accounting income
    b.   Incremental cash flow; sunk cost; opportunity cost
    c.   Net working capital changes
    d.   Salvage value
    e.   Replacement decision
    f.   Replacement chain
    g.   Equivalent annual annuity
    h.   Abandonment value
    i.   Real rate of return, k_r, versus nominal rate of return, k_n
    j.   Cash flow estimation bias
    k.   Managerial options

10-2 Operating cash flows rather than accounting profits are listed in Table 10-2. What is the basis for this emphasis on cash flows as opposed to net income?

10-3 Why is it true, in general, that a failure to adjust expected cash flows for expected inflation biases the calculated NPV downward?

10-4 Suppose a firm is considering two mutually exclusive projects. One has a life of 6 years and the other a life of 10 years. Would the failure to employ some type of replacement chain analysis bias an NPV analysis against one of the projects? Explain.

10-5 Look at Table 10-5 and answer these questions:
  a. Why is the salvage value shown on Line 12 reduced for taxes on Line 13?
  b. Why is depreciation on the old machine deducted on Line 8 to get Line 9?
  c. What would happen if the new machine permitted a *reduction* in net working capital?
  d. Why are the cost savings on Line 6 reduced by multiplying the before-tax figure by $(1 - T)$, whereas the change in depreciation figure on Line 9 is multiplied by T?

Self-Test Problems (Solutions Appear in Appendix D)

ST-1 **(New project analysis)** You have been asked by the president of the Farr Construction Company to evaluate the proposed acquisition of a new earth mover. The mover's basic price is $50,000, and it would cost another $10,000 to modify it for special use. Assume that the mover falls into the MACRS 3-year class, it would be sold after 3 years for $20,000, and it would require an increase in net working capital (spare parts inventory) of $2,000. The earth mover would have no effect on revenues, but it is expected to save the firm $20,000 per year in before-tax operating costs, mainly labor. The firm's marginal federal-plus-state tax rate is 40 percent.
  a. What is the net cost of the earth mover? (That is, what are the Year 0 cash flows?)
  b. What are the operating cash flows in Years 1, 2, and 3?
  c. What are the additional (nonoperating) cash flows in Year 3?
  d. If the project's cost of capital is 10 percent, should the earth mover be purchased?

ST-2 **(Replacement project analysis)** The Erickson Toy Corporation currently uses an injection molding machine that was purchased 2 years ago. This machine is being depreciated on a straight line basis toward a $500 salvage value, and it has 6 years of remaining life. Its current book value is $2,600, and it can be sold for $3,000 at this time. Thus, the annual depreciation expense is ($2,600 − $500)/6 = $350 per year.

The firm is offered a replacement machine which has a cost of $8,000, an estimated useful life of 6 years, and an estimated salvage value of $800. This machine falls into the MACRS 5-year class. The replacement machine would permit an output expansion, so sales would rise by $1,000 per year; even so, the new machine's much greater efficiency would still cause operating expenses to decline by $1,500 per year. The new machine would require that inventories be increased by $2,000, but accounts payable would simultaneously increase by $500.

The firm's marginal federal-plus-state tax rate is 40 percent, and its cost of capital is 15 percent. Should it replace the old machine?

Problems

10-1 **(Depreciation effects)** John Barnard, great-grandson of the founder of Tallman Tile Products and current president of the company, believes in simple, conservative accounting. In keeping with his philosophy, he has decreed that the company shall use alternative straight line depreciation, based on the MACRS class lives, for all newly acquired assets. Your boss, the financial vice-president and the only non-family officer, has asked you to develop an exhibit which shows how much this policy costs the company in terms of market value. Mr. Barnard is interested in increasing the value of the firm's stock because he fears a family stockholder revolt which might remove him from office. For your exhibit, assume that the company spends $50 million each year on new capital projects, that the projects have on average a 10-year class life, that the company has a 10 percent cost of debt, and that its tax rate is 34 percent. (Hint: Show how much the NPV of projects in an average year would increase if Tallman used the standard MACRS recovery allowances. Also, ignore the half-year convention on the straight line calculation.)

10-2   **(New project analysis)** You have been asked by the president of your company to evaluate the proposed acquisition of a new spectrometer for the firm's R&D department. The equipment's basic price is $70,000, and it would cost another $15,000 to modify it for special use by your firm. The spectrometer, which falls into the MACRS 3-year class, would be sold after 3 years for $30,000. Use of the equipment would require an increase in net working capital (spare parts inventory) of $4,000. The spectrometer would have no effect on revenues, but it is expected to save the firm $25,000 per year in before-tax operating costs, mainly labor. The firm's marginal federal-plus-state tax rate is 40 percent.
   a.   What is the net cost of the spectrometer? (That is, what is the Year 0 net cash flow?)
   b.   What are the net operating cash flows in Years 1, 2, and 3?
   c.   What is the additional (nonoperating) cash flow in Year 3?
   d.   If the project's cost of capital is 10 percent, should the spectrometer be purchased?

10-3   **(New project analysis)** The Ritchie Company is evaluating the proposed acquisition of a new milling machine. The machine's base price is $180,000, and it would cost another $25,000 to modify it for special use by your firm. The machine falls into the MACRS 3-year class, and it would be sold after 3 years for $80,000. The machine would require an increase in net working capital (inventory) of $7,500. The machine would have no effect on revenues, but it is expected to save the firm $75,000 per year in before-tax operating costs, mainly labor. Ritchie's marginal tax rate is 34 percent.
   a.   What is the net cost of the machine for capital budgeting purposes? (That is, what is the Year 0 net cash flow?)
   b.   What are the operating cash flows in Years 1, 2, and 3?
   c.   What is the additional (nonoperating) cash flow in Year 3?
   d.   If the project's cost of capital is 10 percent, should the machine be purchased?
   (Do Parts e, f, g, and h only if you are using the computerized diskette.)
   e.   Determine the NPV if the cost of capital were (1) to rise to 12 percent or (2) to fall to 8 percent.
   f.   There is some uncertainty about the salvage value. It could be as low as $50,000 or as high as $90,000. What would the NPV be at those two salvage value levels? (Assume k = 10 percent.) Should this uncertainty affect the decision to invest? What salvage value (to the nearest thousand) would make you indifferent to the project?
   g.   Return to the original salvage value of $80,000. What would be the project's NPV if the corporate tax rate were increased to 46 percent?
   h.   Return the tax rate to 34 percent. Now assume that the manufacturer of the machine calls you with bad news: The base price of the machine has increased to $200,000. What does this do to the project's NPV? At what cost (to the nearest hundred) would Ritchie be indifferent to the project?

10-4   **(Replacement analysis)** The Durst Equipment Company purchased a machine 5 years ago at a cost of $100,000. It had an expected life of 10 years at the time of purchase and an expected salvage value of $10,000 at the end of the 10 years. It is being depreciated by the straight line method toward a salvage value of $10,000, or by $9,000 per year.

A new machine can be purchased for $150,000, including installation costs. Over its 5-year life, it will reduce cash operating expenses by $50,000 per year. Sales are not expected to change. At the end of its useful life, the machine is estimated to be worthless. MACRS depreciation will be used, and it will be depreciated over its 3-year class life rather than its 5-year economic life.

The old machine can be sold today for $65,000. The firm's tax rate is 34 percent. The appropriate discount rate is 15 percent.

a.   If the new machine is purchased, what is the amount of the initial cash flow at Year 0?

b.   What incremental operating cash flows will occur at the end of Years 1 through 5 as a result of replacing the old machine?

c.   What incremental nonoperating cash flow will occur at the end of Year 5 if the new machine is purchased?

d.   What is the NPV of this project? Should the firm replace the old machine?

10-5   (Replacement analysis) The Orange Fizz Company is contemplating the replacement of one of its bottling machines with a newer and more efficient one. The old machine has a book value of $500,000 and a remaining useful life of 5 years. The firm does not expect to realize any return from scrapping the old machine in 5 years, but it can sell it now to another firm in the industry for $200,000. The old machine is being depreciated toward a zero salvage value, or by $100,000 per year, using the straight line method.

The new machine has a purchase price of $1.2 million, an estimated useful life and MACRS class life of 5 years, and an estimated salvage value of $175,000. It is expected to economize on electric power usage, labor, and repair costs, and also to reduce the number of defective bottles. In total, an annual savings of $275,000 will be realized if it is installed. The company is in the 40 percent federal-plus-state tax bracket, and it has a 10 percent cost of capital.

a.   What is the initial cash outlay required for the new machine?

b.   Calculate the annual depreciation allowances for both machines, and compute the change in the annual depreciation expense if the replacement is made.

c.   What are the operating cash flows in Years 1 to 5?

d.   What is the cash flow from the salvage value in Year 5?

e.   Should the firm purchase the new machine? Support your answer.

f.   In general, how would each of the following factors affect the investment decision, and how should each be treated?

(1) The expected life of the existing machine decreases.

(2) The cost of capital is not constant but is increasing.

(Do Parts g, h, and i only if you are using the computerized diskette.)

g.   The firm may be able to purchase an alternative new bottling machine from another supplier. Its purchase price would be $1,050,000, and its salvage value would be $250,000. This machine has a lower annual operating savings of $210,000. Should the firm purchase this machine?

h.   If the salvage value on the alternative new machine were $200,000 rather than $250,000, how would this affect the decision?

i.   With everything as in Part h, assume that the cost of capital declined from 10 percent to 8 percent. How would this affect the decision?

10-6   (Unequal lives) Lanser Clothes, Inc., is considering the replacement of its old, fully depreciated knitting machine. Two new models are available: Machine 190-3, which has a cost of $190,000, a 3-year expected life, and after-tax cash flows (labor savings and depreciation) of

$87,000 per year; and Machine 360-6, which has a cost of $360,000, a 6-year life, and after-tax cash flows of $98,300 per year. Knitting machine prices are not expected to rise, because inflation will be offset by cheaper components (microprocessors) used in the machines. Assume that Lanser's cost of capital is 14 percent.

a.   Should the firm replace its old knitting machine, and, if so, which new machine should it use?

b.   Suppose the firm's basic patents will expire in 9 years, and the company expects to go out of business at that time. Assume further that the firm depreciates its assets using the straight line method, that its marginal federal-plus-state tax rate is 40 percent, and that the used machines can be sold at their book values. Under these circumstances, should the company replace the old machine and, if so, which new model should the company purchase?

10-7   **(Abandonment value)** The Merville Milk Company recently purchased a new delivery truck. The new truck cost $22,500, and it is expected to generate net after-tax operating cash flows, including depreciation, of $6,250 per year. The truck has a 5-year expected life. The expected abandonment values (salvage values after tax adjustments) for the truck are given below. The company's cost of capital is 10 percent.

Year	Annual Operating Cash Flow	Abandonment Value
0	($22,500)	$22,500
1	6,250	17,500
2	6,250	14,000
3	6,250	11,000
4	6,250	5,000
5	6,250	0

a.   Should the firm operate the truck until the end of its 5-year life, or, if not, what is its optimal economic life?

b.   Would the introduction of abandonment values, in addition to operating cash flows, ever *reduce* the expected NPV and/or IRR of a project?

10-8   **(Inflation adjustments)** The Rowell Company is considering an average-risk investment in a mineral water spring project that has a cost of $150,000. The project will produce 1,000 cases of mineral water per year indefinitely. The current sales price is $138 per case, and the current cost per case (all variable) is $105. The firm is taxed at a rate of 34 percent. Both prices and costs are expected to rise at a rate of 6 percent per year. The firm uses only equity, and it has a cost of capital of 15 percent. Assume that cash flows consist only of after-tax profits, since the spring has an indefinite life and will not be depreciated.

a.   Should the firm accept the project? (Hint: The project is a perpetuity, so you must use the formula for a perpetuity to find the NPV.)

b.   If total costs consisted of a fixed cost of $10,000 per year and variable costs of $95 per unit, and if only the variable costs were expected to increase with inflation, would this make the project better or worse? Continue with the assumption that the sales price will rise with inflation.

10-9   **(Inflation adjustments)** The Apilado Company is evaluating an average-risk capital project having both a 3-year economic and MACRS class life. The net investment outlay at Time 0 is $18,800. The expected end-of-year cash flows, expressed in Time 0 dollars, are listed below: (Ignore salvage value and Year 4 depreciation.)

	Year 1	Year 2	Year 3
Revenues	$30,000	$30,000	$30,000
Variable costs	15,000	15,000	15,000
Fixed costs	6,500	6,500	6,500
Depreciation	6,204	8,460	2,820

The firm has a marginal federal-plus-state tax rate of 40 percent. Apilado's current cost of debt is 12 percent, and its cost of equity is 16 percent. These costs include an estimated inflation premium of 6 percent. The firm's target capital structure is 50 percent debt and 50 percent equity.

a.   What is the firm's nominal WACC? Its real WACC?

b.   What are the project's relevant real cash flows? What discount rate should be utilized when calculating a project's NPV based upon real cash flows? Why?

c.   What is the NPV for this project? Should this project be accepted? What might have occurred if you had used the *nominal* WACC with *real* cash flows?

d.   Now assume that all revenues and costs, except depreciation, are expected to increase at the inflation rate of 6 percent. What are the project's nominal cash flows and NPV based on these flows? Why is this NPV different from the NPV calculated in Part c?

(Do Part e only if you are using the computerized diskette.)

e.   Assume that the firm's management anticipates a rate of inflation resulting in a 6 percent inflation premium for Year 1 through Year 3. Based upon this assumption, the firm accepts the project. However, suppose the firm actually experiences nonneutral inflation such that revenues increase by only 6 percent, while variable and fixed costs increase by 7.5 percent. What are the actual after-tax cash flows in this case? What effect would the acceptance of the project coupled with unanticipated nonneutral inflation have had upon the value of the firm?

f.   If a company, in its capital budgeting process, bases its cash flows on sales prices and unit costs as of the time it analyzes the project, (1) would this tend to produce systematic errors in its capital budgeting evaluations, (2) would any such error be more serious for long-term or short-term projects, and (3) if you do think that systematic errors are likely to occur, how could they be corrected?

Mini Case

John Crockett Furniture Company is considering adding a new line to its product mix, and the capital budgeting analysis is being conducted by Joan Samuels, a recently graduated finance major. The production line would be set up in unused space in Crockett's main plant. The machinery's invoice price would be approximately $200,000; another $10,000 in shipping charges would be required; and it would cost an additional $30,000 to install the equipment. Further, the firm's inventories would have to be increased by $25,000 to handle the new line, but its accounts payable would rise by $5,000. The machinery has an economic life of 4 years, and Crockett has obtained a special tax ruling which places the equipment in the MACRS 3-year class. The machinery is expected to have a salvage value of $25,000 after 4 years of use.

The new line would generate $125,000 in incremental net revenues (before taxes and excluding depreciation) in each of the next 4 years. The firm's tax rate is 40 percent, and its overall weighted average cost of capital is 10 percent.

a.   Set up, without numbers, a time line for the project's cash flows.

b.   (1) Construct incremental operating cash flow statements for the project's 4 years of operations.

    (2) Does your cash flow statement include any financial flows such as interest expense or dividends? Why or why not?

c. (1) Suppose the firm had spent $100,000 last year to rehabilitate the production line site. Should this cost be included in the analysis? Explain.

    (2) Now assume that the plant space could be leased out to another firm at $25,000 a year. Should this be included in the analysis? If so, how?

    (3) Finally, assume that the new product line is expected to decrease sales of the firm's other lines by $50,000 per year. Should this be considered in the analysis? If so, how?

d. Disregard the assumptions in Part c. What is Crockett's net investment outlay on this project? What is the net nonoperating cash flow at the time the project is terminated? Based on these cash flows, what are the project's NPV, IRR, MIRR, and payback? Do these indicators suggest that the project should be undertaken?

e. Assume now that the project is a replacement project rather than a new, or expansion, project. Describe how the analysis would differ for a replacement project.

f. Explain what is meant by cash flow estimation bias. What are some steps that Crockett's management could take to eliminate the incentives for bias in the decision process?

g. Do you think it likely that the project being considered here might have managerial option value over and above the indicated NPV? If so, how might this be handled?

h. Assume that inflation is expected to average 5.0 percent over the next 4 years. Does it appear that Crockett's cash flow estimates are real or nominal? That is, are all the cash flows stated in the Time 0 dollars or have the cash flows been increased to account for expected inflation? Further, would it appear that the 10 percent cost of capital is a nominal or real rate? Does it appear that the current NPV is biased because of inflation effects? If so, in what direction, and how could any bias be removed?

i. In an unrelated analysis, Joan was asked to choose between the following two mutually exclusive projects:

| | **Expected Net Cash Flow** | |
Year	Project S	Project L
0	($100,000)	($100,000)
1	60,000	33,500
2	60,000	33,500
3	—	33,500
4	—	33,500

The projects provide a necessary service, so whichever one is selected is expected to be repeated into the foreseeable future. Both projects have a 10.0 percent cost of capital.

    (1) What is each project's initial NPV without replication?

    (2) Now apply the replacement chain approach to determine the projects' extended NPVs. Which project should be chosen?

    (3) Repeat the analysis using the equivalent annual annuity approach.

    (4) Now assume that the cost to replicate Project S in 2 years will increase to $105,000 because of inflationary pressures. How should the analysis be handled now, and which project should be chosen?

j. Crockett is also considering another project which has a physical life of 3 years; that is, the machinery will be totally worn-out after 3 years. However, if the project were abandoned prior to the end of 3 years, the machinery would have a positive salvage (or abandonment) value. Here are the project's estimated cash flows:

Year	Initial Investment and Operating Cash Flows	End-of-Year Net Abandonment Value
0	($5,000)	$5,000
1	2,100	3,100
2	2,000	2,000
3	1,750	0

Using the 10 percent cost of capital, what is the project's NPV if it is operated for the full 3 years? Would the NPV change if the company planned to abandon the project at the end of Year 2? At the end of Year 1? What is the project's optimal (economic) life?

Selected Additional References and Cases

Several articles have been written regarding the implications of the Accelerated Cost Recovery System (ACRS). Among them are the following:

Angell, Robert J., and Tony R. Wingler, "A Note on Expensing Versus Depreciating Under the Accelerated Cost Recovery System," *Financial Management,* Winter 1982, 34–35.

McCarty, Daniel E., and William R. McDaniel, "A Note on Expensing Versus Depreciating Under the Accelerated Cost Recovery System: Comment," *Financial Management,* Summer 1983, 37–39.

For further information on replacement analysis, as well as other aspects of capital budgeting, see the texts by Bierman and Smidt, by Grant, Ireson, and Leavengood, by Levy and Sarnat, and by Seitz referenced in Chapter 9.

Three additional papers on the impact of inflation on capital budgeting are the following:

Bailey, Andrew D., and Daniel L. Jensen, "General Price Level Adjustments in the Capital Budgeting Decision," *Financial Management,* Spring 1977, 26–32.

Mehta, Dileep R., Michael D. Curley, and Hung-Gay Fung, "Inflation, Cost of Capital, and Capital Budgeting Procedures," *Financial Management,* Winter 1984, 48–54.

Rappaport, Alfred, and Robert A. Taggart, Jr., "Evaluation of Capital Expenditure Proposals Under Inflation," *Financial Management,* Spring 1982, 5–13.

For additional insights into unequal life analysis, see

Emery, Gary W., "Some Guidelines for Evaluating Capital Investment Alternatives with Unequal Lives," *Financial Management,* Spring 1982, 15–19.

For an interesting discussion on cash flow estimation and abandonment biases, see

Statman, Meir, and David Caldwell, "Applying Behavioral Finance to Capital Budgeting: Project Terminations," *Financial Management,* Winter 1987, 7–13.

Statman, Meir, and Tyzoon T. Tyebjee, "Optimistic Capital Budgeting Forecasts: An Experiment," *Financial Management,* Autumn 1985, 27–33.

The Brigham-Gapenski casebook contains the following cases which focus on Chapter 9 and 10 material:

Case 13, "McReath Corporation (A)" and Case 15, "Adams Wineries, Inc. (A)," which focus on cash flow estimation, but also include capital budgeting decision methods.

The Harrington casebook contains the following relevant cases:

"Massalin Particulares," which illustrates capital budgeting in an inflationary environment.

"Federal Reserve Bank of Richmond (A)," which describes three mutually exclusive methods of automating savings bond processing.

"Metalcrafters, Inc.," which illustrates cash flow estimation and ranking methods.

CHAPTER 11

Risk Analysis and The Optimal Capital Budget

In 1990, Gillette introduced the Sensor, its first new nondisposable razor in decades. Founder King C. Gillette invented the first safety razor in 1903, and the company followed up with such revolutionary designs as the Blue Blade in 1932 and the Trac II in 1971. With twin blades mounted on tiny springs so they can move independently—allowing them to reach every nook and cranny on a man's face—Sensor is being touted as providing the smoothest and closest shave man has ever known. Gillette believes that shavers will buy the new razor by the millions.

The new razor had better be a big hit, because Gillette had spent more than $200 million in the previous 10 years to develop it and to begin production, plus an additional $110 million on roll out advertising in 1990. Thus, Gillette has placed its biggest bet in history on the success of Sensor, yet if it is to substantially increase Gillette's profits, Sensor must perform a marketing miracle by halting a 15-year trend towards inexpensive, disposable razors. At twice the cost of disposables, Sensor will be a hard sell.

All this came at a time when Gillette needed a lot of help. Though it boasts some of the world's best-known brand names—including Foamy shaving cream, Right Guard deodorant, Oral B toothbrushes, and Papermate and Flair pens—the company became a takeover target in the late 1980s because stockholders were unhappy with its sluggish growth. Efforts to spur growth by diversifying into such disjointed businesses as computer accessories, eyewear, hearing aids, and beauty centers hurt the company more than it helped it. Still, Gillette executives expect those investments to pay off in the 1990s, and if the new razor is a hit, it will support management's claim that its strategies will pay off for shareholders over the long run. However, if the Sensor flops, the raiders will probably make another attack, and stockholders will probably back them.

The Sensor project clearly poses great risks for Gillette, and when it decided to develop and market the new razor, management took account of the risks involved. Executives at Gillette asked questions such as "What would happen if Sensor is unable to convert shavers from disposables?" and "What would the impact be if Schick markets a competing product?" Showing how these questions can be answered is one aspect of project risk analysis, the primary topic of this chapter.

R ISK analysis is important in all financial decisions, especially those relating to capital budgeting. As we saw in Chapter 5, the higher the risk associated with a security, the higher the rate of return needed to compensate for the risk, and this situation is as true for capital assets as for securities. In this chapter we discuss procedures (1) for assessing risk in a capital budget context, (2) for incorporating risk into capital budgeting decisions, and (3) for determining a firm's optimal capital budget.

INTRODUCTION TO PROJECT RISK

Three separate and distinct types of project risk can be defined: (1) *stand-alone risk*, which views the risk of a project in isolation, hence without regard to portfolio effects; (2) *within-firm risk*, also called *corporate risk*, which views the risk of a project within the context of the firm's portfolio of projects; and (3) *market risk*, which views a project's risk within the context of the firm's stockholders' diversification in the general stock market. As we shall see, a particular project might have highly uncertain returns, thus have high stand-alone risk, yet taking it on might not have much effect on either the firm's corporate risk or the risk of its owners, once diversification is taken into account.

Figure 11-1 provides a framework for analyzing the riskiness of a project. In the remainder of this section, we discuss the figure, and in following sections, we discuss how the different types of risk may be quantified and used in actual capital budgeting decisions. Here are nine points related to the figure:

1.   Risk in Figure 11-1 and throughout the chapter relates to uncertainty about *future* events, and in capital budgeting, this means the *future* profitability of a project. For certain types of projects, it is possible to look back at historical data and to statistically analyze the riskiness of the investment. This is often true when the investment involves an expansion decision; for example, if Sears were opening a new

Figure 11-1   Project Risk Analysis

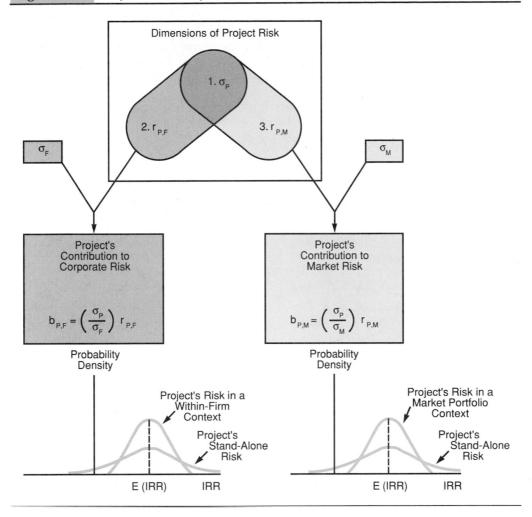

store, if Citibank were opening a new branch, or if GM were expanding its Chevrolet plant, then past experience could be used as a starting point for assessing future risk. Similarly, a company that is considering going into a new business might be able to look at historical data on existing firms in that industry to get an idea about the riskiness of its proposed investment. However, there are times when it is impossible to obtain historical data regarding proposed investments; for example, if GM were considering the production of an electric auto, not much relevant historical data for assessing the riskiness of the project would be available. Rather, GM would have to rely primarily on the judgment of its executives, and they, in turn, would have to rely on their experience in developing, manufacturing, and marketing new products. *We will try to quantify risk analysis, but you must recognize at the outset that some of the data used in the analysis will necessarily be based on subjective judgments rather than on hard statistical observations.*

2.   In Figure 11-1, and in risk analysis generally, we shall use the terms which are defined here. Note that these terms and concepts are drawn directly from portfolio analysis as set forth back in Chapters 4 and 5, so you should refer back to those chapters if you are hazy on portfolio concepts. Here are the key terms:

σ_P = standard deviation of the profitability of the project in question, measured as the standard deviation of the project's IRR. σ_P is a measure of the project's *stand-alone risk.*

$r_{P,F}$ = correlation coefficient between the rate of return on the project and the rate of return on the firm's other assets. What we want to know here is this: "Will this project be profitable at the same time the firm's other assets are also profitable, or are its returns likely to be independent of (or even negatively correlated with) returns on the firm's other assets? This correlation can be determined statistically for certain types of projects, but for many others it must be assessed subjectively.

$r_{P,M}$ = correlation coefficient between the rate of return on the project and returns on a stock market index, or "the market." If this correlation, which generally must be assessed subjectively on the basis of judgment and experience, is positive, then the project will tend to produce high returns if the economy, and most stocks, are also doing well.

σ_F = standard deviation of the rate of return on the firm's assets before it takes on the project in question, measured as (Net income + Depreciation + Interest) / (Debt + Equity). Note that the firm's average rate of return is, in effect, a sort of average of IRRs on past projects, and if σ_F is low, then the firm is stable, and its *corporate risk* is relatively low, while if σ_F is high, then the firm has a high degree of corporate risk, and its chances of going bankrupt are higher than if σ_F were low. The value of σ_F for past years can be measured statistically, but changes in the firm's situation may make its *expected future corporate riskiness* different from its past risk, in which case a subjectively estimated σ_F would be preferable for use in the analysis.

σ_M = standard deviation of the market's returns. This value is measured using historical data, and it is about 15 percent.

$b_{P,F}$ = *within-firm beta coefficient* of the project, which is found (conceptually) by regressing the project's returns against returns on the firm excluding the project. If you think of the project as a stock, and the firm as the market, then $b_{P,F}$ is found (conceptually) the same way stock betas were found back in Chapter 5. Note also that we can use this formula, which was developed in Chapter 5, to calculate the within-firm beta:

$$b_{P,F} = \left(\frac{\sigma_P}{\sigma_F}\right) r_{P,F}.$$

Here we see that the project's within-firm beta is a function of its stand-alone risk, σ_P, the riskiness of the firm's other assets, σ_F, and the correlation coefficient between the returns on the project and the firm's other assets. Further, the within-firm beta is a measure of the project's contribution to the firm's *corporate risk*, just as a stock's market beta is a measure of its contribution to the risk faced by a well-diversified investor who holds a broad portfolio of stocks.

$b_{P,M}$ = beta coefficient of the project within the context of a broad portfolio of stocks, which could (conceptually) be found by regressing the project's returns against returns on the market. Again, we can express $b_{P,M}$ as an equation:

$$b_{P,M} = \left(\frac{\sigma_P}{\sigma_M}\right) r_{P,M}.$$

This is the project's *market beta*, and it is a measure of the contribution of the project to the risk borne by the firm's stockholders, who are assumed to hold well-diversified portfolios.

3.   Now look carefully at Figure 11-1. The upper box shows that there are three dimensions to a project's risk: (1) the standard deviation of the project's forecasted returns, σ_P, (2) the correlation of those returns with the firm's other assets, $r_{P,F}$, and (3) the correlation of the project's returns with the stock market, $r_{P,M}$. As shown in the center-left panel, two of the project's risk attributes, σ_P and $r_{P,F}$, combine with the standard deviation of returns on the firm's other assets, σ_F, to determine the project's contribution to the firm's corporate risk, or its *within-firm risk*. Then, as shown in the center-right panel, two of the project's risk attributes, σ_P and $r_{P,M}$, combine with the riskiness of the market, σ_M, to determine the project's contribution to the riskiness of a well-diversified investor's portfolio, or the project's *market risk*.

4.   We see that it is especially important, when assessing a project's riskiness, to measure the project's stand-alone risk, σ_P, because that element is used in all aspects of capital budgeting risk analysis, along with the project's correlation with either the rest of the firm or with the market, or both correlations, depending on whether we want to measure corporate risk, market risk, or both types of risk.

5.   Most projects are positively correlated with the firm's other assets, with the correlation being highest for projects in the firm's core business and less high (but still positive) for investments outside the core. However, the correlation coefficient is rarely +1.0. This being the case, some of most projects' stand-alone risk will be diversified away, and the larger the firm, the greater this effect is likely to be. Therefore, in the probability distribution graph shown at the lower-left corner of Figure 11-1, we show a flatter distribution for the illustrative project's stand-alone risk than for its risk within the context of the firm's portfolio of assets; this shows that the project's within-firm risk is less than its stand-alone risk.

6.   Most projects are also positively correlated with other assets in the economy — most corporate assets have high returns when the economy is strong, and vice versa — but again the correlation is usually not perfect, so the typical project's stand-alone risk is also greater than its market risk. Hence, in the lower-right graph we drew the probability distribution curve for the project's stand-alone risk flatter than its distribution within a market portfolio context.

7.   If a project's within-firm beta, $b_{P,F}$, is equal to 1.0, then the project has the same degree of corporate risk as an average project. If $b_{P,F}$ is greater than 1.0, the project has more than average corporate risk, and vice versa if $b_{P,F}$ is less than 1.0. A higher than average within-firm risk would probably lead to the use of a higher than aver-

age WACC, but there is no precise formula for specifying how much higher — the adjustment is a matter of judgment.

8.   If the project's market beta, $b_{P,M}$, is equal to the firm's market beta, then the project has the same degree of market risk as an average project. If $b_{P,M}$ is greater than the firm's beta, then the project has more than average market risk, and vice versa if $b_{P,M}$ is less than the corporate beta. A higher than average project market beta, where "average" is defined as the firm's beta, would lead to an upward adjustment in the WACC, and the CAPM can be used to make the adjustment. We discuss this adjustment process later in the chapter.

9.   People occasionally argue that stand-alone and corporate risk as we have defined them are not important — if a firm seeks to maximize shareholders' wealth, the only relevant risk is market risk. This position is not correct, for the following reasons:

    a.   Undiversified stockholders, including the owners of small businesses, are more concerned about corporate risk than about market risk.

    b.   Many financial theorists argue that investors, even those who are well diversified, consider factors other than market risk when setting required returns. One such factor is the risk of financial distress, which depends on a firm's corporate risk. Empirical studies of the determinants of required rates of return generally find both market and corporate risk to be important.

    c.   The firm's stability is important to all the firm's other stakeholders, including its managers, workers, customers, suppliers, creditors, and the community in which it operates. Firms that are in serious danger of bankruptcy, or even of suffering low profits and reduced output, have difficulty attracting and retaining good managers and workers. Also, both suppliers and customers are reluctant to depend on weak firms, and such firms have difficulty borrowing money except at high interest rates. These factors will tend to reduce risky firms' profitability, hence the prices of their stocks.

For these reasons, corporate risk is also important, even to well-diversified stockholders.

Self-Test Questions

What are the three types of project risk, and how are they measured?

How are these three types related?

Why should managers be concerned with a project's corporate risk as well as its market risk?

STAND-ALONE RISK

A project's stand-alone risk is of little interest in and of itself. It is relevant only to not-for-profit firms (firms without shareholders) with a single project, or to single project firms with undiversified shareholders. However, as we saw earlier, stand-alone risk is an important determinant (along with the correlation coefficients) of both within-firm and market risk. Therefore, firms spend a great deal of time and effort on assessing stand-alone risk.

The starting point for analyzing a project's stand-alone risk involves determining the uncertainty inherent in the project's cash flows. This analysis can be handled in a number of ways, ranging from informal judgments to complex economic and statistical analyses involving large-scale computer models. To illustrate what is involved, let's refer back to the Robotics International Corporation appliance-control computer project that we discussed in Chapter 10. Most of the individual cash flows in Tables 10-1, 10-2, and 10-3, which produced the expected net cash flows for the project as set forth in Table 10-4, are subject to uncertainty. For example, sales for 1994 were projected at 25,000 units to be sold at a net price of $2,200 per unit, or $55 million in total. However, unit sales would almost certainly be somewhat higher or lower than 25,000, and the sales price would probably be different from $2,200 per unit. In effect, the sales quantity and price estimates are really expected values taken from probability distributions, as are many of the other values listed in Tables 10-1 through 10-3. The distributions could be relatively "tight," reflecting small standard deviations and low risk, or they could be "flat," denoting a great deal of uncertainty about the variable in question, hence a high degree of stand-alone risk.

The nature of the individual cash flow distributions, and their correlations with one another, determine the nature of the project's NPV and IRR distributions, and thus the project's stand-alone risk. In the following section, we discuss four techniques for assessing a project's stand-alone risk: (1) sensitivity analysis, (2) scenario analysis, (3) Monte Carlo simulation, and (4) decision tree analysis.

Sensitivity Analysis

Intuitively, we know that many of the variables which determine a project's cash flows are subject to some type of probability distribution rather than known with certainty. We also know that if a key input variable such as units sold changes, so will the project's NPV and IRR. *Sensitivity analysis is a technique which indicates exactly how much the NPV or IRR will change in response to a given change in a single input variable, other things held constant.*

Sensitivity analysis begins with a *base case* situation developed using the expected input values. To illustrate, consider the data given in Table 10-2 in Chapter 10, where projected cash flow statements for RIC's appliance-control computer project are shown. The values for unit sales, sales price, fixed costs, and variable costs are the *expected,* or *base case, values,* and the resulting $12,075,384 NPV shown in Table 10-4 is called the *base case NPV.* Now we ask a series of "what if" questions: "What if unit sales fall 20 percent below the expected level?" "What if the sales price per unit falls?" "What if variable costs are 70 percent of dollar sales rather than the expected 65 percent?" *Sensitivity analysis is designed to provide the decision maker with answers to questions such as these.*

In a sensitivity analysis, we usually change each variable by several specific percentages above and below the expected value, holding other things constant, then calculate new NPVs, and finally plot the derived NPVs against the variable that was

Figure 11-2   Sensitivity Analyses (Thousands of Dollars)

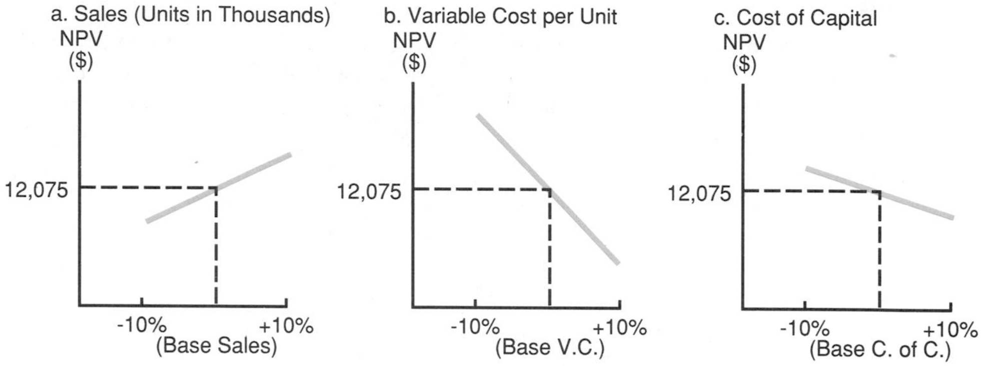

Change from Base Level (%)	Net Present Value		
	Units Sold	**Variable Cost/Unit**	**Cost of Capital**
−10	$ 7,944	$20,287	$13,772
−5	10,010	16,181	12,905
0	12,075	12,075	12,075
+5	14,141	7,970	11,281
+10	16,207	3,864	10,521

changed. Figure 11-2 shows the computer project's sensitivity graphs for three of the key input variables. The table below the graphs gives the NPVs that were used to construct the graphs. The slopes of the lines in the graphs show how sensitive the project's NPV is to changes in each of the inputs: the steeper the slope, the more sensitive the NPV is to a change in the variable. Here we see that the project's NPV is very sensitive to changes in variable costs, fairly sensitive to changes in sales volume, and relatively insensitive to changes in the cost of capital.

If we were comparing two projects, the one with the steeper sensitivity lines would be regarded as riskier because a relatively small error in estimating a variable such as the variable cost per unit would produce a large error in the project's projected NPV. Thus, sensitivity analysis can provide useful insights into the riskiness of a project.

Before we move on, note these two additional points about sensitivity analysis. First, computer spreadsheet models are ideally suited for performing sensitivity analyses, because such models automatically recalculate NPV when an input value is changed. We used a *Lotus 1-2-3* model to conduct the analyses represented in Figure 11-2, both the tabular data and the graphs. Second, we could have plotted all of the sensitivity lines on one graph; this would have facilitated direct comparisons of the sensitivities among different input variables.

Scenario Analysis

Although sensitivity analysis is probably the most widely used risk analysis technique, it does have some limitations. Consider, for example, a proposed coal mine whose NPV is highly sensitive to changes in output and sales prices. However, if a utility company has contracted to buy a fixed amount of coal at a fixed price per ton, plus inflation adjustments, then the mining venture may be quite safe in spite of its steep sensitivity lines. *In general, a project's stand-alone risk depends on both (1) the sensitivity of its NPV to changes in key variables and (2) the range of likely values of these variables as reflected in their probability distributions.* Because sensitivity analysis considers only the first factor, it is incomplete.

One risk analysis technique that considers both the sensitivity of NPV to changes in key variables and also the range of likely variable values is *scenario analysis.* Here the financial analyst asks operating managers to pick a "bad" set of circumstances (low unit sales, low sales price, high variable cost per unit, high construction cost, and so on), an average, or "most likely" set, and a "good" set. The NPVs under the "bad" and "good" conditions are then calculated and compared to the base case NPV.

As an example, let us return to the appliance-control computer project. Assume that RIC's managers are fairly confident of their estimates of all the project's cash flow variables except price and unit sales. Further, suppose they regard a drop in unit sales below 15,000, or a rise above 35,000 units, as being extremely unlikely. Similarly, they expect the sales price as set in the marketplace to fall within the range of $1,700 to $2,700. Thus, 15,000 units at a price of $1,700 defines the lower bound, or the *worst case scenario,* while 35,000 units at a price of $2,700 defines the upper bound, or the *best case scenario.* Remember that the most likely values (which are the same as the base case values in this example) are 25,000 units and a price of $2,200. Also, note that the indicated sales prices are for 1994, with future years' prices expected to rise because of inflation.

To complete the scenario analysis, we use the worst case variable values to obtain the worst case NPV and the best case variable values to obtain the best case NPV.[1] We performed the analysis using a *Lotus* model, and Table 11-1 summarizes the results. We see that the most likely case forecasts a positive NPV; the worst case produces a negative NPV; and the best case results in a very large positive NPV. We can now use these results to determine the expected NPV, standard deviation of NPV, and coefficient of variation of NPV. For this, we need an estimate of the probabilities of occurrence of the three scenarios. Suppose management estimates that there is a 25 percent probability of the worst case occurring, a 50 percent probability of the most likely case, and a 25 percent probability of the best case. Of course, it is *very difficult* to estimate scenario probabilities accurately.

---

[1] We could have included worst and best case values for fixed and variable costs, the inflation rate, salvage values, and so on. For illustrative purposes, we limited the changes to only two variables. Also, note that we are treating sales price and quantity as independent variables; that is, a low sales price could occur when unit sales were low, and a high sales price could be coupled with high unit sales, or vice versa. As we discuss in the next section, it is relatively easy to vary these assumptions if the facts of the situation suggest a different set of conditions.

Table 11-1 Scenario Analysis

Scenario	Probability of Outcome	Sales Volume (Units)	Sales Price	NPV (Thousands)
Worst case	0.25	15,000	$1,700	($10,079)
Most likely case	0.50	25,000	2,200	12,075
Best case	0.25	35,000	2,700	41,752
			Expected NPV =	$13,956
			σ_{NPV} =	$18,421

Note: Variables other than unit sales and sales price were set at their expected values.

Table 11-1 contains a discrete probability distribution of returns just like those we dealt with in Chapter 4, except that the returns are measured in dollars (NPV) rather than in percentages (rate of return). The expected NPV (in thousands of dollars) is

$$0.25(-\$10,079) + 0.50(\$12,075) + 0.25(\$41,752) = \$13,956.$$

Note that the expected NPV is *not* the same as the base case NPV, $12,075 (in thousands). This is because the two uncertain variables, sales volume and sales price, are multiplied together to get dollar sales, and this process causes the NPV distribution to be skewed to the right. (A big number times another big number produces a very big number, which in turn causes the average, or expected value, to be increased.) The standard deviation of NPV is $18,421 (in thousands of dollars):[2]

---

[2]If we had a probability distribution for the net cash flows for each year of a project's life, then we could calculate the expected net cash flow for each year, CF_t, and the variance of that cash flow, σ_t^2. We could then calculate the expected NPV as

$$E(NPV) = \sum_{t=0}^{n} \frac{CF_t}{(1 + k)^t}. \qquad (11\text{-}1)$$

If the net cash flow distributions across time were normal and were not correlated with one another (intertemporally independent), then the standard deviation of the NPV would be calculated as follows:

$$\text{Independent cash flow case: } \sigma_{NPV} = \left[\sum_{t=0}^{n} \frac{\sigma_t^2}{(1 + k)^{2t}} \right]^{1/2}. \qquad (11\text{-}2)$$

If the net cash flow distributions from one year to the next were normal and were completely dependent on one another (intertemporally dependent) such that the correlation coefficient between them is 1.0, then σ_{NPV} would be calculated as

$$\text{Dependent cash flow case: } \sigma_{NPV} = \sum_{t=0}^{n} \frac{\sigma_t}{(1 + k)^t}. \qquad (11\text{-}3)$$

See Frederick S. Hillier, "The Derivation of Probabilistic Information for the Evaluation of Risky Investments," *Management Science,* April 1963, 443–457. Although Hillier's approach to finding projects' standard deviations is relatively simple, it is rarely used in practice because (1) many project cash flow distributions are not normal and (2) most project cash flow distributions over time are neither totally independent nor perfectly positively correlated. Still, Hillier's model does show that if a project's cash flows are independent across time (that is, fluctuate randomly from year to year), the project is less risky than if cash flows are dependent, because for a given set of σ_t, Equation 11-2 produces a lower σ_{NPV} than Equation 11-3.

$$\sigma_{NPV} = [0.25(-\$10,079 - \$13,956)^2 + 0.50(\$12,075 - \$13,956)^2$$

$$+ 0.25(\$41,752 - \$13,956)^2]^{1/2} = \$18,421.$$

Finally, the project's coefficient of variation of NPV is 1.3:

$$CV_{NPV} = \frac{\sigma_{NPV}}{E(NPV)} = \frac{\$18,421}{\$13,956} = 1.3.$$

The project's coefficient of variation of NPV can be compared with the coefficient of variation of RIC's "average" asset to get an idea of the relative corporate riskiness of the appliance-control computer project. RIC's existing assets have an aggregate coefficient of variation of about 1.0. Thus, on the basis of this stand-alone total risk measure, RIC's managers would conclude that the appliance-control computer project is riskier than the firm's "average" project.

While scenario analysis provides useful information about a project's stand-alone risk, it is limited in that it only considers a few discrete outcomes (NPVs) for the project, although there are in reality an infinite number of possibilities. In the next section, we describe a method of assessing a project's stand-alone risk which deals with this problem.

Monte Carlo Simulation

Monte Carlo simulation, so named because this type of analysis grew out of work on the mathematics of casino gambling, ties together sensitivities and input variable probability distributions.[3] However, simulation requires a relatively powerful software package, while scenario analysis can be done using a PC with only a spreadsheet program, or even with a calculator.

The first step in a computer simulation is to specify the probability distribution of each uncertain cash flow variable such as sales price and sales quantity. Continuous distributions, which allow analysts to specify only a mean and standard deviation, or a lower limit, most likely value, and upper limit, are usually used for this purpose. Once this has been done, the simulation proceeds as follows:

1. The simulation software chooses at random a value for each uncertain variable, based on its specified probability distribution. For example, a value for unit sales would be chosen.

2. The value selected for each uncertain variable, along with values for the certain variables such as the tax rate and depreciation charges, are then used by the model to determine the net cash flows for each year, and these cash flows are then used to determine the project's NPV for this particular computer run.

3. Steps 1 and 2 are repeated many times, say 1,000, resulting in 1,000 NPVs, which make up a probability distribution with its own expected value and standard deviation.

---

[3]The use of simulation analysis in capital budgeting was first reported by David B. Hertz, "Risk Analysis in Capital Investments," *Harvard Business Review,* January-February 1964, 95–106.

Table 11-2   Summary of Simulation Results

	Probability of NPV Being Greater than the Indicated Value (Thousands of Dollars)								
Probability	**0.90**	**0.80**	**0.70**	**0.60**	**0.50**	**0.40**	**0.30**	**0.20**	**0.10**
NPV	($2,631)	$2,509	$5,999	$9,133	$11,956	$15,095	$17,930	$21,457	$26,045

NPV Sample Statistics (Thousands of Dollars)		
Mean	**Standard Deviation**	**Skewness Coefficient**
$12,078	$10,686	0.08

Using this procedure, we can perform a simulation analysis on RIC's appliance-control computer project. As in our scenario analysis, we have simplified the illustration by specifying the distributions for only two key variables, unit sales and sales price. For all the other variables, we merely specified their expected values.

In our simulation analysis, we assumed that sales price can be represented by a continuous normal distribution. Further, suppose the expected value is $2,200, and the actual sales price is not likely to vary by more than $500 from the expected value, that is, to fall below $1,700 or rise above $2,700. We know that in a normal distribution, the expected value plus or minus three standard deviations will encompass virtually the entire distribution, so three standard deviations of the sales price would be about $500. Therefore, as a reasonable approximation, we assumed that $\sigma_{\text{Sales price}} = \$500/3 = \$166.67 \approx \$167$, so we tell the computer to assume that the sales price distribution is normal, with an expected value of $2,200 and a standard deviation of $167.

Next, we assumed that the estimated distribution of unit sales is also symmetric with an expected value of 25,000 units, and sales could be as high as 40,000 units, given our production capacity, if demand is strong, but if public acceptance is poor, sales could be as low as 10,000 units. We could have again specified a normal distribution, but in the case of unit sales, we felt that a triangular distribution, with a most likely (and expected) value of 25,000, a lower limit of 10,000, and an upper limit of 40,000 is most appropriate.

We used these data plus a *Lotus* add-in program called @ *RISK* to conduct the simulation. The output is summarized in Table 11-2, and the resulting NPV probability distribution is plotted in Figure 11-3. There is a 90 percent probability that NPV will exceed − $2,631,000. Thus, there is a 10 percent probability of NPV being equal to or less than − $2,631,000. It is not shown in the table, but there is about a 14 percent chance that the project would have a negative NPV, hence an 86 percent probability of an NPV greater than zero. Also, note that the simulation output includes the NPV's expected value (mean) and standard deviation. Thus, the project's

---

Figure 11-3   NPV Probability Distribution (Thousands of Dollars)

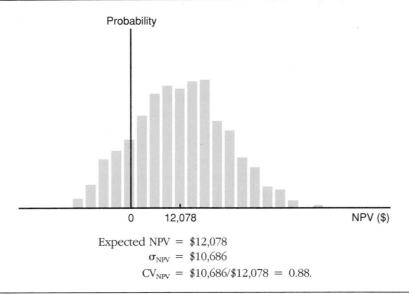

Expected NPV = $12,078

σ_{NPV} = $10,686

CV_{NPV} = $10,686/$12,078 = 0.88.

---

coefficient of variation of NPV can be calculated, and the project's stand-alone risk can be estimated in the same way as in our discussion of scenario analysis.[4]

In spite of its obvious appeal, simulation analysis has not been as widely used in industry as one might expect. One of the major problems is specifying each uncertain variable's probability distribution and the correlations among the distributions. Mechanically, it is easy to incorporate any type of correlation among variables into a simulation analysis; for example, @ *RISK* permits us to specify both intervariable and intertemporal correlations. However, it is *not* easy to specify what the correlations should be. Indeed, people who have tried to obtain such relationships from the operating managers who must estimate them have eloquently emphasized the difficulties involved. Clearly, the problem is not insurmountable, and simulation is being used in business with increasing frequency. Still, it is important

---

[4]Note that the standard deviation of NPV in the simulation is much smaller than the standard deviation we obtained in the scenario analysis. In the scenario analysis, we assumed that the low unit sales figure would be coupled with the low sales price for the worst case, and high values for each for the best case. That is, we assumed that these variables were *dependent* on one another, so high unit sales would mean high price, and vice versa. Thus, we ended up with only 3 NPVs, and a 25 percent probability of the worst (or best) case occurring.

In the simulation, we assumed that unit sales and price are *independent* of one another. Thus, in the simulation a high unit sales could be picked, and in the same run the computer could choose a low sales price. When the two variables are independent, the probability of a very low unit sales coupled with a very low sales price is remote. Further, in a simulation there are many possible values for each uncertain variable, while in a scenario analysis there is a discrete number (3 in our example). These two differences led to a lower standard deviation in the simulation analysis.

not to underestimate the difficulty of obtaining valid estimates of variables' probability distributions, and correlations among the distributions.[5]

Another problem with both scenario and simulation analyses is that even when the analysis has been completed, no clear-cut decision rule emerges. We end up with an expected NPV and a distribution about this expected value, which we can use to judge the project's stand-alone risk. However, the analysis provides no mechanism to indicate whether a project's profitability as measured by its expected NPV is sufficient to compensate for its risk as measured by σ_{NPV} or CV_{NPV}.

Finally, since scenario and simulation analyses focus on a project's stand-alone risk, they ignore the effects of diversification, both among projects within the firm and by investors in their personal investment portfolios. Thus, an individual project may have highly uncertain returns when evaluated on a "stand-alone" basis, but if those returns are not correlated with the returns on the firm's other assets or with the returns on a stock portfolio, then the project may not be very risky in terms of either within-firm or market risk. Indeed, if the project's returns are negatively correlated with the returns on the firm's other assets, then it may decrease the firm's corporate risk, and the larger its σ_{NPV}, the more it will reduce the firm's overall risk. Similarly, if a project's returns are not positively correlated with the stock market, then even a project with highly variable returns might not be regarded as risky by well-diversified stockholders, who are normally more concerned with market risk than with stand-alone or within-firm risk.

Decision Tree Analysis

Up to this point, we have focused primarily on techniques for estimating a project's stand-alone riskiness. Although this is an integral part of capital budgeting, managers are much more concerned about *reducing* risk than they are about *measuring* it. Often, project expenditures are not made at one point in time, but, rather, are made over a period of years, which gives managers the opportunity to reevaluate decisions and either invest additional funds or cancel (abandon) the project. Projects that require capital outlays over several years are often evaluated using *decision trees*.

For example, suppose Robotics International Corporation is considering the production of industrial robots for the television manufacturing industry. The net investment for this project will be broken down into three stages, as set forth in Figure 11-4.

Stage 1. At t = 0, which in this case is sometime in the near future, conduct a $500,000 study of the market potential for using robots in television assembly lines.

Stage 2. If it appears that a sizable market for television assembly robots does exist, then at t = 1 spend $1,000,000 to design and fabricate several prototype ro-

---

[5]For an interesting discussion of the pros and cons of simulation analysis, see Wilbur G. Lewellen and Michael S. Long, "Simulation versus Single-Value Estimates in Capital Expenditure Analysis," *Decision Sciences,* October 1972, 19–33. For more insight into the difficulties involved in estimating probability distributions and correlations in practice, see K. Larry Hastie, "One Businessman's View of Capital Budgeting," *Financial Management,* Winter 1974, 36–43. Hastie was treasurer of Bendix Corporation.

Figure 11-4 Robotics International Corporation: Decision Tree Analysis
(Thousands of Dollars)

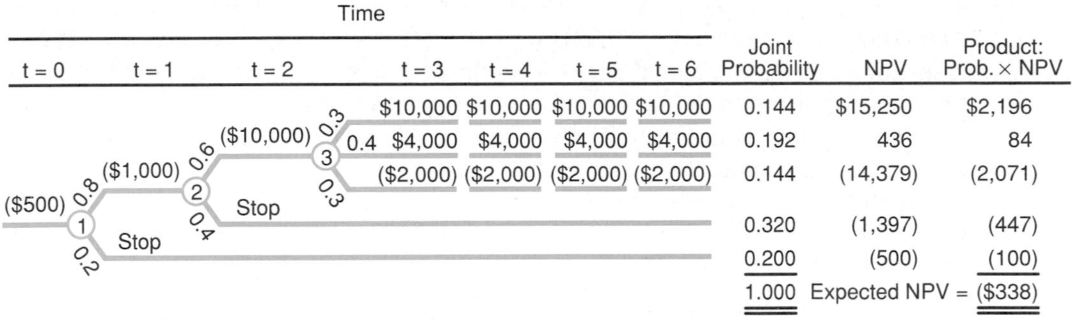

Time							Joint Probability	NPV	Product: Prob. × NPV
t = 0	t = 1	t = 2	t = 3	t = 4	t = 5	t = 6			
			$10,000	$10,000	$10,000	$10,000	0.144	$15,250	$2,196
		($10,000)	$4,000	$4,000	$4,000	$4,000	0.192	436	84
	($1,000)		($2,000)	($2,000)	($2,000)	($2,000)	0.144	(14,379)	(2,071)
($500)		Stop					0.320	(1,397)	(447)
	Stop						0.200	(500)	(100)
							1.000	Expected NPV =	($338)

bots. These robots would then be evaluated by television industry engineers, and their reactions would determine whether RIC would proceed with the project.

Stage 3. If reaction to the prototype robots is good, then at t = 2 build a production plant at a net cost of $10,000,000. If this stage were reached, managers estimate that the project would generate net cash flows over the following 4 years which depend on how well the final product was accepted by TV manufacturers.

A decision tree such as the one in Figure 11-4 is often used to analyze such multistage, or sequential, decisions. Here, we assume that one year goes by between decisions. Each circle represents a decision point, or stage. The dollar value to the left of each decision point represents the net investment required at that decision point, and the cash flows shown under t = 3 to t = 6 represent the cash inflows if the project is pushed on to completion. Each diagonal line represents a branch of the decision tree, and each branch has an estimated probability. For example, if RIC decides to "go" with the project at Decision Point 1, it will have to spend $500,000 on a marketing study. Management estimates that there is a probability of 0.8 that the study will produce favorable results, leading to the decision to move on to Stage 2, and a 0.2 probability that the marketing study will produce negative results, indicating that the project should be canceled after Stage 1. If the project is stopped here, the cost to the company will be $500,000 for the initial marketing study, and it will be a loss.

If the marketing study is undertaken, and if it does yield positive results, then RIC will spend $1,000,000 on the prototype robot at Decision Point 2. Management estimates (before even making the initial $500,000 investment) that there is a 60 percent probability that the television engineers will find the robot useful and a 40 percent probability that they will not like it. These are conditional probabilities; that is, they are conditioned upon reaching Decision Point 2.

If the engineers accept the robot, RIC will then spend the final $10,000,000 to build the plant and go into production, while if the engineers do not like the prototype, the project will be dropped. If RIC does go into production, the operating cash flows over the project's 4-year life will depend on how well the market accepts the final product. There is a 30 percent chance that acceptance will be quite good and net cash flows will be $10,000,000 per year, a 40 percent probability of $4,000,000 each year, and a 30 percent chance of a $2,000,000 loss per year. These cash flows are shown under Years 3 through 6. Also, note that RIC could elect to terminate or abandon the project even after it goes into operation.

The joint probabilities shown in Figure 11-4 give the probability of occurrence of each final outcome. Each joint probability is obtained by multiplying together all probabilities on a particular branch. For example, the probability that the company will, if Stage 1 is undertaken, move through Stages 2 and 3, and that a strong demand will produce $10,000,000 of inflows over 4 years, is $(0.8)(0.6)(0.3) = 0.144 = 14.4\%$.

The NPV of each final outcome is also given in Figure 11-4. The company has a cost of capital of 11.5 percent, and management assumes initially that all projects have average risk. The NPV of the top (most favorable) outcome is about $15,250 (in thousands of dollars):

$$\text{NPV} = -\$500 - \frac{\$1,000}{(1.115)^1} - \frac{\$10,000}{(1.115)^2} + \frac{\$10,000}{(1.115)^3} + \frac{\$10,000}{(1.115)^4} + \frac{\$10,000}{(1.115)^5} + \frac{\$10,000}{(1.115)^6}$$

$$= \$15,250.$$

Other NPVs were calculated similarly.

The last column in Figure 11-4 gives the product of the NPV for each branch times the joint probability of that branch, and the sum of the NPV products is the expected NPV of the project. Based on the expectations set forth in Figure 11-4 and a cost of capital of 11.5 percent, the project's expected NPV is $-\$338,000$.

Since the expected NPV is negative, it would appear that RIC should reject the project, but that conclusion is not necessarily correct. First, recall that management assumed that the project is of average risk, hence used the unadjusted cost of capital to evaluate it. However, the company should now consider whether this project is more, less, or about as risky as an average project. The expected NPV is a negative $338,000, and the standard deviation of that NPV is $7,991,000, so the coefficient of variation is quite large. This suggests that the project is highly risky in terms of stand-alone risk. Note also that there is a $0.144 + 0.320 + 0.200 = 0.664$ probability of incurring a loss. Based on all this, the project appears to be unacceptable. However, there are two other considerations: (1) The project can be abandoned, and this option could have a considerable impact on the analysis. We discuss this point in the next section. (2) As we discussed in Chapter 10, the project could have some other managerial option value that is not captured in the DCF analysis.

Self-Test Questions

Define stand-alone risk.

Briefly describe the mechanics of sensitivity analysis, scenario analysis, Monte Carlo simulation, and decision tree analysis.

What are the advantages and disadvantages of each type of stand-alone risk analysis?

THE IMPACT OF ABANDONMENT ON NPV AND STAND-ALONE RISK

In Chapter 10 we introduced the concept of abandonment value. We now illustrate how the possibility of abandonment can affect a project's risk as well as its expected NPV. Suppose RIC is not contractually bound to continue the project once operations have begun. Thus, if sales are poor and cash flows amount to only − $2,000 during the first year of operations, and a similar cash flow situation is expected for the remainder of the project's life, RIC can abandon the project at the beginning of Year 4 rather than continue to suffer losses over the next 3 years. (In this case, low first year cash flows signify that the product is not well received in the market, hence that future sales will be poor. In other cases, the cash flows could vary from year to year depending on economic conditions, in which case low first year sales and cash flows might be followed by high cash flows in subsequent years.)

The ability to abandon the project changes the branch of the decision tree in Figure 11-4 that contains the series of $2,000 losses. It now looks like this:

	Joint Probability	NPV	Product: Prob. × NPV
③ 0.3 ($2,000) ④ Stop	0.144	(10,883)	(1,567)

Changing this branch to reflect the abandonment alternative eliminates the $2 million cash losses in Years 4, 5, and 6, and thus causes the NPV for the branch to be less negative. This increases the project's expected NPV from − $338,000 to about $166,000, and also lowers its standard deviation from $7,991,000 to $7,157,000. Thus, abandonment possibilities changed the project's NPV from negative to positive, and also lowered its stand-alone risk as measured by either the standard deviation or the coefficient of variation.

Here are some additional points to note concerning decision tree analysis and abandonment possibilities:

1.   Managers can reduce project risk if they can structure the decision process to include several decision points rather than just one. To illustrate, if RIC were to make a total commitment at t = 0, signing contracts that would in effect require completion of the project, it might save some money and accelerate the project, but in doing so it would substantially increase the project's riskiness.

2.   Once production begins, if the firm can shut down or spin off the operation, this could dramatically reduce its risk. Indeed, firms do this frequently. To illustrate, Woolworth recently liquidated every one of its 336 Woolco discount stores in the United States. These stores had been operating at a loss, and Woolworth abandoned the entire division, selling off the stores piecemeal. In another example, General Motors recently sold several of its plants which produce parts required in its autos. These plants were sold to non-union companies, hence the buyers were able to produce the parts using low-cost labor. GM ended up getting the parts at a lower cost than when they were produced in GM-owned plants. Similar spin-offs have occurred in many industries. Such managerial options must be considered when major capital budgeting decisions are being made.

3. The cost of abandonment is generally reduced if the firm has alternative uses for the project's assets. If RIC could use its TV robot production equipment for the planned expansion of its auto robot production facilities, then the TV robot project could be more easily abandoned, hence its riskiness would be reduced.

4. Finally, note that capital budgeting is a dynamic process. Virtually all inputs to a capital budgeting decision change over time, and firms must periodically review both their capital expenditure plans and their ongoing projects. In the RIC example, conditions might change between Decision Points 1 and 2, and if so, this new information should be used to develop revised probability and cash flow estimates.

A dramatic example of both good and bad abandonment decisions is nuclear power plant construction. When the demand for electric power dropped sharply in the late 1970s, and construction costs rose in the aftermath of the Three Mile Island accident, some utilities reexamined their nuclear plant construction plans and decided to cancel plants. This required write-offs amounting to millions of dollars. Other companies decided to keep building, and they ended up losing literally billions of dollars.

The key concept to remember is that decisions can often be structured with multiple decision points; if so, and if the company has the willpower to admit it when a project is not working out as initially planned, then risks can be reduced, and expected cash flows can be increased.

Self-Test Questions

How can the possibility of abandonment affect a project's profitability and stand-alone risk?

What are the costs and benefits of structuring large capital budgeting decisions in stages rather than as a single go, no-go decision?

WITHIN-FIRM, OR CORPORATE, RISK

In a previous section, we described four methods for measuring a project's stand-alone risk. However, we know that the type of risk that is generally most relevant to managers, employees, creditors, and suppliers is the project's within-firm, or corporate, risk, while a project's market risk is most relevant to well-diversified stockholders. A project's corporate risk is the contribution of the project to the firm's overall total risk, or, put another way, the impact of the project on the variability of the firm's consolidated cash flows. Corporate risk is a function of both the project's standard deviation and its correlation with the returns on the firm's other assets, so a project with a high standard deviation would have relatively low corporate risk if its returns were uncorrelated or negatively correlated with those from the firm's other assets.

Conceptually, corporate risk can be thought of within a characteristic line framework. Remember that a stock's market risk characteristic line is the plot of the stock's market returns versus the returns on some market index, say the S&P 500. Further, the slope of a stock's characteristic line is its beta coefficient, which measures the stock's market risk. Now, if we consider a firm to be a portfolio of individual assets, then we can think of a project's corporate risk characteristic line as being the plot of the project's returns (in this case accounting returns, since no market returns can be measured on individual projects) versus the returns on the entire firm, which are made up of all the firm's individual asset returns, except the project being evaluated. The slope of such a characteristic line would be the project's *corporate risk beta*.

A project with a corporate risk beta of 1.0 would be just as risky as the firm's average asset; a project with a corporate risk beta greater than 1.0 would be riskier than the firm's average asset; and a beta less than 1.0 would signify relatively low corporate risk. Note (from Figure 11-1) that the corporate risk beta equals $(\sigma_P/\sigma_F)r_{P,F}$, where σ_P is the project's standard deviation of returns, σ_F is the firm's standard deviation of returns, and $r_{P,F}$ is the correlation coefficient between the two sets of returns. Thus, we see that a project's corporate, or within-firm, risk depends on the project's standard deviation of returns, on the standard deviation of the entire firm's returns, and on the correlation coefficient between those returns. A project with a relatively large standard deviation and a high correlation will have more corporate risk than a project with a relatively low standard deviation and a low, or negative, correlation. However, a large standard deviation is desirable if the project's returns are negatively correlated with the firm's other returns, because then the larger the σ_P, the larger the negative beta in absolute terms, hence the lower the project's corporate risk.

In practice, it is often difficult to estimate the returns distribution for a single project with any confidence, but the distributions for firms and divisions are more easily estimated. Thus, the corporate risk characteristic line is seldom used for individual projects, but it is used to estimate the relative risk of divisions within a firm. Therefore, the transition from a project's stand-alone risk to its within-firm risk is usually made subjectively. We know that if the project is in the same line of business as the firm's other projects, which is normally the case, then high stand-alone risk translates into high corporate risk, because the correlation coefficient will also be high. On the other hand, if the project is not in the same line of business, then it is possible that the correlation may be low, and in that case the project's stand-alone risk will overstate its corporate risk. In the final analysis, senior managers must use informed judgment when assessing projects' riskiness.

Self-Test Questions

Define within-firm, or corporate, risk.

Can a project's corporate risk be different from its stand-alone risk?

Briefly describe how a project's corporate risk might be measured, at least in theory.

What are the three primary determinants of a project's corporate risk?

MARKET RISK

The types of risk analysis discussed thus far provide insights into a project's stand-alone and corporate risk. However, as we noted, these methods do not focus on a project's market risk, which should be the most relevant type of risk to equity investors. Further, the methods described to this point are subjective rather than objective in the sense that while they help assess a project's riskiness, they do not specify which projects should be accepted and which rejected. In this section, we discuss how the CAPM might be used to help overcome those shortcomings. Of course, the CAPM has shortcomings of its own, but it does provide some useful insights into capital budgeting risk analysis.

Overview

To begin, recall that the Security Market Line expresses the risk/return relationship as follows:

$$k_s = k_{RF} + (k_M - k_{RF})b_i.$$

For example, if RIC's beta $= 1.8$, $k_{RF} = 8\%$, and $k_M = 13\%$, then the firm's cost of equity is 17.0 percent:

$$k_s = 8\% + (13\% - 8\%)1.8$$

$$= 8\% + (5\%)1.8 = 17.0\%.$$

Further, if RIC's cost of debt is 10 percent, if its marginal federal-plus-state tax rate is 40 percent, and if its target capital structure calls for 50 percent debt and 50 percent common equity, then its WACC is 11.5 percent:

$$WACC = k_a = w_d k_d(1 - T) + w_s k_s$$

$$= 0.5(10\%)(0.60) + 0.5(17\%)$$

$$= 3.0\% + 8.5\% = 11.5\%.$$

This suggests that investors would be willing to give RIC money to invest in average-risk projects that are financed in the usual manner if the company could earn 11.5 percent or more on this money. In this case, the term "average risk" means projects which have *market* risk—which is the risk that concerns the stockholders who supply capital to the company—similar to that of the firm's existing assets.

Now recall that a firm is a portfolio of assets, and its beta as established in the market is an average of its assets' betas. Therefore, if taking on a particular project will cause a change in RIC's 1.8 beta coefficient, then taking on the project will also cause a change in the company's cost of equity. For example, the appliance-control computer project might have a beta, if financed at the target capital structure, of 2.5, so taking it on would cause the overall corporate beta to rise, and it will end up somewhere between the original beta of 1.8 and the new project's beta of 2.5. The new corporate beta will depend on the relative size of the investment in the appliance-control computer project versus the company's investment in other assets. If 80 percent of RIC's total funds would be in other assets with an average beta of

1.8, and 20 percent in the new project with a beta of 2.5, then the new corporate beta would be 1.94, up from 1.8:

$$\text{New } b = 0.8(1.8) + 0.2(2.5) = 1.94.$$

This increase in RIC's market risk would cause the stock price to decline *unless the increased beta were offset by a higher expected overall rate of return.* Specifically, taking on the new project would cause the required rate of return on equity to rise from 17.0 to 17.7 percent,

$$k_s = 8\% + (5\%)1.94 = 17.7\%,$$

and the overall corporate cost of capital would rise from 11.5 to 11.85 percent:

$$\text{WACC} = k_a = 0.5(10\%)(0.60) + 0.5(17.7\%) = 11.85\%.$$

Therefore, to keep the appliance-control project from lowering the value of the firm, RIC's expected overall rate of return would have to rise from 11.5 to 11.85 percent.

If investments in RIC's original assets must earn 11.5 percent, how much must the new project earn in order for the new overall rate of return to equal 11.85 percent? We know that if it completes the new project, RIC would have 80 percent of its assets invested in other assets which must earn 11.5 percent, that 20 percent of its assets would be in the new project which must earn X percent, and that the average required rate of return would be 11.85 percent. Therefore,

$$0.8(11.5\%) + 0.2X = 11.85\%$$

$$0.2X = 11.85\% - 9.20\%$$

$$X = 2.65\%/0.2 = 13.25\%.$$

Therefore, the appliance-control computer project must have an overall expected return of 13.25 percent if the corporation is to earn its new cost of capital.

In summary, if RIC takes on the new project, its corporate beta would rise from 1.8 to 1.94; its cost of equity would increase from 17.0 to 17.7 percent; its weighted average cost of capital would rise from 11.5 to 11.85 percent; and the new project would have to earn at least 13.25 percent for RIC to earn its overall cost of capital.

This line of reasoning leads to the conclusion that if the beta coefficient for each project, b_i, could be determined, then an individual project's weighted average cost of capital, $\text{WACC}_i = k_{ai}$, could be found as follows:

1. Find Project i's required rate of return on equity, k_{si}:

$$k_{si} = k_{RF} + (k_M - k_{RF})b_i.$$

2. Use k_{si} to find the project's overall required rate of return, $k_{ai} = \text{WACC}_i$:

$$\text{WACC}_i = k_{ai} = w_d k_d(1 - T) + w_s k_{si}.$$

Applying these two steps to RIC's new project gives this result:

$$k_{si} = 8\% + (5\%)2.5 = 20.5\%,$$

and

$$\text{WACC}_i = k_{ai} = 0.5(10\%)(0.60) + 0.5(20.5\%) = 13.25\%.$$

We see that the required rate of return on the appliance-control computer project is the same using this "short-cut" method as it was when we developed the project's cost of capital by solving for X in the equation $11.85\% = 0.8(11.5) + 0.2X$. Note, however, that both solutions disregard any effects of the new project on either the firm's capital structure or its cost of debt; implicitly, we assumed that the cost of the debt used to support the new project, and the financing mix, would be the same as for the firm's existing assets.

Techniques for Measuring Market Risk

In Chapter 8, when we discussed the estimation of firms' betas, we indicated that it is difficult to estimate "true future betas" for common stocks. The estimation of *project* betas is even more difficult and more fraught with uncertainty, primarily because individual operating assets pay no dividends and have no quoted market prices; thus, we cannot calculate historical market-return betas for use in the analysis. However, two approaches have been used for estimating the betas of individual assets: (1) the pure play method and (2) the accounting beta method.

The Pure Play Method. In the *pure play method,* the company tries to find one or more nonintegrated, single-product companies in the same line of business as the project being evaluated.[6] For example, suppose RIC could find several existing single-product firms that produced appliance-control computer systems. Further, suppose RIC believes that its new project would be subject to the same risks as those of the other firms. It could then determine the betas of these firms by the regular regression process, average them, and use this average as a proxy for the project's beta.

To illustrate, assume that RIC's analysts have identified three publicly owned companies engaged only in the production and distribution of appliance-control computer systems. Further, assume that the average beta of these firms is 2.5. Then, the appliance-control project's cost of equity and its weighted average cost of capital are:

$$k_{si} = 8\% + (13\% - 8\%)2.50 = 20.5\%.$$

$$k_{ai} = 0.5(10\%)(0.60) + 0.5(20.5\%) = 13.25\%.$$

These values are consistent with those we calculated earlier.[7]

---

[6]One important article on this subject is Russell J. Fuller and Halbert S. Kerr, "Estimating the Divisional Cost of Capital: An Analysis of the Pure-Play Technique," *Journal of Finance,* December 1981, 997–1009. Fuller and Kerr used the method to estimate divisional betas and then tested the results empirically. They concluded that the pure play method is a valid technique for estimating the betas of major sub-parts of a firm.

[7]Our discussion here is somewhat simplified. The proxy betas reflect each proxy firm's capital structure and tax rate. If the proxy firms' average capital structure or tax rate is different from the financing mix that the evaluating firm would use, then the proxy beta must be adjusted to account for this difference. We will discuss a procedure for making this adjustment in Chapter 13.

The pure play approach is often difficult to implement because it is difficult to find pure play proxy firms. For our illustration, we assumed the existence of three pure play proxies. In reality, there is no pure play appliance-control computer system manufacturer. In fact, most systems are made by GE, Honeywell, and other large, multidivisional firms, and their control systems operations are combined with their other operations in a manner that makes it impossible to ascertain market betas for their appliance-control computer systems. However, there are times when the method is feasible. For example, when IBM was considering going into personal computers, it was able to get data on Apple Computer and several other essentially pure play personal computer companies. Similarly, Pillsbury is able to employ this technique when it is considering capital budgeting decisions in its Burger King, Godfather's Pizza, Steak and Ale, and Bennigan's divisions.

The Accounting Beta Method. As previously noted, it is generally not possible to find single-product, publicly traded firms suitable for the pure play approach. When this is the case, companies sometimes use the *accounting beta method*. As you know, betas are normally found by regressing the returns on a particular company's stock against returns on a stock market index. However, one could run a regression of the company's basic earning power (EBIT/Total assets) against the average basic earning power for a large sample of stocks such as the NYSE or the S&P 500. Such data are readily available from Standard & Poor's Compustat tapes. Betas determined in this manner, using accounting data rather than stock market data, are called *accounting betas*.

Historical accounting betas can be calculated for all types of companies (publicly owned or privately held, or even not for profit), for divisions, or even for certain types of large projects. But how good are accounting betas as proxies for market betas? Many studies have addressed this issue.[8] Although the results vary, most studies do support the conclusion that firms with high accounting betas tend to have high market betas, whereas firms with low accounting betas tend to have low market betas. However, the correlations are generally only in the 0.5 to 0.6 range, so accounting-determined betas provide only rough approximations for market-determined betas, market risk, and consequently the cost of capital.

Note that the accounting beta method described here is similar to the procedure discussed earlier to estimate a project's within-firm, or corporate, risk. The only difference is that when measuring corporate risk, the regression is run on the firm's returns rather than on the average return of firms in a stock index. Also, the accounting beta technique can be used to estimate different divisions' within-firm risk. Here the firm's overall accounting rate of return would be used as the benchmark, and the results would reflect the degree of correlation between different divisions.

---

[8]The original work on this subject was William H. Beaver and James Manegold, "The Association between Market-Determined Measures of Systematic Risk: Some Further Evidence," *Journal of Financial and Quantitative Analysis,* June 1975, 231–284. That study, and many subsequent ones, are summarized in George Foster, *Financial Statement Analysis* (Englewood Cliffs, N.J.: Prentice-Hall, 1986).

Self-Test Questions

What is the difference between corporate risk and market risk?

Briefly describe two techniques that can be used to estimate a project's market risk.

Summarize your views regarding both the relevance and the ease of determining a project's stand-alone risk, corporate risk, and market risk.

RISK-ADJUSTED DISCOUNT RATES VERSUS CERTAINTY EQUIVALENTS

Thus far, we have seen that capital budgeting can affect a firm's market risk, its corporate risk, or both. We have also seen that it is exceedingly difficult to quantify either type of risk. In other words, it may be possible to reach the general conclusion that one project is riskier than another (in either the market or the corporate or the stand-alone sense), but it is difficult to develop a really good *measure* of project risk. Further, this lack of precision in measuring project risk makes it difficult to incorporate differential risk into capital budgeting decisions.

Still, two methods have been developed for incorporating project risk into the capital budgeting decision process. One is the *certainty equivalent* method, in which the expected cash flows in each year are adjusted to reflect project risk — risky cash flows are scaled down, and the riskier the flows, the lower their certainty equivalent values. Then, the stream of certainty equivalent cash flows is discounted by the risk-free rate. The second procedure is the *risk-adjusted discount rate* method, in which differential project risk is dealt with by changing the discount rate — average-risk projects are discounted at the firm's WACC, above-average risk projects are discounted at a higher cost of capital, and below-average risk projects are discounted at a rate below the firm's WACC.

Risk-adjusted discount rates lump together the pure time value of money as represented by the risk-free rate and risk as represented by a risk premium: $k = k_{RF} + RP$. On the other hand, the certainty equivalent approach keeps risk and the time value of money separate because risk is incorporated in the numerator of the NPV equation rather than in the denominator. This separation gives a theoretical advantage to certainty equivalents, because the compounding of the risk premium over time implies that risk is increasing over time.[9] However, the risk-adjusted discount rate method is more frequently used in practice because it is far easier to estimate suitable discount rates based on current market data than it is to derive certainty equivalent cash flows. Further, if risk is perceived to be an increasing function of time, then using a risk-adjusted discount rate is a valid procedure.[10]

A firm using the risk-adjusted discount rate approach for its capital budgeting decisions will have an overall cost of capital that reflects its overall market-

---

[9]See Alexander A. Robichek and Stewart C. Myers, "Conceptual Problems in the Use of Risk-Adjusted Discount Rates," *Journal of Finance,* December 1966, 727–730.

[10]See Houng-Yhi Chen, "Valuation under Uncertainty," *Journal of Financial and Quantitative Analysis,* September 1967, 313–326.

determined riskiness. This rate should be used for "average" projects, that is, projects which have the same risk as the firm's existing assets. Lower rates should be used for less risky projects, and higher rates should be used for riskier projects. Further, as typically applied in practice, the risk-adjusted discount rate approach uses a constant discount rate.

Consciously or unconsciously, such use of a constant k assumes that risk increases with time, and it therefore imposes a relatively severe burden on long-term projects. This means that short-payoff alternatives will tend to be selected over those with longer payoffs when, for example, there are alternative ways of performing a given task.

However, there may be a substantial number of projects for which distant returns are *not* more risky than short-term returns. For example, the estimated returns on a water pipeline serving a developing community may be quite uncertain in the short run, because the rate of growth of the community is uncertain. However, the water company may be quite sure that in time the community will be fully developed and will utilize the full capacity of the pipeline. Similar situations could exist in many public projects—water projects, highway programs, schools, and so forth; in public utility investment decisions; and when industrial firms are building plants, or retailers are building stores, to serve growing geographic markets.

To the extent that the implicit assumption of rising risk over time reflects the facts, then a constant discount rate may be appropriate. Indeed, in the vast majority of business situations, risk undoubtedly is an increasing function of time, so a constant risk-adjusted discount rate is generally reasonable. However, one should be aware of the relationships described in this section and avoid the pitfall of unwittingly penalizing long-term projects when they are not, in fact, more risky than short-term projects.

Self-Test Questions

Describe how the certainty equivalent approach is used to incorporate risk into the capital budgeting decision.

Describe how the risk-adjusted discount rate approach is used.

Which approach is best conceptually? Which is easiest to apply in practice?

If a constant risk-adjusted discount rate is used to evaluate cash flows in all years, what does this imply about the perceived risk of cash flows in different years?

INCORPORATING RISK AND CAPITAL STRUCTURE INTO CAPITAL BUDGETING DECISIONS

Because of implementation problems with the certainty equivalent approach, firms generally use the risk-adjusted discount rate method to incorporate risk into the capital budgeting process—average-risk projects are discounted at the firm's WACC, above-average-risk projects are discounted at a higher cost of capital, and below-average-risk projects are discounted at a rate below the firm's WACC. Unfortunately, since risk cannot generally be measured precisely, there is no good way of specifying exactly *how much* higher or lower these discount rates should be—given the present state of the art, risk adjustments are necessarily judgmental, and somewhat arbitrary.

Capital structure must also be taken into account if a firm finances different assets in different ways. For example, one division might have a lot of real estate, which is well suited as collateral for loans, whereas some other division might have most of its capital tied up in special-purpose machinery, which is not good collateral. As a result, the division with the real estate might have a higher *debt capacity* than the machinery division, and thus an optimal capital structure which contains a higher percentage of debt. In this case, the division with more real estate contributes more to the overall debt capacity of the firm, and management might calculate its WACC using a higher debt ratio than for the other division.

Although the process is not exact, many companies use a two-step procedure to develop risk-adjusted discount rates for use in capital budgeting: (1) *Divisional costs of capital* are established for each of the major operating divisions on the basis of each division's estimated riskiness and debt capacity. (2) Within each division, all projects are classified into three categories—high risk, average risk, and low risk—and then each division uses its basic divisional WACC as the discount rate for average-risk projects, reduces the divisional WACC by one or two percentage points when evaluating low-risk projects, and raises the WACC by several percentage points for high-risk projects. For example, if a division's basic WACC is estimated to be 10 percent, then a 12 percent discount rate might be used for a high-risk project and a 9 percent rate for a low-risk project. Average-risk projects, which constitute about 80 percent of most capital budgets, would be evaluated at the 10 percent divisional cost of capital. This procedure is far from precise, but it does at least recognize that different divisions have different characteristics, hence different costs of capital, and it also accounts for differential project riskiness within divisions.

Self-Test Question

How do most firms incorporate differences in risk and debt capacity into the capital budgeting decision process?

RISKY CASH OUTFLOWS

In Chapter 9 we stated that some projects are evaluated on the basis of minimizing the present value of future costs rather than on the basis of the projects' NPVs. This is done because (1) it is often impossible to allocate revenues to a particular project that must be undertaken if the firm is to continue in operation (such as a pollution control project), and (2) it is appropriate to focus on comparative costs when two projects will produce exactly the same revenues. For example, suppose Duke Power must build a new generating plant to provide electricity in North and South Carolina. Several alternative types of plants are available, but they have different initial costs, different lives, and different operating costs (mainly fuel). There is no question about building some type of plant, because Duke Power's franchise agreement with the states requires it to supply electricity to consumers in the region. In this case, the decision will be based on the *present values of expected future costs.*

Some projects also have large cash outflows which occur at the end of the projects' lives. For example, in 1990 Toronto Development Company (TDC) was offered the opportunity to use a large city-owned warehouse along the lake, to refurbish it, and to lease space to others for a period of 10 years. During the 10 years, TDC would receive large cash inflows. However, at the end of the 10-year period, TDC would be required to raze the building and to develop the site as a park, at a cost estimated at $5 million. However, the cost could be much higher or lower, depending on conditions at the time.

In the case of both Duke Power's generating plant and TDC's warehouse-to-park project, risk adjustments must be made to future cash *outflows* (rather than inflows), and *the risk adjustment for a risky cash outflow is generally the exact opposite of that for an inflow.*

Consider again the Duke Power example. Suppose Duke is choosing between a coal-fired plant and a nuclear plant. The coal plant has a lower initial cost but a much higher annual operating cost. Also, the coal plant has a zero expected salvage value—removal costs are expected to equal the scrap value of the plant—while the cost of disassembling and disposing of the radioactive nuclear plant will be quite high, and very uncertain. Further, nuclear plants are less reliable than coal plants, and, hence, costly shut-downs and mid-life repairs may be necessary. There is also more uncertainty about nuclear plants' construction costs, in-service timing, and service lives. For all these reasons, there is a good basis for regarding the nuclear plant as being riskier than the coal plant in both the corporate and market risk senses.

Both nuclear and coal plants generally take a number of years to build, and they have expected lives of about 30 years. However, for simplicity, we shall assume that both plants have a 1-year construction period and a 5-year operating life. Further, we shall disregard inflation, and we also assume that the two plants have an equal capacity and that the electricity produced by both plants would be sold at the same price per unit.

Table 11-3 gives the projected costs associated with the two power plants: the investment costs at Year 0, and the operating costs plus nuclear decommissioning cost in Years 1 to 5. We assume that Duke Power's overall WACC, before it announces plans for a new generating plant, is 10 percent. If this discount rate were used to find the present value of future costs, we see from Table 11-3 that the plants would be judged equal. However, if Duke recognizes that the nuclear plant is more risky, and it therefore evaluates this project with a 12 percent cost of capital, then the nuclear plant's present value of future costs declines to $2,973 million, while at a still higher rate of 15 percent, the nuclear plant's costs drop to only $2,916 million. Thus, the riskier the nuclear plant is judged to be, the better it looks!

The two alternative investments have the same expected revenue stream, and, at a 10 percent cost of capital, the same present value of future costs, hence the same calculated NPV. Now we want to reflect the nuclear plant's higher risk, so we raise its discount rate, and that makes the nuclear plant look better. Something is ob-

	Table 11-3	Expected Costs: Coal versus Nuclear Power Plants (Millions of Dollars)

Year	Coal Plant	Nuclear Plant
0	($1,500)	($2,500)
1	(400)	(10)
2	(400)	(10)
3	(400)	(10)
4	(400)	(10)
5	(400)	(10) + (770) = (780)

PV of costs at: 10% ($3,016)   ($3,016)

               12%   n.a.   (2,973)

               15%   n.a.   (2,916)

Correct analysis: PV_{Coal} (at 10%) = ($3,016).

$PV_{Nuclear}$ (at 7%) = ($3,090).

Therefore, build the coal plant.

viously wrong. If we want to penalize a cash outflow for higher-than-average risk, then that outflow must have a *higher* present value, not a *lower* value. *Therefore, a cash outflow that has higher-than-average risk must be evaluated with a lower-than-average cost of capital.*

Recognizing this situation, Duke Power might discount the nuclear plant's costs at a 7 percent rate versus a 10 percent rate for the coal plant. In that case, the coal plant, with a PV cost of $3,016 million versus $3,090 million for the nuclear plant, would be chosen. This example illustrates both the problem that a negative outflow can cause and an approach for dealing with the problem.[11]

Self-Test Questions

Describe some "real world" situations in which risk adjustments must be applied to cash outflows.

How does the risk-adjustment process differ for cash outflows as compared to the process for cash inflows?

---

[11]The negative outflow problem could arise in a conventional NPV analysis as well as a PV of future costs analysis. For example, in the Toronto Development Company illustration, if the cash outflow at the end of the project's life was judged to be more risky than the cash inflows during the project's life, and if the outflow was discounted at a high risk-adjusted discount rate, then this would incorrectly bias the evaluation toward acceptance of the project. For more on the effects of negative cash flows, see Wilbur G. Lewellen, "Some Observations on Risk-Adjusted Discount Rates," *Journal of Finance,* September 1977, 1331–1337; and a comment on that paper by Stephen E. Celec and Richard H. Pettway, plus a reply by Lewellen, in the September 1979 issue of the *Journal,* 1061–1066. Pettway and Celec's analysis leads to a risk adjustment process similar to the one contained in this section. Lewellen points out that even though an outflow may be risky in the stand-alone risk sense, this outflow may have correlations with the firm's other cash flows and/or the returns on the market such that its within-firm and/or market risk is equal to or even less than the firm's average risk.

OUR VIEW OF PROJECT RISK ANALYSIS

From our discussion of project risk assessment and incorporation, it should be apparent that project risk analysis is far from precise. First, there are three types of project risk that can be considered, and a project can be highly risky in one sense, say, corporate risk, but not very risky in another, say, market risk. Second, none of these risks can be measured very precisely. To help place all the issues in perspective, we present our view of the process in this section.

To begin, should managers place most emphasis on a project's stand-alone, corporate, or market, risk? First, note that stand-alone risk is truly relevant only to a not-for-profit start-up firm which is evaluating its first project. Thus, in most situations, a project's riskiness is measured better by its within-firm risk, which takes into account the firm's whole portfolio of assets, than by its stand-alone risk. Second, well-diversified stock investors should be concerned primarily with market risk, managers should be concerned primarily with stock price maximization, and these two factors should lead to the conclusion that market risk should be given the most weight in capital budgeting decisions within investor-owned firms. However, stockholders are concerned about costs related to financial distress, and these costs are not captured by market risk. Further, managers should be and are concerned about the firm's other stakeholders (bondholders, suppliers, employees, customers, and so on), and this implies that corporate risk should be taken into account. Thus, managers should consider both a project's corporate risk and its market risk when making capital budgeting decisions.

In many cases it is impossible to assess quantitatively a project's market risk, or even its corporate risk, and managers are often left with only an assessment of a project's stand-alone risk. In most situations, the project being evaluated will be in the same line of business as the firm's other projects, and most firms' profitability is highly correlated with the national economy. Thus, stand-alone, corporate, and market risk are usually highly correlated, hence a project with a high degree of stand-alone risk, say, as measured by the coefficient of variation of NPV, will also have high corporate and market risk. This suggests that managers can get a feel for the relative risk of most projects on the basis of the scenario, simulation, and/or decision tree analyses conducted to estimate the project's stand-alone risk.

The firm's overall WACC provides the starting point for estimating a project's risk-adjusted discount rate. If all projects had equal risk and equal debt capacity, then all projects would be evaluated at the firm's WACC. However, larger firms typically have several divisions that vary in risk, and projects within divisions can also have risk differences. The first step in developing a project cost of capital calls for adjusting the firm's WACC to reflect divisional risk and debt capacity. Divisions with above-average risk or below-average debt capacity would have a divisional WACC above the firm's overall WACC, while divisions with below-average risk or above-average debt capacity would have a lower than average WACC. (Of course, the combined divisional WACCs must equal the firm's overall WACC.) A project is then assigned to a risk category on the basis of its own risk relative to the division's average risk. If a project is riskier than average for the division, then its risk-adjusted discount rate is set above the divisional WACC, and the opposite holds true if the project has below-average risk. (Remember that the risk adjustment process is reversed if the adjustment is being made to cash outflows.) Also, adjustments should be made when projects have debt capacities which differ widely from the divisional average. The most difficult part of this process is judging how large the divisional and project adjustments should be. If it is possible to assess the project's market risk, then the project's beta and the CAPM can be used to estimate the size of the adjustment. However, in most situations the adjustment is judgmental, and often a range of two to five percentage points is used.

The end result of the process is a project discount rate and an NPV which incorporates, to the extent possible, the project's debt capacity and at least one aspect of the project's relative riskiness. Managers also must consider other possible risk factors that may not have been included in the analysis. For example, if the project could lead to litigation against the firm, then the project has additional riskiness that should be taken into account—a number of drug and asbestos companies have learned this, to their regret. Conversely, if the project can easily be abandoned, or if the assets can easily be converted to other uses within the firm, then it might be less risky than it appears in a standard analysis. Such additional factors must be considered subjectively in making the final accept/reject decision. Typically, if the project involves new products and is large relative to the firm's average project, then these additional risk factors will be very important to the final decision—one large mistake can bankrupt a firm, and "bet the company" decisions are not made lightly. On the other hand, if the project being considered is a small replacement project, then the decision would be made almost exclusively on the basis of a straight numerical analysis.

Ultimately, capital budgeting decisions require a mix of objective and subjective analyses of the factors that will determine a project's risk, debt capacity, and profitability. The process is not precise, and often there is a temptation to ignore risk considerations because they are so nebulous. However, despite the imprecision and subjectiveness, a project's risk should be assessed and incorporated into the capital budgeting process. Anything less would be tantamount to ignoring one of the basic principles of finance—projects with higher risk require higher expected returns.

Self-Test Questions

Is project risk analysis a precise process?

Describe the process by which a project's risk and debt capacity are considered in capital budgeting decisions.

Describe some qualitative risk factors that managers should consider in the capital budgeting decision process that may not be included in the quantitative risk analysis.

THE OPTIMAL CAPITAL BUDGET

In Chapter 8, we developed the concept of the weighted average cost of capital (WACC). Then, in Chapters 9 and 10, and up to this point in Chapter 11, we have discussed how the cost of capital is used in project evaluations. However, capital budgeting and the cost of capital are actually interrelated—we cannot determine the cost of capital until we determine the size of the capital budget, and we cannot determine the size of the capital budget until we determine the cost of capital. Therefore, as we show in the next sections, *the cost of capital and the capital budget must be determined simultaneously.* Swift, Inc., a Midwestern grocery wholesaler, is used to illustrate the concepts involved.

The Investment Opportunity Schedule (IOS)

Consider first Figure 11-5, which gives some information on Swift's potential capital projects for next year. The tabular data show each project's cash flows, IRR, and payback. The graph is defined as the firm's *investment opportunity schedule (IOS)*, which is a plot of each project's IRR, in descending order, versus the dollars of new capital required to finance it (the cash flow at $t = 0$). For example, Project B has an IRR of 38.5 percent, shown on the vertical axis, and a cost of $100,000, shown on the horizontal axis.[12] Notice also that Projects A and B are mutually exclusive. Thus, Swift has two possible IOS schedules: the one defined by the solid line, which contains Project B plus C, D, E, and F, and the one defined by the dotted line, which contains Project A plus C, D, E, and F. Beyond $600,000, the two IOS schedules are identical. Thus, the two alternative schedules differ only in that one contains B and has C ranked second while the other contains A, in which case C ranks first because $IRR_C > IRR_A$. For now, we assume that all six projects have the same risk as Swift's "average" project.

The Marginal Cost of Capital (MCC) Schedule

In Chapter 8, we discussed the concept of the weighted average cost of capital (WACC). However, the value of the WACC depends on the amount of new capital raised—the WACC will, at some point, rise if more and more capital is raised during a given year. This increase occurs because (1) flotation costs (including any "signaling" costs and supply/demand imbalance costs associated with stock issues) cause the cost of new equity to be higher than the cost of retained earnings, and (2) higher rates of return on debt, preferred stock, and common stock may be required to induce additional investors to supply capital to the firm.

Suppose Swift's cost of retained earnings is 15.0 percent, while its cost of new common stock is 16.8 percent. The company's target capital structure calls for 40 percent debt and 60 percent common equity; its marginal federal-plus-state tax rate is 40 percent; and its before-tax cost of debt is 10 percent. Thus, Swift's WACC using retained earnings as the common equity component is 11.4 percent:

$$WACC_1 = k_a = w_d(k_d)(1 - T) + w_s k_s$$

$$= 0.4(10\%)(0.6) + 0.6(15\%) = 11.4\%.$$

---

[12]Do not be concerned at this point by the fact that we use IRR in this analysis rather than MIRR or NPV. The fact is, we cannot calculate either MIRR or NPV until we know k, and we are using this analysis to develop a first-approximation estimate of k. Later on, we could switch to MIRR or NPV, but such a switch is not necessary for this type of analysis.

Figure 11-5   Swift, Inc.: IOS Schedules

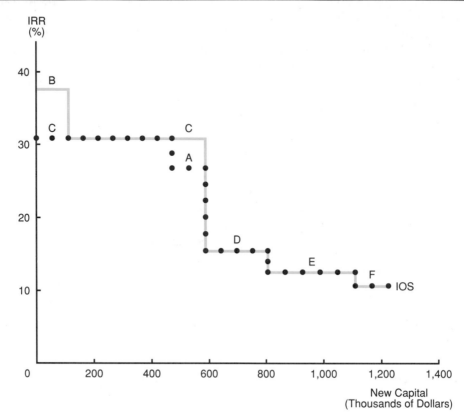

Potential Capital Projects

Year	Aª	Bª	C	D	E	F
0	($100,000)	($100,000)	($500,000)	($200,000)	($300,000)	($100,000)
1	10,000	90,000	190,000	52,800	98,800	58,781
2	70,000	60,000	190,000	52,800	98,800	58,781
3	100,000	10,000	190,000	52,800	98,800	—
4	—	—	190,000	52,800	98,800	—
5	—	—	190,000	52,800	—	—
6	—	—	190,000	52,800	—	—
IRR	27.0%	38.5%	30.2%	15.2%	12.0%	11.5%
Payback	2.2	1.2	2.6	3.8	3.0	1.7

ªProjects A and B are mutually exclusive.

Swift is forecasting $240,000 of retained earnings plus $300,000 in depreciation cash flow during the planning period, hence the firm's retained earnings break point is $700,000:

$$\text{Break point} = \$240,000/0.6 + \$300,000 = \$400,000 + \$300,000 = \$700,000.$$

After $700,000 of new capital has been raised, Swift's WACC increases to 12.5 percent:

$$WACC_2 = k_a = 0.4(10\%)(0.6) + 0.6(16.8\%) \approx 12.5\%.$$

Thus, each dollar has a weighted average cost of 11.4 percent until the company has raised a total of $700,000. This $700,000 will consist of $300,000 of depreciation cash flow with a cost of 11.4 percent, $160,000 of new debt with an after-tax cost of 6 percent, and $240,000 of retained earnings with a cost of 15 percent. However, if the company raises $700,001 or more, each additional dollar will contain 60 cents of equity obtained by selling new common stock, so k_a = WACC rises from 11.4 to 12.5 percent.

Combining the MCC and IOS Schedules

Now that we have estimated the MCC schedule, we can use it to determine the base discount rate for the capital budgeting process; *that is, we can use the MCC schedule to find the cost of capital for use in determining an average-risk project's net present value*. To do this, we combine the IOS and MCC schedules on the same graph, as in Figure 11-6, and then analyze this consolidated figure.

Finding the Marginal Cost of Capital. Just how far down its IOS curve should Swift go? That is, which of the firm's available projects should it accept? *First, Swift should accept all independent projects that have rates of return in excess of the cost of the capital that will be used to finance them, and it should reject all others.* Projects E and F should be rejected, because they would have to be financed with capital that has a cost of 12.5 percent, and at that cost of capital, we know that these projects must have negative NPVs since their IRRs are below their costs of capital. Therefore, Swift's capital budget should consist of either A or B, plus C and D, and the firm should thus raise and invest a total of $800,000.[13]

The preceding analysis, as summarized in Figure 11-6, reveals a very important point: The average-risk cost of capital used in the capital budgeting process is actually determined at the intersection of the IOS and MCC schedules. This cost is called the firm's *marginal cost of capital (MCC),* and if it is used as the firm's WACC, then the firm will make correct accept/reject decisions, and its level of financing and investment will be optimal. If it uses any other rate for average-risk projects, its capital budget will not be optimal.

---

[13]Note that if the MCC schedule cuts through a project, and if that project must be accepted in total or else rejected, then we can calculate the average cost of the capital that will be used to finance the project (some at the higher WACC and some at the lower WACC) and compare that average WACC to the project's IRR.

Figure 11-6 Swift, Inc.: Combined IOS and MCC Schedules

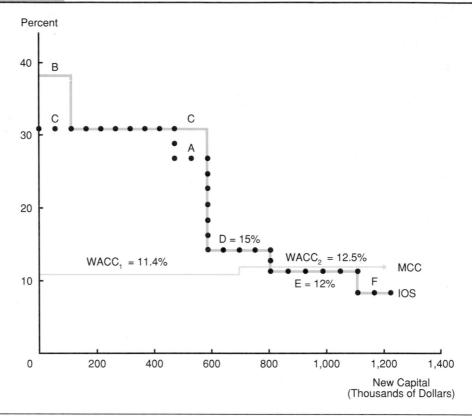

If Swift had fewer good investment opportunities, then its IOS schedule would be shifted to the left, possibly causing the intersection to occur at the $WACC_1 =$ 11.4% portion of the MCC curve. Then, Swift's MCC would be 11.4 percent, and average-risk projects would be evaluated at that rate. Conversely, if the firm had more and better investment opportunities, its IOS would be shifted to the right, and if the shift is very far to the right, then Swift might have to raise its MCC above 12.5 percent, because its higher capital requirements could lead to further increases in capital costs. Thus, we see that the discount rate used for evaluating average-risk projects is influenced by the set of projects available. We have, of course, abstracted from differential project riskiness in this section, because we assumed that all of Swift's projects are equally risky.

Choosing between Mutually Exclusive Projects. We have not, at this point, actually determined Swift's optimal capital budget. We know that it should total $800,000, and that Projects C and D should be included, but we do not know which of the mutually exclusive projects, A or B, should be made part of the final budget. How can we choose between A and B? We know that in general the final set of projects should be the one which has the highest total NPV, as this set will increase the value of the firm by the largest amount. We also know that Projects C and D should be included in the final set, so their contributions to the total NPV will be the same regardless of whether we choose Project A or Project B. This narrows our analysis to the NPVs of A and B. The project with the higher NPV should be chosen.

Notice that Figure 11-5 contained the projects' paybacks and IRRs, but no NPVs or MIRRs. We were not able to determine the NPVs or MIRRs at that point, because we did not know Swift's marginal cost of capital. Now, in Figure 11-6, we see that the last dollar raised will cost 12.5 percent, so Swift's marginal cost of capital is 12.5 percent. Therefore, assuming the projects both have average risk, we can use a 12.5 percent discount rate to find $NPV_A = \$34{,}431$ and $NPV_B = \$34{,}431$. Thus, in our example, Swift should be indifferent between the two mutually exclusive projects, according to the NPV criterion. To break the tie, assume for the sake of argument that Project B is selected because of its faster payback and higher IRR.

Self-Test Questions

Define a firm's marginal cost of capital.

On what basis is the choice made between mutually exclusive projects?

CAPITAL RATIONING

Under ordinary circumstances, capital budgeting is, in essence, an application of this classic economic principle: A firm should expand to the point where its marginal return is just equal to its marginal cost. However, under some circumstances, a firm may deviate from this principle and place an absolute limit on the size of its capital budget. This is called *capital rationing,* and we discuss this topic in Appendix 11A.

Self-Test Question

Define capital rationing.

ESTABLISHING THE OPTIMAL CAPITAL BUDGET IN PRACTICE

The procedures set forth in the preceding sections are conceptually correct, and it is important that you understand the logic of this process. However, Swift (and most other companies) actually uses a more judgmental, less quantitative process for establishing its final capital budget:

Step 1. The financial vice-president obtains a reasonably good fix on the firm's IOS schedule from the director of capital budgeting, and a reasonably good estimate of the MCC schedule from the treasurer. These two schedules are then combined, as in Figure 11-6, to get a reasonably good approximation of the corporation's marginal cost of capital (the cost of capital at the intersection of the IOS and MCC schedules).

Step 2. The corporate MCC is scaled up or down for each division to reflect the division's capital structure and risk characteristics. Swift, for example, assigns a factor of 0.9 to its stable, low-risk canned vegetables division but a factor of 1.1 to its more risky gourmet frozen foods group. Therefore, if the corporate MCC is determined to be 12.5 percent, the cost for the canned vegetables division is 0.9(12.5%) = 11.25%, while that for the gourmet frozen foods division is 1.1(12.5%) = 13.75%.

Step 3. Each project within each division is classified into one of three groups—high risk, average risk, and low risk—and the same 0.9 and 1.1 factors are used to adjust the divisional MCCs. For example, a low-risk project in the canned vegetables division would have a cost of capital of 0.9(11.25%) = 10.13%, rounded to 10 percent, if the corporate cost of capital were 12.5 percent, while a high-risk project in the gourmet frozen foods division would have a cost of 1.1(13.75%) = 15.13%, rounded to 15 percent.

Step 4. Each project's NPV is then determined, using its risk-adjusted project cost of capital. The optimal capital budget consists of all independent projects with positive risk-adjusted NPVs plus those mutually exclusive projects with the highest positive risk-adjusted NPVs.

These steps implicitly assume that the projects taken on have, on average, about the same debt capacity and risk characteristics, and consequently the same weighted average cost of capital, as the firm's existing assets. If this is not true, then the corporate MCC determined in Step 1 will not be correct, and it will have to be adjusted. However, given all the measurement errors and uncertainties inherent in the entire cost of capital/capital budgeting process, it would be unrealistic to push the adjustment process very far.

This type of analysis may seem more precise than the data warrant. Nevertheless, the procedure does force the firm to think carefully about each division's relative risk, about the risk of each project within the divisions, and about the relationship between the total amount of capital raised and the cost of that capital. Further, the procedure forces the firm to adjust its capital budget to reflect capital market conditions—if the cost of debt and equity rise, this fact will be reflected in the cost of capital used to evaluate projects, and projects that would be marginally acceptable when capital costs were low would (correctly) be ruled unacceptable when capital costs were high.

Self-Test Questions

Describe the general procedures that most firms follow when establishing optimal capital budgets.

What key assumption is implicit in these procedures?

MULTINATIONAL
FINANCE
Risk Analysis of Foreign Capital Projects

Although the same basic principles of capital budgeting analysis apply to both foreign and domestic operations, there are three crucial differences: (1) cash flow estimation is generally much more difficult for overseas investments; (2) foreign cash flows are in foreign currencies, so exchange rate fluctuations add to the riskiness of overseas investments; and (3) the possibility of deliberate government acts that reduce or divert cash flows adds another dimension to risk analysis for foreign investments. In this section, we briefly discuss risk analysis of foreign capital projects.

The first issue to be addressed in foreign project analysis is the definition of the relevant cash flows. Is the relevant flow the net cash generated by the foreign subsidiary, or is it the incremental cash flows that will be sent back to the U.S. parent company? As long as there are no restrictions on the repatriation of cash flows, these two cash flow streams will be the same. However, if there are local withholding taxes on dividends, restrictions on return of capital, or other blockages of international cash flows, both the timing and magnitude of the cash flows sent back to the parent company will be different from the operating cash flows of the project. The parent corporation cannot use cash flows blocked in a foreign country to pay current dividends to its shareholders, nor does it have the flexibility to reinvest the capital in its other subsidiaries. Hence, from the perspective of the parent organization, *the relevant capital budgeting cash flows are the dollar cash flows that are expected to be turned over to the parent.*

As we discussed in Chapter 10, the foreign currency cash flows to be turned over to the parent must be converted into U.S. dollar values by translating them at expected future exchange rates. Sensitivity or simulation analyses should be conducted to ascertain the effects of exchange rate uncertainty.

Sovereignty risk also differentiates international investment decisions from domestic capital budgeting. Sovereignty refers to the supreme and independent political authority of a nation to do as it pleases within its own borders. Since foreign subsidiaries are physically located within the jurisdiction of the host country, they are subject to rules and regulations established by local government authorities, no matter how arbitrary and unfair such regulations appear to be. Sovereignty risk includes both the possibility of expropriation or nationalization without adequate compensation and the possibility of unanticipated restrictions of cash flows to the parent company, such as tighter controls on repatriation of dividends or higher taxes. The risk of expropriation of U.S. assets abroad is small in traditionally friendly and stable countries, such as the United Kingdom, Switzerland, or Japan. However, risk may be substantial in Eastern European nations as they emerge from Communist control, in many Pacific Rim countries, in Africa, and in South America.

If a company's management has a serious concern that a given country might expropriate foreign assets, it simply will not make significant investments in that country. Expropriation is viewed as a catastrophic or ruinous event, and managers have been shown to be extraordinarily risk averse in the presence of ruinous loss possibilities. However, companies can take three major steps to reduce the potential loss from expropriation: (1) financing the subsidiary with local sources of capital, (2) structuring operations so that the subsidiary has value only as a part of the integrated corporate system, and (3) obtaining insurance against economic losses from expropriation from a source such as the Overseas Private Investment Corporation (OPIC). In the latter case, insurance premiums would have to be added to the project's cost.

SUMMARY

This chapter discussed three issues in capital budgeting: (1) assessing risk, (2) incorporating risk into the capital budgeting decision process, and (3) determining the optimal capital budget. The key concepts covered are summarized next.

- A project's *stand-alone risk* is the risk the project would have if it were the firm's only asset and if the firm's stockholders held only that one stock. Stand-alone risk is measured by the variability of the asset's expected returns. Stand-alone risk is often used as a proxy for both market and corporate risk, because (1) market and corporate risk are difficult to measure and (2) the three types of risk are usually highly correlated.

- *Within-firm,* or *corporate, risk* reflects the effects of a project on the firm's risk, and it is measured by the project's effect on the firm's earnings variability. Stockholder diversification is not taken into account.

- *Market risk* reflects the effects of a project on the riskiness of the stockholders' well-diversified portfolios. In theory, market risk should be the most relevant type of risk.

- *Corporate risk* is important because it influences the firm's ability to use low-cost debt, to maintain smooth operations over time, and to avoid crises that might consume management's energy and disrupt employees, customers, suppliers, and the community.

- *Sensitivity analysis* is a technique which shows how much an output variable such as NPV will change in response to a given change in an input variable such as sales, other things held constant.

- *Scenario analysis* is a risk analysis technique in which the best and worst case NPVs are compared with the project's expected NPV.

- *Monte Carlo simulation* is a risk analysis technique in which a computer is used to simulate all probable future events and thus to estimate the profitability distribution and riskiness of a project.

- Projects that require capital outlays in stages over several years are often evaluated using *decision trees.* Sensitivity analysis, scenario analysis, Monte Carlo simulation, and decision trees all measure stand-alone risk.

- The ability to *abandon* a project can increase the project's return and decrease its riskiness.

- The *pure play method* and the *accounting beta method* can be used to estimate betas for large projects or for divisions.

- Either *certainty equivalents* or *risk-adjusted discount rates* can be used to incorporate risk into the decision process. In practice, firms normally use risk-adjusted discount rates.

- The *risk-adjusted discount rate* is that rate which is used to evaluate a particular project. The discount rate is increased for projects which are riskier than the firm's average project, and it is decreased for less risky projects.

- When evaluating *risky cash outflows,* the risk adjustment process is generally reversed, that is, lower rates are used to discount more risky outflows.

- *Capital rationing* occurs when management places a constraint on the size of the firm's capital budget during a particular period.

- The *investment opportunity schedule (IOS)* is a graph of the firm's investment opportunities, listed in descending order of IRR.

- The *marginal cost of capital (MCC) schedule* is a graph of the firm's weighted average cost of capital versus the amount of funds raised.

- The MCC schedule is combined with the IOS schedule, and the intersection defines the firm's *marginal cost of capital.*

This chapter completes our discussion of capital budgeting decisions. In the next chapter, we begin our discussion of capital structure decisions.

Questions

11-1   Define each of the following terms:
    a.   Stand-alone risk; within-firm (corporate) risk; market risk
    b.   Sensitivity analysis
    c.   Simulation analysis
    d.   Scenario analysis
    e.   Decision tree analysis
    f.   Coefficient of variation versus standard deviation
    g.   Project beta versus corporate beta
    h.   Accounting beta versus stock market beta
    i.   Pure play method of estimating divisional betas
    j.   Corporate diversification versus stockholder diversification
    k.   Certainty equivalent
    l.   Risk-adjusted discount rate; project cost of capital
    m. IOS schedule; MCC schedule; marginal cost of capital

11-2   Differentiate between (a) simulation analysis, (b) optimistic-pessimistic-most likely analysis, and (c) sensitivity analysis. If AT&T were considering two investments, one calling for the expenditure of $100 million to develop a satellite communications system and the other involving the expenditure of $5,000 for a new truck, on which one would the company be more likely to use simulation?

11-3   Distinguish between market risk, within-firm (or corporate) risk, and stand-alone risk for a project being considered for inclusion in the capital budget. Which type do you feel should be given the greatest weight in capital budgeting decisions?

11-4   Suppose Lima Locomotive Company, which has a high beta and also a great deal of total risk, merged with Homestake Mining, which has a low beta but relatively high total risk. What would the merger do to the cost of capital in the consolidated company's locomotive division and its gold mining division?

11-5   Suppose a firm estimates its MCC and IOS schedules for the coming year and finds that they intersect at the point 10 percent, $10 million. What cost of capital should be used to evaluate average-risk projects, high-risk projects, and low-risk projects?

11-6   The MCC and IOS schedules can be thought of as "bands" rather than as lines to show that they are not known with certainty but, rather, are merely estimates of the true MCC and IOS schedules.
    a.   Do you think that the bands would be wider for the MCC or for the IOS schedule? In answering this question, visualize each point on the MCC and IOS schedules as being the expected value of a probability distribution.

b. For the IOS schedule, would the band, or confidence interval, associated with each project be identical? If not, what would this imply, and how might it affect the firm's capital budgeting analysis?

Self-Test Problems (Solutions Appear in Appendix D)

ST-1 **(Corporate risk analysis)** The staff of Porter Manufacturing has estimated the following net cash flows and probabilities for a new manufacturing process:

	Net Cash Flow		
Year	P = 0.2	P = 0.6	P = 0.2
0	($100,000)	($100,000)	($100,000)
1	20,000	30,000	40,000
2	20,000	30,000	40,000
3	20,000	30,000	40,000
4	20,000	30,000	40,000
5	20,000	30,000	40,000
5*	0	20,000	30,000

Line 0 is the cost of the process, Lines 1-5 are operating cash flows, and Line 5* contains the estimated salvage values. The firm's marginal cost of capital (MCC) for an average-risk project is 10 percent.

a. Assume that the project has average risk. Find the project's base case NPV. (Hint: Use expected values for the net cash flow in each year.)

b. Find the best case and worst case NPVs. What is the probability of occurrence of the worst case if the cash flows are perfectly dependent (perfectly positively correlated) over time? If they are independent over time?

c. Assume that all the cash flows are perfectly positively correlated; that is, there are only three possible cash flow streams over time: (1) the worst case, (2) the most likely case, and (3) the best case, with probabilities of 0.2, 0.6, and 0.2, respectively. These cases are represented by each of the columns in the table. Find the expected NPV, its standard deviation, and its coefficient of variation.

d. The coefficient of variation of the firm's average project is in the range 0.8 to 1.0. If the coefficient of variation of a project being evaluated is greater than 1.0, 2 percentage points are added to the firm's MCC. Similarly, if the coefficient of variation is less than 0.8, 1 percentage point is deducted from the MCC. What is the project's cost of capital? Should the firm accept or reject the project?

ST-2 **(Optimal capital budget)** Wolfe Enterprises has the following capital structure, which it considers to be optimal under the present and forecasted conditions:

Debt	30%
Common equity	70
Total capital	100%

For the coming year, management expects to realize net earnings of $56,000, plus $35,000 in depreciation cash flow. The past dividend policy of paying out 50 percent of earnings will continue. Present commitments from its banker will allow the firm to borrow at a rate of 8 percent.

The company's federal-plus-state tax rate is 40 percent; the current market price of its stock is $50 per share; its *last* dividend was $1.85 per share; and its expected constant growth rate is 8 percent. External equity (new common) can be sold at a flotation cost of 15 percent.

The firm has the following investment opportunities for the next period:

Project	Cost	IRR
A	$50,000	12%
B	15,000	11
C	20,000	10
D	50,000	9

Management asks you to help them determine what projects (if any) should be undertaken. You proceed with this analysis by following these steps:

a.   Calculate the WACC using both retained earnings and new common stock.
b.   Graph the IOS and MCC schedules.
c.   Which projects should the firm accept?
d.   What implicit assumptions about project risk are embodied in this problem? If you learned that Projects A and B were of above-average risk, yet the firm chose the projects which you indicated in Part c, how would this affect the situation?
e.   The problem stated that the firm pays out 50 percent of its earnings as dividends. How would the analysis change if the payout ratio were changed to 0 percent? To 100 percent?

Problems

11-1   **(Risky cash outflows)** Northeast Utilities is deciding if it should build an oil or a coal generating plant. Its MCC is 8 percent for low-risk projects, 10 percent for projects of average risk, and 12 percent for high-risk projects. Management believes that an oil plant is of average risk, but that a coal plant is of high risk due to the problem of acid rain. The cash *outflows* required to construct each plant are listed here. The revenues, fuel costs, and other operating costs are expected to be the same under both plans:

	Construction Costs (Thousands of Dollars)	
Year	Coal Plant	Oil Plant
0	($ 100)	($ 400)
1	(500)	(1,000)
2	(1,500)	(1,000)
3	(1,500)	(1,000)
4	(1,500)	(1,500)
5	(1,000)	(1,000)
6	(500)	(200)

Which type of plant should be constructed?

11-2   **(Sequential decisions)** The Haugen Yacht Company (HYC), a prominent sailboat builder in Florida, may design a new 30-foot sailboat based on the "winged" keels first introduced on the 12-meter yachts that raced for the America's Cup.

First, HYC would have to invest $10,000 at t = 0 for the design and model tank testing of the new boat. HYC's managers believe that there is a 60 percent probability that this phase will be successful and the project will continue. If Stage 1 is not successful, the project will be abandoned with zero salvage value.

The next stage, if undertaken, would consist of making the molds and producing two prototype boats. This would cost $500,000 at t = 1. If the boats test well, HYC would go into production. If they do not, the molds and prototypes could be sold for $100,000. The managers estimate that the probability is 80 percent that the boats will pass testing, and that Stage 3 will be undertaken.

Stage 3 consists of converting an unused production line to produce the new design. This would cost $1,000,000 at t = 2. If the economy is strong at this point, the net value of sales would be $3,000,000, while if the economy is weak, the net value would be $1,500,000. Both net values occur at t = 3, and each state of the economy has a probability of 0.5. HYC's marginal cost of capital is 12 percent.

a.   Assume that this project has average risk. Construct a decision tree and determine the project's expected NPV.

b.   Find the project's standard deviation of NPV and coefficient of variation (CV) of NPV. If HYC's average project had a CV of between 1.0 and 2.0, would this project be of high, low, or average stand-alone risk?

11-3   **(Divisional market risk adjustments)** SureGrip Rubber Company has two divisions: (1) the tire division, which manufactures tires for new autos; and (2) the recap division, which manufactures recapping materials that are sold to independent tire recapping shops throughout the United States. Since auto manufacturing fluctuates with the general economy, the tire division's earnings contribution to SureGrip's stock price is highly correlated with returns on most other stocks. If the tire division were operated as a separate company, its beta coefficient would be about 1.60. The sales and profits of the recap division, on the other hand, tend to be countercyclical, since recap sales boom when people cannot afford to buy new tires. The recap division's beta is estimated to be 0.40. Approximately 75 percent of SureGrip's corporate assets are invested in the tire division and 25 percent are in the recap division.

Currently, the rate of interest on Treasury bonds is 10 percent, and the expected rate of return on an average share of stock is 15 percent. SureGrip uses only common equity capital, hence it has no debt outstanding.

a.   What is the required rate of return on SureGrip's stock?

b.   What discount rate should be used to evaluate capital budgeting projects? Explain your answer fully, and in the process, illustrate your answer with a project which costs $100,000, has a 10-year life, and provides expected after-tax net cash flows of $20,000 per year.

11-4   **(Scenario and sensitivity analysis)** Your firm, Agrico, is considering the purchase of a tractor which will have a net cost of $30,000, will increase pre-tax operating cash flows exclusive of depreciation effects by $10,000 per year, and will be depreciated on a straight line basis to zero over 5 years at the rate of $6,000 per year, beginning the first year. (Annual cash flows will be $10,000, reduced by taxes, plus the tax savings that result from $6,000 of depreciation.) The board of directors, however, is having a heated debate as to whether the tractor will actually last 5 years. Specifically, Charles Cornwell insists that he knows of some that have lasted only 4 years. Jim Adams agrees with Cornwell, but he argues that most tractors do give 5 years of service. Jane Wright, on the other hand, says she has seen some last as long as 8 years.

a.   Given this discussion, the board asks you to prepare a scenario analysis to ascertain the importance of the uncertainty about the tractor's life. Assume a 40 percent marginal federal-plus-state tax rate, a zero salvage value, and a marginal cost of capital of 10 percent. (Hint: The MACRS alternate straight-line depreciation is based on the class life of the tractor and is not affected by the actual life. Also, ignore the half-year convention for this problem.)

(Do Parts b and c only if you are using the computerized diskette.)

b.   The board would also like to know how changes in the cost of capital affect the analysis. Assume that the machine's life is 5 years, and analyze the effects of a change in the cost of capital to 8 percent or to 12 percent. Is the project very sensitive to changes in the cost of capital?

c. The board would like to determine the sensitivity of the project's NPV to changes in certain variables. First, they would like to examine the effect of changes in pre-tax operating revenues upon NPV. Calculate the project's NPV at plus 10, 20, and 30 percent of the estimated $10,000 pre-tax revenues, as well as minus 10, 20, and 30 percent of this figure. (Hold all other variables constant.) Second, calculate the effect upon NPV of various project lives. (Hint: Hold all other variables constant, and try lives ranging from 1 to 10 years.) Finally, examine NPV while changing the cost of capital. (Once again, hold all other variables constant at their original levels.) Plot a separate sensitivity diagram for each variable examined.

11-5 **(Simulation)** Hettenhouse Supplies Corporation (HSC) manufactures medical products for hospitals, clinics, and nursing homes. HSC may introduce a new type of X-ray scanner designed to identify certain types of cancers in their early stages. There are a number of uncertainties about the proposed project, but the following data are believed to be reasonably accurate.

	Probability	Value	Random Numbers
Developmental costs	0.3	$2,000,000	00–29
	0.4	4,000,000	30–69
	0.3	6,000,000	70–99
Project life	0.2	3 years	00–19
	0.6	8 years	20–79
	0.2	13 years	80–99
Sales in units	0.2	100	00–19
	0.6	200	20–79
	0.2	300	80–99
Sales price	0.1	$13,000	00–09
	0.8	13,500	10–89
	0.1	14,000	90–99
Cost per unit (excluding developmental costs)	0.3	$5,000	00–29
	0.4	6,000	30–69
	0.3	7,000	70–99

HSC uses a cost of capital of 15 percent to analyze average-risk projects, 12 percent for low-risk projects, and 18 percent for high-risk projects. These risk adjustments reflect primarily the uncertainty about each project's NPV and IRR as measured by the coefficients of variation of NPV and IRR. HSC is in the 40 percent federal-plus-state income tax bracket.

a. What is the expected IRR for the X-ray scanner project? Base your answer on the expected values of the variables. Also, assume the after-tax "profits" figure you develop is equal to annual cash flows. All facilities are leased, so depreciation may be disregarded. Can you determine the value of σ_{IRR} short of actual simulation or a fairly complex statistical analysis?

b. Assume that HSC uses a 15 percent cost of capital for this project. What is the project's NPV? Could you estimate σ_{NPV} without either simulation or a complex statistical analysis?

c. Show the process by which a computer would perform a simulation analysis for this project. Use the random numbers 44, 17, 16, 58, 1; 79, 83, 86; and 19, 62, 6 to illustrate the process with the first computer run. Actually calculate the first-run NPV and IRR. Assume that the cash flows for each year are independent of cash flows for other years. Also, assume that the computer operates as follows: (1) A developmental cost and a project life are estimated for the first run. (2) Next, sales volume, sales price, and cost per unit are estimated and used to derive a cash flow for the first year. (3) Then, the next three random numbers are used to estimate sales volume, sales price, and cost per unit for the second year, hence the cash flow for the second year. (4) Cash flows for other years are developed similarly, on out to the first run's estimated life. (5) With the developmental cost and the cash flow stream established, NPV and IRR for the first run are derived and stored in the computer's memory. (6) The process is repeated to generate perhaps 500 other NPVs and IRRs. (7) Frequency distributions for NPV and IRR are plotted by the computer, and the distributions' means and standard deviations are calculated.

d. Does it seem a little strange to conduct a risk analysis such as the one here *after* having already established a cost of capital for use in the analysis? What might be done to improve this situation?

e. In this problem, we assumed that the probability distributions were all independent of one another. It would have been possible to use conditional probabilities where, for example, the probability distribution for cost per unit would vary from trial to trial, depending on the unit sales for the trial. Also, it would be possible to construct a simulation model such that the sales distribution in Year t would depend on the sales level attained in Year t − 1. Had these modifications been made in this problem, do you think the standard deviation of the NPV distribution would have been larger (riskier) or smaller (less risky) than where complete independence is assumed?

f. Name two *major* difficulties not mentioned earlier that occur in the kind of analysis discussed in this problem.

11-6 **(Simple optimal capital budget)** The Shalit Corporation's present capital structure, which is also its target capital structure, calls for 50 percent debt and 50 percent common equity. The firm has only one potential project, an expansion program with a 10.2 percent IRR and a cost of $20 million but which is completely divisible; that is, Shalit can invest any amount up to $20 million. The firm expects to retain $2 million of earnings next year and to generate $2 million in depreciation cash flow. It can raise up to $5 million in new debt at a before-tax cost of 8 percent, and all debt after the first $5 million will have a cost of 10 percent. The cost of retained earnings is 12 percent and the firm can sell any amount of new common stock desired at a constant cost of new equity of 15 percent. The firm's marginal federal-plus-state tax rate is 40 percent. What is the firm's optimal capital budget?

11-7 **(Optimal capital budget)** The management of Finnerty Phosphate Industries (FPI) is planning next year's capital budget. FPI projects its net income at $7,500, and its payout ratio is 40 percent. Depreciation is forecasted at $3,000. The company's earnings and dividends are growing at a constant rate of 5 percent; the last dividend, D_0, was $0.90; and the current stock price is $8.59. FPI's new debt will cost 14 percent. If FPI issues new common stock, flotation costs will be 20 percent. FPI is at its optimal capital structure, which is 40 percent debt and 60 percent equity, and the firm's marginal tax rate is 40 percent. FPI has the following independent, indivisible, and equally risky investment opportunities:

Project	Cost	IRR
A	$15,000	17%
B	20,000	14
C	15,000	16
D	12,000	15

What is FPI's optimal capital budget?

11-8   **(Risk-adjusted optimal capital budget)** Refer to Problem 11-7. Management neglected to incorporate project risk differentials into the analysis. FPI's policy is to add 2 percentage points to the cost of capital of those projects significantly more risky than average and to subtract 2 percentage points from the cost of capital of those which are substantially less risky than average. Management judges Project A to be of high risk, Projects C and D to be of average risk, and Project B to be of low risk. No projects are divisible. What is the optimal capital budget after adjustment for project risk?

Mini Case 1

(Risk analysis) The Chapter 10 Mini Case contains the details of a new-project capital budgeting evaluation being conducted by Joan Samuels at the John Crockett Furniture Company. However, in the initial analysis the riskiness of the project was not considered. The base case, or expected, cash flow estimates as they were estimated in Chapter 10 (in thousands of dollars) are given next. Crockett's overall cost of capital (WACC) is 10.0 percent.

			Year		
	0	1	2	3	4
Investment in:					
Fixed assets	($240)				
Net working capital	(20)				
Unit sales		1,250	1,250	1,250	1,250
Sales price (dollars)		$200	$200	$200	$200
Gross revenue		$250	$250	$250	$250
Cash operating costs (50%)		125	125	125	125
Operating profit		$125	$125	$125	$125
Depreciation		79	108	36	17
EBIT		$ 46	$ 17	$ 89	$108
Taxes (40%)		18	7	36	43
Net operating income		$ 28	$ 10	$ 53	$ 65
Add back depreciation		79	108	36	17
Net operating cash flow		$107	$118	$ 89	$ 82
Salvage value					$ 25
Tax on SV (40%)					(10)
Recovery of NWC					20
Net cash flow	($260)	$107	$118	$ 89	$117

NPV at 10% cost of capital = $82
IRR   = 23.8%
MIRR   = 17.8%

As Joan's assistant, you have been directed to answer the following questions.

a.   What does the term "risk" mean in the context of capital budgeting, to what extent can risk be quantified, and when risk is quantified, is the quantification based primarily on statistical analysis of historical data or on subjective, judgmental estimates?

b.   (1)   What are the three types of risk that are relevant in capital budgeting?
     (2)   How is each of these risk types measured, and how do they relate to one another?
     (3)   How is each type of risk used in the capital budgeting process?
c.   (1)   What is sensitivity analysis?
     (2)   Perform a sensitivity analysis on the unit sales, salvage value, and cost of capital for the project. Assume that each of these variables can vary from its base case, or expected, value by plus and minus 10, 20, and 30 percent. Include a sensitivity diagram, and discuss the results.
     (3)   What is the primary weakness of sensitivity analysis? What is its primary usefulness?
d.   Assume that Joan Samuels is confident of her estimates of all the variables that affect the project's cash flows except unit sales: If product acceptance is poor, unit sales would be only 900 units a year, while a strong consumer response would produce sales of 1,600 units. In either case, cash costs would still amount to 50 percent of revenues. Joan believes that there is a 25 percent chance of poor acceptance, a 25 percent chance of excellent acceptance, and a 50 percent chance of average acceptance (the base case).
     (1)   What is the worst case NPV? The best case NPV?
     (2)   Use the worst, most likely, and best case NPVs and probabilities of occurrence to find the project's expected NPV, standard deviation, and coefficient of variation.
e.   (1)   Assume that Crockett's average project has a coefficient of variation in the range of 0.2–0.4. Would the new furniture line be classified as high risk, average risk, or low risk? What type of risk is being measured here?
     (2)   Based on common sense, how highly correlated do you think that the project would be to the firm's other assets? (Give a correlation coefficient, or range of coefficients, based on your judgment.)
     (3)   How would this correlation coefficient and the previously calculated σ combine to affect the project's contribution to corporate, or within-firm, risk? Explain.
f.   (1)   Based on your judgment, what do you think the project's correlation coefficient would be with the general economy and thus with returns on "the market"?
     (2)   How would this correlation affect the project's market risk?
g.   (1)   Crockett typically adds or subtracts 3 percentage points to the overall cost of capital to adjust for risk. Should the new furniture line be accepted?
     (2)   Are there any subjective risk factors that should be considered before the final decision is made?
h.   Define scenario analysis and simulation analysis, and discuss their principal advantages and disadvantages.
i.   (1)   Crockett's target capital structure is 50 percent debt and 50 percent common equity; its cost of debt is 12 percent; the risk-free rate is 10 percent; the market risk premium is 6 percent; and the firm's tax rate is 40 percent. If Joan's estimate of the new project's beta is 1.2, what is the project's market risk, and what is its cost of capital based on the CAPM?
     (2)   How does the project's market risk compare with the firm's overall market risk?
     (3)   How does the project's market risk compare with its stand-alone risk?
     (4)   Briefly describe two methods that Joan could conceivably have used to estimate the project's market beta. How feasible do you think those procedures would actually be in this case?
     (5)   What are the advantages and disadvantages of focusing on a project's market risk?
j.   As a completely different project, Crockett is also evaluating two different production line systems for its overstuffed furniture line. Plan W requires more workers but less capital, while Plan C requires more capital but fewer workers. Both systems have estimated

3-year lives. Since the production line choice has no impact on revenues, Joan will base her decision on the relative costs of the two systems as set forth next:

	Expected Net Costs	
Year	Plan W	Plan C
0	($500)	($1,000)
1	(500)	(300)
2	(500)	(300)
3	(500)	(300)

(1) Assume initially that the two systems are both of average risk. Which one should be chosen?

(2) Now assume that the worker-intensive plan (W) is judged to be riskier than average, because future wage rates are very difficult to forecast. Under this condition, which system should be chosen?

(3) What is Plan W's IRR?

Mini Case 2

(Optimal capital budget) Ron Redwine, financial manager of Blum Industries, is developing the firm's optimal capital budget for the coming year. He has identified the five potential projects shown below. Projects B and B* are mutually exclusive, while the remainder are independent. Neither B nor B* are essential to the firm's operations, so replication is not mandatory.

Project	Cost	CF_{1-N}	Life (N)	IRR	NPV
A	$400,000	$119,326	5	15%	
B	200,000	56,863	5	13	
B*	200,000	35,397	10	12	
C	100,000	27,057	5	11	
D	300,000	79,139	5	10	

The following information was developed for purposes of determining Blum's weighted average cost of capital (WACC):

Interest rate on new debt	8.0%
Tax rate	40.0%
Debt ratio	60.0%
Current stock price, P_0	$20.00
Last dividend, D_0	$2.00
Expected growth rate, g	6.0%
Flotation cost on common, F	19.0%
Expected addition to retained earnings	$200,000

The firm adjusts for differential project risk by adding or subtracting 2.0 percentage points to the firm's marginal cost of capital.

a. Calculate the WACC, and then plot the company's IOS and MCC schedules. What is the firm's marginal cost of capital for capital budgeting purposes?

b. Assume initially that all five projects are of average risk. What is Blum's optimal capital budget? Explain your answer fully.

c.   Now assume that the retained earnings break point occurred at $900,000 of new capital. What effect would this have on the firm's MCC schedule and its optimal capital budget?

d.   Now suppose it was discovered that the firm has $200,000 of depreciation cash flow that had not been included in the analysis thus far. Discuss how this might affect the firm's MCC schedule and its optimal capital budget.

e.   Now disregard the $200,000 of depreciation cash flow, and return to the situation in Part a, with the $500,000 break point. Suppose Project A is reexamined, and it is judged to be a high-risk project, while Projects C and D are, upon reexamination, judged to have low risk. Projects B and B* remain average-risk projects. How would these changes affect Blum's optimal capital budget?

f.   In reality, companies like Blum have hundreds of projects to evaluate each year, hence it is generally not practical to draw the IOS and MCC schedules which include every potential project. Now suppose this situation exists for Blum. Suppose also that the company has 3 divisions, L, A, and H, with low, average, and high risk, respectively, and that the projects within each division can also be grouped into three risk categories. Describe how Blum might go about structuring its capital budgeting decision process and choosing its optimal set of projects. For this purpose, assume that Blum's overall WACC is estimated to be 11.0 percent. As part of your answer, find appropriate divisional and project hurdle rates when differential risk is considered.

Selected Additional References and Cases

The literature on risk analysis in capital budgeting is vast; here is a small but useful selection of additional references that bear directly on the topics covered in this chapter:

Ang, James S., and Wilbur G. Lewellen, "Risk Adjustment in Capital Investment Project Evaluations," *Financial Management,* Summer 1982, 5–14.

Bower, Richard S., and Jeffrey M. Jenks, "Divisional Screening Rates," *Financial Management,* Autumn 1975, 42–49.

Butler, J. S., and Barry Schachter, "The Investment Decision: Estimation Risk and Risk Adjusted Discount Rates," *Financial Management,* Winter 1989, 13–22.

Fama, Eugene F., "Risk-Adjusted Discount Rates and Capital Budgeting under Uncertainty," *Journal of Financial Economics,* August 1977, 3–24.

Findlay, M. Chapman, III, Arthur E. Gooding, and Wallace Q. Weaver, Jr., "On the Relevant Risk for Determining Capital Expenditure Hurdle Rates," *Financial Management,* Winter 1976, 9–16.

Gehr, Adam K., Jr., "Risk-Adjusted Capital Budgeting Using Arbitrage," *Financial Management,* Winter 1981, 14–19.

Gup, Benton E., and S. W. Norwood III, "Divisional Cost of Capital: A Practical Approach," *Financial Management,* Spring 1982, 20–24.

Lessard, Donald R., and Richard S. Bower, "An Operational Approach to Risk Screening," *Journal of Finance,* May 1973, 321–338.

Myers, Stewart C., and Samuel M. Turnbull, "Capital Budgeting and the Capital Asset Pricing Model: Good News and Bad News," *Journal of Finance,* May 1977, 321–333.

Robichek, Alexander A., "Interpreting the Results of Risk Analysis," *Journal of Finance,* December 1975, 1384–1386.

Sick, Gordon A., "A Certainty-Equivalent Approach to Capital Budgeting," *Financial Management,* Winter 1986, 23–32.

Weaver, Samuel C., Peter J. Clemmens III, Jack A. Gunn, and Bruce D. Danneburg, "Divisional Hurdle Rates and the Cost of Capital," *Financial Management*, Spring 1989, 18–25.

Yagil, Joseph, "Divisional Beta Estimation under the Old and New Tax Laws," *Financial Management,* Winter 1987, 16–21.

The Brigham-Gapenski casebook contains the following cases which focus on capital budgeting under uncertainty:

Case 14, "McReath Corporation (B)" and Case 16, "Adams Wineries, Inc. (B)," which illustrate project risk analysis.

Case 17, "Analog Equipment Company," which focuses on sequential investments and decision trees.

Case 19, "Worldwide Petroleum, Inc., " which illustrates multinational risk analysis.

The Harrington casebook contains the following applicable cases:

"Interchemical Consumer Products Division," which focuses on simulation analysis.

"Alaska Interstate," which illustrates a variety of ways to measure the riskiness of a conglomerate's subsidiaries.

"The Jacobs Division," which focuses on the riskiness of mutually exclusive alternatives.

APPENDIX 11A

Capital Rationing

As we discussed in Chapter 11, under ordinary circumstances a firm should expand to the point where its marginal return is just equal to its marginal cost. A simplified view of the concept is shown in Figure 11A-1. Here we assume that the firm has five equally risky and independent investment opportunities which would cost a total of $23 million. Its cost of capital is assumed to be constant at 10 percent, implying that the firm can raise all the money it wants at a cost of 10 percent. Under these conditions, the firm would accept Projects V, W, and X, since they all have IRRs greater than the cost of capital, hence NPVs greater than zero. It would reject Y and Z because they have IRRs less than k, indicating negative NPVs. This decision would maximize the value of the firm and the wealth of its stockholders.

Firms ordinarily operate in the manner depicted in the graph—they accept all independent projects having positive NPVs, reject those with negative NPVs, and choose between mutually exclusive investments on the basis of the higher NPV. However, some firms set an absolute limit on the size of their capital budgets such that the size of the budget is less than the level of investment called for by the NPV (or IRR) criterion. This is called *capital rationing,* and it is the topic of this appendix.

Reasons for Capital Rationing

The principal reason for capital rationing is that some firms are reluctant to engage in external financing (either borrowing or selling stock). One management, recalling the plight of firms with substantial amounts of debt during recent credit crunches, may simply refuse to use

Figure 11A-1 The Typical Capital Budgeting Situation

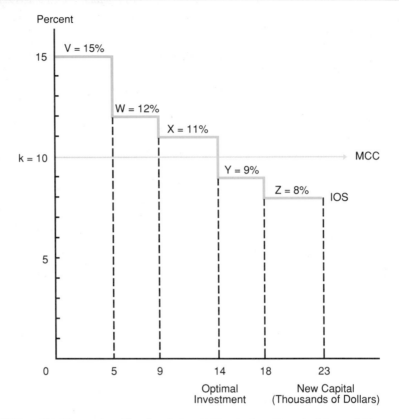

Note: If IRR > 10%, NPV is positive. Therefore, Projects V, W, and X have NPV > 0, while Y and Z have NPV < 0.

debt. Another management, which has no objection to selling debt, may not want to sell equity capital for fear of losing some measure of voting control. Still others may refuse to use any form of outside financing, considering safety and control to be more important than additional profits. These are all cases of capital rationing, and they result in limiting the rate of expansion to a slower pace than would be dictated by "purely rational wealth-maximizing behavior."

We should make three points here. First, a decision to hold back on expansion is not necessarily irrational. If the owners/managers of a privately held firm have what they consider to be plenty of income and wealth, then it might be quite rational for them to "trim their sails," relax, and concentrate on enjoying what they have already earned rather than on earning still more. Such behavior would not, however, be appropriate for a publicly owned firm.

Second, it is not correct to interpret as capital rationing a situation where the firm is willing to sell additional securities at the going market price but finds that it cannot because the market simply will not absorb more of its issues. Rather, such a situation indicates that the weighted average cost of capital is rising. If more acceptable investments are indicated than can be financed, then the marginal cost of capital being used is too low and should be raised.

Third, firms sometimes set a limit on capital expenditures, not because of a shortage of funds, but because of limitations on other resources, especially managerial talent. A firm might, for example, feel that its personnel development program is sufficient to handle an expansion of no more than 10 percent a year, and then set a limit on the capital budget to insure that expansion is held to that rate. This is not capital rationing — rather, it involves a downward reevaluation of project returns if growth exceeds some limit; that is, expected rates of return are, after some point, a decreasing function of the level of expenditures.

Project Selection under Capital Rationing

How should projects be selected under conditions of true capital rationing? First, note that if a firm truly rations capital, its value is not being maximized: If management were maximizing, then they would move to the point where the marginal project's NPV was zero, and capital rationing as defined would not exist. So, if a firm uses capital rationing, it has ruled out value maximization. The firm may, however, want to maximize value *subject to the constraint that the capital ceiling not be exceeded.* Constrained maximization behavior will, in general, result in a lower value than following unconstrained maximization, but some type of constrained maximization may produce reasonably satisfactory results. *Linear programming* is one method of constrained maximization that has been applied to capital rationing. Much work has been done in this area, and linear programming may, in the future, be widely applied in capital budgeting.[1]

If the firm does face capital rationing, and if the constraint cannot be lifted, what can the financial manager do? The objective should be to select projects, subject to the capital rationing constraint, such that the sum of the projects' NPVs is maximized. Linear programming can be used, or if there are not too many projects involved, the financial manager can simply enumerate all the sets of projects that meet the budget constraint and then select the set with the largest total NPV.

The complexities involved in a capital rationing situation are indicated in Table 11A-1. Here we assume that the firm is considering a total of eight potential projects; all are independent and have average risk. The firm has a 10 percent cost of capital, but management has decided to limit capital expenditures during the year to the amount of money that can be generated internally, $500,000. In the table, the projects are listed in the descending order of their NPVs, but their IRRs and profitability indices (PIs) are also shown.

If it is to maximize the value of the firm, management must choose the set of projects with the greatest total NPV, subject to the constraint that total expenditures must not exceed

---

[1]For further information on mathematical programming solutions to capital rationing, and for a review and analysis of the literature on this issue, see H. Martin Weingarten, "Capital Rationing: n Authors in Search of a Plot," *Journal of Finance,* December 1977, 1403–1431; and Stephen P. Bradley and Sherwood C. Frey, Jr., "Equivalent Mathematical Programming Models of Pure Capital Rationing," *Journal of Financial and Quantitative Analysis,* June 1978, 345–361.

Table 11A-1	Illustration of Capital Rationing					
Project Number	Project Cost, or Outlay, at t = 0	Project Life (Years)	Cash Flow per Year	NPV at the 10% Cost of Capital	IRR	Profitability Index
1	$400,000	20	$58,600	$98,894	13.5%	1.25
2	250,000	10	55,000	87,951	17.7	1.35
3	100,000	8	24,000	28,038	17.3	1.28
4	75,000	15	12,000	16,273	13.7	1.22
5	75,000	6	18,000	3,395	11.5	1.05
6	50,000	5	14,000	3,071	12.4	1.06
7	250,000	10	41,000	1,927	10.2	1.01
8	250,000	3	99,000	(3,802)	9.1	0.98

$500,000. With only eight projects in total, we can try all different combinations and, by "brute force," determine the set which maximizes NPV. This set is optimal:[2]

Project	Cost	NPV
2	$250,000	$87,951
3	100,000	28,038
4	75,000	16,273
5	75,000	3,395
	$500,000	$135,657

This analysis seems simple enough, but there are three factors which complicate it greatly in realistic situations:

1. **Number of projects.** In the example, we have only eight projects, so it is easy to simply list all the combinations whose costs do not exceed $500,000 and then see which combination provides the greatest total NPV. For a large firm with thousands of projects, this would be a tedious process, although computer programs are available to solve such problems. However, the other problems listed next are more serious.

2. **Project risk.** In our example, we assumed that the eight projects are equally risky, hence have the same cost of capital. If this was not the case, and if the number of projects was so large as to preclude hand analysis, then it would be difficult, if not impossible, to reach an optimal solution, because the computer programs currently available cannot deal efficiently with projects having differential risks.

3. **Multiple time constraints.** Our example also assumed a single-time-period capital constraint. Yet, realistically, when capital rationing is practiced, the constraints usually extend for several years. However, the funds available in future years depend on cash throw-offs from investments made in earlier years. Thus, the constraint in Year 2 depends on the invest-

---

[2]Note that in capital rationing the goal in project selection is to get the "biggest bang for the buck." Since this is measured by the profitability index (PI), one way to determine the optimal set is by accepting projects in descending order of PIs, but recognizing that some high-PI projects might have to be rejected because insufficient funds are available.

ments made in Year 1, and so on. For example, we might have investment funds of $500,000 per year available from external sources for 1991 through 1995 plus the cash flows from investments made in previous years. To solve this type of multiperiod problem, we need information on both investment opportunities and funds availability in future years, and not just on the situation in the current year. Also, the NPV we seek to maximize is the sum of the present values of the NPVs in each year over the time horizon being analyzed, say 1991 to 1995. In such a situation, we might even choose Project 8 in Table 11A-1, in spite of its negative NPV, because it has rapid cash throw-offs. In fact, if excellent investment opportunities are expected to be available in 1992, 1993, and 1994, taking Project 8 might be part of the best long-run strategy.

A Better Approach to Capital Rationing

Our main conclusion thus far about capital rationing—which means deliberately foregoing projects with positive NPVs—is that practicing it is irrational for any firm which seeks to maximize its stockholders' wealth. Also, while mathematical programming methods are available to help solve the simpler cases of capital rationing so that management can make the best of a bad situation, programming methods are really not capable of dealing with all the complexities encountered in the real world.

Fortunately, there is a better method for handling the types of situations that give rise to capital rationing. Usually, capital rationing occurs when the firm believes that it will encounter severe problems if it attempts to raise capital beyond some specified amount. For example, the interest rate it would have to pay would rise sharply if it attempted to increase its existing lines of credit. Such situations can be rationally handled by increasing the firm's WACC as the amount of capital raised increases. In effect, in terms of Figure 11A-1, the MCC schedule would begin to rise beyond some amount of capital, resulting in a higher MCC, and this higher MCC should be used as the discount rate when determining a project's NPV.

PART IV

Capital Structure and Dividend Policy

CHAPTER 12

Capital Structure Theory

A June 18, 1990, *Fortune* article called "Hard Lessons from the Debt Decade" reported that the debt ratio of the average U.S. nonfinancial company had risen from 34 percent in 1980 to 48 percent in 1990. Also, it is not uncommon for debt ratios to rise to 90 percent in leveraged buyouts. When questioned about this trend, a number of respected business and academic leaders concluded that corporations are using too much debt. For example, Henry Kaufman, a well-known Wall Street worrier whose nickname is "Dr. Gloom," argued that debt levels are so high that an otherwise minor economic setback could turn into a major recession. However, John Paulus, Morgan Stanley's chief economist, countered that debt is the cheapest source of capital, that Japanese and German firms use far more debt than U.S. companies, and that if U.S. firms are to compete effectively in global markets, they should use even more debt. Still others questioned *Fortune*'s basic data. Robert Taggart, a finance professor at Boston College, argued that accounting data like those *Fortune* used provide limited information about a firm's true debt usage, and that market value debt ratios are the only measures that make sense.

Fortune also noted that, while the median rating of companies followed by Standard & Poor's, a leading bond rating agency, was A in 1980, it had dropped to BB, which is "junk" level, by 1990. However, *Fortune* also noted that in 1980 most smaller, riskier companies were simply unable to obtain capital in the public bond markets, hence they did not have rated debt, whereas by 1990 the development of the junk bond market has made public capital available to such companies, so the sample companies tracked by Standard & Poor's have changed over time.

ONE of the most perplexing issues facing financial managers is the relationship between capital structure and stock price. How much debt financing, as opposed to equity financing, should a firm use? Should different industries, and different firms within industries, have different capital structures, and, if so, what are the factors that lead to these differences? We will devote two chapters to these issues. First, in this chapter, we lay the theoretical groundwork by providing a framework for thinking about capital structure issues. Then, in Chapter 13, we discuss the various approaches that financial managers use when they establish target capital structures.

Our study of capital structure theory leads to the following conclusions: (1) There does exist an optimal capital structure, or at least an optimal range of structures, for every firm. (2) However, financial theory is not powerful enough at this point to enable us to locate a firm's optimal structure with precision. (3) The optimal capital structure is not set in isolation; rather, it depends on a set of factors which include the firm's dividend policy, its capital investment opportunities, and investors' preferences for different types of securities at each point in time. (4) Small deviations from the optimal capital structure do not have a significant influence on a firm's value, hence managers are generally willing to depart temporarily from the target capital structure in response to fluctuations in operating and/or capital market conditions.

Although capital structure theory does not provide a complete answer to the question of optimal capital structure, it does provide many insights into the value of debt financing versus equity financing. Thus, an understanding of capital structure theory will aid a manager in establishing his or her firm's target capital structure.

THE MODIGLIANI-MILLER MODELS

Until 1958, capital structure theories were little more than loose assertions about investor behavior rather than carefully constructed models which could be tested by formal statistical studies. In what has been called the most influential set of financial papers ever published, Franco Modigliani and Merton Miller (MM) addressed the capital structure issue in a rigorous, scientific fashion, and they set off a chain of research that continues to this day.[1]

Assumptions

To begin, MM made the following assumptions, some of which were later relaxed:

1. Firms' business risk can be measured by σ_{EBIT}, and firms with the same degree of business risk are said to be in a *homogeneous risk class.*

---

[1]See Franco Modigliani and Merton H. Miller, "The Cost of Capital, Corporation Finance and the Theory of Investment," *American Economic Review,* June 1958, 261–297; "The Cost of Capital, Corporation Finance and the Theory of Investment: Reply," *American Economic Review,* September 1958, 655–669; "Taxes and the Cost of Capital: A Correction," *American Economic Review,* June 1963, 433–443; and "Reply," *American Economic Review,* June 1965, 524–527. In a 1979 survey of Financial Management Association members, the original MM article was judged to have had the greatest impact on the field of finance of any work ever published. See Philip L. Cooley and J. Louis Heck, "Significant Contributions to Finance Literature," *Financial Management,* Tenth Anniversary Issue 1981, 23–33.

2. All present and prospective investors have identical estimates of each firm's future EBIT; that is, investors have *homogeneous expectations* about expected future corporate earnings and the riskiness of those earnings. This assumption is comparable to our use of the "marginal investor" in earlier chapters when we discussed the DCF model and market equilibrium ($\hat{k}_s = k_s$).

3. Stocks and bonds are traded in *perfect capital markets*. This assumption implies, among other things, (a) that there are no brokerage costs and (b) that investors (both individuals and institutions) can borrow at the same rate as corporations.

4. The debt of firms and individuals is riskless, so the interest rate on debt is the risk-free rate. Further, this situation holds regardless of how much debt a firm (or an individual) uses.

5. All cash flows are perpetuities; that is, the firm is a zero-growth firm with an "expectationally constant" EBIT, and its bonds are perpetuities. "Expectationally constant" means that investors expect EBIT to be constant, but, after the fact, the realized level could be different from the expected level.

MM without Taxes

MM first performed their analysis under the assumption that there are no corporate or personal income taxes. On the basis of the preceding assumptions, and in the absence of corporate taxes, MM stated and algebraically proved two propositions:[2]

Proposition I. The value of any firm is established by capitalizing its expected net operating income (EBIT when T = 0) at a constant rate which is appropriate for the firm's risk class:

$$V_L = V_U = \frac{\text{EBIT}}{\text{WACC}} = \frac{\text{EBIT}}{k_{sU}}. \tag{12-1}$$

Here the subscripts L and U designate levered (a firm that uses debt financing) and unlevered (a firm that uses no debt financing) firms in a given risk class, and the constant rate, k_{sU} = WACC, is the required rate of return for an unlevered, or all-equity, firm.

Since V as established by the Proposition I equation is a constant, *then under the MM model, when there are no taxes, the value of the firm is independent of its leverage.* This also implies (1) that the weighted average cost of capital to any firm, leveraged or not, is completely independent of its capital structure, and (2) that the WACC for all firms in a risk class is equal to the cost of equity to an unlevered firm in that same risk class.

Proposition II. The cost of equity to a levered firm, k_{sL}, is equal to (1) the cost of equity to an unlevered firm in the same risk class, k_{sU}, plus (2) a risk premium whose size depends on both the differential between the costs of equity and debt to an unlevered firm and the amount of leverage used:

$$k_{sL} = k_{sU} + \text{Risk premium} = k_{sU} + (k_{sU} - k_d)(D/S). \tag{12-2}$$

---

[2]MM actually stated three propositions, but the third one is not material to our discussion here.

Here D = market value of the firm's debt, S = market value of the firm's equity, and k_d = constant cost of debt. *Proposition II states that as the firm's use of debt increases, its cost of equity also rises, and in a mathematically precise manner.*

Taken together, the two MM propositions imply that the inclusion of more debt in the capital structure will not increase the value of the firm, because the benefits of cheaper debt will be exactly offset by an increase in the riskiness, hence in the cost, of equity. *Thus, the MM theory implies that in a world without taxes, both the value of a firm and its overall cost of capital are unaffected by its capital structure.*

MM's Arbitrage Proof

MM used an *arbitrage proof* to support their propositions.[3] They showed that, under their assumptions, if two companies differed only (1) in the way they are financed and (2) in their total market values, then investors would sell shares of the higher valued firm, buy those of the lower valued firm, and continue this process until the companies had exactly the same market value. To illustrate, assume that two firms, Firm L (for levered) and Firm U (for unlevered), are identical in all important respects except financial structure. Firm L has $4,000,000 of 7.5 percent debt, while Firm U uses only equity. Both firms have EBIT = $900,000, and σ_{EBIT} is the same for both firms, so they are in the same risk class.

MM assumed that all firms are in a zero-growth situation; that is, EBIT is expected to remain constant, and all earnings are paid out as dividends. Under this assumption, the total market value of a firm's common stock, S, is a perpetuity whose value is found as follows:

$$S = \frac{Dividends}{k_s} = \frac{Net\ income}{k_s} = \frac{(EBIT - k_dD)(1 - T)}{k_s}. \qquad (12\text{-}3)$$

Equation 12-3 is merely the value of a perpetuity, with the numerator being the net income available to common stockholders, which is all paid out as dividends, while the denominator is the cost of common equity. In MM's zero-tax world, the tax rate, T, is zero; thus, Equation 12-3 becomes simply $(EBIT - k_dD)/k_s$.

In the initial situation, before any arbitrage occurs, assume that both firms have the same equity capitalization rate: $k_{sU} = k_{sL} = 10\%$. Under this condition, according to Equation 12-3, the following situation would exist:

Firm U:

$$\begin{matrix} \text{Value of} \\ \text{Firm U's} \\ \text{stock} \end{matrix} = S_U = \frac{EBIT - k_dD}{k_{sU}} = \frac{\$900,000 - \$0}{0.10} = \$9,000,000.$$

$$\begin{matrix} \text{Total market} \\ \text{value of} \\ \text{Firm U} \end{matrix} = V_U = D_U + S_U = \$0 + \$9,000,000 = \$9,000,000.$$

---

[3]By *arbitrage* we mean the simultaneous buying and selling of essentially identical assets at different prices. The buying increases the price of the undervalued asset, and the selling decreases the price of the overvalued asset. Arbitrage operations will continue until prices have been adjusted to the point where the arbitrageur can no longer earn a profit. At this point, the markets are in equilibrium.

Firm L:

$$\text{Value of Firm L's stock} = S_L = \frac{\text{EBIT} - k_d D}{k_{sL}}$$

$$= \frac{\$900,000 - 0.075(\$4,000,000)}{0.10} = \$6,000,000.$$

$$\text{Total market value of Firm L} = V_L = D_L + S_L = \$4,000,000 + \$6,000,000 = \$10,000,000.$$

Thus, before arbitrage, and assuming that $k_{sU} = k_{sL}$, the value of the levered Firm L exceeds that of unlevered Firm U.

MM argued that this is a disequilibrium situation which cannot persist. To see why, suppose you owned 10 percent of L's stock, so the market value of your investment was $0.10(\$6,000,000) = \$600,000$. According to MM, you could increase your total investment income without increasing your exposure to risk. For example, suppose you (1) sold your stock in L for $600,000, (2) borrowed an amount equal to 10 percent of L's debt ($400,000), and then (3) bought 10 percent of U's stock for $900,000. Notice that you would receive $1 million from the sale of your 10 percent of L's stock plus your borrowing, and you would be spending only $900,000 on U's stock, so you would have an extra $100,000, which MM assumed you would invest in riskless debt to yield 7.5 percent, or $7,500 annually.

Now consider your income positions:

Old Income:	10% of L's $600,000 equity income		<u>$60,000</u>
New Income:	10% of U's $900,000 equity income	$90,000	
	Less 7.5% interest on $400,000 loan	(30,000)	$60,000
	Plus 7.5% interest on extra $100,000		7,500
	Total new investment income		<u>$67,500</u>

Thus, your net investment income from common stock would be exactly the same as before, $60,000, but you would have $100,000 left over for investment in riskless debt, which would increase your income by $7,500. Therefore, the total return on your $600,000 net worth would rise to $67,500. Further, your risk, according to MM, would be the same as before; you would have simply substituted $400,000 of "home-made" leverage for your 10 percent share of Firm L's $4 million of corporate leverage, hence neither your "effective" debt nor your risk would have changed. Thus, you would have increased your income without raising your risk, which is obviously a desirable thing to do.

MM argued that this arbitrage process would actually occur, with sales of L's stock driving its price down, and purchases of U's stock driving its price up, until the market values of the two firms were equal. Until this equality was established, gains could be obtained by switching from one stock to the other, so the profit motive would force the equality to be reached. When equilibrium was established, the values of Firms L and U, and their weighted average costs of capital, would be equal. Thus, according to Modigliani and Miller, both a firm's value and its WACC must be independent of capital structure under equilibrium conditions.

Note that each of the assumptions listed at the beginning of this section is necessary for the arbitrage proof to work. For example, if the companies are not identical in business risk, then the arbitrage process could not be envoked. We will discuss further implications of the assumptions later in the chapter.

MM with Corporate Taxes

MM's original work, published in 1958, assumed zero taxes. In 1963, they published a second article which included corporate tax effects. With corporate income taxes, they concluded that leverage will increase a firm's value, because interest on debt is a tax-deductible expense, hence more of a leveraged firm's operating income flows through to investors. The MM propositions when corporations are subject to income taxes follow.

Proposition I. The value of a levered firm is equal to (1) the value of an unlevered firm in the same risk class plus (2) the gain from leverage, which is the value of the tax savings and which equals the corporate tax rate times the amount of debt the firm uses:

$$V_L = V_U + TD. \tag{12-1a}$$

The important point here is that when corporate taxes are introduced, the value of the levered firm exceeds that of the unlevered firm by the amount TD. Note also that the differential increases as the use of debt increases, so a firm's value is maximized at virtually 100 percent debt financing.

The value of the unlevered firm can be found by using Equation 12-3. With zero debt, then $D = \$0$, and the value of the firm is its equity value. Thus,

$$S = V_U = \frac{EBIT(1 - T)}{k_{sU}}. \tag{12-4}$$

Proposition II. The cost of equity to a levered firm is equal to (1) the cost of equity to an unlevered firm in the same risk class plus (2) a risk premium whose size depends on the differential between the costs of equity and debt to an unlevered firm, the amount of financial leverage used, and the corporate tax rate:

$$k_{sL} = k_{sU} + (k_{sU} - k_d)(1 - T)(D/S). \tag{12-2a}$$

Notice that Equation 12-2a is identical to the corresponding without-tax equation, 12-2, except for the term $(1 - T)$ in 12-2a. Since $(1 - T)$ is less than 1.0, the imposition of corporate taxes causes the cost of equity to rise at a slower rate than it did in the absence of taxes. It is this characteristic, along with the fact that the effective cost of debt is reduced, that produces the Proposition I result, namely, the increase in firm value as leverage increases.

Illustration of the MM Models

To illustrate the MM models, assume that the following data and conditions hold for Fredrickson Water Company, an old, established firm that supplies water to business and residential customers in several no-growth upstate New York metropolitan areas.

1. Fredrickson currently has no debt; it is an all-equity company.

2. Expected EBIT = $2,400,000. EBIT is not expected to increase over time, so Fredrickson is in a no-growth situation.

3. Fredrickson pays out all of its income as dividends.

4. If Fredrickson begins to use debt, it can borrow at a rate k_d = 8%. This borrowing rate is constant, and it is independent of the amount of debt used. Any money raised by selling debt would be used to retire common stock, so Fredrickson's assets would remain constant.

5. The risk of Fredrickson's assets, and thus its EBIT, is such that its shareholders require a rate of return, k_{sU}, of 12 percent if no debt is used.

With Zero Taxes. To begin, assume that there are no taxes, so T = 0%. At any level of debt, Proposition I (Equation 12-1) can be used to find Fredrickson's value, $20 million:

$$V_L = V_U = \frac{EBIT}{k_{sU}} = \frac{\$2.4 \text{ million}}{0.12} = \$20.0 \text{ million.}$$

If Fredrickson uses $10 million of debt, its stock value must be $10 million:

$$S = V - D = \$20 \text{ million} - \$10 \text{ million} = \$10 \text{ million.}$$

We can also find Fredrickson's cost of equity, k_{sL}, and its WACC at a debt level of $10 million. First, we use Proposition II (Equation 12-2) to find k_{sL}, Fredrickson's leveraged cost of equity:

$$k_{sL} = k_{sU} + (k_{sU} - k_d)(D/S)$$

$$= 12\% + (12\% - 8\%)(\$10 \text{ million}/\$10 \text{ million})$$

$$= 12\% + 4.0\% = 16.0\%.$$

Now we can find the company's weighted average cost of capital:

$$WACC = (D/V)(k_d)(1 - T) + (S/V)k_s$$

$$= (\$10/\$20)(8\%)(1.0) + (\$10/\$20)(16.0\%) = 12.0\%.$$

Fredrickson's value and cost of capital based on the MM model with zero taxes at various debt levels are shown in Panel a of Figure 12-1. Here we see that in an MM world without taxes, financial leverage does not matter: the value of the firm and its overall cost of capital are independent of the amount of debt financing.

With Corporate Taxes. To illustrate the MM model with corporate taxes, assume that all of the previous assumptions hold except these two:

1. Expected EBIT = $4,000,000.

2. Fredrickson has a 40 percent federal-plus-state tax rate, so T = 40%.

Note that, other things held constant, the introduction of corporate taxes would lower Fredrickson's value, so we increased its EBIT from $2.4 million to $4 million to make the comparison between the two models easier.

Figure 12-1 Effects of Leverage: MM Models (Millions of Dollars)

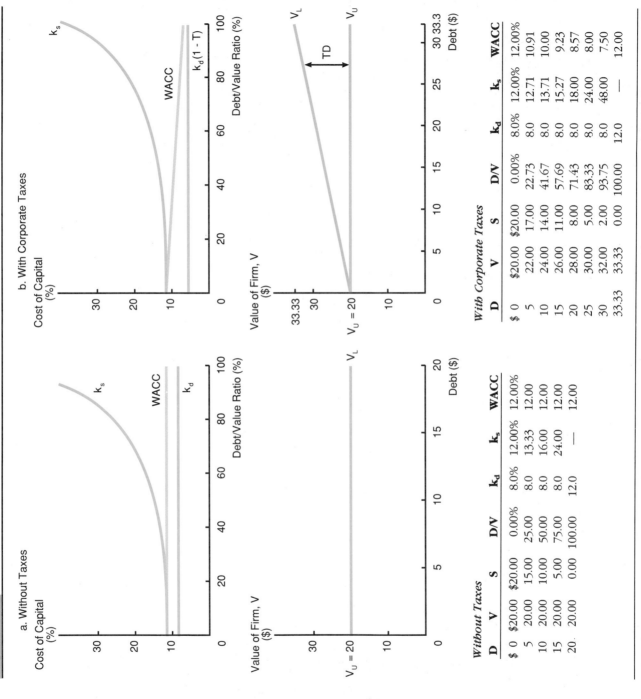

Without Taxes

D	V	S	D/V	k_d	k_s	WACC
$ 0	$20.00	$20.00	0.00%	8.0%	12.00%	12.00%
5	20.00	15.00	25.00	8.0	13.33	12.00
10	20.00	10.00	50.00	8.0	16.00	12.00
15	20.00	5.00	75.00	8.0	24.00	12.00
20	20.00	0.00	100.00	12.0	—	12.00

With Corporate Taxes

D	V	S	D/V	k_d	k_s	WACC
$ 0	$20.00	$20.00	0.00%	8.0%	12.00%	12.00%
5	22.00	17.00	22.73	8.0	12.71	10.91
10	24.00	14.00	41.67	8.0	13.71	10.00
15	26.00	11.00	57.69	8.0	15.27	9.23
20	28.00	8.00	71.43	8.0	18.00	8.57
25	30.00	5.00	83.33	8.0	24.00	8.00
30	32.00	2.00	93.75	8.0	48.00	7.50
33.33	33.33	0.00	100.00	12.0	—	12.00

When Fredrickson has zero debt but pays taxes, Equation 12-4 can be used to find its value, $20 million:

$$V_U = \frac{EBIT(1 - T)}{k_{sU}} = \frac{\$4 \text{ million}(0.6)}{0.12} = \$20.0 \text{ million.}$$

With $10 million of debt in a world with taxes, we see by Proposition I (Equation 12-1a) that Fredrickson's total market value rises to $24 million:

$$V_L = V_U + TD = \$20 \text{ million} + 0.4(\$10 \text{ million}) = \$24 \text{ million.}$$

Therefore, the value of Fredrickson's stock must be $14 million:

$$S = V - D = \$24 \text{ million} - \$10 \text{ million} = \$14 \text{ million.}$$

We can also find Fredrickson's cost of equity, k_{sL}, and its WACC at a debt level of $10 million. First, we use Proposition II (Equation 12-2a) to find k_{sL}, the leveraged cost of equity:

$$k_{sL} = k_{sU} + (k_{sU} - k_d)(1 - T)(D/S)$$

$$= 12\% + (12\% - 8\%)(0.6)(\$10 \text{ million}/\$14 \text{ million})$$

$$= 12\% + 1.71\% = 13.71\%.$$

Now we can find the company's weighted average cost of capital:

$$WACC = (D/V)(k_d)(1 - T) + (S/V)k_s$$

$$= (\$10/\$24)(8\%)(0.6) + (\$14/\$24)(13.71\%) = 10.0\%.$$

Fredrickson's value and cost of capital at various debt levels with corporate taxes are also shown in Figure 12-1, but in Panel b. Here we see that in an MM world with corporate taxes, financial leverage does matter: the value of the firm is maximized, and its overall cost of capital is minimized, if it uses virtually 100 percent debt financing. Further, we see that the increase in value is due solely to the tax deductibility of interest payments, which causes both the cost of debt and the increase in the cost of equity with leverage to be reduced by $(1 - T)$.[4]

---

[4]In the limiting case, where the firm used 100 percent debt financing, the bondholders would own the entire company; thus, they would have to bear all the business risk. (Up until this point, MM assume that the stockholders bear all the risk.) If the bondholders bear all the risk, then the capitalization rate on the debt should be equal to the equity capitalization rate at zero debt, $k_d = k_{sU} = 12\%$.

The income stream to the stockholders in the all-equity case was $CF_U = \$4,000,000(1 - T) = \$2,400,000$, and the value of the firm was

$$V_U = \frac{\$2,400,000}{0.12} = \$20,000,000.$$

With all debt, the entire $4,000,000 of EBIT would be used to pay interest charges—k_d would be 12%, so $I = 0.12(Debt) = \$4,000,000$. Taxes would be zero, and investors (bondholders) would get the entire $4,000,000 of operating income; they would not have to share it with the government. Thus, at 100 percent debt, the value of the firm would be

$$V_L = \frac{\$4,000,000}{0.12} = \$33,333,333 = D.$$

There is, of course, a transition problem in all this—MM assume that $k_d = 8\%$ regardless of how much debt the firm has until debt reaches 100 percent, at which point k_d jumps to 12 percent, the cost of equity. As we shall see later in the chapter, k_d realistically rises as the use of financial leverage increases.

Self-Test Questions

What is the single most important conclusion of the MM zero-tax model?

What is the single most important conclusion of the MM model with corporate taxes?

How does Proposition I differ in the two models?

How does Proposition II differ in the two models?

What is the underlying cause of the "gain from leverage" in the MM with corporate taxes model?

THE MILLER MODEL

Although MM included *corporate* taxes in the second version of their model, they did not extend the model to analyze the effects of *personal* taxes. However, in his 1976 presidential address to the American Finance Association, Merton Miller did introduce a model designed to show how leverage affects firms' values when both personal and corporate taxes are taken into account.[5] To explain Miller's model, let us begin by defining T_c as the corporate tax rate, T_s as the personal tax rate on income from stocks, and T_d as the personal tax rate on income from debt. Note that stock returns come partly as dividends and partly as capital gains, so T_s is a weighted average of the effective tax rates on dividends and capital gains, while essentially all debt income comes from interest, which is effectively taxed at an investor's top rate.

With personal taxes included, *and under the same set of assumptions used in the earlier MM models,* the value of an unlevered firm is found as follows:

$$V_U = \frac{EBIT(1 - T_c)(1 - T_s)}{k_{sU}}. \tag{12-5}$$

The $(1 - T_s)$ term adjusts for personal taxes. Therefore, the numerator shows how much of the firm's operating income is left after the unlevered firm itself pays corporate income taxes and its investors subsequently pay personal taxes on their equity income. Since the introduction of personal taxes lowers the usable income to investors, personal taxes reduce the value of the unlevered firm, other things held constant.

Miller's results can be obtained from an arbitrage proof similar to the one we presented earlier. However, we shall use an alternative approach here. To begin, we partition the levered firm's annual cash flows, CF_L, into those going to the stockholders and those going to the bondholders, considering both corporate and personal taxes:

$$
\begin{aligned}
CF_L &= \quad \text{Net CF to stockholders} \quad + \text{Net CF to bondholders} \\
&= (EBIT - I)(1 - T_c)(1 - T_s) + \quad I(1 - T_d).
\end{aligned} \tag{12-6}
$$

Here I is the annual interest payment. Equation 12-6 can be rearranged as follows:

$$CF_L = [EBIT(1 - T_c)(1 - T_s)] - [I(1 - T_c)(1 - T_s)] + [I(1 - T_d)]. \tag{12-6a}$$

---

[5]See Merton H. Miller, "Debt and Taxes," *Journal of Finance,* May 1977, 261–275.

The first term in Equation 12-6a is identical to the after-tax cash flow of an unlevered firm as shown in Equation 12-5, and its present value is found by discounting the perpetual cash flow by k_{sU}. The second and third terms, which reflect leverage, result from the cash flows associated with interest payments, and these two cash flows are assumed to have a risk equal to that of the basic interest payment stream, hence their present values are obtained by discounting at the cost of debt, k_d. (Remember, these are all perpetual cash flows, so the basic perpetuity valuation model, $V = CF/k$, applies.) Combining the present values of the three terms, we obtain this value for the levered firm:

$$V_L = \frac{EBIT(1 - T_c)(1 - T_s)}{k_{sU}} - \frac{I(1 - T_c)(1 - T_s)}{k_d} + \frac{I(1 - T_d)}{k_d}. \tag{12-7}$$

The first term in Equation 12-7 is identical to V_U as set forth in Equation 12-5, and we can consolidate the second two terms to produce this equation:

$$V_L = V_U + \frac{I(1 - T_d)}{k_d}\left[1 - \frac{(1 - T_c)(1 - T_s)}{(1 - T_d)}\right]. \tag{12-7a}$$

Now recognize that the after-tax perpetual interest payment divided by the required rate of return on debt, $I(1 - T_d)/k_d$, equals the market value of the debt, D. Substituting D into the preceding equation, and rearranging, we obtain this very important expression, called the Miller Model:

$$\text{Miller Model: } V_L = V_U + \left[1 - \frac{(1 - T_c)(1 - T_s)}{(1 - T_d)}\right]D. \tag{12-8}$$

The Miller Model defines the value of a levered firm in a world with both corporate and personal taxes.

The Miller Model has several important implications:

1.   The term in brackets,

$$\left[1 - \frac{(1 - T_c)(1 - T_s)}{(1 - T_d)}\right],$$

when multiplied by D, represents the gain from leverage. The bracketed term replaces the factor $T = T_c$ in the earlier MM model with corporate taxes, $V_L = V_U + TD$.

2.   If we ignore all taxes, that is, if $T_c = T_s = T_d = 0$, then the bracketed term reduces to zero, so in that case Equation 12-8 is the same as the original MM model without taxes.

3.   If we ignore personal taxes, that is, if $T_s = T_d = 0$, then the bracketed term reduces to $[1 - (1 - T_c)] = T_c$, so Equation 12-8 is the same as the MM model with corporate taxes.

4.   If the effective personal tax rates on stock and bond incomes were equal, that is, if $T_s = T_d$, then $(1 - T_s)$ and $(1 - T_d)$ would cancel, and the bracketed term would again reduce to T_c.

5. If $(1 - T_c)(1 - T_s) = (1 - T_d)$, then the bracketed term would go to zero, and the value of using leverage would also be zero. This implies that the tax advantage of debt to the firm would be exactly offset by the personal tax advantage of equity. Under this condition, capital structure would have no effect on a firm's value or its cost of capital, so we would be back to MM's original zero-tax theory.

6. Because taxes on capital gains are deferred, the effective tax rate on stock income is normally less than the effective tax rate on bond income. This being the case, what would the Miller model predict as the gain from leverage? To answer this question, assume that the tax rate on corporate income is $T_c = 34\%$, the effective rate on bond income is $T_d = 28\%$, and the effective rate on stock income is $T_s = 20\%$.[6] Using these values in the Miller model, we find that a levered firm's value increases over that of an unlevered firm by 27 percent of the market value of corporate debt:

$$
\begin{aligned}
\text{Gain from leverage} &= \left[1 - \frac{(1 - T_c)(1 - T_s)}{(1 - T_d)}\right]D \\
&= \left[1 - \frac{(1 - 0.34)(1 - 0.20)}{(1 - 0.28)}\right]D \\
&= [1 - 0.73]D = 0.27(D).
\end{aligned}
$$

Note that the MM model with corporate taxes would indicate a gain from leverage of $T_c(D) = 0.34D$, or 34 percent of the amount of corporate debt. Thus, with these assumed tax rates, adding personal taxes to the model lowers the benefit from corporate debt financing. In general, whenever the effective tax rate on stock income is less than the effective rate on bond income, the Miller model produces a lower gain from leverage than is produced by the MM with corporate taxes model.

In his paper, Miller argued that firms in the aggregate would issue a mix of debt and equity securities such that the before-tax yields on corporate securities and the personal tax rates of the investors who bought these securities would adjust until an equilibrium was reached. At the equilibrium, $(1 - T_d)$ would equal $(1 - T_c)(1 - T_s)$, so, as we noted earlier in Point 5, the tax advantage of debt to the firm would be exactly offset by personal taxation, and capital structure would have no effect on a firm's value or its cost of capital. Thus, according to Miller, the conclusions derived from the original Modigliani-Miller zero-tax model are correct!

Others have extended and tested Miller's 1977 analysis. Generally, these extensions disagree with Miller's conclusion that there is no advantage to the use of corporate debt. In the United States, even though the differential rate on dividends and capital gains was eliminated by the new tax law, the effective tax rate on stock income is probably less than the effective tax rate on bond income due to the deferral of

---

[6]Note that in a follow-on article, Miller and Scholes describe how investors could, theoretically, shelter or delay income from stock to the point where the effective personal tax rate on such income is essentially zero. See Merton H. Miller and Myron S. Scholes, "Dividends and Taxes," *Journal of Financial Economics,* December 1978, 333–364. However, the 1986 changes in the tax law eliminated most of the shelters Miller and Scholes discussed.

taxes on capital gains. Thus, it appears that $(1 - T_c)(1 - T_s)$ is less than $(1 - T_d)$, and there is an advantage to the use of corporate debt. However, Miller's work does show that personal taxes offset some of the benefits of corporate debt, so the tax advantages of corporate debt are less than were implied by the earlier MM model that considered only corporate taxes.

As we note in the next section, there are a number of problems with both the MM and the Miller models, so one should not put much trust in results such as those in our examples.

Self-Test Questions

How does the Miller model differ from the MM model with corporate taxes?

What are the implications of the Miller model if $T_c = T_s = T_d = 0$?

What are the implications if $T_s = T_d = 0$?

Considering the current tax structure in the United States, what is the primary implication of the Miller model?

CRITICISMS OF THE MM AND MILLER MODELS

The conclusions of each capital structure model follow logically from its initial assumptions: if its assumptions are correct, then its conclusions must be reached. However, both academicians and financial executives have voiced concern over the validity of the MM and Miller models, and virtually no firms follow their recommendations. The MM zero-tax model leads to the conclusion that capital structure doesn't matter, but we observe some regularities in structure within industries. Further, when used with "reasonable" tax rates, both the MM model with corporate taxes and the Miller model lead to the conclusion that firms should use 100 percent debt financing. That situation is not observed in practice except by firms whose equity has been eroded by operating losses. People who disagree with the MM and Miller theories and their suggestions for financial policy generally attack them on the grounds that their assumptions do not reflect actual market conditions. Some of the main objections include the following:

1.   Both MM and Miller assume that personal and corporate leverage are perfect substitutes. However, an individual investing in a levered firm has less loss exposure, which means a more *limited liability,* than if he or she used "homemade" leverage. For example, in our earlier illustration of the MM arbitrage argument, it should be noted that only the $600,000 our investor had in Firm L would be lost if that firm went bankrupt. However, if the investor engaged in arbitrage transactions and employed "homemade" leverage to invest in Firm U, then he or she could lose $900,000—the original $600,000 investment plus the $400,000 loan less the $100,000 investment in riskless bonds. This increased personal risk exposure would tend to restrain investors from engaging in arbitrage, and that could cause the equi-

librium values of V_L, V_U, k_{sL}, and k_{sU} to be different from those specified by the models. Restrictions on institutional investors, who dominate capital markets today, may also retard the arbitrage process, because most institutional investors cannot legally borrow to buy stocks, hence they are prohibited from engaging in home-made leverage.

2.   Brokerage costs were assumed away by MM and Miller, making the switch from L to U costless. However, brokerage and other transaction costs do exist, and they too impede the arbitrage process.

3.   MM initially assumed that corporations and investors can borrow at the risk-free rate. Although risky debt has been introduced into the analysis by others, to reach the MM and Miller conclusions it is still necessary to assume that both corporations and investors can borrow at the same rate. Although major institutional investors probably can borrow at the corporate rate, many institutions are not allowed to borrow to buy securities. Further, most individual investors probably must borrow at higher rates than those paid by large corporations.

4.   In his article, Miller concluded that an equilibrium would be reached, but to reach his equilibrium the tax benefit from corporate debt (a) must be the same for all firms, and (b) must be constant for an individual firm regardless of the amount of leverage used. However, we know that the tax benefit varies from firm to firm: Highly profitable companies gain the maximum tax benefit from leverage, while the benefits to firms that are struggling are much smaller. Further, some firms have other tax shields such as high depreciation, pension plan contributions, and operating loss carry-forwards, and these shields reduce the tax savings value of interest payments.[7] It also appears simplistic to assume that the expected tax shield is unaffected by the amount of debt financing used. Higher leverage increases the probability that the firm cannot effectively use the full tax shield in the future, because higher leverage increases the probability of future unprofitability and consequently lower tax rates. All things considered, it appears likely that the interest tax shield from corporate debt is more valuable to some firms than to others.

5.   MM and Miller assume that there are no costs associated with financial distress. Further, they ignore agency costs. These topics are discussed in the next section.

Self-Test Questions

Should we accept one of the models presented thus far (MM with zero taxes, MM with corporate taxes, or Miller) as being correct? Why or why not?

Which of the assumptions used in the models is most worrisome to you, and what does "worrisome" mean in this context?

---

[7]For a discussion of the impact of tax shields other than debt financing, see Harry DeAngelo and Ronald W. Masulis, "Optimal Capital Structure under Corporate and Personal Taxation," *Journal of Financial Economics,* March 1980, 3–30.

FINANCIAL DISTRESS AND AGENCY COSTS

Some of the assumptions inherent in the MM and Miller models can be relaxed, and when this is done, their basic conclusions remain unchanged.[8] However, as we discuss next, when financial distress and agency costs are added, the MM and Miller results are altered significantly.

Financial Distress Costs

A number of firms experience financial distress each year, and some of them are forced into bankruptcy. Financial distress includes but is not restricted to bankruptcy, and when it occurs, several things can happen:

1. Arguments between claimants often delay the liquidation of assets. Bankruptcy cases can take many years to settle, and during this time machinery rusts, buildings are vandalized, inventories become obsolete, and the like.

2. Lawyer's fees, court costs, and administrative expenses can absorb a large part of the firm's value. Together, the costs of physical deterioration plus legal fees and administrative expenses are called the *direct costs* of bankruptcy.

3. Managers and other employees generally lose their jobs when a firm fails. Knowing this, the management of a firm that is in financial distress may take actions which keep it alive in the short run but which also dilute long-run value. For example, the firm may defer maintenance of machinery, sell off valuable assets at bargain prices to raise cash, or cut costs so much that the quality of its products is impaired and the firm's long-run market position is eroded.

4. Both customers and suppliers of companies that are experiencing financial difficulties are aware of the problems that can arise, and they often take "evasive action" that further damages the troubled firm. For example, Eastern Airlines, as it struggled to deal with its unions and avoid liquidation in 1990, was having trouble making sales because potential customers were worried about buying a seat for a future flight and then having the company shut down before they could take the trip. Some potential customers were also worried that the company might cut back on maintenance expenditures, and its suppliers were reluctant to grant normal credit terms, or to gear up to supply Eastern with parts and other materials on a long-term basis. Further, Eastern was having great difficulty obtaining capital. Finally, Eastern had trouble attracting and retaining the highest-quality workers, as most workers with a choice prefer employment with a more stable airline to one that could go out of business at any time.

---

[8]For example, see Robert A. Haugen and James L. Pappas, "Equilibrium in the Pricing of Capital Assets, Risk-Bearing Debt Instruments, and the Question of Optimal Capital Structure," *Journal of Financial and Quantitative Analysis,* June 1971, 943–954; Joseph Stiglitz, "A Re-Examination of the Modigliani-Miller Theorem," *American Economic Review,* December 1969, 784–793; and Mark E. Rubenstein, "A Mean-Variance Synthesis of Corporate Financial Theory," *Journal of Finance,* March 1973, 167–181.

Table 12-1 Fredrickson Water Company: Expected Costs of Financial Distress

		Amount of Debt			
	$0	$5 Million	$10 Million	$20 Million	$30 Million
Probability of financial distress	0.0	0.05	0.15	0.50	0.95
PV of expected costs of financial distress[a]	$0	$250,000	$750,000	$2,500,000	$4,750,000

[a]$5 million times the indicated probability.

Nonoptimal managerial actions associated with financial distress, as well as the costs imposed by customers, suppliers, and capital providers, are called the *indirect costs* of financial distress. Of course, these costs may be incurred by a firm in financial distress even if it does not go into bankruptcy: bankruptcy is just one point on the continuum of financial distress.

All things considered, the direct and indirect costs associated with financial distress are high.[9] Further, financial distress typically occurs only if a firm has debts — debt-free firms do not usually experience financial distress. *Therefore, the greater the use of debt financing, and the larger the fixed interest charges, the greater the probability that a decline in earnings will lead to financial distress, hence the higher the probability that the costs of financial distress will be incurred.*

An increase in the probability of financial distress lowers the current value of a firm and raises its cost of capital. To see why, suppose we estimate that Fredrickson Water will incur financial distress costs of $7 million if it fails at some future date, and that the *present value* of this possible future cost is $5 million. Further, the probability of financial distress increases with leverage, causing the expected present value cost of financial distress to rise from zero at zero debt to $4.75 million at $30 million of debt as shown in Table 12-1.

These expected costs of financial distress must be subtracted from the values we previously calculated in Part b of Figure 12-1 to find the firm's value at various amounts of leverage: they would reduce the values of V and S and, as a result, would raise k_s and the WACC. For example, at $20 million of debt, we would obtain the values in Table 12-2.[10] These changes would, of course, then have carry-through

---

[9]See Edward I. Altman, "A Further Empirical Investigation of the Bankruptcy Cost Question," *Journal of Finance,* September 1984, 1067–1089. On the basis of a sample of 26 bankrupt companies, Altman found that bankruptcy costs often exceed 20 percent of firm value.

[10]To find k_s and the WACC in Table 12-2, simply transpose Equation 12-3 and then apply the definition for the WACC:

$$k_s = \frac{(EBIT - k_dD)(1 - T)}{S} = \frac{[\$4 - 0.08(\$20)](1 - 0.4)}{\$5.5} = 26.18\%.$$

$$k_a = WACC = (D/V)(k_d)(1 - T) + (S/V)(k_s)$$
$$= (\$20/\$25.5)(8\%)(0.6) + (\$5.5/\$25.5)(26.18\%)$$
$$= 3.76\% + 5.65\% = 9.41\%.$$

Table 12-2   Fredrickson Water Company: Effects of Financial Distress
(Millions of Dollars)

	Values at D = $20 Million with Financial Distress Effects Ignored: Pure MM	Values at D = $20 Million with Financial Distress Effects Considered: Modified MM
V	$28.00	$28.00 − $2.5 = $25.5
S	$8.00	$8.00 − $2.5 = $5.5
k_s	18.00%	26.18%
WACC	8.57%	9.41%

effects on the graphs in Panel b of Figure 12-1—most important, they would (1) reduce the decline of the WACC line and (2) reduce the slope of the V_L line.

The effects of financial distress are also felt by a firm's bondholders. Firms experiencing financial distress have a higher probability of defaulting on debt payments, so the expectation of financial distress influences bond investors' required rates of return: The higher the probability of financial distress, the higher the required return on debt. Thus, as a firm uses more and more debt financing, hence increasing the probability of distress, the value of k_d also increases, causing several elements in Panel b of Figure 12-1 to change.

Agency Costs

We introduced the concept of agency costs in Chapter 1. One type of agency cost is associated with the use of debt, and it involves the relationship between a firm's stockholders and its bondholders. In the absence of any restrictions, a firm's management would be tempted to take actions that would benefit stockholders at the expense of bondholders. For example, if Fredrickson Water were to sell only a small amount of debt, then this debt would have relatively little risk, hence a high bond rating and a low interest rate. Yet, having sold the low-risk debt, Fredrickson could then issue more debt secured by the same assets as the original debt. This would raise the risks faced by *all bondholders,* cause k_d to rise, and consequently cause the original bondholders to suffer capital losses. Similarly, suppose that after issuing a substantial amount of debt, Fredrickson decided to restructure its assets, selling off assets with low business risk and acquiring assets that were more risky but that also had higher expected rates of return. If things worked out well, the stockholders would benefit. If things went sour, most of the loss in a highly leveraged firm would fall on the bondholders. In other words, the stockholders would be playing a game of "heads, I win; tails, you lose" with the bondholders.

Because of the possibility that stockholders might try to take advantage of bondholders in these and other ways, bonds are protected by restrictive covenants. These covenants hamper the corporation's legitimate operations to some extent. Further, the company must be monitored to insure that the covenants are being obeyed, and the costs of monitoring are passed on to the stockholders in the form of higher debt costs. The costs of lost efficiency plus monitoring are what we mean here by *agency costs,* and these costs increase the cost of debt to the firm and reduce the value of the equity, and thus reduce the advantage of debt.[11]

Firm Value and the Cost of Capital with Financial Distress and Agency Costs

If the MM model with corporate taxes were correct, a firm's value would rise continuously as it moved from zero debt toward 100 percent debt: the equation $V_L = V_U + TD$ shows that TD, hence V_L, is maximized if D is at a maximum. Recall that the rising component of value, TD, results directly from the tax shelter provided by interest on the debt. However, the following factors, which were ignored by MM, could cause V_L to decline as the level of debt rises: (1) the present value of costs associated with potential future financial distress, and (2) the present value of agency costs. Therefore, MM's relationship between a firm's value and its use of leverage should look like this:

$$V_L = V_U + TD - \begin{pmatrix} \text{PV of} \\ \text{expected} \\ \text{financial} \\ \text{distress costs} \end{pmatrix} - \begin{pmatrix} \text{PV of} \\ \text{agency} \\ \text{costs} \end{pmatrix}. \qquad \textbf{(12-9)}$$

The relationship expressed in Equation 12-9 is graphed in Figure 12-2. The tax shelter effect totally dominates until the amount of debt reaches Point A. After Point A, financial distress and agency costs become increasingly important, offsetting some of the tax advantages. At Point B, the marginal tax shelter benefits of additional debt are exactly offset by the disadvantages of debt, and beyond Point B, the disadvantages outweigh the tax benefits.

Equation 12-8, the Miller Model, can also be modified to reflect financial distress and agency costs. The equation would be identical to Equation 12-9, except that the gain from leverage term, TD, would reflect the addition of personal taxes. In either the MM or Miller models, the gain from leverage can at least be roughly estimated, but the value reduction resulting from potential financial distress and agency costs is almost entirely subjective. We know that these costs must increase as leverage rises, but we simply do not know the specific functional relationships.

Self-Test Questions

Describe some types of financial distress and agency costs.

How are these costs related to the use of financial leverage?

How are the basic MM with corporate taxes and Miller models affected by the inclusion of financial distress and agency costs?

---

[11]Jensen and Meckling point out that there are also agency costs between outside equity holders and management. See "Theory of the Firm: Managerial Behavior, Agency Costs, and Ownership Structure," *Journal of Financial Economics,* October 1976, 305–360. Their study further suggests that (1) bondholder agency costs increase as the debt ratio increases, but (2) outside stockholder agency costs move in reverse fashion, falling with increased use of debt.

Figure 12-2   Net Effects of Leverage on the Value of the Firm

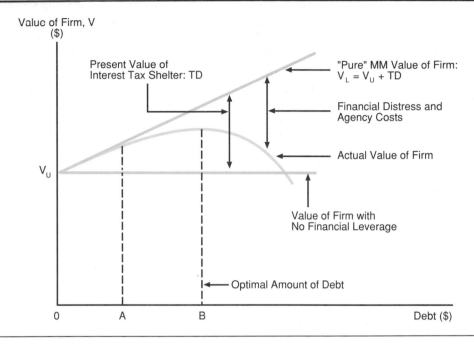

REVIEW OF THE TRADEOFF MODELS

Both the MM with corporate taxes and Miller models as modified to reflect financial distress and agency costs can be described as *tradeoff models*. That is, the optimal capital structure is found by balancing the tax shield benefits of leverage against the financial distress and agency costs of leverage, so the costs and benefits are "traded off" against one another.

Implications of the Models

The tradeoff models are not capable of specifying precise optimal capital structures, but they do enable us to make three statements about debt usage:

1.   Higher-risk firms, as measured by the variability of returns on the firm's assets, ought to borrow less than lower-risk firms, other things equal. The greater this variability, the greater the probability of financial distress at any level of debt, hence the greater the expected costs of distress. Thus, firms with lower business risk can borrow more before the expected costs of distress offset the tax advantages of borrowing.

2.   Firms that employ tangible assets such as real estate and standard production machinery should borrow more than firms whose value is derived either from in-

tangible assets such as patents and goodwill, or from growth opportunities. The costs of financial distress depend not only on the probability of incurring distress, but also on what happens if distress occurs. Specialized assets, intangible assets, and growth opportunities are more likely to lose value if financial distress occurs than are standardized, tangible assets.

3.   Firms that are currently paying taxes at the highest rate, and that are likely to continue to do so in the future, should carry more debt than firms with current and/or prospectively lower tax rates. High corporate tax rates lead to greater benefits from debt financing, hence high-rate firms can carry more debt, other factors held constant, before the tax shield is offset by financial distress and agency costs.

According to the tradeoff models, each firm should set its target capital structure such that its costs and benefits of leverage are balanced at the margin, because such a structure will maximize its value. We would expect to find actual target structures that are consistent with the three points just noted. Further, we would generally expect to find that firms within an industry have similar capital structures, because such firms have roughly the same types of assets, business risks, and profitability.

The Empirical Evidence

The tradeoff models have intuitive appeal because they lead to the conclusion that both no debt and all debt are bad, while a "moderate" debt level is good. However, we must ask ourselves whether these models explain actual behavior. If they do not, then we must search for other explanations or else assume that managers, hence investors, are acting irrationally, an assumption that we are unwilling to make.

The tradeoff models do have some empirical support.[12] For example, firms that have primarily tangible assets tend to borrow more heavily than firms whose value stems from intangibles and/or growth opportunities. However, there is other empirical evidence which refutes the tradeoff models. First, several studies have examined models of financing behavior to see if firms' financing decisions reflect adjustment toward a target capital structure. These studies provide some evidence that this occurs, but the explanatory power of the models is very low, suggesting that tradeoff models capture only a part of actual behavior. Second, no study has clearly demonstrated that a firm's tax rate has a predictable, material effect on its capital structure. In fact, firms used debt financing long before corporate income taxes even existed. Finally, actual debt ratios tend to vary widely across apparently similar firms, whereas the tradeoff models suggest that the use of debt should be relatively consistent within industries.

All in all, the empirical support for the tradeoff models is not strong, which suggests that other factors not incorporated into these models are also at work. In other words, the tradeoff models do not tell the full story.

---

[12]For examples of the empirical research in this area, see Robert Taggart, "A Model of Corporate Financing Decisions," *Journal of Finance,* December 1977, 1467–1484; and Paul Marsh, "The Choice between Equity and Debt: An Empirical Study," *Journal of Finance,* March 1982, 121–144.

Self-Test Questions

What is a tradeoff model of capital structure?

What implications do the tradeoff models have regarding capital structure?

Does the empirical evidence fully support the tradeoff models?

ASYMMETRIC INFORMATION THEORY

In the early 1960s, Professor Gordon Donaldson of Harvard University conducted an extensive survey of how corporations actually establish their capital structures.[13] Here is a summary of his findings:

1.   Firms prefer to finance with internally generated funds; that is, retained earnings and depreciation.

2.   Firms set their target dividend payout ratios based on (a) their expected future investment opportunities and (b) their expected future cash flows. The target payout ratio is set at a level such that retained earnings plus depreciation will meet capital expenditure requirements under normal conditions.

3.   Dividends are "sticky" in the short run—firms are reluctant to make major changes in the dollar dividend, and they are especially reluctant to cut the dividend. Thus, in any given year, depending on realized cash flows and actual investment opportunities, a firm may or may not have sufficient internally generated funds to cover its capital expenditures.

4.   If the firm has more internal cash flow than is needed for expansion purposes, then it will invest in marketable securities or else use the funds to retire debt. If it has insufficient internal cash flow to finance non-postponable new projects, then it will first draw down its marketable securities portfolio, and if still more funds are needed, then the firm will go to the external capital markets, first issuing debt, then convertible bonds, and then common stock only as a last resort. *Thus, Donaldson observed a "pecking order" of financing, not the balanced approach that is called for under the tradeoff models.*

Professor Stewart Myers noted the inconsistency between Donaldson's findings and the tradeoff models, and that led him to propose a new theory.[14] First, Myers noted that Donaldson's pecking order findings led away from rather than toward a well-defined capital structure. Equity is raised in two forms, and one form, retained earnings, is at the top of the pecking order, while the other, new common stock, is at the bottom.

---

[13]Gordon Donaldson, *Corporate Debt Capacity: A Study of Corporate Debt Policy and the Determination of Corporate Debt Capacity* (Boston: Harvard Graduate School of Business Administration, 1961).

[14]Stewart C. Myers, "The Capital Structure Puzzle," *Journal of Finance,* July 1984, 575–592. It is interesting to note that, like the Miller Model, Myers' paper was presented as a presidential address to the American Finance Association.

Next, Myers noted that the tradeoff models assume that all market participants have homogeneous expectations, which implies (1) that all participants have the same information set and (2) that any changes in operating income are purely random as opposed to anticipated by some parties. Myers had the insight to see that if the homogeneous expectations assumption is relaxed, and asymmetric (or different) information by different groups of market participants is admitted, Donaldson's results could be explained in a logical manner. Myers' work resulted in what is now called the *asymmetric information theory* of capital structure.

The basis for the theory, as articulated by Myers, rests on the existence of asymmetric information. To illustrate, assume that a firm has 10,000 common shares outstanding at a current price of $19 per share, so the market value of its equity is $190,000. However, its managers have better information about the firm's prospects than stockholders, and the managers believe that the actual share value based on existing assets is $21, giving the equity a total "true" market value of $210,000. Such information asymmetry could easily exist, for managers often know more about their firms' prospects than do current and potential investors.[15]

Suppose further that the firm now identifies a new project which requires external financing of $100,000 and which has an estimated net present value (NPV) of $5,000. (Remember that a project's NPV is a residual value over its costs, and that this residual accrues to the shareholders.) This project is unanticipated by the firm's investors, so the $5,000 NPV has not been incorporated into the firm's $190,000 equity market value. Should the firm accept the project? To begin, assume that the firm plans to sell new equity to raise the $100,000 to finance the project. Several possibilities are set forth next:

1. **Symmetric information.** First, as a point of departure, consider the situation where management can convey its information to the public, hence all investors *do* have the same information as management regarding existing asset values. Under these conditions, the stock would be selling at $21 per share, so the firm would have to sell $100,000/$21 = 4,762 new shares to finance the project. Acceptance of the project would result in a new stock price of $21.34:

$$\text{New stock price} = \frac{\text{Original market value} + \text{New money raised} + \text{NPV}}{\text{Original shares} + \text{New shares}}$$

$$= \frac{\$210,000 + \$100,000 + \$5,000}{10,000 + 4,762} = \$21.34.$$

Clearly, both old and new shareholders would benefit if the project were accepted.

2. **Asymmetric information prior to stock issue.** Now consider the situation where our firm's management can in no way inform investors about the stock's "true" value. Perhaps it is necessary to hold back such information to maintain a competitive edge, or perhaps SEC regulations cause management to refrain from "touting" the stock price prior to the new issue (if things did not work out as ex-

---

[15]This assumption is contrary to the strong-form efficient markets hypothesis (EMH) presented in Chapter 7, but few observers—including people who believe ardently in weak-form and semistrong-form efficiency—are willing to accept strong-form efficiency.

pected, new shareholders might sue the managers who had provided the rosy forecast). In this situation, new stock would fetch only $19 per share, so the company
would have to sell $100,000/$19 = 5,263 shares in order to raise the required
$100,000. If this were done, this new price would result if the project were accepted
and then the information asymmetry was removed:

$$\text{New stock price} = \frac{\text{New market value} + \text{New money raised} + \text{NPV}}{\text{Original shares} + \text{New shares}}$$

$$= \frac{\$210,000 + \$100,000 + \$5,000}{10,000 + 5,263} = \$20.64.$$

Under this condition, the project should not be undertaken. If the project were not
accepted, so no new shares were sold, then the price of the stock would rise to $21
when the information asymmetry is removed. The sale of new stock at $19 per share
would lead to a $0.36 loss to the firm's existing shareholders and to a $1.64 gain to
the new shareholders.

3. **A more profitable project.** Suppose now that the project had an NPV of
$20,000, and other conditions were unchanged. Now the firm's stock price would
rise to $21.62 if it undertook the project.

$$\text{New stock price} = \frac{\$210,000 + \$100,000 + \$20,000}{10,000 + 5,263} = \$21.62.$$

Under these conditions, the firm should take on the project. Note, though, that most
of the positive NPV would go to the new stockholders, who would pay $19 per share
and thus would enjoy a capital gain of $2.62 versus a gain of only $0.62 for the
original stockholders.

4. **Dark clouds on the horizon.** Now suppose an entirely different situation
faced the firm. Stockholders think the firm is worth $19 per share, but the firm's
managers think (a) that outside investors are entirely too optimistic about the firm's
growth opportunities, (b) that investors are not properly recognizing proposed legislation which will require large, nonearning investments in pollution control equipment, and (c) that investors do not fully anticipate the need for new R&D expenditures which may be required to keep the firm's products competitive. If all of these
bad events materialize, profit margins will be under pressure, cash flows will be
down, and the company will not be able to carry safely its present level of debt.
Moreover, the stock price will fall sharply, and it will be extremely difficult to raise
the capital that will be necessary to assure the firm's survival.

Faced with these conditions, management might well conclude that the "true"
value of the firm's stock is only $17 per share, and further decide to sell a new issue
of 10,000 shares at a price of $19, raising $190,000 and using the funds to retire debt
or to support this year's capital budget. This action would increase the "true" value
of the stock from $17 to $18:

$$\text{New "true" value} = \frac{\text{Old "true" market value} + \text{New money}}{\text{Original shares} + \text{New shares}}$$

$$= \frac{\$170,000 + \$190,000}{10,000 + 10,000} = \$18.00.$$

Current stockholders will, if management's expectations come true, suffer a loss when the bad news becomes known, but the sale of new stock would reduce that loss. (Note: Management would have to word the prospectus for the new issue carefully, pointing out the potential problems. However, virtually all prospectuses are filled with cautionary language, so investors cannot tell from them what management really expects.)

5. **Finance the original $5,000 NPV project with debt.** If the firm used debt to finance the original $100,000 project, *and then the information asymmetry was removed,* the new stock price would be $21.50:

$$\text{New stock price} = \frac{\text{New market value} + \text{NPV}}{\text{Original shares}}$$

$$= \frac{\$210,000 + \$5,000}{10,000} = \$21.50.$$

Thus, if debt financing were used, all of the "true" value of the firm's existing assets, plus the NPV of the new project, would accrue to the original shareholders. If stock financing were used, we saw that the value of the original stock would end up at $20.64 rather than $21, the true value without the new investment.

What does all this suggest about corporate financial policy? First, in a world where asymmetric information exists, corporations should issue new shares only (1) if they have extraordinarily profitable investments that cannot be postponed or financed by debt, or (2) if management thinks the shares are overvalued. Second, investors recognize this and tend to mark down a company's share prices when it announces plans to issue new shares, because chances are that the announcement is signaling bad news, not good news. Third, the financing pecking order that Donaldson observed is rational when asymmetric information exists — it pays to retain a large fraction of earnings, and to keep the equity ratio up and the debt ratio down, so as to maintain some "reserve borrowing capacity" which can be used to support the capital budget if and when an unusually large volume of positive NPV projects come along, or if problems arise which require outside capital.[16]

Note that the degree of information asymmetry and its impact on investors' perceptions differ substantially across firms. To illustrate, the degree of asymmetry is typically much greater in the drug and semiconductor industries than in the retailing and trucking industries, because success in the drug and semiconductor industries depends on secretive proprietary research and development. Thus, managers in these industries hold significantly more information about their firms' prospects than do outside analysts and investors. Also, emerging firms with limited capital and good growth opportunities are recognized as having to use external financing, so the announcement of new stock offerings are not viewed with as much concern by

---

[16]Flotation costs also play a role in capital structure theory. In general, flotation costs are smaller on debt issues than on equity issues, and this provides an additional rationale for using debt rather than outside equity. We will discuss this issue in more detail in Chapter 15.

investors as are new offerings by mature firms with limited growth opportunities. Thus, although the asymmetric information theory is applicable to all firms, its impact on managerial decisions varies from firm to firm and over time.

Self-Test Questions

Briefly explain the asymmetric information theory.

What does this theory suggest about capital structure decisions?

Is the asymmetric information theory equally applicable to all firms at all times?

OUR VIEW OF CAPITAL STRUCTURE THEORY

The great contribution of the tradeoff models of MM, Miller, and their followers is that these models identified the specific benefits and costs of using debt—the tax effects, financial distress costs, and so on. Prior to these models, no capital structure theory existed, and we had no systematic way of analyzing the effects of debt financing.

The tradeoff model is summarized graphically in Figure 12-3. The top graph shows the relationships between the debt ratio and the cost of debt, cost of equity, and the WACC. Both k_s and $k_d(1 - T_c)$ rise steadily with increases in leverage, but the rate of increase accelerates at higher debt levels, reflecting agency costs and the increased probability of financial distress and its attendant costs. The WACC first declines, then hits a minimum at D/V*, and then begins to rise. Note that the value of D in D/V* in the upper graph is D*, the level of debt in the lower graph that maximizes the firm's value. Thus, a firm's WACC is minimized and its value is maximized at the same capital structure. Also note that the general shapes of the curves apply regardless of whether we are using the MM with corporate taxes model, the Miller model, or a variant of these models.

Unfortunately, it is extremely difficult for financial managers to actually quantify the costs and benefits of debt financing to their firms, so it is virtually impossible to pinpoint D/V*, the capital structure that truly maximizes a firm's value. Most experts believe such a structure exists for every firm, but that it changes substantially over time as the nature of the firm and the capital markets change. Most experts also believe that, as shown in Figure 12-3, the relationship between firm value and leverage is relatively flat; thus, relatively large deviations from the optimum can occur without materially affecting a firm's value.

Now consider the asymmetric information theory. Because of asymmetric information, investors know less about a firm's prospects than do its managers. Further, managers try to maximize value for current stockholders, not new ones, so if the firm has excellent prospects, management will not want to issue new shares, but if things look bleak, then a new stock offering may be sold. Therefore, investors take a stock offering to be a signal of bad news, so stock prices tend to decline when new issues are announced. As a result, new equity financing can be very expensive, and this fact must be incorporated into the capital structure decision. Its effect is to

Figure 12-3   Effects of Leverage: The Tradeoff View

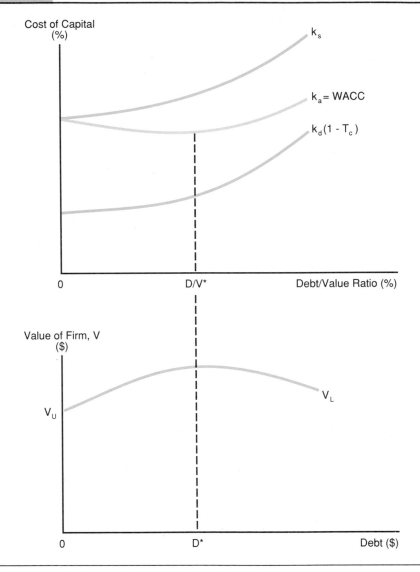

motivate firms to maintain a reserve borrowing capacity, which permits future in-vestment opportunities to be financed by debt when internal funds are insufficient.

By combining the two theories, we obtain this possible explanation for firms' behavior: (1) Debt financing provides benefits because of the tax deductibility of interest. Hence, firms should have some debt in their capital structures. (2) How-ever, financial distress and agency costs place limits on debt usage—beyond some point, these costs offset the tax advantage of debt. (3) Finally, because of asymmetric information, firms maintain a borrowing capacity reserve in order to take advantage of good investment opportunities, and, at the same time, avoid having to issue stock at distressed prices.

All this may sound reasonable, but how should financial decisions actually be made in practice? The answer is rather unclear, and many factors must be considered when choosing a capital structure. This topic will be covered in the next chapter.

Self-Test Questions

Summarize the tradeoff and asymmetric information theories of capital structure.

Can the tradeoff theory and the asymmetric information theory coexist, that is, can they both help explain capital structure choices, or are they mutually exclusive? Explain.

Does capital structure theory provide managers with a model that prescribes a precise optimal capital structure for each firm?

SUMMARY

This chapter presented the major elements of capital structure theory. The key concepts covered are listed next.

- In 1958, *Franco Modigliani and Merton Miller (MM)* startled the academic community by proving, under a restrictive set of assumptions including zero taxes, that capital structure is irrelevant—a firm's value is not affected by its financing mix.

- *MM* later added *corporate taxes* to their model, leading to the conclusion that capital structure does matter, and that firms should use almost 100 percent debt financing in order to maximize value.

- MM's model with corporate taxes illustrates that the benefits of debt financing stem solely from the *tax deductibility of interest payments.*

- Much later, Miller extended the model to include *personal taxes.* The introduction of personal taxes reduces, but does not eliminate, the benefits of debt financing. Thus, the *Miller model* also prescribes 100 percent debt financing.

- The addition of financial distress and agency costs to either the MM tax model or the Miller model results in a *tradeoff model.* Here the marginal costs and benefits of debt financing are balanced against one another, and the result is an optimal capital structure that falls somewhere between zero and 100 percent debt.

- The *asymmetric information theory,* which is based on the assumption that managers have better information than investors, postulates that there is a preferred order of financing: first retained earnings (and depreciation), then debt, and finally, as a last resort only, new common stock.

- The asymmetric information theory prescribes that firms maintain a *borrowing capacity reserve* so that they can always issue debt on reasonable terms rather than being forced into a new equity issue at the wrong time.

- There is clearly some value to debt financing, and firms use different amounts of debt depending on their tax rates, their asset structures, and their inherent riskiness.

- Unfortunately, capital structure theory does not provide neat, clean answers to the question of the optimal capital structure. Thus, many factors must be considered when actually choosing a firm's target capital structure, and the final decision will be based on both analysis and judgment.

In the next chapter, we will examine some additional issues which provide further insights into the capital structure decision.

Questions

12-1 Define each of the following terms:
    a.   Leverage
    b.   MM Proposition I without taxes; with corporate taxes
    c.   MM Proposition II without taxes; with corporate taxes
    d.   Miller model
    e.   Financial distress costs; agency costs
    f.   Tradeoff model
    g.   Asymmetric information theory

12-2 Explain why agency costs would probably be more of a problem for a large, publicly owned firm that uses both debt and equity capital than for a small, unleveraged, owner-managed firm.

12-3 The stock of Gentech Company is currently selling at its low for the year, but management feels that the stock price is only temporarily depressed because of investor pessimism. The firm's capital budget this year is so large that the use of new outside equity is contemplated. However, management does not want to sell new stock at the current low price and is therefore considering a temporary departure from the firm's "optimal" capital structure by borrowing the funds it would otherwise have raised in the equity markets. Does this seem to be a wise move? Does this action conform to any of the theories presented in the chapter?

12-4 Explain, verbally, how MM use the arbitrage process to prove the validity of Proposition I. Also, list the major MM assumptions and explain why each of these assumptions is necessary in the arbitrage proof.

12-5 A utility company is supposed to be allowed to charge prices high enough to cover all costs, including its cost of capital. Public service commissions are supposed to take actions to stimulate companies to operate as efficiently as possible in order to keep costs, hence prices, as low as possible. Some time ago, AT&T's debt ratio was about 33 percent. Some people (Myron J. Gordon in particular) argued that a higher debt ratio would lower AT&T's cost of capital and permit it to charge lower rates for telephone service. Gordon thought an optimal debt ratio for AT&T was about 50 percent. Do the theories presented in the chapter support or refute Gordon's position?

Self-Test Problem (Solutions Appear in Appendix D)

ST-1 **(MM with financial distress costs)** B. Gibbs, Inc., is an unlevered firm, and it has constant expected operating earnings (EBIT) of $2 million per year. The firm's tax rate is 40 percent, and its market value is V = S = $12 million. Management is considering the use of some debt financing. (Debt would be issued and used to buy back stock, so the size of the firm would remain constant.) Since interest expense is tax deductible, the value of the firm would tend to increase as debt is added to the capital structure, but there would be an offset in the form of a rising risk of financial distress. The firm's analysts have estimated, as an approximation, that the present value of any future financial distress costs is $8 million, and that the probability of distress would increase with leverage according to the following schedule:

Value of Debt	Probability of Financial Distress
$ 2,500,000	0.00%
5,000,000	1.25
7,500,000	2.50
10,000,000	6.25
12,500,000	12.50
15,000,000	31.25
20,000,000	75.00

a. What is the firm's cost of equity and weighted average cost of capital at this time?
b. According to the "pure" MM with-tax model, what is the optimal level of debt?
c. What is the optimal capital structure when financial distress costs are included?
d. Plot the value of the firm, with and without distress costs, as a function of the level of debt.

Problems

12-1 **(MM without taxes)** Companies U and L are identical in every respect except that U is unlevered while L has $10 million of 5 percent bonds outstanding. Assume (1) that all of the MM assumptions are met, (2) that there are no corporate or personal taxes, (3) that EBIT is $2 million, and (4) that the cost of equity to Company U is 10 percent.
a. What value would MM estimate for each firm?
b. What is k_s for Firm U? For Firm L?
c. Find S_L, and then show that $S_L + D = V_L = \$20$ million.
d. What is the WACC for Firm U? For Firm L?
e. Suppose $V_U = \$20$ million and $V_L = \$22$ million. According to MM, do these values represent an equilibrium? If not, explain the process by which equilibrium would be restored.

12-2 **(MM with corporate taxes)** Refer to Problem 12-1. Assume that all the facts hold, except that both firms are subject to a 40 percent federal-plus-state corporate tax rate.
a. What value would MM now estimate for each firm? (Use Proposition I.)
b. What is k_s for Firm U? Firm L?
c. Find S_L, and then show that $S_L + D = V_L$ results in the same value as obtained in Part a.
d. What is the WACC for Firm U? For Firm L?

12-3   **(Miller model)** Refer to Problems 12-1 and 12-2. Assume that all facts hold, except that both corporate and personal taxes apply. Assume that both firms must pay a federal-plus-state corporate tax rate of $T_c = 40\%$, and that investors in both firms face a tax rate of $T_d = 28\%$ on debt income and $T_s = 20\%$, on average, on stock income.

    a.   What is the value of the unlevered firm, V_U? (Note that V_U is now reduced by the personal tax on stock income, hence $V_U \neq \$12$ million as in Problem 12-2a.)

    b.   What is the value of V_L?

    c.   What is the gain from leverage in this situation? Compare this with the gain from leverage in Problem 12-2.

    d.   Set $T_c = T_s = T_d = 0$. What is the value of the levered firm? The gain from leverage?

    e.   Now suppose $T_s = T_d = 0$. What are the value of the levered firm and the gain from leverage?

    f.   Assume that $T_d = 28\%$, $T_s = 28\%$, and $T_c = 40\%$. Now what are the value of the levered firm and the gain from leverage?

12-4   **(MM with and without taxes)** European Partners Limited (EPL) is just about to commence operations as an international trading company. The firm will have book assets of $10 million, and it expects to earn a 16 percent return on these assets before taxes. However, because of certain tax arrangements with foreign governments, EPL will not pay any taxes, that is, its tax rate will be zero. Management is trying to decide how to raise the required $10 million. It is known that the capitalization rate for an all-equity firm in this business is 11 percent, that is, $k_{sU} = 11\%$. Further, EPL can borrow at a rate $k_d = 6\%$. Assume that the MM assumptions apply.

    a.   According to MM, what will be the value of EPL if it uses no debt? If it uses $6 million of 6 percent debt?

    b.   What are the values of the WACC and k_s at debt levels of $D = \$0$, $D = \$6$ million, and $D = \$10$ million? What effect does leverage have on firm value? Why?

    c.   Assume the initial facts of the problem ($k_d = 6\%$, EBIT $= \$1.6$ million, $k_{sU} = 11\%$), but now assume that a 40 percent federal-plus-state corporate tax rate exists. Find the new market values for EPL with zero debt and with $6 million of debt, using the MM formulas.

    d.   What are the values of the WACC and k_s at debt levels of $D = \$0$, $D = \$6$ million, and $D = \$10$ million, assuming a 40 percent corporate tax rate? Plot the relationships between the value of the firm and the debt ratio, and between capital costs and the debt ratio.

    e.   What is the maximum dollar amount of debt financing that can be used? What is the value of the firm at this debt level? What is the cost of this debt?

    f.   How would each of the following factors tend to change the values you plotted in your graph?

        (1) The interest rate on debt increases as the debt ratio rises.

        (2) At higher levels of debt, the probability of financial distress rises.

12-5   **(Agency costs)** Until recently, the Crary Company carried a triple-A bond rating and was strong in every respect. However, a series of problems has afflicted the firm: It is currently in severe financial distress, and its ability to make future payments on outstanding debt is questionable. If the firm were forced into bankruptcy at this time, the common stockholders would almost certainly be wiped out. Although the firm has limited financial resources, its cash flows (primarily from depreciation) are sufficient to support one of two mutually exclusive investments, each costing $150 million and having a 10-year expected life. These projects have the same market risk, but different total risk as measured by the variance of returns. Each project has the following after-tax cash inflows for 10 years:

	Annual Cash Inflows	
Probability	Project A	Project B
0.5	$30,000,000	$10,000,000
0.5	35,000,000	50,000,000

Assume that both projects have the same market risk as the firm's "average" project. The firm's weighted average cost of capital is 15 percent.

a. What is the expected annual cash inflow from each project?

b. Which project has the greater total risk?

c. Which project would you choose if you were a stockholder? Why?

d. Which project would the bondholders prefer to see management select? Why?

e. If the choices conflict, what "protection" do the bondholders have against the firm's making a decision that is contrary to their interests?

f. Who bears the cost of this "protection"? How is this cost related to leverage and the optimal capital structure?

12-6 **(MM with financial distress costs)** Magee, Inc., currently has no debt. An in-house research group has just been assigned the job of determining whether the firm should change its capital structure. Because of the importance of the decision, management has also hired the investment banking firm of Stanley Morgan & Company to conduct a parallel analysis of the situation. Mr. Smith, the in-house analyst, who is well versed in modern finance theory, has decided to carry out the analysis using the MM framework. Mr. Jones, the Stanley Morgan consultant, who has a good knowledge of capital market conditions and is confident of his ability to predict the firm's debt and equity costs at various levels of debt, has decided to estimate the optimal capital structure as that structure which minimizes the firm's weighted average cost of capital. The following data are relevant to both analyses:

$$\text{EBIT} = \$4 \text{ million per year, in perpetuity.}$$

$$\text{Federal-plus-state tax rate} = 40\%.$$

$$\text{Dividend payout ratio} = 100\%.$$

$$\text{Current required rate of return on equity} = 12\%.$$

The cost of capital schedule predicted by Mr. Jones follows:

	At a Debt Level of (Millions of Dollars)							
	$0	$2	$4	$6	$8	$10	$12	$14
Interest rate (%)	—	8.0	8.3	9.0	10.0	11.0	13.0	16.0
Cost of equity (%)	12.0	12.25	12.75	13.0	13.15	13.4	14.65	17.0

Mr. Smith estimated the present value of financial distress costs at $8 million. Additionally, he estimated the following probabilities of financial distress:

	At a Debt Level of (Millions of Dollars)							
	$0	$2	$4	$6	$8	$10	$12	$14
Probability of financial distress	0	0	0.05	0.07	0.10	0.17	0.47	0.90

a. What level of debt would Mr. Jones and Mr. Smith recommend as optimal?

b. Comment on the similarities and differences in their recommendations.

12-7 (MM with financial distress costs) The Wallace Corporation is an unlevered firm, and it has constant expected operating earnings (EBIT) of $2 million per year. Wallace's federal-plus-state tax rate is 40 percent, its cost of equity is 10 percent, and its market value is V = S = $12 million. Management is considering the use of debt which would cost the firm 8.0 percent regardless of the amount used. (Debt would be issued and used to buy back stock, so the size of the firm would remain constant.) Since interest expense is tax deductible, the value of the firm would tend to increase as debt is added to the capital structure, but there would be an offset in the form of rising risk of financial distress. The firm's analysts have estimated, as an approximation, that the present value of any future financial distress costs is $8 million, and that the probability of distress would increase with leverage according to the following schedule:

Value of Debt	Probability of Distress
$ 0	0.0%
2,500,000	2.5
5,000,000	5.0
7,500,000	10.0
10,000,000	25.0
12,500,000	50.0
15,000,000	75.0

a. According to the "pure" MM with corporate taxes model, what is the optimal level of debt? (Consider only those debt values listed in the table.)

b. What is the optimal capital structure when financial distress costs are included?

(Do Parts c, d, e, and f only if you are using the computerized diskette.)

c. Plot the value of the firm, with and without financial distress costs, as a function of the level of debt.

d. Assume that the firm's unlevered cost of equity is 8 percent. What is the firm's optimal capital structure now? (From this point on, include financial distress costs in all your analyses.)

e. Return to the base case k_{sU} of 10 percent. Now assume that the firm's tax rate increases to 60 percent. What effect does this change have on the firm's optimal capital structure?

f. Return to the base case tax rate of 40 percent. Assume that the estimated present value of financial distress costs is only $5 million. Now what is the firm's optimal capital structure?

Mini Case

Donald Cheney, the CEO of Cheney Electronics, is concerned about his firm's level of debt financing. The company uses short-term debt to finance its temporary working capital needs, but it does not use any permanent (long-term) debt. Other electronics companies average about 30 percent debt, and Mr. Cheney wonders why the difference occurs, and what its effects are on stock prices. To gain some insights into the matter, he poses the following questions to you, his recently hired assistant:

a. *Business Week* recently ran an article on companies' debt policies, and the names Modigliani and Miller (MM) were mentioned several times as leading researchers on the theory of capital structure. Briefly, who are MM, and what assumptions are embedded in the MM and Miller models?

b.   Assume that Firms U and L are in the same risk class, and that both have EBIT = $500,000. Firm U uses no debt financing, and its cost of equity is k_{sU} = 14%. Firm L has $1 million of debt outstanding at a cost of k_d = 8%. There are no taxes. Assume that the MM assumptions hold, and then:
   (1) Find V, S, k_s, and k_a = WACC for Firms U and L.
   (2) Graph (a) the relationships between capital costs and leverage as measured by D/V, and (b) the relationship between value and D.

c.   Using the data given in Part b, but now assuming that firms L and U are both subject to a 40 percent corporate tax rate, repeat the analysis called for in b(1) and b(2) under the MM with-tax model.

d.   Now suppose investors are subject to the following tax rates: T_d = 30% and T_s = 25%.
   (1) What is the gain from leverage according to the Miller model?
   (2) How does this gain compare to the gain in the MM model with corporate taxes?
   (3) What does the Miller model imply about the effect of corporate debt on the value of the firm, that is, how do personal taxes affect the situation?

e.   What capital structure policy recommendations do the three theories (MM without taxes, MM with corporate taxes, and Miller) suggest to financial managers? Empirically, do firms appear to follow any one of these guidelines?

f.   What are financial distress and agency costs? How does the addition of these costs change the MM and Miller models? (Express your answer in words, in equation form, and in graphical form.)

g.   Briefly describe the asymmetric information theory of capital structure.

h.   Are the tradeoff and asymmetric information theories mutually exclusive? What do you believe that capital structure theory prescribes for financial managers? What insights does capital structure theory provide regarding the factors that influence firms' optimal capital structures?

Selected Additional References and Cases

The body of literature on capital structure—and the number of potential references—is huge. Therefore, only a sampling can be given here. For an extensive review of the recent literature, as well as a detailed bibliography, see

Beranek, William, "Research Directions in Finance," *Quarterly Review of Business and Economics,* Spring 1981, 6–24.

The major theoretical works on capital structure theory are discussed in an integrated framework in

Copeland, Thomas E., and J. Fred Weston, *Financial Theory and Corporate Policy* (Reading, Mass.: Addison-Wesley, 1988).

The Fall 1988 issue of The Journal of Economic Perspectives *contains five interesting and very readable articles which review the MM propositions after 30 years of debate and testing.*

In addition to Miller's work, the effect of personal taxes on capital structure decisions has been addressed by

Gordon, Myron J., and Lawrence I. Gould, "The Cost of Equity Capital with Personal Income Taxes and Flotation Costs," *Journal of Finance,* September 1978, 1201–1212.

For a recent article on the asymmetric information theory, see

Baskin, Jonathon, "An Empirical Investigation of the Pecking Order Hypothesis," *Financial Management,* Spring 1989, 26–35.

Some other references of note include the following:

Ben-Horim, Moshe, Shalom Hockman, and Oded Palmon, "The Impact of the 1986 Tax Reform Act on Corporate Financial Policy," *Financial Management,* Autumn 1987, 29–35.

Bradley, Michael, Gregg A. Jarrell, and E. Han Kim, "On the Existence of an Optimal Capital Structure: Theory and Evidence," *Journal of Finance,* July 1984, 857–878.

Conine, Thomas E., Jr., "Debt Capacity and the Capital Budgeting Decision: Comment," *Financial Management,* Spring 1980, 20–22.

Crutchley, Claire E., and Robert S. Hansen, "A Test of the Agency Theory of Managerial Ownership, Corporate Leverage, and Corporate Dividends," *Financial Management,* Winter 1989, 36–46.

Ferri, Michael, and Wesley H. Jones, "Determinants of Financial Structure: A New Methodological Approach," *Journal of Finance,* June 1979, 631–644.

Flath, David, and Charles R. Knoeber, "Taxes, Failure Costs, and Optimal Industry Capital Structure," *Journal of Finance,* March 1980, 89–117.

Kelly, William A., Jr., and James A. Miles, "Capital Structure Theory and the Fisher Effect," *The Financial Review,* February 1989, 53–73.

Lee, Wayne Y., and Henry H. Barker, "Bankruptcy Costs and the Firm's Optimal Debt Capacity: A Positive Theory of Capital Structure," *Southern Economic Journal,* April 1977, 1453–1465.

Martin, John D., and David F. Scott, "Debt Capacity and the Capital Budgeting Decision: A Revisitation," *Financial Management,* Spring 1980, 23–26.

Miller, Merton H., "The Modigliani-Miller Propositions after Thirty Years," *Journal of Applied Corporate Finance,* Spring 1989, 6–18.

Pinegar, J. Michael, and Lisa Wilbricht, "What Managers Think of Capital Structure Theory: A Survey," *Financial Management,* Winter 1989, 82–91.

Scherr, Frederick C., "A Multiperiod Mean-Variance Model of Optimal Capital Structure," *The Financial Review,* February 1987, 1–31.

Schneller, Meir I., "Taxes and the Optimal Capital Structure of the Firm," *Journal of Finance,* March 1980, 119–127.

Taggart, Robert A., Jr., "Taxes and Corporate Capital Structure in an Incomplete Market," *Journal of Finance,* June 1980, 645–659.

There has been considerable discussion in the literature concerning a financial leverage clientele effect. Many theorists postulate that firms with low leverage are favored by high-tax bracket investors and vice versa. Two articles on this subject are

Harris, John M., Jr., Rodney L. Roenfeldt, and Philip L. Cooley, "Evidence of Financial Leverage Clienteles," *Journal of Finance,* September 1983, 1125–1132.

Kim, E. Han, "Miller's Equilibrium, Shareholder Leverage Clienteles, and Optimal Capital Leverage," *Journal of Finance,* May 1982, 301–319.

For a very readable discussion of the many issues involved in capital structure theory, see

"A Discussion of Corporate Capital Structure," *Midland Corporate Finance Journal,* Fall 1985, 19–48.

Case 7, "Raymond Aluminum Products," in the Brigham-Gapenski casebook, focuses on capital structure theory.

CHAPTER 13

Capital Structure Policy

At the 1989 annual meeting of the Financial Management Association, one panel session consisted of financial managers from Hershey Foods, Bell Atlantic, and EG&G, who discussed how their firms set capital structure policy. Although there were minor differences among the participants, several themes came through loud and clear.

First, in practice it is impossible to specify a point value for a firm's optimal capital structure. Indeed, it is even difficult to specify a range for the optimal capital structure. Thus, financial managers are primarily concerned about whether their firms are overleveraged or underleveraged, and much less concerned about the precise optimal level of debt. Second, a firm's capital structure can vary widely from the theoretical optimum and yet have little impact on the value of the firm. This suggests that, unless the firm's capital structure is obviously way off the mark, capital structure decisions should be secondary in importance to other decisions, especially capital investment decisions, which have a far greater potential for affecting a firm's value.

Because of these points, firms focus more on identifying a "prudent" level of debt than on setting a precise optimal level. A prudent level of debt should capture most of the benefits of debt financing, and, at the same time, (1) keep financial risk at a manageable level, (2) ensure financing flexibility, and (3) maintain a desirable credit rating. Thus, a prudent level of debt will protect the company against financial distress under all reasonable economic scenarios, will ensure access to capital and money markets, and will maintain a bond rating consistent with the firm's financing policy. For example, a minimum debt rating of A is required if the firm is to issue commercial paper.

> This panel session reinforced our view that establishing a proper capital structure is an imprecise process at best, and one which involves a combination of quantitative analysis and informed judgment.

IN Chapter 12, we discussed the major capital structure theories and the insights they provide to financial managers. Now, in Chapter 13, we discuss some additional concepts that are relevant to capital structure decisions, and we consider how financial managers make capital structure decisions in practice.

BUSINESS AND FINANCIAL RISK

In Chapters 4 and 5, when we examined risk from the viewpoint of the individual investor, we distinguished between *market risk,* which is measured by the firm's beta coefficient, and *total risk,* which includes both market risk and an element of risk which can be eliminated by diversification. Now we introduce two new dimensions of risk: (1) *business risk,* or the riskiness of the firm's assets if it uses no debt, and (2) *financial risk,* the additional risk placed on the common stockholders as a result of the firm's decision to use debt.[1] Conceptually, the firm has a certain amount of risk inherent in its operations: this is its business risk. If the firm uses debt, then it in effect partitions its investors into two groups and concentrates most of its business risk on one class of investors—the common stockholders. However, the common stockholders are compensated for their higher risk by a higher expected return. Business and financial risk can be examined within a total risk framework, which ignores the benefits of diversification, or within a market risk framework, where part of the business and financial risk is eliminated by diversification.

Self-Test Question

Explain the difference between business risk and financial risk.

BUSINESS AND FINANCIAL RISK: A TOTAL RISK PERSPECTIVE

We begin our discussion of business risk and financial risk with a focus on total risk. A market risk perspective is provided in the next major section.

---

[1]Using preferred stock also adds to financial risk. To simplify matters somewhat, we concentrate on debt and common equity in this chapter.

Business Risk

Business risk, in a total risk sense, is measured by the uncertainty inherent in projections of a firm's future return on assets (ROA). We could measure ROA in several ways, but for purposes of capital structure analysis, the following definition is most appropriate:

$$\text{Return on assets} \atop (\text{ROA}) = \frac{\text{Return to investors}}{\text{Assets}} = \frac{\text{Net income to common stockholders } + \text{ Interest payments}}{\text{Assets}}.$$

Further, since a firm's assets must be equal to the capital that has been invested in the form of debt and equity, assets equal investment, and we can rewrite the rate of return equation as the return on investment, ROI:

$$\text{Return on} \atop \text{investment} \atop (\text{ROI}) = \frac{\text{Net income to common stockholders } + \text{ Interest payments}}{\text{Investment}}.$$

Thus, business risk can be measured by the standard deviation of either ROA or ROI.

Note also that if a firm uses no debt, then its interest payments will be zero, its assets will be all-equity financed, and its return on investment will equal its return on equity, ROE:

$$\text{ROI (zero debt)} = \text{ROE} = \frac{\text{Net income to common stockholders}}{\text{Common equity}}.$$

Therefore, the business risk of a *leverage-free* firm can be measured by the standard deviation of its expected ROE, σ_{ROE}.

To illustrate all this, consider Strasburg Electronics Company, a debt-free (unlevered) firm. Figure 13-1 gives some clues about the company's business risk. The top graph shows the trend in the firm's ROE from 1980 through 1990; this graph gives both security analysts and Strasburg's management an idea of the degree to which ROE has varied in the past and consequently might vary in the future. This graph also shows that Strasburg's ROE is growing slowly because of inflation, so the relevant variability of ROE is the dispersion about the trend line.

The lower graph shows the beginning-of-year subjectively estimated probability distribution of Strasburg's ROE for 1990, based on the trend line in the top section of Figure 13-1. As both graphs indicate, Strasburg's actual ROE in 1990 was only 8 percent, well below the expected value of 12 percent—1990 was a bad year.

Strasburg's past fluctuations in ROE were caused by many factors—booms and recessions in the national economy, successful new products introduced both by Strasburg and by its competitors, labor strikes, price controls, a fire in Strasburg's main plant, and so on. Similar events will doubtless occur in the future, and when they do, the realized ROE will be higher or lower than the projected level. Further, there is always the possibility that a long-term disaster might strike, permanently depressing the company's earning power; for example, a competitor might intro-

Figure 13-1 Strasburg Electronics: Trend in ROE, 1980–1990 and Subjective Probability Distribution of ROE, 1990

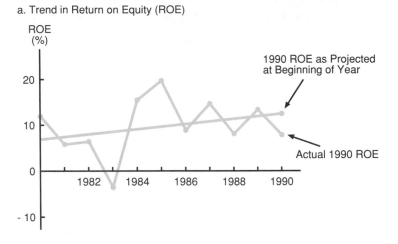

a. Trend in Return on Equity (ROE)

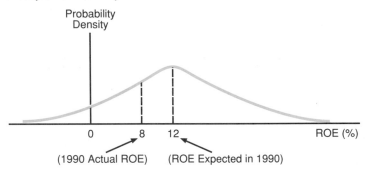

b. Subjective Probability Distribution of ROE

duce a new product that would permanently lower Strasburg's earnings. This uncertainty regarding Strasburg's future ROE is defined as the company's *basic business risk.*

Business risk varies not only from industry to industry, but also among firms in a given industry. Further, business risk can change over time. For example, the electric utilities were regarded for years as having little business risk, but a combination of events in the 1970s and 1980s altered the utilities' situation, producing sharp declines in their ROEs and greatly increasing the industry's business risk. Now, food processors and grocery retailers are frequently given as examples of industries with low business risk, while cyclical manufacturing industries such as steel are regarded as having especially high business risk. Also, smaller companies, and those that are dependent on a single product, are often regarded as having a high degree of business risk.[2]

Business risk depends on a number of factors; the more important ones are listed next:

1.   **Demand variability.** The more stable the demand for a firm's products, other things held constant, the lower its business risk.

2.   **Sales price variability.** Firms whose products are sold in highly volatile markets are exposed to more business risk than similar firms whose output prices are more stable.

3.   **Input cost variability.** Firms whose input costs are highly uncertain are exposed to a high degree of business risk.

4.   **Ability to adjust output prices for changes in input costs.** Some firms are better able than others to raise their own output prices when input costs rise. The greater the ability to adjust output prices to reflect cost conditions, the lower the degree of business risk, other things held constant.

5.   **The extent to which costs are fixed: operating leverage.** If a high percentage of a firm's costs are fixed, hence do not decline when demand falls off, then the firm is exposed to a relatively high degree of business risk. This factor is called *operating leverage,* and it is discussed at length in the next section.

Each of these factors is determined partly by the firm's industry characteristics, but each of them is also controllable to some extent by management. For example, most firms can, through their marketing policies, take actions to stabilize both unit sales and sales prices. However, this stabilization may require firms to spend a great deal on advertising and/or price concessions in order to get commitments from their customers to purchase fixed quantities at fixed prices in the future. Similarly, firms such as Strasburg Electronics can reduce the volatility of future input costs by negotiating long-term labor and materials supply contracts, but they may have to agree to pay prices above the current spot price level to obtain these contracts.[3]

Operating Leverage

As noted above, business risk depends in part on the extent to which a firm builds fixed costs into its operations — if fixed costs are high, even a small decline in sales can lead to a large decline in ROE, so, other things held constant, the higher a firm's fixed costs, the greater its business risk. Higher fixed costs are generally associated with more highly automated, capital intensive firms and industries. Also, businesses

---

[2]We have avoided any discussion of market versus company-specific risk in this section. We note now (1) that any action which increases business risk in the total risk sense will generally also increase a firm's beta coefficient, and (2) that a part of business risk as we define it here will generally be company-specific, hence subject to elimination by diversification by the firm's stockholders. This point is discussed at some length in the next major section.

[3]For example, in 1990 utilities could buy coal in the spot market for about $30 per ton. Under a 5-year contract, coal cost about $50 per ton. Clearly, the price for reducing uncertainty was high!

that employ highly skilled workers who must be retained and paid even during recessions have relatively high fixed costs.

If a high percentage of a firm's total costs are fixed, then the firm is said to have a high degree of *operating leverage*. In physics, leverage implies the use of a lever to raise a heavy object with a small force. In politics, if people have leverage, their smallest word or action can accomplish a lot. *In business terminology, a high degree of operating leverage, other factors held constant, implies that a relatively small change in sales results in a large change in ROE.*

Figure 13-2 illustrates the concept of operating leverage by comparing the results that Strasburg would achieve if it used different degrees of operating leverage. Plan A calls for a relatively small amount of fixed costs, $20,000. Here the firm would not have much automated equipment, so its depreciation, maintenance, property taxes, and so on would be low, but the total operating costs line has a relatively steep slope, indicating that variable costs per unit are higher than they would be if the firm used more operating leverage. Plan B calls for a higher level of fixed costs, $60,000. Here the firm uses automated equipment (with which one operator can turn out a few or many units at the same labor cost) to a much larger extent. The breakeven point is higher under Plan B: Breakeven occurs at 60,000 units under Plan B versus only 40,000 units under Plan A.

We can calculate the breakeven quantity by recognizing that breakeven occurs when ROE = 0, and, hence, when earnings before interest and taxes (EBIT) = 0:

$$EBIT = 0 = PQ - VQ - F. \qquad \text{(13-1)}$$

Here P is average sales price per unit of output, Q is units of output, V is variable cost per unit, and F is fixed operating costs.[4] We can solve Equation 13-1 for the breakeven quantity, Q_{BE}:

$$Q_{BE} = \frac{F}{P - V}. \qquad \text{(13-1a)}$$

Thus, for Plan A,

$$Q_{BE} = \frac{\$20,000}{\$2.00 - \$1.50} = 40,000 \text{ units,}$$

and for Plan B,

$$Q_{BE} = \frac{\$60,000}{\$2.00 - \$1.00} = 60,000 \text{ units.}$$

How does operating leverage affect business risk? *Other things held constant, the higher a firm's operating leverage, the higher its business risk.* This point is demonstrated in Figure 13-3, where we develop probability distributions for ROE under Plans A and B.

---

[4]This definition of breakeven does not include any fixed financial costs, because Strasburg is an unlevered firm. If there were fixed financial costs, the firm would suffer an accounting loss at the operating breakeven point. Thus, Equation 13-1 defines the *operating* breakeven level of sales. We will introduce financial costs shortly.

Figure 13-2   Strasburg Electronics: Illustration of Operating Leverage

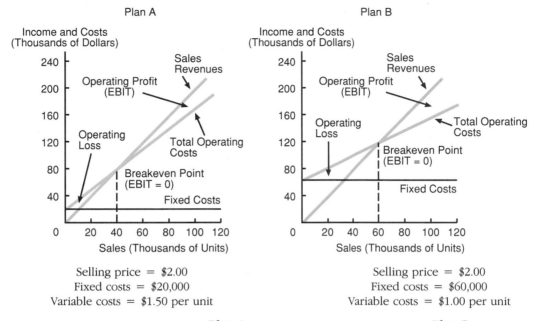

Selling price = $2.00
Fixed costs = $20,000
Variable costs = $1.50 per unit

Selling price = $2.00
Fixed costs = $60,000
Variable costs = $1.00 per unit

Prob-ability	Units Sold, Q	Sales	Plan A Operating Costs	EBIT	NI	ROE	Plan B Operating Costs	EBIT	NI	ROE
0.03	0	$ 0	$ 20,000	($20,000)	($12,000)	(6.9%)	$ 60,000	($ 60,000)	($36,000)	(20.6%)
0.07	40,000	80,000	80,000	0	0	0.0	100,000	(20,000)	(12,000)	(6.9)
0.15	60,000	120,000	110,000	10,000	6,000	3.4	120,000	0	0	0.0
0.50	110,000	220,000	185,000	35,000	21,000	12.0	170,000	50,000	30,000	17.1
0.15	160,000	320,000	260,000	60,000	36,000	20.6	220,000	100,000	60,000	34.3
0.07	180,000	360,000	290,000	70,000	42,000	24.0	240,000	120,000	72,000	41.1
0.03	220,000	440,000	350,000	90,000	54,000	30.9	280,000	160,000	96,000	54.9
Expected value				$35,000	$21,000	12.0%		$50,000	$30,000	17.1%
Standard deviation				$23,249	$13,949	8.0%		$46,497	$27,898	15.9%

Notes:
a. Strasburg Electronics has a 40 percent federal-plus-state tax rate.
b. The firm uses no debt financing.
c. Assets = equity = $175,000.

The left-hand section of Figure 13-3 graphs the probability distribution of sales that was presented in tabular form in Figure 13-2. The sales probability distribution depends on how demand for the product varies, and not on whether the product is manufactured by Plan A or by Plan B. Therefore, the same sales probability distribution applies to both production plans; this distribution has expected sales of $220,000, and it ranges from zero to about $450,000, with $\sigma_{Sales} = \$92,995$.

Figure 13-3   Strasburg Electronics: Analysis of Business Risk

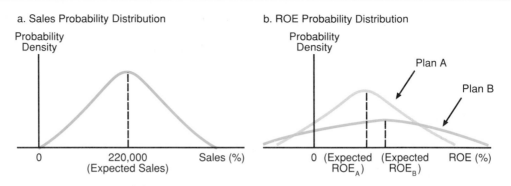

a. Sales Probability Distribution

Probability Density

0   220,000   Sales (%)
         (Expected Sales)

b. ROE Probability Distribution

Probability Density

Plan A

Plan B

0   (Expected   (Expected   ROE (%)
      ROE$_A$)   ROE$_B$)

Note: We are using continuous distributions to approximate the discrete distributions contained in Figure 13-2. Using data from Figure 13-2, we calculate $\sigma_{Sales} = \$92,995$.

We use the sales probability distribution, together with the operating costs at each sales level, to develop graphs of the ROE probability distributions under Plans A and B. These are shown in the right-hand section of Figure 13-3. Plan B has a higher expected ROE, but this plan also entails a much higher probability of large losses. Clearly, Plan B, the one with more fixed costs and a higher degree of operating leverage, is riskier. *In general, holding other factors constant, the higher the degree of operating leverage, the greater the firm's business risk as measured by the standard deviation of its expected ROE.*

To what extent can firms control their operating leverage? To a large extent, operating leverage is determined by technology. Electric utilities, telephone companies, airlines, steel mills, and chemical companies simply *must* have heavy investments in fixed assets; this results in high fixed costs and operating leverage. Grocery stores, on the other hand, generally have significantly lower fixed costs, hence lower operating leverage. Still, although industry factors do exert a major influence, all firms do have some control over their operating leverage. For example, an electric utility can expand its generating capacity by building either a nuclear reactor or a coal-fired plant. The nuclear plant would require a larger investment and have higher fixed costs, but its variable operating costs would be relatively low. The coal plant, on the other hand, would require a smaller investment and would have lower fixed costs, but the variable costs (for coal) would be high. Thus, by its capital budgeting decisions, a utility (or any other company) can influence its operating leverage, hence its basic business risk.

The concept of operating leverage was, in fact, originally developed for use in capital budgeting. Mutually exclusive projects which involve alternative methods for producing a given product often have different degrees of operating leverage, and thus different breakeven points and different degrees of risk. Strasburg Electronics and many other companies regularly undertake a type of breakeven analysis (the sensitivity analysis discussed in Chapter 11) for each proposed project as a part of their regular capital budgeting process. Still, once a corporation's operating leverage has been established, this factor exerts a major influence on its capital structure decision. This point is covered next.

Financial Risk

Financial risk is the additional risk placed on the common stockholders as a result of the decision to finance with debt and/or preferred stock. Conceptually, a firm has a certain amount of risk inherent in its operations—this is its business risk, which is defined as the uncertainty inherent in projections of future ROE, assuming that the firm is solely financed with common stock. If a firm uses debt and preferred stock (financial leverage), this concentrates its business risk on the common stockholders. To illustrate, suppose 10 people decide to form a corporation to manufacture steel roof trusses. There is a certain amount of business risk in the operation. If the firm is capitalized only with common equity, and if each person buys 10 percent of the stock, then each investor shares equally in the business risk. However, suppose the firm is capitalized with 50 percent debt and 50 percent equity, with five of the investors putting up their capital as debt and the other five putting up their money as equity. In this case, those investors who put up the equity will have to bear all of the business risk, so the common stock will be twice as risky as it would have been had the firm been financed only with equity. Thus, the use of debt, or *financial leverage,* concentrates the firm's business risk on its stockholders.

To illustrate the concentration of business risk, again consider Strasburg Electronics. Strasburg has $175,000 in assets and is all-equity financed.[5] If the firm were using Plan A from Figure 13-2, then its expected ROE would be 12.0 percent with a standard deviation of 8.0 percent. Now suppose the firm decides to change its capital structure by issuing $87,500 of debt at $k_d = 10\%$ and using these funds to replace $87,500 of equity. Its expected return on equity (which would now be only $87,500) would rise from 12 to 18 percent:

Expected EBIT (unchanged)	$35,000
Interest (10% on $87,500 of debt)	8,750
Earnings before taxes	$26,250
Taxes (40%)	10,500
Net income	$15,750
Expected ROE = $15,750/$87,500 =	18%

Thus, the use of debt would "leverage up" the expected ROE from 12 percent to 18 percent.

---

[5]A firm in business for at least 10 years would likely have far more than $175,000 in assets. We are purposely keeping Strasburg Electronics small so that we may focus on the concepts without being overwhelmed by the numbers. Also note that, to be consistent with capital structure theory, we should be working with market values of securities rather than book values of assets. We are using book values at this point to simplify the illustration, but we will discuss market value relationships later in the chapter. In this regard, see Haim Levy and Robert Brooks, "Financial Break-Even Analysis and the Value of the Firm," *Financial Management,* Autumn 1986, 22–26.

However, financial leverage also increases risk to the equity investors. For example, suppose EBIT actually turned out to be $5,000 rather than the expected $35,000. If the firm used no debt, then ROE would decline from 12.0 percent to 1.7 percent. However, with debt financing, ROE would fall from 18.0 to −2.6 percent:

	Zero Debt	$87,500 of Debt
Actual EBIT	$5,000	$5,000
Interest (10%)	0	8,750
Earnings before taxes	$5,000	−$3,750
Taxes (40%)	2,000	− 1,500
Net income	$3,000	−$2,250
Actual ROE	1.7%	−2.6%
Expected ROE	12.0%	18.0%

A more complete analysis of the effects of leverage on Strasburg's ROE is illustrated in Figure 13-4. The two lines in the top graph show the level of ROE that would exist at different levels of EBIT under the two different capital structures. The lines were plotted from data developed as described previously, and they show that the greater the use of financial leverage, the more sensitive ROE is to changes in EBIT.

The lower panel of Figure 13-4 shows the effects of leverage on the firm's ROE probability distribution. With zero debt, the company would have an expected ROE of 12 percent, and a relatively tight distribution. With 50 percent debt, the expected ROE would rise to 18 percent, but the ROE distribution would be much flatter, indicating a larger standard deviation of returns (σ_{ROE}) and a more risky situation for the equity investors. In fact, the standard deviation of ROE is 8.0 percent at zero debt, but exactly twice as high, 16.0 percent, at 50 percent debt.

Our conclusions from this analysis may be stated as follows:

1. The use of debt generally increases the expected ROE; this situation occurs whenever the expected return on assets (measured by EBIT/Total assets) exceeds the cost of debt.

2. σ_{ROE} assuming zero financial leverage, $\sigma_{ROE(U)}$, is a measure of the firm's business risk, and σ_{ROE} at any debt level, $\sigma_{ROE(L)}$, is a measure of the risk borne by stockholders. $\sigma_{ROE(U)} = \sigma_{ROE(L)}$ if the firm does not use any financial leverage. However, if the firm does use debt, then $\sigma_{ROE(L)} > \sigma_{ROE(U)}$ because business risk is being concentrated on the stockholders.

3. The difference between $\sigma_{ROE(U)}$, which is both the firm's business risk and the risk that stockholders would bear if no financial leverage were used, and $\sigma_{ROE(L)}$, which is the risk stockholders in leveraged firms actually face, is a measure of the risk-increasing effects of financial leverage:

$$\text{Risk from financial leverage} = \sigma_{ROE(L)} - \sigma_{ROE(U)}.$$

In our example,

$$\text{Risk from financial leverage} = 16.0\% - 8.0\% = 8.0\%.$$

Figure 13-4   Strasburg Electronics: Effects of Financial Leverage on ROE

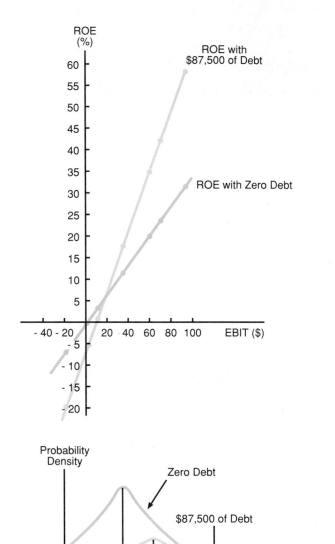

4.   Operating leverage and financial leverage normally work in the same way; they both increase expected ROE, but they also increase the risk borne by stockholders.[6] Operating leverage affects the firm's business risk, financial leverage affects the firm's financial risk, and both influence the firm's total risk.

Self-Test Questions

How can business risk be measured in a total risk context?

What are some determinants of business risk?

How can financial risk be measured within a total risk framework?

What is operating leverage? What are the similarities between operating leverage and financial leverage?

BUSINESS AND FINANCIAL RISK: A MARKET RISK PERSPECTIVE

Thus far our discussion of business and financial risk has focused on total risk. We have used $\sigma_{ROE(U)}$ as the measure of business risk and $\sigma_{ROE(L)}$ as the measure of the total risk borne by the stockholders in leveraged firms. Thus, in the total risk sense, $\sigma_{ROE(L)} - \sigma_{ROE(U)}$ is a measure of financial risk. Recall, though, that part of a firm's total risk can be eliminated if its stockholders diversify their own portfolios. This point is addressed in this section, where we shift our focus from total risk to *market, or beta, risk.*

In an important article, Robert Hamada combined the CAPM with the MM after-tax model to obtain this expression for k_{sL}, the cost of equity to a leveraged firm:[7]

$$k_{sL} = \frac{\text{Risk-free}}{\text{rate}} + \frac{\text{Business risk}}{\text{premium}} + \frac{\text{Financial risk}}{\text{premium}}$$

$$= k_{RF} + (k_M - k_{RF})b_U + (k_M - k_{RF})b_U(1 - T)(D/S). \tag{13-2}$$

Here b_U is the beta coefficient the firm would have if it used no financial leverage, and the other terms are as defined in previous chapters. In effect, Equation 13-2 partitions the required rate of return on the stock of a leveraged firm into three components: k_{RF}, the risk-free rate, which compensates shareholders for the time value of money; a premium for business risk as reflected by the term $(k_M - k_{RF})b_U$; and a premium for financial risk as reflected by the third term,

---

[6]Note that for operating leverage to benefit shareholders, the firm must be operating at a sales level above the breakeven point, and for financial leverage to be of benefit, the cost of debt must be less than the return on assets as measured by EBIT/Total assets. Normally, when managers make operating and financing decisions, they expect the firm to be operating above the breakeven point, and they expect the return on assets to exceed the cost of debt.

[7]See Robert S. Hamada, "Portfolio Analysis, Market Equilibrium, and Corporation Finance," *Journal of Finance,* March 1969, 13–31. Note that Thomas Conine and Maurry Tamarkin have extended Hamada's work to include risky debt. See "Divisional Cost of Capital Estimation: Adjusting for Leverage," *Financial Management,* Spring 1985, 54–58.

$(k_M - k_{RF})b_U(1 - T)(D/S)$. If a firm has no financial leverage $(D = \$0)$, then the financial risk premium term would be zero (the third term would drop out) and equity investors would be compensated only for business risk.

As we saw in the last chapter, the MM model with corporate taxes does not hold exactly, and we also know that the CAPM does not fully describe investor behavior. Therefore, Equation 13-2 must be regarded as an approximation. Nevertheless, Equation 13-2 can provide financial managers with some useful insights. As an illustration, assume that Firm U, an unlevered company with $b_U = 1.5$ and \$100,000 of equity $(S = \$100,000)$, is considering replacing \$20,000 of equity with debt. If $k_{RF} = 10\%$, $k_M = 15\%$, and $T = 34\%$, then Firm U's current unlevered required rate of return on equity would be 17.5 percent:

$$k_{sU} = 10\% + (15\% - 10\%)1.5$$

$$= 10\% + 7.5\% = 17.5\%.$$

This shows that the business risk premium is 7.5 percentage points. If the firm were to add \$20,000 of debt to its capital structure, then its new value, according to MM, would be $V_L = V_U + TD = \$100,000 + 0.34(\$20,000) = \$106,800$, and its k_s, using Equation 13-2, would rise to 18.64 percent:

$$k_{sL} = 10\% + (15\% - 10\%)1.5 + (15\% - 10\%)1.5(1 - 0.34)(\$20,000/\$86,800)$$

$$= 10\% + 7.5\% + 1.14\% = 18.64\%.$$

Thus, adding \$20,000 of debt to the capital structure would result in a financial risk premium on the stock of 1.14 percentage points, which would be added to the business risk premium of 7.5 percentage points.

Hamada also showed that Equation 13-2 can be used to analyze the effect of a firm's financial leverage on its beta. We know that under the CAPM, the SML can be used to determine a firm's required rate of return on equity:

$$\text{SML: } k_{sL} = k_{RF} + (k_M - k_{RF})b_L.$$

Now, by equating the SML equation with Equation 13-2, we obtain:

$$k_{RF} + (k_M - k_{RF})b_L = k_{RF} + (k_M - k_{RF})b_U + (k_M - k_{RF})b_U(1 - T)(D/S)$$

$$(k_M - k_{RF})b_L = (k_M - k_{RF})b_U + (k_M - k_{RF})b_U(1 - T)(D/S)$$

$$b_L = b_U + b_U(1 - T)(D/S), \qquad \textbf{(13-3)}$$

or

$$b_L = b_U[1 + (1 - T)(D/S)]. \qquad \textbf{(13-3a)}$$

Thus, under the MM and CAPM assumptions, the beta of a levered firm is equal to the beta the firm would have if it used zero debt, adjusted upward by a factor that depends on (1) the corporate tax rate and (2) the amount of financial leverage employed.[8] Therefore, the firm's market risk, which is measured by b_L, depends on

---

[8]If a firm uses preferred stock financing, then Equation 13-3 becomes

$$b_L = b_U + b_U(P/S) + b_U(1 - T)(D/S),$$

where P = market value of preferred stock. Here, the unlevered beta is adjusted upward by the preferred stock as well as the debt financing.

both the firm's business risk as measured by b_U and its financial risk as measured by $b_L - b_U = b_U(1 - T)(D/S)$.

To continue our illustration, if Firm U were to replace \$20,000 of equity with debt, its beta would increase from 1.5 to 1.728, according to Equation 13-3a:

$$b_L = b_U[1 + (1 - T)(D/S)]$$

$$= 1.5[1 + (1 - 0.34)(20,000/\$86,800)]$$

$$= 1.5(1.152) = 1.728.$$

We can confirm the Equation 13-2 value of $k_{sL} = 18.64\%$ by using $b_L = 1.728$ in the SML:

$$k_{sL} = k_{RF} + (k_M - k_{RF})b_L$$

$$= 10\% + (15\% - 10\%)1.728 = 18.64\%.$$

These relationships can be used to help estimate a company's or a division's cost of equity. In both instances, we proceed by obtaining betas for similar publicly traded firms and then "lever them up or down" to make them consistent with our own firm's (or division's) capital structure and tax rate. The result is an estimate of our firm's (or division's) beta, given (1) its business risk as measured by the betas of other firms in the same industry and (2) its financial risk as measured by its own capital structure and tax rate.

Self-Test Questions

According to Hamada, the required rate of return on a stock consists of three elements. What are they?

How is business risk measured within a market risk framework?

How is financial risk measured within a market risk framework?

What is the relationship between levered and unlevered betas according to Hamada?

ESTIMATING THE TARGET CAPITAL STRUCTURE: A SIMPLIFIED EXAMPLE

We saw in Chapter 12 that the tax benefit/financial distress tradeoff theory leads to the conclusion that each firm has an optimal capital structure, one which maximizes its value and minimizes its weighted average cost of capital. In this section, we present an illustration which demonstrates many of the points discussed in Chapter 12.

Hill Software Systems

Hill Software Systems (HSS) was founded in 1980 to develop and market a new type of operating system for personal computers. The basic program was written and patented by Mark Hill, HSS's founder. Hill owns a majority of the stock, although a

Table 13-1 Data on Hill Software Systems

Balance Sheet as of December 31, 1990

Current assets	$ 500,000	Debt	$	0
Net fixed assets	500,000	Common equity (1.0 million shares outstanding)		1,000,000
Total assets	$1,000,000	Total claims		$1,000,000

Income Statement for 1990

Sales		$20,000,000
Fixed operating costs	$ 4,000,000	
Variable operating costs	12,000,000	16,000,000
Earnings before interest and taxes (EBIT)		$ 4,000,000
Interest		0
Taxable income		$ 4,000,000
Taxes (40% federal-plus-state)		1,600,000
Net income		$ 2,400,000

Other Data

1. Earnings per share = EPS = $2,400,000/1,000,000 shares = $2.40.
2. Dividends per share = DPS = $2,400,000/1,000,000 shares = $2.40. Thus, the company has a 100 percent payout ratio.
3. Book value per share = $1,000,000/1,000,000 shares = $1.
4. Market price per share = P_0 = $20. Thus, the stock sells at 20 times its book value.
5. Price/earnings ratio = P/E = $20/2.40 = 8.33 times.
6. Dividend yield = DPS/P_0 = $2.40/$20 = 12%.

significant portion is held by institutional investors. The company has no debt, and HSS's key financial data are shown in Table 13-1. Assets are carried at a book value of $1 million; hence, the common equity also has a balance sheet value of $1 million. However, these balance sheet figures are not very meaningful because (1) the asset figures do not include any value for patents and (2) the fixed assets were purchased several years ago at lower than today's prices.

Mark Hill will retire shortly, and he is planning to sell a major part of his interest in the company to the public, using the proceeds of the sale to diversify his personal portfolio. As a part of the planning process, the question of capital structure has arisen. Should the firm continue its policy of using no debt, or should it recapitalize? And if it does decide to substitute debt for equity, how far should it go? As in all such decisions, the correct answer is that *it should choose that capital structure which maximizes the value of the company*. If the company's total market value is maximized, so will be the price of its stock, and its cost of capital will simultaneously be minimized.

To simplify the analysis, we assume that the long-run demand for HSS's products is not expected to grow; hence, its EBIT is expected to continue at $4 million. (However, future sales may turn out to be different from the expected level, so realized

Figure 13-5 HSS's Cost of Debt and Equity and Beta

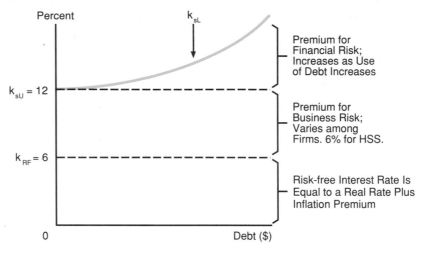

Amount Borrowed[a] (1)	Interest Rate on All Debt, k_d (2)	Estimated Beta Coefficient of Stock, b[b] (3)	Required Rate of Return on Stock, k_s[c] (4)
$ 0	—	1.50	12.0%
2,000,000	8.0%	1.55	12.2
4,000,000	8.3	1.65	12.6
6,000,000	9.0	1.80	13.2
8,000,000	10.0	2.00	14.0
10,000,000	12.0	2.30	15.2
12,000,000	15.0	2.70	16.8
14,000,000	18.0	3.25	19.0

[a]HSS is unable to borrow more than $14 million because of limitations on interest coverage in its corporate charter.
[b]Note that the beta coefficient estimates do not correspond to Hamada's equation (Equation 13-3a). The estimates here are subjective estimates furnished by investment bankers.
[c]We assume here that k_{RF} = 6% and k_M = 10%. Therefore, at zero debt, k_s = 6% + (10% − 6%) 1.5 = 12%. Other values of k_s are calculated similarly.

EBIT may be more or less than the expected $4 million.) Also, since the company has no need for new capital, all of its income will be paid out as dividends.

Now assume that HSS's treasurer consults with the firm's investment bankers and learns that debt can be sold, but the more debt used, the riskier the debt, and, of course, the higher the interest rate, k_d. Also, the bankers state that the more debt HSS uses, the greater the riskiness of its stock, hence the higher its required rate of return on equity, k_s. Estimates of k_d, beta, and k_s at different debt levels are given in Figure 13-5, along with a graph of the relationship between k_s and debt level.

Given the data in Table 13-1, along with those in Figure 13-5, we can determine HSS's total market value, V, at different capital structures, and we can then use this information to establish the company's stock price as a function of its capital structure. These equations, which were developed in earlier chapters, are used in the analysis:[9]

$$V = D + S. \tag{13-4}$$

$$S = \frac{\text{Net income after taxes}}{k_s} = \frac{(\text{EBIT} - k_d D)(1 - T)}{k_s}. \tag{13-5}$$

$$P_0 = \frac{\text{DPS}}{k_s} = \frac{\text{EPS}}{k_s}. \tag{13-6}$$

$$\text{WACC} = (D/V)(k_d)(1 - T) + (S/V)(k_s). \tag{13-7}$$

We first substitute values for k_d, D, and k_s into Equation 13-5 to obtain values for S, the market value of common equity, at each level of debt, D, and we then sum S and D to find the total value of the firm. Table 13-2 and Figure 13-6, which plots selected data from the table, were developed by this process. The values shown in Columns 1, 2, and 3 of the table were taken from Figure 13-5, while those in Column 4 were obtained by solving Equation 13-5 at different debt levels. The values for the firm given in Column 5 were obtained by summing Columns 1 and 4, D + S = V.

To see how the stock prices shown in Column 6 were developed, visualize this series of events:

1.   Initially, HSS has no debt. The firm's value is $20 million, or $20 for each of its 1 million shares. (See the top line of Table 13-2.)

2.   Management announces a decision to change the capital structure; legally, the firm *must* make an explicit announcement or run the risk of having stockholders sue the directors.

3.   The values shown in Columns 1 through 5 of Table 13-2 are estimated as described previously. The major institutional investors, and the large brokerage companies which advise individual investors, have analysts just as capable of making these estimates as the firm's management. These analysts would start making their own estimates as soon as HSS announced the planned change in leverage, and they would presumably reach similar conclusions to those of the HSS analysts.

4.   HSS's stockholders initially own the entire company. (There are not yet any bondholders.) They see, or are told by their advisor-analysts, that very shortly the value of the enterprise will rise from $20 million to some higher amount, presumably the maximum attainable, or $21,727,000. Thus, they anticipate that the value of the firm will increase by $1,727,000.

5.   This additional $1,727,000 will accrue to the firm's current stockholders. Since there are 1 million shares of stock, each share will rise in value by $1.73, or from $20 to $21.73.

---

[9]Note that Equations 13-4 through 13-7 do not stem from a particular capital structure theory—they do not require acceptance of MM, Miller, or any other theory. Rather, they are definitions and basic DCF valuation equations for perpetual cash flows.

Table 13-2 HSS's Value, Stock Price, and Cost of Capital at Different Debt Levels

Value of Debt, D (in Millions) (1)	k_d (2)	k_s (3)	Value of Stock, S (in Millions) (4)	Value of Firm, V (in Millions) (1) + (4) = (5)	Stock Price, P_0 (6)	D/V (7)	k_a = WACC (8)
$ 0.0	—	12.0%	$20.000	$20.000	$20.00	0.0%	12.0%
2.0	8.0%	12.2	18.885	20.885	20.89	9.6	11.5
4.0	8.3	12.6	17.467	21.467	21.47	18.6	11.2
6.0	**9.0**	**13.2**	**15.727**	**21.727**	**21.73**	**27.6**	**11.0**
8.0	10.0	14.0	13.714	21.714	21.71	36.8	11.1
10.0	12.0	15.2	11.053	21.053	21.05	47.5	11.4
12.0	15.0	16.8	7.857	19.857	19.86	60.4	12.1
14.0	18.0	19.0	3.158	17.158	17.16	81.6	12.3

Notes:

a. The data in Columns 1 through 3 were taken from Figure 13-5.

b. The values for S in Column 4 were found by use of Equation 13-5:

$$S = \frac{\text{Net income}}{k_s} = \frac{(EBIT - k_dD)(1 - T)}{k_s}.$$

For example, at D = $0,

$$S = \frac{(\$4.0 - 0)(0.6)}{0.12} = \frac{\$2.4}{0.12} = \$20.0 \text{ million,}$$

and at D = $6.0,

$$S = \frac{[\$4.0 - 0.09(\$6.0)](0.6)}{0.132} = \frac{\$2.076}{0.132} = \$15.727 \text{ million.}$$

c. The values for V in Column 5 were obtained as the sum of D + S. For example, at D = $6.0, V = $6.0 + $15.727 = $21.727 million.

d. The stock prices shown in Column 6 are equal to the value of the firm as shown in Column 5 divided by the original number of shares outstanding, which in this case is 1 million. The logic behind this procedure is explained in the text.

e. Column 7 is found by dividing Column 1 by Column 5. For example, at D = $6.0, D/V = $6.0/$21.727 = 27.6%.

f. Column 8 is found by use of Equation 13-7. For example, at D = $6.0,

$$WACC = (D/V)(k_d)(1 - T) + (S/V)(k_s)$$
$$= (0.276)(9\%)(0.6) + (0.724)(13.2\%) = 11.0\%.$$

g. At $14.0 million of debt, EBIT declines from $4 million to $3.52 million.

h. The row in boldface indicates the optimal amount of debt.

6. This price increase will occur *before* the transaction is completed. Suppose, for example, that the stock price remained at $20 after the announcement of the recapitalization plan. Shrewd investors would immediately recognize that the stock's price will soon go up to $21.73, and they would place orders to buy at any price below $21.73. This buying pressure would quickly run the price up to $21.73, at which point it would remain constant. Thus, $21.73 is the *equilibrium stock price* for HSS once the decision to recapitalize is announced.

Figure 13-6 Relationship between HSS's Capital Structure,
Cost of Capital, and Stock Price

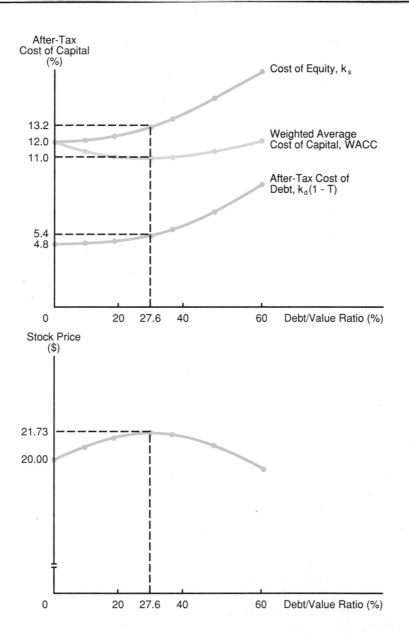

7.   The firm sells $6 million of bonds at an interest rate of 9 percent. This money is used to buy stock at the market price, which is now $21.73, so 276,116 shares are repurchased:

$$\text{Shares repurchased} = \frac{\$6,000,000}{\$21.73} = 276,116.$$

8.   The value of the stock after the 276,116 shares have been repurchased is $15,727,000, as shown in Column 4 of Table 13-2. There are $1,000,000 - 276,116 = 723,884$ shares still outstanding, so the value per share of the remaining stock is

$$\text{Value per share} = \frac{\$15,727,000}{723,884} = \$21.73.$$

This confirms our earlier calculation of the equilibrium stock price.

9.   The same process was used to find stock prices at other capital structures; these prices are given in Column 6 of Table 13-2 and plotted in the lower graph of Figure 13-6. *Since the maximum price occurs when HSS uses $6 million of debt, its optimal capital structure calls for $6 million of debt.* Note that $6 million of debt corresponds to a firm value of $21.727 million. Thus, the optimal market value capital structure, D/V*, is $6/$21.727 = 27.6%.

10.   In this example, we assumed that EBIT would decline from $4 million to $3.52 million if the firm's debt rose to $14 million. The reason for the decline is that, at this very high level of debt, managers and employees would be worried about the firm's failing and about losing their jobs; suppliers would not sell to the firm on normal credit terms; orders would be lost because of customers' fears that the company might go bankrupt and thus be unable to deliver; and so on. EBIT is independent of financial leverage at "reasonable" debt levels, but at extreme degrees of leverage, EBIT is adversely affected.

11.   Quite obviously, the situation in the real world is much more complex, and less exact, than this example suggests. Most important, different investors will have different estimates for EBIT and k_s, hence will form different expectations about the equilibrium stock price. This means that HSS might have to pay more than $21.73 to repurchase its shares, or perhaps that the shares could be bought at a lower price. These changes would cause the optimal amount of debt to be somewhat higher or lower than $6 million. Still, $6 million represents our best estimate as to the optimal debt level, so it is the level we should use as our target capital structure.

12.   The WACC for the various levels of debt is shown in Column 8 of Table 13-2. It can be seen that the minimum cost of capital, 11.0 percent, corresponds to the level of debt at which the value of the firm and its stock price are maximized, $6.0 million.

The stock price and cost of capital relationships developed in Table 13-2 are graphed in Figure 13-6. Here we see that HSS's stock price is maximized, and its weighted average cost of capital is minimized, at the same D/V ratio, 27.6 percent.

Extensions of the Example

In the preceding section, we examined the effects of debt financing on its stock price if HSS went from zero debt to some positive level of debt. Now we will examine the general effects of a change from one debt level to some other level, using this equation:

$$P_1 = \frac{\text{Ending value of firm} - \text{Beginning value of debt}}{\text{Beginning number of shares}}. \qquad \textbf{(13-8)}$$

Note that the beginning value of debt could be zero, so Equation 13-8 is general in the sense that it could apply to any analysis, zero initial debt or not. In this section, we explain the logic of Equation 13-8, and we illustrate it with three different cases.

Example 1: Zero Initial Debt. Suppose we wish to determine what would happen to HSS's stock price if it went from zero debt to $4 million of debt. This requires us to find new values of V and P, V_1 and P_1, with $4 million of debt:

$$V_1 = D_1 + S_1 = D_1 + \frac{(\text{EBIT} - k_d D)(1 - T)}{k_s}$$

$$= \$4,000,000 + \frac{(\$4,000,000 - \$332,000)(0.6)}{0.126}$$

$$= \$4,000,000 + \$17,466,667 = \$21,466,667.$$

$$P_1 = \frac{\text{Ending value} - \text{Beginning debt}}{\text{Beginning shares}} = \frac{\$21,466,667 - \$0}{1,000,000}$$

$$= \$21.47, \text{ versus } P_0 = \$20 \text{ with zero debt.}$$

As explained previously, this stock price would exist *as soon as investors learned of the recapitalization plans, before the plans were actually carried out.* Stockholders would recognize that the company will have a value of $21,466,667 very shortly, and this value will belong entirely to them because they will receive the $4,000,000 brought in by the sale of bonds as payment for shares repurchased. Note also that management must inform all stockholders of the planned recapitalization. If you were a stockholder, you would certainly not be willing to sell your stock back to the company at $20 per share if you expected to see the stock price rise to $21.47. You and the other stockholders would insist on receiving as much if you sold your stock back to the company as you would end up with if you chose not to sell it.[10]

---

[10]Indeed, if you and other stockholders were silly enough to sell at $20 per share, then the $4 million of debt could be used to buy and retire even more shares, so the remaining shares would be worth even more than $21.47. In fact, the stock would, under these conditions, be worth $21.83:

$$P_1 = \frac{S_1}{n_1} = \frac{\$17,466,667}{1,000,000 - (\$4,000,000/\$20)} = \$21.83.$$

Of course, you might be afraid that the recapitalization plan would fall through, so you might be willing to sell out for slightly less than $21.47, say for $21, figuring that $21 in the hand is better than $21.47 in the bush.

Once the plan had been carried out, the shares outstanding would decline from 1,000,000 to 813,694:

$$\text{New shares} = \text{Old shares} - \text{Shares repurchased}$$

$$n_1 = n_0 - \text{Shares repurchased}$$

$$= n_0 - \frac{\text{Incremental debt}}{\text{Price per share}}$$

$$= 1{,}000{,}000 - \frac{\$4{,}000{,}000}{\$21.47}$$

$$= 1{,}000{,}000 - 186{,}306$$

$$= 813{,}694 \text{ shares after repurchase.}$$

Check on stock price:

$$P_1 = \frac{\text{New value of equity}}{\text{New shares outstanding}} = \frac{S_1}{n_1} = \frac{\$17{,}466{,}667}{813{,}694} = \$21.47.$$

Had we made similar calculations, but used $6 million of debt, the resulting stock price would have been $21.73 as shown in Table 13-2.

Example 2: $4 Million Initial Debt. Now assume that HSS had actually made the move to $4 million of debt, and management is now considering another increase in leverage. What would happen to HSS's stock price if it increased its leverage from $4 million to $6 million of debt? Assume that its old debt must be retired if new debt is issued, so the entire $6 million of debt will have a cost of 9 percent (from Figure 13-5). Now the analysis will begin with these initial values:

$$\text{Initial debt value} = D_0 = \$4{,}000{,}000.$$

$$\text{Initial stock value} = S_0 = \$17{,}466{,}667.$$

$$\text{Initial total value} = V_0 = \$21{,}466{,}667.$$

$$\text{Initial stock price} = P_0 = \$21.47.$$

$$\text{Initial number of shares} = n_0 = 813{,}694.$$

The new equilibrium total value will be

$$V_1 = D_1 + S_1$$

$$= \$6{,}000{,}000 + \frac{(\$4{,}000{,}000 - \$540{,}000)(0.6)}{0.132}$$

$$= \$6{,}000{,}000 + \$15{,}727{,}273 = \$21{,}727{,}273,$$

and the new equilibrium stock price will be

$$P_1 = \frac{V_1 - D_0}{n_0} = \frac{\$21{,}727{,}273 - \$4{,}000{,}000}{813{,}694}$$

$$= \frac{\$17{,}727{,}273}{813{,}694} = \$21.79.$$

Thus, HSS could increase the value of its stock from $21.47 to $21.79 by increasing its leverage from $4 million to $6 million.[11] This second round of debt financing would increase the stockholders' gain by ($21.79 − $21.47)813,694 = $260,382.

Example 3: Nonreplacement of Old Debt. Now assume that HSS again plans to increase its leverage from $4 million to $6 million, but that the old debt need not be retired. Here, the $4 million in old debt would remain in force, carrying a coupon rate of 8.3 percent. As before, assume that the new debt issue of $2 million would have a cost of 9 percent. Assuming the same initial values as in Example 2, the new equilibrium values are calculated as follows:

1. $$S_1 = \frac{\left[\text{EBIT} - \left(\begin{array}{c}\text{Cost of}\\\text{old debt}\end{array}\right)\left(\begin{array}{c}\text{Amount of}\\\text{old debt}\end{array}\right) - \left(\begin{array}{c}\text{Cost of}\\\text{new debt}\end{array}\right)\left(\begin{array}{c}\text{Amount of}\\\text{new debt}\end{array}\right)\right](1 - T)}{k_s}$$

$$= \frac{[\$4,000,000 - (0.083)(\$4,000,000) - (0.09)(\$2,000,000)](0.6)}{0.132}$$

$$= \frac{(\$3,488,000)(0.6)}{0.132} = \$15,854,545.$$

2.   The old debt has a book value of $4,000,000. However, because more debt is to be issued, the risk of the old debt will rise and consequently its market value will fall to $3,688,889:

$$D_0' = \frac{0.083(\$4,000,000)}{0.09} = \$3,688,889 \text{ versus } \$4,000,000.$$

3.   The loss suffered by the old bondholders is $311,111:

$$D_0 - D_0' = \$4,000,000 - \$3,688,889 = \$311,111.$$

4.   The new value of the firm will be

$$V_1 = D_1 + S_1 = D_0' + \text{New debt} + S_1$$

$$= \$3,688,889 + \$2,000,000 + \$15,854,545 = \$21,543,434.$$

5.   The new equilibrium stock price will be

$$P_1 = \frac{\$21,543,434 - \$3,688,889}{813,694} = \$21.943.$$

6.   The stockholders will have an aggregate gain calculated as follows:

$$\text{Stockholders' gain} = (P_1 - P_0)n_0$$

$$= (\$21.943 - \$21.467)(813,694) = \$387,318.$$

---

[11]Notice the slight difference in equilibrium stock prices at $6 million of debt: $21.73 in the first example versus $21.79 now. This difference demonstrates two points: (1) If HSS could move to its optimal capital structure in stages, it could repurchase shares at a lower average price than the equilibrium price of $21.73, and (2) if it could buy back shares at a lower price, its final price would be higher because more shares could be repurchased for a given expenditure (debt raised), hence fewer shares would be outstanding in the end.

7.   Of the stockholders' $387,318 gain, $311,111 will have "come out of the hides of the old bondholders," while $76,207 will have come as a "true gain from leverage" as a result of tax savings net of costs associated with financial distress:

$$\text{True gain from leverage} = V_1 - V_0$$

$$= \$21,543,434 - \$21,466,667 = \$76,767.$$

(There are rounding errors in these calculations.)

Thus, HSS could increase the value of its stock from $21.47 to $21.94 by increasing its leverage from $4 million to $6 million if it did not have to refund its initial lower-cost debt. Of course, this gain to stockholders would come mostly at the expense of the old bondholders. The addition of $2 million of new debt would increase the riskiness of all the firm's securities. The stockholders would be compensated, as would the new bondholders, but the old bondholders would still be receiving coupon payments of only 8.3 percent, even though the new debt increased the riskiness of HSS's bonds to the point where $k_d = 9\%$.[12] Therefore, the value of the old debt would fall, and there would be a transfer of wealth from the old bondholders to HSS's stockholders. Because of the possibility of such events, bond indentures often limit the amount of debt a firm can issue.

The Effect of Financial Leverage on EPS

Thus far we have focused on the impact of leverage on a firm's total value and its stock price. Before we leave the HSS illustration, we should also take a look at how leverage affects earnings per share (EPS); this is done in Table 13-3. The top third of the table gives operating income data. It begins by recognizing that HSS's future EBIT is not known with certainty. Expected EBIT is $4 million, but the realized EBIT could be less than or greater than $4 million. To simplify matters, we have assumed a discrete distribution of sales, thus EBIT, with only three possible outcomes. Notice that here EBIT is assumed not to depend on financial leverage.[13]

The middle third of Table 13-3 shows the situation that would exist if HSS continues to use no debt. Net income after taxes is divided by the 1 million shares outstanding to calculate EPS. If sales were as low as $10 million, EPS would be zero, but EPS would rise to $4.80 at sales of $30 million.

---

[12]The $2 million of additional debt might actually have a cost somewhat below 9 percent. This is because retention of the old debt at 8.3 percent would result in lower total interest payments at the new debt level than if the entire $6 million of debt had cost 9 percent. Given equal business risk, the lower interest payments would lower the probability of financial distress, and thus lower the riskiness of the new debt. Additionally, lower distress risk would mean that equity holders might have a required return somewhat less than the 13.2 percent indicated in Table 13-2. However, these gains all come at the expense of the existing bondholders—the addition of new debt makes the old debt more risky, yet the old debtholders will not be compensated for the additional risk. Our analysis does not include these effects; they would, of course, be extremely hard to measure with any degree of confidence.

[13]As we discussed earlier, capital structure does affect EBIT at very high debt levels. For example, we assumed that HSS's EBIT would fall from $4 million to $3.52 million if the level of debt rose to $14 million. However, debt in Table 13-3 is limited to $10 million, so the "excessive leverage effect on EBIT" is not present in this particular example.

Table 13-3   HSS's EPS at Different Amounts of Debt
(Millions of Dollars Except per-Share Figures)

Operating Income (EBIT)

Probability of indicated sales	0.2	0.6	0.2
Sales	$10.00	$20.00	$30.00
Fixed costs	4.00	4.00	4.00
Variable costs (60% of sales)	6.00	12.00	18.00
Total costs (except interest)	$10.00	$16.00	$22.00
Earnings before interest and taxes (EBIT)	$ 0.00	$ 4.00	$ 8.00

Zero Debt

Less interest	0.00	0.00	0.00
Earnings before taxes	$ 0.00	$ 4.00	$ 8.00
Less taxes (40%)	0.00	1.60	3.20
Net income	$ 0.00	$ 2.40	$ 4.80
Earnings per share on 1 million shares (EPS)	$ 0.00	$ 2.40	$ 4.80
Expected EPS		$ 2.40	
Standard deviation of EPS[a]		$ 1.52	
Coefficient of variation of EPS[a]		0.63	

$10 Million of Debt

Less interest (0.12 × $10,000,000)	1.20	1.20	1.20
Earnings before taxes	($1.20)	$ 2.80	$ 6.80
Less taxes (40%)[b]	(0.48)	1.12	2.72
Net income	($0.72)	$ 1.68	$ 4.08
Earnings per share on 524,940 shares (EPS)[c]	($1.37)	$ 3.20	$ 7.77
Expected EPS		$ 3.20	
Standard deviation of EPS[a]		$ 2.90	
Coefficient of variation of EPS[a]		0.91	

[a]Procedures for calculating the standard deviation and the coefficient of variation were discussed in Chapter 4.

[b]Assume tax credit on losses. If credits were not available, expected EPS would be lower, and risk higher, at high debt levels.

[c]Shares outstanding is determined as follows:

$$\text{Shares} = \text{Original shares} - \frac{\text{Debt}}{\text{Stock price}} = 1,000,000 - \frac{\text{Debt}}{\text{Stock price}},$$

where the stock price is taken from Table 13-2, Column 6. With $10 million of debt, P = $21.05. After the recapitalization, 524,940 shares will remain outstanding:

$$\text{Shares} = 1,000,000 - \frac{\$10,000,000}{\$21.05} = 524,940.$$

EPS figures can also be calculated using this formula:

$$\text{EPS} = \frac{(\text{EBIT} - k_dD)(1 - T)}{\text{Original shares} - \text{Debt/Price}}.$$

For example, at D = $10 million,

$$\text{EPS} = \frac{[\$4,000,000 - (0.12)(\$10,000,000)](0.6)}{1,000,000 - \$10,000,000/\$21.05} = \frac{\$1,680,000}{524,940} = \$3.20.$$

The EPS at each sales level is next multiplied by the probability of that sales level to obtain the expected EPS, which is $2.40 if HSS uses no debt. We also calculate the standard deviation of EPS and its coefficient of variation to get an idea of the firm's total risk at a zero debt ratio: $\sigma_{EPS} = \$1.52$, and $CV_{EPS} = 0.63$.

The lower third of Table 13-3 shows the financial results that would occur if the company decided to use $10 million of debt. The interest rate on the debt, 12 percent, is taken from Figure 13-5. With $10 million of 12 percent debt outstanding, the company's interest expense is $1.2 million per year. This is a fixed cost, and it is deducted from EBIT as calculated in the top section. Next, taxes are taken out, and we work on down to the EPS figures that would result at each sales level. With $10 million of debt, EPS would be −$1.37 if sales were as low as $10 million; it would rise to $3.20 if sales were $20 million; and it would soar to $7.77 if sales were as high as $30 million.

Continuous approximations of the EPS distributions under the two financial structures are graphed in Figure 13-7. Although expected EPS is much higher if the firm uses financial leverage, the graph makes it clear that the risk of low or even negative EPS is also higher if debt is used. Figure 13-7 shows clearly that using leverage involves a risk/return tradeoff—higher leverage increases expected earnings per share, but using more leverage also increases the firm's risk. It is this increasing risk that causes k_s and k_d to increase at higher amounts of financial leverage.

The relationship between expected EPS and financial leverage is plotted in the top section of Figure 13-8. Here we see that expected EPS first rises as the use of debt increases—interest charges rise, but the decreasing number of shares out-

Figure 13-7   Probability Distribution of EPS for HSS with Different Amounts of Financial Leverage

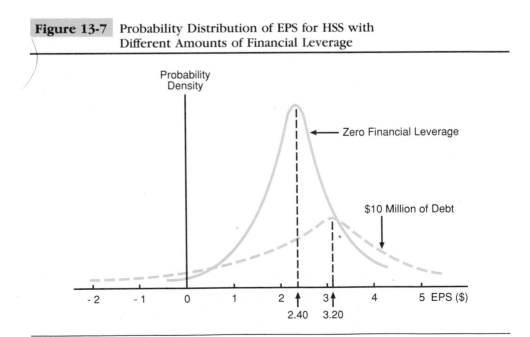

Figure 13-8   Relationship between HSS's Expected EPS and Stock Price

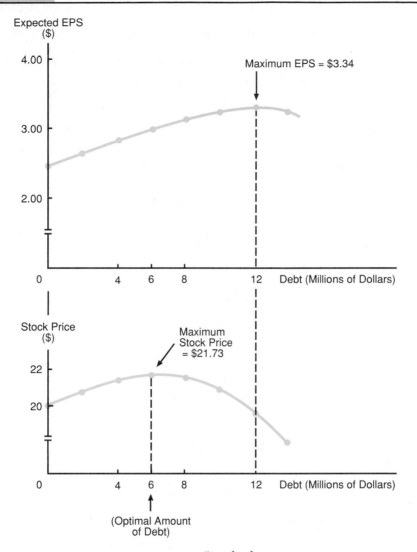

Debt	Expected EPS	Standard Deviation of EPS	Coefficient of Variation	Stock Price[b]
$ 0	$2.40[a]	$1.52[a]	0.63[a]	$20.00
2,000,000	2.55	1.68	0.66	20.89
4,000,000	2.70	1.87	0.69	21.47
6,000,000	2.87	2.09	0.73	21.73
8,000,000	3.04	2.40	0.80	21.71
10,000,000	3.20[a]	2.90[a]	0.91[a]	21.05
12,000,000	3.34	3.83	1.15	19.86
14,000,000	3.26	5.20	1.60	17.16

[a]These values are taken from Table 13-3. Values at other debt levels were calculated similarly.
[b]Stock prices are from Table 13-2.

standing as debt is substituted for equity still causes EPS to increase. However, EPS peaks when $12 million of debt is used. Beyond this amount, interest rates rise rapidly, and EBIT begins to fall, so EPS is depressed in spite of the falling number of shares outstanding. Risk as measured by the coefficient of variation of EPS shown in the fourth column of the data in Figure 13-8 rises continuously, and at an increasing rate, as debt is substituted for equity.

Does the same amount of debt maximize both price and EPS? The answer is *no*. As we can see from the lower graph in Figure 13-8, HSS's stock price is maximized with $6 million of debt, while the upper graph shows that expected EPS is maximized by using $12 million of debt. *Since management is primarily interested in maximizing the value of the stock, the optimal capital structure calls for the use of $6 million of debt.*

Problems with the HSS Analysis

The Hill Software Systems example illustrated the effects of leverage on firm value, stock prices, earnings per share, and debt values. However, the example was obviously simplified to facilitate the discussion, and we cannot overemphasize the difficulties that are encountered when one attempts to use this type of analysis in practice. First, the capitalization rates (k_d and especially k_s) are very difficult to estimate. The cost of debt at different debt levels can generally be estimated with some degree of confidence, but cost of equity estimates must be viewed as very rough approximations.[14]

Second, the mathematics of the valuation process make the outcomes very sensitive to the input estimates. Thus, fairly small errors in the estimates of k_d, k_s, and EBIT can lead to large errors in estimated EPS and stock price.

Third, our example was restricted to the case of a no-growth firm. In view of the input requirements to model even a simple no-growth situation, and the still greater requirements for the growth model, it is unrealistic to think that a precise optimal capital structure can really be identified.

Finally, many firms are not publicly owned, and that causes still more difficulties. If a privately held firm's owner never plans to have his or her firm go public, then potential market value data are really irrelevant. However, an analysis based on market values for a privately owned firm is very useful if the owner is interested in knowing how the firm's market value would be affected by leverage should the decision be made to go public.

---

[14]The statistical relationship between k_s and financial leverage has been studied extensively by using both cross-sectional and time series data. In the cross-sectional studies, a sample of firms is analyzed, with multiple regression techniques used in an attempt to "hold constant" all factors other than financial leverage that might influence k_s. The general conclusion of the cross-sectional studies is that k_s rises as leverage increases, but statistical problems preclude us from specifying the functional relationship with much confidence.

In the time series studies, a single firm's k_s is analyzed over time in an attempt to see how k_s changes in response to changes in its debt ratio. Here again, "other factors" do not remain constant, so it is impossible to specify exactly how k_s is affected by financial leverage.

Self-Test Questions

What are the key assumptions used in the Hill Software Systems example?

Briefly describe the steps involved in finding Hill's optimal capital structure.

Why is the stock price higher when the firm adds debt in increments rather than a single step, even when the existing issue is retired?

Why is the stock price higher when the existing issue remains outstanding rather than being refunded?

What problems are there with the procedures used in the Hill example for estimating "real world" optimal capital structures?

SOME CONSIDERATIONS IN THE CAPITAL STRUCTURE DECISION

Since one cannot determine precisely the optimal capital structure, managers must apply judgment along with quantitative analysis. The judgmental analysis involves several different factors, and in one situation a particular factor might have great importance, while the same factor might be relatively unimportant in another situation. This section discusses some of the more important judgmental issues that should be taken into account.

Long-Run Viability

Managers of large firms, especially those providing vital services such as electricity or telephone service, have a responsibility to provide *continuous* service, so they must refrain from using leverage to the point where the firm's long-run viability is endangered. Long-run viability may conflict with stock price maximization and cost of capital minimization.[15]

Managerial Conservatism

Well-diversified investors have eliminated most, if not all, of the diversifiable risk from their portfolios. Therefore, the typical investor can tolerate some chance of financial distress, because a loss on one stock would probably be offset by random gains on other stocks in his or her portfolio. However, managers often view financial distress with more concern—they are typically not well diversified, and their ca-

---

[15]Recognizing this fact, most public service commissions require utilities to obtain their approval before issuing long-term securities, and Congress has empowered the SEC to supervise the capital structures of public utility holding companies. However, in addition to concern over the firms' safety, which suggests low debt ratios, both managers and regulators recognize a need to keep all costs as low as possible, including the cost of capital. Since a firm's capital structure affects its cost of capital, regulatory commissions and utility managers try to select capital structures that minimize utilities' cost of capital, subject to the constraint that a firm's ability to finance needed construction projects is not endangered.

reers, and thus the present value of their expected earnings, can be seriously affected by the onset of financial distress. Thus, it is not difficult to imagine that managers might be more "conservative" in their use of leverage than the average stockholder would desire. If this is true, then managers would set somewhat lower target capital structures than the ones which maximize expected stock prices. The managers of a publicly owned firm would never admit this, for unless they owned voting control, they would quickly be removed from office. However, in view of the uncertainties about what constitutes the value-maximizing structure, management could always say that the target capital structure employed is, in its judgment, the value-maximizing structure, and it would be difficult to prove otherwise.[16]

Lender and Rating Agency Attitudes

Regardless of a manager's own analysis of the proper leverage for his or her firm, there is no question but that lenders' and rating agencies' attitudes are frequently important determinants of financial structures. In the majority of cases, the corporation discusses its financial structure with lenders and rating agencies, and gives much weight to their advice. Also, if a particular firm's management is so confident of the future that it seeks to use leverage beyond the norms for its industry, its lenders may be unwilling to accept such debt increases, or may do so only at a high price.

One of the primary measures of the risk of financial distress used by lenders and rating agencies is *coverage ratios.* Accordingly, managements give considerable weight to such ratios as the *times-interest-earned (TIE) ratio,* which is defined as EBIT divided by total interest charges. The lower this ratio, the higher the probability that a firm will encounter financial distress.

Table 13-4 shows how HSS's expected TIE ratio declines as its use of debt increases. At zero debt, the TIE ratio is undefined, but it is almost infinitely high at very low debt levels. When $2 million of debt is used, the expected TIE is a high 25 times, but the interest coverage ratio declines rapidly as debt rises. Note, however, that these coverages are expected values—the actual TIE will be higher if sales exceed the expected $20 million level, but lower if sales fall below $20 million.

The variability of the TIE ratio is highlighted in Figure 13-9, which shows the probability distributions of the ratio at $8 million and $12 million of debt. The expected TIE is much higher if only $8 million of debt is used. Even more important, with less debt there is a much lower probability of a TIE of less than 1.0, the level at which the firm is not earning enough to meet its required interest payment and is thus seriously exposed to the threat of bankruptcy.

---

[16]It is, of course, possible for a particular manager to be less conservative than his or her firm's average stockholder. However, this condition is less likely to occur than is excessive managerial conservatism, which is just another manifestation of the agency problem. If excessive conservatism exists, then managers, as agents of the stockholders, are not acting in the best interests of their principals. However, when managers become the primary owners of a company, such as in managerial buyouts (MBOs), they often become very aggressive in their use of financial leverage. By using extreme amounts of debt, they take on a great deal of risk, but, in the process, they open the door for big payoffs.

Table 13-4   HSS's Expected Times-Interest-Earned Ratio
at Different Amounts of Debt

Amounts of Debt (in Millions)	Expected TIE[a]
$ 0	Undefined
2	25.0
4	12.1
6	7.4
8	5.0
10	3.3
12	2.2

[a]TIE = EBIT/Interest. Example: TIE = $4,000,000/$1,200,000 = 3.3 at $10 million of debt. Data are from Table 13-1 and Figure 13-5.

Another ratio that is often used by lenders and rating agencies is the *fixed charge coverage (FCC) ratio*. This is a better measure than the TIE ratio because it recognizes that there are fixed charges other than interest payments which could lead to financial distress. The FCC ratio is defined as follows:

$$FCC = \frac{EBIT + Lease\ payments}{Interest + \left(\begin{array}{c}Lease \\ payments\end{array}\right) + \left(\dfrac{Sinking\ fund\ payments}{1 - T}\right)}.$$

Figure 13-9   Probability Distributions of Times-Interest-Earned Ratio
for HSS with Different Capital Structures

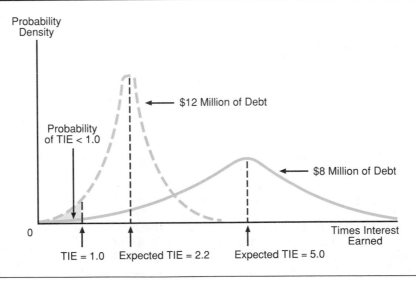

Note that the sinking fund payments are "grossed up" in recognition of the fact that these payments must be made with after-tax dollars (net income) because sinking fund payments are not tax deductible.

If HSS had $1 million of lease payments and $1 million of sinking fund payments, its FCC ratio at a debt level of $10 million would be 1.3:

$$\text{FCC} = \frac{\$4{,}000{,}000 \; + \; \$1{,}000{,}000}{\$1{,}200{,}000 \; + \; \$1{,}000{,}000 \; + \; \dfrac{\$1{,}000{,}000}{0.6}}$$

$$= \frac{\$5{,}000{,}000}{\$3{,}866{,}667} = 1.3.$$

Thus, the coverage of total fixed charges is considerably less than the 3.3 times-interest-earned coverage at the same $10 million debt level.

Borrowing Capacity Reserve

When we discussed the asymmetric information theory in Chapter 12, we noted that firms should maintain a borrowing capacity reserve, which preserves the ability to issue debt at favorable terms. For example, suppose Firm Y had just successfully completed an R&D program, and its internal projections forecast much higher earnings in the immediate future. However, the new earnings are not yet anticipated by investors, hence are not reflected in the price of its stock. Firm Y would not want to issue stock—it would prefer to finance with debt until the higher earnings materialized and were reflected in the stock price, at which time it could sell an issue of common stock, retire the debt, and return to its target capital structure. Similarly, if the financial manager felt that interest rates were temporarily low, but were likely to rise fairly soon, he or she might want to issue long-term bonds and thus "lock in" the favorable rates for many years. To maintain this borrowing capacity reserve, firms generally use less debt under "normal" conditions, hence presenting a stronger financial picture, than they otherwise would. This is not suboptimal from a long-run standpoint, although it might appear so if viewed strictly on a short-run basis.

Note too that firms' debt contracts often specify that no new debt can be issued unless certain ratios exceed minimum levels. Very frequently, the TIE ratio is required to exceed 2 or 2.5 times as a condition for the issuance of additional debt. With this in mind, look back at Figure 13-9 and note that, if it used $12 million of debt, HSS's TIE would be less than 2.0 almost half the time, whereas the probability of a coverage less than 2.0 would be quite small if it used only $8 million of debt.

Control

The effect that its choice of securities has on a management's control position may also influence its capital structure decision. If a firm's management just barely has majority control (just over 50 percent of the stock), but it is not in a position to buy any more stock, debt may be the choice for new financings. On the other hand, a management group that is not concerned about voting control may decide to use equity rather than debt if the firm's financial situation is so weak that the use of debt might subject the company to serious risk of default. If the firm gets into serious difficulties, the creditors (through covenants in the debt agreements) will assume control and perhaps force a management change. This has happened to Chrysler, Navistar International (formerly International Harvester), Braniff, Continental Illinois Bank, and a number of other companies in recent years. However, if too little debt is used, management runs the risk of a takeover, where some other company or management group tries to persuade stockholders to turn over control to the new group, which may plan to boost earnings and stock prices by using financial leverage. This happened to Lenox, the china company, and to many other firms in the 1980s. In general, control considerations do not necessarily suggest the use of debt or of equity, but if management does not have majority control, the effects of capital structure on control will certainly be taken into account.

Additional Considerations

In addition to those factors just listed, the following considerations are also relevant to the capital structure decision:

Asset Structure. Firms whose assets are suitable as security for loans tend to use debt rather heavily. Thus, real estate companies tend to be highly leveraged, but companies involved in technological research employ relatively little debt. Also, if the firm's assets carry high business risk, then it will be less able to use financial leverage than a firm with low business risk. Accordingly, factors such as sales stability and operating leverage, which influence business risk, also influence firms' optimal capital structures.

Growth Rate. Other factors the same, faster growing firms must rely more heavily on external capital—slow growth can be financed with retained earnings, but rapid growth generally requires the use of external funds. As postulated in the information asymmetry theory, firms first turn to debt financing to meet external funding needs. Further, the flotation costs involved in selling common stock exceed those incurred when selling debt. Thus, rapidly growing firms tend to use somewhat more debt than do slower-growth companies.

Profitability. One often observes that firms with very high rates of return on investment use relatively little debt. This behavior is consistent with the information asymmetry theory, and the practical reason seems to be that highly profitable firms such as IBM, 3M, and Kodak simply do not need to do much debt financing— their high rates of return enable them to do most of their financing with retained earnings.

Taxes. Interest is a deductible expense, while dividends are not deductible, so the higher a firm's corporate tax rate, the greater the advantage of using corporate debt.

Self-Test Questions

Is the capital structure decision mostly objective (made on the basis of numerical analysis) or mostly subjective (judgmental, with many factors considered)?

Briefly discuss some of the factors that managers should consider when setting the firm's target capital structure.

AN APPROACH TO SETTING THE TARGET CAPITAL STRUCTURE

Thus far in Chapters 12 and 13, we have discussed (1) several theories of capital structure, (2) a method of analysis based on these theories (including a discussion of the very severe problems one encounters with such an application of the theory), and (3) a myriad of factors which influence the capital structure decisions of most firms. In this section, we describe a pragmatic approach to setting the target capital structure. Our approach requires judgmental assumptions, but it also allows managers to see how alternative capital structures would affect future profitability, coverage, and external financing requirements under a variety of assumptions.

The starting point for the analysis is a forecasting model that is set up to test the effects of capital structure changes. Here is a brief description of one model and how it has been used. Basically, the *Lotus 1-2-3* model generates forecasted data based on inputs supplied by the financial manager. Each data item can be fixed, or it can be allowed to vary from year to year. The required data include the most recent balance sheet and income statement, plus the following items, all of which represent either expectations or policy variables:

1. Annual growth rates in unit sales
2. Annual inflation rates
3. Corporate tax rate
4. Variable costs as a percentage of sales
5. Fixed costs
6. Interest rate on already outstanding (or embedded) debt
7. Marginal component costs of capital
8. Capital structure percentages
9. Dividend growth rate
10. Long-term dividend payout ratio

The model uses the input data to forecast balance sheets and income statements for five years. Further, the model calculates and displays other information such as external financing requirements, ROE, EPS, DPS, times interest earned, stock price, and WACC for projected future years.

The financial manager begins by entering base year values and data on expected unit sales growth rates, expected inflation rates, and so on. These inputs are used by the model to forecast operating income and asset requirements which, in general, will *not* depend on the financing decision. Next, the financial manager must consider the financing mix. Our model permits as inputs both the debt/equity mix and the debt maturity mix. By debt maturity mix, we mean the proportion of short-term versus long-term debt. Further, the manager must estimate as best he or she can the effects of the capital structure on the component costs, and then must enter these cost rate estimates. A higher debt ratio will lead to increases in the costs of all components, and vice versa if less debt is used. With all inputs entered, the model then completes the forecasted financial statements and generates projected stock prices.

Next, the model's output must be reviewed and analyzed. Since we are focusing on the capital structure decision, we would pay particular attention to the forecasted EPS, coverage, and external funding requirements, as well as the projected stock price. Finally, the model is used to analyze alternative scenarios. This analysis takes two forms: (1) changing the financing inputs to get some idea of how the financing mix affects the key outputs, and (2) changing the operating inputs to see how the basic business risk of the firm affects the key outputs under various financing strategies.

The model can generate the output "answers" quite easily, but it remains up to the financial manager to assign input values, to interpret the output, and, finally, to set the target capital structure. The final decision is based on all the factors we have discussed in Chapters 12 and 13, and the decision maker must judge which factors are most relevant to his or her firm. Reaching a decision is not easy, but a capital structure forecasting model such as the one we use at least permits managers to analyze the effects of alternative courses of action, which is an essential element of good decision making.

It should be noted again that, although capital structure decisions do affect the prices of companies' stocks, those effects are relatively small in comparison to the effects of operating decisions. A company's ability to identify (or create) market opportunities, and to produce and sell products efficiently, is the primary determinant of success. Financial arrangements can facilitate or hamper operations, but the best of financial plans cannot overcome deficiencies in the operations area. These opinions are supported by empirical studies, which generally find a weak statistical relationship between capital structure and stock price. The opinions are also supported by runs of our computer model, which show stock price to be affected significantly by changes in unit sales, sales prices, fixed costs, and variable costs, but not to be affected much by changes in capital structure. This last point can also be seen from the HSS example discussed earlier. Refer again to Table 13-2. Hill Software Systems' stock price is maximized at a D/V ratio of 27.6 percent. However, at a much lower D/V of 18.6 percent, the firm's stock price drops only from $21.73 to $21.47, or by a slight 1.2 percent, while if D/V rises to 36.8 percent, HSS's stock price hardly drops at all. Thus, HSS could set its target D/V ratio anywhere in the range from 18.6 to 36.8 percent and still come very close to maximizing firm value.

Self-Test Questions

Briefly describe the elements of a financial forecasting model that could be used to help set the target capital structure.

How critical is the optimal capital structure decision to the financial performance of the firm, that is, how important are small deviations from the optimal structure?

Should the target capital structure be thought of as a single point or as a range?

VARIATIONS IN CAPITAL STRUCTURES AMONG FIRMS

As might be expected, wide variations in the use of financial leverage occur both among industries and among the individual firms in each industry. Table 13-5 illustrates differences for four industries, ranked in descending order of the amount of common equity used as shown in Column 1.[17]

The drug and steel companies do not use much debt (their common equity ratios are high); the uncertainties inherent in industries that are cyclical, oriented toward research, or subject to huge product liability suits render the heavy use of leverage unwise. Retailers and utility companies, on the other hand, use debt relatively heavily, but for different reasons. Retailers use short-term debt to finance inventories and long-term debt secured by mortgages on their stores. The utilities have traditionally used large amounts of debt, particularly long-term debt—their fixed assets make good security for mortgage bonds, and their relatively stable sales make it safe for them to carry more debt than would be true for firms with more business risk.

Particular attention should be given to the times-interest-earned (TIE) ratio, because it gives a measure of how safe the debt is and how vulnerable the company is to financial distress. TIE depends on three factors: (1) the percentage of debt, (2) the interest rate on the debt, and (3) the company's profitability. Imbedded interest rates are fairly similar across the firms in the four industries, but the ROEs are quite different. Thus, the retailing industry, which uses much more debt than the steel industry (50.6 percent versus 36.8 percent), still has a TIE close to the steels because of its much higher profitability.

Wide variations in capital structures also exist among firms within given industries—for example, although the average common equity ratio in 1989 for the drug industry was 71.8 percent, ICN Pharmaceuticals' equity ratio was less than 40 percent, but Bristol-Myers's ratio was over 90 percent. Thus, factors unique to individual firms, including managerial attitudes, do play an important role in setting target capital structures.

Self-Test Questions

Why does the average capital structure vary from industry to industry?

Do all firms within an industry have roughly the same capital structure and debt maturity mix?

---

[17]Information on capital structures and financial strength is available from a multitude of sources. We used the *Compustat* Industrial Data Tapes to develop Table 13-5, but other published sources include *The Value Line Investment Survey, Robert Morris Associates Annual Studies,* and *Dun & Bradstreet Key Business Ratios.*

Table 13-5 Capital Structure Percentages, 1989: Four Industries
Ranked by Common Equity Ratios

Industry	Common Equity (1)	Preferred Stock (2)	Total Debt (3)	Long-Term Debt (4)	Short-Term Debt (5)	Times-Interest-Earned Ratio (6)	Return on Equity (7)
Drugs	71.8%	1.5%	26.7%	16.0%	10.7%	10.5×	24.5%
Steel	63.2	0.0	36.8	32.2	4.6	4.0	10.7
Retailing	48.1	1.3	50.6	36.1	14.5	3.8	15.7
Utilities	43.3	6.0	50.7	46.9	3.8	2.4	9.2
Composite (average of all industries, not just those listed above)	40.3%	1.7%	58.0%	35.4%	22.6%	2.2×	13.7%

Note: These ratios are based on accounting (or book) values. Stated on a market value basis, the equity percentages would rise because most stocks sell at prices that are much higher than their book values.

Source: *Compustat* Industrial Data Tape, 1990.

CAPITAL STRUCTURE AND MERGERS

One of the most exciting developments in the financial world during the 1980s was the high level of mergers and LBOs. Mergers and LBOs will be discussed at length in Chapter 24, but it is useful to make several points now: (1) very often the acquiring firm issues debt and uses it to buy the target firm's stock; (2) the new debt effectively changes the enterprise's capital structure; and (3) the value enhancement resulting from the use of debt is often sufficient to cover the premium offered for the stock and still leave a profit for the acquiring company.

The profit potential of these transactions has led to the creation of companies whose major function is to acquire other companies through debt-financed takeovers. The managers of these acquiring companies have made huge personal fortunes, and shrewd individual investors, including a few finance professors, have selected stock portfolios heavily weighted with prime acquisition targets and have done well in the market. Of course, the managements of firms with low leverage ratios who do not want to be taken over can be expected to react by attempting to find their optimal debt levels and then issuing debt and repurchasing stock, thus bringing their firms' actual debt ratios up to the levels that maximize the prices of their stocks, which will make these companies less attractive acquisition targets. This is called *restructuring,* and a great deal of it has been going on lately. CBS, for example, did this when it was fighting off an acquisition attempt by Ted Turner, and Phillips Petroleum did likewise to fend off T. Boone Pickens.

Like many developments in business, the use of leverage in mergers and LBOs was carried to excessive lengths during the 1980s, so many observers expect debt ratios to decline somewhat during the 1990s. However, as the following section on international finance indicates, it may turn out that global competition will lead to an even greater use of debt.

Self-Test Question

What impact has the high level of merger and LBO activity had on managerial capital structure decisions?

MULTINATIONAL FINANCE
International Differences in Capital Structures

Significant differences have been observed in the capital structures of U.S. corporations in comparison to their German and Japanese counterparts. For example, the Organization for Economic Cooperation and Development (OECD) recently reported that, on average, Japanese firms use 85 percent debt to total assets (in book value terms), German firms use 64 percent, and U.S. firms use 55 percent. Of course, different countries use somewhat different accounting conventions with regard to (1) reporting assets on a historical versus a replacement cost basis, (2) treatment of leased assets, (3) pension plan funding, and (4) capitalizing versus expensing R&D costs, and these differences make comparisons difficult. Still, even after adjusting for accounting differences, researchers find that Japanese and German firms use considerably more financial leverage than U.S. companies.

Why do international differences exist? Since taxes are thought to be a major reason for using debt, the effects of differential tax structures in the three countries have been examined. The interest on corporate debt is deductible in each country, and individuals must pay taxes on dividends and interest received. However, capital gains are not taxed in either Germany or Japan. The conclusions from this analysis are as follows: (1) From a tax standpoint, corporations should be equally inclined to use debt in all three countries. (2) Since capital gains are not taxed in Germany or Japan, but are taxed in the United States, and since capital gains are associated more with stocks than with bonds, investors in Germany and Japan should show a preference for stocks as compared with U.S. investors. (3) Tax-related investor preferences should lead to relatively low equity capital costs in Germany and Japan, and this, in turn, should cause German and Japanese firms to use more equity capital than their U.S. counterparts. Of course, this is exactly the opposite of the actual capital structures, so differ-

ential tax laws cannot explain the observed capital structure differences.

If tax rates cannot explain differential capital structures, what else might explain the observed differences? Another possibility is differences in financial distress costs—actual bankruptcy, and even the threat of potential bankruptcy, imposes a costly burden on firms with large amounts of debt. Note, though, that financial distress costs are dependent on the *probability* of distress. Now recall our discussion of *agency costs* in Chapter 1. There we saw that agency costs arise from two agency relationships: (1) the relationship between shareholders and managers, and (2) the relationship between bondholders and shareholders. In the United States, equity agency costs are comparatively low—corporations produce quarterly reports, pay quarterly dividends, and must comply with relatively stringent audit requirements. These conditions are less prevalent in the other countries. Conversely, debt agency costs are probably lower in Germany and Japan than in the United States. In these countries, the bulk of corporate debt consists of bank loans as opposed to publicly issued bonds, but, more important, the banks are closely linked to the corporations which borrow from them. German and Japanese banks often (1) hold major equity positions in their debtor corporations, (2) vote the shares of individual shareholders for whom banks hold shares in trust, and (3) have bank officers sit on the boards of debtor corporations. Given these close relationships, the banks are much more directly involved with the debtor firms' affairs, and as a result they are also more accommodating in the event of financial distress than U.S. bondholders would be. This, in turn, suggests that a given amount of debt brings with it a lower threat of financial distress for a German or a Japanese firm than for a U.S. firm with the same amount of business risk. Thus, an analysis of both financial distress and equity agency costs leads to the conclusion that U.S. firms ought to have more equity and less debt than firms in Japan and Germany.

Note also that U.S. banks are not permitted to own stocks—they can only own debt, for the most part. Thus, legal as well as cultural differences may account for the observed differences in capital structure in the United States, Germany, and Japan.

We cannot state that one financial system is better or worse than another in the sense of making the firms in one country more efficient than those in another. However, as U.S. firms become increasingly involved in worldwide operations, they must become increasingly aware of worldwide conditions, and they must be prepared to adapt to conditions in the various countries in which they do business.

SUMMARY

In this chapter, we discussed a variety of topics related to capital structure decisions. The key concepts covered are listed next.

- *Business risk* is the inherent riskiness in a firm's operations if it uses no debt. *Financial risk* is the additional risk that is concentrated on the shareholders when debt financing is used. Business and financial risk can be viewed from either a *total risk* or *market risk* perspective.

- Within a *total risk framework,* business risk can be measured by $\sigma_{ROE(U)}$, total risk can be measured by $\sigma_{ROE(L)}$, and financial risk can be measured by Total risk − Business risk $= \sigma_{ROE(L)} - \sigma_{ROE(U)}$.

- *Robert Hamada* combined the CAPM with MM (with corporate taxes) and produced the following equation:

$$k_{sL} = k_{RF} + (k_M - k_{RF})b_U + (k_M - k_{RF})b_U(1 - T)(D/S).$$

This equation shows that the required rate of return on a levered company's stock is equal to the risk-free rate, which compensates investors for the time value of money, plus a premium for business risk, plus a premium for financial risk.

- Within a *market risk framework*, business risk can be measured by b_U, market risk can be measured by b_L, and financial risk can be measured by $b_L - b_U = b_U(1 - T)(D/S)$.

- *If a firm has perpetual cash flows*, then a relatively simple model can be used to value the firm at different capital structures. In theory, this model can be used to find the capital structure that maximizes stock price. However, the inputs to the model are very difficult, if not impossible, to estimate. Further, most firms are growing, hence they do not have perpetual cash flows.

- Since one cannot determine the optimal capital structure with quantitative models, managers must conduct a *qualitative analysis* which involves many different factors. Among these factors are long-run viability, managerial conservatism, lender and rating agency attitudes, reserve borrowing capacity, control, asset structure, profitability, and taxes.

- Firms generally have *computerized planning models* that are used for financial planning. These models, if built to include alternative capital structures and capital costs, can be used to get some feel for the impact of capital structure changes on a firm's financial condition.

- Wide variations in capital structure exist, both among industries and among individual firms within industries. The variations among industries can be explained to a large extent by the economic nature of the industry.

- The heavy use of financial leverage in mergers and LBOs has prompted many CEOs to reevaluate their firm's capital structures. This has led to a wave of *restructurings,* in which debt is issued and the proceeds distributed to shareholders by special dividends or stock repurchases.

- Significant differences occur in the capital structures of U.S. firms versus firms in other countries. These differences seem to be due to the differences in financial institutions and market structures among countries.

Questions

13-1 Define each of the following terms:
   a. Capital structure; optimal capital structure; target capital structure
   b. Business risk; financial risk
   c. Operating leverage; financial leverage
   d. Breakeven point
   e. Hamada equation
   f. Reserve borrowing capacity

13-2 What term refers to the uncertainty inherent in projections of future ROE(U)?

13-3 Firms with relatively high nonfinancial fixed costs are said to have a high degree of what?

13-4 "One type of leverage affects both EBIT and EPS. The other type affects only EPS." Explain this statement.

13-5 What is the relationship between market risk and leverage?

13-6 Why is the following statement true? "Other things being the same, firms with relatively stable sales are able to carry relatively high debt ratios."

13-7 Why do public utility companies usually have capital structures that are different from those of retail firms?

13-8 Some economists believe that swings in business cycles will not be as wide in the future as they have been in the past. Assuming that they are correct, what effect might this added stability have on the types of financing used by firms in the United States? Would your answer be true for all firms?

13-9 Why is EBIT generally considered to be independent of financial leverage? Why might EBIT actually be influenced by financial leverage at high debt levels?

13-10 If a firm with no debt could buy back and retire its stock at the pre-announcement price, would its final stock price be higher than that resulting from the procedure outlined in the chapter? Would it be fair for a firm to buy back its stock without telling stockholders that stock was being repurchased?

13-11 How might increasingly volatile inflation rates, interest rates, and bond prices affect the optimal capital structure for corporations?

13-12 If a firm went from zero debt to successively higher levels of debt, why would you expect its stock price to first rise, then hit a peak, and then begin to decline?

13-13 Why is the debt level that maximizes a firm's expected EPS generally higher than the debt level that maximizes its stock price?

Self-Test Problems (Solutions Appear in Appendix D)

ST-1 **(Operating leverage and breakeven)** Daines Scientific, Inc., produces satellite earth stations which sell for $100,000 each. The firm's fixed costs, F, are $2 million; 50 earth stations are produced and sold each year; profits total $500,000; and the firm's assets (all equity financed) are $5 million. The firm estimates that it can change its production process, adding $4 million to investment and $500,000 to fixed operating costs. This change will (1) reduce variable costs per unit by $10,000 and (2) increase output by 20 units, but (3) the sales price on all units will have to be lowered to $95,000 to permit sales of the additional output. The firm has tax loss carry-forwards that cause its tax rate to be zero, its cost of equity is 15 percent, and it uses no debt.
   a.   Should the firm make the change?
   b.   Would the firm's operating leverage increase or decrease if it made the change? What about its breakeven point?
   c.   Would the new situation expose the firm to more or less business risk than the old one?

ST-2 **(Optimal capital structure)** Suppose, some years later, Daines Scientific found itself in this situation: (1) EBIT = $4 million; (2) tax rate, T = 35%; (3) value of debt, D = $2 million; (4) k_d = 10%; (5) k_s = 15%; and (6) shares of stock outstanding, n = 600,000. The firm's market is stable, and it expects no growth, so all earnings are paid out as dividends. The debt consists of perpetual bonds.
   a.   What is the total market value of the firm's stock, S, its price per share, P_0, and the firm's total market value, V?
   b.   What is the firm's weighted average cost of capital?
   c.   The firm can increase its debt by $8 million, to a total of $10 million, using the new debt to buy back and retire some of its shares. Its interest rate on all debt will be 12 percent (it will have to call and refund the old debt), and its cost of equity will rise from 15 to 17 percent. EBIT will remain constant. Should the firm change its capital structure?
   d.   If the firm did not have to refund the $2 million of old debt, how would this have affected things? Assume the new and the old debt are equally risky, with k_d = 12%, but the coupon rate on the old debt is 10 percent.
   e.   What is the firm's TIE ratio under the original conditions and under the conditions in Part c?

Problems

13-1 **(Business and financial risk: total)** Here are the estimated ROE distributions for Firms A, B, and C:

	Probability				
	0.1	**0.2**	**0.4**	**0.2**	**0.1**
Firm A: ROE_A	0.0%	5.0%	10.0%	15.0%	20.0%
Firm B: ROE_B	(2.0)	5.0	12.0	19.0	26.0
Firm C: ROE_C	(5.0)	5.0	15.0	25.0	35.0

   a.   Calculate the expected value and standard deviation for Firm C's ROE. ROE_A = 10.0%, σ_A = 5.5%; ROE_B = 12.0%, σ_B = 7.7%.

b.   Discuss the relative riskiness of the three firms' returns. (Assume that these distributions are expected to remain constant over time.)

c.   Now suppose all three firms have the same standard deviation of basic earning power (EBIT/Total assets), $\sigma_A = \sigma_B = \sigma_C = 5.5\%$. What can we tell about the financial risk of each firm?

13-2   **(Business and financial risk: market)** Air Tampa has just been incorporated, and its board of directors is currently grappling with the question of optimal capital structure. The company plans to offer commuter air services between Tampa and smaller surrounding cities. Jaxair has been around for a few years, and it has about the same basic business risk as Air Tampa would have. Jaxair's market-determined beta is 1.8, and it has a current market value debt ratio (total debt/total assets) of 50 percent and a federal-plus-state tax rate of 40 percent. Air Tampa expects only to be marginally profitable at start up, hence its tax rate would only be 25 percent. Air Tampa's owners expect that the total book and market value of the firm's stock, if it uses zero debt, would be $10 million.

a.   Estimate the beta of an unlevered firm in the commuter airline business based on Jaxair's market-determined beta. (Hint: Jaxair's market-determined beta is a levered beta. Use Equation 13-3a and solve for b_U.)

b.   Now assume that $k_{RF} = 10\%$ and $k_M = 15\%$. Find the required rate of return on equity for an unlevered commuter airline. What is the business risk premium for this industry?

c.   Air Tampa is considering three capital structures: (1) $2 million debt, (2) $4 million debt, and (3) $6 million debt. Estimate Air Tampa's k_s for these debt levels. What is the financial risk premium at each level?

d.   Calculate Air Tampa's k_s and financial risk premium at $6 million debt assuming its federal-plus-state tax rate is now 40 percent. Compare this with your corresponding answer to Part c. (Hint: The increase in the tax rate causes V_U to drop to $8 million.)

13-3   **(Capital structure analysis)** The following data reflect the current financial conditions of Boyer Corporation:

Value of debt (book = market)	$1,000,000
Market value of equity	$5,257,143
Sales, last 12 months	$12,000,000
Variable operating costs (50% of sales)	$6,000,000
Fixed operating costs	$5,000,000
Tax rate, T (federal-plus-state)	40%

At the current level of debt, the cost of debt, k_d, is 8 percent and the cost of equity, k_s, is 10.5 percent. Management questions whether or not the capital structure is optimal, so the financial vice-president has been asked to consider the possibility of issuing $1 million of additional debt and using the proceeds to repurchase stock. It is estimated that if the leverage were increased by raising the level of debt to $2 million, the interest rate on new debt would rise to 9 percent and k_s would rise to 11.5 percent. The old 8 percent debt is senior to the new debt, and it would remain outstanding, continue to yield 8 percent, and have a market value of $1 million. The firm is a zero-growth firm, with all of its earnings paid out as dividends.

a.   Should the firm increase its debt to $2 million?

b.   If the firm decided to increase its level of debt to $3 million, its cost of the additional $2 million of debt would be 12 percent and k_s would rise to 15 percent. The original 8 percent of debt would again remain outstanding, and its market value would remain at $1 million. What level of debt should the firm choose: $1 million, $2 million, or $3 million?

c.   The market price of the firm's stock was originally $20 per share. Calculate the new equilibrium stock prices at debt levels of $2 million and $3 million.

d.   Calculate the firm's earnings per share if it uses debt of $1 million, $2 million, and $3 million. Assume that the firm pays out all of its earnings as dividends. If you find that EPS increases with more debt, does this mean that the firm should choose to increase its debt to $3 million, or possibly higher?

e.   What would happen to the value of the old bonds if the firm uses more leverage and the old bonds are not senior to the new bonds?

13-4 **(Capital structure analysis)** ABC, Inc., has no debt outstanding, and its financial position is given by the following data:

Assets (book = market)	$3,000,000
EBIT	$500,000
Cost of equity, k_s	10%
Stock price, P_0	$15
Shares outstanding, n	200,000
Tax rate, T (federal-plus-state)	40%

The firm is considering selling bonds and simultaneously repurchasing some of its stock. If it uses $900,000 of debt, its cost of equity, k_s, will increase to 11 percent to reflect the increased risk. Bonds can be sold at a cost, k_d, of 7 percent. ABC is a no-growth firm. Hence, all its earnings are paid out as dividends, and earnings are expectationally constant over time.

a.   What effect would this use of leverage have on the value of the firm?

b.   What would be the price of ABC's stock?

c.   What happens to the firm's earnings per share after the recapitalization?

d.   The $500,000 EBIT given previously is actually the expected value from the following probability distribution:

Probability	EBIT
0.10	($ 100,000)
0.20	200,000
0.40	500,000
0.20	800,000
0.10	1,100,000

What is the probability distribution of EPS with zero debt and with $900,000 of debt? Which EPS distribution is riskier?

e.   Determine the probability distributions of times interest earned for each debt level. What is the probability of not covering the interest payment at the $900,000 debt level?

13-5 **(Capital structure analysis)** Cooley Printing, Inc., has a total market value of $100 million, consisting of 1 million shares selling for $50 per share and $50 million of 10 percent perpetual bonds now selling at par. The company's EBIT is $13.24 million, and its tax rate is 15 percent. Cooley can change its capital structure by either increasing its debt to $70 million or decreasing it to $30 million. If it decides to *increase* its use of leverage, it must call its old bonds and issue new ones with a 12 percent coupon. If it decides to *decrease* its leverage, it will call in its old bonds and replace them with new 8 percent coupon bonds. The company will sell or repurchase stock at the new equilibrium price to complete the capital structure change.

The firm pays out all earnings as dividends; hence, its stock is a zero growth stock. If it increases leverage, k_s will be 16 percent. If it decreases leverage, k_s will be 13 percent.

a.   What is the firm's cost of equity at present?

b.   Should the firm change its capital structure?

c.   Suppose the tax rate is changed to 34 percent. This would lower after-tax income and also cause a decline in the price of the stock and the total value of the equity, other things held constant. Calculate the new stock price (at $50 million of debt).

d.   Continue the scenario of Part c, but now reexamine the question of the optimal amount of debt. Does the tax rate change affect your decision about the optimal use of financial leverage?

e.   Go back to Part b; that is, assume T = 15%. How would your analysis of the capital structure change be modified if the firm's presently outstanding debt could not be called, and it did not have to be replaced; that is, if the $50 million of 10 percent debt continued even if the company issued new 12 percent bonds?

f.   Suppose these probabilities for EBIT exist: P[EBIT = $5 million] = 0.2; P[EBIT = $15 million] = 0.6; and P[EBIT = $25 million] = 0.2. Under the assumptions of Part e, what are (1) expected EPS and σ_{EPS}, and (2) expected TIE and σ_{TIE}, assuming an increase in book value of debt to $70 million?

13-6 **(Pro forma analysis)** The C.S. Grant Company is currently all-equity financed, but the firm is considering a change to 50 percent debt financing. The debt would cost 12 percent, and would be used to repurchase shares currently selling at $25 per share. Grant now has 40,000 shares outstanding and $1,000,000 in total assets. Its pro forma income statement for 1991, assuming zero debt usage, is as follows:

Sales	$900,000
Operating costs	750,000
EBIT	$150,000
Taxes (40%)	60,000
Net income	$ 90,000

a.   What is the firm's expected EPS for 1991 using zero debt? At a debt level of $500,000?

b.   Assume that operating costs remain at 83.33 percent of sales over a wide range of sales levels. Further, the 1991 pro forma income statement is based on expected sales of $900,000, but the actual sales distribution is as follows:

Probability	Sales
0.10	$ 500,000
0.15	700,000
0.50	900,000
0.15	1,100,000
0.10	1,300,000

Find the EPS at each sales level for both zero debt and 50 percent debt financing.

c.   Make a plot of EPS versus sales level for both financing alternatives. Place the plots on the same set of axes. Interpret this graph.

(Do Parts d and e only if you are using the computerized diskette.)

d.   At a zero debt level, Grant's expected ROE = $90,000/$1,000,000 = 9.0%, while at $500,000 of debt, expected ROE = $54,000/$500,000 = 10.8%. Determine the firm's ROE at each debt level for every possible sales level. Plot the two ROE distributions.

e.   Now, assume that the $500,000 debt financing would cost 15 percent. Repeat the Part d analysis. Is there a significant difference? Why?

13-7 **(Subjective analysis)** You have been hired as a financial consultant by two firms, Alpha Industries (Firm A) and Zed Corporation (Firm Z). Firm A is in the fast-growing microcomputer retail sales industry, while Firm Z manufactures office equipment such as pencil sharpeners, staplers, and tape dispensers. Your task is to recommend the optimal capital structure for the two firms. Discuss the factors that would influence your decision, and specifically how each of these factors apply to each firm. Here are some additional points about the two firms: (1) Firm A generally leases its stores, while Firm Z purchases its plants.

(2) Firm A's stock is widely held, while the family of Firm Z's founder holds 40 percent of its stock.

(3) Firm Z has a significant amount of accelerated depreciation expense each year, while Firm A has almost none.

(4) Firm A has demonstrated high growth and profitability over the last few years. On the other hand, Firm Z's growth has averaged a modest 5 percent per year, and its profit margins and ROEs have been unspectacular.

Mini Case

Assume you have just been hired as business manager of PizzaPalace, a pizza restaurant located adjacent to campus. The company's EBIT was $500,000 last year, and since the university's enrollment is capped, EBIT is expected to remain constant (in real terms) over time. Since no expansion capital will be required, PizzaPalace plans to pay out all earnings as dividends. The management group owns about 50 percent of the stock, and the stock is traded in the over-the-counter market.

The firm is currently financed with all equity; it has 100,000 shares outstanding; and $P_0 = \$20$ per share. When you took your MBA corporate finance course, your instructor stated that most firms' owners would be financially better off if the firms used some debt. When you suggested this to your new boss, he encouraged you to pursue the idea. As a first step, assume that you obtained from the firm's investment banker the following estimated costs of debt and equity for the firm at different debt levels (in thousands of dollars):

Amount Borrowed	k_d	k_s
$ 0	—	15.0%
250	10.0%	15.5
500	11.0	16.5
750	13.0	18.0
1,000	16.0	20.0

If the company were to recapitalize, debt would be issued, and the funds received would be used to repurchase stock. PizzaPalace is in the 40 percent state-plus-federal corporate tax bracket.

a. (1) What is business risk? What factors influence a firm's business risk?
    (2) What is operating leverage, and how does it affect a firm's business risk?
b. (1) What is meant by financial leverage and financial risk?
    (2) How does financial risk differ from business risk?
c. How are financial and business risk measured in a total risk framework? In a market risk framework?
d. Now, to develop an example which can be presented to PizzaPalace's management as an illustration, consider two hypothetical firms: Firm U, which uses no debt, and Firm L, which uses $10,000 of 12 percent debt. Both firms have $20,000 in assets and a 40 percent tax rate, and the following EBIT probability distribution applies to both for the coming year:

Probability	EBIT
0.25	$2,000
0.50	3,000
0.25	4,000

(1) Construct partial income statements, which start with EBIT, for the two firms at each level of EBIT.

(2) Now calculate the ratio of EBIT to total assets, which is the *basic earning power* ratio; the ROI, which is (net income + interest) divided by (debt + equity); the ROE; and the times-interest-earned (TIE) ratio for both firms at each level of EBIT.

(3) What does this example illustrate concerning the impact of financial leverage on risk and expected rate of return?

e.   With the above points in mind, now consider the optimal capital structure for PizzaPalace.

(1) What valuation equations can you use in the analysis?

(2) Could either the MM or the Miller capital structure theories be applied directly in this analysis, and if you presented an analysis based on these theories, how do you think the owners would respond?

f.   (1) Describe briefly, without using any numbers, the sequence of events that would take place if PizzaPalace does recapitalize.

(2) What would be the new stock price if PizzaPalace recapitalized and used these amounts of debt: $250,000; $500,000; $750,000?

(3) How many shares would remain outstanding after recapitalization under each debt scenario?

(4) Considering only the levels of debt discussed, what is PizzaPalace's optimal capital structure?

g.   (1) Assume now that the firm has recapitalized with $250,000 of debt, and that currently S = $1,839,000, D = $250,000, P = $20.89, and n = 88,030. The debt has a "poison put" which requires that it be paid off if additional debt is issued. What would PizzaPalace's stock price be if it now increased its debt to $500,000 by issuing $500,000 of new debt and using half to refund the old issue and half to repurchase stock?

(2) Now assume that PizzaPalace issues an additional $250,000 of debt, but it does not have to refund the old issue. What would happen to its stock price? Assume also that the new and old issues have the same priority of claims.

h.   It is also useful to determine the effect of any proposed recapitalization on EPS. Calculate the EPS at debt levels of $0, $250,000, $500,000, and $750,000, assuming that the firm begins at zero debt and recapitalizes to each level in a single step. Is EPS maximized at the same level that maximizes stock price?

i.   Calculate the firm's WACC at each debt level. What is the relationship between the WACC and the stock price?

j.   Suppose you discovered that PizzaPalace had more business risk than you originally estimated. Describe how this would affect the analysis. What if the firm had less business risk than originally estimated?

k.   Would it make sense to do an analysis similar to the PizzaPalace analysis for most firms? Why or why not? What type of analysis do you think a firm should actually use to help set its optimal, or target, capital structure? What other factors should managers consider when setting the target capital structure?

Selected Additional References and Cases

Chapter 12 provided references on the theory of capital structure; the references listed here are oriented more toward applications than theory.

Donaldson's work on the setting of debt targets is old but still relevant:

Donaldson, Gordon, "New Framework for Corporate Debt Capacity," *Harvard Business Review,* March-April 1962, 117–131.

———, "Strategy for Financial Emergencies," *Harvard Business Review,* November-December 1969, 67–79.

Definitive references on the empirical relationships between capital structure and (1) the cost of debt, (2) the cost of equity, (3) earnings, and (4) the price of a firm's stock are virtually nonexistent — statistical problems make the precise estimation of these relationships extraordinarily difficult, if not impossible. One good way to get a feel for the issues involved is to obtain a set of the cost of capital testimonies filed in a major utility rate case — such testimony is available from state public utility commissions, the Federal Communications Commission, the Federal Energy Regulatory Commission, and utility companies themselves. For an academic discussion of the issues, see

Caks, John, "Corporate Debt Decisions: A New Analytical Framework," *Journal of Finance,* December 1978, 1297–1315.

Gordon, Myron J., *The Cost of Capital to a Public Utility* (East Lansing, Mich.: Division of Research, Graduate School of Business Administration, Michigan State University, 1974).

Hamada, Robert S., "The Effect of the Firm's Capital Structure on the Systematic Risk of Common Stocks," *Journal of Finance,* May 1972, 435–452.

Masulis, Ronald W., "The Impact of Capital Structure Change on Firm Value: Some Estimates," *Journal of Finance,* March 1983, 107–126.

Piper, Thomas R., and Wolf A. Weinhold, "How Much Debt is Right for Your Company," *Harvard Business Review,* July-August 1982, 106–114.

Shalit, Sol S., "On the Mathematics of Financial Leverage," *Financial Management,* Spring 1975, 57–66.

Shiller, Robert J., and Franco Modigliani, "Coupon and Tax Effects on New and Seasoned Bond Yields and the Measurement of the Cost of Debt Capital," *Journal of Financial Economics,* September 1979, 297–318.

For some insights into how practicing financial managers view the capital structure decision, see

Pinegar, J. Michael, and Lisa Wilbricht, "What Managers Think of Capital Structure Theory: A Survey," *Financial Management,* Winter 1989, 82–91.

Scott, David F., and Dana J. Johnson, "Financing Policies and Practices in Large Corporations," *Financial Management,* Summer 1982, 51–59.

To learn more about the link between market risk and operating and financial leverage, see

Callahan, Carolyn M., and Rosanne M. Mohr, "The Determinants of Systematic Risk: A Synthesis," *The Financial Review,* May 1989, 157–181.

Gahlon, James M., and James A. Gentry, "On the Relationship between Systematic Risk and the Degrees of Operating and Financial Leverage," *Financial Management,* Summer 1982, 15–23.

Prezas, Alexandros P., "Effects of Debt on the Degrees of Operating and Financial Leverage," *Financial Management,* Summer 1987, 39–44.

See the following three articles for additional insights into the relationship between industry characteristics and financial leverage:

Bowen, Robert M., Lane A. Daley, and Charles C. Huber, Jr., "Evidence on the Existence and Determinants of Inter-Industry Differences in Leverage," *Financial Management,* Winter 1982, 10–20.

Scott, David F., Jr., and John D. Martin, "Industry Influence on Financial Structure," *Financial Management,* Spring 1975, 67–73.

Long, Michael, and Ileen Malitz, "The Investment-Financing Nexus: Some Empirical Evidence," *Midland Corporate Finance Journal,* Fall 1985, 53–59.

For a more thorough discussion of the international implications of capital structure, see

Rutterford, Janette, "An International Perspective on the Capital Structure Puzzle," *Midland Corporate Finance Journal,* Fall 1985, 60–72.

The following cases contain many of the concepts we present in Chapters 12 and 13.

In Brigham, Eugene F., and Louis C. Gapenski, *Cases in Financial Management* (Hinsdale, Ill.: Dryden, 1990):

Case 8, "Floral Concepts, Inc.," which shows the effects of financial leverage on EPS and stock price.

Case 9, "Southern Skylights, Inc.," which illustrates how operating and financial leverage interact to affect firm value.

Case 10, "Quick Prints, Inc." which presents a situation similar to the Hill Software Systems example in the text.

Case 11, "Town & Country Mortgage Company," which concentrates on the impact of financial leverage on firm value and WACC.

In Harrington, Diana, *Cases in Financial Decision Making* (Hinsdale, Ill.: Dryden 1989):

"Marriott," which illustrates several ways to measure debt capacity when determining the optimal capital structure.

CHAPTER 14

Dividend Policy

On December 21, 1989, American Telephone & Telegraph (AT&T) Company announced that it would pay a quarterly dividend of $0.30 per share on February 1, 1990, to stockholders of record on December 29. The February dividend would continue AT&T's payout at the rate of $1.20 per year, which has held constant since the company's breakup in 1984.

Although one might expect the dividend announcement to be warmly greeted by analysts and investors, AT&T's stock price actually dropped by $1.25, because many analysts and investors had expected the company to announce a dividend increase. The analysts said that AT&T's annual dividend of $1.20 a share is no longer high enough, given AT&T's comeback in the last 18 months after years of internal turmoil and cost-containment problems. AT&T earned $1.25 per share in 1984, when the current dividend was set, but in 1990 the company is expected to earn about twice that amount. However, an AT&T spokesman said the current dividend is in line with the company's plan to keep its payout ratio at about 40 to 50 percent of earnings.

Still, some analysts thought AT&T might be signaling that 1990 will be a tough year for profits. "I'm getting a sense that earnings will be flat," said Robert B. Morris III, an analyst at Goldman Sachs. Mr. Morris had expected AT&T to raise its annual dividend by 12 to 16 cents per share. "I'm disappointed," he said, "I was hoping that they would at least provide an indication that they were confident of earnings growth in 1990 and reward patient shareholders who haven't seen a dividend increase since 1983."

"Put this on record," said Jack B. Grubman, telecommunications analyst at Paine Webber, "Whoever advised Bob Allen (AT&T's chairman) not to raise the dividend should be fired immediately, because he cost the company almost $3 billion in market capitalization to save it $120 million in dividends." Mr. Grubman had been forecasting a $1.50 jump in share price on the basis of a dividend increase announcement, and the $1.25 price drop versus a predicted $1.50 rise translates into a $2.75 billion decline in market value, given the firm's one billion shares outstanding.

DIVIDEND policy, which is the decision to pay out earnings as dividends or to retain and reinvest them in the firm, has three key elements: (1) What fraction of earnings should be paid out, on average, over time? This is the *target payout policy* decision. (2) Should the firm attempt to maintain a steady, stable dividend growth rate, or should it vary its dividend payments from year to year depending on its internal needs for funds and on its cash flows? (3) What dollar amount should the firm pay in current dividends? These three elements are the primary focus of this chapter, but we also examine two related issues, stock repurchases and stock splits.

DIVIDENDS VERSUS CAPITAL GAINS: WHAT DO INVESTORS PREFER?

The target payout ratio should be based in large part on investors' preferences for dividends versus capital gains—would the marginal investor prefer to have the firm distribute its income as dividends or plow earnings back into the business to produce capital gains? This preference can be considered in terms of the constant growth stock valuation model:

$$\hat{P}_0 = \frac{D_1}{k_s - g}.$$

This equation shows that if the company increases the payout ratio and thus raises D_1, the numerator will increase, and that, taken alone, would cause the stock price to rise. However, if D_1 is raised, then less money will be available for reinvestment, the expected growth rate will decline, and that would tend to depress the stock's price. Thus, any change in payout policy will have two opposing effects, and the firm must seek to strike that balance between current dividends and future growth which maximizes the price of the stock.

In this section we examine three theories of investor preference: (1) the dividend irrelevance theory, (2) the "bird-in-the-hand" theory, and (3) the tax differential theory.

Dividend Irrelevance: Modigliani and Miller

In an important theoretical article on dividend policy, Merton Miller and Franco Modigliani (MM) argued that dividend policy has no effect on either the price of a firm's stock or its cost of capital — MM stated that dividend policy is *irrelevant*.[1] They reasoned that the value of a firm is determined by its basic earning power and its risk class, and, therefore, that a firm's value depends on its asset investment policy rather than on how earnings are split between dividends and retained earnings. MM demonstrated, under a particular set of assumptions, that if a firm pays higher dividends, then it must sell more stock to new investors, and that the share of the value of the company given up to new investors is exactly equal to the dividends paid out. For example, if IBM's capital budget calls for $1 billion of equity financing in 1991, and if the company expects $1 billion of earnings, then (1) it could pay all of its earnings out as dividends and finance the equity requirement by selling $1 billion of new stock, (2) it could retain the entire $1 billion of earnings, sell no new stock, and provide stockholders with a capital gain of $1 billion, or (3) it could pick a payout anywhere between 0 and 100 percent and thus provide stockholders with a total of $1 billion in dividends and capital gains.

MM proved their proposition theoretically, but only under these five assumptions: (1) There are no personal or corporate income taxes. (2) There are no stock flotation or transaction costs. (3) Dividend policy has no effect on the firm's cost of equity. (4) The firm's capital investment policy is independent of its dividend policy. (5) Investors and managers have the same set of information (symmetric information) regarding future investment opportunities.

The MM assumptions are not realistic, and they obviously do not hold precisely. Firms and investors do pay income taxes, firms do incur flotation costs, investors do incur transactions costs, and both taxes and transactions costs could cause k_s to be affected by dividend policy. Further, managers often have better information than outside investors. Thus, the MM conclusions on dividend irrelevance may not be valid under "real world" conditions.

"Bird-in-the-Hand" Theory: Gordon and Lintner

In some respects, the most critical assumption inherent in MM's dividend irrelevance theory is that dividend policy does not affect investors' required rates of return on equity, k_s. This issue has been hotly debated in academic circles. Myron Gordon and John Lintner, on the one hand, argued that k_s increases as the dividend payout is reduced, because investors can be more sure of receiving dividend payments than the income from capital gains which are expected to result from retaining earnings.[2] They say, in effect, that investors value a dollar of expected dividends more highly

---

[1]See Merton H. Miller and Franco Modigliani, "Dividend Policy, Growth, and the Valuation of Shares," *Journal of Business,* October 1961, 411–433.

[2]See Myron J. Gordon, "Optimal Investment and Financing Policy," *Journal of Finance,* May 1963, 264–272; and John Lintner, "Dividends, Earnings, Leverage, Stock Prices, and the Supply of Capital to Corporations," *Review of Economics and Statistics,* August 1962, 243–269.

than a dollar of expected capital gains because the dividend yield component, D_1/P_0, is less risky than the g component in the total expected return equation, $\hat{k}_s = D_1/P_0 + g$.

On the other hand, MM argued that investors are indifferent between D_1/P_0 and g, hence k_s is not affected by dividend policy. MM called the Gordon-Lintner argument the "bird-in-the-hand fallacy" because, in MM's view, many if not most investors are going to reinvest their dividends in the same or similar firms anyway, and, in any event, the riskiness of the firm's cash flows to investors in the long run is determined only by the riskiness of its cash flows from operating assets, and not by its dividend payout policy.[3]

Tax Differential Theory: Litzenberger and Ramaswamy

A third theory, based on tax effects, was supported by Litzenberger and Ramaswamy.[4] In Chapter 2, where we summarized key aspects of U.S. tax laws, we pointed out that up until 1986, only 40 percent of long-term capital gains were taxed. Thus, an investor in the 50 percent marginal tax bracket paid a 50 percent tax rate on his or her dividend income, but only $(0.4)(0.5) = 20\%$ on long-term capital gains. Further, by not selling stock, the investor could defer realization of the capital gains and payment of the tax, and since a dollar paid in the future is less valuable than a dollar paid today, the tax deferral feature provided yet another advantage to capital gains. Under current (1990) tax laws, capital gains and dividend income are taxed at the same rate, but the deferral feature still exists.

To illustrate the tax advantage of capital gains, suppose an individual investor in the 28 percent tax bracket is considering the purchase of two stocks: Stock G, which is a "growth stock" with a 10 percent capital gains yield and a 5 percent dividend yield, and Stock I, which is an "income stock" with a 5 percent capital gains yield and a 10 percent dividend yield. Both stocks sell for $10, have the same risk, and are constant growth stocks; thus, $\hat{k}_G = \hat{k}_I$ = Dividend yield + Capital gains yield = 15% on a before tax basis.

Table 14-1 shows the expected after-tax rates of return on Stocks G and I for selected holding periods. For all holding periods longer than one year, the after-tax yield on Stock G is greater than the after-tax yield on Stock I. Further, the after-tax yield differentials increase as the holding period increases. Stock G has the higher after-tax yield because a larger percentage of its return comes from capital gains, and these taxes are deferred until the end of the holding period. Of course, under the old tax laws, when capital gains were taxed at only 40 percent of the rate on dividends and the taxes were also deferred, the yield differentials were far more pronounced. Note, too, that President Bush wants to reinstate the capital gains rate, and he may be successful.

---

[3]Academicians other than MM have also rebutted the "bird-in-the-hand" theory. For example, see Michael Brennan, "A Note on Dividend Irrelevance and the Gordon Valuation Model," *Journal of Finance,* December 1971, 1115–1121.

[4]Robert H. Litzenberger and Krishna Ramaswamy, "The Effects of Personal Taxes and Dividends on Capital Asset Prices," *Journal of Financial Economics,* June 1979, 163–196.

Table 14-1   After-Tax Rates of Return: Stock G and Stock I

	Holding Period in Years					
Stock	1	2	3	4	5	∞
G	10.80%	10.94%	11.07%	11.20%	11.32%	13.60%
I	10.80	10.87	10.94	11.00	11.07	12.20
Yield differential	0.00	0.07	0.13	0.20	0.25	1.40

Note: The after-tax rates of return were calculated as follows:
(1) Determine the after-tax dollar dividend for each year during the holding period; (2) calculate the after-tax capital gain and the end-of-holding-period cash flow; and (3) calculate the IRR of the resulting cash flow stream, which is the expected after-tax rate of return. For example, Stock G's after-tax rate of return for a two-year holding period was found in this way:
a. Stock G sells for $10 and has a 5 percent dividend yield. Thus, D_1 = $10(0.05) = $0.50 and D_2 = $D_1(1 + g)$ = $0.50(1.10) = $0.55. T = 28% and $(1 - T)$ = 0.72, so the after-tax dividend stream is D_{1AT} = $0.50(0.72) = $0.36 and D_{2AT} = $0.55(0.72) = $0.396.
b. $\hat{P}_2 = P_0(1 + g)^2 = \$10(1.10)^2 = \$12.10$. Thus, the Year 2 capital gain is $12.10 − $10.00 = $2.10, the tax is $2.10(0.28) = $0.588, and the after-tax proceeds from the sale are $12.10 − $0.588 = $11.512.
c. The after-tax cash flows are CF_0 = −$10.00, CF_1 = $0.36, and CF_2 = $0.396 + $11.512 = $11.908. The IRR of this stream, which is Stock G's expected after-tax rate of return, is 10.94 percent.

Tax-paying investors with long holding periods would recognize that Stock G offers a higher after-tax return than Stock I, and thus would bid up the price of G relative to I. For example, Stock G's price might rise to $10.25, while Stock I's might fall to $9.75. The end result would be a higher before-tax yield on Stock I than on Stock G, but equal after-tax returns to the marginal investor. If investors in the aggregate behave as described in this section, the result would be higher pre-tax required rates of return on high dividend yield stocks than on low dividend yield stocks.

Self-Test Questions

Describe MM's dividend irrelevance theory.

What is the "bird-in-the-hand" theory?

Describe the tax differential theory.

TESTS OF THE THREE THEORIES

In the preceding section, we presented three theories of investor preference for dividends:

1. MM argued that dividend policy is irrelevant; that is, dividend policy does not affect a firm's value or its cost of capital. Thus, according to MM, there is no optimal dividend policy—one dividend policy is as good as any other.

2. Gordon and Lintner disagreed with MM, arguing that dividends are less risky than capital gains, so a firm should set a high dividend payout ratio and offer a high dividend yield in order to maximize its value. MM disagreed, and they called this the "bird-in-the-hand fallacy."

3.   Litzenberger and Ramaswamy, whose position is the reverse of Gordon-Lintner, stated that since dividends are effectively taxed at higher rates than capital gains, investors should require higher rates of return on stocks with high dividend yields. According to this theory, a firm should pay a low (or zero) dividend in order to maximize its value.

These three theories offer contradictory advice to corporate managers. MM say dividend policy doesn't matter, Gordon-Lintner say set a high payout, and the tax differential advocates say set a low payout. Which theory should we believe?

Two primary types of empirical tests have been conducted in an attempt to determine the true relationship between dividend policy and required returns. In theory, one could take a sample of companies which have different dividend policies, thus different dividend yield and growth rate components, and plot them in graphs such as those shown in Figure 14-1. Here we show three possible results. Only one result could actually exist, but we show three possibilities on one graph. If the plot resembled the center line in the graph, then, for the sample of firms, $\hat{k}_s = k_s = D_1/P_0 + g =$ a constant 13.3% regardless of the dividend payout. Both the X- and Y-axes have an intercept of 13.3 percent, and in this case, the total return would be a constant whether it comes entirely as a dividend yield (the Y-axis intercept), entirely as expected capital gains (the X-axis intercept), or as any combination of the two. The line has a slope of -1.0, and if the test actually resulted in this line, then it would support the MM irrelevance hypothesis.

Figure 14-1   Alternative Theories of the Effects of Dividend Policy

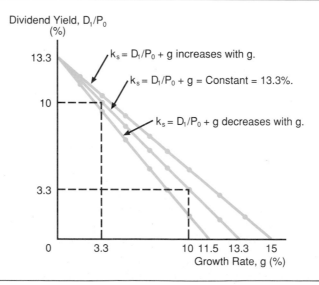

If the plot looked like the upper line in Figure 14-1, with a slope less negative (less steep) than -1.0 (say -0.8), then the test would support the Gordon-Lintner "bird-in-the-hand" hypothesis. Here investors would require a larger total return if the company provided a larger capital gains component, g, than dividend yield, D_1/P_0. An all-dividend stock would have $k_s = 13.3\%$, while a stock which provides only capital gains would have $k_s = 15.0\%$. Thus, more than 1 percent of additional g is required to offset a 1 percent reduction in the lower-risk dividend yield.

Finally, if the tax differential theory were correct, the plot would resemble the lower line in Figure 14-1, with a slope more negative (steeper) than -1.0 (say -1.2). Here the deferral of capital gains taxes causes investors to favor capital gains over dividends. In this situation, an all-dividend stock might have $k_s = 13.3\%$, while a similar stock whose returns all come as capital gains might have $k_s = 11.5\%$. Thus, less than 1 percent of additional g would be required to offset a 1 percent reduction in dividend yield.

In fact, when such tests have been conducted with reasonably good data, the slope of the regression line is found to be about -1.0. This seems to refute both Gordon-Lintner and tax differential advocates, and to support MM. However, statistical problems prevent us from saying that these tests *prove* that MM are right and that dividend policy does not affect k_s. The two statistical problems are these: (1) For a valid statistical test, things other than dividend policy must be held constant; that is, the sample companies must differ only in their dividend payout policies. (2) We must be able to measure with a high degree of accuracy the expected growth rates for the sample firms.[5] Neither of these two conditions actually holds: We cannot find a set of publicly owned firms that differ only in their dividend policies, nor can we obtain precise estimates of the growth rates which the marginal investor expects. Therefore, we cannot determine with much precision what effect, if any, dividend policy has on the cost of equity. Our conclusion is that this particular type of test is not capable of solving the dividend policy riddle.

Researchers have also studied the dividend yield effect from a CAPM perspective. They hypothesized that required returns are a function of both market risk, as measured by beta, and dividend yield. If so, then a stock's required return, k_i, could be expressed as follows:

$$k_i = k_{RF} + (k_M - k_{RF})b_i + (D_i - D_M)\lambda_i. \qquad (14\text{-}1)$$

Here, D_i is the dividend yield of Stock i, D_M is the dividend yield of an average stock, and λ_i is the dividend impact coefficient. Researchers have tested Equation 14-1 by regressing historical values of k_{RF}, k_M, D_i, and D_M against historical values of k_i. If the coefficient of λ_i turns out to be zero, dividend yield would not appear to affect required returns, and MM would be supported. If λ_i were positive, then investors would appear to require a higher return on stocks with high dividend yields, as the tax differential theory predicts. If λ_i were negative, this would support Gordon-Lintner.

---

[5]Also, the expected future growth rate must be constant, or we must measure g as an average of expected future growth rates. This complicates the problem of estimating the correct growth for use in the empirical tests.

The results of this line of research have been mixed. Litzenberger and Ramaswamy showed, using NYSE data from 1936 through 1977, that stocks with high dividend yields did have higher total returns than did stocks with low dividend yields, after adjusting for market risk.[6] Their study indicated that investors' required rates of return increased about 0.24 percentage points for every percentage point increase in dividend yield. However, other studies have reached contradictory conclusions; namely, that the λ_i term is zero and consequently that dividend yield has no effect on required returns.[7] (Of course, when these studies were conducted, capital gains and dividend income were taxed at different rates.)

The major problem with the CAPM studies is that they used historical earned rates of return as proxies for expected future returns, and with such a poor proxy, the tests are almost bound to have mixed results. Thus, these CAPM empirical tests, like the pure DCF-based tests, have not led to definitive conclusions as to which dividend theory is most correct. The issue is still unresolved.

Self-Test Questions

What are the two types of empirical tests that have been used to try to identify the correct dividend policy theory?

What are the general results of the empirical tests?

OTHER DIVIDEND POLICY ISSUES

Before we discuss dividend policy in practice, we need to examine two other issues that could affect our views toward the three theories presented above. These issues are (1) the information content, or signaling, hypothesis, and (2) the clientele effect.

Information Content, or Signaling, Hypothesis

When MM set forth their dividend irrelevance theory, they assumed, among other things, that everyone—investors and managers alike—had identical expectations about the firm's future earnings and dividend stream. In reality, however, investors have conflicting opinions regarding both the level of future dividend payments and the degree of uncertainty inherent in those payments, and managers often have better information about future prospects than public stockholders. This is the same sort of *asymmetric information* situation that we discussed in Chapter 12 in connection with the announcement of new stock issues.

It has been observed that an increase in the dividend is often accompanied by an increase in the price of the stock, while a dividend cut generally leads to a stock price decline. This could suggest that investors, in the aggregate, prefer dividends to capital gains. However, MM argued differently. They noted the well-established fact

---

[6]See Litzenberger and Ramaswamy, op. cit.

[7]For example, see Fischer Black and Myron Scholes, "The Effects of Dividend Yield and Dividend Policy on Common Stock Prices and Returns," *Journal of Financial Economics,* May 1974, 1–22.

that corporations are reluctant to cut dividends, hence do not raise dividends unless they anticipate equal or higher earnings in the future. Thus, MM argued that a higher-than-normal dividend increase is a "signal" to investors that the firm's management forecasts good future earnings.[8] Conversely, a dividend reduction, or a smaller-than-normal increase, is a signal that management is forecasting poor earnings in the future. Thus, MM claimed that investors' reactions to changes in dividend policy do not necessarily show that investors prefer dividends to retained earnings. Rather, the fact that price changes follow dividend actions simply indicated to MM that there is an important *information,* or *signaling, content* in dividend announcements.

The AT&T example at the beginning of the chapter illustrated how investors could interpret a failure to declare a dividend increase as a negative signal. To illustrate the devastating impact of a dividend omission, consider the case of Clabir Corporation, a conglomerate with an odd mixture of businesses ranging from the manufacture of tank ammunition to the production of food products such as the Klondike ice cream bar. Clabir had been troubled by losses in its defense business, and in December 1987 the firm announced an annual dividend cut from 72 cents to only 16 cents a share. After this bad news had been digested, the stock was selling for about $3.00 a share in February 1988. Then, Clabir announced that it planned to completely omit dividends for the coming year. Although the near-term cash flow loss to stockholders was relatively small, only 16 cents in annual dividends, the firm's stock price dropped almost immediately from $3.00 to $1.00. Clearly, investors viewed the dividend announcement as a signal that the company was in for very rough times ahead, and this caused them to lower their expectations about Clabir's future profitability, and hence to cut the value of its stock.

Like most other aspects of dividend policy, empirical studies of signaling effects have been inconclusive. There clearly is some information content in dividend announcements. However, it is difficult to tell whether stock price changes that follow increases or decreases in dividends reflect only signaling effects or both signaling and dividend preference effects, because major dividend policy changes typically include both a change in the percentage payout ratio and a change in the dollars of dividends paid.

Signaling effects must be considered when a firm is contemplating a change in dividend policy as a result of changed economic conditions. Later in the chapter we will look at a method for determining a firm's target payout ratio. If that analysis suggests that a change in the payout ratio is desirable, signaling effects might constrain the firm's ability to move quickly to the new policy. As one executive put it, "Dividends, like diamonds, are forever."

---

[8]Stephen Ross has suggested that managers can use capital structure as well as dividends to give signals concerning firms' future prospects. For example, a firm with good earnings prospects can carry more debt than a similar firm with poor earnings prospects. This theory, called *incentive-signaling,* rests on the premise that signals with cash-based variables (either debt interest or dividends) cannot be mimicked by unsuccessful firms because such firms do not have the future cash-generating power to maintain the announced interest or dividend payment. Thus, investors are more likely to believe a glowing verbal report when it is accompanied by a dividend increase or a debt-financed expansion program. See Stephen A. Ross, "The Determination of Financial Structure: The Incentive-Signaling Approach," *The Bell Journal of Economics,* Spring 1977, 23–40.

Clientele Effect

Different groups, or *clienteles,* of stockholders prefer different dividend payout policies. For example, some stockholders such as retired individuals and university endowment funds prefer current income, so they would want the firm to pay out a high percentage of its earnings. Such investors are often in a low or even zero tax bracket, so taxes are of no concern. On the other hand, stockholders in their peak earning years prefer reinvestment, because they have no need for current investment income and would simply reinvest any dividends received, after first paying income taxes on the dividend income.

If the firm retains and reinvests income, rather than paying dividends, those stockholders who need current income would be disadvantaged. They would receive capital gains, but they would be forced to go to the trouble and expense of selling off some of their shares to obtain cash. Also, some institutional investors (or trustees for individuals) may be precluded from selling stock and then "spending capital." The other group, the stockholders who are saving rather than spending dividends, would favor the low dividend policy, for the more the firm pays out in dividends, the more these stockholders will have to pay in current taxes and the more trouble and expense they will have to go through to reinvest their after-tax dividends. Thus, investors who want current investment income should own shares in high dividend payout firms, while investors with no need for current investment income should own shares in low dividend payout firms. For example, investors seeking high current income might invest in electric utilities, which averaged a 71 percent payout from 1985 through 1989, while those favoring growth could invest in the semiconductor industry, which averaged a low 18 percent payout.

To the extent that stockholders can shift their investments among firms, a firm can change from one dividend payout policy to another and then let stockholders who do not like the new policy sell to other investors who do. However, switching may be inefficient because of (1) brokerage costs, (2) the likelihood that stockholders who are selling will have to pay capital gains taxes (the "lock-in effect"), and (3) a possible shortage of investors who like the firm's newly adopted dividend policy. Thus, management might be reluctant to change its dividend policy, because such changes might cause current shareholders to sell their stock, forcing the stock price down. Such a price decline might be temporary, but it might also be permanent—if few new investors are attracted by the new dividend policy, then the stock price would remain depressed. Of course, it is possible that the new policy would attract an even larger clientele than the firm had previously, in which case the stock price would rise.

Evidence from several studies suggests that there is in fact a clientele effect.[9] MM and others have argued that one clientele is as good as any other, so the existence of a clientele effect does not necessarily imply that one dividend policy is better than any other. MM may be wrong, though, and neither they nor anyone else

---

[9]For example, see R. Richardson Pettit, "Taxes, Transactions Costs and the Clientele Effect of Dividends," *The Journal of Financial Economics,* December 1977, 419–436.

has offered proof that the aggregate makeup of investors permits firms to disregard clientele effects. This issue, like most others in the dividend arena, is still up in the air.

Self-Test Questions

Briefly describe the information content, or signaling, hypothesis.

What is the clientele effect?

How could the signaling hypothesis and the presence of dividend clienteles affect the dividend policy decision?

DIVIDEND STABILITY

As we noted at the beginning of the chapter, the decision as to how stable a firm's dividend should be is an important issue. Firms' profits and cash flows vary over time, as do their investment opportunities. Taken alone, this suggests that corporations should vary their dividends over time, increasing them when cash flows are large and the need for funds is low, and lowering them when cash is in short supply relative to investment opportunities. However, many stockholders rely on dividends to meet expenses, and they would be seriously inconvenienced if the dividend stream were unstable. Further, reducing dividends to make funds available for investment could send incorrect signals, and that could drive down the price of the stock. Thus, maximizing stock price requires a firm to balance its internal needs for funds against the needs and desires of its owners, the stockholders.

How should this balance be struck, that is, how stable and dependable should a firm attempt to make its dividends? It is impossible to give a definitive answer to this question, but the following points are relevant:

1.   Virtually every publicly owned company makes a 5- to 10-year financial forecast, and projected earnings and dividends are a part of these forecasts. Such forecasts are not made public—they are used for internal planning purposes. However, security analysts construct similar forecasts and make them available to investors; see the *Value Line Report* for an example. Further, every internal 5- to 10-year corporate forecast we have seen for a "normal" company projects a trend of higher earnings and dividends, and every long-run forecast constructed by a security analyst for a "normal" company shows exactly the same thing. Of course, both managers and investors know that economic conditions may cause actual results to differ from forecasted results.

2.   Years ago, when inflation was not persistent, the term "stable dividend policy" meant a policy of paying the same dollar dividend year after year. AT&T was a prime example of a company with a stable dividend policy—it paid $9 per year ($2.25 per quarter) for 25 straight years. Today, most companies and stockholders expect earnings to grow over time as a result of earnings retention and inflation. Further, dividends are normally expected to grow more or less in line with earnings. Thus, today

a "stable dividend policy" generally means increasing the dividend at a reasonably steady rate. For example, Rubbermaid made this statement in its 1988 Annual Report:

> Dividends per share were increased in 1988 for the 34th consecutive year . . . Our goal is to increase sales, earnings, and earnings per share by 15% per year, while achieving a 21% return on beginning shareholders' equity. It is also the Company's objective to pay approximately 30% of current year's earnings as dividends, which will permit us to retain sufficient capital to provide for future growth.

Rubbermaid used the word "approximately" in discussing its payout ratio, because even if earnings vary a bit from the target level, the company still plans to increase the dividend by the target growth rate, thus forcing the payout ratio to vary from the target level. Note also that even though the dividend growth rate is not specified directly in the statement, analysts can calculate the growth rate and see that it is the same 15 percent as indicated for sales and earnings:

$$g = b \, (\text{ROE})$$

$$= (1 - \text{Payout}) \, (\text{ROE})$$

$$= 0.7(21\%) \approx 15\%.$$

Companies with volatile earnings and cash flows would be reluctant to make a commitment to increase the dividend each year, so they would not make such a statement. Even so, most companies would like to be able to exhibit the kind of stability Rubbermaid has shown, and they try to come as close to it as they can.

Dividend stability has two components: (1) How dependable is the growth rate, and (2) how dependable is the current dividend, that is, can we count on at least receiving the current dividend in the future? The most stable policy, from an investor's standpoint, is that of a firm whose dividend growth rate is predictable—such a company's total return (dividend yield plus capital gains yield) should be relatively stable over the long run, and its stock should be a good hedge against inflation. The second most stable policy is one of a firm whose investors can be reasonably sure that the current dividend will not be reduced—it may not grow at a steady rate, but management will probably be able and willing to avoid cutting the current dividend. The least stable dividend policy is one of a firm whose earnings and cash flows are so volatile that investors cannot count on the company to maintain the current dividend over the typical business cycle.

3.   Most observers believe that dividend stability is desirable, even though statistical problems prevent empirical tests from proving the point. If this position is correct, then investors would prefer a stock that pays more predictable dividends to one that has the same expected present value of dividends but pays them in a more erratic manner. This means that the cost of equity will be minimized, and the stock price maximized, if a firm stabilizes its dividends as much as possible, given its own cash flows and its requirements for capital.

Self-Test Questions

What does the term "stable dividend policy" mean?

Has this meaning changed over time?

What are the two components of dividend stability?

ESTABLISHING THE DIVIDEND POLICY IN PRACTICE

In the preceding sections we have seen that investors may or may not prefer dividends to capital gains but that they do seem to prefer predictable to unpredictable dividends. Given this situation, how should firms set their basic dividend policies? For example, how should a company like Rubbermaid establish its policy of paying some specific percentage of earnings? Rubbermaid's target is 30 percent, but why not 40 percent, 50 percent, or some other percentage? In this section, we describe how the long-run target payout should be established.

Residual Dividend Model

The optimal payout ratio is a function of four factors: (1) investors' preferences for dividends versus capital gains, (2) the firm's investment opportunities, (3) the firm's target capital structure, and (4) the availability and cost of external capital. The last three elements are combined in what we call the *residual dividend model,* under which a firm follows these four steps when deciding its target payout ratio: (1) It determines the optimal capital budget; (2) it determines the amount of equity needed to finance that budget given its target capital structure; (3) it uses retained earnings to supply this equity to the extent possible; and (4) it pays dividends only if more earnings are available than are needed to support the optimal capital budget. The word *residual* implies "leftover," and the residual policy implies that dividends are paid out of "leftover" earnings.

We saw in Chapter 8 that the cost of retained earnings is an *opportunity cost* which reflects rates of return available to equity investors. If a firm's stockholders could buy other stocks of equal risk and obtain a 12 percent dividend-plus-capital-gains yield, then 12 percent is the firm's cost of retained earnings. The cost of new outside equity raised by selling common stock is higher because of the costs of floating the issue, including both underwriting costs and any downward price pressure resulting from "negative signals" investors might get from the announcement of a stock offering.

Also, most firms have a target capital structure that calls for at least some debt, so new financing is done partly with debt and partly with equity. As long as the firm finances with the optimal mix, using the proper amounts of debt and equity, and provided it uses only internally generated equity (retained earnings), then its marginal cost of each new dollar of capital will be minimized. Internally generated equity is available for financing a certain amount of new investment, but beyond that amount, the firm must turn to more expensive new common stock. At the point where new stock must be sold, the cost of equity, and consequently the weighted average cost of capital (WACC), rises.

These concepts, which were developed in Chapters 8 and 11, are illustrated in Figure 14-2 with data from the Dallas Oil Company (DOC). DOC has a WACC of 10 percent as long as its equity is from retained earnings, but its MCC schedule begins to rise at the point where new stock must be sold. DOC has $60 million of earnings and a 40 percent optimal debt ratio. Provided it does not pay any cash dividends, DOC can make net investments (investments in addition to asset replacements financed from depreciation) of $100 million, consisting of $60 million from retained

Figure 14-2   Dallas Oil Company: Marginal Cost of Capital Schedule

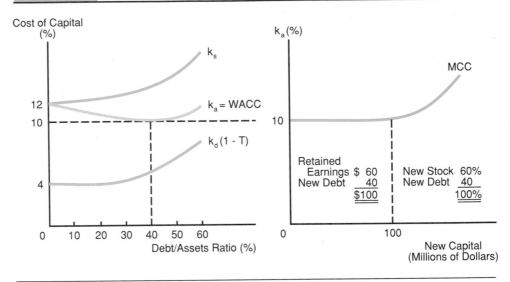

earnings plus $40 million of new debt supported by the retained earnings, at a 10 percent cost of capital. Therefore, its WACC is potentially constant at 10 percent up to $100 million of capital. Beyond $100 million, the WACC rises as the firm begins to use more expensive new common stock.

Of course, if DOC does not retain all of its earnings, its WACC will begin to rise before $100 million. For example, if DOC retained only $30 million, then its WACC would begin to rise at $30 million retained earnings + $20 million debt = $50 million.

Now suppose DOC's director of capital budgeting constructs several investment opportunity schedules and plots them on a graph. In Figure 14-3, we combine these investment opportunity schedules with the cost of capital schedule. The point where the relevant IOS curve cuts the MCC curve defines the firm's marginal cost of capital and its optimal level of new investment. When investment opportunities are relatively bad (IOS_B), the optimal level of investment is $40 million; when opportunities are normal (IOS_N), $70 million should be invested; and when opportunities are relatively good (IOS_G), DOC should make new investments in the amount of $150 million.

If IOS_G is the appropriate schedule, the company should raise and invest $150 million. DOC has $60 million in earnings and a 40 percent target debt ratio. Thus, it can finance $100 million, consisting of $60 million of retained earnings plus $40 million of new debt, at an average cost of 10 percent if it retains all of its earnings. The remaining $50 million will include external equity and thus have a higher cost. If DOC pays out part of its earnings in dividends, it will have to begin to use costly new common stock earlier than need be, so its MCC schedule will rise earlier than

Figure 14-3   Dallas Oil Company: Combined IOS and MCC Schedules

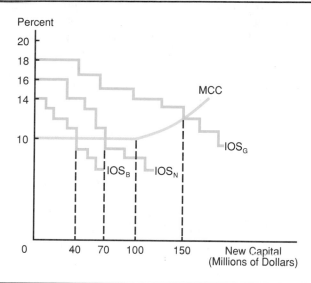

it otherwise would. *This suggests that, under the conditions of IOS_G, DOC should retain all of its earnings. According to the residual policy, DOC's payout ratio should be zero if IOS_G applies.*

Under the normal conditions of IOS_N, however, DOC should invest only $70 million. How should this investment be financed? First, notice that if DOC retained all of its earnings, $60 million, it would need to sell only $10 million of new debt. However, if DOC retained $60 million and sold only $10 million of new debt, it would move away from its target capital structure. To stay on target, DOC must finance 60 percent of the required $70 million by equity—retained earnings—and 40 percent by debt; this means DOC must retain $42 million and sell $28 million of new debt. If DOC retains only $42 million of its $60 million total earnings, it must distribute the residual, $18 million, to its stockholders. Thus, its optimal payout ratio under IOS_N is $18/$60 = 30%.

Under the conditions shown in IOS_B, DOC should invest only $40 million. Because it has $60 million in earnings, it could finance the entire $40 million out of retained earnings and still have $20 million available for dividends. Should this be done? Under our assumptions, this would not be a good decision, because DOC would move away from its optimal capital structure. To stay at the 40 percent target debt/assets ratio, DOC must retain $24 million of earnings and sell $16 million of debt. When the $24 million of retained earnings is subtracted from the $60 million total earnings, DOC is left with a residual of $36 million, the amount that should be paid out in dividends. Thus, the payout ratio as prescribed by the residual policy is $36/$60 = 60%.

Since both the IOS schedule and the earnings level will surely vary from year to year, strict adherence to the residual dividend policy would result in dividend variability—one year the firm might declare zero dividends because investment opportunities were good, but the next year it might pay a large dividend because investment opportunities were poor. Similarly, fluctuating earnings would also lead to variable dividends even if investment opportunities were stable over time. As we noted earlier, variable dividend payments are less desirable than stable dividends, and varying the dividend payments could also lead to false signals and a loss of investor confidence in the firm. Therefore, the residual model can be used as a guide for establishing the long-run target payout ratio, but the model should not be adhered to strictly on a year-to-year basis.

Companies use the graphic residual model as presented to gain an understanding of the determinants of an optimal dividend policy, but they typically use a financial forecasting model as the basis for the target payout ratio. Most larger corporations have a corporate model which is used to forecast their financial statements over the next 5 years or so. Information on projected capital expenditures and working capital requirements is programmed into the model, along with sales forecasts, profit margins, depreciation, and the other elements required to forecast corporate cash flows. The target capital structure is also specified, and the model is designed to show the amount of debt and equity that will be required to meet the forecasted capital requirements while maintaining the target capital structure.

Then, dividend payments are introduced. Naturally, the larger the payout ratio, the greater the required external equity. Most companies then use the model to find a dividend pattern over the forecast period (generally 5 years) that will result in sufficient equity being obtained to support the capital budget without the firm's having to sell new common stock or to move the capital structure ratios outside the optimal range. The end result might include a statement, in a memo from the financial vice-president to the chairman of the board, such as the following:

> We have forecasted the total market demand for our products, what our share of the market is likely to be, and our required investment in capital assets and working capital if we are to meet our forecasted demand. Using this information, we have developed projected balance sheets and income statements for the period 1991–1995.
>
> Our 1990 dividends will total $50 million, or $2 per share. On the basis of our projected earnings, cash flows, and capital requirements, we can increase the dividend by 8 percent per year. This is consistent with a payout ratio of 42 percent, on average, over the forecast period. Any faster dividend growth rate (or higher payout) would require dividend payments so large that we would have to sell common stock, cut the capital budget, or raise the debt ratio. Any slower growth rate would lead to a buildup of the common equity ratio. Therefore, I recommend that the board increase the dividend for 1991 to $2.16, and that it plan for a similar 8 percent increase in the future.
>
> Events could and undoubtedly will occur over the next 5 years that will lead to differences between our forecasts and actual results. If and when changes occur, we will want to reexamine our position. However, I am confident that we can meet our random cash shortfalls by increasing our borrowings—we have some unused debt capacity which gives us flexibility in this regard.
>
> We ran the corporate model under several recession scenarios. If the economy really crashes, our earnings will not cover the dividend. However, in all "reasonable" scenarios cash flows do cover the dividend. I know you are concerned about getting the

dividend up to a level where we might have to cut it under bad economic conditions, and I share this concern. Our model runs indicate, though, that the $2.16 dividend can be maintained—we would have to increase the dividend to over $3 before we would really be exposed to the possible need for an actual cut.

I might also note that *Value Line* and most other analysts' reports are forecasting our dividend growth rate in the 6 to 8 percent range. Thus, if we go to $2.16, we will be at the high end of the range, which should give our stock a boost. With takeover rumors so widespread, getting the stock price up a bit would make us all breathe a little easier.

This company, like Rubbermaid, has very stable operations, so it can plan its dividends with a fairly high degree of confidence. Other companies, especially those in cyclical industries such as autos, have difficulty maintaining in bad times a dividend that is really too low in good times. Such companies—and General Motors is an example—set a very low "regular" dividend and then supplement it with an "extra" dividend when times are good. General Motors has followed this *low-regular-dividend-plus-extras* policy in the past. The company announced a low regular dividend that it was sure could be maintained "through hell or high water," and stockholders could count on receiving this dividend under all conditions. Then, when times were good and profits and cash flows were high, the company paid a clearly noted extra dividend. Investors recognized that the extras might not be maintained in the future, so they did not interpret them as a signal that GM's earnings were going up permanently, nor did they take the elimination of the extra as a negative signal.

Earnings, Cash Flows, and Dividends

We normally think of earnings as being the primary determinant of dividends, but in reality cash flows are even more important. This situation is revealed in Figure 14-4, which gives data for Chevron Corporation from 1972 through 1990. Chevron's dividends increased steadily from 1972 to 1981; during that period both earnings and cash flows were rising, as was the price of oil. After 1981, oil prices declined sharply, pulling earnings down. Cash flows, though, remained relatively high.

Chevron acquired Gulf Oil in 1984, and it issued over $10 billion of debt to finance the acquisition. Interest on the debt hurt earnings immediately after the merger, as did certain write-offs connected with the merger. Further, Chevron's management wanted to pay off the new debt as fast as possible. All of this influenced the company's decision to raise the dividend very slowly from 1984 through 1987.

Now look at Columns 4 and 6, which show payout ratios based on earnings and on cash flows. The earnings payout is quite volatile—dividends ranged from 26 percent to 113 percent of earnings. The cash flow payout, on the other hand, is much more stable—it ranged from 19 percent to 33 percent of cash flows. Further, the correlation between dividends and cash flows was 0.92 versus only 0.50 between dividends and earnings. Thus, dividends clearly depend more on cash flows, which reflect the company's *ability* to pay dividends, than on current earnings, which are heavily influenced by accounting practices and which do not necessarily reflect the ability to pay dividends.

Figure 14-4   Chevron: Earnings, Cash Flow, and Dividends, 1972–1990

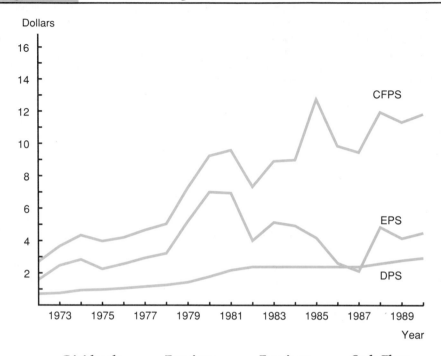

Year (1)	Dividends per Share (2)	Earnings per Share (3)	Earnings Payout (4)	Cash Flow per Share (5)	Cash Flow Payout (6)
1972	$0.73	$1.61	45%	$ 2.72	27%
1973	0.78	2.49	31	3.68	21
1974	0.96	2.86	34	4.36	22
1975	1.00	2.28	44	4.00	25
1976	1.08	2.59	42	4.22	26
1977	1.18	2.98	40	4.68	25
1978	1.28	3.24	40	5.06	25
1979	1.45	5.22	28	7.29	20
1980	1.80	7.02	26	9.26	19
1981	2.20	6.96	32	9.61	23
1982	2.40	4.03	60	7.35	33
1983	2.40	5.15	47	8.93	27
1984	2.40	4.94	49	9.00	27
1985	2.40	4.19	57	12.76	19
1986	2.40	2.63	91	9.86	24
1987	2.40	2.13	113	9.47	25
1988	2.60	4.86	53	11.97	22
1989	2.80	4.16	67	11.33	25
1990 (est.)	2.95	4.50	66	11.85	25

Payment Procedures

Dividends are normally paid quarterly, and, if conditions permit, the dividend is increased once each year. For example, Kodak paid $0.50 per quarter in 1989, or at an annual rate of $2.00. In common financial parlance, we say that in 1989 Kodak's *regular quarterly dividend* was $0.50, and its *annual dividend* was $2.00.

The actual payment procedure is as follows:

1.   **Declaration date.** On the declaration date — say, on November 14 — the directors meet and declare the regular dividend, issuing a statement similar to the following: "On November 14, 1990, the directors of the XYZ Company met and declared the regular quarterly dividend of 50 cents per share, payable to holders of record on December 7, payment to be made on January 2, 1991." For accounting purposes, the declared dividend becomes an actual liability on the declaration date, and if a balance sheet were constructed, the amount ($0.50) × (Number of shares outstanding) would appear as a current liability, and retained earnings would be reduced by a like amount.

2.   **Holder-of-record date.** At the close of business on the holder-of-record date, December 7, the company closes its stock transfer books and makes up a list of shareholders as of that date. If XYZ Company is notified of the sale and transfer of some stock before 5 P.M. on December 7, then the new owner receives the dividend. However, if notification is received on or after December 8, the previous owner of the stock gets the dividend check.

3.   **Ex-dividend date.** Suppose Jean Buyer buys 100 shares of stock from John Seller on December 5. Will the company be notified of the transfer in time to list Buyer as the new owner and thus pay the dividend to her? To avoid conflict, the securities industry has set up a convention of declaring that the right to the dividend remains with the stock until four business days prior to the holder-of-record date; on the fourth day before that date, the right to the dividend no longer goes with the shares. The date when the right to the dividend leaves the stock is called the *ex-dividend date*. In this case, the ex-dividend date is December 4:

	Friday,	November 30, Buyer would receive dividend
Ex-dividend date:	Monday,	December 3, Seller will receive dividend
	Tuesday,	December 4
	Wednesday,	December 5
	Thursday,	December 6
Holder-of-record date:	Friday,	December 7

Therefore, if Buyer is to receive the dividend, she must buy the stock on or before November 30. If she buys it on December 3 or later, Seller will receive the dividend because he will be the official holder of record.

The XYZ dividend amounts to $0.50, so the ex-dividend date is important. Barring fluctuations in the stock market, one would normally expect the price of a stock to drop by approximately the amount of the dividend on the ex-dividend date. Thus, if XYZ closed at $30½ on Friday, November 30, it would probably open at about $30 on Monday, December 3.

4. **Payment date.** The company actually mails the checks to the holders of record on January 2, the payment date.

Self-Test Questions

Explain the residual dividend model.

How do firms use planning models to help set dividend policy?

Are earnings or cash flows more critical to the dividend decision?

Explain the procedures used to actually pay the dividend.

DIVIDEND REINVESTMENT PLANS

During the 1970s, most large companies instituted *dividend reinvestment plans,* or *DRPs,* whereby stockholders can automatically reinvest their dividends in the stock of the paying corporation.[10] Today it is estimated that about 1,000 companies offer DRPs, and, although participation rates vary considerably, on average about 25 percent of the firm's shareholders are enrolled. There are two types of DRPs: (1) plans which involve only "old stock" that is already outstanding, and (2) plans which involve newly issued stock. In either case, the stockholder must pay income taxes on the amount of the dividends, even though stock rather than cash is received.

Under both types of DRP, the stockholder must choose between continuing to receive dividend checks or using the dividends to buy more stock in the corporation. Under the "old stock" type of plan, if the stockholder elects reinvestment, a bank, acting as trustee, takes the total funds available for reinvestment (less a fee), purchases the corporation's stock on the open market, and allocates the shares purchased to the participating stockholders' accounts on a pro rata basis. The transactions costs of buying shares (brokerage costs) are low because of volume purchases, so these plans benefit small stockholders who do not need cash dividends for current consumption.

The "new stock" type of DRP provides for dividends to be invested in newly issued stock; hence, these plans raise new capital for the firm. AT&T, Xerox, Union Carbide, and many other companies have had new stock plans in effect in recent years, using them to raise substantial amounts of new equity capital. No fees are charged to stockholders, and some companies offer stock at a discount of 3 to 5 percent below the actual market price. The companies absorb these costs as a trade-off against flotation costs that would be incurred if stocks were sold through investment bankers rather than through the dividend reinvestment plans. Discussions

---

[10]See Richard H. Pettway and R. Phil Malone, "Automatic Dividend Reinvestment Plans," *Financial Management,* Winter 1973, 11–18, for an excellent discussion of the subject.

with corporate treasurers suggest that many other companies are seriously considering establishing or switching to new-stock DRPs.[11]

Self-Test Questions

What are dividend reinvestment plans?

What are their advantages and disadvantages from both the stockholders' and the firm's perspectives?

OTHER FACTORS THAT INFLUENCE DIVIDEND POLICY

In earlier sections, we described the major theories and issues concerning the effect of dividend policy on the value of a firm, and we discussed the residual dividend model for setting a long-run target payout ratio. In this section, we discuss several other factors that affect the dividend decision.

1. **Bond indentures.** Debt contracts often restrict dividend payments to earnings generated after the loan was granted. Also, debt contracts frequently stipulate that no dividends can be paid unless the current ratio, the times-interest-earned ratio, and other safety ratios exceed stated minimums.

2. **Preferred stock restrictions.** Typically, common dividends cannot be paid if the company has omitted (passed) its preferred dividend. The preferred arrearages must be satisfied before common dividends can be resumed.

3. **Impairment of capital rule.** Dividend payments cannot exceed the balance sheet item "retained earnings." This legal restriction, known as the "impairment of capital rule," is designed to protect creditors. (*Liquidating dividends* can be paid out of capital, but they must be indicated as such and must not reduce capital below limits stated in the firm's debt contracts.)

4. **Availability of cash.** Cash dividends can only be paid with cash. Thus, a shortage of cash in the bank can restrict dividend payments. However, unused borrowing capacity can offset this factor.

5. **Penalty tax on improperly accumulated earnings.** To prevent wealthy individuals from using corporations to avoid personal taxes, the Tax Code provides

---

[11]One interesting aspect of DRPs is that they are forcing corporations to reexamine their basic dividend policies. A high participation rate in a DRP suggests that stockholders might be better off if the firm simply reduced cash dividends to save stockholders some personal income taxes. Quite a few firms are surveying their stockholders to learn more about their preferences and to find out how they would react to a change in dividend policy. A more rational approach to basic dividend policy decisions may emerge from this research.

Note that companies use or stop the use of new-stock DRPs depending on their need for equity capital. Thus, both Union Carbide and AT&T recently stopped offering a new-stock DRP with a 5 percent discount because their needs for equity capital declined, but Xerox recently began such a plan. Other companies have continued their DRPs, but eliminated the price discount. For example, Travellers Corporation, a diversified insurance company, recently eliminated its 5 percent discount. The discount was halted because the DRP had become a "relatively expensive source of capital," a spokeswoman said.

for a special surtax on improperly accumulated income. Thus, if the IRS can demonstrate that the dividend payout ratio is being deliberately held down to help stockholders avoid personal taxes, heavy penalties will be imposed on the firm. However, as a practical matter, the penalty has been applied only to privately owned firms.

6.   **Control.** If management is concerned about maintaining control, it may be reluctant to sell new stock, hence it may retain more earnings than it otherwise would. This factor is especially important for small, closely held firms.

Self-Test Question

What are some factors that influence a firm's dividend policy decision?

OUR VIEW OF THE DIVIDEND POLICY DECISION

In many ways, our discussion of dividend policy parallels our discussion of capital structure: We have presented the relevant theories and issues, and have listed some additional factors that influence dividend policy, but we have not come up with any hard and fast guidelines that managers should follow. It should be apparent from our discussion that dividend policy decisions are truly exercises in informed judgment, not decisions that can be made on the basis of a precise mathematical model.

In practice, dividend policy is not an independent decision—the dividend decision is made jointly with capital structure and capital expenditure decisions. The underlying reason for this joint decision process is asymmetric information, which influences managerial actions in two ways:

1.   In general, managers do not want to issue new common stock. First, new common stock involves issuance costs—commissions, fees, and so on—that may be avoided by using retained earnings to finance the firm's equity needs. Also, as we discussed in Chapter 12, the potential for asymmetric information causes investors to view new common stock sales as negative signals, causing investors to lower their expectations regarding the firm's future prospects. The end result is that the announcement of a new stock issue is usually followed by a decrease in the firm's stock price. Considering the total costs involved, including both issuance and asymmetric information costs, managers strongly prefer to use retained earnings as their primary source of equity financing.

2.   Because of asymmetric information, analysts and investors view dividend changes as an important means for a manager to signal his or her beliefs about the future prospects of the firm. Thus, dividend decreases, or worse yet, omissions, generally have a significant negative effect on a firm's stock price. Since managers recognize this, they want to set dollar dividends low enough so that there is only a remote chance that the payment will have to be reduced in the future.

The effects of asymmetric information on dividend policy are clear. To the extent possible, managers should avoid both new common stock sales and dividend cuts, because both actions tend to lower stock price. Thus, in setting dividend policy, managers should first consider the firm's future investment opportunities relative to its projected internal sources of funds, because the amount of capital required for new investment dictates the firm's future equity requirements. The firm's target capital structure also plays a part, but because the optimal capital structure is a *range,* firms can vary the actual capital structure somewhat from year to year. Since it is best to avoid issuing new common stock, a long-term payout ratio is set which, for planning purposes, will permit the firm to meet all its equity capital requirements with retentions. In effect, managers use the residual dividend model to set dividends, but in a long-term framework. Finally, the current dollar dividend is set so that there is an extremely low probability that the dividend, once set, will ever have to be lowered or omitted.

Of course, the dividend decision is made during the planning process, so there is uncertainty about future investment opportunities and operating cash flows. Thus, the actual payout ratio in any year may be above or below the firm's long-range target, but the dollar dividend will be maintained, or increased as planned, unless the firm's financial condition deteriorates to the point where planned policy simply cannot be maintained. A steady or increasing stream of dividends over the long run signals that the firm's financial condition is under control. Further, investor uncertainty is decreased by stable dividends, so a steady dividend stream reduces the negative effect of a new stock issue, should one become absolutely necessary.

In general, firms with superior investment opportunities set a lower payout than firms with poor investment opportunities, because firms with strong growth opportunities require more equity capital to support growth. The degree of uncertainty also influences the decision. If there is a great deal of uncertainty in the forecasts of *free cash flows*, which are defined here as the firm's operating cash flows minus mandatory equity investment requirements, then it is best to be conservative and to set a lower current dollar dividend, because the chances of future earnings' being less than forecasted are high. Also, firms with postponable investment opportunities can afford to set a higher dollar dividend, because in times of stress investments can be postponed for a year or two, thus increasing the cash available for dividends. Finally, firms which have a flat WACC curve, when WACC is plotted against the debt ratio as in the left panel of Figure 14-2, can also afford to set a higher payout ratio, because they can, in times of stress, more easily issue additional debt to maintain the capital budgeting program without having to cut dividends or issue stock.

In practice, dividend policy is a dynamic process, because most firms only have a single opportunity to set the dividend payment from scratch. Therefore, for the average firm, today's dividend policy decision is constrained by the policies that have been followed in the past, and setting a policy for the next 5-year planning period necessarily begins with a review of the current dividend situation.

Although we have outlined a rational process which managers can use to set their firms' dividend policies, dividend policy still remains one of the most judgmental decisions that a manager must make. For this reason, dividend policy is always set by the board of directors—the financial staff does various types of analyses, and the financial vice-president may make a recommendation, but the board makes the final dividend policy decision.

Self-Test Question

Describe the dividend policy decision process. Be sure to discuss all the factors that influence the decision.

STOCK REPURCHASES

As an alternative to paying cash dividends, a firm may distribute income to stockholders by *repurchasing its own stock,* and stock that has been repurchased by a firm is called *treasury stock.* If some of the outstanding stock is repurchased and held as treasury stock, fewer shares will remain outstanding. Assuming the repurchase does not adversely affect the firm's earnings, the earnings per share on the remaining shares will increase, resulting in a higher market price per share, which means that capital gains will have been substituted for dividends.

Companies have been repurchasing their stock in record amounts in recent years. In 1989 alone, GE announced a stock buyback of 174 million shares valued at $10.0 billion; IBM announced a $5 billion buyback of 50.1 million shares; and 11 other corporations announced buybacks of $1.0 billion or more.

Most very large repurchase programs are part of a general corporate restructuring, wherein certain major assets, such as whole divisions or subsidiaries, are sold off, or where the debt ratio is increased substantially. Asset sales and the issuance of new debt both bring in additional capital, and this capital can then be distributed to stockholders through a major, one-time stock repurchase. A repurchase that is part of a corporate restructuring is quite different from a "regular" repurchase, where the repurchase is merely a substitute for cash dividends as a method for distributing operating income to shareholders.

The effects of a "regular" repurchase can be illustrated with data on American Development Corporation (ADC). The company expects to earn $4.4 million in 1991, and 50 percent of this amount, or $2.2 million, will be available for distribution to common shareholders. There are 1,100,000 shares outstanding. ADC could use the $2.2 million to repurchase 100,000 of its shares through a tender offer for $22 a share, or it could pay a cash dividend of $2 a share.[12] The current stock price is $20 per share.

---

[12]Stock repurchases are commonly made in three ways. First, a publicly owned firm can simply buy its own stock through a broker on the open market. Second, it can issue a *fixed price tender,* under which it permits stockholders to send in (that is, "tender") their shares to the firm in exchange for a specified price per share. When tender offers are made, the firm generally indicates that it will buy up a specified number of shares within a particular time period (usually one month); if more shares are tendered than the company wishes to purchase, then purchases are made on a pro rata basis. Third, the firm can use a *Dutch-auction tender,* where it announces that it will spend, say, $10 million to repurchase stock, and it then sets a range of prices at which shares can be tendered, say, from $20 to $25 per share if the stock currently sells for $20. Stockholders who elect to tender can choose a price anywhere in the specified range, but the lower the price chosen, the higher the probability of getting cash. The company completes the Dutch-auction tender by using the lowest price which spends the allocated money. All stockholders who tendered at or below the selected price will get cash for their shares, while all others will have their shares returned. Finally, the firm can purchase a block of shares from one or more large holders on a negotiated basis. If a negotiated purchase is employed, care should be taken to insure that these stockholders do not receive preferential treatment not available to other stockholders.

The effect of the repurchase on ADC's EPS and stock price can be determined in the following way:

1.   Current EPS $= \dfrac{\text{Total earnings}}{\text{Number of shares}} = \dfrac{\$4.4 \text{ million}}{1.1 \text{ million}} = \$4$ per share.

2.   Current P/E ratio $= \dfrac{\$20}{\$4} = 5\times$, assumed to remain constant.

3.   EPS after repurchase of 100,000 shares $= \dfrac{\$4.4 \text{ million}}{1 \text{ million}} = \$4.40$ per share.

4.   Expected stock price after repurchase $= (\text{P/E})(\text{EPS}) = (5)(\$4.40) = \$22$ per share.

5.   Expected capital gains per remaining share $= \$22 - \$20 = \$2.00$.

It should be noticed from this example that investors would receive benefits of $2 per share in any case, either in the form of a $2 cash dividend or a $2 increase in the stock price. This result occurs because we assumed (1) that shares could be repurchased at exactly $22 a share and (2) that the P/E ratio would remain constant. If shares could be bought for less than $22, the repurchase would be even better for *remaining* stockholders, but the reverse would hold if ADC paid more than $22 a share. Furthermore, the P/E ratio might change as a result of the repurchase, rising if investors viewed the repurchase favorably and falling if they viewed it unfavorably. Some factors that might affect P/E ratios are considered next.

Advantages of Repurchases from the Stockholder's Viewpoint

1.   Repurchase announcements may be viewed as positive signals by investors because the repurchase could be motivated by management's belief that the firm's shares are undervalued. For example, Teledyne, a $3.5 billion conglomerate, currently earns about $300 million per year, yet it did not pay a cash dividend for over 26 years. Profits were, however, used to repurchase stock and thus to stimulate price growth. Teledyne's stock rose from $4 to $355, so the company was clearly doing something right! During that period, the number of shares outstanding shrunk from 83 million to fewer than 12 million. Teledyne finally began paying dividends in 1987, starting with an annual dollar payout of $4.02.

2.   The stockholder has a choice—to sell or not to sell. On the other hand, one must accept a dividend payment and pay the tax. Thus, Teledyne stockholders who wanted cash could sell some of their shares, and those who did not need cash could simply retain their stock and defer their tax liabilities.

Advantages of Repurchases from Management's Viewpoint

1.   As noted earlier, dividends are "sticky" in the short run because managements are reluctant to raise dividends if the new dividend cannot be maintained in the future—because of signaling effects, managements dislike cutting cash dividends. Hence, if the excess cash flow is thought to be only *temporary*, management may prefer to make the distribution in the form of a share repurchase rather than to declare a cash dividend which they believe cannot be maintained.

2.   Repurchased stock can be used for acquisitions or released when stock options are exercised, when convertibles are converted, or when warrants are exercised. Discussions with financial managers indicate that they often like to use repurchased stock rather than newly issued stock for these purposes so as to avoid dilution of per-share earnings. To illustrate the first two points, Rockwell International, a major manufacturer of aerospace, automotive, and electronic products, recently announced a $500 million stock repurchase program that reduced its common shares outstanding by about 8 percent. This buyback was financed from earnings from B1-B bomber sales, a source which will not continue indefinitely. Further, some analysts speculated that the repurchased stock might eventually be used to acquire another firm.

3.   Repurchases are the only practical alternative when management has decided to undertake a major restructuring such as a large asset sale, a substantial increase in the debt ratio, or a combination of the two. For example, at one time American Standard (a major plumbing supply company) had virtually no long-term debt outstanding. The company decided that its optimal capital structure called for the use of considerably more debt, but even if it had financed only with debt, it would have taken years to get the debt ratio up to the new target. What should the company do? It decided to sell long-term debt and to use the proceeds to repurchase its common stock, thus producing an immediate large change in its capital structure.

4.   Treasury stock can be resold in the open market if the firm needs additional funds.[13]

Disadvantages of Repurchases from the Stockholder's Viewpoint

1.   The price of the stock might benefit more from cash dividends than from repurchases, because cash dividends are generally thought to be relatively dependable, but repurchases are not. Further, if a firm announced a regular, dependable repurchase program, the improper accumulation tax would become more of a threat. Although Teledyne apparently had no problems in this regard, Teledyne's repurchases were irregular, which makes a difference.

2.   The *selling* stockholders may not be fully aware of all the implications of a repurchase, or they may not have all the pertinent information about the corporation's present and future activities. However, firms generally announce a repurchase program before embarking on it to avoid potential lawsuits from selling stockholders.

---

[13]Another interesting use of stock repurchases was St. Joe Minerals' strategy of repurchasing its own stock to thwart an attempted takeover. Seagram Company was attempting to acquire a controlling interest in St. Joe through a tender offer of $45 a share. St. Joe's management countered with a tender offer of its own for seven million shares at $60 per share, to be financed by the sale of several divisions plus borrowings. Similarly, Texaco bought back over $1 billion of its stock from the Bass brothers of Texas, who were rumored to be planning a takeover of Texaco. Texaco paid the Bass brothers a premium of about 40 percent over the market price. Some Texaco stockholders sued management, arguing that Texaco's management was giving away corporate assets in order to preserve their own jobs. This type of payment is called "greenmail."

3.   The corporation may pay too high a price for the repurchased stock, to the disadvantage of remaining stockholders. If the shares are inactively traded, and if the firm seeks to acquire a relatively large amount of its own stock, the price may be bid above its equilibrium price. If so, the price will fall after the firm ceases its repurchase operations.

Disadvantages of Repurchases from Management's Viewpoint

1.   Some people have argued that firms which repurchase substantial amounts of stock often have poorer growth rates and fewer good investment opportunities than firms which do not engage in repurchases. If the announcement of a repurchase program is taken as a signal that the firm has especially unfavorable growth opportunities, then there could be an adverse impact on the price of its stock. However, if the firm really does have a shortage of good investment opportunities, then it would be better for management to distribute funds to investors, who could then redeploy the funds elsewhere in the market, than to invest the funds in the business in poor projects. There is, in our view, little empirical support for the position that stockholders dislike repurchases.[14]

2.   Repurchases might involve some risk from a legal standpoint. If the Internal Revenue Service could establish that the repurchases were primarily for the avoidance of taxes on dividends, then penalties could be imposed on the firm under the improper accumulation of earnings provision of the Tax Code. Such actions have been brought against privately held companies, but we know of no case involving a publicly owned firm, even though some firms have retired over one-half of their outstanding stock.

3.   The SEC could raise questions if it appears that the firm may be manipulating the price of its shares. This factor, in particular, keeps firms from doing much repurchasing if they plan offerings of other types of securities in the near future, or if they contemplate merger negotiations in which their stock would be exchanged for that of the acquired company.

Conclusions on Stock Repurchases

When all the pros and cons on stock repurchases are totaled, where do we stand? Our conclusions may be summarized as follows:

1.   Repurchases on a regular, dependable basis may not be feasible because of uncertainties both about the tax treatment of such a program and about such factors as the market price of the shares, how many shares would be tendered, and so forth.

2.   However, repurchases do offer tax deferral advantages over dividends for the stockholders who do not tender their shares, so this procedure should be given careful consideration on the basis of the firm's unique situation.

---

[14]In fact, there is some evidence that the stocks of companies which repurchased large quantities of their common stock in the 10 years from 1974 through 1983 had above-average stock price appreciation. See "Beating the Market By Buying Back Stock," *Fortune*, April 29, 1985, 42–48.

3.   Repurchases can be especially valuable to a firm that is restructuring and consequently wants to increase significantly its debt ratio within a short period, or to dispose of cash generated from the sale of assets.

Self-Test Questions

Briefly describe the mechanics of a stock repurchase.

What are some potential benefits from stock repurchases?

Are there any drawbacks to stock repurchases?

STOCK DIVIDENDS AND STOCK SPLITS

Stock dividends and stock splits are related to the firm's cash dividend policy. The rationale for stock dividends and splits can best be explained through an example; we will use the Nashville Company, a large multimedia entertainment company specializing in country and western music, in our illustrations.

Nashville's markets are expanding, and as the company continues to grow and to retain earnings, its book value per share should also grow. More important, its earnings per share and stock price should also rise. The company began its life with only a few thousand shares outstanding. After some years of growth, each share had a very high EPS and DPS. When a "normal" P/E ratio was applied to the stock, the derived market price was so high that few people could afford to buy a "round lot" of 100 shares. This limited the demand for the stock, thus keeping the total market value of the firm below what it would have been if more shares, at lower prices, were outstanding. To correct this situation, Nashville "split its stock" as described next.

Stock Splits

Although there is little empirical evidence to support the contention, there is nevertheless a widespread belief in financial circles that an *optimal price range* exists for stocks. "Optimal" means that if the price is in this range, the price/earnings ratio, hence the value of the firm, will be maximized. Many observers, including Nashville's management, believe that the best range for most New York Stock Exchange stocks is from $20 to $80 per share. Companies whose shares are owned largely by institutions tend to move toward the high end of the range, while those owned largely by individuals, such as the public utilities, generally operate in the lower end of the range. Companies with average institutional ownership, like Nashville Company, cluster in the $30 to $50 range. Accordingly, if the price of Nashville's stock rose to $80, management would probably declare a two-for-one stock split, thus doubling the number of shares outstanding, halving the earnings and dividends per share, and thereby lowering the price of the stock. Each stockholder would have more shares, but each share would be worth less. If the post-split price were $40, Nashville's stockholders would be exactly as well off as they were before the split.

If the price of the stock were to stabilize above $40, stockholders would be better off. Stock splits can be of any size. For example, the stock could be split two-for-one, three-for-one, 1.5-for-one, or in any other way.[15]

Ford Motor Company, in late 1987, announced the largest quarterly dividend increase in the firm's history, along with a 2-for-1 stock split. At the time of the announcement, Ford's stock was selling at about $94 a share. Wall Street analysts said they had expected Ford to take these actions in view of the stock's soaring price and relatively modest dividend. "I thought it was overdue," said David Healy, a well-known security analyst. "Generally, they split the stock when it gets into the $50 to $70 range." Individual investors "would rather buy two shares for $47 each than one for $94," Mr. Healy said. The quarterly dividend on the old shares was increased 33 percent to $1.00 a share, up from 75 cents. After the split, which occurred in January 1988, the quarterly dividend was readjusted to 50 cents, producing a $2.00 annual dividend, up from $1.50.

Stock splits can also be used to increase the "float," or the number of shares held by outsiders. For example, Care Corporation, a nursing home operator, recently declared a 4-for-1 split, in large part because about 60 percent of the company's 500,000 shares outstanding were controlled by insiders and relatives, leaving only 200,000 shares for trading by others. The split increased the float to 800,000 which, according to the firm's management, increased the trading activity in the stock. Note, though, that academic studies have suggested that stock splits actually lower trading volume when measured on a proportional basis, primarily because brokerage commissions are increased.[16]

Stock Dividends

Stock dividends are similar to stock splits in that they divide the pie into smaller slices without affecting the fundamental position of the current stockholders. On a 5 percent stock dividend, the holder of 100 shares would receive an additional 5 shares (without cost); on a 20 percent stock dividend, the same holder would receive 20 new shares; and so on. Again, the total number of shares is increased, so earnings, dividends, and price per share all decline.

If a firm wants to reduce the price of its stock, should a stock split or a stock dividend be used? Stock splits and large stock dividends are generally used after a sharp price run-up, when a large price reduction is sought. Small stock dividends are occasionally used on a regular annual basis to keep the stock price more or less constrained. For example, if a firm's earnings and dividends are growing at about 10 percent per year, the price would tend to go up at about that same rate, and the

---

[15]*Reverse splits,* which reduce the shares outstanding, can even be used. For example, a company whose stock sells for $5 might employ a one-for-five reverse split, exchanging one new share for five old shares and raising the value of the shares to about $25, which is within the "acceptable" range. LTV Corporation did this after several years of losses had driven its stock price down below the optimal range.

[16]Commissions are generally higher on a trade of, say, 500 shares at $10 per share than on a trade of 100 shares at $50 a share, even though the dollar value of the trades is the same. For a further discussion of the effects of stock splits on market liquidity, see Thomas E. Copeland, "Liquidity Changes Following Stock Splits," *Journal of Finance,* March 1979, 115–141.

price would soon be outside the desired trading range. For this company, a 10 percent annual stock dividend would maintain the stock price within the optimal trading range.

Although the economic effects of stock splits and stock dividends are virtually identical, accountants treat them somewhat differently. For a discussion of the accounting treatment, see any financial accounting text.

Price Effects

If a company splits its stock or declares a stock dividend, will this action increase the market value of its stock? Several empirical studies have sought to answer this question, and in general here are their findings.[17]

1.   On average, the price of a company's stock rises shortly after it announces a stock split or dividend.

2.   However, these price increases are more the result of the fact that investors take stock splits/dividends as signals of higher earnings and dividends than of a desire for stock dividends/splits per se. Since only those companies whose managements think things look good tend to use stock splits/dividends, the announcement of a stock split is taken as a signal that earnings and cash dividends are likely to rise. Thus, the price increases that are associated with stock splits/dividends are probably the result of signals of favorable prospects for earnings and dividends, not a desire for stock splits/dividends per se.

3.   It has been observed that if a company announces a stock split or dividend, its price will tend to rise. However, if during the next few months it does not announce an increase in earnings and dividends, then its stock price will drop back to the earlier level.

4.   As we noted earlier, brokerage commissions are higher in percentage terms on lower-priced stocks. This means that it is more expensive to trade low-priced than high-priced stocks, and this in turn means that stock splits reduce the liquidity of a company's shares. This particular piece of evidence suggests that stock splits/ dividends are actually harmful, although a lower price does mean that more investors can afford to make round lot (100 shares) purchases, which carry lower commissions than do odd lot (less than 100 shares) purchases.

What do we conclude from all this? From a pure economic standpoint, stock dividends and splits are just additional pieces of paper. However, they do provide management with a relatively low-cost way of signaling that the firm's prospects look good. Further, we should note that since few large, publicly owned stocks sell at prices above several hundred dollars, we simply do not know what the effect would be if IBM, Xerox, Hewlett-Packard, and other highly successful firms had never split

---

[17]See Eugene F. Fama, Lawrence Fisher, Michael C. Jensen, and Richard Roll, "The Adjustment of Stock Prices to New Information," *International Economic Review,* February 1969, 1–21; Mark S. Grinblatt, Ronald M. Masulis, and Sheridan Titman, "The Valuation Effects of Stock Splits and Stock Dividends," *Journal of Financial Economics,* December 1984, 461–490; C. Austin Barker, "Evaluation of Stock Dividends," *Harvard Business Review,* July–August 1958, 99–114; and Copeland op. cit.

their stocks, and consequently had sold at prices in the thousands or even tens of thousands of dollars. All in all, it probably makes sense to employ stock dividends/splits when a firm's prospects are favorable, especially if the price of its stock has gone beyond the normal trading range.[18]

Self-Test Questions

What are stock dividends and stock splits?

What impact do stock dividends and splits have on stock price? Why?

In what situations should managers consider the use of stock dividends? In what situations should they consider the use of stock splits?

SUMMARY

Dividend policy involves the decision to pay out earnings versus retaining them for reinvestment in the firm, and dividend policy decisions can have either favorable or unfavorable effects on the price of the firm's stock. The key factors influencing a firm's dividend policy are as follows:

- The *dividend policy decision* involves three questions: (1) What fraction of earnings should be paid out, on average, over time? (2) Should the firm maintain a steady, stable dividend growth rate? (3) What dollar amount should the firm pay in current dividends?

- Miller and Modigliani developed the *dividend irrelevance theory,* which holds that a firm's dividend policy has no effect either on the value of the firm or on its cost of capital.

- The *bird-in-the-hand theory,* advocated by Gordon and Lintner, holds that the value of the firm will be maximized by a high dividend payout ratio, because investors regard actual dividends as being less risky than potential capital gains.

- The *tax differential theory,* advocated by Litzenberger and Ramaswamy, holds that the value of the firm will be maximized by a low dividend payout, because investors pay lower effective taxes on capital gains than on dividends.

- Because *empirical tests* of the three theories *have been inconclusive,* academicians simply cannot tell corporate managers with any degree of precision how a change in dividend policy will affect stock prices and capital costs. Thus, actually determining the optimal dividend policy is extremely difficult.

- Dividend policy should also reflect the *information content of dividends (signaling)* and the *clientele effect.* The information content, or signaling, hypothesis states that investors regard dividend changes as a signal of management's fore-

---

[18]It is interesting to note that Berkshire Hathaway, which is controlled by billionaire Warren Buffett, one of the most successful financiers of the twentieth century, has never had a stock split, and its stock sells on the NYSE for about $7,000 per share. Perhaps Berkshire Hathaway's total market value would be even higher if it had a 200:1 split, but we would not want to debate Buffett on the point!

cast of future earnings. The clientele effect suggests that a firm will attract investors who like the firm's dividend policy, hence a change in dividend policy will lead to a change in the set of stockholders.

- In practice, most firms try to follow a policy of paying a *steadily increasing dividend*. This policy provides investors with a stable, dependable income, and, if the signaling theory is correct, it also gives investors information about management's expectations for earnings growth.

- Most firms use the *residual dividend model* to set a long-run target payout ratio which permits the firm to satisfy its equity requirements with retained earnings.

- A *dividend reinvestment plan (DRP)* allows stockholders to have the company automatically use their dividends to purchase additional shares of the firm's stock. DRPs are popular with investors who do not need current income because the plans allow stockholders to acquire additional shares without incurring normal brokerage fees.

- Other factors, such as *legal constraints, investment opportunities, availability and cost of funds from other sources,* and *taxes,* are considered by managers when they establish dividend policies.

- Under a *stock repurchase plan,* a firm buys back some of its outstanding stock, thereby decreasing the number of shares, which in turn increases both EPS and the stock price. Repurchases are useful for making major changes in a firm's capital structure, as well as for allowing stockholders to delay paying taxes on their share of the firm's profits.

- A *stock split* is an action taken by a firm to increase the number of shares outstanding. Normally, splits reduce the price per share in proportion to the increase in shares because splits merely "divide the pie into smaller slices." A *stock dividend* is a dividend paid in additional shares of stock rather than in cash. Both stock dividends and splits are used to keep stock prices within an "optimal" range.

Questions

14-1   Define each of the following terms:
   a.   Dividend policy
   b.   Dividend irrelevance theory
   c.   "Bird-in-the-hand" theory
   d.   Tax differential theory
   e.   Residual dividend model
   f.   Constraints on dividend policy
   g.   Clientele effect
   h.   Information content of dividends; signaling
   i.   Extra dividend
   j.   Ex-dividend date
   k.   Dividend reinvestment plans (each of two types)
   l.   Stock split; stock dividend
   m.   Stock repurchase

14-2   As an investor, would you rather invest in a firm that has a policy of maintaining (a) a constant payout ratio, (b) a constant dollar dividend per share, (c) a target dividend growth rate, or (d) a constant regular quarterly dividend plus a year-end extra when earnings are sufficiently high or corporate investment needs are sufficiently low? Explain your answer, stating how these policies would affect your k_s.

14-3   How would each of the following changes probably affect aggregate (that is, the average for all corporations) payout ratios? Explain your answers.
   a.   An increase in the personal income tax rate. An increase in the corporate tax rate.
   b.   A liberalization in depreciation for federal income tax purposes, that is, faster tax write-offs.
   c.   A rise in interest rates.
   d.   An increase in corporate profits.
   e.   A decline in investment opportunities.
   f.   Reinstatement of a differential (lower) capital gains tax rate.

14-4   Discuss the pros and cons of having the directors formally announce what a firm's dividend policy will be in the future.

14-5   Most firms would like to have their stock selling at a high P/E ratio and also have an extensive public ownership (many different shareholders). Explain how stock dividends or stock splits may help achieve these goals.

14-6   What is the difference between a stock dividend and a stock split? As a stockholder, would you prefer to see your company declare a 100 percent stock dividend or a two-for-one split? Assume that either action is feasible.

14-7   "The cost of retained earnings is less than the cost of new outside equity capital. Consequently, it is totally irrational for a firm to sell a new issue of stock and to pay dividends during the same year." Discuss this statement.

14-8   Would it ever be rational for a firm to borrow money in order to pay dividends? Explain.

14-9   Union representatives have presented arguments similar to the following: "Corporations such as General Motors retain about half of their profits for financing needs. If they financed by selling stock instead of by retaining earnings, they could raise wages substantially and still earn enough to pay the same dividend to their shareholders. Therefore, their profits are too high." Evaluate this statement.

14-10   "Executive salaries have been shown to be more closely correlated to the size of the firm than to its profitability. If a firm's board of directors is controlled by management instead of by outside directors, this might result in the firm's retaining more earnings than can be justified from the stockholders' point of view." Discuss the statement, being sure (a) to use Figure 14-3 in your answer and (b) to explain the implied relationship between dividend policy and stock prices.

Problems

14-1   **(Dividend theories)** Modigliani and Miller (MM), on the one hand, and Gordon and Lintner (GL), on the other, have expressed strong views regarding the effect of dividend policy on a firm's cost of capital and value.
   a.   In essence, what are the MM and the GL views regarding the effect of dividend policy on cost of capital and value? Illustrate your answer with a graph.
   b.   How does the tax differential model differ from the views of MM and GL?
   c.   According to the text, which position (MM, GL, or tax differential) has received statistical confirmation from empirical tests?

  d.   How could GL use the fact that dividend increase announcements are often followed by stock price increases to support their "bird-in-the-hand" theory? How could MM use the information content, or signaling, hypothesis to counter these arguments?

  e.   How could MM's opponents use the clientele effect concept to counter MM's arguments? If you were debating MM's opponents, how would you counter them?

14-2   **(Residual dividend model)** One position expressed in the literature is that firms should set their dividends as a residual, after using income to support new investment.

  a.   Explain what the residual dividend model implies, illustrating your answer with a graph showing how different conditions could lead to different dividend payout ratios.

  b.   Could the residual dividend model be consistent with (1) a constant dividend growth rate policy, (2) a constant payout policy, and/or (3) a low-regular-plus-extras policy? Explain.

  c.   In Chapters 12 and 13, we considered the relationship between capital structure and the cost of capital. If the WACC versus debt ratio plot were shaped like a sharp V, would this have a different implication for the importance of setting dividends according to the residual model than if the ratio relationship were shaped like a shallow bowl (or a U)?

  d.   Companies A and B both have IOS schedules which intersect their MCC schedules at a point which, under the residual policy, calls for a 20 percent payout. In both cases, a 20 percent payout would require a cut in the annual dividend from $2 to $1. One company cut its dividend and accepted all projects, while the other did not cut its dividend and accepted less than the optimal number of projects. One company had a relatively steep IOS curve, while the other had a relatively flat IOS. Explain which company had the steep, and which the flat, IOS.

14-3   **(Stock dividends and splits)** More NYSE companies had stock dividends and stock splits during 1983 and 1984 than ever before. What events in these years could have made stock splits and dividends so popular? Explain the rationale that a financial vice president might give the board of directors to support a stock split/dividend recommendation.

14-4   **(Residual dividend model)** Baranek Manufacturing Corporation (BMC) has an all-equity capital structure which includes no preferred stock. It has 200,000 shares of $2 par value common stock outstanding.

  When BMC's founder, who was also its research director and most successful inventor, died unexpectedly in 1991, BMC was left suddenly and permanently with materially lower growth expectations and relatively few attractive new investment opportunities. Unfortunately, there was no way to replace the founder's contributions to the firm. Previously, BMC had found it necessary to plow back most of its earnings to finance growth, which has been averaging 12 percent per year. Future growth at a 5 percent rate is considered realistic, but that level would call for an increase in the dividend payout. Further, it now appears that new investment projects with at least the 14 percent rate of return required by BMC's stockholders (k_s = 14%) would amount to only $800,000 for 1991 in comparison to a projected $2,000,000 of net income after taxes. If the existing 20 percent dividend payout were continued, retained earnings would be $1.6 million in 1991, but as noted, investments which yield the 14 percent cost of capital amount to only $800,000.

  The one encouraging thing is that the high earnings from existing assets are expected to continue and net income of $2 million is still expected for 1991. Given the dramatically changed circumstances, BMC's management is reviewing the firm's dividend policy.

  a.   Assuming that the acceptable 1991 investment projects would be financed entirely by earnings retained during the year, calculate DPS in 1991 assuming BMC uses the residual payment model.

b.   What payout ratio does this imply for 1991?

c.   If the increased payout ratio is maintained for the foreseeable future, what should be the present intrinsic value of the common stock? How does this compare with the price that should have prevailed under the assumptions existing just prior to the news about the death of the founder? If the two values of $\hat{P}_0$ are different, comment on why.

14-5   **(Dividend policy and capital structure)** The Tennessee Bourbon Company (TBC) has for many years enjoyed a moderate but stable growth in sales and earnings. However, bourbon consumption has been falling recently, primarily because of an increasing use of lighter alcoholic beverages such as vodka and wines. Anticipating further declines in sales for the future, TBC's management hopes eventually to move almost entirely out of the liquor business and into a newly developed, diversified product line in growth-oriented industries. The company is especially interested in the prospects for pollution-control devices, because its research department has already done much work in this area. Right now the company estimates that an investment of $24 million is necessary to purchase new facilities and to begin operations on these products, but the investment could be earning a return of about 18 percent within a short time. The only other available investment opportunity totals $9.6 million, is expected to return about 11.2 percent, and is indivisible, that is, it must be accepted in its entirety or else be rejected.

The company is expected to pay a $2.00 dividend on its 7 million outstanding shares, the same as its dividend last year. The directors might, however, change the dividend if there are good reasons for doing so. Net income for the year is expected to be $22.5 million; the common stock is currently selling for $45; the firm's target debt ratio (debt/assets ratio) is 45 percent; and its tax rate is 34 percent. The costs of various forms of financing are listed below:

New bonds: $k_d = 11\%$. This is a before-tax rate.

New common stock sold at $45 per share will net $41.

Required rate of return on retained earnings: $k_s = 14\%$.

a.   Calculate TBC's expected payout ratio, the break point where its MCC schedule rises, and its marginal cost of capital above and below the point of exhaustion of retained earnings at the current payout. (Hint: k_s is given, and D_1/P_0 can be found. Then, knowing k_s and D_1/P_0, and assuming constant growth, g can be determined.)

b.   How large should TBC's capital budget be for the year?

c.   What is an appropriate dividend policy for the firm? How should the capital budget be financed?

d.   How might risk factors influence TBC's cost of capital, capital structure, and dividend policy?

e.   What assumptions, if any, do your answers to Questions a-d make about investors' preferences for dividends versus capital gains, that is, their preferences regarding the D_1/P_0 and g components of k_s?

(Do Part f only if you are using the computerized diskette.).

f.   Assume that TBC's management is considering a change in its capital structure to include more debt, and thus it would like to analyze the effects of an increase in the debt ratio to 60 percent. However, the treasurer believes that such a move would cause lenders to increase the required rate of return on new bonds to 12 percent and k_s would rise to 14.5 percent. How would this change affect the optimal capital budget? If k_s rose to 16 percent, would the low-return project be acceptable? Would the project selection be affected if the dividend were reduced to $1.25 from $2.00, still assuming $k_s = 16$ percent?

14-6   **(Stock repurchases)** Goldware, Inc., has earnings this year of $16.5 million, 50 percent of which is required to take advantage of the firm's excellent investment opportunities. The firm has 2,062,500 shares outstanding, selling currently at $32 per share. Greg Beaumont, a major stockholder (187,500 shares), has expressed displeasure with a great deal of managerial policy. Management has approached him about selling his holdings back to the firm, and he has expressed a willingness to do this at a price of $32 a share. Assuming that the market uses a constant P/E ratio of 4 in valuing the stock, should the firm buy Beaumont's shares? Assume that dividends will not be paid on Beaumont's shares if they are repurchased. (Hint: Calculate the ex-dividend price of the stock with and without the repurchase, and add to these values the dividends received to determine the remaining shareholders' value per share.)

Mini Case

Information Systems, Inc. (ISI), was founded 5 years ago by Michael Taylor and Karen Black, who are still its only stockholders. ISI has now reached the stage where outside equity capital is necessary if the firm is to grow with the industry and still maintain its target capital structure of 60 percent equity and 40 percent debt. Therefore, Taylor and Black have decided to take the company public. Until now, Taylor and Black have routinely invested all earnings in the firm, so dividend policy had not been an issue. However, as a publicly owned firm, they will have to decide on a dividend policy.

Assume that you were recently hired by Arthur Adamson & Company, a national consulting firm which has been asked to help ISI prepare its public offering. Tom Nickols, the senior consultant in your group, has asked you to make a presentation to Taylor and Black in which you review the theory of dividend policy and discuss the following questions.

a. (1) What is meant by the term "dividend policy?"
(2) What are the three elements of dividend policy?

b. (1) What are the three major theories regarding stockholders' preferences for dividends versus capital gains?
(2) What do the three theories indicate regarding the actions management should take regarding dividend policy?

c.   Construct a graph with dividend yield on the Y-axis and capital gains yield on the X-axis. Now assume that if the company paid out all earnings as dividends, it would have a required rate of return of 15.0 percent. Plot dividend yield versus capital gains yield for alternative payout policies under each dividend policy theory. Explain your plots.

d.   Has empirical testing been able to prove which theory, if any, is most correct?

e.   What is the information content, or signaling, hypothesis, and how does it constrain dividend policy?

f.   What is the clientele effect, and how does it constrain dividend policy?

g. (1) What is the residual dividend model? Assume that ISI plans to spend $800,000 on capital investments during the coming year; its optimal capital structure calls for 60 percent equity and 40 percent debt, and its net income is forecasted at $600,000. Construct a graph which shows what the total dollar dividend and the payout ratio would be if the firm used the residual model.
(2) How would a change in net income affect the dividend?
(3) How would a change in investment opportunities affect the dividend?
(4) Assume that the firm also forecasts $100,000 of depreciation cash flow. How would these funds impact the residual analysis, still assuming $600,000 in net income?
(5) What are the advantages and disadvantages of the residual model? (*Hint:* Think about both signaling and the clientele effect.)

h.   What are the two primary dividend payment policies? What are their advantages and disadvantages?

i.   What is a dividend reinvestment plan? What are the two major types of plans, and when should each type be used?

j.   Describe how most firms set their dividend policies in practice.

k.   What is a stock repurchase? Discuss the advantages and disadvantages of stock repurchases.

l.   What is a stock dividend, and how does it differ from a stock split? When should a firm consider issuing a stock dividend? When should a firm consider splitting its stock?

Selected Additional References and Cases

Dividend policy has been studied extensively by academicians. The first major academic work, and still a classic that we recommend highly, is Lintner's analysis of the way corporations actually set their dividend payment policies:

Lintner, John, "Distribution of Incomes of Corporations among Dividends, Retained Earnings, and Taxes," *American Economic Review,* May 1956, 97–113.

The effects of dividend policy on stock prices and capital costs have been examined by many researchers. The classic theoretical argument that dividend policy is important, and that stockholders like dividends, was set forth by Gordon, while Miller and Modigliani (MM) developed the notion that dividend policy is not important. Many researchers have extended both Gordon's and MM's theoretical arguments, and have attempted to test the effects of dividend policy in a variety of ways. Although statistical problems have precluded definitive conclusions, the following articles, among others, have helped to clarify the issues:

Brennan, Michael, "Taxes, Market Valuation, and Corporate Financial Policy," *National Tax Journal,* Spring 1975, 417–427.

Hayes, Linda S., "Fresh Evidence That Dividends Don't Matter," *Fortune,* May 4, 1981, 351–354.

Lewellen, Wilbur G., Kenneth L. Stanley, Ronald C. Lease, and Gary G. Schlarbaum, "Some Direct Evidence on the Dividend Clientele Phenomenon," *Journal of Finance,* December 1978, 1385–1399.

Mukherjee, Tarun, and Larry M. Austin, "An Empirical Investigation of Small Bank Stock Valuation and Dividend Policy," *Financial Management,* Spring 1980, 27–31.

On stock dividends and stock splits, see

Baker, H. Kent, and Patricia L. Gallagher, "Management's View of Stock Splits," *Financial Management,* Summer 1980, 73–77.

Copeland, Thomas E., "Liquidity Changes Following Stock Splits," *Journal of Finance,* March 1979, 115–141.

On repurchases, see

Finnerty, Joseph E., "Corporate Stock Issue and Repurchase," *Financial Management,* Autumn 1975, 62–71.

Netter, Jeffry M., and Mark L. Mitchell, "Stock-Repurchase Announcements and Insider Transactions after the October 1987 Stock Market Crash," *Financial Management,* Autumn 1989, 84–96.

Pugh, William, and John S. Jahera, Jr., "Stock Repurchases and Excess Returns: An Empirical Examination," *The Financial Review,* February 1990, 127–142.

Stewart, Samuel S., Jr., "Should a Corporation Repurchase Its Own Stock?" *Journal of Finance,* June 1976, 911–921.

Wansley, James W., William R. Lane, and Salil Sarkar, "Managements' View on Share Repurchase and Tender Offer Premiums," *Financial Management,* Autumn 1989, 97–110.

Woolridge, J. Randall, and Donald R. Chambers, "Reverse Splits and Shareholder Wealth," *Financial Management,* Autumn 1983, 5–15.

For a survey of managers' views on dividend policy, see

Baker, H. Kent, Gail E. Farrelly, and Richard B. Edelman, "A Survey of Management Views on Dividend Policy," *Financial Management,* Autumn 1985, 78–84.

Other pertinent articles include

Asquith, Paul, and David W. Mullins, Jr., "Signalling with Dividends, Stock Repurchases, and Equity Issues," *Financial Management,* Autumn 1986, 27–44.

Born, Jeffrey A., "Insider Ownership and Signals—Evidence from Dividend Initiation Announcement Effects," *Financial Management,* Spring 1988, 38–45.

Brealey, Richard A., "Does Dividend Policy Matter?" *Midland Corporate Finance Journal,* Spring 1983, 17–25.

Fehrs, Donald H., Gary A. Benesh, and David R. Peterson, "Evidence of a Relation between Stock Price Reactions Around Cash Dividend Changes and Yields," *Journal of Financial Research,* Summer 1988, 111–123.

Ghosh, Chinmoy, and J. Randall Woolridge, "An Analysis of Shareholder Reaction to Dividend Cuts and Omissions," *Journal of Financial Research,* Winter 1988, 281–294.

Healy, Paul M., and Krishna G. Palepu, "How Investors Interpret Changes in Corporate Financial Policy," *Journal of Applied Corporate Finance,* Fall 1989, 59–64.

Miller, Merton H., "Behavioral Rationality in Finance: The Case of Dividends," *Midland Corporate Finance Journal,* Winter 1987, 6–15.

Peterson, Pamela P., David R. Peterson, and Norman H. Moore, "The Adoption of New-Issue Dividend Reinvestment Plans and Shareholder Wealth," *Financial Review,* May 1987, 221–232.

Woolridge, J. Randall, and Chinmoy Ghosh, "Dividend Cuts: Do They Always Signal Bad News?" *Midland Corporate Finance Journal,* Summer 1985, 20–32.

The following cases from the Brigham-Gapenski casebook focus on the issues contained in this chapter:

Case 20, "Northern Paper Company," which examines many dividend policy issues.

Case 21, "Lawson Manufacturing Company," which illustrates the dividend policy decision.

The Harrington casebook contains the following applicable case:

"New Hampshire Savings Bank Corporation," which illustrates the traditional arguments set forth as the board of directors attempt to establish the company's dividend policy.

PART V

Long-Term Financing Decisions

CHAPTER 15

Common Stock, Preferred Stock, and the Investment Banking Process

A recent issue of *Fortune* contained a cover story called "Inside the Deal that Made Bill Gates $350,000,000." The story presented a rare inside view of the five months of negotiation that culminated in Microsoft Corporation's going public.

Microsoft, a Seattle-based software maker for personal computers that is best known for developing the disk operating system (DOS) for IBM's PC line, was cofounded in 1975 by William H. Gates III, a Harvard dropout. By the mid-1980s, its archcompetitors, Lotus Development and Ashton-Tate, along with numerous other microcomputer software companies, had already gone public, while Microsoft remained privately held. Unlike its competitors, Microsoft was not dominated by venture capitalists eager to harvest some of their gains. Further, the business had lots of cash, and the firm needed no outside money to expand. Most important, however, was Bill Gates's attitude toward selling stock to the public. "The whole process looks like a pain," he said, "and an ongoing pain once you're public. People get confused because the stock price doesn't reflect your financial performance. And to have a stock trader call up the chief executive and ask him questions is uneconomic — the ball bearings shouldn't be asking the driver about the grease."

However, a public offering was just a matter of time. To attract the best managers and programmers, Gates had been selling them shares, and it was estimated that over 500 people would own shares by 1987, enough to require SEC registration. Once registered, the stock in effect would have a public market, but one so narrow that trading would be difficult. Since it would have to register anyway, Microsoft decided it might as well sell enough shares to enough investors to create a liquid market.

On March 13, 1986, Microsoft sold 2,300,000 shares of new stock, and existing shareholders (including Bill Gates) sold an additional 600,000 shares, at a price of $21 per share. At 9:35 A.M., Microsoft's stock traded publicly on the over-the-counter market for the first time at a price of $25.75. By the end of the first day of trading, 2.5 million shares had changed hands, and Microsoft's stock price was $27.75. Microsoft and its original shareholders raised $61 million. Bill Gates got only $1.6 million for the shares he sold, but going public established a market value of $350 million on the 45 percent stake he retained. The deal made Gates, at the age of 30, one of the 100 richest Americans. Further, the stock sale set up Microsoft (and Gates) for more success, and by 1990 Gates's net worth was over $2 billion.

Initial public offerings, or IPOs, do not always work out as well as Microsoft's. Success or failure for an equity issue is a function of many factors. We discuss the primary ones in this chapter.

IN Part III we examined the analysis financial managers employ when making decisions regarding the investment in long-term (or fixed) assets, and in Part IV we discussed capital structure and dividend decisions. With this background, we now turn our attention to specific types of long-term capital. Any decision to acquire new assets necessitates the raising of new capital, and, generally, long-term assets are financed with long-term capital. In this chapter, we consider in some detail the decisions financial managers must make regarding stock financings. As a part of this analysis, we also examine in detail the procedures used to raise new long-term capital, or the investment banking process.

BALANCE SHEET ACCOUNTS AND DEFINITIONS

Legal and accounting terminology is vital to both investors and financial managers if they are to avoid misinterpretations and possibly costly mistakes. Therefore, we begin our analysis of common stock with a discussion of accounting and legal issues. Consider first Table 15-1, which shows the common equity section of American Chemical Company's balance sheet. American's owners, its stockholders, have autho-

Table 15-1   American Chemical Company: Stockholders' Equity
Accounts as of December 31, 1990

Common stock (30 million shares authorized, 25 million shares outstanding, $1 par)	$ 25,000,000
Additional paid-in capital	50,000,000
Retained earnings	375,000,000
Total common stockholders' equity (or common net worth)	$450,000,000

$$\text{Book value per share} = \frac{\text{Total common stockholders' equity}}{\text{Shares outstanding}} = \frac{\$450,000,000}{25,000,000} = \$18.$$

rized management to issue a total of 30 million shares, and management has thus far actually issued (or sold) 25 million shares. Each share has a *par value* of $1; this is the minimum amount for which new shares can be issued.[1]

American Chemical is an old company—it was established back in 1912. Its initial equity capital consisted of 3,000 shares sold at the $1 par value, so on its first balance sheet the total stockholders' equity was $3,000. The initial paid-in capital and retained earnings accounts showed zero balances. Over the years American has retained some of its earnings, and the firm has issued new stock to raise capital from time to time. During 1990, American earned $60 million, paid $50 million in dividends, and retained $10 million. The $10 million was added to the $365 million accumulated *retained earnings,* shown on the year-end 1989 balance sheet, to produce the $375 million retained earnings at year-end 1990. Thus, since its inception in 1912, American has retained, or plowed back, a total of $375 million. This is money that belongs to the stockholders and that they could have received in the form of dividends. Instead, the stockholders chose to let management reinvest the $375 million in the business.

Now consider the $50 million *additional paid-in capital.* This account shows the difference between the stock's par value and what new stockholders paid when they bought newly issued shares. As we noted, American was formed in 1912 with 3,000

---

[1]A stock's par value is an arbitrary figure that indicates the minimum amount of money stockholders have put up, or must put up in the event of bankruptcy. Actually, the firm could legally sell new shares at below par, but any purchaser would be liable for the difference between the issue price and the par value in the event the company went bankrupt. Thus, if American sold an investor 10,000 shares at 40 cents per share, for $4,000, then the investor would have to put up an additional $6,000 if the company later went bankrupt. This contingent liability effectively precludes the sale of new common stock at prices below par.

Also, we should point out that firms are not required to establish a par value for their stock. Thus, American could have elected to use "no par" stock, in which case the common stock and additional paid-in capital accounts could have been consolidated under one account called *common stock,* which would show a 1990 balance of $75 million.

Table 15-2   Effects of 1920 Stock Sale on American Chemical's Equity Accounts

Before Sale of Stock

Common stock (3,000 shares outstanding, $1 par)	$ 3,000
Additional paid-in capital	0
Retained earnings	6,000
Total stockholders' equity	$ 9,000
Book value per share = $9,000/3,000 =	$3.00

After Sale of Stock

Common stock (5,000 shares outstanding, $1 par)	$ 5,000
Additional paid-in capital ($4 − $1) × 2,000 shares	6,000
Retained earnings	6,000
Total stockholders' equity	$17,000
Book value per share = $17,000/5,000 =	$3.40

shares issued at the $1 par value; thus, the first balance sheet showed a zero balance for additional paid-in capital. By 1920 the company had demonstrated its profitability and was earning 50 cents per share. Further, it had built up the retained earnings account to a total of $6,000, so the total stockholders' equity was $3,000 of par value plus $6,000 of retained earnings = $9,000, and the *book value per share* was $9,000/3,000 shares = $3. American had also borrowed heavily, and, even though it had retained most of its earnings, the company's debt ratio had risen to an unacceptable level, precluding further use of debt without an infusion of equity.

The company had profitable investment opportunities, so in order to take advantage of them, management decided to issue another 2,000 shares of stock. The market price at the time was $4 per share, which was eight times the 50 cents earnings per share (the price/earnings ratio was 8×). This $4 market value per share was well in excess of the $1 par value and also higher than the $3 book value per share, demonstrating that par value, book value, and market value are not necessarily equal. Had the company lost money since its inception, it would have had negative retained earnings, the book value would have been below par, and the market price might well have been below book.

Table 15-2 shows how the 1920 stock sale affected American's common equity accounts. A total of 2,000 new shares were sold to investors at the market price of $4 per share. Each share brought in $4, of which $1 represented the par value, and $3 represented the excess of the sale price above par. Since 2,000 shares were involved, a total of $2,000 was added to common stock, and $6,000 was entered in additional paid-in capital. Notice also that book value per share rose from $3 to $3.40; whenever stock is sold at a price above book, the book value increases, and vice versa if stock is sold below book.[2] Similar transactions have taken place down through the years to produce the current situation, as shown earlier in Table 15-1.[3]

Self-Test Questions

Explain how the balance sheet is affected when a company issues new common stock.

Does it matter if new common stock is sold for more or less than its par value? Than its book value?

LEGAL RIGHTS AND PRIVILEGES OF COMMON STOCKHOLDERS

The common stockholders are the owners of a corporation, and as such they have certain rights and privileges. The most important of these rights are discussed in this section.

Control of the Firm

The stockholders have the right to elect the firm's directors, who in turn elect the officers who will manage the business. In a small firm, the major stockholder typically assumes the positions of president and chairman of the board of directors. In a large, publicly owned firm, the managers typically have some stock, but their personal holdings are insufficient to allow them to exercise voting control. Thus, the managements of most publicly owned firms can be removed by the stockholders if they decide a management team is not effective.

Various state and federal laws stipulate how stockholder control is to be exercised. First, corporations must hold an election of directors periodically, usually once a year, with the vote taken at the annual meeting. Frequently, one third of the

---

[2]The effects of stock sales on book value are not important for industrial firms, but they are *very* important for utility companies, whose allowable earnings per share are in effect determined by regulators as a percentage of book value. Thus, if a utility's stock is selling below book and the company sells stock to raise new equity, this will dilute the book value per share of its existing stockholders and drive down their allowable earnings per share, which in turn will drive down the market price. Most U.S. electric utilities' stocks sold below book value during the late 1970s and early 1980s. The firms needed to raise large amounts of capital, including equity, since they had to keep their capital structures in balance. This meant selling stock at prices below book, which tended to depress the market value of the stock still further.

[3]Stock dividends, stock splits, and stock repurchases (the reverse of stock issues) also affect the capital accounts. These topics were discussed in Chapter 14.

directors are elected each year for a three-year term. Each share of stock has one vote; thus, the owner of 1,000 shares has 1,000 votes. Stockholders can appear at the annual meeting and vote in person, but typically they transfer their right to vote to a second party by means of a *proxy*. Management always solicits stockholders' proxies and usually gets them. However, if earnings are poor and stockholders are dissatisfied, an outside group may solicit the proxies in an effort to overthrow management and take control of the business. This is known as a *proxy fight*.

The question of control has become a central issue in finance in recent years. The frequency of proxy fights has increased, as have attempts by one corporation to take over another by purchasing a majority of the outstanding stock. This latter action, which is called a *takeover,* is discussed in detail in Chapter 24. Managers who do not have majority control (over 50 percent) of their firms' stocks are very concerned about proxy fights and takeovers, and many of them are attempting to get stockholder approval for changes in their corporate charters that would make takeovers more difficult. Managements seeking such changes generally cite a fear that the firm will be picked up at a bargain price, but it often appears that managers' concern over their own positions is an even more important consideration.

The Preemptive Right

Common stockholders often have the right, called the *preemptive right,* to purchase any new shares sold by the firm. In some states the preemptive right is mandatory; in others it is necessary to specifically insert it into the charter.

The purpose of the preemptive right is twofold. First, it protects the present stockholders' power of control. If it were not for this safeguard, the management of a corporation under criticism from stockholders could secure its position by issuing a large number of additional shares and purchasing these shares itself. Management would thereby gain control of the corporation and frustrate the current stockholders.

The second, and by far the more important, reason for the preemptive right is that it protects stockholders against a dilution of value. For example, suppose 1,000 shares of common stock, each with a price of $100, were outstanding, making the total market value of the firm $100,000. If an additional 1,000 shares were sold at $50 a share, or for $50,000, this would raise the total market value of the firm to $150,000. When the total market value is divided by the new total shares outstanding, a value of $75 a share is obtained. The old stockholders thus lose $25 per share, and the new stockholders have an instant profit of $25 per share. Thus, selling common stock at a price below the market value would dilute its price and would transfer wealth from the present stockholders to those who purchase the new shares. The preemptive right prevents such occurrences.

Self-Test Questions

How do shareholders exercise their right of control?

What is the preemptive right, and what is its purpose?

TYPES OF COMMON STOCK

Although most firms have only one type of common stock, in some instances *classified stock* is used to meet the special needs of the company. Generally, when special classifications of stock are used, one type is designated *Class A,* another *Class B,* and so on. Small, new companies seeking to obtain funds from outside sources frequently use different types of common stock. For example, when Genetic Research, Inc., went public in 1990, its Class A stock was sold to the public and paid a dividend, but carried no voting rights for five years. Its Class B stock was retained by the organizers of the company and carried full voting rights for five years, but dividends could not be paid on the Class B stock until the company had established its earning power by building up retained earnings to a designated level. Because of the use of classified stock, the public was able to take a position in a conservatively financed growth company without sacrificing income, while the founders retained absolute control during the crucial early stages of the firm's development. At the same time, outside investors were protected against excessive withdrawals of funds by the original owners. As is often the case in such situations, the Class B stock was also called *founders' shares.*

Note that "Class A," "Class B," and so on, have no standard meanings. Most firms have no classified shares, but a firm that does could designate its Class B shares as founders' shares and its Class A shares as those sold to the public, while another could reverse these designations. Other firms could use the A and B designations for entirely different purposes.

General Motors recently introduced yet another type of common stock. When GM acquired Hughes Aircraft for $5 billion, it paid in part with a new Class H common, GMH, which had limited voting rights and whose dividends were tied to Hughes's performance as a GM subsidiary. The reasons for the new stock were reported to be that: (1) GM wanted to limit voting privileges on the new classified stock because of management's concern about a possible takeover, and (2) Hughes employees wanted to participate more directly in Hughes's own performance than would have been possible through regular GM stock.

GM's deal posed a problem for the NYSE, which had a rule against listing any company's common stock if the company had any nonvoting common stock outstanding. GM made it clear that it was willing to delist if the NYSE did not change its rules. The NYSE concluded that such arrangements as GM had made were logical and were likely to be made by other companies in the future, so it changed its rules to accommodate GM.

Self-Test Question

Name several types of common stock, and explain their uses.

THE MARKET FOR COMMON STOCK

Some companies are so small that their common stock is not actively traded—it is owned by only a few people, usually the companies' managers. Such companies are said to be *privately held,* or *closely held,* and the stock is said to be *closely held stock.*

On the other hand, the stocks of most larger companies are owned by many investors, most of whom are not active in management. Such companies are said to be *publicly owned,* and their stock is said to be *publicly held stock.*

The stocks of smaller, publicly owned firms are not listed on an exchange; they trade in the *over-the-counter (OTC)* market. The companies and their stocks are said to be *unlisted.* However, most larger, publicly owned companies apply for listing on an exchange. These companies and their stocks are said to be *listed.* As a general rule, companies are first listed on a regional exchange, such as the Pacific Coast or Midwest, then they move up to the American (AMEX), and finally, if they grow large enough, to the "Big Board," the New York Stock Exchange (NYSE). Thousands of stocks are traded in the OTC market, but in terms of market value of both outstanding and daily transactions, the NYSE dominates, with about 60 percent of the business. However, as we discuss next, electronic hookups between OTC market participants are giving them many of the advantages formerly enjoyed solely by the organized exchanges, so the OTC market has been growing more rapidly than the exchanges in recent years.

Institutional investors such as pension trusts, insurance companies, and mutual funds own about 40 percent of all common stocks. However, the institutions buy and sell relatively actively, so they account for about 80 percent of all transactions. Thus, the institutions have a heavy influence on the prices of individual stocks — in a real sense, institutional investors determine the price levels of individual stocks.

We can classify stock market transactions into three distinct categories:

1. Initial Public Offerings by Privately Held Firms: The New Issue Market.

As we discussed in the chapter opener, Microsoft Corporation, a major developer of computer software (including the operating system for the IBM PC line) decided to sell about $50 million of stock to raise capital and to create a liquid market. At the time, Microsoft was owned by its management and a handful of private investors. Microsoft's action is defined as *going public* — whenever stock in a closely held corporation is offered to the public for the first time, the company is said to be going public. The market for stock that is in the process of going public is often called the *new issue market,* and the issue is called an *initial public offering (IPO).*

The market for IPOs varies widely from year to year. For example, new public issues totaled 550 in 1987, but only 245 in 1989. The large decline in the number of new issues was attributed to the stock market crash of October 1987, which led to lower equity prices, fear of further losses, and a reduced investor demand for stocks. Companies that had planned to go public were turned off by the depressed valuations and sluggish market conditions. For example, ComputerLand Corporation, one of the leading computer retailers, cancelled its planned 1988 initial public offering because of poor market conditions. Said a company spokesman: "We realized the stock wasn't going to command the price we thought it deserved."

Firms can go public without raising any additional capital. For example, in its early days the Ford Motor Company was owned exclusively by the Ford family. When Henry Ford died, he left a substantial part of his stock to the Ford Foundation. When the Foundation later sold some of this stock to the general public, the Ford Motor Company went public, even though the company raised no capital in the transaction.

2.   **Additional Shares Sold by Established, Publicly Owned Companies: The Primary Market.** In 1989, Chase Manhattan raised $441 million by issuing new common stock. Since the shares sold were newly created, Chase's issue was defined as a *primary market* offering, but since the firm was already publicly held, the offering was not an IPO. As we discussed in Chapters 12 and 14, firms prefer to obtain equity by retaining earnings because of the flotation costs and market pressure associated with the sale of new common stock. Thus, only 3 percent of the new securities issued in 1989 were common stock. Still, if a company requires more equity funds than can be generated from retained earnings, a stock sale may be required. The Chase sale was the largest new stock issue in 1989, but it paled in comparison to the $10.0 billion stock repurchase announced by GE. In fact, there were 26 announced stock buybacks in 1989 that were larger than Chase's new issue, and over the past several years, stock buybacks have significantly outnumbered the relatively rare new stock issues, causing the aggregate amount of stock available to investors to diminish. This process has been accelerated by the large numbers of mergers and LBOs that have taken place recently, all of which remove stock from the markets.[4]

3.   **Outstanding Shares of Established, Publicly Owned Companies: The Secondary Market.** If the owner of 100 shares of Chase Manhattan sells his or her stock, the trade is said to have occurred in the *secondary market*. Thus, the market for outstanding shares, or *used shares,* is defined as the secondary market. Over 11.5 million shares of Chase were bought and sold on the NYSE in 1989, and Chase did not receive a dime from these transactions.

Self-Test Questions

What is an initial public offering (IPO)?

What are some differences in the situation when Chase Manhattan sells shares in the primary market and when its shares are sold in the secondary market?

THE DECISION TO GO PUBLIC

Most businesses begin life as proprietorships or partnerships, and then, as the more successful ones grow, at some point they find it desirable to convert into corporations. Initially, these new corporations' stocks are generally owned by the firm's officers, key employees, and/or a very few investors who are not actively involved in management. However, if growth continues, at some point the company may decide to go public. As described earlier, Microsoft Corporation decided to take this step in 1986. The advantages and disadvantages of public ownership are discussed next.

---

[4]Note, however, that equity values increase when companies retain earnings and that new shares are created when firms split their stock or pay stock dividends. Thus, even though repurchases exceed new stock offerings, this does not necessarily mean that total shares outstanding, or their value, is decreasing.

Advantages of Going Public

1.   **Permits Diversification.** As a company grows and becomes more valuable, its founders often have most of their wealth tied up in the company. By selling some of their stock in a public offering, they can diversify their holdings, thereby reducing somewhat the riskiness of their personal portfolios.

2.   **Increases Liquidity.** The stock of a closely held firm is illiquid: it has no ready market. If one of the owners wants to sell some shares to raise cash, it is hard to find a ready buyer, and even if a buyer is located, there is no established price on which to base the transaction. These problems do not exist with publicly owned firms.

3.   **Facilitates Raising New Corporate Cash.** If a privately held company wants to raise cash by a sale of new stock, it must either go to its existing owners, who may not have any money or not want to put any more eggs in this particular basket, or else shop around for wealthy investors. However, it is usually quite difficult to get outsiders to put money into a closely held company, because if the outsiders do not have voting control (over 50 percent of the stock), the inside stockholders/ managers can run roughshod over them. The insiders can pay or not pay dividends, pay themselves exorbitant salaries, have private deals with the company, and so on. For example, the president might buy a warehouse and lease it to the company at a high rental, get the use of a Rolls Royce, and enjoy frequent "all-the-frills" travel to conventions. The insiders can even keep the outsiders from knowing the company's actual earnings, or its real worth. There are not many positions more vulnerable than that of an outside stockholder in a closely held company, and for this reason, it is hard for closely held companies to raise new equity capital. Going public, which brings with it both public disclosure of information and regulation by the Securities and Exchange Commission (SEC), greatly reduces these problems, making people more willing to invest in the company, and thus making it easier for the firm to raise capital.

4.   **Establishes a Value for the Firm.** For a number of reasons, it is often useful to establish a firm's value in the marketplace. For one thing, when the owner of a privately owned business dies, state and federal inheritance tax appraisers must set a value on the company for estate tax purposes. Often, these appraisers set too high a value, which creates an obvious problem. However, a company that is publicly owned has its value established with little room for argument. Similarly, if a company wants to give incentive stock options to key employees, it is useful to know the exact value of those options. Finally, for a number of reasons, employees much prefer to own stock, or options on stock, that is publicly traded.

Disadvantages of Going Public

1.   **Cost of Reporting.** A publicly owned company must file quarterly and annual reports with the SEC and/or with various state agencies. These reports can be costly, especially for small firms.

2. **Disclosure.** Management may not like the idea of reporting operating data, because such data will then be available to competitors. Similarly, the owners of the company may not want people to know their net worth, and since a publicly owned company must disclose the number of shares owned by its officers, directors, and major stockholders, it is easy enough for anyone to multiply shares held by price per share to estimate the net worth of the insiders.

3. **Self-Dealings.** The owners/managers of closely held companies have many opportunities for various types of questionable but legal self-dealings, including the payment of high salaries, nepotism, personal transactions with the business (such as a leasing arrangement), and not-truly-necessary fringe benefits. Such self-dealings, which are often designed to minimize taxes, are much harder to arrange if a company is publicly owned.

4. **Inactive Market/Low Price.** If the firm is very small, and if its shares are not traded with much frequency, its stock will not really be liquid, and the market price may not be representative of the stock's true value. Security analysts and stockbrokers simply will not follow the stock, because there will just not be sufficient trading activity to generate sufficient sales commissions to cover the costs of following the stock.

5. **Control.** Because of the dramatic increase in tender offers and proxy fights in the 1980s, the managers of publicly owned firms who do not have voting control must be concerned about maintaining control. Further, there is pressure on such managers to produce annual earnings gains, even when it might be in the shareholders' best long-term interests to adopt a strategy that might penalize short-term earnings but benefit earnings in future years. These factors have led a number of public companies to "go private" in "leveraged buyout" deals where the managers borrow the money to buy out the nonmanagement stockholders. We discuss the decision to go private in a later section.

Conclusions on Going Public

It should be obvious from this discussion that there are no hard-and-fast rules regarding if or when a company should go public. This is an individual decision that should be made on the basis of the company's and its stockholders' own unique circumstances.

If a company does decide to go public, either by the sale of newly issued stock to raise new capital or by the sale of stock by the current owners, the key issue is setting the price at which shares will be offered to the public. The company and its current owners want to set the price as high as possible—the higher the offering price, the smaller the fraction of the company the current owners will have to give up to obtain any specified amount of money. On the other hand, potential buyers will want the price set as low as possible. We will return to the establishment of the offering price later in the chapter, after we have described some other aspects of common stock financing.

Self-Test Questions

What are the major advantages of going public?

What are the major disadvantages?

THE DECISION TO LIST

The decision to go public is truly a milestone in a company's life—it marks a major transition in the relationship between the firm and its owners. The decision to *list* the stock and have it trade on an exchange rather than in the over-the-counter market, on the other hand, is not a major event. The company will have to file a few new reports with an exchange and to abide by the rules of the exchange; stockholders will generally purchase or sell shares through a stockbroker who acts as an *agent* rather than a *dealer;* and the stock's price will be quoted in the newspaper under a stock exchange rather than in the over-the-counter section. These are not very significant differences.

In order to have its stock listed, a company must apply to an exchange, pay a relatively small fee, and meet the exchange's minimum requirements. These requirements relate to the size of the company's net income as well as to the number of shares outstanding and in the hands of outsiders (as opposed to the number held by insiders, who generally do not trade their stock very actively). Also, the company must agree to disclose certain information to the exchange; this information is designed to help the exchange track trading patterns and thus to try to ensure that no one is attempting to manipulate the price of the stock.[5] The size qualifications increase as one moves from the regional exchanges to the AMEX and on to the NYSE.

Assuming a company qualifies, many people believe that listing is beneficial both to it and to its stockholders. Listed companies receive a certain amount of free advertising and publicity, and their status as a listed company may enhance their prestige and reputation. This may have a beneficial effect on the sales of the products of the firm. Investors respond favorably to increased information, increased liquidity, and confidence that the quoted price is not being manipulated. By providing investors with these benefits in the form of listing their companies' stocks, financial managers may be able to lower their firms' cost of equity and increase the value of their stock.[6]

---

[5]It is illegal for anyone to attempt to manipulate the price of a stock. During the 1920s, and earlier, syndicates would buy and sell stocks back and forth at rigged prices so the public would believe that a particular stock was worth more or less than its true value. The exchanges, with the encouragement and support of the SEC, utilize sophisticated computer programs to help spot any irregularities that suggest manipulation, and they require disclosures to help identify manipulators. This same system helps to identify illegal insider trading.

[6]Due to improvements in telecommunications and computer technologies, the differences between the OTC and the exchanges have become less distinct. As a result, some very large companies such as MCI and Apple, which almost certainly would have been listed on the NYSE in earlier days, have elected to remain in the OTC market.

Self-Test Question

What are the major advantages and disadvantages to a company listing its stock on an exchange?

PROCEDURES FOR SELLING NEW COMMON STOCK

If stock is to be sold to raise new capital, the new shares may be sold in one of five ways: (1) on a pro rata basis to existing stockholders through a rights offering, (2) through investment bankers to the general public in a public offering, (3) to a single buyer (or a very small number of buyers) in a private placement, (4) to employees through employee stock purchase plans, or (5) through a dividend reinvestment plan. We discussed dividend reinvestment plans in Chapter 14; the other methods of selling stock are considered in the following sections.

Rights Offerings

As discussed earlier, common stockholders often have the *preemptive right* to purchase any additional shares sold by the firm. If the preemptive right is contained in a particular firm's charter, the company must offer any newly issued common stock to existing stockholders. If the charter does not prescribe a preemptive right, the firm can choose to sell to its existing stockholders or to the public at large. If it sells to the existing stockholders, the stock flotation is called a *rights offering*. Each stockholder is issued an option to buy a certain number of new shares, and the terms of the option are listed on a certificate called a *stock purchase right,* or simply a *right.* If a stockholder does not wish to purchase any additional shares in the company, then he or she can sell the rights to some other person who does want to buy the stock.[7]

Public Offerings

If the preemptive right exists in a company's charter, it must sell new stock through a rights offering. If the preemptive right does not exist, the company can choose between a rights offering and a *public offering.* We discuss procedures for public offerings later in the chapter.

Private Placements

In a *private placement,* securities are sold to one or a few investors, generally institutional investors. Private placements are most common with bonds, but they also occur with stocks. The primary advantages of private placements are (1) lower flo-

---

[7]For more details on the mechanics of a rights offering, see Eugene F. Brigham and Louis C. Gapenski, *Intermediate Financial Management,* 3rd Edition, Chapter 12.

tation costs and (2) greater speed, since the shares do not have to go through the SEC registration process.

The most common type of private placement occurs when a company places debt directly with a financial institution, usually an insurance company. For example, J.C. Penney recently sold $700 million in private placement bonds to eight insurance companies led by Prudential. In fact, Prudential has begun sending salespeople to call on businesses — not to sell them policies, but to sell them on borrowing privately from Prudential.

One particular type of private stock placement that is occurring with increasing frequency is the situation in which a large company makes an equity investment in a smaller supplier. For example, IBM invested close to $500 million in Rolm, a telecommunications equipment manufacturer, and a similar amount in Intel, a semiconductor manufacturer. In both instances, (1) the companies needed capital for expansion, (2) IBM was engaged in joint development ventures with the companies, and thus wanted them to be financially strong, and (3) the companies had strong, independent managements, who would probably have resisted an attempt by IBM to take full control. So, IBM (1) bought stock that gave it an ownership in the 15 to 25 percent range, (2) agreed to limit its ownership to no more than 30 percent, and (3) simultaneously executed operating contracts for joint ventures with Rolm and Intel. Similar arrangements are quite common, and some of them go back many years. For example, Sears, Roebuck has for many years supplied equity capital to some of its major suppliers, including Johnson Controls, which furnishes Sears with "Die-Hard" batteries, and with DeSoto Chemical, which supplies most of the paints that Sears sells.

The primary disadvantage of a private placement is that the securities generally will not have gone through the SEC registration process, so they cannot be sold except to another large, "sophisticated" purchaser in the event the original buyer wants to sell them. However, the SEC has recently ruled that any institution with a portfolio of $100 million or more can buy and sell private placement securities. Since there are many institutions with assets that exceed this limit, private placements are expected to boom in the 1990s. Today, private placements constitute almost 40 percent of all nonbank debt financing.

Employee Purchase Plans and ESOPs

Many companies have plans that allow employees to purchase stock on favorable terms. First, under executive incentive stock option plans, key managers are given options to purchase stock. These managers generally have a direct, material influence on the company's fortunes, so if they perform well, the stock will go up, and the options will become valuable. Second, there are plans for lower-level employees. For example, IBM permits employees who are not participants in its stock option plan to allocate up to 10 percent of their salaries to its stock purchase plan, and the funds are then used to buy newly issued shares at 85 percent of the market value on the purchase date. Often, the company's contribution (in IBM's case, the 15 percent discount) is not vested in an employee until five years after the purchase date. This type of plan is designed both to improve employee performance and to reduce turnover.

A third type of plan is related to the second one, but here the stock bought for employees is purchased out of a share of the company's profits. Congress has sought to encourage such plans through tax policy—under an *Employee Stock Ownership Plan (ESOP),* companies can claim a tax credit equal to a percentage of wages, provided that the funds are used to buy newly issued stock for the benefit of employees. The amount of the credit varies from year to year, depending on the whims of Congress: currently it is ½ of 1 percent of total wages. Firms have been jumping on the ESOP bandwagon in record numbers in recent years—over 10,000 companies now have ESOPs covering over 12 million employees.

ESOPs have been hailed by some as a miracle tonic that will invigorate a tiring manufacturing economy, but critics claim that ESOPs represent a desperate move by managers who would rather give the company to employees than succumb to raiders. Others call ESOPs tax dodges, some call them socialistic, and some call them "people's capitalism." All parties can muster some evidence to support their claims, but the ESOP trend is still too new for anyone to be sure who is right.

In a typical ESOP start-up, a company borrows money to buy its own stock, either from treasury stock or on the open market, and places the stock in the hands of the ESOP trustee, who then allocates the stock ownership to the firm's employees on the basis of relative salaries. Then, after the ESOP is initially funded, stock contributions are made out of annual earnings. Often, ESOPs are set up to supplement or to replace entirely the employees' retirement programs. ESOPs often have one thing in common with LBOs—more debt and hence higher financial leverage. However, the similarity ends there. While an LBO usually makes owners out of a small group of managers, an ESOP makes an owner out of practically everyone on the payroll.

The advantages of ESOPs are as follows:

1. **Tax Breaks.** Companies get a triple tax deduction on ESOPs—they can deduct (1) the interest on the debt used to buy the stock for the ESOP, (2) some of the principal payments on the ESOP-funding debt, and (3) the dividends they pay on the ESOP-held shares.

2. **Anti-takeover Defense.** The more of a company's stock the ESOP holds, the better equipped a company is to fend off a raider, because the ESOP's trustee is presumably more inclined to support current management over a raider who may fire many of the current employees.

3. **Pension Cost Control.** When a company uses an ESOP to reduce or even replace its conventional pension plan, it can save heavily. Some companies drop their retirement medical benefits, telling employees that they can dip into their ESOP accounts to buy medical coverage.

4. **Productivity Enhancement.** Once the employees are owners as well as workers, they are presumably motivated to become more productive and concerned about product quality. However, studies have shown that ESOPs help little toward

increased productivity unless executives are willing to give workers a strong and genuine role in running the company.

Although their advantages are very real, ESOPs do have some potential disadvantages:

1. **Balance of Power.** ESOPs transform workers into a large bloc of shareholders with intimate knowledge about the company. If a firm's managers alienate the employee-owners, workers could vote their shares in favor of a raider.

2. **Legal Considerations.** The Labor Department and the courts are on the lookout for ESOP abuses. If they perceive an ESOP to be a hastily constructed takeover defense, designed primarily to protect current management, they could reject the ESOP plan. Also, ESOP laws could be changed by Congress at any time to make them less favorable to the firm.

3. **Retiree Benefits.** The more that retirees' benefits are tied to an ESOP, the more dependent retirees become on the price of the company's stock. That leaves retirees vulnerable to the whims of Wall Street as well as to management mistakes.

Although employee purchase plans are designed more to provide incentives to help improve employee performance than to raise capital, the fact is that these plans can produce a surprisingly large amount of new equity. Note, though, that companies may choose to repurchase shares on the open market rather than issue new shares. The decision to use newly issued shares or repurchased shares depends upon the company's need for funds in a given year. Still, employee purchase plans provide the potential for raising equity regardless of whether they are actually used for this purpose each and every year.

Self-Test Questions

What is a rights offering?

What is a private placement? What are its primary advantages over a public offering?

Briefly describe employee purchase plans.

What is an Employee Stock Ownership Plan (ESOP)? What are its major advantages and disadvantages?

ADVANTAGES AND DISADVANTAGES OF COMMON STOCK FINANCING

In this section we briefly discuss the advantages and disadvantages of common stock financing.

Advantages of Common Stock Financing

1. Common stock does not entail fixed charges. If the company generates the earnings, it can pay common stock dividends. This is very much in contrast to interest on debt, which must be paid regardless of the level of earnings.

2.   Common stock carries no fixed maturity date—it is permanent capital which does not have to be "paid back."

3.   Since common stock provides a cushion against losses to the firm's creditors, the sale of common stock increases the creditworthiness of the firm.

4.   Common stock can, at times, be sold more easily than debt. It appeals to certain investor groups because (1) it typically carries a higher expected return than does preferred stock or debt, (2) it provides investors with a better hedge against inflation than does preferred stock or bonds, and (3) returns from capital gains on common stock are not taxed until the gains are realized.

Disadvantages of Common Stock Financing

1.   The sale of common stock normally extends voting rights, or even control, to the additional stock owners who are brought into the company. For this reason, additional equity financing is often avoided by small firms, whose owner-managers may be unwilling to share control of their companies with outsiders. Note, though, that firms can use special classes of common stock that do not carry voting rights.

2.   The use of debt enables the firm to acquire funds at a fixed cost, whereas the use of common stock means that more stockholders will share in the firm's net profits.

3.   The costs of underwriting and distributing common stock are usually higher than the costs of underwriting and distributing preferred stock or debt.

4.   As we discussed in Chapters 12 and 14, the sale of new common stock may be perceived by investors as a negative signal, hence may cause the stock price to fall.

Self-Test Questions

What are the advantages of common stock financing?

What are some disadvantages of common stock financing?

THE DECISION TO GO PRIVATE

In a *going private* transaction, the entire equity of a publicly held firm is purchased by a small group of investors which usually includes the firm's current senior management.[8] In some of these transactions, the current management group acquires all of the equity of the new company. In others, current management participates in the ownership with a small group of outside investors who typically place directors on the now private firm's board and arrange for the financing needed to purchase the publicly held stock. Such deals almost always involve substantial borrowing, often

---

[8]See Harry DeAngelo, Linda DeAngelo, and Edward M. Rice, "Going Private: The Effects of a Change in Corporate Ownership," *Midland Corporate Finance Journal,* Summer 1984, 35–43, for a more complete discussion of going private. The discussion in this section draws heavily from their work.

up to 90 percent, and thus are commonly known as *leveraged buyouts (LBOs)* or *leveraged managerial buyouts (MBOs)*.

Regardless of the structure of the deal, going private initially affects the right-hand side of the balance sheet, the liabilities and capital, and not the assets — going private simply rearranges the ownership structure. Thus, going private involves no obvious operating economies, yet the new owners are generally willing to pay a large premium over the stock's current price in order to take the firm private. For example, in 1989 the managers of Hospital Corporation of America (HCA) paid $51 a share to outside (public) shareholders although the stock was only selling for about $31 before the LBO offer was made. It is hard to believe that the managers of a company, who have the best information about the firm's potential profitability, would knowingly pay too much for the firm. Thus, HCA's management must have regarded the firm as being grossly undervalued or else thought that it could significantly boost the firm's value under private ownership. This suggests that going private can increase the value of some firms sufficiently to enrich both managers and public stockholders. The primary advantages to going private are (1) administrative cost savings, (2) increased managerial incentives, (3) increased managerial flexibility, (4) increased shareholder participation, and (5) increased use of financial leverage, which of course reduces taxes. We will discuss each of these advantages in more detail in the following paragraphs.

1. **Administrative Cost Savings.** Because going private takes the stock of a firm out of public hands, it saves on costs associated with securities registration, annual reports, SEC and exchange reporting, responding to stockholder inquiries, and so on. More important, the top management of private firms are free from meetings with security analysts, government bodies, and other outside parties. Byron C. Radaker, CEO of Congoleum Corporation, a company that went private in the early 1980s, estimated the cost savings to his company from going private at between $6 million and $8 million per year.

2. **Increased Managerial Incentives.** An even larger potential gain comes from the improvement in the incentives for high-level managerial performance. Their increased ownership means that the firm's managers will benefit more directly from their own efforts, hence managerial efficiency tends to increase after going private. If the firm is highly successful, its managers can easily see their personal net worth increase 10 or 20 fold, while if the firm fails, its managers will end up with nothing. Further, as we saw back in Chapter 13, a highly leveraged position will tend to drive the firm toward the extremes — large losses or large profits. The managers of companies that have gone through an LBO tell us that heavy interest payments, combined with a knowledge that success will bring large wealth, does a lot to improve decisions.

3. **Increased Managerial Flexibility.** Another source of value stems from the increased flexibility available to managers of private firms. These managers do not have to worry about what a drop in next quarter's earnings will do to the firm's stock price, hence they can focus on long-term, strategic actions that ultimately will have the greatest positive impact on the firm's value. Managerial flexibility concerning asset sales is also greater in a private firm, since such sales do not have to be justified to a large number of shareholders with potentially diverse interests.

4.   **Increased Shareholder Participation.** Going private typically results in replacing a dispersed, largely passive group of public shareholders with a small group of new investors who play a much more active role in managing the firm. These new equity investors take a substantial position in the private firm, hence have a greater motivation to monitor management and to provide incentives to management than do the typical stockholders of a public corporation. Further, the new nonmanagement equity investors, such as KKR, are typically represented on the board, and they bring both sophisticated financial expertise and hard-nosed attitudes to the new firm. These outsiders don't have old buddies running money-losing operations, so they are more willing to force major operating changes than is an entrenched management. For example, within a few weeks after KKR won the battle for RJR Nabisco, the much touted but unprofitable Premier "smokeless" cigarette project was abandoned.

5.   **Increased Financial Leverage.** Going private usually entails a drastic increase in the firm's use of debt financing, which has two effects. First, the firm's taxes are reduced because interest payments are tax deductible, so more of the operating income flows through to investors. Second, the increased debt servicing requirements provide managers with an incentive to increase revenues and/or reduce costs to insure that the firm has sufficient cash flow to meet its obligations—a highly leveraged firm simply cannot afford any fat.

One might ask why all firms are not privately held. The answer is that, while there are real benefits to private ownership, there are also benefits to being publicly owned. Most notably, public corporations have access to large amounts of equity capital on advantageous terms, and for most companies, the advantage of access to public capital markets dominates the advantages of going private. Also, note that most companies which go private end up going public again after several years of operation as private firms. During the private phase, management typically sheds inefficient businesses, cuts costs throughout the corporation, and, generally, rationalizes operations. These actions increase the value of the firm to investors. Once the company has been "straightened up," going public allows the private equityholders to recover their investment, take their profit, and move on to new ventures.

Note too that the examples set by LBO companies are not lost on companies that maintain their publicly owned status. Thus, companies such as Phillips Petroleum and Union Carbide have changed their operations to the point where they resemble LBO companies. This has increased their value and thus made them less attractive to KKR and other LBO specialists, and this has benefitted both managements and shareholders. Thus far, LBOs seem to have provided a net advantage to the economy. However, the final chapter has not been written, and the high degree of leverage may ultimately prove harmful.

Self-Test Questions

What is meant by the term "going private"?

What are the main benefits of going private?

Why don't all firms go private to capture these benefits?

PREFERRED STOCK

Preferred stock is a hybrid—it is similar to bonds in some respects and to common stock in other ways. Accountants generally view preferred stock as equity and show it on the balance sheet as an equity account. However, financial managers view preferred stock as being somewhere between debt and common equity—it imposes a fixed charge and thus increases the firm's financial leverage, yet if the preferred dividend is not paid, this does not force the company into bankruptcy. We first describe the basic features of preferred, after which we describe some recent innovations in preferred stock financing.

Basic Features

Preferred stock generally has a par (or liquidating) value, usually either $25 or $100. The dividend is indicated as a percentage of par, as so many dollars per share, or sometimes both ways. For example, several years ago Mississippi Power Company sold 150,000 shares of $100 par value preferred stock for a total of $15 million. This preferred had a stated annual dividend of $12 per share, so the preferred dividend yield was $12/$100 = 0.12, or 12 percent, at the time of issue. The dividend was set when the stock was issued; it will not be changed in the future. Therefore, if the required rate of return on preferred, k_p, changes from 12 percent after the issue date—as it did—then the market price of the preferred stock will go up or down. Currently, k_p for Mississippi Power's preferred is 9 percent, and the price of the preferred has risen to $12/0.09 = $133.33.

If the preferred dividend is not earned, the company does not have to pay it. However, most preferred issues are *cumulative,* meaning that the cumulative total of all unpaid preferred dividends must be paid before dividends can be paid on the common stock. Unpaid preferred dividends are called *arrearages.*[9]

Preferred stock normally has no voting rights. However, most preferred issues stipulate that the preferred stockholders can elect a minority of the directors—say 3 out of 10—if the preferred dividend is passed (omitted). Jersey Central Power & Light, one of the companies that owned a share of the Three Mile Island (TMI) nuclear plant, has preferred stock outstanding which can even elect a *majority* of the directors if the preferred dividend is passed for four successive quarters. Jersey Central kept paying its preferred dividends even during the dark days following the TMI accident. Had the preferred only been entitled to elect a minority of the directors, the dividend would probably have been passed.

Even though nonpayment of preferred dividends will not bankrupt a company, corporations issue preferred with every intention of paying the dividends. Even if passing the dividend does not give the preferred stockholders control of the company, failure to pay a preferred dividend precludes payment of common dividends

---

[9]Dividends in arrears do not earn interest; thus, arrearages do not increase in a compound interest sense. They only grow from continued nonpayment of the preferred dividend. Also, many preferred stocks accrue arrearages for only a limited number of years, not indefinitely. Often, only three years of arrearages accrue; the cumulative feature ceases after three years, but the dividends in arrears until that point continue in force.

and, in addition, makes it difficult for a firm to raise capital by selling bonds, and virtually impossible to sell more preferred or common stock. However, having preferred stock outstanding does give the firm that experiences temporary problems a chance to overcome its difficulties; had bonds been used instead of preferred stock, the company might have been forced into bankruptcy before it could straighten out its problems. Thus, from the viewpoint of the issuing corporation, preferred stock is less risky than bonds.

Investors, on the other hand, regard preferred stock as being riskier than bonds for two reasons: (1) Preferred stockholders' claims are subordinated to those of bondholders in the event of liquidation, and (2) bondholders are more likely to continue receiving income during hard times than are preferred stockholders. Accordingly, investors require a higher after-tax rate of return on a given firm's preferred stock than on its bonds. However, recall that 70 percent of preferred dividends are exempt from the corporate tax; this makes preferred stock attractive to corporate investors. In recent years, high-grade preferred stock, on average, has sold on a lower pre-tax yield basis than have high-grade bonds. As an example, in May 1990, Du Pont's preferred stock had a market yield of about 8.3 percent, whereas its bonds provided a yield of 9.3 percent, or 1.0 percentage points *more* than its preferred. The tax treatment accounted for this differential; the *after-tax yield* to corporate investors was greater on the preferred stock than on the bonds.[10]

About half of all preferred stock issued in recent years has been convertible into common stock. For example, Enron Corporation issued preferred stock which stipulated that one share of preferred could be converted into three shares of common, at the option of the preferred stockholder. Convertibles are discussed at length in Chapter 18.

Some preferred stocks are similar to perpetual bonds in that they have no maturity date. However, many preferred shares do have a sinking fund provision, often one which calls for the retirement of 2 percent of the issue each year, meaning that the issue will "mature" in a maximum of 50 years. Also, many preferred issues are callable by the issuing corporation. This feature, if exercised, can also limit the life of the preferred.[11]

Nonconvertible preferred stock is virtually all owned by corporations, which can take advantage of the 70 percent dividend exclusion to obtain a higher after-tax yield on preferred stock than on bonds. Individuals should not own preferred stocks

---

[10]The after-tax yield on a 9.3 percent bond to a corporate investor that is paying a 34 percent marginal tax rate is $9.3\%(1 - T) = 9.3\%(0.66) = 6.14\%$. The after-tax yield on an 8.3 percent preferred stock is $8.3\%(1 - \text{Effective } T) = 8.3\%[1 - (0.30)(0.34)] = 7.45\%$. Also, note that the tax law prohibits firms from issuing debt and then using the proceeds to purchase another firm's preferred or common stock. If debt financing is used for stock purchases, then the 70 percent dividend exclusion is reduced. This provision is designed to prevent firms from engaging in "tax arbitrage," or the use of tax-deductible debt to purchase largely tax-exempt preferred stock.

[11]Prior to the late 1970s, virtually all preferred stock was perpetual, and almost no issues had sinking funds or call provisions. Then, insurance company regulators, worried about the unrealized losses the companies had been incurring on preferred holdings as a result of rising interest rates, put into effect some regulatory changes which essentially mandated that insurance companies buy only limited life preferreds. From that time on, virtually no new issues have been perpetuities. This example illustrates the way the nature of securities changes as a result of changes in the economic environment.

(except convertible preferreds)—they can get higher yields on safer bonds, so it is not logical for them to hold preferreds. As a result of this ownership pattern, the volume of preferred stock financing is geared to the supply of money in the hands of insurance companies and other corporate investors who are looking for tax-favored investments. When the supply of such money is plentiful, the prices of preferred stocks are bid up, their yields fall, and investment bankers suggest to companies that they consider issuing preferred stock.

Recent Innovations

Several important innovations in preferred stock financing have occurred in recent years. We will discuss two of these here: (1) floating, or adjustable rate, preferred and (2) money market, or market auction, preferred.

Adjustable-rate preferred stocks (ARPs) were introduced in 1982. These stocks, instead of paying fixed dividends, have their dividends tied to the rate on Treasury securities. The ARPs, which are issued mainly by large commercial banks, were touted as nearly perfect short-term corporate investments since (1) only 30 percent of the dividends are taxable to corporations, and (2) the floating rate feature was supposed to keep the issue trading at near par. The new security proved to be so popular as a short-term investment for firms with idle cash that mutual funds which invest in these securities sprouted like weeds (the funds, in turn, were purchased by corporations). However, the ARPs still had some price volatility due (1) to changes in the riskiness of the issues (some big banks which had issued ARPs, such as Continental Illinois, ran into serious loan default problems) and (2) to the fact that Treasury yields exhibited significant fluctuations between dividend rate adjustments dates. Thus, the ARPs had too much price instability for the liquid asset portfolios of many corporate investors.

In 1984, Shearson Lehman Brothers introduced *money market,* or *market auction, preferred.* Here is how they work: The underwriter conducts an auction on the issue every 7 weeks (to get the 70 percent exclusion from taxable income, buyers must hold the stock at least 46 days). Any holders who want to sell their shares can put them up for auction at par value. Buyers then submit bids in the form of the yields they are willing to accept over the next 7-week period. The yield that is set on the issue for the next period is the lowest yield necessary to sell all the shares being offered at that auction. The buyers pay the sellers the par value, hence holders are virtually assured that their shares can be sold at par. The issuer then has to pay the dividend rate over the next 7-week period as determined by the auction. From the holder's standpoint, market auction preferred is a low-risk, largely tax-exempt, 7-week maturity security which can be sold between auction dates at close to par value. However, if there are not enough buyers to match the sellers, then the auction can fail. This has occurred several times recently. For example, an auction of MCorp, a Texas bank holding company, preferred stock recently failed. Analysts attributed the failure to the downgrading of MCorp's preferred stock from double-A to single-B.

Adjustable-rate and market auction preferreds, although initially issued exclusively by banks, are also now being issued by nonfinancial corporations. For example, Texas Instruments recently issued $225 million of market auction preferred. About the only thing investors do not seem to like about ARPs and auction market preferreds is that, as stock, they are more vulnerable to an issuer's financial problems than debt would be, as evidenced by the MCorp example.

Advantages and Disadvantages of Preferred Stock Financing

There are both advantages and disadvantages to selling preferred stock. Here are the major advantages from the issuers' standpoint:

1.   In contrast to bonds, the obligation to make preferred dividend payments is not contractual in nature, and the passing (omission) of preferred dividends cannot force a firm into bankruptcy.

2.   By selling preferred stock, the firm avoids the dilution of common equity that occurs when common stock is sold.

3.   Since preferred stock often has no maturity, and since preferred sinking fund payments, if present, are typically spread over a long period, preferred issues avoid the cash flow drain from repayment of principal that is inherent in debt issues.

These are the major disadvantages:

1.   Preferred stock dividends are not deductible as a tax expense to the issuer, hence the after-tax cost of preferred is typically higher than the after-tax cost of debt.

2.   Although preferred dividends can be passed, investors expect them to be paid, and firms intend to pay the dividends if conditions permit. Thus, preferred dividends are truly a fixed payment, and the use of preferred stock, like debt, increases the financial risk of the firm and thus increases the cost of all financing.

Self-Test Questions

Should preferred stock be considered as equity or debt financing? Explain.

Who are the major purchasers of nonconvertible preferred stock? Why?

Briefly explain the mechanics of adjustable-rate and market auction preferred stock.

What are the advantages and disadvantages of preferred stock financing to the issuer?

REGULATION AND THE INVESTMENT BANKING PROCESS

In this section, we describe the regulation of securities markets, the way securities are issued, and the role of investment bankers in the process.

Regulation of Securities Markets

Sales of new securities, and also sales in the secondary markets, are regulated by the *Securities and Exchange Commission (SEC)* and, to a lesser extent, by each of the 50 states. Here are the primary elements of SEC regulation:

1.   The SEC has jurisdiction over all interstate offerings of new securities to the public in amounts of $1.5 million or more.

2.   Newly issued securities must be registered with the SEC at least 20 days before they are publicly offered. The *registration statement* provides financial, legal, and technical information about the company to the SEC, and the *prospectus* summarizes this information for investors. SEC lawyers and accountants analyze both the registration statement and the prospectus; if the information is inadequate or misleading, the SEC will delay or stop the public offering.

3.   After the registration has become effective, new securities may be offered, but any sales solicitation must be accompanied by the prospectus. Preliminary, or *"red herring," prospectuses* may be distributed to potential buyers during the 20-day waiting period, but no sales may be finalized during this time. The "red herring" prospectus contains all the key information that will appear in the final prospectus except the price, which is generally set after the market closes the day before the new securities are actually offered to the public.

4.   If the registration statement or prospectus contains misrepresentations or omissions of material facts, any purchaser who suffers a loss may sue for damages. Severe penalties may be imposed on the issuer or its officers, directors, accountants, engineers, appraisers, underwriters, and all others who participated in the preparation of the registration statement or prospectus.

5.   The SEC also regulates all national stock exchanges, and companies whose securities are listed on an exchange must file annual reports similar to the registration statement with both the SEC and the exchange.

6.   The SEC has control over corporate *insiders.* Officers, directors, and major stockholders must file monthly reports of changes in their holdings of the stock of the corporation. Any short-term profits from such transactions must be turned over to the corporation.

7.   The SEC has the power to prohibit manipulation by such devices as pools (large amounts of money used to buy or sell stocks to artificially affect prices) or wash sales (sales between members of the same group to record artificial transaction prices).

8.   The SEC has control over the form of the proxy and the way the company uses it to solicit votes.

Control over the flow of credit into security transactions is exercised by the Board of Governors of the Federal Reserve System. The Fed exercises this control through *margin requirements,* which specify the maximum percentage of the purchase price of a security that can be borrowed. If a great deal of margin borrowing has been going on, then a decline in stock prices can result in inadequate coverages; this forces the stockbrokers to issue *margin calls,* which in turn require investors either to put up more money or to have their margined stock sold to pay off their loans. Such forced sales further depress the stock market and can set off a downward spiral. The margin requirement has been 50 percent since 1974.

States also have some control over the issuance of new securities within their boundaries. This control is usually exercised by a "corporation commissioner" or someone with a similar title. State laws relating to security sales are called *blue sky laws,* because they were put into effect to keep unscrupulous promoters from selling securities that offered the "blue sky" but which actually had little or no asset backing.

The securities industry itself realizes the importance of stable markets, sound brokerage firms, and the absence of stock manipulation. Therefore, the various exchanges work closely with the SEC to police transactions on the exchanges and to maintain the integrity and credibility of the system. Similarly, the *National Association of Securities Dealers (NASD)* cooperates with the SEC to police trading in the OTC market. These industry groups also cooperate with regulatory authorities to set net worth and other standards for securities firms, to develop insurance programs to protect the customers of brokerage houses, and the like.

In general, government regulation of securities trading, as well as industry self-regulation, is designed to insure that investors receive information that is as accurate as possible, that no one artificially manipulates the market price of a given stock, and that corporate insiders do not take advantage of their position to profit in their companies' stocks at the expense of other stockholders. Neither the SEC, the state regulators, nor the industry itself can prevent investors from making foolish decisions or from having "bad luck," but they can and do help investors obtain the best data possible for making sound investment decisions.

The Investment Banking Process

The investment banking process takes place in two stages.

Stage I Decisions. At Stage I, the firm itself makes some initial, preliminary decisions, including the following:

1. **Dollars to Be Raised.** How much new capital is needed?

2. **Type of Securities Used.** Should common, preferred, bonds, or hybrid securities, or a combination, be used? Further, if common stock is to be issued, should it be done as a rights offering or by a direct sale to the general public?

3. **Competitive Bid versus a Negotiated Deal.** Should the company simply offer a block of its securities for sale to the highest bidder, or should it negotiate a deal with an investment banker? These two procedures are called *competitive bids* and *negotiated deals,* respectively. Only about 100 of the largest firms listed on the NYSE, whose securities are already well known to the investment banking community, are in a position to use the competitive bidding process. The investment banks must do a large amount of investigative work in order to bid on an issue unless they are already quite familiar with the firm, and such costs would be too high to make it worthwhile unless the banker were sure of getting the deal. Therefore, except for the largest firms, offerings of stock or bonds are generally on a negotiated basis.

4. **Selection of an Investment Banker.** If the issue is to be negotiated, the firm must select an investment banker. This can be an important decision for a firm that is going public. On the other hand, an older firm that has already "been to market" will have an established relationship with an investment banker. However, it is easy to change bankers if the firm is dissatisfied. Different investment banking houses are

better suited for different companies. The older, larger "establishment houses" such as Morgan Stanley deal mainly with companies such as AT&T, IBM, and Exxon. Other bankers such as Drexel Burnham Lambert (which went bankrupt in 1990) handle more speculative issues. Some houses specialize in new issues, while others are not well suited to handle such issues because their brokerage clients are relatively conservative. (Investment banking firms sell new issues largely to their own regular brokerage customers, so the nature of these customers has a major effect on the ability of the house to do a good job for a corporate client.) Table 15-3 lists the top ten global underwriters for 1989 as measured by the dollar amount of securities underwritten.

Stage II Decisions. Stage II decisions, which are made jointly by the firm and its selected investment banker, include the following:

1. **Reevaluating the Initial Decisions.** The firm and its banker will reevaluate the initial decisions regarding the size of the issue and the type of securities to use. For example, the firm may have decided initially to raise $50 million by selling common stock, but the investment banker may convince management that it would be better off, in view of current market conditions, to limit the stock issue to $25 million and to raise the other $25 million as debt.

2. **Best Efforts or Underwritten Issues.** The firm and its investment banker must decide whether the banker will work on a *best efforts* basis or will *underwrite* the issue. In a best efforts sale, the banker does not guarantee that the securities will be sold or that the company will get the cash it needs, only that it will put forth its best efforts to sell the issue. On an underwritten issue, the company does get a guarantee, because the banker agrees to buy the entire issue and then resell the

Table 15-3 Top Ten Global Underwriters	
	Total Amount Managed (In Billions of Dollars)
1. Merrill Lynch	51.9
2. First Boston	47.4
3. Goldman Sachs	46.3
4. Salomon Brothers	36.0
5. Morgan Stanley	35.9
6. Nomura Securities	34.2
7. Shearson Lehman	27.1
8. Prudential-Bache	17.9
9. Drexel Burnham	17.0
10. Yamaichi Securities	16.0

Source: *The Wall Street Journal,* January 2, 1990.

stock to its customers. Therefore, the banker bears significant risks in underwritten offerings. For example, on one IBM bond issue, interest rates rose sharply, and bond prices fell, after the deal had been set but before the investment bankers could sell the bonds to ultimate purchasers. The bankers lost somewhere between $10 million and $20 million. Had the offering been on a best efforts basis, IBM would have been the loser.

3. **Banker's Compensation and Other Expenses.** The investment banker's compensation must be negotiated. Also, the firm must estimate the other underwriting expenses it will incur in connection with the issue—lawyers' fees, accountants' costs, printing and engraving, and so on. In an underwritten issue, the banker will buy the issue from the company at a discount below the price at which the securities are to be offered to the public, with this "spread" being set to cover the banker's costs and to provide a profit.

Table 15-4 gives an indication of the issuance costs associated with public issues of bonds, preferred stock, and common stock. As the table shows, costs as a percentage of the proceeds are higher for stocks than for bonds, and costs are higher for small than for large issues. The relationship between size of issue and flotation cost is due primarily to the existence of fixed costs—certain costs must be incurred regardless of the size of the issue, so the percentage flotation cost is quite high for small issues.

Also, it should be noted that when companies go public to raise new capital, the new shares are typically underpriced. Thus, the stock closes on the first day of trading at a price above the issue price. Underpricing represents a potentially large cost to existing shareholders, as shown in the initial public offerings section of Table 15-4. Further, the investment bankers frequently take part of their compensation in the form of options to buy stock in the firm. For example, Glasgo Technologies, Inc., recently went public with a $10 million issue by selling 1 million shares at a price of $10 per share. Its investment bankers bought the stock from the company at a price of $9.75 per share, so the direct underwriting fee was only 1,000,000($10.00 − $9.75) = $250,000, or 2.5 percent, but they also received a 5-year option to buy 200,000 shares at a price of $10 per share. If the stock should go up to $15 per share, which the bankers expected it to do, then the investment banking firm would make a $1 million profit, which would in effect be an additional underwriting fee.

4. **Setting the Offering Price.** If the company is already publicly owned, the offering price will be based upon the existing market price of the stock or the yield on the bonds. Typically, for common stock, the investment banker buys the securities at a prescribed number of points below the closing price on the last day of registration. For example, suppose that in October 1990, the stock of Microwave Telecommunications, Inc. (MTI) had a current price of $28.50 per share, and the stock had traded between $25 and $30 per share during the previous three months. Suppose further that MTI and its underwriter agreed that the investment banker would buy 10 million new shares at $1 per share below the closing price on the last day of registration. If the stock closed at $25 on the day the SEC released the issue, MTI would receive $24 per share. Typically, such agreements have an escape clause that provides for the contract to be voided if the price of the securities drops below

Table 15-4   Issuance Costs for Underwritten, Nonrights Offerings
(Expressed as Percentage of Gross Proceeds)

Size of Issue (Millions of Dollars)	Bonds			Preferred Stock		
	Underwriting Commission	Other Expenses	Total Costs	Underwriting Commission	Other Expenses	Total Costs
Under 1.0	10.0%	4.0%	14.0%	—	—	—
1.0–1.9	8.0	3.0	11.0	—	—	—
2.0–4.9	4.0	2.2	6.2	—	—	—
5.0–9.9	2.4	0.8	3.2	1.9%	0.7%	2.6%
10.0–19.9	1.2	0.7	1.9	1.4	0.4	1.8
20.0–49.9	1.0	0.4	1.4	1.4	0.3	1.7
50.0 and over	0.9	0.2	1.1	1.4	0.2	1.6

Notes:

a. Small issues of preferred are rare, so no data on issues below $5 million are given.

b. Flotation costs tend to rise somewhat when interest rates are cyclically high, indicating that money is in relatively tight supply, hence investment bankers will have a relatively hard time placing issues with permanent investors. Thus, the figures shown in this table represent averages, as flotation costs actually vary somewhat over time.

c. Underpricing is shown as a separate cost component for initial public offerings because it has been measured and is reasonably predictable. Underpricing also exists for common stock offerings by companies that already have publicly traded stock, but the effects are unstable and difficult to measure; these effects are discussed later in the chapter.

some predetermined figure. In the illustrative case, this "upset" price might be set at $24 per share. Thus, if the closing price of the shares on the last day of registration had been $23.50, MTI would have had the option of withdrawing from the agreement.

The investment banker will have an easier job if the issue is priced relatively low, but the issuer of the securities naturally wants as high a price as possible. Some conflict of interest on price therefore arises between the investment banker and the issuer. If the issuer is financially sophisticated and makes comparisons with similar security issues, the investment banker will be forced to price close to the market.

As we discussed in Chapter 12, the announcement of a new stock offering by a mature firm is often taken as a negative signal — if the firm's prospects were very good, management would not want to issue new stock and thus share the rosy future with new stockholders, so the announcement of a new offering is taken as bad news. Consequently, the price will probably fall when the announcement is made, so the offering price will probably have to be set at a price substantially below the pre-announcement market price. Consider Figure 15-1, in which d_0 is the estimated market demand curve for MTI's stock and S_0 is the number of shares currently outstanding. Initially, there are 50 million shares outstanding, and the equilibrium price of the stock is $28.60 per share, determined as follows:

$$\hat{P}_0 = \frac{D_1}{k_s - g} = \frac{\$2.00}{0.12 - 0.05} \approx \$28.60.$$

Table 15-4   *(continued)*

Common Stock: Additional Shares			Common Stock: Initial Public Offerings			
Underwriting Commission	Other Expenses	Total Costs	Underwriting Commission	Other Expenses	Underpricing Costs	Total Costs
13.0%	9.0%	22.0%	9.8%	9.6%	12.3%	31.7%
11.0	5.9	16.9	9.8	9.6	12.3	31.7
8.6	3.8	12.4	9.4	6.6	6.9	22.9
6.3	1.9	8.1	8.0	4.3	5.5	17.8
5.1	0.9	6.0	7.2	2.1	7.0	16.3
4.1	0.5	4.6	7.2	2.1	7.0	16.3
3.3	0.2	3.5	7.2	2.1	7.0	16.3

Sources: Securities and Exchange Commission, *Cost of Flotation of Registered Equity Issues* (Washington, D.C.: U.S. Government Printing Office, December 1974); Pettway, Richard H., "A Note on the Flotation Costs of New Equity Capital Issues of Electric Companies," *Public Utilities Fortnightly,* March 18, 1982; Hansen, Robert, "Evaluating the Costs of a New Equity Issue," *Midland Corporate Finance Journal,* Spring 1986; Ritter, Jay R., "The Costs of Going Public," *Journal of Financial Economics,* December 1987; and informal surveys of common stock, preferred stock, and bond issues conducted by the authors.

Figure 15-1   Microwave Telecommunications, Inc.: Estimated Common Stock Demand Curves

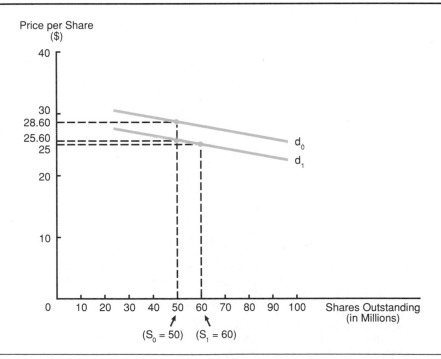

The values shown for D_1, k_s, and g are the *estimates of the marginal investor*. Investors who do not now own MTI's stock probably, on average, regard the stock as being more risky, thus assign it a higher value for k_s, or perhaps they estimate the company's growth rate as being lower than do people who now own the stock, and so they use g < 5 percent when calculating the stock's intrinsic value. In any event, people who do not now own the stock think the stock is worth less than $28.60.

When MTI announces that it is going to sell another 10 million shares, this is taken as a negative signal. Consequently, the demand curve for the stock drops from d_0 to d_1, and the price falls. The new equilibrium price, if 50 million shares were outstanding, and if the marginal investor now expects MTI's growth rate to be 4.2 percent, would be about $25.60:

$$\hat{P}_0 = \frac{\$2.00}{0.12 - 0.042} \approx \$25.60.$$

However, if MTI is to sell another 10 million shares of stock, it will either have to attract investors who would not be willing to own the stock at the $25.60 per share price or else induce present stockholders to buy additional shares. There are two ways this can be accomplished: (1) by reducing the offering price of the stock or (2) by "promoting" or "advertising" the company and thus shifting the demand curve for its stock back to the right.[12] If the demand curve does not shift at all from d_1, we see from Figure 15-1 that the only way the 10 million additional shares could be sold would be by setting the offering price at about $25 per share. However, if the investment banker could promote the stock sufficiently to shift the demand curve back up to d_0, then the offering price could be set much closer to the pre-announcement equilibrium price of $28.60 per share.[13]

The extent to which the demand curve can be shifted depends primarily on two factors: (1) what investors think the company can do with the money brought in by the stock sale and (2) how effectively the brokers promote the issue. If investors can be convinced that the new money will be invested in highly profitable projects that will substantially raise earnings and the earnings growth rate, then the demand curve shift will occur, and the stock price might actually go above $28.60. Even if investors do not radically change their expectations about the company's fundamental factors, the fact that MTI's stock is brought to their attention may shift the demand curve. The extent to which this promotion campaign is successful in shifting the demand curve depends, of course, upon the effectiveness of the investment banking firm. Therefore, the effectiveness of different investment bankers, as perceived by MTI's financial manager, will be an important factor in the choice of an underwriter.

---

[12]It should be noted that investors can buy newly issued stock without paying normal brokerage commissions, and brokers are quick to point this out to potential purchasers. Thus, if an investor were to buy MTI's stock at $28 per share in the regular market, the commission would be about 1 percent, or 28 cents per share. If the stock were purchased in an underwriting, this commission would be avoided.

It should also be noted that for years many academicians argued that the demand curve for a firm's stock is either horizontal or has an extremely slight downward slope, and that signaling effects are minimal. Most corporate treasurers, on the other hand, have long felt that both effects exist for mature companies, and recent empirical studies confirm the treasurers' position. For example, see Andrei Shleifer, "Do Demand Curves for Stocks Slope Down?" *Journal of Finance,* July 1986, 579–590.

[13]Note that the supply curve is a vertical line, first at 50 million and then, after the new issue, at 60 million.

One final point is that *if pressure from the new shares and/or negative signaling effects drives down the price of the stock, all shares outstanding, not just the new shares, are affected.* Thus, if MTI's stock should fall from $28.60 to $25 per share as a result of the financing, and if the price should remain at that new level, then the company would incur a loss of $3.60 on each of the 50 million shares previously outstanding, or a total market value loss of $180 million. This loss, like underwriting expenses, is a flotation cost, and it should be considered as a cost associated with the stock issue. However, if the company's prospects really were poorer than investors thought, then the price decline would have occurred sooner or later anyway. On the other hand, if the company's prospects are really not all that bad (the signal was incorrect), then over time MTI's demand curve will move back to d_0, or even above d_0, so the company would not suffer a permanent loss anywhere close to $180 million.

If the company is "going public," there will be no established price or demand curve, so the bankers will have to estimate the *equilibrium price* at which the stock will sell after issue. Note that if the offering price is set below the true equilibrium price, the stock will rise sharply after the issue, and the company and its selling stockholders will have given away too much stock to raise the required capital. If the offering price is set above the true equilibrium price, either the issue will fail or, if the bankers succeed in selling the stock to their retail clients, these clients will be unhappy when the stock subsequently falls to its equilibrium level. Therefore, it is important that the equilibrium price be closely approximated, although it is hard to estimate this price.

Selling Procedures. Once the company and its investment banker have decided how much money to raise, the types of securities to issue, and the basis for pricing the issue, they will prepare and file an SEC *registration statement* and a *prospectus.* It generally takes about 20 days for the issue to be approved by the SEC. The final price of the stock (or the interest rate on a bond issue) is set at the close of business the day the issue clears the SEC, and the securities are offered to the public the following day.

Investors are required to pay for securities within 10 days, and the investment banker must pay the issuing firm within four days of the official commencement of the offering. Typically, the banker sells the stock within a day or two after the offering begins, but on occasion, the banker miscalculates, sets the offering price too high, and thus is unable to move the issue. At other times, the market declines during the offering period, forcing the banker to reduce the price of the stock or bonds. In either instance, on an underwritten offering the firm receives the price that was agreed upon, so the banker must absorb any losses that are incurred.

Because they are exposed to large potential losses, investment bankers typically do not handle the purchase and distribution of issues single-handedly unless the issue is a very small one. If the sum of money involved is large, investment bankers form *underwriting syndicates* in an effort to minimize the risk each banker carries. The banking house which sets up the deal is called the *lead,* or *managing, underwriter.*

In addition to the underwriting syndicate, on larger offerings still more investment bankers are included in a *selling group,* which handles the distribution of securities to individual investors. The selling group includes all members of the underwriting syndicate plus additional dealers who take relatively small percentages of the total issue, from the members of the underwriting syndicate. Thus, the underwriters act as *wholesalers,* while members of the selling group act as *retailers.* The number of houses in a selling group depends partly upon the size of the issue. For example, the one set up when Communications Satellite Corporation (Comsat) went public consisted of 385 members.

A new selling procedure has recently emerged which does not require an underwriting syndicate. In this type of sale, called an *unsyndicated stock offering,* the managing underwriter, acting alone, sells the issue entirely to institutional investors, thus bypassing both retail stockbrokers and individual investors. In recent years, about 50 percent of all stock sold has been by unsyndicated offerings. Behind this phenomenon is a simple motivating force: money. The fees that issuers pay on a syndicated offering, which includes commissions paid to retail brokers, can run at least a full percentage point higher than those on unsyndicated offerings. Further, although total fees are lower if there is no syndicate, managing underwriters usually come out ahead because they do not have to share the fees with an underwriting syndicate. Recent issuers of unsyndicated stock include Transamerica Corporation and Public Service Company of New Mexico. However, some types of stock do not appeal to institutional investors, so not all firms can use unsyndicated offers.

Shelf Registrations. The selling procedures described previously, including the 20-day waiting period between registration with the SEC and sale of the issue, apply to most security sales. However, it should be noted that large, well-known public companies which issue securities frequently may file a *master registration statement* with the SEC and then update it with a *short-form statement* just prior to each individual offering. Further, the company can decide at 10 A.M. to sell securities and have the sale completed before noon. This procedure is known as *shelf registration* because, in effect, the company puts its new securities "on the shelf" and then sells them to investors when it feels the market is "right." Firms with less than $150 million in stock held by outside investors cannot use shelf registrations. The rationale for this distinction is to protect investors who may not be able to get adequate financial data about a little-known company in the short time between announcement of a shelf issue and its sale. Shelf registrations have two advantages over standard registrations: (1) lower flotation costs and (2) more control over the timing of the issue.

Maintenance of the Secondary Market In the case of a large, established firm such as IBM or GM, the investment banking firm's job is finished after it has disposed of the stock and turned the net proceeds over to the issuing firm. However, in the case of a small company going public for the first time, the investment banker is under some obligation to maintain a market in the shares after the issue has been completed. Such stocks are typically traded in the over-the-counter market, and the lead underwriter generally agrees to "make a market" in the stock so as to keep it reasonably liquid. The company wants a good market to exist for its stock, as do the stockholders. Therefore, if the banking house wants to do business with the company in the future, to keep its own brokerage customers happy, and to have future referral business, it will hold an inventory and help to maintain an active secondary market in the stock.

Self-Test Questions

What are the key features of securities markets regulation?

What is the difference between Stage I and Stage II decisions?

What is the difference between a best efforts and an underwritten issue?

What are some potential problems encountered when setting the offering price on a stock issue?

Briefly explain the selling procedures used on a new securities issue.

What is a shelf registration? What are the advantages of shelf registrations over standard registrations?

SUMMARY

This chapter is more descriptive than analytical, but a knowledge of the issues discussed here is essential to an understanding of finance. The key concepts covered are listed next.

- *Stockholders' equity* consists of the firm's common stock, additional paid-in capital (funds received in excess of the par value), and retained earnings (earnings not paid out as dividends).

- *Book value per share* is equal to stockholders' equity divided by the number of shares of stock outstanding. A stock's book value is often different from its par value and its market value.

- A *proxy* is a document which gives one person the power to act for another person, typically the power to vote shares of common stock. A *proxy fight* occurs when an outside group solicits stockholders' proxies in order to vote a new management team into office.

- Stockholders often have the right to purchase any additional shares sold by the firm. This right, called the *preemptive right,* protects the control of the present stockholders and prevents dilution of the value of their stock.

- Although most firms use only one type of common stock, in some instances several *classes of stock* are issued.

- The major *advantages of common stock financing* are as follows: (1) there is no obligation to make fixed payments, (2) common stock never matures, (3) the use of common stock increases the creditworthiness of the firm, (4) stock can often be sold more easily than debt, and (5) using stock helps the firm maintain its reserve borrowing capacity.

- The major *disadvantages of common stock financing* are (1) it extends voting privileges to new stockholders, (2) new stockholders share in the firm's profits,

(3) the costs of issuing stock are high, (4) using stock can raise the firm's cost of capital, and (5) dividends paid on common stock are not tax deductible.

■ A *closely held corporation* is one that is owned by a few individuals who are typically associated with the firm's management.

■ A *publicly owned corporation* is one that is owned by a relatively large number of individuals who are not actively involved in its management.

■ *Going public* facilitates stockholder diversification, increases liquidity of the firm's stock, makes it easier for the firm to raise capital, and establishes a value for the firm. However, reporting costs are high, operating data must be disclosed, management self-dealings are harder to arrange, the price may sink to a low level if the stock is not traded actively, and public ownership may make it harder for management to maintain control of the firm.

■ The decision to *list* the stock on a major exchange is not as critical as the decision to go public.

■ New common stock may be sold in five ways: (1) on a pro rata basis to existing stockholders through a *rights offering,* (2) through investment bankers to the general public in a *public offering,* (3) to a single buyer, or a small number of buyers, in a *private placement,* (4) to employees through an *employee purchase plan,* and (5) to shareholders through a *dividend reinvestment plan.*

■ Securities markets are regulated by the *Securities and Exchange Commission (SEC).*

■ An *investment banker* assists in the issuing of securities by helping the firm determine the size of the issue and the type of securities to be used, by establishing the selling price, by selling the issue, and, in some cases, by maintaining an after-market for the stock.

■ *Preferred stock* is a hybrid — it is similar to bonds in some respects and to common stock in other ways.

■ The 1980s spawned two innovations in preferred stock financing: (1) *floating rate preferred* and (2) *money market, or market auction, preferred.*

Questions

15-1   Define each of the following terms:
   a.   Common equity; additional paid-in capital; retained earnings
   b.   Par value; book value per share; market value per share
   c.   Proxy; proxy fight
   d.   Preemptive right
   e.   Classified stock; founders' shares
   f.   Closely held corporation; publicly owned corporation
   g.   Over-the-counter (OTC) market; organized security exchange
   h.   Primary market; secondary market
   i.   Going public; new issue market; initial public offering (IPO)
   j.   Rights offering

   k.   Public offering; private placement
   l.   Employee purchase plan; ESOP
   m.   Securities and Exchange Commission (SEC); registration statement; shelf registration; "blue sky" laws; margin requirement; insiders
   n.   Prospectus; "red herring" prospectus
   o.   National Association of Securities Dealers (NASD)
   p.   Cumulative dividends; arrearages
   q.   Floating rate preferred stock
   r.   Best efforts arrangement; underwritten arrangement
   s.   Spread; flotation costs; offering price
   t.   Underwriting syndicate; lead, or managing, underwriter; selling group

15-2   Examine Table 15-1. Suppose American Chemical sold 2 million shares, with the company netting $25 per share. Construct a pro forma statement of the equity accounts to reflect this sale.

15-3   Is it true that the "flatter," or more nearly horizontal, the demand curve for a particular firm's stock, and the less important investors regard the signaling effect of the offering, the more important the role of investment bankers when the company sells a new issue of stock?

15-4   The SEC attempts to protect investors who are purchasing newly issued securities by making sure that the information put out by a company and its investment bankers is correct and is not misleading. However, the SEC does not provide an opinion about the real value of the securities; hence, an investor might pay too much for some new stock and consequently lose heavily. Do you think the SEC should, as a part of every new stock or bond offering, render an opinion to investors on the proper value of the securities being offered? Explain.

15-5   How do you think each of the following items would affect a company's ability to attract new capital and the flotation costs involved in doing so?
   a.   A decision to list a company's stock; the stock now trades in the over-the-counter market.
   b.   A decision of a privately held company to go public.
   c.   The increasing institutionalization of the "buy side" of the stock and bond markets.
   d.   The trend toward "financial conglomerates" as opposed to stand-alone investment banking houses.
   e.   Elimination of the preemptive right.
   f.   The introduction of "shelf registrations" in 1981.

15-6   Before entering a formal agreement, investment bankers carefully investigate the companies whose securities they underwrite; this is especially true of the issues of firms going public for the first time. Since the bankers do not themselves plan to hold the securities but intend to sell them to others as soon as possible, why are they so concerned about making careful investigations?

15-7   It is frequently stated that the primary purpose of the preemptive right is to allow individuals to maintain their proportionate share of the ownership and control of a corporation.
   a.   How important do you suppose this consideration is for the average stockholder of a firm whose shares are traded on the New York or American Stock Exchanges?
   b.   Is the preemptive right likely to be of more importance to stockholders of publicly owned or closely held firms? Explain.
   c.   Is a firm likely to get a wider distribution of shares if it sells new stock through a preemptive rights offering to existing stockholders or directly to underwriters?
   d.   Why would management be interested in getting a wider distribution of its shares?

Problems

15-1 **(Book value per share)** The Lange Music Company had the following balance sheet at the end of 1990.

Lange Music Company:
Balance Sheet as of
December 31, 1990

		Accounts payable	$ 48,000
		Notes payable	54,000
		Long-term debt	108,000
		Common stock (30,000 shares authorized, 20,000 shares outstanding)	270,000
		Retained earnings	225,000
Total assets	$705,000	Total liabilities and equity	$705,000

a. What is the book value per share of the firm's common stock?

b. Suppose the firm sold the remaining authorized shares and netted $22.50 per share from the sale. What would be the new book value per share?

15-2 **(Profit or loss on new stock issue)** Security Brokers, Inc., specializes in underwriting new issues by small firms. On a recent offering of Millar, Inc., the terms were as follows:

Price to public:	$5 per share
Number of shares:	3 million
Proceeds to Millar:	$14,000,000

The out-of-pocket expenses incurred by Security Brokers in the design and distribution of the issue were $300,000. What profit or loss would Security Brokers incur if the issue were sold to the public at an average price of

a. $5 per share?

b. $6 per share?

c. $4 per share?

15-3 **(Underwriting and flotation expenses)** The Lee Company, whose stock price is now $25, needs to raise $20 million in common stock. Underwriters have informed the firm's management that they must price the new issue to the public at $22 per share because of a downward-sloping demand curve. The underwriters' compensation will be 5 percent of the issue price, so Lee will net $20.90 per share. The firm will also incur expenses in the amount of $150,000.

How many shares must the firm sell to net $20 million after underwriting and flotation expenses?

15-4 **(New stock issue)** The Ewert Gem Company, a small jewelry manufacturer, has been successful and has enjoyed a good growth trend. Now Ewert is planning to go public with an issue of common stock, and it faces the problem of setting an appropriate price on the stock. The company and its investment bankers believe that the proper procedure is to select several similar firms with publicly traded common stock and to make relevant comparisons.

Several jewelry manufacturers are reasonably similar to Ewert with respect to product mix, asset composition, and debt/equity proportions. Of these companies, Groth Jewelers and Hill Fashions are most similar. When analyzing the following data, assume that 1985 and 1990 were reasonably "normal" years for all three companies—that is, these years were neither especially good nor especially bad in terms of sales, earnings, and dividends. At the time of the analysis, k_{RF} was 8 percent and k_M was 12 percent. Groth is listed on the AMEX and Hill on the NYSE, while Ewert will be traded in the OTC market.

	Groth	Hill	Ewert (Totals)
Earnings per share			
1990	$ 4.50	$ 7.50	$1,200,000
1985	3.00	5.50	816,000
Price per share			
1990	$36.00	$65.00	—
Dividends per share			
1990	$ 2.25	$ 3.75	$ 600,000
1985	1.50	2.75	420,000
Book value per share, 1990	$30.00	$55.00	$ 9 million
Market/book ratio, 1990	120%	118%	—
Total assets, 1990	$28 million	$ 82 million	$20 million
Total debt, 1990	$12 million	$ 30 million	$11 million
Sales, 1990	$41 million	$140 million	$37 million

a. Assume that Ewert has 100 shares of stock outstanding. Use this information to calculate earnings per share (EPS), dividends per share (DPS), and book value per share for Ewert. (Hint: Ewert's 1990 EPS = $12,000.)

b. Calculate earnings and dividend growth rates for the three companies. (Hint: Ewert's EPS growth rate is 8 percent.)

c. On the basis of your answer to Part a, do you think Ewert's stock would sell at a price in the same "ballpark" as that of Groth and Hill, that is, in the range of $25 to $100 per share?

d. Assuming that Ewert's management can split the stock so that the 100 shares could be changed to 1,000 shares, 100,000 shares, or any other number, would such an action make sense in this case? Why?

e. Now assume that Ewert did split its stock and has 400,000 shares. Calculate new values for EPS, DPS, and book value per share. (Hint: Ewert's new 1990 EPS is $3.00.)

f. Return on equity (ROE) can be measured as EPS/book value per share or as total earnings/total equity. Calculate ROEs for the three companies for 1990. (Hint: Ewert's 1990 ROE = 13.3%.)

g. Calculate dividend payout ratios for the three companies for both years. (Hint: Ewert's 1990 payout ratio is 50%.)

h. Calculate debt/total assets ratios for the three companies for 1990. (Hint: Ewert's 1990 debt ratio is 55%.)

i. Calculate the P/E ratios for Groth and Hill for 1990. Are these P/Es reasonable in view of relative growth, payout, and ROE data? If not, what other factors might explain them? (Hint: Groth's P/E = 8×.)

j. Now determine a range of values for Ewert's stock price, with 400,000 shares outstanding, by applying Groth's and Hill's P/E ratios, price/dividends ratios, and price/book value ratios to your data for Ewert. For example, one possible price for Ewert's stock is (P/E Groth)(EPS Ewert) = 8($3) = $24 per share. Similar calculations would produce a range of prices based on both Groth's and Hill's data. (Hint: Our range was $24 to $27.)

k. Using the equation $k = D_1/P_0 + g$, find approximate k values for Groth and Hill. Then use these values in the constant growth stock price model to find a price for Ewert's stock. (Hint: We averaged the EPS and DPS g's for Ewert.)

l.   At what price do you think Ewert's shares should be offered to the public? You will want to select a price that will be low enough to induce investors to buy the stock but not so low that it will rise sharply immediately after it is issued. Think about relative growth rates, ROEs, dividend yields, and total returns ($k_s = D_1/P_0 + g$).

Mini Case

Randy's, a family-owned restaurant chain operating in Alabama, has grown to the point where expansion throughout the entire Southeast is feasible. The proposed expansion would require the firm to raise about $15 million in new capital. Because Randy's currently has a debt ratio of 50 percent, and also because the family members already have all their personal wealth invested in the company, the family would like to sell common stock to the public to raise the $15 million. However, the family does want to retain voting control. You have been asked to brief the family members on the issues involved by answering the following questions:

a.   What are the primary advantages of financing with stock rather than bonds? What are the disadvantages to financing with stock?

b.   Is the stock of Randy's currently publicly held or privately owned? Would this situation change if the stock sale were made?

c.   What is classified stock? Would there be any advantages to the family in designating the stock currently outstanding as "founders' shares"? What type of common stock should Randy's sell to the public to allow the family to retain control of the business?

d.   Would the stock sale be an initial public offering (IPO)? What would be the advantages to the family members of having the firm go public? Would there be any disadvantages? If you were a key employee, but not a family member, or a potential key employee being interviewed as a part of the expansion process, how would the decision affect you?

e.   What does it mean for a stock to be listed? Do you think that Randy's stock would be listed shortly after the company goes public? If not, where would the stock trade?

f.   What is a rights offering? Would it make sense for Randy's to use a rights offering to raise the $15 million? Even if you do not think a rights offering should be employed, could one be used?

g.   What is the difference between a private placement and a public offering? What are the advantages and disadvantages of each type of placement? Which type would be most suitable for Randy's?

h.   What is meant by going private? Assume for the sake of this question that Randy's previously went public. What are the advantages and disadvantages of the firm's going private?

i.   How does preferred stock differ from both common equity and debt? Briefly describe the features of floating rate (or adjustable rate) preferred stock.

j.   (1) Would Randy's be likely to sell the $15 million of stock by itself or through an investment banker?

        (2) If an investment banker were used, would the sale most likely be on the basis of a competitive bid or a negotiated deal?

        (3) If it were a negotiated deal, would it most likely be done on a best efforts or an underwritten basis? In each case, explain your answer.

k.   Without doing any calculations, describe the procedure by which the company and its investment banker would determine the price at which the stock would be offered to the public.

l.   Suppose the decision were made to issue 1.5 million shares at $10 per share. What would be the approximate flotation cost on the issue? Would the cost be higher or lower if the firm were already publicly owned? Would there be a difference in costs between a best efforts and an underwritten offering?

m. If some of the family members wanted to sell some of their own shares in order to diversify their holdings at the same time the company was selling new shares to raise capital, would this be feasible?

Selected Additional References and Cases

For a wealth of facts and figures on a major segment of the stock market, see New York Stock Exchange, Fact Book (New York: published annually).

For both a description of the stock markets and some further facts and figures, see the investment textbooks referenced in Chapter 5. For a discussion of the current state of investment banking and trends in the industry, see

Hayes, S. L., "The Transformation of Investment Banking," *Harvard Business Review,* January-February 1979, 153–170.

Rogowski, Robert, and Eric Sorensen, "The New Competitive Environment of Investment Banking: Transactional Finance and Concession Pricing of New Issues," *Midland Corporate Finance Journal,* Spring 1986, 64–71.

For additional insights on the benefits of listing, see

Edelman, Richard B., and H. Kent Baker, "Liquidity and Stock Exchange Listing," *The Financial Review,* May 1990, 231–249.

Other good references on specific aspects of equity financing include the following:

Block, Stanley, and Marjorie Stanley, "The Financial Characteristics and Price Movement Patterns of Companies Approaching the Unseasoned Securities Market in the Late 1970s," *Financial Management,* Winter 1980, 30–36.

Bowyer, John W., and Jess B. Yawitz, "Effect of New Equity Issues on Utility Stock Prices," *Public Utilities Fortnightly,* May 22, 1980, 25–28.

Fabozzi, Frank J., "Does Listing on the AMEX Increase the Value of Equity?" *Financial Management,* Spring 1981, 43–50.

Hansen, Robert S., and John M. Pinkerton, "Direct Equity Financing: A Resolution to a Paradox," *Journal of Finance,* June 1982, 651–665.

Ibbotson, Roger G., Jody L. Sindelar, and Jay R. Ritter, "Initial Public Offerings," *Journal of Applied Corporate Finance,* Summer 1988, 37–45.

Jurin, Bruce, "Raising Equity in an Efficient Market," *Midland Corporate Finance Journal,* Winter 1988, 53–60.

Logue, Dennis, and Robert A. Jarrow, "Negotiation versus Competitive Bidding in the Sale of Securities by Public Utilities," *Financial Management,* Autumn 1978, 31–39.

Muscarella, Chris J., and Michael R. Vetsuypens, "The Underpricing of 'Second' Initial Public Offerings," *The Journal of Financial Research,* Fall 1989, 183–192.

For more information on shelf registration, see

Bhagat, Sanjai, "The Evidence on Shelf Registration," *Midland Corporate Finance Journal,* Spring 1984, 6–12.

For an excellent discussion of the various procedures used to raise capital, see

Smith, Clifford W., Jr., "Raising Capital: Theory and Evidence," *Midland Corporate Finance Journal,* Spring 1986, 6–22. Also, Pages 72–76 of the Spring 1986 issue of the *Midland*

Corporate Finance Journal contain a bibliography of recent articles pertaining to investment banking and capital acquisition.

For additional discussions on preferred stock, see

Alderson, Michael J., Keith C. Brown, and Scott L. Lummer, "Dutch Auction Rate Preferred Stock," *Financial Management,* Summer 1987, 68–73.

Fooladi, Iraj, and Gordon S. Roberts, "On Preferred Stock," *Journal of Financial Research,* Winter 1986, 319–324.

Wansley, James W., Fayez A. Elayan, and Brian A. Maris, "Preferred Stock Returns, CreditWatch, and Preferred Stock Rating Changes," *The Financial Review,* May 1990, 265–285.

Winger, Bernard J., et al., "Adjustable Rate Preferred Stock," *Financial Management,* Spring 1986, 48–57.

The Spring 1990 issue of Financial Management *is devoted to Employee Stock Ownership Plans (ESOPs).*

The following cases from the Brigham-Gapenski casebook focus on the issues contained in this chapter:

Case 22, "Golden Gate Savings and Loan," which illustrates the decision to go public.

Case 23, "Synergistics, Inc.," which emphasizes the investment banking process.

Case 24, "Williamsburg Furniture Company," which focuses on the analysis of a rights offering.

The Harrington casebook contains the following applicable case:

"Hop-In Food Stores, Incorporated," which focuses on a firm's decision to go public.

CHAPTER 16

Long-Term Debt

On any given day, corporations go to the markets for vast amounts of new debt capital, and they use many types and forms of securities. To illustrate, during one week in February 1990, *The Wall Street Journal* announced the following debt-related actions: (1) Arco Chemical issued $225 million of 9.80 percent, 30-year debentures. The noncallable issue was priced at 1.24 percentage points above a 30-year Treasury bond. Merrill Lynch was the lead underwriter on the issue, which was rated A by Standard & Poor's and A2 by Moody's. (2) Norfolk and Western Railway issued $35 million of Equipment Trust Certificates. The certificates, which are backed by rolling stock of the issuer, mature from 1991 through 2005 and were priced to yield from 8.56 percent for the 1-year certificate to 9.15 percent for the 15-year certificate. (3) Duke Power announced the March 1, 1990, redemption (call) of its First and Refunding Mortgage Bonds, due 2015. Each bond, which carried a coupon of 12⅝ percent, would be redeemed by the Trustee, Morgan Guaranty Trust, for $1,095.00, plus accrued interest of $10.52 per $1,000 principal amount. Interest would cease to accrue on the bonds after the redemption date. (4) Kaiser Aluminum raised $722 million in short-term bank debt from a group of 19 banks, led by Bank of America. Ten of the 19 participating banks were foreign, including the Nippon Credit Bank, the Toronto-Dominion Bank, and the State Bank of South Australia. (5) Standard & Poor's and Moody's announced their ratings on $1.25 billion of new senior notes to be issued by RJR Nabisco. Although RJR had hoped that the notes would be rated as investment-grade debt, Standard & Poor's rated the issue at BB and Moody's assigned a rating of Ba3, meaning that the issue was rated as junk. (6) Hyundai Motors announced a $70 million Eurobond issue with warrants. The bonds have a coupon rate of only 1.5 percent, but each $5,000 bond carries a warrant that entitles the holder to purchase shares of Hyundai common stock at a price that investors expect to be less than the market price during the 1991 exercise period.

Why did these companies use so many different types of debt? How are bond ratings determined, and how do they affect a company's cost of debt? How does a company decide when to call a bond, or, at the time of issue, whether to make the bond callable? These are some of the issues discussed in this chapter.

AS noted in Chapters 12 and 13, the use of debt financing is generally required to maximize the value of the firm. In this chapter, we discuss long-term debt, including its different forms, typical provisions in debt contracts, swaps, securitization, bond ratings, refunding operations, and the various factors that influence a firm's decision to use debt financing at a particular point in time.

TRADITIONAL DEBT INSTRUMENTS

There are many types of long-term debt: amortized and nonamortized, publicly issued or privately placed, secured and unsecured, marketable and nonmarketable, callable and noncallable, and so on. In this section, we review briefly the traditional long-term debt instruments and then, in the next section, we discuss some important recent innovations in long-term debt financing.

Term Loans

A *term loan* is a contract under which a borrower agrees to make a series of interest and principal payments, on specific dates, to a lender.[1] Investment bankers are generally not involved: Term loans are negotiated directly between the borrowing firm and a financial institution—generally a bank, an insurance company, or a pension fund. Although the maturities of term loans vary from 2 to 30 years, most are for periods in the 3- to 15-year range.

Term loans have three major advantages over public offerings—*speed, flexibility,* and *low issuance costs.* Also, because they are negotiated directly between the lender and the borrower, formal documentation is minimized. The key provisions of the loan can be worked out much more quickly, and with more flexibility, than can those for a public issue, and it is not necessary for a term loan to go through the Securities and Exchange Commission registration process. A further advantage

---

[1]If the interest and maturity payments required under a term loan agreement are not met on schedule, the borrowing firm is said to have *defaulted,* and it can then be forced into bankruptcy. See Appendix 16A for a discussion of bankruptcy.

of term loans over publicly held debt has to do with future flexibility: If a bond issue is held by many different bondholders, it is virtually impossible to alter the terms of the agreement, even though new economic conditions may make such changes desirable. With a term loan, the borrower can generally negotiate with the lender to work out modifications in the contract.

The interest rate on a term loan can be either fixed for the life of the loan or variable. If it is fixed, the rate used will be close to the rate on bonds of equivalent maturity for companies of comparable risk. If the rate is variable, it is usually set at a certain number of percentage points over the prime rate, the commercial paper rate, the T-bill rate, or the London Interbank Offered Rate (LIBOR). Then, when the index rate goes up or down, so does the rate on the outstanding balance of the term loan. In 1990, about 60 percent of the dollar amount of term loans made by banks had floating rates, up from virtually zero in 1970. Most of the money banks lend to corporations is "bought" in the certificate of deposit market, and if CD rates rise along with other market rates, banks need to raise the rates they earn in order to meet their own interest costs. With the increased volatility of interest rates in recent years, banks have rightly become reluctant to make long-term, fixed rate loans.

Term loans are actually private placements of debt (as we discussed in Chapter 15), as opposed to public offerings of bonds. Typically, bonds are sold by large, well-known companies with strong financial positions. Thus, bond buyers do not need to spend much time and effort gathering information about the issuer since buyers are well aware of the company and its bond rating. Further, most bonds are not amortized, that is, no principal payments are made during the life of the issue. On the other hand, private placements usually involve smaller companies whose credit conditions must be analyzed. Credit assessment can be done easily by large banks, insurance companies, and the like, but individual investors and small institutional investors do not have this capability. Also, private placements (term loans) are usually amortized in equal installments over the life of the loan. Private placements are often called *story credit,* because each placement has a "story" which explains the company's need for funds.

Bonds

Like a term loan, a bond is a long-term contract under which a borrower agrees to make payments of interest and principal, on specific dates, to the holder of the bond. Although bonds are similar to term loans, a bond issue is generally advertised, offered to the public, and actually sold to many different investors. Indeed, thousands of individual and institutional investors may participate when a firm such as New York Telephone sells a bond issue, while there is generally only one lender in the case of a term loan.[2] Although bonds are generally issued with maturities in the range of 20 to 30 years, shorter maturities, such as 7 to 10 years, are occasionally used, as are 40-year maturities. Unlike term loans, a bond's interest rate is generally

---

[2]However, for very large term loans, 20 or more financial institutions may form a syndicate to grant the credit. Also, it should be noted that a bond issue can be sold to one lender (or to just a few); in this case, the issue would be a private placement.

fixed, although in recent years, there has been an increase in the use of various types of floating rate bonds.

Mortgage Bonds. Under a *mortgage bond,* the corporation pledges certain real assets as security for the bond. To illustrate, suppose McLaughlin Container Company needs $10 million to purchase land and to build a plant. Bonds in the amount of $4 million, secured by a mortgage on the property, are issued. If McLaughlin defaults on the bonds, the bondholders could foreclose on the plant and sell it to satisfy their claims.

McLaughlin could, if it so chose, also issue *second mortgage bonds* secured by the same $10 million plant. In the event of liquidation, the holders of these second mortgage bonds would have a claim against the property only after the first mortgage bondholders had been paid off in full. Thus, second mortgages are sometimes called *junior mortgages,* or *junior liens,* because they are junior in priority to claims of *senior mortgages,* or *first mortgage bonds.*

Most major corporations' first mortgage indentures (discussed in detail later in the chapter) were written 20, 30, 40, or more years ago. These indentures are generally "open ended," meaning that new bonds may be issued from time to time under the existing indenture. However, the amount of new bonds that can be issued is virtually always limited to a specified percentage of the firm's total "bondable property," which generally includes all plant and equipment. For example, Savannah Electric Company can issue first mortgage bonds which total up to 60 percent of its fixed assets. If fixed assets totaled $100 million, and if Savannah Electric had $50 million of first mortgage bonds outstanding, then it could, by the 60 percent of property test, issue another $10 million of bonds.

In recent years, Savannah Electric has at times been unable to issue any new first mortgage bonds because of another indenture provision: Its times-interest-earned (TIE) ratio was below 2.5, the minimum coverage that it must maintain in order to sell new bonds. Thus, Savannah Electric passed the property test but failed the coverage test; hence, it could not issue first mortgage bonds, and it had to finance with other securities. Since first mortgage bonds carry lower rates of interest than junior long-term debt, this restriction was a costly one.

Savannah Electric's neighbor, Georgia Power Company, has more flexibility under its indenture; its interest coverage requirement is only 2.0 versus Savannah's 2.5 requirement. In hearings before the Georgia Public Service Commission, it was suggested that Savannah Electric should change its indenture coverage to 2.0 so that it could issue more first mortgage bonds. However, this was simply not possible — the holders of the outstanding bonds would have to approve the change, and it is inconceivable that they would vote for a change that would seriously weaken their position.

Debentures. A *debenture* is an unsecured bond, and as such, it has no lien against specific property as security for the obligation. Debenture holders are, therefore, general creditors whose claims are protected by property not otherwise pledged. In practice, the use of debentures depends on the nature of the firm's assets and its general credit strength. If its credit position is exceptionally strong, the firm can issue debentures—it simply does not need specific security. AT&T and IBM have both financed mainly through debentures; they are such strong corporations that they do not have to put up property as security for their debt issues. Debentures are also issued by companies in industries where it would not be practical to provide security through a mortgage on fixed assets. Examples of such industries are the large mail-order houses and commercial banks, which characteristically hold most of their assets in the form of inventory or loans, neither of which is satisfactory security for a mortgage bond. Finally, companies that have used up their capacity to borrow in the mortgage market may be forced to use debentures. These companies' debentures will be quite risky, and their interest rates will be correspondingly high.

Subordinated Debentures. The term *subordinate* means "below," or "inferior." Thus, *subordinated debt* has claims on assets in the event of bankruptcy only after senior debt has been paid off. Debentures may be subordinated either to designated notes payable—usually bank loans—or to all other debt. In the event of liquidation or reorganization, holders of subordinated debentures cannot be paid until senior debt, as named in the debentures' indenture, has been paid. The subordinated debenture of a company that has used up its ability to employ mortgage bonds is normally quite risky, and these debentures carry interest rates that are up to six percentage points above the rate on top quality debt. Precisely how subordination works, and how it strengthens the position of senior debtholders, is shown in Appendix 16A.

Other Types of Bonds. Several other types of bonds are used often enough to warrant mention. First, *convertible bonds* are securities that are convertible into shares of common stock, at a fixed price, at the option of the bondholder. Basically, convertibles provide their holders with a chance for capital gains in exchange for a lower coupon rate, while the issuing firm gets the advantage of the low coupon rate. Bonds issued with *warrants* are similar to convertibles. Warrants are options which permit the holder to buy stock for a stated price. Therefore, if the price of the stock rises, the holder of the warrant will earn a capital gain. Bonds that are issued with warrants, like convertibles, carry lower coupon rates than straight bonds. Both warrants and convertibles are discussed in detail in Chapter 18.

Income bonds pay interest only when the interest is earned. Thus, these securities cannot bankrupt a company, so from a corporation's standpoint, they are less risky than "regular" bonds. However, from an investor's standpoint, they are riskier than regular bonds. Another type of bond that has been discussed in the United States, but which has not yet been used here to any extent, is the *indexed,* or *purchasing power, bond,* which is popular in Brazil, Israel, and a few other countries long plagued by high inflation. The interest rate paid on these bonds is based on an inflation index such as the Consumer Price Index, and the interest paid rises when the inflation rate rises, thus protecting bondholders against inflation. Mexico has used bonds whose interest rate is pegged to the price of oil to finance the development of its huge petroleum reserves; since oil prices and inflation are correlated, these bonds offer some protection to investors against inflation.

Some companies may be in a position to benefit from the sale of either *development bonds* or *pollution control bonds*. State and local governments may set up both *industrial development agencies* and *pollution control agencies*. These agencies are allowed, under certain circumstances, to sell *tax-exempt bonds,* then to make the proceeds available to corporations for specific uses deemed (by Congress) to be in the public interest. Thus, an industrial development agency in Florida might sell bonds to provide funds for a paper company to build a plant in the Florida Panhandle, where unemployment is high. Similarly, a Detroit pollution control agency might sell bonds to provide Ford with funds to be used to purchase pollution control equipment. In both cases, the income from the bonds would be tax exempt to the holders, so the bonds would sell at relatively low interest rates. Note, however, that these bonds are guaranteed by the corporation that will use the funds, not by a governmental unit, so their rating reflects the credit strength of the corporation.

Self-Test Questions

Describe the primary features of the following debt instruments:

1. Term loan; bond
2. Mortgage bond; first mortgage bond; junior mortgage
3. Debenture; subordinated debenture
4. Convertible bond; bond with warrants; income bond
5. Indexed bond; development bond; pollution control bond

RECENT INNOVATIONS IN BOND FINANCING

The last decade witnessed many innovations in long-term debt financing. We will discuss seven in this section. The first three—zero coupon bonds, floating rate bonds, and bonds that are redeemable at par—are a result of the extreme volatility in interest rates which has characterized the last decade. The fourth, so called "junk bonds," gained popularity (some observers might say notoriety) as a source of takeover financing. The fifth and sixth, project financing and securitization, permit a firm to tie a debt issue to a specific asset. The final innovation, swaps, permits firms to change the nature of their debt obligations by trading with other firms.

Zero (or Very Low) Coupon Bonds

Zero (or very low) coupon bonds are offered at a substantial discount below their par values; hence, they are also called *original issue discount bonds (OIDs)*. This type of bond was first used in a major way in 1981, and in recent years IBM, Alcoa, J. C. Penney, ITT, Cities Service, GMAC, Martin-Marietta, and many other companies have used them to raise billions of dollars. We include a discussion of these securities both to illustrate how they are analyzed and also to demonstrate how quickly financial markets react to changes in the economic environment.

An example will help clarify what zero coupon bonds are and how they are analyzed. In 1990 Carson Foods issued $100 million (par value) of "zeroes." They have no coupons, pay no interest, and mature after 5 years, in 1995, at which time holders will be paid $1,000 per bond. The bonds were originally issued at a price of $571.74 per $1,000 bond. The semiannual interest rate which causes $571.74 to grow to $1,000 over 5 years (10 periods) is 5.75 percent, which is equivalent to a nominal annual return of $2 \times 5.75\% = 11.5\%$. Since most bonds pay interest semi-annually, and since people normally compare the yield on a zero with yields on "regular" bonds, it is important to calculate the zero's yield in the same manner as we would for a coupon bond—find the semiannual rate, $k_d/2$, and then multiply by 2 to obtain the nominal annual rate. Even though the effective annual rate is $(1.0575)^2 - 1.0 = 0.1183 = 11.83\%$, 11.5 percent is the rate that should be used when comparing Carson's zeroes to reported yields on semiannual coupon bonds, and 11.5 percent is the rate that would be quoted in the bond market.

Carson received about $57 million, after underwriting expenses, for the issue, but it will have to pay back $100 million in 1995. The advantages to Carson include the following: (1) No cash outlays are required for either interest or principal until the bond matures; (2) the zeroes have a relatively low yield to maturity (Carson would have had to pay approximately 12 percent rather than 11.5 percent had it issued regular coupon bonds at par); and (3) Carson receives an annual tax deduction, which means that the bonds provide a positive cash flow in the form of tax savings over their life. However, there are also two disadvantages to Carson: (1) The bond is, in effect, simply not callable; since it would have to be called at its $1,000 par value, Carson cannot refund it if interest rates should fall. (2) Carson will have a very large, nondeductible cash outlay coming due in 1995.

There are two principal advantages to investors in zero coupon bonds: (1) They have no danger whatever of a call, and (2) investors are guaranteed a "life of bond" yield (11.5 percent in the Carson case) irrespective of what happens to interest rates—the holders of Carson's bonds do not have to worry about reinvestment rate risk, which means having to reinvest coupons received at low rates if interest rates should fall, which would result in a realized yield to maturity of less than 11.5 percent.[3] This second feature is extremely important to pension funds, life insurance companies, and other institutions which make actuarial contracts based on assumed reinvestment rates. For such investors, the risk of declining interest rates, and the subsequent inability to reinvest cash inflows at the assumed rate, is greater than the risk of an increase in rates and the accompanying fall in bond values.

To illustrate, suppose an insurance company or pension fund administrator signed a contract to pay $100,000 in five years in exchange for a lump sum premium of $61,391 today. The premium was based on the assumption that the company could invest the $61,391 at a return of 10 percent. If the $61,391 were invested in regular coupon bonds paying a 10 percent coupon rate, then the accumulated value five years hence would be equal to the required $100,000 only if all coupon payments could be reinvested at 10 percent over the next five years. If interest rates

---

[3]Recently a number of municipal governments have begun using zeroes to obtain funds for low-income housing projects. However, unlike most corporate zeroes, the muni zeroes permit the issuers to pay them off in advance at a compounded amount equal to $X(1 + k)^n$, where X is the original purchase price, k is the original yield to maturity, and n is the number of periods since issue. Corporations can also issue such callable zeroes, although investors insist on higher base yields because such callability removes the main advantage of zeroes to investors.

were to fall, then the accumulated amount would fall short of the required $100,000. Note, however, that if the $61,391 were invested in a zero coupon bond with a 10 percent yield, the insurance company would be sure of ending up with the required $100,000 regardless of what happened to interest rates in the future. Thus, the insurance company or pension fund would have been "immunized" against a decline in interest rates.[4]

One might think there would be a tax advantage to investors in zero coupon bonds in that income would come in the form of capital gains rather than interest income, hence be taxed at maturity, but this is not true in the United States. The IRS has ruled that original-issue discounts must be amortized and treated as ordinary income. Further, all zero coupon bonds must be registered, and the issuing corporation must send both the registered owner and the IRS a Form 1099 each year indicating the amount of the amortized discount. However, according to investment bankers who have handled the underwritings, this is not a material issue, because taxable zeroes have been sold exclusively to tax-exempt organizations, principally pension funds and Individual Retirement Plans (IRAs).[5] Yet, since pension funds are by far the largest purchasers of corporate bonds, the potential market for zero coupon bonds is by no means small.

To analyze a zero coupon bond and to compare it with a coupon bond, a corporate treasurer (or pension fund administrator) must employ the valuation models developed in Chapter 7. Consider again Carson's bonds. Someone buying Carson's zeroes would pay $571.74 per bond at t = 0 and receive $1,000 at the end of ten semiannual periods. The periodic interest rate is 5.749943 percent, the rate that causes $571.74 to grow to $1,000 over 10 periods as found with a financial calculator. Table 16-1 shows how interest charges associated with the bond are calculated. The values shown in Column 3 will be reported to the IRS by Carson for each bondholder, and the bondholders (if they pay taxes) must declare these amounts as income, even though they receive no cash each year. Carson, on the other hand, can deduct the amounts shown in Column 3, calling them "amortization of discount on bonds." Note particularly that the discount is not amortized using the straight line method; rather, amortization is calculated on the basis of the compound interest method. The periodic amortization is tax deductible, hence will save Carson T(Amortization) = 0.34(Amortization) in taxes each six months. These savings are shown in Column 4 of Table 16-1.

Thus, Carson received $571.74 at Period 0; it must repay $1,000 after 5 years (Period 10); and it receives tax benefits during the interim. The after-tax cash flows look like this:

---

[4]The best way to measure a bond's sensitivity to interest rate changes is by its *duration*, which is a measure of the "average date" that a bondholder will receive cash flows (interest and principal) on the bond. A zero coupon bond, with only one cash inflow, has a duration equal to its maturity, while a coupon bond has a duration that is less than its maturity. For a complete discussion of duration and its usefulness in immunization, see Jimmy Hilliard and Joseph F. Sinkey, Jr., "Duration Analysis as a Tool for Predicting Interest-Sensitive Cash Flows," *Journal of Financial Education,* Fall 1989, 1–7.

[5]This statement refers to sales within the United States. There was also a strong market for zero coupon bonds issued by U.S. companies in Europe and the Far East, especially in Japan, where the appreciation of the bonds was treated as capital gains income rather than as interest income. Japan subsequently modified its tax laws and now treats the amortized discount as interest.

Period	After-Tax Cash Flows
0	$571.74
1	11.18
2	11.82
3	12.50
4	13.22
5	13.98
6	14.78
7	15.63
8	16.53
9	17.48
10	$18.49 - 1,000 = -981.51$

The internal rate of return (IRR) of the above cash flow stream is the after-tax periodic cost of the zero coupon bond. This rate, $k_d/2$, is 3.795 percent, so the after-tax cost of the issue is 2(3.795%) = 7.59%.

If Carson had sold a semiannual payment coupon bond, its pre-tax cost would have been 12 percent. Its after-tax interest payments would have been (Coupon/2) $(1 - T) = (\$120/2)(0.66) = \$39.60$, and its after-tax cost of debt would have been $k_d = 12\%(1 - T) = 7.92\%$. Thus, on an after-tax basis, the zero coupon bond has a lower cost to Carson than would a regular coupon bond, 7.59 percent for the zero

Table 16-1 Calculation of Zero Coupon Bond Interest

Semiannual Period (1)	Beginning Investment Value (2)	Calculated Interest (3)	Tax Savings (4)
1	$571.74	$32.87	$11.18
2	604.61	34.77	11.82
3	639.38	36.76	12.50
4	676.14	38.88	13.22
5	715.02	41.11	13.98
6	756.13	43.48	14.78
7	799.61	45.98	15.63
8	845.59	48.62	16.53
9	894.21	51.42	17.48
10	945.63	54.37	18.49
		$428.26	$145.61

Notes:
a. The periodic interest rate is 5.749943 percent.
b. The amounts shown in Column 3 are found by multiplying the beginning investment value shown in Column 2 times 0.05749943.
c. The investment value shown in Column 2 is the previous period's investment value plus interest, Column 2 plus Column 3.
d. The sum of Column 3, $428.26, is the total calculated interest, and $428.26 + $571.74 = $1,000.00.
e. The tax savings shown in Column 4 is the interest, or amortization, charge multiplied by Carson's marginal tax rate of 34 percent.

versus 7.92 percent for the coupon bond.[6] For a purchaser, of course, the reverse is true. A tax-exempt bond buyer would receive the yield to maturity, which is 11.5 percent for the zero coupon bond and 12.0 percent for the coupon bond. Purchasers apparently believed that call protection plus the interest rate immunization were worth the 0.5 percentage point cost.

In 1983, several brokerage houses introduced a new security based on separating, or "stripping," the interest coupons from the principal amount of a Treasury bond. Merrill Lynch first introduced the concept with its Treasury Investment Growth Receipts (TIGRs, or "tigers"). To back its first TIGRs, Merrill Lynch bought $500 million face value of 30-year Treasury bonds, which it placed in trust. Then, Merrill Lynch in effect stripped off the coupons that mature each six months over the next 30 years, and used the $2 \times 30 = 60$ sets of coupons to back 60 series of TIGRs that mature at six-month intervals, on the dates the coupon payments on the Treasury bonds come due. The investor receives nothing until the maturity date he or she selects, be it six months or 30 years away. Sold at a discount, the TIGR is redeemed at face value at maturity—the more distant the maturity, the deeper the discount. Thus, with the introduction of TIGRs, insurance companies and pension funds were offered a default-free substitute for zero coupon corporate bonds, and thus far, the substitute has been more attractive to investors than the original product.

Floating (or Adjustable) Rate Debt

In the late 1970s and early 1980s, inflation pushed interest rates up to unprecedented levels. These rising interest rates caused sharp declines in the prices of long-term bonds. Even supposedly "risk-free" U.S. Treasury bonds lost fully half their value, and a similar situation occurred with corporate bonds, mortgages, and other fixed rate, long-term securities. The lenders who held the fixed rate debt were of course hurt very badly. Bankruptcies (or forced mergers to avoid bankruptcy) were commonplace in the banking and especially in the savings and loan industries. Pension fund asset values declined, requiring corporations to increase contributions to their plans, which in turn hurt profits. The value of insurance company reserves plummeted, causing those companies severe problems, including the bankruptcy of Baldwin-United, a $9 billion diversified insurance firm.

As a result of all this, many lenders became extremely reluctant to lend money at fixed rates on a long-term basis, and they would do so only at high rates. There is normally a *maturity risk premium* embodied in long-term interest rates—this is a risk premium designed to offset the risk of declining bond prices if interest rates rise. Prior to the 1970s, this maturity risk premium is estimated to have been about one percentage point, meaning that, under "normal" conditions, a firm might expect to pay about one percentage point more to borrow on a long-term basis than on a short-term basis. However, in the late 1970s and early 1980s, the maturity risk pre-

---

[6]Note that the compound interest method of amortization used on original issue discount bonds results in an after-tax cost to the issuer which is equal to the after-tax cost of a coupon bond with the same yield to maturity. A coupon bond with an 11.5 percent YTM has an after-tax cost of 0.66(11.5%) = 7.59%, which is the same as we calculated by examining the actual cash flows.

mium is estimated to have jumped to about three percentage points. This made long-term debt very expensive relative to short-term debt.

Lenders were able and willing to lend on a short-term basis, but corporations were rightly reluctant to borrow short-term to finance long-term assets — this is, as we shall see in Chapter 19, extremely dangerous. Therefore, we had a situation where lenders did not want to lend on a long-term basis, but corporations had a need for long-term money. The problem was solved by the introduction of long-term, floating rate debt. A typical floating rate issue works like this: The coupon rate is set for, say, the first six months after issue, after which it is adjusted every six months on the basis of some market rate. For example, Gulf Oil recently sold a floating rate bond that was pegged at 35 basis points above the rate on 30-year Treasury bonds. Other issues are tied to short-term rates. Additional provisions have been included in floating rate issues; for example, some may, after several years, be converted to fixed rate debt, whereas others have a stated cap on how high the rate can go, or a stated floor on how low the rate can go. A provision that includes both a cap and a floor is called a "collar."

Floating rate debt is advantageous to lenders because (1) the market value of the debt is stabilized and (2) the lender receives an income level which permits it to meet its own obligations (for example, a bank which owns floating rate bonds can use the interest it earns to pay interest on its own floating rate deposits). Floating rate debt is also advantageous to borrowing corporations because, with this security, they can obtain debt with a long maturity yet not have to continue paying high rates if rates fall in the future. Of course, if interest rates increase after a floating rate note has been signed, then the borrower would have been better off issuing conventional, fixed-rate debt.[7]

Bonds That Are Redeemable at Par

Bonds that are *redeemable at par* at the holder's option also protect the holder against a rise in interest rates. If rates rise, the price of fixed-rate debt declines. However, if the holders have the option of turning their bonds in and having them redeemed at par, they are protected against rising rates. Examples of such debt include Transamerica's $50 million issue of 25-year, 8½ percent bonds. The bonds are not callable by the company, but holders can turn them in for redemption at par five years after the date of issue. If interest rates have risen, holders will turn in the bonds and reinvest the proceeds at a higher rate. This feature enabled Transamerica to sell the bonds with an 8½ percent coupon at a time when other similarly rated bonds had yields of 9 percent.

In late 1988, the corporate bond markets were sent into turmoil by a leveraged buyout of RJR Nabisco. RJR's bonds dropped in value by 20 percent within days of the LBO announcement, and the prices of many industrial corporate bonds also plunged, because investors feared that a boom in LBOs would load up many companies with excessive debt, leading to lower bond ratings and declining bond prices. All this led to a resurgence of concern about *event risk*, which is the risk that some

---

[7]For a general discussion of floating rate debt, see Kenneth R. Marks and Warren A. Law, "Hedging against Inflation with Floating-Rate Notes," *Harvard Business Review,* March-April 1980, 106–112.

sudden action, such as an LBO, will occur and increase the credit risk of the company, hence lower the firm's bond rating and the value of its outstanding bonds. Investors' concern over event risk meant that those firms deemed most likely to face events that could harm bondholders suddenly had to pay dearly to raise new debt capital, if they could raise it at all. In an attempt to control debt costs, a new type of protective covenant devised to minimize event risk was developed. This covenant, called a *super poison put,* enables a bondholder to turn in, or "put" a bond back to the issuer at par in the event of a takeover, merger, or major recapitalization.

Poison puts had actually been around since 1986, when the leveraged buyout trend took off. However, the earlier puts proved to be almost worthless because they allowed investors to "put" their bonds back to the issuer at par value only in the event of an *unfriendly* takeover, but almost all takeovers were eventually approved by the target firm's board, hence what started as a hostile takeover generally ended up as a friendly takeover. Also, the earlier poison puts failed to protect investors from voluntary recapitalizations, in which a company loads up on debt to pay a big, one-time dividend to stockholders or to buy back its own stock. The "super" poison puts that were used following the RJR buyout announcement protected against both of these actions. It is too early to say whether super poison puts are here to stay, but their use does provide a good illustration of how quickly the financial community reacts to changes in the marketplace.

Junk Bonds

A *junk bond* is a high-risk, high-yield bond.[8] There are two types of junk bonds: (1) Bonds that were originally sound, but which became high-risk when the issuer got into financial trouble after the bond was issued. These bonds, called "fallen angels," generally have "reasonable" coupons but sell at deep discounts and thus have high yields to maturity to reflect their now-high risk. (2) Bonds that were quite risky at the time of issue. These bonds are almost always debentures, are generally subordinated to other debt, and are either issued to finance a leveraged buyout or a merger, or are issued by a company that is in deep trouble. Thus, the bonds KKR issued to finance the RJR buyout were junk bonds, and RJR's outstanding bonds were transformed from investment-grade bonds to junk bonds (fallen angels) by the LBO.

In all new issue junk bond deals, the debt ratio is extremely high, so the bondholders must bear as much risk as stockholders normally would. The bonds' yields reflect this fact—the yields on RJR's bonds rose from about 9.5 percent to about 12 percent in a matter of days as a result of the buyout.

The emergence of junk bonds as an important type of new debt is another example of the way the investment banking industry adjusts to—and facilitates—new developments in capital markets. In the 1980s, mergers and takeovers increased dramatically. People like T. Boone Pickens and Ted Turner thought that certain old-line, established companies were financed too conservatively and were run ineffi-

---

[8]For an excellent discussion of junk bonds, see Kevin J. Perry and Robert A. Taggart, Jr., "The Growing Role of Junk Bonds in Corporate Finance," *Journal of Applied Corporate Finance,* Spring 1988, 37–45. This section draws heavily from their work.

ciently, and they wanted to take over these companies and restructure them. To help finance these takeovers, the investment banking firm of Drexel Burnham Lambert had the idea of persuading certain institutions to purchase high-yield bonds. Drexel developed expertise in putting together deals that would be attractive to the institutions yet feasible in the sense that cash flow projections indicated that the issuing firms could meet their required interest payments. The fact that interest on the bonds is tax deductible, combined with the much higher debt ratios of the restructured firms, also increased after-tax cash flows and helped make the whole deal feasible.

Do junk bonds have a role in corporate finance aside from takeovers and LBOs? In Chapter 12, we discussed the asymmetric information theory of capital structure, which implies that companies should first use retained earnings plus debt supported by retained earnings, then use "reserve borrowing capacity" debt, and only issue new common stock as a last resort, after all the debt capacity has been exhausted. The development of the junk bond market has effectively extended the limits of firms' debt capacities beyond the earlier limits, and as a result, in spite of all the publicity surrounding the use of junk bonds in mergers and acquisitions, statistics show that well over half of the junk bond issues in recent years have been used for normal expansion purposes.

The phenomenal growth of the junk bond market has been impressive, but controversial. In early 1989, Drexel Burnham Lambert, the leading junk bond investment banker, agreed to pay a $650 million fine for various securities law violations. The firm also agreed to fire "junk bond king" Michael Milken, the true developer of the market, and to withhold his 1988 bonus, said to exceed $200 million. Further, a grand jury indicted Mr. Milken on charges of fraud, and in April 1990 he agreed to a settlement that included $600 million in fines and penalties. These events badly tarnished the junk bond market, which had already come under severe criticism, rightly or wrongly, for improperly fueling the takeover fires. Additionally, the realization that high leverage can spell trouble—as when Campeau, with $3 billion in junk financing, filed for bankruptcy in early 1990—has slowed the growth in the junk bond market.

The final blow came when Drexel Burnham Lambert declared bankruptcy in 1990 and promptly began liquidation. The bankruptcy (1) removed the leading dealer from the market and thus drastically reduced the liquidity of junk bonds and (2) created an instant oversupply as Drexel attempted to unload its inventory on the market. The final verdict on junk bonds is not yet in, but it appears that junk bonds will play a much smaller role in corporate financings in the 1990s than they did in the 1980s.

Project Financing

In recent years, many large projects such as the Alaska pipeline have been financed by what is called *project financing*.[9] We can only present an overview of the concept, for in practice it involves very complicated provisions and can take many forms.

---

[9]For an excellent discussion of project financing, see John W. Kensinger and John D. Martin, "Project Finance: Raising Money the Old-Fashioned Way," *Journal of Applied Corporate Finance,* Fall 1988, 69–81.

Project financing has been used to finance energy explorations, oil tankers, refineries, and utility power plants. Generally, one or more firms will sponsor the project, putting up the required equity capital, while the remainder of the financing is furnished by lenders or lessors.[10] Most often, a separate legal entity is formed to operate the project. The single most important feature of project financing is that normally the project's creditors do not have full recourse against the sponsors. In other words, the lenders and lessors must be paid from the project's cash flows, plus the sponsors' equity in the project, for the creditors have no claims against the sponsors' other assets or cash flows. Often the sponsors write "comfort" letters, giving general assurances that they will strive diligently to make the project successful, but these letters are not legally binding and therefore represent only a moral commitment. Therefore, in project financing the lenders and lessors must focus their analysis on the inherent merits of the project plus the equity cushion provided by the sponsors.[11]

Project financing is not a new development. Indeed, back in 1299, the English Crown negotiated a loan with Florentine merchant bankers that was repaid with one year's output from the Devon silver mines. Essentially, the Italians were allowed to operate the mines for one year, paying all the operating costs and mining as much ore as they could. The Crown made no guarantees as to how much ore could be mined, or the value of the refined silver. A more current example involved GE Capital, the credit arm of General Electric, which recently arranged a $72 million project financing to build an aluminum can plant. The plant is owned by several beverage makers, but it is operated independently, and GE Capital must depend on the cash flows from the plant to repay the loan. About half of all project financings in recent years have been for electric generating plants, including both plants owned by electric utilities and cogeneration plants operated by industrial companies. Project financings are generally characterized by large size and a high degree of complexity. However, since project financing is tied to a specific project, it can be tailored to meet the specific needs of both the creditors and the sponsors. In particular, the financing can be structured so that both the funds provided during the construction phase and the subsequent repayments match the timing of the project's projected cash outflows and inflows.

Project financing offers several potential benefits over conventional debt financing. For one, project financing usually restricts the usage of the project's cash flows, which means that the lenders, rather than the managers, can decide whether to reinvest excess cash flows or to use them to reduce the loan balance by more than

---

[10]A lessor is an individual or firm that owns buildings and equipment and then leases them to another firm. Leasing is discussed in Chapter 17.

[11]In another type of project financing, each sponsor guarantees its share of the project's debt obligations. Here the creditors would also consider the creditworthiness of the sponsors in addition to the project's own prospects. It should be noted that project financing with multiple sponsors in the electric utility industry has led to problems when one or more of the sponsors has gotten into financial trouble. For example, Long Island Lighting, one of the sponsors in the Nine Mile Point nuclear project, became unable to meet its commitments to the project, which forced other sponsors to shoulder an additional burden or else see the project cancelled and lose all their investment up to that point. Utility executives have stated that this default, and others, will make companies reluctant to enter into similar projects in the future.

the minimum required. Conferring this power on the lenders reduces their risks. Project financings also have advantages for borrowers. First, because risks to the lenders are reduced, the interest rate built into a project financing deal may be relatively low. Second, since suppliers of project financing capital have no recourse against the sponsoring firms' other assets and cash flows, project financings insulate the firm's other assets from risks associated with the project being financed. Managers may be more willing to take on a very large, risky project if they know that the company's existence would not be threatened if it fails.

Project financings increase the number and type of investment opportunities, hence they make capital markets "more complete." At the same time, project financings reduce the costs to investors of obtaining information and monitoring the borrower's operations. To illustrate, consider an oil and gas exploration project that is funded using project financing. If the project were financed as an integral part of the firm's normal operations, investors in all the firm's outstanding securities would need information on the project. By isolating the project, the need for information is confined to the investors in the project financing, and they need to monitor only the project's operations, and not those of the entire firm.

Project financings also permit firms whose earnings are below the minimum requirements specified in their existing bond indentures to obtain additional debt financing. In such situations, lenders look only at the merits of the new project, and its cash flows may support additional debt even though the firm's existing assets would not. Project financings also permit managers to reveal proprietary information to a smaller group of investors, hence project financings increase the ability of a firm to maintain confidentiality. Finally, project financings can improve incentives for key managers by enabling them to take direct ownership stakes in the operations under their control. By establishing separate projects, companies can provide incentives that are much more directly based upon individual performance than is typically possible within a large corporation.

Securitization

As the term is generally used, a *security* refers to a publicly traded financial instrument, as opposed to a privately placed instrument. Thus, securities have greater liquidity than otherwise similar instruments that are not traded in an open market. In recent years, procedures have been developed to *securitize* various types of debt instruments, thus increasing their liquidity, lowering the cost of capital to borrowers, and generally increasing the efficiency of the financial markets.[12]

Securitization has occurred in two major ways. First, some debt instruments that were formerly never traded in a broad market are now widely traded, with the change being due to decisions by certain financial institutions to "make a market," which means to stand willing to buy or sell the security, and to hold an inventory of the security in order to balance buy and sell orders. This occurred many years ago in the case of common stocks and investment-grade bonds. More recently, it

---

[12]The Fall 1988 issue of the *Journal of Applied Corporate Finance* is devoted to securitization. For additional discussion, see any of its excellent articles.

occurred in the commercial paper market, in which large, financially strong firms issue short-term, unsecured debt in lieu of obtaining bank loans. The commercial paper market has grown from about $50 billion outstanding in the mid-1970s to over $350 billion today, and this market permits borrowers to finance working capital needs at lower cost than bank loans.

Another example of securitization is the junk bond market. Before this market developed, firms with high credit risk were forced to obtain debt financing on a private placement basis, typically supplied by the firm's commercial bank. It was difficult for firms to shop around for the best rate, because lenders who were not familiar with them were unwilling to spend the time and money necessary to determine the feasibility of the loan, and lenders were also reluctant (and hence charged a higher rate) because of the illiquidity of privately placed debt. Then, Michael Milken developed procedures for analyzing the repayment feasibility of junk bonds, and Drexel Burnham Lambert put its reputation and credibility behind these issues and made a market for them in case a purchaser needed to cash out. Subsequently, Morgan Stanley, Merrill Lynch, Salomon Brothers, and the other major investment bankers entered the junk bond market, and today it has "securitized" much of the old private placement market for below-investment-grade debt.

The second major development in securitization involves the pledging of specific assets, *asset securitization,* or the creation of *asset-backed securities.* The oldest type of asset securitization is the mortgage-backed security. Here, individual home mortgages are combined into pools, and then securities are created which use the pool of mortgages as collateral. The financial institution that originated the mortgage generally continues to act as collection agent, but the mortgage itself is sold to other investors. The securitization of mortgages has created a national mortgage market with many players, hence it has benefited borrowers. The development has also benefited lenders, for the original lending institution, often a savings and loan, no longer owns the relatively long-term mortgage, hence it is better able to match the maturity of its assets (loans) with its liabilities (savings accounts and certificates of deposit). Today, many different types of assets are being used as collateral for securitization, including auto loans and accounts receivable.

The asset securitization process involves the pooling and repackaging of loans secured by relatively homogeneous, small-dollar assets into liquid securities. In the past, such financing was provided by a single lending institution, which would write the loan, structure the terms, absorb the credit and interest rate risk, provide the capital, and service the collections. Under securitization, several different institutions are involved, with each playing a different functional role. A savings and loan might originate the loan, an investment banker might pool the loans and structure the security, a federal agency might insure against credit risk, a second investment banker might sell the securities, and a pension fund might be the investor which supplies the final capital.

The process of securitization has, in general, lowered costs and increased the availability of funds to borrowers, decreased risks to lenders, and created new investment opportunities for many investors. With these potential benefits, we predict that securitization will continue to expand in the future.

Swaps

As its name implies, a *swap* is an exchange.[13] In finance, a swap is an exchange of cash payment obligations, in which each party to the swap, often called a "counterparty," prefers the payment type or pattern of the other party. In other words, swaps occur because the parties involved prefer the terms of someone else's debt contract, and the swap enables each party to obtain a better payment obligation. Generally, one party has a fixed rate obligation and the other a floating rate obligation, or one obligation is denominated in one currency and the other in another currency.

The earliest swaps were *currency swaps,* in which one company, say, with a debt obligation in British pounds, trades its interest payment obligation with another company that had dollar-denominated debt. To illustrate, suppose a U.S. firm is expanding into England. It might prefer to issue debt denominated in pounds to fund the venture—this would remove any currency risk, since the cash flows generated by the project and available to service the debt would be in pounds. However, the firm may not be well known in England, and thus it might have trouble placing debt there at a reasonable cost because of the time and effort English lenders would have to expend to gather the necessary credit information. In this case, it might be cheaper for the firm to issue debt denominated in dollars in the United States to fund the British effort, and then to arrange a currency swap. In the swap, the U.S. firm would agree to make interest payments in pounds to a counterparty who, in return, would agree to pay the firm a series of interest payments in dollars, which would then be used to service the original dollar-denominated debt. The firm would, in effect, have converted dollar-denominated debt to pound-denominated debt, and the exchange rate risk would have been removed, because the source of the cash flows for the interest payments would be the firm's British operation, whose cash flows would be denominated in pounds. If the firm had not engaged in the swap, then the pounds generated by the British operation would have to be converted to dollars to make the interest payments to the U.S. bondholders, and a change in the exchange rate could increase the effective cost of the debt, and perhaps render the entire operation unprofitable. The motivation for the counterparty would be similar, but a mirror image of the first party; for example, the counterparty might be a British firm expanding into the United States.

The earliest currency swaps were custom-tailored products which involved matching two firms that wanted to trade a given principal amount of debt denominated in two different currencies. The swaps were typically arranged by a financial intermediary, usually a commercial or investment banker, and a great deal of time was spent matching the counterparties and developing terms that were mutually agreeable to the participants. The intermediaries themselves typically were not counterparties in the early deals—they merely arranged the swap and were paid a fee for their efforts. However, the swap market has evolved considerably over the last

---

[13]For more information on swaps, see Clifford W. Smith, Jr., Charles W. Smithson, and Lee Macdonald Wakeman, "The Evolving Market for Swaps," *Midland Corporate Finance Journal,* Winter 1986, 20–32; and Mary E. Ruth and Steve R. Vinson, "Managing Interest Rate Uncertainty Amidst Change," *Public Utilities Fortnightly,* December 22, 1988, 28–31.

decade, and now there are several different types of swaps. In addition to currency swaps, some of the more common types are (1) interest rate swaps, in which the counterparties trade fixed-rate debt for floating-rate debt; (2) basis rate swaps, in which the counterparties both hold floating-rate debt, but the basis differs, say, with one being tied to the T-bill rate and the other tied to the commercial paper rate; and (3) timing swaps, where, for example, one party would trade a stream of quarterly payments to a counterparty which makes annual payments.

Other major changes have occurred in the swaps market. First, standardized contracts have been developed for the most common types of swaps, and this had two effects: (1) Standardized contracts lower the time and effort involved in arranging swaps, and thus lower transactions costs. (2) The development of standardized contracts has led to a secondary market for swaps, which increased the liquidity and efficiency of the swaps market. Thus, swaps are becoming a commodity-type item, and a number of international banks now make markets in swaps and offer quotes on several standard types. Finally, the intermediaries now take counterparty positions in swaps, and thus it is not necessary to find another firm with matching needs before a swap transaction can be completed. The intermediary would generally find a final counterparty for the swap at a later date, so intermediary positioning helps make the swap market more operationally efficient.

To further illustrate a swap transaction, consider the following situation. An electric utility currently has outstanding a 5-year floating rate note tied to the prime rate. The prime rate could rise significantly over the period, so the note carries a high degree of interest rate risk to the utility. The utility could, however, enter into a swap with a counterparty, say Citibank, wherein the utility would pay Citibank a fixed series of interest payments over the 5-year period, and Citibank would make the company's required floating rate payments. As a result, the utility would have converted a floating rate loan to a fixed rate loan, and the risk of rising interest rates would have been passed from the utility to Citibank. Note, though, that a bank's income tends to rise as interest rates rise, so Citibank's risk is actually lower if it has floating as opposed to fixed rate obligations.

Longer-term swaps can also be made. Recently, Citibank entered into a 17-year swap in an electricity cogeneration project financing deal. The project's sponsors were unable to obtain fixed rate financing on reasonable terms, and they were afraid that interest rates might rise to the point where the project would be unprofitable. The project's sponsors were, however, able to borrow from local banks on a floating rate basis and to arrange a simultaneous swap with Citibank for a fixed rate obligation.

Self-Test Questions

What are zero coupon bonds? What are their advantages and disadvantages for issuers and purchasers?

What is the difference between fixed rate and floating rate debt? What are the advantages and disadvantages of floating rate debt for issuers and purchasers?

What are super poison puts, and how do they lower event risk?

Briefly describe the characteristics and role of junk bonds.

What is project financing? What are its advantages and disadvantages?

What is meant by securitization? What are the advantages of securitization to borrowers? What are the advantages to lenders?

What is a swap? Briefly describe the mechanics of (1) a fixed rate to floating rate swap and (2) a currency swap.

DEBT CONTRACT PROVISIONS

A firm's managers are most concerned about (1) the effective cost of debt and (2) any provisions which might restrict the firm's future actions. In this section, we discuss features which could affect either the cost of the firm's debt or its future flexibility.

Bond Indentures

An *indenture* is a legal document that spells out the rights of both bondholders and the issuing corporation, and a *trustee* is an official (usually of a bank) who represents the bondholders and makes sure that the terms of the indenture are carried out. The indenture may be several hundred pages in length, and it will include *restrictive covenants* that cover such points as the conditions under which the issuer can pay off the bonds prior to maturity, the level at which the issuer's times-interest-earned ratio must be maintained if the company is to issue additional debt, and restrictions against the payment of dividends unless earnings meet certain specifications. Overall, these covenants relate to the agency problem first discussed in Chapter 1, and they are designed to insure, insofar as possible, that the firm does not change its financial policies in a way that would cause the quality of its bonds to deteriorate after they have been issued.

The trustee is responsible for trying to keep the covenants from being violated and for taking appropriate action if a violation does occur. What constitutes "appropriate action" varies with the circumstances. It might be that to insist on immediate compliance would result in bankruptcy and possibly large losses on the bonds. In such a case, the trustee might decide that the bondholders would be better served by giving the company a chance to work out its problems and thus avoid forcing it into bankruptcy.

The Securities and Exchange Commission (1) approves indentures and (2) makes sure that all indenture provisions are met before allowing a company to sell new securities to the public. Also, it should be noted that the indentures of most larger corporations were actually written in the 1930s or 1940s, and that many issues of new bonds sold since then were covered by the same indenture. The interest rates on the bonds, and perhaps also the maturities, varied depending on market conditions at the time of each issue, but bondholders' protection as spelled out in the indenture was the same for all bonds of the same type.[14]

Call Provisions

A *call provision* gives the issuing corporation the right to call a bond (or preferred stock) for redemption. If it is used, the call provision generally states that the company must pay an amount greater than the par value for the bond. The additional sum required, defined as the *call premium,* is typically set equal to one year's interest if the bond is called during the first year, with the premium declining at a constant rate of I/n each year thereafter, where I = annual interest and n = original maturity in years. For example, the call premium on a $1,000 par value, 20-year, 10 percent bond would generally be $100 if it were called during the first year, $95 during the second year (calculated by reducing the $100, or 10 percent, premium by one-twentieth), and so on.

The call privilege is valuable to the firm but potentially detrimental to the investor, especially if the bond is issued in a period when interest rates are cyclically high. This point was illustrated in Chapter 7, and it causes the interest rate on a new issue of callable bonds to exceed that on a new issue of noncallable bonds. For example, on February 1, 1990, Great Falls Timber Company sold an issue of A-rated bonds to yield 10.375 percent. These bonds were callable immediately. On the same day, Midwest Milling Company sold an issue of A-rated bonds to yield 10 percent. Midwest's bonds were noncallable for 10 years. (This is known as a *deferred call.*) Investors were apparently willing to accept a 0.375 percent lower interest rate on Midwest's bonds for the assurance that the relatively high (by historical standards) rate of interest would be earned for at least 10 years. Great Falls, on the other hand, had to incur a 0.375 percent higher annual interest rate to obtain the option of calling the bonds in the event of a subsequent decline in interest rates. We discuss the analysis for determining when to call an issue in Appendix 16B.

Sinking Funds

A *sinking fund* is a provision that provides for the systematic retirement of a bond issue (or an issue of preferred stock). Typically, the sinking fund provision requires a firm to call and retire a portion of its bonds each year. On some occasions, the firm may be required to deposit money with a trustee, who invests the funds and then uses the accumulated sum to retire the entire bond issue when it matures. Sometimes the stipulated sinking fund payment is tied to the sales or earnings of the current year, but usually it is a mandatory fixed amount. If it is mandatory, a failure to meet the sinking fund requirement causes the bond issue to be thrown into default, which may force the company into bankruptcy.

In most cases, the firm is given the right to handle the sinking fund in either of two ways:

---

[14]A firm will have different indentures for each of the major types of bonds it issues. For example, one indenture will cover its first mortgage bonds, another its debentures, and a third its convertible bonds.

1. It may call in for redemption (at par value) a certain percentage of the bonds each year—for example, it might be able to call 2 percent of the total original amount of the issue at a price of $1,000 per bond. The bonds are numbered serially, and the ones called for redemption are determined by a lottery. (For bonds issued in denominations of $100,000 or more, the specified percentage of the holder's par value is called.)

2. It may buy the required amount of bonds on the open market.

The firm will choose the least cost method. Therefore, if interest rates have risen, causing bond prices to fall, the company will elect to use the option of buying bonds in the open market at a discount. Otherwise, it will call them. Note that a call for sinking fund purposes is quite different from a refunding call. A sinking fund call requires no call premium, but only a small percentage of the issue is callable in any one year.

Although the sinking fund is designed to protect the bondholders by assuring that the issue is retired in an orderly fashion, it must be recognized that the sinking fund may at times work to the detriment of bondholders. If, for example, the bond carries a 13 percent interest rate, and if yields on similar securities have fallen to 9 percent, then the bond will sell above par. A sinking fund call at par would thus greatly disadvantage those bondholders whose bonds were called. On balance, however, securities that provide for a sinking fund and continuing redemption are regarded as being safer than bonds without sinking funds, so adding a sinking fund provision to a bond issue will lower the interest rate on the bond.

Self-Test Questions

What is a bond indenture? A restrictive covenant?

What is a call provision? What impact does a call provision have on an issue's required rate of return?

What is a sinking fund? How are bonds retired for sinking fund purposes? What impact does a sinking fund have on an issue's required rate of return? How do sinking funds differ from call provisions?

BOND RATINGS

Since the early 1900s, bonds have been assigned quality ratings that reflect their probability of going into default. The two major rating agencies are Moody's Investors Service (Moody's) and Standard & Poor's Corporation (S&P). These agencies' rating designations are shown in Table 16-2.[15]

The triple and double A bonds are extremely safe. Single A and triple B bonds are strong enough to be called "investment grade," and they are the lowest rated

---

[15]In the discussion to follow, reference to the S&P code is intended to imply the Moody's code as well. Thus, for example, triple B bonds means both BBB and Baa bonds; double B bonds, both BB and Ba bonds.

Table 16-2   Comparison of Bond Ratings

	High Quality		Investment Grade		Substandard		Speculative		
Moody's	Aaa	Aa	A	Baa	Ba	B	Caa	to	C
S&P	AAA	AA	A	BBB	BB	B	CCC	to	D

Note: Both Moody's and S&P use "modifiers" for bonds rated below triple A. S&P uses a plus and minus system; thus, A+ designates the strongest A rated bonds and A− the weakest. Moody's uses a 1, 2, or 3 designation, with 1 denoting the strongest and 3 the weakest; thus, within the double A category, Aa1 is the best, Aa2 is average, and Aa3 is the weakest. Triple A bonds have no modifiers in either system.

bonds that many banks and other institutional investors are permitted by law to hold. Double B and lower bonds are speculations; they are junk bonds with a fairly high probability of going into default, and many financial institutions are prohibited from buying them.

Bond Rating Criteria

Although the rating assignments are subjective, they are based on both qualitative characteristics such as "quality of management" and quantitative factors such as the debt ratio, the coverage ratio, and so forth. Analysts at the rating agencies have consistently stated that no precise formula is used to set a firm's rating—many factors are taken into account, but not in a mathematically precise manner. Statistical studies have borne out this contention. Researchers who have tried to predict bond ratings on the basis of quantitative data have had only limited success, indicating that the agencies do indeed use a good deal of subjective judgment to establish a firm's rating.[16]

Importance of Bond Ratings

Bond ratings are important both to firms and to investors. First, a bond's rating is an indicator of its risk, so the rating has a direct, measurable influence on the bond's interest rate and the firm's cost of debt capital. Second, most bonds are purchased by institutional investors, not by individuals, and many of these institutions are restricted to investment-grade securities. Thus, if a firm's bonds fall below BBB, it will have a harder time trying to sell new bonds, since many potential purchasers will not be allowed to buy them.

As a result of their higher risk and more restricted market, lower-grade bonds have much higher required rates of return, k_d, than do high-grade bonds. This point

---

[16]See Robert S. Kaplan and Gabriel Urwitz, "Statistical Models of Bond Ratings: A Methodological Inquiry," *Journal of Business,* April 1979, 231–261; and Ahmed Belkaoui, *Industrial Bonds and the Rating Process* (London: Quorum Books, 1983).

is highlighted in Figure 16-1, which gives the yields on three types of bonds, and the risk premiums for AAA and BBB bonds, in June 1963, in June 1975, and again in April 1989.[17] Note first that the riskless rate, or vertical axis intercept, rose 5.17 percentage points from 1963 to 1989, reflecting the increase in realized and anticipated inflation. Second, the slope of the line also rose, indicating increased investor risk aversion from 1963 to 1989, but risk aversion declined from 1975 to 1989. Thus, the penalty for having a low credit rating varies over time. Occasionally, as in 1963, it is not too severe, but at other times, as in 1975, it is quite large.[18]

Changes in Ratings

A change in a firm's bond rating will have a significant effect on its ability to borrow long-term capital, and on the cost of that capital. Rating agencies review outstanding bonds on a periodic basis, occasionally upgrading or downgrading a bond as a result of its issuer's changed circumstances. Also, an announcement that a company plans to sell a new debt issue, or to merge with another company and to pay for the acquisition by exchanging bonds for the stock of the acquired company, will trigger an agency review and possibly lead to a rating change. For example, in January 1989, when Texaco and financier Carl Icahn reached an agreement which precluded him from making a bid for Texaco, S&P placed Texaco's bonds on "CreditWatch" with "positive implications." CreditWatch is an S&P publication which lists bonds that it is actively reviewing for a possible rating change in response to some development, and investors are warned that the rating may be changed upon completion of the review. CreditWatch listings are published in *The Wall Street Journal,* and the pub-

---

[17]The term *risk premium* ought to reflect only the difference in the expected (and required) returns between two securities that results from differences in their risk. However, the difference between *yields to maturity* on different types of bonds consists of (1) a true risk premium; (2) a liquidity premium, which reflects the fact that U.S. Treasury bonds are more readily marketable than most corporate bonds; (3) a call premium, because most Treasury bonds are not callable, while corporate bonds are; and (4) an expected loss differential, which reflects the probability of loss on the corporate bonds. As an example of the latter point, suppose the yield to maturity on a BBB bond were 10 percent versus 7 percent on government bonds, but there is a 5 percent probability of total default loss on the corporate bond. In this case, the expected return on the BBB bond would be $0.95(10\%) + 0.05(0\%) = 9.5\%$, and the risk premium would be 2.5 percent, not the full 3.0 percentage point difference in "promised" yields to maturity. Therefore, the risk premiums given in Figure 16-1 overstate somewhat the true (but unmeasurable) risk premiums.

[18]The relationship graphed here is akin to the Security Market Line developed in Chapter 5, although bond ratings rather than beta coefficients are used to measure risk. A word about the scaling of the horizontal axis and about the placement of the points is in order. (1) We have shown a linear fit, although there is no theoretical reason to think that yields plotted against bond ratings are necessarily linear. (2) We have shown the interval on the horizontal axis between AAA and BBB to be equal to that between U.S. Government bonds and AAA, but this is an arbitrary scaling. (3) Finally, on an accurate, large-scale graph, it would be clear that the plotted points for the AAA and BBB bonds are not precisely on straight lines as they appear in the graph; however, they are sufficiently close to warrant our analysis.

   Attempts have been made to calculate beta coefficients for bonds and to plot bonds on the same SML that is used for common stocks. However, these results have not been successful—bonds do not plot on the same linear SML as stocks.

Figure 16-1 Relationship between Bond Ratings
and Bond Yields, 1963, 1975, and 1989

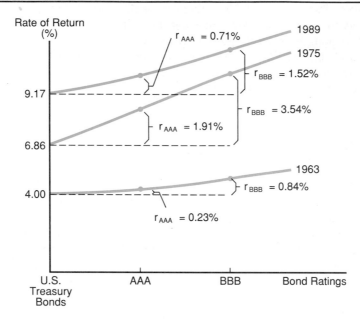

r_{AAA} = risk premium on AAA bonds.
r_{BBB} = risk premium on BBB bonds.

	Long-Term Government Bonds (Default-Free) (1)	AAA Corporate Bonds (2)	BBB Corporate Bonds (3)	Risk Premiums	
				AAA (4) = (2) − (1)	BBB (5) = (3) − (1)
June 1963	4.00%	4.23%	4.84%	0.23%	0.84%
June 1975	6.86	8.77	10.40	1.91	3.54
April 1989	9.17	9.88	10.69	0.71	1.52

Sources: *Federal Reserve Bulletin,* December 1963 and December 1975; *Federal Reserve Statistical Release,* April 1989.

lication itself may be subscribed to or read in many libraries. It spells out in detail what S&P sees as going on, and it is updated frequently.[19]

If a firm's situation has deteriorated somewhat, but its bonds have not been reviewed and downgraded, then it may choose to use a term loan or short-term debt rather than to finance through a public bond issue. This will perhaps postpone

---

[19]Rating agencies do review ratings without being prompted by the company. However, most reviews associated with new issues are actually requested by the company, not because the company wants a review but because the investment bankers make such a review a condition of their handling the offering. Note also that a company must pay the agency to have its bonds rated. It has been suggested that such

a rating agency review until the situation has improved. For example, a number of public utilities delayed bond issues in the early 1980s, financing with short-term debt until electric rate increases could be obtained to raise interest coverage ratios to acceptable levels. After rate increases were put into effect and coverages improved, the companies sold bonds and used the proceeds to retire the excess short-term debt.

Self-Test Questions

What are the two major rating agencies?

What are some criteria the rating agencies use when they assign ratings?

What impact does its bond rating have on the cost of debt to the issuing firm?

ADVANTAGES AND DISADVANTAGES OF LONG-TERM DEBT FINANCING

From the issuer's viewpoint, there are several advantages and disadvantages to long-term debt financing. The major advantages are as follows:

1. The cost of debt is independent of earnings, so debtholders do not participate if profits soar. There is, however, a flip side to this argument—if profits fall, the bondholders must still be paid their interest.

2. The risk-adjusted component cost of debt is lower than that of common stock.

3. The owners of the corporation do not have to share control when debt financing is used.

The major disadvantages are as follows:

1. Since debt service (interest plus scheduled principal repayments) is a fixed charge, a reduction in revenues may result in insufficient cash flow to meet debt service requirements. This can lead to bankruptcy.

2. As discussed in Chapters 12 and 13, financial leverage increases the firm's riskiness, hence increases the costs of both debt and equity.

3. Debt normally has a fixed maturity, hence the firm must repay the principal at some future time.

4. In a long-term contractual relationship, it is necessary for the indenture provisions to be much more stringent than in a short-term credit agreement. Thus, the firm will be subject to more restrictions than if it had borrowed on a short-term basis or had issued common stock.

---

payments might lead to a favorable bias in ratings. However, there is no evidence whatever of any bias on the part of the major rating agencies. The value of their service, hence the rating agencies' incomes, depends almost entirely on their credibility, so there is every reason to expect the agencies to maintain strict objectivity.

5. There is a limit to the amount of funds which can be raised at a "reasonable" rate. Widely accepted lending standards dictate that the debt ratio should not exceed certain limits, and when debt goes beyond these limits, its cost becomes exhorbitant.

Self-Test Questions

What are the major advantages to long-term debt financing?

What are the major disadvantages?

FACTORS THAT INFLUENCE LONG-TERM FINANCING DECISIONS

As we show in this section, many factors influence a firm's long-term financing decisions. It is impossible to rank the factors in order of importance, because their relative importance varies (1) among firms at any point in time and (2) for any given firm over time.

Capital Structure Considerations

One of the most important considerations in any financing decision is the way the firm's actual capital structure compares to its target capital structure. Remember that firms establish an optimal, or target, capital structure (or at least a range) and, over time, finance in accordance with this target. Of course, in any one year, few firms finance exactly in accordance with their target capital structures, primarily because of flotation costs: Smaller issues of new securities have proportionally larger flotation costs, so firms tend to issue long-term debt sporadically, while retained earnings are generated continuously.

Note that making fewer, but larger, security offerings would cause a firm's capital structure to fluctuate about its optimal level rather than stay right on target. However, (1) small fluctuations about the optimal capital structure have little effect on a firm's weighted average cost of capital, (2) investors would recognize that this action is prudent, and (3) the firm would save substantial amounts of flotation costs by financing in this manner. So, firms tend, over the long haul, to finance in accordance with their target capital structures, but flotation costs plus the factors discussed in the following sections do influence the specific financing decisions in any given year.

We should also point out that firms can, and often do, arrange financings in advance. Thus, if a firm concluded that it would need $8 million of debt over a 2-year period, it might arrange with one or more pension funds to lend it $4 million in each of the next 2 years, with the second $4 million being firmly committed by the lenders at the time the first $4 million is borrowed. Such financings can reduce flotation costs, because the lenders need to make only one detailed credit analysis. Similarly, larger firms can use shelf registrations, which we discussed in Chapter 15, to hold down financing costs even while they sell relatively small blocks of securities. Both commitment financings and shelf registrations make it possible for firms to adhere reasonably closely to their optimal capital structures without incurring unduly high flotation costs.

Maturity Matching

Assume that Consolidated Tools, a Cincinnati machine tool manufacturer, made the decision to float a single $25 million nonconvertible bond issue to help finance its 1991 capital budget. It must next choose a maturity for the issue, taking into consideration both the shape of the yield curve, management's own expectations about future interest rates, and the maturity of the assets being financed. To illustrate how asset maturities affect the choice of debt maturities, suppose Consolidated's capital projects consist primarily of new, automated milling and stamping machinery for its Cincinnati plant. This machinery has an expected economic life of 10 years (even though it falls into the MACRS 5-year class life). Should Consolidated finance the debt portion of this equipment with 5-year, 10-year, 20-year, or 30-year debt, or some other maturity?

Note that some of the new capital for the machinery will come from common and perhaps preferred stock, both of which are generally considered to be permanent capital. Of course, preferred stock can have a sinking fund or be redeemable, and common stock can always be repurchased on the open market or by a tender offer, so the effective maturity of preferred and common stock can be reduced significantly. On the other hand, debt maturities can be specified at the time of issue. If Consolidated financed its capital budget with 10-year sinking fund bonds, it would be matching asset and liability maturities. The cash flows resulting from the new machinery could be used to make the interest and sinking fund payments on the issue, so the bonds would be retired as the machinery wore out. If Consolidated had used one-year debt, it would have to pay off this debt with cash flows derived from assets other than the machinery in question. Conversely, if it used 20-year or 30-year debt, it would have to service the debt long after the assets that were purchased with the funds raised had been scrapped and had ceased providing cash flows. This would worry the lenders.

Of course, the one-year debt could probably be rolled over year after year, out to the 10-year asset maturity. However, if interest rates rose, Consolidated would have to pay a higher rate when it rolled over its debt, or if the company experienced difficulties, it might even be unable to refund the debt at any reasonable rate. On the other hand, if Consolidated financed 10-year assets with 20-year or 30-year bonds, it would still have (1) a liability after the 10-year life of the asset, but (2) it would have generated some excess cash from the assets over their 10-year life. The question then would be this: Can we reinvest the accumulated cash flows at a rate which will enable us to pay off the bonds over their remaining 20-year or 30-year life? This strategy clearly imposes uncertainty on the firm, since it cannot know at the time it sells the bonds if profitable capital investment opportunities will be available 10 years later.

For all these reasons, the best all-around financing strategy is to match debt maturities with asset maturities. In recognition of this fact, firms generally do place great emphasis on maturity matching, and this factor often dominates the debt portion of the financing decision.

Effects of Interest Rate Levels and Forecasts

Financial managers also consider interest rate levels and forecasts, both absolute and relative, when making financing decisions. For example, if long-term interest rates are high by historical standards and are expected to fall, managers will be reluctant to issue long-term debt and thus lock in those costs for long periods. We already know that one solution to this problem is for firms to use a call provision—callability permits refunding of the issue should interest rates drop, but there is a cost, because the firm must pay more for callable debt. Alternatively, the firm could finance with short-term debt whenever long-term rates were historically high, and then, assuming that interest rates subsequently fall, sell a long-term issue to replace the short-term debt. Of course, this strategy has its risks: If interest rates move even higher, the firm will be forced to renew its short-term debt at higher and higher rates, or to replace the short-term debt with a long-term bond which costs even more than it would have when the original decision was made.

One could argue, and many do, that capital markets are efficient. If so—and most evidence supports the efficient markets hypothesis—then it is impossible to predict what future interest rates will be because these rates will be determined by information which is not now known. Thus, under the efficient markets hypothesis, it would be unproductive for firms to try to "beat the market" by forecasting future capital costs and then acting on these forecasts. According to this view, financial managers ought to arrange their capital structures in such a manner that they can ride out almost any economic storm, and this generally calls for (1) using some "reasonable" mix of debt and equity and (2) using debt with maturities which match the maturities of the assets being financed.

Although we personally support the view dictated by the efficient markets hypothesis, there is no question that many managers disagree. They are influenced by current cost levels and forecasts, and they act accordingly. One manifestation of this behavior is the heavy use of shelf registrations. Some firms use shelf registrations because managers believe that financing "windows" exist. In the volatile interest rate environment that has characterized recent years, a company might decide to issue bonds when the rate is 12 percent but then find, 6 weeks later when it has SEC approval to go ahead with the issue, that rates are up to 13 percent. If it had "bonds on the shelf," it could have gone ahead and sold the issue while the low-cost window was open. (Another way to protect against rising rates is to hedge against this possibility by use of interest rate futures. We discuss futures markets and the use of futures in Chapter 18.)

In early September of 1983, the interest rate on AAA corporate bonds was about 12.5 percent, up from 11.5 percent in April. Exxon's investment bankers advised the company to tap the Eurobond market for relatively cheap fixed-rate financing.[20] At the time, Exxon could issue its bonds in London at 0.4 percentage points *below*

---

[20]See the "Multinational Finance" section at the end of this chapter for a discussion of Eurobonds.

comparable maturity U.S. Treasury bonds. However, one of Exxon's officers was quoted as saying, "I say so what. The absolute level of rates is too high. Our people would rather wait." The managers of Exxon, as well as many other companies, were betting that the next move in interest rates would be down. This belief was also openly expressed by executives of ITT, Ontario Hydro, and RCA, among others.

These attitudes confirm that many firms base their financing decisions on expectations about future interest rates. It is easy to be right on one interest rate call—if you predict a decline in interest rates, you have a 50-50 chance of being correct. However, the success of a strategy based on forecasting rates requires that those forecasts be right more often than they are wrong, and it is very difficult to find someone with a long-term track record which is better than 50-50. Finance would be easy if we could predict future interest rates accurately. Unfortunately, predicting future interest rates with consistent accuracy is somewhere between difficult and impossible—people who make a living selling interest rate forecasts say it is difficult; many others say it is impossible.

Information Asymmetries

Earlier in the chapter, we discussed bond ratings and the effects of changes in ratings on the cost and availability of capital. If a firm's current financial condition is poor, its managers may be reluctant to issue new long-term debt because (1) a new debt issue would probably trigger a review by the rating agencies, and (2) debt issued when a firm is in poor financial condition would probably cost more and have more severe restrictive covenants than debt issued from strength. Further, in Chapter 12, we pointed out that firms are reluctant to use new common stock financing, especially when this might be taken as a negative signal. Thus, a firm that is in a weakened condition, but which is forecasting a better time in the future, would be inclined to delay permanent financing of any type until things improved. Conversely, a firm that is strong now, but which forecasts a potentially bad time in the period just ahead, would be motivated to finance long term now rather than to wait. Each of these scenarios implies that the capital markets are either inefficient or that investors do not have the same information regarding the firm's future as does its financial manager. The second situation is undoubtedly true at times, and possibly the first one is also true in rare cases.

The firm's earnings outlook, and the extent to which forecasted higher earnings per share are reflected in stock prices, also has an effect on the choice of securities. If a successful R&D program has just been concluded, and as a result management forecasts higher earnings than do most investors, then the firm would not want to issue common stock. It would use debt and then, once earnings rise and push up the stock price, sell common to restore the capital structure to its target level.

Amount of Financing Required

Obviously, the amount of financing required will influence the financing decision. This is mainly due to flotation costs. A $5 million debt financing would most likely be done with a term loan or a privately placed bond issue, while a firm seeking $100 million of new debt would most likely use a public offering.

Availability of Collateral

Generally, secured debt will be less costly than unsecured debt. Thus, firms with large amounts of fixed assets which have a ready resale value are likely to use a relatively large amount of debt, especially mortgage bonds. Additionally, each year's financing decision would be influenced by the amount of qualified assets available as security for new bonds.

Self-Test Questions

What are some factors that financial managers should consider when making long-term financing decisions?

How do information asymmetries affect financing decisions?

MULTINATIONAL FINANCE
The International Bond Markets

Thus far, we have concentrated on the U.S. capital markets, where U.S. firms raise most of their long-term capital. However, many firms, both multinational and domestic, raise large sums of debt capital in the international markets. For example, General Electric recently raised over $1 billion in the Eurobond market. These bonds were dollar denominated but issued in Europe to European holders of dollars. What was the big attraction that caused GE to look to Europe for its borrowing needs? As you might suspect, the answer is lower cost. To illustrate, GE's issue cost the firm only 20 basis points more than the U.S. Treasury was paying on its bonds. Had it borrowed in the U.S. bond market, GE, a triple-A-rated firm, would have paid at least 50 basis points over Treasury rates.

Any bond sold outside the country of the borrower is called an *international bond,* but it is necessary to distinguish further between two types of international bonds: (1) foreign bonds and (2) Eurobonds.

Foreign Bonds

Borrowers sometimes raise long-term debt capital in the domestic capital market of a foreign country. For instance, Bell Canada may need U.S. dollars to finance the operations of its subsidiaries in the United States. If it decides to raise the needed capital in the domestic U.S. bond market, the bond would be underwritten by a syndicate of U.S. investment bankers, would be denominated in (that is, pays interest and principal in

terms of) U.S. dollars, and would be sold to investors in the United States in accordance with SEC and applicable state regulations. Except for the foreign headquarters of the borrower — Canada — this bond would be indistinguishable from bonds issued by equivalent U.S. corporations. Since Bell Canada is a foreign corporation, though, this bond would be called a *foreign bond.* Formally, a foreign bond is a bond that is (1) issued by a foreign borrower, (2) underwritten by a syndicate whose members all come from the country where the funds are raised, (3) denominated in the currency of that same country, and (4) sold entirely within that country. Foreign bonds sold in the United States are sometimes called "Yankee bonds," while foreign bonds sold by U.S. and European firms in Japan are often referred to as "Samurai bonds."

Eurobonds

The second type of international bond is the *Eurobond,* which is internationally syndicated and is denominated in a currency *other than* that of the country in which it is sold. For example, when GE sold U.S. dollar-denominated bonds in Europe, through investment bankers who operate worldwide, to people who paid for the bonds with dollars, that was a Eurobond issue. The institutional arrangements by which Eurobonds are brought to market are different from those for most other bond issues. To a corporation issuing a Eurobond, perhaps the most important feature of the process is the far lower level of required disclosure than would usually be found for bonds issued in domestic markets, particularly in the United States. Also, governments tend not to apply as strict a set of regulations to securities denominated in foreign currencies, but sold in domestic markets to investors holding foreign currencies, as they would for home-currency securities. This often leads to lower total transaction costs for the issue.

Investors also like Eurobonds for several reasons. Generally, they are issued in bearer form rather than as registered bonds, so the names and nationalities of investors are not recorded. Individuals who desire anonymity, whether for privacy reasons or for less worthy motives such as tax evasion, find Eurobonds to their liking. Similarly, most governments do not withhold tax on interest payments associated with Eurobonds. If the investor requires an effective yield of 10 percent, a Eurobond that is exempt from tax withholding would need a coupon rate of 10 percent. Another type of bond—for instance, a domestic issue subject

to a 30 percent withholding tax on interest—would need a coupon rate of roughly 14.3 percent to yield an after-withholding rate of 10 percent. Investors who desire secrecy would not want to file for a refund of the tax, so they would prefer to hold the Eurobond.

Over half of all Eurobonds are denominated in U.S. dollars; bonds in German marks and Dutch guilders account for most of the rest. Although centered in Europe, Eurobonds are truly international. Their underwriting syndicates include investment bankers from all parts of the world, and the bonds are sold to investors not only in Europe but also in such faraway places as Bahrain and Singapore. Up to a few years ago, Eurobonds were issued solely by multinational firms, by international financial institutions, and by national governments. Today, however, the Eurobond market is also being tapped by purely domestic U.S. firms, such as electric utilities, that are going overseas to lower their debt costs.

SUMMARY

This chapter described the characteristics, advantages, and disadvantages of the major types of long-term debt securities. The key concepts covered are listed next.

- *Term loans* and *bonds* are long-term debt contracts under which a borrower agrees to make a series of interest and principal payments on specific dates to the lender. A term loan is generally sold to one (or a few) lenders, while a bond is typically offered to the public and sold to many different investors.

- There are many different types of bonds, including *mortgage bonds, debentures, convertibles, bonds with warrants, income bonds, putable bonds,* and *purchasing power (indexed) bonds.* The return required on each type of bond is determined by the bond's riskiness.

- A bond's *indenture* is a legal document that spells out the rights of the bondholders and of the issuing corporation. A *trustee* is assigned to make sure that the terms of the indenture are carried out.

- A *call provision* gives the issuing corporation the right to redeem the bonds prior to maturity under specified terms, usually at a price greater than the maturity value (the difference is a *call premium*). A firm will typically call a bond and refund it if interest rates fall substantially.

- A *sinking fund* is a provision which requires the corporation to retire a portion of the bond issue each year. The purpose of the sinking fund is to provide for the orderly retirement of the issue. No call premium is paid to the holders of bonds called for sinking fund purposes.

- Some recent innovations in long-term financing include *zero coupon bonds,* which pay no annual interest but which are issued at a discount; *floating rate debt,* whose interest payments fluctuate with changes in the general level of interest rates; and *junk bonds,* which are high-risk, high-yield instruments used by firms which are poor credit risks. Other innovations include *project financing, bonds that are redeemable at par, securitization,* and *swaps.*

- Bonds are assigned *ratings* which reflect the probability of their going into default. The higher a bond's rating, the lower its interest rate.

- A firm's long-term financing decisions are influenced by its *target capital structure,* the *maturity of its assets,* current and forecasted *interest rate levels,* the firm's current and forecasted *financial condition,* and the suitability of its *assets for use as collateral.*

- U.S. firms often find that they can raise long-term capital at a lower cost outside the United States by selling bonds in the *international capital markets.* International bonds may be either *foreign bonds,* which are exactly like regular domestic bonds except that the issuer is a foreign company, or *Eurobonds,* which are bonds sold in a foreign country but denominated in the currency of the issuing company's home country.

Two related issues are discussed in Appendixes 16A and 16B: bankruptcy and reorganization, and refunding operations.

Questions

16-1 Define each of the following terms:
   a.   Story credit
   b.   Term loan; bond
   c.   Mortgage bond
   d.   Debenture; subordinated debenture
   e.   Convertible bond; warrant; income bond; indexed, or purchasing power, bond
   f.   Indenture; restrictive covenant
   g.   Trustee
   h.   Call provision; sinking fund
   i.   Zero coupon bond; original issue discount bond (OID)
   j.   Floating rate bond
   k.   Junk bond
   l.   Project financing
   m.   Securitization
   n.   Swaps
   o.   Poison put; super poison put
   p.   Bond rating; rating agency; investment-grade bonds
   q.   Maturity matching

16-2 What effect would each of the following items have on the interest rate a firm must pay on a new issue of long-term debt? Indicate whether each factor would tend to raise, lower, or have an indeterminate effect on the interest rate, and then explain *why.*
   a.   The firm uses bonds rather than a term loan.
   b.   The firm uses nonsubordinated debentures rather than first mortgage bonds.
   c.   The firm makes its bonds convertible into common stock.

    d.   The firm makes its debentures subordinate to its bank debt. What will the effect be
        (1) On the cost of the debentures?
        (2) On the cost of the bank debt?
        (3) On the average cost of total debt?
    e.   The firm sells income bonds rather than debentures.
    f.   The firm must raise $100 million, all of which will be used to construct a new plant, and is debating the sale of first mortgage bonds or debentures. If it decides to issue $50 million of each type, as opposed to $75 million of first mortgage bonds and $25 million of debentures, how will this affect
        (1) The cost of debentures?
        (2) The cost of mortgage bonds?
        (3) The average cost of the $100 million?
    g.   The firm puts a call provision on its new issue of bonds.
    h.   The firm uses zero coupon bonds rather than coupon bonds.
    i.   The firm includes a sinking fund on its new issue of bonds.
    j.   The firm's bonds are downgraded from A to BBB.
    k.   The firm adds a super poison put provision on its new bond issue.

16-3 Rank the following securities from lowest (1) to highest (9) in terms of their riskiness for an investor. All securities (except the government bond) are for a given firm. If you think two or more securities are equally risky, indicate so.
    a.   Income bond   _____
    b.   Subordinated debentures — noncallable   _____
    c.   First mortgage bond — no sinking fund   _____
    d.   Common stock   _____
    e.   U.S. Treasury bond   _____
    f.   First mortgage bond — with sinking fund _____
    g.   Subordinated debentures — callable   _____
    h.   Amortized term loan   _____
    i.   Nonamortized term loan   _____

16-4 A sinking fund can be set up in one of two ways:
        (1) The corporation makes annual payments to the trustee, who invests the proceeds in securities (frequently government bonds) and uses the accumulated total to retire the bond issue at maturity.
        (2) The trustee uses the annual payments to retire a portion of the issue each year, either calling a given percentage of the issue by a lottery and paying a specified price per bond or buying bonds on the open market, whichever is cheaper.
    Discuss the advantages and disadvantages of each procedure from the viewpoint of both the firm and the bondholders.

16-5 Draw an SML graph. Put dots on the graph to show (approximately) where you think a particular company's (a) common stock and (b) bonds would lie. Now put on dots to represent a riskier company's stock and bonds.

16-6 Suppose you work for the treasurer of a large, profitable corporation. Your company has some surplus funds to invest. You can buy these securities:
        (1) Aaa-rated Exxon 20-year bonds which sell at par and yield 12 percent.
        (2) Aa-rated Exxon preferred stock which yields 10 percent.
        (3) Ca-rated Eastern Airlines bonds which yield 16 percent.
        (4) C-rated Eastern Airlines preferred stock which yields 17 percent.
        (5) A-rated Alabama Power floating rate preferred stock which currently yields 9 percent.
        (6) Treasury bills which yield 8.5 percent.

    a.   Does it appear that these securities are in equilibrium?

    b.   If these were your only choices, which would you recommend? Why?

Self-Test Problem   (Solutions Appear in Appendix D)

ST-1   **(Sinking funds)** The California Development Commission has just issued a $100 million, 10-year, 12 percent bond with semiannual coupon payments. A sinking fund will retire the issue over its life. Sinking fund payments are of equal amounts and will be made *semiannually,* and the proceeds will be used to retire bonds as the payments are made. Assume that the bonds will be called at par for sinking fund purposes.

    a.   How large must each semiannual sinking fund payment be?

    b.   What will happen, under the conditions of the problem thus far, to the company's debt service requirements per year for this issue over time?

    c.   Now suppose the Commission had set its sinking fund so that *equal annual amounts,* payable at the end of each year, were paid into a sinking fund trust held by a bank, with the proceeds being used to buy government bonds that pay 9 percent interest. The payments, plus accumulated interest, must total $100 million at the end of 10 years, and the proceeds will be used to retire the bonds at that time. How large must the annual sinking fund payment now be?

    d.   What are the annual cash requirements for covering bond service costs under the trusteeship arrangement described in Part c? (Note: Interest must be paid on the outstanding bonds but not on bonds that have been retired.)

    e.   Now assume that the Commission has the option of buying the bonds on the open market. What would have to happen to interest rates to cause the company to buy bonds on the open market rather than call them under the original sinking fund plan?

Problems

16-1   **(Loan amortization)** Suppose a firm is setting up an amortized term loan. What are the annual payments for a $10 million loan under the following terms:

    a.   9 percent, 5 years?

    b.   9 percent, 10 years?

    c.   12 percent, 5 years?

    d.   12 percent, 10 years?

16-2   **(Amortization schedule)** Set up an amortization schedule for a $1 million, 3-year, 10 percent loan.

16-3   **(Yield to call)** Five years ago Sinkey Company sold a 20-year bond issue with a 17 percent coupon rate and a 10 percent constant call premium. Today the firm called the bonds. The bonds originally were sold at their face value of $1,000. Compute the realized rate of return for investors who purchased the bonds when they were issued and will surrender them today in exchange for the call price.

16-4   **(Perpetual bond analysis)** In 1936 the Canadian government raised $55 million by issuing bonds at a 3 percent annual rate of interest. Unlike most bonds issued today, which have a specific maturity date, these bonds can remain outstanding forever; they are, in fact, perpetuities.

    At the time of issue, the Canadian government stated in the bond indenture that cash redemption was possible at face value ($100) on or after September 1966; in other words, the bonds were callable at par after September 1966. Believing that the bonds would in fact be called, many investors purchased these bonds in 1965 with expectations of receiving $100 in 1966 for each perpetual bond they had. In 1965 the bonds sold for $55, but a rush of buyers drove the price to just below the $100 par value by 1966. Prices fell dramatically, however, when the Canadian government announced that these perpetual bonds were indeed perpetual and would not be paid off. A new, 30-year supply of coupons was sent to each bondholder.

The bonds' market price declined to $42 in December 1966. Because of their severe losses, hundreds of Canadian bondholders formed the Perpetual Bond Association to lobby for face value redemption of the bonds, claiming that the government had reneged on an implied promise to redeem the bonds. Government officials in Ottawa insisted that claims for face value payment were nonsense, for the bonds were and always had been clearly identified as perpetuals. One Ottawa official stated, "Our job is to protect the taxpayer. Why should we pay $55 million for less than $25 million worth of bonds?"

The issue heats up again every few years, and it recently resurfaced once more. Here are some questions relating to the Canadian issue that will test your understanding of bonds in general:

a. Would it make sense for a business firm to issue bonds such as the Canadian bonds described here? Would it matter whether the firm were a proprietorship or a corporation?

b. Suppose the U.S. government today sold $100 million each of these four types of bonds: 5-year bonds, 50-year bonds, "regular" perpetuities, and Canadian-type (callable) perpetuities. What do you think the relative order of interest rates would be? In other words, rank the bonds from the one with the lowest to the one with the highest rate of interest. Explain your answer.

c. (1) Suppose that because of pressure by the Perpetual Bond Association you believe that the Canadian government will redeem this particular perpetual bond issue in 5 years. Which course of action would be more advantageous to you if you owned the bonds: (a) sell your bonds today at $42, or (b) wait 5 years and have them redeemed? Assume that similar-risk bonds earn 8 percent today and that interest rates are expected to remain at this level for the next 5 years.

(2) If you had the opportunity to invest your money in bonds of similar risk, at what rate of return would you be indifferent to the choice of selling your perpetuals today or having them redeemed in 5 years — that is, what is the expected yield to maturity on the Canadian bonds?

d. Show mathematically the perpetuities' value if they yield 7.15 percent, pay $3 interest annually, and are considered "regular" perpetuities. Show what would happen to the price of bonds if the going interest rate fell to 2 percent.

e. Are the Canadian bonds more likely to be valued as "regular" perpetuities if the going rate of interest is above or below 3 percent? Why?

f. Do you think the Canadian government would have taken the same action with regard to retiring the bonds if the interest rate had fallen rather than risen after they were issued?

g. Do you think the Canadian government was "fair" or "unfair" in its actions? Give the pros and cons, and justify your reason for thinking that one outweighs the other. Would it matter if the bonds had been sold to "sophisticated" as opposed to "naive" purchasers?

16-5 **(Zero coupon bond)** Suppose Mid-State Insurance Company needs to raise $400 million, and its investment bankers have indicated that 10-year zero coupon bonds could be sold at a YTM of 12 percent while a 14 percent yield would be required on *annual* payment coupon bonds sold at par. Mid-State's tax rate is 34 percent. (Assume that the discount can be amortized by the issuer using the straight line method. This cannot be done under current tax laws, but assume it anyway.)

a. How many $1,000 par value bonds would Mid-State have to sell under each plan?

b.   What would be the after-tax YTM on each type of bond (1) to a holder who is tax exempt and (2) to a taxpayer in the 50 percent federal-plus-state bracket?

c.   What would be the after-tax cost of each type of bond to Mid-State?

d.   Why would investors be willing to buy the zero coupon bonds?

e.   Why might Mid-State turn down the offer to issue zero coupon bonds?

(Do Part f only if you are using the computerized diskette.)

f.   Redo Parts a, b, and c assuming that the YTM on zero coupon bonds falls to 10 percent and that on annual coupon bonds falls to 12 percent. As in the previous analysis, the after-tax yield to investors on the annual coupon bond exceeds that of the zero coupon bond. Has the differential between the annual and zero coupon bond yields changed? Would investors be more willing to purchase the zero coupon bond under the original assumptions or under the new assumptions? If the before-tax YTM were 10 percent on each type of bond, what would the after-tax YTMs be to zero and to 50 percent taxpayers, what would the after-tax cost be to the company, and what type of investors would be likely to hold the zeros and what type the regular coupon bonds?

Mini Case

Hospital Development Corporation (HDC) needs $10 million to build a regional testing laboratory in Birmingham. Once the lab is completed and fully operational, which should take about 5 years, HDC will sell it to a health maintenance organization (HMO). HDC tentatively plans to raise the $10 million by selling 5-year bonds, and its investment bankers have stated that either regular or zero coupon bonds can be used. Regular coupon bonds would have annual payment coupons of 12 percent, and zero coupon bonds would also be priced to yield 12 percent. Either bond would be callable after 3 years, on the anniversary date of the issue, at a premium of 6 months' interest for regular bonds or 5 percent over the accrued value on the call date for zero coupon bonds. HDC's federal-plus-state tax rate is 40 percent.

As assistant to HDC's treasurer, you have been assigned the task of making a recommendation as to which type of bonds to issue. As part of your analysis, you have been asked to answer the following questions.

a.   What is the difference between a bond and a term loan? What are the advantages of a term loan over a bond?

b.   Suppose HDC issues bonds and uses the medical center as collateral for the issue. What type of bond would this be? Suppose that instead of using a secured bond, HDC had decided to sell debentures. How would this affect the interest rate that HDC would have to pay on the debt?

c.   What is a bond indenture? What are some examples of provisions the bondholders would probably require HDC to include in its indenture?

d.   HDC's bonds will be callable after 3 years. If the bonds were not callable, would the interest rate required be higher or lower than 12 percent? What would be the effect on the rate if the bonds were callable immediately? What are the advantages to HDC of making the bonds callable?

e.   (1) If its indenture included a sinking fund provision which required HDC to retire one-fifth of the bonds each year, would this provision raise or lower the interest rate required on the bonds?

     (2) How would the sinking fund operate?

     (3) Why might HDC's investors require it to use a sinking fund? For this particular issue, would it make sense to include a sinking fund?

f.   If HDC were to issue zero coupon bonds, what initial price would cause the zeros to yield 12 percent? How many $1,000 par value zeros would HDC have to sell to raise the needed $10 million? How many regular 12 percent coupon bonds would HDC have to sell?

g.   Set up a time line which shows the accrued value of the zeros at the end of each year, along with the annual after-tax cash flows from the zeros to an investor in the 28 percent tax bracket and to HDC.

h.   What would the after-tax yield to maturity be on each type of bond to an investor in the 28 percent tax bracket? What would the after-tax cost of debt be to HDC?

i.   If interest rates were to fall, causing HDC to call the bonds (either the coupon or the zero) at the end of Year 3, what would be the after-tax yield to call on each type of bond to an investor in the 28 percent tax bracket?

j.   HDC is an A-rated firm. Suppose HDC's bond rating was (1) lowered to triple B or (2) raised to double A. What would be the effect of these changes on the interest rate required on HDC's new long-term debt and on the market value of the company's outstanding debt?

k.   What are some of the factors a firm such as HDC should consider when deciding whether to issue long-term debt, short-term debt, or equity? Why might long-term debt be HDC's best choice in this situation?

l.   Describe the key features of the following securities and transactions:

   (1) Junk bonds
   (2) Project financing
   (3) Swaps
   (4) Securitization
   (5) Bonds that are redeemable at par

Selected Additional References and Cases

The investment textbooks listed in the Chapter 5 references provide useful information on bonds, as well as the markets in which they are traded. In addition, the following articles offer useful insights:

Allen, David S., Robert E. Lamy, and G. Rodney Thompson, "Agency Costs and Alternative Call Provisions: An Empirical Investigation," *Financial Management,* Winter 1987, 37–44.

Arak, Marcelle, Arturo Estrella, Laurie Goodman, and Andrew Silver, "Interest Rate Swaps: An Alternative Explanation," *Financial Management,* Summer 1988, 12–18.

Backer, Morton, and Martin L. Gosman, "The Use of Financial Ratios in Credit Downgrade Decisions," *Financial Management,* Spring 1980, 53–56.

Barrett, W. Brian, Andrea J. Heuson, and Robert W. Kolb, "The Differential Effects of Sinking Funds on Bond Risk Premia," *Journal of Financial Research,* Winter 1986, 303–312.

Clark, John J., with Brenton W. Harries, "Some Recent Trends in Municipal and Corporate Securities Markets: An Interview with Brenton W. Harries, President of Standard & Poor's Corporation," *Financial Management,* Spring 1976, 9–17.

Einzig, Robert, and Bruce Lange, "Swaps at Transamerica: Applications and Analysis," *Journal of Applied Corporate Finance,* Winter 1990, 48–58.

Ferri, Michael G., "An Empirical Examination of the Determinants of Bond Yield Spreads," *Financial Management,* Autumn 1978, 40–46.

Gentry, James A., David T. Whitford, and Paul Newbold, "Predicting Industrial Bond Ratings with a Probit Model and Funds Flow Components," *The Financial Review,* August 1988, 269–286.

Goodman, Laurie S., "The Uses of Interest Rate Swaps in Managing Corporate Liabilities," *Journal of Applied Corporate Finance,* Winter 1990, 35–47.

Hsueh, L. Paul, and David S. Kidwell, "Bond Ratings: Are Two Better than One?" *Financial Management,* Spring 1988, 46–53.

Johnson, James M., Robert A. Pari, and Leonard Rosenthal, "The Impact of In-Substance Defeasance on Bondholder and Shareholder Wealth," *Journal of Finance,* September 1989, 1049–1057.

Kalotay, Andrew J. "Sinking Funds and the Realized Cost of Debt," *Financial Management,* Spring 1982, 43–54.

———, "Innovations in Corporation Finance: Deep Discount Private Placements," *Financial Management,* Spring 1982, 55–57.

Kao, Chihwa, and Chunchi Wu, "Sinking Funds and the Agency Costs of Corporate Debt," *The Financial Review,* February 1990, 95–113.

Pinches, George E., J. Clay Singleton, and Ali Jahankhani, "Fixed Coverage as a Determinant of Electric Utility Bond Ratings," *Financial Management,* Summer 1978, 45–55.

Roach, Stephen S., "Living with Corporate Debt," *Journal of Applied Corporate Finance,* Spring 1989, 19–29.

Smith, Clifford W., and J. B. Warner, "On Financial Contracting: An Analysis of Bond Covenants," *Journal of Financial Economics,* June 1979, 117–161.

Turnbull, Stuart M., "Swaps: A Zero Sum Game," *Financial Management,* Spring 1987, 15–21.

Weinsten, Mark I., "The Seasoning Process of New Corporate Bond Issues," *Journal of Finance,* December 1978, 1343–1354.

Zwick, Burton, "Yields on Privately Placed Corporate Bonds," *Journal of Finance,* March 1980, 23–29.

References on bond refunding include the following:

Ang, James S., "The Two Faces of Bond Refunding," *Journal of Finance,* June 1975, 869–874.

———, "The Two Faces of Bond Refunding: Reply," *Journal of Finance,* March 1978, 354–356.

Dyl, Edward A. and Michael D. Joehnk, "Refunding Tax Exempt Bonds," *Financial Management,* Summer 1976, 59–66.

Emery, Douglas R., "Overlapping Interest in Bond Refunding: A Reconsideration," *Financial Management,* Summer 1978, 19–20.

Finnerty, John D., "Refunding High-Coupon Debt," *Midland Corporate Finance Journal,* Winter 1986, 59–74.

Harris, Robert S., "The Refunding of Discounted Debt: An Adjusted Present Value Analysis," *Financial Management,* Winter 1980, 7–12.

Kalotay, Andrew J., "On the Advanced Refunding of Discounted Debt," *Financial Management,* Summer 1978, 14–18.

———, "On the Structure and Valuation of Debt Refundings," *Financial Management*, Spring 1982, 41–42.

Kraus, Alan, "An Analysis of Call Provisions and the Corporate Refunding Decision," *Midland Corporate Finance Journal,* Spring 1983, 46–60.

Laber, Gene, "The Effect of Bond Refunding of Discounted Debt," *Financial Management,* June 1979, 795–799.

———, "Implications of Discount Rates and Financing Assumptions for Bond Refunding Decisions," *Financial Management,* Spring 1979, 7–12.

———, "Repurchases of Bonds through Tender Offers: Implications for Shareholder Wealth," *Financial Management,* Summer 1978, 7–13.

Livingston, Miles, "The Effect of Bond Refunding on Shareholder Wealth: Comment," *Journal of Finance,* June 1979, 801–804.

———, "Bond Refunding Reconsidered: Comment," *Journal of Finance,* March 1980, 191–196.

Mayor, Thomas H., and Kenneth G. McCoin, "Bond Refunding: One or Two Faces?" *Journal of Finance,* March 1978, 349–353.

Ofer, Ahron R., and Robert A. Taggart, Jr., "Bond Refunding: Reconsidered: Reply," *Journal of Finance,* March 1980, 197–200.

Riener, Kenneth D., "Financial Structure Effects of Bond Refunding," *Financial Management,* Summer 1980, 18–23.

Yawitz, Jess B., and James A. Anderson, "The Effect of Bond Refunding on Shareholder Wealth," *Journal of Finance,* December 1977, 1738–1746.

———, "The Effect of Bond Refunding on Shareholder Wealth: Reply," *Journal of Finance,* June 1979, 805–809.

Zeise, Charles H., and Roger K. Taylor, "Advance Refunding: A Practitioner's Perspective," *Financial Management,* Summer 1977, 73–76.

For more information on Eurodollar bonds, see

Kidwell, David S., M. Wayne Marr, and G. Rodney Thompson, "Eurodollar Bonds: Alternative Financing for U.S. Companies," *Financial Management,* Winter 1985, 18–27; and the same authors' correction in the Spring 1986 issue of *Financial Management.*

The following Brigham-Gapenski case focuses on the topics covered in this chapter:

Case 25, "West Coast Electric," which illustrates the bond refunding decision.

The following Harrington case is also relevant:

"Bearings Inc. (A) and Bearings Inc. (B)," which illustrate the choice between debt and equity financing.

APPENDIX 16A

Bankruptcy and Reorganization

Bankruptcy is a way of life in the United States. Such well-known companies as Texaco, Penn Central, Eastern Airlines, Revco, W. T. Grant, A. H. Robins, Allis Chalmers, Coleco, and Dart Drugs have filed for bankruptcy for various reasons. Debtholders have a prior claim to a

---

This appendix was co-authored by Arthur L. Herrmann of the University of Hartford.

firm's income, and to its assets in the event of bankruptcy, over common and preferred stockholders. Also, different classes of debtholders are accorded different treatments in the event of bankruptcy, so it is important that one know who gets what if a firm fails. Finally, firms in financial distress can often survive "bad times" by a reorganization rather than resorting to a formal declaration of bankruptcy. These topics are discussed in this appendix.[1]

Federal Bankruptcy Laws

The bankruptcy process begins when a debtor is unable to meet scheduled payments to creditors or when the firm's cash flow projections indicate that it will soon be unable to do so. As the situation develops, these central issues arise:

1. Is the firm's inability to meet scheduled debt payments a temporary cash flow problem, or is it a permanent problem caused by long-term economic trends?

2. If the problem is a temporary one, then an agreement which gives the firm time to recover and to satisfy everyone will be worked out. However, if basic long-run asset values have declined, economic losses will have occurred. In this event, who should bear the losses?

3. Is the company "worth more dead than alive"—that is, would the business be more valuable if it were maintained and continued in operation or if it were liquidated and sold off in pieces?

4. Should the firm file for formal bankruptcy, or should it try to use informal procedures?

5. Who should control the firm while it is being rehabilitated or liquidated? Should the existing management be left in control, or should a trustee be placed in charge of operations?

Our bankruptcy laws were first enacted in 1898, modified substantially in 1938, changed again in 1978, and further fine-tuned in 1984. The 1978 act was a major revision designed to streamline and expedite proceedings, and it consists of eight odd-numbered chapters (the even-numbered chapters were deleted in the revision). Chapters 1, 3, and 5 contain general provisions applicable to the other chapters; Chapter 7 details the procedures to be followed when liquidating a firm; Chapter 9 deals with financially distressed municipalities; Chapter 11 is the business reorganization chapter; Chapter 13 covers the adjustment of debts for "individuals with regular income"; and Chapter 15 sets up a system of trustees who help administer proceedings under the new act. When you read in the paper that a firm, such as Eastern Airlines in 1989, has "filed for court protection under Chapter 11," this means that the company is bankrupt and is trying to reorganize. Under Chapter 11, a company is protected from creditor lawsuits while it works out a court-approved plan to meet its debt obligations.

Our bankruptcy law is flexible, and it provides much scope for informal negotiations between a company and its creditors and stockholders. The case is opened by the filing of a petition with a federal district bankruptcy court. The petition may be either voluntary or involuntary—that is, it may be filed either by the firm's management or by its creditors. A committee of unsecured creditors is then appointed by the court to negotiate with management for a reorganization, which may include the restructuring (that is, lengthening maturities, reducing the interest rate, and/or reducing the principal) of debt and other claims against the firm. At the time of its Chapter 11 filing, Eastern had thousands of creditors, and they

---

[1]Much of the current work in this area is based on writings by Edward I. Altman. For a summary of his work, and that of others, see Edward I. Altman, "Bankruptcy and Reorganization," in *Financial Handbook,* Edward I. Altman, ed. (New York: Wiley, 1986), Chapter 35.

want to get as much of their claims as possible, but they may conclude that they will come out better if they accept less than the full amount owed them, because the alternative might be a "fire sale" liquidation rather than maintenance of the firm as a going concern.

In one reorganization plan (March 1990), Eastern proposed giving its unsecured creditors 10 percent of what they are owed in cash, another 70 percent paid out over 10 years with no interest, and the remaining 20 percent would be exchanged for special preferred stock convertible into common shares which would give the creditors 40 percent ownership. A trustee will be appointed by the court if that is deemed to be in the best interests of the creditors and stockholders (one was appointed for Eastern); otherwise, the existing management will retain control. If no fair and feasible reorganization can be agreed on by the creditors and the company, and agreed on by the court, then the firm will be liquidated under the procedures spelled out in Chapter 7.

Liquidation Procedures

If a company is too far gone to be reorganized, it must be liquidated. Liquidation should occur if a business is worth more "dead than alive," or if the possibility of restoring it to financial health is so remote that the creditors would face a high risk of even greater losses if operations were to continue. Note that very few large firms are ever liquidated—they are either reorganized or taken over by another firm, because the losses incurred in a liquidation are just too big.

Chapter 7 of the 1978 Bankruptcy Act is designed to accomplish these three objectives: (1) provide safeguards against the withdrawal of assets by the owners of the bankrupt firm; (2) provide for an equitable distribution of the assets among the creditors; and (3) allow insolvent debtors to discharge all their obligations and start over unhampered by a burden of prior debt.

The distribution of assets in a liquidation under Chapter 7 of the Bankruptcy Act is governed by the following priority of claims:

1. **Secured creditors, who are entitled to the proceeds of the sale of specific property pledged for a lien or a mortgage.** If the proceeds do not fully satisfy the secured creditors' claims, the remaining balance of such claims is treated as a general creditor claim. (See Item 9)

2. **Trustee's costs to administer and operate the bankrupt firm.**

3. **Expenses incurred after an involuntary liquidation has begun but before a trustee is appointed.**

4. **Wages due workers if earned within three months prior to the filing of the petition in bankruptcy.** The amount of wages is limited to $2,000 per person.

5. **Claims for unpaid contributions to employee benefit plans that should have been paid within six months prior to filing.** However, these claims, plus wages in Item 4, may not exceed the $2,000-per-wage-earner limit.

6. **Unsecured claims for customer deposits, not to exceed a maximum of $900 per individual.**

7. **Taxes due to federal, state, county, and any other government agency.**

8. **Unfunded pension plan liabilities.** Unfunded pension plan liabilities have a claim above that of the general creditors for an amount up to 30 percent of the book value of the common and preferred equity; any remaining unfunded pension claims rank with the general creditors.

9. **General, or unsecured, creditors.** Holders of trade credit, unsecured loans, the unsatisfied portion of secured loans and unfunded pension plan liabilities, and debenture bonds are classified as *general creditors*. Holders of subordinated debt also fall into this category, but they must turn over required amounts to the holders of senior debt, as discussed later in this section.

10. **Preferred stockholders, who can receive an amount up to the par value of the preferred stock.**

11. **Common stockholders, who receive the remaining funds, if any.**

To illustrate the way this priority system works, consider the balance sheet of Midwest Steel, Inc., shown in Table 16A-1. The assets have a book value of $90 million. The claims are indicated on the right-hand side of the balance sheet. Note that the debentures are subordinate to the notes payable to banks. Midwest filed for bankruptcy under Chapter 11, and no fair and feasible reorganization could be arranged. Therefore, the trustee was ordered by the court to liquidate the firm under Chapter 7.

The assets as reported in the balance sheet in Table 16A-1 were greatly overstated; they were, in fact, worth less than half of the $90 million at which they were carried. The following amounts were realized on liquidation:

From sale of current assets	$28,000,000
From sale of fixed assets	5,000,000
Total proceeds	$33,000,000

The distribution of proceeds is shown in Table 16A-2. The first mortgage holders receive the $5 million in net proceeds from the sale of fixed assets. Since there were $6 million of first mortgage bonds, those bondholders are still owed $1 million. This unsatisfied claim is

---

Table 16A-1 Midwest Steel, Inc.: Balance Sheet at Liquidation (Thousands of Dollars)

Current assets	$80,000	Accounts payable	$20,000
Net fixed assets	10,000	Notes payable (to bank)	10,000
		Accrued wages, 1,400 @ $500	700
		U.S. taxes	1,000
		State and local taxes	300
		Current liabilities	$32,000
		First mortgage	$ 6,000
		Second mortgage	1,000
		Subordinated debentures[a]	8,000
		Total long-term debt	$15,000
		Preferred stock	$ 2,000
		Common stock	26,000
		Paid-in capital	4,000
		Retained earnings	11,000
		Total equity	$43,000
Total assets	$90,000	Total claims	$90,000

[a]Subordinated to $10 million in notes payable to the bank.

Table 16A-2   Midwest Steel, Inc.: Distribution of Liquidation Proceeds

Distribution to Priority Claimants

1. Proceeds from sale of assets	$33,000,000
2. First mortgage, paid from sale of fixed assets	5,000,000
3. Fees and expenses of administration of bankruptcy	6,000,000
4. Wages due workers earned within three months prior to filing of bankruptcy petition	700,000
5. Taxes	1,300,000
6. Available to general creditors	$20,000,000

Distribution to General Creditors

Claims of General Creditors	Amount of Claim[a] (1)	Application of 50 Percent[b] (2)	After Subordination Adjustment[c] (3)	Percentage of Original Claim Received[d] (4)
Unsatisfied portion of first mortgage	$ 1,000,000	$ 500,000	$ 500,000	92%
Unsatisfied portion of second mortgage	1,000,000	500,000	500,000	50
Notes payable	10,000,000	5,000,000	9,000,000	90
Accounts payable	20,000,000	10,000,000	10,000,000	50
Subordinated debentures	8,000,000	4,000,000	0	0
	$40,000,000	$20,000,000	$20,000,000	

[a]Column 1 is the claim of each class of general creditor. Total claims equal $40 million.
[b]From Line 6 in the upper section of the table, we see that $20 million is available for general creditors. This sum, divided by the $40 million of total claims, indicates that general creditors will initially receive 50 cents on the dollar; this is shown in Column 2.
[c]The debentures are subordinated to the notes payable, so $4 million must be reallocated from debentures to notes payable. This adjustment is made in Column 3.
[d]Column 4 shows the results of dividing the amount in Column 3 by the original claim amount given in Column 1, except for the first mortgage, where the $5 million received from the sale of fixed assets is included.

added to that of the other general creditors. After payment to the first mortgage bondholders come the fees and expenses of administration, which are typically about 20 percent of gross proceeds; in this example, they are $6 million. Next in priority are wages due workers, which total $700,000, and taxes due, which amount to $1.3 million.

Thus far, the priority claimants have been allocated $13 million of the $33 million of available cash, leaving $20 million for the general creditors. In this case, there were no claims for unpaid benefit plans or unfunded pension liabilities; if there had been, they would have had priority over the general creditors.

The claims of the general creditors total $40 million. Since $20 million is available, claimants would initially be allocated 50 percent of their claims, as shown in Column 2 of Table 16A-2, before the subordination adjustment. The subordination agreement requires the subordinated debentures to turn over to the holders of the notes payable all amounts received until the notes are satisfied. In this situation, the claim of the notes payable is $10 million, but only $5 million is available; the deficiency is therefore $5 million. After transfer of

$4 million from the subordinated debentures, there remains a deficiency of $1 million on the notes; this amount will remain unsatisfied.

Note that 92 percent of the first mortgage bonds' claim and 90 percent of the bank claim are satisfied, whereas a maximum of 50 percent of other unsecured claims will be satisfied. These figures illustrate (1) the advantage of having a secured claim and (2) the usefulness of the subordination provision to the security to which the subordination is made. The claims of the subordinated debentures, the preferred stock, and the common stock are completely wiped out. Studies of bankruptcy liquidations reveal that unsecured creditors receive on average about 15 cents on the dollar, whereas common stockholders generally receive nothing.

Informal Procedures

Both reorganization and liquidation can be accomplished without a formal bankruptcy court filing. In this section, we briefly discuss these informal procedures.

Informal Reorganization. In the case of a fundamentally sound company whose financial difficulties appear to be temporary, the creditors generally prefer to work directly with the company, helping it to recover and reestablish itself on a sound financial basis. Such voluntary plans usually require some type of restructuring of the firm's debt, which involves either postponing payment of debt obligations or reducing creditor claims, or both. These procedures are designed to keep the debtor in business and to avoid the court costs associated with formal bankruptcy. Although creditors may not obtain immediate payment and may even have to accept less than is owed them, they often recover more money, and sooner, than if formal bankruptcy is declared. Also, for both trade creditors and bankers, chances are good that a customer will be preserved.

We should point out that informal voluntary settlements are not reserved for small firms. Navistar International (formerly International Harvester) avoided formal bankruptcy proceedings by getting its creditors to agree to restructure some $3.5 billion of debt. Likewise, Chrysler's creditors accepted both an extension of maturities and a reduction of accounts to help it through its bad years.

Informal Liquidation. *Assignment* is an informal procedure for liquidating debts, and it usually yields creditors a larger amount than they would receive in a formal Chapter 7 liquidation. However, assignments are feasible only if the firm is small, and its affairs are not too complex. An assignment calls for title to the debtor's assets to be transferred to a third person, known as an *assignee* or *trustee*. The assignee is instructed to liquidate the assets through a private sale or a public auction, and then to distribute the proceeds among the creditors on a pro rata basis. The assignment does not automatically discharge the debtor's obligations. However, the debtor may have the assignee write on the check to each creditor the requisite legal language to make endorsement of the check acknowledgment of full settlement of the claim.

Assignment has some advantages over Chapter 7 liquidation, which involves more time, legal formality, and expense. The assignee has more flexibility in disposing of property than does a bankruptcy trustee. Action can be taken sooner, before the inventory becomes obsolete or the machinery rusts, and, since the assignee is often familiar with the channels of trade in the debtor's business, better results may be achieved. However, an assignment does not automatically result in a full and legal discharge of all the debtor's liabilities, nor does it protect the creditors against fraud.

APPENDIX 16B

Refunding Operations

A great deal of long-term debt was sold during the period from 1979 through 1984 at interest rates going up to 18 percent for double A companies. Because the period of call protection on much of this debt is, or soon will be, ending, many companies are analyzing the pros and cons of bond refundings. Refunding decisions actually involve two separate questions: (1) Is it profitable to call an outstanding issue in the current period and replace it with a new issue; and (2) even if refunding is currently profitable, would the expected value of the firm be increased even more if the refunding were postponed to a later date? We consider both questions in this section.

Note that the decision to refund a security is analyzed in much the same way as a capital budgeting expenditure. The costs of refunding (the investment outlays) are (1) the call premium paid for the privilege of calling the old issue, (2) the tax savings from writing off the unexpensed flotation costs on the old issue, and (3) the net interest that must be paid while both issues are outstanding (the new issue is often sold one month before the refunding to insure that the funds will be available). The annual cash flows, in a capital budgeting sense, are the interest payments that are saved each year plus the net tax savings which the firm receives for amortizing the flotation expenses. For example, if the interest expense on the old issue is $1,000,000 whereas that on the new issue is $700,000, the $300,000 reduction in interest savings constitutes an annual benefit.[1]

The net present value method is used to analyze the advantages of refunding: the future cash flows are discounted back to the present, and then this discounted value is compared with the cash outlays associated with the refunding. The firm should refund the bond if the present value of the savings exceeds the cost — that is, if the NPV of the refunding operation is positive.

In the discounting process, the after-tax cost of the new debt, k_{db} should be used as the discount rate. The reasons for this are (1) there is relatively little risk to the savings — cash flows in a refunding are known with relative certainty, which is quite unlike the situation with cash flows in most capital budgeting decisions, and (2) the cash outlay required to refund the old issue is generally obtained by increasing the amount of the new issue (see Footnote 4).

The easiest way to examine the refunding decision is through an example. Microchip Computer Company has outstanding a $60 million bond issue which has a 15 percent annual coupon and 20 years remaining to maturity. This issue, which was sold 5 years ago, had flotation costs of $3 million, which the firm has been amortizing on a straight line basis over the 25-year original life of the issue. The bond has a call provision which makes it possible for the company to retire the bonds at this time by calling them in at a 10 percent call premium. Investment bankers have assured the company that it could sell an additional $60 million to $70 million worth of new annual coupon 20-year bonds at an interest rate of 12

---

[1]During the early 1980s, there was a flurry of work on the pros and cons of refunding bond issues that had fallen to deep discounts as a result of rising interest rates. At such times, the company could go into the market, buy its debt at a low price, and retire it. The difference between the bonds' par value and the price the company paid would be reported as income, and taxes would have to be paid on it. The results of the research on the refunding of discount issues suggest that bonds should not, in general, be refunded after a rise in rates. See Andrew J. Kalotay, "On the Structure and Valuation of Debt Refundings," *Financial Management,* Spring 1982, 41–42; and Robert S. Harris, "The Refunding of Discounted Debt: An Adjusted Present Value Analysis," *Financial Management,* Winter 1980, 7–12.

percent. To insure that the funds required to pay off the old debt will be available, the new bonds would be sold one month before the old issue is called, so for one month, interest would have to be paid on two issues. Current short-term interest rates are 11 percent; for the one-month overlap period, proceeds from the new issue will be invested in short-term securities. Predictions are that long-term interest rates are unlikely to fall below 12 percent.[2] Flotation costs on a new refunding issue would amount to $2,650,000. Microchip's marginal tax rate is 34 percent. Should the company refund the $60 million of 15 percent bonds?

The following steps outline the decision process; the steps are summarized in worksheet form in Table 16B-1.

Step 1.   Determine the Investment Outlay Required to Refund the Issue.
a. Call premium

$$\text{Before tax: } 0.10(\$60,000,000) = \$6,000,000.$$

$$\text{After tax: } \$6,000,000(1 - T) = \$6,000,000(0.66)$$

$$= \$3,960,000.$$

Although Microchip must expend $6 million on the call premium, this is a deductible expense in the year the call is made. Since the company is in the 34 percent tax bracket, it saves $6,000,000 − $3,960,000 = $2,040,000 in taxes. Therefore, the after-tax cost of the call is only $3.96 million. This amount is shown as a cost, or outflow, on Line 1 of Table 16B-1.

b. Flotation costs on new issue

Flotation costs on the new issue are $2,650,000, as shown on Line 2 of the worksheet. For tax purposes, flotation costs must be amortized over the life of the new bond, or 20 years. Therefore, the annual tax deduction is

$$\frac{\$2,650,000}{20} = \$132,500.$$

Since Microchip is in the 34 percent tax bracket, it has a tax savings of $132,500(0.34) = $45,050 a year for 20 years. This is an annuity of $45,050 for 20 years. In a refunding analysis, all cash flows should be discounted at the after-tax cost of new debt, in this case $12\%(1 - T) = 12\%(0.66) = 7.92\%$. The present value of the tax savings, discounted at 7.92 percent, is $444,953, which is shown on Line 7 as an inflow.

c. Flotation costs on old issue

The old issue has an unamortized flotation cost of $(20/25)(\$3,000,000) = \$2.4$ million at this time. If the issue is retired, the unamortized flotation cost may be recognized immediately as an expense, thus creating an after-tax savings of $2,400,000(0.34) = $816,000, which is shown on Line 3 of the worksheet. The firm will, however, no longer receive a tax deduction of $120,000 a year for 20 years, or an after-tax benefit of $40,800 a year. The present value of this tax savings, discounted at 7.92 percent, is $402,976, which is shown on Line 8 as an opportunity cost of the refunding. It is important to note that because of the refunding, the old flotation costs provide an immediate tax saving

---

[2]The firm's management has estimated that there is a 75 percent probability that interest rates will remain at their present level of 12 percent or else rise; there is only a 25 percent probability that they will fall further.

Table 16B-1   Bond Refunding Decision Worksheet

	Amount before Tax	Amount after Tax	Present Value at 7.92%
Investment Outlay: t = 0			
1. Call premium on old issue	($6,000,000)	($3,960,000)	($ 3,960,000)
2. Flotation costs on new issue	(2,650,000)	(2,650,000)	(2,650,000)
3. Tax savings on old issue			
flotation costs	2,400,000	816,000	816,000
4. Extra interest cost on old issue	(750,000)	(495,000)	(495,000)
5. Interest earned on short-term			
investment	550,000	363,000	363,000
6. Net investment outlay at t = 0			($ 5,926,000)
Annual Flotation Cost Tax Effects: t = 1 − 20			
7. Annual benefit from new issue			
flotation costs	$132,500	$45,050	$ 444,953
8. Annual lost benefit from old			
issue flotation costs	(120,000)	(40,800)	(402,976)
9. PV of amortization tax effects			$ 41,977
Savings Due to Refunding: t = 1 − 20			
10. Interest payment on old issue	$9,000,000	$5,940,000	
11. Interest payment on new issue	7,200,000	4,752,000	
12. Net interest savings		$1,188,000	$11,733,727
NPV of Refunding Decision			$ 5,849,704

rather than annual savings over the next 20 years. Thus, the $816,000 − $402,976 = $413,024 net savings simply reflects the difference between the present value of benefits received in the future without the refunding versus an immediate benefit if the refunding occurs.

d.   Additional interest

One month "extra" interest on the old issue, after taxes, costs $495,000:

$$(Dollar\ amount)(1/12\ of\ 15\%)(1 − T) = Interest\ cost$$

$$(\$60,000,000)(0.0125)(0.66) = \$495,000.$$

However, the proceeds from the new issue can be invested in short-term securities for one month. Thus, $60 million invested at a rate of 11 percent will return $363,000 in after-tax interest:

$$(\$60,000,000)(1/12\ of\ 11\%)(1 − T) = Interest\ earned$$

$$(\$60,000,000)(0.009167)(0.66) = \$363,000.$$

These figures are reflected in Lines 4 and 5.

e. Total after-tax investment outlay

The total investment outlay required to refund the bond issue, which will be financed by debt, is thus $5,926,000.[3] This is shown on Line 6 of Table 16B-1.

Step 2. Calculate the PV of the Flotation Cost Tax Effects.

The net effect of the amortization of the flotation costs on the old and new issues is $41,977 in savings on a present value basis. This amount is shown on Line 9.

Step 3. Calculate the PV of the Annual Interest Savings.

a. Interest on old bond, after tax

The annual after-tax interest on the old issue is $5,940,000:

$$(\$60,000,000)(0.15)(0.66) = \$5,940,000.$$

This is shown on Line 10.

b. Interest on new bond, after tax

The new issue has an annual after-tax cost of $4,752,000:

$$(\$60,000,000)(0.12)(0.66) = \$4,752,000.$$

This is shown on Line 11.

c. Annual savings

Thus, the annual after-tax savings is $1,188,000:

Interest on old bond, after tax	$5,940,000
Interest on new bond, after tax	(4,752,000)
Annual net savings	$1,188,000

This is shown on Line 12.

d. PV of annual savings

The PV of $1,188,000 per year at 7.92 percent for 20 years is $11,733,727. This is also shown on Line 12.

Step 4. Determine the NPV of the Refunding.

Net investment outlay	($ 5,926,000)
Amortization tax effects	41,977
Interest savings	11,733,727
NPV from refunding	$ 5,849,704

Since the net present value of the refunding is positive, it would be profitable to refund the old bond issue.

---

[3]The net cash investment outlay (in this case, about $6 million) is usually obtained by increasing the amount of the new bond issue. Thus, the new issue would be about $66 million. However, the interest on the additional debt *should not* be deducted at Step 2 because the net investment outlay itself will be deducted at Step 3. If additional interest on the $6 million were deducted at Step 2, then interest would, in effect, be deducted twice. The situation here is exactly like that in regular capital budgeting decisions. Even though some debt may be used to finance a project, interest on that debt is not subtracted when developing the annual cash flows. Rather, the annual cash flows are discounted by the project's cost of capital.

Several other points should be noted. First, since the cash flows are based on differences between contractual obligations, their risk is the same as that of the underlying obligations. Therefore, the present values of the cash flows should be found by discounting at the firm's least risky rate—its after-tax cost of marginal debt. Second, since the refunding operation is advantageous to the firm, it must be disadvantageous to bondholders; they must give up their 15 percent bonds and reinvest in new ones that yield 12 percent. This points out the danger of the call provision to bondholders, and it also explains why bonds without a call provision command higher prices than callable bonds. Third, although it is not emphasized in the example, we assumed that the firm raises the investment required to undertake the refunding operation (the $5,926,000 shown on Line 6 of Table 16B-1) as debt. This should be feasible, since the refunding operation will improve the interest coverage ratio even though, if the investment outlay is raised as debt, a larger amount of debt will be outstanding.[4] Fourth, we set up our example in such a way that the new issue had the same maturity as the remaining life of the old issue. Often, the old bonds have only a relatively short time to maturity (say, 5 to 10 years), while the new bonds would have a longer maturity (say, 25 to 30 years). In this situation, a replacement chain analysis is required. Although the interest savings benefit occurs over a much shorter period, refunding now pushes future flotation costs out further into the future, and this value can most easily be captured by a replacement chain analysis. Fifth, refunding decisions are well suited for analysis with a spreadsheet program such as *Lotus 1-2-3*. The spreadsheet is easy to set up, and once it is, it is easy to vary the assumptions, especially the assumption about the interest rate on the new issue, and to see the way such changes affect the NPV.

One final point should be addressed: Although our analysis shows that the refunding would increase the value of the firm, would refunding *at this time* truly maximize the firm's expected value? Note that if interest rates continue to fall, then the company might be better off waiting, for this could increase the NPV of the refunding operation even more. The mechanics of calculating the NPV of a refunding are simple, but the decision on *when* to refund is not a simple one at all, because it requires a forecast of future interest rates. Thus, refund now versus waiting for a possibly more favorable future refunding is a judgmental decision.

To illustrate the timing decision, assume that Microchip's managers forecast that long-term interest rates have a 50 percent probability of remaining at their present level of 12 percent over the next year. However, there is a 25 percent probability that rates could fall to 10 percent, and a 25 percent probability that they could rise to 14 percent. Further, assume that short-term rates are expected to remain one percentage point below long-term rates, and that the call premium would be reduced by one-twentieth if the call were delayed for one year.

The refunding analysis could then be repeated, as previously, but assuming it would take place one year from now. Thus, the old bonds would have only 19 years remaining to

---

[4]See Ahron R. Ofer and Robert A. Taggart, Jr., "Bond Refunding: A Clarifying Analysis," *Journal of Finance,* March 1977, 21–30, for a discussion of how the method of financing the refunding affects the analysis. Ofer and Taggart prove that (1) if the refunding investment outlay is to be raised as debt, the after-tax cost of debt is the proper discount rate, while (2) if these funds are to be raised as common equity, then the before-tax cost of debt is the proper rate. Since a profitable refunding will virtually always raise the firm's debt-carrying capacity (because total interest charges after the refunding will be lower than before the refunding), it is more logical to use debt than either equity or a combination of debt and equity to finance the operation. Therefore, firms generally do use additional debt to finance refunding operations, so we assume debt financing for the costs of refunding and discount at the after-tax cost of debt.

maturity. We performed the analysis and found the NPV distribution of refunding one year from now:

Probability	Long-Term Interest Rate	NPV of Refunding One Year from Now
25%	10%	$15,328,674
50	12	5,770,191
25	14	(2,158,208)

At first blush, it would seem reasonable to calculate the expected NPV of refunding next year in terms of the probability distribution. However, that would not be correct. If interest rates did rise to 14 percent, Microchip would not refund the issue; therefore, the actual NPV if rates rise to 14 percent would be zero. The expected NPV from refunding one year hence is, therefore, 0.25($15,328,674) + 0.50($5,770,191) + 0.25($0) = $6,717,264 versus $5,849,704 if refunding occurred today.

Even though the expected NPV of refunding in one year is higher, Microchip's managers would probably decide to refund today. The $5,849,704 represents a certain increase in firm value, whereas the $6,717,264 is only an expected increase, plus proper comparison requires that the $6,717,264 be discounted back one year to today. Microchip's managers should opt to delay refunding only if the expected NPV from later refunding is sufficiently above today's certain NPV to compensate for the risk and time value involved.

The refunding analysis could be extended by (1) including possible refunding at more than one future point in time, and (2) specifying future interest rates by a continuous rather than a discrete distribution. However, the essence of the timing decision would remain the same.

CHAPTER 17

Lease Financing

Some of the biggest players in the airline business these days have never issued a ticket or had to land on a runway. They are the aircraft lease companies—the merchant bankers of aviation—whose role in financing aircraft sales is helping cash-strapped airlines respond more quickly to market changes. Among the major players in aircraft leasing are GPA Group, a closely held company based in Shannon, Ireland, and International Lease Finance of Beverly Hills. Leasing companies currently buy about 50 percent of new commercial aircraft. GPA Group already owns about 200 airplanes, and has over 600 more on order for delivery in the 1990s.

Aircraft leasing companies purchase airplanes from manufacturers such as Boeing, Airbus Industries, and McDonnell Douglas, and then lease them, often on a relatively short-term basis, to carriers such as American, Pan Am, KLM, and Lufthansa. For years, banks, insurance companies, and aircraft manufacturers have offered long-term, financial leases to airlines, but in recent years, aircraft lease companies have offered short-term, operating leases. Such leases, which range from a few months to five years, separate the risks and rewards of owning from those of operating a plane. The airline industry is currently undergoing major changes due to deregulation, and companies are constantly dropping and adding routes as competition and travel patterns change. However, certain types of aircraft are better suited for some routes than others, and operating leases permit an airline to quickly restructure its fleet to optimize the aircraft mix for the routes currently being flown. If the company had purchased all its aircraft, it would be hampered in its ability to quickly respond to changing market conditions. The leasing companies lease to all types of airlines, both domestic and foreign companies, and there is usually another airline interested in leasing an aircraft when its lease is dropped by a competitor. Because leasing companies have become specialists at matching airlines with available aircraft, they are quite good at managing the changing demand for different types of aircraft. This permits them to offer lease terms that are attractive to the airlines.

FIRMS generally own fixed assets and report them on their balance sheets, but it is the *use* of buildings and equipment that is important, not their ownership per se. One way of obtaining the use of facilities and equipment is to buy them, but an alternative is to lease them. Prior to the 1950s, leasing was generally associated with real estate—land and buildings. Today, however, it is possible to lease virtually any kind of fixed asset, and currently about 30 percent of all new capital equipment acquired by businesses is financed through lease arrangements.

TYPES OF LEASES

Leasing takes several different forms, the four most important being (1) sale-and-leaseback arrangements, (2) operating leases, (3) financial, or capital, leases, and (4) combination leases.

Sale-and-Leaseback Arrangements

Under a *sale-and-leaseback arrangement,* a firm that owns land, buildings, or equipment sells the property to another firm and simultaneously executes an agreement to lease the property back for a stated period under specific terms. The capital supplier could be an insurance company, a commercial bank, a specialized leasing company, the finance arm of an industrial firm, or an individual investor. The sale-and-leaseback plan is an alternative to a mortgage.

Note that the seller, or *lessee,* immediately receives the purchase price put up by the buyer, or *lessor.*[1] At the same time, the seller-lessee retains the use of the property. The parallel to borrowing is carried over to the lease payment schedule. Under a mortgage loan arrangement, the lender would normally receive a series of equal payments just sufficient to amortize the loan and to provide a specified rate of return on the outstanding loan balance. Under a sale-and-leaseback arrangement, the lease payments are set up exactly the same way—the payments are just sufficient to return the full purchase price to the investor, plus a stated return on the lessor's investment.

---

[1] The term *lessee* is pronounced "less-ee," not "lease-ee," and *lessor* is pronounced "less-or."

Operating Leases

Operating leases, sometimes called *service leases,* generally provide for both *financing* and *maintenance.* IBM was one of the pioneers of the operating lease contract, and computers and office copying machines, together with automobiles and trucks, are the primary types of equipment involved in operating leases. Ordinarily, these leases require the lessor to maintain and service the leased equipment, and the cost of the maintenance is built into the lease payments.

Another important characteristic of operating leases is the fact that they are *not fully amortized.* In other words, the payments required under the lease contract are not sufficient to recover the full cost of the equipment. However, the lease contract is written for a period considerably less than the expected economic life of the leased equipment, and the lessor expects to recover all costs either by subsequent renewal payments, by re-leasing the equipment to other lessees, or by sale of the equipment.

A final feature of operating leases is that they frequently contain a *cancellation clause* which gives the lessee the right to cancel the lease and to return the equipment before the expiration of the basic lease agreement. This is an important consideration to the lessee, for it means that the equipment can be returned if it is rendered obsolete by technological developments or if it is no longer needed because of a decline in the lessee's business.

Financial, or Capital, Leases

Financial leases, sometimes called *capital leases,* are differentiated from operating leases in that (1) they *do not* provide for maintenance service, (2) they *are not* cancellable, and (3) they *are* fully amortized (that is, the lessor receives rental payments equal to the full price of the leased equipment plus a return on investment). In a typical arrangement, the firm that will use the equipment (the lessee) selects the specific items it requires, and then it negotiates the price and delivery terms with the manufacturer. The user firm then arranges to have a leasing company (the lessor) buy the equipment from the manufacturer or the distributor, and the user firm simultaneously executes an agreement to lease the equipment from the financial institution. The terms of the lease call for full amortization of the lessor's investment, plus a rate of return on the unamortized balance which is close to the percentage rate the lessee would have paid on a secured term loan. For example, if the lessee would have to pay 10 percent for a term loan, then a rate of about 10 percent would be built into the lease contract.

The lessee is generally given an option to renew the lease at a reduced rate upon expiration of the basic lease. However, the basic lease usually cannot be cancelled unless the lessor is completely paid off. Also, the lessee generally pays the property taxes and insurance on the leased property. Since the lessor receives a return *after,* or *net of,* these payments, this type of lease is often called a "net, net" lease.

Financial leases are almost the same as sale-and-leaseback arrangements, the major difference being that the leased equipment is new and the lessor buys it from a manufacturer or a distributor instead of from the user-lessee. A sale and leaseback may, then, be thought of as a special type of financial lease. Both sale-and-leaseback arrangements and financial leases are analyzed in the same manner.

Combination Leases

Many lessors now offer leases under a wide variety of terms. Therefore, in practice, leases often do not fit exactly into the operating lease or financial lease category, but, rather, combine some features of each. Such leases are called *combination leases*. To illustrate, cancellation clauses are normally associated with operating leases, but many of today's financial leases also contain cancellation clauses. However, in financial leases these clauses generally include prepayment provisions whereby the lessee must make penalty payments sufficient to enable the lessor to recover the unamortized investment cost of the leased property.

Self-Test Questions

What is a sale-and-leaseback transaction?

What is the difference between an operating lease and a financial, or capital, lease?

What is a combination lease?

TAX EFFECTS

The full amount of the annual lease payment is a tax-deductible expense for the lessee *provided that the Internal Revenue Service agrees that a particular contract is a genuine lease and not simply an installment loan called a lease.* This makes it important that a lease contract be written in a form acceptable to the IRS. A lease that complies with all of the IRS requirements is called a *guideline,* or *tax-oriented, lease,* because the lease meets all of the IRS guidelines, and the tax benefits of ownership (depreciation and investment tax credits when they are available) belong to the lessor. The main provisions of the tax guidelines are as follows:

1. The lease term (including any extensions or renewals at a fixed rental rate) must not exceed 80 percent of the estimated useful life of the equipment at the commencement of the lease transaction. Thus, at the end of the lease the equipment must have an estimated remaining life equal to at least 20 percent of its original life. Further, the remaining useful life must not be less than one year. This requirement limits the maximum term of a lease to 80 percent of the asset's useful life. Note that an asset's useful life is normally much longer than its MACRS class life.

2. The equipment's estimated residual value (in constant dollars without adjustment for inflation) at the expiration of the lease must equal at least 20 percent of its value at the start of the lease. This requirement can have the effect of limiting the maximum lease term.

3.   Neither the lessee nor any related party can have the right to purchase the property from the lessor at a fixed price predetermined at the lease's inception. However, the lessee can be given a fair market value purchase option.

4.   Neither the lessee nor any related party can pay or guarantee payment of any part of the price of the leased equipment. Simply put, the lessee cannot make any investment in the equipment, other than through the lease payments.

5.   The leased equipment must not be "limited use" property, defined as equipment that can only be used by the lessee or a related party at the end of the lease.

The reason for the IRS's concern about lease terms is that, without restrictions, a company could set up a "lease" transaction calling for very rapid payments, which would be tax deductions. The effect would be to depreciate the equipment over a much shorter period than its MACRS class life. For example, suppose a firm planned to acquire a $2 million computer which had a 3-year MACRS class life. The annual depreciation allowances would be $660,000 in Year 1, $900,000 in Year 2, $300,000 in Year 3, and $140,000 in Year 4. If the firm were in the 40 percent federal-plus-state tax bracket, the depreciation would provide a tax saving of $264,000 in Year 1, $360,000 in Year 2, $120,000 in Year 3, and $56,000 in Year 4, for a total savings of $800,000. At a 6 percent discount rate, the present value of these tax savings would be $757,441.

Now suppose the firm could acquire the computer through a 1-year lease arrangement with a leasing company for a payment of $2 million, with a 1-dollar purchase option. If the $2,000,000 payment were treated as a lease payment, it would be fully deductible, so it would provide a tax saving of 0.4($2,000,000) = $800,000 versus a present value of only $757,441 for the depreciation shelters. Thus, the lease payment and the depreciation would both provide the same total amount of tax savings (40% of $2 million, or $800,000), but the savings would come in faster, hence have a higher present value, with the 1-year lease. Therefore, if just any type of contract could be called a lease and given tax treatment as a lease, then the timing of the tax shelters could be speeded up as compared with ownership depreciation tax shelters. This speedup would benefit companies, but it would be costly to the government. For this reason, the IRS has established the rules described above for defining a lease for tax purposes.

Even though leasing can be used only within limits to speed up the effective depreciation schedule, there are still times when very substantial tax benefits can be derived from a leasing arrangement. For example, if a firm like Tucson Electric has a very large construction program which has generated so many investment tax credits and so much accelerated depreciation that it has no current tax liabilities, then depreciation shelters are not very useful. In this case, a leasing company set up by profitable companies like IBM and Philip Morris can buy the equipment, receive the depreciation shelters, and then share these benefits with the lessee by charging lower lease payments. This point will be discussed in detail later in the chapter, but the point to be made now is that if firms are to obtain tax benefits from leasing, the lease contract must be written in a manner that will qualify it as a true lease under IRS guidelines. If there is any question about the legal status of the contract, the financial manager must be sure to have the firm's lawyers and accountants check the latest IRS regulations.[2]

Note that a lease which does not meet the tax guidelines is called a *non-tax-oriented lease.* For this type of lease, the lessee can only deduct the interest portion of each lease payment. However, the lessee is effectively the owner of the leased equipment; thus the lessee can take the tax depreciation.

Self-Test Questions

What is the difference between a tax-oriented lease and a non-tax-oriented lease?

What are some lease provisions that would cause a lease to be classified as a non-tax-oriented lease?

Why is it necessary for the IRS to place limits on lease provisions?

FINANCIAL STATEMENT EFFECTS

Under certain conditions, neither the leased assets nor the liabilities under the lease contract appear on the firm's balance sheet. For this reason, leasing is often called *off-balance sheet* financing. This point is illustrated in Table 17-1 by the balance sheets of two hypothetical firms, B and L. Initially, the balance sheets of both firms are identical, and they both have debt ratios of 50 percent. Next, each firm decides to acquire a fixed asset costing $100. Firm B borrows $100 and buys the asset, so both an asset and a liability go on its balance sheet, and its debt ratio rises from 50 to 75 percent. Firm L leases the equipment. The lease may call for fixed charges as high or even higher than the loan, and the obligations assumed under the lease may be equally or more dangerous from the standpoint of potential bankruptcy, but the firm's debt ratio remains at only 50 percent.

To correct this problem, the Financial Accounting Standards Board issued FASB Statement 13, which requires that, for an unqualified audit report, firms that enter into financial (or capital) leases must restate their balance sheets to report the leased asset as a fixed asset and the present value of the future lease payments as a liability. This process is called *capitalizing the lease,* and its net effect is to cause Firms B and L to have similar balance sheets, both of which will, in essence, resemble the one shown for Firm B.[3]

---

[2]Under the Economic Recovery Tax Act of 1981, Congress relaxed the normal IRS rules to permit *safe harbor leases,* which had virtually no IRS restrictions and which were explicitly designed to permit the transfer of tax benefits from low-profit companies which could not use them to high-profit companies which could. The point of safe harbor leases was to provide incentives for capital investment to companies which had little or no tax liability — under safe harbor leasing, companies with a low tax liability could sell the benefit to companies in a high marginal tax bracket. In 1981 and 1982, literally billions of dollars were paid by such profitable firms as IBM and Philip Morris for the tax shelters of such unprofitable ones as Ford and Eastern Airlines. However, in 1983, Congress sharply curtailed the use of safe harbor leases.

[3]FASB Statement 13, "Accounting for Leases," spells out in detail both the conditions under which the lease must be capitalized and the procedures for capitalizing it.

Table 17-1   Balance Sheet Effects of Leasing

Before Asset Increase				After Asset Increase							
Firms B and L				Firm B, which Borrows and Buys				Firm L, which Leases			
Current assets	$ 50	Debt	$ 50	Current assets	$ 50	Debt	$150	Current assets	$ 50	Debt	$ 50
Fixed assets	50	Equity	50	Fixed assets	150	Equity	50	Fixed assets	50	Equity	50
	$100		$100		$200		$200		$100		$100
Debt/assets ratio:			50%				75%				50%

The logic behind Statement 13 is as follows. If a firm signs a financial lease contract, its obligation to make lease payments is just as binding as if it had signed a loan agreement — the failure to make lease payments can bankrupt a firm just as fast as the failure to make principal and interest payments on a loan. Therefore, for all intents and purposes, a financial lease is identical to a loan.[4] This being the case, if a firm signs a financial lease agreement, this has the effect of raising its true debt ratio, and thus its true capital structure is changed. Therefore, if the firm had previously established a target capital structure, and if there is no reason to think that the optimal capital structure has changed, then using lease financing requires additional equity support exactly like debt financing.

If disclosure of the lease in our Table 17-1 example were not made, then Firm L's investors could be deceived into thinking that its financial position is stronger than it really is. Thus, even before FASB Statement 13 was issued in 1976, firms were required to disclose the existence of long-term leases in footnotes to their financial statements. At that time, it was debated as to whether or not investors recognized fully the impact of leases and, in effect, would see that Firms B and L were in essentially the same financial position. Some people argued that leases were not fully recognized, even by sophisticated investors. If this were the case, then leasing could alter the capital structure decision in a really significant manner — a firm could increase its true leverage through a lease arrangement, and this procedure would have a smaller effect on its cost of conventional debt, k_d, and on its cost of equity, k_s, than if it had borrowed directly and reflected this fact on its balance sheet. These benefits of leasing would accrue to existing investors at the expense of new investors who would, in effect, be deceived by the fact that the firm's balance sheet did not reflect its true liability situation.

---

[4]There are, however, certain legal differences between loans and leases. In the event of liquidation in bankruptcy, a lessor is entitled to take possession of the leased asset, and if the value of the asset is less than the required payments under the lease, the lessor can enter a claim (as a general creditor) for one year's lease payments. In a reorganization, the lessor receives the asset plus three years' lease payments if needed to cover the value of the lease. The lender under a secured loan arrangement has a security interest in the asset, meaning that if it is sold, the lender will be given the proceeds, and the full unsatisfied portion of the lender's claim will be treated as a general creditor obligation. It is not possible to state, as a general rule, whether a supplier of capital is in a stronger position as a secured creditor or as a lessor. Usually, one position is regarded as being about as good as the other at the time the financial arrangements are being made.

The question of whether investors were truly deceived was debated but never resolved. Those who believed strongly in efficient markets thought that investors were not deceived and that footnotes were sufficient, while those who questioned market efficiency thought that all leases should be capitalized. Statement 13 represents a compromise between these two positions, though one that is tilted heavily toward those who favor capitalization.

A lease is classified as a capital lease, hence is capitalized and shown directly on the balance sheet, if one or more of the following conditions exist:

1.   Under the terms of the lease, ownership of the property is effectively transferred from the lessor to the lessee.

2.   The lessee can purchase the property at less than its true market value when the lease expires.

3.   The lease runs for a period equal to or greater than 75 percent of the asset's life. Thus, if an asset has a 10-year life and the lease is written for 8 years, the lease must be capitalized.

4.   The present value of the lease payments is equal to or greater than 90 percent of the initial value of the asset.[5]

These rules, together with strong footnote disclosure rules for operating leases, are sufficient to insure that no one will be fooled by lease financing; thus, leases are regarded as debt for capital structure purposes, and they have the same effects as debt on k_d and k_s. Therefore, leasing is not likely to permit a firm to use more financial leverage than could be obtained with conventional debt.

Self-Test Questions

Why is lease financing sometimes referred to as off-balance sheet financing?

What is the intent of FASB Statement 13?

What is the difference in the balance sheet treatment of a lease that is capitalized and one that is not?

EVALUATION BY THE LESSEE

Leases are evaluated by both the lessee and the lessor. The lessee must determine whether leasing an asset is less costly than buying the asset, and the lessor must decide what the lease payments must be to produce a reasonable rate of return. This section focuses on the analysis by the lessee.

---

[5]The discount rate used to calculate the present value of the lease payments must be the lower of (1) the rate used by the lessor to establish the lease payments (this rate is discussed later in the chapter) or (2) the rate of interest which the lessee would have to pay for new debt with a maturity equal to that of the lease. Also, note that any maintenance payments embedded in the lease payment must be stripped out prior to checking this condition.

In the typical case, the events leading to a lease arrangement follow the sequence described next. We should note that a degree of uncertainty exists regarding the theoretically correct way to evaluate lease-versus-purchase decisions, and some very complex decision models have been developed to aid in the analysis. However, the simple analysis given here leads to the correct decision in all the cases we have ever encountered.

1. The firm decides to acquire a particular building or piece of equipment; this decision is based on regular capital budgeting procedures. The decision to acquire the machine is not at issue in the typical lease analysis—this decision was made previously as part of the capital budgeting process. In a lease analysis, we are concerned simply with whether to obtain the use of the machine by lease or by purchase. However, if the effective cost of capital obtained by leasing is substantially lower than the cost of debt, then the cost of capital used in capital budgeting would have to be recalculated, and perhaps projects formerly deemed unacceptable might become acceptable.

2. Once the firm has decided to acquire the asset, the next question is how to finance its acquisition. Well-run businesses do not have excess cash lying around, so capital to finance new assets must be obtained from some source.

3. Funds to purchase the asset could be obtained by borrowing, by retaining earnings, or by selling new equity. Alternatively, the asset could be leased. Because of the capitalization/disclosure provision for leases, leasing normally has the same capital structure effect as borrowing.

As indicated earlier, a lease is comparable to a loan in the sense that the firm is required to make a specified series of payments and that a failure to meet these payments could result in bankruptcy. Thus, the most appropriate comparison is the cost of lease financing versus the cost of debt financing.[6]

To illustrate the basic elements of lease analysis, consider this simplified example. The Thompson-Grammatikos Company (TGC) requires the use of a 2-year asset that costs $100, and the company must choose between leasing and buying the asset. If the asset is purchased, the bank would lend TGC the $100 at a rate of 10 percent on a 2-year, simple interest loan. Thus, the firm would have to pay the bank $10 in interest at the end of each year, plus return the $100 in principal at the end of Year 2. For simplicity, assume that TGC could depreciate the asset over 2 years for tax purposes by the straight line method if it is purchased, resulting in tax depreciation of $50 in each year. Also for simplicity, assume the asset's value at the end of 2 years (the residual value) is estimated to be $0.

Alternatively, the firm could lease the asset under a guideline lease for 2 years for a payment of $55 at the end of each year. TGC's tax rate is 40 percent. The analysis for the lease-versus-borrow decision consists of (1) estimating the cash flows

---

[6]Note that the analysis should compare the cost of leasing to the cost of debt financing *regardless* of how the asset is actually financed. The asset may be purchased with available cash if not leased, but since leasing is a substitute for debt financing, the appropriate comparison would still be to debt financing.

associated with borrowing and buying the asset, that is, the flows associated with debt financing, (2) estimating the cash flows associated with leasing the asset, and (3) comparing the two financing methods to determine which has the lower cost. Here are the borrow-and-buy flows:

Cash Flows if TGC Buys	Year 0	Year 1	Year 2
Equipment cost	($100)		
Loan amount	100		
Interest expense		($10)	($ 10)
Tax savings from interest		4	4
Principal repayment			(100)
Tax savings from depreciation		20	20
Net cash flow	$ 0	$14	($ 86)

The net cash flow is zero in Year 0, positive in Year 1, and negative in Year 2. The operating cash flows are not shown, but they must, of course, be positive or else TGC would not want to acquire the asset. Since the operating cash flows will be the same regardless of whether the asset is leased or purchased, they can be ignored.

Here are the cash flows associated with the lease:

Cash Flows if TGC Leases	Year 0	Year 1	Year 2
Lease payment		($55)	($55)
Tax savings from payment	—	22	22
Net cash flow	$0	($33)	($33)

Note that the two sets of cash flows reflect the tax deductibility of interest expense, depreciation, and lease payments, as appropriate. Thus, the net cash flows include the tax savings from these items. If the lease had not met IRS guidelines, then ownership would effectively reside with the lessee, and TGC would depreciate the asset for tax purposes whether it was leased or purchased. Further, only the implied interest portion of the lease payment would be tax deductible. Thus, the analysis for a nonguideline lease would consist of simply comparing the after-tax financing flows on the loan with the after-tax lease payment stream.

To compare the cost streams of buying and leasing, we must put them on a present value basis. As we explain later, the correct discount rate is the after-tax cost of debt, which for TGC is 10%(1 − 0.4) = 6.0%. Applying this rate, we find the present value cost of buying to be $63.33, and the present value cost of leasing to be $60.50. Since leasing has the lower present value of costs, the company should lease the asset.

The example shows the general approach that we use in lease analysis, and it also illustrates a concept that can simplify the cash flow estimation process. Look back at the loan-related cash flows if TGC buys the asset. The after-tax loan-related flows are − $6 in Year 1 and − $106 in Year 2. When these flows are discounted to Year 0 at the 6.0 percent after-tax cost rate, their present value is − $100, the negative of the loan amount. This equality results because we first used the cost of debt to estimate the future financing flows, and we then used this same rate to discount the flows back to the present, all on an after-tax basis. Here is the cash flow stream after the Year 0 loan amount and the related Year 1 and Year 2 flows have been removed:

Cash Flows if TGC Buys	Year 0	Year 1	Year 2
Cost of asset	($100)		
Tax savings from depreciation		$20	$20
Net cash flow	($100)	$20	$20

The present value cost of buying here is, of course, $63.33, the same number we found earlier. This result will always occur regardless of the specific terms of the debt financing—as long as the discount rate is the after-tax cost of debt, the cash flows associated with the loan can be ignored.

Now we examine a more realistic example, one for the Anderson Equipment Company, which is conducting a lease analysis on some assembly line equipment that it will procure in the coming year. The following data have been developed:

1.   Anderson plans to acquire an automated assembly line with a 10-year life and a cost of $10 million, delivered and installed. However, Anderson plans to use the equipment for only 5 years, for it will discontinue the product line at that time.

2.   Anderson can borrow the required $10 million at a before-tax cost of 10 percent.

3.   The equipment's estimated scrap value is $50,000 after 10 years of use, but its estimated salvage value after only 5 years of use is $1,000,000. Thus, if Anderson buys the equipment, it would expect to receive $1,000,000 before taxes when the equipment is sold in 5 years. Note that in leasing, the asset's value at the end of the lease period is generally called its *residual value*.

4.   Anderson can lease the equipment for 5 years at a rental charge of $2,750,000, payable at the beginning of each year, but the lessor will own the equipment upon the expiration of the lease. (The lease payment schedule is established by the potential lessor, as described in the next major section, and Anderson can accept it, reject it, or negotiate.)

5.   The lease contract stipulates that the lessor will maintain the equipment at no additional charge to Anderson. However, if Anderson borrows and buys, it will have to bear the cost of maintenance, which will be performed by the equipment manufacturer at a fixed contract rate of $500,000 per year, payable at the beginning of each year.

6.   The equipment falls in the MACRS 5-year class life, Anderson's marginal tax rate is 40 percent, and the lease qualifies as a guideline lease.

NPV Analysis

Table 17-2 shows the steps involved in a complete NPV lease analysis. Part I of the table is devoted to the costs of borrowing and buying. Here, Line 1 gives the equipment's cost; Line 2 shows the maintenance expense; Line 3 gives the maintenance tax savings; Line 4 contains the depreciation tax savings, which is the depreciation expense times the tax rate; Lines 5 and 6 contain the residual value cash flows; Line 7 contains the net cash flows; and Line 8 shows the net present value of these flows, discounted at 6 percent.

Table 17-2   Anderson Equipment Company: NPV Analysis
(Thousands of Dollars)

I. Cost of Owning (Borrowing and Buying)

	Year 0	Year 1	Year 2	Year 3	Year 4	Year 5
1. Net purchase price	($10,000)					
2. Maintenance cost	(500)	($500)	($ 500)	($500)	($500)	
3. Maintenance tax savings	200	200	200	200	200	
4. Depreciation tax savings		800	1,280	760	480	$ 440
5. Residual value						1,000
6. Residual value tax						(160)
7. Net cash flow	($10,300)	$500	$ 980	$460	$180	$1,280

8. PV cost of owning = ($7,471)

II. Cost of Leasing

	Year 0	Year 1	Year 2	Year 3	Year 4	Year 5
9. Lease payment	($2,750)	($2,750)	($2,750)	($2,750)	($2,750)	
10. Payment tax savings	1,100	1,100	1,100	1,100	1,100	
11. Net cash flow	($1,650)	($1,650)	($1,650)	($1,650)	($1,650)	$0

12. PV cost of leasing = ($7,367)

III. Cost Comparison

13. Net advantage to leasing (NAL) = PV cost of owning − PV cost of leasing = $7,471 − $7,367 = $104.

Notes:
a. The net cash flows shown in Lines 7 and 11 are discounted at the lessee's after-tax cost of debt, 6.0 percent.
b. The MACRS depreciation allowances are 0.20, 0.32, 0.19, 0.12, and 0.11 in Years 1 through 5, respectively. Thus, the depreciation expense is 0.20($10,000) = $2,000 in Year 1, and so on. The depreciation tax savings in each year is merely 0.4 (Depreciation).
c. The residual value is $1,000 while the book value is $600. Thus, Anderson would have to pay 0.4($1,000 − $600) = $160 in taxes, producing a net after-tax residual value of $1,000 − $160 = $840. These amounts are shown in Lines 5 and 6 in the cost of owning analysis.
d. In practice, a lease analysis such as this would be done using a spreadsheet program such as *Lotus 1-2-3.*
e. In the NAL equation on Line 13, the PV costs are stated as positive values.

Part II of Table 17-2 contains an analysis of the cost of leasing. The lease payments, shown on Line 9, are $2,750,000 per year; this rate, which includes maintenance, was established by the prospective lessor and offered to Anderson Equipment. If Anderson accepts the lease, the full amount will be a deductible expense, so the tax savings, shown on Line 10, is 0.40(Lease payment) = 0.40($2,750,000) = $1,100,000. Thus, the after-tax cost of the lease payment is Lease payment − Tax savings = $2,750,000 − $1,100,000 = $1,650,000. This amount is shown on Line 11, Years 0 through 4.

The next step is to compare the net cost of owning with the net cost of leasing. However, we must first put the annual cash flows of leasing and borrowing on a common basis. This requires converting them to present values, which brings up the question of the proper rate at which to discount the costs. We know that the riskier the cash flows, the higher will be the discount rate used to find present values. This same principle was observed in our discussion of capital budgeting, and it also applies in lease analysis. Just how risky are the cash flows under consideration here? Most of them are relatively certain, at least when compared with the types of cash flow estimates that were developed in capital budgeting. For example, the loan payment schedule is set by contract, as is the lease payment schedule. The depreciation expenses are also established by law and not subject to change, and the $500,000 annual maintenance cost is fixed by contract as well. The tax savings are somewhat uncertain, but they will be as projected so long as Anderson's marginal tax rate remains at 40 percent. The residual value is the least certain of the cash flows, but even here, Anderson's management is fairly confident because the estimated residual value distribution is relatively tight.

Since the cash flows under the lease and under the borrow-and-purchase alternatives are both relatively certain, they should be discounted at a relatively low rate. Most analysts recommend that the company's cost of debt be used, and this rate seems reasonable in our example. Further, since the interest on the loan would be tax deductible, *the after-tax cost of debt, which is 6.0 percent, should be used.* Accordingly, we discount the net cash flows in Lines 7 and 11 using a rate of 6.0 percent. The resulting present values are $7,471,000 for the cost of owning and $7,367,000 for the cost of leasing, as shown in Lines 8 and 12. The financing method that produces the smaller present value of costs is the one that should be selected. We define the net advantage to leasing (NAL) as follows:

$$NAL = PV \text{ cost of owning} - PV \text{ cost of leasing.}$$

$$= \quad \$7,471,000 \quad - \quad \$7,367,000$$

$$= \quad \$104,000$$

The PV cost of owning exceeds the PV cost of leasing, so the NAL is positive. Therefore, Anderson should lease the equipment.[7]

---

[7]The more complicated methods which exist for analyzing leasing generally focus on the issue of the discount rate that should be used to discount the cash flows. Conceptually, we could assign a separate discount rate to each individual cash flow component, then find the present values of each of the cash flow components, and finally sum these present values to determine the net advantage or disadvantage to leasing. This approach has been taken by Stewart C. Myers, David A. Dill, and Alberto J. Bautista (MDB) in "Valuation of Financial Lease Contracts," *Journal of Finance,* June 1976, 799–819, among others. MDB correctly note that procedures like the one presented in this chapter are valid only if (1) leases and loans are viewed by investors as being equivalent and (2) all cash flows are equally risky, hence appropriately discounted at the same rate. The first assumption is valid today for virtually all financial leases, and even where it is not, no one knows how to adjust properly for any capital structure effects that leases might have. (MDB, and others, have presented an adjustment formula, but it is based on the assumption that the Modigliani-Miller leverage argument, with no financial distress costs, is correct. Since even MM do not regard the pure MM model as being correct, the MDB formula cannot be correct.) Regarding the second assumption, it is generally believed that all of the cash flows in Table 17-2 except the residual value are of about the same degree of risk, at least to the extent that we are able to evaluate risk. Therefore, the procedures used in Table 17-2 normally meet the MDB assumption; hence, the Table 17-2 analysis is usually correct.

Regarding the residual value, advocates of multiple discount rates often point out that the residual value is more uncertain than are the other cash flows and thus recommend discounting it at a higher rate. However, there is no way of knowing precisely how much to increase the after-tax cost of debt to account for the increased riskiness of the residual value cash flow. Further, in a CAPM sense, all cash flows could be equally risky even though individual items such as the residual value might have more or less total variability than others.

IRR Analysis

Anderson's lease-versus-purchase decision could also be analyzed using the IRR approach. Here we know the after-tax cost of debt, 6.0 percent, so we can find the *after-tax cost rate implied in the lease contract* and compare it with the cost of the loan. Signing a lease is similar to signing a loan contract—the firm has the use of equipment, but it must make a series of payments under either type of contract. We know the rate built into the loan; it is 6.0 percent after taxes for Anderson. There is an equivalent cost rate built into the lease. If the equivalent after-tax cost rate in the lease is less than the after-tax interest rate on the debt, then there is an advantage to leasing.

Table 17-3 sets forth the cash flows needed to determine the equivalent loan cost. Here is an explanation of the table:

1.   The net cost to purchase the equipment, which is avoided if Anderson leases, is shown on Line 1 as a positive cash flow (an inflow) at Year 0. If Anderson leases, it avoids having to pay the net purchase price for the equipment—the lessor pays that cost, so Anderson saves $10 million. That is a positive cash flow at Year 0.

2.   Next, we must determine what Anderson must give up (or "pay back") if it leases. As we saw in the last section, Anderson must make annual lease payments of $2,750,000, which amount to $1,650,000 on an after-tax basis. These amounts are reported as cash outflows on Line 2, Years 0 through 4.

3.   If Anderson elects to lease, it will have to give up the right to depreciate the asset. The lost depreciation tax savings, which represent an opportunity cost of leasing, are shown as outflows on Line 3, Years 1 through 5.

4.   If Anderson decides to lease rather than borrow and buy, it will avoid the maintenance cost of $500,000 per year, or $300,000 after taxes. This is shown on Line 4 as an inflow, or benefit of leasing.

5.   If Anderson leases the equipment, it will have to give up the net after-tax residual value of $840,000. This is also an opportunity cost of leasing, and it is shown on Line 5 as an outflow in Year 5.

Table 17-3   Anderson Equipment Company: IRR Analysis
              (Thousands of Dollars)

	Year 0	Year 1	Year 2	Year 3	Year 4	Year 5
1. Avoided net purchase price	$10,000					
2. After-tax lease payment	(1,650)	($1,650)	($1,650)	($1,650)	($1,650)	
3. Loss of depreciation tax savings		(800)	(1,280)	(760)	(480)	($ 440)
4. Avoided after-tax maintenance cost	300	300	300	300	300	
5. Loss of after-tax residual value						(840)
6. Net cash flow	$ 8,650	($2,150)	($2,630)	($2,110)	($1,830)	($1,280)

$$\text{NPV} = \sum_{t=0}^{5} \frac{\text{NCF}_t}{(1 + k_L)^t} = 0 \text{ when } k_L = \text{IRR} = 5.5\%.$$

6.   Line 6 shows the annual net cash flows. If Anderson leases, there is an inflow at Year 0 followed by outflows in Years 1 to 5. Note that the Line 6 net cash flows are simply the net cash flows of leasing rather than buying, or Line 11 − Line 7 in Table 17-2.

By inputting the cash flows on Line 6 of Table 17-3 into the cash flow register of a calculator and then pressing the IRR button, we can find the IRR for the stream; it is 5.5 percent, and this is the equivalent after-tax cost rate implied in the lease contract. If Anderson leases, it is using up $10 million of its debt capacity, and the implied cost rate is 5.5 percent. Since this cost rate is less than the 6.0 percent after-tax cost of a regular loan, this IRR lease analysis confirms the NPV analysis: Anderson should lease rather than buy the equipment. The NPV and IRR approaches will always lead to the same decision. Thus, one method is as good as the other from a decision standpoint.[8]

Self-Test Questions

Explain how the cash flows are structured when estimating the net advantage to leasing.

What discount rate should be used in the lessee's analysis? Why?

Define the term "net advantage to leasing."

What is the economic significance of a lease's IRR?

EVALUATION BY THE LESSOR

Thus far we have considered leasing only from the lessee's viewpoint. It is also useful to analyze the transaction as the lessor sees it: Is the lease a good investment for the party who must put up the money? The lessor will generally be a specialized leasing company, a bank or bank affiliate, an individual or group of individuals, or a manufacturer such as IBM that uses leasing as a sales tool. The specialized leasing companies are often owned by profitable companies such as General Electric, which owns General Electric Capital, the largest leasing company in existence. Investment banking houses such as Merrill Lynch also set up and/or work with specialized leasing companies, where brokerage clients' money is made available to leasing customers in deals which permit the investors to share in the tax shelters provided by the lease.

Any potential lessor needs to know the rate of return on the capital invested in the lease, and this information is also useful to the prospective lessee: Lease terms on large leases are generally negotiated, so the lessor and the lessee should know one another's position. The lessor's analysis involves (1) determining the net cash outlay, which is usually the invoice price of the leased equipment less any lease

---

[8]Note that the net cash flows shown on Line 6 of Table 17-3 are the incremental cash flows to Anderson if it leases rather than borrows and buys. Thus, the NPV of these flows is the net advantage to leasing. When discounted at a rate of 6.0 percent, the NPV of the Line 6 flows is $103,389, which, except for a rounding error, is the same as we obtained in the Table 17-2 NPV analysis.

payments made in advance; (2) determining the periodic cash inflows, which consist of the lease payments minus both income taxes and any maintenance expense the lessor must bear; (3) estimating the after-tax residual value of the property when the lease expires; and (4) determining whether the rate of return on the lease exceeds the lessor's opportunity cost of capital or, equivalently, whether the NPV of the lease exceeds zero.

To illustrate the lessor's analysis, we assume the same facts as for the Anderson Equipment Company lease, as well as this situation: (1) The potential lessor is a wealthy individual whose current income is in the form of interest, and whose marginal federal-plus-state income tax rate, T, is 40 percent. (2) The investor can buy bonds that have a 9 percent yield to maturity, providing an after-tax yield of $(9\%)(1 - T) = (9\%)(0.6) = 5.4\%$. This is the after-tax return that the investor can obtain on alternative investments of similar risk. (3) The before-tax residual value is $1,000,000. Since the asset will be depreciated to a book value of $600,000 at the end of the 5-year lease, $400,000 of this $1 million will be taxable at the 40 percent rate because of the recapture of depreciation rule, so the lessor can expect to receive $840,000 after taxes from the sale of the equipment after the lease expires.

The NPV of the lease from the investor's standpoint is developed in Table 17-4. Here we see that the lease as an investment has a net present value of $26,000. On a present value basis, the investor who invests in the lease rather than in the 9 percent bonds (5.4 percent after taxes) is better off by $26,000, indicating that the investor should be willing to write the lease. Since we saw earlier that the lease is also advantageous to Anderson Equipment Company, the transaction should be completed.

The investor can also calculate the lease investment's IRR based on the net cash flows shown on Line 9 of Table 17-4. The IRR of the lease, which is that discount

Table 17-4   Lease Analysis from the Lessor's Viewpoint (Thousands of Dollars)

	Year 0	Year 1	Year 2	Year 3	Year 4	Year 5
1. Net purchase price	($10,000)					
2. Maintenance cost	(500)	($ 500)	($ 500)	($ 500)	($ 500)	
3. Maintenance tax savings	200	200	200	200	200	
4. Depreciation tax savings		800	1,280	760	480	$ 440
5. Lease payment	2,750	2,750	2,750	2,750	2,750	
6. Tax on lease payment	(1,100)	(1,100)	(1,100)	(1,100)	(1,100)	
7. Residual value						1,000
8. Tax on residual value						(160)
9. Net cash flow	($ 8,650)	$2,150	$2,630	$2,110	$1,830	$1,280

$$NPV = \sum_{t=0}^{5} \frac{NCF_t}{(1 + k)^t} = \$26 \text{ when } k = 5.4\%.$$

$$IRR: NPV = 0 = \sum_{t=0}^{5} \frac{NCF_t}{(1 + IRR)^t}. \quad IRR = 5.5\%.$$

rate which forces the NPV of the lease to zero, is 5.5 percent. Thus, the lease provides a 5.5 percent after-tax return to this 40 percent tax rate investor. This exceeds the 5.4 percent after-tax return on 9 percent bonds. So, using either the IRR or the NPV method, the lease would appear to be a satisfactory investment.[9]

Setting the Lease Payment

In the preceding sections we evaluated the lease assuming that the lease payments had already been specified. However, as a general rule, in large leases the parties will sit down and work out an agreement as to the size of the lease payments, with these payments being set so as to provide the lessor with some specific required rate of return. In situations where the lease terms are not negotiated, which is often the case for small leases, the lessor must still go through the same type of analysis, setting terms which provide a target rate of return, and then offering these terms to the potential lessee on a take-it-or-leave-it basis.

Competition among leasing companies forces lessors to build market-related returns into their lease payment schedules. To illustrate all this, suppose the potential lessor described earlier, after examining other alternative investment opportunities, decides that the 5.5 percent return on the Anderson Equipment Company lease is too low, and that the lease should provide an after-tax return of 6.0 percent. What lease payment schedule would provide this return?

To answer this question, note again that Table 17-4 contains the lessor's cash flow analysis. If the basic analysis is computerized, it is very easy to change the lease payment until the lease's NPV = $0 or, equivalently, its IRR = 6.0 percent. We did this with our *Lotus 1-2-3* lease evaluation model, and found that the lessor must set the lease payment at $2,788,591.50 to obtain an expected after-tax rate of return of 6.0 percent. However, if this lease payment is not acceptable to the lessee, Anderson Equipment Company, then it may not be possible to strike a deal.

Note that a lease payment of $2,788,591.50 would drive Anderson's NAL down to exactly zero. Leasing is not always a zero sum game, but if the inputs to the lessee and the lessor are identical, then a positive NAL to the lessee implies an equal but negative NPV to the lessor. However, conditions are often such that leasing can provide net benefits to both parties. This situation arises because of differentials, generally in taxes, estimated residual values, or the ability to bear the residual value risk. We will explore this issue in detail in a later section.

Leveraged Lease Analysis

When leasing began, only two parties were involved in a lease transaction—the lessor, who put up the money, and the lessee. In recent years, however, a new type of lease, the *leveraged lease,* has come into widespread use. Under a leveraged lease, the lessor arranges to borrow part of the required funds, generally giving the lender

[9]Note that the lease investment is actually slightly more risky than the alternative bond investment because the residual value cash flow is less certain than a principal repayment. Thus, the lessor would probably require an expected return somewhat above the 5.4 percent promised on a bond investment.

a first mortgage on the plant or equipment being leased. The lessor still receives the tax benefits associated with accelerated depreciation. However, the lessor now has a riskier position, because of the use of financial leverage.

Such leveraged leases, often with syndicates of wealthy individuals seeking tax shelters acting as owner-lessors, are an important part of the financial scene today. Incidentally, whether or not a lease is leveraged is not important to the lessee; from the lessee's standpoint, the method of analyzing a proposed lease is unaffected by whether or not the lessor borrows part of the required capital.

The example in Table 17-4 is not set up as a leveraged lease. However, it would be easy enough to modify the analysis if the lessor borrows all or part of the required $10 million, making the transaction a leveraged lease. First, we would add a set of lines to Table 17-4 to show the financing cash flows. The interest component would represent another tax deduction, while the loan repayments would constitute additional cash outlays. The "initial cost" would be reduced by the amount of the loan. With these changes made, a new NPV and IRR could be calculated and used to evaluate whether or not the lease represents a good investment.

To illustrate, assume that the lessor can borrow $5 million of the $10 million net purchase price at a rate of 9 percent on a 5-year simple interest loan. Table 17-5 contains the lessor's leveraged lease NPV analysis. The NPV of the leveraged lease investment based on the net cash flows shown on Line 3 is $26,000, which is the same as the $26,000 NPV for the unleveraged lease. Note, though, that the lessor has spent only $3.65 million on this lease. Therefore, the lessor could invest in a total of 2.37 similar leveraged leases for the same $8.65 million investment required to finance a single unleveraged lease, producing a total net present value of 2.37($26,000) = $61,620.

The effect of leverage on the lessor's return is also reflected in the leveraged lease's IRR. The IRR is that discount rate which equates the sum of the present values of the Line 3 cash flows to zero. We find the IRR of the leveraged lease to be about 8.5 percent, which is substantially higher than the 5.5 percent after-tax return on the unleveraged lease.[10]

Typically, leveraged leases provide lessors with higher expected rates of return (IRRs) and higher NPVs per dollar of invested capital than unleveraged leases. However, such leases are also riskier for the same reason that any leveraged investment is riskier. Since leveraged leases are a relatively new development, no standard methodology has been developed for analyzing them in a risk/return framework. However, sophisticated lessors are now developing simulations similar to those described in Chapter 11. Then, given the apparent riskiness of the lease investment, the lessor can decide whether the returns built into the contract are sufficient to compensate for the risk involved.

---

[10]Note two additional points concerning the leveraged lease analysis. First, in this situation, leveraging had no impact on the lessor's per-lease NPV. This is because the cost of loan to the lessor (5.4 percent after taxes) equals the discount rate, hence the leveraging cash flows are netted out on a present value basis. Second, the leveraged lease has multiple IRRs, one at 0.0 percent and another at approximately 8.5 percent.

Table 17-5 Leveraged Lease Analysis (Thousands of Dollars)

	Year 0	Year 1	Year 2	Year 3	Year 4	Year 5
1. Net cash flow from Table 17-4	($8,650)	$2,150	$2,630	$2,110	$1,830	$1,280
2. Leveraging cash flows[a]	5,000	(270)	(270)	(270)	(270)	(5,270)
3. Net cash flow	($3,650)	$1,880	$2,360	$1,840	$1,560	($3,990)

$$\text{NPV} = \sum_{t=0}^{5} \frac{NCF_t}{(1 + k)^t} = \$26 \text{ when k } = 5.4\%.$$

[a]The lessor borrows $5 million at t = 0 and repays it at t = 5. Interest expense, payable at the end of each year, is $0.09(\$5,000) = \$450$, but it is tax deductible, so the after-tax interest cash flow is $-\$450(1 - T) = -\$450(0.6) = -\$270$.

Self-Test Questions

What discount rate is used in a lessor's NPV analysis?

What is the economic interpretation of the lessor's IRR?

What is a leveraged lease? What is the usual impact of leveraging on the lessor's expected return? On the lessor's risk?

OTHER ISSUES IN LEASE ANALYSIS

The basic methods of analysis used by lessees and lessors were presented in the previous sections. However, some other issues warrant discussion.

Estimated Residual Value

It is important to note that the lessor owns the property upon expiration of a lease; thus, the lessor has claim to the asset's residual value. Superficially, it would appear that if residual values are expected to be large, owning would have an advantage over leasing. However, this apparent advantage does not hold up. If expected residual values are large—as they may be under inflation for certain types of equipment and also if real property is involved—competition between leasing companies and other financing sources, as well as competition among leasing companies themselves, will force leasing rates down to the point where potential residual values are fully recognized in the lease contract. Thus, the existence of large residual values on equipment is not likely to result in materially higher costs for leasing.

Increased Credit Availability

As noted earlier, leasing is sometimes said to have an advantage for firms that are seeking the maximum degree of financial leverage. First, it is sometimes argued that firms can obtain more money, and for longer terms, under a lease arrangement than under a loan secured by a specific piece of equipment. Second, since some leases do not appear on the balance sheet, lease financing has been said to give the firm a stronger appearance in a *superficial* credit analysis and thus to permit the firm to use more leverage than would be possible if it did not lease.

There may be some truth to these claims for smaller firms. However, now that firms are required to capitalize financial leases and to report them on their balance sheets, this point is of questionable validity for any firm large enough to have audited financial statements.

Depreciation Tax Savings

If a firm is unprofitable, or if it is expanding so rapidly and generating so much depreciation that its taxable income is driven down to zero, then it may be worthwhile for it to enter a lease arrangement with a high tax bracket lessor. Here the lessor (a bank, a leasing company, or an individual) will get to use the depreciation tax shelter and in return give the lessee a reduction in lease charges. Railroads and airlines have been large users of leasing for this reason in recent years, as have unprofitable industrial companies such as USX Corporation (formerly U.S. Steel). Tax considerations (including the AMT discussed below) are one of the driving forces behind financial leases today.

Computer Models

Lease analysis, like capital budgeting analysis, is particularly well suited for computer analysis. Both the lessee and lessor can create computer models for their analyses. Setting the analysis up on a computer is especially useful when negotiations are under way, and when investment banking houses such as Merrill Lynch are working out a leasing deal between a group of investors and a company, the analysis is always computerized.

Leasing under the 1986 Tax Act

The 1986 Tax Act contained three provisions that reduced the potential advantages of leasing: (1) The investment tax credit (ITC) was eliminated. Prior to 1987, many leases were signed for the primary purpose of transferring ITCs from zero tax bracket corporations such as Eastern Airlines to high-bracket investors such as IBM. (2) Under the 1986 Act, depreciation tax rates were effectively lowered. Thus, the potential depreciation benefits which could be passed on to high-tax-bracket lessors were lowered. (3) Tax rates were lowered, generally from 46 percent to 34 percent for corporations, and from 50 percent to 28 percent for individuals. The first two factors lower the tax shelters that are available for transfer from low-bracket to high-bracket investors, while the third lowers the economic value of any such transfer (because the tax saving is equal to the deduction times the tax rate).

We used our lease analysis models to analyze a number of recent lease deals made under the new and old tax laws. Invariably, the advantage of leasing was lower under the new law, often so much lower that the lease deal was simply not worthwhile after giving consideration to the expenses of setting up the lease. This suggested that the volume of leasing should fall as a result of the new tax law. However, another feature of the new law—the Alternative Minimum Tax (AMT) on corporations—actually stimulated leasing. Corporations are permitted to use accelerated depreciation and other tax shelters to hold down their actual taxes paid, but then to use straight line depreciation for stockholder reporting and hence to report high profits. Thus, IBM, GE, and other profitable companies have reported high earnings yet paid little or no federal income taxes in recent years. The AMT, which is figured at approximately 20 percent of *reported* profits, is designed to force profitable companies to pay at least some taxes.

Many companies have forecasted that they will be exposed to heavy tax liabilities under the AMT, and they are looking for ways to reduce reported income. Leasing can be beneficial here—use a relatively short period for the lease and consequently have a high annual payment, and the result will be low reported profits, hence a low AMT liability. Note that in this case the lease payments would not necessarily have to qualify as a deductible expense for regular tax purposes—all that is needed is that they be used to hold down reported income as shown in the annual report.

We have not attempted to set up a model to deal with AMT considerations. However, people in the leasing industry have designed such models, and they are generating a substantial amount of new leasing business as a direct result of the AMT.

Self-Test Questions

Does leasing lead to increased credit availability?

What impacts has the Tax Reform Act of 1986 had on leasing?

WHY FIRMS LEASE

Up to this point, we have noted that tax rate or other differentials are generally necessary to make leasing attractive to both the lessee and lessor. If the lessee and lessor are facing different tax situations, including the alternative minimum tax, then it may be possible to structure a lease that is beneficial to both parties. However, there are other reasons why firms might want to lease an asset rather than buy it.

For example, in the opening section of the chapter we discussed leasing in the airline industry, and we saw that a key reason for leasing is operating flexibility—leasing provides airlines with the ability to quickly alter their fleet compositions at relatively low cost in response to changing market conditions.

Leasing is also an attractive alternative for many high-technology items that are subject to rapid and unpredictable technological obsolescence. Say a small rural hospital wants to buy a magnetic resonance imaging (MRI) device. If it buys the MRI equipment, it is exposed to the risk of technological obsolescence. In a short time some new technology might make the current system almost worthless, and this large economic depreciation could make the whole project unprofitable. Since it does not use much equipment of this nature, the hospital would bear a great deal of risk if it buys the MRI device. Conversely, a lessor that specializes in state-of-the-art medical equipment might be exposed to significantly less risk. By purchasing and then leasing many different items, the lessor benefits from diversification. Of course, over time some items will probably lose more value than the lessor expected, but this will be offset by other items that retained more value than was expected. Also, since such a leasing company will be especially familiar with the market for used medical equipment, it can get a better price in the resale market than could a remote rural hospital. For these reasons, leasing can reduce the risk of technological obsolescence.

Leasing can also be attractive when a firm is uncertain about the demand for its products or services, and thus about how long the equipment will be needed. Again, consider the hospital industry. Hospitals often offer services that are dependent on a single staff member—for example, a physician who does liver transplants. To support the physician's practice, the hospital might have to invest millions of dollars in equipment that can be used only for this particular procedure. The hospital will charge for the use of the equipment, and if things go as expected, the investment will be profitable. However, if the physician dies or leaves the hospital staff, and if no other qualified physician can be recruited to fill the void, then the project is dead, and the equipment becomes useless to its owner. In this case, a lease with a cancellation clause would permit the hospital to simply return the equipment. The lessor would charge something for the cancellation clause, and this would lower the expected profitability of the project, but it would provide the hospital with an option to abandon the equipment, and such an option could have a value that exceeds the incremental cost of the cancellation clause. The leasing company would be willing to write this option because it is in a better position to remarket the equipment, either by writing another lease or by selling it outright.

Some companies also find leasing attractive because the lessor is able to provide services on favorable terms. For example, Virco Manufacturing, a company that makes school desks and other furniture, recently leased 25 truck tractors and 140 trailers which it uses to ship furniture from its plant. The lease agreement, with a large leasing company which specializes in purchasing, maintaining, and then re-selling trucks, permitted the replacement of an aging fleet that Virco had built up over seven years. "We are pretty good at manufacturing furniture, but we aren't very good at maintaining a truck fleet," said Virco's CFO.

There are other reasons that might influence a firm to lease an asset rather than buy it. Often, these reasons are difficult to quantify, hence they cannot be easily incorporated into an NPV or IRR analysis. Nevertheless, a sound lease analysis must begin with a quantitative analysis, and then qualitative factors can be considered before making the final lease-or-buy decision.

Self-Test Questions

Describe some economic factors which might provide an advantage to leasing.

Would it ever make sense to lease an asset that has a negative NAL? Explain.

SUMMARY

In this chapter, we discussed the leasing decision from the standpoints of both the lessee and lessor. The key concepts covered are listed below.

- The four most important types of lease agreement are (1) *sale and leaseback,* (2) *operating lease,* (3) *financial,* or *capital, lease,* and (4) *combination lease.*

- The IRS has specific guidelines that apply to lease arrangements. A lease that meets these guidelines is called a *guideline,* or *tax-oriented, lease,* because the IRS permits the lessor to deduct the asset's depreciation and allows the lessee to deduct the lease payments. A lease that does not meet the IRS guidelines is called a *non-tax-oriented lease.* In these leases, ownership effectively resides with the lessee rather than the lessor.

- *FASB Statement 13* spells out the conditions under which a lease must be *capitalized* (shown directly on the balance sheet) as opposed to shown only in the notes to the financial statements. Generally, leases that run for a period equal to or greater than 75 percent of the asset's life must be capitalized.

- The lessee's analysis consists basically of a comparison of the costs associated with leasing the asset and the costs associated with owning the asset. There are two analytical techniques that can be used: (1) the *net advantage to leasing (NAL or PV of costs) method,* and (2) the *internal rate of return (IRR) method.*

- One of the key issues in the lessee's analysis is the appropriate discount rate. Since the cash flows in a lease analysis are known with relative certainty, the appropriate discount rate is the *lessee's after-tax cost of debt.* A higher discount rate may be used on the *residual value* if it is substantially riskier than the other flows.

- The lessor evaluates the lease as an *investment.* If the lease's NPV is greater than zero or its IRR is greater than the lessor's opportunity cost, then the lease should be written.

- In a *leveraged lease,* the lessor borrows part of the funds required to buy the asset. Generally, the asset is pledged as collateral for the loan.

- Leasing is motivated by differentials between lessees and lessors. Some of the more common reasons for leasing are (1) *tax rate differentials,* (2) leases in which the lessee faces the *alternative minimum tax (AMT),* and (3) leases in which the lessor is better able to bear the *residual value risk* than the lessee.

Questions

17-1   Define each of the following terms:
   a.   Lessee; lessor
   b.   Sale and leaseback; operating lease; financial lease; combination lease; leveraged lease
   c.   "Off-balance sheet" financing; capitalizing
   d.   FASB Statement 13
   e.   Guideline lease
   f.   Residual value

    g.   Lessee's analysis; lessor's analysis

    h.   Alternative minimum tax (AMT)

17-2 Distinguish between operating leases and financial leases. Would you be more likely to find an operating lease employed for a fleet of trucks or for a manufacturing plant?

17-3 Would you be more likely to find that lessees are in high or low income tax brackets as compared to lessors?

17-4 Commercial banks moved heavily into equipment leasing during the early 1970s, acting as lessors. One major reason for this invasion of the leasing industry was to gain the benefits of accelerated depreciation and the investment tax credit on leased equipment. During this same period, commercial banks were investing heavily in municipal securities, and they were also making loans to real estate investment trusts (REITs). In the mid-1970s, these REITs got into such serious difficulty that many banks suffered large losses on their REIT loans. Explain how its investments in municipal bonds and REITs could reduce a bank's willingness to act as a lessor.

17-5 One alleged advantage of leasing voiced in the past is that it kept liabilities off the balance sheet, thus making it possible for a firm to obtain more leverage than it otherwise could have. This raised the question of whether or not both the lease obligation and the asset involved should be capitalized and shown on the balance sheet. Discuss the pros and cons of capitalizing leases and related assets.

17-6 Suppose there were no IRS restrictions on what constituted a valid lease. Explain, in a manner that a legislator might understand, why some restrictions should be imposed. Illustrate your answer with numbers.

17-7 What are the advantages and disadvantages of leveraged leases from the standpoint of (a) the lessee, (b) the equity investor in the lease, and (c) the supplier of the debt capital?

17-8 Suppose Congress enacted new tax law changes that would (1) permit equipment to be depreciated over a shorter period, (2) lower corporate tax rates, and (3) reinstate the investment tax credit. Discuss how each of these potential changes would affect the relative volume of leasing versus conventional debt in the U.S. economy.

17-9 In our example, we assumed that the lease could not be cancelled. What effect would a cancellation clause have on the lessee's analysis? On the lessor's analysis?

Self-Test Problem   (Solutions Appear in Appendix D)

ST-1 **(Lease versus buy)** The Randolph Teweles Company (RTC) has decided to acquire a new truck. One alternative is to lease the truck on a 4-year guideline contract for a lease payment of $10,000 per year, with payments to be made at the *beginning* of each year. The lease would include maintenance. Alternatively, RTC could purchase the truck outright for $40,000, financing the purchase by a bank loan for the net purchase price and amortizing the loan over a 4-year period at an interest rate of 10 percent per year. Under the borrow-to-purchase arrangement, RTC would have to maintain the truck at a cost of $1,000 per year, payable at year-end. The truck falls into the MACRS 3-year class. It has a residual value of $10,000, which is the expected market value after 4 years, when RTC plans to replace the truck irrespective of whether it leases or buys. RTC has a marginal federal-plus-state tax rate of 40 percent.

    a.   What is RTC's PV cost of leasing?

    b.   What is RTC's PV cost of owning? Should the truck be leased or purchased?

    c.   The appropriate discount rate for use in the analysis is the firm's after-tax cost of debt. Why?

    d.   The residual value is the least certain cash flow in the analysis. How might RTC incorporate differential riskiness on this cash flow into the analysis?

Problems

17-1   **(Balance sheet effects)** Two companies, Electroway and Levin Corporation, began operations with identical balance sheets. A year later, both required additional manufacturing capacity at a cost of $50,000. Electroway obtained a 5-year, $50,000 loan at an 8 percent interest
rate from its bank. Levin, on the other hand, decided to lease the required $50,000 capacity
for 5 years, and an 8 percent return was built into the lease. The balance sheet for each
company, before the asset increases, follows:

		Debt	$ 50,000
		Equity	100,000
Total assets	$150,000	Total claims	$150,000

a.   Show the balance sheets for both firms after the asset increase and calculate each firm's
      new debt ratio. (Assume that the lease is not capitalized.)
b.   Show how Levin's balance sheet would look immediately after the financing if it capital-
      ized the lease.
c.   Would the rate of return (1) on assets and (2) on equity be affected by the choice of
      financing? How?

17-2   **(Lease versus buy)** J. Grant Industries must install $1 million of new machinery in its Texas
plant. It can obtain a bank loan for 100 percent of the required amount. Alternatively, a Texas
investment banking firm which represents a group of investors believes that it can arrange
for a lease financing plan. *Assume* that these facts apply:
    (1)   The equipment falls in the MACRS 3-year class.
    (2)   Estimated maintenance expenses are $50,000 per year.
    (3)   The firm's tax rate is 34 percent.
    (4)   If the money is borrowed, the bank loan will be at a rate of 14 percent, amortized
          in 3 equal installments at the end of each year.
    (5)   The tentative lease terms call for payments of $320,000 at the end of each year for
          3 years. The lease is a guideline lease.
    (6)   Under the proposed lease terms, the lessee must pay for insurance, property taxes,
          and maintenance.
    (7)   Grant must use the equipment if it is to continue in business, so it will almost
          certainly want to acquire the property at the end of the lease. If it does, then under
          the lease terms it can purchase the machinery at its fair market value at that time.
          The best estimate of this market value is the $200,000 residual value, but it could be
          much higher or lower under certain circumstances.
To assist management in making the proper lease-versus-buy decision, you are asked to answer the following questions:
a.   Assuming that the lease can be arranged, should the firm lease or borrow and buy the
      equipment? Explain. (Hint: In this situation, the firm plans to use the asset beyond the
      term of the lease. Thus, the residual value becomes a *cost* to leasing in Year 3. Also, there
      is no Year 3 residual value tax consequence, as the firm cannot immediately deduct the
      Year 3 purchase price from taxable income.)
b.   Consider the $200,000 estimated residual value. Is it appropriate to discount it at the
      same rate as the other cash flows? What about the other cash flows—are they all equally
      risky? (Hint: Riskier cash flows are normally discounted at higher rates, but when the
      cash flows are *costs* rather than *inflows,* the normal procedure must be reversed.)
    (Do Parts c and d only if you are using the computerized diskette.)
c.   Determine the lease payment at which Grant would be indifferent to buying or leasing;
      that is, the lease payment which equates the PV cost of leasing to that of buying. (Hint:
      Use trial-and-error.)

d.   Using the $320,000 lease payment, what would be the effect if the firm's tax rate fell to zero?

17-3   **(Lessor's analysis)** The Benton Company has decided to acquire some new R&D equipment. One alternative is to lease the equipment on a 4-year guideline contract for a lease payment of $11,500 per year, payments to be made at the *beginning* of each year. The lease, which would include maintenance, is being offered by LePage Credit Corporation, a local leasing company. LePage would purchase the equipment outright for $40,000, and would have to pay the local dealer $1,000 at the beginning of each year to provide maintenance service. The equipment falls into the MACRS 3-year class; and it has a residual value of $10,000, which is the expected market value after 4 years. The lessor's marginal state-plus-federal tax rate is 40 percent. The analysts at LePage compare the returns on potential leases with returns available on comparable maturity commercial loans which the firm also writes. Currently, LePage is charging 9 percent on 4-year commercial loans.

a.   What is the NPV on the lease investment?

b.   Should LePage write the lease? Why?

(Do Parts c, d, e, g, and h only if you are using the computerized diskette.)

c.   Assume that interest rates rise, and LePage can now earn 16 percent (before taxes) on its commercial loans. How does this affect the lease analysis?

d.   What lease payment must LePage charge to be indifferent between writing the lease and loaning at 16 percent?

e.   Return to the original situation. Suppose there is a 25 percent chance that the residual value will be only $5,000, and another 25 percent probability that the residual value will be $15,000. There is a 50 percent probability that the residual value will be $10,000. What is LePage's best case and worst case NPV? Suppose that the LePage analysts account for differential risk by increasing the residual value discount rate. What residual value discount rate forces NPV = $0 when the residual value is $10,000?

f.   Now suppose that LePage can leverage the lease. LePage could borrow up to $30,000 using the truck as collateral on a term loan at an 8 percent rate. Should LePage leverage the lease? Should LePage leverage the lease at 9 percent?

g.   Refer back to Part f. Suppose that the loan for $30,000 may only be obtained at a rate of 16 percent. What is the new NPV to the lessor of the leveraged lease? Should LePage leverage the lease under these circumstances? Why?

h.   If LePage were able to borrow only $15,000 for this project due to restrictive covenants contained in a previous loan agreement, would it be beneficial to leverage the lease at 8 percent? At 9 percent? At 16 percent?

17-4   **(Lessee's analysis)** As part of its overall plant modernization and cost reduction program, Southern Fabrics' management has decided to install a new automated weaving loom. In the capital budgeting analysis of this equipment, the IRR of the project was found to be 29 percent versus a project required return of 14 percent.

The loom has an invoice price of $100,000, including delivery and installation charges. The funds needed could be borrowed from the bank through a 4-year amortized loan at a 15 percent interest rate, with payments to be made at the end of each year. In the event the loom is purchased, the manufacturer will contract to maintain and service it for a fee of $8,000 per year paid at the end of each year. The loom falls in the MACRS 5-year class, and Southern's marginal federal-plus-state tax rate is 40 percent.

Brooks Automation, Inc., maker of the loom, has offered to lease the loom to Southern for $30,500 upon delivery and installation (at t = 0) plus 4 additional annual lease payments of $30,500 to be made at the end of Years 1 to 4. (Note that there are 5 lease payments in total.) The lease agreement includes maintenance and servicing. Actually, the loom has an expected life of 8 years, at which time its expected salvage value is zero; however, after 4 years, its market value is expected to equal its book value. Southern plans to build an entirely new plant in 4 years, so it has no interest in either leasing or owning the proposed loom for more than that period.

a.   Should the loom be leased or purchased?

(Do the remainder of the problem only if you are using the computerized diskette.)

b.   Southern's managers disagree on the appropriate discount rate to be used in the analysis. What effect would a discount rate change have on the lease-versus-purchase decision?

c.   The salvage value is clearly the most uncertain cash flow in the analysis. What effect would a salvage value risk adjustment have on the analysis? (Assume that the appropriate salvage value pre-tax discount rate is 18 percent.)

d.   The original analysis assumed that the firm would not need the loom after 4 years. Now assume that the firm will continue to use it after the lease expires. Thus, if it leased, Southern would have to buy the asset after 4 years at the then existing market value, which is assumed to equal the book value. What effect would this requirement have on the basic analysis?

e.   Under the original lease terms, it was to Southern's advantage to purchase the loom. However, if you had analyzed the lease from the lessor's viewpoint, you would have found that it was more profitable for Brooks Automation to lease the machine than to sell it — in fact, the manager of Brooks has found that the company can lower the lease payment to $30,000 and still make more by leasing the machine than by selling it. With an annual lease payment of $30,000, should the loom be leased or bought?

f.   Perform the lease analysis assuming that Southern's marginal tax rate is (1) 0 percent and (2) 50 percent. Assume a lease payment of $30,500 and a 15 percent pre-tax discount rate. What effect, if any, would the lessee's tax rate have on the lease-buy decision?

Mini Case

Lewis Securities, Inc., has decided to acquire a new data and quotation system for its Richmond home office. The system receives current market prices and other information from several on-line data services, then either displays the information on a screen or stores it for later retrieval by the firm's brokers. The system also permits customers to call up current quotes on terminals in the lobby.

The equipment costs $1,000,000, and, if it were purchased, Lewis could obtain a term loan for the full purchase price at a 10 percent interest rate. The equipment is classified as a special-purpose computer, so it falls into the MACRS 3-year class. If the system were purchased, a 4-year maintenance contract could be obtained at a cost of $20,000 per year, payable at the *beginning* of each year. The equipment would be sold after 4 years, and the best estimate of its residual value at that time is $100,000. However, since real-time display system technology is changing rapidly, the actual residual value is uncertain.

As an alternative to the borrow-and-buy plan, the equipment manufacturer informed Lewis that Consolidated Leasing would be willing to write a 4-year guideline lease on the equipment, including maintenance, for payments of $280,000 at the *beginning* of each year. Lewis's marginal federal-plus-state tax rate is 40 percent. You have been asked to analyze the lease-versus-purchase decision, and in the process to answer the following questions:

a.   (1) Why is leasing sometimes referred to as "off-balance sheet" financing?
     (2) What is the difference between a capital lease and an operating lease?
     (3) What impact does leasing have on a firm's capital structure?

b.   (1) What is the present value cost of owning the equipment? (*Hint:* Set up a table whose bottom line is a "time line" which shows the net cash flows over the period t = 0 to t = 4, and then find the PV of these net cash flows, or the PV cost of owning.)

(2) Explain the rationale for the discount rate you used to find the PV.

c. What is Lewis's present value cost of leasing the equipment? (*Hint:* Again, construct a time line.)

d. What is the net advantage to leasing (NAL)? Does your analysis indicate that Lewis should buy or lease the equipment? Explain.

e. What is the IRR of the lease from the lessee's standpoint? What is the economic meaning of this IRR?

f. Now assume that the equipment's residual value could be as low as $0 or as high as $200,000, but that $100,000 is the expected value. Since the residual value is riskier than the other cash flows in the analysis, this differential risk should be incorporated into the analysis. Describe how this could be accomplished. (No calculations are necessary, but explain how you would modify the analysis if calculations were required.) What effect would increased uncertainty about the residual value have on Lewis's lease-versus-purchase decision?

g. The lessee compares the cost of owning the equipment with the cost of leasing it. Now put yourself in the lessor's shoes. In a few sentences, how should you analyze the decision to write or not write the lease?

h. (1) Assume that the lease payments were actually $300,000 per year, that Consolidated Leasing is also in the 40 percent tax bracket, and that it also forecasts a $100,000 residual value. Also, to furnish the maintenance support, Consolidated would have to purchase a maintenance contract from the manufacturer at the same $20,000 annual cost, again paid in advance. Consolidated Leasing can obtain an expected 10.0 percent pre-tax return on investments of similar risk. What would Consolidated's NPV and IRR of leasing be under these conditions?

(2) What do you think the lessor's NPV would be if the lease payment were set at $280,000 per year? (*Hint:* The lessor's cash flows would be a "mirror image" of the lessee's cash flows.)

i. Now assume that the lessor can leverage the $300,000 payment lease by borrowing $500,000 of the $1,000,000 purchase price on a 4-year balloon note bearing a 10.0 percent simple interest rate. The lender requires only interest payments (at the end of each year) during the life of the note, with the full $500,000 principal to be repaid at maturity. What is the NPV of the leveraged lease? What is its rate of return? What factors, besides the NPV and the IRR, should the lessor consider before deciding to leverage the lease? Should it be leveraged?

j. Lewis's management has been considering moving to a new downtown location, and they are concerned that these plans may come to fruition prior to the expiration of the lease. If the move occurs, Lewis would buy or lease an entirely new set of equipment, and hence management would like to include a cancellation clause in the lease contract. What impact would such a clause have on the riskiness of the lease from Lewis's standpoint? From the lessor's standpoint? If you were the lessor, would you insist on changing any of the lease terms if a cancellation clause were added? Should the cancellation clause contain any restrictive covenants and/or penalties of the type contained in bond indentures or provisions similar to call premiums?

Selected Additional References and Cases

For a description of lease analysis in practice, as well as a comprehensive bibliography of the leasing literature, see

O'Brien, Thomas J., and Bennie H. Nunnally, Jr., "A 1982 Survey of Corporate Leasing Analysis," *Financial Management,* Summer 1983, 30–36.

Many of the theoretical issues surrounding lease analysis are discussed in the following articles:

Finucane, Thomas J., "Some Empirical Evidence on the Use of Financial Leases," *The Journal of Financial Research,* Fall 1988, 321–333.

Hockman, Shalom, and Ramon Rabinovitch, "Financial Leasing under Inflation," *Financial Management,* Spring 1984, 17–26.

Levy, Haim, and Marshall Sarnat, "Leasing, Borrowing, and Financial Risk," *Financial Management,* Winter 1979, 47–54.

Lewellen, Wilbur G., Michael S. Long, and John J. McConnell, "Asset Leasing in Competitive Capital Markets," *Journal of Finance,* June 1976, 787–798.

Miller, Merton H., and Charles W. Upton, "Leasing, Buying, and the Cost of Capital Services," *Journal of Finance,* June 1976, 761–786.

Schall, Lawrence D., "The Evaluation of Lease Financing Opportunities," *Midland Corporate Finance Journal,* Spring 1985, 48–65.

Leveraged lease analysis is discussed in these articles:

Athanasopoulos, Peter J., and Peter W. Bacon, "The Evaluation of Leveraged Leases," *Financial Management,* Spring 1980, 76–80.

Dyl, Edward A., and Stanley A. Martin, Jr., "Setting Terms for Leveraged Leases," *Financial Management,* Winter 1977, 20–27.

Grimlund, Richard A., and Robert Capettini, "A Note on the Evaluation of Leveraged Leases and Other Investments," *Financial Management,* Summer 1982, 68–72.

Perg, Wayne F., "Leveraged Leasing: The Problem of Changing Leverage," *Financial Management,* Autumn 1978, 47–51.

The Summer 1987 issue of Financial Management *contains articles by H. Martin Weingartner, Roger L. Cason, and Lawrence D. Schall which focus on the impact of asset life uncertainty on lease analysis.*

The Option Pricing Model (OPM) has recently been used in lease analysis by

Copeland, Thomas E., and J. Fred Weston, "A Note on the Evaluation of Cancellable Operating Leases," *Financial Management,* Summer 1982, 60–67.

Lee, Wayne Y., John D. Martin, and Andrew J. Senchack, "The Case for Using Options to Evaluate Salvage Values in Financial Leases," *Financial Management,* Autumn 1982, 33–41.

For a discussion of the impact of the AMT on lease decisions, see

"The Effect of the Corporate Alternative Minimum Tax: Amount, Duration, and Effect on the Lease versus Buy Decision," *The Journal of Equipment Lease Financing,* Spring 1989, 7–26.

The Brigham-Gapenski casebook contains the following cases which deal with lease analysis:

Case 26, "Barngrover Chemical Company," which examines the lease decision from the perspectives of both the lessee and lessor.

Case 27, "Atlas Research Company," which examines the same issues as Case 26.

CHAPTER 18

Options, Warrants, Convertibles, and Futures

In May 1989, Ashland Oil Company sold $200 million of 25-year subordinated debentures with a coupon rate of 6¾ percent. At the time, Ashland was paying about 10 percent on its commercial paper and about 11 percent on its first mortgage bonds. How was Ashland able to issue subordinated debentures with such a low coupon rate? The answer is easy—the issue was convertible, and each debenture could be converted into the firm's common stock at a rate of $51.34 of debentures for each common share. Thus, a $1,000 par value bond could be converted into about 20 common shares. The stock, which is traded on the Big Board (the New York Stock Exchange), closed at $40.75 on the day the convertibles were sold. If Ashland's stock price rises in the future, the value of the convertible debentures will also rise. In effect, each purchaser of an Ashland convertible debenture was paying $1,000 to buy (1) a fixed-income security with a yield of 6¾ percent, plus (2) an option to buy Ashland's common stock, and the option will provide a capital gain if the firm's stock price increases sufficiently over time.

Convertibles and warrants are specialized types of options used in corporate financing. Ashland's convertibles appealed to investors because these securities provided a steady income stream well above the 4 percent dividend yield on Ashland's common stock and also offered a potential for capital gains. The bonds were attractive to the company because they saved interest expense and also because they offered the possibility of replacing debt with equity in the future. Of course, there are also disadvantages to both Ashland and the buyers of the convertibles, and we will discuss these in detail in this chapter.

The attractiveness of convertible bonds, which accounted for about 2 percent of all securities issued during 1989, depends on investors' beliefs about future stock prices. During bull markets, convertibles are extremely popular — in the bull market of 1986 and early 1987, convertibles represented about 5 percent of all securities issued. However, after the October 1987 crash, investors wouldn't touch convertible issues. In general, the same holds for bonds with warrants.

THUS far our discussion of long-term financing has concentrated on common and preferred stock, on various types of debt, and on lease financing. In this chapter, we shall see how a company can use warrants and convertibles to make its securities attractive to a broader range of investors, thereby increasing the potential supply of capital. We also introduce options and futures markets, and we illustrate how these markets provide a method for locking in future financing costs.

OPTIONS

Both warrants and convertibles are types of option securities, and options themselves represent an important part of today's financial scene. Therefore, we begin the chapter by discussing both the rapidly growing option markets and option pricing theory. An *option* is a contract which gives its holder the right to buy (or sell) an asset at some predetermined price within a specified period of time. *Pure options* are instruments that (1) are created by outsiders (generally exchanges which specialize in options) rather than the firm, (2) are bought and sold primarily by investors, and (3) are of greater importance to investors than to financial managers. However, financial managers should understand option theory, because such an understanding will help them structure warrant and convertible financings. Additionally, option theory provides some useful insights into other facets of corporate finance.

Option Types and Markets

There are many types of options and option markets.[1] To illustrate how options work, suppose you owned 100 shares of IBM, which, on February 13 sold for $126 per share. You could give (or sell) to someone else the right to buy the 100 shares at any time during the next 2 months at a price of, say, $130 per share. The $130 is called the *striking,* or *exercise, price.* Such options exist, and they are traded on a

---

[1]For an in-depth treatment of options, see Robert C. Radcliffe, *Investment Concepts, Analysis, and Strategy* (Glenview, Ill.: Scott, Foresman, 1990).

Table 18-1   February 13 Listed Options Quotations (CBOE)

NYSE Close	Strike Price	Calls — Last Quote			Puts — Last Quote		
		February	March	April	February	March	April
IBM							
126	120	6¼	7⅜	9¼	¹⁄₁₆	¹¹⁄₁₆	1³⁄₁₆
126	125	1⅞	4	5¾	⁹⁄₁₆	2¹⁄₁₆	2¾
126	130	³⁄₁₆	1¹¹⁄₁₆	3⅛	4	4⅞	5¼
Delta							
56	60	⅛	1	1⅝	r	r	r
Merck							
62	60	2¼	3⅛	4	³⁄₁₆	¾	1⅛

Note: r means not traded on February 13.

number of exchanges, with the Chicago Board Options Exchange (CBOE) being the oldest and the largest. This type of option is defined as a *call option,* because the purchaser has a "call" on 100 shares of stock. The seller of an option is defined as the *writer.* An investor who "writes" call options against stock held in his or her portfolio is said to be selling *covered options.* Options sold without the stock to back them up are called *naked options.* When the exercise price exceeds the current stock price, the option is said to be *out-of-the-money.* When the exercise price is less than the current price of the underlying stock, the option is *in-the-money.*

You can also buy an option which gives you the right to *sell* a stock at a specified price within some future period—this is called a *put option.* For example, suppose you think IBM's stock price is likely to decline from its current level of $126 sometime during the next 2 months. For $275 you could buy a 2-month put option giving you the right to sell 100 shares (which you would not necessarily own) at a price of $125 per share ($125 is the striking price). If you bought a 100-share contract for $275 and then IBM's stock actually fell to $115, your put option would be worth ($125 − $115)(100) = $1,000. After subtracting the $275 you paid for the option, your profit (before taxes and commissions) would be $725.

Table 18-1 contains an extract from the February 14 *Wall Street Journal* Listed Options Quotations Table. This extract, which focuses on IBM, Delta, and Merck options, reflects the trading which occurred on the previous day. On February 13, Delta's April (2-month), $60 call option sold on the CBOE for $1⅝. Thus, for $1.625(100) = $162.50 you could buy options that would give you the right to purchase 100 shares of Delta at a price of $60 per share at any time during the next 2 months.[2] If the stock price stayed below $60 during that period, you would lose

---

[2]Actually, the *expiration date,* which is the last date that the option can be exercised, is the third Friday of the exercise month. Thus, the April options actually have a term somewhat more than 2 months. Also, note that option contracts are generally written in 100-share multiples.

your $162.50, but if it rose to $75, then your $162.50 investment would have grown to ($75 − $60)(100) = $1,500. That translates into a very healthy annualized rate of return. Incidentally, if the stock price did go up, you would probably not actually exercise your options and buy the stock—rather, you would sell the options, which would then have a value of at least $1,500 versus the $162.50 you paid, to another option buyer.

Option trading is one of the hottest financial activities in the United States today. In addition to options on individual stocks, options are also available on several stock indexes such as the NYSE Index and the S&P 100 Index, permitting one to bet on a rise or fall in the general market as well as on individual stocks such as Delta. The leverage involved makes it possible for speculators with just a few dollars to make a fortune almost overnight. Also, investors with sizable portfolios can sell options against their stocks and earn the value of the option (less brokerage commissions), even if the stock's price remains constant. Further, options can be used to create hedges which protect the value of an individual stock or portfolio. We will discuss hedging strategies in more detail later in the chapter.[3]

Corporations such as Delta and IBM, on whose stocks options are written, have nothing to do with the option market. The corporations do not raise money in the option market, nor do they have any direct transactions in it, and option holders do not vote for corporate directors (unless they exercise their options to purchase the stock, which few actually do) or receive dividends. There have been studies by the SEC and others as to whether option trading stabilizes or destabilizes the stock market, and whether this activity helps or hinders corporations seeking to raise new capital. The studies have not been conclusive, but option trading does seem to be here to stay, and many regard it as the most exciting game in town.

Factors That Affect the Value of a Call Option

An analysis of Table 18-1 provides some insights into call option valuation. First, we can see that there are at least three factors which affect a call option's value: (1) For a given striking price, the higher the stock's market price in relation to the strike price, the higher will be the call option price. Thus, Delta's $60 April call option sells for $1.625, whereas Merck's $60 April option sells for $4.00 because Merck's current stock price is $62 versus $56 for Delta. (2) For a given stock price, the higher the striking price, the lower will be the call option price. Thus, all of IBM's call options, regardless of exercise month, decline as the striking price increases. (3) The longer the option period, the higher will be the option price, because the longer the time before expiration, the greater the chance that the stock price will climb substantially above the exercise price. Thus, for all striking prices, option prices increase as the expiration date is lengthened.

---

[3]It should be noted that insiders who trade illegally generally buy options rather than stock because options increase the profit potential. Note, though, that it is illegal to use insider information for personal gain, and an insider would be taking advantage of the option seller. Insider trading, in addition to being unfair and essentially equivalent to stealing, hurts the economy: Investors lose confidence in the capital markets and raise their required returns because of an increased element of risk, which raises the cost of capital and thus reduces the level of investment.

Expiration Value versus Option Price

How is the actual price of a call option determined in the market? We shall, shortly, present a widely used model (the Black-Scholes model) for pricing call options, but first it is useful to establish some basic concepts. To begin, we define a call option's *expiration value* as follows:

$$\text{Expiration value} = \frac{\text{Current price}}{\text{of the stock}} - \text{Striking price.}$$

For example, if a stock sells for $50, and its option has a striking price of $20, then the expiration value is $30. The expiration value can be thought of as the value of the option if it expired today. Note that the calculated expiration value of a call option could be negative, but realistically the minimum value of an out-of-the-money option is zero. Note also that an option's expiration value can be thought of as its first approximation value, because it provides a starting point for valuing the option.

Now consider Figure 18-1, which presents some data on Space Technology, Inc. (STI), a company which recently went public and whose stock has fluctuated widely during its short history. The third column in the tabular data shows the expiration values for STI's call option when the stock was selling at different prices; the fourth column gives the actual market prices for the option; and the fifth column shows the premium of the actual option price over its expiration value. At any stock price below $20, the expiration value is zero; above $20, each $1 increase in the price of the stock brings with it a $1 increase in the option's expiration value. Note, however, that the actual market price of the option lies above the expiration value at each price of the common stock, but the premium declines as the price of the common stock increases. For example, when the common stock sold for $20 and the option had a zero expiration value, its actual price, and the premium, was $9. Then, as the price of the stock rose, the *expiration value's increase* matched the stock's increase dollar for dollar, but the *market price* of the option climbed less rapidly, so the premium declined. The premium was $9 when the stock sold for $20 a share, but it declined to $1 by the time the stock price had risen to $73 a share. Beyond this point, the premium virtually disappeared.

Why does this pattern exist? Why should the option ever sell for more than its expiration value, and why does the premium decline as the price of the stock increases? The answer lies in the speculative appeal of options — they enable someone to gain a high degree of personal leverage when buying securities. To illustrate, *suppose STI's option sold for exactly its expiration value.* Now suppose you were thinking of investing in the company's common stock at a time when it was selling for $21 a share. If you bought a share and the price rose to $42, you would have made a 100 percent capital gain. However, had you bought the option at its expiration value ($1 when the stock was selling for $21), your capital gain would have been $22 − $1 = $21 on a $1 investment, or 2,100 percent! At the same time, your total loss potential with the option would be only $1 versus a potential loss of $21 if you purchased the stock. The huge capital gains potential, combined with the loss limitation, is clearly worth something — the exact amount it is worth to investors is the amount of the premium. Note, however, that buying the option is riskier than

Figure 18-1   Space Technology, Inc.:
Option Price and Expiration Value

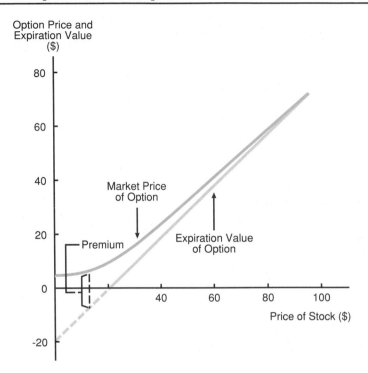

Price of Stock (1)	Striking Price (2)	Expiration Value of Option (1) − (2) = (3)	Market Price of Option (4)	Premium (4) − (3) = (5)
$20.00	$20.00	$ 0.00	$ 9.00	$9.00
21.00	20.00	1.00	9.75	8.75
22.00	20.00	2.00	10.50	8.50
35.00	20.00	15.00	21.00	6.00
42.00	20.00	22.00	26.00	4.00
50.00	20.00	30.00	32.00	2.00
73.00	20.00	53.00	54.00	1.00
98.00	20.00	78.00	78.50	0.50

buying STI's stock, because there is a higher probability of losing money on the option. If STI's stock price remains at $21, you would break even on the stock (ignoring transaction costs), but you would lose your entire $1 option investment.

Why does the premium decline as the price of the stock rises? Part of the answer is that both the leverage effect and the loss protection feature decline at high stock prices. For example, if you were thinking of buying STI stock when its price was $73 a share, the expiration value of the option would be $53. If the stock price doubled to $146, the expiration value of the option would go from $53 to $126. The percentage capital gain on the stock would still be 100 percent, but the percentage gain on the option would now be only 138 percent versus 2,100 percent in the earlier case. Notice also that the potential loss on the option is much greater when the option is selling at high prices. These two factors, the declining leverage impact and the increasing danger of losses, help explain why the premium diminishes as the price of the common stock rises.

In addition to the stock price and the exercise price, the price of an option depends on three other factors: (1) the option's term to maturity, (2) the variability of the stock price, and (3) the risk-free rate. We will explain precisely how these factors affect option prices later, but for now, note these points:

1.   The longer an option has to run, the greater its value and the larger its premium. If an option expires at 4 P.M. today, there is not much chance that the stock price will go way up, so the option must sell at close to its expiration value, and its premium must be small. On the other hand, if the expiration date is a year away, the stock price could rise sharply, pulling the option's value up with it.

2.   An option on an extremely volatile stock will be worth more than one on a very stable stock. If the stock price rarely moves, then there is only a small chance of a large gain. However, if the stock price is highly volatile, the option could easily become very valuable. At the same time, losses on options are limited, so large declines in a stock's price do not have a corresponding bad effect on option holders. Therefore, the more volatile a stock, the higher is the value of its options.

Because of Points 1 and 2, in a graph such as Figure 18-1, if everything else were constant, then the longer an option's life, the higher its market price line would be above the expiration value line. Similarly, the more volatile the price of the under- lying stock, the higher is the market price line. We will see precisely how these factors, and also the risk-free rate, affect option values when we discuss the option pricing model.

Self-Test Questions

What is an option? A call option? A put option?

Define a call option's expiration value. Why is the actual market price of a call option usually above its expiration value?

What are some factors which affect a call option's value?

INTRODUCTION TO OPTION PRICING

In the next section, we will discuss a well-known option pricing model, but it is useful first to go through a simple example. Assume that 1-year call options are available on Butler Company, a Midwestern firm which owns 32 McDonald's fran- chises. Each option has an exercise price of $35, and Butler's stock is now selling for $40 a share. Assume further that when the options expire 1 year hence, Butler's shares will be selling at one of only two possible prices, $30 or $50. Under these simple conditions, what is the value of a call option on Butler's stock?

To answer this question, we proceed as follows:

1.   **Examine the payoffs at maturity.** At expiration, the stock price will be either $30 or $50, and the value of the option at expiration will depend on Butler's stock price. Thus, we have the following situation at expiration:

	Stock Price	**Option Value**	
Low	$30	$ 0	(option is worthless)
High	50	15	(expiration value)
Range	$20	$15	

2.   **Create the same range of payoffs.** Note that the range of payoffs as shown in Step 1 is $20 for a stock investment (either a $30 or $50 payoff) and $15 for an option investment (either a $0 or $15 payoff). The ranges would be identical on the two investments if you could buy 0.75 shares of Butler's stock. In this situation, the payoff matrix would look like this:

	Stock Price	**Value of 0.75 Shares**	**Option Value**
Low	$30	$22.50	$ 0
High	50	37.50	15
Range	$20	$15.00	$15

3.   **Create a riskless hedge.** You can now create a riskless portfolio by buying 0.75 shares of Butler's stock and selling 1 call option. The sale of the call option will not affect the final portfolio value if the price of the stock declines, but this sale will lower the portfolio's value if the price rises. Here is the resulting payoff matrix:

	Stock Price	**Value of 0.75 Shares**	**+**	**Effect of the Call on Portfolio Value**	**=**	**Value of Portfolio**
Low	$30	$22.50	+	$ 0	=	$22.50
High	50	37.50	+	(15)	=	22.50

If the stock price at expiration is $30, the stock investment returns $22.50, but the call will not be exercised, hence it will not affect the portfolio's value. On the other hand, if the stock price is $50 at expiration, the value of the stock investment would be $37.50, but the holder of the call would exercise his or her option. Thus, you must provide one share at the exercise price, $35, which you must purchase at the market price of $50, hence you will incur a $15 loss. Therefore, regardless of what happens to the price of the stock, your portfolio's return is $22.50—you have created a riskless portfolio by buying the stock and writing (selling) a call option on that stock.

4.   **Valuing the call option.** To this point, we have not specified what price you would charge to write (sell) the call. However, we have seen that your riskless portfolio will provide a sure $22.50 at option expiration in 1 year. If the risk-free

rate is 8 percent, the value of the portfolio today is $22.50/1.08 = $20.83. Since Butler's stock is currently selling at $40 a share, creating the riskless portfolio would require a stock investment of 0.75($40) = $30. Since your total investment outlay to create the riskless portfolio must be equal to or less than $20.83, the present value of the portfolio, you must be able to sell the call option for at least $30 − $20.83 = $9.17 in order to break even. Assuming that competition exists in the options market, $9.17 will be the equilibrium price of the option.

Clearly, this example is unrealistic—Butler's stock price could be almost anything after 1 year, and you cannot purchase 0.75 shares of stock. But the example does illustrate that investors can, in principle, create riskless portfolios by buying stocks and selling call options against those stocks, and the return on such portfolios would be the risk-free rate. If call options are not priced to reflect this condition, arbitrageurs will actively trade stocks and options until option prices do reflect such equilibrium conditions. In the next section, we discuss the Black-Scholes Option Pricing Model, which is based on the general premise we developed here—the creation of a riskless portfolio—but which is much more applicable to "real-world" option pricing because it allows for a wide range of ending stock prices.

Self-Test Questions

Describe how a risk-free portfolio can be created using stocks and options.

How can such a portfolio be used to help estimate a call option's value?

THE BLACK-SCHOLES OPTION PRICING MODEL (OPM)

The *Black-Scholes Option Pricing Model (OPM)* was developed in 1973, just as the rapid growth in options trading began.[4] This model, which has actually been programmed into the permanent memories of some hand-held calculators, is widely used by option traders. Our interest, however, lies in the insights that option theory provides in valuing all securities subject to contingent claims, including warrants, convertibles, and even the equity of a levered firm.

In deriving their option pricing model, which estimates the value of a call option, Black and Scholes made the following assumptions:

1. The stock underlying the call option provides no dividends or other distributions during the life of the option.

2. There are no transaction costs in buying or selling either the stock or the option.

3. The short-term, risk-free interest rate is known and is constant during the life of the option.

4. Any purchaser of a security may borrow any fraction of the purchase price at the short-term, risk-free interest rate.

---

[4]See Fischer Black and Myron Scholes, "The Pricing of Options and Corporate Liabilities," *Journal of Political Economy,* May/June 1973, 637–659.

5.   Short selling is permitted without penalty, and the short seller will receive immediately the full cash proceeds of today's price for a security sold short.[5]

6.   The call option can be exercised only on its expiration date.

7.   Trading in all securities takes place in continuous time, and the stock price moves randomly in continuous time.

The derivation of the Black-Scholes Option Pricing Model rests on the concept of a riskless hedge such as the one we set up in the last section. By buying shares of a stock and simultaneously selling call options on that stock, an investor can create a risk-free investment position, where gains on the stock will exactly offset losses on the option, and vice versa. This riskless hedged position must earn a rate of return equal to the risk-free rate; otherwise, an arbitrage opportunity would exist, and people trying to take advantage of this opportunity would drive the price of the option to the equilibrium level as specified by the Black-Scholes model.

The Black-Scholes model consists of the following three equations:

$$V = P[N(d_1)] - Xe^{-k_{RF}t} [N(d_2)]. \tag{18-1}$$

$$d_1 = \frac{\ln(P/X) + [k_{RF} + (\sigma^2/2)]t}{\sigma\sqrt{t}}. \tag{18-2}$$

$$d_2 = d_1 - \sigma\sqrt{t}. \tag{18-3}$$

Here

V = current value of a call option with time t until expiration.

P = current price of the underlying stock.

$N(d_i)$ = probability that a deviation less than d_i will occur in a standard normal distribution. Thus, $N(d_1)$ and $N(d_2)$ represent areas under a standard normal distribution function.

X = exercise, or striking, price of the option.

e = exponential function ≈ 2.7183.

k_{RF} = risk-free interest rate.

t = time until the option expires (the option period).

$\ln(P/X)$ = natural logarithm of P/X.

σ^2 = variance of the rate of return on the stock.

Note that the value of the option is a function of the variables we discussed earlier: (1) P, the stock's price; (2) t, the option's time to expiration; (3) X, the striking price;

---

[5]Suppose an investor (or speculator) does not now own any IBM stock. If the investor anticipates a rise in the stock price and consequently buys IBM stock, he or she is said to have *gone long* in IBM. On the other hand, if the investor thinks IBM's stock is likely to fall, he or she could *go short*, or *sell IBM short*. Since the short seller has no IBM stock, he or she would have to borrow the shares sold short from a broker. If the stock price falls, the short seller could, later on, buy shares on the open market and pay back the ones borrowed from the broker. The short seller's profit, before commissions and taxes, would be the difference between the price received from the short sale and the price paid later to purchase the replacement stock.

(4) σ^2, the variance of the underlying stock; and (5) k_{RF}, the risk-free rate. We do not derive the Black-Scholes model—the derivation involves some extremely complicated mathematical statistics that go far beyond the scope of this text. However, it is not difficult to use the model, and under the assumptions set forth previously, if the option price is different from the one found by Equation 18-1, this would provide the opportunity for arbitrage profits, which would, in turn, force the option price back to the value indicated by the model.[6] As we noted earlier, the Black-Scholes model is widely used by traders, so actual option prices do conform reasonably well to values derived from the model.

In essence, the first term of Equation 18-1, $P[N(d_1)]$, can be thought of as the expected present value of the terminal stock price, while the second term, $Xe^{-k_{RF}t}[N(d_2)]$, can be thought of as the present value of the exercise price. However, rather than try to figure out exactly what the equations mean, it is more productive to work out some values and to see how changes in the inputs affect the value of a call option.

OPM Illustration

The current stock price, P, the exercise price, X, and the time to maturity, t, of the option can be obtained from a newspaper such as *The Wall Street Journal*. The risk-free rate, k_{RF}, used in the OPM is the yield on Treasury bills with a maturity date equal to the option expiration date. The stock price variance, σ^2, can be estimated by calculating the variance of the percentage change in daily stock prices for the past year, that is, the variance of $(P_t - P_{t-1})/P_t$ on a daily basis.

Assume that the following information has been obtained:

P = $20.

X = $20.

 t = 3 months or 0.25 years.

k_{RF} = 12% = 0.12.

σ^2 = 0.16.

Given this information, we can now use the OPM by solving Equations 18-1 through 18-3. Since d_1 and d_2 are required inputs for Equation 18-1, we solve Equations 18-2 and 18-3 first:

$$d_1 = \frac{\ln(\$20/\$20) + [0.12 + (0.16/2)](0.25)}{0.40(0.50)}$$

$$= \frac{0 + 0.05}{0.20} = 0.25.$$

$$d_2 = d_1 - 0.20 = 0.05.$$

Note that $N(d_1) = N(0.25)$ and $N(d_2) = N(0.05)$ represent areas under a standard normal distribution function. From Table A-5 in Appendix A at the end of the book,

---

[6]*Programmed trading,* in which stocks are bought and options are sold, or vice versa, is an example of arbitrage between stocks and options.

Table 18-2   Effects of OPM Factors on the Value of a Call Option

Case	Input Factors					V
	P	X	t	k_{RF}	σ^2	
Base case	$20	$20	0.25	12%	0.16	$1.88
Increase P by $5	**25**	20	0.25	12	0.16	5.81
Increase X by $5	20	**25**	0.25	12	0.16	0.39
Increase t to 6 months	20	20	**0.50**	12	0.16	2.81
Increase k_{RF} to 16%	20	20	0.25	**16**	0.16	1.99
Increase σ^2 to 0.25	20	20	0.25	12	**0.25**	2.27

we see that the value $d_1 = 0.25$ implies a probability of $0.0987 + 0.5000 = 0.5987$, so $N(d_1) = 0.5987$. Similarly, $N(d_2) = 0.5199$. We can use those values to solve Equation 18-1:

$$V = \$20[N(d_1)] - \$20e^{-(0.12)(0.25)}[N(d_2)]$$

$$= \$20[N(0.25)] - \$20(0.9704)[N(0.05)]$$

$$= \$20(0.5987) - \$19.41(0.5199)$$

$$= \$11.97 - \$10.09 = \$1.88.$$

Thus, the value of the option, under the assumed conditions, is $1.88. Suppose the actual option price were $2.25. Arbitrageurs could simultaneously sell the option and buy the underlying stock, and earn a riskless profit. Such trading would occur until the price of the option was driven to $1.88. The reverse would occur if the option sold for less than $1.88. Thus, investors would be unwilling to pay more than $1.88 for the option, and they could not buy it for less, so $1.88 is the *equilibrium value* of the option.

To see how each of the five OPM factors affects the value of the option, V, consider Table 18-2. Here the top row shows the base case input values and the resulting option value, $V = \$1.88$. The base case input values are those we used earlier to illustrate how to solve the OPM. In each of the subsequent rows, one factor is increased, while the values of the other four are held constant at their base case levels. The value of the call option is given in the last column. Now consider the effects of a change in each factor:

1. **Current stock price.** As the current stock price, P, increases from $20 to $25, the option value increases from $1.88 to $5.81. Thus, the value of the option increases as the stock price increases, but by less than the stock price increase, $3.93 versus $5.00. Note, though, that the percentage increase in the option value, ($5.81 − $1.88)/$1.88 = 209%, far exceeds the percentage increase in the stock price, ($25 − $20)/$20 = 25%.

2. **Exercise price.** As the exercise price, X, increases from $20 to $25, the value of the option declines. Again, though, the decrease in the option value is less

than the exercise price increase, but the percentage change in the option value, ($0.39 − $1.88)/$1.88 = −79%, exceeds the percentage change in the exercise price, ($25 − $20)/$20 = 25%.

3. **Option period.** As time to expiration increases from t = 3 months (or 0.25 years) to t = 6 months (or 0.50 years), the value of the option increases from $1.88 to $2.81. This result occurs because the value of the option depends on the chances for an increase in the price of the underlying stock, and the longer the option has to go, the higher the stock price may climb. Thus, other factors held constant, a 6-month option is worth more than a 3-month option.

4. **Risk-free rate.** The next factor is the risk-free rate, k_{RF}. As the risk-free rate increases from 12 to 16 percent, the value of the option increases slightly, from $1.88 to $1.99. Equations 18-1, 18-2, and 18-3 suggest that the principal effect of an increase in k_{RF} is to reduce the present value of the exercise price, $Xe^{-k_{RF}t}$, hence to increase the current value of the option.[7] The risk-free rate also plays a role in determining the values of the normal distribution functions $N(d_1)$ and $N(d_2)$, but this effect is of secondary importance. Indeed, option prices in general are not very sensitive to interest rate changes, at least not to changes within the ranges normally encountered.

5. **Variance.** As the variance increases from the base case level of 0.16 to 0.25, the value of the option increases from $1.88 to $2.27. That is, if all other factors are held constant, the riskier the underlying security, the more valuable will be the option. This result is logical. First, if you bought an option to buy a stock that sells at its exercise price, and if $\sigma^2 = 0$, then there would be a zero probability of the stock price going up, hence a zero probability of making any money on the option. On the other hand, if you bought an option on a high-variance stock, there would be a fairly high probability that the stock price would go way up, hence that you would make a large profit on the option. Of course, the price of a high-variance stock could go way down, but as an option holder, your losses would be limited to the price paid to buy the option—only the right-hand side of the stock's probability distribution counts. Put another way, an increase in the price of the stock helps options holders more than a decrease hurts them; thus, the greater the variance, the greater is the value of the option. All of this makes options on risky stocks more valuable than those on safer, low-variance stocks.

This concludes our discussion of options and option pricing theory. The next section discusses how option pricing theory can be used to help think about financial decisions, while the following two major sections describe warrants and convertibles, the primary types of option securities issued by firms.

---

[7]At this point, you may be wondering why the first term in Equation 18-1, $P[N(d_1)]$, is not discounted. In fact, it has been, because the current stock price, P, already represents the present value of the expected expiration date stock price. In other words, P is a discounted value, and the discount rate used in the market to determine today's stock price includes the risk-free rate. Thus, Equation 18-1 can be thought of as the present value of the end-of-option-period spread between the stock price and the striking price, adjusted for the probability that the stock price will be higher than the striking price.

Self-Test Questions

What is the purpose of the Black-Scholes Option Pricing Model?

Explain what a "riskless hedge" is, and how the riskless hedge concept is used in the Black-Scholes OPM.

Describe the impact that an increase in each of the following factors would have on the value of a call option:

1. Stock price
2. Exercise price
3. Option period
4. Risk-free rate
5. Stock price variance

OPTION PRICING: IMPLICATIONS FOR CORPORATE FINANCIAL POLICY

The equity of a levered firm can be thought of as a call option: When a firm issues debt, this is in a sense equivalent to the shareholders selling the assets of the firm to the debtholders, who pay for the assets with cash but also give the stockholders an implied call option with a striking price equal to the principal value of the debt plus interest. If the company is successful, the stockholders will "buy the company back" by exercising their call, which means paying the principal and interest on the debt. If the company is not successful, stockholders will default on the loan, which amounts to not exercising their call and thus giving the company to the creditors.

As an illustration, suppose the One-Shot Corporation is just being formed to make a 1-year investment in producing and marketing presidential campaign buttons. The firm requires an investment of $10,000, of which $7,500 will be obtained by selling debt with a 10 percent interest rate, and the other $2,500 will be raised by selling common stock. All cash distributions to debtholders and stockholders are to be made at the end of 1 year. After this year is over, the value of the firm will depend primarily on which candidates make it through the primary elections, plus a small value in the collector's market. Here is the estimated probability distribution of the firm's value:

Probability	Value
0.7	$20,000
0.2	5,000
0.1	0
1.0	

Thus, the expected value of the firm at the end of the year is 0.7($20,000) + 0.2($5,000) + 0.1($0) = $15,000.

The expected value, if it could be realized, would provide the shareholders with $6,750 before taxes on their $2,500 investment:

Expected value		$15,000
Less:		
Debt principal	$7,500	
Debt interest	750	8,250
Before-tax return		$ 6,750

However, the expected value is not achievable: The value of the firm will be $0 or $5,000 or $20,000. If the value is either $0 or $5,000, the shareholders will not exercise their call option; instead, they will default. The debtholders would then be entitled to the value of the firm, and the equity holders would receive nothing. However, if the firm's value turns out to be $20,000, the shareholders would exercise the call option by paying off the $8,250 principal and interest, and then pocket the remaining $11,750 before taxes. Thus, equity ownership can be viewed as a call option. In this illustration, an equity investment of $2,500 (the current price of the call) entitles the shareholders to purchase the assets of the firm from the debtholders for $8,250 (the exercise price). This insight has been applied to several of the traditional issues of corporate finance.[8] We look at one issue here, investment decisions, and we will examine the implications of option analysis for mergers in Chapter 24.

Start with a levered firm which has a large portfolio of Treasury bills. Suppose management sold the bills (which are riskless) and used the proceeds to purchase a risky asset that increased the firm's earnings variance, yet had no effect on the firm's beta coefficient. Since the equity can be viewed as a call option, the increased variance would increase the market value of the equity without increasing its market risk. The risk of bankruptcy would increase, but shareholders would have increased their chances of greater gains while their losses would still be limited to the amount of their investment. However, any gains to shareholders come at the expense of the debtholders. In general, we can see that increasing a firm's riskiness by changing its asset mix benefits the stockholders at the expense of the debtholders. This point is made clear by applying option pricing theory.

Options are important in the investments area, so students of investments need to have a knowledge of how they are used and priced in the market. Further, option theory helps us understand the nature of option-like securities such as warrants and convertibles. However, the role of option theory in financial management decision making is less clear. As we have seen, it is possible to use option theory to gain insights into the effects of asset investments on the value of the firm's debt and equity. However, these insights are really rather obvious, and one can see the general effects of asset risk changes more easily just by thinking about them than by working through the OPM. Still, it may be that the OPM approach can in the future lead to a more precise quantification of certain effects, which would be useful in structuring contracts and in other types of financial policy decisions. Also, we noted

---

[8]For example, see Dan Galai and Ronald Masulis, "The Option Pricing Model and the Risk Factor of Stock," *The Journal of Financial Economics,* January/March 1976, 53–82. Galai and Masulis combine the CAPM with the OPM. Thus, the assumptions of both models underlie their analysis.

in Chapter 10 that the Black-Scholes OPM is being used in some industries to value the managerial options inherent in some capital projects. In any event, it is safe to predict that option pricing theory will play a greater role in financial management decision making in the future, so students of corporate finance need to be aware of the progress in this area.

Self-Test Questions

Describe how the equity of a levered firm can be thought of as a call option.

What does option pricing theory tell us about how changes in assets might affect the value of a firm's debt and equity?

WARRANTS

A *warrant* is an option issued by a company which gives the warrant's owner the right to buy a stated number of shares of the company's stock at a specified price. Generally, warrants are distributed with debt, and they are used to induce investors to buy a firm's long-term debt at a lower interest rate than would otherwise be required. For example, when Infomatics Corporation, a rapidly growing high-tech company, wanted to sell $50 million of 20-year bonds in 1990, the company's investment banker informed the financial vice president that the bonds would be difficult to sell, and that an interest rate of 10 percent would be required. However, as an alternative the banker suggested that investors might be willing to buy the bonds with a coupon rate of only 8 percent if the company would offer 20 warrants with each $1,000 bond, each warrant entitling the holder to buy one share of common stock at a price of $22 per share. The stock was selling for $20 per share at the time, and the warrants would expire in the year 2000 if they had not been exercised previously.

Why would investors be willing to buy Infomatics Corporation's bonds at a yield of only 8 percent in a 10 percent market just because warrants were also offered as part of the package? It is because the warrants are long-term options which have value as discussed earlier, and this value offsets the low interest rate on the bonds and makes the package of low-yield bonds plus warrants attractive to investors.

Initial Market Price of Bond with Warrants

The Infomatics bonds, if they had been issued as straight debt, would have carried a 10 percent interest rate. However, with warrants attached, the bonds were sold to yield 8 percent. Someone buying the bonds at their $1,000 initial offering price would thus be receiving a package consisting of an 8 percent, 20-year bond plus 20 warrants. Since the going interest rate on bonds as risky as those of Infomatics was 10 percent, we can find the straight-debt value of the bonds, assuming an annual coupon for ease of illustration, as follows:

$$\text{Value} = \sum_{t=1}^{20} \frac{\$80}{(1.10)^t} + \frac{\$1,000}{(1.10)^{20}}$$

$$= \$681.09 + \$148.64 = \$829.73.$$

Thus, a person buying the bonds in the initial underwriting would pay \$1,000 and receive in exchange a straight bond worth about \$830 plus 20 warrants presumably worth about \$1,000 − \$830 = \$170:

$$\begin{array}{ccc}
\text{Price paid for} & = & \text{Straight-debt} + \text{Value of} \\
\text{bond with warrants} & & \text{value of bond} \quad \text{warrants}
\end{array}$$

$$\$1,000 \quad = \quad \$830 \quad + \quad \$170.$$

Since investors receive 20 warrants with each bond, each warrant has an implied value of \$170/20 = \$8.50.

The key issue in setting the terms of a bond-with-warrants offering is valuing the warrants. The straight-debt value of the bond can be estimated quite accurately. However, it is much more difficult to estimate the value of the warrants. Even the Black-Scholes OPM provides only a rough estimate because (1) its parameters are not easily estimated and (2) it assumes no dividends on the underlying stock, which is not generally a reasonable assumption for a long-term option. If, in setting the terms, the warrants are overvalued relative to their true market value, then it will be difficult to sell the issue at its par value. Conversely, if the warrants are undervalued, then investors who subscribe to the issue will receive a windfall profit, since they can sell the warrants in the market for more than they implicitly paid for them, and this windfall profit would come out of the pockets of Infomatics's stockholders.

Use of Warrants in Financing

In the past, warrants have generally been used by small, rapidly growing firms as "sweeteners" when they were selling either debt or preferred stock. Such firms are frequently regarded by investors as being highly riskly. Their bonds could be sold only if they were willing to pay extremely high rates of interest and also to accept very restrictive indenture provisions. To avoid this, firms such as Infomatics often offered warrants along with the bonds. However, several years ago, AT&T raised \$1.57 billion by selling bonds with warrants. This was the largest financing of any type ever undertaken by a business firm, and it marked the first use ever of warrants by a large, strong corporation.[9]

---

[9]It is interesting to note that before the AT&T issue, the New York Stock Exchange's stated policy was that warrants could not be listed because they were "speculative" instruments rather than "investment" securities. When AT&T issued warrants, however, the Exchange changed its policy, agreeing to list warrants that met certain requirements. Many other warrants have since been listed.

It is also interesting to note that, prior to the sale, AT&T's treasury staff, working with Morgan Stanley analysts, estimated the value of the warrants as a part of the underwriting decision. The package was supposed to sell for a total price in the neighborhood of \$1,000. The bond value could be determined accurately, so the trick was to estimate the equilibrium value of the warrant under different possible exercise prices and years to expiration, and then to use that exercise price and life that caused Bond value + Warrant value ≈ \$1,000. Using the option pricing model, the AT&T/Morgan Stanley analysts set terms which caused the warrant to sell on the open market at a price that was only 35¢ away from the estimated price.

Getting warrants along with bonds enables investors to share in the company's growth, if it does in fact grow and prosper; therefore, investors are willing to accept a lower bond interest rate and less restrictive indenture provisions. A bond with warrants has some characteristics of debt and some characteristics of equity. It is a hybrid security that provides the financial manager with an opportunity to expand the firm's mix of securities and to appeal to a broader group of investors.

Virtually all warrants today are *detachable.* Thus, after a bond with attached warrants is sold, the warrants can be detached and traded separately from the bond. Further, when these warrants are exercised, the bond issue (with its low coupon rate) remains outstanding, so the warrants bring in additional funds to the firm while leaving its interest costs relatively low.

The exercise price is generally set at from 10 to 30 percent above the market price of the stock on the date the bond is issued. If the firm does grow and prosper, and if its stock price rises above the exercise price at which shares may be purchased, warrant holders could exercise their warrants and buy stock at the stated price. However, without some incentive, warrants would never be exercised prior to maturity—their value in the market would be greater than their exercise value, hence holders would sell rather than exercise. There are three conditions which encourage holders to exercise their warrants: (1) Warrant holders will surely exercise warrants and buy stock if the warrants are about to expire and the market price of the stock is above the exercise price. (2) Warrant holders will tend to exercise voluntarily and buy stock if the company raises the dividend on the common stock by a sufficient amount. No dividend is earned on the warrant, so it provides no current income. However, if the common stock pays a high dividend, it provides an attractive dividend yield. This induces warrant holders to exercise their option to buy the stock. (3) Warrants sometimes have *stepped-up exercise prices,* which prod owners into exercising them. For example, the Williamson Scientific Company has warrants outstanding with an exercise price of $25 until December 31, 1995, at which time the exercise price rises to $30. If the price of the common stock is over $25 just before December 31, 1995, many warrant holders will exercise their options before the stepped-up price takes effect.

Another desirable feature of warrants is that they generally bring in funds only if funds are needed. If the company grows, it will probably need new equity capital. At the same time, growth will cause the price of the stock to rise, the warrants to be exercised, and the firm to obtain additional cash. If the company is not successful and cannot profitably employ additional money, the price of its stock will probably not rise sufficiently to induce exercise of the warrants.

The Component Cost of Bonds with Warrants

When Infomatics issued its debt with warrants, the firm received $50 million, or $1,000 for each bond. Simultaneously, the company assumed an obligation to pay $80 interest for 20 years plus $1,000 at the end of 20 years. The cost of the money would have been 10 percent if no warrants had been attached, but each Infomatics bond had 20 warrants, each of which entitles its holder to buy one share of Infomatics stock for $22. A cost rate must be assigned to the warrants to determine the total cost of the issue. As we shall see, the total cost is well above 8 percent.

Assume that Infomatics's stock price, which is now $20, is expected to grow, and does grow, at 10 percent per year. When the warrants expire 10 years from now, the stock price will be $20(1.10)^{10} = $51.87. Assuming the warrants had not been exercised during the 10-year period, the company would then have to issue one share of stock worth $51.87 for each warrant exercised, and in return, Infomatics would receive the exercise price, $22. Thus, a purchaser of the bonds, if he or she holds the complete package, will make a profit in Year 10 of $51.87 − $22 = $29.87 for each common share issued. Since each bond has 20 warrants attached, investors would have a gain of 20($29.87) = $597.40 per bond at the end of Year 10. Here is a time line of the cash flow stream to an investor:

0	1		9	10	11		20
− $1,000	+ $80	. . .	+ $80	+ $ 80.00	+ $80	. . .	+ $ 80
				+ 597.40			+ 1,000
				+ $677.40			+ $1,080

The IRR of this stream is 10.7 percent, which is the investor's overall rate of return on the issue. This return is 70 basis points higher than the return on straight debt, which reflects the fact that the issue is riskier to investors than a straight-debt issue because some of the return is expected to come in the form of stock price appreciation, and that part of the return may not materialize.

The expected rate of return to investors is, of course, also the before-tax cost of the issue to the company—this was true of common stocks, straight bonds, and preferred stocks, and it is also true of bonds sold with warrants. In thinking about this, note that the investor's Year 10 gain of $597.40 does not just appear out of thin air—the company is giving the warrant holders the right to buy for $22 a share of stock with a market value of $51.87. That obviously dilutes the value of the stock, so Infomatics's original shareholders are incurring an opportunity cost which is exactly equal to the warrant holders' gain.

The cost of warrants can also be illustrated in terms of the effect on earnings per share (EPS). Suppose Infomatics had 1,000,000 common shares outstanding just prior to the expiration of the warrants. Further, assume that the company earns 13.5 percent on its market value equity, so earnings per share are 0.135($51.87) = $7, and total earnings are 1,000,000($7) = $7,000,000. Now, if there were 100,000 warrants outstanding at expiration, exercise of these warrants would bring in 100,000($22) = $2,200,000 of new equity funds, and the number of shares would increase by 100,000. Assuming that the earning power of the $2.2 million of new assets was also 13.5 percent, then 0.135($2,200,000) = $297,000 of new earnings would be produced, making the new total earnings $7,000,000 + $297,000 = $7,297,000. When that new total earnings figure is divided by the new total shares outstanding (1,000,000 + 100,000 = 1,100,000), we get a new EPS of $6.63:

$$\text{New EPS} = \$7,297,000/1,100,000 = \$6.63.$$

Thus, exercise of the warrants results in a dilution of EPS from $7 to $6.63, or by $0.37. This $0.37 EPS dilution is a real cost, it is borne by Infomatics's original shareholders, and it must be considered when calculating the cost of the bonds with warrants.

Self-Test Questions

What is a warrant?

Describe how a new bond issue with warrants is valued.

How are warrants used in corporate financing?

The use of warrants lowers the coupon rate on the corresponding debt issue. Does this mean that the component cost of debt plus warrants is less than the cost of straight debt? Explain.

CONVERTIBLES

Convertible securities are bonds or preferred stocks which, under specified terms and conditions, can be exchanged for common stock at the option of the holder. Unlike the exercise of warrants, which brings in additional funds to the firm, conversion does not bring in additional capital: Debt (or preferred stock) is simply replaced on the balance sheet by common stock. Of course, the reduction of the debt or preferred stock will improve the financial strength of the company and make it easier to raise additional fixed charge capital, but that requires a separate action.

Conversion Ratio and Conversion Price

One of the most important provisions of a convertible security is the *conversion ratio, CR,* defined as the number of shares of stock a bondholder will receive upon conversion. Related to the conversion ratio is the *conversion price, P_c,* which is the effective price the company will receive for the common stock when conversion occurs. The relationship between the conversion ratio and the conversion price can be illustrated by the Silicon Valley Software Company's convertible debentures, issued at their $1,000 par value in July of 1990. At any time prior to maturity on July 15, 2010, a debenture holder can exchange a bond for 20 shares of common stock; therefore, the conversion ratio, CR, is 20. The bond has a par value of $1,000, so the holder would be relinquishing the right to receive $1,000 at maturity if he or she converts. Dividing the $1,000 par value by the 20 shares received gives a conversion price of $P_c = \$50$ a share:

$$\text{Conversion price} = P_c = \frac{\text{Par value of bond given up}}{\text{Shares received}}$$

$$= \frac{\$1,000}{\text{CR}} = \frac{\$1,000}{20} = \$50.$$

Conversely, by solving for CR, we obtain the conversion ratio:

$$\text{Conversion ratio} = \text{CR} = \frac{\$1,000}{P_c} = \frac{\$1,000}{\$50} = 20 \text{ shares.}$$

Once CR is set, the value of P_c is established, and vice versa.

Like a warrant's exercise price, the conversion price is characteristically set at from 10 to 30 percent above the prevailing market price of the common stock at the time the convertible issue is sold. Exactly how the conversion price is established can best be understood after examining some of the reasons firms use convertibles.

Generally, the conversion price and conversion ratio are fixed for the life of the bond, although sometimes a stepped-up conversion price is used. For example, the 1990 convertible debentures for Breedon Industries are convertible into 12.5 shares until 2000; into 11.76 shares from 2000 until 2010; and into 11.11 shares from 2010 until maturity in 2020. The conversion price thus starts at $80, rises to $85, and then goes to $90. Breedon's convertibles, like most, become callable after a 10-year call-protection period.

Another factor that may cause a change in the conversion price and ratio is a standard feature of almost all convertibles—the clause protecting the convertible against dilution from stock splits, stock dividends, and the sale of common stock at prices below the conversion price. The typical provision states that if common stock is sold at a price below the conversion price, then the conversion price must be lowered (and the conversion ratio raised) to the price at which the new stock was issued. Also, if the stock is split, or if a stock dividend is declared, the conversion price must be lowered by the percentage amount of the stock dividend or split. For example, if Breedon Industries were to have a two-for-one stock split during the first 10 years of its convertible's life, the conversion ratio would automatically be adjusted from 12.5 to 25, and the conversion price lowered from $80 to $40. If this protection were not contained in the contract, a company could completely thwart conversion by the use of stock splits and stock dividends. Warrants are similarly protected against dilution.

The standard protection against dilution from selling new stock at prices below the conversion price can, however, get a company into trouble. For example, assume that Breedon's stock was selling for $65 per share in 1990 at the time of the convertible issue. Further, suppose the market went sour, and Breedon's stock price dropped to $50 per share. A new common stock sale now would require the company to lower the conversion price on the convertible debentures from $80 to $50. That would raise the value of the convertibles and, in effect, transfer wealth from current shareholders to the convertible holders. Potential problems such as this must be kept in mind by firms considering the use of convertibles or bonds with warrants.

Convertible Bond Model

In the spring of 1990, Silicon Valley Software was evaluating the use of the convertible bond issue described earlier. The issue would consist of 20-year convertible bonds which would sell at a price of $1,000 per bond; this $1,000 would also be the bond's par (and maturity) value. The bonds would pay a 10 percent annual coupon interest rate, or $100 per year. Each bond would be convertible into 20 shares of stock, so the conversion price would be $1,000/20 = $50. The stock was expected to pay a dividend of $2.80 during the coming year, and it sold at $35 per share. Further, the stock price was expected to grow at a constant rate of 8 percent per year. Therefore, $k_s = \hat{k}_s = D_1/P_0 + g = \$2.80/\$35 + 8\% = 8\% + 8\% = 16\%$. If the bonds were not made convertible, they would have to offer a yield of 13 percent, given their riskiness and the general level of interest rates. The convertible bonds would not be callable for 10 years, after which they could be called at a price of $1,050, with this price declining by $5 per year thereafter. If, after 10 years, the conversion value exceeds the call price by at least 20 percent, management would probably call the bonds.

Figure 18-2 shows the expectations of both an average investor and the company:[10]

1.   The horizontal line at M = $1,000 represents the par (and maturity) value. Also, $1,000 is the price at which the bond is initially offered to the public.

2.   The bond is protected against call for 10 years. It is initially callable at a price of $1,050, and the call price declines thereafter by $5 per year. Thus, the call price is represented by the solid section of the line V_0M''.

3.   Since the convertible has a 10 percent coupon rate, and since the yield on a nonconvertible bond of similar risk was stated to be 13 percent, the "straight bond" value of the convertible, B_t, must be less than par. At the time of issue, assuming an annual coupon, B_0 is $789:

$$B_0 = \sum_{t=1}^{20} \frac{\$100}{(1.13)^t} + \frac{\$1,000}{(1.13)^{20}} = \$789.$$

Note, however, that the bond's straight-debt value must be $1,000 just prior to maturity, so the bond's straight-debt value rises over time. B_t follows the line B_0M'' in the graph.

4.   The bond's initial conversion value, or the value of the stock the investor would receive if the bonds were converted at t = 0, is $700: The bond's conversion value is $P_t(CR)$, so at t = 0, conversion value = $P_0(CR)$ = $35(20 \text{ shares})$ = $700. Since the stock's price is expected to grow at an 8 percent rate, the conversion value of the bond should rise over time. For example, in Year 5 it should be $P_5(CR)$ = $\$35(1.08)^5(20)$ = $1,029. The expected conversion value over time is given by the line C_t in Figure 18-2.

5.   The actual market price of the bond can never fall below the higher of its straight-debt value or its conversion value. If the market price were below the straight-bond value, those who wanted bonds would recognize the bargain and buy the convertible as a bond. If the market price were below the conversion value, people would buy the convertibles, turn them in for stock, and sell the stock at a profit. Therefore, the higher of the bond value and conversion value curves in the graph represents a *floor price* for the bond. In Figure 18-2, the floor price is represented by the thicker shaded line B_0XC_t.

6.   In fact, the bond's market value will typically exceed its floor value. It will exceed the straight-bond value because the option to convert is worth something—a 10 percent bond with conversion possibilities is worth more than a 10 percent

---

[10]For a more complete discussion of how this model can be used to structure the terms of a convertible offering, see Eugene F. Brigham, "An Analysis of Convertible Debentures: Theory and Some Empirical Evidence," *Journal of Finance,* March 1966, 35–54; and M. Wayne Marr and G. Rodney Thompson, "The Pricing of New Convertible Bond Issues," *Financial Management,* Summer 1984, 31–37.

Figure 18-2   Silicon Valley Software:
Convertible Bond Model

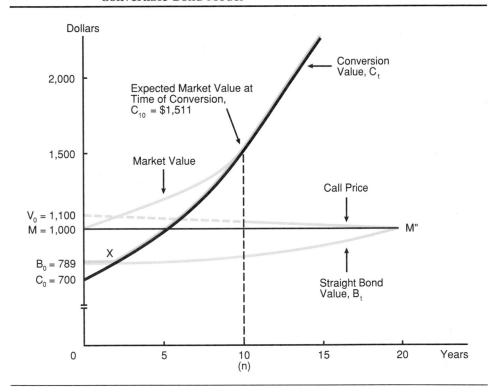

bond without this option. The actual price will also exceed the conversion value because holding the convertible is equivalent to holding a call option, and, prior to expiration, the option's true value is higher than its expiration (or conversion) value. We cannot say exactly where the market value line will lie, but it will typically be above the floor set by the straight bond and conversion value lines.

7.   At some point, the market value line will hit the conversion value line. This convergence will occur for two reasons. First, the stock should pay higher and higher dividends as the years go by, but the interest payments on the convertible are fixed. For example, Silicon's convertibles would pay $100 in interest annually, while the dividends on the 20 shares received upon conversion would initially be $20($2.80) = 56. However, at an 8 percent growth rate, the dividends after 10 years would be up to $120.90, while the interest would still be $100. Thus, at some point, rising dividends could be expected to push against the fixed interest payments, causing the premium to disappear and investors to convert voluntarily. Second, once the bond becomes callable, its market value cannot get very far above the higher of the conversion value and the call price without exposing investors to the danger of a call. For example, suppose that 10 years after issue (when the bonds were callable),

the market value of the bonds was $1,600, the conversion value was $1,500, and the call price was $1,050. If the company called the bonds the day after you bought 10 bonds for $16,000, you would be forced to convert into stock worth only $15,000, so you would suffer a loss of $100 per bond, or $1,000, in one day. Recognizing this danger, you and other investors would simply not pay much of a premium over the higher of the call price or the conversion value once the bond becomes callable. Therefore, in Figure 18-2, we assume that the market value line hits the conversion value line in Year 10, when the bond becomes callable.

8. We can let n represent the year when investors expect conversion to occur, either voluntarily because of rising dividends or because the company calls the convertibles to strengthen its balance sheet by substituting equity for debt. In our example, we assume that $n = 10$, the first call date. Had the company used a lower initial conversion value, or a lower expected growth rate for the stock, such that C_{10} was less than V_{10}, n would have been greater than 10, the first call date.

9. Since $n = 10$, the expected market value at Year 10 is $35(1.08)^{10}(20) = \$1,511$. An investor can find the expected rate of return on the convertible bond, k_c, by finding the IRR of the following cash flow stream:

The solution is $k_c = IRR = 12.8$ percent.

10. The return on a convertible is expected to come partly from interest income and partly from capital gains; in this case, the total return is 12.8 percent, with 10 percent representing interest income and 2.8 percent representing the expected capital gain. The interest component is relatively assured, while the capital gain component is more risky. On a new straight bond, all of the return is in the form of interest. Therefore, a convertible's expected return is more risky than that of a straight bond, so k_c should be larger than the cost of straight debt, k_d. Thus, it would seem that the expected rate of return on Silicon's convertibles, k_c, should lie between its cost of straight debt, $k_d = 13\%$, and its cost of common stock, $k_s = 16\%$.

Investment bankers use the type of model described here, plus a knowledge of the market, to set the terms on convertibles (the conversion ratio and the coupon interest rate) such that the security will just "clear the market" at its $1,000 offering price. In this example, the required conditions do not seem to hold—the calculated rate of return on the convertible is only 12.8 percent, which is less, rather than more, than the 13 percent cost of straight debt. Therefore, it would appear that the terms on the bond must be made more attractive to investors. Silicon Valley Software would have to increase the coupon interest rate on the convertible to a level above 10 percent, raise the conversion ratio above 20 (and thereby lower the conversion price from $50 to a level closer to the current $35 market price of the stock), or use a combination of these two such that the expected rate of return on the convertible ends up between 13 and 16 percent.[11]

Use of Convertibles in Financing

Convertibles have two important advantages from the issuer's standpoint. (1) Convertibles, like bonds with warrants, offer a company the chance to sell debt with lower interest rates and less restrictive covenants in exchange for a chance to participate in the company's success if it does well. (2) In a sense, convertibles provide a way to sell common stock at prices higher than those currently prevailing. Some companies actually want to sell common stock, and not debt, but feel that the price of their stock is temporarily depressed. Management may know, for example, that earnings are depressed because of start-up costs associated with a new project, but they expect earnings to rise sharply during the next year or so, pulling the price of the stock up with them. Such a management might think that if it sold stock now, it would be giving up more shares than necessary to raise a given amount of money. However, if it set the conversion price 20 to 30 percent above the present market price of the stock, then 20 to 30 percent fewer shares would be given up when the bonds were converted than would be required if stock were sold directly at the current time. Notice, however, that management is counting on the stock's price to rise above the conversion price to make the bonds attractive in conversion. If earnings do not rise and pull the stock price up, hence conversion does not occur, then the company will be saddled with debt in the face of low earnings, which could be disastrous.

How can the company be sure that conversion will occur if the price of the stock rises above the conversion price? Typically, convertibles contain a call provision that enables the issuing firm to force bondholders to convert. Suppose the conversion price is $50, the conversion ratio is 20, the market price of the common stock has risen to $60, and the call price on the convertible bond is $1,050. If the company calls the bond, bondholders can either convert into common stock with a market value of 20($60) = $1,200 or allow the company to redeem the bond for $1,050. Naturally, bondholders prefer $1,200 to $1,050, so conversion occurs. The call provision therefore gives the company a way to force conversion, provided the market price of the stock is greater than the conversion price. Note, however, that most convertibles have a fairly long period of call protection—10 years is typical. Therefore, if the company wants to be able to force conversion fairly early, then it will have to set a short call protection period. This will, in turn, require that it set a higher coupon rate or a lower conversion price.

From the standpoint of the issuer, convertibles have three important disadvantages. (1) Although the use of a convertible security does give the issuer the opportunity to sell common stock at a price higher than the price at which it could be sold currently, if the common stock greatly increases in price, the issuing firm would

---

[11]In this discussion, we ignore the tax advantages to investors of the deferral of taxes on capital gains. This factor could explain why k_c is less than k_d.

probably find that it would have been better off if it had used straight debt in spite of its higher cost and then later sold common stock and refunded the debt. (2) Convertibles typically have a low coupon interest rate, and the advantage of this low-cost debt will be lost when conversion occurs. (3) If the company truly wants to raise equity capital, and if the price of the stock does not rise sufficiently after the bond is issued, then the company will be stuck with debt. This debt will, however, have a low interest rate.

To illustrate the third disadvantage, consider what happened after the October 1987 stock market crash. Prior to the crash, many firms, especially small technology companies, had issued convertibles because the rising stock market had made convertibles attractive to investors and therefore an inexpensive form of financing. For example, Seagate Technology, which manufactures hard disk drives for personal computers such as the IBM PC, issued $288 million of convertible bonds with a coupon rate of 6.75 percent and a conversion price of $42.50. The stock price at the time of the issue was $30, and straight debt would have cost the company about 11 percent. By mid-November of 1987, the firm's stock price had fallen to only $11.875 per share, and in the spring of 1990, the stock was trading at about $18. As a result, the convertible holders are stuck with low-yielding bonds, while Seagate is saddled with too much long-term debt on its balance sheet, and it cannot issue new common stock without lowering the conversion price and thus giving a tremendous break to the convertible bondholders. At the time of issue, both the company and its investors were anticipating a relatively quick conversion. One investment banker has said that some convertible issuers do so "without a serious consideration of the downside" and that "convertible issuers with depressed stock prices are stuck with a form of debt in sheep's clothing."

Self-Test Questions

What is the difference between a convertible bond and a bond with warrants?

What is the conversion ratio? The conversion price? The straight bond value?

What is meant by a convertible's floor value?

What are the advantages and disadvantages of convertibles to issuers? To investors?

REPORTING EARNINGS WHEN WARRANTS OR CONVERTIBLES ARE OUTSTANDING

If warrants or convertibles are outstanding, a firm could theoretically report earnings per share in one of three ways:

1. *Simple EPS,* where earnings available to common stockholders are divided by the average number of shares actually outstanding during the period.

2. *Primary EPS,* where earnings available are divided by the average number of shares that would have been outstanding if warrants and convertibles "likely to be converted in the near future" had actually been exercised or converted. Earnings

are pro formed by "backing out" the interest on the convertibles. Accountants have a formula which basically compares the conversion or exercise price with the actual market value of the stock to determine the likelihood of conversion when deciding on the need to use this adjustment procedure.

3.   *Fully diluted EPS,* which is similar to primary EPS except that *all* warrants and convertibles are assumed to be exercised or converted, regardless of the likelihood of exercise or conversion.

Simple EPS is virtually never reported by firms which have warrants or convertibles likely to be exercised or converted, but the SEC requires that primary and fully diluted earnings be shown. For firms with large amounts of option securities outstanding, there can be a substantial difference between the primary and fully diluted EPS figures. The purpose of the provision is, of course, to give investors a more accurate picture of the firm's true profit position.

Self-Test Questions

What are the three possible methods for reporting EPS when warrants and convertibles are outstanding?

Which methods are most used in practice?

Why should investors be concerned about a firm's outstanding warrants and convertibles?

FUTURES

Recent years have been characterized by record capital markets volatility. To illustrate, in June 1982, AA bonds were yielding 15.3 percent, while the same bonds yielded 8.9 percent in May 1986, 10.2 percent in April 1989, and 9.7 percent in February 1990. Further, it is not unusual for long-term rates to move by over 100 basis points within a 2- or 3-month period; indeed, a 100 basis point increase occurred during the first quarter of 1990. At the same time, the level of stock prices has bounced around like a rubber ball. All this instability in the capital markets has made corporate financing much more difficult than it was in the 1950s, 1960s, and 1970s.

Although the evidence strongly indicates that managers can forecast their own firms' internal conditions better than outside investors, no one has been able to make consistent forecasts of either interest rates or the general level of stock prices. If one believes that it is impossible to forecast future capital costs, then the major concern should be to minimize the adverse effects of deviations in capital costs from today's "spot" costs. The use of futures contracts can help in this regard.[12]

---

[12]Our discussion of futures is necessarily limited in scope. For a more detailed description of futures and their use in financial management, see Daniel R. Siegel and Diane F. Siegel, *Futures Markets* (Hinsdale, Ill.: Dryden Press, 1990).

Futures Markets and Contracts

Most financial and real asset transactions occur in what is known as the *spot,* or *cash, market,* where the asset is delivered immediately (or within a few days). *Futures,* or *futures contracts,* on the other hand, call for the purchase or sale of a financial or real asset at some future date, but at a price which is fixed today.

In 1990, futures contracts were available on more than 30 real and financial assets traded on 14 U.S. exchanges, the largest of which are the Chicago Board of Trade (CBT) and the Chicago Mercantile Exchange (CME). Futures contracts are divided into two classes, *commodity futures* and *financial futures.* Commodity futures, which cover various grains, oilseeds, livestock, meats, fibers, metals, and wood, were first traded in the United States in the middle of the 1800s. Financial futures, which were first traded in 1975, include Treasury bills, Treasury notes and bonds, certificates of deposit, Eurodollar deposits, foreign currencies, and stock indexes.

To illustrate how futures contracts work, consider the CBT's contract on Treasury bonds. The basic contract is for $100,000 of a hypothetical 8 percent coupon, semiannual payment, Treasury bond with 20 years to maturity. Table 18-3 shows an extract from the Treasury bond futures prices which appeared in the May 7 issue of *The Wall Street Journal.*

The first column gives the delivery month; the next three columns give the opening, high, and low prices on that contract for that day. The opening price for the June future, 100-20, means 100 plus 20/32, or 100.625 percent of par. Column 5 gives the settlement price, which is typically the price at the close of trading. Column 6 reports the change in the settlement price from the preceding day—the June contract dropped by 13/32. Column 7 gives the yield on the 8 percent bonds at the settlement price, while Column 8 reports the change in the settlement yield from the previous trading day. Finally, Column 9 shows the "open interest," which is the number of contracts outstanding.

To illustrate, we focus on the Treasury bonds for December delivery. The settlement price on May 6 was 98-30, or 98 plus 30/32 percent of the $100,000 contract value. Thus, the futures price closed at 98.9375 percent, or at 0.989375($100,000) = $98,937.50. The contract price declined by 10/32 of one percent of $100,000, or by $312.50, from the previous day. The settlement yield on the contract was 8.108 percent, and the yield increased by 0.032 percentage points from the previous day. Finally, there were 5,207 contracts outstanding on the December futures, represent-

Table 18-3   May 6 Futures Prices

Treasury Bonds (CBT) — $100,000; pts. 32nds of 100%

(1)	Open (2)	High (3)	Low (4)	Settle (5)	Change (6)	Yield Settle (7)	Yield Change (8)	Open Interest (9)
June	100-20	101-11	100-07	100-16	−13	7.950	+.041	188,460
Sept	99-25	100-18	99-16	99-24	−11	8.025	+.034	42,622
Dec	99-00	99-24	98-24	98-30	−10	8.108	+.032	5,207

ing a total value of about $520 million. Thus, on May 6, futures contracts for December delivery (7-month futures) of this hypothetical bond sold for $98,937.50 for 100 bonds with a par value of $100,000, which translates to a yield to maturity of about 8.1 percent.[13] This yield reflects investors' beliefs in May about the interest rate level which will prevail in December. The spot yield on T-bonds on May 6 was about 7.9 percent, so the marginal trader in the futures market was predicting a 20 basis point increase in yields over the next 7 months.

Suppose now that three months later, on August 6, interest rates in the futures market had fallen from the May levels, say from 8.1 to 7.5 percent. Falling interest rates mean rising bond prices, so the December contract would now be worth about $105,138. Thus, the contract's value would have increased by $105,138 − $98,938 = $6,200.

When futures contracts are purchased, the purchaser does not have to put up the full amount of the purchase price; rather, the purchaser is required to post an initial *margin,* which for CBT Treasury bond contracts is $3,000 per $100,000 contract. However, investors are required to maintain a certain value in the margin account, called a *maintenance margin.* If the value of the contract declines, then the owner may be required to add additional funds to the margin account, and the more the contract value falls, the more money must be added. The value of the contract is checked at the end of every working day, and margin account adjustments are made at that time. If an investor purchased a contract in May, and then sold it in August, he or she would have made a profit of $6,200 on a $3,000 investment, or a return of over 200 percent in only three months. It is clear, therefore, that futures contracts offer a considerable amount of leverage. Of course, if interest rates had risen, then the value of the contract would have declined, and the investor could easily have lost his or her $3,000, or more.

Commodity futures contracts are sometimes settled by the actual delivery of the commodity—for example, a wheat farmer might sell in April a futures contract for 5,000 bushels of wheat for October delivery, and then deliver 5,000 bushels of wheat to satisfy the contract. The purchaser of the contract might be General Mills. The price would have been established in April, so the farmer would know how much he would get for his wheat, and General Mills would know its cost for flour. Financial futures, on the other hand, are virtually never settled by delivery of the securities involved. Rather, the transaction is completed by reversing the trade, which amounts to selling the contract back to the original seller.[14] The actual gains and losses on the contract are realized when the futures contract is closed.

---

[13]The yield is calculated by solving for k_d in the following equation:

$$\$989.375 = \sum_{t=1}^{40} \frac{\$40}{(1 + k_d/2)^t} + \frac{\$1,000}{(1 + k_d/2)^{40}}.$$

Recall that the hypothetical bond is assumed to be a semiannual payment, 8 percent coupon bond with a 20-year maturity.

[14]The buyers and sellers of financial futures contracts do not actually trade with one another, even though a contract cannot be bought without a seller, and vice versa. Each trader's contractual obligation is with the futures exchange. This feature helps to guarantee the fiscal integrity of the trade. Incidentally, commodities futures traded on the exchanges are settled in the same way as financial futures, but in the case of commodities much of the contracting is done off the exchange, between farmers and processors, and there actual deliveries occur.

Futures versus Options

Futures contracts and options are similar to one another—so similar that people often confuse the two. Therefore, it is useful to compare the two instruments.

A *futures contract* is a definite agreement on the part of one party to buy something on a specific date and at a specific price, and the other party agrees to sell on the same terms. No matter how low or how high the price goes, the two parties must settle the contract at the agreed-upon price. An *option,* on the other hand, merely gives someone the right to buy (a call option) or sell (a put option), but the holder of the option does not have to complete the transaction.

Note also that options exist for individual stocks and for "bundles" of stocks such as those in the S&P or Value Line index, whereas futures are used for commodities, debt securities, and stock indexes. The two types of instruments can be used for the same purposes. One is not necessarily better or worse than another—they are simply different.

Hedging

Futures markets are used for both speculation and hedging. Speculation involves betting on future price movements, and futures are used because the inherent leverage in the contract enhances expected returns. Hedging, on the other hand, is done by a firm or individual engaged in a business where a price change could negatively affect profits. For example, rising interest rates and commodity (raw material) prices can hurt profits, as can adverse currency fluctuations. Of course, one party to a futures contract could be a speculator, the other a hedger. Thus, to the extent that they broaden the market and make hedging possible, speculators decrease risks in the economy.

There are two basic types of hedges: (1) *long hedges,* in which futures contracts are bought in anticipation of (or to guard against) price increases, and (2) *short hedges,* where a firm or individual sells futures contracts to guard against price declines. Recall that rising interest rates lower bond prices and thus the value of bond futures contracts. Therefore, if a firm or individual needs to guard against an *increase* in interest rates, a futures contract that makes money if rates rise should be used. That means selling, or going short, on the futures contract. To illustrate, assume that Carson Foods plans to issue $10,000,000 of 20-year bonds in September to support a capital expenditure program. The interest rate would be 10 percent if the bonds were issued today, May 6, and at that rate, the project being financed has a positive NPV. However, Carson's financial manager fears that interest rates may rise over the next four months, and that, when the issue is actually sold, it may have a cost substantially above 10 percent, which would make the project a bad investment. Carson can protect itself against such a rise in rates by hedging in the futures market.

In this situation, Carson would be hurt by an increase in interest rates, hence Carson would use a short hedge. It would choose a futures contract on the security most similar to the one Carson plans to issue, long-term bonds. In this case, Carson would probably choose to hedge with Treasury bond futures. Since it plans to issue $10,000,000 of bonds, Carson would sell $10,000,000/$100,000 = 100 Treasury bond contracts for delivery in September. In doing so, Carson would have to put up 100($3,000) = $300,000 in margin money, and also pay brokerage commissions. We can see from Table 18-3 that each September contract has a value of 99 plus 24/32 percent, so the total value of the 100 contracts is 0.9975($100,000)(100) = $9,975,000. Now suppose the interest rate on Carson's debt rises by 100 basis points, to 11 percent, over the next four months. Carson's own 10 percent coupon bonds would bring only about $920 per bond, because investors now require an 11 percent return. Thus, Carson would lose $80 per bond times 10,000 bonds, or $800,000, as a result of delaying the financing. However, the increase in interest rates would also bring about a change in the value of Carson's short position in the futures market. Since interest rates have increased, the futures contract value would fall, and if the interest rate on the futures contract also increased by a full percentage point, from 8.025 to 9.025 percent, the contract value would fall to $9,059,000. Carson would then close its position in the futures market by repurchasing for $9,059,000 the contracts which it sold short for $9,975,000, giving it a profit of $916,000, less commissions.

Thus, Carson has, if we ignore commissions and the opportunity cost of the margin money, offset the loss on the bond issue. In fact, Carson more than offset the loss, pocketing an additional $116,000 in our example. Of course, if in our example interest rates had fallen, Carson would have lost on its futures position. However, this loss would have been offset by the fact that Carson could now sell its bonds at a lower yield. If futures contracts existed on Carson's own debt, then the firm could construct a *perfect hedge,* in which gains on the futures contract would exactly offset losses due to rising interest rates. In reality, it is virtually impossible to construct perfect hedges, because in most cases the underlying asset is not identical to the futures asset.

Similarly, if Carson had been planning an equity offering, and if its stock tended to move fairly closely with one of the stock indexes on which futures are written, the company could have hedged against falling stock prices by selling short the index future. Alternatively, if options on Carson Foods were traded in the option market, then options, rather than futures, could be used to hedge against falling stock prices.

The futures and option markets permit flexibility in the timing of financial transactions, because the firm can be protected, at least partially, against changes that occur between the present and the time when a particular transaction will be completed. There is, however, a cost for this protection, and it is the commissions plus the opportunity cost of the margin money. Whether or not the protection is worth the cost is a matter of judgment, and it depends on management's risk aversion as well as the company's strength and ability to assume the risk of changing interest rates and stock prices. In theory, the reduction in risk resulting from a hedge transaction has a value exactly equal to the cost of the hedge. Thus, a firm should be indifferent to hedging. However, many firms believe that hedging is worthwhile. Trammell Crow, a large Texas real estate developer, recently used T-bill futures to lock in interest costs on floating rate construction loans, while Dart & Kraft used Eurodollar futures to protect its marketable securities portfolio. Merrill Lynch, Salomon Brothers, and the other investment banking houses hedge in the futures and option markets to protect themselves when they are engaged in major underwritings. Similarly, institutional investors engage in hedging activities to protect their bond portfolios against interest rate increases, their stock portfolios against market declines, and their foreign holdings against adverse exchange rate movements. We will discuss the use of the futures market again when we examine inventory management.

It is interesting to note that Eurodollars recently surpassed Treasury bonds as the most traded futures contract. Currently, about 60,000 Eurodollar futures contracts, with a face value of $60 billion, are traded daily on the Chicago Mercantile Exchange. The Eurodollar futures market can provide protection against volatility in short-term interest rates, since the value of a Eurodollar deposit is tied to the London Interbank Offered Rate (LIBOR), the rate to which most floating rate corporate loans are tied. Rapid growth in the Eurodollar futures market will continue, because Eurodollars now make up the largest pool of short-term funds in the world, totaling more than $2 trillion, and this pool is growing due to the U.S. trade deficit and the increasing globalization of business. The Eurodollar futures contract was originally devised to serve the hedging needs of institutional investors (banks and securities firms) which make a market in interest rate swaps, but now the market is used also by nonfinancial companies to reduce interest rate risk.

Self-Test Questions

What is a futures contract?

What is the difference between futures and options?

Explain how a company can use the futures market to hedge against rising interest rates.

SECURITIES INNOVATION

In recent years an avalanche of new types of securities has hit the markets, and the trend shows no sign of letting up. Each new offering is heralded by the investment bank that developed it as a boon to both issuers and investors. Yet there are critics who contend that the development of new securities has contributed little, if any, economic gain to anyone except the investment banks that sell them.

Two primary factors have fueled the rush to innovation. First, the investment banking business has become increasingly competitive, and the development of a new security usually means increased business and profits, both for the firm and for the individuals who developed it. Second, the last decade has been an era of unprecedented volatility: Interest rates, tax laws, and regulation are now changing much more rapidly than in the past, and new financial products are needed to cope with the changing economic environment. For example, adjustable rate preferred stock was specifically developed to eliminate investors' exposure to losses in principal as interest rates change, and at the same time to provide a tax shelter to corporate investors in high tax brackets.

The development of new securities has presented an almost overwhelming number of financial alternatives to financial managers, and it is necessary for managers to evaluate the merits of each alternative before making a decision. It is not enough that a security be different—it must also enable issuers or investors to do something that they could not previously do, or permit them to do the same things in a more cost-effective way.[15] Value is created in new securities in a number of ways. For example, value can be created if the new security reallocates risk from one class of investors to another class that is less risk sensitive and thus requires a smaller risk premium. Interest rate swaps are an example of this type of value creation. Value can also be created if a new security reduces the transactions costs paid to third parties, or increases the liquidity to investors. The development of the junk bond market illustrates these points. Taxes also present an opportunity for value creation. If taxes can be reduced to investors without increasing the corporate tax liability, or vice versa, then value can be created (or at least transferred). Leasing provides a good example of this point.

Not all innovations are successful. Shearson Lehman Hutton recently unveiled a new product called *unbundled stock units,* which it proposed to create and sell initially for four companies: American Express, Dow Chemical, Pfizer, and Sara Lee. Common stock has traditionally offered investors three sources of value: (1) the current dollar dividend, (2) potential increases in the dollar dividend, and (3) potential capital appreciation in stock price. In the unbundled stock unit concept, a portion of the firm's common stock, say 20 percent, would be broken into those three parts which would trade separately on the NYSE. To illustrate, consider the offering planned for Pfizer. At the time, Pfizer's stock was trading at about $56 a share and paying $2 in annual dividends. A stockholder who tendered his or her shares would receive the following for each share tendered:

1. A 30-year bond that pays $2 annually in interest and has a maturity value of $150.

2. A share of preferred stock that initially pays no dividend, but which pays a dividend that matches any common stock dividend increases above the $2 current dividend for the next 30 years. For example, if Pfizer paid $3 in common dividends in 1995, the preferred would receive a $3 − $2 = $1 dividend. The preferred stock would be redeemed after 30 years for $250.

3. An equity appreciation certificate that entitles the holder to any rise in stock price above $150 after 30 years. Thus, if Pfizer's stock rose to $200 in 30 years, the appreciation certificate would be worth $200 − $150 = $50.

From an investor's standpoint, the new securities created the same cash flow as the common stock, but without voting rights. However, the new securities in the aggregate would have less risk because, while the common dividend could be cut or omitted, the interest payment on the bond portion of the package could not be lowered. Further, once trading began, an investor need not hold all three securities —he or she could hold only the securities that provided the desired risk/return combination.

---

[15]For a more complete discussion of securities innovation, see John D. Finnerty, "Securities Innovation: Where Is the Value Added?" *Financial Management Collection,* Winter 1988, 1–7.

The initial investor reaction to unbundled stock units was mixed. "This sounds like an interesting way to get the stock price up, and if it works, then it's a good thing to do," said one analyst. However, other analysts were not as supportive. One trader said she would be reluctant to swap her common shares for the new securities. "What happens if you change your opinion on Pfizer?" she asked. "I couldn't be sure that the liquidity would be there." Shearson pushed hard to sell the new product, but a lukewarm response by institutional investors and an adverse ruling by the SEC regarding accounting for the new securities tolled the death knell for the product, and three months later Shearson announced that the idea was dead.

Undoubtedly, many opportunities remain for innovation, and new ones will arise as the economy continues to change. Such innovation will offer opportunities for financial managers to lower their companies' costs of capital, hence to increase their shareholders' wealth. However, the increase in the number of financing possibilities, and the increasing complexity of the new securities, will make it more important than ever that corporate decision makers keep up with developments in the financial world, and learn how to use (or when to avoid using) the new products.

Self-Test Questions

What is meant by securities innovation?

What are some factors that can create value in new types of securities?

SUMMARY

In this chapter, we first discussed options, then warrants and convertibles, and finally futures and how futures can be used to hedge against undesirable market movements. The key concepts covered are listed next.

- *Pure options* are financial instruments that (1) are created by exchanges rather than firms, (2) are bought and sold primarily by investors, and (3) are of greater importance to investors than to financial managers. However, an understanding of options will help financial managers understand warrants and convertibles, which are option-type securities issued by firms.

- The two primary types of options are (1) *call options,* which give the holder the right to purchase a common stock at a given price (the *exercise* or *striking price*) for a given period of time, and (2) *put options,* which give the holder the right to sell a stock at a given price for a given period of time.

- The *Black-Scholes Option Pricing Model (OPM)* can be used to estimate the value of a call option.

- A *warrant* is a long-term call option issued along with a bond. Warrants are generally detachable from the bond, and they trade separately in the markets. When warrants are exercised, the firm receives additional equity capital, and the original bonds remain outstanding.

- A *convertible* security is a bond or preferred stock which can be exchanged for common stock at the option of the holder. When a security is converted, debt or preferred stock is replaced with common stock, and no money changes hands.

- Warrants and convertibles are *"sweeteners"* which are used to make the underlying debt or preferred stock issue more attractive to investors. Although the coupon rate on the debt or dividend yield on the preferred stock is lower when options are part of the issue, the overall cost of the issue is higher than the cost of straight debt or preferred, because the addition of warrants or convertibility makes the issue riskier.

- *Financial futures* permit firms to create hedge positions to protect themselves against the damage done by fluctuating interest rates, stock prices, and exchange rates.

- In recent years, a large number of new securities have been introduced. Such *securities innovation* provides opportunities for financial managers to lower their firms' costs of capital.

In the next chapter, we turn our attention to short-term financial planning and then discuss in detail cash and marketable securities, inventories, and receivables.

Questions

18-1 Define each of the following terms:
   a.   Option; call option; put option
   b.   Striking price; exercise price; variance
   c.   Warrant; detachable warrant
   d.   Expiration value
   e.   Stepped-up price
   f.   Convertible security
   g.   Conversion ratio; conversion price; conversion value
   h.   "Sweetener"
   i.   Simple EPS; primary EPS; fully diluted EPS
   j.   Futures; hedging
   k.   Securities innovation

18-2 Why do options typically sell at prices higher than their expiration values?

18-3 What effect does the trend in stock prices (subsequent to issue) have on a firm's ability to raise funds through (a) convertibles and (b) warrants?

18-4 If a firm expects to have additional financial requirements in the future, would you recommend that it use convertibles or bonds with warrants? What factors would influence your decision?

18-5 How does a firm's dividend policy affect each of the following?
   a.   The value of its long-term warrants.
   b.   The likelihood that its convertible bonds will be converted.
   c.   The likelihood that its warrants will be exercised.

18-6 Evaluate the following statement: "Issuing convertible securities represents a means by which a firm can sell common stock at a price above the existing market."

18-7 Why do corporations often sell convertibles on a rights basis?

18-8 Suppose a company simultaneously issues $50 million of convertible bonds with a coupon rate of 10 percent and $50 million of straight bonds with a coupon rate of 14 percent. Both bonds have the same maturity. Does the fact that the convertible issue has the lower coupon rate suggest that it is less risky than the straight bond? Is the cost of capital lower on the convertible than on the straight bond? Explain.

Problems

18-1 **(Black-Scholes OPM)** Cotner Software Corporation (CSC) options are actively traded on one of the regional exchanges. CSC's current stock price is $10, with a 0.16 instantaneous variance of returns. The current 6-month risk-free rate is 12 percent.
   a. What is the value of CSC's 6-month option with an exercise price of $10 according to the Black-Scholes model?
   b. What would be the effect on the option price if CSC redeployed its assets and thereby reduced its variance of returns to 0.09?
   (Do Parts c and d only if you are using the computerized diskette.)
   c. Assume that CSC returns to its initial asset structure; that is, its stock return variance is 0.16. Now assume that CSC's current stock price is $15. What effect does the stock price increase have on the option value?
   d. Return to base case (Part a) values. Now assume that the striking price is $15. What is the new option value?

18-2 **(Warrants)** Maese Industries, Inc., has warrants outstanding that permit the holders to purchase one share of stock per warrant at a price of $25.
   a. Calculate the expiration value of the firm's warrants if the common sells at each of the following prices: (1) $20, (2) $25, (3) $30, (4) $100.
   b. At what approximate price do you think the warrants would actually sell under each condition indicated above? What premium is implied in your price? Your answer is a guess, but your prices and premiums should bear reasonable relationships to one another.
   c. How would each of the following factors affect your estimates of the warrants' prices and premiums in Part b?
      (1) The life of the warrant.
      (2) Expected variability (σ_p) in the stock's price.
      (3) The expected growth rate in the stock's EPS.
      (4) The company announces a change in dividend policy: Whereas it formerly paid no dividends, henceforth it will pay out *all* earnings as dividends.
   d. Assume the firm's stock now sells for $20 per share. The company wants to sell some 20-year, annual interest, $1,000 par value bonds. Each bond will have attached 50 warrants, each exercisable into one share of stock at an exercise price of $25. The firm's straight bonds yield 12 percent. Regardless of your answer to Part b, assume that each warrant will have a market value of $3 when the stock sells at $20. What coupon interest rate, and dollar coupon, must the company set on the bonds with warrants if they are to clear the market?

18-3 **(Convertible premiums)** The Tsetsekos Company was planning to finance an expansion in the summer of 1990. The principal executives of the company all agreed that an industrial company such as theirs should finance growth by means of common stock rather than by debt. However, they felt that the price of the company's common stock did not reflect its true worth, so they decided to sell a convertible security. They considered a convertible debenture but feared the burden of fixed interest charges if the common stock did not rise in price to make conversion attractive. They decided on an issue of convertible preferred stock, which would pay a dividend of $2.10 per share.

The common stock was selling for $42 a share at the time. Management projected earnings for 1990 at $3 a share and expected a future growth rate of 10 percent a year in 1991 and beyond. It was agreed by the investment bankers and the management that the common stock would sell at 14 times earnings, the current price/earnings ratio.

a.   What conversion price should be set by the issuer? The conversion ratio will be 1.0; that is, each share of convertible preferred can be converted into one share of common. Therefore, the convertible's par value (and also the issue price) will be equal to the conversion price, which in turn will be determined as a percentage over the current market price of the common. Your answer will be a guess, but make it a reasonable one.

b.   Should the preferred stock include a call provision? Why?

18-4   **(Convertible bond analysis)**   In June 1976, U.S. Steel (now USX Corporation) sold $400 million of convertible bonds, the largest issue on record. The bonds had a 25-year maturity, a 5¾ percent coupon rate, and were sold at their $1,000 par value. The conversion price was set at $62.75 against a current price of $55 per share of common. The bonds were subordinated debentures, and they were given an A rating; straight nonconvertible debentures of the same quality yielded about 8¾ percent at the time.

a.   Calculate the premium on the bonds, that is, the percentage excess of the conversion price over the current stock price.

b.   What is U.S. Steel's annual interest savings on the convertible issue versus a straight debt issue?

c.   Look up U.S. Steel's (USX's) current stock price in the paper. On the basis of this price, do you think it likely that the bonds would have been converted? (Calculate the value of the stock one would receive by converting a bond.)

d.   The bonds originally sold for $1,000. If interest rates on A-rated bonds had remained constant at 8¾ percent, what do you think would have happened to the price of the convertible bonds?

e.   Now suppose the price of U.S. Steel's common stock had fallen from $55 on the day the bonds were issued to $32.75 at present. (At the time this problem was written, that is exactly what had happened.) Suppose also that the rate of interest had fallen from 8¾ to 5¾ percent. (This had not happened when the problem was being written — the interest rate on A-rated bonds was about 10 percent.) Under these conditions, what do you think would have happened to the price of the bonds?

f.   Set up a graphic model to illustrate how investors valued the U.S. Steel convertibles in 1976. How well were these expectations realized?

18-5   **(Warrant/convertible decisions)**   The Howland Carpet Company has grown rapidly during the past 5 years. Recently its commercial bank urged the company to consider increasing its permanent financing. Its bank loan under a line of credit has risen to $250,000, carrying an 8 percent interest rate. Howland has been 30 to 60 days late in paying trade creditors.

Discussions with an investment banker have resulted in the decision to raise $500,000 at this time. Investment bankers have assured the firm that the following alternatives are feasible (flotation costs will be ignored):

- *Alternative 1:* Sell common stock at $8.

- *Alternative 2:* Sell convertible bonds at an 8 percent coupon, convertible into 100 shares of common stock for each $1,000 bond (that is, the conversion price is $10 per share).

- *Alternative 3:* Sell debentures at an 8 percent coupon, each $1,000 bond carrying 100 warrants to buy common stock at $10.

John L. Howland, the president, owns 80 percent of the common stock and wishes to maintain control of the company. One hundred thousand shares are outstanding. The following are extracts of Howland's latest financial statements:

Balance Sheet

		Current liabilities	$400,000
		Common stock, par $1	100,000
		Retained earnings	50,000
Total assets	$550,000	Total claims	$550,000

Income Statement

Sales	$1,100,000
All costs except interest	990,000
EBIT	$ 110,000
Interest	20,000
EBT	$ 90,000
Taxes (40%)	36,000
Net income	$ 54,000
Shares outstanding	100,000
Earnings per share	$0.54
Price/earnings ratio	15.83 ×
Market price of stock	$8.55

a. Show the new balance sheet under each alternative. For Alternatives 2 and 3, show the balance sheet after conversion of the bonds or exercise of the warrants. Assume that half of the funds raised will be used to pay off the bank loan and half to increase total assets.
b. Show Mr. Howland's control position under each alternative, assuming that he does not purchase additional shares.
c. What is the effect on earnings per share of each alternative, if it is assumed that profits before interest and taxes will be 20 percent of total assets?
d. What will be the debt ratio under each alternative?
e. Which of the three alternatives would you recommend to Howland, and why?

18-6 **(Convertible bond model)** Niendorf Incorporated needs to raise $25 million to construct production facilities for a new model diskette drive. The firm's straight non-convertible debentures currently yield 14 percent. Its stock sells for $30 per share; the last dividend was $2; and the expected growth rate is a constant 9 percent. Investment bankers have tentatively proposed that the firm raise the $25 million by issuing convertible debentures. These convertibles would have a $1,000 par value, carry a coupon rate of 10 percent, have a 20-year maturity, and be convertible into 20 shares of stock. The bonds would be noncallable for 5 years, after which they would be callable at a price of $1,075; this call price would decline by $5 per year in Year 6 and each year thereafter. Management has called convertibles in the past (and presumably it will call them again in the future), once they were eligible for call, when the bonds' conversion value was about 20 percent above the bonds' par value (not their call price).
a. Draw an accurate graph similar to Figure 18-2 representing the expectations set forth above. (Assume an annual coupon.)
b. What is the expected rate of return on the proposed convertible issue?

c. Do you think that these bonds could be successfully offered to the public at par? That is, does $1,000 seem to be an equilibrium price in view of the stated terms? If not, suggest the type of change that would have to be made to cause the bonds to trade at $1,000 in the secondary market, assuming no change in capital market conditions.

d. Suppose the projects outlined here work out on schedule for 2 years, but then the firm begins to experience extremely strong competition from Japanese firms. As a result, Niendorf's expected growth rate drops from 9 percent to zero. Assume that the dividend at the time of the drop is $2.38. The company's credit strength is not impaired, and its value of k_s is also unchanged. What would happen (1) to stock price and (2) to the convertible bond's price? Be as precise as you can.

18-7 **(Futures)** Refer back to Table 18-3. It is now May 6. The Barry Greene Company plans to negotiate a 5-year, $100,000 semiannual interest loan in December. However, its managers are concerned about rising interest rates, and plan to use the futures market to hedge against this possibility. Discussions with their lenders indicate that the loan rate would be 10 percent if the loan were negotiated today.

a. Suppose the company planned to use T-bond futures for the hedge. Would the firm buy or sell futures contracts? How many contracts would be involved?

b. Assume that interest rates on all securities increased by 2 percentage points from May to December. What impact would the rate rise have on the value of the firm's loan? On its futures position? Overall?

c. Did the firm create a perfect hedge? Explain.

d. Now assume that interest rates dropped by 2 percentage points. What impact does the hedge now have on the pending financing transaction? Does this imply that firms should not hedge future financings?

Mini Case

Paul Duncan, financial manager of EduSoft, Inc., is facing a dilemma. The firm was founded 5 years ago to provide educational software for the rapidly expanding primary and secondary school markets. Although EduSoft has done well, the firm's founder believes that an industry shakeout is imminent. To survive, EduSoft must grab market share now, and this will require a large infusion of new capital.

Because he expects earnings to continue rising sharply and looks for the stock price to follow suit, Mr. Duncan does not think it would be wise to issue new common stock at this time. On the other hand, interest rates are currently high by historical standards, and with the firm's B rating, the interest payments on a new debt issue would be prohibitive. Thus, he has narrowed his choice of financing alternatives to two securities: (1) bonds with warrants or (2) convertible bonds. As Duncan's assistant, you have been asked to help in the decision process by answering the following questions:

a. What is a call option? How can a knowledge of call options help a financial manager to better understand warrants and convertibles?

b. Consolidated Energy Industries (CEI) has options listed on the CBOE. The following table gives the option prices for its 6-month, $20 strike price call option at 3 different stock prices:

Stock Price	Option Price
$20	$ 5
30	13
40	21

    (1) What are the option's expiration values, and the premiums, at each stock price? Why do call options sell for more than their expiration values?

    (2) Assume that CEI's stock price increased from $20 to $30. What rate of return would this provide to a stock investor? To an option investor? What is the loss potential on the stock and on the option if the stock price remains at $20?

    (3) Now assume that CEI's stock price increased from $30 to $40. What rate of return would a stock investor receive? An option investor? What is the loss potential on the stock? On the option? Why does the premium over the expiration value decline as the stock price increases?

c.   One of the firm's alternatives is to issue a bond with warrants attached. EduSoft's current stock price is $20, and its investment banker estimates that the cost of a 20-year, annual coupon bond without warrants would be 12 percent. The bankers suggest attaching 50 warrants, each with an exercise price of $25, to each $1,000 bond. It is estimated that each warrant, when detached and traded separately, would have a value of $3.

    (1) What coupon rate should be set on the bond with warrants if the total package is to sell for $1,000?

    (2) Suppose the bonds were issued and the warrants immediately traded on the open market for $5 each. What would this imply about the terms of the issue? Did the company "win" or "lose"?

    (3) When would you expect the warrants to be exercised? Assume they have a 10-year life, that is, they expire 10 years after issue.

    (4) Will the warrants bring in additional capital when exercised? If so, how much, and what type of capital?

    (5) Since warrants lower the cost of the accompanying debt issue, shouldn't all debt be issued with warrants? What is the expected return to the holders of the bond with warrants (or the expected cost to the company) if the warrants are expected to be exercised in 5 years, when EduSoft's stock price is expected to be $36.75? How would you expect the cost of the bond with warrants to compare with the cost of straight debt? With the cost of common stock?

d.   As an alternative to the bond with warrants, Mr. Duncan is considering convertible bonds. The firm's investment bankers estimate that EduSoft could sell a 20-year, 10.5 percent annual coupon, callable convertible bond for its $1,000 par value, whereas a straight debt issue would require a 12 percent coupon. The convertibles would be call protected for 5 years, the call price would be $1,100, and the company would probably call the bonds as soon as possible after their conversion value exceeds $1,200. Note, though, that the call must occur on an issue date anniversary. EduSoft's current stock price is $20, its last dividend was $1.48, and the dividend is expected to grow at a constant 8 percent rate. The convertible could be converted into 40 shares of EduSoft stock at the owner's option.

    (1) What conversion price is built into the bond?

    (2) What is the convertible's straight debt value? What is the implied value of the convertibility feature?

    (3) What is the formula for the bond's expected conversion value in any year? What is its conversion value at Year 0? At Year 10?

    (4) What is meant by the "floor value" of a convertible? What is the convertible's expected floor value at Year 0? At Year 10?

    (5) Assume that EduSoft intends to force conversion by calling the bond as soon as possible after its conversion value exceeds 20 percent above its par value, or 1.2($1,000) = $1,200. When is the issue expected to be called? (*Hint:* Recall that the call must be made on an anniversary date of the issue.)

    (6) What is the expected cost of capital for the convertible to EduSoft? Does this cost appear to be consistent with the riskiness of the issue?

e. EduSoft's market value capital structure is as follows (in millions of dollars):

Debt	$ 50
Equity	50
	$100

If the company raises $20 million in additional capital by selling (1) convertibles or (2) bonds with warrants, what would its WACC be, and how would those figures compare to its current WACC? EduSoft's tax rate is 40 percent.

f. Mr. Duncan believes that the costs of both the bond with warrants and the convertible bond are close enough to one another to call them even, and also consistent with the risks involved. Thus, he will make his decision based on other factors. What are some of the factors which he should consider?

g. (Unrelated question) Explain briefly why the equity of a levered firm can be thought of as a call option. What does option pricing theory indicate will happen to shareholders' wealth if the firm increases the riskiness of its asset mix? What happens to bondholders' wealth?

h. (Unrelated question) What is the futures market? Explain how futures contracts can be used to hedge against rising interest rates.

Selected Additional References and Cases

The investment texts listed in Chapter 5 provide extended discussions of options, warrants, convertibles, and futures.

The original Black-Scholes article tested the OPM to see how well predicted prices conformed to market values. For additional empirical tests, see

Galai, Dan, "Tests of Market Efficiency of the Chicago Board Options Exchange," *Journal of Business,* April 1977, 167–197.

Gultekin, N. Bulent, Richard J. Rogalski, and Seha M. Tinic, "Option Pricing Model Estimates: Some Empirical Results," *Financial Management,* Spring 1982, 58–69.

MacBeth, James D., and Larry J. Merville, "An Empirical Examination of the Black-Scholes Call Option Pricing Model," *Journal of Finance,* December 1979, 1173–1186.

Quite a bit of work has also been done on warrant pricing. Two of the more prominent articles are

Galai, Dan, and Mier I. Schneller, "The Pricing of Warrants and the Value of the Firm," *Journal of Finance,* December 1978, 1333–1342.

Schwartz, Eduardo S., "The Valuation of Warrants: Implementing a New Approach," *Journal of Financial Economics,* January 1977, 79–93.

For more insights into convertible pricing and use, see

Alexander, Gordon J., and Roger D. Stover, "Pricing in the New Issue Convertible Debt Market," *Financial Management,* Fall 1977, 35–39.

Alexander, Gordon J., Roger D. Stover, and D. B. Kuhnau, "Market Timing Strategies in Convertible Debt Financing," *Journal of Finance,* March 1979, 143–155.

Brennan, Michael, "The Case for Convertibles," *Issues in Corporate Finance* (New York: Stern Stewart Putnam & Macklis, 1983), 102–111.

Ingersoll, Jonathan E., "A Contingent Claims Valuation of Convertible Securities," *Journal of Financial Economics,* May 1977, 289–322.

————, "An Examination of Corporate Call Policies on Convertible Securities," *Journal of Finance,* May 1977, 463–478.

Janjigian, Vahan, "The Leverage Changing Consequences of Convertible Debt Financing," *Financial Management,* Autumn 1987, 15–21.

For additional insights into the use of financial futures for hedging, see

Bacon, Peter W., and Richard Williams, "Interest Rate Futures Trading: A New Tool for the Financial Manager," *Financial Management,* Spring 1976, 32–38.

Block, Stanley B., and Timothy J. Gallagher, "The Use of Interest Rate Futures and Options by Corporate Financial Managers," *Financial Management,* Autumn 1986, 73–78.

McCabe, George M., and Charles T. Franckle, "The Effectiveness of Rolling the Hedge Forward in the Treasury Bill Futures Market," *Financial Management,* Summer 1983, 21–29.

The following cases cover issues presented in this chapter:

Case 28, "Weaver Foods, Inc.," in the Brigham-Gapenski casebook, which illustrates convertible bond valuation.

"Van Dusen Air," in the Harrington casebook, which focuses on a financing decision that includes convertible debentures.

PART VI

Short-Term Financial Management

CHAPTER 19

Short-Term Financial Planning and Financing

In early 1990, Campeau Corporation, the owner of the Allied and Federated department store chains, filed for protection from creditors under Chapter 11 of the Bankruptcy Act. Thus, the cloud of bankruptcy descended over such well-known retailers as Abraham & Straus, Bloomingdale's, Bon Marche, Burdine's, Jordan Marsh, Maas Brothers, Rich's, and Stern's.

In the fall of 1989, several months before the bankruptcy filing, Campeau's suppliers were deeply concerned. For example, consider the situation faced by St. Gillian Group, a dress manufacturer that sells about $25 million of its clothes to Campeau's stores. In November St. Gillian showed its spring fashions, and department store buyers, including those from Campeau's stores, placed orders for delivery in the busy March and April season. On the basis of such orders, St. Gillian must purchase the fabrics and manufacture and ship the dresses. Since manufacturers are typically paid 10 days after the month in which they ship, payment on clothes shipped to Campeau stores in March would not be due until April 10, even though St. Gillian would incur the manufacturing costs during January and February.

Orders from Campeau retailers used to be cause for celebration, but this was not the case in late 1989. "The dress business has always been a gamble, but it's never been like this," said Jon Levy, St. Gillian's president. "The few million dollars that I could lose today is nothing against what I could lose on the spring line. I'm buying fabric right now for clothes to be delivered in March and April. What happens to me if Campeau collapses between now and then?" "Everybody is worried about the possibility of cancellations," said another manufacturer's representative. "The buyers who work for the various Campeau chains may lose their jobs. The stores they work for may be sold. What this will mean for manufacturers is anybody's guess."

Because of concerns over Campeau's creditworthiness, some manufacturers were asking for bank letters of credit to support Campeau's orders. "We're being paid today, but we're worried about tomorrow and will want letters of credit," said one manufacturer's sales director. As for Mr. Levy at St. Gillian, he said he will maintain his credit lines with the various Campeau stores unless they miss a payment. "If they slip for 10 cents for 10 minutes, I'll stop," he said.

THE immediate concern of the clothing manufacturers involved building up inventories that might never be sold; that is, incurring production costs that might never be recaptured by sales revenue. This is just one aspect of *short-term financial planning,* a very important part of every firm's planning process. Short-term financial planning involves decisions relating to cash flows expected in the near future, say in the coming year. Although most cash flows stem from transactions involving current assets and current liabilities, short-term financial planning must also consider the impact of cash flows that arise from long-term asset and liability transactions such as fixed asset purchases, bond and stock sales, and dividend payments.

About 60 percent of a financial manager's time is devoted to short-term decision making, and many finance students' first assignment on the job will involve short-term financial planning. For these reasons, short-term financial planning is an essential topic of study. Chapter 19 provides an overview of short-term financial planning and discusses short-term financing. Chapter 20 focuses on cash and marketable securities, and Chapter 21 covers inventories and receivables.

SHORT-TERM FINANCIAL PLANNING TERMINOLOGY

The primary purpose of short-term financial planning is to insure that the firm maintains its *liquidity.* As used here, "liquidity" means the ability to meet obligations as they become due. A firm that is liquid can by definition support its operational goals, since it has the funds that are needed to make payments to its workers, suppliers, tax collectors, investors, and so on. Conversely, a firm that is illiquid cannot easily generate the cash needed to make these payments, and thus its operations suffer. In some situations, illiquidity may only be temporary, but in other cases it may be the first symptom of severe problems that could ultimately lead to bankruptcy.

It is useful to begin the discussion of short-term financial planning by reviewing some basic definitions and concepts:

1.   *Working capital,* sometimes called *gross working capital,* simply refers to current assets.

2.   *Net working capital* is defined as current assets minus current liabilities.

3.   The *current ratio,* which is computed by dividing current assets by current liabilities, is intended to measure a firm's liquidity. However, a high current ratio does not insure that a firm will have the cash required to meet its needs. If inventories are not sold, or if receivables are not collected in a timely manner, then the apparent safety reflected in a high current ratio could be illusory.

4.   The *quick ratio,* or *acid test,* which also attempts to measure liquidity, is current assets less inventories, divided by current liabilities. The quick ratio removes inventories from current assets because they are the least liquid of current assets. It is thus an "acid test" of a company's ability to meet its current obligations. However, like the current ratio, the quick ratio could give a false signal regarding a firm's liquidity position.

5.   The *days liquidity on hand ratio* is another liquidity measure. It is defined as liquid assets (cash, marketable securities, and receivables) divided by projected daily cash operating expenses, and it measures the number of days that the firm can operate solely on the basis of its present liquid assets. Daily cash operating expenses are best obtained from the projected cash budget, but a reasonable proxy can be obtained by dividing the annual cost of goods sold plus selling and administrative expenses plus other cash costs by 360 (or 365). This ratio recognizes, at least partially, that true liquidity stems from cash flows rather than stocks of assets, although it still focuses on the stock of liquid assets rather than on the inflow of cash.

6.   The *days cash on hand ratio,* defined as cash plus marketable securities, divided by daily cash operating expenses, is similar to the days liquidity on hand ratio, but it is even more restrictive in its interpretation of "liquidity." The days cash on hand ratio recognizes that cash and marketable securities are the only absolutely liquid assets.

7.   By far the best and most comprehensive picture of a firm's liquidity position is obtained by examining its *cash budget.* This statement, which forecasts cash inflows and outflows, focuses on what really counts, the firm's ability to generate cash inflows in a timely manner sufficient to meet its required cash outflows. We will discuss cash budgeting in detail in Chapter 20.

8.   *Current asset management* involves the administration, within policy guidelines, of current assets, including the financing of those assets.

9.   *Liquidity management* involves the planned acquisition and use of liquid resources over time to meet cash obligations as they become due. Liquidity management is more encompassing than current asset management, as liquidity management includes planned sales of fixed assets, issuance of long-term securities, and all other long-term activities which affect the firm's liquidity.

Table 19-1   Foxcraft Printing Company: Balance Sheets as of
December 31, 1990, and June 30, 1991 (Thousands of Dollars)

	Actual 12/31/90	Projected 6/30/91		Actual 12/31/90	Projected 6/30/91
Cash and marketable securities	$ 20	$ 20	Accounts payable	$ 30	$ 50
Accounts receivable	80	20	Accrued wages	15	10
Inventories	100	200	Accrued taxes	15	10
			Notes payable	50	80
			Current portion of long-term debt	40	40
Current assets	$200	$240	Current liabilities	$150	$190
Fixed assets	500	500	Long-term debt	150	140
			Stockholders' equity	400	410
Total assets	$700	$740	Total claims	$700	$740

We must be careful to distinguish between (1) those current liabilities which are specifically used to finance current assets and (2) those which represent either current maturities of long-term debt or financing associated with a construction program which will, after the project is completed, be funded with the proceeds of a long-term security issue. The first category of liabilities is considered part of both current asset and liquidity management, while the second is part of liquidity management only.

Table 19-1 contains the December 31, 1990, and projected June 30, 1991, balance sheets of Foxcraft Printing Company, a manufacturer of greeting cards. Note that, according to the definitions given, Foxcraft's December 31 working capital is $200,000, and its net working capital is $200,000 − $150,000 = $50,000. Also, Foxcraft's year-end current ratio is 1.33, and its quick ratio is 0.67. Finally, if the firm's daily cash operating expenses are $10,000, then its end-of-year days liquidity on hand ratio is 10 days, and its days cash on hand is 2.

Note that the total current liabilities of $150,000 includes the current portion of long-term debt, which is $40,000. This account is unaffected by changes in current asset management decisions, since it is a function of past long-term financing decisions. Thus, even though we define long-term debt coming due in the next accounting period as a current liability, it is not a short-term decision variable. Similarly, if Foxcraft were building a new factory and financing this construction with short-term loans which were to be converted to a mortgage bond when the building was completed, the construction loans would be segregated out with regard to current asset management. Although these accounts are not current asset decision variables, they cannot be ignored, and they must be considered as a part of Foxcraft's liquidity management program.

Self-Test Questions

In the context of this chapter, what is meant by the term "liquidity"?

Define the following terms:
1. Working capital
2. Net working capital
3. Current ratio
4. Quick ratio
5. Days liquidity on hand
6. Days cash on hand

Are all current liability accounts relevant to current asset management decisions? Explain.

What is the difference between liquidity management and current asset management?

THE REQUIREMENT FOR EXTERNAL CURRENT ASSET FINANCING

The manufacture of greeting cards is a seasonal business. In June of each year, Foxcraft begins producing Christmas cards for sale in the July-November period, and by December 31, it has sold most of its Christmas and New Year's cards, so its inventories are relatively low. However, most of its buyers purchase on credit, so the year-end receivables are at a seasonal high. Now look in Table 19-1 at Foxcraft's projected balance sheet for June 30, 1991. Here we see that June inventories will be relatively high ($200,000 versus $100,000 the previous December), as will accounts payable ($50,000 versus $30,000), but receivables are projected to be relatively low ($20,000 versus $80,000).

Now consider what happens to Foxcraft's current assets and current liabilities over the period from December 1990 to June 1991. Current assets increase from $200,000 to $240,000, so the firm must raise $40,000—a net increase on the left side of the balance sheet must be financed by an increase on the right-hand side. However, the higher volume of both purchases and labor expenditures associated with increased production to build inventories will cause payables and accruals to increase *spontaneously,* on net, by $10,000—from $30,000 + $15,000 + $15,000 = $60,000 to $50,000 + $10,000 + $10,000 = $70,000. This leaves a $30,000 projected current asset financing requirement, which we assume will be obtained from the bank as a short-term loan. Therefore, on June 30, 1991, we show notes payable of $80,000, up from $50,000 on December 31, 1990.

These fluctuations for Foxcraft resulted from seasonal factors. Similar fluctuations in current asset requirements, hence in financing needs, can occur over business cycles—typically, financing needs contract during recessions, and they expand during booms.

Self-Test Question

Describe how both seasonal and cyclical sales fluctuations influence current asset levels and financing requirements.

THE CASH CONVERSION CYCLE

The concept of the *cash conversion cycle* is important in short-term financial planning. We can illustrate the process with data from Real Time Corporation (RTC), which in late 1990 introduced a new super-minicomputer that can perform 15 million instructions per second and that will sell for $250,000. RTC anticipated a demand for 100 of the new machines. The following are the steps in the cash conversion cycle:

1.   RTC will order and then receive the materials that it needs to produce the 100 computers. Because RTC and most other firms purchase materials on credit, this transaction will create an account payable, but the decision will have no immediate cash flow effect.

2.   Labor will be used to convert the materials into finished computers. However, wages will not be fully paid at the time the work is done, so accrued wages will build up.

3.   The finished computers will be sold, usually on credit, so sales will create receivables, not immediate cash inflows.

4.   At some point during the cycle, RTC must pay off its accounts payable and accrued wages. Because these payments must normally be made before RTC has collected cash from its receivables, a net cash outflow will occur, and this outflow must be financed.

5.   The cash conversion cycle will be completed when RTC's receivables have been collected; at this point, the company will be in a position to pay off the credit that was used to finance production. It will at that point take its profit, and it can then repeat the cycle.

The *cash conversion cycle model* has been developed to formalize the steps outlined above.[1] The following are some terms used in the model:

1.   *Inventory conversion period,* which is the average length of time required to convert materials into finished goods and then to sell these goods. Note that the inventory conversion period can be calculated as 360 divided by the inventory turnover ratio based on cost of goods sold. For example, if the cost of goods sold is $10 million and average inventories are $2 million, then the inventory turnover ratio is

---

[1]See Verlyn D. Richards and Eugene J. Laughlin, "A Cash Conversion Cycle Approach to Liquidity Analysis," *Financial Management,* Spring 1980, 32–38. A similar approach was set forth earlier by Lawrence J. Gitman, "Estimating Corporate Liquidity Requirements: A Simplified Approach," *The Financial Review,* 1974, 79–88.

$10 million/$2 million = 5, and the inventory conversion period is 360/5 = 72 days.

$$\text{Inventory conversion period} = \frac{360}{\text{Cost of goods sold/Inventory}}$$

$$= \frac{360}{\$10 \text{ million/}\$2 \text{ million}}$$

$$= 360/5 = 72 \text{ days.}$$

Thus, it takes an average of 72 days to convert materials into finished goods and then to sell those goods.

2. *Receivables collection period,* which is the average length of time required to convert the firm's receivables into cash, that is, to collect cash following a sale. The receivables collection period is also called days sales outstanding (DSO) or average collection period (ACP), and it is calculated as Receivables/Sales per day = Receivables/(Sales/360). If receivables are $1 million and sales are $15 million, the receivables collection period is

$$\frac{\text{Receivables}}{\text{collection period}} = \frac{\text{Receivables}}{\text{Sales/360}} = \frac{\$1 \text{ million}}{\$15 \text{ million/360}} = 24 \text{ days.}$$

Thus, it takes 24 days after a sale to convert the receivables into cash.

3. *Payables deferral period,* which is the average length of time between the purchase of materials and labor and the payment of cash for them. For example, the firm might on average have 30 days to pay for labor and materials.

4. *Cash conversion cycle,* which nets out the three periods just defined and which therefore equals the length of time between the firm's actual cash expenditures on productive resources (materials and labor) and its own cash receipts from the sale of products (that is, the length of time between paying for labor and materials and collecting on receivables). The cash conversion cycle thus equals the length of time the firm has funds tied up in current assets.

We can now use these definitions to analyze the cash conversion cycle. First, the concept is diagrammed in Figure 19-1. Each component is given a number, and the cash conversion cycle can be expressed by this equation:

$$
\begin{array}{ccccccc}
(1) & + & (2) & - & (3) & = & (4) \\
\text{Inventory} & & \text{Receivables} & & \text{Payables} & & \text{Cash} \\
\text{conversion} & + & \text{collection} & - & \text{deferral} & = & \text{conversion} \,. \\
\text{period} & & \text{period} & & \text{period} & & \text{cycle}
\end{array}
$$

To illustrate, suppose it takes Real Time an average of 72 days to convert raw materials to computers and to make a sale and another 24 days to collect on receivables, while 30 days normally elapse between receipt of raw materials and payment of the associated account payable. In this case, the cash conversion cycle would be 66 days:

$$72 \text{ days} + 24 \text{ days} - 30 \text{ days} = 66 \text{ days.}$$

Figure 19-1   The Cash Conversion Cycle Model

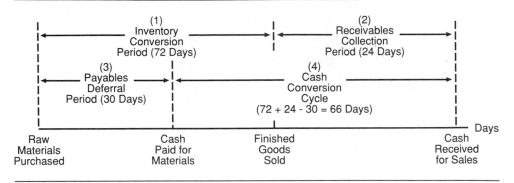

To look at it another way,

Receipts delay   − Payment delay = Net delay
(72 days + 24 days) −   30 days   = 66 days.

Given these data, RTC knows when it starts producing a computer that it will have to finance the costs of manufacturing the computer for a 66-day period. The firm's goal should be to shorten its cash conversion cycle as much as possible without hurting operations. This would improve profits, because the longer the cash conversion cycle, the greater the need for external financing, and such financing has a cost.

The cash conversion cycle can be shortened (1) by reducing the inventory conversion period, that is, by processing and selling goods more quickly; (2) by reducing the receivables collection period by speeding up collections; or (3) by lengthening the payables deferral period by slowing down its own payments. To the extent that these actions can be taken *without increasing costs or depressing sales,* they should be carried out.

Note that the cash conversion cycle can also be expressed as the following equation:

$$\text{Cash conversion cycle} = 360 \left[\frac{\text{Inventory}}{\text{Cost of sales}} + \frac{\text{Receivables}}{\text{Sales}} - \frac{\text{Payables} + \text{Accruals}}{\text{Cash operating expenses}} \right].$$

In this form, we see clearly that an increase in either inventories or receivables lengthens the cash conversion cycle, assuming no change in sales, cost of goods sold, or cash operating expenses. Since any decision which lengthens the cash conversion cycle also increases financing requirements, inventory and receivables decisions must take account of the potential impact on the firm's cash conversion cycle.

We can illustrate the benefits of shortening the cash conversion cycle by looking again at Real Time Corporation. Suppose RTC must spend $200,000 on materials and labor to produce one computer, and it can turn out three computers per day. Thus, it must invest $600,000 for each day's production. This investment must be financed for 66 days—the length of the cash conversion cycle—so the company's working capital financing needs will be $66 \times \$600,000 = \$39.6$ million. If RTC could reduce the cash conversion cycle to 50 days, say by deferring payment of its accounts payable an additional 16 days, or by speeding up either the production process or the collection of its receivables, it could reduce its working capital financing requirements by $9.6 million. We see, then, that actions which affect the inventory conversion period, the receivables collection period, and the payables deferral period all affect the cash conversion cycle, hence they influence the firm's need for current assets and current asset financing. You should keep the cash conversion cycle concept in mind as you go through the remainder of this chapter and the other chapters on short-term financial management.

Self-Test Questions

Briefly describe the steps involved in the cash conversion cycle.

What is the cash conversion cycle model? How can it be used to improve current asset management?

CURRENT ASSET INVESTMENT AND FINANCING POLICIES

We should mention at the outset that short-term financial decisions are conceptually similar to long-term decisions, such as capital structure and capital budgeting decisions, in that they are made within a risk/return tradeoff framework. However, finance theorists have not been totally successful in applying the goal of shareholder wealth maximization to current asset decisions in the sense of showing how a specific current asset decision affects stock values. Thus, there is no strong theoretical foundation which provides direction to financial managers.

Current asset financial policy involves two basic questions: (1) What is the appropriate level for current assets, both in total and by specific accounts? (2) How should current assets be financed?

Alternative Current Asset Investment Policies

Figure 19-2 shows three alternative policies regarding the total amount of current assets carried. Essentially, these policies differ in that different amounts of current asset are carried to support a given level of sales. The line with the steepest slope represents a relaxed policy, where relatively large amounts of cash, marketable securities, and inventories are carried, and where sales are stimulated by the use of a credit policy that provides liberal financing to customers and a corresponding high level of receivables. Conversely, with the restricted (or "lean-and-mean") policy, the holdings of cash, securities, inventories, and receivables are minimized. The moderate policy is between the two extremes.

Under conditions of certainty—when sales, costs, lead times, payment periods, and so on, are known for sure—all firms would hold only minimal levels of current

Figure 19-2   Alternative Current Asset Investment Policies
(Millions of Dollars)

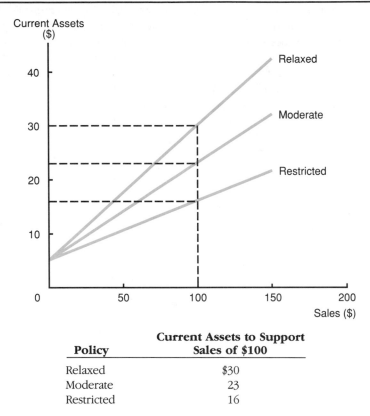

Policy	Current Assets to Support Sales of $100
Relaxed	$30
Moderate	23
Restricted	16

Note: The sales/current assets relationship is shown here as being linear, but the relationship is often curvilinear.

assets. Any larger amounts would increase the need for external funding without a corresponding increase in profits, while any smaller holdings would involve late payments to labor and suppliers, lost sales and production inefficiencies because of inventory shortages, and lost sales due to an overly restrictive credit policy.

However, the picture changes when uncertainty is introduced. Here the firm requires some minimum amount of cash and inventories based on expected payments, expected sales, expected order lead times, and so on, plus additional amounts, or *safety stocks*, which enable it to deal with ex post departures from the expected values. Similarly, accounts receivable levels are determined by credit terms, and the tougher the credit terms, the lower the receivables for any given level of sales. With a restricted current asset investment policy, the firm would hold minimal levels of safety stocks for cash and inventories, and it would have a tight credit policy even though this meant running the risk of a decline in sales. A restricted, lean-and-mean current asset investment policy generally provides the highest expected return on investment, but it entails the greatest risk, while the converse is true under a relaxed policy. The moderate policy falls in between the two extremes in terms of expected risk and return.

In terms of the cash conversion cycle, a restricted investment policy would tend to reduce the inventory conversion and receivables collection periods, hence result in a relatively short cash conversion cycle. Conversely, a relaxed policy would create higher levels of inventories and receivables, longer inventory conversion and receivables collection periods, and a relatively long cash conversion cycle. A moderate policy would produce a cash conversion cycle which falls between the two extremes.

As we will see in the next two chapters, companies can often reduce current assets without adversely affecting sales or operating costs through the use of just-in-time inventory procedures and the like. It should also be noted that the profit penalty for holding current assets is very much dependent upon how they are financed. Therefore, corporate policy with regard to the level of current assets is never set all by itself—it is always established in conjunction with the firm's current asset financing policy, which we consider next.

Alternative Current Asset Financing Policies

Most businesses experience seasonal and/or cyclical fluctuations. For example, construction firms have peaks in the spring and summer, retailers peak around Christmas, and the manufacturers who supply both construction companies and retailers follow similar patterns. Similarly, virtually all businesses must build up current assets when the economy is strong, but they then sell off inventories and have net reductions of receivables when the economy slacks off. Still, current assets rarely drop to zero, and this realization has led to the development of the idea of *permanent current assets.* Applying this idea to Foxcraft, Table 19-1 suggests that, at this stage in its life, Foxcraft's total assets fluctuate between $700,000 and $740,000. Thus, Foxcraft has $700,000 in permanent assets, composed of $500,000 of fixed assets and $200,000 in permanent current assets, plus *seasonal,* or *temporary, current assets* which fluctuate from zero to a maximum of $40,000. The manner in which the permanent and temporary current assets are financed defines the firm's *current asset financing policy.*

Maturity Matching Approach. One policy is to match asset and liability maturities as shown in Panel a of Figure 19-3. This strategy minimizes the risk that the firm will be unable to pay off its maturing obligations. To illustrate, suppose Foxcraft borrows on a 1-year basis and uses the funds obtained to build and equip a plant. Cash flows from the plant (profits plus depreciation) would almost never be sufficient to pay off the loan at the end of only one year, so the loan must be renewed. If for some reason the lender refuses to renew the loan, then Foxcraft would have problems. Had the plant been financed with long-term debt, however, the required loan payments would have been better matched with cash flows from profits and depreciation, and the problem of renewal would not have arisen.

At the limit, a firm could attempt to match exactly the maturity structure of its assets and liabilities. Inventory expected to be sold in 30 days could be financed

Figure 19-3   Alternative Current Asset Financing Policies

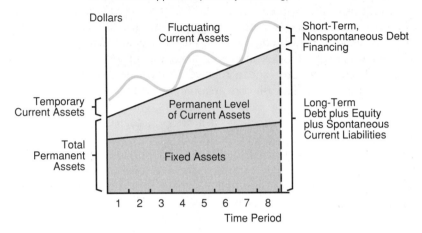

a. Moderate Approach (Maturity Matching)

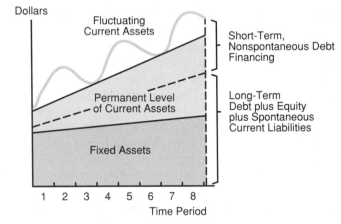

b. Relatively Aggressive Approach

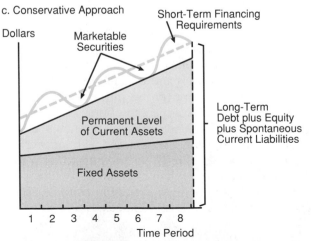

c. Conservative Approach

with a 30-day bank loan; a machine expected to last for 5 years could be financed by a 5-year loan; a 20-year building could be financed by a 20-year mortgage bond; and so forth. Actually, of course, two factors prevent this exact maturity matching: (1) there is uncertainty about the lives of assets, and (2) some common equity must be used, and common equity has no maturity. To illustrate the uncertainty factor, Foxcraft might finance inventories with a 30-day loan, expecting to sell the inventories and to use the cash generated to retire the loan. But if sales were slow, the cash would not be forthcoming, and the use of short-term credit could end up causing a problem. Still, if Foxcraft makes an attempt to match asset and liability maturities, we would define this as a moderate current asset financing policy.

Aggressive Approach. Panel b of Figure 19-3 illustrates the situation for a relatively aggressive firm which finances all of its fixed assets with long-term capital but part of its permanent current assets with short-term, nonspontaneous credit. A look back at Table 19-1 will show that Foxcraft actually follows this strategy. Assuming that the $40,000 current portion of long-term debt will be refinanced with new long-term debt, Foxcraft has $500,000 in fixed assets and $590,000 of long-term capital, leaving only $90,000 of long-term capital to finance $200,000 in permanent current assets. Additionally, Foxcraft has a minimum of $60,000 of "costless" spontaneous short-term credit consisting of payables and accruals. Thus, Foxcraft uses $50,000 of short-term notes payable to help finance its permanent level of current assets.

Returning to Figure 19-3, note that we used the term "relatively" in the title for Panel b, because there can be different *degrees* of aggressiveness. For example, the dashed line in Panel b could have been drawn *below* the line designating fixed assets, indicating that all of the permanent current assets and part of the fixed assets were financed with short-term credit; this would be a highly aggressive, extremely nonconservative position, and the firm would be very much subject to dangers from rising interest rates as well as to loan renewal problems. However, short-term debt is often cheaper than long-term debt, and some firms are willing to sacrifice safety for the chance of higher profits.

Conservative Approach. As shown in Panel c of Figure 19-3, the dashed line could also be drawn *above* the line designating permanent current assets, indicating that permanent capital is being used to finance all permanent asset requirements and also to meet some or all of the seasonal demands. In the situation depicted in our graph, the firm uses a small amount of short-term, nonspontaneous credit to meet its peak requirements, but it also meets a part of its seasonal needs by "storing liquidity" in the form of marketable securities during the off-season. The humps above the dashed line represent short-term financing; the troughs below the dashed line represent short-term security holdings. Panel c represents a very safe, conservative current asset financing policy.

Self-Test Questions

What are three alternative current asset investment policies? Which one is best?

What are three alternative current asset financing policies? Which one is best?

ADVANTAGES AND DISADVANTAGES OF SHORT-TERM FINANCING

The three possible financing policies described above were distinguished by the relative amounts of short-term debt used under each policy. The aggressive policy called for the greatest use of short-term debt, while the conservative policy called for the least. Maturity matching fell in between. Although using short-term credit is generally riskier than using long-term credit, short-term credit does have some significant advantages. The pros and cons of short-term financing are considered in this section.

Speed

A short-term loan can be obtained much faster than long-term credit. Lenders will insist on a more thorough financial examination before extending long-term credit, and the loan agreement will have to be spelled out in considerable detail because a lot can happen during the life of a 10- or 20-year loan. Therefore, if funds are needed in a hurry, the firm should look to the short-term markets.

Flexibility

If its needs for funds are seasonal or cyclical, a firm may not want to commit itself to long-term debt for three reasons: (1) Flotation costs are generally high when raising long-term debt but trivial for short-term credit. (2) Although long-term debt can be repaid early, provided the loan agreement includes a prepayment provision, prepayment penalties can be expensive. Accordingly, if a firm thinks its need for funds may diminish in the near future, it should choose short-term debt for the flexibility it provides. (3) Long-term loan agreements always contain provisions, or covenants, which constrain the firm's future actions. Short-term credit agreements are generally much less onerous in this regard.

Cost of Long-Term versus Short-Term Debt

The yield curve is normally upward sloping, indicating that interest rates are generally lower on short-term than on long-term debt. Thus, under normal conditions, interest costs at the time the funds are obtained will be lower if the firm borrows on a short-term rather than a long-term basis.

Risk of Long-Term versus Short-Term Debt

Even though short-term debt is often less expensive than long-term debt, short-term credit subjects the firm to more risk than does long-term financing. This occurs for two reasons: (1) If a firm borrows on a long-term basis, its interest costs will be relatively stable over time, but if it uses short-term credit, its interest expense will fluctuate widely, at times going quite high. For example, the short-term rate banks charge large corporations more than tripled over a two-year period in the 1980s, rising from 6.25 to 21 percent. Many firms that had borrowed heavily on a short-term basis simply could not meet their rising interest costs, and as a result bankruptcies hit record levels during that period. (2) If a firm borrows heavily on a short-term basis, it may find itself unable to repay this debt, and it may be in such a weak financial position that the lender will not extend the loan; this too could force the firm into bankruptcy. Braniff Airlines, which failed during a credit crunch in the 1980s, is an example.

Another good example of the riskiness of short-term debt is provided by Transamerica Corporation, a major financial services company. Transamerica's chairman, Mr. Beckett, described how his company was moving to reduce its dependency on short-term loans whose costs vary with short-term interest rates. According to Mr. Beckett, Transamerica had reduced its variable-rate (short-term) loans by about $450 million over a two-year period. "We aren't going to go through the enormous increase in debt expense again that had such a serious impact (on earnings)," he said. The company's earnings fell sharply because money rates rose to record highs. "We were almost entirely in variable-rate debt," he said, but currently "about 65 percent is fixed rate and 35 percent variable. We've come a long way, and we'll keep plugging away at it." Transamerica's earnings were badly depressed by the increase in short-term rates, but other companies were even less fortunate—they simply could not pay the rising interest charges, and this forced them into bankruptcy.

Self-Test Questions

What are some advantages of short-term debt over long-term debt as a source of capital?

Are there any disadvantages to short-term debt?

SOURCES OF SHORT-TERM FINANCING

Statements about the flexibility, cost, and riskiness of short-term versus long-term debt depend, to a large extent, on the type of short-term credit that is actually used. There are numerous sources of short-term funds, and in the following sections we describe four major types: (1) accruals, (2) accounts payable (trade credit), (3) bank loans, and (4) commercial paper. In addition, we discuss the cost of bank loans and the factors that influence a firm's choice of a bank.

ACCRUALS

Firms generally pay employees on a weekly, biweekly, or monthly basis, so the balance sheet will typically show some accrued wages. Similarly, the firm's own estimated income taxes, the social security and income taxes withheld from employee payrolls, and the sales taxes collected are generally paid on a weekly, monthly, or quarterly basis, so the balance sheet will typically show some accrued taxes along with accrued wages.

Accruals increase automatically, or spontaneously, as a firm's operations expand. Further, this type of debt is "free" in the sense that no explicit interest is paid on funds raised through accruals. However, a firm cannot ordinarily control its accruals: The timing of wage payments is set by economic forces and industry custom, while tax payment dates are established by law. Thus, firms use all the accruals they can, but they have little control over the levels of these accounts.

Self-Test Questions

What types of short-term credits are classified as accruals?

What is the cost of accruals?

How much control do financial managers have over the dollar amount of accruals?

ACCOUNTS PAYABLE (TRADE CREDIT)

Firms generally make purchases from other firms on credit, recording the debt as an *account payable.* Accounts payable, or *trade credit,* is the largest single category of short-term debt, representing about 40 percent of the current liabilities of the average nonfinancial corporation. The percentage is somewhat larger for smaller firms: Because small companies often do not qualify for financing from other sources, they rely especially heavily on trade credit.[2]

Trade credit is a spontaneous source of financing in the sense that it arises from ordinary business transactions. For example, suppose a firm makes average purchases of $2,000 a day on terms of net 30, meaning that it must pay for goods 30 days after the invoice date. On average, it will owe 30 times $2,000, or $60,000, to its suppliers. If its sales, and consequently its purchases, were to double, then its accounts payable would also double, to $120,000. Simply by growing, the firm would have spontaneously generated an additional $60,000 of financing. Similarly, if the terms under which it bought were extended from 30 to 40 days, its accounts payable would expand from $60,000 to $80,000. Thus, lengthening the credit period, as well as expanding sales and purchases, generates additional financing.

The Cost of Trade Credit

Firms that sell on credit have a *credit policy* that includes certain *terms of credit.* For example, Microchip Electronics sells on terms of 2/10, net 30, meaning that a 2 percent discount is given if payment is made within 10 days of the invoice date, with the full invoice amount being due and payable within 30 days if the discount is not taken.

---

[2]In a credit sale, the seller records the transaction as a receivable; the buyer, as a payable. We will examine accounts receivable as an asset investment in Chapter 21. Our focus in this chapter is on accounts payable, a liability item. We might also note that if a firm's accounts payable exceed its receivables, it is said to be *receiving net trade credit,* whereas if its receivables exceed its payables, it is *extending net trade credit.* Smaller firms frequently receive net credit; larger firms generally extend it.

Suppose Personal Computer Company (PCC) buys an average of $12 million of electronic components from Microchip each year, less a 2 percent discount, for net purchases of $11,760,000/360 = $32,666.67 per day. For simplicity, suppose Microchip is PCC's only supplier. If PCC takes the discount, paying at the end of the tenth day, its payables will average (10)($32,666.67) = $326,667; PCC will, on average, be receiving $326,667 of credit from its only supplier, Microchip Electronics.

Now suppose PCC decides *not* to take the discount; what will happen? First, PCC will begin paying invoices after 30 days, so its accounts payable will increase to 30($32,666.67) = $980,000.[3] Microchip will now be supplying PCC with an *additional* $653,333 of credit. PCC could use this additional credit to pay off bank loans, to expand inventories, to increase fixed assets, to build up its cash account, or even to increase its own accounts receivable.

Personal's new credit from Microchip has a cost—PCC is foregoing a 2 percent discount on its $12 million of purchases, so its costs will rise by $240,000 per year. Dividing this $240,000 by the additional credit, we find the implicit cost of the added trade credit as follows:

$$\text{Approximate percentage cost} = \frac{\$240,000}{\$653,333} = 36.7\%.$$

Assuming that PCC can borrow from its bank (or from other sources) at an interest rate less than 36.7 percent, it should not expand its payables by foregoing discounts.

The following equation can be used to calculate the approximate percentage cost, on an annual basis, of not taking discounts:

$$\begin{matrix}\text{Approximate} \\ \text{percentage} \\ \text{cost}\end{matrix} = \frac{\text{Discount percent}}{100 - \begin{matrix}\text{Discount} \\ \text{percent}\end{matrix}} \times \frac{360}{\begin{matrix}\text{Days credit is} \\ \text{outstanding}\end{matrix} - \begin{matrix}\text{Discount} \\ \text{period}\end{matrix}}. \quad \textbf{(19-1)}$$

The numerator of the first term, Discount percent, is the cost per dollar of credit, while the denominator in this term, 100 − Discount percent, represents the funds made available by not taking the discount. Thus, the first term is the periodic cost of the trade credit, while the second term shows how many times each year this cost is incurred. To illustrate the equation, the approximate cost of not taking a discount when the terms are 2/10, net 30, is computed as follows:

$$\text{Approximate percentage cost} = \frac{2}{98} \times \frac{360}{20} = 0.0204(18)$$

$$= 0.367 = 36.7\%.$$

In effective annual interest terms, the rate is even higher. The discount amounts to interest, and with terms of 2/10, net 30, the firm gains use of the funds for

---

[3]A question arises here: Should accounts payable reflect gross purchases or purchases net of discounts? Although generally accepted accounting principles permit either treatment on the grounds that the difference is not material, most accountants prefer to record payables net of discounts, and then to report the higher payments that result from not taking discounts as an additional expense, called "discounts lost." *Thus, we show accounts payable net of discounts even if the company does not expect to take the discount.*

$30 - 10 = 20$ days, so there are $360/20 = 18$ "interest periods" per year. Remember that the first term in Equation 19-1, (Discount percent)/(100 − Discount percent) = $0.02/0.98 = 0.0204$, is the periodic interest rate. This rate is paid 18 times each year, so the effective annual rate cost of trade credit is

$$\text{Effective annual rate} = (1.0204)^{18} - 1.0 = 1.438 - 1.0 = 43.8\%.$$

Thus, the 36.7 percent approximate cost calculated with Equation 19-1 understates the true cost of trade credit.

Notice, however, that the cost of trade credit can be reduced by paying late. Thus, if PCC could get away with paying in 60 days rather than in the specified 30, then the effective credit period would become $60 - 10 = 50$ days, and the approximate cost would drop from 36.7 percent to $(2/98)(360/50) = 14.7\%$. The effective annual rate would drop from 43.8 to 15.7 percent:

$$\text{Effective annual rate} = (1.0204)^{7.2} - 1.0 = 1.157 - 1.0 = 15.7\%.$$

In periods of excess capacity, firms may be able to get away with late payments, but they will also suffer a variety of problems associated with "stretching" accounts payable and being branded a "slow payer" account. These problems are discussed later in the chapter.

The cost of the additional trade credit that results from not taking discounts can be worked out for other purchase terms. Some illustrative costs are shown below:

	Cost of Additional Credit if the Cash Discount Is Not Taken	
Credit Terms	**Approximate Cost**	**Effective Cost**
1/10, net 20	36%	44%
1/10, net 30	18	20
2/10, net 20	73	107
3/15, net 45	37	44

As these figures show, the cost of not taking discounts can be substantial. Incidentally, throughout the chapter, we assume that payments are made either on the *last day* for taking discounts or on the *last day* of the credit period, unless otherwise noted. It would be foolish to pay, say, on the fifth day or on the twentieth day if the credit terms were 2/10, net 30.

Effects of Trade Credit on the Financial Statements

A firm's policy with regard to taking or not taking discounts can have a significant effect on its financial statements. To illustrate, let us assume that PCC is just beginning its operations. On the first day, it makes net purchases of $32,666.67. This amount is recorded on its balance sheet under accounts payable.[4] The second day it buys another $32,666.67. The first day's purchases are not yet paid for, so at the end of the second day, accounts payable total $65,333.34. Accounts payable increase by

---

[4] Inventories also increase by $32,666.67, but we are not now concerned with inventories. Again note that both inventories and receivables are recorded net of discounts regardless of whether discounts are taken.

Table 19-2 PCC's Financial Statements with Different Trade Credit Policies

	Take Discounts; Borrow from Bank	Do Not Take Discounts; Use Maximum Trade Credit
I. Balance Sheets		
Cash	$ 500,000	$ 500,000
Receivables	1,000,000	1,000,000
Inventories	2,000,000	2,000,000
Fixed assets	2,980,000	2,980,000
Total assets	$ 6,480,000	$ 6,480,000
Accounts payable	$ 326,667	$ 980,000
Notes payable	653,333	0
Accruals	500,000	500,000
Common equity	5,000,000	5,000,000
Total claims	$ 6,480,000	$ 6,480,000
II. Income Statements		
Sales	$15,000,000	$15,000,000
Less: Purchases	11,760,000	11,760,000
Labor	2,000,000	2,000,000
Interest	65,333	0
Discounts lost	0	240,000
Net income before tax	$ 1,174,667	$ 1,000,000
Tax (40%)	469,867	400,000
Net income	$ 704,800	$ 600,000

another $32,666.67 on the third day, for a total of $98,000, and after 10 days, accounts payable are up to $326,667.

If PCC takes discounts, then on the 11th day it will have to pay for the $32,666.67 of purchases made on the first day, which will reduce accounts payable. However, it will buy another $32,666.67, which will increase payables. Thus, after the 10th day of operations, PCC's balance sheet will level off, showing a balance of $326,667 in accounts payable, assuming that the company pays on the 10th day in order to take discounts.

Now suppose PCC decides not to take discounts. In this case, on the 11th day it will add another $32,666.67 to payables, but it will not pay for the purchases made on the 1st day. Thus, the balance sheet figure for accounts payable will rise to 11($32,666.67) = $359,333.37. This buildup will continue through the 30th day, at which point payables will total 30($32,666.67) = $980,000. On the 31st day, PCC will buy another $32,667 of goods, which will increase accounts payable, but it will also pay for the purchases made the 1st day, which will reduce payables. Thus, the balance sheet item accounts payable will stabilize at $980,000 after 30 days, assuming PCC does not take discounts.

Table 19-2, Part I, shows PCC's balance sheet, after it reaches a steady state, under the two trade credit policies. Total assets are unchanged by this policy decision, and we also assume that the accruals and common equity accounts are unchanged. The differences show up in accounts payable and notes payable; when PCC elects to take discounts and thus gives up some of the trade credit it otherwise could have obtained, it will have to raise $653,333 from some other source. It could have sold more common stock, or it could have used long-term bonds, but it chose to use bank credit, which has a 10 percent cost and is reflected in the notes payable account.

Part II of Table 19-2 shows PCC's income statement under the two policies. If the company does not take discounts, then its interest expense will be zero, but it will have a $240,000 expense for discounts lost. On the other hand, if it does take discounts, it will incur an interest expense of $65,333, but it will avoid the cost of discounts lost. Since discounts lost exceed the interest expense, the take-discounts policy results in a higher net income and, thus, in a higher stock price.

Components of Trade Credit: Free versus Costly

On the basis of the preceding discussion, trade credit can be divided into two components: (1) *free trade credit,* which involves credit received during the discount period and which for PCC amounts to 10 days' net purchases, or $326,667, and (2) *costly trade credit,* which involves credit in excess of the free credit, and whose cost is an implicit one based on the foregone discounts.[5] PCC could obtain $653,333, or 20 days' net purchases, of nonfree trade credit at a cost of approximately 37 percent. *Financial managers should always use the free component, but they should use the costly component only after analyzing the cost of this capital to make sure that it is less than the cost of funds which could be obtained from other sources.* Under the terms of trade found in most industries, the costly component will involve a relatively high percentage cost, so stronger firms will avoid using it.

We noted earlier that firms sometimes can and do deviate from the stated credit terms, thus altering the percentage cost figures cited earlier. For example, a California manufacturing firm that buys on terms of 2/10, net 30, makes a practice of paying in 15 days (rather than 10), but it still takes discounts. Its treasurer simply waits until 15 days after receipt of the goods to pay, and then writes a check for the invoiced amount less the 2 percent discount. The company's suppliers want its business, so they tolerate this practice. Similarly, a Wisconsin firm that also buys on terms of 2/10, net 30, does not take discounts, but it pays in 60 rather than in 30 days, thus "stretching" its trade credit. As we saw earlier, both practices reduce the cost of trade credit. Neither of these firms is "loved" by its suppliers, and neither could continue these practices in times when suppliers were operating at full capacity and had order backlogs, but these practices can and do reduce the costs of trade credit during times when suppliers have excess capacity.

---

[5]There is some question as to whether any credit is really "free," because the supplier will have a cost of carrying receivables which must be passed on to the customer in the form of higher prices. Still, if suppliers sell on standard terms such as 2/10, net 30, and if the base price cannot be negotiated downward for early payment, then for all intents and purposes, the 10 days of trade credit is indeed "free."

Self-Test Questions

What is trade credit?

What is the difference between free trade credit and costly trade credit?

What is the formula for finding the approximate cost of trade credit? What is the formula for the effective annual cost?

How does the cost of costly trade credit generally compare with the cost of short-term bank loans?

SHORT-TERM BANK LOANS

Commercial banks, whose loans generally appear on firms' balance sheets under the notes payable account, are second in importance to trade credit as a source of short-term financing.[6] The banks' influence is actually greater than it appears from the dollar amounts they lend, because banks provide *nonspontaneous* funds. As a firm's financing needs increase, it requests its bank to provide the additional funds. If the request is denied, the firm may be forced to abandon attractive growth opportunities. The key features of bank loans are discussed in the following paragraphs.

Maturity

Although banks do make longer-term loans, *the bulk of their lending is on a short-term basis* — about two-thirds of all bank loans mature in a year or less. Bank loans to businesses are frequently written as 90-day notes, so the loan must be repaid or renewed at the end of 90 days. Of course, if a borrower's financial position has deteriorated, the bank may well refuse to renew the loan. This can mean serious trouble for the borrower.

Promissory Note

When a bank loan is approved, the agreement is executed by signing a *promissory note*. The note specifies (1) the amount borrowed; (2) the percentage interest rate; (3) the repayment schedule, which can involve either a lump sum or a series of installments; (4) any collateral that might have to be put up as security for the loan; and (5) any other terms and conditions to which the bank and the borrower may have agreed. When the note is signed, the bank credits the borrower's checking account with the amount of the loan, while on the borrower's balance sheet, both cash and notes payable increase.

---

[6]Although commercial banks remain the primary source of short-term loans, other sources are available. For example, in 1990 GE Capital Corporation (GECC) had over $2 billion in commercial loans outstanding. Firms such as GECC, which was initially established to finance consumers' purchases of GE's durable goods, often find business loans to be more profitable than consumer loans.

Compensating Balances

Banks sometimes require regular borrowers to maintain an average demand deposit (checking account) balance equal to from 10 to 20 percent of the face amount of the loan. This is called a *compensating balance,* and such balances raise the effective interest rate on the loans. For example, if a firm needs $80,000 to pay off outstanding obligations, but if it must maintain a 20 percent compensating balance, then it must borrow $100,000 to obtain a usable $80,000. If the stated interest rate is 8 percent, the effective cost is actually 10 percent: $8,000 interest divided by $80,000 of usable funds equals 10 percent.[7]

Line of Credit

A *line of credit* is a formal or informal understanding between the bank and the borrower indicating the maximum credit the bank will extend to the borrower. For example, on December 31 a bank loan officer might indicate to a financial manager that the bank regards the firm as being "good" for up to $80,000 during the forthcoming year. If on January 10 the financial manager signs a promissory note for $15,000 for 90 days, this would be called "taking down" $15,000 of the total line of credit. This amount would be credited to the firm's checking account at the bank, and before repayment of the $15,000, the firm could borrow additional amounts up to a total of $80,000 outstanding at any one time.

Revolving Credit Agreement

A *revolving credit agreement* is a formal line of credit often used by large firms. To illustrate, in 1990 Texas Petroleum Company negotiated a revolving credit agreement for $100 million with a group of banks. The banks were formally committed for 4 years to lend the firm up to $100 million if the funds were needed. Texas Petroleum, in turn, paid an annual commitment fee of one-quarter of 1 percent on the unused balance of the commitment to compensate the banks for making the commitment. Thus, if Texas Petroleum did not take down any of the $100 million commitment during a year, it would still be required to pay a $250,000 annual fee, normally in monthly installments of $20,833.33. If it borrowed $50 million on the first day of the agreement, the unused portion of the line of credit would fall to $50 million, and the annual fee would fall to $125,000. Of course, interest would also have to be paid on the money Texas Petroleum actually borrowed. As a general rule, the rate of interest on "revolvers" is pegged to the prime rate, so the cost of the

---

[7]Note, however, that the compensating balance may be set as a minimum monthly *average,* and if the firm would maintain this average anyway, the compensating balance requirement would not raise the effective interest rate. Also, note that these *loan* compensating balances are added to any compensating balances that the firm's bank may require for *services performed,* such as clearing checks.

loan varies over time as interest rates change.[8] Texas Petroleum's rate was set at prime plus 0.5 percentage points.

Note that a revolving credit agreement is very similar to a line of credit. However, there is an important distinguishing feature: The bank has a *legal obligation* to honor a revolving credit agreement, and it receives a commitment fee. Neither the legal obligation nor the fee exists under a less formal line of credit.

Self-Test Question

Define each of the following terms as they might be used in a bank loan agreement:
1. Maturity
2. Promissory note
3. Compensating balance
4. Line of credit
5. Revolving credit agreement

THE COST OF BANK LOANS

The cost of bank loans varies for different types of borrowers at a given point in time, and for all borrowers over time. Interest rates are higher for riskier borrowers, and rates are also higher on smaller loans because of the fixed costs involved in making and servicing loans. If a firm can qualify as a "prime risk" because of its size and financial strength, it can borrow at the *prime rate,* which has traditionally been the lowest rate banks charge. Rates on other loans tend to be scaled up from the prime rate.

Bank rates vary widely over time depending on economic conditions and Federal Reserve policy. When the economy is weak, then (1) loan demand is usually

---

[8]Each bank sets its own prime rate, but, because of competitive forces, most banks' prime rates are identical. Further, most banks follow the rate set by the large New York City banks, and they, in turn, generally follow the rate set by Citibank, the largest bank in the United States. Citibank had a policy of setting the prime rate each week at $1\frac{1}{4}$ to $1\frac{1}{2}$ percentage points above the average rate on large certificates of deposit (CDs) during the three weeks immediately preceding. CD rates represent the "price" of money in the open market, and they rise and fall with the supply and demand of money, so CD rates are "market-clearing" rates. By tying the prime rate to CD rates, the banking system insured that the prime rate would also be a market-clearing rate.

However, in recent years the prime rate has been held relatively constant even during periods when open market rates fluctuated. Also, in recent years many banks have been lending to the very strongest companies at rates below the prime rate. As we discuss later in this chapter, larger firms have ready access to the commercial paper market, and if banks want to do a significant volume of business with these larger companies, they must match or at least come close to the commercial paper rate. As competition in financial markets increases, as it has been doing because of the deregulation of banks and other financial institutions, "administered" rates such as the prime rate must give way to flexible, negotiated rates based on market forces.

slack, and (2) the Fed also makes plenty of money available to the system. As a result, rates on all types of loans are relatively low. Conversely, when the economy is booming, loan demand is typically strong, and the Fed restricts the money supply; the result is high interest rates. As an indication of the kinds of fluctuations that can occur, the prime rate during 1980 rose from 11 percent in August to 21 percent in December. Interest rates on other bank loans also vary, but generally they are kept in phase with the prime rate.

Interest rates on bank loans are calculated in three ways: (1) *simple interest,* (2) *discount interest,* and (3) *add-on interest.* These three methods are explained in the next sections.

Regular, or Simple, Interest

In a *simple interest* loan, the borrower receives the face value of the loan and repays the principal and interest at maturity. For example, in a simple interest loan of $10,000 at 12 percent for one year, the borrower receives the $10,000 upon approval of the loan and pays back the $10,000 principal plus $10,000(0.12) = $1,200 in interest at maturity (one year later). The 12 percent is the stated, or nominal, rate. On this 1-year loan, the effective annual rate is also 12 percent:

$$\text{Effective annual rate}_{\text{Simple}} = \frac{\text{Interest}}{\text{Amount received}} = \frac{\$1,200}{\$10,000} = 12\%.$$

On a simple interest loan of one year or more, the nominal rate equals the effective rate. However, if the loan had a term of less than one year, say 90 days, then the effective annual rate would be calculated as follows:

$$\text{Effective annual rate}_{\text{Simple}} = \left(1 + \frac{k_{\text{Nom}}}{m}\right)^m - 1.0$$
$$= (1 + 0.12/4)^4 - 1.0 = 12.55\%.$$

Here k_{Nom} is the nominal, or stated, rate and m is the number of loan periods per year, or $360/90 = 4$. The bank gets the interest sooner than under a 1-year loan, hence the effective rate is higher.

Discount Interest

In a *discount interest* loan, the bank deducts the interest in advance (*discounts* the loan). Thus, the borrower receives less than the face value of the loan. On a 1-year, $10,000 loan with a 12 percent (nominal) rate, discount basis, the interest (discount) is $10,000(0.12) = $1,200, so the borrower obtains the use of only $10,000 - $1,200 =

$8,800. The effective annual rate is 13.64 percent versus 12 percent on a 1-year simple interest loan:[9]

$$\text{Effective annual rate}_{\text{Discount}} = \frac{\text{Interest}}{\text{Amount received}}$$

$$= \frac{\text{Interest}}{\text{Face value} - \text{Interest}}$$

$$= \frac{\$1,200}{\$10,000 - \$1,200} = 13.64\%.$$

An alternative procedure for finding the effective annual rate on a discount interest loan is

$$\text{Effective annual rate}_{\text{Discount}} = \frac{\text{Nominal rate (\%)}}{1.0 - \text{Nominal rate (fraction)}}$$

$$= \frac{12\%}{1.0 - 0.12} = \frac{12\%}{0.88} = 13.64\%.$$

If the discount loan is for a period of less than one year, its effective annual rate is found as follows:

$$\text{Effective annual rate}_{\text{Discount}} = \left(1.0 + \frac{\text{Interest}}{\text{Face value} - \text{Interest}}\right)^{m} - 1.0.$$

For example, if we borrow $10,000 face value at a nominal rate of 12 percent, discount interest, for 3 months, then m = 12/3 = 4, and the interest payment is $(0.12/4)(\$10,000) = \$300$, so

$$\text{Effective annual rate}_{\text{Discount}} = \left(1.0 + \frac{\$300}{\$10,000 - \$300}\right)^{4} - 1.0$$

$$= 0.1296 = 12.96\%$$

Thus, discount interest imposes less of a penalty on shorter-term than on longer-term loans.

---

[9]Note that if the borrowing firm actually requires $10,000 of cash, it must borrow $11,363.64:

$$\text{Face value} = \frac{\text{Funds required}}{1.0 - \text{Nominal rate (fraction)}}$$

$$= \frac{\$10,000}{1.0 - 0.12} = \frac{\$10,000}{0.88} = \$11,363.64.$$

Now, the borrower will receive $11,363.64 - 0.12(\$11,363.64) = \$10,000$. Increasing the face value of the loan does not change the effective rate of 13.64 percent on the $10,000 of usable funds.

Installment Loans: Add-On Interest

Lenders typically charge *add-on interest* on automobile and other types of small installment loans. The term "add-on" means that the interest is calculated based on the nominal rate and then added to the amount received to obtain the loan's face value. To illustrate, suppose you borrow $10,000 on an add-on basis at a nominal rate of 12 percent to buy a car, with the loan to be repaid in 12 monthly installments. At a 12 percent nominal rate, you will pay a total interest charge of $1,200. However, since the loan is paid off in monthly installments, you have the use of the full $10,000 for only the first month, and the amount actually advanced by the lender declines until, during the last month, only $\frac{1}{12}$ of the original loan will still be outstanding. Thus, you are paying $1,200 for the use of only about half the loan's face amount, as the average outstanding balance of the loan is only about $5,000. Therefore, we can approximate the effective rate as follows:

$$\text{Approximate effective annual rate}_{\text{Add-on}} = \frac{\text{Interest}}{(\text{Amount received})/2}$$

$$= \frac{\$1,200}{\$10,000/2} = 24.0\%.$$

To determine the precise effective rate under add-on, we proceed as follows:

1.   The total amount to be repaid is $10,000 of principal, plus $1,200 of interest, or $11,200.

2.   The monthly payment is $11,200/12 = $933.33.

3.   The bank is, in effect, buying a 12-period annuity of $933.33 for $10,000, so $10,000 is the present value of the annuity:

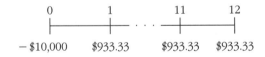

4.   The IRR of this cash flow stream (or the interest rate on a 12-period annuity) is 1.788% = 0.01788, which is the monthly rate.

5.   The effective annual rate is found as follows:[10]

$$\text{Effective annual rate}_{\text{Add-on}} = (1 + k_d)^{12} - 1.0$$

$$= (1.01788)^{12} - 1.0$$

$$= 1.2370 - 1.0 = 23.7\%.$$

---

[10]Note that if an installment loan is paid off ahead of schedule, additional complications arise. For a discussion of this point, see Dick Bonker, "The Rule of 78," *Journal of Finance,* June 1976, 877–888.

Simple Interest with Compensating Balances

Compensating balances tend to raise the effective rate on a loan. To illustrate this, suppose a firm needs $10,000 to pay for some equipment that it recently purchased. A bank offers to lend the company money for one year at a 12 percent simple rate, but the company must maintain a *compensating balance (CB)* equal to 20 percent of the loan amount. If the firm did not take the loan, it would keep no deposits with the bank. What is the effective annual rate on the loan?

First, note that if the firm requires $10,000, it must, assuming it does not have current cash to use as the compensating balance, borrow $12,500:

$$\text{Face value} = \frac{\text{Funds required}}{1.0 - \text{CB (fraction)}} = \frac{\$10,000}{1.0 - 0.20} = \$12,500.$$

The interest paid at the end of the year will be $12,500(0.12) = $1,500, but the firm will only get the use of $10,000. Therefore, the effective annual rate is 15 percent:

$$\text{Effective annual rate}_{\text{Simple/CB}} = \frac{\text{Interest}}{\text{Amount received}}$$

$$= \frac{\$1,500}{\$10,000} = 15\%.$$

An alternative formulation is

$$\text{Effective annual rate}_{\text{Simple/CB}} = \frac{\text{Nominal rate (\%)}}{1.0 - \text{CB (fraction)}}$$

$$= \frac{12\%}{1.0 - 0.2} = 15\%.$$

Discount Interest with Compensating Balances

The analysis can be extended to the case where compensating balances are required and the loan is on a discount basis. In this situation, if a firm required $10,000 for one year and a 20 percent compensating balance (CB) is required on a 12 percent discount loan, it must borrow $14,705.88:

$$\text{Face value} = \frac{\text{Funds required}}{1.0 - \text{Nominal rate (fraction)} - \text{CB (fraction)}}$$

$$= \frac{\$10,000}{1.0 - 0.12 - 0.2} = \$10,000/0.68 = \$14,705.88.$$

The firm would record this $14,705.88 as a note payable offset by these asset accounts. (Note that a small rounding error occurs.)

To cash account	$10,000.00
Prepaid interest (12% of $14,705.88)	1,764.71
Compensating balance (20% of $14,705.88)	2,941.18
	$14,705.89

Now the effective annual rate is 17.65 percent:

$$\text{Effective annual rate}_{\text{Discount/CB}} = \frac{\text{Nominal rate}}{1.0 - \text{Nominal rate (fraction)} - \text{CB (fraction)}}$$

$$= \frac{12\%}{1.0 - 0.12 - 0.2} = 12\%/0.68 = 17.65\%.$$

In our example, compensating balances and discount interest combined to push the effective rate of interest up from 12 to 17.65 percent. Note, however, that in our analysis we assumed that the compensating balance requirement forced the firm to increase its bank deposits. Had the company had transactions balances which could be used to supply all or part of the compensating balances, the effective annual rate would have been less than 17.65 percent. Also, if the firm earns interest on its bank deposits, including the compensating balance, then the effective annual rate would be further decreased.

Self-Test Questions

What are some different ways that banks can calculate interest on loans?

What is a compensating balance? What effect does a compensating balance requirement have on the effective interest rate on a loan?

CHOOSING A BANK

Individuals whose only contact with their bank is through the use of its checking services generally choose a bank for the convenience of its location and the competitive cost of its services. However, a business that borrows from banks must look at other criteria, and a potential borrower seeking banking relations should recognize that important differences exist among banks. Some of these differences are considered next.

Willingness to Assume Risks

Banks have different basic policies toward risk. Some banks are inclined to follow relatively conservative lending practices, while others engage in what are properly termed "creative banking practices." These policies reflect partly the personalities of officers of the bank and partly the characteristics of the bank's deposit liabilities. Thus, a bank with fluctuating deposit liabilities in a static community will tend to be a conservative lender, while a bank whose deposits are growing with little interruption may follow "liberal" credit policies. A large bank with broad diversification over geographic regions or across industries can obtain the benefit of combining and averaging risks. Thus, marginal credit risks that might be unacceptable to a small bank or to a specialized unit bank can be pooled by a branch banking system to reduce the overall risk of a group of marginal accounts.

Advice and Counsel

Some bank loan officers are active in providing counsel and in stimulating development loans to firms in their early and formative years. Certain banks have specialized departments which make loans to firms expected to grow and thus to become more important customers. The personnel of these departments can provide valuable counseling to customers: The bankers' experience with other firms in growth situations may enable them to spot, and then to warn their customers about, developing problems.

Loyalty to Customers

Banks differ in the extent to which they will support the activities of the borrower in bad times. This characteristic is referred to as the degree of *loyalty* of the bank. Some banks may put great pressure on a business to liquidate its loans when the firm's outlook becomes clouded, whereas others will stand by the firm and work diligently to help it get back on its feet. An especially dramatic illustration of this point was Bank of America's bailout of Memorex Corporation. The bank could have forced Memorex into bankruptcy, but instead it loaned the company additional capital and helped it survive a bad period. Memorex's stock price subsequently rose on the New York Stock Exchange from $1.50 to $68, so Bank of America's help was indeed substantial.

Specialization

Banks differ greatly in their degrees of loan specialization. Larger banks have separate departments that specialize in different kinds of loans—for example, real estate loans, farm loans, and commercial loans. Within these broad categories, there may be a specialization by line of business, such as steel, machinery, cattle, or textiles. The strengths of banks are also likely to reflect the nature of the business and the economic environment in which they operate. For example, some California banks have become specialists in lending to electronics companies, while many Midwestern banks are agricultural specialists. A sound firm can obtain more creative cooperation and more active support by going to the bank that has the greatest experience and familiarity with its particular type of business. The financial manager should therefore choose a bank with care. A bank that is excellent for one firm may be unsatisfactory for another.

Maximum Loan Size

The size of a bank can be an important factor. Since the maximum loan a bank can make to any one customer is limited to 15 percent of the bank's capital accounts (capital stock plus retained earnings), it is generally not appropriate for large firms to develop borrowing relationships with small banks.

Other Services

Banks also provide cash management services (see Chapter 20), assist with electronic funds transfers, help firms obtain foreign exchange, and the like, and such services should be taken into account when selecting a bank. Also, if the firm is a small business whose manager owns most of its stock, the bank's willingness and ability to provide trust and estate services should also be considered.

Self-Test Question

What are some of the factors that should be considered when choosing a bank?

COMMERCIAL PAPER

Commercial paper is a type of unsecured promissory note issued by large, strong firms, and it is sold primarily to other business firms, to insurance companies, to pension funds, to money market mutual funds, and to banks. Although the amount of commercial paper outstanding is smaller than bank loans outstanding, this form of financing has grown rapidly in recent years. In early 1990, there was approximately $500 billion of commercial paper outstanding, versus about $650 billion of bank loans to businesses.

Maturity and Cost

Maturities of commercial paper generally vary from one to nine months, with an average of about five months.[11] The rate on commercial paper fluctuates with supply and demand conditions — it is determined in the marketplace, varying daily as conditions change. Recently, commercial paper rates have generally ranged from 1½ to 2½ percentage points below the stated prime rate, and about ½ of a percentage point above the T-bill rate. For example, on February 22, 1990, the average rate on 3-month commercial paper was 8.1 percent, the stated prime rate was 10.0 percent, and the 6-month T-bill rate was about 7.8 percent. Also, since compensating balances are not required for commercial paper, the *effective* cost differential may be wider.[12]

---

[11]The maximum maturity without SEC registration is 270 days. Also, commercial paper can only be sold to "sophisticated" investors; otherwise, SEC registration would be required even for maturities of 270 days or less.

[12]However, this factor is offset to some extent by the fact that firms issuing commercial paper are required by commercial paper dealers to have unused revolving credit agreements to back up their outstanding commercial paper, and fees must be paid on these lines. In other words, to sell $1 million of commercial paper, a firm must have revolving credit available to pay off the paper when it matures, and commitment fees on this unused credit line (about ½ percent) increase the effective cost of the paper. Note also that commercial paper and T-bill rates are quoted on a discount basis, whereas the prime rate is on an annual yield basis.

Use of Commercial Paper

The use of commercial paper is restricted to a comparatively small number of concerns that are exceptionally good credit risks. Dealers prefer to handle the paper of firms whose net worth is $100 million or more and whose annual borrowing exceeds $10 million. One potential problem with commercial paper is that a debtor who is in temporary financial difficulty may receive little help, because commercial paper dealings are generally less personal than are bank relationships. Thus, banks are generally more able and willing to help a good customer weather a temporary storm than is a commercial paper dealer. On the other hand, using commercial paper permits a corporation to tap a wide range of credit sources, including financial institutions outside its own area and industrial corporations across the country, and this can reduce interest costs.

Self-Test Questions

What is commercial paper?

What types of companies can use commercial paper to meet their short-term financing needs?

How does the cost of commercial paper compare to the cost of short-term bank loans? To the cost of Treasury bills?

SECURED SHORT-TERM LOANS

Thus far, we have not addressed the question of whether or not loans are secured. Commercial paper loans are never secured by specific collateral, but all the other types of loans can be if this is deemed necessary or desirable. Given a choice, it is ordinarily better to borrow on an unsecured basis, since the bookkeeping costs of secured loans are often high. However, weak firms may find (1) that they can borrow only if they put up some type of security to protect the lender, or (2) that by using some security they can borrow at a much lower rate.

Several different kinds of collateral can be employed, including marketable stocks or bonds, land or buildings, equipment, inventory, and accounts receivable. Marketable securities make excellent collateral, but few firms hold portfolios of stocks and bonds. Similarly, both real property (land and buildings) and equipment are good forms of collateral, but they are generally used as security for long-term loans rather than for short-term loans. Therefore, most secured short-term business borrowing involves the use of accounts receivable and/or inventories as collateral.

To understand the use of security, consider the case of an Orlando hardware dealer who wanted to modernize and expand his store. He requested a $200,000 bank loan. After examining his business's financial statements, the bank indicated (1) that it would lend him a maximum of $100,000, and (2) that the interest rate would be 13 percent. The owner had a substantial personal portfolio of stocks, so he offered to put up $300,000 of high-quality stocks to support the $200,000 loan. The bank then granted the full $200,000 loan, and at a rate of only 11 percent. The store owner might also have used his inventories or receivables as security for the loan, but processing costs would have been high.

In the past, state laws varied greatly with regard to the use of security in financing. Today, however, all states except Louisiana operate under the *Uniform Commercial Code,* which standardizes and simplifies the procedure for establishing loan security. The heart of the Uniform Commercial Code is the *Security Agreement,* a standardized document, or form, on which the specific assets that are pledged are stated. The assets can be items of equipment, accounts receivable, or inventories. Secured short-term loans involve quite a bit of paperwork and administrative costs, which makes them relatively expensive. However, this is often the only type of financing available to weaker firms. In the following two sections, we briefly describe procedures for using accounts receivable and inventories as security for short-term credit.[13]

Accounts Receivable Financing

Accounts receivable financing involves either the pledging of receivables or the selling of receivables (factoring). The *pledging of accounts receivable* is characterized by the fact that the lender not only has a claim against the receivables but also has recourse to the borrower: If the person or the firm that bought the goods does not pay, the selling firm must take the loss. Therefore, the risk of default on the accounts receivable pledged remains with the borrower. Also, the buyer of the goods is not ordinarily notified about the pledging of the receivables, and the financial institution that lends on the security of accounts receivable is generally either a commercial bank or one of the large industrial finance companies such as General Electric Capital Corporation (GECC).

Factoring, or *selling accounts receivable,* involves the purchase of accounts receivable by the lender, generally without recourse to the borrower. Under factoring, the buyer of the goods is typically notified of the transfer and is asked to make payment directly to the financial institution. Since the factoring firm assumes the risk of default on bad accounts, it must do a credit check. Accordingly, factors can provide not only money but also a credit department for the borrower. Incidentally, the same banks and other financial institutions that make loans against pledged receivables also serve as factors. Thus, depending on the circumstances and the wishes of the borrower, a financial institution will provide either form of receivables financing.[14]

---

[13]For a more complete description of accounts receivable and inventory financing, see Eugene F. Brigham and Louis C. Gapenski, *Intermediate Financial Management,* 3rd ed., Chapter 16.

[14]In the latter half of the 1980s, several large companies such as Ford and General Motors began to sell "collateralized bonds" secured by packages of accounts receivable. The holders of these bonds receive monthly payments made with cash flows from the repayment of auto or other loans. The bonds have relatively short maturities, and the principal buyers are pension funds and other institutional investors. These new securities serve the same purpose as traditional receivables financing, but they have opened a whole new source of funds to corporate borrowers.

Inventory Financing

A substantial amount of credit is secured by business inventories. If a firm is a relatively good credit risk, the mere existence of the inventory may be a sufficient basis for an unsecured loan. However, if the firm is a relatively poor risk, the lending institution may insist upon security, which can take the form of a blanket lien against all inventory or either trust receipts or warehouse receipts against specific inventory items.

The *inventory blanket lien* gives the lending institution a lien against all the borrower's inventories. However, the borrower is free to sell inventories, so the value of the collateral can be reduced below the level that existed when the loan was granted. Because of the inherent weakness of the blanket lien, another procedure for inventory financing was developed—the *security instrument* (also called a *trust receipt*), which is an instrument acknowledging that the goods are held in trust for the lender. When trust receipts are used, the borrowing firm, upon receiving funds from the lender, signs and delivers a trust receipt for the goods. The goods can be stored in a public warehouse or held on the premises of the borrower. The trust receipt acknowledges that the goods are held in trust for the lender and that any proceeds from the sale of trust goods must be transmitted to the lender at the end of each day. Automobile dealer financing is one of the best examples of trust receipt financing.

Like trust receipts, *warehouse receipt* financing uses inventory as security. A *public warehouse* is an independent third-party operation engaged in the business of storing goods. Items which must age, such as tobacco and liquor, are often financed and stored in public warehouses. The borrower cannot remove the goods until the lender has been repaid, so the warehouse operation protects the lender. However, at times a public warehouse is not practical because of the bulkiness of goods and the expense of transporting them to and from the borrower's premises. In such cases, a *field warehouse* may be established at the borrower's place of business. To provide inventory supervision, the lending institution employs a third party, a field warehousing company, which acts as an agent for the lending institution.

Self-Test Questions

What are some types of current assets that are pledged as security for short-term loans?

What is the difference between pledging receivables and factoring receivables?

Explain the differences among blanket liens, trust receipts, and warehouse receipts.

SUMMARY

This chapter examined short-term financial planning and financing. The key concepts covered are listed next.

- The essence of short-term financial planning is assuring that the optimal amount of current assets is on hand, and that the firm's liquidity position is adequate to meet cash obligations as they become due.

- The *inventory conversion period* is the average length of time required to convert raw materials into finished goods and then to sell them.

- The *receivables collection period* is the average length of time required to convert the firm's receivables into cash, and it is equal to the days sales outstanding.

- The *payables deferral period* is the average length of time between the purchase of raw materials and labor, and paying for them.

- The *cash conversion cycle* is the length of time between paying for raw materials purchased and receiving cash from the sale of finished goods. The cash conversion cycle can be calculated as follows:

$$
\begin{array}{c}
\text{Inventory} \\
\text{conversion} \\
\text{period}
\end{array}
+
\begin{array}{c}
\text{Receivables} \\
\text{conversion} \\
\text{period}
\end{array}
-
\begin{array}{c}
\text{Payables} \\
\text{deferral} \\
\text{period}
\end{array}
=
\begin{array}{c}
\text{Cash} \\
\text{conversion.} \\
\text{cycle}
\end{array}
$$

- Under a *relaxed current asset investment policy,* a firm holds relatively large amounts of each type of current asset. A *restricted current asset investment policy* entails holding minimal amounts of these items.

- *Permanent current assets* are those current assets that the firm holds even during slack times, whereas *temporary current assets* are the additional current assets that are needed during seasonal or cyclical peaks. The methods used to finance permanent and temporary current assets define the firm's *current asset financing policy.*

- A *moderate* approach to current asset financing involves matching, to the extent possible, the maturities of assets and liabilities, so that temporary current assets are financed with short-term nonspontaneous debt and permanent current assets and fixed assets are financed with long-term debt or equity, plus spontaneous debt. Under an *aggressive* approach, some permanent current assets and perhaps even some fixed assets are financed with short-term debt. A *conservative* approach would be to use long-term capital to finance all permanent assets and some of the temporary current assets.

- The advantages of short-term credit are (1) the *speed* with which short-term loans can be arranged, (2) increased *flexibility,* and (3) the fact that short-term *interest rates* are generally *lower* than long-term rates. The principal disadvantage of short-term credit is the *extra risk* that the borrower must bear because (1) the lender can demand payment on short notice and (2) the cost of the loan will increase if interest rates rise.

- *Short-term credit* is defined as any liability originally scheduled for payment within one year. The four major sources of short-term credit are (1) accruals, (2) accounts payable, (3) loans from commercial banks and finance companies, and (4) commercial paper.

- *Accruals,* which are continually recurring short-term liabilities, represent free, spontaneous credit.

- *Accounts payable,* or *trade credit,* is the largest category of short-term debt. This credit arises spontaneously as a result of purchases on credit. Firms should use all the *free trade credit* they can obtain, but they should use *costly trade credit* only if it is less expensive than other forms of short-term debt. Suppliers often offer discounts to customers who pay within a stated discount period. The following equation may be used to calculate the approximate percentage cost, on an annual basis, of not taking discounts:

$$\begin{array}{c} \text{Approximate} \\ \text{percentage} \\ \text{cost} \end{array} = \frac{\text{Discount percent}}{100 - \begin{array}{c}\text{Discount}\\\text{percent}\end{array}} \times \frac{360}{\begin{array}{c}\text{Days credit}\\\text{is outstanding}\end{array} - \begin{array}{c}\text{Discount}\\\text{period}\end{array}}.$$

- *Bank loans* are an important source of short-term credit. Interest on bank loans may be quoted as *simple interest, discount interest,* or *add-on interest.* The effective rate on a discount or add-on loan always exceeds the stated nominal rate.

- When a bank loan is approved, a *promissory note* is signed. It specifies: (1) the amount borrowed, (2) the percentage interest rate, (3) the repayment schedule, (4) the collateral, and (5) any other conditions to which the parties have agreed.

- Banks sometimes require borrowers to maintain *compensating balances,* which are deposit requirements set at between 10 and 20 percent of the loan amount. Compensating balances raise the effective rate of interest on bank loans.

- *Lines of credit* are formal or informal understandings between the bank and the borrower indicating the maximum amount of credit the bank will extend to the borrower.

- A *revolving credit agreement* is a formal line of credit often used by large firms; it involves a *commitment fee.*

- *Commercial paper* is unsecured short-term debt issued by large, financially strong corporations. Although the cost of commercial paper is lower than the cost of bank loans, commercial paper's maturity is limited to 270 days, and it can be used only by large firms with exceptionally strong credit ratings.

- Sometimes a borrower will find that it is necessary to borrow on a *secured basis,* in which case the borrower pledges assets such as real estate, securities, equipment, inventories, or accounts receivable as collateral for the loan.

- Accounts receivable financing involves either *pledging* or *factoring receivables.* Under a pledging arrangement the lender not only gets a claim against the receivables but also has recourse to the borrower. Factoring receivables involves the purchase of accounts receivable by the lender, generally without recourse to the borrower.

- There are three primary methods of inventory financing: An *inventory blanket lien* gives the lender a lien against all of the borrower's inventories. A *trust receipt* is an instrument that acknowledges that the goods are held in trust for the lender. *Warehouse receipt financing* is an arrangement under which the lender employs a third party to exercise control over the borrower's inventory and to act as the lender's agent.

In the next two chapters we examine short-term financial planning in more detail. In Chapter 20 we discuss cash and marketable securities, and in Chapter 21 we cover accounts receivable and inventory.

Questions

19-1 Define each of the following terms:
   a. Cash conversion cycle; cash conversion cycle model
   b. Current asset investment policies; current asset financing policies
   c. Permanent current assets versus temporary current assets
   d. "Flexibility" as a reason for using short-term debt
   e. Trade credit; free trade credit; costly trade credit
   f. "Stretching" accounts payable
   g. Promissory note; line of credit; revolving credit agreement
   h. Compensating balance; a compensating balance which *does not* increase the cost of a loan
   i. Prime rate
   j. Simple interest; discount interest; add-on interest; revolving credit interest
   k. Commercial paper; commercial paper rate
   l. Secured loan; trust receipt; field warehouse; pledging; factoring

19-2 "Firms can control their accruals within fairly wide limits; depending on the cost of accruals, financing from this source can be increased or decreased." Discuss.

19-3 Is it true that both trade credit and accruals represent a spontaneous source of capital to finance growth? Explain.

19-4 Is it true that most firms are able to obtain some "free" trade credit, and that additional trade credit is often available, but at a cost? Explain.

19-5 What kinds of firms use commercial paper? Could Pappa Gus's Corner Grocery borrow in the commercial paper market?

19-6 From the standpoint of the borrower, is long-term or short-term credit riskier? Explain. Would it ever make sense to borrow on a short-term basis if short-term rates were above long-term rates?

19-7 If long-term credit exposes a borrower to less risk, why would people or firms borrow on a short-term basis?

19-8 Suppose a firm can borrow at the prime rate and also sell commercial paper.
   a. If the prime rate is 9 percent, what is a reasonable estimate for the cost of commercial paper?
   b. If a substantial cost differential exists, why might a firm such as this one actually borrow some of its funds from both markets?

Self-Test Problem   (Solutions Appear in Appendix D)

ST-1 **(Trade credit versus bank credit)** The Boisjoly Company buys on terms of 1/10, net 30, but it has not been taking discounts and has actually been paying in 60 days rather than 30 days. The firm's balance sheet follows (in thousands of dollars):

Cash	$ 50	Accounts payable[a]	$ 500
Accounts receivable	450	Notes payable	50
Inventories	750	Accruals	50
Current assets	$1,250	Current liabilities	$ 600
		Long-term debt	150
Fixed assets	750	Common equity	1,250
Total assets	$2,000	Total claims	$2,000

[a]Stated net of discounts.

Now the firm's suppliers are threatening to stop shipments unless the company begins making prompt payments (that is, pays in 30 days or less). The firm can borrow on a 1-year note (call this a current liability) from its bank at a rate of 15 percent, discount interest, with a 20 percent compensating balance required. (All of the cash now on hand is needed for transactions; it cannot be used as part of the compensating balance.)

a.   Determine what action the firm should take by calculating (1) the cost of nonfree trade credit, and (2) the cost of the bank loan.

b.   Based on your decision in Part a, construct a pro forma balance sheet. (Hint: You will need to include an account called "prepaid interest" under current assets.)

Problems

19-1 **(Cost of trade credit)** Suppose a firm makes purchases of $3,000,000 per year under terms of 2/10, net 30. It takes discounts.

a.   What is the average amount of accounts payable, net of discounts? (Assume the $3.0 million purchases are net of discounts; that is, gross purchases are $3,061,224, discounts are $61,224, and net purchases are $3.0 million. Also, use 360 days in a year.)

b.   Is there a cost for the trade credit it uses?

c.   If it did not take discounts, what would be its average payables, and what would be the cost of this nonfree trade credit?

d.   What would its cost of not taking discounts be if it "stretched" its payments to 40 days?

19-2 **(Trade credit versus bank credit)** O'Connor Corporation projects an increase in sales from $2 million to $2.5 million, but the company needs an additional $300,000 of current assets to support this expansion. The money can be obtained from the bank at an interest rate of 10 percent. Alternatively, the firm can finance the expansion by no longer taking discounts, thus increasing accounts payable. O'Connor purchases under terms of 1/10, net 30, but it currently can delay payment for an additional 30 days, paying in 60 days and thus becoming 30 days past due, without a penalty.

a.   Based strictly on an interest rate comparison, how should the firm finance its expansion?

b.   What additional qualitative factors should be considered in reaching a decision?

19-3 **(Accounts payable)** The Kretovich Copper Corporation had sales of $3,000,000 last year and earned a 5 percent return, after taxes, on sales. Although its terms of purchase are 20 days, its accounts payable represent 60 days' purchases. Suppliers are threatening to cut off the firm's purchases, so the firm's president is seeking to increase the company's bank borrowings in order to become current (that is, have 20 days payables outstanding) in meeting its trade obligations. The company's balance sheet is shown below (in thousands of dollars):

Cash	$ 25	Accounts payable	$ 300
Accounts receivable	125	Bank loans	250
Inventory	650	Accruals	125
Current assets	$ 800	Current liabilities	$ 675
Land and buildings	250	Mortgage on real estate	250
Equipment	250	Common stock, par 10¢	125
		Retained earnings	250
Total assets	$1,300	Total claims	$1,300

a. How much financing is needed to eliminate past-due accounts payable?

b. Would you as a bank loan officer make the loan? Why?

c. Suppose the firm had these choices for raising the needed capital:

   (1) Borrow from the bank on a line of credit. The loan would be written as a 90-day, discount interest loan with a nominal rate of 12 percent. A 20 percent compensating balance would be required.

   (2) Negotiate with suppliers and arrange to buy on terms of 0.75/10, net 30.

   (3) Sell subordinated convertible debentures with a 10 percent annual coupon rate. The firm's stock currently sells for $30; the conversion price would be $35; the expected growth rate is 10 percent; and the convertibles would not be callable for 10 years, and then they would be callable at par. The convertibles would initially sell at par.

   Which of these borrowing methods would you recommend, and why? What would Kretovich's key ratios be just after the new financing had been put into effect?

19-4 **(Cash conversion cycle)** A firm has an average age of accounts receivable of 53 days, an average age of accounts payable of 42 days, and an average age of inventory of 70 days.

a. What is the length of the firm's cash conversion cycle?

b. If the firm's annual sales are $1,323,000, what is its investment in accounts receivable?

19-5 **(Alternative credit sources)** Water Park, Incorporated (WPI), estimates that as a result of the seasonal nature of its business, it will require an additional $350,000 of cash for the month of July. WPI has the following four alternatives available for raising the needed funds:

   (1) Establish a 1-year line of credit for $350,000 with a commercial bank. The commitment fee will be 0.5 percent per year on the unused portion, and the interest charge on the used funds will be 12 percent per year. Assume that the funds are needed only in July, and that there are 30 days in July and 360 days in the year.

   (2) Forego the trade discount of 3/10, net 40, on $350,000 of purchases during July.

   (3) Issue $350,000 of 30-day commercial paper at an 11.4 percent annual interest rate. The total transactions fee, including the cost of a backup credit line, on using commercial paper is 0.5 percent of the amount of the issue.

   (4) Issue $350,000 of 60-day commercial paper at an 11.0 percent annual interest rate, plus a transactions fee of 0.5 percent. Since the funds are required for only 30 days, the excess funds ($350,000) can be invested in marketable securities for the month of August earning 10.8 percent annually. The total transactions cost of purchasing and selling the marketable securities is 0.4 percent of the amount of the issue.

a. What is the cost of each financing arrangement?

b. Is the source with the lowest expected cost necessarily the one to select? Why or why not?

19-6 **(Working capital financing policy)** Three companies — Aggressive, Between, and Conservative — have different working capital management policies as implied by their names. For example, Aggressive employs only minimal current assets, and it finances almost entirely with current liabilities plus equity. This "tight-ship" approach has a dual effect. It keeps total assets low, which tends to increase return on assets; but because of stock-outs and credit rejections, total sales are reduced, and since inventory is ordered more frequently and in smaller quantities, variable costs are increased. Condensed balance sheets for the three companies are presented next.

	Aggressive	Between	Conservative
Current assets	$150,000	$200,000	$300,000
Fixed assets	200,000	200,000	200,000
Total assets	$350,000	$400,000	$500,000
Current liabilities (cost = 12%)	$200,000	$100,000	$ 50,000
Long-term debt (cost = 10%)	0	100,000	200,000
Total debt	$200,000	$200,000	$250,000
Equity	150,000	200,000	250,000
Total claims	$350,000	$400,000	$500,000
Current ratio	0.75:1	2:1	6:1

The cost of goods sold functions for the three firms are as follows:

$$\text{Cost of goods sold} = \text{Fixed costs} + \text{Variable costs.}$$

Aggressive: Cost of goods sold = $200,000 + 0.70(Sales).
Between: Cost of goods sold = $270,000 + 0.65(Sales).
Conservative: Cost of goods sold = $385,000 + 0.60(Sales).

Because of the working capital differences, sales for the three firms under different economic conditions are expected to vary as indicated here:

	Aggressive	Between	Conservative
Strong economy	$1,200,000	$1,250,000	$1,300,000
Average economy	900,000	1,000,000	1,150,000
Weak economy	700,000	800,000	1,050,000

a.   Construct income statements for each company for strong, average, and weak economies using the following format:

- Sales

- Less cost of goods sold

- Earnings before interest and taxes (EBIT)

- Less interest expense

- Taxable income

- Less taxes (at 40%)

- Net income

b.   Compare the basic earning power (EBIT/Assets) and return on equity (Net income/Equity) for the companies. Which company is best in a strong economy? In an average economy? In a weak economy?

(Do Parts c, d, and e only if you are using the computerized diskette.)

c.   Suppose, with sales at the normal-economy level, short-term interest rates rose to 25 percent. How would that affect the three firms?

d.   Suppose that because of production slowdowns caused by inventory shortages, the aggressive company's variable cost ratio rises to 80 percent. What would happen to its ROE, assuming a normal economy and a short-term rate of 12 percent?

e.   What considerations for management of current assets are indicated by this problem?

Mini Case

Lee Barenbaum was recently hired as the financial manager of Discount Computer Company (DCC), which owns five computer retail stores. His first assignment is to develop a rational current asset investment and financing policy, and he has identified three potential alternative policies: (1) a "lean and mean" (LM) policy which calls for a minimum amount of current assets and for the use of a substantial amount of short-term debt, (2) a "fat cat" (FC) policy which calls for a high level of current assets and a primary reliance on long-term as opposed to short-term debt, and (3) a moderate policy which falls between the two extremes. Barenbaum estimates that DCC's balance sheet would look like this under the three policies (in thousands of dollars):

	Balance Sheet		
	LM	**Moderate**	**FC**
Current assets	$300	$400	$500
Net fixed assets	400	400	400
Total assets	$700	$800	$900
Short-term debt (8.0%)	$400	$200	$ 0
Long-term debt (10.0%)	0	200	400
Common equity	300	400	500
Total claims	$700	$800	$900

Assume that short-term debt would have a cost of 8 percent, while long-term debt would cost 10 percent regardless of the policy chosen. (In reality, the policies would lead to different debt costs because of differences in financial risk.) Variable costs are expected to be 60 percent of sales regardless of which policy is adopted, but fixed costs would increase if more current assets were held because of higher storage and insurance costs. Annual fixed costs would be $200,000 under a "lean and mean" policy, $210,000 with a moderate policy, and $220,000 under a "fat cat" policy.

Because its current asset policy would influence DCC's ability to respond in a timely manner to its customers' needs, expected sales would vary under different economic scenarios as follows (in thousands of dollars):

	Sales under Each Current Asset Policy		
Economy	**LM**	**Moderate**	**FC**
Strong	$1,000	$1,050	$1,100
Average	800	900	1,000
Weak	600	750	900

As Barenbaum's assistant, you have been asked to draft a report which answers the following questions:

a.   (1) What is the cash conversion cycle?

(2) Suppose DCC has an inventory conversion period of 90 days; that is, on average it takes 90 days from ordering/receipt of inventory to sale of the item. Once a sale is

made, payment is, on average, received in 30 days. Finally, DCC pays for its inventories, on average, 20 days after ordering/receipt. What is DCC's cash conversion cycle?

(3) How can Barenbaum use the concept of the cash conversion cycle to help improve the firm's short-term financial management?

b.   What are the two basic issues that must be decided in formulating current asset policy? Explain how a firm that is willing to take relatively high risks would set these two policies, and then contrast them with the policies of a highly risk-averse firm.

c.   Construct income statements for DCC for the "lean and mean" (LM) policy, assuming an average economy. Also, calculate ROE. Use the following format (in thousands of dollars):

Income Statements with Each Policy

	LM	Moderate	FC
Sales		$900	$1,000
Cost of goods sold	_____	750	820
EBIT		$150	$ 180
Interest expense	_____	36	40
Taxable income		$114	$ 140
Taxes (40%)	_____	46	56
Net income	══════	$ 68	$ 84
ROE	══════	17.1%	16.8%

d.   The ROEs under a weak and strong economy are shown below:

		ROE	
Economy	**LM**	**Moderate**	**FC**
Weak	1.6%	8.1%	12.0%
Strong	33.6	26.1	21.6

Explain in words why these results occur.

e.   Assume that there is a 50 percent chance for an average economy and a 25 percent chance for either a strong or a weak economy. What is the *expected* ROE under each policy? Are the policies equally risky? Explain.

f.   Now assume that, after Barenbaum has established DCC's current asset policy, the Federal Reserve reacts to increasing inflationary expectations and begins to tighten monetary policy. As a result, long-term rates increase slightly, but short-term rates climb rapidly. If DCC were following the "fat cat" policy, it would have locked in its 10.0 percent long-term debt cost. However, if it were following the "lean and mean" policy, and if short-term rates increased by 4 percentage points, then this would push DCC's short-term debt cost up to 12.0 percent. What impact would this have on the firm's profitability under each of the current asset policies, in an average economy, as measured by ROE?

g.   Like most small companies, DCC has three primary sources of short-term debt: trade credit, bank loans, and accruals. One supplier, which supplies DCC with $25,000 of materials a year (gross purchases), offers terms of 3/10, net 60.

(1) What are DCC's net average daily purchases from this supplier?

(2) What is the average level of DCC's accounts payable to this supplier if the discount is taken? If the discount is not taken? What are the amounts of free trade credit and costly trade credit under each discount policy?

(3) What is the approximate cost of the costly trade credit? What is the effective annual cost?

h. In discussing a possible loan with the firm's banker, Barenbaum has found that the bank is willing to lend DCC up to $400,000 for one year at an 8 percent nominal, or stated, rate. However, he forgot to ask what the specific terms would be.

(1) Assume that the firm would borrow $400,000. What would be the effective interest rate if the loan were a simple interest loan? If the loan had been for 6 months rather than for a year, would that have affected the effective annual rate?

(2) What would be the effective rate if the loan were a discount interest loan? What would be the face amount of a loan large enough to net the firm $400,000 in usable funds?

(3) Now assume that the terms call for an installment (add-on) loan with equal monthly payments. What would be (a) the monthly payment, (b) the approximate cost rate of the loan, and (c) the effective annual rate?

(4) Now assume that the bank charges simple interest, but it requires the firm to maintain a 20 percent compensating balance. How much must DCC borrow to obtain its needed $400,000 yet still meet its compensating balance requirement? What is the effective annual rate on the loan?

(5) Now assume that the bank charges discount interest and also requires the compensating balance. How much must DCC borrow, and what is the effective annual rate under these terms?

(6) Now assume all the conditions in Part (4), that is, a 20 percent compensating balance on an 8 percent simple interest loan, but assume also that DCC has $50,000 of cash balances which it normally holds for transactions purposes and which can be used as part of the required compensating balance. How does this affect (a) the size of the required loan and (b) the effective cost of the loan?

i. What are accruals? What is the cost of accruals to DCC? How much accrual financing should DCC use? How much control does DCC have over its level of accruals?

j. What is commercial paper? Could DCC use commercial paper as a source of short-term financing? If it could, what would be the cost of this capital (approximately)?

k. What are secured short-term loans? What types of assets are normally used as security for short-term loans? Why do firms use secured financing?

(1) What is the procedure for pledging receivables? For factoring receivables?

(2) What are blanket liens? Trust receipts? Warehouse receipts?

Selected Additional References and Cases

The following books focus on short-term financial management:

Gallinger, George W., and P. Basil Healy, *Liquidity Analysis and Management* (Reading, Mass.: Addison-Wesley, 1987).

Hill, Ned C., and William L. Sartoris, *Short-Term Financial Management* (New York: Macmillan, 1988).

Smith, Keith V., and George W. Gallinger, *Readings on Short-term Financial Management* (St. Paul: West, 1988).

The following articles provide more information on short-term financial management:

Gentry, James A., "State of the Art of Short-Run Financial Management," *Financial Management,* Summer 1988, 41–57.

Gentry, James A., R. Vaidyanathan, and Hei Wai Lee, "A Weighted Cash Conversion Cycle," *Financial Management,* Spring 1990, 90–99.

Lambrix, R. J., and S. S. Singhvi, "Managing the Working Capital Cycle," *Financial Executive,* June 1979, 32–41.

Maier, Steven F., and James H. Vander Weide, "A Practical Approach to Short-Run Financial Planning," *Financial Management,* Winter 1978, 10–16.

Merville, Larry J., and Lee A. Tavis, "Optimal Working Capital Policies: A Chance-Constrained Programming Approach," *Journal of Financial and Quantitative Analysis,* January 1973, 47–60.

Smith, Keith V., and Brian Belt, "Working Capital Management in Practice: An Update," Krannert Graduate School of Management Working Paper Number 951, March 1989.

Yardini, Edward E., "A Portfolio-Balance Model of Corporate Working Capital," *Journal of Finance,* May 1979, 535–552.

For more on trade credit, see

Brosky, John J., *The Implicit Cost of Trade Credit and Theory of Optimal Terms of Sale* (New York: Credit Research Foundation, 1969).

Schwartz, Robert A., "An Economic Analysis of Trade," *Journal of Financial and Quantitative Analysis,* September 1974, 643–658.

For more on bank lending and commercial credit in general, see

Campbell, Tim S., "A Model of the Market for Lines of Credit," *Journal of Finance,* March 1978, 231–243.

Stone, Bernell K., "Allocating Credit Lines, Planned Borrowing, and Tangible Services over a Company's Banking System," *Financial Management,* Summer 1975, 65–78.

For a discussion of effective yields, see

Glasgo, Philip W., William J. Landes, and A. Frank Thompson, "Bank Discount, Coupon Equivalent, and Compound Yields," *Financial Management,* Autumn 1982, 80–84.

Finnerty, John D., "Bank Discount, Coupon Equivalent, and Compound Yields: Comment," *Financial Management,* Summer 1983, 40–44.

The following case is appropriate for use with this chapter:

Case 30, "Baxter Furniture Company," in the Brigham-Gapenski casebook, which illustrates how changes in current asset policy affect expected profitability and risk.

CHAPTER 20

Cash and Marketable Securities

Cash is the oil that lubricates the wheels of business. Without adequate oil, machines grind to a halt, and a business with inadequate cash will do likewise. On the other hand, carrying cash is expensive; since it is a non-earning asset, a firm that holds cash beyond its minimum requirements is lowering its potential earnings.

Cash management is developing into a very professional, highly refined activity. The following excerpt from a Union California Bank (UCB) advertisement illustrates what is involved:

> Using any lockbox will accelerate cash flow. But a UCB Lock Box System does it with maximum efficiency. One difference is our unique city-wide zip code system for California lockbox customers. It speeds the receipt of your lockbox mail by several hours.
>
> Another difference: We work around the clock, seven days a week. So you can be sure your funds will be deposited, regardless of absenteeism or seasonal work loads.
>
> A third difference: We're the only West Coast bank using helicopters to speed collections of checks, thus reducing float.
>
> Also, using our computerized optimization models, we can determine how many lockboxes you should use, where they should be located, and how much money you'll save with them.
>
> Finally—you need not keep idle cash balances to guard against a failure to receive expected payments or to be ready for unexpected outflows. We can arrange a line of credit for you, let you know by 11 A.M. how much (if any) you need to borrow to cover the checks that have cleared, and have the

money in your account by 4 P.M. Or, if your account has net inflows on a given day, we will use these funds to reduce your loan balance or to purchase securities, as you direct. With this service, you'll never have funds sitting idle.

The cost is surprisingly low. Call us, and let us show you how UCB can make your cash work harder.

For some companies, these ideas make good sense. However, firms sometimes go too far with their cash management systems. For example, the general practice in the securities brokerage business (until Merrill Lynch lost a major suit and agreed to stop doing it) was to write checks to customers located east of the Mississippi on a West Coast bank and checks to customers located west of the river on an East Coast bank. This slowed down payment of checks, deprived customers of the use of their money, and gave the brokerage firms the use of billions of dollars of their customers' money for extended periods of time. According to the SEC, this practice, although it increased brokerage firms' profits by millions of dollars each year, was "inconsistent with a broker-dealer's obligation to deal fairly with its customers."

APPROXIMATELY 1.5 percent of the average industrial firm's assets are held in the form of cash, which is defined as demand deposits plus currency. In addition, sizable holdings of near-cash short-term marketable securities such as U.S. Treasury bills (T-bills), bank certificates of deposit (CDs), money market funds, and floating rate preferred stock are often reported on corporations' financial statements. Moreover, cash and marketable securities balances vary widely both across industries and between firms within a given industry. In this chapter, we analyze the factors that determine firms' cash and marketable securities balances, and we describe the most commonly used types of marketable securities. The lessons to be learned from this chapter apply to the cash holdings of individuals and nonprofit organizations, including government agencies.

CASH MANAGEMENT

Cash is often called a "nonearning asset." It is needed to pay for labor and raw materials, to buy fixed assets, to pay taxes, to service debt, to pay dividends, and so on. However, cash itself (and also commercial checking accounts) earns no interest. Thus, the goal of the cash manager is to minimize the amount of cash the firm must hold in order to conduct its normal business activities, yet, at the same time, have sufficient cash (1) to take trade discounts, (2) to maintain its credit rating, and (3) to meet unexpected cash needs. We begin our discussion of cash management with the cash budget.

Self-Test Question

What is the goal of cash management?

THE CASH BUDGET

The firm estimates its needs for cash as a part of its general budgeting, or forecasting, process. First, it forecasts both fixed asset and inventory requirements, along with the times when payments must be made. This information is combined with projections about the delay in collecting accounts receivable, tax payment dates, dividend and interest payment dates, and so on. All of this information is summarized in the *cash budget,* which shows the firm's projected cash inflows and outflows over some specified period. Generally, firms use a monthly cash budget forecasted over the next year, plus a more detailed daily or weekly cash budget for the coming month. The monthly cash budget is used for planning purposes and the daily or weekly budget for actual cash control.

We shall illustrate the process with a monthly cash budget covering the last six months of 1991 for the Foxcraft Printing Company, a leading producer of greeting cards. Foxcraft's birthday and get-well cards are sold year-round, but the bulk of the company's sales occurs from July through November, with a peak in September, when retailers are stocking up for Christmas and New Year's. All sales are made on terms that allow a cash discount for payments made within 10 days, and if the discount is not taken, the full amount is due in 40 days. However, like most other companies, Foxcraft finds that some of its customers delay payment up to 90 days. Experience shows that on 20 percent of the sales, payment is made during the month in which the sale is made; on 70 percent of the sales, payment is made during the first month after the month of the sale; and on 10 percent of the sales, payment is made during the second month after the month of the sale. Foxcraft offers a 2 percent discount for payments received within 10 days of sales. Virtually all payments received in the month of sale are discount sales.

Rather than produce at a uniform rate throughout the year, Foxcraft prints cards immediately before they are required for delivery. Paper, ink, and other materials amount to 70 percent of sales, and these items are bought the month before the company expects to sell the finished product. Its own purchase terms permit Foxcraft to delay payment on purchases for one month. Accordingly, if July sales are forecasted at $10 million, then purchases during June will amount to $7 million, and this amount will actually be paid in July.

Such other cash expenditures as wages and rent are also built into the cash budget, and Foxcraft must make tax payments of $2 million on September 15 and on December 15, while payment for a new plant must be made in October. Assuming that the company's target cash balance is $2.5 million, and that it has $3 million on July 1, what are Foxcraft's monthly cash requirements for the period from July through December?[1]

---

[1]Setting the target cash balance is an important part of cash management. We will discuss this topic in the next section.

The monthly cash requirements are worked out in Table 20-1. Section I of the table provides a worksheet for calculating both collections on sales and payments on purchases. Line 1 gives the sales forecast for the period from May through December. (May and June sales are necessary to determine collections for July and August.) Next, on Lines 2 through 5 cash collections are given. Line 2 shows that 20 percent of the sales during any given month are collected during that month. Customers who pay in the first month, however, typically take the discount, so the cash collected in the month of sale is reduced by 2 percent; for example, collections during July for the $10 million of sales in that month will be 20 percent times sales less the 2 percent discount = (0.2)(0.98)($10,000,000) = $1,960,000. Line 3 shows the collections on the previous month's sales, or 70 percent of sales in the preceding month; for example, in July, 70 percent of the $5,000,000 June sales, or $3,500,000, will be collected. Line 4 gives collections from sales two months earlier, or 10 percent of sales in that month; for example, the July collections for May sales are (0.10)($5,000,000) = $500,000. The collections during each month are summed and shown on Line 5; thus, the July collections represent 20 percent of July sales (minus the discount) plus 70 percent of June sales plus 10 percent of May sales, or $5,960,000 in total.

Next, payments for purchases of raw materials are shown. July sales are forecasted at $10 million, so Foxcraft will purchase $7 million of materials in June (Line 6) and pay for these purchases in July (Line 7). Similarly, Foxcraft will purchase $10.5 million of materials in July to produce cards to meet August's forecasted sales of $15 million.

With Section I completed, Section II can be constructed. Cash from collections is shown on Line 8. Lines 9 through 14 list payments made during each month, and these payments are summed on Line 15. The difference between cash receipts and cash payments (Line 8 minus Line 15) is the net cash gain or loss during the month; for July there is a net cash loss of $2,140,000, as shown on Line 16.

In Section III, we first determine Foxcraft's cash balance at the start of each month, assuming no borrowing is done; this is shown on Line 17. We assume that Foxcraft will have $3 million on hand on July 1. The beginning cash balance (Line 17) is then added to the net cash gain or loss during the month (Line 16) to obtain the cumulative cash that would be on hand if no financing were done (Line 18); at the end of July, Foxcraft forecasts a cumulative cash balance of $860,000 in the absence of borrowing.

The target cash balance, $2.5 million, is then subtracted from the cumulative cash balance to determine the firm's borrowing requirements, shown in parentheses, or its surplus cash. Because Foxcraft expects to have cumulative cash, as shown on Line 18, of only $860,000 in July, it will have to borrow $1,640,000 to bring the cash account up to the target balance of $2,500,000. Assuming that this amount is indeed borrowed, loans outstanding will total $1,640,000 at the end of July. (We assume that Foxcraft did not have any loans outstanding on July 1 because its beginning cash balance exceeded the target balance.) The cash surplus or required loan balance is given on Line 20; a positive value indicates a cash surplus, whereas a negative value indicates a loan requirement. Note that the surplus cash or loan requirement shown on Line 20 is a *cumulative amount*. Thus, Foxcraft must borrow

Table 20-1 Foxcraft Printing Company: Cash Budget (Thousands of Dollars)

	May	Jun	Jul	Aug	Sep	Oct	Nov	Dec
I. Collections and Purchases Worksheet								
(1) Sales (gross)[a]	$5,000	$5,000	$10,000	$15,000	$20,000	$10,000	$10,000	$5,000
Collections:								
(2) During month of sale: (0.2)(0.98)(month's sales)			1,960	2,940	3,920	1,960	1,960	980
(3) During first month after sale: 0.7 (previous month's sales)			3,500	7,000	10,500	14,000	7,000	7,000
(4) During second month after sale: 0.1 (sales 2 months ago)			500	500	1,000	1,500	2,000	1,000
(5) Total collections (2+3+4)			$ 5,960	$10,440	$15,420	$17,460	$10,960	$8,980
Purchases:								
(6) 0.7 (next month's sales)		$7,000	$10,500	$14,000	$ 7,000	$ 7,000	$ 3,500	
(7) Payments (1-month lag)			$ 7,000	$10,500	$14,000	$ 7,000	$ 7,000	$3,500
II. Cash Gain or Loss for Month								
(8) Collections (from Section I)			$ 5,960	$10,440	$15,420	$17,460	$10,960	$8,980
(9) Purchases (from Section I)			$ 7,000	$10,500	$14,000	$ 7,000	$ 7,000	$3,500
(10) Wages and salaries			750	1,000	1,250	750	750	500
(11) Rent			250	250	250	250	250	250
(12) Other expenses			100	150	200	100	100	50
(13) Taxes					2,000			2,000
(14) Payment for plant construction						5,000		
(15) Total payments			$ 8,100	$11,900	$17,700	$13,100	$ 8,100	$6,300
(16) Net cash gain (loss) during month (Line 8 − Line 15)			($ 2,140)	($ 1,460)	($ 2,280)	$ 4,360	$ 2,860	$2,680
III. Cash Surplus or Loan Requirement								
(17) Cash at start of month if no borrowing is done[b]			$ 3,000	$ 860	($ 600)	($ 2,880)	$ 1,480	$4,340
(18) Cumulative cash (cash at start, +gain or −loss = Line 16 + Line 17)			$ 860	($ 600)	($ 2,880)	$ 1,480	$ 4,340	$7,020
(19) Target cash balance			2,500	2,500	2,500	2,500	2,500	2,500
(20) Cumulative surplus cash or loans outstanding to maintain $2,500 target cash balance: (Line 18 − Line 19)[c]			($ 1,640)	($ 3,100)	($ 5,380)	($ 1,020)	$ 1,840	$4,520

[a]Although the budget period is July through December, sales and purchases data for May and June are needed to determine collections and payments during July and August.

[b]The amount shown on Line 17 for the first budget period month, the $3,000 balance on July 1, is assumed to be on hand initially. The values shown for each of the following months on Line 17 are equal to the cumulative cash as shown on Line 18 for the preceding month; for example, the $860 shown on Line 17 for August is taken from Line 18 in the July column.

[c]When the target cash balance of $2,500 (Line 19) is deducted from the cumulative cash balance (Line 18), a resulting negative figure on Line 20 represents a required loan, whereas a positive figure represents surplus cash. Loans are required from July through October, and surpluses are expected during November and December. Note also that firms can borrow or pay off loans on a daily basis, so the $1,640 borrowed during July would be done on a daily basis, as needed, and during October the $5,380 loan that existed at the beginning of the month would be reduced daily to the $1,020 ending balance, which in turn would be completely paid off during November.

$1,640,000 in July; it has a cash shortfall during August of $1,460,000 as reported on Line 16, so its total loan requirement at the end of August is $1,640,000 + $1,460,000 = $3,100,000, as reported on Line 20. Foxcraft's arrangement with the bank permits it to increase its outstanding loans on a daily basis, up to a prearranged maximum, just as you could increase the amount you owe on a credit card. Foxcraft will use any surplus funds it generates to pay off its loans, and because the loan can be paid down at any time, on a daily basis, the firm will never have both a cash surplus and an outstanding loan balance.

This same procedure is used in the following months. Sales will peak in September, accompanied by increased payments for purchases, wages, and other items. Receipts from sales will also go up, but the firm will still be left with a $2,280,000 net cash outflow during the month. The total loan requirement at the end of September will hit a peak of $5,380,000, the cumulative cash plus the target cash balance. This amount is also equal to the $3,100,000 needed at the end of August plus the $2,280,000 cash deficit for September.

Sales, purchases, and payments for past purchases will fall sharply in October, but collections will be the highest of any month because they will reflect the high September sales. As a result, Foxcraft will enjoy a healthy $4,360,000 net cash gain during October. This net gain can be used to pay off borrowings, so loans outstanding will decline by $4,360,000, to $1,020,000.

Foxcraft will have another cash surplus in November, which will permit it to pay off all of its loans. In fact, the company is expected to have $1,840,000 in surplus cash by the month's end, and another cash surplus in December will swell the excess cash to $4,520,000. With such a large amount of unneeded funds, Foxcraft's treasurer will certainly want to invest in interest-bearing securities, or to put the funds to use in some other way.

Before concluding our discussion of the cash budget, we should make some additional points:

1.   Our cash budget example does not reflect interest on loans or income from the investment of surplus cash. This refinement could easily be added.

2.   If cash inflows and outflows are not uniform during the month, we could seriously understate the firm's peak financing requirements. The data in Table 20-1 show the situation expected on the last day of each month, but on any given day during the month it could be quite different. For example, if all payments had to be made on the fifth of each month, but collections came in uniformly throughout the month, the firm would need to borrow much larger amounts than those shown in Table 20-1. In this case, we would have to prepare a cash budget identifying requirements on a daily basis.

3.   Since depreciation is a noncash charge, it does not appear on the cash budget other than through its effect on taxes paid.

4.   Since the cash budget represents a forecast, all the values in the table are *expected* values. If actual sales, purchases, and so on, are different from the forecasted levels, then the projected cash deficits and surpluses will also be incorrect. Thus,

Foxcraft might end up needing to borrow larger amounts than are indicated on Line 20, so it should arrange a line of credit in excess of that amount.

5. Computerized spreadsheet programs such as *Lotus 1-2-3* are particularly well suited for constructing and analyzing the cash budget, especially with respect to the sensitivity of cash flows to changes in sales levels, collection periods, and the like. We could change any assumption, say the projected monthly sales or the time that customers pay, and the cash budget would automatically and instantly be recalculated. This would show us exactly how the firm's borrowing requirements would change if various other things changed. Also, with a computer model, it is easy to add features like interest paid on loans, interest earned on marketable securities, and so on.

6. Finally, we should note that the target cash balance probably will be adjusted over time, rising and falling with seasonal patterns and with long-term changes in the scale of the firm's operations. Thus, Foxcraft will probably plan to maintain larger cash balances during August and September than at other times, and as the company grows, so will its required cash balance. Factors that influence the target cash balance are discussed in the next section. Also, the firm might even set the target cash balance at zero—this could be done if it carried a portfolio of marketable securities which could be sold to replenish the cash account, or if it had an arrangement with its bank that permitted it to borrow the funds it needed on a daily basis. In that event, the cash budget would simply stop with Line 18, and the amounts on that line would represent the projected loans outstanding or surplus cash. Note, though, that most firms would find it difficult to operate with a zero-balance bank account, just as you would, and the costs of such an operation would in most instances offset the opportunity cost associated with maintaining a positive cash balance. Therefore, most firms do set a positive target cash balance.

Self-Test Questions

What is the purpose of a cash budget?

What are the three major sections of a cash budget?

Suppose a firm's cash flows do not occur uniformly throughout the month. What impact would this have on the validity of a monthly cash budget?

How is uncertainty handled in a cash budget?

Is depreciation reflected in a cash budget? Explain.

SETTING THE TARGET CASH BALANCE

When we discussed Foxcraft Printing Company's cash budget, we assumed that it has a $2.5 million target cash balance. In this section, we discuss four methods for setting and controlling the target cash balance: (1) the Baumol model, (2) the Miller-Orr model, (3) the Stone model, and (4) Monte Carlo simulation.

The Baumol Model

William Baumol first noted that cash balances are in many respects similar to inventories, and that the EOQ inventory model that we develop in Chapter 21 can be used to establish the target cash balance.[2] Baumol's model assumes (1) that the firm uses cash at a steady, predictable rate, say $1 million per week, and (2) that the firm's cash inflows from operations also occur at a steady, predictable rate, say $900,000 per week, so (3) its net cash outflows, or net need for cash, also occur at a steady rate, in this case, $100,000 per week.[3] Under these steady-state assumptions, the firm's cash balance will resemble an inventory balance, which is conceptually identical to the inventory position shown in Figure 21-2 in Chapter 21.

If our illustrative firm started at Time 0 with a cash balance of C = $300,000, and if its outflows exceeded its inflows by $100,000 per week, then (1) its cash balance would drop to zero at the end of Week 3, and (2) its average cash balance would be C/2 = $300,000/2 = $150,000. At the end of Week 3, the firm would have to replenish its cash balance, either by selling marketable securities, if it has any, or by borrowing.

If C were set at a higher level, say $600,000, then the cash supply would last longer (six weeks), so the firm would have to sell securities (or borrow) less frequently, but its average cash balance would rise from $150,000 to $300,000. Since a "transactions cost" must be incurred to sell securities (or to borrow), establishing large cash balances will lower the transaction costs associated with cash management. On the other hand, cash provides no income, so the larger the average cash balance, the higher the opportunity cost, or the return that could have been earned on marketable securities held in lieu of cash (or the higher the interest expense on borrowings). The situation is analogous to the one for inventories presented in Figure 21-1, and the optimal cash balance is found in the same way as in the EOQ model, but with a different set of variables:

C = amount of cash raised by selling marketable securities or by borrowing.
  C/2 = average cash balance.

C* = optimal amount of cash to be raised by selling marketable securities or by borrowing.
  C*/2 = optimal average cash balance.

F = fixed costs of making a securities trade or of borrowing.

T = total amount of net new cash needed for transactions over the entire period (usually a year, but some other period if cash needs are seasonal).

k = opportunity cost of holding cash (equals the rate of return foregone on marketable securities or the cost of borrowing to hold cash).

---

[2]See William J. Baumol, "The Transactions Demand for Cash: An Inventory Theoretic Approach," *Quarterly Journal of Economics,* November 1952, 545–556.

[3]Although our hypothetical firm is experiencing a $100,000 weekly cash shortfall, it is not necessarily headed toward bankruptcy. The firm could, for example, be highly profitable and have high earnings, but be expanding so rapidly that it is subject to chronic cash shortages that must be made up by borrowing or by selling common stock. Similarly, the firm could be in the construction business and therefore receive major cash inflows at wide intervals, but have net cash outflows of $100,000 per week between major inflows.

The total costs of cash balances consist of a holding, or opportunity, cost plus a transactions cost:[4]

$$\text{Total costs} = \text{Holding cost} + \text{Transactions cost}$$

$$= \frac{C}{2}(k) + \frac{T}{C}(F). \quad \text{(20-1)}$$

To minimize total costs, we differentiate Equation 20-1 with respect to C and set the derivative equal to zero:

$$\frac{d(\text{Total costs})}{dC} = \frac{k}{2} - \frac{(T)(F)}{C^2} = 0. \quad \text{(20-2)}$$

Finally, we solve for C*, the optimal cash transfer:

$$\frac{k}{2} = \frac{(F)(T)}{C^2}$$

$$C^2 = \frac{2(F)(T)}{k}$$

$$C^* = \sqrt{\frac{2(F)(T)}{k}}. \quad \text{(20-3)}$$

Equation 20-3 is the Baumol model for determining optimal cash balances. To illustrate its use, suppose F = $150; T = 52 weeks × $100,000 per week = $5,200,000; and k = 15% = 0.15. Then

$$C^* = \sqrt{\frac{2(\$150)(\$5,200,000)}{0.15}} = \$101,980.$$

Therefore, the firm should sell securities (or borrow) in the amount of $101,980 when its cash balance approaches zero, thus building its cash balance back up to $101,980. If we divide T by C*, we have the number of transactions per year: $5,200,000/$101,980 = 50.99 ≈ 51, or about once a week. The firm's average cash balance would be $101,980/2 = $50,990 ≈ $51,000.

Notice that the optimal transfer amount, hence the target cash balance, increases less than proportionately with increases in transactions. For example, if the firm's size and consequently its net new cash needs increased by 100 percent, from $5.2 million to $10.4 million per year, average cash balances would increase by only 41 percent, from $51,000 to $72,000. This suggests that there are economies of scale in the holding of cash balances, and this, in turn, gives larger firms an edge over smaller ones.[5]

Also, note that the lower the value of F, the cost of making a securities trade or of borrowing, the lower the optimal cash balance. Computers, electronic wire trans-

---

[4]Total costs can be expressed on a before-tax basis or on an after-tax basis. Both methods lead to the same conclusions regarding target cash balances and comparative costs. Here, for simplicity, we present the model on a before-tax basis.

[5]This edge may, of course, be more than offset by other factors—after all, cash management is only one aspect of running a business.

Figure 20-1   Concept of the Miller-Orr Model

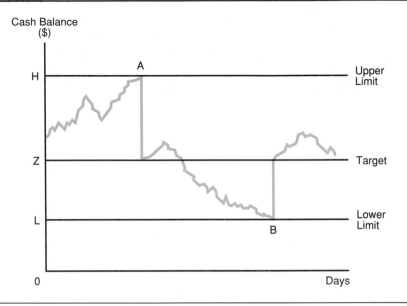

fers, and other technological changes have lowered F in recent years, so required cash balances have been falling.

Finally, firms often find it desirable to hold "safety stocks" of cash designed to reduce the probability of a cash shortage to some specified level. However, if a firm is able to sell securities or to borrow on short notice—and most larger firms can do either in a matter of a couple of hours simply by making a telephone call—then the safety stock of cash can be quite low.

The Baumol model is obviously simplistic in many respects. Most important, it assumes relatively stable, predictable cash inflows and outflows, and it does not take account of any seasonal or cyclical trends. Other models have been developed to deal with uncertainty in the cash flows and with trends. Three of these models are discussed next.

The Miller-Orr Model

Merton Miller and Daniel Orr developed a model for setting the target cash balance which incorporates uncertainty in the cash inflows and outflows.[6] They assumed that the distribution of daily net cash flows is approximately normal. Each day, the net

---

[6]See Merton H. Miller and Daniel Orr, "A Model of the Demand for Money by Firms," *Quarterly Journal of Economics,* August 1966, 413–435.

cash flow could be the expected value or some higher or lower value drawn from a normal distribution. Thus, the daily net cash flow follows a trendless random walk.

Figure 20-1 shows how the Miller-Orr model operates over time. The model sets higher and lower control limits, H and L respectively, and a target cash balance, Z. When the cash balance reaches H, such as at Point A, then H − Z dollars are transferred from cash to marketable securities, that is, the firm purchases H − Z dollars of securities. Similarly, when the cash balance hits L, as at Point B, then Z − L dollars are transferred from marketable securities to cash. The lower limit, L, is set by management depending on how much risk of a cash shortfall the firm is willing to accept, and this, in turn, depends both on access to borrowings and on the consequences of a cash shortfall.

Given L as set by management, the Miller-Orr model determines the target cash balance and the upper limit. We will not show their derivations here, but Miller-Orr found these values for Z and H:

$$Z = \left[\frac{3F\sigma^2}{4k}\right]^{1/3} + L, \qquad\qquad (20\text{-}4)$$

and

$$H = 3\left[\frac{3F\sigma^2}{4k}\right]^{1/3} + L = 3Z - 2L. \qquad\qquad (20\text{-}5)$$

Additionally, the average cash balance is

$$\text{Average cash balance} = \frac{4Z - L}{3}. \qquad\qquad (20\text{-}6)$$

Here,

Z = target cash balance.

H = upper limit.

L = lower limit.

F = fixed transactions cost.

k = opportunity cost on a daily basis.

σ^2 = variance of net daily cash flows.

To illustrate, suppose F is $150, the opportunity cost is k = 15 percent annually, and the standard deviation (σ) of daily net cash flows is $1,000. The daily opportunity cost and variance of daily net cash flows are, thus,

$$(1 + k)^{360} - 1.0 = 0.15$$

$$(1 + k)^{360} = 1.15$$

$$1 + k = 1.00039$$

$$k = 0.00039,$$

and

$$\sigma^2 = (1,000)^2 = 1,000,000.$$

Further, assume that management sets the lower limit, L, at zero because it can arrange transfers quickly. Substituting these values into Equations 20-4, 20-5, and 20-6 gives Z = \$6,607, H = \$19,821, and an average cash balance of \$8,809:

$$Z = \left[\frac{3(150)(1,000,000)}{4(0.00039)} \right]^{1/3} + \$0$$

$$= (288,461,500,000)^{1/3} = \$6,607,$$

and

$$H = 3(\$6,607) - 2(\$0) = \$19,821,$$

and

$$\text{Average cash balance} = \frac{4(\$6,607) - \$0}{3} = \$8,809.$$

Several other points should be noted about the Miller-Orr model:

1. The target cash balance is *not* midway between the upper and lower limits. Therefore, the cash balance will, on average, hit the lower limit more often than the upper limit. Placing the target cash balance midway between the limits would minimize transactions costs, but placing the target cash balance lower than midway decreases opportunity costs. In their derivation of the model, Miller and Orr find, assuming L = \$0, that a target of H/3 minimizes total costs.

2. The target cash balance, and consequently the acceptable range, increases with both F and σ^2; a higher F makes it more costly to hit either limit, and a larger σ^2 causes the firm to hit the limits more frequently.

3. The target cash balance decreases with increases in k, because the higher the value of k, the more costly it is to hold cash.

4. The lower limit need not be set at zero. It could be greater than zero because of compensating balance requirements or because of management's desire to maintain a cash safety stock.

5. The Miller-Orr model has been tested by several firms. It performed as well or better than intuitive cash management rules. However, it starts to break down when the firm has multiple cash alternatives rather than a single type of marketable security such as T-bills.

6. The Miller-Orr model assumes that the distribution of net cash flows is symmetric about the expected net cash flow. Similar models could be derived with other assumptions concerning the net cash flow distribution. For example, the model could be adjusted for seasonal trends. Here the distribution of cash flows would not be normal, but would reflect a greater probability of either increasing or decreasing the cash balance, depending on whether the firm was moving into or away from the peak season. The target cash balance in these cases would not be a third of the way between the lower and upper limits.

Figure 20-2   Concept of the Stone Model

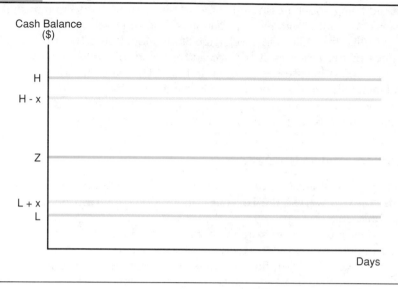

The Stone Model

The Stone model, which focuses more on managing cash balances than on setting the target balance, is similar to the Miller-Orr model.[7] However, the Stone model views the higher and lower control limits as guidelines to be considered in light of the cash flows expected in the next several days. Figure 20-2 presents the concept of the Stone model. Like the Miller-Orr model, Z represents the target cash balance and H and L are the higher and lower control limits, respectively. Note, though, that the Stone model has inner and outer control limits — H and L are the outer limits, while H − x and L + x are the inner limits. Although the control limits in the Miller-Orr model trigger immediate action, the control limits in the Stone model do not.

To illustrate the Stone model, suppose that the cash balance reaches H in Figure 20-2, the outer higher control limit. Instead of automatically transferring the amount H − Z from cash into marketable securities, the cash manager now considers the firm's cash flow forecast for the next several days, say 5. If the expected cash balance after 5 days remains above the inner limit, H − x, then a cash transfer is made which would bring the expected balance 5 days hence down to the target, Z. However, if the forecasted cash balance falls below the inner limit, no action is taken. The decision process at the lower limit is similar. The main feature of the Stone model is that any action taken reflects expectations about future cash flows and their impact on the firm's cash balance. Thus, hitting the higher outer control limit would

---

[7]See Bernell K. Stone, "The Use of Forecasts and Smoothing in Control-Limit Models for Cash Management," *Financial Management,* Spring 1972, 72–84.

not trigger a transfer from cash if the firm anticipated that the next several days would bring about a cash drain. The whole idea here is to minimize the number of transfers by incorporating expectations of future flows.

Unlike the Miller-Orr model, the Stone model offers no guidance for setting the values of the target cash balance and the control limits. However, the Miller-Orr model could be used to set Z and H, and L, x, and the forecast period could be judgmentally set. A key point here is that these values should not be treated as fixed parameters. Cash needs vary according to cyclical and seasonal trends, and cash balance models should be adjusted to reflect these trends.

Monte Carlo Simulation

Monte Carlo simulation can also be used to set the target cash balance.[8] To illustrate this concept, we use the Foxcraft Printing Company cash budget presented earlier in Table 20-1.

Sales and collections are the driving forces in the cash budget. In the Table 20-1 cash budget, we used expected values for sales, and these values were used to derive most of the other cash flow forecasts. Now we repeat the cash budget, but with the assumption that sales are subject to a probability distribution about the expected value. Specifically, we assumed that the distribution of sales for each month is normal, with a coefficient of variation (CV) of 0.10 and a standard deviation which varies with the sales level. In effect, we assumed that the relative variability of sales is constant from month to month. Thus in May, when expected sales are $5 million, the standard deviation of sales is $500,000:

$$CV = 0.10 = \frac{\sigma_{Sales}}{Expected\ sales} = \frac{\sigma_{Sales}}{\$5,000,000}$$

$$\sigma_{Sales} = 0.10\ (Sales) = 0.10(\$5,000,000) = \$500,000.$$

Similarly, the standard deviation of sales in the peak month of September is found to be $2 million, and so forth.

Of course, collections are based on actual sales rather than on expected sales, so the collections pattern will reflect realized sales. If we assume that the sales realized in any month will not change Foxcraft's expectations for future sales, then purchases in any month will be based on 70 percent of next month's expected sales, but with upward or downward adjustments to reflect excess inventories on hand due to the current month's sales being less than expected or to inventory shortages that result from above-normal sales. Other payments, such as wages, rent, and so on, were assumed to be fixed for the analysis, although uncertainty could be built into them, too.

Based on these assumptions, we used @ *RISK* add-in software, along with *Lotus 1-2-3,* to conduct a Monte Carlo simulation of Foxcraft's cash budget. The simulation analysis focuses on Line 16 of Table 20-1, the net cash gain (loss) during the month.

---

[8]See Eugene M. Lerner, "Simulating a Cash Budget," in *Readings on the Management of Working Capital,* 2nd ed., Keith V. Smith, ed. (St. Paul, Minn.: West, 1980).

Table 20-2   Foxcraft Printing Company: Cash Budget Simulation
(Thousands of Dollars)

Month	Net Cash Flow from Table 20-1	Net Cash Flow: At Least the Indicated Amount with the Indicated Probability				
		90%	70%	50%	30%	10%
July	($2,140)	($2,897)	($2,454)	($2,161)	($1,832)	($1,354)
August	(1,460)	(2,810)	(2,043)	(1,512)	(885)	(130)
September	(2,280)	(4,088)	(2,989)	(2,302)	(1,587)	(489)
October	4,360	2,407	3,606	4,394	5,097	6,268
November	2,860	1,737	2,324	2,868	3,328	4,002
December .	2,680	1,753	2,259	2,661	3,077	3,651

Notes:

a. The value ($2,897) in the 90% column indicates that there is a 90% probability that the cash flow in July will be at least − $2,897 and a 10% probability that the cash flow will be less than − $2,897.

b. The net cash flows shown in the first column were taken from Line 16 of Table 20-1. These values should, theoretically, equal the values shown in the 50 percent column. The deviations are caused by randomness in the simulation runs.

Table 20-2 summarizes the results and compares the range of likely cash gains or losses with the point estimates taken from Line 16 of Table 20-1.

Now suppose Foxcraft's managers want to be 90 percent confident that the firm will not run out of cash during July. They would set the beginning-of-month balance at $2,897,000 (rather than $2,500,000), because there is a 90 percent probability that the July cash flow will be no worse than a $2,897,000 net outflow. Thus, with a beginning cash balance of $2,897,000, there would be only a 10 percent probability that the firm would run out of cash during July. This type of analysis could be extended for the other months, and it could be used in lieu of the fixed $2.5 million as the target beginning-of-month cash balance.

Note that in our simulation we assumed that sales are independent from month to month. Alternatively, we could have assumed some type of dependence such that a lower-than-expected sales level in July would signal a trend toward lower sales in the following months. This type of dependency would increase the firm's uncertainty with regard to cash flows in any given month and, consequently, increase the required cash balance needed to provide any prescribed level of confidence regarding running out of cash.

Other Factors Influencing the Target Cash Balance

Firms actually set their target cash balances as the larger of (1) their transactions balances plus precautionary (safety stock) balances or (2) their required compensating balances as determined by their agreements with banks. Transactions balances and precautionary balances depend upon the firm's volume of business, the degree of uncertainty inherent in its forecasts of cash inflows and outflows, and its ability to borrow on short notice to meet cash shortfalls. Consider again the cash budget shown for Foxcraft Printing Company in Table 20-1, where the target cash balance is shown on Line 19. Other factors held constant, the target cash balance would increase if Foxcraft expanded, whereas it would decrease if Foxcraft contracted. Similarly, Foxcraft could afford to operate with a smaller target balance if it could forecast better and thus be more certain that inflows would come in as scheduled and that no unanticipated outflows such as might result from uninsured fire losses, lawsuits, and the like, would occur.

Statistics are not available on whether transactions balances or compensating balances actually control most firms' target cash balances, but compensating balance requirements do often dominate, especially during periods of high interest rates and tight money.[9]

Self-Test Questions

Briefly describe the Baumol model. If you are familiar with the EOQ inventory model, how is it related to the Baumol model?

Briefly describe the Miller-Orr model. How does the Miller-Orr model differ from the Baumol model?

Briefly describe the Stone model. How does it differ from the Miller-Orr model?

Describe how simulation analysis can be used to help establish the target cash balance.

CASH MANAGEMENT TECHNIQUES

Cash management has changed significantly over the last 20 years as a result of two factors. First, interest rates have been trending up, pushing up the opportunity cost of holding cash and forcing financial managers to search for more efficient ways of managing the firm's cash. Second, new technologies, particularly computerized electronic funds transfer mechanisms, have provided a means to optimize cash transactions on a real-time basis.

Most cash management activities are performed jointly by the firm and its primary bank, but the financial manager is responsible for the effectiveness of the cash management program. Cash management techniques fall generally into five categories: (1) synchronizing cash flow, (2) using float, (3) accelerating collections, (4) determining where and when funds are needed, and getting available funds to the right place, and (5) controlling disbursements. Most business is conducted by

---

[9]This point is underscored by an incident that occurred at a professional finance meeting. A professor presented a scholarly paper that used operations research techniques to determine "optimal cash balances" for a sample of firms. He then reported that actual cash balances of the firms greatly exceeded their "optimal" balances, suggesting inefficiency and the need for more refined techniques. The discussant of the paper made her comments short and sweet. She reported that she had written and asked the sample firms why they had so much cash. They uniformly replied that their cash holdings were set by compensating balance requirements. The model was useful to determine the optimal cash balance in the absence of compensating balance requirements, but it was precisely those requirements that determined actual balances. Since the model did not include compensating balances as a determinant of cash balances, its usefulness was questionable.

large firms, many of which operate regionally, nationally, or even worldwide. They collect cash from many sources and make payments from a number of different points. For example, companies like IBM, General Motors, and Hewlett-Packard have manufacturing plants all around the world, even more sales offices, and bank accounts in virtually every city where they do business. Their collection points are typically spread out, following sales patterns. Some disbursements are made from local offices, but most disbursements are made in the areas where manufacturing occurs, or from the home office (dividend and interest payments, taxes, debt repayments, and the like). Thus, a major corporation might have hundreds or even thousands of bank accounts, and since there is no reason to think that inflows and outflows will balance in each account, a system must be in place to transfer funds from where they are to where they are needed, to arrange loans to cover net corporate shortfalls, and to invest without delay net corporate surpluses. We discuss the most commonly used techniques for accomplishing these tasks in the following sections.

Cash Flow Synchronization

If you as an individual were to receive income once a year, you would probably put it in the bank, draw down your account periodically, and have an average balance during the year equal to about half your annual income. If you received income monthly instead of once a year, you would operate similarly, but now your average balance would be much smaller. If you could arrange to receive income daily and to pay rent, tuition, and other charges on a daily basis, and if you were quite confident of your forecasted inflows and outflows, then you could hold a very small average cash balance.

Exactly the same situation holds for business firms—by improving their forecasts and by arranging things so that their cash receipts coincide with required cash outflows, firms can reduce their transactions balances to a minimum. Recognizing this point, utility companies, oil companies, credit card companies, and so on arrange to bill customers, and to pay their own bills, on regular "billing cycles" throughout the month. This improves the *synchronization of cash flows,* which in turn enables a firm to reduce its cash balances, decrease its bank loans, lower interest expenses, and boost profits.

Using Float

Float is defined as the difference between the balance shown in a firm's (or individual's) checkbook and the balance on the bank's records. Suppose a firm writes, on the average, checks in the amount of $5,000 each day, and it takes six days for these checks to clear and to be deducted from the firm's bank account. This will cause the firm's own checkbook to show a balance $30,000 smaller than the balance on the bank's records; this difference is called *disbursement float.* Now suppose the firm also receives checks in the amount of $5,000 daily, but it loses four days while they are being deposited and cleared. This will result in $20,000 of *collections float.* In total, the firm's *net float*—the difference between $30,000 positive disbursement float and the $20,000 negative collections float—will be $10,000.

If the firm's own collection and clearing process is more efficient than that of the recipients of its checks—which is generally true of larger, more efficient firms—then the firm could actually show a *negative* balance on its own books but have a *positive* balance on the records of its bank. Some firms indicate that they *never* have positive book cash balances. One large manufacturer of construction equipment stated that while its account, according to its bank's records, shows an average cash balance of about $20 million, its *book* cash balance is *minus* $20 million—it has $40 million of net float. Obviously the firm must be able to forecast its disbursements and collections accurately in order to make such heavy use of float.

E. F. Hutton provides an example of pushing cash management too far. Hutton did business with banks all across the country, and it had to keep compensating balances in these banks. The sizes of the required compensating balances were known, and any excess funds in these banks were sent electronically, on a daily basis, to concentration banks, where they were immediately invested in interest-bearing securities. However, rather than waiting to see what the end-of-day balances actually were, Hutton began estimating inflows and outflows, and it transferred out for investment the *estimated* end-of-day excess. But then Hutton got greedy—it began to deliberately overestimate its deposits and underestimate clearings of its own checks, thereby deliberately overstating the estimated end-of-day balances. As a result, Hutton was chronically overdrawn at its local banks, and it was in effect earning interest on funds which really belonged to those local banks. It is entirely proper to forecast what your bank will have recorded as your balance and then to make decisions based on the estimate, even if that balance is different from the balance your own books show. However, it is illegal to forecast an overdrawn situation but then to tell the bank that you forecast a positive balance.[10]

Basically, a firm's net float is a function of its ability to speed up collections on checks received and to slow down collections on checks written. Efficient firms go to great lengths to speed up the processing of incoming checks, thus putting the funds to work faster, and they try to stretch their own payments out as long as possible.

Acceleration of Receipts

Financial managers have searched for ways to collect receivables faster since credit transactions began. Although cash collection is the financial manager's responsibility, the speed with which checks are cleared is dependent on the banking system. Several techniques are now used both to speed collections and to get funds where they are needed. Included are lockbox services, pre-authorized debits, and concentration banking.

---

[10]A question raised during the Hutton investigation was this: "Why didn't the banks recognize that Hutton was systematically overdrawing its account and call the company to task?" The answer is that some banks, with tight controls, did exactly that—they refused to let Hutton get away with the practice. Other banks were lax. Still other banks apparently let Hutton get away with being chronically overdrawn out of fear of losing its business: Hutton used its economic muscle to force the banks to let it get away with an illegal act. In many people's opinion, the banks were as much at fault as Hutton. Still, in business dealings, honesty is presumed, and Hutton was dishonest in its dealings with the banks. This dishonesty severely damaged Hutton's reputation, cost the company profits totaling hundreds of millions of dollars, cost its top managers their jobs, and contributed to the ultimate demise of the company.

Lockboxes. *Lockboxes* are one of the oldest cash management tools. The concept was first used on a large scale by RCA, but now virtually all banks that offer cash management services also offer lockbox services. In a lockbox system, incoming checks are sent to post office boxes rather than to corporate headquarters. For example, a firm headquartered in New York City might have its West Coast customers send their payments to a box in San Francisco, its customers in the Southwest send their checks to Dallas, and so on, rather than having all checks sent to New York City. Several times a day a local bank will collect the contents of the lockbox and deposit the checks into the company's local account. The bank would then provide the firm with a daily record of the receipts collected, usually via an electronic data transmission system in a format that permits on-line updating of the firm's receivables accounts.

A lockbox system reduces the time required for a firm to receive incoming checks, to deposit them, and to get them cleared through the banking system so that the funds are available for use. This time reduction occurs because mail time and check collection time are both reduced if the lockbox is located in the geographic area where the customer is located. Lockbox services can often increase the availability of funds by one to four days over the "regular" system.

Pre-Authorized Debits. A *pre-authorized debit* allows funds to be automatically transferred from a customer's account to the firm's account on specified dates. These transactions are also called "checkless" or "paperless" transactions since they are accomplished without using traditional paper checks. However, a record of payment does appear on both parties' bank statements. Pre-authorized debiting accelerates the transfer of funds because mail and check-clearing time are totally eliminated. Although pre-authorized debits are efficient, and they appear to be the trend of the future, the pace of acceptance by payers has been much slower than originally predicted. Of course, a payer who uses a pre-authorized debit system loses the disbursement float that is inherent in the paper-based system.

Concentration Banking. Lockbox systems and pre-authorized debits, although efficient in speeding up collections, result in the firm's cash being spread around among many banks. The primary purpose of *concentration banking* is to mobilize funds from decentralized receiving locations, whether they be lockboxes or decentralized company locations, into one or more central cash pools. The cash manager then uses these pools for short-term investing or reallocation among the firm's banks.

In a typical concentration system, the firm's collection banks record deposits received each day. Then, based on disbursement needs, the corporate cash manager transfers the funds from these collection points to a concentration bank. Concentration accounts allow firms to take maximum advantage of economies of scale in cash management and investment.

One of the keys to concentration banking is the ability to quickly transfer funds from collecting banks to concentration banks. One commonly used transfer tool is the *depository transfer check (DTC)*. Here's how it works: Collection banks report the amounts deposited daily to a central data collection service, which operates a nationwide data processing network. This information is then transmitted at a specified time to the firm's concentration bank. The concentration bank, based on preset cash balance targets for the collection accounts, automatically produces DTCs drawn against the collection banks; this transfers funds to the concentration bank.

A relatively new development in funds transfer is the *electronic depository transfer,* sometimes called an *ACH-DTC.* The ACH stands for automated clearinghouse, which is a communications network that provides a means of sending data from one financial institution to another. Instead of using paper checks, magnetic tape files are processed by the ACH, and all entries for a particular bank are placed on a single file which is sent to that bank. Some banks send and receive their data on tapes, while others have direct computer links to the ACH. There are actually 32 regional ACH associations, but all of the ACH facilities, except for the New York ACH, are operated by the Federal Reserve System. All ACHs guarantee one-day clearing regardless of the location of the bank on which the check was written. The ACH network sorts all transactions daily, the entries are then forwarded for processing the following day, and the processing accomplishes the actual transfer.

In addition to the automated clearinghouses, the Federal Reserve wire system can be used for cash concentration or for other cash transfers. This system is used to move large sums that occur on a sporadic basis, such as would occur if a firm borrowed $10 million in the commercial paper market.

Disbursement Control

Accelerated collections represent one side of cash management, and controlling funds outflow is the flip side of the coin. Of course, efficient cash management can only result if both inflows and outflows are effectively managed.

Payables Centralization. No single action controls cash outflow more effectively than centralization of payables. This permits the financial manager to evaluate the payments coming due for the entire firm and to schedule cash transfers to meet these needs on a company-wide basis. Centralized disbursement also permits more efficient monitoring of payables and float balances. Of course, there are also disadvantages to a centralized disbursement system—regional offices may not be able to make prompt payment for services rendered, which can create ill will and raise the company's operating costs. More than one firm has saved a few pennies by using a cheaper check-disbursing system but lost far more as a result of higher operating costs caused by ill will.

Zero-Balance Accounts. *Zero-balance accounts (ZBAs)* are special disbursement accounts having a zero-dollar balance on which checks are written. Typically, a firm establishes several ZBAs in the concentration bank and funds them from a master account. As checks are presented to a ZBA for payment, funds are automatically transferred from the master account. If the master account goes negative, it is replenished by borrowing from the bank against a line of credit, by borrowing in the commercial paper market, or by selling some T-bills from the marketable securities portfolio. Zero-balance accounts simplify the control of disbursements and cash balances, hence reduce the amount of idle (non-interest-bearing) cash.

Controlled Disbursement Accounts. Whereas zero-balance accounts are typically established at concentration banks, *controlled disbursement accounts* can be set up at any bank. In fact, controlled disbursement accounts were initially used only in relatively remote banks, hence this technique was originally called *remote disbursement.* The basic technique is simple: Controlled disbursement accounts are not funded until the day's checks are presented against the account. The key to controlled disbursement is the ability of the bank having the account to report the total daily amount of checks received for clearance by 11 A.M., New York time. This early notification gives financial managers sufficient time (1) to wire funds to the controlled disbursement account to cover the checks presented for payment and (2) to invest excess cash at midday, when money market trading is at a peak.

Self-Test Questions

What is float? How do firms use float to increase cash management efficiency?

What are some methods that can be used to accelerate a firm's receipts?

What are some techniques for controlling disbursements?

MATCHING THE COSTS AND BENEFITS OF CASH MANAGEMENT

Although a number of techniques have been discussed to reduce cash balance requirements, implementing these procedures is not a costless operation. How far should a firm go in making its cash operations more efficient? As a general rule, the firm should incur these expenses so long as the marginal returns exceed the marginal costs.

For example, suppose that by establishing a lockbox system a firm can reduce its investment in cash by $1 million without increasing the risk of running short of cash. Further, suppose the firm borrows at a cost of 12 percent. The lockbox system will release $1 million, which can be used to reduce bank loans and thus save $120,000 per year. If the costs of setting up and operating the lockbox system are less than $120,000, the move is a good one, but if the costs exceed $120,000, the improvement in efficiency is not worth the cost. It is clear that larger firms, with larger cash balances, can better afford to hire the personnel necessary to maintain tight control over their cash positions. Cash management is one element of business operations in which economies of scale are present.

Very clearly, the value of careful cash management depends upon the costs of funds invested in cash, which in turn depend upon the current rate of interest. In the 1980s, with interest rates at relatively high levels, firms were devoting a great deal of care to cash management.[11]

---

[11]Banks have also placed considerable emphasis on developing and marketing cash management services. Because of scale economies, banks can generally provide these services to smaller companies at lower costs than companies can achieve by operating in-house cash management systems.

Self-Test Questions

How far should a firm go in its cash management effort; that is, how much should be spent on cash management?

Would large firms use different cash management systems than small firms?

MARKETABLE SECURITIES MANAGEMENT

Realistically, cash and marketable securities management cannot be separated — management of one implies management of the other. In the first part of the chapter, we focused on cash management. Now we turn to marketable securities.

Rationale for Holding Marketable Securities

Marketable securities typically provide much lower yields than firms' operating assets; for example, in 1990 IBM held a $6.1 billion portfolio of marketable securities that yielded about 8 percent, while its operating assets provided a return of about 18 percent. Why would a company such as IBM have such large holdings of low-yielding assets? There are two basic reasons for these holdings: (1) They serve as a substitute for cash balances, and (2) they are used as a temporary investment. These points are considered next.

Marketable Securities as a Substitute for Cash. Some firms hold portfolios of marketable securities in lieu of larger cash balances, liquidating part of the portfolio to increase the cash account when cash outflows exceed inflows. In such situations, the marketable securities could be used as a substitute for transactions balances, for precautionary balances, for speculative balances, or for all three. In most cases, the securities are held primarily for precautionary purposes — most firms prefer to rely on bank credit to make temporary transactions or to meet speculative needs, but they may still hold some liquid assets to guard against a possible shortage of bank credit.

IBM a few years ago had substantially more marketable securities than it does today. Those large liquid balances had been built up primarily as a reserve for possible damage payments resulting from pending antitrust suits. When it became clear that IBM would win most of the suits, its liquidity needs declined, and the company spent some of the funds on other assets, including repurchases of its own stock. This is a prime example of a firm's building up its precautionary balances to handle possible emergencies.

Marketable Securities Held as a Temporary Investment. Temporary investments in marketable securities generally occur in one of the following two situations:

1. **When the firm must finance seasonal or cyclical operations.** If the firm has a conservative financing policy as we defined it back in Chapter 19, in Panel c of Figure 19-3, then its long-term capital will exceed its permanent assets, and mar-

Figure 20-3 Alternative Methods of Financing a Continuous Construction Program

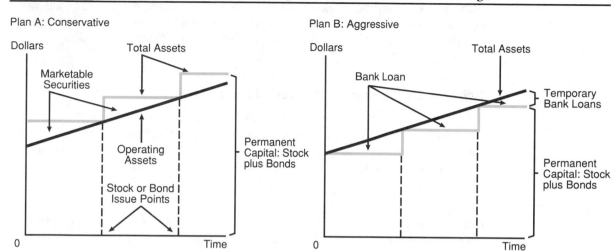

ketable securities will be held when inventories and receivables are low. On the other hand, with a highly aggressive policy it will never carry any securities, and it will borrow heavily to meet peak needs. With a moderate policy, where maturities are matched, permanent assets will be matched with long-term financing, most seasonal increases in inventories and receivables will be met by short-term loans, and the firm will also carry marketable securities at certain times.

2. **When the firm must meet some known financial requirements.** Marketable securities are frequently built up immediately preceding quarterly corporate tax payment dates. Further, if a major plant construction program is planned for the near future, if an acquisition is planned, or if a bond issue is about to mature, a firm may build up its marketable securities portfolio to provide the required funds. For example, Commonwealth Edison, the electric utility serving Chicago, has a permanent, ongoing construction program, generating a continuous need for new capital. Since there are substantial fixed costs involved in stock or bond flotations, these securities are issued infrequently and in large amounts.

During the 1960s, Commonwealth followed the practice of selling bonds and stock *before* the capital was needed, investing the proceeds in marketable securities, and then liquidating the securities to finance plant construction. Plan A in Figure 20-3 illustrates this procedure. However, during the 1970s and early 1980s, Commonwealth encountered financial stress. It was forced to use up its liquid assets and to switch to its present policy of financing plant construction with short-term bank loans and then selling long-term securities to retire the bank loans when they have built up to some target level. This policy is illustrated by Plan B of Figure 20-3.

Plan A is the more conservative, less risky one. First, the company is minimizing its liquidity problems because it has no short-term debt hanging over its head. Second, it is sure of having the funds available to meet construction payments as they come due. On the other hand, firms generally have to pay higher interest rates when they borrow than the return they receive on marketable securities, so following the less risky strategy has a cost. Again, we are faced with a risk/return tradeoff.

Criteria for Selecting Marketable Securities

A wide variety of securities and investment strategies, differing in terms of default risk, interest rate risk, liquidity risk, and expected rate of return, are available to firms that choose to hold marketable securities. In this section, we first consider the characteristics of different securities, and then we discuss how financial managers select the specific instruments held in their marketable securities portfolios.

Default Risk.   The risk that a borrower will be unable to make interest or principal payments is known as *default* (or *credit*) *risk*. If the borrower is the U.S. Treasury, default risk is essentially zero, so Treasury securities are risk free with regard to default risk. Corporate securities, and bonds issued by state and local governments, are subject to some degree of default risk, and they are rated with regard to their chances of going into default.

Event Risk.   The probability that some event, such as a recapitalization or a leveraged buyout (LBO), will occur which suddenly increases a firm's default risk, hence lowers the value of its outstanding bonds, is called *event risk*. Bonds issued by industrial and service companies generally have more event risk than bonds issued by regulated companies such as banks or electric utilities. Also, long-term securities are affected more by unfavorable events than are short-term securities. Treasury securities do not carry any event risk, barring national disaster.

Interest Rate Risk.   Bond prices vary with changes in interest rates. Further, the prices of long-term bonds are much more sensitive to shifts in interest rates than are the prices of short-term securities—they have much more *interest rate risk*. Therefore, even Treasury securities are not free of all risk; they are subject to risk due to interest rate fluctuations. Thus, if Foxcraft's treasurer purchased at par $1 million of 25-year U.S. government bonds paying 9 percent interest, and if interest rates rose to 14.5 percent, then the market value of the bonds would fall from $1 million to approximately $638,000—a loss of almost 40 percent. (This actually happened from 1980 to 1982.) Had 90-day Treasury bills been held, the capital loss resulting from the change in interest rates would have been negligible.

Purchasing Power Risk.   Another type of risk is *purchasing power risk,* or the risk that inflation will reduce the purchasing power of a given sum of money. This risk is important both to firms and to individual investors during times of inflation, and it is generally regarded as being lower on assets whose returns can be expected to rise during inflation than on assets whose returns are fixed. Thus, real estate and common stocks are often thought of as being better "hedges against inflation" than are bonds and other long-term, fixed-income securities.

Liquidity, or Marketability, Risk. An asset that can be sold on short notice for close to its quoted market price is defined as being highly *liquid*. If Foxcraft purchased $1 million of infrequently traded bonds issued by a relatively obscure company, it would probably have to accept a price reduction to sell the bonds on short notice. On the other hand, if Foxcraft bought $1 million worth of U.S. Treasury bonds, or bonds issued by AT&T, General Motors, or Exxon, it would be able to dispose of them almost instantaneously at close to the current market price. These latter bonds are said to have very little *liquidity risk*. Note, though, that although Treasury bonds and AT&T bonds may be liquid, their value will decline if they have long maturities and interest rates rise.

Returns on Securities. As we know from earlier chapters, the higher a security's risk, the higher is its expected and required rate of return. Thus, corporate treasurers, like other investors, must make a tradeoff between risk and return when choosing investments for their marketable securities portfolios. Since the liquidity portfolio is generally held for a specific known need, or else for use in emergencies, the firm might be financially embarrassed should the portfolio decline in value. Accordingly, the marketable securities portfolio is generally confined to safe, highly liquid, short-term securities issued by either the U.S. government or the very strongest corporations. However, the cash managers of larger firms with substantial marketable security holdings often use sophisticated hedging strategies which permit them to take low-risk positions in risky assets.

Types of Marketable Securities

Table 20-3 lists the major types of securities available for investment, with yields as of June 10, 1977, February 10, 1982, and March 1, 1990. Depending on how long they will be held, the financial manager decides upon a suitable set of securities, and a suitable maturity pattern, for the firm's portfolio. Because the securities' characteristics change with shifts in financial market conditions, it would be misleading to attempt to give detailed descriptions of them here.

It should be noted that larger corporations, with large amounts of surplus cash, tend to own directly Treasury bills, commercial paper, and CDs, as well as Euromarket securities. Smaller firms, on the other hand, are more likely to invest through a money market or preferred stock mutual fund, because the small firm's volume of investment simply does not warrant its hiring specialists to manage the portfolio and to make sure that the securities held mature (or can be sold) at the same time cash is required. Firms can use a mutual fund and then literally write checks on the fund to meet cash needs as they arise. Interest rates on mutual funds are somewhat lower than rates on direct investments of equivalent risk because of management fees, but for smaller companies net returns may well be higher on money funds.

Table 20-3   Securities Available for Investment of Surplus Cash

Security	Typical Maturity at Time of Issue	Approximate Yields		
		6/10/77	2/10/82	3/1/90
Suitable to Hold as Near-Cash Reserve				
U.S. Treasury bills[a]	91 days to 1 year	4.8%	15.1%	7.7%
Commercial paper[a]	Up to 270 days	5.5	15.3	8.1
Negotiable certificates of deposit (CDs) of U.S. banks	Up to 1 year	6.0	15.5	7.8
Money market mutual funds	Instant liquidity	5.1	14.0	7.5
Floating rate and market auction preferred stock[b]	Instant liquidity	N.A.	N.A.	5.6
Eurodollar time deposits	Up to 1 year	6.1	16.2	8.5
Not Suitable to Hold as Near-Cash Reserve				
U.S. Treasury notes	3 to 10 years	6.8	14.8	8.5
U.S. Treasury bonds	Up to 30 years	7.6	14.6	8.6
Corporate bonds (AAA)[c]	Up to 40 years	8.2	16.0	9.4
State and local government bonds (AAA)[c,d]	Up to 30 years	5.7	12.8	7.2
Preferred stocks (AAA)[c,d]	30 years to perpetual	7.5	14.0	8.5
Common stocks of other corporations	Unlimited	Variable	Variable	Variable
Common stock of the firm in question	Unlimited	Variable	Variable	Variable

[a]Treasury bills and commercial paper are sold at a discount but are paid off at par upon maturity, so their returns are quoted on a *discount basis rate*. To obtain an interest rate which can be compared to quoted yields on coupon bonds—called a *yield basis rate*—we use the following formula:

$$\frac{\text{Yield basis rate}}{\text{(Effective annual rate)}} = \frac{365(\text{Discount basis rate})}{360 - (\text{Discount basis rate})(\text{Days to maturity})}.$$

To illustrate, if we assume a 3-month (91-day) maturity, the T-bills' 7.7 percent discount basis rate on March 1, 1990, translates into a yield basis rate (or effective annual rate) of 7.96 percent:

$$\text{Yield basis rate} = \frac{365(0.077)}{360 - 0.077(91)}$$

$$= 0.0796 = 7.96\%.$$

See Robert C. Radcliffe, *Investment Concepts, Analysis, and Strategy* (Glenview, Ill.: Scott, Foresman, 1990), for a further discussion.

[b]Floating rate and market auction preferred stock are recent innovations in near-cash securities. They are held by corporations (often through money funds designed for this purpose) because of the 70 percent dividend tax exclusion.

[c]Rates shown for corporate and state/local government bonds, and for preferred stock, are for longer maturities rated AAA. Lower-rated securities have higher yields. The slope of the yield curve determines whether shorter- or longer-term securities of a given rating would have higher yields.

[d]Rates are lower on state/municipal government bonds because the interest they pay is exempt from federal income taxes, and for preferred stocks because 70 percent of the dividends paid on them is exempt from federal taxes for corporate owners, who own most preferred stocks.

Self-Test Questions

Why do firms hold marketable securities?

What criteria are applied when selecting securities for a firm's liquid asset portfolio?

What are some securities commonly held as marketable securities?

MULTINATIONAL FINANCE
Cash Management in Multinational Corporations

The objectives of cash management in a multinational corporation are similar to those in a purely domestic corporation—namely (1) to speed up collections and to slow down disbursements as much as is feasible, hence to maximize net float; (2) to shift cash from those parts of the business where it is not needed to parts where it is needed as rapidly as possible; and (3) to obtain the highest possible risk-adjusted rate of return on temporary cash balances. Multinational companies use the same general procedures for achieving these goals as domestic firms, but because of longer distances and more serious mail delays, lockbox systems and electronic funds transfers are especially important.

Although multinational and domestic corporations have the same objectives and use similar procedures, the multinational corporation faces a more complex task. First, domestic governments often place restrictions on transfers of funds out of the country, so although IBM can transfer money from its Salt Lake City office to its New York concentration bank just by pressing a few buttons, a similar transfer from its Buenos Aires office is far more complex. Buenos Aires funds are denominated in australs (Argentina's equivalent of the dollar), so the australs must be converted to dollars before the transfer. If there is a shortage of

dollars in Argentina, or if the Argentinean government wants to conserve available dollars to use for the purchase of strategic materials, then conversion, hence the transfer, may be blocked. Even if no dollar shortage exists in Argentina, the government may still restrict funds outflows if those funds represent profits or depreciation rather than payments for purchased materials or equipment. The reason is that many countries, especially the less developed countries, want profits reinvested in the country in which they were made in order to stimulate economic growth.

Once it has been determined what funds can be transferred out of the various nations in which a multinational corporation operates, it is important to get those funds to locations where they will earn the highest returns. Whereas domestic corporations tend to think in terms of the alternatives listed in Table 20-3, multinationals are more likely to be aware of investment opportunities all around the world. Most multinational corporations use one or more global concentration banks, located in money centers such as London, New York, Tokyo, Zurich, or Singapore, and their staffs in those cities, working with international bankers, know of and are able to take advantage of the best rates available anywhere in the world.

SUMMARY

In this chapter, we discussed cash and marketable securities. First, we examined the cash budget; then we discussed several ways to set the target cash balance; and then we examined some cash management techniques. Finally, we discussed marketable securities. The key concepts covered are listed next.

- The *primary goal of cash management* is to reduce the amount of cash held to the minimum necessary to conduct business. Some cash is necessary so the firm (1) can take trade discounts, (2) can maintain its credit rating, and (3) can meet unexpected cash needs.

- A *cash budget* is a schedule showing projected cash inflows and outflows over some period. The cash budget is used to predict cash surpluses and shortages, and thus it is the primary cash management planning tool.

- Four methods can be used to set a firm's *target cash balance:* (1) the Baumol model, (2) the Miller-Orr model, (3) the Stone model, and (4) Monte Carlo simulation.

- The *Baumol model* balances the opportunity cost of holding cash against the transactions costs associated with replenishing the cash account.

- The *Miller-Orr model* takes account of the uncertainty inherent in a firm's cash inflows and outflows, and it sets upper and lower limits on the cash balance which trigger transactions into or out of the cash account.

- The *Stone model* extends the Miller-Orr model by considering the cash flows expected in the near future before making any transfers triggered by the upper and lower limits.

- *Monte Carlo simulation* provides a probability distribution of net cash flows which can be used to set a target balance which holds the probability of a shortfall to an acceptable level.

- *Cash management techniques* generally fall into five categories: (1) synchronizing cash flow, (2) using float, (3) accelerating collections, (4) determining where and when funds will be needed, and insuring that they are available at the right place at the right time, and (5) controlling disbursements.

- Two techniques that can be used to speed up collections are (1) *lockboxes* and (2) *pre-authorized debits.* Then, a *concentration banking system* consolidates the collections into a centralized pool that can be managed more efficiently than a large number of individual accounts.

- Three techniques for controlling disbursements are (1) *payables centralization,* (2) *zero-balance accounts,* and (3) *controlled disbursement accounts.*

- The implementation of a sophisticated cash management system is costly, and all cash management actions must be evaluated to insure that the benefits exceed the costs.

- Firms can reduce their cash balances by holding *marketable securities,* which can be sold on short notice at close to their true values. Marketable securities serve both as a substitute for cash and as a temporary investment for funds that will be needed in the near future. Safety is the primary consideration when treasurers select marketable securities.

- *Multinational corporations* have the same cash management objective as domestic corporations, and multinationals use the same cash management techniques. However, cash management in a multinational firm is much more complex because of the geographic distances and multiple currencies involved.

In the next chapter, we continue our discussion of short-term financial management by examining receivables and inventories.

Questions

20-1   Define each of the following terms:
   a.   Cash budget; net cash gain (loss)
   b.   Target cash balance
   c.   Baumol model
   d.   Miller-Orr model
   e.   Stone model
   f.   Monte Carlo simulation

g.   Synchronized cash flows
h.   Disbursement float; collection float; net float
i.   Lockbox plan
j.   Pre-authorized debits
k.   Concentration banking
l.   Payables centralization
m.   Zero-balance accounts
n.   Controlled disbursement accounts
o.   Marketable securities; near-cash reserves
p.   Default risk; event risk; interest rate risk; purchasing power risk; liquidity (marketability) risk

20-2   How can better methods of communication reduce the necessity for firms to hold large cash balances?

20-3   Explain how each of the following factors would probably affect a firm's target cash balance, assuming all other factors are held constant.
a.   The firm institutes a new billing procedure which better synchronizes its cash inflows and outflows.
b.   The firm develops a new forecasting technique which improves its sales forecasts.
c.   The firm reduces its portfolio of U.S. Treasury bills.
d.   The firm arranges for a line of credit on its checking account.
e.   The firm borrows a large amount of money from its bank and also begins to pay suppliers twice as frequently as in the past, so it must write far more checks that it did in the past even though the dollar totals of checks written have not changed.
f.   Interest rates on Treasury bills rise from 5 percent to 10 percent.

20-4   Would a lockbox plan make more sense for a firm that makes sales all over the United States or for a firm with the same volume of business but whose customers are concentrated in its home city?

20-5   Would a corporate treasurer be more tempted to invest the firm's liquid asset portfolio in long-term as opposed to short-term securities when the yield curve was upward sloping or downward sloping?

20-6   What does the term *liquidity* mean? Which would be more important to a firm that held a portfolio of marketable securities as a precautionary balance against the possibility of losing a major lawsuit—liquidity or rate of return? Explain.

20-7   Firm A's management is very conservative, while Firm B's is more aggressive. Is is true that, other things the same, Firm B would probably have larger holdings of marketable securities? Explain.

20-8   Is it true that interest rate risk refers to the risk that a firm will be unable to pay the interest on its bonds? Explain.

20-9   When selecting securities for portfolio investments, corporate treasurers must make a tradeoff between risk and returns. Is it true that most treasurers are willing to assume a fairly high exposure to risk to gain higher expected returns?

Self-Test Problem (Solutions Appear in Appendix D)

ST-1   **(Lockbox analysis)** Tysseland Company has grown from a small Boston firm with customers concentrated in New England to a large, national firm serving customers throughout the United States. However, all operations, including the central billing system, have remained in Boston. On average, 5 days elapse from the time customers mail payments until Tysseland is able to receive and process the checks so that it can use the money. To shorten the collection period, Tysseland is considering the installation of a lockbox system consisting of 30 local depository banks, or lockbox operators, and 8 regional concentration banks. The fixed cost of operating the system is estimated to be $14,000 per month. Under this system, customers' checks would be received by the lockbox operator 1 day after they are mailed, and daily collections would average $30,000 at each location. The collections would be transferred daily to the regional concentration banks.

One transfer mechanism involves having the local depository banks use "mail depository transfer checks," or DTCs, to move the funds to the concentration banks; the alternative is to use electronic ("wire") transfers. A DTC would cost only 75 cents, but it would take 2 days to get funds to the concentration bank and thus make them available to Tysseland. Therefore, float time under the DTC system would be 1 day for mail plus 2 days for transfer, or 3 days total, down from 5 days under the present system where no concentration banking is used. A wire transfer would cost $11, but funds would be available immediately, so float time would be only 1 day.

If Tysseland's opportunity cost is 11 percent, should it initiate the lockbox/concentration banking system? If so, which transfer method should be used? (Assume that there are 52 × 5 = 260 working days, hence transfers from each lockbox, in a year.)

Problems

20-1 **(Cash budgeting)** Neil and Terry Sicherman recently leased space in the Southside Mall and opened a new business, Sicherman's Coin Shop. Business has been good, but the Sichermans have frequently run out of cash. This has necessitated late payment on certain orders, and this, in turn, is beginning to cause a problem with suppliers. The Sichermans plan to borrow money from the bank to have cash ready as needed, but first they need a forecast of just how much they must borrow. Accordingly, they have asked you to prepare a cash budget for the critical period around Christmas, when needs will be especially high.

Sales are made on a *cash basis only*. The Sichermans' purchases must be paid for the following month. The Sichermans pay themselves a salary of $4,800 per month, and the rent is $2,000 per month. In addition, the Sichermans must make a tax payment of $12,000 in December. The current cash on hand (on December 1) is $400, but the Sichermans have agreed to maintain an end-of-month bank balance of $6,000, their target cash balance. (Disregard till cash, which is insignificant because the Sichermans keep only a small amount on hand in order to lessen the chances of robbery.)

The estimated sales and purchases for December, January, and February are shown next. Purchases during November amounted to $140,000.

	Sales	Purchases
December	$160,000	$40,000
January	40,000	40,000
February	60,000	40,000

a. Prepare a cash budget for December, January, and February.
b. Now suppose the Sichermans were to start selling on a credit basis on December 1, giving customers 30 days to pay. All customers accept these terms, and all other facts in the problem are unchanged. What would the company's loan requirements be at the end of December in this case?

20-2 **(Cash budgeting)** The Torrence Company is planning to request a line of credit from its bank. The following sales forecasts have been made for 1991 and 1992:

May 1991	$150,000
June	150,000
July	300,000
August	450,000
September	600,000
October	300,000
November	300,000
December	75,000
January 1992	150,000

Collection estimates were obtained from the credit and collection department as follows: collected within the month of sale, 10 percent; collected the month following the month of sale, 85 percent; and collected the second month following the month of sale, 5 percent. Payments for labor and raw materials are typically made during the month following the month in which these costs are incurred. Total labor and raw materials costs are estimated for each month as follows (payments are made the following month):

May 1991	$ 75,000
June	75,000
July	105,000
August	735,000
September	255,000
October	195,000
November	135,000
December	75,000

General and administrative salaries will amount to approximately $29,250 a month; lease payments under long-term lease contracts will be $9,750 a month; depreciation charges will be $39,000 a month; miscellaneous expenses will be $2,925 a month; income tax payments of $68,250 will be due in both September and December; and a progress payment of $195,000 on a new research laboratory must be paid in October. Cash on hand on July 1 will amount to $143,000, and a minimum cash balance of $97,500 should be maintained throughout the cash budget period.

a.   Prepare a monthly cash budget for the last six months of 1991. How much money will Torrence need to borrow (or how much will it have available to invest) each month?

b.   Suppose receipts from sales come in uniformly during the month—that is, cash payments come in 1/30 each day—but all outflows are paid on the fifth of the month. Would this have an effect on the cash budget—in other words, would the cash budget you have prepared be valid under these assumptions? If not, what could be done to make a valid estimation of financing requirements? No calculations are required, although calculations can be used to illustrate the effects.

c.   Torrence produces on a seasonal basis, just ahead of sales. Without making any calculations, discuss how the company's current ratio and debt ratio (Total debt/Total assets) would vary during the year assuming all financial requirements were met by short-term bank loans. Could changes in these ratios affect the firm's ability to obtain bank credit?

d.   If you prepared the cash budget in Part a correctly, you would show a surplus at the end of July, which increases by the end of August. Suggest some alternative investments for this money. Be sure to consider the pros and cons of long-term versus short-term debt instruments, and the appropriateness of investing in common stock.

e.   Would your choice of securities in Part d be affected if the cash budget showed continuous cash surpluses versus alternating surpluses and deficits?

(Do Parts f, g, and h only if you are using the computerized diskette.)

f.   By offering a 2 percent cash discount for paying within the month of sale, the credit
manager has revised the collection percentages to 50 percent, 35 percent, and 15 percent,
respectively. How will this affect the loan requirements?

g.   Return the payment percentages to their base case values and the discount to zero. Now
suppose sales fall to only 70 percent of the forecasted level. Production is maintained, so
cash outflows are unchanged. How does this affect Torrence's financial requirements?

h.   Return sales to the forecasted level (100%), and suppose collections slow down to 5%,
20%, and 75% for the three months, respectively. How does this affect financial requirements? If Torrence went to a cash-only sales policy, how would that affect requirements,
other factors held constant?

20-3 **(Baumol model)** You have just been hired as the cash manager of the Lamm Company.
Your first task is to determine the target cash balance. The firm expects to need $1,000,000 of
net new cash during the coming year. This requirement occurs at a relatively constant rate
over the year. The firm plans to meet this cash requirement by borrowing from Bank A at an
annual interest rate of 10 percent. The fixed cost of transferring funds from the bank is $50
per transfer.

a.   Assume that the firm will not carry a cash "safety stock." What average cash balance is
indicated by the Baumol model? How many cash transfers are expected over the year?

b.   Suppose the firm wants to maintain a $5,000 cash "safety stock," which is currently on
hand. What would be the new average cash balance?

20-4 **(Baumol model)** The Koehl Company has accumulated $100,000 in excess cash. However,
it is expected that the firm will need the entire amount to cover cash outflows anticipated to
occur evenly over the coming year. Koehl has the funds invested in commercial paper that
pays 10 percent annually. The cost of transferring funds is $50 per transaction.

a.   What is Koehl's target cash balance according to the Baumol model? What is the firm's
total cost of cash balances?

b.   As Koehl's cash manager, you are concerned about whether the Baumol model is on a
before-tax or after-tax basis. Koehl's federal-plus-state tax rate is 40 percent. What are the
firm's target cash balance and total costs of cash balances on an *after-tax* basis?

c.   Koehl is considering putting its excess cash in a floating rate preferred stock mutual fund.
The fund pays 10 percent annually, but only 30 percent of its dividends are taxable. What
effect would this decision have on the firm's target cash balance and cost of cash balances?

20-5 **(Miller-Orr model)** The Pettijohn Corporation has estimated that the standard deviation of
its daily net cash flows is $2,500. The firm pays $50 in transaction costs to transfer funds into
and out of commercial paper that pays 7.465 percent annual interest. The firm uses the Miller-
Orr model to set its target cash balance. Additionally, the firm has decided to maintain a
$10,000 minimum cash balance (lower limit).

a.   What is the firm's target cash balance?

b.   What are the upper and lower limits?

c.   What are Pettijohn's decision rules? (That is, when is a transaction called for, and what is
the transaction?)

d.   What is the firm's expected average cash balance?

20-6 **(Lockbox system)** Bacon, Inc., began operations 5 years ago as a small firm serving customers in the Seattle area. However, its reputation and market area grew quickly, so that today
Bacon has customers throughout the entire United States. Despite its broad customer

base, Bacon has maintained its headquarters in Seattle and keeps its central billing system there. Bacon's management is considering an alternative collection procedure to reduce its mail time and processing float. On average, it takes 5 days from the time customers mail payments until Bacon is able to receive, process, and deposit them. Bacon would like to set up a lockbox collection system, which it estimates would reduce the time lag from customer mailing to deposit by 3 days—bringing it down to 2 days. Bacon receives an average of $700,000 in payments per day.

a.   How many days of collection float now exist (Bacon's customers' disbursement float) and what would it be under the lockbox system? What reduction in cash balances could Bacon achieve by initiating the lockbox system?

b.   If Bacon has an opportunity cost of 9 percent, how much is the lockbox system worth on an annual basis?

c.   What is the maximum monthly charge Bacon should pay for the lockbox system?

20-7 **(Lockbox system)** D. Hurst and Sons, Inc., operates a mail-order firm doing business on the East Coast. Hurst receives an average of $500,000 in payments per day. On average it takes 4 days from the time customers mail checks until Hurst receives and processes them. Hurst is considering the use of a lockbox system to reduce collection and processing float. The system will cost $10,000 per month and will consist of 10 local depository banks and a concentration bank located in Atlanta. Under this system, customers' checks should be received at the lockbox locations 1 day after they are mailed, and they will be transferred to Atlanta using wire transfers costing $15 each. Assume that Hurst has an opportunity cost of 10 percent and that there are $52 \times 5 = 260$ working days, hence 260 transfers from each lockbox location, in a year.

a.   What is the total cost of operating the lockbox system?

b.   What is the benefit of the lockbox system to Hurst?

c.   Should Hurst initiate the system?

(Do Parts d and e only if you are using the computerized diskette.)

d.   Would the system be beneficial if Hurst could operate it with only 8 lockbox locations while achieving the same reduction in float?

e.   Suppose interest rates rise so that Hurst can now earn 11 percent on its invested funds. What would be the benefit (or loss) of operating the lockbox system with 10 lockbox locations? 8 locations?

Mini Case

Bruce Vogel, financial manager of SkiWear, Inc., a manufacturer of high-fashion ski clothes, is currently forecasting the company's cash needs for the second half of the year. SkiWear's sales are highly seasonal, with most of its sales occurring in the fall, just prior to the start of the ski season. The firm's marketing department forecasts sales as follows:

May	$200,000	August	$450,000	November	$200,000
June	250,000	September	600,000	December	100,000
July	300,000	October	800,000	January	100,000

The firm's credit terms are 2/10, net 30, and the credit department provided Bruce with the following collections estimates: 20 percent of dollar sales will be collected in the month of sale (these are the discount sales); 70 percent will be collected the month following the sale; 9 percent will be collected 2 months following the sale; and 1 percent will end up as bad debt losses.

Wages and material costs are related to production, and hence to sales. The cost accountants have estimated production costs as follows:

June	$175,000	August	$325,000	October	$125,000
July	250,000	September	425,000	November	75,000

Note, however, that payments for wages and materials are typically made in the month after the costs are incurred.

Administrative salaries are projected at $25,000 a month; lease payments amount to $20,000 a month; and miscellaneous expenses total $10,000 a month. Quarterly tax payments of $125,000 must be made in September and December, and $250,000 will be needed in October to pay for a new fabric cutting machine.

Bruce expects the firm to have $50,000 on hand at the beginning of July, and he wants to start each month with that amount on hand. As Bruce's assistant, you have been asked to answer the following questions:

a.   Complete the following collections worksheet (Part I of the cash budget):

	Jul	Aug	Sep	Oct	Nov	Dec
Sales	$300,000	$450,000	$600,000	$800,000	$200,000	$100,000
Collections: This month			117,600	156,800	39,200	19,600
Last month			315,000	420,000	560,000	140,000
2 months ago			27,000	40,500	54,000	72,000
			$459,600	$617,300	$653,200	$231,600

b.   Fill in the missing cells in the following cash budget. What is SkiWear's maximum loan requirement? What is the firm's maximum surplus cash balance?

II. Cash Gain or Loss	Jul	Aug	Sep	Oct	Nov	Dec
Receipts:						
Collections	$251,800	$320,700			$653,200	$231,600
Payments:						
Labor/raw materials	$175,000	$250,000			$125,000	$ 75,000
Admin salaries	25,000	25,000			25,000	25,000
Lease payments	20,000	20,000			20,000	20,000
Misc expenses	10,000	10,000			10,000	10,000
Taxes	0	0		0	0	125,000
Equipment	0	0	0		0	0
Total payments	$230,000	$305,000			$180,000	$255,000
Net cash gain (loss)	$ 21,800	$ 15,700			$473,200	($ 23,400)

III. Cash Surplus or Loan						
Beginning-of-month cash without loans	$50,000	$71,800			($70,600)	402,600
Cumulative = NCG(L) + Beginning cash	71,800	87,500			402,600	379,200
Target balance	50,000	50,000			50,000	50,000
Surplus (loan)	$ 21,800	$37,500			$352,600	$329,200

c. (1) Depreciation amounts to $1,200,000 per year, or $100,000 per month. Should this expense be explicitly included in the cash budget? Why or why not?

   (2) Suppose the outflows all occur on the 5th day of each month, but the inflows all occur on the 25th day. This situation occurs because of the credit terms used by SkiWear and its suppliers. How would this affect July's cash budget? What could be done to incorporate such nonuniform flows into the cash budget?

   (3) SkiWear's cash budget's only receipts are collections. What are some other types of inflows that could occur? List both fairly regular cash inflows and also some cash inflows that could be forecasted, but which would have to be planned for (negotiated with someone).

   (4) Like most firms, SkiWear plans to "sweep" its excess cash balances into marketable securities. Further, SkiWear would have to pay interest on its short-term borrowings. Explain how these flows could be incorporated into the cash budget. Be specific — say exactly where lines would be added to the budget, and exactly what the entries on those lines would be and how they would then be carried through to the remainder of the statement.

d. (1) The cash budget is a *forecast,* so many of the flows are expected values rather than amounts known with certainty. If actual sales, hence collections and production, were different from the forecasted levels, then the surpluses and deficits would also be incorrect. What would you expect the general impact on the cash budget to be if sales were 20 percent *above* those originally forecasted? What if sales were 20 percent *below* those originally forecasted? In answering these questions, think about how production would be adjusted, how your answer would be affected (a) if production could be adjusted to reflect the new sales with no lags, and (b) if production could not be adjusted at all during the forecast period, and (c) how production would *probably* actually be adjusted.

   (2) How could sensitivity analysis, scenario analysis, or Monte Carlo simulation be used to help forecast the net cash inflows and required beginning-of-month cash balances?

e. SkiWear's annual cash requirements average about $3,000,000 per year. It costs about $5 per transaction to transfer funds between the cash account and the marketable securities account, and the current interest rate on marketable securities is about 10 percent. Use the Baumol model to answer the following questions:

   (1) To the nearest thousand dollars, what is the optimal transfer amount between cash and marketable securities?

   (2) What would the firm's average cash balance be if it determined this balance with the Baumol model?

   (3) How many transfers would be made in a year?

   (4) Are economies of scale in cash management implicit in the Baumol model?

   (5) What assumptions underlie the Baumol model?

f. Now consider the Miller-Orr model. SkiWear's lower limit is set at $20,000, and the standard deviation of its daily cash flow is $2,000. The firm's annual opportunity cost is 10 percent, and the transfer charge is $5.

   (1) What is the firm's optimal transfer point (Z) according to the Miller-Orr model?

   (2) What are the upper and lower limits?

   (3) What is the firm's average cash balance?

   (4) What are SkiWear's cash management decision rules according to the Miller-Orr model?

   (5) How does the average cash balance under the Miller-Orr model compare with that under the Baumol target? Which model would you be more inclined to use? Why?

g. Describe the Stone model. How is it similar to the Miller-Orr model? How does it differ?

h. If the cash budget is correct, SkiWear will generate large surpluses in November and December, and these surpluses will be invested in marketable securities. Assume that the cash surpluses will be required for expansion purposes during the coming year.

    (1) What are the characteristics of the securities that should be used in the marketable security portfolio? What are some securities that you would recommend?

    (2) Suppose you learned that the surplus cash flows shown in SkiWear's cash budget would probably *not* be needed during the next year — long-range forecasts indicate that the company will probably continue to generate cash surpluses, although there is always a chance that something will go wrong, and that some cash will be required. Would this cause you to change your recommendation as to what SkiWear should plan to do with its surplus cash? Explain.

Additional References and Cases

Perhaps the best way to get a good feel for the current state of the art in cash management is to look through recent issues of The Journal of Cash Management, *a relatively new publication aimed at professionals in the field.*

For more information on cash management in general, see

Beehler, Paul J., *Contemporary Cash Management* (New York: Wiley, 1983).

Driscoll, Mary C., *Cash Management: Corporate Strategies for Profit* (New York: Wiley, 1983).

Key references on cash balance models include the following:

Daellenbach, Hans G., "Are Cash Management Optimization Models Worthwhile?" *Journal of Financial and Quantitative Analysis,* September 1974, 607–626.

Miller, Merton H., and Daniel Orr, "The Demand for Money by Firms: Extension of Analytic Results," *Journal of Finance,* December 1968, 735–759.

Mullins, David Wiley, Jr., and Richard B. Homonoff, "Applications of Inventory Cash Management Models," in *Modern Developments in Financial Management,* Stewart C. Myers, ed. (New York: Praeger, 1976).

Stone, Bernell K., "The Use of Forecasts for Smoothing in Control-Limit Models for Cash Management," *Financial Management,* Spring 1972, 72–84.

For more information on float management, see

Batlin, C. A., and Susan Hinko, "Lockbox Management and Value Maximization," *Financial Management,* Winter 1981, 39–44.

Gitman, Lawrence J., D. Keith Forrester, and John R. Forrester, Jr., "Maximizing Cash Disbursement Float," *Financial Management,* Summer 1976, 32–41.

Nauss, Robert M., and Robert E. Markland, "Solving Lockbox Location Problems," *Financial Management,* Spring 1979, 21–31.

The following articles provide more information on cash concentration systems:

Stone, Bernell K., and Ned C. Hill, "Cash Transfer Scheduling for Efficient Cash Concentration," *Financial Management,* Autumn 1980, 35–43.

———, "The Design of a Cash Concentration System," *Journal of Financial and Quantitative Analysis,* September 1981, 301–322.

Stone, Bernell K., and Tom W. Miller, "Daily Cash Forecasting with Multiplicative Models of Cash Flow Patterns," *Financial Management,* Winter 1987, 45–54.

For greater insights into compensating balance requirements, see

Campbell, Tim S., and Leland Brendsel, "The Impact of Compensating Balance Requirements on the Cash Balances of Manufacturing Corporations," *Journal of Finance,* March 1977, 31–40.

Frost, Peter A., "Banking Services, Minimum Cash Balances, and the Firm's Demand for Money," *Journal of Finance,* December 1970, 1029–1039.

For more information on marketable securities, see any of the investment textbooks referenced in Chapter 4, or see

Brown, Keith C., and Scott L. Lummer, "A Reexamination of the Covered Call Option Strategy for Corporate Cash Management," *Financial Management,* Summer 1986, 13–17.

Kamath, Ravindra R., et al, "Management of Excess Cash: Practices and Developments," *Financial Management,* Autumn 1985, 70–77.

Stigum, M., *The Money Market: Myth, Reality, and Practice* (Homewood, Ill.: Dow Jones-Irwin, 1978).

Van Horne, J. C., *Financial Market Rates and Flows* (Englewood Cliffs, N.J.: Prentice-Hall, 1984).

Zivney, Terry L., and Michael J. Alderson, "Hedged Dividend Capture with Stock Index Options," *Financial Management,* Summer 1986, 5–12.

The following cases from the Brigham-Gapenski casebook focus on cash management:

Case 32, "Standard Uniform Company," which focuses on the target cash balance decision.

Case 33, "Broske Enterprises," which illustrates the mechanics of the cash budget and the rationale behind its use.

The following case in the Harrington casebook considers cash management:

"Austin Limited," which examines changes in a firm's cash disbursement system.

CHAPTER 21

Accounts Receivable and Inventory

Most security analysts were forecasting Xerox's sales and earnings to fall during the recent recession. But it did not happen—earnings rose 10 percent on a 23 percent sales gain. The secret, analysts learned, was that Xerox had instituted a major change in its credit policy—it had built up a pool of cash which it then loaned to its customers at bargain rates in order to increase sales of its products. Profits on the added sales more than offset the cost to Xerox of the low-rate loans, boosting the company's net income at a time when its competitors' profits were falling.

Xerox liberalized its credit policy and gained, but other companies, faced with different conditions, have increased their profits by tightening or even eliminating credit. For example, Atlantic Richfield Company (Arco) recently eliminated the use of credit cards at all of its service stations. Its management believed (1) that customers were very sensitive to gasoline prices; (2) that the cost of extending credit to customers amounted to about 4 cents per gallon; (3) that if it eliminated credit sales it could cut gas prices at the pump by 3 cents a gallon, which would boost profit per gallon by 1 cent and at the same time double its number of customers; and (4) that consequently it would enjoy a substantial increase in net profits. The plan worked beautifully, and it contributed to Arco's overall success.

Besides their credit policies, companies are also very much concerned with inventory policies. The cost of money used to buy and carry inventories is about 15 percent for many firms, and storage, insurance, pilferage, and obsolescence amount to another 10 to 15 percent. Thus, holding $100 of inventory for a year has a cost in the range of $25 to $30. With these high costs, holding excessive inventories can literally ruin a company. On the other hand, inventory shortages lead to lost sales, to production interruptions, and to customer ill will, so shortages can be just as harmful as excesses.

Many firms today are using computerized inventory control models to match stocks on hand with forecasted sales levels, and they are coordinating closely with suppliers to reduce average inventory levels. For example, Huffy Corporation, the largest U.S. bicycle manufacturer, was able to reduce its peak spring inventory from $69 million to $36 million through a better inventory control process. Huffy is saving millions of dollars in interest and storage costs by keeping a pared-down inventory, with no adverse effect on sales. However, such a policy is not without dangers—if bicycle sales surge, Huffy's inventories might not be sufficient to meet demand, causing the company to lose sales to its rivals, who are continuing to carry higher inventories. Note, though, that if sales fall, Huffy will be in a better position than its rivals, and if consumers begin to demand bicycles of different styles, Huffy will be able to adapt more easily than its competitors, who will be stuck with obsolete bicycles.

Our goal in this chapter is to examine the factors that companies like Xerox, Arco, and Huffy consider when they establish credit and inventory policies. From the standpoint of profitability, no decisions have a greater effect.

SINCE the typical firm has about 20 percent of its assets in receivables and another 20 percent in inventories, its effectiveness in managing these two accounts is obviously important to its profitability and risk—and thus to its stock price. Techniques for managing receivables and inventories are covered in this chapter.

RECEIVABLES MANAGEMENT

Firms would, in general, rather sell for cash than on credit, but competitive pressures force most firms to offer credit. Thus, goods are shipped, inventories are reduced, and an account receivable is created. Eventually, the customer will pay the account, at which time (1) the firm will receive cash and (2) its receivables will decline. Carrying receivables has both direct and indirect costs, but it also has an important benefit—granting credit will increase sales. The optimal credit policy is the one which maximizes the firm's net cash flows over time, giving consideration to the risk assumed.

Receivables management begins with the decision of whether or not to grant credit. In this section, we discuss the manner in which a firm's receivables build up, and we also present several alternative means of monitoring receivables. A monitoring system is important, because without it, receivables will build up to excessive levels, cash flows will decline, and bad debts will offset the profits on sales. Corrective action is often needed, and the only way to know whether the situation is getting out of hand is to set up and then follow a good receivables control system.

The Accumulation of Receivables

The total amount of accounts receivable outstanding at any given time is determined by two factors: (1) the volume of credit sales and (2) the average length of time between sales and collections. For example, suppose the Boston Lumber Company (BLC), a wholesale distributor of lumber products, opens a warehouse on January 1 and, starting the first day, makes sales of $1,000 each day. (For simplicity, we assume that all sales are on credit.) Customers are given 10 days in which to pay. At the end of the first day, accounts receivable will be $1,000; they will rise to $2,000 by the end of the second day; and by January 10, they will have risen to 10($1,000) = $10,000. On January 11, another $1,000 will be added to receivables, but payments for sales made on January 1 will reduce receivables by $1,000, so total accounts receivable will remain constant at $10,000. In general, once the firm's operations have stabilized, this situation will exist:

$$\frac{\text{Accounts}}{\text{receivable}} = \frac{\text{Credit sales}}{\text{per day}} \times \frac{\text{Length of}}{\text{collection period}}$$

$$= \quad \$1,000 \quad \times \quad 10 \text{ days} \quad = \$10,000.$$

If either credit sales or the collection period changes, such changes will be reflected in accounts receivable.

Notice that the $10,000 investment in receivables must be financed. To illustrate, suppose that when the store opened on January 1, BLC's shareholders had put up $800 as common stock and used this money to buy the goods sold the first day. The $800 worth of inventory will be sold for $1,000; thus, BLC's gross profit on the $800 investment is $200 or 25 percent. In this situation, the initial balance sheet would be as follows:[1]

Inventories	$800	Common equity	$800
Total assets	$800	Total claims	$800

At the end of the day, the balance sheet would look like this:

Accounts receivable	$1,000	Common equity	$ 800
Inventories	0	Retained earnings	200
Total assets	$1,000	Total claims	$1,000

---

[1]Note that the firm would need other assets such as cash, fixed assets, and a permanent stock of inventory. Also, overhead costs and taxes would have to be deducted, so retained earnings would be less than the figures shown here. We abstract from these details here so that we may focus on receivables.

In order to remain in business, BLC must replenish inventories. To do so requires that $800 of goods be purchased, and this requires $800 in cash. Assuming that BLC borrows the $800 from the bank, the balance sheet at the start of the second day will be as follows:

Accounts receivable	$1,000	Notes payable to bank	$ 800
Inventories	800	Common equity	800
		Retained earnings	200
Total assets	$1,800	Total claims	$1,800

At the end of the second day, the inventories will have been converted to receivables, and the firm will have to borrow another $800 to restock for the third day.

This process will continue, provided the bank is willing to lend the necessary funds, until the beginning of the eleventh day, when the balance sheet reads as follows:

Accounts receivable	$10,000	Notes payable to bank	$ 8,000
Inventories	800	Common equity	800
		Retained earnings	2,000
Total assets	$10,800	Total claims	$10,800

From this point on, $1,000 of receivables will be collected every day, and $800 of these funds can be used to purchase new inventories.

This example should make it clear (1) that accounts receivable depend jointly on the level of credit sales and the collection period, (2) that any increase in receivables must be financed in some manner, but (3) that the entire amount of receivables does not have to be financed because the profit portion ($200 of each $1,000 of sales) does not represent a cash outflow. In our example, we assumed bank financing, but, as noted in Chapter 19, there are many alternative ways to finance current assets.

Monitoring the Receivables Position

The optimal credit policy, hence the optimal level of accounts receivable, depends on the firm's own unique operating conditions. For example, a firm with excess capacity and low variable production costs should extend credit more liberally, and carry a higher level of receivables, than a firm operating at full capacity on a slim profit margin. However, even though optimal credit policies vary among firms, or even for a single firm over time, it is still useful to analyze the effectiveness of the firm's credit policy in an overall, aggregate sense. Investors—both stockholders and bank loan officers—should pay close attention to accounts receivable management, for, as we shall see, one can be misled by reported financial statements and later suffer serious losses on an investment.

When a credit sale is made, the following events occur: (1) Inventories are reduced by the cost of goods sold, (2) accounts receivable are increased by the sales price, and (3) the difference is profit, which is added to retained earnings. If the sale is for cash, the profit is definitely earned, but if the sale is on credit, the profit is not actually earned unless and until the account is collected. Firms have been known to encourage "sales" to very weak customers in order to report high profits. This could boost the firm's stock price, at least until credit losses begin to lower earnings, at which time the stock price will fall. Analyses along the lines suggested in the following sections will detect any such questionable practice, as well as any unconscious deterioration in the quality of accounts receivable. Such early detection could help both investors and bankers avoid losses.[2]

Days Sales Outstanding (DSO). Suppose Super Sets, Inc., a television manufacturer, sells 200,000 television sets a year at a sales price of $198 each. Further, assume that all sales are on credit, with terms of 2/10, net 30. Finally, assume that 70 percent of the customers take discounts and pay on Day 10, while the other 30 percent pay on Day 30.

Super Sets' *days sales outstanding (DSO),* sometimes called the *average collection period (ACP),* is 16 days:

$$DSO = ACP = 0.7(10 \text{ days}) + 0.3(30 \text{ days}) = 16 \text{ days.}$$

Super Sets' *average daily sales (ADS),* assuming a 360-day year, is $110,000:

$$ADS = \frac{\text{Annual sales}}{360} = \frac{(\text{Units sold})(\text{Sales price})}{360} = \frac{200,000(\$198)}{360}$$

$$= \frac{\$39,600,000}{360} = \$110,000.$$

If the company had made cash as well as credit sales, we would have concentrated on credit sales only, and calculated average daily *credit* sales.

Super Sets' accounts receivable, assuming a constant, uniform rate of sales all during the year, will at any point in time be $1,760,000:[3]

$$\text{Receivables} = (ADS)(DSO) = (\$110,000)(16) = \$1,760,000.$$

Finally, note that its DSO is a measure of the average length of time it takes Super Sets' customers to pay off their credit purchases, and the DSO is often compared with an industry average DSO. For example, if all television manufacturers sell on the same credit terms, and if the industry average DSO is 25 days versus Super Sets' 16-day DSO, then Super Sets either has a higher percentage of discount customers or else its credit department is exceptionally good at ensuring prompt payment.

The DSO can also be compared with the firm's own credit terms. For example, suppose Super Sets' DSO had been running at a level of 35 days versus its 2/10, net

---

[2]Accountants are increasingly interested in these matters. Investors have sued several of the major accounting firms for substantial damages when (1) profits were overstated and (2) it could be shown that the auditors should have conducted an analysis along the lines described here and then should have reported the results to stockholders in their audit opinion letter.

[3]Note that the DSO can be calculated, given a firm's accounts receivable balance and its average daily credit sales, as follows:

$$DSO = \frac{\text{Receivables}}{ADS} = \frac{\$1,760,000}{\$110,000} = 16 \text{ days.}$$

Table 21-1   Aging Schedules

Age of Account (Days)	Super Sets		Wonder Vision	
	Value of Account	Percentage of Total Value	Value of Account	Percentage of Total Value
0-10	$1,232,000	70%	$ 825,000	47%
11-30	528,000	30	460,000	26
31-45	0	0	265,000	15
46-60	0	0	179,000	10
Over 60	0	0	31,000	2
Total receivables	$1,760,000	100%	$1,760,000	100%

30 credit terms. With a 35-day DSO, some customers would obviously be taking more than 30 days to pay their bills. In fact, if some customers were paying within 10 days to take advantage of the discount, the others would, on average, have to be taking much longer than 35 days. One way to check this possibility is to use an aging schedule as described in the next section.

Aging Schedules. An *aging schedule* breaks down a firm's receivables by age of account. Table 21-1 contains the December 31, 1990, aging schedules of two television manufacturers, Super Sets and Wonder Vision. Both firms offer the same credit terms, 2/10, net 30, and both show the same total receivables. However, Super Sets' aging schedule indicates that all of its customers pay on time—70 percent pay on Day 10 while 30 percent pay on Day 30. Wonder Vision's schedule, which is more typical, shows that many of its customers are not abiding by its credit terms—some 27 percent of its receivables are more than 30 days past due, even though Wonder Vision's credit terms call for full payment by Day 30.

Aging schedules cannot be constructed from the type of summary data that are reported in financial statements; they must be developed from the firm's accounts receivable ledger. However, well-run firms have computerized their accounts receivable records, so it is easy to determine the age of each invoice, to sort electronically by age categories, and thus to generate an aging schedule. Although changes in aging schedules over time do provide more information than does the corporate DSO taken alone, and although aging schedules are valuable for monitoring individual accounts, there is a better way to monitor the aggregate performance of the credit department, as we demonstrate in the next section.

The Payments Pattern Approach. The primary point in analyzing the aggregate accounts receivable situation is to see if customers are slowing down their payments. If so, the firm will have to increase its receivables financing, which will increase its cost of carrying receivables. Further, the payment slowdown may signal an increase in bad debt losses down the road. The DSO and aging schedules are useful in monitoring credit operations, but both are affected by increases and decreases in a

Table 21-2   Receivables Data (Thousands of Dollars)

Month (1)	Credit Sales (2)	Receivables (3)	Based on Quarterly Data		Based on Year-to-Date Data	
			ADS[a] (4)	DSO[b] (5)	ADS (6)	DSO (7)
January	$ 60	$ 54				
February	60	90				
March	60	102	$2.00	51 days	$2.00	51 days
April	60	102				
May	90	129				
June	120	174	3.00	58	2.50	70
July	120	198				
August	90	177				
September	60	132	3.00	44	2.67	49
October	60	108				
November	60	102				
December	60	102	2.00	51	2.50	41

[a]ADS = Average daily sales.

[b]DSO = Days sales outstanding.

firm's level of sales. Thus, changes in sales levels, including normal seasonal or cyclical changes, can change a firm's DSO and aging schedule even though its customers' payment behavior has not changed at all. For this reason, a procedure called the *payments pattern approach* has been developed to measure any changes that might be occurring in customers' payment behavior.[4] To illustrate the payments pattern approach, consider the credit sales of Hanover Manufacturing Company, a small manufacturer of hand tools which commenced operations in January 1990. Table 21-2 contains Hanover's credit sales and receivables data for 1990. Column 2 shows that Hanover's credit sales are seasonal, with the lowest sales in the fall and winter months and the highest sales during the summer.

Now assume that 10 percent of Hanover's customers pay in the same month that the sale is made, that 30 percent pay in the first month following the sale, that 40 percent pay in the second month, and that the remaining 20 percent pay in the third month. Further, assume that Hanover's customers have the same payment behavior throughout the year; that is, they always take the same length of time to pay. On the basis of this payment pattern, Column 3 of Table 21-2 contains Hanover's receivables balance at the end of each month. For example, during January, Hanover has $60,000 in sales. Ten percent of the customers paid during the month of sale, so the receiv-

---

[4]See Wilbur G. Lewellen and Robert W. Johnson, "A Better Way to Monitor Accounts Receivable," *Harvard Business Review,* May-June 1972, 101–109; and Bernell Stone, "The Payments-Pattern Approach to the Forecasting and Control of Accounts Receivable," *Financial Management,* Autumn 1976, 65–82.

Table 21-3   Aging Schedules (Thousands of Dollars)

Age of Accounts (Days)	Value and Percentage of Total Value of Accounts Receivable at the End of Quarter Ending							
	March 31		June 30		September 30		December 31	
0–30	$ 54	53%	$108	62%	$ 54	41%	$ 54	53%
31–60	36	35	54	31	54	41	36	35
61–90	12	12	12	7	24	18	12	12
	$102	100%	$174	100%	$132	100%	$102	100%

ables balance at the end of January was $60,000 − 0.1($60,000) = (1.0 − 0.1)($60,000) = 0.9($60,000) = $54,000. By the end of February, 10% + 30% = 40% of the customers had paid for January's sales, and 10 percent had paid for February's sales. Thus, the receivables balance at the end of February was 0.6($60,000) + 0.9($60,000) = $90,000. By the end of March, 80 percent of January's sales had been paid, 40 percent of February's had been paid, and 10 percent of March's sales had been paid, so the receivables balance was 0.2($60,000) + 0.6($60,000) + 0.9($60,000) = $102,000; and so on.

Columns 4 and 5 give Hanover's average daily sales (ADS) and days sales outstanding (DSO) respectively, as these measures would be calculated from quarterly financial statements. For example, in the April-June quarter, ADS = ($60,000 + $90,000 + $120,000)/90 = $3,000, and the end-of-quarter (June 30) DSO = $174,000/$3,000 = 58 days. Columns 6 and 7 also show ADS and DSO, but here they are calculated on the basis of accumulated sales throughout the year. For example, at the end of June, ADS = $450,000/180 = $2,500 and DSO = $174,000/$2,500 = 70 days. (For the entire year, sales are $900,000; ADS = $2,500, and DSO at year-end = 41 days. These last two figures are shown in the lower right corner of the table.)

The data in Table 21-2 illustrate two major points. First, when the level of sales changes, this leads to changes in the DSO, which suggests that customers are paying faster or slower, even though we know that customers' payment patterns are actually not changing at all. The rising monthly sales trend causes the calculated DSO to rise, whereas falling sales (as in the third quarter) cause the calculated DSO to fall, even though nothing is changing with regard to when customers pay. Second, we see that the DSO depends on an averaging procedure, but regardless of whether quarterly, semiannual, or annual data are used, the DSO is still unstable even though payment patterns are *not* changing. Therefore, it is difficult to use the DSO as a monitoring device if the firm's sales exhibit seasonal or cyclical patterns.

Seasonal or cyclical variations also make it difficult to interpret aging schedules. Table 21-3 contains Hanover's aging schedules at the end of each quarter of 1990. At the end of June, Table 21-2 showed that Hanover's receivables balance was $174,000. Eighty percent of April's $60,000 of sales had been collected, 40 percent of May's $90,000 of sales had been collected, and 10 percent of June's $120,000 of sales had been collected. Thus, the end-of-June receivables balance consisted of

Table 21-4   Uncollected Balances Schedules (Thousands of Dollars)

Quarter	Sales	Remaining Receivables	Receivables/Sales
Quarter 1:			
January	$ 60	$ 12	20%
February	60	36	60
March	60	54	90
		$102	170%
Quarter 2:			
April	$ 60	$ 12	20%
May	90	54	60
June	120	108	90
		$174	170%
Quarter 3:			
July	$120	$ 24	20%
August	90	54	60
September	60	54	90
		$132	170%
Quarter 4:			
October	$ 60	$ 12	20%
November	60	36	60
December	60	54	90
		$102	170%

0.2($60,000) = $12,000 of April sales, 0.6($90,000) = $54,000 of May sales, and 0.9($120,000) = $108,000 of June sales. Note again that Hanover's customers had not changed their payment patterns. However, rising sales during the second quarter created the impression of faster payments when judged by the percentage aging schedule, and falling sales after July created the opposite appearance. Thus, neither the DSO nor the aging schedule provides the financial manager with an accurate picture of customers' payment patterns if sales fluctuate during the year or are trending up or down.

With this background, we can now examine another basic tool, the *uncollected balances schedule,* as shown in Table 21-4. At the end of each quarter, the dollar amount of receivables remaining from each of the three month's sales is divided by that month's sales to obtain three receivables-to-sales ratios. For example, at the end of the first quarter, $12,000 of the $60,000 January sales, or 20 percent, are still outstanding; 60 percent of February sales are still out; and 90 percent of March sales are uncollected. Exactly the same situation is revealed at the end of each of the next three quarters. Thus, Table 21-4 shows that Hanover's customers' payment behavior has remained constant.

Recall that at the beginning of the example we assumed the existence of a constant payments pattern. In a normal situation, the firm's customers' payments pattern would probably vary somewhat over time. Such variations would be shown in the last column of the uncollected balances schedule. For example, suppose customers began, in the second quarter, to pay their accounts slower. That might cause the second quarter uncollected balances schedule to look like this (in thousands of dollars):

Quarter 2, 1990	Sales	Remaining Receivables	Receivables/Sales
April	$ 60	$ 16	27%
May	90	70	78
June	120	110	92
		$196	197%

We see that the receivables-to-sales ratios are now higher than in the corresponding months of the first quarter. This causes the total uncollected balances percentage to rise from 170 to 197 percent, which in turn should alert Hanover's managers that customers are paying slower than they did earlier in the year.

The uncollected balances schedule permits a firm to monitor its receivables better, and it can also be used to forecast future receivables balances. When Hanover's pro forma 1991 quarterly balance sheets are constructed, management can use the receivables-to-sales ratios, coupled with 1991 sales estimates, to project each quarter's receivables balance. For example, with projected sales as given below, and using the same payments pattern as in 1990, Hanover's projected end-of-June 1991 receivables balance would be as follows:

Quarter 2, 1991	Projected Sales	Receivables/Sales	Projected Receivables
April	$ 70,000	20%	$ 14,000
May	100,000	60	60,000
June	140,000	90	126,000
		Total projected receivables =	$200,000

The payments pattern approach permits us to remove the effects of seasonal and/or cyclical sales variation and to construct an accurate measure of customers' payments patterns. Thus, it provides financial managers with better aggregate information than such crude measures as the days sales outstanding or the aging schedule. Managers should use the payments pattern approach to monitor collection performance as well as to project future receivables requirements.

Use of Computers in Receivables Management

Except possibly in the inventory and cash management areas, nowhere in the typical firm have computers had more of an impact than in accounts receivable management. A well-run business will use a computer system to record sales, to send out bills, to keep track of when payments are made, to alert the credit manager when an account becomes past due, and to ensure that actions are taken to collect past due accounts (for example, to prepare form letters requesting payment) automatically. Additionally, the payment history of each customer can be summarized and used to help establish credit limits for customers and classes of customers, and the data on each account can be aggregated and used for the firm's accounts receivable monitoring system. Finally, historical data can be stored in the firm's data base and used to develop inputs for studies related to credit policy changes, as we discuss in the next section.

Self-Test Questions

Explain how a new firm's receivables balance is built up over time.

Define days sales outstanding (DSO). What can be learned from it? Does it have any deficiencies when used to monitor collections over time?

What is an aging schedule? What can be learned from it? Does it have any deficiencies when used to monitor collections over time?

What is the uncollected balances schedule? What advantages does it have over the DSO and the aging schedule for monitoring receivables? How can it be used to forecast a firm's receivables balance?

CREDIT POLICY

The success or failure of a business depends primarily on the demand for its products—as a rule, the higher its sales, the larger its profits and the higher the value of its stock. Sales, in turn, depend on a number of factors, some exogenous but others under the control of the firm. The major controllable variables which affect demand are sales prices, product quality, advertising, and *the firm's credit policy*. Credit policy, in turn, consists of these four variables:

1.   The *credit period,* which is the length of time buyers are given to pay for their purchases.

2.   The *credit standards,* which refer to the minimum financial strength of acceptable credit customers, and the amount of credit available to different customers.

3.   The firm's *collection policy,* which is measured by its toughness or laxity in following up on slow-paying accounts.

4.   Any *discounts* given for early payment, including the discount amount and period.

The credit manager has the responsibility for administering the firm's credit policy. However, because of the pervasive importance of credit, the credit policy itself is normally established by the executive committee, which usually consists of the president and the vice-presidents in charge of finance, marketing, and production.

Self-Test Question

What are the four credit policy variables?

SETTING THE CREDIT PERIOD AND STANDARDS

A firm's regular credit terms, which include the *credit period,* might call for sales on a 2/10, net 30 basis to all "acceptable" customers. Its *credit standards* would be applied to determine which customers are qualified for the regular credit terms, and the amount of credit available to each customer. The focal point when considering credit standards is the likelihood that a given customer will pay slowly, or end up as a bad debt loss. This requires a measurement of *credit quality,* which is defined in terms of the probability of default. The probability estimate for a given customer is, for the most part, a subjective judgment, but credit evaluation is a well-established practice, and a good credit manager can make reasonably accurate judgments regarding the probability of default by different classes of customers.

Credit-Scoring Systems

Although most credit decisions are subjective, many firms now use a sophisticated statistical method called *multiple discriminant analysis (MDA)* to assess credit quality. MDA is similar to multiple regression analysis. The dependent variable is, in essence, the probability of default, and the independent variables are factors associated with financial strength and the ability to pay off the debt if credit is granted. For example, if a firm such as Sears evaluated consumers' credit quality, then the independent variables in the credit scoring system would be such factors as these: (1) Does the credit applicant own his or her own home? (2) How long has the applicant worked on his or her current job? (3) What is the applicant's outstanding debt in relation to his or her annual income? (4) Does the potential customer have a history of paying his or her debts on time?

One major advantage of an MDA credit-scoring system is that a customer's credit quality is expressed in a single numerical value, rather than as a subjective assessment of various factors. This is a tremendous advantage for a large firm which must evaluate many customers in many different locations using many different credit analysts, for without an automated procedure, the firm would have a hard time applying equal standards to all credit applicants. Therefore, most credit card companies, department stores, oil companies, and the like use credit-scoring systems to determine who gets how much credit, as do the larger building supply chains and manufacturers of electrical products, machinery, and so on.

Multiple discriminant analysis will be discussed in detail in Appendix 22A in connection with financial statement analysis. For now, we will briefly describe the concept. Suppose Hanover Manufacturing has historical information on 500 of its customers, all of whom are retail businesses. Of these 500, assume that 400 have always paid on time, but the other 100 either paid late or, in some cases, went bankrupt and did not pay at all. Further, the firm has historical data on each customer's quick ratio, times-interest-earned ratio, debt ratio, years in existence, and so on. Multiple discriminant analysis relates the experienced record (or historical probability) of late payment or nonpayment with various measures of a firm's financial condition, and MDA assigns weights for the critical factors. In effect, MDA produces an equation that looks much like a regression equation, and when data on a customer are plugged into the equation, then a credit score for that customer is produced.

For example, suppose Hanover's multiple discriminant analysis indicates that the critical factors affecting prompt payment are its customers' times-interest-earned ratio (TIE), quick ratio, debt/assets ratio, and number of years in business. Here is the discriminant function:

$$\text{Score} = 3.5(\text{TIE}) + 10.0(\text{Quick ratio}) - 25.0(\text{Debt/Assets}) + 1.3(\text{Years in business}).$$

Further, assume that a score less than 40 indicates a poor credit risk, 40-50 indicates an average credit risk, and a score above 50 signifies a good credit risk. Now, suppose a firm with the following conditions applies for credit:

$$\text{TIE} = 4.2$$

$$\text{Quick ratio} = 3.1$$

$$\text{Debt/assets} = 0.30$$

$$\text{Years in business} = 10$$

This firm's credit score would be $3.5(4.2) + 10.0(3.1) - 25.0(0.30) + 1.3(10) = 51.2$. Therefore, it would be considered a good credit risk, and consequently it would be offered favorable credit terms.

Sources of Credit Information

Two major sources of credit information are available. The first is a set of *credit associations,* which are local groups that meet frequently and which correspond with one another to exchange information on credit customers. These local groups have also banded together to create Credit Interchange, a system developed by the National Association of Credit Management for assembling and distributing information about debtors' past performance. The interchange reports show the paying records of different debtors, the industries from which they are buying, and the geographic areas in which they are making purchases. The second source of external information is the work of the *credit-reporting agencies,* which collect credit information and sell it for a fee. The best known of these agencies are Dun & Bradstreet (D&B) and TRW, Incorporated. D&B, TRW, and other agencies provide factual data that can be used in credit analysis, and they also provide ratings similar to those available on corporate bonds.[5]

---

[5]For additional information, see *Credit Management,* a publication of the National Association of Credit Management; and also see Peter Nulty, "An Upstart Takes on Dun & Bradstreet," *Fortune,* April 9, 1979, 98–100.

Managing a credit department requires fast, accurate, up-to-date information, and to help get such information, the National Association of Credit Management (a group with 43,000 member firms) persuaded TRW to develop a computer-based telecommunication network for the collection, storage, retrieval, and distribution of credit information. The TRW system contains credit data on over 120 million individuals, and it electronically transmits credit reports which are available within seconds to its thousands of subscribers. Dun & Bradstreet has a similar electronic system which covers businesses, plus another service which provides more detailed reports through the U.S. mail.

A typical business credit report would include the following pieces of information:

1. A summary balance sheet and income statement.

2. A number of key ratios, with trend information.

3. Information obtained from the firm's suppliers telling whether it has been paying promptly or slowly, and whether it has recently failed to make any payments.

4. A verbal description of the physical condition of the firm's operations.

5. A verbal description of the backgrounds of the firm's owners, including any previous bankruptcies, lawsuits, divorce settlement problems, and the like.

6. A summary rating, ranging from A for the best credit risks down to F for those that are deemed likely to default.

Although a great deal of credit information is available, it must still be processed in a judgmental manner. Computerized information systems can assist in making better credit decisions, but, in the final analysis, most credit decisions are really exercises in informed judgment. Even credit scoring systems require judgment in deciding where to draw the lines, given the set of derived scores.

Self-Test Questions

What is a credit-scoring system?

What are some sources of credit information?

SETTING THE COLLECTION POLICY

Collection policy refers to the procedures the firm follows to collect past-due accounts. For example, a letter may be sent to customers when a bill is 10 days past due; a more severe letter, followed by a telephone call, may be used if payment is not received within 30 days; and the account may be turned over to a collection agency after 90 days.

The collection process can be expensive in terms of both out-of-pocket expenditures and lost goodwill, but at least some firmness is needed to prevent an undue lengthening of the collection period and to minimize outright losses. Again, a balance must be struck between the costs and benefits of different collection policies.

Changes in collection policy influence sales, the collection period, the bad debt loss percentage, and the percentage of customers who take discounts. The effects of a change in collection policy, along with changes in the other credit policy variables, will be analyzed later in the chapter.

Self-Test Question

What does the term "collection policy" mean, and what impact does it have on sales and profitability?

CASH DISCOUNTS

The last element in the credit policy decision, the use of *cash discounts* for early payment, is analyzed by balancing the costs and benefits of different cash discounts. For example, a firm might decide to change its credit terms from "net 30," which means that customers must pay within 30 days, to "2/10, net 30," which means that it will allow a 2 percent discount if payment is received within 10 days, while the full invoice price must otherwise be paid within 30 days. This change should produce two benefits: (1) It should attract new customers who consider discounts to be a type of price reduction, and (2) the discounts should cause a reduction in the days sales outstanding, since some established customers will pay more promptly in order to take advantage of the discount. Offsetting these benefits is the dollar cost of the discounts taken.[6] The optimal discount is established at the point where the marginal costs and benefits are exactly offsetting. The methodology for analyzing changes in the discount is developed later in the chapter.

If sales are seasonal, a firm may use *seasonal dating* on discounts. For example, Slimware, Inc., a swimsuit manufacturer, sells on terms of 2/10, net 30, May 1 dating. This means that the effective invoice date is May 1, even if the sale was made back in January. The discount may be taken up to May 10; otherwise the full amount must be paid on May 30. Slimware produces throughout the year, but retail sales of bathing suits are concentrated in the spring and early summer, and by offering seasonal dating, the company induces some of its customers to stock up early, saving Slimware storage costs and also "nailing down sales."

Self-Test Questions

How can cash discounts be used to influence sales volume and collections?

What is seasonal dating?

---

[6]Note that some firms offer discounts only to customers who pay cash on the spot, because the cost of giving such discounts is offset by the reduction in receivables accounting costs.

OTHER FACTORS INFLUENCING CREDIT POLICY

In addition to the factors discussed in the previous section, several other conditions also influence a firm's overall credit policy.

Profit Potential

Thus far, we have emphasized the costs of granting credit. *However, if it is possible to sell on credit and also to assess a carrying charge on the receivables that are outstanding, then credit sales can actually be more profitable than cash sales.* This is especially true for consumer durables (autos, appliances, clothing, and so on), but it is also true for certain types of industrial equipment. Thus, GM's General Motors Acceptance Corporation (GMAC) unit, which finances automobiles, is highly profitable, as is Sears, Roebuck's credit subsidiary.[7] Some encyclopedia companies are even reported to lose money on cash sales but to more than make up these losses from the carrying charges on their credit sales; obviously, such companies would rather sell on credit than for cash!

The carrying charges on outstanding credit are generally about 18 percent on a nominal interest rate basis: 1.5 percent per month, so $1.5\% \times 12 = 18\%$. This is equivalent to an effective annual rate of $(1.015)^{12} - 1.0 = 19.6\%$. Except in the type of situation that occurred in the early 1980s, when short-term interest rates rose to unprecedented levels, having receivables outstanding that earn over 18 percent is highly profitable.

Legal Considerations

It is illegal, under the Robinson-Patman Act, for a firm to charge prices that discriminate between customers unless these differential prices are cost-justified. The same holds true for credit—it is illegal to offer more favorable credit terms to one customer or class of customers than to another, unless the differences are cost-justified.

Credit Instruments

Most credit is offered on *open account,* which means that the only formal evidence of credit is an invoice which accompanies the shipment and which the buyer signs to indicate that goods have been received. Then, the buyer and the seller each record the purchase on their books of account. Under certain circumstances, the selling firm may require the buyer to sign a *promissory note* evidencing the credit obligation. Promissory notes are useful (1) if the order is very large; (2) if the seller anticipates the possibility of having trouble collecting, because a note is a stronger legal claim than a simple signed invoice; or (3) if the buyer wants a longer-than-usual time in which to pay for the order, because in that case interest should be charged, and interest charges can be built into a promissory note.

---

[7]Companies that do a large volume of sales financing typically set up subsidiary companies called *captive finance companies* to do the actual financing. Thus, General Motors, Chrysler, and Ford all have captive finance companies, as do Sears, Roebuck and Montgomery Ward.

Another instrument used in trade credit, especially in international trade, is the *commercial draft*. Here the seller draws up a draft—which is a sort of combination check and a promissory note—calling for the buyer to pay a specific amount to the seller by a specified date. This draft is then sent to the buyer's bank, along with the shipping invoices necessary to take possession of the goods. The bank forwards the draft to the buyer, who signs it and returns it to the bank. The bank then delivers the shipping documents to its customer, who at this point can claim the goods. If the draft is a *sight draft,* then upon delivery of the shipping documents and acceptance of the draft by the buyer, the bank actually withdraws money from the buyer's account and forwards it to the selling firm. If the draft is a *time draft,* payable on a specific future date, then the bank returns it to the selling firm. In this case, the draft is called a *trade acceptance,* and it amounts to a promissory note that the seller can hold for future payment or use as collateral for a loan. The bank, in such a situation, has served as an intermediary, making sure that the buyer does not receive title to the goods until the note (or draft) has been executed for the benefit of the seller.

A seller who lacks confidence in the ability or willingness of the buyer to pay off a time draft may refuse to ship without a guarantee of payment by the buyer's bank. Presumably, the bank knows its customer, and, for a fee, the bank will guarantee payment of the draft. In this instance, the draft is called a *banker's acceptance.* Such instruments are widely used, especially in foreign trade. They have a low degree of risk if guaranteed by a strong bank, and there is a ready market for acceptances, making it easy for the seller of the goods to sell the instrument to raise immediate cash. (Banker's acceptances are sold at a discount below face value, and then paid off at face value when they mature, so the discount amounts to interest on the acceptance. The effective interest rate on a strong banker's acceptance is a little above the Treasury bill rate of interest.)

Another type of credit instrument is the *conditional sales contract,* under which the seller retains legal ownership of the goods until the buyer has completed payment. Conditional sales contracts are used primarily for such items as machinery, dental equipment, and the like, which are often purchased on an installment basis over a period of two or three years. The significant advantage of a conditional sales contract is that it is easier for the seller to repossess the equipment in the event of default than it would be if title had passed. This feature makes possible some credit sales that otherwise would not be feasible. Conditional sales contracts generally have a market interest rate built into their payment schedules.

Self-Test Questions

How do profit potential and legal considerations affect a firm's credit policy?

Define and illustrate the following terms and credit instruments:
1. Open account
2. Promissory note
3. Commercial draft
4. Sight draft
5. Trade acceptance
6. Conditional sales contract

ANALYZING PROPOSED CHANGES IN CREDIT POLICY

If the firm's credit policy is *eased* by such actions as lengthening the credit period, relaxing credit standards, following a less tough collection policy, or offering cash discounts, then sales should increase: *Easing the credit policy stimulates sales.* Of course, if credit policy is eased and sales rise, then costs will also rise because more labor, materials, and so on will be required to produce the additional goods. Additionally, receivables outstanding will also increase, which will increase carrying costs, and bad debt and/or discount expenses may also rise. Thus, the key question when deciding on a proposed credit policy change is this: Will sales revenues rise more than costs, including credit-related costs, causing cash flow to increase, or will the increase in sales revenues be more than offset by the higher costs?

Table 21-5 illustrates the general idea behind credit policy analysis. Column 1 shows the projected 1991 income statement for Monroe Manufacturing under the assumption that the firm's current credit policy is maintained throughout the year. Column 2 shows the expected effects of easing the credit policy by extending the credit period, offering larger discounts, relaxing credit standards, and easing collection efforts. Specifically, Monroe is analyzing the effects of changing its credit terms from 1/10, net 30, to 2/10, net 40, relaxing its credit standards, and putting less pressure on slow-paying customers. Column 3 shows the projected 1991 income statement incorporating the expected effects of an easing in credit policy. The generally looser policy is expected to increase sales and lower collection costs, but discounts and several other types of costs would rise. The overall, bottom-line effect is a $7 million increase in projected net income. In the following paragraphs, we explain how the numbers in the table were calculated.

Monroe's annual sales are $400 million. Under its current credit policy, 50 percent of those customers who pay do so on Day 10 and take the discount, 40 percent pay on Day 30, and 10 percent pay late, on Day 40. Thus, Monroe's days sales outstanding is $(0.5)(10) + (0.4)(30) + (0.1)(40) = 21$ days, and discounts total $(0.01)(\$400,000,000)(0.5) = \$2,000,000$.

The cost of carrying receivables is equal to the average receivables balance times the variable cost percentage times the cost of money used to carry receivables. The firm's variable cost ratio is 70 percent, and its pre-tax cost of capital invested in receivables is 20 percent. Thus, its cost of carrying receivables is $3 million:

$$(\text{DSO})\left(\begin{array}{c}\text{Sales}\\\text{per}\\\text{day}\end{array}\right)\left(\begin{array}{c}\text{Variable}\\\text{cost}\\\text{ratio}\end{array}\right)\left(\begin{array}{c}\text{Cost}\\\text{of}\\\text{funds}\end{array}\right) = \text{Cost of carrying receivables}$$

$$(21)(\$400,000,000/360)(0.70)(0.20) = \$3,266,667 \approx \$3 \text{ million.}$$

Only variable costs enter this calculation because this is the only cost element in receivables that must be financed. We are seeking the cost of carrying receivables, and variable costs represent the firm's investment in the cost of goods sold.

Even though Monroe spends $5 million annually to analyze accounts and to collect bad debts, 2.5 percent of sales will never be collected. Bad debt losses therefore amount to $(0.025)(\$400,000,000) = \$10,000,000$.

Monroe's new credit policy would be 2/10, net 40 versus the old policy of 1/10, net 30, so it would call for a larger discount and a longer payment period, as well as

Table 21-5   Monroe Manufacturing Company:
Analysis of Changing Credit Policy
(Millions of Dollars)

	Projected 1991 Net Income under Current Credit Policy (1)	Effect of Credit Policy Change (2)	Projected 1991 Net Income under New Credit Policy (3)
Gross sales	$400	+ $130	$530
Less discounts	2	+ 4	6
Net sales	$398	+ $126	$524
Production costs, including overhead	280	+ 91	371
Profit before credit costs and taxes	$118	+ $ 35	$153
Credit-related costs:			
Cost of carrying receivables	3	+ 2	5
Credit analysis and collection expenses	5	− 3	2
Bad debt losses	10	+ 22	32
Profit before taxes	$100	+ $ 14	$114
State-plus-federal taxes (50%)	50	+ 7	57
Net income	$ 50	+ $ 7	$ 57

Note: The above statements include only those cash flows incremental to the credit policy decision.

a relaxed collection effort and lower credit standards. The company believes that these changes will lead to a $130 million increase in sales, to $530 million per year. Under the new terms, management believes that 60 percent of the customers who pay will take the 2 percent discount, so discounts will increase to $(0.02)($530,000,000)(0.60)$ $= \$6,360,000 \approx \$6$ million. Half of the nondiscount customers will pay on Day 40, and the remainder on Day 50. The new DSO is thus estimated to be 24 days:

$$(0.6)(10) + (0.2)(40) + (0.2)(50) = 24 \text{ days.}$$

Also, the cost of carrying receivables will increase to $5 million:

$$(24)(\$530,000,000/360)(0.70)(0.20) = \$4,946,667 \approx \$5 \text{ million.}[8]$$

---

[8]Since the credit policy change will result in a longer DSO, the firm will have to wait longer to receive its profit on the goods it sells. Therefore, the firm will incur an opportunity cost due to not having the cash from these profits available for investment. The dollar amount of this opportunity cost is equal to the old sales per day times the change in DSO times the contribution margin $(1 -$ Variable cost ratio) times the firm's cost of carrying receivables, or

$$\text{Opportunity cost} = (\text{Old sales}/360)(\Delta \text{DSO})(1 - v)(k)$$
$$= (\$400/360)(3)(0.3)(0.20)$$
$$= \$0.2 = \$200,000.$$

For simplicity, we have ignored this opportunity cost in our analysis. For a more complete discussion of credit policy change analysis, see Eugene F. Brigham and Louis C. Gapenski, *Intermediate Financial Management*, 3rd ed., Chapter 19.

The company plans to reduce its annual credit analysis and collection expenditures to $2 million. The reduced credit standards and the relaxed collection effort are expected to raise bad debt losses to about 6 percent of sales, or to $(0.06)(\$530,000,000) = \$31,800,000 \approx \$32,000,000$, which is an increase of $22 million from the previous level.

The combined effect of all the changes in credit policy is a projected $7 million annual increase in net income. There would, of course, be corresponding changes on the projected balance sheet—the higher sales would necessitate somewhat larger cash balances, inventories, and, depending on the capacity situation, perhaps more fixed assets. Accounts receivable would of course also increase. Since these asset increases would have to be financed, certain liabilities and/or equity would have to be increased.

The $7 million expected increase in net income is, of course, an estimate, and the actual effects of the change could be quite different. In the first place, there is uncertainty—perhaps quite a lot—about the projected $130 million increase in sales. Conceivably, if the firm's competitors matched its changes, sales would not rise at all. Similar uncertainties must be attached to the number of customers who would take discounts, to production costs at higher or lower sales levels, to the costs of carrying additional receivables, and to bad debt losses. In the final analysis, the decision will be based on judgment, especially concerning the risks involved, but the type of quantitative analysis set forth above is essential to the process.

Self-Test Questions

Describe the procedure for evaluating a change in credit policy.

Do you think that credit policy decisions are made more on the basis of numerical analyses or on judgmental factors?

INVENTORIES

Inventories, which may be classified as (1) *raw materials,* (2) *work-in-process,* and (3) *finished goods,* are an essential part of virtually all business operations. As is the case with accounts receivable, inventory levels depend heavily upon sales. However, whereas receivables build up *after* sales have been made, inventories must be acquired *ahead* of sales. This is a critical difference, and the necessity of forecasting sales before establishing target inventory levels makes inventory management a difficult task. Also, since errors in the establishment of inventory levels quickly lead either to lost sales or to excessive carrying costs, inventory management is as important as it is difficult.

Inventory management techniques are covered in depth in production management courses, but since financial managers have a responsibility both for raising the capital needed to carry inventory and for the overall profitability of the firm, we need to cover the basics of inventory management here. Two examples will make clear the types of issues involved in inventory management, and the problems poor inventory control can cause.

Retail Clothing Store

Chicago Discount Clothing Company (CDCC) must order swimsuits for summer sales in January, and it must take delivery by April to be sure of having enough suits to meet the heavy May-June demand. Bathing suits come in many styles, colors, and sizes, and if CDCC stocks incorrectly, either in total or in terms of the style-color-size distribution, then the store will have trouble. It will lose potential sales if it stocks too few suits, and it will be forced to lower prices and take losses if it stocks too many or the wrong types.

The effects of inventory changes on the balance sheet are important. For simplicity, assume that CDCC has a $10,000 base stock of inventories, financed by common stock. Its balance sheet is as follows:

Inventories (base stock)	$10,000	Common stock	$10,000
Total assets	$10,000	Total claims	$10,000

Now it anticipates that it will sell $5,000 worth of swimsuit inventory this summer. Dollar sales will actually be greater than $5,000, since CDCC makes about $200 in profits for every $1,000 of inventory sold. CDCC finances its seasonal inventory with bank loans, so its pre-summer balance sheet would look like this:

Inventories (seasonal)	$ 5,000	Notes payable to bank	$ 5,000
Inventories (base stock)	10,000	Common stock	10,000
Total assets	$15,000	Total claims	$15,000

If everything works out as planned, sales will be made, inventories will be converted to cash, the bank loan will be retired, and the company will earn a profit. The balance sheet, after a successful season, might look like this:

Cash	$ 1,000	Notes payable to bank	$ 0
Inventories (seasonal)	0	Common stock	10,000
Inventories (base stock)	10,000	Retained earnings	1,000
Total assets	$11,000	Total claims	$11,000

The company is now in a highly liquid position and is ready to begin a new season.

But suppose the season had not gone well, and CDCC had only sold $1,000 of its inventory. As fall approached, the balance sheet would look like this:

Cash	$ 200	Notes payable to bank	$ 4,000
Inventories (seasonal)	4,000	Common stock	10,000
Inventories (base stock)	10,000	Retained earnings	200
Total assets	$14,200	Total claims	$14,200

Now suppose the bank insists on repayment of the $4,000 outstanding on the loan, and it wants cash, not swimsuits. But if the swimsuits did not sell well in the summer, how will out-of-style suits sell in the fall? Assume that CDCC is forced to mark the suits down to half their cost in order to sell them to raise cash to repay the bank loan. The result will be as follows:

Cash	$ 2,200	Notes payable to bank	$ 4,000
Inventories (base stock)	10,000	Common stock	10,000
		Retained earnings	(1,800)
Total assets	$12,200	Total claims	$12,200

At this point, CDCC is in serious trouble. It does not have the cash to pay off the loan, and the firm's shareholders have lost $1,800 of their equity. If the bank will not extend the loan, and if other sources of cash are not available, CDCC will have to mark down its base stock prices in an effort to stimulate sales, and if this does not work, CDCC could be forced into bankruptcy. Clearly, poor inventory decisions can spell trouble.

Appliance Manufacturer

Now consider a different type of situation, that of Housepro Corporation, a well-established appliance manufacturer, whose inventory position, in millions of dollars, follows:

Raw materials	$ 200
Work-in-process	200
Finished goods	600
Total inventories	$1,000

Suppose Housepro anticipates that the economy is about to get much stronger and that the demand for appliances will rise sharply. If it is to share in the expected boom, Housepro will have to increase production. This means it will have to increase inventories, and, since the inventory buildup must precede sales, additional financing will be required—some liability account, perhaps notes payable, would have to be increased in order to support the additional inventory.

Proper inventory management requires close coordination among the sales, purchasing, production, and finance departments. The sales/marketing department is generally the first to spot changes in demand. These changes must be worked into the company's purchasing and manufacturing schedules, and the financial manager must arrange any financing that will be needed to support the inventory buildup. Improper coordination among departments, poor sales forecasts, or both, can lead to disaster.

Self-Test Questions

Why is good inventory management essential to a firm's success?

What departments should be involved in inventory decisions?

INVENTORY MANAGEMENT

Inventory management focuses on four basic questions. (1) How many units should be ordered (or produced) at a given time? (2) At what point should inventory be ordered (or produced)? (3) What inventory items warrant special attention? (4) Can inventory cost changes be hedged? The remainder of the chapter is devoted to providing answers to these four questions.

Self-Test Question

What four basic questions are addressed by the inventory manager?

INVENTORY COSTS

The goal of inventory management is to provide at the lowest total cost the inventories required to sustain operations. The first step in inventory management is to identify all the costs involved in purchasing and maintaining inventories. Table 21-6 gives à listing of the typical costs that are associated with inventories. In the table, we have broken down costs into three categories: those associated with carrying

Table 21-6   Costs Associated with Inventories

	Approximate Annual Cost as a Percentage of Inventory Value
I. Carrying Costs	
Cost of capital tied up	12.0%
Storage and handling costs	0.5
Insurance	0.5
Property taxes	1.0
Depreciation and obsolescence	12.0
Total	26.0%
II. Ordering, Shipping, and Receiving Costs	
Cost of placing orders, including production and set-up costs	Varies
Shipping and handling costs	2.5%
III. Costs of Running Short	
Loss of sales	Varies
Loss of customer goodwill	Varies
Disruption of production schedules	Varies

Note: These costs vary from firm to firm, from item to item, and also over time. The figures shown are U.S. Department of Commerce estimates for an average manufacturing firm. Where costs vary so widely that no meaningful numbers can be assigned, we simply report "Varies."

inventories, those associated with ordering and receiving inventories, and those associated with running short of inventories.

Although they may well be the most important element, we shall at this point disregard the third category of costs—the costs of running short. These costs are dealt with by adding safety stocks, as we will discuss later. Similarly, we shall discuss quantity discounts in a later section. The costs that remain for consideration at this stage, then, are carrying costs and ordering, shipping, and receiving costs.

Carrying Costs

Carrying costs generally rise in direct proportion to the average amount of inventory carried. Inventories carried, in turn, depend on the frequency with which orders are placed. To illustrate, if a firm sells S units per year, and if it places equal-sized orders N times per year, then S/N units will be purchased with each order. If the inventory is used evenly over the year, and if no safety stocks are carried, then the average inventory, A, will be:

$$A = \frac{\text{Units per order}}{2} = \frac{S/N}{2}. \qquad\qquad (21\text{-}1)$$

For example, if S = 120,000 units in a year, and N = 4, then the firm will order 30,000 units at a time, and its average inventory will be 15,000 units:

$$A = \frac{S/N}{2} = \frac{120,000/4}{2} = \frac{30,000}{2} = 15,000 \text{ units.}$$

Just after a shipment arrives, the inventory will be 30,000 units; just before the next shipment arrives, it will be zero; and on average, 15,000 units will be carried.

Now assume the firm purchases its inventory at a price P = $2 per unit. The average inventory value is, thus, (P)(A) = $2(15,000) = $30,000. If the firm has a cost of capital of 10 percent, it will incur $3,000 in financing charges to carry the inventory for one year. Further, assume that each year the firm incurs $2,000 of storage costs (space, utilities, security, taxes, and so forth), that its inventory insurance costs are $500, and that it must mark down inventories by $1,000 because of depreciation and obsolescence. The firm's total costs of carrying the $30,000 average inventory is thus $3,000 + $2,000 + $500 + $1,000 = $6,500, and the annual percentage cost of carrying the inventory is $6,500/$30,000 = 0.217 = 21.7%.

Defining the annual percentage carrying cost as C, we can, in general, find the annual total carrying cost, TCC, as the percentage carrying cost, C, times the price per unit, P, times the average number of units, A:

$$TCC = \text{Total carrying cost} = (C)(P)(A). \qquad\qquad (21\text{-}2)$$

In our example,

$$TCC = (0.217)(\$2)(15,000) \approx \$6,500.$$

Ordering Costs

Although we assume that carrying costs are entirely variable and rise in direct proportion to the average size of inventories, ordering costs are usually fixed. For example, the costs of placing and receiving an order—interoffice memos, long-distance telephone calls, setting up a production run, and taking delivery—are essentially fixed regardless of the size of an order, so this part of inventory cost is simply the fixed cost of placing and receiving orders times the number of orders placed per year.[9] We define the fixed costs associated with ordering inventories as F, and if we place N orders per year, the total ordering cost is given by Equation 21-3:

$$\text{Total ordering cost} = \text{TOC} = (F)(N). \qquad \textbf{(21-3)}$$

Here TOC = total ordering cost, F = fixed costs per order, and N = number of orders placed per year.

Equation 21-1 may be rewritten as N = S/2A, and then substituted into Equation 21-3:

$$\text{Total ordering cost} = \text{TOC} = F\left(\frac{S}{2A}\right). \qquad \textbf{(21-4)}$$

To illustrate the use of Equation 21-4, if F = $100, S = 120,000 units, and A = 15,000 units, then TOC, the total annual ordering cost, is $400:

$$\text{TOC} = \$100\left(\frac{120,000}{30,000}\right) = \$100(4) = \$400.$$

Total Inventory Costs

Total carrying cost, TCC, as defined in Equation 21-2, and total ordering cost, TOC, as defined in Equation 21-4, may be combined to find total inventory costs, TIC, as follows:

$$\text{Total inventory costs} = \text{TIC} = \quad \text{TCC} \quad + \quad \text{TOC}$$
$$= (C)(P)(A) + F\left(\frac{S}{2A}\right). \qquad \textbf{(21-5)}$$

---

[9]Note that, in reality, both carrying and ordering costs can have variable and fixed cost elements, at least over certain ranges of average inventory. For example, security and utilities charges are probably fixed in the short run over a wide range of inventory levels. Similarly, labor costs in receiving inventory could be tied to the quantity received, hence could be variable. To simplify matters, we treat all carrying costs as variable and all ordering costs as fixed. However, if these assumptions do not fit the situation at hand, the cost definitions can be changed. For example, one could add another term for shipping costs if there are economies of scale in shipping, such that the cost of shipping a unit is smaller if shipments are larger. However, in most situations, shipping costs are not sensitive to order size, so total shipping costs are simply the shipping cost per unit times the units ordered (and sold) during the year. Under this condition, shipping costs are not influenced by inventory policy, hence they may be disregarded for purposes of determining the optimal inventory level and the optimal order size.

Recognizing that the average inventory carried is A = Q/2, or one-half the size of each order quantity, Q, we may rewrite Equation 21-5 as follows:

$$TIC = \quad TCC \quad + \quad TOC$$
$$= (C)(P)\left(\frac{Q}{2}\right) + (F)\left(\frac{S}{Q}\right). \qquad \textbf{(21-6)}$$

Here we see that total carrying cost equals average inventory in units, Q/2, multiplied by unit price, P, times the percentage annual carrying cost, C. Total ordering cost equals the number of orders placed per year, S/Q, multiplied by the fixed cost of placing and receiving an order, F. We will use this equation in the next section to develop the optimal inventory ordering quantity.

Self-Test Questions

What are the three categories of inventory costs?

What are some specific inventory carrying costs? As defined here, are these costs fixed or variable?

What are some inventory ordering costs? As defined here, are these costs fixed or variable?

THE ECONOMIC ORDERING QUANTITY (EOQ) MODEL

Inventories are obviously necessary, but it is equally obvious that a firm's profitability will suffer if it has too much or too little inventory. How can we determine the optimal inventory level? One commonly used approach is based on the *economic ordering quantity (EOQ)* model, which is described next.

Derivation of the EOQ Model

Figure 21-1 illustrates the basic premise on which the EOQ model is built, namely, that some costs rise with larger inventories while other costs decline, and there is an optimal order size (and associated average inventory) which minimizes the total costs of inventories. First, as noted earlier, the average investment in inventories depends on how frequently orders are placed and the size of each order—if we order every day, average inventories will be much smaller than if we order once a year. Further, as Figure 21-1 shows, the firm's carrying costs rise with larger orders: Larger orders mean larger average inventories, so warehousing costs, interest on funds tied up in inventory, insurance, and obsolescence costs will all increase. However, ordering costs decline with larger orders and inventories: The cost of placing orders, suppliers' production setup costs, and order handling costs will all decline if we order infrequently and consequently hold larger quantities.

If the carrying and ordering cost curves in Figure 21-1 are added, the sum represents total inventory costs, TIC. The point where the TIC is minimized represents the *economic ordering quantity (EOQ),* and this, in turn, determines the optimal average inventory level.

Figure 21-1   Determination of the Optimal Order Quantity

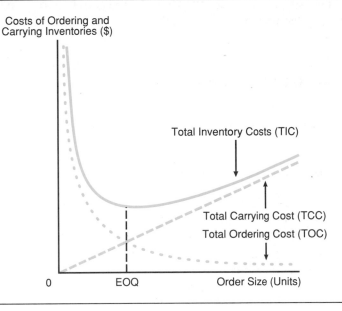

The EOQ is found by differentiating Equation 21-6 with respect to ordering quantity, Q, and setting the derivative equal to zero:

$$\frac{d(TIC)}{dQ} = \frac{(C)(P)}{2} - \frac{(F)(S)}{Q^2} = 0.$$

Now, solving for Q, we obtain:

$$\frac{(C)(P)}{2} = \frac{(F)(S)}{Q^2}$$

$$Q^2 = \frac{2(F)(S)}{(C)(P)}$$

$$EOQ = \sqrt{\frac{2(F)(S)}{(C)(P)}}. \qquad \textbf{(21-7)}$$

Here

EOQ = economic ordering quantity, or the optimum quantity to be ordered each time an order is placed.

F = fixed costs of placing and receiving an order.

S = annual sales in units.

C = annual carrying costs expressed as a percentage of average inventory value.

P = purchase price the firm must pay per unit of inventory.

Equation 21-7 is the EOQ model.[10] The assumptions of the model, which will be relaxed shortly, include the following: (1) sales can be forecasted perfectly, (2) sales are evenly distributed throughout the year, and (3) orders are received when expected.

EOQ Model Illustration

To illustrate the EOQ model, consider the following data, supplied by Cotton Tops, Inc., a distributor of custom-designed T-shirts which sells to concessionaires at Daisy World:

S = annual sales = 26,000 shirts per year.

C = percentage carrying cost = 25 percent of inventory value.

P = purchase price per shirt = $4.92 per shirt. (The sales price is $9, but this is irrelevant for our purposes here.)

F = fixed cost per order = $1,000. Cotton Tops designs and distributes the shirts, but the actual production is done by another company. The bulk of this $1,000 cost is the labor cost for setting up the equipment for the production run, which the manufacturer bills separately from the $4.92 cost per shirt.

Substituting these data into Equation 21-7, we obtain an EOQ of 6,500 units:

$$EOQ = \sqrt{\frac{2(F)(S)}{(C)(P)}} = \sqrt{\frac{(2)(\$1,000)(26,000)}{(0.25)(\$4.92)}}$$
$$= \sqrt{42,276,423} \approx 6,500 \text{ units.}$$

With an EOQ of 6,500 shirts and annual usage of 26,000 shirts, Cotton Tops will place 26,000/6,500 = 4 orders per year. Notice that average inventory holdings depend directly on the EOQ: This relationship is illustrated graphically in Figure 21-2, where we see that average inventory = EOQ/2. Immediately after an order is received, 6,500 shirts are in stock. The usage rate, or sales rate, is 500 shirts per week (26,000/52 weeks), so inventories are drawn down by this amount each week. Thus, the actual number of units held in inventory will vary from 6,500 shirts just after an order is received to zero just before a new order arrives. With a 6,500 beginning balance, a zero ending balance, and a uniform sales rate, inventories will average one-half the EOQ, or 3,250 shirts, during the year. At a cost of $4.92 per shirt, the average investment in inventories will be (3,250)($4.92) ≈ $16,000. If inventories are financed by bank loans, the loan will vary from a high of $32,000 to a low of $0, but the average amount outstanding over the course of a year will be $16,000.

---

[10]The EOQ model can also be written as

$$EOQ = \sqrt{\frac{2(F)(S)}{C^*}},$$

where C^* is the annual carrying cost per unit expressed in *dollars*.

Figure 21-2   Inventory Position without Safety Stock

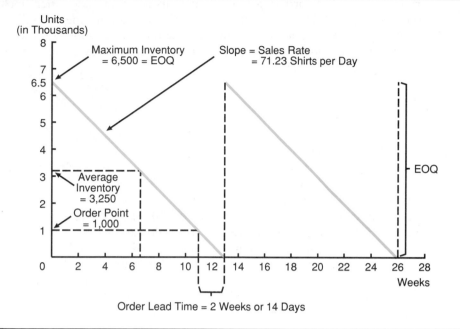

Order Lead Time = 2 Weeks or 14 Days

Notice that the EOQ, hence average inventory holdings, rises with the square root of sales. Therefore, a given increase in sales will result in a less-than-proportionate increase in inventories, so the inventory/sales ratio will tend to decline as a firm grows. For example, Cotton Tops' EOQ is 6,500 shirts at an annual sales level of 26,000, and the average inventory is 3,250 shirts, or $16,000. However, if sales were to increase by 100 percent, to 52,000 shirts per year, the EOQ would rise only to 9,195 units, or by 41 percent, and the average inventory would rise by this same percentage. This suggests that there are economies of scale in holding inventories.[11]

Finally, look at Cotton Tops' total inventory costs for the year, assuming that the EOQ is ordered each time. Using Equation 21-6, we find total inventory costs are $8,000:

$$
\begin{aligned}
\text{TIC} &= \text{TCC} &+&\quad \text{TOC} \\
&= (C)(P)\left(\frac{Q}{2}\right) &+&\quad (F)\left(\frac{S}{Q}\right) \\
&= 0.25(\$4.92)\left(\frac{6,500}{2}\right) &+&\quad (\$1,000)\left(\frac{26,000}{6,500}\right) \\
&\approx \quad \$4,000 &+&\quad \$4,000 \quad = \$8,000
\end{aligned}
$$

[11]Note, however, that these scale economies relate to each particular item, not to the entire firm. Thus, a large distributor with $500 million of sales might have a higher inventory/sales ratio than a much smaller distributor if the small firm has only a few high-sales-volume items while the large firm distributes a great many low-volume items.

Note these two points: (1) The $8,000 total inventory cost represents the total of carrying costs and ordering costs, but this amount does *not* include the 26,000($4.92) = $127,920 annual purchasing cost of the inventory itself. (2) As we see both in Figure 21-1 and in the numbers just preceding, at the EOQ, total carrying cost (TCC) equals total ordering cost (TOC). This property is not unique to our Cotton Tops illustration; it always holds.

Setting the Order Point

If a two-week lead time is required for production and shipping, what is Cotton Tops' order point level? If we use a 52-week year, Cotton Tops sells 26,000/52 = 500 shirts per week. Thus, if a two-week lag occurs between placing an order and receiving goods, Cotton Tops must place the order when there are 2(500) = 1,000 shirts on hand. During the two-week production and shipping period, the inventory balance will continue to decline at the rate of 500 shirts per week, and the inventory balance will hit zero just as the order of new shirts arrives.

If Cotton Tops knew for certain that both the sales rate and the order lead time would never vary, it could operate exactly as shown in Figure 21-2. However, sales do change, and production and/or shipping delays are frequently encountered; to guard against these events, the firm must carry additional inventories, or safety stocks, as discussed in the next section.

Self-Test Questions

What is the concept behind the EOQ model?

What is the relationship between total carrying cost and total ordering cost at the EOQ?

What assumptions are inherent in the EOQ model as presented here?

EOQ MODEL EXTENSIONS

The basic EOQ model was derived under several restrictive assumptions. In this section, we relax some of these assumptions and, in the process, extend the model to make it more useful.

The Concept of Safety Stocks

The concept of a *safety stock* is illustrated in Figure 21-3. First, note that the slope of the sales line measures the expected rate of sales. The company *expects* to sell 500 shirts per week, but let us assume that the maximum likely sales rate is twice this amount, or 1,000 units each week. Further, assume that Cotton Tops sets the safety stock at 1,000 shirts, so it initially orders 7,500 shirts, the EOQ of 6,500 plus the 1,000-unit safety stock. Subsequently, it reorders the EOQ whenever the inven-

Figure 21-3   Inventory Position with Safety Stock Included

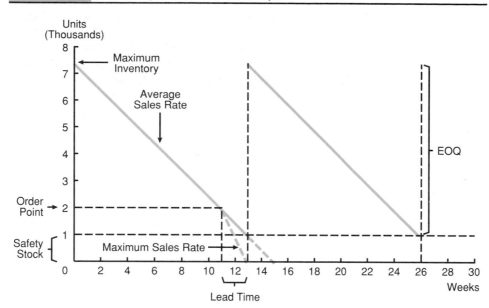

tory level falls to 2,000 shirts, the safety stock of 1,000 shirts plus the 1,000 shirts expected to be used while awaiting delivery of the order.

Notice that the company could, over the two-week delivery period, sell 1,000 units a week, or double its normal expected sales. This maximum rate of sales is shown by the steeper dashed line in Figure 21-3. The condition that makes possible this higher maximum sales rate is the safety stock of 1,000 shirts.

The safety stock is also useful to guard against delays in receiving orders. The expected delivery time is 2 weeks, but with a 1,000-unit safety stock, the company could maintain sales at the expected rate of 500 units per week for an additional 2 weeks if production or shipping delays held up an order.

However, carrying a safety stock has a cost. The average inventory is now EOQ/2 plus the safety stock, or $6,500/2 + 1,000 = 3,250 + 1,000 = 4,250$ shirts, and the average inventory value is now $(4,250)($4.92) = $20,910$. This increase in average inventory causes an increase in annual inventory carrying costs equal to (Safety stock) $(P)(C) = 1,000($4.92)(0.25) = $1,230$.

The optimal safety stock varies from situation to situation, but, in general, it *increases* (1) with the uncertainty of demand forecasts, (2) with the costs (in terms of lost sales and lost goodwill) that result from inventory shortages, and (3) with the probability that delays will occur in receiving shipments. The optimum safety stock *decreases* as the cost of carrying this additional inventory increases.[12]

---

[12]For a more detailed discussion of safety stocks, see Arthur Snyder, "Principles of Inventory Management," *Financial Executive,* April 1964, 13–21.

Quantity Discounts

Now suppose the T-shirt manufacturer offered Cotton Tops a *quantity discount* of 2 percent on large orders. If the quantity discount applied to orders of 5,000 or more, then Cotton Tops would continue to place the EOQ order of 6,500 shirts and take the quantity discount. However, if the quantity discount required orders of 10,000 or more, then Cotton Tops' inventory manager would have to compare the savings in purchase price that would result if its ordering quantity were increased to 10,000 units with the increase in total inventory costs caused by the departure from the 6,500-unit EOQ.

First, consider the total costs associated with Cotton Tops' EOQ of 6,500 units. We found earlier that total inventory costs are $8,000:

$$
\begin{aligned}
\text{TIC} &= & \text{TCC} & & + & & \text{TOC} \\[2mm]
&= & (C)(P)\left(\frac{Q}{2}\right) & & + & & (F)\left(\frac{S}{Q}\right) \\[2mm]
&= & 0.25(\$4.92)\left(\frac{6,500}{2}\right) & & + & & (\$1,000)\left(\frac{26,000}{6,500}\right) \\[2mm]
&\approx & \$4,000 & & + & & \$4,000 & &= \$8,000
\end{aligned}
$$

Now, what would the total inventory costs be if Cotton Tops ordered 10,000 units instead of 6,500? The answer is $8,625:

$$
\begin{aligned}
\text{TIC} &= 0.25(\$4.82)\left(\frac{10,000}{2}\right) & + & (\$1,000)\left(\frac{26,000}{10,000}\right) \\[2mm]
&= \$6,025 & + & \$2,600 & = \$8,625.
\end{aligned}
$$

Notice that when the discount is taken, the price, P, is reduced by the amount of the discount; the new price per unit would be $0.98(\$4.92) = \$4.82$. Also note that when the ordering quantity is increased, carrying costs increase because the firm is carrying a larger average inventory, but ordering costs decrease since the number of orders per year decreases. If we were to calculate total inventory costs at an ordering quantity of 5,000, we would find that carrying costs would be less than $4,000, and ordering costs would be more than $4,000, but the total inventory costs would be more than $8,000, since they are at a minimum when 6,500 units are ordered.[13]

Thus, inventory costs would increase by $8,625 - \$8,000 = \$625$ if Cotton Tops were to increase its order size to 10,000 shirts. *However, this cost increase must be compared with Cotton Tops' savings if it takes the discount.* Taking the discount

---

[13]At an ordering quantity of 5,000 units, total inventory costs are $8,275:

$$
\begin{aligned}
\text{TIC} &= (0.25)(\$4.92)\left(\frac{5,000}{2}\right) + (\$1,000)\left(\frac{26,000}{5,000}\right) \\[2mm]
&= \$3,075 + \$5,200 = \$8,275.
\end{aligned}
$$

would save $0.02(\$4.92) = \$0.0984$ per unit. Over the year, Cotton Tops orders 26,000 shirts, so the annual savings is $\$0.0984(26,000) \approx \$2,558$. Here is a summary:

Reduction in purchase price = $0.02(\$4.92)(26,000)$ = $\$2,558$
Increase in total inventory cost   = $\underline{625}$
Net savings from taking discounts $\underline{\underline{\$1,933}}$

Obviously, the company should order 10,000 units at a time and take advantage of the quantity discount.

Inflation

Moderate inflation—say 3 percent per year—can largely be ignored for purposes of inventory management, but higher rates of inflation must be explicitly considered. If the rate of inflation in the types of goods the firm stocks tends to be relatively constant, it can be dealt with quite easily—simply deduct the expected annual rate of inflation from the carrying cost percentage, C, in Equation 21-7, and use this modified version of the EOQ model to establish the working stock. The reason for making this deduction is that inflation causes the value of the inventory to rise, thus offsetting somewhat the effects of depreciation and other carrying costs factors. Since C will now be smaller, the calculated EOQ, and the average inventory, will increase. However, the higher the rate of inflation, the higher are interest rates, and this factor will cause C to increase, thus lowering the EOQ and average inventories.

On balance, there is no evidence that inflation either raises or lowers the optimal inventories of firms in the aggregate. Inflation should still be explicitly considered, however, for it will raise the individual firm's optimal holdings if the rate of inflation for its own inventories is above average (and is greater than the effects of inflation on interest rates), and vice versa.

Seasonal Demand

For most firms, it is unrealistic to assume that the demand for an inventory item is uniform throughout the year. What happens when there is seasonal demand, as would hold true for an ice cream company? Here the standard annual EOQ model is obviously not appropriate. However, it does provide a point of departure for setting inventory parameters, which are then modified to fit the particular seasonal pattern. The procedure here is to divide the year into the seasons in which annualized sales are relatively constant, say the summer, the spring and fall, and the winter. Then, the EOQ model can be applied separately to each period. During the transitions between seasons, inventories would be either run down or else built up with special seasonal orders.

EOQ Range

Thus far, we have interpreted the EOQ, and the resulting inventory variables, as single point estimates. It can be easily demonstrated that small deviations from the

Table 21-7   EOQ Sensitivity Analysis

Ordering Quantity	Total Inventory Costs	Percentage Deviation from Optimal
3,000	$10,512	+31.4%
4,000	8,960	+12.0
5,000	8,275	+3.4
6,000	8,023	+0.3
6,500	8,000	0.0
7,000	8,019	+0.2
8,000	8,170	+2.1
9,000	8,423	+5.3
10,000	8,750	+9.4

EOQ do not appreciably affect total inventory costs, and, consequently, that the optimal ordering quantity should be viewed more as a range than as a single value.[14]

To illustrate this point, we can examine the sensitivity of total inventory costs to ordering quantity for Cotton Tops, Inc. Table 21-7 contains the results of our sensitivity analysis. We conclude that the ordering quantity could range from 5,000 to 8,000 units without affecting total inventory costs by more than 3.4 percent. Thus, we see that managers can adjust the ordering quantity within a fairly wide range without fear of significantly increasing total inventory costs.

Self-Test Questions

Why are inventory safety stocks required?

Conceptually, how would you evaluate a quantity discount offer from a supplier?

What impact does inflation have on the EOQ?

Can the EOQ model be used when a company faces seasonal demand fluctuations?

What is the impact of minor deviations from the EOQ on total inventory costs?

INVENTORY CONTROL SYSTEMS

The EOQ model, together with safety stock analysis, can be used to establish the proper inventory level, but inventory management also involves the establishment of an *inventory control system.* Inventory control systems run the gamut from very simple to extremely complex, depending on the size of the firm and the nature of its inventories. For example, one simple control procedure is the *redline method* — inventory items are stocked in a bin, a red line is drawn around the inside of the

---

[14]This is somewhat analogous to the optimal capital structure in that small changes in capital structure around the optimum do not have much effect on the firm's weighted average cost of capital.

bin at the level of the order point, and the inventory clerk places an order when the red line shows. The *two-bin method* has inventory items stocked in two bins. When the working bin is empty, an order is placed and inventory is drawn from the second bin. These procedures work well for parts such as bolts in a manufacturing process, or for many items in retail businesses.

Computerized Systems

Larger companies employ *computerized inventory control systems*. The computer starts with an inventory count in memory. As withdrawals are made, they are recorded by the computer, and the inventory balance is revised. When the order point is reached, the computer automatically places an order, and when the order is received, the recorded balance is increased. Retailers such as Wal-Mart have carried this system quite far — each item has a magnetic bar code, and, as an item is checked out, the code is read, a signal is sent to the computer, and the inventory balance is adjusted at the same time the price is fed into the cash register tape. When the balance drops to the order point, an order is placed, in Wal-Mart's case directly from its computers to those of its suppliers.

A good inventory control system is dynamic, not static. A company such as IBM or General Motors stocks hundreds of thousands of different items. The sales (or use) of these various items can rise or fall quite separately from rising or falling overall corporate sales. As the usage rate for an individual item begins to rise or fall, the inventory manager must adjust its balance to avoid running short or ending up with obsolete items. If the change in the usage rate appears to be permanent, then the EOQ should be recomputed, the safety stock level should be reconsidered, and the computer model used in the control process should be reprogrammed.

Just-in-Time Systems

A relatively new approach to inventory control called *just-in-time* has been developed by Japanese firms and is gaining popularity throughout the world. Toyota provides a good example of the just-in-time system. Eight of Toyota's ten factories, along with most of Toyota's suppliers, dot the countryside around Toyota City. Delivery of components is tied to the speed of the assembly line, and parts are generally delivered no more than a few hours before they are used. The just-in-time system reduces the need for Toyota and other manufacturers to carry large inventories, but it requires a great deal of coordination between the manufacturer and its suppliers, both in the timing of deliveries and the quality of the parts.

Not surprisingly, U.S. automobile manufacturers were among the first domestic firms to move toward just-in-time systems. Ford has been restructuring its production system with a goal of increasing its inventory turnover from 20 times a year to 30 or 40 times. Of course, just-in-time systems place considerable pressure on suppliers. GM used to keep a 10-day supply of seats and other parts made by Lear Siegler; now GM sends in orders at four- to eight-hour intervals and expects immediate shipment. A Lear Siegler spokesman stated, "We can't afford to keep things sitting around either," so Lear Siegler has had to be tougher on its own suppliers.

Just-in-time systems are also being adopted by smaller firms. In fact, some production experts say that small companies are better positioned than large ones to use just-in-time methods, because it is easier to redefine job functions and to educate people in small firms. One small-firm example is Fireplace Manufacturers, Inc., a manufacturer of prefabricated fireplaces. The company was recently having cash flow problems, and it was carrying $1.1 million in inventories to support annual sales of about $8 million. The company used just-in-time methods to trim its raw material and work-in-process inventories to $750,000, freeing up $350,000 of cash, even though sales were doubling.

Out-Sourcing

Another important development related to inventories is *out-sourcing,* which is the practice of purchasing components rather than making them in-house. Thus, if General Motors arranged to buy radiators, axles, and other parts from suppliers rather than making them itself, it would be increasing its use of out-sourcing. Out-sourcing is often combined with just-in-time systems to reduce inventory levels. However, perhaps the major reason for out-sourcing has nothing to do with inventory policy —a heavily unionized company like GM can often buy parts from a nonunionized supplier at a lower cost than it would take to make them because of wage-rate differentials.

The Relationship between Production Scheduling and Inventory Levels

A final point relating to inventory levels is *the relationship between production scheduling and inventory levels.* A firm like a greeting card manufacturer has highly seasonal sales. Such a firm could produce on a steady, year-round basis, or it could let production rise and fall with sales. If it established a level production schedule, its inventories would rise sharply during periods when sales were low and then would decline during peak sales periods, but the average inventory held would be substantially higher than if production were geared to rise and fall with sales.

Our discussions of just-in-time systems, out-sourcing, and production scheduling all point out the necessity of coordinating inventory policy with manufacturing/ procurement policies. Companies try to minimize *total production and distribution costs,* and inventory costs are just one part of total costs. Still, they are an important cost, and financial managers should be aware of the determinants of inventory costs and how they can be minimized.

Self-Test Questions

Describe some inventory control systems used in practice.

What are just-in-time systems? What advantages do these inventory systems offer?

What is out-sourcing?

Describe the dependency between production scheduling and inventory levels.

INVENTORY COST HEDGING

In Chapter 18, we discussed the use of financial futures to hedge against changes in interest rate levels. Actually, futures markets were established for many industrial and agricultural commodities long before they began to be used for financial instruments. We can use Porter Electronics, which uses large quantities of copper as well as several precious metals, to illustrate inventory hedging. Suppose that in May 1990, Porter foresaw a need for 100,000 pounds of copper in March 1991 for use in fulfilling a fixed-price contract to supply solar power cells to the U.S. Government. Porter's managers are concerned that a strike by the copper mineworkers' union will occur when the union contract expires in October 1990. A strike would raise the price of copper significantly and possibly turn the expected profit on the solar cell contract into a loss.

Porter could, of course, go ahead and buy the copper now that it will need to fulfill the contract, but if it does, it will incur substantial carrying costs. As an alternative, the company could hedge against increasing copper prices in the futures market. The New York Commodity Exchange trades standard copper futures contracts of 25,000 pounds each. Thus, Porter could buy four contracts (go long) for delivery in March 1991. These contracts were trading in May for about $1.25 per pound. The spot price at that date was about $1.20 per pound. If copper prices do rise appreciably over the next 10 months, the value of Porter's long position in copper futures would increase, thus offsetting some of the price increase in the commodity itself. Of course, if copper prices fall, Porter would lose money on its futures contract, but the company would be buying the copper on the spot market at a cheaper price, so it would make a higher-than-anticipated profit on its sale of solar cells. Thus, hedging in the copper futures market locks in the cost of raw materials and removes some uncertainties, or risks, to which the firm would otherwise be exposed.

Some firms have been using the futures markets for speculation, rather than hedging, and this can lead to disastrous results. For example, when the once-stable aluminum ingot market began fluctuating wildly in the early 1980s, aluminum fabricators did what mining companies had been doing for years—they turned to the futures market to lock in prices. That worked well, but then some companies started speculating. One company, National Aluminum Corporation, lost $41.4 million in futures trading. Basically, National Aluminum bought forward contracts to buy 100,000 tons of ingot for 80 cents a pound, which was far in excess of its planned production needs. When the contracts were near expiration, the price of ingots had dropped below 60 cents a pound, resulting in the $41.4 million loss.

Self-Test Question

Discuss how futures markets can be used to hedge against increasing raw material prices.

MULTINATIONAL FINANCE
International Credit and Inventory Management

Credit Management

Like most other aspects of finance, credit management in the multinational corporation is similar to but more complex than that in a purely domestic business. First, granting credit is riskier in an international context because, in addition to the normal risks of default, the multinational firm must also worry about exchange rate changes between the time a sale is made and the time a receivable is collected. For example, if IBM sold a computer to a Japanese customer for 160 million yen when the exchange rate was 160 yen per $1, IBM would obtain 160,000,000/160 = $1,000,000 for the computer. However, if it sold the computer on 6 months' credit, and if the dollar rose against the yen so that one dollar would now buy 200 yen, IBM would end up realizing only 160,000,000/200 = $800,000 when it collected the receivable.

In addition to being riskier, credit policy is generally more important for a multinational than for a purely domestic firm for two reasons. First, much of the United States' trade is with poorer, less-developed nations, and in such situations granting credit is generally a necessary condition for doing business. Second, and in large part as a result of the first point, nations whose economic health depends upon exports often help their manufacturing firms compete internationally by granting credit to foreign countries. In Japan, for example, the major manufacturing firms have direct ownership ties with large "trading companies" engaged in international trade, as well as with giant commercial banks. In addition, a government agency, the Ministry of International Trade and Industry (MITI), helps Japanese firms identify potential export markets and helps potential customers arrange credit for purchases from Japanese firms. In effect, the huge Japanese trade surpluses are used to finance Japanese exports, thus helping to perpetuate their favorable trade balance. The United States has attempted to counter with the Export-Import Bank, which is funded by Congress, but the fact that the United States expects a balance of payments deficit in 1990 in excess of $100 billion is clear evidence that it has been less successful than others in world markets in recent years.

The huge debt which countries such as Brazil, Mexico, and Argentina owe the international banks, including many U.S. banks, is well known, and this situation illustrates how credit policy (by banks in this case) can go astray. The banks face a particularly sticky problem with these loans, because if a sovereign nation defaults, the banks cannot lay claim to the assets of the country as they could if a corporate customer defaulted. Note too that although the banks' loans to foreign governments are getting most of the headlines, many multinational corporations are also in trouble as the result of granting credit to business customers in the same countries in which the bank loans are on shaky ground.

By pointing out the risks inherent in granting credit internationally, we are by no means suggesting that such credit is necessarily bad. Quite the contrary, for on balance, the potential gains from international operations far outweigh the risks, at least for companies (and banks) that truly have the expertise to engage in these activities.

Inventory Management

Inventory management in a multinational setting is more complex than that in a purely domestic firm for several reasons. First, there is the matter of the physical location of inventories. For example, where should Exxon keep its stockpiles of crude oil and refined products? It has refineries and marketing centers located worldwide, and one alternative is to keep items concentrated in a few strategic spots from which they can then be shipped to the locations where they will be used as needs arise. Such a strategy may minimize the total amount of inventories needed to operate the global business and thus may minimize the firm's total investment in inventories. Note, though, that consideration will have to be given to potential delays in getting goods from central storage locations to user locations all around the world. Both working stocks and safety stocks will have to be maintained at each user location, as well as at the strategic storage centers. Problems like the Iran–Iraq war, which brings with it the potential for a shutdown of production of about 25 percent of the world's oil supply, complicate matters even more.

Exchange rates also influence inventory policy. If a local currency, say the Danish krone, was expected to rise in value against the dollar, a U.S. company operating in Denmark would want to increase stocks of local products before the rise in the krone, and vice versa if the krone was expected to fall.

Another factor that must be considered is the possibility of import or export quotas or tariffs. For example, if Apple Computer Company was obtaining 256K memory chips from Japanese suppliers at bargain prices, but U.S. chipmakers had just charged the Japanese with dumping chips in the U.S. market at prices below cost and were seeking to force the Japanese to raise prices, Apple might decide to increase its chip inventory.[15]

Yet another issue in certain countries is the threat of expropriation. If that threat is large, inventory holdings will be minimized, and goods will be brought in only as needed. Similarly, if the operation involves ex-

traction of raw material such as oil or bauxite, production may be stepped up, and stockpiles moved offshore rather than left close to the production site.

Taxes have two effects on multinational inventory management. First, countries often impose property taxes on assets, including inventories, and when this is done, the tax is based on holdings as of a specific date, say January 1 or March 1. Such rules make it advantageous for a multinational firm (1) to schedule production so that inventories are low on the assessment date, and (2) where assessment dates vary among countries in a region, to hold safety stocks in different countries at different times during the year.

Finally, firms must consider the possibility of at-sea storage. Oil, chemical, grain, and other companies that deal in a bulk commodity that must be stored in some type of tank can often buy tankers at a cost not much greater — or perhaps even cheaper, considering land cost — than land-based facilities. Loaded tankers can then be kept at sea or at anchor in some strategic location. This eliminates the danger of expropriation, minimizes the property tax problem, and maximizes flexibility with regard to shipping to areas where needs are greatest or prices highest.

This discussion has only scratched the surface of inventory management in the multinational corporation. As we noted at the outset, the task is much more complex than for a purely domestic firm, but the greater the degree of complexity, the greater the rewards for superior performance. If you want a challenge along with potentially high rewards, look to the international arena.

---

[15]The term *dumping* warrants explanation, because the practice is so potentially important in international markets. Suppose Japanese chipmakers have excess capacity. A particular chip has a variable cost of $25, and its "fully allocated cost," which is the $25 plus total fixed cost per unit of output, is $40. Now suppose the Japanese firm can sell chips in the United States at $35 per unit, but if it charges $40 it will not make any sales because U.S. chipmakers sell for $35.50. If the Japanese firm sells at $35, it will cover variable cost plus make a contribution to fixed overhead, so selling at $35 makes sense. Continuing, if the Japanese firm can sell in Japan at $40, but U.S. firms are excluded from Japanese markets by import duties or other barriers, the Japanese will have a huge advantage over U.S. manufacturers. The practice of selling goods at lower prices in foreign markets than at home is called "dumping." U.S. firms are required by anti-trust laws to offer the same price to all customers and, therefore, cannot engage in dumping.

SUMMARY

This chapter discussed both receivables and inventories. The key concepts covered are listed below.

- When a firm sells goods to a customer on credit, an *account receivable* is created.

- Firms can use an *aging schedule* and the *days sales outstanding (DSO)* to help keep track of their receivables position and to help avoid the buildup of possible bad debts.

- The *payments pattern approach* is the best way to monitor receivables. The primary tool in this approach is the *uncollected balances schedule*.

- A firm's *credit policy* consists of four elements: (1) credit period, (2) discounts given for early payment, (3) credit standards, and (4) collection policy. The first two, when combined, are called the *credit terms.*

- Two major sources of external credit information are available: *credit associations,* which are local groups that meet frequently and correspond with one another to exchange information on credit customers, and *credit reporting agencies,* which collect credit information and sell it for a fee.

- Additional factors that influence a firm's overall credit policy are (1) *profit potential,* (2) *legal considerations,* and (3) the type of *credit instruments* offered.

- The basic objective of the credit manager is to increase profitable sales by extending credit to worthy customers and therefore adding value to the firm.

- If a firm *eases its credit policy,* its sales should increase. Actions which ease the credit policy include lengthening the credit period, relaxing credit standards and collection policy, and offering cash discounts. Each of these actions, however, increases costs. A firm should ease its credit policy only if the costs of doing so will be more than offset by higher sales revenues.

- *Inventory management* involves determining how much inventory to hold, when to place orders, and how many units to order at a time. Because the cost of holding inventory is high, inventory management is important.

- *Inventory* can be grouped into three categories: (1) raw materials, (2) work-in-process, and (3) finished goods.

- *Inventory costs* can also be divided into three types: carrying costs, ordering costs, and stock-out costs. In general, carrying costs increase as the level of inventory rises, but ordering costs and stock-out costs decline with larger inventory holdings.

- *Total carrying cost (TCC)* is equal to the percentage cost of carrying inventory (C) times the purchase price per unit of inventory (P) times the average number of units held (A): TCC = (C)(P)(A).

- *Total ordering cost (TOC)* is equal to the fixed cost of placing an order (F) times the number of orders placed per year (N): TOC = (F)(N).

- *Total inventory costs (TIC)* are equal to carrying costs plus ordering costs.

- The *economic ordering quantity (EOQ) model* is a formula for determining the order quantity that will minimize total inventory costs:

$$EOQ = \sqrt{\frac{2(F)(S)}{(C)(P)}}.$$

  Here F is the fixed cost per order, S is annual sales in units, C is the percentage cost of carrying inventory, and P is the purchase price per unit.

- The *reorder point* is the inventory level at which new items must be ordered.

- *Safety stocks* are held to avoid shortages (1) if demand becomes greater than expected or (2) if shipping delays are encountered. The cost of carrying safety stocks is equal to the percentage cost of carrying inventories times the purchase price per unit times the number of units held as the safety stock. These costs are separate from those used in the EOQ model.

- Firms use inventory control systems, such as the *red-line method* and the *two-bin method,* as well as *computerized inventory control systems,* to help them keep track of actual inventory levels and to insure that inventory levels are adjusted as sales change. *Just-in-time (JIT)* systems are also used to hold down inventory costs and, simultaneously, to improve the production process.

Questions

21-1 Define each of the following terms:
   a.   Account receivable
   b.   Aging schedule; days sales outstanding (DSO)
   c.   Payments pattern approach; uncollected balances schedule
   d.   Credit policy; credit period; credit standards; collection policy
   e.   Cash discounts
   f.   Seasonal dating
   g.   Open account; promissory note; commercial draft; sight draft; time draft; trade acceptance; banker's acceptance; conditional sales contract
   h.   Carrying costs; ordering costs; total inventory costs
   i.   Economic ordering quantity (EOQ); EOQ model; EOQ range
   j.   Reorder point; safety stock
   k.   Red-line method; two-bin method; computerized inventory control system
   l.   Just-in-time systems

21-2 Is it true that when one firm sells to another on credit, the seller records the transaction as an account receivable while the buyer records it as an account payable and that, disregarding discounts, the receivable typically exceeds the payable by the amount of profit on the sale?

21-3 What are the four elements in a firm's credit policy? To what extent can firms set their own credit policies as opposed to having to accept policies that are dictated by "the competition"?

21-4 Suppose a firm makes a purchase and receives the shipment on February 1. The terms of trade as stated on the invoice read "2/10, net 40, May 1 dating." What is the latest date on which payment can be made and the discount still be taken? What is the date on which payment must be made if the discount is not taken?

21-5 What is the days sales outstanding (DSO) for a firm whose sales are $2,880,000 per year and whose accounts receivable are $312,000? (Use 360 days per year.) Is it true that if this firm sells on terms of 3/10, net 40, its customers probably all pay on time?

21-6 Is it true that if a firm calculates its days sales outstanding (DSO) it has no need for an aging schedule?

21-7 Firm A had no credit losses last year, but 1 percent of Firm B's accounts receivable proved to be uncollectible and resulted in losses. Should Firm B fire its credit manager and hire A's?

21-8 Indicate by a +, −, or 0 whether each of the following events would probably cause accounts receivable (A/R), sales, and profits to increase, decrease, or be affected in an indeterminate manner:

	A/R	Sales	Profits
a. The firm tightens its credit standards.	_____	_____	_____
b. The terms of trade are changed from 2/10, net 30, to 3/10, net 30.	_____	_____	_____
c. The terms are changed from 2/10, net 30, to 3/10, net 40.	_____	_____	_____
d. The credit manager gets tough with past-due accounts	_____	_____	_____

21-9 Indicate by a +, −, or 0 whether each of the following events would probably cause average annual inventories (the sum of the inventories held at the end of each month of the year divided by 12) to rise, fall, or be affected in an indeterminate manner:

a.   Our suppliers switch from delivering by train to air freight.   _____

b.   We change from producing just in time to meet seasonal sales to steady, year-round production. (Sales peak at Christmas.)   _____

c.   Competition in the markets in which we sell increases.   _____

d.   The rate of general inflation increases.   _____

e.   Interest rates rise; other things are constant.   _____

Self-Test Problems (Solutions Appear in Appendix D)

ST-1 **(Credit policy)** The McCue Company expects to have sales of $10 million this year under its current operating policies. Its variable costs as a percentage of sales are 80 percent, and its cost of capital is 16 percent. Currently the firm's credit policy is net 25 (no discount for early payment). However, its DSO is 30 days, and its bad debt loss percentage is 2 percent. McCue spends $50,000 per year to collect bad debts, and its federal-plus-state-plus-local tax rate is 50 percent.

   The credit manager is considering two alternative proposals, given below, for changing the firm's credit policy. Find the expected change in net income, taking into consideration anticipated changes in carrying costs for accounts receivable, the probable bad debt losses, and the discounts likely to be taken, for each proposal. Should a change in credit policy be made?

Proposal 1: Lengthen the credit period by going from net 25 to net 30. The bad debt collection expenditures will remain constant. Under this proposal, sales are expected to increase by $1 million annually, and the bad debt loss percentage on *new* sales is expected to rise to 4 percent (the loss percentage on old sales should not change). In addition, the DSO is expected to increase from 30 to 45 days on all sales.

Proposal 2: Shorten the credit period by going from net 25 to net 20. Again, collection expenses will remain constant. The anticipated effects of this change are (1) a decrease in sales of $1 million per year, (2) a decline in the DSO from 30 to 22 days, and (3) a decline in the bad debt loss percentage to 1 percent on all sales.

ST-2 **(EOQ model)** The Bertin Breads Company buys and then sells (as bread) 2.6 million bushels of wheat annually. The wheat must be purchased in multiples of 2,000 bushels. Ordering costs, which include grain elevator removal charges of $3,500, are $5,000 per order. Annual carrying costs are 2 percent of the purchase price per bushel of $5. The company maintains a safety stock of 200,000 bushels. The delivery time is 6 weeks.

a. What is the EOQ?

b. At what inventory level should a reorder be placed to prevent having to draw on the safety stock?

c. What are the total inventory costs?

d. The wheat processor agrees to pay the elevator removal charges if Bertin Breads will purchase wheat in quantities of 650,000 bushels. Would it be to the firm's advantage to order under this alternative?

Problems

21-1 (Receivables investment) Provencial, Inc., sells on terms of 2/10, net 30. Total sales for the year are $600,000. Forty percent of the customers pay on the tenth day and take discounts; the other 60 percent pay, on average, 40 days after their purchases.

a. What is the days sales outstanding?

b. What is the average amount of receivables?

c. What would happen to the average investment in receivables if Provencial toughened up on its collection policy with the result that all nondiscount customers paid on the thirtieth day?

21-2 (Easing credit terms) Butler Auto Parts is considering changing its credit terms from 2/15, net 30, to 3/10, net 30, in order to speed collections. At present, 60 percent of the firm's customers take the 2 percent discount. Under the new terms, discount customers are expected to rise to 70 percent. Regardless of the credit terms, half of the customers who do not take the discount are expected to pay on time, while the remainder will pay 10 days late. The change does not involve a relaxation of credit standards; therefore, bad debt losses are not expected to rise above their present 2 percent level. However, the more generous cash discount terms are expected to increase sales from $1 million to $1.2 million per year. The firm's variable cost ratio is 75 percent, the interest rate on funds invested in accounts receivable is 12 percent, and its tax rate is 40 percent.

a. What is the days sales outstanding before and after the change?

b. Calculate the discount costs before and after the change.

c. Calculate the dollar cost of carrying receivables before and after the change.

d. Calculate the bad debt losses before and after the change.

e. What is the incremental profit from the change in credit terms? Should the firm change its credit terms?

(Do Part f only if you are using the computerized diskette.)

f. (1) Suppose the sales forecast is lowered to $1,100,000. Should the firm change its credit policy? What if the sales forecast dropped to $1,036,310?

(2) Suppose the payment pattern of customers remains unchanged with the new credit plan; that is, 60 percent still take the discount, 20 percent pay on time, and 20 percent pay late. Also, the variable cost ratio rises to 78 percent. How does all this affect the decision, assuming the sales forecast remains at $1,200,000?

21-3 (Credit analysis) Wolfe Distributors makes all sales on a credit basis, selling on terms of 2/10, net 30. Once a year it evaluates the creditworthiness of all its customers. The evaluation procedure ranks customers from 1 to 5, with 1 indicating the "best" customers. Results of the ranking are as follows:

Customer Category	Percentage of Bad Debts	Days Sales Outstanding	Credit Decision	Annual Sales Lost Due to Credit Restrictions
1	None	10	Unlimited credit	None
2	1.0	12	Unlimited credit	None
3	3.0	20	Limited credit	$365,000
4	9.0	60	Limited credit	$182,500
5	16.0	90	Limited credit	$230,000

The variable cost ratio is 75 percent. The cost of capital invested in receivables is 15 percent. What would be the effect on the profitability of extending unlimited credit to each of the Categories 3, 4, and 5? (Hint: Determine the effect of changing each policy separately on the income statement. In other words, find the change in sales, change in production costs, change in receivables and cost of carrying receivables, change in bad debt costs, and so forth, down to the change in net profits. Assume a tax rate of 40 percent.)

21-4 **(Tightening credit terms)** Mary Considine, the new credit manager of the Hunt Corporation, was alarmed to find that Hunt sells on credit terms of net 90 days while industrywide credit terms have recently been lowered to net 30 days. On annual credit sales of $2.5 million, Hunt currently averages 95 days of sales in accounts receivable. Considine estimates that tightening the credit terms to 30 days would reduce annual sales to $2,375,000, but accounts receivable would drop to 35 days of sales and the savings on investment in them should more than overcome any loss in profit.

Hunt's variable cost ratio is 85 percent, and taxes are 40 percent. If the interest rate on funds invested in receivables is 18 percent, should the change in credit terms be made?

21-5 **(Monitoring of receivables)** The Doug French Company, a small manufacturer of cordless telephones, began operations on January 1, 1990. Its credit sales for the first 6 months of operations were as follows:

Month	Credit Sales
January	$ 50,000
February	100,000
March	120,000
April	105,000
May	140,000
June	160,000

Throughout this entire period, the firm's credit customers maintained a constant payments pattern: 20 percent paid in the month of sale, 30 percent paid in the month following the sale, and 50 percent paid in the second month following the sale.

a.   What was French's receivables balance at the end of March and at the end of June?

b.   Assume 90 days per calendar quarter. What were the average daily sales (ADS) and days sales outstanding (DSO) for the first quarter and for the second quarter? What were the cumulative ADS and DSO for the first half-year?

c.   Construct an aging schedule as of June 30. Use 0-30, 31-60, and 61-90 day account ages.

d.   Construct the uncollected balances schedule for the second quarter as of June 30.

21-6 **(Relaxing collection efforts)** The Dill Corporation has annual credit sales of $1.6 million. Current expenses for the collection department are $35,000, bad debt losses are 1.5 percent, and the days sales outstanding is 30 days. The firm is considering easing its collection efforts such that collection expenses will be reduced to $22,000 per year. The change is expected to increase bad debt losses to 2.5 percent and to increase the days sales outstanding to 45 days. In addition, sales are expected to increase to $1,625,000 per year.

Should the firm relax collection efforts if the opportunity cost of funds is 16 percent, the variable cost ratio is 75 percent, and taxes are 40 percent?

21-7   **(Economic ordering quantity)** The Dimkoff Garden Center sells 90,000 bags of lawn fertilizer annually. The optimal safety stock (which is on hand initially) is 1,000 bags. Each bag costs the firm $1.50, inventory carrying costs are 20 percent, and the cost of placing an order with its supplier is $15.
   a.   What is the economic ordering quantity?
   b.   What is the maximum inventory of fertilizer?
   c.   What will be the firm's average inventory?
   d.   How often must the company order?

21-8   **(EOQ and total ordering costs)** The following inventory data have been established for the Zocco Corporation:
   1.   Orders must be placed in multiples of 100 units.
   2.   Annual sales are 338,000 units.
   3.   The purchase price per unit is $3.
   4.   Carrying cost is 20 percent of the purchase price of goods.
   5.   Cost per order placed is $24.
   6.   Desired safety stock is 14,000 units; this amount is on hand initially.
   7.   Two weeks are required for delivery.
      a.   What is the EOQ?
      b.   How many orders should the firm place each year?
      c.   At what inventory level should a reorder be made? (Hint: Reorder point = Safety stock + (Weeks to deliver × Weekly usage) − Goods in transit.)
      d.   Calculate the total costs of ordering and carrying inventories if the order quantity is (1) 4,000 units, (2) 4,800 units, or (3) 6,000 units. What are the total costs if the order quantity is the EOQ?
      (Do Part e only if you are using the computerized diskette.)
      e.   What are the EOQ and total inventory costs if
         (1)   Sales increase to 500,000 units?
         (2)   Fixed order costs increase to $30? Sales remain at 338,000 units.
         (3)   Purchase price increases to $4? Leave sales and fixed costs at original values.

Mini Case

Section I: Receivables Management. Rich Jackson, a recent finance graduate, is planning to go into the wholesale building supply business with his brother, Jim, who majored in building construction. The firm would sell primarily to general contractors, and it would start operating next January. Sales would be slow during the cold months, rise during the spring, and then fall off again in the summer, when new construction in the area slows. Sales estimates for the first 6 months are as follows (in thousands of dollars):

January	$100	March	$300	May	$200
February	200	April	300	June	100

The terms of sale are net 30, but because of special incentives the brothers expect 30 percent of the customers (by dollar value) to pay on the 10th day following the sale, 50 percent to pay on the 40th day, and the remaining 20 percent to pay on the 70th day. No bad debt losses are expected, because Jim, the building construction expert, knows which contractors are having financial problems.

a. Assume that, on average, the brothers expect annual sales of 18,000 items at an average price of $100 per item. (Use a 360-day year.)

(1) What is the firm's expected days sales outstanding (DSO)?

(2) What is its expected average daily sales (ADS)?

(3) What is its expected average accounts receivable level?

(4) Assume that the firm's profit margin is 25 percent. How much of the receivables balance must be financed? What would the firm's balance sheet figures for accounts receivable, notes payable, and retained earnings be at the end of one year if notes payable are used to finance the investment in receivables? Assume that the cost of carrying receivables had been deducted when the 25 percent profit margin was calculated.

(5) If bank loans cost 12 percent, what is the annual dollar cost of carrying the receivables?

b. What are some factors which influence (1) a firm's receivables level and (2) the dollar cost of carrying receivables?

c. Assuming that the monthly sales forecasts given previously are accurate, and that customers pay exactly as was predicted, what would the receivables level be at the end of each month? *To reduce calculations, assume that 30 percent of the firm's customers pay in the month of sale, 50 percent pay in the month following the sale, and the remaining 20 percent pay in the second month following the sale. Note that this is a different assumption than was made earlier.* Use the following format:

Month	Sales	End-of-Month Receivables	Quarterly Sales	ADS	DSO = (A/R)/(ADS)
Jan	$100	$ 70			
Feb	200	160			
Mar	300	250	$660	$6.67	37.5
Apr	$300				
May	200				
Jun	100				

d. What is the firm's forecasted average daily sales for the first 3 months? For the entire half-year? The days sales outstanding is commonly used to measure receivables performance. What DSO is expected at the end of March? At the end of June? What does the DSO indicate about customers' payments? Is DSO a good management tool in this situation? If not, why not?

e. Construct aging schedules for the end of March and the end of June (use the format given below). Do these schedules properly measure customers' payment patterns? If not, why not?

Age of Account (Days)	Mar A/R	Mar %	Jun A/R	Jun %
0–30	$210	84%		
31–60	40	16		
61–90	0	0	___	___
	$250	100%		

f.   Construct the uncollected balances schedules for the end of March and the end of June. Use the format given next. Do these schedules properly measure customers' payment patterns?

Month	Sales	Contribution to A/R	A/R-to-Sales Ratio	Month	Sales	Contribution to A/R	A/R-to-Sales Ratio
Jan	$100	$ 0	0%	Apr			
Feb	200	40	20	May			
Mar	300	210	70	Jun			

g.   Assume that it is now July of Year 1, and the brothers are developing pro forma financial statements for the following year. Further, assume that sales and collections in the first half-year matched the predicted levels. Using the Year 2 sales forecasts as shown next, what are next year's pro forma receivables levels for the end of March and for the end of June?

Month	Predicted Sales	Predicted A/R-to-Sales Ratio	Predicted Contribution to Receivables
Jan	$150	0%	$ 0
Feb	300	20	60
Mar	500	70	350
	Projected March 31 A/R balance =		$410
Apr	$400		
May	300		
Jun	200		
	Projected June 30 A/R balance =		

h.   Assume now that it is several years later. The brothers are concerned about the firm's current credit terms, which are now net 30, which means that contractors buying building products from the firm are not offered a discount, and they are supposed to pay the full amount in 30 days. Gross sales are now running $1,000,000 a year, and 80 percent (by dollar volume) of the firm's *paying* customers generally pay the full amount on Day 30, while the other 20 percent pay, on average, on Day 40. Two percent of the firm's gross sales end up as bad debt losses.

The brothers are now considering a change in the firm's credit policy. The change would entail (1) changing the credit terms to 2/10, net 20, (2) employing stricter credit standards before granting credit, and (3) enforcing collections with greater vigor than in the past. Thus, cash customers and those paying within 10 days would receive a 2 percent discount, but all others would have to pay the full amount after only 20 days. The brothers believe that the discount would both attract additional customers and encourage some existing customers to purchase more from the firm—after all, the discount amounts to a price reduction. Of course, these customers would take the discount and, hence, would pay in only 10 days. The net expected result is for sales to increase to $1,100,000; for 60 percent of the paying customers to take the discount and pay on the 10th day; for 30 percent to pay the full amount on Day 20; for 10 percent to pay late on Day 30; and for bad debt losses to fall from 2 percent to 1 percent of gross sales. The firm's operating cost ratio will remain unchanged at 75 percent, and its cost of carrying receivables will remain unchanged at 12 percent.

To begin the analysis, describe the four variables which make up a firm's credit policy, and explain how each of them affects sales and collections. Then use the information given in Part h to answer Parts i through n.

i. Under the current credit policy, what is the firm's days sales outstanding (DSO)? What would the expected DSO be if the credit policy change were made?

j. What is the dollar amount of the firm's current bad debt losses? What losses would be expected under the new policy?

k. What would be the firm's expected dollar cost of granting discounts under the new policy?

l. What is the firm's current dollar cost of carrying receivables? What would it be after the proposed change?

m. What is the incremental after-tax profit associated with the change in credit terms? Should the company make the change? (Assume a tax rate of 40 percent.)

	New	Old	Difference
Gross sales		$1,000,000	
Less discounts	_____	0	_____
Net sales		$1,000,000	
Production costs	_____	750,000	_____
Profit before credit costs and taxes		$ 250,000	
Credit-related costs:			
Carrying costs		8,000	
Bad debt losses	_____	20,000	_____
Profit before taxes		$ 222,000	
Taxes (40%)	_____	88,880	_____
Net income	=====	$ 133,200	=====

n. Suppose the firm makes the change, but its competitors react by making similar changes to their own credit terms, with the net result being that gross sales remain at the current $1,000,000 level. What would the impact be on the firm's post-tax profitability?

Section II: Inventory Management. Andria Mullins, financial manager of Webster Electronics, has been asked by the firm's CEO, Fred Weygandt, to evaluate the company's inventory control techniques and to lead a discussion of the subject with the senior executives. Andria plans to use as an example one of Webster's "big ticket" items, a customized computer microchip which the firm uses in its laptop computer. Each chip costs Webster $200, and in addition it must pay its supplier a $1,000 setup fee on each order. Further, the minimum order size is 250 units; Webster's annual usage forecast is 5,000 units; and the annual carrying cost of this item is estimated to be 20 percent of the average inventory value.

Andria plans to begin her session with the senior executives by reviewing some basic inventory concepts, after which she will apply the EOQ model to Webster's microchip inventory. As her assistant, she has asked you to help her by answering the following questions:

a. Why is inventory management vital to the financial health of most firms?

b. What assumptions underlie the EOQ model?

c. Write out the formula for the total costs of carrying and ordering inventory, and then use the formula to derive the EOQ model.

d. What is the EOQ for custom microchips? What are total inventory costs if the EOQ is ordered?

e. What is Webster's added cost if it orders 400 units at a time rather than the EOQ quantity? What if it orders 600 per order?

f.   Suppose it takes 2 weeks for Webster's supplier to set up production, make and test the chips, and deliver them to Webster's plant. Assuming certainty in delivery times and usage, at what inventory level should Webster reorder? (Assume a 52-week year, and assume that Webster orders the EOQ amount.)

g.   Of course, there is uncertainty in Webster's usage rate as well as in delivery times, so the company must carry a safety stock to avoid running out of chips and having to halt production. If a 200-unit safety stock is carried, what effect would this have on total inventory costs? What is the new reorder point? What protection does the safety stock provide if usage increases, or if delivery is delayed?

h.   Now suppose Webster's supplier offers a discount of 1 percent on orders of 1,000 or more. Should Webster take the discount? Why or why not?

i.   For many firms, inventory usage is not uniform throughout the year, but, rather, follows some seasonal pattern. Can the EOQ model be used in this situation? If so, how?

j.   How would these factors affect an EOQ analysis?

(1) The use of just-in-time procedures.

(2) The use of air freight for deliveries.

(3) The use of a computerized inventory control system, wherein as units were removed from stock an electronic system automatically reduced the inventory account and, when the order point was hit, automatically sent an electronic message to the supplier placing an order. The electronic system insures that inventory records are accurate, and that orders are placed promptly.

(4) The manufacturing plant is redesigned and automated. Computerized process equipment and state-of-the-art robotics are installed, making the plant highly flexible in the sense that the company can switch from the production of one item to another at a minimum cost and quite quickly. This makes short production runs more feasible than under the old plant setup.

Selected Additional References and Cases

Recent articles which address credit policy and receivables management include the following:

Atkins, Joseph C., and Yong H. Kim, "Comment and Correction: Opportunity Cost in the Evaluation of Investment in Accounts Receivable," *Financial Management,* Winter 1977, 71–74.

Ben-Horim, Moshe, and Haim Levy, "Management of Accounts Receivable under Inflation," *Financial Management,* Spring 1983, 42–48.

Dyl, Edward A., "Another Look at the Evaluation of Interest in Accounts Receivable," *Financial Management,* Winter 1977, 67–70.

Gallinger, George W., and A. James Ifflander, "Monitoring Accounts Receivable Using Variance Analysis," *Financial Management,* Winter 1986, 69–76.

Gentry, James A., and Jesus M. De La Garza, "A Generalized Model for Monitoring Accounts Receivable," *Financial Management,* Winter 1985, 28–38.

Hill, Ned C., and Kenneth D. Riener, "Determining the Cash Discount in the Firm's Credit Policy," *Financial Management,* Spring 1979, 68–73.

Kim, Yong H., and Joseph C. Atkins, "Evaluating Investments in Accounts Receivable: A Wealth Maximizing Framework," *Journal of Finance,* May 1978, 403–412.

Oh, John S., "Opportunity Cost in the Evaluation of Investment in Accounts Receivable," *Financial Management,* Summer 1976, 32–36.

Roberts, Gordon S., and Jeremy A. Viscione, "Captive Finance Subsidiaries: The Manager's View," *Financial Management,* Spring 1981, 36–42.

Sachdeva, Kanwal S., and Lawrence J. Gitman, "Accounts Receivable Decisions in a Capital Budgeting Framework," *Financial Management,* Winter 1981, 45–49.

Walia, Tinlochan S., "Explicit and Implicit Cost of Changes in the Level of Accounts Receivable and the Credit Policy Decision of the Firm," *Financial Management,* Winter 1977, 75–78.

Weston, J. Fred, and Pham D. Tuan, "Comment on Analysis of Credit Policy Changes," *Financial Management,* Winter 1980, 59–63.

The following cases from the Brigham-Gapenski casebook focus on the credit policy decision:

Case 34, "Kiddyland Clothes, Inc.," which deals with credit policy changes.

Case 35, "Richard's Nursery, Inc.," which focuses on receivables management.

The textbooks referenced in Chapter 19 include detailed discussions of inventory management.

The following articles and books provide additional insights into the problems of inventory management:

Arvan, L., and L. N. Moses, "Inventory Management and the Theory of the Firm," *American Economic Review,* March 1982, 186–193.

Bierman, H., Jr., C. P. Bonini, and W. H. Hausman, *Quantitative Analysis for Business Decisions* (Homewood, Ill.: Irwin, 1977).

Brooks, L. D., "Risk-Return Criteria and Optimal Inventory Stocks," *Engineering Economist,* Summer 1980, 275–299.

Followill, Richard A., Michael Schellenger, and Patrick H. Marchand, "Economic Order Quantities, Volume Discounts, and Wealth Maximization," *The Financial Review,* February 1990, 143–152.

Kallberg, Jarl G., and Kenneth L. Parkinson, *Current Asset Management: Cash, Credit, and Inventory* (New York: Wiley, 1984).

Magee, John F., "Guides to Inventory Policy, I," *Harvard Business Review,* January-February 1956, 49–60.

———, "Guides to Inventory Policy, II," *Harvard Business Review,* March-April 1956, 103–116.

———, "Guides to Inventory Policy, III," *Harvard Business Review,* May-June 1956, 57–70.

Mehta, Dileep R., *Working Capital Management* (Englewood Cliffs, N.J.: Prentice-Hall, 1974).

Shapiro, A., "Optimal Inventory and Credit Granting Strategies under Inflation and Devaluation," *Journal of Financial and Quantitative Analysis,* January 1973, 37–46.

Smith, Keith V., *Guide to Working Capital Management* (New York: McGraw-Hill, 1979).

The Brigham-Gapenski casebook has a useful case on inventory management:

Case 31, "Bayside Marine Corporation" which focuses on the EOQ model and safety stocks.

PART VII

Financial Analysis and Planning

CHAPTER 22

Financial Statement Analysis

The "bottom line" in a company's income statement is its net income, or reported profits. This figure is the basis for dividends, and it is used to determine managers' bonuses. Further, accountants are paid high salaries to make sure income is reported "correctly." One would think, then, that the profit figure a company reports would be unambiguous and trustworthy. However, that is not always the case—companies can and do "play games" so as to influence the numbers they report. To illustrate, an article which appeared in the April 24, 1989, issue of *Fortune,* "Cute Tricks on the Bottom Line," made these points:

1. The net incomes reported in annual reports generally meet the accounting industry's guidelines. However, managers view accounting guidelines not as standards to be met but as obstacles to be overcome, and they are always on the alert for new ways of getting around the guidelines. To put it another way, companies obey the letter but not the spirit of the law.

2. The temptation to stretch the truth hits companies of all sizes, even giant blue chips such as General Motors. For example, GM reported record earnings in 1988, enabling its managers to realize huge bonuses. However, almost 40 percent of its reported "profits" resulted not from operations but from "financial wizardry." One such piece of wizardry was an increase from 35 to 45 years in the life over which GM's plants are depreciated; this added $790 million to GM's reported profits, but nothing to its true income or cash flows.

3. Managers know that investors like a steady earnings uptrend and that they dislike negative surprises, so what happens if a company gets lucky some year and has a huge one-time gain? It could report a sharp increase

in this year's profits, which would be hard to top next year, or it could "bank" the windfall in a special reserve for later use. To illustrate, Bank of America has in recent years sold several divisions, including Charles Schwab, the discount brokerage firm, and it realized sizable profits on these transactions. Then, in March 1989, the bank announced to its stockholders that it expected to lose about $600 million on loans to vocational students, but it told stockholders not to worry, because it just happened to have enough income from "special items" to offset the effects of these loans.

Are accounting tricks such as these "good" or "bad," and should managers attempt to "manage earnings"? On the one hand, if the underlying trend in reported earnings is really stable, then managers' attempts to report stabilized profits could provide more meaningful information than would "pure" numbers. On the other hand, actions such as those of GM and Bank of America could be obscuring the true picture. In any event, you should be aware that accounting numbers must always be viewed with at least some skepticism.

FINANCIAL analysis is of vital concern to corporate managers, security analysts, investors, and lenders, all of whom use it for a variety of purposes. As an indication of its importance, a recent U.S. Commerce Department survey showed that the highest salaries for corporate employees in the 25 to 30 age group went to people engaged in financial analysis and control—they beat out engineers, marketers, and all the rest. Further, this situation extends on up the ladder—throughout the United States, and indeed the world, efficiency and cost control are the keys to success, so people with those skills are increasingly taking over the top spots in industry.

The focus of any financial analysis depends on its purpose, which may range from a total analysis of a firm's strengths and weaknesses to a relatively simple analysis of its short-term liquidity. Since the foundation of most types of financial analysis is the firm's financial statements, we concentrate on statement analysis in this chapter. Note, though, that its financial statements reflect what has happened in the past, and that the really interesting question is where the firm will go in the future. Therefore, analysts invariably use the types of analysis discussed in this chapter as a springboard for predicting and planning for the future, which is the subject of the next chapter.

FINANCIAL STATEMENTS AND REPORTS

A corporate *annual report* provides a verbal description of the firm's operating results during the past year and a discussion of new developments that will affect its future operations. More important, the report presents several financial statements, including three basic financial statements—the *income statement,* the *balance sheet,* and the *statement of cash flows.* Taken together, these statements give an accounting picture of the firm's operations and its financial position. Detailed data are provided for the two or three most recent years, along with brief historical summaries of key operating statistics for the past 5 or 10 years.[1]

Table 22-1 contains the 1990 and 1989 income statements for Southern Metals Company, a major producer of fabricated aluminum products, and Table 22-2 presents its balance sheets for those same years. Some points about the income statement and balance sheet are worth noting:

1. **Earnings and dividends.** Southern earned $110 million for its common stockholders in 1990, and it paid out $90 million in common dividends. EPS was $2.20, and DPS was $1.80.

2. **Cash flows.** Southern's cash flow from operations is approximately equal to net income plus any noncash expenses. In 1990, the cash flow after preferred dividends was $110 million net income plus $100 million depreciation expense, for a total cash flow of $210 million. Depreciation does not really *provide* funds; it is simply a noncash charge which is added back to net income to obtain an estimate of the cash flow from operations. However, if the firm made no sales and hence paid no taxes, then depreciation would certainly not provide cash flows.

3. **Cash versus other assets.** Although the assets are all stated in terms of dollars, only cash represents actual money. We see from Table 22-2 that Southern can write checks at present for a total of $50 million (versus current liabilities of $300 million due within a year). The noncash current assets will presumably be converted to cash within a year, but they do not represent cash on hand.

4. **Liabilities versus stockholders' equity.** The claims against assets are of two types—liabilities, or money the company owes, and the stockholders' ownership position.[2] The equity, or net worth, is a residual; for 1990,

$$\begin{array}{ccccc} \text{Assets} & - & \text{Liabilities} & = & \text{Stockholders' equity} \\ \$2{,}000{,}000{,}000 & - & \$1{,}100{,}000{,}000 & = & \$900{,}000{,}000. \end{array}$$

Liabilities consist of $300 million of current liabilities plus $800 million of long-term debt. Suppose assets decline in value. For example, suppose some of the accounts receivable are written off as bad debts. Liabilities remain constant, so the value of the equity declines. Therefore, the risk of asset value fluctuations is borne largely by the stockholders, and specifically by the common stockholders. Note, however, that if asset values rise, these benefits accrue exclusively to the common stockholders.

---

[1]Firms also provide quarterly reports, but these are much less comprehensive than the annual reports. In addition, larger firms file even more detailed statements, giving the particulars of each major division or subsidiary, with the Securities and Exchange Commission (SEC). These reports, called *10-K reports,* are made available to stockholders upon request to a company's secretary. Finally, many larger firms also publish *statistical supplements,* which give financial statement data and key ratios going back about 10 years. Like the 10-K, statistical supplements may be obtained from the corporate secretary.

[2]One could divide liabilities into (1) debts owed to specific firms or individuals and (2) other items such as deferred taxes and reserves. We do not make this distinction, so the terms *debt* and *liabilities* are used synonymously.

Table 22-1   Southern Metals Company: Income Statements for the Years Ended December 31 (Millions of Dollars, Except for Per Share Data)

	1990	1989
Net sales	$3,000	$2,850
Costs and expenses:		
Labor and materials	2,544	2,413
Depreciation	100	90
Selling	22	20
General and administrative	40	35
Lease payments	28	28
Total costs	$2,734	$2,586
Net operating income, or earnings before interest and taxes (EBIT)	$ 266	$ 264
Less interest expense:		
Interest on notes payable	8	2
Interest on first mortgage bonds	40	42
Interest on debentures	18	3
Total interest	$ 66	$ 47
Earnings before taxes	$ 200	$ 217
Taxes (at 40%)	80	87
Net income before preferred dividends	$ 120	$ 130
Dividends to preferred stockholders	10	10
Net income available to common stockholders	$ 110	$ 120
Disposition of net income:		
Dividends to common stockholders	$ 90	$ 80
Addition to retained earnings	$ 20	$ 40
Per share of common stock:		
Stock price	$28.50	$29.00
Earnings per share (EPS)[a]	$ 2.20	$ 2.40
Dividends per share (DPS)[a]	$ 1.80	$ 1.60

[a]There are 50 million common shares outstanding; see Table 22-2. EPS is based on earnings after preferred dividends, that is, on net income available to common stockholders. Calculations of EPS and DPS for 1990 are as follows:

$$\text{EPS} = \frac{\text{Net income available to common stockholders}}{\text{Shares outstanding}} = \frac{\$110,000,000}{50,000,000} = \$2.20.$$

$$\text{DPS} = \frac{\text{Dividends paid to common stockholders}}{\text{Shares outstanding}} = \frac{\$90,000,000}{50,000,000} = \$1.80.$$

5.   Breakdown of the stockholders' equity account. Note that the equity section is divided into four accounts—preferred stock, common stock, additional paid-in capital, and retained earnings. The retained earnings account is built up over time by the firm's "saving" a part of its earnings rather than paying all earnings out as dividends. The other three accounts arose from the sale of stock by the firm to raise capital. Accountants generally assign a *par value* to common stock—Southern's common stock has a par value of $1. Now suppose Southern were to sell 1 million additional shares at a price of $30 per share. The company would raise $30 million,

Table 22-2   Southern Metals Company: December 31
Balance Sheets (Millions of Dollars)

Assets	1990	1989	Liabilities and Equity	1990	1989
Cash	$ 50	$ 55	Accounts payable	$ 60	$ 30
Marketable securities	0	25	Notes payable	100	60
Accounts receivable	350	315	Accrued wages	10	10
Inventories	300	215	Accrued taxes	130	120
Total current assets	$ 700	$ 610	Total current liabilities	$ 300	$ 220
Gross plant and equipment	1,800	1,470	First mortgage bonds	500	520
Less depreciation	500	400	Debentures	300	60
Net plant and equipment	$1,300	$1,070	Total long-term debt	$ 800	$ 580
			Stockholders' equity:		
			Preferred stock		
			(1,000,000 shares, 10% preferred,		
			$100 par value)	100	100
			Common stock		
			(50,000,000 shares, $1 par value)	50	50
			Additional paid-in capital	90	90
			Retained earnings	660	640
			Total common equity	$ 800	$ 780
			Total stockholders' equity	900	880
Total assets	$2,000	$1,680	Total claims	$2,000	$1,680

Notes:

a. The first mortgage bonds have a sinking fund requirement of $20 million a year.

b. Southern had $28 million in uncapitalized lease payments in both 1989 and 1990; see Table 22-1.

and the cash account would go up by this amount. Of the total, $1 million would be added to common stock, and $29 million would be added to paid-in capital. Thus, after the sale, common stock would show $51 million, additional paid-in capital would show $119 million, and there would be 51 million shares outstanding.

6.   **The time dimension.** The balance sheet may be thought of as a snapshot of the firm's financial position *at a point in time*—for example, on December 31, 1990. The income statement, on the other hand, reports on operations *over a period of time*—for example, during the calendar year 1990.

7.   **Retained earnings.** The balance sheet account for retained earnings indicates how much of its past earnings the firm has reinvested. Further, firms retain earnings primarily to expand the business, which means investing in plant and equipment, inventories, and so on, and *not* in a bank account. *Thus, retained earnings as reported on the balance sheet do not represent cash and are not "available" for the payment of dividends or anything else.*[3]

---

[3]Also, recall from your accounting course the difference between accrual and cash accounting. Even though a company reports record earnings and shows an increase in the retained earnings account, it may still be short of cash.

Statement of Cash Flows

Twenty years ago, most annual reports contained a statement called the "sources and uses of funds statement." The purpose of the statement was to report where the firm had obtained funds during the past year and how it had used them. For example, had it obtained most of its funds from such sources as bank loans, or as retained earnings, and had it used those funds to retire bonds, to build new plants, to build up inventories, or to pay dividends? One could look at the statement and see the total sources and total uses (which were equal), and how funds were obtained and used, but there was no summary figure which could be used to judge whether the company ended the year in a stronger or weaker position.

Gradually, in accordance with generally accepted accounting principles, companies changed the name of the statement to "statement of changes in financial position." The same basic sources and uses were listed, but a focal point, or bottom line, was provided—the statement was prepared to show not just total sources and uses but also the change in net working capital (current assets minus current liabilities). It was believed—generally correctly—that if its net working capital increased, then the firm's financial position was strengthened.

Recently, the Financial Accounting Standards Board (FASB) issued Statement 95, which requires companies to use a new format for the statement, one that focuses on cash rather than net working capital. The new statement, called the *statement of cash flows,* is organized into three sections: (1) operating activities, (2) investing activities, and (3) financing activities. FASB adopted the new format because it provides information in the most useful way for financial analysis.

The starting point in preparing a statement of cash flows is to determine the change in each balance sheet account, and then to record it as either a source or a use of funds in accordance with the following rules:

Sources: 1.   Any increase in a liability or equity account. Borrowing and issuing common stock are examples.

2.   Any decrease in an asset account. Selling some inventories is an example.

Uses: 1.   Any decrease in a liability or equity account. Paying off a loan is an example.

2.   Any increase in an asset account. Buying fixed assets is an example.

Thus, sources of funds include bank loans, retained earnings, and new issues of stock, as well as money generated by selling assets, collecting receivables, and even drawing down the cash account. Uses include acquiring fixed assets, building up inventories, paying off debts, and repurchasing stock.

Table 22-3 shows the changes in Southern Metals' balance sheet accounts during the calendar year 1990, with each change designated as a source or a use. Sources and uses each total $470 million.[4] Note that Table 22-3 does not contain any sum-

---

[4]Adjustments must normally be made if fixed assets were sold or retired during the year. Southern had no sales of fixed assets or major retirements during 1990.

Table 22-3   Changes in Balance Sheet Accounts (Millions of Dollars)

	Balance Sheets		Change	
	12/31/90	12/31/89	Source	Use
Cash	$ 50	$ 55	$ 5	
Marketable securities	0	25	25	
Accounts receivable	350	315		$ 35
Inventories	300	215		85
Gross plant and equipment	1,800	1,470		330
Accumulated depreciation[a]	500	400	100	
Accounts payable	60	30	30	
Notes payable	100	60	40	
Accrued wages	10	10		
Accrued taxes	130	120	10	
Mortgage bonds	500	520		20
Debentures	300	60	240	
Preferred stock	100	100		
Common stock	50	50		
Additional paid-in capital	90	90		
Retained earnings	660	640	20	
			$470	$470

[a]Depreciation is a *contra-asset,* and not an asset. Hence, an increase in depreciation is a source of funds.

---

mary accounts such as total current assets or net plant and equipment. If we included summary accounts in Table 22-3, and then used these accounts to prepare the statement of cash flows, we would be "double counting."

The data contained in Table 22-3 are next used as inputs to the formal statement of cash flows. Note that every item in the "change" columns of Table 22-3 is carried over to Table 22-4 except retained earnings: The statement of cash flows reports net income as a source and dividends as a use, rather than netting these items out and just reporting the increase in retained earnings. Also, cash and marketable securities are combined in Table 22-4. Like most large companies, Southern regards its marketable securities as cash equivalents, so with regard to financial position, cash and marketable securities are combined.

Table 22-4 pinpoints the sources and uses of Southern's cash and marketable securities. The top part shows cash generated by and used in operations — for Southern, operations provided $220 million in cash flow (net income plus depreciation), but required an $80 million increase in net working capital, for a net cash flow from operations of $140 million.

By far the heaviest use of funds was to increase fixed assets, and this is shown in the next section of the table, "Cash Flow from Investing Activities."

Southern's financing activities as shown in the third section included borrowing from banks (notes payable) and the sale of debentures, but it paid off part of its

Table 22-4   Statement of Cash Flows (Millions of Dollars)

Cash Flow from Operating Activities		
Net income	$120	
Additions (sources of cash):		
Depreciation	100	
Increase in accounts payable	30	
Increase in accrued taxes	10	
Subtractions (uses of cash):		
Increase in accounts receivable	($ 35)	
Increase in inventories	(85)	
Net cash flow from operations		$140
Cash Flow from Investing Activities		
Acquisition of fixed assets		($330)
Cash Flow from Financing Activities		
Increase in notes payable	$ 40	
Increase in debentures	240	
Repayment of mortgage bonds	(20)	
Common and preferred dividends paid	(100)	
Net cash flow from financing		$160
Net increase (decrease) in cash and cash equivalents		($ 30)
Cash and cash equivalents at beginning of year		$ 80
Cash and cash equivalents at end of year		$ 50

mortgage bonds through sinking fund operations. Thus, in net, Southern raised $260 million from the capital markets during 1990. However, Southern also paid $100 million of dividends on its common and preferred stock, so there was a $160 million net cash inflow from financing activities.

When all these items are totaled, we see that Southern had a $30 million net cash outflow during 1990, which was met by selling off marketable securities ($25 million) and reducing cash balances ($5 million), as shown in Table 22-3.

Southern's statement of cash flows shows nothing unusual or alarming. It does show a $30 million cash drain, which resulted primarily from the purchase of fixed assets, but, more important, it also shows that Southern's operations are inherently profitable, generating $140 million in cash in 1990. Had the statement showed an operating cash drain in a situation where fixed assets did not increase (that is, where the addition to gross fixed assets equaled depreciation charges), then we would have had something to worry about, because such a drain would be much more likely to continue and to bleed the company to death unless the problem was corrected.

Sophisticated security analysts, loan officers, and corporate raiders pay close attention to the statement of cash flows. Finance is, after all, a cash-flow-oriented discipline, and this statement gives a good picture of the annual cash flows generated by the business. A bank loan officer could examine Table 22-4 (or, better yet, a series of such tables going back for perhaps the last 5 years and projected out several years into the future) to get an idea of whether or not the business could generate the necessary cash to pay off a requested loan. If projected cash flows appear sufficient, then the loan will be granted. If the cash flows are questionable, then the banker will pay close attention to the balance sheet, attempting to determine whether the assets would bring enough in a liquidation to satisfy the loan.

Free Cash Flow

The statement of cash flows provides an important financial measure called *free cash flow*. Free cash flow has many different definitions, depending on the purpose of the analysis, but, in general, it is the cash flow that remains after considering all anticipated cash inflows and outflows, including capital expenditures and asset sales. The bottom line of the statement of cash flows, the net increase (decrease) in cash and cash equivalents, can be viewed as the firm's basic free cash flow. For Southern Metals Company, the basic free cash flow for 1990 was − $30 million. Thus, if Southern Metals were acquired at the beginning of 1990, and if the new management carried out actions identical to those taken by Southern's management over the year, the end result would be a negative free cash flow.

Now suppose that in 1989 a raider was forecasting Southern's free cash flow for 1990. The raider might opt to omit the firm's common dividends, thus saving $90 million. Further, the raider might plan to invest only $200 million in new fixed assets, with the belief that $130 million was nonessential. Finally, the raider might plan to sell off one of Southern's inefficient plants, netting $100 million in cash from the transaction. With these plans, the raider would estimate Southern's 1990 free cash flow as − $30 + $90 + $130 + $100 = $290 million. This cash flow would be available to the raider for other purposes, typically to make interest payments on the heavy debt load used to make the acquisition. In the extreme, a raider might even add back the $80 million in taxes, giving a free cash flow of $370 million. This can be done when the raider plans to use so much debt that the interest payments will drive taxable income down to zero (or even negative).

Free cash flow analysis has always been important, but perhaps raiders such as T. Boone Pickens and LBO companies such as KKR have done more than anyone to highlight the importance of such analysis. Pickens, KKR, and others have made a science of looking at a company such as Gulf Oil, analyzing each of its many parts on a separate basis to determine the cash flows attributable to each part, setting values on those parts, and then adding up the calculated values of each part to determine the *break-up value* of the firm. Both raiders and LBO companies work with investment banking houses like Morgan Stanley, which use the cash flow projections to ascertain how much debt the operation can support, and then line up purchasers of such debt to provide the funds needed to enable the raiders to make offers for the target companies.

Managers have, of course, always been interested in their companies' free cash flows, but the actions of raiders and LBO companies have heightened that interest enormously. Companies now know (1) that their values are very much dependent on free cash flows (as well as reported accounting profits), because the higher the cash flows, the more someone can bid for the company, and (2) that if their assets are not providing as much free cash flow as they could under more efficient management, then again, raiders will attempt to take over the company and either install better managers or break up the company and sell its assets to companies who can operate those assets better.

We will consider the takeover phenomena in more depth in Chapter 24, but first, in the remainder of this chapter, we shall discuss techniques for analyzing a firm's financial statements in order to pinpoint its strengths and weaknesses.

Self-Test Questions

What three basic financial statements are included in a firm's annual report?

What are the three sections in a statement of cash flows?

Why did the Financial Statement Accounting Board change the format from the statement of changes in financial position to the statement of cash flows?

What is free cash flow? How do raiders and LBO companies use free cash flows when analyzing a potential acquisition?

RATIO ANALYSIS

Financial statements report both on a firm's position at a point in time and on its operations over some past period. However, the real value of financial statements lies in the fact that they can be used to help predict the firm's future earnings and dividends. From an investor's standpoint, *predicting the future is what financial statement analysis is all about,* while from management's standpoint, *financial statement analysis is useful both as a way to anticipate future conditions and, more important, as a starting point for planning actions that will influence the future course of events.*

An analysis of the firm's financial ratios is generally the first step in a financial analysis. The ratios are designed to show relationships between financial statement accounts. For example, Firm A might have debt of $5,248,760 and interest charges of $419,900, while Firm B might have debt of $52,647,980 and interest charges of $3,948,600. The true burden of these debts, and the companies' ability to repay them, can be ascertained by comparing each firm's debt to its assets, and the interest it pays versus the income it has available for payment of interest. Such comparisons are made by *ratio analysis.*

In the paragraphs which follow, we will calculate the 1990 financial ratios for Southern Metals Company. We will also evaluate those ratios in relation to the industry averages. Note that all dollar amounts in the ratio calculations are in millions.

Liquidity Ratios

One of the first concerns of most financial analysts is liquidity: Will the firm be able to meet its maturing obligations? Southern has debts totaling $300 million that must be paid off within the coming year. Will Southern have trouble satisfying those obligations? A full liquidity analysis requires the use of cash budgets, but, by relating the amount of cash and other current assets to the current obligations, ratio analysis provides a quick, easy-to-use, approximate measure of liquidity. Two commonly used *liquidity ratios* are discussed next.

Current Ratio. The *current ratio* is computed by dividing current assets by current liabilities:

$$\text{Current ratio} = \frac{\text{Current assets}}{\text{Current liabilities}} = \frac{\$700}{\$300} = 2.3 \text{ times.}$$

$$\text{Industry average} = 2.5 \text{ times.}$$

Current assets normally include cash, marketable securities, accounts receivable, and inventories. Current liabilities consist of accounts payable, short-term notes payable, current maturities of long-term debt, accrued income taxes, and other accrued expenses (principally wages).

If a company is getting into financial difficulty, it will begin paying its bills (accounts payable) more slowly, building up bank loans, and so on. If these current liabilities rise faster than current assets, then the current ratio will fall, and this could spell trouble. Since the current ratio provides the best single indicator of the extent to which the claims of short-term creditors are covered by assets which are expected to be converted to cash in a period roughly corresponding to the maturity of the claims, it is one commonly used measure of short-term solvency.

Southern's current ratio is slightly below the average for the industry, 2.5, but it is not low enough to cause concern. It appears that Southern is about in line with most other aluminum producers. Since current assets are scheduled to be converted to cash in the near future, it is highly probable that they could be liquidated at close to their stated value. With a current ratio of 2.3, Southern could liquidate current assets at only 43 percent of book value and still pay off current creditors in full.[5]

Although industry average figures are discussed later in some detail, it should be stated at this point that an industry average is not a magic number that all firms should strive to maintain — in fact, some very well-managed firms will be above the average while other good firms will be below it. However, if a firm's ratios are far removed from the average for its industry, the analyst must be concerned about why this variance occurs. Thus, a deviation below the industry average should signal the analyst to check further.

Quick, or Acid Test, Ratio. The *quick,* or *acid test, ratio* is calculated by deducting inventories from current assets and dividing the remainder by current liabilities:

$$\text{Quick, or acid test, ratio} = \frac{\text{Current assets} - \text{Inventories}}{\text{Current liabilities}} = \frac{\$400}{\$300} = 1.3 \text{ times.}$$

$$\text{Industry average} = 1.1 \text{ times.}$$

---

[5]$1/2.3 = 0.43$, or 43 percent. Note that $0.43(\$700) = \$300$, the amount of current liabilities.

Inventories are typically the least liquid of a firm's current assets, hence they are the assets on which losses are most likely to occur in the event of liquidation. Therefore, a measure of the firm's ability to pay off short-term obligations without relying on the sale of inventories is important.

The industry average quick ratio is 1.1, so Southern's 1.3 ratio compares favorably with other firms in the industry. If the accounts receivable can be collected, the company can pay off its current liabilities even if it cannot sell its inventory.[6]

Asset Management Ratios

A second group of ratios, the *asset management ratios,* is designed to measure how effectively the firm is managing its assets. These ratios are designed to answer this question: Does the total amount of each type of asset as reported on the balance sheet seem reasonable, too high, or too low in view of current and projected operating levels? Southern and other companies must borrow or raise equity capital to acquire assets. If they have too many assets, then their interest expenses will be too high and their profits will be depressed. On the other hand, if assets are too low, then profitable sales may be lost.

Inventory Turnover. The *inventory turnover ratio,* also called the *inventory utilization ratio,* is defined as sales divided by inventories:

$$\text{Inventory turnover, or utilization, ratio} = \frac{\text{Sales}}{\text{Inventory}} = \frac{\$3,000}{\$300} = 10 \text{ times.}$$

$$\text{Industry average} = 9.3 \text{ times.}$$

As a rough approximation, each item of Southern's inventory is sold out and re-stocked, or "turned over," 10 times per year.[7]

Southern's turnover of 10 times compares favorably with an industry average of 9.3 times. This suggests that the company does not hold excessive stocks of inventory; excess stocks are, of course, unproductive, yet they must be financed in the same way as productive assets. Southern's high inventory turnover ratio also reinforces our faith in the current ratio. If the turnover had been low—say, 3 or 4 times—we would wonder whether the firm was holding damaged or obsolete goods not actually worth their stated value.

Two problems arise in calculating and analyzing the inventory turnover ratio. First, sales are stated at market prices, so if inventories are carried at cost, as they

---

[6]Two other liquidity ratios that are widely used are (1) the days liquidity on hand and (2) the days cash on hand ratios. These ratios were discussed in Chapter 19.

[7]"Turnover" is a term that originated many years ago with the old Yankee peddler, who would load up his wagon with goods, then go off on his route to peddle his wares. The merchandise was defined as his "working capital," because it was what he actually sold, or "turned over," to produce his profits, while his "turnover" was the number of trips he took each year. Annual sales divided by inventory equaled turnover, or trips per year. If he made 10 trips per year, stocked 100 pans, and made a gross profit of $5 per pan, then his annual gross profit would be $(100)(\$5)(10) = \$5,000$. If he sped up and made 20 trips per year, his gross profit would double, other things held constant.

generally are, then the calculated turnover overstates the true turnover ratio. There-fore, it would be more appropriate to use cost of goods sold in place of sales in the numerator of the formula. However, established compilers of financial ratio statistics, such as Dun & Bradstreet, use the ratio of sales to inventories carried at cost, so to develop a figure that can be compared with those published by Dun & Bradstreet and similar organizations, it is necessary to measure inventory utilization with sales in the numerator, as we do here.

The second problem lies in the fact that sales occur over the entire year, whereas the inventory figure is for one point in time. This makes it better to use an average inventory measure.[8] If it were determined that the firm's business is highly seasonal, or if there has been a strong upward or downward sales trend during the year, it would become essential to make some such adjustment. To maintain com-parability with industry averages, however, we did not use the average inventory figure.

Days Sales Outstanding. The *days sales outstanding (DSO),* also called the *aver-age collection period (ACP),* is used to appraise accounts receivable, and it is com-puted by dividing average daily sales into accounts receivable to find the number of days' sales tied up in receivables. Thus, the DSO represents the average length of time that the firm must wait after making a sale before receiving cash. The calcula-tions for Southern show a DSO of 42.0 days, slightly above the 36.2-day industry average.[9]

$$DSO = \begin{array}{c} \text{Days} \\ \text{sales} \\ \text{outstanding} \end{array} = \frac{\text{Receivables}}{\text{Average sales per day}} = \frac{\text{Receivables}}{\text{Annual sales/360}}$$

$$= \frac{\$350}{\$3,000/360} = \frac{\$350}{\$8.333} = 42.0 \text{ days.}$$

$$\text{Industry average} = 36.2 \text{ days.}$$

The DSO can also be evaluated by comparison with the terms on which the firm sells its goods. For example, Southern's sales terms call for payment within 30 days, so the 42.0-day collection period indicates that customers, on the average, are not paying their bills on time. If the trend in the collection period over the past few years had been rising, but the credit policy had not changed, this would be even

---

[8]Preferably, the average inventory value would be calculated by summing the monthly figures during the year and dividing by 12. If monthly data are not available, one can add the beginning and ending figures and divide by 2; this will adjust for growth but not for seasonal effects.

[9]Because information on credit sales is generally unavailable, total sales must be used. Since all firms may not have the same percentage of credit sales, there is a chance that the days sales outstanding will be somewhat in error. Also, note that by convention the financial community generally uses 360 rather than 365 as the number of days in the year for purposes such as these. Finally, it would be better to use *average* receivables, either an average of the monthly figures or (Beginning + Ending)/2 = ($315 + $350)/2 = $332.5 in the formula. Had the annual average been used, Southern's DSO would have been $332.5/$8.333 = 39.9 days. The 39.9-day figure is the more accurate one, but since the industry average was based on year-end receivables, we used 42.0 days for our comparison.

stronger evidence that steps should be taken to expedite the collection of accounts receivable.

As we know from our discussion in Chapter 21, the DSO does have weaknesses from the standpoint of appraising a company's credit management program. Therefore, the problems we discussed in Chapter 21 should be kept in mind with regard to this ratio.

Fixed Asset Turnover. The *fixed asset turnover ratio,* also called the *fixed asset utilization ratio,* measures the utilization of plant and equipment, and it is the ratio of sales to fixed assets:

$$\text{Fixed asset turnover, or utilization, ratio} = \frac{\text{Sales}}{\text{Net fixed assets}}$$

$$= \frac{\$3,000}{\$1,300} = 2.3 \text{ times.}$$

$$\text{Industry average} = 3.1 \text{ times.}$$

Southern's ratio of 2.3 times compares poorly with the industry average of 3.1 times, indicating that the firm is not using its fixed assets to as high a percentage of capacity as are the other firms in the industry. The financial manager should bear this in mind when production people request funds for new capital investments.

A major potential problem exists with the use of the fixed asset turnover ratio for comparative purposes. Recall that all assets except cash and accounts receivable reflect the historical cost of the assets. Inflation has caused the value of many assets that were purchased in the past to be seriously understated. Therefore, if we were comparing an old firm which had acquired many of its fixed assets years ago at low prices with a new company which had acquired its fixed assets only recently, then the old firm would probably report a higher turnover. However, this would be more reflective of the inability of accountants to deal with inflation than of any inefficiency on the part of the new firm. The accounting profession is trying to devise ways of making financial statements more reflective of current rather than historical values. If balance sheets were stated on a current basis, this would eliminate the problem of comparisons, but at the moment the problem still exists. Since financial analysts typically do not have the data necessary to make adjustments, they simply recognize that a problem exists and deal with it judgmentally. In Southern's case, the issue is not a serious one because all firms in the industry have been expanding at about the same rate, so the balance sheets of the comparison firms are indeed comparable.[10]

---

[10]See FASB #33, *Financial Reporting and Changing Prices* (September 1979), for a discussion of the effects of inflation on financial statements and what the accounting profession is trying to do to provide better and more useful balance sheets and income statements. We discuss the impact of inflation on financial statements in more depth later in the chapter.

Total Asset Turnover. The final asset management ratio, the *total asset turnover ratio,* measures the turnover, or utilization, of all of the firm's assets; it is calculated by dividing sales by total assets:

$$\text{Total asset turnover, or utilization, ratio} = \frac{\text{Sales}}{\text{Total assets}} = \frac{\$3,000}{\$2,000} = 1.5 \text{ times.}$$

$$\text{Industry average} = 1.8 \text{ times.}$$

Southern's ratio is somewhat below the industry average, indicating that the company is not generating a sufficient volume of business given the size of its total asset investment. Sales should be increased, some assets should be disposed of, or a combination of these steps should be taken.

Debt Management Ratios

The extent to which a firm uses debt financing, or *financial leverage,* has three important implications. (1) By raising funds through debt, the owners can maintain control of the firm with a limited investment. (2) Creditors look to the equity, or owner-supplied funds, to provide a margin of safety: If the owners have provided only a small proportion of total financing, then the risks of the enterprise are borne mainly by its creditors. (3) If the firm earns more on investments financed with borrowed funds than it pays in interest, then the return on the owners' capital is magnified, or "leveraged."

When they examine a company's financial statements, analysts develop two different types of debt management ratios: (1) They check balance sheet ratios to determine the extent to which borrowed funds have been used to finance assets; the debt/assets ratio is used for this purpose. (2) They review income statement ratios to determine the number of times fixed charges are covered by operating profits. These two sets of ratios are complementary, and most analysts use both types.

Total Debt to Total Assets. The ratio of total debt to total assets, generally called the *debt ratio,* measures the percentage of total funds provided by creditors:

$$\text{Debt ratio} = \frac{\text{Total debt}}{\text{Total assets}} = \frac{\$1,100}{\$2,000} = 55.0\%.$$

$$\text{Industry average} = 40.1\%.$$

Debt is defined to include both current liabilities and long-term debt. Creditors prefer low debt ratios, since the lower the ratio, the greater the cushion against creditors' losses in the event of liquidation. The owners, on the other hand, may seek high leverage either to magnify earnings or because selling new stock would mean giving up some degree of control.

Southern's debt ratio is 55 percent; this means that its creditors have supplied more than half the firm's total financing. Since the average debt ratio for this industry is about 40 percent, Southern would find it difficult to borrow additional funds without first raising more equity capital. Creditors would be reluctant to lend the firm more money, and management would probably be subjecting the firm to the risk of bankruptcy if it sought to increase the debt ratio any further by borrowing additional funds.[11]

Times Interest Earned. The *times-interest-earned (TIE) ratio* is determined by dividing earnings before interest and taxes (EBIT) by the interest charges:

$$\text{Times-interest-earned (TIE) ratio} = \frac{\text{EBIT}}{\text{Interest charges}} = \frac{\$266}{\$66} = 4.0 \text{ times.}$$

$$\text{Industry average} = 6.2 \text{ times.}$$

The TIE ratio measures the extent to which operating income can decline before the firm's earnings are less than its annual interest costs. Failure to pay interest can bring legal action by the firm's creditors, possibly resulting in bankruptcy. Note that earnings *before* interest and taxes is used in the numerator. Because interest is a deductible cost, the ability to pay current interest is not affected by taxes.

Southern's interest is covered 4 times. Since the industry average is 6.2 times, the company is covering its interest charges by a relatively low margin of safety. Thus, the TIE ratio reinforces our conclusion based on the debt ratio, namely, that the company would face some difficulties if it attempted to borrow additional funds.

Fixed Charge Coverage. The *fixed charge coverage ratio* is similar to the times-interest-earned ratio, but it is more inclusive in that it recognizes that firms incur fixed long-term obligations other than interest payments under lease and debt contracts.[12] Leasing has become widespread in certain industries in recent years, making this ratio preferable to the times-interest-earned ratio for many purposes. Fixed charges are defined as interest plus annual long-term lease payments plus sinking fund payments, and the fixed charge coverage ratio is defined as follows:

$$\frac{\text{Fixed charge}}{\text{coverage ratio}} = \frac{\text{EBIT} + \text{Lease payments}}{\text{Interest charges} + \text{Lease payments} + \dfrac{\text{Sinking fund payments}}{1 - T}}$$

$$= \frac{\$266 + \$28}{\$66 + \$28 + \$20/0.6} = \frac{\$294}{\$127.33} = 2.3 \text{ times.}$$

$$\text{Industry average} = 4.0 \text{ times.}$$

---

[11]The ratio of debt to equity is also used in financial analysis. The debt-to-assets (D/A) and debt-to-equity (D/E) ratios are simply transformations of each other:

$$\text{D/E} = \frac{\text{D/A}}{1 - \text{D/A}}, \text{ and D/A} = \frac{\text{D/E}}{1 + \text{D/E}}.$$

Both ratios increase as a firm of a given size (total assets) uses a greater proportion of debt, but D/A rises linearly and approaches a limit of 100 percent, while D/E rises exponentially and approaches infinity. Bank analysts often prefer the debt-to-equity ratio, because it indicates explicitly the dollars of creditors' capital per dollar of owners' capital used to finance the company's assets.

[12]Generally, a long-term lease is defined as one that extends for at least 2 years. Thus, rent incurred under a 1-year lease would not be included in the fixed charge coverage ratio, but rental payments under a 2-year or longer lease would be defined as fixed charges and would be included.

Note that the sinking fund payment, since it is paid with after-tax dollars, must be "grossed up" by dividing by $1 - T$. This gives the amount of pre-tax dollars that are required to cover the sinking fund payment.

Southern's fixed charges are covered only 2.3 times, as opposed to an industry average of 4.0 times. Again, this indicates that the firm is somewhat weaker than most other firms in the industry, and it points up the difficulties Southern would likely encounter if it attempted to increase its debt.

Cash Flow Coverage. Southern has outstanding preferred stock which requires the payment of $10 million in dividends per year. To the numerator of the fixed charge coverage ratio we add depreciation, which is a noncash charge, and to the denominator we add the preferred dividends, which are "grossed up" to reflect the fact that they are not tax deductible. These adjustments produce the *cash flow coverage ratio,* which shows the margin by which operating cash flows cover financial requirements:

$$\frac{\text{Cash flow}}{\text{coverage ratio}} = \frac{\text{EBIT} + \text{Lease payments} + \text{Depreciation}}{\text{Interest and lease} + \dfrac{\text{Sinking fund payments}}{1 - T} + \dfrac{\text{Preferred stock dividends}}{1 - T}}$$

$$= \frac{\$266 + \$28 + \$100}{\$94 + \$20/0.6 + \$10/0.6} = \frac{\$394}{\$144} = 2.7 \text{ times.}$$

$$\text{Industry average} = 3.2 \text{ times.}$$

Again, Southern does not come up to industry standards.

Profitability Ratios

Profitability is the net result of a large number of policies and decisions. The ratios examined thus far provide some information about the way the firm is operating, but the *profitability ratios* show the combined effects of liquidity, asset management, and debt management on operating results.

Profit Margin on Sales. The *profit margin on sales,* often just called the *profit margin,* is computed by dividing net income by sales, and it gives the profit per dollar of sales:

$$\text{Profit margin on sales} = \frac{\text{Net income available to common stockholders}}{\text{Sales}} = \frac{\$110}{\$3,000} = 3.7\%.$$

$$\text{Industry average} = 5.1\%.$$

Southern's profit margin is substantially below the industry average of 5.1 percent, indicating that its sales prices are relatively low, that its costs are relatively high, or both.

Basic Earning Power. The *basic earning power ratio* is calculated by dividing earnings before interest and taxes (EBIT) by total assets:

$$\text{Basic earning power ratio} = \frac{\text{EBIT}}{\text{Total assets}} = \frac{\$266}{\$2,000} = 13.3\%.$$

$$\text{Industry average} = 17.2\%.$$

This ratio is useful for comparing firms in different tax situations and with different degrees of financial leverage. Because of its low turnover ratio and low profit margin on sales, Southern is not getting as much operating income out of its assets as is the average metals company.[13]

Return on Assets. The ratio of net income to total assets measures the *return on assets (ROA)* after interest and taxes:

$$\frac{\text{Return on}}{\text{assets (ROA)}} = \frac{\begin{array}{c}\text{Net income available to}\\\text{common stockholders}\end{array}}{\text{Total assets}} = \frac{\$110}{\$2,000} = 5.5\%.$$

$$\text{Industry average} = 9.0\%.$$

Southern's 5.5 percent return is well below the 9.0 percent average for the industry. This low rate results from Southern's low basic earning power plus its above-average use of debt, which causes its interest payments to be high and thus its net income to be low.

Return on Equity. The ratio of net income to common equity measures the *return on equity (ROE),* or the *rate of return on stockholders' investment:*

$$\frac{\text{Return on}}{\text{equity (ROE)}} = \frac{\begin{array}{c}\text{Net income available to}\\\text{common stockholders}\end{array}}{\text{Common equity}} = \frac{\$110}{\$800} = 13.8\%.$$

$$\text{Industry average} = 15.0\%.$$

Southern's 13.8 percent return is below the 15.0 percent industry average, but it is not as far below as the return on total assets. This results from Southern's greater use of debt, a point that is analyzed in detail later in the chapter.

Note that ROE focuses on the return to *common stockholders.* ROE measures the return to the owners of the firm, and since preferred stockholder claims are more like creditor's claims than owner's claims, the preferred stock cash flows are treated like debt flows.[14]

---

[13]Notice that EBIT is earned throughout the year, whereas the total assets figure is as of the end of the year. Therefore, it would be conceptually better to calculate this ratio as EBIT/Average assets = EBIT/[(Beginning assets + Ending assets)/2]. We have not made this adjustment because the published ratios used for comparative purposes do not include it. Incidentally, the same adjustment would also be appropriate for the next two ratios, ROA and ROE.

[14]One other ratio that is often useful is the *return on invested capital,* defined as net income plus interest payments, divided by debt plus equity capital.

Market Value Ratios

A final group of ratios, *market value ratios,* relates the firm's stock price to its earn-ings and book value per share. These ratios give management an indication of what investors think of the company's past performance and future prospects. If the firm's liquidity, asset management, debt management, and profitability ratios are all good, then its market value ratios will be high, and its stock price will probably be as high as can be expected.

Price/Earnings Ratio. The *price/earnings (P/E) ratio* shows how much investors are willing to pay per dollar of reported profits. Southern's stock sells for $28.50, so with an EPS of $2.20, its P/E ratio is 13.0:

$$\text{Price/earnings (P/E) ratio} = \frac{\text{Price per share}}{\text{Earnings per share}} = \frac{\$28.50}{\$2.20} = 13.0 \text{ times.}$$

$$\text{Industry average} = 13.5 \text{ times.}$$

P/E ratios are higher for firms with high growth prospects, other things held con-stant, but they are lower for riskier firms. Southern's P/E ratio is slightly below the average of other metals companies, which suggests that the company is regarded as being somewhat riskier than most, as having poorer growth prospects, or both.

Market/Book Ratio. The ratio of a stock's market price to its book value gives another indication of how investors regard the company. Companies with relatively high rates of return on equity generally sell at higher multiples of book value than those with low returns. Southern's book value per share is $16.00:

$$\text{Book value per share} = \frac{\text{Common equity}}{\text{Shares outstanding}} = \frac{\$800}{50} = \$16.00.$$

Dividing the price per share by the book value gives a *market/book ratio* of 1.8 times:

$$\text{Market/book ratio} = \frac{\text{Market price per share}}{\text{Book value per share}} = \frac{\$28.50}{\$16.00} = 1.8 \text{ times.}$$

$$\text{Industry average} = 2.1 \text{ times.}$$

Investors are willing to pay slightly less for Southern's book value than for that of an average metals fabricator.

The typical railroad, which has a very low rate of return on assets, has a market/book ratio of less than 0.5. On the other hand, very successful firms such as IBM achieve high rates of return on their assets, and they have market values well in excess of their book values. IBM's market/book ratio is about 3.0.

Comparative and Trend Analysis

In our discussion of Southern's ratios, we focused on *comparative analysis;* that is, we compared Southern's ratios with the average ratios for its industry. Another use-ful ratio analysis tool is *trend analysis,* where we analyze the trend of a single ratio

Table 22-5 Southern Metals Company: Summary of Financial Ratios

Ratio	Formula for Calculation	1989	1990	1990 Industry Average	Comment
I. Liquidity					
1. Current	$\dfrac{\text{Current assets}}{\text{Current liabilities}}$	2.8×	2.3×	2.5×	Slightly low; bad trend
2. Quick, or acid test	$\dfrac{\text{Current assets} - \text{Inventories}}{\text{Current liabilities}}$	1.8×	1.3×	1.1×	OK, but bad trend
II. Asset Management					
3. Inventory turnover	$\dfrac{\text{Sales}}{\text{Inventory}}$	13.3×	10.0×	9.3×	OK, but bad trend
4. Days sales outstanding (DSO)	$\dfrac{\text{Receivables}}{\text{Sales}/360}$	39.8 days	42.0 days	36.2 days	Poor; bad trend
5. Fixed asset turnover	$\dfrac{\text{Sales}}{\text{Fixed assets}}$	2.7×	2.3×	3.1×	Low; bad trend
6. Total asset turnover	$\dfrac{\text{Sales}}{\text{Total assets}}$	1.7×	1.5×	1.8×	Low; bad trend
III. Debt Management					
7. Debt to total assets (D/A)	$\dfrac{\text{Total debt}}{\text{Total assets}}$	47.6%	55.0%	40.1%	Very high; bad trend
8. Times interest earned (TIE)	$\dfrac{\text{EBIT}}{\text{Interest charges}}$	5.6×	4.0×	6.2×	Very low; bad trend
9. Fixed charge coverage	$\dfrac{\text{EBIT} + \text{Lease payments}}{\text{Interest charges} + \text{Lease payments} + \dfrac{\text{Sinking fund payments}}{1-T}}$	2.7×	2.3×	4.0×	Very low; bad trend
IV. Profitability					
10. Profit margin on sales	$\dfrac{\text{Net income}^a}{\text{Sales}}$	4.2%	3.7%	5.1%	Low; bad trend
11. Basic earning power (BEP)	$\dfrac{\text{EBIT}}{\text{Total assets}}$	15.7%	13.3%	17.2%	Very low; bad trend
12. Return on assets (ROA)	$\dfrac{\text{Net income}^a}{\text{Total assets}}$	7.1%	5.5%	9.0%	Very low; bad trend
13. Return on equity (ROE)	$\dfrac{\text{Net income}^a}{\text{Common equity}}$	15.4%	13.8%	15.0%	Low; bad trend
V. Market Value					
14. Price/earnings (P/E)	$\dfrac{\text{Price per share}}{\text{Earnings per share}}$	12.1×	13.0×	13.5×	Slightly low
15. Market/book (M/B)	$\dfrac{\text{Market price per share}}{\text{Book value per share}}$	1.9×	1.8×	2.1×	Low

[a] Net income after preferred dividends.

Figure 22-1   Southern Metals Company: Return on Equity (ROE),
1986-1990

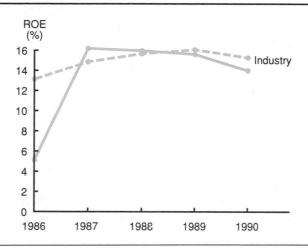

over time. Trend analysis gives clues whether a firm's financial situation is improving, holding constant, or deteriorating. Table 22-5 summarizes Southern's comparative and trend analyses for the past two years.

It is easy to combine comparative and trend analyses in a single graph such as the one shown in Figure 22-1. Here we plotted Southern's ROE and the industry average ROE over the past five years. The graph shows that Southern's ROE has been declining since 1987 even though the industry average has been relatively stable. Other ratios could be analyzed similarly.

Self-Test Questions

Briefly discuss the definitions and interpretation of the following financial ratios:

1. Liquidity ratios
   a. Current
   b. Quick
2. Asset management ratios
   a. Inventory turnover
   b. Days sales outstanding
   c. Fixed asset turnover
   d. Total asset turnover
3. Debt management ratios
   a. Total debt to total assets
   b. Times interest earned
   c. Fixed charge coverage
   d. Cash flow coverage

4. Profitability ratios
    a. Profit margin
    b. Basic earning power
    c. Return on assets
    d. Return on equity

5. Market value ratios
    a. Price/earnings
    b. Market/book

How are trend and comparative analyses used to help appraise a firm's financial ratios?

COMMON SIZE ANALYSIS

In a common size analysis, all income statement items are divided by sales, and all balance sheet items are divided by total assets. Thus, a *common size income statement* shows each item as a percentage of sales, and a *common size balance sheet* shows each item as a percentage of total assets. The significant advantage of common size statements is that they facilitate comparisons of balance sheets and income statements over time and across companies.

Table 22-6 contains Southern's common size income statements, along with the composite statement for the industry. Southern's labor and materials costs are somewhat above average, as is its depreciation. However, Southern's selling expenses are lower than average, which could be one reason why it is not generating sales com-

Table 22-6 Southern Metals Company: Common Size Income Statements

	1989	1990	1990 Industry Average
Net sales	100%	100%	100%
Costs and expenses:			
Labor and materials	85	85	83
Depreciation	3	3	2
Selling	1	1	2
General and administrative	1	1	1
Lease payments	1	1	1
Total costs	91%	91%	89%
Earnings before interest and taxes	9%	9%	11%
Interest expense:			
Interest on notes payable	0	0	0
Interest on first mortgage bonds	1	1	1
Interest on debentures	0	1	0
Total interest	1%	2%	1%
Earnings before taxes	8%	7%	10%
Taxes	3	3	5
Net income (profit margin)	5%	4%	5%

Table 22-7 Southern Metals Company: Common Size Balance Sheets

	1989	1990	1990 Industry Average
Assets			
Cash	3%	2%	2%
Marketable securities	1	0	1
Accounts receivable	19	18	13
Inventories	13	15	20
Total current assets	36%	35%	36%
Gross plant and equipment	88	90	85
Less: Depreciation	24	25	21
Net plant and equipment	64%	65%	64%
Total assets	100%	100%	100%
Liabilities and Equity			
Accounts payable	2%	3%	4%
Notes payable	4	5	3
Accrued wages	1	0	0
Accrued taxes	7	6	7
Total current liabilities	13%	15%	14%
First mortgage bonds	31	25	17
Debentures	4	15	9
Total long-term debt	35%	40%	26%
Preferred equity	6	5	0
Common equity	46	40	60
Total equity	52%	45%	60%
Total claims	100%	100%	100%

mensurate with its asset base, and hence has low asset turnover ratios. Thus, Southern's marketing people may not be sufficiently aggressive. Note also that Southern's interest expenses are relatively high, but its taxes are relatively low because of its low EBIT. The net effect of all these forces is a relatively low profit margin.

Table 22-7 contains Southern's common size balance sheets, along with the industry average. Three striking differences are revealed: (1) Southern's accounts receivable are significantly higher than the industry average, (2) its inventories are significantly lower, and (3) Southern uses far more fixed charge capital (debt and preferred) than the average metals firm.

The conclusions reached in a common size analysis generally parallel those derived from ratio analysis. However, occasionally, a serious deficiency is highlighted only by one of the two analytical techniques. Thus, a thorough financial statement analysis will include both ratio and common size analyses, as well as a Du Pont analysis, our next topic.

Self-Test Questions

How are common size statements created?

What advantage do common size statements have over regular statements?

Is it useful to include in a financial statement analysis both ratio analysis and common size analysis? Explain.

DU PONT ANALYSIS

Figure 22-2, which is called a *modified Du Pont chart* because that company's managers developed the general approach, shows how the profit margin on sales, asset turnover, and financial leverage combine to determine the rate of return on equity. The left-hand side of the chart develops the profit margin on sales. The various expense items are listed, and then summed to obtain Southern's total costs. Subtracting costs from sales yields the company's net income, which when divided by sales indicates that 3.7 percent of each sales dollar is left over for stockholders.

Figure 22-2   Southern Metals Company: Modified Du Pont
Chart (Millions of Dollars)

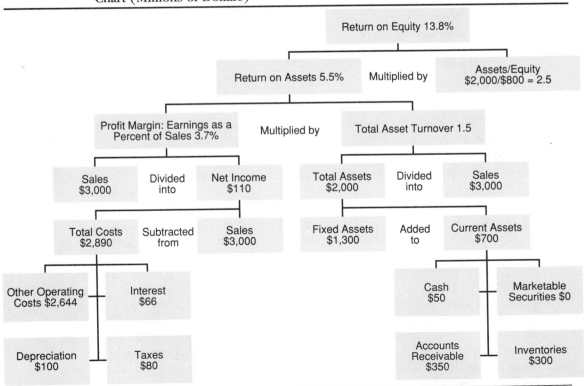

The right-hand side of the chart lists the various categories of assets, which are summed, and then sales are divided by the sum to find the number of times Southern "turns its assets over" each year. Southern's total asset turnover ratio is 1.5 times.

The profit margin times the total asset turnover ratio is defined as the *Du Pont equation*, which gives the rate of return on assets (ROA):

$$\text{ROA} = (\text{Profit margin})(\text{Total asset turnover})$$

$$= \left(\frac{\text{Net income}}{\text{Sales}}\right)\left(\frac{\text{Sales}}{\text{Total assets}}\right) \qquad \textbf{(22-1)}$$

$$= (3.7\%)(1.5) = 5.5\%.$$

Southern made 3.7 percent, or 3.7 cents, on each dollar of sales, and assets were "turned over" 1.5 times during the year, so Southern earned a return of 5.5 percent on its assets.

If Southern used only equity, the 5.5 percent return on assets would equal the rate of return on equity. However, 60 percent of the firm's capital was supplied by creditors and preferred stockholders. Since the 5.5 percent return on assets all goes to common stockholders, who put up only 40 percent of the capital, the return on equity is higher than 5.5 percent. Specifically, the rate of return on assets (ROA) must be multiplied by the *equity multiplier*, which shows the total assets working for each dollar of common equity, to obtain the rate of return on equity (ROE):

$$\text{ROE} = (\text{ROA})\,(\text{Equity multiplier})$$

$$= \left(\frac{\text{Net income}}{\text{Total assets}}\right)\left(\frac{\text{Total assets}}{\text{Common equity}}\right) \qquad \textbf{(22-2)}$$

$$= (5.5\%)(\$2,000/\$800)$$

$$= (5.5\%)(2.5) = 13.8\%.$$

We can combine Equations 22-1 and 22-2 to form the *extended Du Pont equation:*

$$\text{ROE} = \left(\begin{array}{c}\text{Profit}\\\text{margin}\end{array}\right)\left(\begin{array}{c}\text{Total asset}\\\text{turnover}\end{array}\right)\left(\begin{array}{c}\text{Equity}\\\text{multiplier}\end{array}\right)$$

$$= \left(\frac{\text{Net income}}{\text{Sales}}\right)\left(\frac{\text{Sales}}{\text{Total assets}}\right)\left(\frac{\text{Total assets}}{\text{Common equity}}\right) \qquad \textbf{(22-3)}$$

$$= \frac{\text{Net income}}{\text{Common equity}}.$$

For Southern Metals, we thus have

$$\text{ROE} = (3.7\%)(1.5)(2.5) \approx 13.8\%.$$

This 13.8 percent return on equity could, of course, be calculated directly: Net income/Common equity = \$110/\$800 = 13.8%. However, the extended Du Pont equation shows how the profit margin, turnover, and financial leverage interact to determine the return on equity.[15]

Management can use the Du Pont system to analyze ways of improving the firm's performance. On the left, or "profit margin," side of the chart, marketing people can study the effects of raising sales prices (or lowering them to increase volume), of moving into new products or markets with higher margins, and so on, and cost accountants can study the expense items and, working with engineers, purchasing agents, and other operating personnel, seek ways to hold down costs. On the "turn-over" side, financial analysts, working with both production and marketing people, can investigate ways of reducing investments in various types of assets. At the same time, the treasurer can analyze the effects of alternative financing strategies, seeking to hold down interest expenses and the risks of debt while still using debt to increase the rate of return on equity.

Equation 22-3 provides a useful comparison between a firm's performance as measured by ROE and the performance of an average firm in the industry:

$$\text{Southern Metals: ROE} = (3.7\%)(1.5)(2.50) \approx 13.8\%.$$

$$\text{Metals industry: ROE} = (5.1\%)(1.8)(1.67) \approx 15.3\%.$$

We see (1) that the average metals company has a significantly higher profit margin, and thus better control over expenses; (2) that the average firm has a higher total asset turnover, and thus is using its assets more productively; but (3) that Southern has offset some of these advantages with its higher financial leverage, although this increased use of leverage increases Southern's risk.

Self-Test Question

What is the extended Du Pont equation, and how can it be used to make a "first pass" appraisal of a firm's financial condition?

DIVISIONAL ANALYSIS

Thus far we have discussed ratio analysis, and financial analysis generally, on a total corporation basis. Such a consolidated analysis is useful for security analysts and lending officers, but financial managers in large corporations utilize the procedures described in this chapter primarily on a divisional basis. Most U.S. businesses have a large number of *profit centers*; indeed, the 1,000 largest U.S. companies, which produce over half the private sector's goods and services, each have an average of

---

[15]Note that in our Du Pont analysis, we have treated preferred stock as debt. Thus, the relevant net income is that available to common stockholders, and the relevant equity multiplier is Total assets/Common equity. The resulting ROE is, therefore, a measure of return to common stockholders. This treatment is consistent with the facts (1) that the common stockholders have voting control of the firm and (2) that preferred stock, with its fixed dividend payments, is really closer to debt financing than to common stock for purposes of performance analysis. For a specification that treats debt and preferred stock separately, see G. Michael Boyd, "Some Suggestions for a 'New and Improved' Du Pont Model," *Journal of Financial Education*, Fall 1989, 29–32.

25 profit centers. Each profit center has its own asset investments, and each is expected to contribute to the corporation's overall profitability. Each profit center can utilize the Du Pont system to monitor its performance, and these data can be transmitted (often electronically) to corporate headquarters, where financial analysts can keep tabs on the various divisions. If the divisions are all performing well, then the corporation's ROE and market value ratios will also look good. If not, then top management should see to it that corrective actions are taken.

Such a *financial control system*, used with good judgment, is absolutely essential for the proper management of any corporation with sales over a few million dollars. Companies like Du Pont, IBM, GM, and GE, which have had excellent performance over a long period, rely heavily upon such systems. Conversely, when larger companies get into trouble, their difficulties can usually be traced either to a breakdown in their control system or to a failure to heed the signals the system was giving.[16]

Self-Test Questions

What is a profit center?

Should financial analyses performed by corporate managers use consolidated corporate data or divisional (profit center) data? Explain.

SOURCES OF INDUSTRY DATA

The preceding analysis pointed out the need to compare the company in question with other firms in its industry. In this section, we describe some of the sources of industry data.

External Sources

One useful set of comparative data is Dun & Bradstreet (D&B), which, in its *Key Business Ratios,* provides 14 ratios for a large number of industries. Useful ratios can also be found in the *Annual Statement Studies* published by Robert Morris Associates, which is the national association of bank loan officers. The Federal Trade

---

[16]An extended discussion of financial controls would go beyond the scope of this book, but we should point out a few problems with such systems: (1) Different divisions will have assets of different ages. This will affect depreciation, hence profits, and also the investment base, hence ROA and ROE. (2) Frequently, one division sells to another, and the transfer price used in such intercorporate sales will have a major effect on the divisions' relative profitability. (3) The allocation of corporate overheads will affect relative profitability. (4) Certain types of investments may have no payoff for a number of years, and if divisional managers are rewarded only on the basis of short-term results, this may bias decisions against long-run projects. (5) Certain divisions have more debt capacity than others, yet borrowing is generally done at the corporate level; this must be taken into account.

These are just a few of the problems that arise when one attempts to utilize a system of divisional financial controls. Some top managers, when faced with these problems, have just given up and let their division managers operate autonomously. However, this is a sure path to corporate destruction. Well-run corporations recognize and deal with these problems.

Commission's *Quarterly Financial Report* gives a set of ratios for manufacturing firms by industry group and size of firm. Trade associations also compile industry average financial ratios.

Each of the listed organizations uses a somewhat different set of ratios, designed for its own purposes. For example, D&B deals mainly with small firms, many of which are proprietorships, and it is concerned largely with the creditors' viewpoint. Accordingly, D&B's ratios emphasize current assets and liabilities, and it provides no market value ratios whatever. Therefore, when you select a comparative data source, be sure that your emphasis is similar to that of the organization whose data you use, or else recognize the limitations of its ratios for your purposes. Additionally, there are often minor definitional differences in the ratios presented by different sources —for example, one may report ROE as net income divided by year-end common equity (Value Line does this) while another may divide by average common equity (Salomon Brothers does this). Therefore, before mixing ratios from different sources, be sure to verify the exact definitions of the ratios used. From this discussion, it is apparent that the structure of a financial ratio analysis is dictated to a large degree by the extent and type of industry data available.

Internal Sources

Larger firms will generally create their own comparative data using a computerized data base supplied by a financial services firm. For example, Standard and Poor's Compustat Services, Inc., markets a number of data tapes and diskettes, covering several thousand industrial and nonindustrial companies.

To illustrate, the *Compustat* primary industry file consists of data on approximately 900 companies. For most companies, annual data are available for the past 20 years, and quarterly data for the last 20 quarters. The data, which are picked up from reports filed with the SEC, are in the form of annual report statements, and the records are updated on a weekly basis to reflect new data as companies report them. Firms which subscribe to the *Compustat* service can use this data base to create up-to-date, tailor-made statistics that best serve their individual needs.

Self-Test Questions

What are some external sources of comparative industry data?

Explain how a firm could create its own comparative industry financial data base.

PROBLEMS IN FINANCIAL STATEMENT ANALYSIS

In our earlier discussion of the ratios, we mentioned some of the problems one encounters in financial statement analysis. In this section, we discuss some of the additional problems and limitations.

Development of Comparative Data

Many large firms operate a number of different divisions in quite different industries, and in such cases, it is difficult to develop meaningful industry averages. This tends to make financial statement analysis more useful for small firms with single product lines than for large, multiproduct companies.

Additionally, most firms want to be better than average (although half will be above and half below the median), so merely attaining average performance is not necessarily good. As a target for high-level performance, it is preferable to look at the industry leaders' ratios. Compilers of ratios such as D&B and Robert Morris Associates generally report industry ratios in quartiles. For example, D&B might report that 25 percent of the firms in the aluminum industry have a current ratio above 4.8, that the median is 2.5, and that 25 percent are below 1.6. This gives the analyst an idea of the distribution of ratios within an industry, and he or she can make better judgments about how the firm in question compares with the top firms in its industry.

Distortion of Comparative Data

Inflation has badly distorted firms' balance sheets. Further, reported profiles are affected because past inflation affects both depreciation charges and the cost of inventory included in the cost of goods sold. Thus, a financial statement analysis for one firm over time, or a comparative analysis of firms of different ages or which use different accounting methods, must be interpreted with caution and judgment. Inflation's effects are discussed in detail in a later section.

Seasonal factors can also distort ratio analysis. For example, the inventory turnover ratio for a food processor will be radically different if the balance sheet figure used for inventory is the one just before versus just after the close of the canning season. Receivables, and also current liabilities, are often affected similarly. These problems can be minimized by using 12-month average figures for balance sheet items.

Notes to Financial Statements

Information which can significantly affect a firm's financial condition is often contained in the notes to its financial statements. These notes contain information on the firm's pension plan, on its noncapitalized lease agreements, on its recent acquisitions and divestitures, on its accounting policies, and so forth. For example, the notes to Southern's financial statements contain the following information:

1.   Inventories are valued at the lower of cost or market, with costs determined by the last-in, first-out (LIFO) method.

2.   Receivables were reduced by $51.3 million in 1990 and by $42.7 million in 1989 to allow for doubtful accounts.

3.   Noncancelable operating lease commitments are $26.8 million for 1991, $23.3 million for 1992, and $21.1 million for 1993.

4.   As of December 31, 1990, the firm had a $968.2 million actuarial present value of vested pension benefits and $881.6 million in pension fund assets, so its unfunded pension liability was $86.6 million.

Clearly, this information has a bearing on Southern's financial position, and it should be considered, either directly or indirectly, by the financial analyst. The decreasing lease commitment means that, other factors held constant, Southern's fixed charge coverage ratio will improve in the future unless it signs new lease contracts. The unfunded pension liability means that the book value of the equity is in a sense overstated, so the general creditors' position is weaker than it would appear at first glance. Other potential problems might be revealed in a more detailed analysis. Indeed, professional analysts occasionally use the footnote information to recast financial statements on a common basis before they even begin to develop and compare ratios, and to these analysts the notes are especially vital.

Interpretation of Results

It is difficult to generalize about whether a particular ratio is "good" or "bad." For example, a high quick ratio may show a strong liquidity position, which is good, or an excessive amount of cash, which is bad because cash is a nonearning asset. Similarly, a high asset turnover ratio may denote either a firm that uses its assets efficiently or one that is undercapitalized and simply cannot afford to buy enough assets. Also, firms often have some ratios which look "good" and others which look "bad," making it difficult to tell whether the firm is, on balance, in a strong or a weak position. For this reason, ratio analysis is normally used as an input to judgmental decisions. However, in Appendix 22A we discuss multiple discriminant analysis, a procedure which can be used to assign weights to different ratios and which can thus permit us to quantify a company's overall financial strength.

Differences in Accounting Treatment

Different accounting practices can distort ratio comparisons. For example, firms can use different accounting conventions to value the cost of goods sold and the ending inventories. During inflationary periods these differences can lead to ratio distortions. Other accounting practices can also create distortions. For example, if one firm uses short-term, noncapitalized leases to obtain a substantial amount of its productive equipment, then its reported assets may be low relative to its sales. At the same time, if the lease liability is not shown as a debt, then leasing may artificially improve the debt and turnover ratios. Again, this problem has been reduced but not eliminated by the requirement that firms capitalize most large nonoperating leases.

Window Dressing

Firms sometimes employ *window dressing* techniques to make their financial statements look better to analysts. To illustrate, a Chicago builder borrowed on a two-year note on December 29, 1990, held the proceeds of the loan as cash for a few days, and then paid off the loan ahead of time on January 4, 1991. This improved his current and quick ratios, and made his year-end 1990 balance sheet look good. However, the improvement was strictly temporary; a week later, the balance sheet was back at the old level.

On an even larger scale, E. F. Hutton and several other brokerage houses followed the practice of recording checks they had written, but which had not yet been cleared through the banking system, as current liabilities rather than simply deducting them from reported cash balances. Hutton had been systematically overdrawing its bank accounts, and the question was raised, during investigations into this practice, why its negative cash balances did not alert its bankers that something was amiss. It turned out that, presumably to avoid having to report negative cash, Hutton recorded checks received as cash, but it recorded checks written as current liabilities rather than as deductions from cash.

Financial statement analysis is useful, but analysts should be aware of the problems discussed in this section and then must make adjustments as necessary. Financial statement analysis conducted in a mechanical, unthinking manner is dangerous; however, used intelligently and with good judgment, it can provide useful insights into a firm's operations.

Effects of Inflation

The high inflation rates of the late 1970s and early 1980s drew increased attention to the need to assess both the impact of inflation on business and the success of management in coping with it. Numerous reporting methods have been proposed to adjust accounting statements for inflation, but no consensus has been reached either on how to do this or even on the practical usefulness of the resulting data. Nevertheless, the Financial Accounting Standards Board issued Statements 33, 82, and 89, which encourage but do not require businesses to disclose supplementary data to reflect the effects of general inflation.

Financial Statement Effects. Traditionally, financial statements have been prepared on the basis of historical costs, that is, the actual number of dollars paid for each asset purchased. However, inflation has caused the purchasing power of dollars to change over time, and as a result financial statements can be badly distorted. To illustrate, a $100,000 expenditure on industrial land in 1990 would, in general, purchase far less acreage than a $100,000 expenditure in 1950, so adding 1990 dollars and 1950 dollars is much like adding apples and oranges. Nevertheless, this is done when the typical balance sheet is constructed. To help eliminate this disparity, the assets acquired in different years may be restated in *constant* dollars, each of which has equal purchasing power.

To reflect the effects of inflation, and thus to express operating results in dollars of comparable purchasing power, FASB encourages companies to show in annual reports what it characterizes as "income from continuing operations" calculated as if all its depreciable assets had been purchased with current-year dollars, and consequently its depreciation were based on higher-valued assets. Such an adjustment comes closer to showing what profits might be in the long run, when the old, undervalued assets have been replaced with new, inflated-value assets, and depreciation is correspondingly higher.

FASB also encourages firms to present a supplementary five-year comparison of selected financial data in current dollars. Operating revenues, net income, and cash dividends per common share are typically restated in constant dollars. This allows investors to see what portion of growth stems from inflation effects as opposed to true economic growth.

Effects of Inflation on Ratio Analysis. If a ratio analysis is based on "regular" financial statements, unadjusted for inflation, then distortions can creep in. Obviously, there will be a tendency for the value of the fixed assets to be understated, and inventories will also be understated if the firm uses last-in, first-out (LIFO) accounting. At the same time, increasing rates of inflation will lead to increases in interest rates, which in turn will cause the value of the outstanding long-term debt to decline. Further, profits will vary from year to year as the inflation rate changes, and these variations will be especially severe if inventory is charged to cost of goods sold based on the first-in, first-out (FIFO) method.

These factors tend to make ratio comparisons over time for a given company, and across companies at any point in time, less reliable than would be the case in the absence of inflation. This is especially true if a company changes its accounting procedures (say, from straight-line to accelerated depreciation, or from FIFO to LIFO), or if various companies in a given industry use different accounting methods. Analysts can attempt to restate financial statements to put everything on a common basis, but, at best, this can only reduce the problem, not eliminate it. Indeed, with the present state of the art, financial analysts cannot do much more than base their financial statement analysis of a firm on its existing accounting data. However, analysts ought to recognize that there are weaknesses in this approach, and they should apply judgment in interpreting the data.

Self-Test Questions

Explain how each of the following factors could present problems to an analyst conducting a financial statement analysis:
1. Development of comparative data
2. Seasonal/cyclical data distortions
3. Differences in accounting treatment
4. Window dressing
5. Inflation

Should analysts consider the information contained in the notes to the financial statements when analyzing a firm's financial condition? Explain.

SUMMARY

The primary purposes of this chapter were (1) to describe the basic financial statements and (2) to discuss techniques used by investors and managers to analyze them. The key concepts covered are listed next.

- The three basic statements contained in the annual report are the *balance sheet,* the *income statement,* and the *statement of cash flows.* Investors use the information contained in these statements to form expectations about the future levels of earnings and dividends, and about the riskiness of these expected values.

- *Financial statement analysis* generally begins with the calculation of a set of *financial ratios* designed to reveal the relative strengths and weaknesses of a company as compared to other companies in the same industry, and to show whether the firm's position has been improving or deteriorating over time.

- *Liquidity ratios* show the relationship of a firm's current assets to its current obligations, and thus indicate the firm's ability to meet its maturing debts.

- *Asset management ratios* measure how effectively a firm is managing its assets.

- *Debt management ratios* reveal (1) the extent to which the firm is financed with debt and (2) the extent to which operating cash flows cover debt service and other fixed charge requirements.

- *Profitability ratios* show the combined effects of liquidity, asset management, and debt management on operating results.

- *Market value ratios* relate the firm's stock price to its earnings and book value per share.

- Ratios are analyzed using *comparative analysis,* in which a firm's ratios are compared with industry averages (or another firm), and *trend analyses,* in which a firm's ratios are examined over time.

- In a *common size analysis,* a firm's income statement and balance sheet are expressed in percentages. This facilitates comparisons between firms of different sizes and for a single firm over time.

- The *Du Pont system* is designed to show how the profit margin on sales, the total asset turnover ratio, and the use of debt interact to determine the rate of return on equity.

- Financial statement analysis is not without problems. Some of the major difficulties are (1) *development of comparative data,* (2) *distortion of comparative data,* (3) *interpretation of results,* (4) *window dressing,* and (5) *effects of inflation.*

Financial statement analysis has limitations, but used with care and judgment, it can provide a sound picture of a firm's financial condition.

Questions

22-1 Define each of the following terms:
    a.   Annual report; income statement; balance sheet
    b.   Statement of cash flows; statement of changes in financial position; sources and uses of funds statement
    c.   Liquidity ratios; current ratio; quick, or acid test, ratio
    d.   Asset management ratios; inventory turnover ratio; days sales outstanding (DSO); fixed asset turnover ratio; total asset turnover ratio

e. Financial leverage; debt ratio; times-interest-earned (TIE) ratio; fixed charge coverage ratio; cash flow coverage ratio

f. Profitability ratios; profit margin on sales; basic earning power ratio; return on assets (ROA); return on equity (ROE)

g. Market value ratios; price/earnings (P/E) ratio; market/book (M/B) ratio; dividend payout ratio; book value per share

h. Trend analysis; comparative analysis

i. Common size analysis

j. Du Pont chart; Du Pont equation

k. Window dressing; seasonal effects on ratios

22-2 What three basic financial statements are contained in most annual reports?

22-3 Is it true that if a "typical" firm reports $20 million of retained earnings on its balance sheet, its directors could declare a $20 million cash dividend without any qualms whatsoever?

22-4 Financial ratio analysis is conducted by four groups of analysts: managers, equity investors, long-term creditors, and short-term creditors. What is the primary emphasis of each of these groups in evaluating ratios?

22-5 Why would the inventory turnover ratio be more important to a grocery store than to a shoe repair store?

22-6 Profit margins and turnover ratios vary from one industry to another. What are some industry characteristics that help explain these variations?

22-7 How does inflation distort ratio analysis comparisons both for one company over time (trend analysis) and when different companies are compared? Are only balance sheet items or both balance sheet and income statement items affected?

22-8 If a firm's ROE is low and management wants to improve it, explain how using more debt might help. Explain how it might hurt.

22-9 Suppose a firm used debt to leverage up its ROE, and in the process its EPS was also boosted. Would this necessarily lead to an increase in the price of the firm's stock? Assume the payout ratio remains constant.

22-10 How might (a) seasonal factors and (b) different growth rates distort a comparative ratio analysis? Give some examples. How might these problems be alleviated?

22-11 Indicate the effects of the transactions listed next on total current assets, the current ratio, and net income. Use + to indicate an increase, − to indicate a decrease, and 0 to indicate either no effect or an indeterminate effect. Be prepared to state any necessary assumptions, and assume an initial current ratio of more than 1.0. (Note: A good accounting background is necessary to answer some of these questions; if yours is not strong, just answer the questions you can handle.)

		Total Current Assets	Current Ratio	Net Income
a.	Cash is acquired through issuance of additional common stock.	_____	_____	_____
b.	Merchandise is sold for cash.	_____	_____	_____
c.	Federal income tax due for the previous year is paid.	_____	_____	_____
d.	A fixed asset is sold for less than book value.	_____	_____	_____

		Total Current Assets	Current Ratio	Net Income
e.	A fixed asset is sold for more than book value.	_____	_____	_____
f.	Merchandise is sold on credit.	_____	_____	_____
g.	Payment is made to trade creditors for previous purchases.	_____	_____	_____
h.	A cash dividend is declared and paid.	_____	_____	_____
i.	Cash is obtained through short-term bank loans.	_____	_____	_____
j.	Short-term notes receivable are sold at a discount.	_____	_____	_____
k.	Marketable securities are sold below cost.	_____	_____	_____
l.	Advances are made to employees.	_____	_____	_____
m.	Current operating expenses are paid.	_____	_____	_____
n.	Short-term promissory notes are issued to trade creditors for past due accounts receivable.	_____	_____	_____
o.	Ten-year notes are issued to pay off accounts payable.	_____	_____	_____
p.	A fully depreciated asset is retired.	_____	_____	_____
q.	Accounts receivable are collected.	_____	_____	_____
r.	Equipment is purchased with short-term notes.	_____	_____	_____
s.	Merchandise is purchased on credit.	_____	_____	_____
t.	The estimated taxes payable are increased.	_____	_____	_____

Self-Test Problems   (Solutions Appear in Appendix D)

ST-1   **(Debt ratio)** Glasgo & Co. had earnings per share of $4 last year, and it paid a $2 dividend. Book value per share at year-end was $40, while total retained earnings increased by $12 million during the year. The firm has no preferred stock, and no new common stock was issued during the year. If the firm's year-end debt (which equals its total liabilities) was $120 million, what was the company's year-end debt/assets ratio?

ST-2   **(Ratio analysis)** The following data apply to the Jason B. Smith Company (millions of dollars):

Cash and marketable securities	$100.00
Fixed assets	$283.50
Sales	$1,000.00
Net income	$50.00
Quick ratio	2.0 ×
Current ratio	3.0 ×
DSO	40 days
ROE	12%

The firm has no preferred stock—only common equity, current liabilities, and long-term debt.

a.   Find the firm's (1) accounts receivable, (2) current liabilities, (3) current assets, (4) total assets, (5) ROA, (6) common equity, and (7) long-term debt.

b.   In Part a, you should have found the firm's accounts receivable = $111.1 million. If the firm could reduce its DSO from 40 days to 30 days while holding other things constant, how much cash would it generate? If this cash were used to buy back common stock (at book value) and thus reduced the amount of common equity, how would this affect (1) the ROE, (2) the ROA, and (3) the total debt/total assets ratio?

Problems

22-1 **(Ratio analysis)** Data for the Stendardi Computer Company and its industry averages follow.
a.   Calculate the indicated ratios for Stendardi.
b.   Construct the Du Pont equation for both the firm and the industry.
c.   Outline the firm's strengths and weaknesses as revealed by your analysis.
d.   Suppose the firm had doubled its sales as well as its inventories, accounts receivable, and common equity during 1990. How would that information affect the validity of your ratio analysis? (Hint: Think about averages and the effects of rapid growth on ratios if averages are not used. No calculations are needed.)

Balance Sheet as of December 31, 1990

Cash	$ 155,000	Accounts payable	$ 258,000
Receivables	672,000	Notes payable	168,000
Inventory	483,000	Other current liabilities	234,000
Total current assets	$1,310,000	Total current liabilities	$660,000
Net fixed assets	585,000	Long-term debt	513,000
		Common equity	722,000
Total assets	$1,895,000	Total liabilities and equity	$1,895,000

Income Statement for Year Ended December 31, 1990

Sales		$3,215,000
Cost of goods sold:		
Materials	$1,434,000	
Labor	906,000	
Heat, light, and power	136,000	
Indirect labor	226,000	
Depreciation	83,000	2,785,000
Gross profit		$ 430,000
Selling expenses		230,000
General and administrative expenses		60,000
Earnings before interest and taxes		$ 140,000
Interest expense		49,000
Net income before taxes		$ 91,000
Federal and state income taxes (40%)		36,400
Net income		$ 54,600

Ratio	Stendardi	Industry Average
Current assets/Current liabilities	————	2.0×
Days sales outstanding	————	35 days
Sales/Inventories	————	6.7×
Sales/Total assets	————	2.9×
Net income/Sales	————	1.2%
Net income/Total assets	————	3.4%
Net income/Equity	————	8.5%
Total debt/Total assets	————	60.0%

22-2 **(Liquidity ratios)** The Edelman Company has $1,750,000 in current assets and $700,000 in current liabilities. Its initial inventory level is $500,000, and it will raise funds as additional notes payable and use them to increase inventory. How much can the firm's short-term debt (notes payable) increase without violating a current ratio of 2 to 1? What will be the firm's quick ratio after it has raised the maximum amount of short-term funds?

22-3 **(Ratio calculations)** The Jackson Company had a quick ratio of 1.4, a current ratio of 3.0, an inventory turnover of 6 times, total current assets of $675,000, and cash and marketable securities of $100,000 in 1990. What were the firm's annual sales and its DSO for that year?

22-4 **(Balance sheet analysis)** Complete the balance sheet and sales information shown for Jones Software Company using the following financial data:

Debt ratio: 50%
Quick ratio: 0.80×
Total asset turnover: 1.5×
Days sales outstanding: 36 days
Gross profit margin: 25%
Inventory turnover ratio: 5×

Balance Sheet and Sales Data

Cash	————	Accounts payable	————
Accounts receivable	————	Long-term debt	40,000
Inventories	————	Common stock	————
Fixed assets	————	Retained earnings	65,000
Total assets	200,000	Total claims	————
Sales	————	Cost of goods sold	————

22-5 **(Du Pont analysis)** The Riener Furniture Company, a manufacturer and wholesaler of high-quality home furnishings, has been experiencing low profitability in recent years. As a result, the board of directors has replaced the president of the firm with a new president, Don Sorenson, who has asked you to make an analysis of the firm's financial position using the Du Pont system. The most recent industry average ratios and the firm's financial statements are shown next.

Industry Average Ratios

Current ratio	2×	Sales/Fixed assets	6×
Debt/Total assets	30%	Sales/Total assets	3×
Times interest earned	7×	Net profit on sales	3%
Sales/Inventory	10×	Return on assets	9%
Days sales outstanding	24 days	Return on equity	12.9%

Balance Sheet as of
December 31, 1990
(Millions of Dollars)

Cash	$ 30	Accounts payable	$ 30
Marketable securities	22	Notes payable	30
Net receivables	44	Other current liabilities	14
Inventories	106	Total current liabilities	$ 74
Total current assets	$202	Long-term debt	16
Gross fixed assets	$150	Total liabilities	$ 90
Less depreciation	52	Common stock	$ 76
Net fixed assets	$ 98	Retained earnings	134
		Total stockholders' equity	$210
Total assets	$300	Total liabilities and equity	$300

Income Statement for Year Ended
December 31, 1990
(Millions of Dollars)

Net sales	$530
Cost of goods sold	440
Gross profit	$ 90
Selling expenses	49
Depreciation expense	8
Interest expense	3
Total expenses	$ 60
Net income before tax	$ 30
Taxes (40%)	12
Net income	$ 18

a. Calculate those ratios that you think would be useful in this analysis.
b. Construct a Du Pont equation for the firm, and compare the company's ratios to the composite ratios for the industry as a whole.
c. Do the balance sheet accounts or the income statement figures seem to be primarily responsible for the low profits?
d. Which specific accounts seem to be most out of line in relation to other firms in the industry?
e. If the firm had a pronounced seasonal sales pattern, or if it grew rapidly during the year, how might that affect the validity of your ratio analysis? How might you correct for such potential problems?

22-6 **(Statement of cash flows)** The consolidated balance sheets for the Trivoli Lumber Company at the beginning and end of 1990 follow. The company bought $150 million worth of fixed assets during 1990, and the charge for depreciation was $30 million. Earnings after taxes were $76 million, and the company paid out $20 million in dividends.
a. Fill in the amount of source or use in the appropriate column.

**Balance Sheets at
Beginning and End of 1990
(Millions of Dollars)**

	Jan 1	Dec 31	Change Source	Change Use
Cash	$ 30	$ 14	_____	_____
Marketable securities	22	0	_____	_____
Net receivables	44	60	_____	_____
Inventories	106	150	_____	_____
Total current assets	$202	$224	_____	_____
Gross fixed assets	150	300	_____	_____
Less depreciation	(52)	(82)	_____	_____
Net fixed assets	$ 98	$218	_____	_____
Total assets	$300	$442	_____	_____
Accounts payable	$ 30	$ 36	_____	_____
Notes payable	30	6	_____	_____
Other current liabilities	14	30	_____	_____
Long-term debt	16	52	_____	_____
Common stock	76	128	_____	_____
Retained earnings	134	190	_____	_____
Total liabilities and equity	$300	$442	_____	_____

Note: Total sources must equal total uses.

b. Prepare a statement of cash flows.
c. Briefly summarize your findings.

22-7 **(Du Pont analysis)** The Swift Electronic Corporation's balance sheets for 1990 and 1989 are as follows (in millions of dollars):

	1990	1989
Cash	$ 21	$ 45
Marketable securities	0	33
Receivables	90	66
Inventories	225	159
Total current assets	$336	$303
Gross fixed assets	450	225
Less accumulated depreciation	(123)	(78)
Net fixed assets	$327	$147
Total assets	$663	$450
Accounts payable	$ 54	$ 45
Notes payable	9	45
Accruals	45	21
Total current liabilities	$108	$111
Long-term debt	78	24
Common stock	192	114
Retained earnings	285	201
Total long-term capital	$555	$339
Total liabilities and equity	$663	$450

Additionally, Swift's 1990 income statement is as follows (in millions of dollars):

Sales	$1,365
Cost of goods sold	888
General expenses	300
EBIT	$ 177
Interest	10
EBT	$ 167
Taxes (40%)	67
Net income	$ 100

a.   What was the firm's dividend payout ratio in 1990?
b.   The following extended Du Pont equation shows the industry average for 1990:

$$\text{Profit margin} \times \text{Asset turnover} \times \text{Equity multiplier} = \text{ROE}$$

$$6.52\% \quad \times \quad 1.82 \quad \times \quad 1.77 \quad = 21.00\%.$$

Construct the firm's 1990 extended Du Pont equation. What does the Du Pont analysis indicate about the firm's expense control, asset utilization, and debt utilization? What is the industry's debt-to-assets ratio?
c.   Construct the firm's 1990 statement of cash flows. What does it suggest about the company's operations?

22-8   **(Ratio trend analysis)** The Shrieves Corporation's forecasted 1991 financial statements are given next, along with some industry average ratios.
a.   Calculate the firm's 1991 forecasted ratios, compare them with the industry average data, and comment briefly on the firm's projected strengths and weaknesses.
(Do Part b only if you are using the computerized diskette.)
b.   Suppose the firm is considering installing a new computer system which would provide tighter control of inventory, accounts receivable, and accounts payable. If the new system is installed, the following data are projected rather than the data now given in certain balance sheet and income statement categories:

Cash	$81,000
Accounts receivable	$400,000
Inventory	$750,000
Other fixed assets	$91,000
Accounts payable	$300,000
Accruals	$133,000
Retained earnings	$279,710
Cost of goods sold	$3,510,000
Administrative and selling expenses	$228,320
P/E ratio	6×

(1)   How does this affect the projected ratios and the comparison to the industry averages?
(2)   If the new computer system were either more efficient or less efficient and caused the cost of goods sold to decrease or increase by $150,000 from the new projections, what effect would that have on the company's position?

Pro Forma Balance Sheet as of December 31, 1991

Cash	$ 72,000
Accounts receivable	439,000
Inventory	894,000
Total current assets	$1,405,000
Land and building	238,000
Machinery	132,000
Other fixed assets	61,000
Total assets	$1,836,000
Accounts payable	$ 432,000
Accruals	170,000
Total current liabilities	$ 602,000
Long-term debt	404,290
Common stock	575,000
Retained earnings	254,710
Total liabilities and equity	$1,836,000

Pro Forma Income Statement for 1991

Sales	$4,290,000
Cost of goods sold	3,580,000
Gross operating profit	$ 710,000
Administrative and selling expenses	236,320
Depreciation	159,000
Miscellaneous	134,000
Taxable income	$ 180,680
Taxes (40%)	72,272
Net income	$ 108,408
Number of shares outstanding	23,000

Per Share Data:

EPS	$4.71
Cash dividends	$0.95
P/E ratio	5×
Market price (average)	$23.57

Industry Financial Ratios (1991)[a]

Quick ratio	1.0×
Current ratio	2.7×
Inventory turnover[b]	7×
Days sales outstanding	32 days
Fixed asset turnover[b]	13.0×
Total asset turnover[b]	2.6×
Return on total assets	9.1%
Return on equity	18.2%
Debt ratio	50%
Profit margin on sales	3.5%
P/E ratio	6×
M/B ratio	1.09×

[a]Industry average ratios have been constant for the past four years.
[b]Based on year-end balance sheet figures.

Mini Case

Lori Campbell was recently hired as a financial analyst by Jackson Industries, an Oklahoma-based manufacturer of mobile homes. Her first task is to conduct a financial statement analysis of the firm covering the past 2 years. As a starting point, Lori obtained the following historical data:

Balance sheets	1989	1990
Cash	$ 57,600	$ 52,000
Accounts receivable	351,200	402,000
Inventory	715,200	836,000
Total current assets	$1,124,000	$1,290,000
Gross fixed assets	$ 491,000	$ 527,000
Less: Accumulated depreciation	146,200	166,200
Net fixed assets	$ 344,800	$ 360,800
Total assets	$1,468,800	$1,650,800
Accounts payable	$ 145,600	$ 175,200
Notes payable	200,000	225,000
Accruals	136,000	140,000
Total current liabilities	$ 481,600	$ 540,200
Long-term debt	323,432	424,612
Common stock	460,000	460,000
Retained earnings	203,768	225,988
Total equity	$ 663,768	$ 685,988
Total claims	$1,468,800	$1,650,800

Income statements		
Sales	$3,432,000	$3,850,000
Cost of goods sold	2,864,000	3,250,000
Other expenses	340,000	430,300
Depreciation	18,900	20,000
EBIT	$ 209,100	$ 149,700
Interest expense	62,500	76,000
EBT	$ 146,600	$ 73,700
Taxes (40%)	58,640	29,480
Net income	$ 87,960	$ 44,220

Other data		
December 31 stock price	$8.50	$6.00
Number of shares outstanding	100,000	100,000
Dividend per share	$0.22	$0.22
Annual lease payment	$40,000	$40,000

Lori also developed the following industry average data for 1990:

Ratio	Industry Average
Current	2.7×
Quick	1.0×
Inventory turnover	7.0×
Days sales outstanding (DSO)	32.0 days
Fixed asset turnover	10.7×
Total asset turnover	2.6×
Debt ratio	50.0%
TIE	2.5×
Fixed charge coverage	2.1×
Profit margin	3.5%
Basic earning power	19.1%
ROA	9.1%
ROE	18.2%
P/E	14.2×
M/B	1.40×

See if you can answer the following questions that Lori developed:

a.   Apply the extended Du Pont equation (ROE = Profit margin × Total asset turnover × Equity multiplier) to Jackson's 1989 and 1990 data to obtain a general overview of the firm's financial condition.

b.   Prepare a statement of cash flows for the firm for 1990. Interpret the statement. (*Hint:* Note that Jackson's cash balance declined by $5,600 in 1990.)

c.   Define the term "liquidity" within a financial statement analysis context. What are Jackson's current and quick ratios? Assess the firm's liquidity position.

d.   What are Jackson's inventory turnover, days sales outstanding, fixed asset turnover, and total asset turnover? How do the firm's asset utilization ratios stack up against the industry averages?

e.   What are Jackson's debt, times-interest-earned, and fixed charge coverage ratios? How does Jackson compare with the industry with respect to financial leverage?

f.   Calculate and interpret Jackson's profitability ratios, that is, its profit margin, basic earning power, return on assets (ROA), return on equity (ROE), and return on investors' capital.

g.   Analyze Jackson's market value ratios, that is, its price/earnings and market/book ratios.

h.   While financial statement analysis can provide useful information concerning a company's operations and financial condition, it does have some inherent problems and limitations that necessitate care and judgment. Discuss the most important of these problems and limitations.

i.   (*Answer this question only if Appendix 22A has been assigned.*) What is multiple discriminant analysis (MDA)? Apply MDA as developed by Edward Altman to assess Jackson's probability of bankruptcy as it appeared in 1989 and in 1990.

Selected Additional References and Cases

The effects of alternative accounting policies on both financial statements and ratios based on these statements are discussed in the investment textbooks referenced in Chapter 4, and also in the many excellent texts on financial statement analysis. For example, see

Gibson, Charles H., and Patricia A. Frishkoff, *Financial Statement Analysis* (Boston: Kent, 1986).

Hawkins, David F., *Corporate Financial Reporting and Analysis* (Homewood, Ill.: Irwin, 1986).

For further information on the relative usefulness of various financial ratios, see

Chen, Kung H., and Thomas A. Shimerda, "An Empirical Analysis of Useful Financial Ratios," *Financial Management,* Spring 1981, 51–60.

Considerable work has been done to establish the relationship between bond ratings and financial ratios. For one example, see

Belkaoui, Ahmed, *Industrial Bonds and the Rating Process* (London: Quorum Books, 1983).

For sources of ratios and common size statements, see the following:

Dun & Bradstreet, *Key Business Ratios* (New York: Updated annually).

Financial Research Associates, *Financial Studies of the Small Business* (Arlington, Va.: Updated annually).

Robert Morris Associates, *Annual Statement Studies* (Philadelphia: Updated annually).

For a better understanding of multiple discriminant analysis and its use in financial analysis, see

Collins, Robert A., "An Empirical Comparison of Bankruptcy Prediction Models," *Financial Management,* Summer 1980, 52–57.

Eisenbeis, Robert A., "Pitfalls in the Application of Discriminant Analysis in Business Finance and Economics," *Journal of Finance,* June 1977, 875–900.

Joy, O. Maurice, and John O. Tollefson, "On the Financial Application of Discriminant Analysis," *Journal of Financial and Quantitative Analysis,* December 1975, 723–739.

Pinches, George E., "Factors Influencing Classification Results from Multiple Discriminant Analysis," *Journal of Business Research,* December 1980, 429–456.

Scott, Elton, "On the Financial Application of Discriminant Analysis: Comment," *Journal of Finance and Quantitative Analysis,* March 1978, 201–205.

Tollefson, John O., and O. Maurice Joy, "Some Clarifying Comments on Discriminant Analysis," *Journal of Financial and Quantitative Analysis,* March 1978, 197–200.

The following Brigham-Gapenski cases focus on financial analysis:

Case 36, "Southeast Trailer Company (A)," which illustrates the use of ratio analysis in the evaluation of a firm's existing and potential financial positions.

Case 37, "Pennsylvania Box Company," which also illustrates ratio analysis.

APPENDIX 22A

Multiple Discriminant Analysis

As we discussed in Chapter 22, one of the problems with ratio analysis is the interpretation of results—some ratios might look "good" while other ratios look "bad," and it might thus be difficult to reach a conclusion on an action such as approving or denying a loan for the company. *Multiple discriminant analysis (MDA)* is a statistical procedure that can help one interpret ratios and use them for decision purposes. Discriminant analysis is similar to regression analysis, and it identifies those factors which seem to have an important bearing on the likelihood of some future event. For example, when we first discussed MDA in Chapter 21, we listed several factors associated with an individual's being a good or bad credit risk. In this section, we discuss MDA in more detail, and we illustrate its application to bankruptcy prediction.[1]

The Basics of Multiple Discriminant Analysis

Suppose a bank loan officer wants to segregate corporate loan applications into those likely to default and those not likely to default. Assume that data for some past period are available on a group of firms which includes both companies that went bankrupt and companies that did not. For simplicity, we assume that only the current ratio and the debt/assets ratio are analyzed. These ratios for our sample of firms are given in Columns 2 and 3 at the bottom of Figure 22A-1. The Xs in the graph represent firms that went bankrupt, while the dots represent firms that remained solvent. For example, Point A in the upper left section is the point for Firm 2, which had a current ratio of 3.0 and a debt ratio of 20 percent, and a dot to indicate that the firm did not go bankrupt. Point B, in the lower right section, represents Firm 19, which had a current ratio of 1.0, a debt ratio of 60 percent, and an X to indicate that it did go bankrupt.

   The objective of discriminant analysis is to construct a boundary line through the graph such that, if the firm is to the left of the line, it is not likely to become insolvent, whereas it is likely to go bankrupt if it falls to the right. This boundary line is called the *discriminant function,* and in our example it takes this form:

$$Z = a + b_1(\text{Current ratio}) + b_2(\text{Debt ratio}).$$

Here Z is called the *Z score,* a is a constant term, and b_1 and b_2 indicate the effect of the current ratio and the debt ratio on the probability of a firm's going bankrupt.

   Although a full discussion of discriminant analysis would go well beyond the scope of this book, some useful insights may be gained by observing these points:

1.   The discriminant function is fitted (that is, the values of a, b_1, and b_2 are obtained) using historical data for a sample of firms that either went bankrupt or did not during some past period. When the data in the lower part of Figure 22A-1 were fed into a "canned" discriminant analysis program (the computing centers of most universities and large corporations have such programs), the following discriminant function was obtained:

$$Z = -0.3877 - 1.0736(\text{Current ratio}) + 0.0579(\text{Debt ratio}).$$

2.   This equation was plotted on Figure 22A-1 as the locus of points for which Z = 0. All combinations of current ratios and debt ratios shown on the line result in Z = 0.[2] Companies that lie to the left of the line (and also have Z values less than zero) are not likely to go

---

[1]This section is based largely on the work of Edward I. Altman, especially these two papers: (1) "Financial Ratios, Discriminant Analysis, and the Prediction of Corporate Bankruptcy," *Journal of Finance,* September 1968, 589–609; and (2) with Robert G. Haldeman and P. Narayanan, "Zeta Analysis: A New Model to Identify Bankruptcy Risk of Corporations," *Journal of Banking and Finance,* June 1977, 29–54.

[2]To plot the boundary line, let D/A = 0% and 80%, and then find the current ratio that forces Z = 0 at those two values. For example, at D/A = 0,

$$Z = -0.3877 - 1.0736(\text{Current ratio}) + 0.0579(0) = 0$$

$$0.3877 = -1.0736(\text{Current ratio})$$

$$\text{Current ratio} = 0.3877/(-1.0736) = -0.3611.$$

Thus, -0.3611 is the vertical axis intercept. Similarly, the current ratio at D/A = 80% is found to be 3.9533. Plotting these two points on Figure 22A-1, and then connecting them, provides the discriminant boundary line, which is the line that best partitions the companies into bankrupt and nonbankrupt. It should be noted that nonlinear discriminant functions may also be used.

Figure 22A-1   Discriminant Boundary between Bankrupt and Solvent Firms

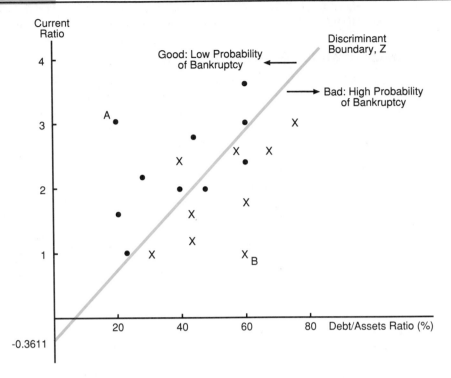

Firm Number (1)	Current Ratio (2)	Debt/Assets Ratio (3)	Did Firm Go Bankrupt? (4)	Z Score (5)	Probability of Bankruptcy (6)
1	3.6	60%	No	−0.780	17.2%
2(A)	3.0	20	No	−2.451	0.8
3	3.0	60	No	−0.135	42.0
4	3.0	76	Yes	0.791	81.2
5	2.8	44	No	−0.847	15.5
6	2.6	56	Yes	0.062	51.5
7	2.6	68	Yes	0.757	80.2
8	2.4	40	Yes[a]	−0.649	21.1
9	2.4	60	No[a]	0.509	71.5
10	2.2	28	No	−1.129	9.6
11	2.0	40	No	−0.220	38.1
12	2.0	48	No[a]	0.244	60.1
13	1.8	60	Yes	1.153	89.7
14	1.6	20	No	−0.948	13.1
15	1.6	44	Yes	0.441	68.8
16	1.2	44	Yes	0.871	83.5
17	1.0	24	No	−0.072	45.0
18	1.0	32	Yes	0.391	66.7
19(B)	1.0	60	Yes	2.012	97.9

Figure 22A-2   Probability Distributions of Z Scores

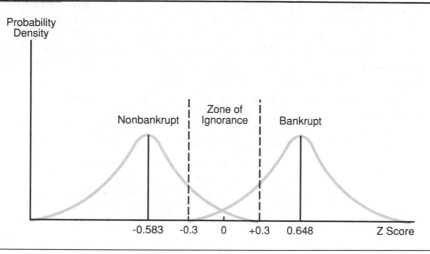

bankrupt, while those to the right (and have Z greater than zero) are likely to fail. It may be seen from the graph that one X, indicating a failing company, lies to the left of the line, while two dots, indicating nonbankrupt companies, lie to the right of the line. Thus, the discriminant analysis failed to properly classify three companies.

3.   If we have determined the parameters of the discriminant function, then we can calculate the Z score for other companies, say loan applicants at a bank. The Z scores for our hypothetical companies, along with their probabilities for going bankrupt, are given in Columns 5 and 6 of Figure 22A-1. The higher the Z score, the worse the company looks from the standpoint of bankruptcy. Here is an interpretation:

$Z = 0$:   50-50 probability of future bankruptcy (say within two years). The company lies exactly on the boundary line.

$Z < 0$:   If Z is negative, there is less than a 50 percent probability of bankruptcy. The smaller (more negative) the Z score, the lower is the probability of bankruptcy. The computer output from MDA programs gives this probability, and it is shown in Column 6 of Figure 22A-1.

$Z > 0$:   If Z is positive, the probability of bankruptcy is greater than 50 percent, and the larger Z is, the greater is the probability of bankruptcy.

Figure 22A-1 footnote:
[a]Denotes a misclassification. Firm 8 had $Z = -0.649$, so MDA predicted no bankruptcy, but it did go bankrupt. Similarly, MDA predicted bankruptcy for Firms 9 and 12, but they did not go bankrupt. The following tabulation shows bankruptcy and solvency predictions versus actual results:

	Z Positive: MDA Predicts Bankruptcy	Z Negative: MDA Predicts Solvency
Went bankrupt	8	1
Remained solvent	2	8

The model did not perform perfectly, as two predicted bankruptcies remained solvent, and one firm that was expected to remain solvent went bankrupt. Thus, the model misclassified 3 out of 19 firms, or 16 percent of the sample. Its success rate was 84 percent.

4.   The mean Z score of the companies that did not go bankrupt is -0.583, while that for the bankrupt firms is $+0.648$. These means, along with approximations of the Z score probability distributions of the two groups, are shown in Figure 22A-2. We may interpret this graph as indicating that if Z is less than about -0.3, there is a very small probability that the firm will go bankrupt, whereas if Z is greater than $+0.3$, there is only a small probability that it will remain solvent. If Z is in the range ± 0.3, called the *zone of ignorance,* we are uncertain about how the firm should be classified.

5.   The signs of the coefficients of the discriminant function are logical. Since its coefficient is negative, the larger the current ratio, the lower is a company's Z score, and the lower the Z score, the smaller is the probability of failure. Similarly, high debt ratios produce high Z scores, and this is directly translated into a higher probability of bankruptcy.

6.   Our illustrative discriminant function has only two variables, but other characteristics could be introduced. For example, we could add such variables as the rate of return on assets, the times-interest-earned ratio, the days sales outstanding, the quick ratio, and so forth.[3] Had the rate of return on assets been introduced, it might have turned out that Firm 8 (which failed) had a low ROA, while Firm 9 (which did not fail) had a high ROA. A new discriminant function would be calculated:

$$Z = a + b_1(\text{Current ratio}) + b_2(\text{D/A}) + b_3(\text{ROA}).$$

Firm 8 might now have a positive Z, while Firm 9's Z might become negative. Thus, it is likely that by adding more characteristics we would improve the accuracy of our bankruptcy forecasts. In terms of Figure 22A-2, this would cause each probability distribution to become tighter, would narrow the zone of ignorance, and would lead to fewer misclassifications.

Altman's Model

In a classic paper, Edward Altman applied MDA to a sample of corporations, and he developed a discriminant function that has seen wide use in actual practice. Altman's function was fitted as follows:

$$Z = 0.012X_1 + 0.014X_2 + 0.033X_3 + 0.006X_4 + 0.999X_5.$$

Here

$X_1 =$ net working capital/total assets.
$X_2 =$ retained earnings/total assets.[4]
$X_3 =$ EBIT/total assets.
$X_4 =$ market value of common and preferred stock/book value of debt.[5]
$X_5 =$ sales/total assets.

The first four variables are expressed as percentages rather than as decimals. (For example, if $X_3 = 13.3\%$, then 13.3 is used as its value, and *not* 0.133.) Also, Altman's 50-50 point was

---

[3]With more than two variables, it is difficult to graph the function, but this presents no problem in actual usage because graphs are only used to explain MDA.

[4]Retained earnings is the balance sheet figure, not the addition to retained earnings for the year.

[5][(Shares of common outstanding)(Price per share) + (Shares of preferred)(Price per share of preferred)]/Balance sheet value of total debt, including all short-term liabilities.

2.675, and not 0.0 as in our hypothetical example; his zone of ignorance was from $Z = 1.81$ to $Z = 2.99$; and the *larger* the Z score, the less the probability of bankruptcy.[6]

Altman's function can be used to calculate a Z score for Southern Metals Company based on the data presented previously in Chapter 22 in Tables 22-1 and 22-2. This calculation, ignoring the small amount of preferred stock, is shown next for 1990:

$$X_1 = \$400/\$2,000 = 0.200 = 20.0\% \qquad\qquad 20.0 \times 0.012 = 0.240$$
$$X_2 = \$660/\$2,000 = 0.330 = 33.0\% \qquad\qquad 33.0 \times 0.014 = 0.462$$
$$X_3 = \$266/\$2,000 = 0.133 = 13.3\% \qquad\qquad 13.3 \times 0.033 = 0.439$$
$$X_4 = (50)(\$28.50)/(\$300 + \$800) = 1.295 = 129.5\% \qquad 129.5 \times 0.006 = 0.777$$
$$X_5 = \$3,000/\$2,000 = 1.5 \qquad\qquad\qquad\qquad 1.5 \times 0.999 = \underline{1.499}$$
$$Z = \underline{3.417}$$

Since Southern's Z score of 3.417 is above the 2.99 upper limit of Altman's zone of ignorance, the data indicate that there is virtually no chance that Southern will go bankrupt within the next two years. (Altman's model predicts bankruptcy reasonably well for about two years into the future.)

Altman and his colleagues' later work updated and improved his original study. In their more recent work, they explicitly considered such factors as capitalized lease obligations, and they applied smoothing techniques to level out random fluctuations in the data. The new model was able to predict bankruptcy with a high degree of accuracy for two years into the future, and with a slightly lower but still reasonable degree of accuracy (70 percent) for about five years.

MDA has been used with success to quantify ratio analysis, by credit analysts to establish default probabilities for both consumer and corporate loan applicants, and by portfolio managers considering both stock and bond investments. It can also be used to evaluate a set of pro forma ratios as developed in Chapter 23, or to gain insights into the feasibility of a reorganization plan filed under the Bankruptcy Act. Altman's model has also been used by Morgan Stanley and other investment banking houses to appraise the quality of junk bonds used to finance takeovers and leveraged buyouts. The technique is described in detail in many statistics texts, while several articles cited at the end of Chapter 22 discuss financial applications of MDA. The interested reader is urged to study this literature, for MDA has many potentially valuable applications in finance.

However, when using MDA in practice it is best to create your own discriminant data using a recent sample from the industry in question. It is not reasonable to assume that the financial characteristics of a steel company facing imminent bankruptcy are the same as for a retail grocery chain in the same dire straits. If both of these firms were analyzed using Z scores calculated with the same equation, it might turn out that the grocery chain had a relatively high score, signifying (incorrectly) a low probability of bankruptcy, while the steel company had a relatively low score, indicating (correctly) a high probability of bankruptcy. The misclassification of the grocery company could result from the fact that it has very high sales for the amount of its book assets, and hence X_5, which has the highest coefficient, is much higher than for an average firm in an average industry facing potential bankruptcy. To remove any such industry-unique bias, the MDA analysis should be based on a sample with characteristics similar to the firm being analyzed. Unfortunately, it is often not possible to find enough firms that have recently gone bankrupt to conduct an industry MDA.

---

[6] These differences reflect the software package he used to generate the discriminant function. Altman's program operated from a base of 2.675 rather than 0.0, and his program simply reversed the sign of Z from ours.

CHAPTER 23

Financial Planning and Control

Home Depot, Inc., has a problem that most stores would love—the business at its new store in East Meadow, New York, is so good that the store's 740-car parking lot fills up on weekends, making access difficult for its customers. In just 10 years, Home Depot has become a $2.8 billion chain of 118 stores, most of which are in the Sunbelt. In 1989, Home Depot surpassed Lowe's as the largest home-repair chain in the country. But that is not enough for Home Depot—the firm's goal is to have 350 stores nationwide by 1995, with sales of $10 billion.

Each Home Depot store stocks roughly 30,000 separate items of lumber, tools, lighting, and plumbing supplies, and its prices are 30 percent below the going rate at traditional hardware stores. Although some rival stores may be as well stocked as Home Depot, analysts say that existing chains will have to cut prices if they expect to effectively compete with Home Depot.

In addition to low prices, Home Depot's sales staff gives it another advantage. Consultants say no other company in the industry comes close to Home Depot in hiring and keeping employees who can "hold the hands" of novice repairers. Managers actively recruit workers who have building trades experience, and the firm spends another $400,000 to train the employees for four weeks before a store opens. Then, to keep employees, Home Depot pays from $7 to $11 an hour—well above retailing standards.

How did Home Depot go from nothing to become the top player in the industry in just 10 years? They did it with a good idea, and, just as important, with good planning. Home Depot's capital requirements are enormous, so the company must plan its capital requirements well in advance to ensure that it can get the funds it needs, when it needs them, and on the best possible terms. Forecasting financial requirements is an essential part of any firm's planning process, and the faster the growth rate, the more important the financial forecast. Good financial planning is also important, and perhaps even more important, for smaller, weaker companies. Whereas a firm such as Home Depot, whose stock trades on the New York Stock Exchange, has relatively easy access to the capital markets, a smaller firm may find it difficult, or even impossible, to obtain funds unless its management has time to plan for funds acquisition.

IN the last chapter, we saw how one can analyze financial statements to identify a firm's strengths and weaknesses. Now we consider the actions the firm can take to exploit its strengths and to overcome its weaknesses. As we shall see, managers are vitally concerned with projected, or pro forma, financial statements, and with the effects of alternative policies on these statements. An analysis of such effects is the key ingredient of financial planning. However, a good financial plan cannot, by itself, insure that the firm's goals will be met — the plan must be backed up by a financial control system for monitoring the situation, both to ensure that the plan is carried out properly and to facilitate rapid adjustments if economic and operating conditions change from those built into the plan.

STRATEGIC PLANS

Financial plans are developed within the framework of the firm's overall strategic and operating plans. Thus, we begin our discussion with an overview of the strategic planning process.[1]

Corporate Purpose

The long-run strategic plan should begin with a statement of the *corporate purpose,* which defines the overall mission of the firm. The purpose can be defined either specifically or in general terms. For example, one firm might state that its corporate purpose is "to increase the intrinsic value of the firm's common stock." Another

---

[1]One can take many approaches to corporate planning. For more insights into the corporate planning process, see Benton E. Gup, *Guide to Strategic Planning* (New York: McGraw-Hill, 1980).

might say that its purpose is "to maximize the growth rate in earnings and dividends per share while avoiding excessive risk." Yet another might state that its principal goal is "to provide our customers with state-of-the-art computing systems at the lowest attainable cost, which in our opinion will also maximize benefits to our employees and stockholders."

There should be no conflict between sound operations and stockholders' benefits, but occasionally there is. For example, Varian Associates, Inc., an NYSE company with 1990 sales of about $1.25 billion, was for years regarded as one of the most technologically advanced companies in the electronics devices and semiconductor fields. However, Varian's management was reputed to be more concerned with developing new technology than with marketing it, and the stock price was lower than it had been 10 years earlier. Some of the larger stockholders were intensely unhappy with the state of affairs, and management was faced with the threat of a proxy fight or a forced merger. At that point, management announced a conscious change in policy and stated that it would, in the future, emphasize both technological excellence *and* profitability, rather than focusing primarily on technology. Earnings improved dramatically, and the stock price rose from $6.75 to over $60 in only four years.

The Varian example illustrates both the importance of the corporate purpose as viewed by management and the discipline imposed by the market. Well-run companies need to define an area and then develop competence with regard to meeting the needs of their customers, but they will be forced by the market to translate that competence into earnings.

Corporate Scope

The *corporate scope* defines a firm's lines of business and geographic area of operations. Again, the corporate scope can be spelled out in great detail or put merely in general terms. The steel industry provides a study in contrasts, with some companies such as U.S. Steel (now USX Corporation) diversifying widely, from oil to financial services, and other companies sticking closely to their basic business. Nucor Corporation, an NYSE-listed speciality steel producer, is one which has stuck to its basic business. This statement gives an idea of how Nucor's management defines its scope:

> We are a manufacturing company producing primarily steel products. The major strength of our company is constructing plants economically and operating them efficiently.

A $1,000 investment in Nucor's stock in 1977 would be worth $15,000 in 1990. A similar investment in U.S. Steel would now be worth $700. Factors other than scope of operations affected these results, but scope was surely an important factor.

Corporate Objectives

The corporate purpose and scope outline the general philosophy and approach of the business, but they do not provide managers with operational objectives. The *corporate objectives* set forth specific goals that management strives to attain. Corporate objectives can be quantitative, such as specifying a target market share, a target ROE, or a target earnings per share growth rate, or they can be qualitative, such as "keeping the firm's research and development efforts at the cutting edge of the industry." Multiple goals are often established, and these goals are not static—they should be and are changed when conditions change. The goals should also be challenging, yet realistically attainable, and it is appropriate that management compensation be based on the extent to which objectives are met.

Corporate Strategies

Once a firm has defined its purpose, scope, and objectives, it should develop a strategy designed to help it achieve its stated objectives. *Corporate strategies* are broad approaches rather than detailed plans. For example, one airline may have a strategy of offering "no frills" service between a limited number of cities, while another may plan to offer "staterooms in the sky." Strategies must be attainable and compatible with the firm's purpose, scope, and objectives.

Perhaps the most interesting and important set of strategies that has been developed in recent years is that of AT&T and the Bell operating companies in the wake of the breakup of AT&T. The seven regional telephone holding companies which emerged from the breakup all provide basic local telephone service, but beyond that, they have been developing different strategies which will take them in different directions. Some now sell a broad array of telecommunications equipment, while others have more limited offerings. Some are rapidly diversifying into non-regulated lines of business—Bell Atlantic has spent over $2 billion for this purpose—while others are diversifying at a much slower pace. Others are moving abroad—BellSouth recently won a $220 million contract to build a mobile phone system in Argentina.

The surviving AT&T faces perhaps even greater challenges in setting its corporate strategy. On the one hand, it faces increasing competition in its two major markets, long-distance transmission and telephone equipment manufacturing. Currently, it has most of the industry's capacity in these areas, so to some extent, it can price high and enjoy high short-run profits, but at the expense of an erosion of its share of the business. Alternatively, it can price low and maintain a large market share, but at the expense of short-run (and perhaps also long-run) profits. Also, AT&T must decide on the extent of its foray into the computer business. Its PC6300 clone of the IBM PC has not done very well, and its other computer ventures, such as its Unix operating system, have started slow, but are now beginning to show promise. IBM, meanwhile, has invested heavily in the telecommunications business (both manufacturing and satellite transmissions), and is thus attacking AT&T on its own turf. At the same time, the new Bell companies are all trying to get permission to compete with their former parent in the businesses of long distance service and equipment manufacturing. The AT&T/Bell companies' strategic decisions are more dramatic than most, but they do illustrate the kinds of issues that arise when companies develop their strategic plans.

Self-Test Questions

Briefly describe the nature and use of the following corporate planning tools:

1. Corporate purpose
2. Corporate scope
3. Corporate objectives
4. Corporate strategies

Why do financial planners need to be familiar with the company's overall strategic plan?

OPERATING PLANS

Operating plans can be developed for any time horizon, but most companies use a five-year horizon, and thus the name *five-year plan* has become common. In a five-year plan, the plans are most detailed for the first year, with each succeeding year's plan becoming less specific. The operating plan is intended to provide detailed implementation guidance, based on the corporate strategy, in order to meet the corporate objectives. The five-year plan explains in considerable detail who is responsible for what particular function, and when specific tasks are to be accomplished.

Table 23-1 contains the annual planning schedule of Century Electronics Corporation, a leading manufacturer of telecommunications equipment. This schedule

Table 23-1 Century Electronics Corporation: Annual Planning Schedule

Months	Action
April–May	Planning department analyzes environmental and industry factors. Marketing department prepares sales forecast for each product group.
June–July	Engineering department prepares cost estimates for new manufacturing facilities and plant modernization programs.
August–September	Financial analysts evaluate proposed capital expenditures, divisional operating plans, and proposed sources and uses of funds.
October–November	Five-year plan is finalized by planning department, reviewed by divisional officers, and put into "semi-final" form.
December	Five-year plan is approved by the executive committee and then submitted to the board of directors for final approval.

Table 23-2	Century Electronics Corporation: Five-Year Operating Plan Outline

Chapter 1.   Corporate mission
Chapter 2.   Corporate scope
Chapter 3.   Corporate objectives
Chapter 4.   Projected business environment
Chapter 5.   Corporate strategies
Chapter 6.   Summary of projected business results
Chapter 7.   Product line plans and policies
    a.   Marketing
    b.   Manufacturing
    c.   Finance
       1.   Working capital
          (a)   Overall working capital policy
          (b)   Cash and marketable securities management
          (c)   Inventory management
          (d)   Credit policy and receivables management
       2.   Dividend policy
       3.   Financial forecast
          (a)   Capital budget
          (b)   Cash budget
          (c)   Pro forma financial statements
          (d)   External financing requirements
          (e)   Financial condition analysis
       4.   Accounting plan
       5.   Control plan
    d.   Administrative and personnel
    e.   Research and development
    f.   New products
Chapter 8.   Consolidated corporate plan

illustrates the fact that for larger companies, the planning process is essentially continuous. Next, Table 23-2 outlines the key elements of Century's five-year plan. A full outline would require several pages, but Table 23-2 does at least provide insights into the format and content of a five-year plan. It should be noted that Century, like other large, multidivisional companies, breaks down its operating plan by divisions. Thus, each division has its own goals, mission, and plan for meeting its objectives, and these plans are then consolidated to form the corporate plan.

Self-Test Questions

What is the purpose of a firm's operating plan?

What is the most common time horizon for operating plans?

Briefly describe the contents of a typical operating plan.

THE FINANCIAL PLAN

The financial planning process can be broken down into five steps:

1. Set up a system of projected financial statements which can be used to analyze the effects of the operating plan on projected profits and other financial condition indicators. This system can also be used to monitor operations after the plan has been finalized and put into effect. Rapid awareness of deviations from plans is essential to a good control system, which in turn is essential to corporate success in a changing world.

2. Determine the specific financial requirements needed to support the company's five-year plan. This includes funds for plant and equipment as well as for inventory and receivables buildups, for R&D programs, and for major advertising campaigns.

3. Forecast the financing sources to be used over the next five years. This involves estimating the funds which will be generated internally as well as those which must be obtained from external sources. Any constraints on operating plans imposed by financial limitations which would limit the use of total and/or short-term debt should be incorporated into the plan; examples include restrictions on the debt ratio, the current ratio, and the coverage ratios.

4. Establish and maintain a system of controls governing the allocation and use of funds within the firm. Essentially, this involves making sure that the basic plan is carried out properly.

5. Develop procedures for adjusting the basic plan if the forecasted economic conditions upon which the plan was based do not materialize. For example, if the economy turns out to be stronger than was forecasted when the basic plan was drawn up, then these new conditions must be recognized and reflected in higher production budgets, larger marketing quotas, and the like, and as rapidly as possible. Thus, Step 5 is really a "feedback loop" which triggers modifications to the plan.

The principal components of the financial plan are (1) an analysis of the firm's current financial condition as indicated by an analysis of its most recent statements, (2) a sales forecast, (3) the capital budget, (4) the cash budget, (5) a set of pro forma (or projected) financial statements, and (6) the external financing plan. We have in previous chapters discussed the capital budget, the cash budget, and financial statement analysis. In the remainder of this chapter, we focus on the plan's other elements—the sales forecast, the pro forma financial statements, and the external financing plan.

Self-Test Questions

What are the five steps of the financial planning process?

What are the principal components of a financial plan?

SALES FORECASTS

The *sales forecast* generally starts with a review of sales over the past five to ten years, expressed in a graph such as that in Figure 23-1. The first part of the graph shows actual sales for Century Electronics Corporation from 1981 through 1990. During this 9-year period, sales grew from $200 million to $500 million, or at a compound growth rate of 10.7 percent. However, the growth rate has accelerated sharply in recent years, primarily as a result of the breakup of AT&T and the separation of its manufacturing and telephone operations, which permitted companies like Century to compete for sales to telephone operating companies. Also, Century's R&D program has been especially successful, so when the telecommunications market broke open, the firm was ready.

On the basis of the recent trend in sales, on new product introductions, and on the economics staff's forecast that the national economy will be quite strong during the coming year, Century's planning group projects a 50 percent growth rate during 1991, to a sales level of $750 million. That forecast was developed as follows:

1.   To begin, sales are divided into three major product groups: (1) sales to telephone companies of equipment used in telephone networks; (2) sales of equipment such as PBXs used by hotels, motels, and businesses to route calls among rooms; and (3) sales of electronic components to computer manufacturers. Sales in each of

Figure 23-1   Century Electronics Corporation: 1991 Sales Projection

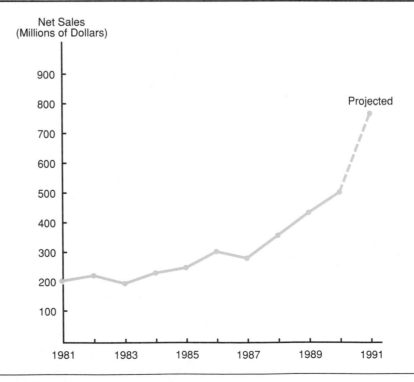

these areas over the past 10 years are plotted, the trend is observed, and a "first approximation forecast," assuming a continuation of past trends, is made.

2.   Next, the level of business activity for each of the company's market areas is forecasted—for example, what will be the level of hotel, motel, and office building construction in 1991? These forecasts are used as a basis for modifying the demand forecasts in each of Century's business areas.

3.   Century next looks at its probable shares of each major market. Consideration is given to such factors as the company's capacity, its competitors' capacity, and new products or product improvements that either Century or its competitors may plan. Pricing strategies are also considered—for example, does the company have plans to raise prices to boost profit margins, or to lower prices to gain market share and economies of scale? Such actions could greatly affect sales forecasts. Also, since Century has some export sales and also faces competition from Japanese and European firms in its U.S. markets, exchange rates and the value of the dollar can have an important influence on its market share.

4.   Advertising campaigns, promotional discounts, credit terms, and the like, also affect sales, so probable developments in these areas must be factored in.

5.   Order backlogs and recent trends in new orders (or cancellations) are taken into account.

6.   Forecasts are made for each product group, both in the aggregate—for example, sales to telephone companies—and on an individual product basis. The individual product sales forecasts are summed and then compared with the aggregate product group forecasts. Differences are reconciled, and the end result is a sales forecast for the company as a whole but with breakdowns by major divisions and for individual products.

If the sales forecast is off, the consequences can be serious. First, if the market expands more than Century has expected and geared up for, then the firm will not be able to meet its customers' needs. Orders will back up, delivery times will lengthen, repairs and installations will be harder to schedule, and customer dissatisfaction will increase. Customers will end up going elsewhere, and Century will lose market share and will have missed a major opportunity. On the other hand, if its projections are overly optimistic, Century could end up with too much plant, equipment, and inventory, and too many employees. This would mean low turnover ratios, high costs for labor, depreciation, and storage, and, possibly, both layoffs and write-offs of obsolete inventory and equipment. All of this would result in a low rate of return on equity, which in turn would depress the company's stock price. If Century had financed the expansion with debt, its problems would, of course, be compounded. Thus, an accurate sales forecast is critical to the well-being of the firm.[2]

---

[2]A sales forecast is actually the *expected value of a probability distribution* of possible levels of sales. Because any sales forecast is subject to a greater or lesser degree of uncertainty, for financial planning purposes we are often just as interested in the degree of uncertainty inherent in the sales forecast (its standard deviation) as we are in the expected value of sales. See "Demand Estimation" in James L. Pappas and Mark Hirschey, *Managerial Economics* (Hinsdale, Ill.: Dryden, 1989), Appendix 4A, for a detailed discussion of procedures for making demand forecasts.

Self-Test Questions

Why is the sales forecast such an important element of the planning process?

What is the starting point for the sales forecast?

What factors must be considered when making a sales forecast?

PERCENTAGE OF SALES FORECASTING

Financial forecasting involves projecting financial statements on the basis of a set of assumed operating conditions. In this section, we present the *percentage of sales* method, a simple but often practical technique for forecasting financial statement variables. The procedure is based on two assumptions: (1) that all assets and some liabilities are tied directly to sales, and (2) that the current levels of most balance sheet items are optimal for the current level of sales. We illustrate the method with Century Electronics Corporation, whose 1990 financial statements are given in Column 1 of Table 23-3. We explain the other columns as we go through this section.

Century operated its fixed assets at full capacity to support the $500 million in sales in 1990; it had no excess manufacturing capacity. Also, its stocks of inventories and its cash balances were in line with its sales of $500 million. Since it was operating at full capacity in 1990, if sales are to increase in 1991, Century will need to increase all its assets. Note also that Century's 1990 profit margin was 4.8 percent, and it distributed one-third of its net income to stockholders as dividends.

If Century's sales increase to $750 million in 1991, what will its pro forma 1991 income statement, balance sheet, and statement of cash flows look like, and how much external financing will the company require during 1991? The first step in the percentage of sales method is to isolate those income statement and balance sheet items that vary directly with sales. Regarding the income statement, increased sales are expected to bring direct increases in all of the variables except interest expense. That is, cost of goods sold and selling and administrative expenses are assumed to be tied directly to sales, but interest expense is a function of financing decisions. Further, Century's federal, state, and local taxes are expected to continue to amount to 40 percent of pre-tax income.

Turning to its balance sheet, since Century was operating at full capacity, fixed assets as well as current assets must increase if sales are to rise. Thus, each asset item must increase if the higher level of sales is to be attained. More cash will be needed for transactions, receivables will be higher, additional inventory must be stocked, and new plant must be added.[3]

If Century's assets are to increase, its liabilities and/or equity must likewise rise —the balance sheet must balance, and increases in assets must be financed in some manner. Accounts payable and accruals will rise *spontaneously* with sales: As sales increase, so will purchases, and larger purchases will result in higher levels of ac-

---

[3]Some assets, such as marketable securities, are not tied directly to operations, so do not vary directly with sales. In fact, marketable securities, if they were held, could be run down to zero, thus reducing external funding requirements.

Table 23-3 Century Electronics Corporation: Financial Projections
(Millions of Dollars, Rounded)

	For the Year Ended 12/31/90 (1)	1991 Projections First Approximation Column 1 × 1.5 (2)	1991 Projections Second Approximation Including Financings (3)
Income Statement			
Net sales	$500	$750	$750
Cost of goods sold	400	600	600
Selling and administrative expenses	52	78	78
EBIT	$ 48	$ 72	$ 72
Interest expense	8	8[a]	17[d]
Earnings before taxes	$ 40	$ 64	$ 55
Taxes (40%)	16	26	22
Net income	$ 24	$ 38	$ 33
Dividends (payout: 33%)	$ 8	$ 8[a]	$ 9[e]
Addition to retained earnings	$ 16	$ 30	$ 24
Balance Sheet	As of 12/31/90		
Cash	$ 10	$ 15	$ 15
Receivables	85	128	128
Inventories	100	150	150
Total current assets	$195	$293	$293
Net fixed assets	150	225	225
Total assets	$345	$518	$518
Accounts payable	$ 40	$ 60	$ 60
Notes payable	10	10[a]	19[f]
Accrued wages and taxes	25	38	38
Total current liabilities	$ 75	$108	$117
Mortgage bonds	72	72[a]	142[g]
Common stock	150	150[a]	181[h]
Retained earnings	48	78[b]	72[i]
Total claims	$345	$408	$512
External funds needed (EFN)		$110[c]	$ 6[j]

[a]This account does not increase spontaneously with sales, so for the first approximation projection, the 1990 balance is carried forward. Later analysis could change the figure shown.

[b]1990 retained earnings plus 1991 addition = $48 + $30 = $78. This figure will change later in the analysis.

[c]EFN is a balancing item found by subtracting projected total claims from projected total assets.

[d]$8 million of interest on the original debt plus $9 million on new debt.

[e]$8 million on old shares plus $1 million on new shares.

[f]$10 million of old 8 percent notes plus $9 million of new 10 percent notes.

[g]$72 million of old 10 percent mortgage bonds plus $70 million of new 12 percent bonds.

[h]$150 million from 1990 statement plus $31 million from sale of new stock.

[i]1990 retained earnings plus projected 1991 addition = $48 + $24 = $72 million.

[j]A third approximation could be developed. *Lotus 1-2-3* models can be written to instantly produce a balance between projected assets and projected claims.

counts payable. Thus, if sales double, accounts payable will also double. Similarly, a higher level of operations will require more labor, so accrued wages will increase, and, assuming profit margins are maintained, an increase in profits will pull up accrued taxes. Retained earnings should also increase, but not in direct proportion to the increase in sales. Neither notes payable, mortgage bonds, nor common stock will rise spontaneously with sales—higher sales do not automatically trigger increases in these items.

We can construct first approximation pro forma financial statements for December 31, 1991, proceeding as follows:

Step 1.   In Table 23-3, Column 2, we multiply those income statement and balance sheet items that vary directly with sales by (1 + Sales growth rate) = 1.50. An item such as interest expense that does not vary directly with sales is simply moved forward from Column 1 to Column 2 to develop the first approximation forecast. Therefore, we insert figures for interest expense, dividends, notes payable, mortgage bonds, and common stock from 1990. Several of these accounts will have to be changed later in the analysis.

Step 2.   We next add the addition to retained earnings estimated for 1991 to the December 31, 1990, balance sheet figure to obtain the December 31, 1991, projected retained earnings. Ignoring any additional interest expense, Century would have a net income of $38 million in 1991. If the firm does not increase its dividend in 1991, the total dividend payment would be $8 million, leaving $38 million − $8 million = $30 million of new retained earnings.[4] Thus, the 1991 balance sheet account retained earnings would be $48 million + $30 million = $78 million.

Step 3.   Next, we sum the balance sheet asset accounts, obtaining a projected total assets figure of $518 million, and we also sum the projected liability and equity items to obtain $408 million. At this point, the balance sheet does not balance: Assets total $518 million, but only $408 million of liabilities and equity is projected. Thus, we have a shortfall, or external funds needed (EFN), of $110 million, which will presumably be raised by bank borrowings and/or by selling securities. (For simplicity, we disregard depreciation by assuming that cash flows generated by depreciation are netted out against fixed asset additions.)

Financing the External Requirements

Century could use short-term notes, mortgage bonds, common stock, or a combination of these securities to make up the $110 million shortfall. Ordinarily, Century would base this choice on its target capital structure, the relative costs of different

---

[4]Normally, companies attempt to "grow" their dividends at a relatively stable rate, and they also have a long-run target payout ratio in mind which is reasonably consistent with the targeted growth rate. However, dividend policy is invariably reviewed as a part of the financial planning process. In its planning, Century begins by holding constant the dollar dividend per share at the earlier year level, but it may modify this figure at a later stage in the process. An alternative first approximation would be to assume the 1990 payout ratio ($8/$24 = 0.33) will be maintained, in which case dividends would be projected at 0.33($38) = $12.7 million as a first approximation.

types of securities, maturity matching considerations, and so on. However, in Century's case, the company's mortgage bond indenture requires it to keep total debt at or below 50 percent of total assets, and also to keep the current ratio at a level of 2.5 or greater. These provisions restrict the financing choices as follows (in millions of dollars):

1.   Restriction on additional debt:

Maximum debt permitted = (0.5)(Total assets) = (0.5)($518) = $259
Subtract debt already projected for December 31, 1991:

		Current liabilities	$108	
		Mortgage bonds	72	$180
Maximum additional debt				$ 79

2.   Restriction on additional current liabilities to maintain a 2.5× current ratio:

$$\frac{\text{Projected current assets}}{\text{Maximum current liabilities}} = 2.5$$

$$\text{Maximum current liabilities} = \frac{\text{Projected current assets}}{2.5} = \$293/2.5 = \qquad \$117$$

Subtract current liabilities already projected   108
Maximum additional current liabilities $ 9

3.   Common equity requirements:

Total external funds needed $110
Maximum additional debt permitted   79
Common equity funds required $ 31

From Table 23-3, we saw that, as a first approximation, Century needs a total of $110 million from external sources. Its bond indenture limits new debt to $79 million, and of that amount, only $9 million can be short-term debt. Thus, assuming that Century wants to make maximum use of debt financing, it must plan to sell common stock in the amount of $31 million, in addition to its debt financing, to cover its financial requirements.

However, the use of external funds will change the first approximation income statement for 1991 as set forth in Column 2 of Table 23-3. First, the issuance of new debt will increase the firm's 1991 interest expense. Second, the sale of new common stock will increase total dividend payments, assuming no cuts in per-share dividends. Century is forecasting that new short-term debt will cost 10 percent, and that new long-term debt will cost 12 percent. Additionally, Century has 10 million shares of common stock outstanding, and it currently sells for $25 per share. Thus, Century's shareholders received $8 million/10 million = $0.80 of dividends per share in 1990, and management has stated that the dividend is not to be cut.

If Century financed in 1991 as outlined above, and if the external financing occurred on January 1, 1991, then its income statement expenses and dividends would increase by the following amounts:

Table 23-4	1991 Pro Forma Statement of Cash Flows, and Selected Ratios (Millions of Dollars)

Cash Flow from Operating Activities

Net income[a]	$33	

Additions (sources of cash):

Increase in accounts payable	$20	
Increase in accruals	13	

Subtractions (uses of cash):

Increase in receivables	(43)	
Increase in inventories	(50)	
Net cash flow from operations		($27)

Cash Flow from Investing Activities

Increase in net fixed assets		($75)

Cash Flow from Financing Activities

Increase in notes payable	$ 9	
Sale of bonds	70	
Sale of common stock	37	
Common dividends paid	(9)	
Net cash flow from financing		$107
Increase (decrease) in cash		$ 5
Cash at beginning of year		10
Cash at end of year		$ 15

Key Ratios Projected for December 31, 1991[b]

1.	Current ratio	2.5×
2.	Total debt/total assets	50%
3.	Rate of return on equity	13.0%

[a]Normally, funds from operations would include depreciation. Here we have assumed that depreciation is reinvested in fixed assets; that is, depreciation is netted out against fixed asset additions.

[b]Other ratios could also be calculated and analyzed, and a Du Pont chart could be developed.

1. Additional interest requirements:

$$\text{Short-term interest} = 0.10(\$9,000,000) \qquad = \$ \ 900,000$$
$$\text{Long-term interest} = 0.12(\$70,000,000) \qquad = \underline{\ 8,400,000}$$
$$\text{Total additional interest} \qquad\qquad \$9,300,000 \approx \$9 \text{ million}$$

2. Additional dividend requirements:

$$\text{New shares} = \$31,000,000/\$25 \text{ per share} = 1,240,000.$$
$$\text{Additional dividends} = \$0.80(1,240,000) = \$992,000 \approx \$1 \text{ million}.$$

The projected 1991 income statement and balance sheet, including financing feedback effects, are shown in Column 3 of Table 23-3. We see that Century is still $6 million short in meeting its financing requirements, because interest and dividends associated with external financing reduced the addition to retained earnings from $30 million, before feedback effects were considered, to $24 million. Century's managers could repeat the preceding process with an additional $6 million of external financing. In this case, the additional $6 million would have to be raised as equity, because Century has already issued debt up to its limit. The addition to retained earnings would be further reduced by additional dividend requirements, but the balance sheet would be closer to being in balance. Successive iterations would continue to reduce the discrepancy. If the budget process were computerized, as would be true for most firms, an exact solution could be reached very rapidly. (We discuss this point later in the chapter.) Otherwise, firms would go through two or three iterations and then stop. At this point, the projected statements would generally be very close to being in balance, and they would certainly be close enough for practical purposes, given the uncertainty inherent in the projections themselves.

For Century, the additional $6 million of new equity would have a minimal feedback effect. Thus, we could use Column 3 of Table 23-3, with $187 million in common stock rather than the $181 million shown, as the projected 1991 income statement and balance sheet. These statements could then be used (1) to create the pro forma statement of cash flows and (2) to check Century's critical financial ratios. This is done in Table 23-4.

Self-Test Questions

Explain the difference between spontaneous and nonspontaneous accounts. Give several examples of each.

Briefly describe how the percentage of sales method can be used to make a first pass forecast of a firm's pro forma financial statements.

What are *financing feedback effects?* What impact do they have on forecasted financial statements?

FACTORS INFLUENCING EXTERNAL FINANCING REQUIREMENTS

The five factors which have the greatest influence on a firm's external funding requirements are (1) its projected sales growth, (2) its initial fixed asset utilization rate, or excess capacity situation, (3) its capital intensity, (4) its profit margin, and (5) its dividend policy. We discuss these factors in this section, but first we present a simple formula for the percentage of sales method that holds when all assets and spontaneous liabilities vary in exact proportion to changes in sales and financing feedbacks are ignored. Although the forecast of capital requirements is normally made by constructing pro forma financial statements as described earlier, this formula is useful to highlight the relationship between sales growth and financial requirements, and to approximate the external funding requirement:

$$
\begin{array}{ccccc}
\text{External} & & \text{Required} & \text{Spontaneous} & \text{Increase in} \\
\text{funds} & = & \text{increase} & - \quad \text{increase in} & - \quad \text{retained} \\
\text{needed} & & \text{in assets} & \text{liabilities} & \text{earnings}
\end{array}
\qquad \textbf{(23-1)}
$$

$$
\text{EFN} = (A/S)\Delta S - (L/S)\Delta S - MS_1(1 - d).
$$

Here

EFN = external funds needed.

A/S = assets that must increase if sales are to increase as a percentage of sales, or required dollar increase in assets per \$1 increase in sales. A/S = \$345/\$500 = 69%, or 0.69, for Century Electronics.

L/S = liabilities that increase spontaneously with sales as a percentage of sales, or spontaneously generated financing per \$1 increase in sales. L/S = (\$40 + \$25)/\$500 = 13.%, or 0.13, for Century.

S_1 = total sales projected for next year. Note that S_0 designates last year's sales. S_1 = \$750 million for Century.

ΔS = change in sales = $S_1 - S_0$ = \$750 million − \$500 million = \$250 million for Century.

M = profit margin, or rate of profits per \$1 of sales. M = \$24/\$500 = 4.8%, or 0.048, for Century.

d = percentage of earnings paid out in dividends, or the dividend payout ratio; d = \$8/\$24 = 33%, or 0.33, for Century. Notice that 1 − d = 1.0 − 0.33 = 0.67, or 67 percent, is the percentage of earnings that Century retains, or its *retention ratio.*

Inserting values for Century into Equation 23-1, we find the approximate external funds needed to be \$116 million:

$$
\begin{aligned}
\text{EFN} &= 0.69(\Delta S) - 0.13(\Delta S) - 0.048(S_1)(1 - 0.33) \\
&= 0.69(\$250 \text{ million}) - 0.13(\$250 \text{ million}) - 0.048(\$750 \text{ million})(0.67) \\
&= \$173 \text{ million} - \$33 \text{ million} - \$24 \text{ million} \\
&= \$116 \text{ million}.
\end{aligned}
$$

To increase sales by \$250 million, Century must increase assets by \$173 million. The \$173 million of new assets must be financed in some manner. Of the total, \$33 million will come from a spontaneous increase in liabilities, while another \$24 million will be obtained from retained earnings. The remaining \$116 million must be

Figure 23-2 Relationship between Growth in Sales and Financial Requirements, Assuming $S_0 = \$500$ Million (Millions of Dollars)

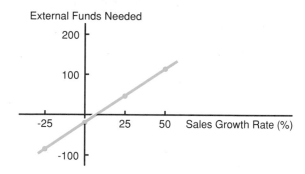

Growth Rate in Sales (1)	Increase (Decrease) in Sales, ΔS (2)	Forecasted Sales, S_1 (3)	External Funds Needed (4)
50%	$250	$750	$116
25	125	625	50
0	0	500	−16
−25	−125	375	−82

Explanation of Columns:

Col. 1: Growth rate in sales, g.

Col. 2: Increase (decrease) in sales: $\Delta S = g(S_0) = g(\$500)$.

Col. 3: Forecasted sales: $S_1 = S_0 + g(S_0) = S_0(1 + g) = \$500(1 + g)$.

Col. 4: External funds needed: EFN $= 0.69(\Delta S) - 0.13(\Delta S) - 0.032(S_1)$.

---

raised from external sources. This value is close to the $110 million external funding requirement developed earlier in Column 2 of Table 23-3[5].

Sales Growth Rate

The faster Century's sales grow, the greater will be its need for external financing. We can use Figure 23-2, which is a plot of Equation 23-1, to roughly quantify the relationship. At very low growth rates, Century will need no external financing; indeed, all required funds can be obtained by spontaneous increases in current liability accounts plus retained earnings, and the company may even generate surplus capital. However, if the company's projected sales growth rate increases beyond a certain level, then it must seek outside financing, and the faster the projected growth

---

[5]The difference reflects assumptions about interest expense and the amount of retained earnings.

rate, the greater will be its outside capital requirements. The reasoning here is as follows:

1.   Increases in sales normally require increases in assets. If sales are not projected to grow, no new assets will be needed.

2.   Any projected asset increases require financing of some type. Some of the required financing will come from spontaneously generated liabilities. Also, assuming a positive profit margin and a payout ratio of less than 100 percent, the firm will generate some retained earnings.

3.   If the sales growth rate is low enough, spontaneously generated funds plus retained earnings will be sufficient to support the asset growth. However, if the sales growth rate exceeds a certain level, then external funds will be needed. If management foresees difficulties in raising this capital—perhaps because it does not want to sell additional stock—then the feasibility of the firm's expansion plans may have to be reconsidered. We discuss this in detail in the next major section.

Capacity Utilization

In determining Century's external financing requirements for 1991, we assumed that its fixed assets were being fully utilized.[6] Thus, any significant increase in sales would require an increase in fixed assets. What would be the effect if Century had been operating its fixed assets at only 70 percent of capacity? Under this condition, fixed assets could remain constant until sales reach that level at which fixed assets were being fully utilized, defined as *capacity sales,* which is calculated as follows:

$$\text{Utilization rate (\% of capacity)} = \frac{\text{Actual sales}}{\text{Capacity sales}},$$

so

$$\text{Capacity sales} = \frac{\text{Actual sales}}{\text{Utilization rate}}.$$

If Century had been operating in 1990 at 70 percent of capacity, then its capacity sales *without any new fixed assets* would be $714 million:

$$\text{Capacity sales} = \frac{\$500 \text{ million}}{0.70} = \$714 \text{ million}.$$

Thus, Century could have increased sales to $714 million with no increase in fixed assets, and to reach its projected sales of $750 million in 1991, it would require only enough new fixed assets to support the sales increase from $714 million to $750 million, or $36 million of new sales.

---

[6]We also assumed that depreciation-generated funds were netted out against fixed asset additions, and that no excess stocks of current assets existed.

Operating at less than full capacity can be incorporated into the pro forma balance sheet as follows:

1.   Calculate the *fixed assets sales growth rate* based on capacity sales rather than on actual sales. If Century had been operating at 70 percent of capacity in 1990, then its capacity sales would be $714 million, and its fixed assets sales growth rate would be ($750 − $714)/$714 = 0.0504.

2.   Use the new sales growth rate to forecast the 1991 level of fixed assets by multiplying the 1990 fixed assets amount by (1 + New sales growth rate). For Century, the 1991 level would be $150 million(1.0504) ≈ $158 million, rather than the $225 million originally projected. Thus, operating at only 70 percent of capacity in 1990 reduces 1991 projected net fixed assets by $225 million − $158 million = $67 million. This decrease in projected assets, in turn, reduces external funding requirements by a like amount. Obviously, operating at less than full capacity has a significant impact on the need for external funds. In terms of Equation 23-1, operating at less than full capacity reduces A/S, the coefficient of the first ΔS term, hence lowers the EFN.

Capital Intensity

The amount of assets required per dollar of sales (total assets/sales) is often called the *capital intensity ratio.* Notice that the capital intensity ratio is the reciprocal of the total asset turnover ratio, and it is also the coefficient of the first term in Equation 23-1. This factor has a major effect on capital requirements to support any level of sales growth. If the capital intensity ratio is low, then sales can grow rapidly without much outside capital. However, if the firm is capital intensive, then even a small growth in output will require a great deal of outside capital.

If a company anticipates that it might have trouble financing its projected capital requirements, then it might, as a part of its strategic planning, consider a reduction in its capital intensity ratio. For example, when faced with a funds shortage in the early 1980s, several U.S. automakers began a policy of purchasing rather than manufacturing certain parts, thus eliminating the need for facilities to manufacture those parts.

Profitability

Profitability is also an important determinant of external funds requirements—the higher the profit margin, the lower the external financing requirement, other factors held constant. Century's profit margin in 1990 was 4.8 percent. Now suppose its profit margin increased to 10 percent through higher sales prices and better expense control. This would increase net income, hence retained earnings (assuming a constant payout), which in turn would decrease the requirement for external funds. In terms of Equation 23-1, a higher profit margin increases the addition to retained earnings, the third term in the equation, hence reduces the EFN.

Because of the relationship between profit margin and external capital requirements, some very rapidly growing firms do not need much external capital. For example, for many years Xerox grew rapidly with very little borrowing or stock sales. However, as the company lost patent protection, and as competition intensified in the copier industry, Xerox's profit margin declined, its needs for external capital rose, and it began to borrow from banks and other sources. IBM and a number of other companies have had similar experiences.

Dividend Policy

Dividend policy also affects external capital requirements, so if Century foresees difficulties in raising capital, it might want to consider a reduction in its dividend payout ratio. However, before making this decision, management should consider the possible effect of a dividend cut on stock price.[7] A dividend cut would also affect the third term in Equation 23-1 by increasing retained earnings.

Before concluding this section, we should note again that, while Equation 23-1 is useful for seeing how the factors listed in this section affect the EFN, the procedures outlined in Table 23-3 are far more useful for making actual forecasts. The equation can be used in very simple situations, but when the various asset and liability accounts do not move exactly with sales, the financial statement method is far better.

Self-Test Questions

Discuss how each of the following factors influences a firm's external funding requirement:
1. Sales growth rate
2. Capacity utilization
3. Capital intensity
4. Profitability
5. Dividend policy

What is the EFN equation? Is it generally used in practice?

SUSTAINABLE GROWTH

We have often mentioned that companies other than start-up firms generally try to avoid issuing new common stock for two reasons: (1) high issuance costs must be incurred to sell common stock, but no such costs are incurred on retained earnings, and (2) information asymmetries lead investors to view stock issues as bad news, and stock prices decline when a new stock issue is announced. These two factors combine to make equity raised by selling stock much more costly than equity obtained by retaining earnings. Therefore, financial planners are often asked this ques-

---

[7]Dividend policy was discussed in detail in Chapter 14. Note that if management believes that dividends are irrelevant, Century could adopt a residual dividend policy and use retained earnings to the maximum extent to meet equity financing requirements. However, if dividends are considered to be relevant, then changes in dividend policy must be assumed to affect stock prices, and the tradeoff between retained earnings financing and new stock financing becomes more complex.

tion: How fast can the firm grow without having to issue new common stock, that is, what is the firm's *sustainable growth rate?* If we make some assumptions, a relatively simple model can be used to answer that question.[8]

We begin by defining these key terms:

M = projected profit margin, or net income divided by sales.

b = target retention rate = 1 − Target payout ratio.

D/E = target debt-to-equity ratio.

A/S = ratio of total assets to sales, the reciprocal of the total asset turnover ratio.

If the firm is operating at full capacity, and if it is currently at its target capital structure, then the sustainable growth rate, g^*, can be found using this equation:

$$g^* = \frac{M(b)(1 + D/E)}{A/S - M(b)(1 + D/E)}. \qquad (23\text{-}2)$$

To illustrate, consider the situation facing Century Electronics Corporation. From the data in Table 23-3 presented earlier in the chapter, Century's 1990 profit margin is Net income/Net sales = $24 million/$500 million = 4.8%, its retention rate is Addition to retained earnings/Net income = $16 million/$24 million = 0.67, its debt-to-equity ratio is Total debt/Total equity = $147 million/$198 million = 0.74, and its assets-to-sales ratio is Total assets/Net sales = $345 million/$500 million = 0.69. If we assume (1) that these values will hold for 1991, (2) that Century's current book value structure is also its target market value target, (3) that depreciation cash flows are being used to replace worn-out assets, and (4) that financing feedback effects are small and hence can be ignored, then the firm's sustainable growth rate is 8.8 percent:

$$g^* = \frac{4.8\%(0.67)(1 + 0.74)}{0.69 - (0.048)(0.67)(1 + 0.74)}$$

$$= \frac{5.60\%}{0.634} = 8.8\%.$$

Thus, Century's sales can grow as much as 8.8 percent in 1991 without requiring the firm to sell new common stock or to increase its use of financial leverage. If you reconstruct Table 23-3 using a 1991 sales forecast of $500(1 + g^*) = $500(1.088) = $544 million, then you would find that Century's 1991 addition to retained earnings would equal $17.5 million and its external funds needed (including spontaneous liabilities) would total $12.9 million. Further, since Century's retained earnings will support $0.74 of additional debt per dollar of retentions, Century's 1991 addition to retained earnings would support 0.74($17.5) ≈ $12.9 million in new debt (including spontaneous liabilities). Thus, all the external funding requirements could be met with debt, and Century would not be forced to issue new common stock.

---

[8]For a more complete discussion of sustainable growth, see Robert C. Higgins, "How Much Growth Can a Firm Afford?" *Financial Management,* Fall 1977, 7–16.

An actual sales growth rate that differs from the sustainable rate has important implications for the firm, and financial managers must actively develop growth targets and financial objectives that are mutually consistent. If the sales growth rate is less than the sustainable rate, then the firm will generate more than enough capital to meet its investment needs, and its financial plans must call for an increase in cash and marketable securities, a reduction in the amount of debt outstanding, a merger program, stock repurchases, or an increase in dividends. Conversely, if the sales growth rate is greater than g^*, then new equity must be sold, financial leverage must be increased, the payout ratio must be reduced, or the growth rate itself must be scaled back.

In Century's actual case, with a forecasted sales growth rate of 50 percent, the firm was forced to plan a new equity issue, although it planned to first use up its available excess debt capacity. Century's managers made a conscious decision to expand beyond its sustainable growth rate in order to gain market share that it could not otherwise capture. However, Century's managers were well aware of its 8.8 percent sustainable growth rate, and of the implications of expanding beyond that rate.

Self-Test Questions

What is meant by sustainable growth?

What are the financial implications of a sales growth rate that exceeds the firm's sustainable rate? Of a growth rate less than the sustainable rate?

PROBLEMS WITH THE PERCENTAGE OF SALES APPROACH

For the percentage of sales method to produce accurate forecasts, each spontaneous asset and liability item must increase in the same proportion as sales. In graph form, this assumption suggests the existence of the type of relationship indicated in Panel a of Figure 23-3, where we graph inventory versus sales. Here the plotted relationship is linear and passes through the origin. Thus, if the company grows and sales double, from $200 million to $400 million, inventories will also double, from $100 million to $200 million.

The assumption of constant ratios is appropriate at times, but there are times when it is incorrect. Three such conditions are described in the following sections.

Economies of Scale

There are economies of scale in the use of many kinds of assets, and when they occur, the ratios are likely to change over time as the size of the firm increases. Often, for example, firms need to maintain base stocks of different inventory items, even if sales levels are quite low. Then, as sales expand, inventories tend to grow less rapidly than sales, so the ratio of inventory to sales declines. This situation is depicted in Panel b of Figure 23-3. Here we see that the inventory/sales ratio is 1.50, or 150 percent, when sales are $200 million, but the ratio declines to 1.00 when sales climb to $400 million.

Figure 23-3   Four Possible Ratio Relationships (Millions of Dollars)

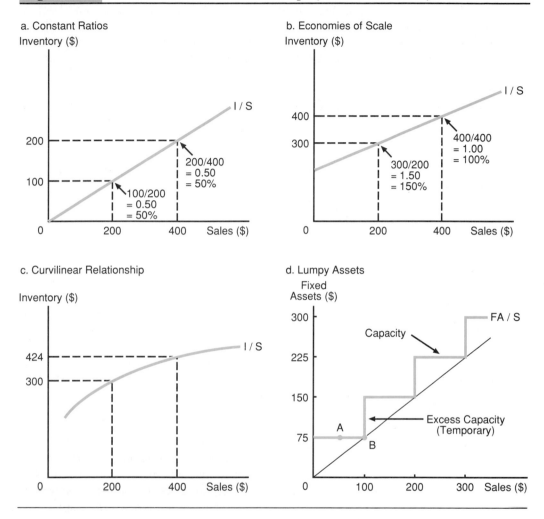

a. Constant Ratios

b. Economies of Scale

c. Curvilinear Relationship

d. Lumpy Assets

Panel b still shows a linear relationship between inventories and sales, but even this is not necessarily the case. Indeed, as we saw in Chapter 21, if a firm employs the EOQ model to establish inventory levels, then inventory will rise with the square root of sales. This type of situation is illustrated in Panel c.

Lumpy Assets

In many industries, technological considerations dictate that if a firm is to be competitive, it must add fixed assets in large, discrete units. For example, in the paper industry, there are strong economies of scale in basic paper mill equipment, so when paper companies expand capacity, they must do so in large increments. This type of situation is depicted in Panel d of Figure 23-3. Here we assume that the plant with the minimum feasible size has a cost of $75 million, and that such a plant can produce enough output to attain a sales level of $100 million per year. If the firm is to be competitive, it simply must have at least $75 million of fixed assets.

This situation has a major effect on the fixed assets/sales (FA/S) ratio at different sales levels, and consequently on financial requirements. At Point A in Panel d, which represents a sales level of $50 million, the fixed assets are $75 million, so the ratio FA/S = $75/$50 = 1.5. However, sales can expand by $50 million, out to $100 million, with no required increase in fixed assets. At that point, represented by Point B, the ratio FA/S = $75/$100 = 0.75. If the firm is operating at full capacity, even a small increase in sales would require the firm to double its plant capacity, so a small projected sales increase would bring with it very large financial requirements.[9]

Cyclical/Seasonal Changes

All of the panels in Figure 23-3 focus on target, or projected, relationships between sales and assets. Actual sales, however, are often different from projected sales, and the actual asset/sales ratio for a given period might be quite different from the optimal ratio. To illustrate, the firm depicted in Panel b might, when its sales are at $200 million and its inventories at $300 million, predict a sales expansion to $400 million and then increase its inventories to $400 million in anticipation of the sales expansion. But suppose a seasonal or cyclical downturn holds sales to only $300 million. In this case, actual inventories would be $400 million versus only about $350 million needed to support sales of $300 million. In this situation, if the firm were forecasting its financial requirements, it should recognize that sales can be expanded by $100 million with no increase in inventories, but that any sales expansion beyond $100 million would require additional financing to build inventories.

If any of the ratios are subject to any of the conditions noted here — and generally many of them are — then the simple percentage of sales method of forecasting financial requirements should not be used. Rather, other techniques must be used to forecast asset and liability item levels and the resulting external financing requirements. Some of these methods are discussed in the following section.

---

[9]Several other points should be noted about Panel d of Figure 23-3. First, if the firm is operating at a sales level of $100 million or less, then any expansion that calls for a sales increase above $100 million would require a *doubling* of fixed assets. Much smaller percentage increases would be involved if the firm were large enough to be operating a number of plants. Second, firms generally go to multiple shifts and take other actions to minimize the need for new fixed asset capacity as they approach Point B. However, these efforts can go only so far, and eventually a fixed asset expansion is required. Third, firms often make arrangements to purchase excess capacity output from other firms in their industry, or to sell excess capacity to other firms. For example, the situation in the electric utility industry is very much like that depicted in Panel d. As a result, when Tampa Electric recently brought a new base load coal-fired plant on line, it had arranged ahead of time to sell half of the plant's output to Florida Power & Light, with the share purchased by FP&L decreasing each year until Tampa Electric's own demand required all of the plant's output.

Self-Test Questions

What is the difference between a proportional relationship between sales and inventory level and a linear relationship? (*Hint:* Use graphs to explain the difference.)

Explain how the following factors can lead to forecasting errors if the percentage of sales method is used:

1. Economies of scale
2. Lumpy assets
3. Cyclical/seasonal changes

OTHER FORECASTING METHODS

In this section, we discuss four other forecasting methods that are commonly used in practice: (1) simple linear regression, (2) curvilinear regression, (3) multiple regression, and (4) miscellaneous other methods.

Simple Linear Regression

Simple linear regression is often used to estimate asset requirements. For example, Century's selling and administrative expenses, receivables, inventories, and net fixed assets over the last 10 years are given in the lower section of Figure 23-4 and plotted as scatter diagrams against sales in the upper section. Estimated regression equations as found using *Lotus 1-2-3* are also shown in the figure. For example, the estimated relationship between inventories and sales (in millions of dollars) is

$$\text{Inventories} = \$22.8 + 0.16(\text{Sales}).$$

The plotted points are quite close to the regression line. In fact, the correlation coefficient between inventories and sales is 0.98, indicating that there is a very strong linear relationship between these two variables. Why might this be the case for Century? According to the EOQ model, inventories should increase with the square root of sales, which would cause the scatter diagram to be nonlinear—the true regression line would rise at a decreasing rate. However, Century has greatly expanded its product line over the last decade, and the base stocks associated with these new products have caused inventories to rise. Also, inflation has had a similar impact on both sales and inventory levels. These three influences—economies of scale in existing products, base stocks for new products, and inflationary effects—are offsetting, resulting in the observed linear relationship between inventories and sales.

We can use the estimated relationship between inventories and sales to forecast 1991 inventory levels. Since 1991 sales are projected at $750 million, 1991 inventories should be $142.8 million:

$$\text{Inventories} = \$22.8 + 0.16(\$750) = \$142.8 \text{ million}.$$

This is $7.2 million less than our earlier forecast based on the percentage of sales method. The difference occurs because the percentage of sales method assumes that

Figure 23-4   Century Electronics Corporation: Simple Linear Regression Models (Millions of Dollars)

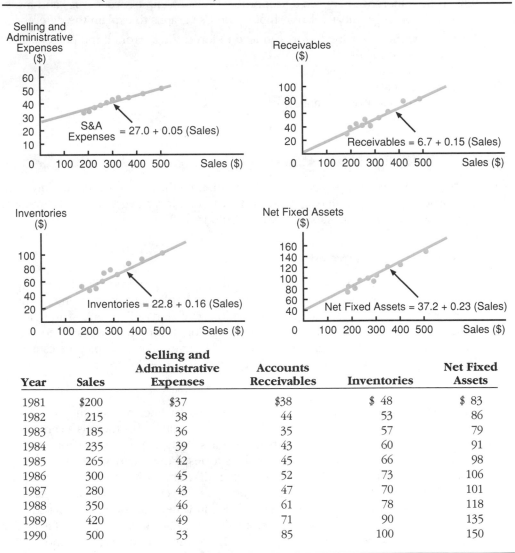

Year	Sales	Selling and Administrative Expenses	Accounts Receivables	Inventories	Net Fixed Assets
1981	$200	$37	$38	$ 48	$ 83
1982	215	38	44	53	86
1983	185	36	35	57	79
1984	235	39	43	60	91
1985	265	42	45	66	98
1986	300	45	52	73	106
1987	280	43	47	70	101
1988	350	46	61	78	118
1989	420	49	71	90	135
1990	500	53	85	100	150

the ratio of inventories to sales remains constant, but the ratio actually declines because the inventories regression line in Figure 23-4 does not pass through the origin.

The other panels in Figure 23-4 illustrate the use of the regression method for forecasting the relationships between sales and (1) selling and administrative expenses, (2) receivables, and (3) net fixed assets. We could insert these specific forecasts into Table 23-3, Columns 2 and 3, and we will use these relationships later in the chapter, when we develop a computerized forecasting model for Century.

Curvilinear Regression

Simple linear regression as discussed previously is based on the assumption that a straight-line relationship exists. Although linear relationships between financial statement variables and sales do exist frequently, this is not a universal rule. For example, if the EOQ relationship had dominated the inventory-sales relationship, the plot of inventory versus sales would have been a concave curve such as the one depicted in Panel c of Figure 23-3 rather than linear. If we forecasted the inventory level needed to support sales of $400 million using the linear relationship, our forecast would be too high.

Firms have in their data bases historical data on their own company by divisions, by product lines, and by individual products. They also have or can easily obtain certain types of data for other firms in their industry. These data can be analyzed using computer programs based on advanced statistical techniques (1) to help determine whether a relationship is curvilinear or linear and (2) to estimate the curvilinear relationship should one exist. Once the best-fit relationship has been estimated, it can be used to project future levels of items such as inventories, given the sales forecast.[10]

Multiple Regression

If the relationship between a variable such as inventories and sales is such that the individual points are widely scattered about the regression line, hence the correlation coefficient is low, then there is a good chance that other factors, in addition to sales, affect the level of that variable. For example, inventory levels might be a function of both sales level and number of different products sold. In this case, we would obtain the best forecast for inventory level by using multiple regression techniques, where inventories would be regressed against both sales and the number of products sold. Then, the projected inventories would be based on forecasts of number of products in addition to total sales. Most computer installations now have complete regression software packages, making it easy to apply multiple and curvilinear regression techniques. One can even do multiple regression analysis with up to 12 independent variables on a PC with *Lotus 1-2 3*.

Other Forecasting Techniques

A final approach to financial forecasting is to develop a specific model for each variable. For example, inventories could be forecasted by using the EOQ model; target cash balances could be forecasted by using the Baumol model; receivables could be forecasted by using the payments pattern approach; and fixed assets could be forecasted on the basis of the firm's capital budget and depreciation schedule. Of course, projected sales demand is still the driving force behind each of these

---

[10]Often, a plot of the data will suggest a nonlinear relationship. The data — inventories in this case — can then be converted to logarithms if it appears that the regression line slopes down, or raised to a power if the slope seems to be increasing. We often use the graphics capabilities of *Lotus 1-2-3* for such analyses. However, for an important forecast such as demand for the output of a power plant, we would use more powerful statistical procedures.

specific forecasts, but given the sales forecast, each item could be analyzed by its own unique forecasting method. Similarly, on the income statement side, a firm could forecast its cost of goods sold by conducting an engineering/production analysis of each major product. Specific item analysis is likely to provide the most accurate forecasts.

Comparison of Forecasting Methods

The percentage of sales method assumes that different financial statement items vary directly (proportionally) with sales. It is the easiest method, but often its forecasts are of questionable accuracy. Regression analysis differs from the percentage of sales method in that regression does not assume constant ratios. This technique can improve on the forecasts for many financial statement items. Note too that curvilinear and multiple regression techniques can provide especially accurate forecasts when relationships (1) are not linear or (2) depend on other variables in addition to sales. Finally, specific item forecasting that utilizes various decision models can be used.

As we move down the list of forecasting methods, accuracy increases, but so do costs. The need to employ more complicated, and consequently more costly, methods varies from situation to situation. As in all applications, the costs of using more refined techniques must be balanced against the benefits of increased accuracy.

Self-Test Questions

Describe each of the following forecasting methods and the circumstances under which it might be used:
1. Simple linear regression
2. Curvilinear regression
3. Multiple regression
4. Specific item forecasting

In what situations might the percentage of sales method be used? When might specific item forecasting be more appropriate?

COMPUTERIZED FINANCIAL PLANNING MODELS

Although the types of financial forecasting described thus far in the chapter can be done with a hand calculator, even the smallest firms now have at least a PC and can employ some type of computerized financial planning model. Such models can be programmed to show the effects of different sales levels, different relationships between sales and operating assets, and even different assumptions about sales prices and input costs (labor, materials, and so forth). Plans are then made regarding how projected financial requirements are to be met—through short-term bank loans, by selling long-term bonds, or by selling new common or preferred stock. Pro forma balance sheets and income statements are generated under the different financing plans, and earnings per share are projected, along with such risk and profitability

Table 23-5   Variable-to-Sales Relationships (Millions of Dollars)

Variable	Relationship to Sales
Cost of goods sold	0.80(Sales)
Administrative and selling expenses	$27.0 + 0.05(Sales)
Cash	0.02(Sales)
Receivables	$6.7 + 0.15(Sales)
Inventories	$22.8 + 0.16(Sales)
Net fixed assets	$37.2 + 0.23(Sales)
Accounts payable	0.08(Sales)
Accrued wages and taxes	0.05(Sales)

measures as the current ratio, the debt/assets ratio, the times-interest-earned ratio, return on assets, and return on equity.

Depending on how these projections look, management may need to modify the initial plan. For example, management might conclude that the projected growth rate must be cut because external capital requirements exceed the firm's ability to raise money. Or management could decide to reduce dividends and thus generate more funds internally. Alternatively, the company might investigate production processes that require fewer fixed assets, or it might consider the possibility of buying rather than manufacturing certain components, thus eliminating some raw materials and work-in-process inventories, as well as certain manufacturing facilities.

The Basic Forecasting Model

To illustrate how computerized forecasting models work, we have constructed a financial statement forecasting model for Century Electronics Corporation using *Lotus 1-2-3*. In the model, we defined the key variables' relationships with sales as shown in Table 23-5; these relationships were developed from historical data using linear regression analysis. Further, we assumed (1) that sales will grow at an annual rate of 50 percent in 1991, at a 25 percent rate in both 1992 and 1993, and at a 15 percent rate in 1994 and 1995; (2) that dividends per share will be increased by 10 percent per year over the next five years; (3) that the stock price will grow at an annual rate of 20 percent during the next five years; (4) that the state-plus-federal income tax rate will be 40 percent for the next five years; (5) that the current ratio cannot fall below 2.5; (6) that the debt ratio cannot exceed 50 percent; (7) that all new financing will occur on January 1 of the year in which it is needed; (8) that new short-term debt will cost 10 percent and new long-term debt will cost 12 percent; and (9) that flotation costs are insignificant and thus can be ignored.

The *Lotus* model automatically performs the financing feedback iterations and generates the 5-year pro forma financial statements along with selected ratios and other information. In effect, it generates a series of forecasted income statements and balance sheets similar to the one for 1991 presented back in Table 23-3. Section a of Table 23-6 presents the following selected output from the model under the

Table 23-6	Century Electronics Corporation: Selected Model Output

	1991	1992	1993	1994	1995
a. Base Case					
EPS	$4.12	$5.50	$7.29	$8.84	$10.66
TIE	5.45×	5.97×	6.40×	7.65×	9.38×
ROA	8.61%	9.59%	10.42%	11.12%	11.79%
ROE	17.22%	19.18%	20.84%	20.73%	20.49%
EFN[a]	$74	$34	$36	($4)	($10)
b. Low-Growth Case					
EPS	$3.50	$4.53	$5.79	$6.73	$7.44
TIE	5.83×	6.20×	6.71×	8.30×	9.31×
ROA	8.14%	8.99%	9.80%	10.45%	10.92%
ROE	15.22%	17.03%	18.49%	18.24%	16.90%
EFN[a]	$38	$20	$20	($15)	($22)

[a]In millions of dollars. Note that, for 1994 and 1995, the external funds needed are negative, indicating that operations are generating excess funds.

assumptions set forth: (1) forecasted earnings per share (EPS), (2) the times-interest-earned (TIE) ratio, (3) the return on assets (ROA), (4) the rate of return on equity (ROE), and (5) the external funds needed (EFN) in each year from 1991 through 1995. We could have displayed the full set of statements as well as more financial ratios, but Table 23-6 is sufficient to show that, under the preceding assumptions, Century's financial condition will be strong and will actually improve over the next five years. However, to support the base case growth in sales, Century must raise a total of over $144 million through external funding over the next three years.

The forecasted situation could look good or bad. In this case, it looks almost too good. Rapidly rising earnings could attract new entry into Century's markets, and this new competition could drive down prices, profit margins, EPSs, and ROEs. Thus, Century might want to reexamine its basic assumptions and to rerun the model using more conservative forecasts as discussed next.

Changing Assumptions and Policies

The most important benefit of computerized financial modeling is that it permits financial managers to see the effects of changing both basic assumptions and specific financial policies. For example, what would Century's financial condition be if competition lowered its growth rate to 30 percent for 1991, to 20 percent for both 1992 and 1993, and then to 10 percent for 1994 and 1995? Section b of Table 23-8 contains selected output data based on these lower sales growth estimates. All other assumptions and financial policies remain as defined by the base case. Here we see that Century's general financial condition and profitability still improve over the next five years, but not as dramatically as in the base case. However, external funding requirements are significantly reduced, to only $78 million over the next three years versus $144 million in the base case.

The pro forma financial statements could be rerun over and over, each time changing one or more assumptions regarding sales growth rates, cost relationships, profit margins, future interest rates, and so on. We could also rerun the model with changes in financial policies, such as increasing or decreasing the dividend growth rate, changing the external financing mix, and so on. Thus, the results of differing assumptions and financial policies could be compared.[11] It is important, however, to note (1) that the financial manager still must interpret the results of alternative financial policies and (2) that the analysis could encompass virtually hundreds of combinations of assumptions and policies, and thus we could generate hundreds of different sets of pro forma financial statements.

One way to reduce the number of different possible scenarios is to perform a sensitivity analysis to determine the effect of each assumption — those assumptions that have little effect on the key financial integrity and profitability ratios need not be changed from their base case levels. Another approach to reducing the number of scenarios is to perform a Monte Carlo simulation analysis. For example, instead of specifying sales growth rates, costs of goods sold, and so on at discrete levels, probability distributions could be specified. Then, the key results would be presented as distributions rather than as point estimates.[12]

Self-Test Questions

Describe briefly how a basic computerized financial planning model would be constructed.

What is the most important benefit of computerized planning models?

One problem with planning models is that they can generate an almost unlimited amount of output. How can financial managers reduce the number of relevant scenarios that must be considered?

FINANCIAL CONTROLS

Financial forecasting and planning is vital to corporate success, but planning is for nought unless the firm has a control system (1) that insures implementation of the planned policies and (2) that provides an information feedback loop which permits rapid adjustments if the market conditions upon which the plan is based change. In a financial control system, the key question is not "How is the firm doing in 1991 as compared with 1990?" Rather, it is "How is the firm doing in 1991 as compared with

---

[11]See Problem 23-4 for an extension of this example. For students with access to *Lotus 1-2-3,* this problem provides an excellent introduction to computerized financial forecasting.

[12]This is a good time to mention the basic axiom of computer modeling: GIGO, which means "garbage in, garbage out." Stated another way, the output of a financial model is no better than the assumptions and other inputs used to construct it. So, when you build models, proceed with caution. Note, though, that one advantage of computer modeling is that it does bring the key assumptions out into the open, where their realism can be examined. One strong advocate of models made this statement: "Critics of our models generally attack our assumptions, but they forget that in their own forecasts, they simply assume the answer."

our forecasts, and if actual results differ from the budget, what can we do to get back on track?"

The basic tools of financial control are *budgets* and *pro forma financial statements*. These documents set forth expected performance, and, hence, they express management's targets. These targets are then compared with actual corporate performance—on a daily, weekly, or monthly basis—to determine the variances, which are defined here as the difference between actual values and target values. Thus, the control system identifies those areas where performance is not meeting target levels. If a division's actuals are better than its targets, this could signify that its manager should be given a raise, but it could also mean that the targets were set too low and thus should be raised in the future. Conversely, failure to meet the financial targets could mean that market conditions are changing, that some managers are not performing up to par, or that the targets were set initially at unrealistic, unattainable levels. In any event, some action should be taken, and perhaps quickly, if the situation is deteriorating rapidly. By focusing on variances, managers can "manage by exception," concentrating on those variables that are most in need of improvement and leaving alone those operations that are running smoothly.[13]

Self-Test Questions

What are the purposes of a financial control system?

What are the basic financial control tools and how do they work?

MULTINATIONAL FINANCE
Currency Exchange Rates

Financial forecasting is more difficult for a multinational corporation than for a purely domestic one because the results for overseas operations must be "translated" from foreign currencies into U.S. dollars. For example, IBM might have correctly forecasted its Japanese subsidiary's results in terms of yen, but then missed the consolidated corporate forecast badly because of an unanticipated change in the rate at which yen can be exchanged into dollars. If the number of dollars a yen would buy rose, IBM's Japanese subsidiary's contribution to consolidated profits would exceed the forecasted level, and vice versa if the value of the yen fell.

Exchange rates also affect unit sales, sales prices, and costs—and thus financial forecasts—in yet another way. To illustrate, suppose Blount-Raulerson Honda, the Gainesville Honda dealer, planned to import 600 autos for model year 1990, at an average cost of 1,600,000 yen each. In the spring of 1989, when these plans were being made, one dollar could be exchanged for 130 yen, so the cost per car was $1,600,000/130 \approx \$12,300$. Assume further that the dealer would incur $1,000 of transportation costs, and that it planned to mark up the cars by another $1,000 and sell them for $14,300 each. Thus, Blount-Raulerson expected a gross profit of $600 \times \$1,000 = \$600,000$.

---

[13]Of course, entire textbooks have been written on financial controls, and much of the subject of financial control overlaps with managerial, or cost, accounting. Here, we want only to emphasize that financial controls are as critical to financial performance as are financial planning and forecasting. We must also add that financial control systems are not costless. Thus, the control system must balance its costs against the savings it is intended to produce.

Suppose, however, that the yen strengthened, and the yen/dollar exchange rate changed from ¥130:$1 to ¥100:$1. That exchange rate change would mean that Blount-Raulerson would have to pay 1,600,000/100 = $16,000 per car, so with the same transportation cost and profit per car, the retail sales price would have to be $18,000. Now something would have to change. If customers were willing to buy 600 cars at a price of $14,300, they would certainly buy fewer cars if prices were raised by 26 percent, to $18,000. Thus, Blount-Raulerson would have to either negotiate a lower price from Honda, cut its profit margin drastically, or sell fewer cars. In fact, Honda dealers all across the United States took all three of these actions in 1987, when a similar increase in the value of the yen occurred. Honda Motors had to lay off workers in Japan, and its profits fell. Toyota, Sony, and other Japanese manufacturers were also hurt by the rise in the value of the yen, but Ford, GM, and other U.S. companies were helped—their sales and profits rose, and they hired new workers to help meet demand.

From the end of World War II to 1971, exchange rates were *fixed* by agreement among the central bankers of the major trading nations. However, since 1971 rates have *floated,* moving up or down depending on supply and demand forces. Here are the exchange rates between dollars and some selected currencies for the past five years.[14]

Units of Foreign Currency Required to Buy One U.S. Dollar

	Mar 1990	Mar 1989	Mar 1988	Mar 1987	Mar 1986
British pound	0.62	0.58	0.55	0.63	0.68
Canadian dollar	1.18	1.20	1.25	1.32	1.40
Japanese yen	152	130	127	151	179
French franc	5.78	6.33	5.69	6.08	7.00
West German mark	1.71	1.87	1.68	1.84	2.28

Consider the Japanese yen. From 1986 to 1988, the dollar *weakened,* or *depreciated,* against the yen —it took fewer yen to buy a dollar in 1988 than it had in 1986. However, from 1988 to 1990, the dollar

---

[14]Typically, the British pound and Canadian dollar are quoted as U.S. dollars required to buy one unit of the foreign currency. Thus, in March 1990 the pound quote would have been 1/0.62 = 1.61 and the Canadian dollar quote would have been 1/1.18 = 0.85. We do not know why this convention exists, but it does.

strengthened, or *appreciated,* against the yen—it took more yen to buy a dollar in 1990 than it had in 1988.

We have already seen the implications of changing exchange rates; the weaker dollar in 1989 vis-à-vis 1986 hurt Japanese manufacturers because it raised the price of Japanese goods in the United States. Conversely, U.S. firms were helped, because U.S. goods became more competitive in world markets. As a corollary, employment rose in the United States, but it fell in Japan and other countries whose currency values rose. Note, though, that the situation from 1989 to 1990 was just the reverse—recent exchange rate changes have hurt U.S. industry and helped Japanese firms.

The preceding discussion focused on the effects of exchange rates on exports and imports between countries, hence on economic conditions within countries. Exchange rate fluctuations also make financial forecasting and planning more difficult. Therefore, many people would like to see the world return to a fixed exchange rate system. However, that probably cannot be done. To understand why, recognize first that exchange rates are simply prices—the price of $1 to a Japanese importer is 152 yen, whereas to a Canadian merchant the price of a U.S. dollar is $1.18 Canadian. Like other prices, exchange rates move up and down in response to changes in supply and demand. Suppose, for illustrative purposes, that the United States traded only with Japan. U.S. importers would order Japanese goods, and they would have to make payment for these goods in yen. Thus, U.S. importers would receive Japanese goods, sell them and receive dollars, and then take those dollars and buy yen in the foreign exchange market to pay the Japanese exporters. If the Japanese were simultaneously buying U.S. goods, Japanese merchants would need U.S. dollars, so they would be buying dollars with yen.

Now suppose U.S. importers want to buy $20 billion of Japanese goods, but Japanese importers want to buy only $10 billion of U.S. goods. There will be a demand for $20 billion of yen but a supply of only $10 billion of yen. The supply of dollars in the foreign exchange market will exceed the demand for dollars, whereas the reverse will be true for the yen. Therefore, the price of the dollar will fall, and the price of the yen will rise. If the initial exchange rate was 152 yen per $1, the dollar might depreciate to a rate of 130 yen per dollar. This change would make U.S. goods less expensive in Japan and Japanese goods more expensive in the United States, and that, in turn, would alter the balance of trade from the $20 billion imports versus $10 billion exports level. Eventually, an equilibrium would be established, with imports equaling exports, but only a freely working floating exchange rate system can bring about an equilibrium.

This discussion has only touched the surface of exchange rates. They are also affected by relative inflation rates in different countries, by capital movements among nations (that is, by net borrowing by the citizens of one nation from those of another), by central bank intervention, and so on. Given the importance of exchange rates—indeed, of international operations generally—business students would be well advised to learn more about international financial systems.

SUMMARY

This chapter described in broad outline how firms project their financial statements and determine their capital requirements. The key concepts covered are listed next.

- The primary planning documents are *strategic plans, operating plans,* and *financial plans.*

- *Financial forecasting* generally begins with a forecast of the firm's sales, in terms of both units and dollars, for some future time period.

- *Pro forma,* or *projected, financial statements* are developed to determine the firm's financial requirements.

- The *percentage of sales method* of forecasting financial statements is based on the assumptions (1) that most balance sheet accounts vary directly with sales and (2) that the firm's existing levels of spontaneous assets and liabilities are optimum for its sales volume.

- A firm can determine the amount of *external funds needed (EFN)* by estimating the amount of assets necessary to support the forecasted level of sales and then subtracting from that amount the forecasted total claims. The firm can then plan to raise the EFN through bank borrowing, by issuing securities, or both.

- Additional external capital means additional interest and/or dividends, which lowers the amount of forecasted retained earnings. Thus, raising external funds creates a *financing feedback* effect which must be incorporated in the forecasting process.

- The *higher a firm's sales growth rate,* the *greater* will be its need for external financing. Similarly, the *larger a firm's dividend payout ratio,* the *greater* its need for external funds.

- A formula can be used to estimate a firm's *sustainable growth rate,* which is the growth rate that can be sustained without issuing new common stock.

- The percentage of sales method cannot be used if *economies of scale* exist, if *excess capacity* exists, or if some assets must be added in *lumpy increments.*

- *Linear regression, curvilinear regression, multiple regression,* and *specific item forecasting techniques* can be used to forecast asset requirements when the percentage of sales method is not appropriate.

- Even the smallest firms now use *computerized financial planning models* to forecast both their financial statements and their external financing needs.

- Financial forecasting is especially difficult for multinational firms, because *exchange rate fluctuations* make it difficult to estimate the dollars that overseas operations will produce.

The type of forecasting described in this chapter is important for several reasons. First, if the projected operating results are unsatisfactory, management can "go back to the drawing board," reformulate its plans, and develop more reasonable targets for the coming year. Second, it is possible that the funds required to meet the sales forecast simply cannot be obtained; if so, it is obviously better to know this in advance and to scale back the projected level of operations than to suddenly run out of cash and have operations grind to a halt. Third, even if the required funds can be raised, it is desirable to plan for their acquisition well in advance.

Questions

23-1   Define each of the following terms:
   a.   Operating plan; five-year plan
   b.   Financial plan
   c.   Sales forecast
   d.   Percentage of sales method
   e.   Spontaneously generated funds
   f.   Dividend payout ratio; retention ratio
   g.   Pro forma financial statement
   h.   External funds needed (EFN)
   i.   Capital intensity ratio
   j.   Lumpy assets
   k.   Sustainable growth
   l.   Simple linear regression; curvilinear regression
   m.   Multiple regression; specific item forecasting
   n.   Computerized financial planning model

23-2   Certain liability and net worth items generally increase spontaneously with increases in sales. Put a check ($\checkmark$) by those items that typically increase spontaneously:

Accounts payable	_____
Notes payable to banks	_____
Accrued wages	_____
Accrued taxes	_____
Mortgage bonds	_____
Common stock	_____
Retained earnings	_____
Marketable securities	_____

23-3   Assume that an average firm in the office supply business has a 6 percent after-tax profit margin, a 40 percent debt/assets ratio, a total assets turnover of 2 times, and a dividend payout ratio of 40 percent. Is it true that if such a firm is to have *any* sales growth (g > 0), it will be forced to borrow or to sell common stock (that is, it will need some external capital even if g is very small)?

23-4 Is it true that computerized corporate planning models were a fad during the 1970s but, because of a need for flexibility in corporate planning, they have been dropped by most firms?

23-5 Suppose a firm makes the following policy changes. If the change means that external financial requirements for any rate of sales growth will increase, indicate this by a +; indicate decreases by a −; and indicate indeterminate and/or no effect by a 0. Think in terms of the immediate, short-run effect on funds requirements.

a. The dividend payout ratio is increased.   _____

b. The firm contracts to buy rather than make certain
    components used in its products.   _____

c. The firm decides to pay all suppliers on delivery, rather
    than after a 30-day delay, in order to take advantage of
    discounts for rapid payment.   _____

d. The firm begins to sell on credit (previously all sales had
    been on a cash basis).   _____

e. The firm's profit margin is eroded by increased
    competition; sales are steady.   _____

f. Advertising expenditures are stepped up.   _____

g. A decision is made to substitute long-term mortgage
    bonds for short-term bank loans.   _____

h. The firm begins to pay employees on a weekly basis
    (previously it had paid at the end of each month).   _____

Self-Test Problem   (Solutions Appear in Appendix D)

ST-1 **(Percentage of sales method)** Strassburg Company's 1990 sales were $72 million. The percentage of sales of each balance sheet item except notes payable, mortgage bonds, and common stock is given below:

Cash	4%
Receivables	25
Inventories	30
Net fixed assets	50
Accounts payable	15
Accruals	5
Profit margin	5

The dividend payout ratio is 60 percent; the December 31, 1989, balance sheet account for retained earnings was $41.80 million; and both common stock and mortgage bonds are constant and equal to the amounts shown on the following balance sheet.

a. Complete the firm's December 31, 1990, balance sheet (in thousands of dollars):

Cash	$	Accounts payable	$
Receivables		Notes payable	6,840
Inventories	———	Accruals	
Total current assets	$	Total current liabilities	$
Net fixed assets		Mortgage bonds	10,000
		Common stock	4,000
		Retained earnings	
Total assets	$	Total claims	$

b. Assume that the company was operating at full capacity in 1990 with regard to all items *except* fixed assets. If the fixed assets had been used to full capacity, the fixed assets/sales ratio would have been 40 percent in 1990. By what percentage could 1991 sales increase over 1990 sales without the need for an increase in fixed assets?

c. Now suppose that 1991 sales increase over 1990 sales by 20 percent. How much additional external capital will be required? Assume that Part b conditions hold and that any required financing is borrowed as notes payable.

d. Suppose the industry percentage of sales averages for receivables and inventories are 20 percent and 25 percent, respectively, and that the firm matches these figures in 1991 and then uses the funds released to reduce equity. (It could pay a special dividend out of retained earnings.) What would this do to the rate of return on year-end 1991 equity? (Assume that Part c conditions hold.)

Problems

23-1 **(Pro forma balance sheet)** A group of investors is planning to set up a new company to manufacture and distribute a novel type of running shoe. To help plan the new operation's financial requirements, you have been asked to construct a pro forma balance sheet for December 31, 1991, the end of the first year of operations. Sales for 1991 are projected at $20 million, and the following are industry average ratios for athletic shoe companies.

Sales to common equity	5×
Current debt to equity	50%
Total debt to equity	80%
Current ratio	2.2×
Net sales to inventory	9×
Accounts receivable to sales	10%
Fixed assets to equity	70%
Profit margin	3%
Dividend payout ratio	30%

a. Complete the pro forma balance sheet below, assuming that the firm maintains industry average ratios.

Cash	$	Current debt	$
Accounts receivable		Long-term debt	
Inventories		Total debt	$
Total current assets	$	Equity	
Fixed assets			
Total assets	$	Total claims	$

b.   If the investor group supplies all of the new firm's equity, how much capital will the group be required to put up during 1991?

23-2   **(Pro forma financial statements)** The 1990 income statement and balance sheet for Welch Industries are given below (in thousands of dollars):

Net sales	$10,000
Cost of goods sold	6,500
Gross profit	$ 3,500
Administrative expenses	1,000
Miscellaneous expenses	500
EBIT	$ 2,000
Interest expense	200
EBT	$ 1,800
Taxes (48%)	864
Net income	$ 936
Dividends	$ 468
Addition to retained earnings	$ 468

Cash	$ 50	Accounts payable	$ 250
Accounts receivable	423	Notes payable	200
Inventory	513	Accruals	50
Total current assets	$ 986	Total current liabilities	$ 500
Net plant	4,014	Long-term debt	1,500
		Common stock	1,500
		Retained earnings	1,500
Total assets	$5,000	Total claims	$5,000

As the firm's financial manager, you want to construct a pro forma income statement, balance sheet, and statement of cash flows for 1991. As a first step, you develop the following relationships between the financial statement variables and sales (in thousands of dollars):

Variable	Relationship to Sales
Cost of goods sold	0.65(Sales)
Administrative expenses	$500 + 0.05(Sales)
Miscellaneous expenses	0.05(Sales)
Cash	0.005(Sales)
Accounts receivable	0.0423(Sales)
Inventory	$200 + 0.03(Sales)
Net plant	0.40(Sales)
Accounts payable	0.025(Sales)
Accruals	0.005(Sales)

Taxes are expected to continue at 48 percent (the firm operates in a very high state and local tax jurisdiction); sales in 1991 are forecasted to increase over 1990 by 30 percent; and fixed assets were fully utilized in 1990. Any external funding required for 1991 will be financed in the proportion of 4 percent notes payable, 36 percent long-term debt, and 60 percent new equity. The firm's stock currently sells for $25 per share, and there are 1,000,000 shares outstanding. Thus, the 1990 DPS was $468,000/1,000,000 = $0.468. However, the firm wants to increase the dividend in 1991 to $0.50 per share. New short-term debt is expected to cost 12 percent, while new long-term debt will cost 14 percent.

a. Construct the initial 1991 pro forma income statement and balance sheet. What is the external financing requirement? How will it be met? (For now, ignore financing feedback effects.)

b. Recast the 1991 pro forma income statement and balance sheet considering financing feedback effects. How much of an external financing shortfall still exists?

c. Perform one more iteration on the pro forma income statement and balance sheet. Construct the pro forma 1991 statement of cash flows. (You should still have a shortfall of $1,000 after the second iteration. Use $1,000 worth of new equity to balance the balance sheet.)

d. The firm's current bond indenture limits the firm to a minimum current ratio of 1.5, a maximum debt ratio of 35 percent, and a minimum times-interest-earned ratio of 8.0. Are any of these restrictions violated in the pro forma statements? If so, how must the financing program be modified to meet these restrictions?

e. What would be the effect on external financing requirements if the firm had been operating at only 80 percent of capacity in 1990? (Note that the net plant account is forecasted using the percentage of sales technique.)

23-3 **(Pro forma financial statements)** The 1990 income statement and balance sheet for O'Brien Pulp and Paper are shown below (in thousands of dollars):

Sales	$500
Operating expenses	320
General expenses	80
EBIT	$100
Interest expense	20
EBT	$ 80
Taxes (50%)	40
Net income	$ 40

Cash	$ 30	Accounts payable	$ 40
Receivables	50	Accruals	20
Inventories	420	Notes payable	20
Net fixed assets	500	Long-term debt	180
		Common stock	200
		Retained earnings	540
Total assets	$1,000	Total claims	$1,000

The firm, which operates in a high-tax environment, has 40,000 shares outstanding, and next year's dividend is forecasted at $0.55 per share. O'Brien has fixed assets sufficient to support a sales level of $750,000. Next year's sales are forecasted to be $700,000. The stock is currently selling at $2.86 per share, and the stock price is expected to be flat over the next year. Any external financing would be met with a mix of 60 percent long-term debt, at an estimated cost of 12.82 percent and 40 percent common equity. No new short-term debt would be used, but the old short-term debt would be rolled over at the current rate.

The relationships between certain financial statement variables and sales are given below (in thousands of dollars):

Variable	Relationship to Sales
General expenses	$30 + 0.10(Sales)
Inventories	$200 + 0.44(Sales)

All other variables are forecasted using the percentage of sales method. The 1990 levels of these variables are appropriate for a sales level of $500,000.

a.   Construct the initial 1991 pro forma income statement and balance sheet, excluding financial feedback effects. What amount of external financing is required? How will it be obtained?

b.   Construct the first iteration pro forma income statement and balance sheet; that is, construct the statements which include financing feedback effects. What is the additional interest expense resulting from external financing? What is the additional dividend payment? How much external financing is still required after this iteration?

23-4   **(Financial forecasting)** Century Electronics Corporation's 1990 financial statements are given below (in millions of dollars):

Income Statement	For the Year Ended December 31, 1990
Net sales	$500
Cost of goods sold	400
Selling and administrative expenses	52
Earnings before interest and taxes	$ 48
Interest expense	8
Earnings before taxes	$ 40
Taxes (40%)	16
Net income	$ 24
Dividends (payout: 33%)	$ 8
Addition to retained earnings	$ 16

Balance Sheet	As of December 31, 1990
Cash	$ 10
Receivables	82
Inventories	103
Total current assets	$195
Net fixed assets	152
Total assets	$347
Accounts payable	$ 40
Notes payable (8%)	8
Accrued wages and taxes	25
Total current liabilities	$ 73
Mortgage bonds (10%)	70
Common stock	150
Retained earnings	54
Total claims	$347

Note: Century's 1990 balance sheet has been recast slightly to reflect the variable relationships given below. Thus, this balance sheet is not an exact duplicate of Table 23-3.

Assume (1) that sales will grow at an annual rate of 50 percent in 1991, at a 25 percent rate in both 1992 and 1993, and at a 15 percent rate in 1994 and 1995; (2) that dividends per share will be increased by 10 percent per year over the next 5 years; (3) that the stock price will grow at an annual rate of 20 percent over the next 5 years; (4) that the state-plus-federal income tax rate will remain at 40 percent; (5) that the current ratio cannot fall below 2.5 and the debt ratio cannot exceed 50 percent; (6) that all new financing will occur on January 1 of the year in which it is needed; (7) that new short-term debt will cost 10 percent and new long-term debt will cost 12 percent; and (8) that 10 million common shares are outstanding and selling at $25 per share.

Further, Century uses the following relationships in its financial forecasting (in millions of dollars):

Variable	Relationship to Sales
Cost of goods sold	0.80(Sales)
Selling and administrative expenses	$27.0 + 0.05(Sales)
Cash	0.02(Sales)
Receivables	$6.7 + 0.15(Sales)
Inventories	$22.8 + 0.16(Sales)
Net fixed assets	$37.2 + 0.23(Sales)
Accounts payable	0.08(Sales)
Accrued wages and taxes	0.05(Sales)

a. Construct Century's 1991 pro forma income statement and balance sheet.
(Do Parts b, c, d, e, and f only if you are using the computerized diskette.)
b. How much will the firm require in external funds each year from 1991 through 1995? How will the firm raise the needed external funds in order to maintain the current ratio and debt ratio requirements given in the problem?
c. What effect will the use of external funds have upon the firm's ROE? Why? (Hint: Think about the three main components of return on equity—that is, asset efficiency, expense control, and debt utilization.)
d. Suppose that management's growth forecasts include the possibility of higher sustained growth in the early years than originally given in the problem. They foresee the possibility of a 35 percent growth rate in Years 2 and 3 followed by a 20 percent growth rate in Years 4 and 5. How does this affect the firm's external funds requirements for 1991-1995?
e. Return to the original scenario. Suppose now that the firm is no longer constrained by a 2.5 current ratio requirement, but rather by a 1.5 current ratio. How does this affect the composition of the firm's external funds financing? What effect does this have upon ROA? ROE? Why?
f. The firm's management is considering increasing dividends at the rate of 25 percent per year. What effect does this have upon the firm's key financial ratios? (Assume a 1.5 current ratio requirement.)

Mini Case

David Steele, financial manager of NorthWest Laboratories, is currently working on the firm's financial forecast for the coming year. NorthWest, which is located in Seattle, produces specialized fertilizers that are used in the apple industry. The firm's income statement and balance sheet for 1990 are given next (in thousands of dollars):

Income Statement

Sales	$7,500
Cost of goods sold	6,000
Administrative expenses	780
Earnings before interest and taxes	$ 720
Interest expense	120
Earnings before taxes	$ 600
Taxes (40%)	240
Net income	$ 360
Dividends (30% payout)	$ 108
Addition to retained earnings	$ 252

Balance Sheet

Cash	$ 300	Accounts payable	$ 200
Receivables	500	Accruals	100
Inventory	1,000	Notes payable	250
Current assets	$1,800	Current liabilities	$ 550
Net fixed assets	4,000	Long-term debt	2,400
		Total debt	$2,950
		Common stock	2,000
		Retained earnings	850
Total assets	$5,800	Total claims	$5,800

NorthWest was operating at full capacity last year, and its sales were $7.5 million. The company's marketing department is forecasting a 20 percent sales increase in the coming year, but the firm does not plan to increase its dollar dividend (it will let the payout ratio decline). David has requested that you, his assistant, help with the company's 1991 financial forecast by answering the following questions:

a. Why is a good sales forecast essential to a good financial forecast? Briefly explain how NorthWest should go about making its sales forecast.

b. Using the percentage of sales forecasting technique, prepare the firm's 1991 pro forma income statement. What are the values for projected net income, dividends, and the addition to retained earnings?

c. Use the percentage of sales method to prepare the firm's 1991 pro forma balance sheet. What is the external funding requirement? What assumptions are embedded in the percentage of sales approach?

d. NorthWest's target capital structure is 50 percent debt and 50 percent common equity. For planning purposes, the firm assumes that any external funds needed will be raised as 10 percent short-term debt (notes payable), 40 percent long-term debt, and 50 percent common stock. What dollar amounts of each type of capital are needed to cover NorthWest's projected cash shortfall? Will financing external funding requirements by the 10/40/50 mix keep NorthWest's capital structure on target over time? Explain.

e. David Steele predicts that new long-term debt will cost 10 percent, that new short-term debt will cost 12 percent, and that new stock could be sold to net $10 per share. NorthWest currently has 100,000 common shares outstanding. What impact would the proposed external financing have on NorthWest's pro forma income statement?

f. Recast the firm's 1991 pro forma balance sheet to reflect financing feedback effects. Are there any external funds required after this iteration? Explain.

g. What sales growth rate can NorthWest achieve without using outside financing, that is, what is its *sustainable growth rate?*

h. What impacts do a firm's dividend policy, profitability, and capital intensity have on its external financing requirements and on its sustainable growth rate?

i. Now assume that NorthWest was operating its fixed assets at only 80 percent of capacity in 1990. What are the firm's external financing requirements in this situation?

j. What are some potential problems with the percentage of sales method? What are some other forecasting methods that could be used to develop projected financial statements?

Selected Additional References and Cases

The heart of successful financial planning is the sales forecast. On this key subject, see

Pan, Judy, Donald R. Nichols, and O. Maurice Joy, "Sales Forecasting Practices of Large U.S. Industrial Firms," *Financial Management,* Fall 1977, 72–77.

Pappas, James L., and Mark Hirschey, *Managerial Economics* (Hinsdale, Ill.: Dryden, 1989).

Computer modeling is becoming increasingly important. For general references, see

Carleton, Willard T., Charles L. Dick, Jr., and David H. Downes, "Financial Policy Models: Theory and Practice," *Journal of Finance,* December 1973, 691–709.

Francis, Jack Clark, and Dexter R. Rowell, "A Simultaneous Equation Model of the Firm for Financial Analysis and Planning," *Financial Management,* Spring 1978, 29–44.

Grinyer, P. H., and J. Wooller, *Corporate Models Today—A New Tool for Financial Management* (London: Institute of Chartered Accountants, 1978).

Pappas, James L., and George P. Huber, "Probabilistic Short-Term Financial Planning," *Financial Management,* Autumn 1973, 36–44.

Traenkle, J. W., E. B. Cox, and J. A. Bullard, *The Use of Financial Models in Business* (New York: Financial Executives' Research Foundation, 1975).

Considerable effort has been expended to develop integrated financial planning models that identify optimal policies. For one example, see

Myers, Stewart C., and Gerald A. Pogue, "A Programming Approach to Corporate Financial Management," *Journal of Finance,* May 1974, 579–599.

For a recent article on control, see

Bierman, Harold, "Beyond Cash Flow ROI," *Midland Corporate Finance Journal,* Winter 1988, 36–39.

The Brigham-Gapenski casebook contains the following applicable cases:

Case 38, "Ceramic Engineering, Inc.," which focuses on using the percentage of sales forecasting equation to forecast future financing requirements.

Case 39, "Real Estate Management Systems Company," which illustrates the construction of pro forma financial statements, including financing feedback effects.

The following case can be found in the Harrington casebook:

"United Telesis Corporation," which illustrates financial forecasting and the estimation of capital requirements.

CHAPTER 24

Mergers, LBOs, Divestitures, and Holding Companies

On November 11, 1989, Ford Motor Company won the battle for Jaguar PLC. By agreeing to pay a whopping $2.5 billion for Britain's leading luxury auto maker, Ford beat out its arch-rival, General Motors, which had earlier announced its own hopes of buying a minority stake in Jaguar. The face-off was expected to be a drawn-out battle of the titans, but it ended before it even began. The Ford/Jaguar announcement, which followed marathon negotiations, occurred before GM had bought even a single share of stock.

But Ford's victory may be costly, leaving GM with the last laugh. Jaguar's earlier talks with GM, amid Ford's unwelcome pursuit of a 15 percent stake in Jaguar, turned the British company's shares into a feverish take-over stock. The share price more than doubled, and Ford was forced to pay over half a billion dollars more than it had expected to pay.

Ford bought a money-losing company which manufactures a mere 50,000 cars a year at an outmoded former aircraft parts plant in Britain's ailing industrial heartland. Its biggest challenge is determining how to take an upscale label, valued for its exclusivity, and sell it to more people without diluting the distinctive Jaguar image. To reap a significant payoff from the Jaguar deal, Ford will have to spend an additional $1.5 billion to help Jaguar launch a less expensive range of so-called "executive cars." This move would put Ford into head-on competition with BMW and with the savvy Japanese auto makers, whose luxury cars have been flooding Europe and the United States.

959

If things go well, however, the acquisition could prove to be a big success. Time and again, Ford has stumbled in its attempts to make itself an elite car maker, particularly in Europe. In 1986, Ford lost a bid to take over Alfa Romeo when Fiat scooped up the troubled firm. Then, shortly before the announcement of the Jaguar deal, Ford broke off talks with Saab about a possible alliance, after concluding that Saab offered little in the way of profit potential or image. At about the same time, Ford abandoned a four-year effort to market its German-built Merkur Scorpio sedan in the United States as a European luxury import. "Ford aspires to sell premium cars, but the Ford name is so synonymous with bread-and-butter that it's impossible," said one analyst.

At the time of the Jaguar announcement, Ford hadn't decided how to fund the all-cash offer. Ford might borrow some of the required $2.5 billion, but it wouldn't have to—the company had $5.8 billion in cash reserves at the end September 1989.

Ford's acquisition of Jaguar was just one of about $400 billion of deals that occurred in 1989. Mergers and leveraged buyouts have been taking place at a feverish pitch over the last decade, and this chapter will help you understand the motivations behind all this activity and the procedures that make mergers work.

MOST corporate growth occurs through *internal expansion,* which takes place when the firm's existing divisions grow through normal capital budgeting activities. However, the most dramatic examples of growth, and often the largest increases in firms' stock prices, are the result of *mergers,* the first topic covered in this chapter. *Leveraged buyouts,* or *LBOs,* occur when a firm's stock is acquired by a small group of investors rather than by another operating company. Since LBOs are similar in many respects to mergers, they are also covered in this chapter. The conditions of corporate life do change over time, and, as a result, firms often find it desirable to *divest,* or sell off, major divisions to other firms that can better utilize the divested assets. Divestitures are also discussed in the chapter. Finally, we discuss the *holding company* form of organization, wherein one corporation owns the stock of one or more other companies.

RATIONALE FOR MERGERS

Many reasons have been proposed by both financial managers and theorists to account for the high level of merger activity in the United States. In this section, we present some of the motives behind corporate mergers.[1]

---

[1]As we use the term, *merger* means any combination that forms one economic unit from two or more previous ones. For legal purposes, there are distinctions among the various ways these combinations can occur, but our focus is on the fundamental business and financial aspects of mergers.

Synergy

The primary motivation for most mergers is to increase the value of the combined enterprise. If Companies A and B merge to form Company C, and if C's value exceeds that of A and B taken separately, then *synergy* is said to exist. Such a merger should be beneficial to both A's and B's stockholders.[2] Synergistic effects can arise from four sources: (1) *operating economies,* which result from economies of scale in management, marketing, production, or distribution; (2) *financial economies,* including lower transactions costs and better coverage by security analysts; (3) *differential efficiency,* which implies that the management of one firm is inefficient, and that the firm's assets will be more productive after the merger; and (4) *increased market power* due to reduced competition. Operating and financial economies are socially desirable, as are mergers that increase managerial efficiency, but mergers that reduce competition are both undesirable and illegal.[3]

Tax Considerations

Tax considerations have stimulated a number of mergers. For example, a firm which is highly profitable and is therefore in the highest corporate tax bracket could acquire a firm with large accumulated tax losses. These losses could then be turned into immediate tax savings rather than carried forward and presumably used in the future.[4] Also, mergers can provide an outlet for excess cash. If a firm has a shortage of internal investment opportunities compared to its cash flow, it could (1) pay an extra dividend, (2) invest in marketable securities, (3) repurchase its own stock, or (4) purchase another firm. If the firm pays an extra dividend, the stockholders would have to pay immediate taxes on the distribution. Marketable securities often provide a good temporary parking place for money, but generally the rate of return on such securities is less than that required by stockholders. A stock repurchase would result in a capital gain for the remaining stockholders, but (1) a repurchase might push up the firm's stock price to a level which is temporarily above the equilibrium price, so the company would have to pay too much for the repurchased shares, which would be disadvantageous to remaining stockholders, and (2) a repurchase designed solely to avoid dividend payment might be challenged by the IRS. However, using

---

[2]If synergy exists, then the whole is greater than the sum of the parts. Synergy is also called the "2 plus 2 equals 5 effect." The distribution of the synergistic gain between A's and B's stockholders is determined by negotiation. This point is discussed later in the chapter.

[3]In the 1880s and 1890s, many mergers occurred in the United States, and some of them were rather obviously directed toward gaining market power rather than increasing operating efficiency. As a result, Congress passed a series of acts designed to insure that mergers are not used as a method of reducing competition. The principal acts include the Sherman Act (1890), the Clayton Act (1914), and the Celler Act (1950). These acts make it illegal for firms to combine in any manner if the combination tends to lessen competition. The acts are enforced by the antitrust division of the Justice Department and by the Federal Trade Commission.

[4]Mergers undertaken only to use accumulated tax losses would probably be challenged by the IRS. However, because many factors are present in any given merger, it is hard to prove that a merger was motivated only, or even primarily, by tax considerations.

surplus cash to acquire another firm has no immediate tax consequences to the acquiring firm or its stockholders, and this fact has motivated a number of mergers.

Purchase of Assets below Their Replacement Cost

Sometimes a firm will be touted as a possible acquisition candidate because the cost of replacing its assets is considerably higher than its market value. For example, in the early 1980s oil companies could acquire reserves cheaper by buying out other oil companies than by doing exploratory drilling. Thus, in 1984 Chevron Corporation acquired Gulf Oil in order to augment its reserves. Similarly, steel companies have stated that it is cheaper to buy an existing steel company than to construct a new mill, and in 1984, LTV (the fourth largest steel company) acquired Republic Steel (the sixth largest) for $700 million in a merger that created the second largest firm in the industry.

At the time the LTV-Republic merger was announced, Republic was selling for less than one-third of its book value. However, the market value of a firm should be based on its earning power, which sets the economic value of its assets. If a firm is fairly valued (that is, if markets are efficient), then its market value, rather than book value, will reflect the economic value of its assets. The real questions, then, were these: Could LTV operate the merged company more efficiently than the two companies had been operating before the merger, or could LTV break up Republic and sell its assets to other producers which could operate them more efficiently? LTV argued that sufficient economies of scale existed to make the merger synergistic. The least efficient plants of both companies would be closed; plants that make similar products (say sheet steel for autos or oil drilling pipe) would be consolidated, and distribution systems would be integrated. If these moves resulted in sizable cost savings, then the merger could be successful. Otherwise, the fact that LTV bought Republic's assets at below their replacement value would be immaterial. The merger appears to have done little for LTV—it has reported losses consistently over the last several years, and ultimately it filed for protection from its creditors under Chapter 11 of the Bankruptcy Act.

Diversification

Managers often claim that diversification is a reason for mergers. They contend that diversification helps to stabilize the firm's earnings stream and thus benefits its owners. Stabilization of earnings is certainly beneficial to employees, suppliers, and customers, but its value is questionable from the standpoint of stockholders. If a stockholder is worried about the variability of a firm's earnings, he or she could diversify more easily than could the firm. Why should Firms A and B merge to stabilize earnings when a stockholder in Firm A could sell half of his or her stock in A and use the proceeds to purchase stock in Firm B? Stockholders can create diversification more easily than can the firm.

Of course, if you were the owner-manager of a closely held firm, it might be nearly impossible for you to sell part of your stock to diversify, because this would dilute your ownership and perhaps also generate a large capital gains tax liability.

In this case, a diversification merger might well be the best way to achieve personal diversification.

We can use option pricing theory to gain some insights into the ways stockholders and debtholders are affected by mergers. In Chapter 18 we discussed the application of option pricing theory to corporate decisions. If we view stock ownership as a call option, then the value of the stock is increased by an increase in earnings variability, but lowered by a decrease in variability. Assume that two firms have the same variability of earnings. If these two firms merge, and their earnings are not perfectly positively correlated, then the earnings of the combined firm will have less variability than the premerger earnings of the separate firms. This decrease in earnings variability would, according to option theory, lower the value of the combined firm's equity. Conversely, the value of the debt would increase, because the probability of default would lessen. According to this approach, using mergers for diversification results in a transfer of wealth from stockholders to debtholders, leaving the total value of the combined firm equal to the sum of the premerger values, assuming no synergistic effects.

However, it is possible for the stockholders to avoid these theoretical losses by financing the merger with debt, or to recoup them by issuing additional debt based on the increased debt capacity of the combined firm, and then using the proceeds to repurchase equity. Also, note that this result depends on the CAPM assumption that only market risk is relevant to stockholders, and that corporate stability has no beneficial effects on operating income. To the extent that these assumptions are not correct, then corporate diversification could benefit stockholders.

Managers' Personal Incentives

Financial economists like to think that business decisions are based only on economic considerations. However, there can be no question that some business decisions are based more on managers' personal motivations than on economic analyses. Many people, business leaders included, like power, and more power is attached to running a larger corporation than a smaller one. Obviously, no executive would ever admit that his or her ego was the primary reason behind a series of mergers, but knowledgeable observers are convinced that egos do play a prominent role in many mergers.

It has also been observed that executive salaries are highly correlated with company size—the bigger the company, the higher the salaries of its top officers. This too could play a role in the aggressive acquisition programs of some corporations.

In recent years many hostile takeovers have occurred, and the managers of the target companies generally lost their jobs, or at least their autonomy. Therefore, managers who own less than 51 percent of the stock in their firms look to devices that will lessen the chances of their firms' being taken over. Mergers can serve as such a device. For example, when Enron was under attack, it arranged to buy Houston Natural Gas Company, paying for Houston primarily with debt. That merger made Enron much larger, hence harder for any potential acquirer to "digest." Also, the much higher debt level resulting from the merger made it harder for any acquiring company to use debt to buy Enron. Such *defensive mergers* are hard to defend on economic grounds. The managers involved invariably argue that synergy, not a desire to protect their own jobs, motivated the acquisition, but there can be no question that many mergers today are indeed designed more for the benefit of managers than for that of stockholders.

Managers' personal incentives as a basis for mergers constitute another example of the agency problem. Of course, there is nothing wrong with executives feeling good about increasing the size of their firms, or with their getting paid a higher salary as a result of growth through mergers—provided the mergers make economic sense from the stockholders' viewpoint. There have been quite a few stockholder suits against managers who resisted hostile takeovers. Perhaps there should be a few such suits against managers who paid too high a price for target companies, hence diluted the wealth of their own shareholders.

Breakup Value

Firms can be valued in many ways, such as by book value, economic value, or replacement value. Recently, analysts and takeover specialists have begun to recognize *breakup value* as another basis for valuation. It is now common to see "expert" analysts on TV business programs giving estimates of a company's breakup value, and often this value is higher than the firm's current market value. If this situation holds, then a takeover specialist could acquire the firm at or even somewhat above its current market value, sell it off in pieces, and earn a substantial profit.

The breakup rationale for mergers is surrounded by controversy. If a firm's assets can be employed more efficiently when split up and sold to other firms that could gain some type of synergy, including better management, then there is economic justification for such actions. However, the breakup of companies is often associated with the closings of headquarters and plants, the loss of jobs, and a resulting economic disruption to employees, suppliers, customers, and even entire communities. Although all of this has some economic cost, the cost is not borne by the shareholders who must make the decision on whether or not to sell the company for breakup. If one takes an altruistic view, breakups should only occur when the economic gains outweigh the economic losses, but the gains can be measured relatively easily while the costs are much more elusive.

Self-Test Questions

Define synergy. Is synergy a valid rationale for mergers? Describe several situations that might produce synergistic gains.

Give two examples of how tax considerations can motivate mergers.

Suppose your firm could purchase another firm for only half of its replacement value. Would this be sufficient justification for the acquisition?

Discuss the merits of diversification as a rationale for mergers.

Can managers' personal incentives motivate mergers? Explain.

What is breakup value? Discuss the pros and cons of breakup-motivated acquisitions.

TYPES OF MERGERS

Economists classify mergers into four groups: (1) horizontal, (2) vertical, (3) congeneric, and (4) conglomerate. A *horizontal merger* occurs when one firm combines with another in its same line of business—for example, when one widget manufacturer acquires another, or one retail food chain merges with a second. The merger of Burroughs and Sperry to form Unisys was a horizontal merger, because both firms manufactured computers and electronics products. An example of a *vertical merger* is a steel producer's acquisition of one of its own suppliers, such as an iron or coal mining firm, or an oil producer's acquisition of a petrochemical firm which uses oil as a raw material. *Congeneric* means "allied in nature or action"; hence, a *congeneric merger* involves related enterprises but not producers of the same product (horizontal) or firms in a producer-supplier relationship (vertical). Examples of congeneric mergers would be American Express's takeover of Shearson Hammill, a stock brokerage firm, or Philip Morris's acquisition of General Foods and Kraft. A *conglomerate merger* occurs when unrelated enterprises combine, as illustrated by Mobil Oil's acquisition of Montgomery Ward.

Operating economies (and also anticompetitive effects) are at least partially dependent on the type of merger involved. Vertical and horizontal mergers generally provide the greatest synergistic operating benefits, but they are also the ones most likely to be attacked by the U.S. Department of Justice. In any event, it is useful to think of these economic classifications when analyzing the feasibility of a prospective merger.

Self-Test Questions

What are the four economic classifications of mergers?

Briefly describe the characteristics of each type of merger.

LEVEL OF MERGER ACTIVITY

Four major "merger waves" have occurred in the United States. The first was in the late 1800s, when consolidations occurred in the oil, steel, tobacco, and other basic industries. The second was in the 1920s, when the stock market boom helped financial promoters consolidate firms in a number of industries, including utilities, communications, and autos. The third was in the 1960s, when conglomerate mergers were the rage. The fourth ran in the 1980s.

The "merger mania" of the 1980s was sparked by seven factors: (1) the relatively depressed condition of the stock market at the beginning of the decade (for example, the Dow Jones Industrial Index in early 1982 was below its 1968 level); (2) the unprecedented level of inflation that existed during the 1970s and early 1980s, which increased the replacement value of firms' assets even while a weak stock market

Table 24-1   The Five Biggest Mergers (Billions of Dollars)

Companies	Year	Value	Premium Paid over Book Value	Type of Transaction
Chevron-Gulf	1984	$13.3	136%	Acquisition for cash
Philip Morris-Kraft	1988	12.9	609	Acquisition for cash
Bristol-Meyers-Squibb	1989	12.7	852	Acquisition for common stock
Texaco-Getty	1984	10.1	191	Acquisition for cash and notes
Beecham Group-Smithkline Beckman	1989	8.3	519	Merger by exchange of stock

reduced their market values; (3) the Reagan administration's stated view that "bigness is not necessarily badness," which resulted in a more tolerant attitude toward large mergers; (4) the general belief among the major natural resource companies that it was cheaper to "buy reserves on Wall Street" through mergers than to explore and find them in the field; (5) the development of an active junk bond market, which helped raiders obtain the capital needed to make tender offers for target firms; (6) attempts to ward off raiders by use of defensive mergers; and (7) the decline of the dollar which has made U.S. firms relatively cheap for foreign firms to acquire, combined with huge U.S. trade deficits, which gave foreign firms large pools of funds to invest in the United States. As seen in Table 24-1, the 1980s wave was by far the largest. However, as we write this (summer 1990), it appears that the "merger mania" is finally cooling off. The primary dampening factors are (1) the near collapse of the junk bond market, (2) a tougher antitrust stance by the Bush administration, and (3) the record high valuation of stocks in general. A sign of changing times was the June 1990 announcement that Coniston Partners, one of the biggest and best corporate raiders, was disbanding its $700 million equity investment pool.

Self-Test Questions

What are the four major merger "waves" that have occurred in the United States?

What are some possible reasons for the current wave? Does it appear that the current wave is dying out?

HOSTILE VERSUS FRIENDLY TAKEOVERS

In the vast majority of merger situations, one firm (generally the larger of the two) simply decides to buy another company, negotiates a price with the management of the target firm, and then acquires the target company. Occasionally, the acquired firm will initiate the action, but it is much more common for a firm to seek acquisitions than to seek to be acquired.[5] Following convention, we shall call a company that seeks to acquire another the *acquiring company* and the one which it seeks to acquire the *target company*.

Once an acquiring company has identified a possible target, it must (1) establish a suitable price, or range of prices, and (2) tentatively set the terms of payment— will it offer cash, its own common stock, bonds, or a mix of securities? Then, the acquiring firm's managers must decide how to approach the target company's managers. If the acquiring firm has reason to believe that the target's management will approve the merger, then it will simply propose a merger and try to work out some suitable terms. If an agreement can be reached, then the two management groups will issue statements to their stockholders indicating that they approve the merger, and the target firm's management will recommend to its stockholders that they agree to the merger. Generally, the stockholders are asked to *tender* (or send in) their shares to a designated financial institution along with a signed power of attorney which transfers ownership of the shares to the acquiring firm. The target firm's stockholders then receive the specified payment, be it common stock of the acquiring company (in which case the target company's stockholders become stockholders of the acquiring company), cash, bonds, or some mix of cash and securities. This is a *friendly merger,* or a *friendly tender offer.*

The recent acquisition of RCA by General Electric typifies a friendly merger. First, the boards of directors of the two firms announced that RCA had agreed to be acquired by GE in an all-cash transaction for $66.50 a share. The merger was approved by shareholders, by the Federal Communications Commission, and by the Justice Department, and then the acquisition was completed. Another example of a friendly merger is Federal Express's recent acquisition of Tiger International, an air freight carrier.

Often, however, the target company's management resists the merger. Perhaps the managers feel that the price offered for the stock is too low, or perhaps they simply want to keep their jobs. In either case, the acquiring firm's offer is said to be *hostile* rather than friendly, and the acquiring firm must make a direct appeal to the target firm's stockholders. In a hostile merger, the acquiring company will again make a tender offer, and again it will ask the stockholders of the target firm to tender their shares in exchange for the offered price. This time, though, the target firm's managers will urge stockholders not to tender their shares, generally stating that the price offered (cash, bonds, or stocks in the acquiring firm) is too low.

The recent battle between Shamrock Holdings and Polaroid illustrates a failed hostile merger attempt. It began in the summer of 1988, when Polaroid's stock was trading in the low $30s. At the time, many analysts had declared that Polaroid was a likely takeover candidate because of its sluggish performance but strong brand

---

[5]However, if a firm is in financial difficulty, if its managers are elderly and do not think that suitable replacements are on hand, or if it needs the support (often the capital) of a larger company, then it may seek to be acquired. Thus, when a number of Texas, Ohio, and Maryland financial institutions were in trouble in the 1980s, they lobbied to get their state legislatures to pass laws that would make it easier for them to be acquired. Out-of-state banks then moved in to help salvage the situation and minimize depositor losses.

name. Also, Polaroid was expected to receive a substantial settlement from its successful suit against Eastman Kodak, which had been found guilty of violating Polaroid's instant camera patents.

Then, Shamrock Holdings, the investment vehicle of the Roy E. Disney family, proposed a friendly takeover, was rebuffed, and made a $45-per-share hostile tender offer. Polaroid responded to the unwanted offer (1) by selling a chunk of its stock to a newly established employee stock ownership plan (ESOP), (2) by selling another chunk to a friendly investor (a *white squire*), and (3) by buying back 22 percent of its outstanding shares at $50 a share. To finance all of this, Polaroid added $536 million in bank debt. Additionally, Polaroid restructured its operations by cutting its work force by 15 percent through a voluntary program of early retirements. Shamrock responded to these actions (1) by initiating a proxy fight to elect a new slate of officers at Polaroid and (2) by filing a court suit challenging the legitimacy of Polaroid's defensive maneuvers.

After nine months of heated exchanges between the companies, an accord was reached in March 1989. Polaroid agreed to pay Shamrock $20 million in compensation for expenses incurred in the battle, and Shamrock signed an agreement promising not to seek control of Polaroid for 10 years. Also, Polaroid agreed to spend $5 million in advertising on Shamrock's radio and television stations, and to distribute to shareholders anywhere between 25 and 50 percent of its pending award from Kodak, depending on the amount of the award. Finally, Shamrock agreed to drop all litigation, as well as its proxy fight. Although defeated, Shamrock ended up making about $35 million before taxes, considering both the cash settlement and the Polaroid shares that it owns. Stanley P. Gold, Shamrock's president, said that the decision to settle was sealed by Delaware court decisions upholding Polaroid's defenses. "It isn't that I went away quietly; I tried as hard as I could," he said. Polaroid ended up with more debt, although it still has a strong balance sheet, and a $36-per-share stock price. Polaroid's president and CEO, I. MacAllister Booth, said "The fundamental changes and initiatives put in place during this period made us stronger, despite the pressure."

The 1988 battle between Campeau Corporation and Federated Department Stores provides a good illustration of a hostile takeover that succeeded—in a sense. On January 25, Campeau, a Toronto-based real estate and department store company which owned such stores as Jordan Marsh, Maas Brothers, Ann Taylor, and Brooks Brothers, made a hostile $47-a-share offer for Federated Department Stores, a Cincinnati-based company that owned Bloomingdale's, Bullock's, Burdine's, Filene's, and I. Magnin, among others. At the same time, Campeau filed suit in a New York federal court challenging Federated's "poison pill" defense, which would allow Federated's shareholders to purchase Campeau's shares at a bargain price should a hostile takeover take place. While waiting for a response from Federated's board, Campeau attempted to coax Federated into a friendly merger by increasing its bid to $61 a share. On February 16, Federated's board rejected the offer, and it also announced that it was weighing various restructuring alternatives.

Under pressure from its shareholders, Federated tentatively accepted Campeau's improved $68-a-share offer on February 29, but this agreement was derailed when R. H. Macy, the large New York–based retailer, made a last-minute bid of $73.80 per share for Federated. On March 2, Federated agreed to be acquired by Macy, but the offer consisted of both cash and securities, and many of Federated's stockholders, who were now dominated by institutional arbitrageurs, were unhappy with the deal. This kept Campeau's interest in Federated alive, even though the Macy deal contained provisions that would make it costly for Federated to back out. Specifically, Federated would be required to pay Macy up to $45 million for expenses incurred in the merger attempt, plus some other penalties. On March 18, the New York court upheld Federated's poison pill, which forced Campeau to seek a friendly merger rather than pushing forward with its hostile tender offer.

During the remainder of March, both Macy and Campeau sweetened their bids, culminating with a $74-a-share all-cash bid from Campeau and a $75.14-a-share cash bid from Macy. Finally, on April 1, Federated agreed to be acquired by Campeau for $74 a share. Macy dropped its bid in return for the right to buy I. Magnin and part of Bullock's for $1.1 billion plus a $60 million payment from Campeau for expenses incurred in the battle. By winning the battle, Robert Campeau, a former factory worker and now the dynamic head of Campeau Corporation, became the new king of American department stores. However, he had to pay top dollar to do it, and he had to finance the takeover with high-cost junk bonds. The win was costly, for Campeau was unable to meet the debt payments in the relatively slow economy that has been especially tough on department stores. After struggling through most of 1989, Campeau was forced to declare bankruptcy in early 1990.

The Campeau-Federated battle demonstrates that a resolved buyer, with access to cash and the will to go as high as needed, will usually prevail in a hostile takeover. However, bids that are too high, and that are financed with debt, may spell disaster for the acquiring firm.

Self-Test Questions

What is the difference between a hostile and a friendly merger?

Describe the mechanics of a typical friendly takeover and of a typical hostile takeover.

MERGER REGULATION

Prior to the mid-1960s, friendly acquisitions generally took place through simple exchange-of-stock mergers, and a proxy fight was the primary weapon used in a hostile control battle. However, in the mid-1960s, corporate raiders began to operate differently. First, they noted that it took a long time to mount a proxy fight—they had to first request a list of the target company's stockholders, be refused, and then get a court order forcing management to turn over the list. During that time, management could think through and then implement a strategy to fend off the raider. As a result, the instigator lost most proxy fights.

Then raiders began saying to themselves, "If we could take an action that would bring the decision to a head quickly, before management could take countermeasures, that would greatly increase the probability of a successful takeover." That led the raiders to turn from proxy fights to tender offers, which had a much shorter response time. For example, the stockholders of a company whose stock was selling for $20 might be offered $27 per share and be given two weeks to accept. The raider, meanwhile, would have accumulated a substantial block of the shares in open market purchases, and additional shares might have been purchased by institutional friends of the raider, who promised to tender their shares in exchange for the tip that a raid was to occur.

Faced with a well-planned raid, managements were generally overwhelmed. The stock might actually still be undervalued at the offered price, but management simply did not have time to get this message across to stockholders, or to find a friendly competing bidder (called a *white knight*), or anything else. This situation was thought to be unfair, and, as a result, Congress passed the Williams Act in 1968. This law had two main objectives: (1) to regulate the way in which acquiring firms can structure takeover offers, and (2) to force acquiring firms to disclose more information about their offers. Basically, Congress wanted to put target managements in a better position to defend against hostile offers. Additionally, Congress believed that shareholders needed easy access to information about tender offers—including information on any securities that might be offered in lieu of cash—in order to make rational tender-versus-don't-tender decisions.

The Williams Act placed the following three major restrictions on the activities of acquiring firms: (1) Acquirers must disclose their current holdings and future intentions within 10 days of amassing at least 5 percent of a company's stock, and they must disclose the source of the funds to be used in the acquisition. (2) The target firm's shareholders must be allowed at least 20 days to tender their shares, that is, the offer must be "open" for at least 20 days. (3) If the acquiring firm increases the offer price during the 20-day open period, all shareholders who tendered prior to the new offer must receive the higher price. In total, these restrictions were intended to reduce the ability of the acquiring firm to surprise management and to stampede target shareholders into accepting the offer. Prior to the Williams Act, offers were generally made on a first-come, first-served basis, and they were often accompanied by an implicit threat to lower the bid price after 50 percent of the shares were in hand. The legislation also gave target managements more time to mount a defense, and it gave rival bidders and white knights a chance to enter the fray and thus help the target's stockholders obtain a better price.

Many states have also passed laws designed to protect firms in their states from hostile takeovers. At first, these laws focused on disclosure requirements, but by the late 1970s, several states had enacted takeover statutes so restrictive that they virtually precluded hostile takeovers. In 1979, when MITE Corporation, a Delaware firm, made a hostile tender offer for Chicago Rivet and Machine Co., a publicly held Illinois corporation, Chicago Rivet sought protection under the Illinois Business Takeover Act. The constitutionality of the Illinois act was contested, and the U.S. Supreme Court found the law unconstitutional. The court ruled that the Illinois law put undue burdens on interstate commerce. The opinion also stated that the market for securities is a national market, and even though the issuing firm was incorporated in Illinois, the State of Illinois could not regulate interstate securities transactions.

The Illinois decision effectively eliminated the first generation of state merger regulations. However, the states kept trying to protect their state-headquartered companies, and in 1987 the U.S. Supreme Court upheld an Indiana law which radically changed the rules of the takeover game. Specifically, the Indiana law first defined "control shares" as enough shares to give an investor 20 percent of the vote, and it went on to state that when an investor buys control shares, those shares can only be voted after approval by a majority of "disinterested shareholders," defined as those who are neither officers nor inside directors of the company, nor associates of the raider. The law also gives the buyer of control shares the right to insist that a shareholders' meeting be called within 50 days to decide whether the shares may be voted. The Indiana law dealt a major blow to raiders, mainly because it slows down the action. Delaware (the state in which most large companies are incorporated) later passed a similar bill, and so did New York and a number of other states.

The new state laws also have some features which protect target stockholders from their own managers. Included are limits on the use of golden parachutes, onerous debt-financing plans, and some types of poison pills. Since these laws do not regulate tender offers per se, but, rather, govern the practices of firms in the state, they have, at least up to this point, withstood all legal challenges.

Self-Test Questions

Is there a need to regulate mergers? Explain.

Do the states play a role in merger regulation, or is it all done at the national level?

MERGER ANALYSIS

In theory, merger analysis is quite simple. The acquiring firm simply performs a capital budgeting analysis to determine whether the present value of the incremental cash flows expected to result from the merger exceeds the price that must be paid for the target company; if the net present value is positive, the acquiring firm should take steps to acquire the target firm. The target company's stockholders, on the other hand, should accept the proposal if the price offered exceeds the present value of the expected future cash flows that would result if it continued to operate independently. Theory aside, however, some difficult issues are involved: (1) the acquiring company must estimate the cash flows that will result from the acquisition; (2) it must also determine what effect, if any, the merger will have on its own required rate of return on equity; (3) it must decide how to pay for the merger—with cash, its own stock, or some other type or package of securities; and (4) having estimated the benefits of the merger, the acquiring and target firms' managers and stockholders must bargain (or fight) over how to share these benefits.

Operating versus Financial Mergers

From the standpoint of financial analysis, there are two basic types of mergers, operating mergers and financial mergers.

1.   An *operating merger* is one in which the operations of two companies are integrated with the expectation of obtaining synergistic effects. To illustrate, Texas Air's 1987 acquisition of People Express resulted in People's planes being repainted and incorporated into Texas Air's Continental Airlines subsidiary.

2.   A pure *financial merger* is one in which the merged companies will not be operated as a single unit and from which no significant operating economies are expected. Coca-Cola's acquisition of Columbia Pictures with $748 million of surplus cash is an example of a financial merger.

Of course, mergers may actually combine these two features. For example, some of RCA's electronics and defense operations were merged with similar GE businesses, but other operations, such as RCA's NBC television network, have been maintained as separate lines of business.

Valuing the Target Firm

To determine the value of the target firm, two key items are needed: (1) a set of pro forma financial statements which develop the incremental cash flows expected from the merger, and (2) a discount rate, or cost of capital, to apply to these projected cash flows.

Pro Forma Cash Flow Statements.   The development of accurate postmerger cash flow forecasts is the most important step in a merger analysis. In a pure financial merger, the postmerger cash flows are simply the sum of the expected cash flows of the two companies if they were to continue to operate independently. However, if the two firms' operations are to be integrated, or if the acquiring firm plans to change the target firm's management in order to get better results, then forecasting future cash flows is a more complex task.

Table 24-2 contains the projected cash flow statements for Apex Corporation, which is being considered as a target by Hightech, a large conglomerate. The projected data are for the postmerger period, so all synergistic effects have been included. Apex currently uses 30 percent debt, but if it were acquired, Hightech would increase Apex's debt ratio to 50 percent. Both Hightech and Apex have 40 percent marginal federal-plus-state tax rates.

The net cash flows shown in Table 24-2 are the flows that would be available to Hightech's stockholders, and these are the basis of the valuation.[6] Of course, the

---

[6]We purposely kept the cash flows relatively simple to help focus on the key issues of the valuation process. In an actual merger valuation, the cash flows would be much more complex, normally including such items as additional capital furnished by the acquiring firm, tax loss carry-forwards, tax effects of plant and equipment valuation adjustments, and cash flows from the sale of some of the subsidiary's assets.

Table 24-2   Hightech Corporation: Projected Postmerger Cash Flow Statements for the Apex Subsidiary as of December 31 (Millions of Dollars)

	1991	1992	1993	1994	1995
Net sales	$105	$126	$151	$174	$191
Cost of goods sold	80	94	111	127	137
Selling and administrative expenses	10	12	13	15	16
EBIT	$ 15	$ 20	$ 27	$ 32	$ 38
Interest[a]	3	4	5	6	6
EBT	$ 12	$ 16	$ 22	$ 26	$ 32
Taxes[b]	4	5	7	9	11
Net income	$ 8	$ 11	$ 15	$ 17	$ 21
Retained by Apex to finance growth[c]	4	4	7	9	12
Cash available to Hightech	$ 4	$ 7	$ 8	$ 8	$ 9
Terminal value[d]					121
Net cash flow[e]	$ 4	$ 7	$ 8	$ 8	$130

[a]Interest payments are estimates based on Apex's existing debt plus additional debt required to increase the debt ratio to 50 percent, plus additional debt required after the merger to finance asset expansion while maintaining the 50 percent target capital structure.

[b]Hightech will file a consolidated tax return after the merger. Thus, the taxes shown here are the full corporate taxes attributable to Apex's operations: there will be no additional taxes on any cash flows passed from Apex to Hightech.

[c]Some of the net income generated by the Apex subsidiary after the merger will be retained to finance Apex's own asset growth, while some will be transferred to Hightech to pay dividends on its stock or for redeployment within the corporation. It is assumed that depreciation-generated funds are used by Apex to replace worn-out and obsolete plant and equipment.

[d]Apex's available cash flows are expected to grow at a constant 10 percent rate after 1995. The value of all post-1995 cash flows as of December 31, 1995, is estimated by use of the constant growth model to be $121 million:

$$V_{1995} = \frac{\$9(1.10)}{0.182 - 0.10} = \$121 \text{ million.}$$

In the next section, we discuss the estimation of the 18.2 percent cost of equity. The $121 million is the PV in 1995 of the stream of cash flows for years 1996 and thereafter.

[e]These are the net cash flows which are available to Hightech by virtue of the acquisition of Apex. These cash flows could be used for dividend payments to Hightech's stockholders, to finance asset expansion in Hightech's other divisions and subsidiaries, and so on.

postmerger cash flows attributable to the target firm are extremely difficult to estimate, and in a complete merger valuation, just as in a complete capital budgeting analysis, the component cash flow probability distributions should be specified, and sensitivity, scenario, and simulation analyses should be conducted. Indeed, in a friendly merger, the acquiring firm would send a team consisting of literally dozens of accountants, engineers, and so forth, to the target firm's headquarters to go over its books, to estimate required maintenance expenditures, to set values on assets such as real estate and petroleum reserves, and the like.

Estimating the Discount Rate. The bottom-line net cash flows shown in Table 24-2 are equity flows, so they should be discounted at the cost of equity rather than at the company's overall cost of capital. Further, the cost of equity used must reflect the riskiness of the net cash flows in the table, hence the appropriate discount rate is Apex's cost of equity, not that of either Hightech or the consolidated postmerger firm.

Apex's market-determined premerger beta was 1.28. However, this reflects its premerger 30 percent debt ratio, while its postmerger debt ratio will increase to 50 percent. The Hamada equations, which were first developed in Chapter 13, can be used to approximate the effects of the leverage change on beta. First, we obtain the unlevered beta of Apex's assets:

$$b_U = \frac{b_L}{1 + (1 - T)(D/E)} = \frac{1.28}{1 + (1 - 0.40)(0.30/0.70)} = \frac{1.28}{1.26} = 1.02.$$

Next, we relever Apex's beta to reflect its new 50 percent debt ratio:

$$b_L = b_U[1 + (1 - T)(D/E)]$$

$$= 1.02[1 + (1 - 0.40)(0.50/0.50)] = 1.02(1.6) = 1.63.$$

Finally, we use the Security Market Line to estimate Apex's postmerger cost of equity. If the risk-free rate is 10 percent and the market risk premium is 5 percent, then Apex's cost of equity, k_s, after the merger with Hightech, would be 18.15 percent:[7]

$$k_s = k_{RF} + (RP_M)b = 10\% + (5\%)1.63 = 18.15\% \approx 18.2\%.$$

Valuing the Cash Flows. The current value of Apex to Hightech is the present value of the cash flows expected to accrue to Hightech, discounted at 18.2 percent (in millions of dollars):

$$V_{1990} = \frac{\$4}{(1.182)^1} + \frac{\$7}{(1.182)^2} + \frac{\$8}{(1.182)^3} + \frac{\$8}{(1.182)^4} + \frac{\$130}{(1.182)^5} \approx \$74.$$

Thus, if Hightech could acquire Apex for $74 million or less, the merger would appear to be acceptable from Hightech's standpoint. Obviously, Hightech would try to buy at as low a price as possible, while Apex would hold out for the highest possible price. The final price is determined by negotiation, with the better negotiator capturing most of the incremental value. *The larger the synergistic benefits, the more room for bargaining, and the higher the probability that the merger will actually be consummated.*[8]

---

[7]In this example, we used the Capital Asset Pricing Model to estimate Apex's cost of equity, and thus we assumed that investors require a premium for market risk only. We could have also conducted a within-firm, or corporate, risk analysis, in which the relevant risk would be the contribution of Apex's cash flows to the total risk of the postmerger firm.

In actual merger situations among large firms, companies almost always hire an investment banker to help develop valuation estimates. For example, when General Electric acquired Utah International, GE hired Morgan Stanley to determine Utah's value. We discussed the valuation process with the Morgan Stanley analyst in charge of the appraisal, and he confirmed that they applied all of the standard procedures discussed in this chapter. Note, though, that merger analysis, like the analysis of any other complex issue, requires judgment, and people's judgments differ as to how much weight to give to different methods in any given situation.

[8]It has been estimated that of all merger negotiations seriously begun, fewer than one-third actually come to fruition. Also, note that in contested merger situations, the company that offers the most will usually make the acquisition, and the company that will gain the greatest synergistic benefits should bid the most.

Postmerger Control

The employment/control situation is often of vital interest in a merger analysis. First, consider the situation in which a small, owner-managed firm sells out to a larger concern. The owner-manager may be anxious to retain a high-status position, and he or she may also have developed a camaraderie with the employees and thus be concerned about keeping operating control of the organization after the merger. Thus, these points are often stressed during the merger negotiations.[9] When a publicly owned firm not controlled by its managers is merged into another company, the acquired firm's management is also worried about its postmerger position. If the acquiring firm agrees to retain the old management, then management may be willing to support the merger and to recommend its acceptance to the stockholders. If the old management is to be removed, then it will probably resist the merger.[10]

Self-Test Questions

What is the difference between an operating and a financial merger?

Describe how the postmerger cash flows are estimated in a merger analysis.

What is the basis for the discount rate in a merger analysis? Describe how this rate might be estimated.

What impact does postmerger control have on a merger analysis?

STRUCTURING THE TAKEOVER BID

The acquiring firm's offer to the target's shareholders can be in the form of cash, stock of the acquiring firm, debt of the acquiring firm, or a combination of the three. The structure of the bid is extremely important, since it affects (1) the capital structure of the postmerger firm, (2) the tax treatment of both the acquiring firm and the target's stockholders, and (3) the types of federal and state regulations to which the

---

[9]The acquiring firm may also be concerned about this point, especially if the target firm's management is quite good. Indeed, a condition of the merger may be that the management team agree to stay on for a period such as five years after the merger. Also, the price paid may be contingent on the acquired firm's performance subsequent to the merger. For example, when International Holdings acquired Walker Products, the price paid was an immediate 100,000 shares of International Holdings stock worth $63 per share plus an additional 30,000 shares each year for the next three years, provided Walker Products earned at least $1 million during each of these years. Since Walker's managers owned the stock and would receive the bonus, they had a strong incentive to stay on and help the firm meet its targets.

Finally, if the managers of the target company are highly competent but do not wish to remain on after the merger, the acquiring firm may build into the merger contract a noncompetitive agreement with the old management. Typically, the acquired firm's principal officers must agree not to affiliate with a new business which is competitive with the one they sold for a specified period, say five years. Such agreements are especially important with service-oriented businesses.

[10]Managements of firms that are thought to be attractive merger candidates occasionally arrange *golden parachutes* for themselves. Golden parachutes are extremely lucrative retirement plans which take effect if a merger is consummated. Thus, when Bendix was acquired by Allied, Bill Agee, Bendix's chairman, "pulled the ripcord of his golden parachute" and walked away with $4 million. If a golden parachute is large enough, it can also function as a poison pill — for example, when the president of a firm worth $10 million would have to be paid $8 million if the firm is acquired. Congress has recently reduced the value of golden parachutes by increasing the tax consequences to the firm, but they seem to persist.

acquiring firm will be subjected. In this section, we focus on how taxes and regulation influence the way in which acquiring firms structure their offers.

The form of payment offered to the target shareholders determines the personal tax treatment of the target's stockholders. Target shareholders do not have to pay taxes on the transaction if they maintain a substantial equity position in the combined firm, defined by the IRS to mean that at least 50 percent of the payment to target shareholders must be in shares (either common or preferred) of the acquiring firm. In such nontaxable offers, target shareholders do not realize any capital gains or losses until the equity securities they receive in the takeover are sold. However, capital gains must be taken and treated as income in the transaction year if an offer consists of over 50 percent cash and/or debt securities.

All other things equal, stockholders prefer nontaxable offers, since they may then postpone the realization of capital gains and the payment of taxes. Most target shareholders are thus willing to sell their stock for a lower price in a nontaxable offer than in a taxable offer. As a result, one might expect nontaxable bids to dominate. However, this is not the case—roughly half of all mergers have been taxable, and, as noted in Table 24-1, two of the top five mergers have been all-cash offers. Prior to 1986, if a firm paid more than book value for a target firm's assets in a taxable merger, it could write up those assets, depreciate the marked-up value for tax purposes, and thus lower the postmerger firm's taxes vis-à-vis the taxes of the two firms operating separately. At the same time, the target firm did not have to pay any taxes on the write-up at the time of the merger.

Under current law, if the acquiring company writes up the target company's assets for tax purposes, then the target company must pay capital gains taxes in the year the merger occurs. (These taxes can be avoided if the acquiring company elects not to write up acquired assets and depreciates them on their old basis.)

Note also that the maximum capital gains tax rate on personal income rose from 20 percent to 28 percent, a 40 percent increase, in 1986. This, of course, means that target companies' stockholders now net out less after a merger than they would have under the old law. When one considers the combined effects of the corporate and personal tax changes, it is clear that the tax treatment of mergers is significantly less favorable today than it was prior to 1987. This means that a lot less money will end up in the pockets of selling stockholders, so they will require larger premiums to sell.

Securities laws also have an effect on the construction of the offer. As we discussed in Chapter 15, the SEC has oversight over the issuance of new securities, including stock or debt issued in connection with a merger. Therefore, whenever a corporation bids for control of another firm through the exchange of equity or debt, the entire process must take place under the scrutiny of the Securities and Exchange Commission. The time required for such reviews allows target managements to implement defensive tactics and other firms to make competing offers, and, as a result, nearly all hostile tender offers are for cash rather than securities.

Self-Test Questions

What are some alternative ways of paying for mergers?

How do taxes influence the payment structure?

How do securities laws affect the payment structure?

THE ROLE OF INVESTMENT BANKERS

The investment banking community is involved with mergers in a number of ways: (1) they help arrange mergers, (2) they help target companies develop and implement defensive tactics, (3) they help value target companies, (4) they help finance mergers, and (5) they speculate in the stocks of potential merger candidates. These merger-related activities have been quite profitable. For example, the investment bankers and lawyers who arranged the Campeau-Federated merger earned fees of about $83 million—First Boston and Wasserstein Perella earned about $29 million from Campeau, and Goldman Sacks, Hellman & Friedman, and Shearson Lehman Hutton received $54 million for representing Federated. No wonder investment banking houses are able to make top offers to finance graduates!

Arranging Mergers

The major investment banking firms have merger and acquisition groups which operate within their corporate finance departments. (Corporate finance departments offer advice, as opposed to underwriting or brokerage services, to business firms.) Members of these groups strive to identify firms with excess cash that might want to buy other firms, companies that might be willing to be bought, and firms that might for a number of reasons be attractive to others. Also, if an oil company, for instance, decided to expand into coal mining, then it might enlist the aid of an investment banker to help it locate and then negotiate with a target coal company. Similarly, dissident stockholders of firms with poor track records might work with investment bankers to oust management by helping to arrange a merger. Investment bankers are reported to have offered packages of financing to corporate raiders, where the package includes both designing the securities to be used in the tender offer, and lining up people and firms who will buy the target firm's stock now, and then tender it once the final offer is made. The financing role is discussed in more detail in a later section.

Investment bankers have also taken some illegal actions in the merger arena. For one thing, they are reported to have *parked stock*—purchasing it for a raider under a guaranteed buy-back agreement—to help the raider avoid the disclosure rules. Some of this came out in connection with recent insider trading scandals.

Developing Defensive Tactics

Target firms that do not want to be acquired generally enlist the help of an investment banking firm, along with a law firm that specializes in helping to block mergers. Defenses include such tactics as (1) changing the bylaws so that only one-third of the directors are elected each year and/or so that a 75 percent approval (a *supermajority*) versus a simple majority is required to approve a merger; (2) trying to convince the target firm's stockholders that the price being offered is too low; (3) raising antitrust issues in the hope that the Justice Department will intervene; (4) repurchasing stock in the open market in an effort to push the price above that being offered by the potential acquirer; (5) getting a white knight who is more acceptable to the target firm's management to compete with the potential acquirer;

(6) getting a white squire who is friendly to current management to buy some of the target firm's shares, and (7) taking a poison pill, as described next.

Poison pills—which occasionally really do amount to virtually committing economic suicide to avoid a takeover—are such tactics as borrowing on terms that require immediate repayment of all loans if the firm is acquired, selling off at bargain prices the assets that originally made the firm a desirable target, granting such lucrative golden parachutes to their executives that the cash drain from these payments would render the merger infeasible, and planning defensive mergers which would leave the firm with new assets of questionable value and a huge debt load to service. Currently, the most popular poison pill is for a company to give its stockholders *stock purchase rights* which allow them to buy at half-price the stock of an acquiring firm, should the firm be acquired. The blatant use of poison pills is constrained by directors' awareness that excessive use could trigger personal suits by stockholders against directors who voted for them, and, perhaps in the near future, by laws that would further limit management's use of pills. Still, investment bankers and antitakeover lawyers are busy thinking up new poison pill formulas, and others are just as actively trying to come up with antidotes.[11]

Another takeover defense that is being used frequently is the employee stock ownership plan (ESOP). ESOPs are designed to give lower-level employees an ownership stake in the firm, and current tax laws provide generous incentives for companies to establish such plans and fund them with the firm's common stock. As we discussed earlier, Polaroid used an ESOP to help fend off Shamrock Holdings' hostile takeover attempt. Also, in early 1989, Procter & Gamble set up an ESOP that, along with an existing profit-sharing plan, eventually will give employees a 20 percent ownership stake in the company. Since the trustees of ESOPs generally support current management in any takeover attempt, and since 85 percent of the votes is generally required to complete a merger, an ESOP can provide an effective defense against a hostile tender offer. Procter & Gamble stated that the ESOP was designed primarily to lower its costs by utilizing the plan's tax advantages and to improve employee's retirement security. However, the company also noted that the ESOP will strengthen its defenses against a takeover.

Establishing a Fair Value

If a friendly merger is being worked out between two firms' managements, it is important to be able to document that the agreed-upon price is a fair one; otherwise, the stockholders of either company may sue to block the merger. Therefore, in many large mergers, each side will hire an investment banking firm to evaluate the target company and to help establish the fair price. For example, General Electric employed Morgan Stanley to determine a fair price for Utah International, as did Royal Dutch to help establish the price it paid for Shell Oil. Even if the merger is

---

[11]It has become extremely difficult and expensive for companies to buy "directors' insurance" which protects the board from losses from such contingencies as stockholders' suits, and even when insurance is available, it often does not pay for losses if the directors did not exercise due caution and judgment. This exposure is making directors extremely leery of actions that might trigger stockholder suits.

not friendly, investment bankers may still be asked to help establish a price. If a surprise tender offer is to be made, the acquiring firm will want to know the lowest price at which it might be able to acquire the stock, while the target firm may seek help in "proving" that the price being offered is too low.[12]

Financing Mergers

Many mergers are financed with the acquiring company's excess cash. At other times, however, the acquiring company has no excess cash, hence requires a source of funds to pay for the target company. Perhaps the single most important factor behind the 1980s merger wave has been the widespread use of junk bonds, and the system that has been developed to market these bonds.

As noted in Chapter 16, Drexel Burnham Lambert was the primary developer of junk bonds, defined as bonds rated below investment grade (BBB/Baa). Prior to Drexel's entry on the scene, it was almost impossible to sell low-grade bonds to raise new capital. Drexel then pioneered a procedure wherein a target firm's situation would be appraised very closely, and a cash flow projection similar to that in Table 24-2 (but much more detailed) would be developed. Part of the cash flow projection would generally include cash flows from major asset sales.

With the cash flows having been forecasted, Drexel's analysts would figure out a debt mix — amount of debt, maturity structure, and interest rate — that could be serviced by the cash flows. With this information, Drexel's junk bond people, operating out of Beverly Hills with a high degree of independence from the New York headquarters, would approach financial institutions (savings and loans, insurance companies, and mutual funds) and wealthy individuals with a financing plan and an offer of a rate of return several percentage points above the rate on more conservative investments. Drexel's early deals worked out well, and the institutions that bought the bonds were quite pleased. These results enabled Drexel to expand its network of investors, and to commit to finance larger and larger mergers (and LBOs). T. Boone Pickens, who went after Phillips, Texaco, and several other oil giants, was an early Drexel customer.

At the present time, to be a successful investment banker in the mergers and acquisitions (M&A) business, a banker must be able to offer a financing package to clients, whether they are acquirers like Campeau who need capital to take over companies like Federated Department Stores or target companies like Union Carbide or CBS trying to finance stock repurchase plans or other defenses against takeovers. Drexel was the leading player in the merger financing game, but since Drexel's declaration of bankruptcy in early 1990, the role of chief takeover financier

---

[12]Such investigations must obviously be done in secret, for if someone knew that Company A was thinking of offering, say, $50 per share for Company T, which was currently selling at $35 per share, then huge profits could be made. One of the biggest scandals to hit Wall Street in the 1980s was the disclosure that Ivan Boesky was buying information from Dennis Levine, a senior member of the investment banking house of Drexel Burnham Lambert, about target companies that Drexel was analyzing for others. Purchases based on such insider information would, of course, raise the prices of the stocks and thus force Drexel's clients to pay more than they otherwise would have had to pay. Levine and Boesky, among others, went to jail for their improper use of inside information, and others may soon follow.

remains unfilled. However, Merrill Lynch, Morgan Stanley, Salomon Brothers, and others are all eager for the title.

Arbitrage Operations

Arbitrage generally means simultaneously buying and selling the same commodity or security in two different markets at different prices, and pocketing a risk-free return. However, the major brokerage houses, as well as some wealthy private investors, are engaged in a different type of arbitrage called *risk arbitrage*. The *arbitrageurs,* or "arbs" as they are called, speculate in the stocks of companies that are likely takeover targets. Vast amounts of capital are required to speculate in a large number of securities and thus reduce risk, and also to make money on narrow spreads, but the large investment bankers have the wherewithal to play the game. To be successful, arbs need to be able to sniff out likely targets, assess the probability of offers reaching fruition, and move in and out of the market quickly and with low transaction costs.

The risk arbitrage business has been rocked by insider trading scandals. Indeed, it was disclosed that the most famous arb of all, Ivan Boesky, had been buying inside information from high-ranked officials of some leading investment banking houses to help make his millions. The Boesky affair slowed down risk arbitrage activity, but it will undoubtedly survive this setback.

Self-Test Questions

What are some defensive tactics that firms can use to resist hostile takeover attempts?

What is the difference between arbitrage and risk arbitrage?

What role did junk bonds play in the merger wave of the 1980s?

WHO WINS: THE EMPIRICAL EVIDENCE

The most recent merger wave has been notable not only for the great number of firms that have combined, but also for the high percentage of hostile takeovers. With all this activity, the following questions have emerged: Do corporate acquisitions create value, and, if so, how is the value shared between the parties involved?

Financial researchers have classified corporate acquisitions as part of "the market for corporate control." Under this concept, management teams are viewed as facing constant competition from other management teams. If the team that currently controls a firm is not maximizing the value of the firm's assets, then an acquisition will likely occur and increase the value of the firm by replacing its poor managers with good managers. Further, under this theory, intense competition will cause managers to combine or divest assets whenever such steps would increase the value of the firm.

Most researchers agree that takeovers increase the wealth of the shareholders of target firms, for otherwise they would not agree to the offer. However, there is a debate as to whether or not mergers benefit the acquiring firm's shareholders. In particular, managements of acquiring firms may be motivated by factors other than shareholder wealth maximization; for example, they may want to merge merely to increase the size of the corporations they manage, since increased size usually brings larger salaries and more job security, perquisites, power, and prestige.

The validity of the competing views on who gains from corporate acquisitions can be tested by examining the stock price changes that occur around a merger or takeover announcement. Such changes in the stock prices of the acquiring and target firms represent market participants' beliefs about the value created by the merger, and about how this value will be divided between the target and acquiring firms' shareholders. As long as the market participants are neither systematically wrong nor biased in their perceptions of the effects of mergers, examining a large sample of stock price movements will shed light on the issue of who gains from mergers.

One cannot simply examine stock prices around merger announcement dates, because other factors influence stock prices. For example, if a merger was announced on a day when the entire market advanced, the fact that the firm in question's price rose would not necessarily signify that the merger created value. Hence, studies examine *abnormal returns* associated with merger announcements, where abnormal returns are defined as that part of a stock price change caused by factors other than changes in the general stock market.

Many studies have examined both acquiring and target firms' stock price responses to mergers and tender offers.[13] Jointly, these studies have covered nearly every acquisition involving publicly traded firms from the early 1960s to the present, and they are remarkably consistent in their results: On average, the stock price of target firms increases by about 30 percent in hostile tender offers, while in friendly mergers the average increase is about 20 percent. However, for both hostile and friendly deals, the stock prices of acquiring firms, on average, remain constant. Thus, the evidence strongly indicates (1) that acquisitions do create value, but (2) that shareholders of target firms reap virtually all of the benefits.

In hindsight, these results are not too surprising. First, target firms' shareholders can always say "no," so they are in the driver's seat. Second, takeovers are a competitive game, so if one potential acquiring firm is not willing to pay full value for a potential target, then another firm will generally jump in with a higher bid. Finally, managements of acquiring firms might well be willing to give up all the value created by the merger, because the merger would enhance the acquiring managers' personal positions with no explicit cost to their shareholders.

It has also been argued that acquisitions may increase shareholder wealth at the expense of bondholders — in particular, concern has been expressed that leveraged buyouts dilute the claims of bondholders. Specific instances can be cited where bonds were downgraded and bondholders did suffer losses as a direct result of an acquisition, but most of the studies find no evidence to support the contention that bondholders generally lose in corporate acquisitions.

---

[13]For an excellent summary of the effects of mergers on value, see Michael C. Jensen and Richard S. Ruback, "The Market for Corporate Control: The Scientific Evidence," *Journal of Financial Economics,* April 1983, 5–50.

Self-Test Questions

Explain how researchers can study the effects of mergers on shareholder wealth.

Do mergers create value? If so, who profits from this value?

Do the research results discussed in this section seem logical? Explain.

CORPORATE ALLIANCES

Mergers are one way for two companies to join forces, but many companies are striking cooperative deals, called *corporate alliances,* which fall far short of merging. These alliances take many forms, from straightforward marketing agreements to joint ownership of world-scale operations. One form of corporate alliance is the *joint venture,* in which parts of companies are joined to achieve specific, limited objectives.[14] A joint venture is controlled by a management team consisting of representatives of the two (or more) parent companies.

Joint ventures have been used often by U.S., Japanese, and European firms to share technology and/or marketing expertise. For example, in 1989 General Electric announced a joint venture with Britain's unrelated General Electric Company to manufacture appliances, medical equipment, and electrical products. In the same month, Whirlpool announced a joint venture with the Dutch electronics giant Philips to produce appliances under Philips's brand names in five European countries. By joining with their foreign counterparts, U.S. firms can get a strong foothold in Europe before 1992, the year that the European community will dismantle its trade barriers and become one unified market. Although alliances are new to some firms, they are established practices to others. For example, Corning Glass now obtains over half its profits from 23 joint ventures, two-thirds of them with foreign companies representing almost all of Europe, as well as Japan, China, South Korea, and Australia.

Self-Test Questions

What is the difference between a merger and a corporate alliance?

What is a joint venture? Give some reasons why joint ventures may be advantageous to the parties involved.

LEVERAGED BUYOUTS

The pros and cons of *leveraged buyouts (LBOs)* were discussed in detail in Chapter 15. To briefly review the concept, in an LBO a small group of equity investors, usually including current management, acquires a firm in a transaction financed

---

[14]Cross-licensing, consortia, joint bidding, and franchising are still other ways for firms to combine resources. For more information on joint ventures, see Sanford V. Berg, Jerome Duncan, and Phillip Friedman, *Joint Venture Strategies and Corporate Innovation* (Cambridge, Mass.: Oelgeschlager, Gunn and Hain, 1982).

largely by borrowing. The debt is serviced with funds generated by the acquired company's operations and, often, by the sale of some of its assets. Generally, the acquiring group plans to run the acquired company for a number of years, boost its sales and profits, and then take it public again as a stronger company. Naturally, the acquiring group expects to make a substantial profit from the LBO, but the inherent risks are great due to the heavy use of financial leverage. To illustrate the profit potential, Kohlberg Kravis Roberts & Company (KKR), the leading LBO specialist firm, has averaged a spectacular 50 percent annual return in recent years on its LBO investments. Potential returns of this magnitude have not gone unnoticed by investors. In 1987, about $35 billion worth of LBOs took place, 1988 brought about LBO deals worth about $45 billion, and in 1989 LBO activity reached $55 billion. As long as realized returns (and investment bankers' fees) remain high, and as long as financing is available, LBOs will continue to be a major force in the economy. However, the recent troubles in the junk bond market will undoubtedly reduce the volume of LBOs.

To illustrate an LBO, consider KKR's $25 billion buyout of RJR Nabisco. RJR, a leading producer of tobacco and food products with brands such as Winston, Camel, Planters, Ritz, Oreo, and Del Monte, was trading at about $55 a share in October 1988. Then, F. Ross Johnson, the company's president and CEO, announced a $75 a share, or $17.6 billion, offer to outside stockholders in a plan to take the firm private. This deal, if completed, would have been the largest-ever business transaction. After the announcement, RJR's stock price soared to $77.25, which indicated that investors thought the final price would be even higher than Johnson's opening bid. Then, a few days later, KKR offered $90 per share, or $20.6 billion, for the firm. The battle between the two bidders raged until late November, when RJR's board accepted KKR's revised bid of cash and securities worth about $106 a share, for a total value of about $25.1 billion. Of course, the investment bankers' fees reflected the record size of the deal—the bankers received almost $400 million, with Drexel Burnham Lambert alone getting over $200 million. Johnson lost his job, but he did walk away with a multimillion dollar golden parachute.

Is RJR worth $25 billion, or did Henry Kravis and his partners let their egos overcome their judgment? It will take several years before the answer is known, but at the time, analysts believed that the deal was workable, but just barely. To meet an estimated $2.5 billion in annual debt payments, KKR is expected to sell off a chunk of Nabisco's food businesses, to lay off employees, to cut advertising and marketing expenses, and to slash spending on new plants. Thus far, things seem to be going well. In 1989, RJR cut more than 2,500 workers from its roles and sold three corporate aircraft. Further, RJR sold its European food units for $2.5 billion; Chun King for $52 million; the Baby Ruth, Butterfinger, and Pearson candy businesses for $370 million; and Del Monte's fresh fruit operations for $900 million. However, a recession, or soaring interest rates, or a prolonged strike could jeopardize the completion of this strategy.

In the highly leveraged world of LBOs, KKR insists that the structure of the buyout is relatively conservative. The new RJR owes banks and bondholders $22.8 billion, while stockholders' equity totals $7.4 billion. That's a 3-to-1 ratio, compared to the 9-to-1 ratio for the average LBO. Still, even the enormous annual cash flows produced by RJR's cigarettes and cookies probably will fall about $400 million short of meeting the annual interest payments over the next few years. On the plus side, RJR will no longer have to pay out $450 million annually in common dividends. Further, the new management team will be highly motivated to make a success of the venture, for if it is successful, they will become *very* wealthy, while if it fails, they will be much worse off than if they had never done the LBO.

LBOs have tended to be disastrous for bondholders, and the RJR deal was no exception. Both Metropolitan Life Insurance Company and ITT Corporation have filed suits against RJR in New York State. RJR bonds lost about 20 percent of their value as a result of the LBO, and this translated into a $40 million loss for Met Life alone. Both suits claim that the value of bondholdings was reduced substantially by the LBO, and ITT's suit goes on to charge that RJR's management knew that the LBO was coming and failed to disclose the information, while Met Life's suit claims that the LBO constituted a breach of trust by RJR's management. Undoubtedly, the outcome of these suits will be some time in coming, but, as we discussed in Chapter 16, the short-term impact of the LBO was a near paralysis of the industrial bond markets and the appearance of "super poison put" restrictive convenants.

Self-Test Questions

What is an LBO?

Have LBOs been profitable in recent years?

What actions do companies typically take to meet the large debt burdens resulting from LBOs?

What impact do LBOs typically have on bondholders?

DIVESTITURES

Although corporations do more buying than selling of productive facilities, a good bit of selling does occur. In this section, we briefly discuss the major types of divestitures, after which we present some recent examples and rationales for divestitures.

Types of Divestitures

There are three primary types of divestitures: (1) sale of an operating unit to another firm, (2) setting up the business to be divested as a separate corporation and then giving (or "spinning off") its stock on a pro rata basis to the divesting firm's stockholders, and (3) outright liquidation of assets.

Sale to another firm generally involves the sale of an entire division or unit, usually for cash but sometimes for stock of the acquiring firm. In a *spin-off,* the firm's existing stockholders are given new stock representing separate ownership rights in the division which was divested. The division establishes its own board of directors and officers, and it becomes a separate company. The stockholders end up owning shares of two firms instead of one, but no cash has been transferred. Finally, in a *liquidation* the assets of a division are sold off piecemeal, rather than as a single entity. To illustrate the different types of divestitures, we present some recent examples in the next section.

Divestiture Illustrations

1.   Esmark, Inc., a holding company which owned such consumer products companies as Swift meats, recently sold off several of its non-consumer-oriented divisions, including petroleum properties for which Mobil and some other oil companies paid $1.1 billion. Investors generally thought of Esmark as a meat packing and consumer products company, and its stock price reflected this image rather than that of a company with large holdings of valuable oil reserves carried at low balance sheet values. Thus, Esmark's stock was undervalued, according to its managers, and the company was in danger of a takeover bid. Selling the oil properties helped Esmark raise its market value from $19 to $45. The Esmark divestiture is an example of a firm's selling assets to another company.

2.   IU International, a multimillion-dollar conglomerate that was listed on the NYSE, spun off three major subsidiaries—Gotaas-Larson, an ocean shipping company involved in petroleum transportation; Canadian Utilities, an electric utility; and Echo Bay Mining, a gold mining company. IU kept its distribution and manufacturing operations. IU's management originally acquired and combined several highly cyclical businesses such as ocean shipping and gold mining with stable ones such as utilities in order to gain overall corporate stability through diversification. The strategy worked reasonably well from an operating standpoint, but it failed in the financial markets. According to its management, IU's very diversity kept it from being classified in any particular industrial group, so security analysts tended not to follow the company and therefore did not understand it or recommend it to investors. (Analysts tend to concentrate on an industry, and they do not like to recommend—and investors do not like to invest in—a company they do not understand.) As a result, IU had a low P/E ratio and a low market price. After the spin-offs, the package of securities rose in market value from $10 to $75, which greatly exceeded general stock market gains.

3.   AT&T was broken up in 1984 to settle a Justice Department antitrust suit f in the 1970s.[15] For almost 100 years AT&T had operated as a holding compan owned Western Electric (its manufacturing subsidiary), Bell Labs (its rese a huge long-distance network system which was operated as a divisior company, and 22 Bell operating companies, such as Pacific Tele Telephone, Southern Bell, and Southwestern Bell. AT&T was r separate companies—a slimmed-down AT&T which kept W and the long-distance operations, plus seven new region panies that were created from the 22 old operating telep.

---

[15]Another forced divestiture involved Du Pont and General Motors. In 192 cial trouble, and Du Pont supplied capital in exchange for 23 percent of the Justice Department won an antitrust suit which required Du Pont to spin off (to its GM stock.

of the seven new telephone companies was then spun off to the old AT&T's stock-holders. A person who held 100 shares of old AT&T stock owned, after the divesti-ture, 100 shares of the "new" AT&T plus 10 shares of each of the seven new oper-ating companies. These 170 shares were backed by the same assets that had previously backed 100 shares of old AT&T common.

The AT&T divestiture resulted from a suit by the Justice Department, which wanted to divide the Bell System into a regulated monopoly segment (the seven regional telephone companies) and a manufacturing/long-distance segment which would be subjected to competition. The breakup was expected to strengthen com-petition and thus speed up technological change in those parts of the telecommu-nications industry that are not natural monopolies.

4.   Woolworth recently liquidated every one of its 336 Woolco discount stores. This made the company, which had had sales of $7.2 billion before the liquidation, 30 percent smaller. Woolco had posted operating losses of $19 million in the year before the liquidation, and its losses in the six months preceding it had climbed to an alarming $21 million. Woolworth's CEO, Edward F. Gibbons, was quoted as say-ing: "How many losses can you take?" Woolco's demise necessitated an after-tax write-off of $325 million, but management believed that it was better to go ahead and "bite the bullet" than to let the losing stores bleed the company to death.

5.   As a result of some imprudent loans to oil companies and to developing nations, Continental Illinois, one of the largest U.S. bank holding companies, was recently threatened with bankruptcy. Continental then sold off several profitable divisions, such as its leasing and credit card operations, to raise funds to cover bad-loan losses and deposit withdrawals. In effect, Continental sold assets in order to stay alive. Ultimately, Continental was bailed out by the Federal Deposit Insurance Corporation and the Federal Reserve, which (1) arranged a $7.5 billion rescue package and (2) provided a blanket guarantee for all of Continental's $40 billion of deposits, which kept deposits in excess of $100,000 from fleeing the bank because of their uninsured status.

The preceding examples illustrate that the reasons for divestitures vary widely. Sometimes the market does not appear to properly recognize the value of a firm's assets when they are held as part of a conglomerate; the Esmark oil divestiture is an example. Similarly, if IU International's management is correct, there are cases in which a company has become so complex and diverse that analysts and investors just do not understand it and consequently ignore it. Other companies need cash either to finance expansion in their primary business lines or to reduce a large debt burden, and divestitures can be used to raise this cash; the RJR Nabisco example in the preceding section illustrates this point. The actions listed also show that running a business is a dynamic process—conditions change, corporate strategies change in response, and, as a result, firms alter their asset portfolios by acquisitions and/or divestitures. Some divestitures, such as Woolworth's liquidation of its Woolco stores, occur in order to unload losing assets that would otherwise drag the company down, while the AT&T example is one of the many instances in which a divestiture is the result of an antitrust settlement. Finally, Continental's actions represent a desperate effort to get the cash needed to stay alive.

Self-Test Questions

What are some reasons that companies divest assets?

What are the three primary types of divestitures?

HOLDING COMPANIES

Holding companies date from 1889, when New Jersey became the first state to pass a law permitting corporations to be formed for the sole purpose of owning the stocks of other companies. Many of the advantages and disadvantages of holding companies are identical to those large-scale operations already discussed in connection with mergers and consolidations. Whether a company is organized on a divisional basis or with subsidiaries kept as separate companies does not affect the basic reasons for conducting a large-scale, multiproduct, multiplant operation. However, as we show next, the use of holding companies to control large-scale operations has some distinct advantages and disadvantages over those of completely integrated divisionalized operations.

Advantages of Holding Companies

1. **Control with fractional ownership.** Through a holding company operation, a firm may buy 5, 10, or 50 percent of the stock of another corporation. Such fractional ownership may be sufficient to give the acquiring company effective working control or substantial influence over the operations of the company in which it has acquired stock ownership. Working control is often considered to entail more than 25 percent of the common stock, but it can be as low as 10 percent if the stock is widely distributed. One financier says that the attitude of management is more important than the number of shares owned: "If they think you can control the company, then you do." In addition, control on a very slim margin can be held through relationships with large stockholders outside the holding company group.

2. **Isolation of risks.** Because the various operating companies in a holding company system are separate legal entities, the obligations of any one unit are separate from those of the other units. Therefore, catastrophic losses incurred by one unit of the holding company system are not translatable into claims on the assets of the other units. However, we should note that while this is a customary generalization, it is not always valid. First, the parent company may feel obligated to make good on the subsidiary's debts, even though it is not legally bound to do so, in order to keep its good name and to retain customers. Examples of this include American Express's payment of over $100 million in connection with a swindle that was the responsibility of one of its subsidiaries, and United California Bank's coverage of its Swiss affiliate's multimillion-dollar fraud loss. Second, a parent company may feel obligated to supply capital to an affiliate in order to protect its initial investment; General Public Utilities' continued support of its subsidiary's Three Mile Island nuclear plant is an example. And, third, when lending to one of the units of a holding company system, an astute loan officer may require a guarantee by the parent holding com-

pany. To some degree, therefore, the assets in the various elements of a holding company are not really separate. Still, a catastrophic loss, as could occur if a drug company's subsidiary distributed a batch of toxic medicine, may be avoided.[16]

Disadvantages of Holding Companies

1. **Partial multiple taxation.** Provided the holding company owns at least 80 percent of a subsidiary's voting stock, the IRS permits the filing of consolidated returns, in which case dividends received by the parent are not taxed. However, if less than 80 percent of the stock is owned, then tax returns cannot be consolidated. Firms that own over 20 percent but less than 80 percent of another corporation can deduct 80 percent of the dividends received, while firms that own less than 20 percent may deduct only 70 percent of the dividends received. This partial double taxation somewhat offsets the benefits of holding company control with limited ownership, but whether the tax penalty is sufficient to offset other possible advantages is a matter that must be decided in individual situations.

2. **Ease of enforced dissolution.** It is relatively easy for the U.S. Department of Justice to require dissolution by disposal of stock ownership of a holding company operation it finds unacceptable. For instance, in the 1950s Du Pont was required to dispose of its 23 percent stock interest in General Motors Corporation, acquired in the early 1920s. Because there was no fusion between the corporations, there were no difficulties, from an operating standpoint, in requiring the separation of the two companies. However, if complete amalgamation had taken place, it would have been much more difficult to break up the company after so many years, and the likelihood of forced divestiture would have been reduced.

Holding Companies as a Leveraging Device

The holding company vehicle has been used to obtain huge degrees of financial leverage. In the 1920s, several tiers of holding companies were established in the electric utility and other industries. In those days, an operating company at the bottom of the pyramid might have $100 million of assets, financed by $50 million of debt and $50 million of equity. Then, a first-tier holding company might own the stock of the operating firm as its only asset and be financed with $25 million of debt and $25 million of equity. A second-tier holding company, which owned the stock of the first-tier company, might be financed with $12.5 million of debt and $12.5 million of equity. Such systems were extended to five or six levels, but with only four holding companies, $100 million of operating assets could be controlled at the top by $3.125 million of equity, and the operating assets would have to provide enough cash income to support $96.875 million of debt. *Such a holding company system is highly leveraged—its consolidated debt ratio is 96.875 percent, even though the individual components only have 50 percent debt/assets ratios.* Because

---

[16]Note, though, that the parent company will still be held accountable for such losses if it is deemed to exercise operating control over the subsidiary. Thus, Union Carbide was held responsible for its subsidiary's Bhopal disaster.

of this consolidated leverage, even a small decline in profits at the operating company level could bring the whole system down like a house of cards.

Self-Test Questions

What is a holding company?

What are some of the advantages of holding companies? What are some of the disadvantages?

MULTINATIONAL FINANCE
International Mergers

In recent years, foreign buyers have been especially active in U.S. takeover deals. To name just a few, in 1990, Bass of Britain bought Holiday Inns, in 1989, Grand Metropolitan of Britain bought Pillsbury, and in 1988, Seagram of Canada acquired Tropicana Products, Bond Holdings of Australia bought Heileman Brewing, and Sony acquired CBS Records.

Foreign companies are interested in U.S. firms for several reasons. First, many companies want to gain a foothold in the U.S. market to avoid being shut out if Congress should pass protectionist legislation. Second, the purchase of an American firm can provide the overseas parent with a tax shelter. For example, the average Japanese firm pays 56 percent of its income in federal and local taxes. If that same firm operates in the United States, the income is generally subject to U.S. taxes of only 34 percent. Third, the decline in the value of the dollar relative to most foreign currencies has made U.S. firms more attractive to foreign purchasers. For example, in early 1988 British retailer Marks & Spencer PLC paid $750 million for American retailer Brooks Brothers. At the prevailing exchange rate of $1.86 per pound, the deal cost Marks & Spencer

403 million pounds. If the purchase had been made in 1985, when a pound was worth only $1.10, it would have cost Marks & Spencer 682 million pounds. Thus, the price of Brooks Brothers to a British company declined by 40.9 percent due to the decline in the value of the dollar. Similar exchange rate drops have occurred in the German mark, the Swiss franc, and the Japanese yen.

Indeed, foreign buyers are literally fighting over U.S. targets. For example, one highly publicized foreign takeover involved a fight between Japan's Bridgestone Corporation and Italy's Pirelli for ownership of Firestone Tire & Rubber Company. Bridgestone began the bidding at $1.25 billion. Then, Pirelli came in, aided by France's Michelin. In the end, Bridgestone won, paying $2.6 billion for Firestone, more than double its original offer.

With the slowdown in the U.S. junk bond market, the continued weakness of the U.S. dollar, and the integration of the European Community, many economists are predicting that the 1990s will be the decade of international mergers.

SUMMARY

This chapter included discussions of mergers, divestitures, holding companies, and LBOs. The key concepts covered are listed next.

- A *merger* occurs when two firms combine to form a single company. The primary motives for mergers are (1) synergy, (2) tax considerations, (3) purchase of assets below their replacement costs, (4) diversification, and (5) gaining control over a larger enterprise.

- Mergers can provide economic benefits through *economies of scale* or through the *concentration of assets* in the hands of more efficient managers. However, mergers also have the potential for reducing competition, and for this reason they are carefully regulated by governmental agencies.

- In most mergers, one company (the *acquiring firm*) initiates action to take over another (the *target firm*).

- A *horizontal merger* occurs when two firms in the same line of business combine.

- A *vertical merger* is the combination of a firm with one of its customers or suppliers.

- A *congeneric merger* involves firms in related industries, but for which no customer-supplier relationship exists.

- A *conglomerate merger* occurs when firms in totally different industries combine.

- In a *friendly merger,* the managements of both firms approve the merger, while in a *hostile merger* the target firm's management opposes the merger.

- An *operating merger* is one in which the operations of the two firms are combined. A *financial merger* is one in which the firms continue to operate separately, hence no operating economies are expected.

- In a *merger analysis,* the key issues to be resolved are (1) the price to be paid for the target firm and (2) the employment/control situation.

- To determine the *value of the target firm,* the acquiring firm must (1) forecast the cash flows that will result after the merger and (2) develop a discount rate to apply to the projected cash flows.

- A *joint venture* is a *corporate alliance* in which two or more companies combine some of their resources to achieve a specific, limited objective.

- A *divestiture* is the sale of some of a company's operating assets. A divestiture may involve (1) selling an operating unit to another firm, (2) *spinning off* a unit as a separate company, or (3) the outright *liquidation* of a unit's assets.

- The *reasons for divestitures* include to settle antitrust suits, to clarify what a company actually does, to enable management to concentrate on a particular type of activity, and to raise capital needed to strengthen the corporation's core business.

- A *holding company* is a corporation which owns sufficient stock in another firm to achieve working control of it. The holding company is also known as the *parent company,* and the companies which it controls are called *subsidiaries,* or *operating companies.*

- Advantages to holding company operations are (1) that control can often be obtained for a smaller cash outlay, (2) that risks may be segregated, and (3) that regulated companies can separate regulated from unregulated assets.

- Disadvantages to holding company operations include (1) tax penalties and (2) the fact that incomplete ownership, if it exists, can lead to control problems.

- A *leveraged buyout (LBO)* is a transaction in which a firm's publicly owned stock is acquired in a mostly debt-financed tender offer, and a privately owned, highly leveraged firm results. Often, the firm's own management initiates the LBO.

- Foreign firms have been acquiring U.S. firms at a record pace in recent years due to *the lower value of the dollar* and *foreigners' desire to gain a foothold in the U.S. market.*

Questions

24-1   Define each of the following terms:
a.   Synergy
b.   Horizontal merger; vertical merger; congeneric merger; conglomerate merger
c.   Friendly merger; hostile merger; defensive merger
d.   Operating merger; pure financial merger
e.   White knight; white squire; poison pill; golden parachute
f.   Leveraged buyout
g.   Joint venture
h.   Divestiture; spin-off
i.   Holding company; operating company; parent company

24-2   The four economic classifications of mergers are (1) horizontal, (2) vertical, (3) congeneric, and (4) conglomerate. Discuss how each type of merger differs in (a) the likelihood of governmental intervention and (b) the possibilities for operating synergy.

24-3   Firm A wants to acquire Firm B. Firm B's management agrees that the merger is a good idea. Might a tender offer be used?

24-4   Distinguish between operating mergers and pure financial mergers.

24-5   Suppose a holding company has subsidiaries which have issued preferred stock and bonds to public investors (all of the subsidiaries' common stock is owned by the holding company). The holding company's major asset is its stock in its subsidiaries, but the parent company does own in its own right certain operating assets. The holding company also issues its own bonds and preferred stock.

    Given this information, describe the relative riskiness of investments in the common, preferred, and bonds both of the holding company itself (the parent) and of the operating subsidiaries. Assume that all the operating assets are equally risky.

24-6   Two large, publicly owned firms are contemplating a merger. No operating synergy is expected. However, since returns on the two firms are not perfectly positively correlated, the standard deviation of earnings would be reduced for the combined corporation. One group of consultants argues that this risk reduction is sufficient grounds for the merger. Another group thinks this type of risk reduction is irrelevant because stockholders could themselves hold the stock of both companies and thus gain the risk reduction benefits without all the hassles and expenses of the merger. Whose position is correct?

Problems

24-1   **(Simple merger analysis)** Mary's House of Beauty wishes to acquire Jane's Nail Emporium for $300,000. Mary expects the merger to provide incremental cash flows of about $55,000 a year for 10 years. She has also calculated her marginal cost of capital for this investment to be 12 percent. Conduct a capital budgeting analysis for Mary to determine whether she should purchase Jane's store.

24-2   **(Merger analysis)** T. S. Hawkey, Inc., a large building materials manufacturer, is evaluating the possible acquisition of the Marvin Laurence Company, a small aluminum siding manufacturer. Hawkey's analysts project the following postmerger cash flows for Laurence (in thousands of dollars):

	1991	1992	1993	1994
Net sales	$250	$288	$312	$338
Selling and administrative expense	25	31	38	40
Interest	12	15	16	18

Cost of goods sold as a percentage of sales: 65%
Terminal growth rate of cash flows available to Hawkey: 8%

If the acquisition is made, it will occur on January 1, 1991. All cash flows are assumed to occur at year-end. Laurence's current market-determined beta is 1.50, but its investment bankers think that its beta would rise to 1.68 if the merger takes place. Depreciation-generated funds would be used to replace worn-out equipment, so they would not be available to Hawkey's shareholders. The risk-free rate is 8 percent, and the market risk premium is 6 percent. The postmerger tax rate would be 40 percent.

a.   What is the appropriate discount rate for valuing the acquisition?

b.   What is Laurence's terminal value? What is the value of the Laurence Company to Hawkey?

(Do Parts c, d, and e only if you are using the computerized diskette.)

c.   If sales in each year were $100,000 higher than the base case amounts, and if the cost of goods sold/sales ratio were 60 percent, what would Laurence be worth to Hawkey?

d.   With sales and the cost of goods sold ratio at the Part c levels, what would Laurence's value be if its beta were 1.8, k_{RF} rose to 10 percent, and RP_M rose to 7 percent?

e.   Leaving all values at the Part d levels, what would the value of the acquisition be if the terminal growth rate rose to 20 percent or dropped to 3 percent?

24-3   **(Merger analysis)** Mehran Electric Corporation is considering a merger with the Rodriguez Lamp Company. Rodriguez is a publicly traded company, and its current beta is 1.40. Rodriguez has barely been profitable, so it has paid only 20 percent in taxes over the last several years. Additionally, Rodriguez uses little debt, having a market value debt ratio of just 25 percent.

If the acquisition is made, Mehran plans to operate Rodriguez as a separate, wholly owned subsidiary. Mehran would pay taxes on a consolidated basis, and thus the federal-plus-state tax rate would increase to 40 percent. Additionally, Mehran would increase the debt capitalization in the Rodriguez subsidiary to a market value of 40 percent of assets. Mehran's acquisition department estimates that Rodriguez, if acquired, would produce the following net cash flows to Mehran's shareholders (in millions of dollars):

Year	Net Cash Flow
1	$1.20
2	1.40
3	1.65
4	1.80
5 and beyond	Constant growth at 5%

These cash flows include all acquisition effects. Mehran's cost of equity is 16 percent, its beta is 1.0, and its cost of debt is 12 percent. The risk-free rate is 10 percent.

a.   What discount rate should be used to discount the given cash flows?

b.   What is the dollar value of Rodriguez to Mehran?

c.   Rodriguez has 1.2 million common shares outstanding. What is the maximum price per share that Mehran should offer for Rodriguez? If the tender offer is accepted at this price, what would happen to Mehran's stock price?

Mini Case

The CompuMax Company, a regional computer retailer, is cash rich due to several consecutive good years. One of the possible uses for the excess funds is an acquisition. Pam Olson, a recent B-school graduate, has been asked to place a value on Pacific Computer Products, Inc., a small mail order hardware and software company that sells nationwide.

Listed next are the estimates of Pacific's earnings potential which Pam developed (in millions of dollars):

	1991	1992	1993	1994
Net sales	$10.0	$20.0	$25.0	$30.0
Cost of goods sold		80 percent of net sales		
Selling/administrative expenses	1.0	1.5	2.0	2.0
Interest expense	0.5	1.0	1.2	1.5
Retentions	0.5	0.5	0.1	0.1

The interest expense listed here includes the interest (1) on Pacific's existing debt, (2) on new debt that CompuMax would issue to help finance the acquisition, and (3) on new debt expected to be issued over time to help finance expansion within the Pacific division. The retentions represent equity funds which are expected to be reinvested within the Pacific division to help finance growth.

Pacific currently uses 20 percent debt financing and pays taxes at a 30 percent rate. The beta coefficients of the large mail order houses average 1.5. If the acquisition takes place, CompuMax would increase Pacific's debt ratio to 50.0 percent. Further, since CompuMax is highly profitable, taxes on the consolidated firm would be 40.0 percent. Pam realizes that Pacific also generates depreciation cash flow, but she believes that these funds would have to be reinvested within the division to replace worn-out equipment.

Pam estimates the risk-free rate to be 10.0 percent, the market risk premium to be 5.0 percent, and the cash flow stream would grow at a constant 7 percent rate after 1994. CompuMax's management is new to the mergers game, so Pam asked you, her assistant, to answer some basic questions about mergers and perform the merger analysis. To structure the task, Pam developed the following questions:

a.   Several reasons have been proposed to justify mergers. Among the more prominent are (1) tax considerations, (2) diversification, (3) control, (4) purchase of assets at below replacement cost, (5) breakup value, and (6) synergy. In general, which of the reasons are economically justifiable? Which are not? Explain.

b.   Briefly describe the differences between a hostile merger and a friendly merger.

c.   Use the data developed previously to construct Pacific's cash flow statements for 1991 through 1994. Why is interest expense deducted in merger cash flow statements whereas it is not normally deducted in capital budgeting cash flow analysis? Why are retentions deducted in the cash flow statement?

d.   Conceptually, what is the appropriate discount rate to apply to the cash flows developed in Part c? What is the numerical estimate? How much faith can be placed in this estimate?

e.   What is the estimated terminal value of the acquisition; that is, what is the estimated value of the Pacific Division's cash flows beyond 1994? What is the value of Pacific to CompuMax? Suppose another firm were evaluating Pacific as an acquisition candidate. Would they obtain the same value? Explain.

f.   Assume that Pacific currently has 10 million shares outstanding. These shares are traded relatively infrequently, but the last trade, made several weeks ago, was at a price of $0.40 per share. Should CompuMax make an offer for Pacific? If so, how much should they offer per share?

g.   There has been considerable research conducted to determine whether mergers really create value, and, if so, how is this value shared between the parties involved? What are the results of this research?

h.   What merger-related activities are undertaken by investment bankers?

Selected Additional References and Cases

Considerable empirical investigation has been conducted to determine whether stockholders of acquiring or acquired companies benefit most from corporate mergers. One of the classic works in this field is

Mandelker, Gershon, "Risk and Return: The Case of Merging Firms," *Journal of Financial Economics,* December 1974, 303–335.

Two of the more recent works are

Black, Bernard S., and Joseph A. Grundfest, "Shareholder Gains from Takeovers and Restructurings Between 1981 and 1986: $162 Billion Is a Lot of Money," *Journal of Applied Corporate Finance,* Spring 1988, 5–15.

Jarrell, Greg A., and Annette B. Poulsen, "The Returns to Acquiring Firms in Tender Offers: Evidence from Three Decades," *Financial Management,* Autumn 1989, 12–19.

For some additional insights into merger returns, see

Elgers, Pieter T., and John J. Clark, "Merger Types and Shareholder Returns: Additional Evidence," *Financial Management,* Summer 1980, 66–72.

Mueller, Dennis C., "The Effects of Conglomerate Mergers," *Journal of Banking and Finance,* December 1977, 315–347.

Wansley, James W., William R. Lane, and Ho C. Yang, "Abnormal Returns to Acquired Firms by Type of Acquisition and Method of Payment," *Financial Management,* Autumn 1983, 16–22.

For an interesting test of the existence of synergy in mergers, see

Haugen, Robert A., and Terence C. Langetieg, "An Empirical Test for Synergism in Merger," *Journal of Finance,* September 1975, 1003–1014.

For more insights into the likelihood of acceptance of a cash tender offer, see

Hoffmeister, J. Ronald, and Edward A. Dyl, "Predicting Outcomes of Cash Tender Offers," *Financial Management,* Winter 1981, 50–58.

Some additional works on tender offers include

Dodd, Peter, and Richard Ruback, "Tender Offers and Stockholder Returns," *Journal of Financial Economics,* November 1977, 351–373.

Kummer, Donald R., and J. Ronald Hoffmeister, "Valuation Consequences of Cash Tender Offers," *Journal of Finance,* May 1978, 505–516.

The following article examines the effect of merger accounting on stock price:

Hong, Hai, Gershon Mandelker, and R. S. Kaplan, "Pooling versus Purchase: The Effects of Accounting for Mergers on Stock Prices," *Accounting Review,* January 1978, 31–47.

The Summer 1984 issue of the Midland Corporate Finance Journal *contains these relevant articles:*

DeAngelo, Harry, Linda DeAngelo, and Edward M. Rice, "Going Private: The Effects of a Change in Corporate Ownership Structure," 35–44.

Hite, Gailen L., and James E. Owers, "The Restructuring of Corporate America: An Overview," 6–16.

Linn, Scott C., and Michael S. Rozeff, "The Corporate Sell-Off," 17–26.

Schipper, Katherine, and Abbie Smith, "The Corporate Spin-Off Phenomenon," 27–34.

Stern, Joel (Moderator), "A Discussion of Corporate Restructuring," 44–79.

The Summer 1989 issue of the Journal of Applied Corporate Finance *also focuses on mergers and acquisitions.*

For a selection of articles on LBOs, see the Spring 1989 issue of the Journal of Applied Corporate Finance.

For a very interesting discussion of many of the important merger issues, see

"A Discussion of Mergers and Acquisitions," *Midland Corporate Finance Journal,* Summer 1983, 21–47.

The following case in the Brigham-Gapenski casebook illustrates merger analysis:

Case 41, "Handyware, Inc.," which focuses on merger valuation.

The following cases in the Harrington casebook focus on Chapter 24 material:

"Philip Morris," which describes the firm's acquisition of Seven-Up.

"Kennecott Corporation," which describes Sohio's potential acquisition of Kennecott.

"Cities Service Company," which considers the acquisition of Cities Service by Occidental Petroleum.

Mathematical Tables

Table A-1   Present Value of $1 Due at the End of n Periods

$$PVIF_{k,n} = \frac{1}{(1 + k)^n}$$

Period	1%	2%	3%	4%	5%	6%	7%	8%	9%	10%
1	.9901	.9804	.9709	.9615	.9524	.9434	.9346	.9259	.9174	.9091
2	.9803	.9612	.9426	.9246	.9070	.8900	.8734	.8573	.8417	.8264
3	.9706	.9423	.9151	.8890	.8638	.8396	.8163	.7938	.7722	.7513
4	.9610	.9238	.8885	.8548	.8227	.7921	.7629	.7350	.7084	.6830
5	.9515	.9057	.8626	.8219	.7835	.7473	.7130	.6806	.6499	.6209
6	.9420	.8880	.8375	.7903	.7462	.7050	.6663	.6302	.5963	.5645
7	.9327	.8706	.8131	.7599	.7107	.6651	.6227	.5835	.5470	.5132
8	.9235	.8535	.7894	.7307	.6768	.6274	.5820	.5403	.5019	.4665
9	.9143	.8368	.7664	.7026	.6446	.5919	.5439	.5002	.4604	.4241
10	.9053	.8203	.7441	.6756	.6139	.5584	.5083	.4632	.4224	.3855
11	.8963	.8043	.7224	.6496	.5847	.5268	.4751	.4289	.3875	.3505
12	.8874	.7885	.7014	.6246	.5568	.4970	.4440	.3971	.3555	.3186
13	.8787	.7730	.6810	.6006	.5303	.4688	.4150	.3677	.3262	.2897
14	.8700	.7579	.6611	.5775	.5051	.4423	.3878	.3405	.2992	.2633
15	.8613	.7430	.6419	.5553	.4810	.4173	.3624	.3152	.2745	.2394
16	.8528	.7284	.6232	.5339	.4581	.3936	.3387	.2919	.2519	.2176
17	.8444	.7142	.6050	.5134	.4363	.3714	.3166	.2703	.2311	.1978
18	.8360	.7002	.5874	.4936	.4155	.3503	.2959	.2502	.2120	.1799
19	.8277	.6864	.5703	.4746	.3957	.3305	.2765	.2317	.1945	.1635
20	.8195	.6730	.5537	.4564	.3769	.3118	.2584	.2145	.1784	.1486
21	.8114	.6598	.5375	.4388	.3589	.2942	.2415	.1987	.1637	.1351
22	.8034	.6468	.5219	.4220	.3418	.2775	.2257	.1839	.1502	.1228
23	.7954	.6342	.5067	.4057	.3256	.2618	.2109	.1703	.1378	.1117
24	.7876	.6217	.4919	.3901	.3101	.2470	.1971	.1577	.1264	.1015
25	.7798	.6095	.4776	.3751	.2953	.2330	.1842	.1460	.1160	.0923
26	.7720	.5976	.4637	.3604	.2812	.2198	.1722	.1352	.1064	.0839
27	.7644	.5859	.4502	.3468	.2678	.2074	.1609	.1252	.0976	.0763
28	.7568	.5744	.4371	.3335	.2551	.1956	.1504	.1159	.0895	.0693
29	.7493	.5631	.4243	.3207	.2429	.1846	.1406	.1073	.0822	.0630
30	.7419	.5521	.4120	.3083	.2314	.1741	.1314	.0994	.0754	.0573
35	.7059	.5000	.3554	.2534	.1813	.1301	.0937	.0676	.0490	.0356
40	.6717	.4529	.3066	.2083	.1420	.0972	.0668	.0460	.0318	.0221
45	.6391	.4102	.2644	.1712	.1113	.0727	.0476	.0313	.0207	.0137
50	.6080	.3715	.2281	.1407	.0872	.0543	.0339	.0213	.0134	.0085
55	.5785	.3365	.1968	.1157	.0683	.0406	.0242	.0145	.0087	.0053

Table A-1   Present Value of $1 Due at the End of n Periods *continued*

Period	12%	14%	15%	16%	18%	20%	24%	28%	32%	36%
1	.8929	.8772	.8696	.8621	.8475	.8333	.8065	.7813	.7576	.7353
2	.7972	.7695	.7561	.7432	.7182	.6944	.6504	.6104	.5739	.5407
3	.7118	.6750	.6575	.6407	.6086	.5787	.5245	.4768	.4348	.3975
4	.6355	.5921	.5718	.5523	.5158	.4823	.4230	.3725	.3294	.2923
5	.5674	.5194	.4972	.4761	.4371	.4019	.3411	.2910	.2495	.2149
6	.5066	.4556	.4323	.4104	.3704	.3349	.2751	.2274	.1890	.1580
7	.4523	.3996	.3759	.3538	.3139	.2791	.2218	.1776	.1432	.1162
8	.4039	.3506	.3269	.3050	.2660	.2326	.1789	.1388	.1085	.0854
9	.3606	.3075	.2843	.2630	.2255	.1938	.1443	.1084	.0822	.0628
10	.3220	.2697	.2472	.2267	.1911	.1615	.1164	.0847	.0623	.0462
11	.2875	.2366	.2149	.1954	.1619	.1346	.0938	.0662	.0472	.0340
12	.2567	.2076	.1869	.1685	.1372	.1122	.0757	.0517	.0357	.0250
13.	.2292	.1821	.1625	.1452	.1163	.0935	.0610	.0404	.0271	.0184
14	.2046	.1597	.1413	.1252	.0985	.0779	.0492	.0316	.0205	.0135
15	.1827	.1401	.1229	.1079	.0835	.0649	.0397	.0247	.0155	.0099
16	.1631	.1229	.1069	.0980	.0708	.0541	.0320	.0193	.0118	.0073
17	.1456	.1078	.0929	.0802	.0600	.0451	.0258	.0150	.0089	.0054
18	.1300	.0946	.0808	.0691	.0508	.0376	.0208	.0118	.0068	.0039
19	.1161	.0829	.0703	.0596	.0431	.0313	.0168	.0092	.0051	.0029
20	.1037	.0728	.0611	.0514	.0365	.0261	.0135	.0072	.0039	.0021
21	.0926	.0638	.0531	.0443	.0309	.0217	.0109	.0056	.0029	.0016
22	.0826	.0560	.0462	.0382	.0262	.0181	.0088	.0044	.0022	.0012
23	.0738	.0491	.0402	.0329	.0222	.0151	.0071	.0034	.0017	.0008
24	.0659	.0431	.0349	.0284	.0188	.0126	.0057	.0027	.0013	.0006
25	.0588	.0378	.0304	.0245	.0160	.0105	.0046	.0021	.0010	.0005
26	.0525	.0331	.0264	.0211	.0135	.0087	.0037	.0016	.0007	.0003
27	.0469	.0291	.0230	.0182	.0115	.0073	.0030	.0013	.0006	.0002
28	.0419	.0255	.0200	.0157	.0097	.0061	.0024	.0010	.0004	.0002
29	.0374	.0224	.0174	.0135	.0082	.0051	.0020	.0008	.0003	.0001
30	.0334	.0196	.0151	.0116	.0070	.0042	.0016	.0006	.0002	.0001
35	.0189	.0102	.0075	.0055	.0030	.0017	.0005	.0002	.0001	*
40	.0107	.0053	.0037	.0026	.0013	.0007	.0002	.0001	*	*
45	.0061	.0027	.0019	.0013	.0006	.0003	.0001	*	*	*
50	.0035	.0014	.0009	.0006	.0003	.0001	*	*	*	*
55	.0020	.0007	.0005	.0003	.0001	*	*	*	*	*

*The factor is zero to four decimal places.

Table A-2   Present Value of an Annuity of $1 per Period for n Periods

$$PVIFA_{k,n} = \sum_{t=1}^{n} \frac{1}{(1 + k)^t} = \frac{1 - \dfrac{1}{(1 + k)^n}}{k} = \frac{1}{k} - \frac{1}{k(1 + k)^n}$$

Number of Periods	1%	2%	3%	4%	5%	6%	7%	8%	9%
1	0.9901	0.9804	0.9709	0.9615	0.9524	0.9434	0.9346	0.9259	0.9174
2	1.9704	1.9416	1.9135	1.8861	1.8594	1.8334	1.8080	1.7833	1.7591
3	2.9410	2.8839	2.8286	2.7751	2.7232	2.6730	2.6243	2.5771	2.5313
4	3.9020	3.8077	3.7171	3.6299	3.5460	3.4651	3.3872	3.3121	3.2397
5	4.8534	4.7135	4.5797	4.4518	4.3295	4.2124	4.1002	3.9927	3.8897
6	5.7955	5.6014	5.4172	5.2421	5.0757	4.9173	4.7665	4.6229	4.4859
7	6.7282	6.4720	6.2303	6.0021	5.7864	5.5824	5.3893	5.2064	5.0330
8	7.6517	7.3255	7.0197	6.7327	6.4632	6.2098	5.9713	5.7466	5.5348
9	8.5660	8.1622	7.7861	7.4353	7.1078	6.8017	6.5152	6.2469	5.9952
10	9.4713	8.9826	8.5302	8.1109	7.7217	7.3601	7.0236	6.7101	6.4177
11	10.3676	9.7868	9.2526	8.7605	8.3064	7.8869	7.4987	7.1390	6.8052
12	11.2551	10.5753	9.9540	9.3851	8.8633	8.3838	7.9427	7.5361	7.1607
13	12.1337	11.3484	10.6350	9.9856	9.3936	8.8527	8.3577	7.9038	7.4869
14	13.0037	12.1062	11.2961	10.5631	9.8986	9.2950	8.7455	8.2442	7.7862
15	13.8651	12.8493	11.9379	11.1184	10.3797	9.7122	9.1079	8.5595	8.0607
16	14.7179	13.5777	12.5611	11.6523	10.8378	10.1059	9.4466	8.8514	8.3126
17	15.5623	14.2919	13.1661	12.1657	11.2741	10.4773	9.7632	9.1216	8.5436
18	16.3983	14.9920	13.7535	12.6593	11.6896	10.8276	10.0591	9.3719	8.7556
19	17.2260	15.6785	14.3238	13.1339	12.0853	11.1581	10.3356	9.6036	8.9501
20	18.0456	16.3514	14.8775	13.5903	12.4622	11.4699	10.5940	9.8181	9.1285
21	18.8570	17.0112	15.4150	14.0292	12.8212	11.7641	10.8355	10.0168	9.2922
22	19.6604	17.6580	15.9369	14.4511	13.1630	12.0416	11.0612	10.2007	9.4424
23	20.4558	18.2922	16.4436	14.8568	13.4886	12.3034	11.2722	10.3711	9.5802
24	21.2434	18.9139	16.9355	15.2470	13.7986	12.5504	11.4693	10.5288	9.7066
25	22.0232	19.5235	17.4131	15.6221	14.0939	12.7834	11.6536	10.6748	9.8226
26	22.7952	20.1210	17.8768	15.9828	14.3752	13.0032	11.8258	10.8100	9.9290
27	23.5596	20.7069	18.3270	16.3296	14.6430	13.2105	11.9867	10.9352	10.0266
28	24.3164	21.2813	18.7641	16.6631	14.8981	13.4062	12.1371	11.0511	10.1161
29	25.0658	21.8444	19.1885	16.9837	15.1411	13.5907	12.2777	11.1584	10.1983
30	25.8077	22.3965	19.6004	17.2920	15.3725	13.7648	12.4090	11.2578	10.2737
35	29.4086	24.9986	21.4872	18.6646	16.3742	14.4982	12.9477	11.6546	10.5668
40	32.8347	27.3555	23.1148	19.7928	17.1591	15.0463	13.3317	11.9246	10.7574
45	36.0945	29.4902	24.5187	20.7200	17.7741	15.4558	13.6055	12.1084	10.8812
50	39.1961	31.4236	25.7298	21.4822	18.2559	15.7619	13.8007	12.2335	10.9617
55	42.1472	33.1748	26.7744	22.1086	18.6335	15.9905	13.9399	12.3186	11.0140

Table A-2   Present Value of an Annuity of $1 per Period for n Periods *continued*

Number of Periods	10%	12%	14%	15%	16%	18%	20%	24%	28%	32%
1	0.9091	0.8929	0.8772	0.8696	0.8621	0.8475	0.8333	0.8065	0.7813	0.7576
2	1.7355	1.6901	1.6467	1.6257	1.6052	1.5656	1.5278	1.4568	1.3916	1.3315
3	2.4869	2.4018	2.3216	2.2832	2.2459	2.1743	2.1065	1.9813	1.8684	1.7663
4	3.1699	3.0373	2.9137	2.8550	2.7982	2.6901	2.5887	2.4043	2.2410	2.0957
5	3.7908	3.6048	3.4331	3.3522	3.2743	3.1272	2.9906	2.7454	2.5320	2.3452
6	4.3553	4.1114	3.8887	3.7845	3.6847	3.4976	3.3255	3.0205	2.7594	2.5342
7	4.8684	4.5638	4.2883	4.1604	4.0386	3.8115	3.6046	3.2423	2.9370	2.6775
8	5.3349	4.9676	4.6389	4.4873	4.3436	4.0776	3.8372	3.4212	3.0758	2.7860
9	5.7590	5.3282	4.9464	4.7716	4.6065	4.3030	4.0310	3.5655	3.1842	2.8681
10	6.1446	5.6502	5.2161	5.0188	4.8332	4.4941	4.1925	3.6819	3.2689	2.9304
11	6.4951	5.9377	5.4527	5.2337	5.0286	4.6560	4.3271	3.7757	3.3351	2.9776
12	6.8137	6.1944	5.6603	5.4206	5.1971	4.7932	4.4392	3.8514	3.3868	3.0133
13	7.1034	6.4235	5.8424	5.5831	5.3423	4.9095	4.5327	3.9124	3.4272	3.0404
14	7.3667	6.6282	6.0021	5.7245	5.4675	5.0081	4.6106	3.9616	3.4587	3.0609
15	7.6061	6.8109	6.1422	5.8474	5.5755	5.0916	4.6755	4.0013	3.4834	3.0764
16	7.8237	6.9740	6.2651	5.9542	5.6685	5.1624	4.7296	4.0333	3.5026	3.0882
17	8.0216	7.1196	6.3729	6.0472	5.7487	5.2223	4.7746	4.0591	3.5177	3.0971
18	8.2014	7.2497	6.4674	6.1280	5.8178	5.2732	4.8122	4.0799	3.5294	3.1039
19	8.3649	7.3658	6.5504	6.1982	5.8775	5.3162	4.8435	4.0967	3.5386	3.1090
20	8.5136	7.4694	6.6231	6.2593	5.9288	5.3527	4.8696	4.1103	3.5458	3.1129
21	8.6487	7.5620	6.6870	6.3125	5.9731	5.3837	4.8913	4.1212	3.5514	3.1158
22	8.7715	7.6446	6.7429	6.3587	6.0113	5.4099	4.9094	4.1300	3.5558	3.1180
23	8.8832	7.7184	6.7921	6.3988	6.0442	5.4321	4.9245	4.1371	3.5592	3.1197
24	8.9847	7.7843	6.8351	6.4338	6.0726	5.4509	4.9371	4.1428	3.5619	3.1210
25	9.0770	7.8431	6.8729	6.4641	6.0971	5.4669	4.9476	4.1474	3.5640	3.1220
26	9.1609	7.8957	6.9061	6.4906	6.1182	5.4804	4.9563	4.1511	3.5656	3.1227
27	9.2372	7.9426	6.9352	6.5135	6.1364	5.4919	4.9636	4.1542	3.5669	3.1233
28	9.3066	7.9844	6.9607	6.5335	6.1520	5.5016	4.9697	4.1566	3.5679	3.1237
29	9.3696	8.0218	6.9830	6.5509	6.1656	5.5098	4.9747	4.1585	3.5687	3.1240
30	9.4269	8.0552	7.0027	6.5660	6.1772	5.5168	4.9789	4.1601	3.5693	3.1242
35	9.6442	8.1755	7.0700	6.6166	6.2153	5.5386	4.9915	4.1644	3.5708	3.1248
40	9.7791	8.2438	7.1050	6.6418	6.2335	5.5482	4.9966	4.1659	3.5712	3.1250
45	9.8628	8.2825	7.1232	6.6543	6.2421	5.5523	4.9986	4.1664	3.5714	3.1250
50	9.9148	8.3045	7.1327	6.6605	6.2463	5.5541	4.9995	4.1666	3.5714	3.1250
55	9.9471	8.3170	7.1376	6.6636	6.2482	5.5549	4.9998	4.1666	3.5714	3.1250

Table A-3   Future Value of $1 at the End of n Periods

$FVIF_{k,n} = (1 + k)^n$

Period	1%	2%	3%	4%	5%	6%	7%	8%	9%	10%
1	1.0100	1.0200	1.0300	1.0400	1.0500	1.0600	1.0700	1.0800	1.0900	1.1000
2	1.0201	1.0404	1.0609	1.0816	1.1025	1.1236	1.1449	1.1664	1.1881	1.2100
3	1.0303	1.0612	1.0927	1.1249	1.1576	1.1910	1.2250	1.2597	1.2950	1.3310
4	1.0406	1.0824	1.1255	1.1699	1.2155	1.2625	1.3108	1.3605	1.4116	1.4641
5	1.0510	1.1041	1.1593	1.2167	1.2763	1.3382	1.4026	1.4693	1.5386	1.6105
6	1.0615	1.1262	1.1941	1.2653	1.3401	1.4185	1.5007	1.5869	1.6771	1.7716
7	1.0721	1.1487	1.2299	1.3159	1.4071	1.5036	1.6058	1.7138	1.8280	1.9487
8	1.0829	1.1717	1.2668	1.3686	1.4775	1.5938	1.7182	1.8509	1.9926	2.1436
9	1.0937	1.1951	1.3048	1.4233	1.5513	1.6895	1.8385	1.9990	2.1719	2.3579
10	1.1046	1.2190	1.3439	1.4802	1.6289	1.7908	1.9672	2.1589	2.3674	2.5937
11	1.1157	1.2434	1.3842	1.5395	1.7103	1.8983	2.1049	2.3316	2.5804	2.8531
12	1.1268	1.2682	1.4258	1.6010	1.7959	2.0122	2.2522	2.5182	2.8127	3.1384
13	1.1381	1.2936	1.4685	1.6651	1.8856	2.1329	2.4098	2.7196	3.0658	3.4523
14	1.1495	1.3195	1.5126	1.7317	1.9799	2.2609	2.5785	2.9372	3.3417	3.7975
15	1.1610	1.3459	1.5580	1.8009	2.0789	2.3966	2.7590	3.1722	3.6425	4.1772
16	1.1726	1.3728	1.6047	1.8730	2.1829	2.5404	2.9522	3.4259	3.9703	4.5950
17	1.1843	1.4002	1.6528	1.9479	2.2920	2.6928	3.1588	3.7000	4.3276	5.0545
18	1.1961	1.4282	1.7024	2.0258	2.4066	2.8543	3.3799	3.9960	4.7171	5.5599
19	1.2081	1.4568	1.7535	2.1068	2.5270	3.0256	3.6165	4.3157	5.1417	6.1159
20	1.2202	1.4859	1.8061	2.1911	2.6533	3.2071	3.8697	4.6610	5.6044	6.7275
21	1.2324	1.5157	1.8603	2.2788	2.7860	3.3996	4.1406	5.0338	6.1088	7.4002
22	1.2447	1.5460	1.9161	2.3699	2.9253	3.6035	4.4304	5.4365	6.6586	8.1403
23	1.2572	1.5769	1.9736	2.4647	3.0715	3.8197	4.7405	5.8715	7.2579	8.9543
24	1.2697	1.6084	2.0328	2.5633	3.2251	4.0489	5.0724	6.3412	7.9111	9.8497
25	1.2824	1.6406	2.0938	2.6658	3.3864	4.2919	5.4274	6.8485	8.6231	10.835
26	1.2953	1.6734	2.1566	2.7725	3.5557	4.5494	5.8074	7.3964	9.3992	11.918
27	1.3082	1.7069	2.2213	2.8834	3.7335	4.8223	6.2139	7.9881	10.245	13.110
28	1.3213	1.7410	2.2879	2.9987	3.9201	5.1117	6.6488	8.6271	11.167	14.421
29	1.3345	1.7758	2.3566	3.1187	4.1161	5.4184	7.1143	9.3173	12.172	15.863
30	1.3478	1.8114	2.4273	3.2434	4.3219	5.7435	7.6123	10.063	13.268	17.449
40	1.4889	2.2080	3.2620	4.8010	7.0400	10.286	14.974	21.725	31.409	45.259
50	1.6446	2.6916	4.3839	7.1067	11.467	18.420	29.457	46.902	74.358	117.39
60	1.8167	3.2810	5.8916	10.520	18.679	32.988	57.946	101.26	176.03	304.48

Table A-3 Future Value of $1 at the End of n Periods *continued*

Period	12%	14%	15%	16%	18%	20%	24%	28%	32%	36%
1	1.1200	1.1400	1.1500	1.1600	1.1800	1.2000	1.2400	1.2800	1.3200	1.3600
2	1.2544	1.2996	1.3225	1.3456	1.3924	1.4400	1.5376	1.6384	1.7424	1.8496
3	1.4049	1.4815	1.5209	1.5609	1.6430	1.7280	1.9066	2.0972	2.3000	2.5155
4	1.5735	1.6890	1.7490	1.8106	1.9388	2.0736	2.3642	2.6844	3.0360	3.4210
5	1.7623	1.9254	2.0114	2.1003	2.2878	2.4883	2.9316	3.4360	4.0075	4.6526
6	1.9738	2.1950	2.3131	2.4364	2.6996	2.9860	3.6352	4.3980	5.2899	6.3275
7	2.2107	2.5023	2.6600	2.8262	3.1855	3.5832	4.5077	5.6295	6.9826	8.6054
8	2.4760	2.8526	3.0590	3.2784	3.7589	4.2998	5.5895	7.2058	9.2170	11.703
9	2.7731	3.2519	3.5179	3.8030	4.4355	5.1598	6.9310	9.2234	12.166	15.917
10	3.1058	3.7072	4.0456	4.4114	5.2338	6.1917	8.5944	11.806	16.060	21.647
11	3.4785	4.2262	4.6524	5.1173	6.1759	7.4301	10.657	15.112	21.199	29.439
12	3.8960	4.8179	5.3503	5.9360	7.2876	8.9161	13.215	19.343	27.983	40.037
13	4.3635	5.4924	6.1528	6.8858	8.5994	10.699	16.386	24.759	36.937	54.451
14	4.8871	6.2613	7.0757	7.9875	10.147	12.839	20.319	31.691	48.757	74.053
15	5.4736	7.1379	8.1371	9.2655	11.974	15.407	25.196	40.565	64.359	100.71
16	6.1304	8.1372	9.3576	10.748	14.129	18.488	31.243	51.923	84.954	136.97
17	6.8660	9.2765	10.761	12.468	16.672	22.186	38.741	66.461	112.14	186.28
18	7.6900	10.575	12.375	14.463	19.673	26.623	48.039	85.071	148.02	253.34
19	8.6128	12.056	14.232	16.777	23.214	31.948	59.568	108.89	195.39	344.54
20	9.6463	13.743	16.367	19.461	27.393	38.338	73.864	139.38	257.92	468.57
21	10.804	15.668	18.822	22.574	32.324	46.005	91.592	178.41	340.45	637.26
22	12.100	17.861	21.645	26.186	38.142	55.206	113.57	228.36	449.39	866.67
23	13.552	20.362	24.891	30.376	45.008	66.247	140.83	292.30	593.20	1178.7
24	15.179	23.212	28.625	35.236	53.109	79.497	174.63	374.14	783.02	1603.0
25	17.000	26.462	32.919	40.874	62.669	95.396	216.54	478.90	1033.6	2180.1
26	19.040	30.167	37.857	47.414	73.949	114.48	268.51	613.00	1364.3	2964.9
27	21.325	34.390	43.535	55.000	87.260	137.37	332.95	784.64	1800.9	4032.3
28	23.884	39.204	50.066	63.800	102.97	164.84	412.86	1004.3	2377.2	5483.9
29	26.750	44.693	57.575	74.009	121.50	197.81	511.95	1285.6	3137.9	7458.1
30	29.960	50.950	66.212	85.850	143.37	237.38	634.82	1645.5	4142.1	10143.
40	93.051	188.88	267.86	378.72	750.38	1469.8	5455.9	19427.	66521.	*
50	289.00	700.23	1083.7	1670.7	3927.4	9100.4	46890.	*	*	*
60	897.60	2595.9	4384.0	7370.2	20555.	56348.	*	*	*	*

*FVIF > 99,999.

Table A-4   Future Value of an Annuity of $1 per Period for n Periods

$$FVIFA_{k,n} = \sum_{t=1}^{n} (1 + k)^{n-t} = \frac{(1 + k)^n - 1}{k}$$

Number of Periods	1%	2%	3%	4%	5%	6%	7%	8%	9%	10%
1	1.0000	1.0000	1.0000	1.0000	1.0000	1.0000	1.0000	1.0000	1.0000	1.0000
2	2.0100	2.0200	2.0300	2.0400	2.0500	2.0600	2.0700	2.0800	2.0900	2.1000
3	3.0301	3.0604	3.0909	3.1216	3.1525	3.1836	3.2149	3.2464	3.2781	3.3100
4	4.0604	4.1216	4.1836	4.2465	4.3101	4.3746	4.4399	4.5061	4.5731	4.6410
5	5.1010	5.2040	5.3091	5.4163	5.5256	5.6371	5.7507	5.8666	5.9847	6.1051
6	6.1520	6.3081	6.4684	6.6330	6.8019	6.9753	7.1533	7.3359	7.5233	7.7156
7	7.2135	7.4343	7.6625	7.8983	8.1420	8.3938	8.6540	8.9228	9.2004	9.4872
8	8.2857	8.5830	8.8923	9.2142	9.5491	9.8975	10.260	10.637	11.028	11.436
9	9.3685	9.7546	10.159	10.583	11.027	11.491	11.978	12.488	13.021	13.579
10	10.462	10.950	11.464	12.006	12.578	13.181	13.816	14.487	15.193	15.937
11	11.567	12.169	12.808	13.486	14.207	14.972	15.784	16.645	17.560	18.531
12	12.683	13.412	14.192	15.026	15.917	16.870	17.888	18.977	20.141	21.384
13	13.809	14.680	15.618	16.627	17.713	18.882	20.141	21.495	22.953	24.523
14	14.947	15.974	17.086	18.292	19.599	21.015	22.550	24.215	26.019	27.975
15	16.097	17.293	18.599	20.024	21.579	23.276	25.129	27.152	29.361	31.772
16	17.258	18.639	20.157	21.825	23.657	25.673	27.888	30.324	33.003	35.950
17	18.430	20.012	21.762	23.698	25.840	28.213	30.840	33.750	36.974	40.545
18	19.615	21.412	23.414	25.645	28.132	30.906	33.999	37.450	41.301	45.599
19	20.811	22.841	25.117	27.671	30.539	33.760	37.379	41.446	46.018	51.159
20	22.019	24.297	26.870	29.778	33.066	36.786	40.995	45.762	51.160	57.275
21	23.239	25.783	28.676	31.969	35.719	39.993	44.865	50.423	56.765	64.002
22	24.472	27.299	30.537	34.248	38.505	43.392	49.006	55.457	62.873	71.403
23	25.716	28.845	32.453	36.618	41.430	46.996	53.436	60.893	69.532	79.543
24	26.973	30.422	34.426	39.083	44.502	50.816	58.177	66.765	76.790	88.497
25	28.243	32.030	36.459	41.646	47.727	54.865	63.249	73.106	84.701	98.347
26	29.526	33.671	38.553	44.312	51.113	59.156	68.676	79.954	93.324	109.18
27	30.821	35.344	40.710	47.084	54.669	63.706	74.484	87.351	102.72	121.10
28	32.129	37.051	42.931	49.968	58.403	68.528	80.698	95.339	112.97	134.21
29	33.450	38.792	45.219	52.966	62.323	73.640	87.347	103.97	124.14	148.63
30	34.785	40.568	47.575	56.085	66.439	79.058	94.461	113.28	136.31	164.49
40	48.886	60.402	75.401	95.026	120.80	154.76	199.64	259.06	337.88	442.59
50	64.463	84.579	112.80	152.67	209.35	290.34	406.53	573.77	815.08	1163.9
60	81.670	114.05	163.05	237.99	353.58	533.13	813.52	1253.2	1944.8	3034.8

Table A-4   Future Value of an Annuity of $1 per Period for n Periods *continued*

Number of Periods	12%	14%	15%	16%	18%	20%	24%	28%	32%	36%
1	1.0000	1.0000	1.0000	1.0000	1.0000	1.0000	1.0000	1.0000	1.0000	1.0000
2	2.1200	2.1400	2.1500	2.1600	2.1800	2.2000	2.2400	2.2800	2.3200	2.3600
3	3.3744	3.4396	3.4725	3.5056	3.5724	3.6400	3.7776	3.9184	4.0624	4.2096
4	4.7793	4.9211	4.9934	5.0665	5.2154	5.3680	5.6842	6.0156	6.3624	6.7251
5	6.3528	6.6101	6.7424	6.8771	7.1542	7.4416	8.0484	8.6999	9.3983	10.146
6	8.1152	8.5355	8.7537	8.9775	9.4420	9.9299	10.980	12.136	13.406	14.799
7	10.089	10.730	11.067	11.414	12.142	12.916	14.615	16.534	18.696	21.126
8	12.300	13.233	13.727	14.240	15.327	16.499	19.123	22.163	25.678	29.732
9	14.776	16.085	16.786	17.519	19.086	20.799	24.712	29.369	34.895	41.435
10	17.549	19.337	20.304	21.321	23.521	25.959	31.643	38.593	47.062	57.352
11	20.655	23.045	24.349	25.733	28.755	32.150	40.238	50.398	63.122	78.998
12	24.133	27.271	29.002	30.850	34.931	39.581	50.895	65.510	84.320	108.44
13	28.029	32.089	34.352	36.786	42.219	48.497	64.110	84.853	112.30	148.47
14	32.393	37.581	40.505	43.672	50.818	59.196	80.496	109.61	149.24	202.93
15	37.280	43.842	47.580	51.660	60.965	72.035	100.82	141.30	198.00	276.98
16	42.753	50.980	55.717	60.925	72.939	87.442	126.01	181.87	262.36	377.69
17	48.884	59.118	65.075	71.673	87.068	105.93	157.25	233.79	347.31	514.66
18	55.750	68.394	75.836	84.141	103.74	128.12	195.99	300.25	459.45	700.94
19	63.440	78.969	88.212	98.603	123.41	154.74	244.03	385.32	607.47	954.28
20	72.052	91.025	102.44	115.38	146.63	186.69	303.60	494.21	802.86	1298.8
21	81.699	104.77	118.81	134.84	174.02	225.03	377.46	633.59	1060.8	1767.4
22	92.503	120.44	137.63	157.41	206.34	271.03	469.06	812.00	1401.2	2404.7
23	104.60	138.30	159.28	183.60	244.49	326.24	582.63	1040.4	1850.6	3271.3
24	118.16	158.66	184.17	213.98	289.49	392.48	723.46	1332.7	2443.8	4450.0
25	133.33	181.87	212.79	249.21	342.60	471.98	898.09	1706.8	3226.8	6053.0
26	150.33	208.33	245.71	290.09	405.27	567.38	1114.6	2185.7	4260.4	8233.1
27	169.37	238.50	283.57	337.50	479.22	681.85	1383.1	2798.7	5624.8	11198.0
28	190.70	272.89	327.10	392.50	566.48	819.22	1716.1	3583.3	7425.7	15230.3
29	214.58	312.09	377.17	456.30	669.45	984.07	2129.0	4587.7	9802.9	20714.2
30	241.33	356.79	434.75	530.31	790.95	1181.9	2640.9	5873.2	12941.	28172.3
40	767.09	1342.0	1779.1	2360.8	4163.2	7343.9	22729.	69377.	*	*
50	2400.0	4994.5	7217.7	10436.	21813.	45497.	*	*	*	*
60	7471.6	18535.	29220.	46058.	*	*	*	*	*	*

*FVIFA > 99,999.

Table A-5   Values of the Areas under the Standard Normal Distribution Function

z	0.00	0.01	0.02	0.03	0.04	0.05	0.06	0.07	0.08	0.09
0.0	.0000	.0040	.0080	.0120	.0160	.0199	.0239	.0279	.0319	.0359
0.1	.0398	.0438	.0478	.0517	.0557	.0596	.0636	.0675	.0714	.0753
0.2	.0793	.0832	.0871	.0910	.0948	.0987	.1026	.1064	.1103	.1141
0.3	.1179	.1217	.1255	.1293	.1331	.1368	.1406	.1443	.1480	.1517
0.4	.1554	.1591	.1628	.1664	.1700	.1736	.1772	.1808	.1844	.1879
0.5	.1915	.1950	.1985	.2019	.2054	.2088	.2123	.2157	.2190	.2224
0.6	.2257	.2291	.2324	.2357	.2389	.2422	.2454	.2486	.2517	.2549
0.7	.2580	.2611	.2642	.2673	.2704	.2734	.2764	.2794	.2823	.2852
0.8	.2881	.2910	.2939	.2967	.2995	.3023	.3051	.3078	.3106	.3133
0.9	.3159	.3186	.3212	.3238	.3264	.3289	.3315	.3340	.3365	.3389
1.0	.3413	.3438	.3461	.3485	.3508	.3531	.3554	.3577	.3599	.3621
1.1	.3643	.3665	.3686	.3708	.3729	.3749	.3770	.3790	.3810	.3830
1.2	.3849	.3869	.3888	.3907	.3925	.3944	.3962	.3980	.3997	.4015
1.3	.4032	.4049	.4066	.4082	.4099	.4115	.4131	.4147	.4162	.4177
1.4	.4192	.4207	.4222	.4236	.4251	.4265	.4279	.4292	.4306	.4319
1.5	.4332	.4345	.4357	.4370	.4382	.4394	.4406	.4418	.4429	.4441
1.6	.4452	.4463	.4474	.4484	.4495	.4505	.4515	.4525	.4535	.4545
1.7	.4554	.4564	.4573	.4582	.4591	.4599	.4608	.4616	.4625	.4633
1.8	.4641	.4649	.4656	.4664	.4671	.4678	.4686	.4693	.4699	.4706
1.9	.4713	.4719	.4726	.4732	.4738	.4744	.4750	.4756	.4761	.4767
2.0	.4773	.4778	.4783	.4788	.4793	.4798	.4803	.4808	.4812	.4817
2.1	.4821	.4826	.4830	.4834	.4838	.4842	.4846	.4850	.4854	.4857
2.2	.4861	.4864	.4868	.4871	.4875	.4878	.4881	.4884	.4887	.4890
2.3	.4893	.4896	.4898	.4901	.4904	.4906	.4909	.4911	.4913	.4916
2.4	.4918	.4920	.4922	.4925	.4927	.4929	.4931	.4932	.4934	.4936
2.5	.4938	.4940	.4941	.4943	.4945	.4946	.4948	.4949	.4951	.4952
2.6	.4953	.4955	.4956	.4957	.4959	.4960	.4961	.4962	.4963	.4964
2.7	.4965	.4966	.4967	.4968	.4969	.4970	.4971	.4972	.4973	.4974
2.8	.4974	.4975	.4976	.4977	.4977	.4978	.4979	.4979	.4980	.4981
2.9	.4981	.4982	.4982	.4982	.4984	.4984	.4985	.4985	.4986	.4986
3.0	.4987	.4987	.4987	.4988	.4988	.4989	.4989	.4989	.4990	.4990

Selected Equations and Data

Chapter 2

	MACRS Class	
Year	3-Year	5-Year
1	33%	20%
2	45	32
3	15	19
4	7	12
5		11
6		6

Chapter 3

$$k = k^* + IP + DRP + LP + MRP.$$

$$k_{RF} = k^* + IP.$$

Chapter 4

$$\text{Expected rate of return} = \hat{k} = \sum_{i=1}^{n} k_i P_i.$$

$$\text{Variance} = \sigma^2 = \sum_{i=1}^{n} (k_i - \hat{k})^2 P_i.$$

$$\text{Standard deviation} = \sigma = \sqrt{\sigma^2} = \sqrt{\sum_{i=1}^{n} (k_i - \hat{k})^2 P_i}.$$

$$\text{Coefficient of variation} = \text{CV} = \frac{\sigma}{\hat{k}}.$$

$$\hat{k}_p = \sum_{i=1}^{n} w_i \hat{k}_i.$$

$$\sigma_p = \sqrt{\sum_{i=1}^{n} (k_{pi} - \hat{k}_p)^2 P_i}.$$

$$\text{Cov(AB)} = \sum_{i=1}^{n} (k_{Ai} - \hat{k}_A)(k_{Bi} - \hat{k}_B)P_i.$$

$$r_{AB} = \frac{\text{Cov(AB)}}{\sigma_A \sigma_B}.$$

$$\sigma_p = \sqrt{x^2 \sigma_A^2 + (1 - x)^2 \sigma_B^2 + 2x(1 - x)r_{AB}\sigma_A\sigma_B}.$$

Chapter 5

$$\text{Capital Market Line (CML): } \hat{k}_p = k_{RF} + \left(\frac{\hat{k}_M - k_{RF}}{\sigma_M}\right)\sigma_p.$$

$$\text{Security Market Line (SML): } k_i = k_{RF} + (k_M - k_{RF})b_i.$$

$$b_p = \sum_{i=1}^{n} x_i b_i.$$

$$b_i = \frac{\text{Cov}(\bar{k}_i, \bar{k}_M)}{\sigma_M^2} = \frac{r_{iM}\sigma_i\sigma_M}{\sigma_M^2} = r_{iM}\left(\frac{\sigma_i}{\sigma_M}\right).$$

Chapter 6

$$FV_n = PV(1 + k)^n = PV(FVIF_{k,n}).$$

$$PV = FV_n\left(\frac{1}{1 + k}\right)^n = FV_n(1 + k)^{-n} = FV_n(PVIF_{k,n}).$$

$$PVIF_{k,n} = \frac{1}{FVIF_{k,n}}.$$

$$FVIFA_{k,n} = [(1 + k)^n - 1]/k.$$

$$PVIFA_{k,n} = [1 - (1/(1 + k)^n)]/k.$$

$$FVA_n = PMT(FVIFA_{k,n}).$$

$$FVA_n \text{ (Annuity due)} = PMT(FVIFA_{k,n})(1 + k).$$

$$PVA_n = PMT(PVIFA_{k,n}).$$

$$PVA_n \text{ (Annuity due)} = PMT(PVIFA_{k,n})(1 + k).$$

$$PV \text{ (Perpetuity)} = \frac{\text{Payment}}{\text{Interest rate}} = \frac{\text{PMT}}{k}.$$

$$FV_n = PV\left(1 + \frac{k_{Nom}}{m}\right)^{mn}.$$

$$\text{Effective annual rate} = \left(1 + \frac{k_{Nom}}{m}\right)^{m} - 1.0.$$

$$FV_n = PVe^{kn}.$$

$$PV = FV_n(e^{-kn}).$$

Chapter 7

$$V = \sum_{t=1}^{n} I\left(\frac{1}{1 + k_d}\right)^{t} + M\left(\frac{1}{1 + k_d}\right)^{n}$$

$$= I\,(PVIFA_{k_d,n}) + M(PVIF_{k_d,n}).$$

$$V = \sum_{t=1}^{2n} \frac{I}{2}\left(\frac{1}{1 + \dfrac{k_d}{2}}\right)^{t} + M\left(\frac{1}{1 + \dfrac{k_d}{2}}\right)^{2n} = \frac{I}{2}(PVIFA_{k_d/2,2n}) + M(PVIF_{k_d/2,2n}).$$

$$V_p = \frac{D_p}{k_p}.$$

$$\hat{P}_0 = PV \text{ of expected future dividends} = \sum_{t=1}^{\infty} \frac{D_t}{(1 + k_s)^{t}}.$$

$$\hat{P}_0 = \frac{D_0(1 + g)}{k_s - g} = \frac{D_1}{k_s - g}.$$

$$\hat{k}_s = \frac{D_1}{P_0} + g.$$

Chapter 8

$$\text{Component cost of debt} = k_d(1 - T).$$

$$\begin{array}{c}\text{Component cost} \\ \text{of preferred stock}\end{array} = k_p = \frac{D_p}{P_n}.$$

$$k_s = \hat{k}_s = \frac{D_1}{P_0} + g.$$

$$k_s = \hat{k}_e = \frac{D_1}{P_0(1 - F)} + g.$$

$$g = b(r).$$

$$WACC = k_a = w_d k_d(1 - T) + w_p k_p + w_s(k_s \text{ or } k_e).$$

Chapter 9

$$NPV = \sum_{t=0}^{n} \frac{CF_t}{(1 + k)^t}.$$

$$IRR: \sum_{t=0}^{n} \frac{CF_t}{(1 + r)^t} = 0.$$

$$PI = \frac{\sum_{t=0}^{n} \frac{CIF_t}{(1 + k)^t}}{\sum_{t=0}^{n} \frac{COF_t}{(1 + k)^t}}.$$

$$MIRR: \sum_{t=0}^{n} \frac{COF_t}{(1 + k)^t} = \frac{\sum_{t=0}^{n} CIF_t(1 + k)^{n-t}}{(1 + MIRR)^n}.$$

Chapter 10

$$k_n = k_r + i + k_r i.$$

$$NPV = \sum_{t=0}^{n} \frac{RCF_t}{(1 + k_r)^t}.$$

Chapter 11

$$CV_{NPV} = \frac{\sigma_{NPV}}{E(NPV)}.$$

$$k_p = k_{RF} + (k_M - k_{RF})b_p.$$

Chapter 12

$$S = \frac{(EBIT - k_d D)(1 - T)}{k_s}.$$

$$k_a = WACC = w_d k_d(1 - T) + w_s k_s$$

$$= \left(\frac{D}{V}\right)k_d(1 - T) + \left(\frac{S}{V}\right)k_s.$$

$$V = \frac{EBIT(1 - T)}{k_a}.$$

$$V_L = V_U = \frac{EBIT}{WACC} = \frac{EBIT}{k_{sU}}.$$

$$k_{sL} = k_{sU} + (k_{sU} - k_d)(D/S).$$

$$V_U = \frac{EBIT(1 - T)}{k_{sU}}.$$

$$V_L = V_U + TD.$$

$$k_{sL} = k_{sU} + (k_{sU} - k_d)(1 - T)(D/S).$$

$$V_L = V_U + TD - \left(\begin{array}{c} \text{PV of} \\ \text{expected} \\ \text{financial distress} \\ \text{costs} \end{array}\right) - \left(\begin{array}{c} \text{PV of} \\ \text{agency} \\ \text{costs} \end{array}\right).$$

$$V_L = V_U + \left[1 - \frac{(1 - T_c)(1 - T_s)}{(1 - T_d)}\right]D.$$

Chapter 13

$$EPS = \frac{(EBIT - k_dD)(1 - T)}{\text{Original shares} - \text{Debt/Price}}.$$

$$FCC = \frac{EBIT + \text{Lease payments}}{\text{Interest} + \left(\begin{array}{c}\text{Lease} \\ \text{payments}\end{array}\right) + \left(\dfrac{\text{Sinking fund payments}}{1 - T}\right)}.$$

$$Q_{BE} = \frac{F}{P - V}.$$

$$k_{sL} = k_{RF} + (k_M - k_{RF})b_U + (k_M - k_{RF})b_U(1 - T)(D/S).$$

$$b_L = b_U[1 + (1 - T)(D/S)].$$

$$P_1 = \frac{V_1 - D_0}{n_0}.$$

$$n_1 = n_0 - \text{Shares repurchased.}$$

Chapter 18

$$V = P[N(d_1)] - Xc^{-k_{RF}t}[N(d_2)].$$

$$d_1 = \frac{\ln(P/X) + [k_{RF} + (\sigma^2/2)]t}{\sigma\sqrt{t}}.$$

$$d_2 = d_1 - \sigma\sqrt{t}.$$

Chapter 19

$$\begin{array}{c}\text{Inventory} \\ \text{conversion} \\ \text{period}\end{array} + \begin{array}{c}\text{Receivables} \\ \text{collection} \\ \text{period}\end{array} - \begin{array}{c}\text{Payables} \\ \text{deferral} \\ \text{period}\end{array} = \begin{array}{c}\text{Cash} \\ \text{conversion.} \\ \text{cycle}\end{array}$$

$$\begin{array}{c}\text{Approximate} \\ \text{percentage cost}\end{array} = \frac{\text{Discount percent}}{100 - \begin{array}{c}\text{Discount} \\ \text{percent}\end{array}} \times \frac{360}{\begin{array}{c}\text{Days credit is} \\ \text{outstanding}\end{array} - \begin{array}{c}\text{Discount} \\ \text{period}\end{array}}.$$

$$\text{Effective rate}_{Simple} = \frac{\text{Interest}}{\text{Amount received}} = \left(1 + \frac{k_{Nom}}{m}\right)^m - 1.0.$$

$$\text{Effective rate}_{Discount} = \frac{\text{Interest}}{\text{Amount received}} = \frac{\text{Nominal rate (\%)}}{1.0 - \text{Nominal rate (fraction)}}.$$

$$\text{Effective rate}_{Simple/CB} = \frac{\text{Interest}}{\text{Amount received}} = \frac{\text{Nominal rate (\%)}}{1.0 - \text{CB (fraction)}}.$$

$$\text{Effective rate}_{Discount/CB} = \frac{\text{Nominal rate (\%)}}{1 - \text{Nominal rate (fraction)} - \text{CB (fraction)}}.$$

$$\text{Approximate effective rate}_{Add-on} = \frac{\text{Interest}}{\text{Amount received}/2}.$$

Chapter 20

$$C^* = \sqrt{\frac{2(F)(T)}{k}}.$$

$$Z = \left[\frac{3F\sigma^2}{4k}\right]^{1/3} + L.$$

$$H = 3\left[\frac{3F\sigma^2}{4k}\right]^{1/3} + L = 3Z - 2L.$$

$$\text{Average cash balance} = \frac{4Z - L}{3}.$$

Chapter 21

$$\text{Cost of carrying receivables} = (DSO)(Sales/360)(v)(k).$$

$$\text{Opportunity cost} = (Old\ sales/360)(\Delta DSO)(1 - v)(k).$$

$$TCC = (C)(P)(A).$$

$$TOC = F\left(\frac{S}{2A}\right) = (F)(N).$$

$$TIC = TCC + TOC$$

$$= (C)(P)\left(\frac{Q}{2}\right) + F\left(\frac{S}{Q}\right).$$

$$EOQ = \sqrt{\frac{2(F)(S)}{(C)(P)}}.$$

Chapter 22

$$\text{ROE} = \left(\frac{\text{Profit}}{\text{margin}}\right)\left(\frac{\text{Total asset}}{\text{turnover}}\right)\left(\frac{\text{Equity}}{\text{multiplier}}\right)$$

$$= \left(\frac{\text{Net income}}{\text{Sales}}\right)\left(\frac{\text{Sales}}{\text{Total assets}}\right)\left(\frac{\text{Total assets}}{\text{Common equity}}\right)$$

$$= \frac{\text{Net income}}{\text{Common equity}}.$$

$$\text{Current ratio} = \frac{\text{Current assets}}{\text{Current liabilities}}.$$

$$\text{Quick, or acid test, ratio} = \frac{\text{Current assets} - \text{Inventories}}{\text{Current liabilities}}.$$

$$\text{Inventory turnover, or utilization, ratio} = \frac{\text{Sales}}{\text{Inventory}}.$$

$$\text{DSO} = \frac{\text{Days sales outstanding}}{} = \frac{\text{Receivables}}{\text{Average sales per day}} = \frac{\text{Receivables}}{\text{Annual sales/360}}.$$

$$\text{Fixed asset turnover, or utilization, ratio} = \frac{\text{Sales}}{\text{Net fixed assets}}.$$

$$\text{Total asset turnover, or utilization, ratio} = \frac{\text{Sales}}{\text{Total assets}}.$$

$$\text{Debt ratio} = \frac{\text{Total debt}}{\text{Total assets}}.$$

$$\text{D/E} = \frac{\text{D/A}}{1 - \text{D/A}}, \text{ and D/A} = \frac{\text{D/E}}{1 + \text{D/E}}.$$

$$\text{Times-interest-earned (TIE) ratio} = \frac{\text{EBIT}}{\text{Interest charges}}.$$

$$\text{Fixed charge coverage ratio} = \frac{\text{EBIT} + \text{Lease obligations}}{\text{Interest charges} + \text{Lease obligations} + \dfrac{\text{Sinking fund payments}}{1 - \text{T}}}.$$

$$\text{Cash flow coverage ratio} = \frac{\text{EBIT} + \text{Lease payments} + \text{Depreciation}}{\text{Interest and lease payments} + \dfrac{\text{Preferred stock dividends}}{1 - \text{T}} + \dfrac{\text{Debt repayment}}{1 - \text{T}}}.$$

$$\text{Profit margin on sales} = \frac{\text{Net income available to common stockholders}}{\text{Sales}}.$$

$$\text{Basic earning power ratio} = \frac{\text{EBIT}}{\text{Total assets}}.$$

$$\text{Return on assets} \atop (\text{ROA}) = \frac{\text{Net income available to common stockholders}}{\text{Total assets}}.$$

$$\text{Return on common} \atop \text{equity (ROE)} = \frac{\text{Net income available to common stockholders}}{\text{Common equity}}.$$

$$\text{Price/earnings} \atop (\text{P/E}) \text{ ratio} = \frac{\text{Price per share}}{\text{Earnings per share}}.$$

$$\text{Book value per share} = \frac{\text{Common equity}}{\text{Shares outstanding}}.$$

$$\text{Market/book ratio} = \frac{\text{Market price per share}}{\text{Book value per share}}.$$

Chapter 23

$$\text{EFN} = (\text{A/S})\Delta\text{S} - (\text{L/S})\Delta\text{S} - \text{MS}_1(1 - d).$$

$$g^* = \frac{\text{M(b)}(1 + \text{D/E})}{\text{A/S} - \text{M(b)}(1 + \text{D/E})}.$$

APPENDIX C

Answers to Selected End-of-Chapter Problems

We present here some intermediate steps and final answers to selected end-of-chapter problems. Please note that your answer may differ slightly from ours due to rounding errors. Also, though we hope not, some of the problems may have more than one correct solution, depending upon what assumptions are made in working the problem. Finally, many of the problems involve some verbal discussion as well as numerical calculations; this verbal material is not presented here.

2-1 $36,290; $113,710.

2-2 a. $61,250.
b. $ 7,800.
c. $ 2,340.

2-3 1993: $0; 1995: $60,000.

2-4 1993: $4,500; but reduced to $0 in 1995.

2-5 a. (1) 1992: $8,355; 1993: $11,355.
(2) 1992: $11,378; 1993: $16,978.

2-6 a. $22,163.
b. 33%; 27%.
d. 18.2%.

2-7 a. 1992: $32,000; 1996: $6,000.
b. $74,120.

2-8   a.   1992: $45,000; 1993: $15,000.
    b.   1992: $6,375.
    c.   1992: $81,125.

3-1   a.   5-year: 8.2%.

3-3   12%.

3-5   a.   8.4%.
    b.   10.4%.
    c.   5-year: 10.9%.

4-1   a.   17.0%.
    b.   17.75%; 1.18.

4-2   a. $1 million.

4-3   a.   A: 13.5%; 4.75; 2.2%; 0.16.
      B: 13.25%; 10.19; 3.2%; 0.24.
      C: 12.0%; 2.0; 1.4%; 0.12.

4-4   a.   12.92%.
    b.   1.69; 1.3%.
    c.   AB: 6.63; 0.94.
      AC: -3.00; -0.97.

4-5   a.   Average $\bar{k}$ A: 11.41%; B: 11.40%; AB: 11.41%.
    b.   A: 21.9%; B: 21.9%; AB: 21.3%.

5-1   a.   14.5%; 16.25%.
    b.   1.0; 1.43.
    c.   17.3%.

5-3   a.   15.6%.
    b.   (1) 16.6%.
       (2) 14.6%.
    c.   (1) 17.0%.
       (2) 12.8%.
    d.   (1) 16.4%.
       (2) 13.0%.

5-4   b.   15.75%.

5-5   b.   X: 10.6%; 13.1%.
      M: 12.1%; 22.6%.
    c.   8.6%.

5-6   a.   0.62.

6-1   a. $324.00.
    b. $349.92.
    c. $277.78.
    d. $257.20.

6-2   a. $647.68.
    b. $1,323.43.
    c. $138.96.
    d. $300.00.

6-3   a.   10.24 years.
    b.   8.04 years.
    c.   6.12 years.
    d.   1 year.

6-4   a. $3,187.48.
    b. $552.56.
    c. $1,000.

6-5   a. $1,228.91.
    b. $432.95.
    c. $1,000.

6-6   a.   A: $1,181.50; B: $1,239.13.
    b.   A: $1,600; B: $1,600.

6-7 $3,638.89.

6-8 $1,000 today.

6-9   a.   14.87%.

6-10 a.   5%.
    b.   5%.
    c.   5%.
    d.   9%.

6-11 20%.

6-12 11.61%.

6-13 12%.

6-14 9%.

6-15 a. $26,497.01.
    b. $20,616.78; $0.

6-16 8.04 years.

6-17 5.19 years.

6-18 a. $352.47.
    b. $358.17.
    c. $361.22.
    d. $225.37.

6-19 a. $111.68.
    b. $110.74.
    c. $177.49.

6-20 a. $2,636.16.
    b. $2,975.50.

6-22 $2,000; $1,000.

6-25 a. $5,121.

7-1   a.   (1) L: $1,388.49; S: $1,037.74.
       (2) L: $1,080.61; S: $1,009.17.
       (3) L: $863.78; S: $982.14.

7-2   a.   (1) 14.01%.
       (2) 4.98%.
    b.   Yes.

7-3   a. $1,233.05.
      b. $905.53.

7-4   a. $1,200.
      b. $800.
      c. $1,000.
      d. $1,170.27; $812.22; $1,000.

7-5   a.   12.9%.
      b.   10.0%.
      c.   9.0%.
      d.   6.9%.

7-6   a. $D_1 = \$2.10; D_2 = \$2.21; D_3 = \$2.32$.
      b. $5.29.
      c. $24.72.
      d. $30.01.
      e. $30.00.

7-7   a.   6.0%.
      b.   3.0%.
      c.   9.0%.

7-8   a.   (1) $7.60.
           (2) $10.00.
           (3) $14.00.
           (4) $46.00.
      b.   (1) Undefined.
           (2) $-\$50$.

7-10 a.   3.4%.
      b.   6.98%.
      c. $853.13.
      d. $1,000.

7-11 $21.60.

7-12 a. $1.80; $2.16; $2.59; $3.11; $3.73.
      b. $71.23.
      c.   2.53%, 7.47%, 10.00%; 3.99%, 6.01%, 10.0%.
      e. $1.73; $1.98; $2.28; $2.62; $3.02; $47.93.
      f. $29.40; $23.25; $15.10.

7-13 a. $36.46; 6.86%; 7.14%.
      e. $55.30; 4.52%; 9.48%.
      f. $29.09; 8.59%; 7.41%.

7-14 a.   9.00%; 7.73%.
      d.   8.20%; 4.58%.
      e.   13.23%; 23.13%.

8-1   a.   10.0%.
      b.   8.0%.
      c.   6.0%.

8-2   10.25%.

8-3   a. $15,000,000.
      b. $3,000,000; $12,000,000.
      c. k_s = 12.0%; k_e = 12.4%.
      d. $6,000,000.
      e.   (1) 8.4%.
           (2) 8.6%.

8-4   a.   4.8%; 12.3%.
      b.   10.05%.
      c. $432,000.
      d.   10.40%.

8-6   a.   8.0%.
      b. $0.864.
      c.   12.0%.
      d. $6 million.
      e. $15 million.
      f.   15%; 12.71%.

9-1 NPV_S = $814.33; NPV_L = $1,675.34.
      IRR_S = 15.24%; IRR_L = 14.67%.
      $MIRR_S$ = 13.77%; $MIRR_L$ = 13.46%.
      PI_S = 1.081; PI_L = 1.067.

9-2   b. IRR_A = 18.1%; IRR_B = 24.0%.
      d.   At k = 10%: $MIRR_A$ = 14.1%; $MIRR_B$ = 15.9%.
           At k = 17%: $MIRR_A$ = 17.6%; $MIRR_B$ = 19.9%.
      e.   14.53%.

9-3   a. $0; −$10,250,000; $1,750,000.
      b.   16.07%.

9-4   a. NPV_A = $18,108,510; NPV_B = $13,946,117.
           IRR_A = 15.03%; IRR_B = 22.26%.
      b. NPV_Δ = $4,162,393; IRR_Δ = 11.71%.

9-7   a.   Undefined.
      b. PV_C = −$911,067; PV_F = −$838,834.

10-2 a. $89,000.
      b. $26,220; $30,300; $20,100.
      c. $24,380.

10-3 a. $212,500.
      b. $72,501; $80,865; $59,955.
      c. $65,179.
      e. $5,766; $23,295.
      f.   −$620; $19,214; $51,000.
      g. $5,256.
      h.   −$52; $199,900.

10-4 a. $88,400.
      b. $46,770; $52,890; $37,590; $33,510; $29,940.
      c.   −$10,000.
      d. $46,051.

10-5 a. $880,000.
      c. $221,000; $278,600; $216,200; $182,600; $177,800.
      d. $133,800.
      e.   NPV = $31,789.
      g.   NPV = $15,296.
      h.   NPV = − $3,331.
      i.   NPV = $37,034.

10-7 a.   3 years.
      b.   No.

10-8 a.   NPV = $106,537.

10-9 a.   11.6%; 5.28%.
      c. $1,392.
      d.   NPV = $768.
      e.   NPV = − $214.

11-1 Oil plant.

11-2 a. $117,779.
      b. $445,060; 3.78; High.

11-3 a.   16.5%.

11-4 a.   5-year NPV = $1,843.
           4-year NPV = − $1,734.
           8-year NPV = $11,107.
      b.   8% NPV = $3,539.
           12% NPV = $280.

11-5 a.   15.3%.
      b. $38,589.

11-6 $10 million.

11-7 $42,000.

11-8 $62,000.

12-1 a. $V_U = V_L$ = $20 million.
      b. k_{sU} = 10.0%; k_{sL} = 15.0%.
      c. S_L = $10 million.
      d. $k_{aU} = k_{aL}$ = 10.0%.

12-2 a. V_U = $12 million; V_L = $16 million.
      b. k_{sU} = 10.0%; k_{sL} = 15.0%.
      c. S_L = 6.0 million.
      d. k_{aU} = 10.0%; k_{aL} = 7.5%.

12-3 a. V_U = 9.6 million.
      b. V_L = $12.93 million.
      c. $3.33 million versus 4.0 million.
      d. V_L = $20.0 million; $0.
      e. V_L = $16.0 million; $4 million.
      f. V_L = $12.64 million; $4 million.

12-4 a. $V_U = V_L = \$14,545,455$.
b. At D = \$6 million: $k_{sL} = 14.51\%$; $k_a = 11.0\%$.
c. $V_U = \$8,727,273$; $V_L = \$11,127,273$.
d. At D = \$6 million: $k_{sL} = 14.51\%$; $k_a = 8.63\%$.
e. D = V = \$14,545,455.

12-5 a. A: \$32.5 million; B: \$30.0 million.
b. Project B.

12-6 a. Jones: \$10.0 million; Smith: \$10.0 million.

12-7 a. \$15 million.
b. D = \$7.5 million; D/V = 52.8%.
d. D = \$7.5 million; D/V = 43.6%.
e. D = \$10.0 million; D/V = 83.3%.
f. D = \$10.0 million; D/V = 67.8%.

13-1 a. 15.0%; 11.0%.

13-2 a. 1.13.
b. 15.65%; 5.65%.
c. k_s = 16.65%; 18.07%; 20.27%.
RP = 1.00%; 2.42%; 4.62%.
d. 20.27%; 4.62%.

13-3 c. \$20.28; \$17.96.

13-4 a. V = \$3,283,636.
b. \$16.42.
c. \$1.81.

13-5 a. 14.0%.
c. \$38.85.

13-6 a. \$2.25; \$2.70.

14-4 a. \$6.00.
b. 60%.
c. \$66.67 versus \$100.00.

14-5 a. 62.22%; \$15.45 million; 11.21%; 10.97%.
b. \$24 million.

15-1 a. \$24.75.
b. \$24.00.

15-2 a. \$700,000.
b. \$3,700,000.
c. − \$2,300,000.

15-3 964,115.

15-4 a. 1990: \$12,000; \$6,000; \$90,000.
b. Ewert: g_{EPS} = 8.0%; g_{DPS} = 7.4%.
e. 1990: \$3.00; \$1.50; \$22.50.
f. Groth: 15.00%; Hill: 13.64%.
g. 1990: Groth: 50%; Hill: 50%.
h. Groth: 43%; Hill: 37%.
i. Groth: 8×; Hill: 8.67×.

16-1 a. $2,570,925.
      b. $1,558,201.
      c. $2,774,097.
      d. $1,769,842.

16-2 PMT = $402,115.

16-3 18.4%.

16-4 c. YTM = 24%.
      d. V = $41.96; $150.00.

16-5 a. Zero: 1,242,236; Annual coupon: 400,000.
      b. Zero: 12%; 5.69%; Annual coupon: 14%; 7%.
      c. Zero: 7.63%; Annual coupon: 9.24%.

17-1 a. Electroway: 50%; Levin: 33%.
      b. D/A = 50%.

17-2 a. NAL = $44,201.
      c. $346,572.
      d. NAL = $122,083.

17-3 a. $2,638.
      c. −$353.
      d. $11,668.
      e. Best case: $5,069; Worst case: $207.

17-4 a. NAL = − $1,461.
      c. NAL = − $698.
      e. NAL = − $190.

18-1 a. $1.41.
      b. $1.14.
      c. $5.65.
      d. $0.18.

18-2 a. (1) − $5, or $0.
           (2) $0.
           (3) $5.
           (4) $75.
      d. 10%; $100.

18-4 a. 14.1%.
      b. $12 million before-tax.

18-5 b. Plan 1: 49%; Plan 2: 53%; Plan 3: 53%.
      c. Plan 1: $0.59; Plan 2: $0.64; Plan 3: $0.88.
      d. Plan 1: 19%; Plan 2: 19%; Plan 3: 50%.

18-6 b. 11.65%.

18-7 b. Net gain = $9,531.
      d. Net loss = $14,628.

19-1 a. $83,333.
   b. No.
   c. $250,000; 36.73%; EAR = 43.84%.
   d. 24.48%; EAR = 27.42%.

19-3 a. $200,000.

19-4 a. 81 days.
   b. $194,775.

19-5 a. $5,104; $10,824; $5,075; $6,417.

20-1 a. February: Surplus cash = $2,000.
   b. $164,400.

20-2 a. September: Loans outstanding = $133,525;
             December: Surplus cash = $47,450.
   f.   December: Loans outstanding = $17,800.
   g.   December: Loans outstanding = $578,050.

20-3 a. $15,811; 32.

20-4 a. $10,000; $1,000.

20-5 a. $20,543.
   b. $41,629; $10,000.

20-6 a. 5 days; 2 days; $2,100,000.
   b. $189,000.
   c. $15,750.

20-7 a. $159,000.
   b. $150,000.
   e. $6,000; $13,800.

21-1 a. 28 days.
   b. $46,667.
   c. $36,667.

21-2 a. DSO_0 = 23 days; DSO_N = 17.5 days.
   b. $24,696; $11,760.
   c. $5,750; $5,250.
   d. $20,000; $24,000.
   e. + $20,138.

21-3 C3: + $46,811; C4: + $15,467; C5: + $8,538.

21-4 ΔNI = + $28,115.

21-5 a. March: $146,000; June: $198,000.
   b. Q1: ADS = $3,000; DSO = 48.7 days; Q2: ADS = $4,500 ; DSO = 44.0 days; Cumulative:
           ADS = $3,750; DSO = 52.8 days.
   c. 0–30 days: 65%; 31–60 days: 35%.
   d. Receivables/Sales = 130%.

21-6 ΔNI = − $3,450.

21-7 a. 3,000 bags.
   b. 4,000 bags.
   c. 2,500 bags.
   d. every 12 days.

21-8 a. 5,200 units.
  b. 65 orders.
  c. Reorder point = 16,600 units.
  d. (1) $11,628.
    (2) $11,530.
    (3) $11,552. At EOQ: $11,520.
  e. (1) 6,300 units.
    (2) 5,800 units.
    (3) 4,500 units.

22-1 b. ROE = 7.6%.

22-2 $350,000; 1.19.

22-3 $2,160,000; 36 days.

22-4 Cash = $18,000; Common stock = $35,000.

22-6 a. Total sources = Total uses = $234.
  b. Decrease in cash and M.S. = $38.

22-7 a. 16%.
  b. D/A = 44%.
  c. Decrease in cash and M.S. = $57.

23-1 a. Total assets = $7.2 million.
  b. $3,580,000.

23-2 a. $489,000.
  b. $20,000.

23-3 a. $52,000.
  b. ≈ $4,000; ≈ $4,000; $6,000.

23-4 a. Total assets = $487 million.
  b. 1991: $74 million.
    1992: $34 million.
    1993: $37 million.
    1994: − $4 million.
    1995: − $10 million.

24-1 NPV = $10,761.

24-2 a. 18.1%.
  b. $386,875; $286,806.
  c. $563,439.
  d. $391,444.
  e. $1,597,764; $324,768.

24-3 a. 19.3%.
  b. $10.37 million.
  c. $8.64; Nothing.

Solutions to Self-Test Problems

Chapter 3

ST-1   a.   Average inflation rate = (4% + 5% + 6% + 7%)/4 = 22%/4 = 5.5% = IP.

      b. $k_{T\text{-bond}}$ = k* + IP + MRP = 3.0% + 5.5% + 0% = 8.5%.

      c.   If the 5-year T-bond rate is 9 percent, then the inflation rate is expected to average approximately 9% − 3% = 6% over the next 5 years. Thus, the Year 5 implied inflation rate is 8.0 percent:

$$6\% = (4\% + 5\% + 6\% + 7\% + IP_5)/5$$

$$30\% = 22\% + IP_5$$

$$IP_5 = 8\%.$$

Chapter 4

ST-1   a.   The realized return in each Period t is estimated as follows:

$$\bar{k}_t = \frac{D_t + P_t - P_{t-1}}{P_{t-1}}.$$

For example, the realized return for Stock A in 1986 was −12.24 percent:

$$\bar{k}_{1986} = \frac{D_{1986} + P_{1986} - P_{1985}}{P_{1985}}$$

$$= \frac{\$1.00 + \$9.75 - \$12.25}{\$12.25}$$

$$= -0.1224 = -12.24\%.$$

The table that follows shows the realized returns for each stock in each year, the averages for the 5 years, and the same data for the portfolio:

Year	Stock A's Return, $\bar{k}_A$	Stock B's Return, $\bar{k}_B$	Portfolio AB's Return, $\bar{k}_{AB}$
1986	−12.24%	−5.00%	−8.62%
1987	23.59	19.46	21.52
1988	35.45	44.10	39.78
1989	5.82	1.19	3.50
1990	28.30	21.11	24.71
$\bar{k}_{Avg}$	16.2%	16.2%	16.2%

b. The standard deviation of returns is estimated as follows:

$$\sigma = \sqrt{\frac{\sum_{t=1}^{n}(\bar{k}_t - \bar{k}_{Avg})^2}{n-1}}.$$

For Stock A, the estimated standard deviation is 19.3 percent:

$$\sigma_A = \sqrt{\frac{(-12.24 - 16.2)^2 + (23.59 - 16.2)^2 + \ldots + (28.30 - 16.2)^2}{5-1}}$$

$$= \sqrt{\frac{1,488.15}{4}} = 19.3\%.$$

The standard deviation of returns for Stock B and for the portfolio are similarly determined, and they are shown here:

	Stock A	Stock B	Portfolio AB
Standard deviation	19.3%	19.3%	18.9%

c. Since the risk reduction from diversification is small (σ_{AB} falls only from 19.3 to 18.9 percent), the most likely value of the correlation coefficient is 0.9. If the correlation coefficient were −0.9, the risk reduction would be much larger. In fact, the correlation coefficient between Stocks A and B is 0.93.

d. If more randomly selected stocks were added to the portfolio; σ_p would decline to somewhere in the vicinity of 15 percent. σ_p would remain constant only if the correlation coefficient were +1.0, which is most unlikely. σ_p would decline to zero only if the correlation coefficient, r, were equal to zero and a large number of stocks were added to the portfolio, or if the proper proportions were held in a two-stock portfolio with r = −1.0.

Chapter 5

ST-1 a. The market risk premium, which is the premium above the risk-free rate required on an average stock, is 5 percentage points:

$$RP_M = (k_M - k_{RF}) = 13.0\% - 8.0\% = 5.0\%.$$

b. Bigbee's required rate of return is 12.0 percent:

$$k_i = k_{RF} + (k_M - k_{RF})b_i$$

$$= 8.0\% + (13.0\% - 8.0\%)0.8$$

$$= 8.0\% + (5\%)0.8 = 8.0\% + 4.0\% = 12.0\%.$$

c.   See the graph below:

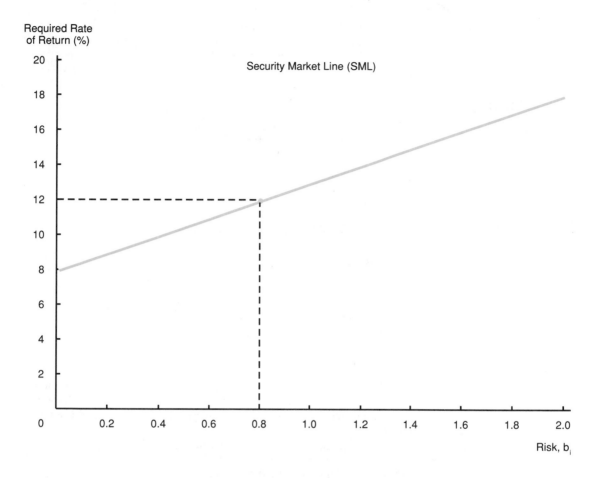

Required Rate
of Return (%)

Security Market Line (SML)

Risk, b_i

d.   If inflation expectations increased by 2 percentage points, then the risk-free rate would increase to 8.0% + 2.0% = 10.0%. However, assuming that there is no change in investors' risk aversion, the required rate of return on the market would also increase by 2 percentage points, to 15.0 percent. Thus, the market risk premium would remain at 15.0% − 10.0% = 5.0%. The effect on Bigbee's stock would be to increase its required rate of return by 2 percentage points:

$$k_i = k_{RF} + (k_M - k_{RF})b_i$$

$$= 10.0\% + (15.0\% - 10.0\%)0.8$$

$$= 10.0\% + (5\%)0.8 = 10.0\% + 4.0\% = 14.0\%.$$

e.   In this situation, Bigbee's required rate of return would be 13.6 percent:

$$k_i = k_{RF} + (k_M - k_{RF})b_i$$

$$= 8.0\% + (7\%)0.8 = 8.0\% + 5.6\% = 13.6\%.$$

f.   If Bigbee's market risk increased to b = 1.2, its required rate of return would rise to 14.0 percent:

$$k_i = k_{RF} + (k_M - k_{RF})b_i$$

$$= 8.0\% + (5\%)1.2 = 8.0\% + 6.0\% = 14.0\%.$$

Chapter 6

ST-1 a.

1/1/91	1/1/92	1/1/93	1/1/94	1/1/95

$1,000   ?

$1,000 is being compounded for 3 years, so your balance on January 1, 1995, is $1,259.71:

$$FV = PV(1 + k)^n = \$1,000(1 + 0.08)^3 = \$1,259.71.$$

b.   The effective annual rate for 8 percent, compounded quarterly, is

$$\text{Effective annual rate} = \left(1 + \frac{0.08}{4}\right)^4 - 1.0$$

$$= (1.02)^4 - 1.0 = 0.0824 = 8.24\%.$$

Therefore, FV = $1,000(1.0824)^3 = $1,268.13.
Alternatively, use FVIF for 2%, 3 × 4 = 12 periods:

$$FV = \$1,000(FVIF_{2\%,12 \text{ periods}}) = \$1,000(1.2682) = \$1,268.20.$$

The future value found by financial calculator is $1,268.24. (Note that since the interest factors are carried to only four decimal places, rounding errors occur. Rounding errors can also occur between regular calculator and financial calculator solutions if intermediate steps are rounded.)

c.

1/1/91	1/1/92	1/1/93	1/1/94	1/1/95
	$250	$250	$250	$250

As you work this problem, keep in mind that the tables assume that payments are made at the end of each period. Therefore, you may solve this problem by finding the future value of an ordinary annuity of $250 for 4 years at 8 percent:

$$PMT(FVIFA_{k,n}) = \$250(4.5061) = \$1,126.53.$$

d.   FV = $1,259.71; k = 8%; n = 4; PMT = ?

$$PMT(FVIFA_{8\%,4 \text{ years}}) = FV$$

$$PMT(4.5061) = \$1,259.71$$

$$PMT = \$1,259.71/4.5061 = \$279.56.$$

Therefore, you would have to make 4 payments of $279.56 each to have a balance of $1,259.71 on January 1, 1995.

ST-2   a.   Set up a time line like those presented earlier, and note that your deposit will grow for 3 years at 8 percent. The fact that it is now January 1, 1991, is irrelevant. The deposit on January 1, 1992, is the PV, and $1,000 = FV. Here is the solution:

$$FV = \$1,000; n = 3; k = 8\%; PV = ?$$

$$PV = FV(PVIF_{8\%,3\ years})$$

$$= \$1,000(0.7938) = \$793.80$$

$$= \text{Initial deposit necessary to accumulate } \$1,000.$$

(Calculator solution = $793.83.)

b.   Here we are dealing with a 4-year ordinary annuity whose first payment occurs one year from today, on 1/1/92, and whose future value must equal $1,000. You should set up a time line to help visualize the situation. Here is the solution:

$$FV = \$1,000; n = 4; k = 8\%; PMT = ?$$

$$FV = PMT(FVIFA_{8\%,4\ years})$$

$$PMT = \frac{FV}{(FVIFA_{8\%,4\ years})}$$

$$= \frac{\$1,000}{4.5061}$$

$$= \$221.92 = \text{Payment necessary to accumulate } \$1,000.$$

c.   This problem can be approached in several ways. Perhaps the simplest is to ask this question: "If I received $750 on 1/1/92 and deposited it to earn 8 percent, would I have the required $1,000 on 1/1/95?" The answer is no:

$$\$750(1.08)(1.08)(1.08) = \$944.78.$$

This indicates that you should let your father make the payments rather than accept the lump sum of $750.

You could also compare the $750 with the PV of the payments:

$$PMT = \$221.92; k = 8\%; n = 4; PV = ?$$

$$PMT(PVIFA_{8\%,4\ years}) = PV$$

$$\$221.92(3.3121) = \$735.02 = \text{PV of the required payments.}$$

This is less than the $750 lump sum offer, so your initial reaction might be to accept the lump sum of $750. However, this would be a mistake. As we saw above, if you were to deposit the $750 on January 1, 1992, at an 8 percent interest rate, to be withdrawn on January 1, 1995, interest would be compounded for only 3 years, from January 1, 1992, to December 31, 1994, and the future value would be only

$$PV(FVIF_{8\%,3\ years}) = \$750(1.2597) = \$944.78.$$

The problem is that when you found the $735.02 PV of the annuity, you were finding the value of the annuity *today*, on January 1, 1991. You were comparing $735.02 today with the lump sum $750 one year from now. This is, of course, invalid. What you should have done was take the $735.02, recognize that this is the PV of an annuity as of January 1,

1991, multiply $735.02 by 1.08 to get $793.82, and compare $793.82 with the lump sum of $750. You would then take your father's offer to make the payments rather than take the lump sum on January 1, 1991.

d. $PV = \$750; FV = \$1,000; n = 3; k = ?$

$$PV(FVIF_{k,3 \text{ years}}) = FV$$

$$FVIF_{k,3 \text{ years}} = \frac{FV}{PV}$$

$$= \frac{\$1,000}{\$750} = 1.3333.$$

Use the Future Value of $1 table (Table A-3 at the end of the book) for 3 periods to find the interest rate corresponding to an FVIF of 1.3333. Look across the Period 3 row of the table until you come to 1.3333. The closest value is 1.3310, in the 10 percent column. Therefore, you would require an interest rate of approximately 10 percent to achieve your $1,000 goal. The exact rate required, found with a financial calculator, is 10.0642 percent.

e. $FV = \$1,000; PMT = \$186.29; n = 4; k = ?$

$$PMT(FVIFA_{k,4 \text{ years}}) = FV$$

$$\$186.29(FVIFA_{k,4 \text{ years}}) = \$1,000$$

$$FVIFA_{k,4 \text{ years}} = \frac{\$1,000}{\$186.29} = 5.3680.$$

Using Table A-4 at the end of the book, we find that 5.3680 corresponds to a 20 percent interest rate. You might be able to find a borrower willing to offer you a 20 percent interest rate, but there would be some risk involved—he or she might not actually pay you your $1,000!

(Calculator solution = 19.9997%.)

f.

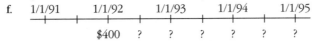

Find the future value of the original $400 deposit:

$$FV = PV(FVIF_{4\%,6}) = \$400(1.2653) = \$506.12.$$

This means that on January 1, 1995, you need an additional sum of $493.88:

$$\$1,000.00 - \$506.12 = \$493.88.$$

This will be accumulated by making 6 equal payments which earn 8 percent compounded semiannually, or 4 percent each 6 months:

$FV = \$493.88; n = 6; k = 4\%; PMT = ?$

$$PMT(FVIFA_{4\%,6}) = FV$$

$$PMT = \frac{FV}{(FVIFA_{4\%,6})}$$

$$= \frac{\$493.88}{6.6330} = \$74.46.$$

g.   Effective annual rate $= \left(1 + \dfrac{k_{Nom}}{m}\right)^{m} - 1.0$

$= \left(1 + \dfrac{0.08}{2}\right)^{2} - 1 = (1.04)^{2} - 1$

$= 1.0816 - 1 = 0.0816 = 8.16\%.$

h.   There is a reinvestment rate risk here, because we assumed that funds will earn an 8 percent return in the bank. In fact, if interest rates in the economy fall, the bank will lower its deposit rate, because it will be earning less when it lends out the funds you deposited with it. If you buy certificates of deposit (CDs) that mature on the date you need the money (1/1/95), you will avoid the reinvestment risk, but that will work only if you are making the deposit today. Other ways of reducing reinvestment rate risk will be discussed later in the text.

ST-3   Bank A's effective annual rate is 8.24 percent:

$$\text{Effective annual rate} = \left(1 + \dfrac{0.08}{4}\right)^{4} - 1.0$$

$$= (1.02)^{4} - 1 = 1.0824 - 1$$

$$= 0.082432 \approx 8.24\%.$$

Now Bank B must have the same effective annual rate:

$$\left(1 + \dfrac{k}{12}\right)^{12} - 1.0 = 0.082432$$

$$\left(1 + \dfrac{k}{12}\right)^{12} = 1.082432$$

$$1 + \dfrac{k}{12} = (1.082432)^{1/12}$$

$$1 + \dfrac{k}{12} = 1.0066227$$

$$\dfrac{k}{12} = 0.0066227$$

$$k = 0.0794724 \approx 7.95\%.$$

Chapter 7

ST-1   a.   The firm's bonds were sold at par; therefore, the original YTM equaled the coupon rate of 12 percent.

b. $V = \displaystyle\sum_{t=1}^{50} \dfrac{\$120/2}{(1 + 0.10/2)^{t}} + \dfrac{\$1,000}{(1 + 0.10/2)^{50}}$

$= \$60(\text{PVIFA}_{5\%,50}) + \$1,000(\text{PVIF}_{5\%,50})$

$= \$60(18.2559) + \$1,000(0.0872)$

$= \$1,095.35 + \$87.20 = \$1,182.55.$

c.

$$\text{Current yield} = \text{Annual coupon payment/Price}$$

$$= \$120/\$1,182.55 = 0.1015 = 10.15\%.$$

$$\text{Capital gains yield} = \text{Total yield} - \text{Current yield}$$

$$= 10\% - 10.15\% = -0.15\%.$$

Alternatively, $V_{1/1/73} = \$1,180.76$, and $(\$1,180.76 - \$1,182.55)/\$1,182.55 = -0.15\%$.

d.

$$\$896.64 = \sum_{t=1}^{19} \frac{\$60}{(1 + k_d/2)^t} + \frac{\$1,000}{(1 + k_d/2)^{19}}.$$

By financial calculator, $k_d/2 = 7.00\%$; thus, the YTM on July 1, 1987, was 14 percent.

e.   Current yield $= \$120/\$896.64 = 13.38\%$.

$$\text{Capital gains yield} = 14\% - 13.38\% = 0.62\%.$$

f.   The following time line illustrates the years to maturity of the bond:

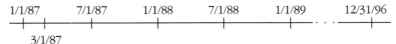

| 1/1/87 | 7/1/87 | 1/1/88 | 7/1/88 | 1/1/89 | 12/31/96 |

3/1/87

Thus, on March 1, 1987, there were 19⅔ periods left before the bond matures. Bond traders actually use the following procedure to determine the price of the bond:

(1) Use a financial calculator to find the price of the bond on the next coupon date, July 1, 1987.

$$V_{7/1/87} = \$60(\text{PVIFA}_{7.75\%,19}) + \$1,000(\text{PVIF}_{7.75\%,19})$$

$$= \$828.87.$$

(2) Add the coupon, $60, to the bond price to get the total value of the bond on the next interest payment date: $828.87 + $60.00 = $888.87.

(3) Discount this total value back to the purchase date:

$$\frac{\text{Value at purchase date}}{\text{(March 1, 1987)}} = \$888.87 \, (\text{PVIF}_{7.75\%,4/6})$$

$$= \$845.20.$$

(4) Therefore, you would have written a check for $845.20 to complete the transaction. Of this amount, $20 = (1/3)($60) would have represented accrued interest and $825.20 would have represented the bond's basic value. This breakdown would affect both your taxes and those of the seller.

ST-2 The first step is to solve for g, the unknown variable, in the constant growth equation. Since D_1 is unknown but D_0 is known, substitute $D_0(1 + g)$ as follows:

$$\hat{P}_0 = P_0 = \frac{D_1}{k_s - g} = \frac{D_0(1 + g)}{k_s - g}$$

$$\$24 = \frac{\$1.60(1 + g)}{0.12 - g}.$$

Solving for g, we find the growth rate to be 5 percent:

$$\$2.88 - \$24g = \$1.60 + \$1.60g$$

$$\$25.60g = \$1.28$$

$$g = 0.05 = 5\%.$$

The next step is to use the growth rate to project the stock price 5 years hence:

$$\hat{P}_5 = \frac{D_0(1 + g)^6}{k_s - g}$$

$$= \frac{\$1.60(1.05)^6}{0.12 - 0.05} = \$30.63.$$

(Alternatively, $\hat{P}_5 = \$24(1.05)^5 = \$30.63$.)
Therefore, the firm's expected stock price 5 years from now, $\hat{P}_5$, is $30.63.

ST-3 a. (1) Calculate the PV of the dividends paid during the supernormal growth period:

$$D_1 = \$1.1500(1.18) = \$1.3570.$$
$$D_2 = \$1.3570(1.18) = \$1.6013.$$
$$D_3 = \$1.6013(1.15) = \$1.8415.$$

$$\text{PV } D_t = \$1.3570/(1.12)^1 + \$1.6013/(1.12)^2 + \$1.8415/(1.12)^3$$

$$= \$3.7989 \approx \$3.80.$$

(2) Find the PV of the stock price at the end of Year 3:

$$\hat{P}_3 = \frac{D_4}{k_s - g} = \frac{D_3(1 + g)}{k_s - g}$$

$$= \frac{\$1.8415(1.06)}{0.12 - 0.06} = \$32.53.$$

$$\text{PV } \hat{P}_3 = \$32.53/(1.12)^3 = \$23.15.$$

(3) Sum the two components to find the value of the stock today:

$$\hat{P}_0 = \$3.80 + \$23.15 = \$26.95.$$

b. $$\hat{P}_1 = \$1.6013/(1.12)^1 + \$1.8415/(1.12)^2 + \$32.53/(1.12)^2$$

$$= \$28.8305 \approx \$28.83.$$

$$\hat{P}_2 - \$1.8415/(1.12)^1 + \$32.53/(1.12)^1$$

$$= \$30.6888 \approx \$30.69.$$

c.

Year	Dividend Yield	+	Capital Gains Yield	=	Total Return
1	$\frac{\$1.3570}{\$26.95} = 5.04\%$		$\frac{\$28.83 - \$26.95}{\$26.95} = 6.98\%$		$\approx 12\%$
2	$\frac{\$1.6013}{\$28.83} = 5.55\%$		$\frac{\$30.69 - \$28.83}{\$28.83} = 6.45\%$		$\approx 12\%$
3	$\frac{\$1.8415}{\$30.69} = 6.00\%$		$\frac{\$32.53 - \$30.69}{\$30.69} = 6.00\%$		$\approx 12\%$

Chapter 8

ST-1 a.   *After-tax cost of debt:*

$$k_d(1 - T) = 12\%(1 - 0.40) = 12\%(0.60) = 7.20\%.$$

Cost of preferred stock:

$$k_p = \frac{D}{P_n} = \frac{\$11}{\$100 - \$5} = \frac{\$11}{\$95} \approx 11.6\%.$$

Cost of retained earnings (using DCF method):

$$k_s = \hat{k}_s = \frac{D_1}{P_0} + g = \frac{D_0(1 + g)}{P_0} + g$$

$$= \frac{\$3.60(1.09)}{\$60} + 9\% \approx 15.5\%.$$

Cost of retained earnings (using CAPM method):

$$k_s = k_{RF} + (k_M - k_{RF})b_i$$

$$= 11\% + (14\% - 11\%)1.51 \approx 15.5\%.$$

Cost of new common stock:

$$k_e = \frac{D_1}{P_0(1.0 - F)} + g = \frac{\$3.924}{\$60(0.9)} + 9\% \approx 16.3\%.$$

Since we are using the DCF k_s estimate as our final estimate for k_s, we can use the DCF k_e estimate as our final estimate for k_e. If this condition did not hold, we would apply the $16.3\% - 15.5\% = 0.8\%$ flotation cost adjustment to the final k_s estimate.

b.   LCI's forecasted retained earnings are $\$17,142.86(1 - 0.30) = \$12,000$. Thus, the retained earnings break point, BP_{RE}, is $\$20,000$:

$$BP_{RE} = \frac{RE}{Equity\ fraction} = \frac{\$12,000}{0.60} = \$20,000.$$

c.   *WACC using retained earnings:*

$$WACC_1 = k_a = w_d k_d(1 - T) + w_p k_p + w_s k_s$$

$$= 0.25(7.20\%) + 0.15(11.6\%) + 0.60(15.5\%) \approx 12.9\%.$$

WACC using new common stock:

$$WACC_2 = k_a = 1.80\% + 1.74\% + 0.60(16.3\%) \approx 13.3\%.$$

d.   See the graph at the top of page D-11.

e.   Depreciation-generated cash flow pushes the retained earnings break point to the right by the amount of depreciation expense. Thus, the break point would shift to $\$20,000 + \$10,000 = \$30,000$.

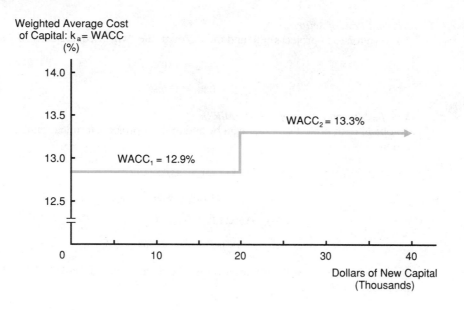

Chapter 9

ST-1 a. *Payback:*

To determine the payback, construct the cumulative cash flows for each project:

	Cumulative Cash Flow	
Year	**Project X**	**Project Y**
0	($10,000)	($10,000)
1	(3,500)	(6,500)
2	(500)	(3,000)
3	2,500	500
4	3,500	4,000

$$\text{Payback}_X = 2 + \frac{\$500}{\$3,000} = 2.17 \text{ years.}$$

$$\text{Payback}_Y = 2 + \frac{\$3,000}{\$3,500} = 2.86 \text{ years.}$$

Net Present Value (NPV):

$$\text{NPV}_X = -\$10,000 + \frac{\$6,500}{(1.12)^1} + \frac{\$3,000}{(1.12)^2} + \frac{\$3,000}{(1.12)^3} + \frac{\$1,000}{(1.12)^4}$$

$$= \$966.01.$$

$$\text{NPV}_Y = -\$10,000 + \frac{\$3,500}{(1.12)^1} + \frac{\$3,500}{(1.12)^2} + \frac{\$3,500}{(1.12)^3} + \frac{\$3,500}{(1.12)^4}$$

$$= \$630.72.$$

Internal Rate of Return (IRR):
To solve for each project's IRR, find the discount rates which equate each NPV to zero:

$$IRR_X = 18.0\%.$$

$$IRR_Y = 15.0\%.$$

Modified Internal Rate of Return (MIRR):
To obtain each project's MIRR, begin by finding each project's terminal value (TV) of cash inflows:

$$TV_X = \$6,500(1.12)^3 + \$3,000(1.12)^2$$

$$+ 3,000(1.12)^1 + \$1,000 = \$17,255.23.$$

$$TV_Y = \$3,500(1.12)^3 + \$3,500(1.12)^2$$

$$+ \$3,500(1.12)^1 + \$3,500 = \$16,727.65.$$

Now, each project's MIRR is that discount rate which equates the PV of the TV to each project's cost, $10,000:

$$MIRR_X = 14.6\%.$$

$$MIRR_Y = 13.7\%.$$

Profitability Index (PI):

$$PI_X = \frac{PV \text{ benefits}}{PV \text{ costs}} = \frac{\$10,966.01}{\$10,000} = 1.10.$$

$$PI_Y = \frac{\$10,630.72}{\$10,000} = 1.06.$$

b. The following table summarizes the project rankings by each method:

	Project That Ranks Higher
Payback	X
NPV	X
IRR	X
MIRR	X
PI	X

Note that all methods rank Project X over Project Y. Additionally, both projects are acceptable under the NPV, IRR, MIRR, and PI criteria. Thus, both projects should be accepted if they are independent.

c. Choose the project with the higher NPV at k = 12%, or Project X. Note that both projects have 4-year lives—if Project X and Project Y had different lives and were repeatable, a different procedure would be required. This point is discussed in Chapter 10.

d. To determine the effects of changing the cost of capital, plot the NPV profiles of each project.

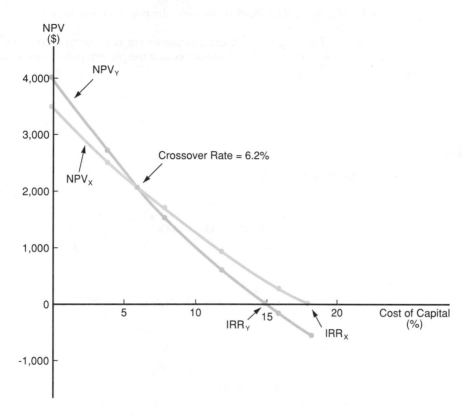

Discount Rate	NPV$_X$	NPV$_Y$
0%	$3,500	$4,000
4	2,546	2,705
8	1,707	1,592
12	966	630
16	307	(206)

The crossover rate occurs at about 6-7 percent. To find this rate exactly, create a Project Δ, which is the difference in cash flows between Projects X and Y:

Year	Project X − Project Y = Project Δ Net Cash Flow
0	$ 0
1	3,000
2	(500)
3	(500)
4	(2,500)

Then find the IRR of Project Δ:

$$IRR_\Delta = \text{Crossover rate} = 6.2\%.$$

Thus, if the firm's cost of capital is less than 6.2 percent, a conflict exists since NPV$_Y$ > NPV$_X$, but IRR$_X$ > IRR$_Y$. Note, however, that when k = 5.0%, MIRR$_X$ = 10.64% and

MIRR$_Y$ = 10.83%, hence the modified IRR ranks the projects correctly, even to the left of the crossover point.

e. The basic cause of the conflict is differing reinvestment rate assumptions between NPV and IRR. The conflict occurs in this situation because the projects differ in their cash flow timing.

Chapter 10

ST-1 a. *Estimated investment requirements:*

Price	($50,000)
Modification	(10,000)
Change in net working capital	(2,000)
Total investment	($62,000)

b. *Operating cash flows:*

		Year 1	Year 2	Year 3
1.	After-tax cost savings	$12,000	$12,000	$12,000
2.	Depreciation*	19,800	27,000	9,000
3.	Depreciation tax savings**	7,920	10,800	3,600
	Net cash flow (1 + 3)	$19,920	$22,800	$15,600

*Depreciable basis = $60,000; the MACRS percentage allowances are 0.33, 0.45, and 0.15 in Years 1, 2, and 3, respectively; hence depreciation in Year 1 = 0.33($60,000) = $19,800, and so on.

**Depreciation tax savings = T(Depreciation) = 0.4($19,800) = $7,920 in Year 1, and so on.

c. *End-of-project cash flows:*

Salvage value	$20,000
Tax on salvage value*	(6,320)
Net working capital recovery	2,000
	$15,680

*Sale price	$20,000
Less book value	4,200
Taxable income	$15,800
Tax at 40%	$ 6,320

Note that Book value = Depreciable basis − Accumulated depreciation = $60,000 − $55,800 = $4,200.

d. *Project NPV:*

$$NPV = -\$62,000 + \frac{\$19,920}{(1.10)^1} + \frac{\$22,800}{(1.10)^2} + \frac{\$31,280}{(1.10)^3}$$

$$= -\$1,547.$$

Since the earthmover has a negative NPV, it should not be purchased.

ST-2 *First determine the net cash flow at t = 0:*

Purchase price	($8,000)
Sale of old machine	3,000
Tax on sale of old machine	(160)*
Change in net working capital	(1,500)**
Total investment	($6,660)

*The market value is $3,000 − $2,600 = $400 above the book value. Thus, there is a $400 recapture of depreciation, and the firm would have to pay 0.40($400) = $160 in taxes.

**The change in net working capital is a $2,000 increase in current assets less a $500 increase in current liabilities, which totals a $1,500 increase in net working capital.

Now, examine the operating cash inflows:

Sales increase	$1,000
Cost decrease	1,500
Pre-tax operating revenue increase	$2,500

After-tax operating revenue increase:

$$\$2,500(1 - T) = \$2,500(0.60) = \$1,500.$$

Depreciation:

Year	1	2	3	4	5	6
New*	$1,600	$2,560	$1,520	$960	$880	$480
Old	350	350	350	350	350	350
Change	$1,250	$2,210	$1,170	$610	$530	$130
Depreciation tax savings**	$ 500	$ 884	$ 468	$244	$212	$ 52

*Depreciable basis = $8,000. Depreciation expense in each year equals depreciable basis times the MACRS percentage allowance of 0.20, 0.32, 0.19, 0.12, 0.11, and 0.06 in Years 1–6, respectively.

**Depreciation tax-savings = T(Δ Depreciation) = 0.4(Δ Depreciation).

Now recognize that at the end of Year 6 the firm would recover its net working capital investment of $1,500, and it would also receive $800 from the sale of the replacement machine. However, since the machine is fully depreciated, the firm must pay 0.40($800) = $320 in taxes on the sale. Note also that by undertaking the replacement now, the firm foregoes the right to sell the old machine for $500 in Year 6; thus, this $500 in Year 6 must be considered as an opportunity cost in that year. There is no tax effect here since the $500 salvage value would equal the old machine's Year 6 book value.

	0	1	2	3	4	5	6
Net investment	($6,660)						
After-tax revenue increase		$1,500	$1,500	$1,500	$1,500	$1,500	$1,500
Depreciation tax savings		500	884	468	244	212	52
Working capital recovery							1,500
Salvage value on new machine							800
Tax on salvage value							(320)
Opportunity cost of old machine							(500)
Net cash flow	($6,660)	$2,000	$2,384	$1,968	$1,744	$1,712	$3,032

The net present value of this incremetal cash flow stream, when discounted at 15 percent, is $1,335. Thus, the replacement should be made.

Chapter 11

ST-1 a. First, find the expected cash flows:

Year	Expected Cash Flow			
0	$0.2(-\$100,000) + 0.6(-\$100,000) + 0.2(-\$100,000) = (\$100,000)$			
1	$0.2(\$20,000)$	$+ 0.6(\$30,000)$	$+ 0.2(\$40,000)$	$= \quad \$30,000$
2				$\$30,000$
3				$\$30,000$
4				$\$30,000$
5				$\$30,000$
5*	$0.2(\$0)$	$+ 0.6(\$20,000)$	$+ 0.2(\$30,000)$	$= \quad \$18,000$

Next, determine the NPV based on the expected cash flows:

$$NPV = -\$100,000 + \frac{\$30,000}{(1.10)^1} + \frac{\$30,000}{(1.10)^2} + \frac{\$30,000}{(1.10)^3}$$

$$+ \frac{\$30,000}{(1.10)^4} + \frac{\$30,000 + \$18,000}{(1.10)^5} = \$24,900.$$

b. For the worst case, the cash flow values from the left-most cash flow column are used to calculate NPV:

$$NPV = -\$100,000 + \frac{\$20,000}{(1.10)^1} + \frac{\$20,000}{(1.10)^2} + \frac{\$20,000}{(1.10)^3}$$

$$+ \frac{\$20,000}{(1.10)^4} + \frac{\$20,000 + \$0}{(1.10)^5} = -\$24,184.$$

Similarly, for the best case, use the values from the right-most column. Here the NPV is $70,259.

If the cash flows are perfectly dependent, then the low cash flow in the first year would mean a low cash flow in every year. Thus, the probability of the worst case occurring is the probability of getting the $20,000 net cash flow in Year 1, or 20 percent. If the cash flows are independent, then the cash flow in each year could be low, high, or average, and the probability of getting all low cash flows would be $0.2(0.2)(0.2)(0.2)(0.2) = 0.2^5 = 0.00032$.

c. Under these conditions, the NPV distribution is

P	NPV
0.2	($24,184)
0.6	26,142
0.2	70,259

Thus, the expected NPV is $0.2(-\$24,184) + 0.6(\$26,142) + 0.2(\$70,259) = \$24,900$. Note that, as is generally the case, the expected NPV is the same as the base case NPV found in Part a. The standard deviation is $29,904:

$$\sigma^2_{NPV} = 0.2(-\$24,184 - \$24,900)^2 + 0.6(\$26,142 - \$24,900)^2$$

$$+ 0.2(\$70,259 - \$24,900)^2$$

$$= \$894{,}261{,}126.$$

$$\sigma_{NPV} = \sqrt{\$894{,}261{,}126} = \$29{,}904.$$

The coefficient of variation, CV, is $\$29{,}904/\$24{,}900 = 1.20$.

d. Since the project's coefficient of variation is 1.20, the project is riskier than average, hence the project's risk-adjusted cost of capital is $10\% + 2\% = 12\%$. Now the project should be evaluated by finding the NPV of the base case as in Part a, but using a 12 percent discount rate. The risk-adjusted NPV is $\$18{,}357$, and thus the project should be accepted.

ST-2 a. *Cost using retained earnings:*

$$k_s = \hat{k}_s = \frac{D_1}{P_0} + g = \frac{(\$1.85)(1.08)}{(\$50)} + 0.08 = 12.0\%.$$

$$\text{WACC}_1 = 0.3(8\%)(0.6) + 0.7(12.0\%) = 9.84\%.$$

Cost using new common stock:

$$k_e = \hat{k}_e = \frac{D_1}{P_0(1 - F)} + g = \frac{(\$1.85)(1.08)}{(\$50)(0.85)} + 0.08 = 12.7\%.$$

$$\text{WACC}_2 = 0.3(8\%)(0.6) + 0.7(12.7\%) = 10.33\%.$$

Break point:

$$\text{Break point} = \frac{\$56{,}000(0.5)}{0.7} + \$35{,}000$$

$$= \$40{,}000 + \$35{,}000 = \$75{,}000.$$

b. The MCC and IOS schedules are shown next:

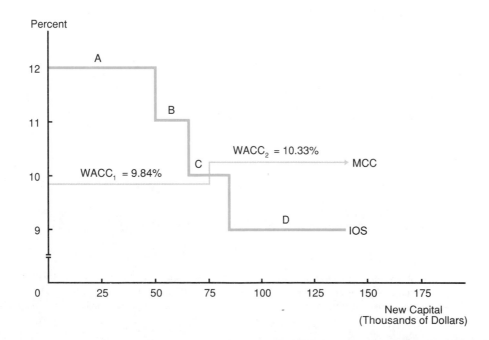

c. From this graph, we conclude that the firm should definitely undertake Projects A and B, assuming that these projects have about "average risk" in relation to the rest of the firm. Now, to evaluate Project C, recognize that one half of its capital would cost 9.84 percent, while the other half would cost 10.33 percent. Thus, the cost of the capital required for Project C is 10.09 percent:

$$0.5(9.84\%) + 0.5(10.33\%) = 10.09\%.$$

Since the cost is greater than Project C's return of 10 percent, the firm should not accept Project C.

d. The solution implicitly assumes (1) that all of the projects are equally risky and (2) that these projects are as risky as the firm's existing assets. If the accepted projects (A and B) were of above-average risk, this could raise the company's overall risk, and hence its cost of capital. Taking on these projects could result in a decline in the company's value.

e. If the payout ratio were lowered to zero, this would shift the break point to the right, from $75,000 to $115,000:

$$\text{Break point} = \frac{\$56,000(1.0)}{0.7} + \$35,000$$

$$= \$80,000 + \$35,000 = \$115,000.$$

As the problem is set up, this would make Project C acceptable. If the payout were changed to 100 percent, the break point would shift to the left, from $75,000 to $35,000:

$$\text{Break point} = \frac{\$56,000(0.0)}{0.7} + \$35,000$$

$$= \$0 + \$35,000 = \$35,000.$$

The optimal capital budget would still consist of Projects A and B. This assumes that the change in payout would not affect k_s or k_d; as we shall see in Chapter 14, this assumption may not be correct.

Chapter 12

ST-1 a.   Value of unlevered firm, $V_U = EBIT(1 - T)/k_{sU}$:

$$\$12 = \$2(1 - 0.4)/k_{sU}$$

$$\$12 = \$1.2/k_{sU}$$

$$k_{sU} = \$1.2/\$12 = 10.0\%.$$

Therefore, $k_{sU} = k_a = 10.0\%$.

b.   Value of levered firm according to MM model with taxes:

$$V_L = V_U + TD.$$

As shown in the following table, value increases continuously with debt, and the optimal capital structure consists of 100 percent debt. Note: The table is not necessary to answer this question, but the data (in millions of dollars) are necessary for Part c of this problem.

Debt, D	V_U	TD	$V_L = V_U + TD$
$ 0	$12.0	$ 0	$12.0
2.5	12.0	1.0	13.0
5.0	12.0	2.0	14.0
7.5	12.0	3.0	15.0
10.0	12.0	4.0	16.0
12.5	12.0	5.0	17.0
15.0	12.0	6.0	18.0
20.0	12.0	8.0	20.0

c. With financial distress costs included in the analysis, the value of the levered firm now is

$$V_L = V_U + TD - PC,$$

where

$$V_U + TD = \text{value according to MM after-tax model.}$$

$$P = \text{probability of financial distress.}$$

$$C = \text{present value of distress costs.}$$

D	$V_U + TD$	P	PC = (P)\$8	$V_L = V_U + TD - PC$
$ 0	$12.0	0	$ 0	$12.0
2.5	13.0	0	0	13.0
5.0	14.0	0.0125	0.10	13.9
7.5	15.0	0.0250	0.20	14.8
10.0	16.0	0.0625	0.50	15.5
12.5	17.0	0.1250	1.00	16.0
15.0	18.0	0.3125	2.50	15.5
20.0	20.0	0.7500	6.00	14.0

Note: All dollar amounts in table are in millions.

Optimal debt level: D = \$12.5 million.

Maximum value of firm: V = \$16.0 million.

Optimal debt/value ratio: D/V = \$12.5/\$16 = 78%.

d. The value of the firm versus debt value with and without financial distress costs is plotted next (millions of dollars):

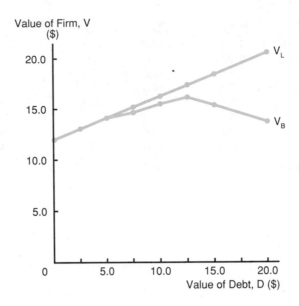

V_L = Value without financial distress costs.
V_B = Value with financial distress costs.

Chapter 13

ST-1 a. (1) Determine the variable cost per unit at present, V:

$$Profit = PQ - VQ - F$$

$$\$500,000 = (\$100,000)(50) - V(50) - \$2,000,000$$

$$50V = \$2,500,000$$

$$V = \$50,000.$$

(2) Determine the new profit level if the change is made:

$$New\ Profit = PQ - VQ - F$$

$$= \$95,000(70) - (\$50,000 - \$10,000)(70) - \$2,500,000$$

$$= \$1,350,000.$$

(3) Determine the incremental profit:

$$Incremental\ profit = \$1,350,000 - \$500,000 = \$850,000.$$

(4) Estimate the approximate rate of return on the new investment:

$$Return = \frac{\Delta Profit}{\Delta Investment} = \frac{\$850,000}{\$4,000,000} = 21.25\%.$$

Since the return exceeds the 15 percent cost of capital, this analysis suggests that Daines should go ahead with the change.

b.   If we measure operating leverage by the ratio of fixed costs to total costs (fixed costs plus total variable costs) at the expected output, then the change would increase operating leverage:

$$\text{Old: } \frac{F}{F + VQ} = \frac{\$2,000,000}{\$2,000,000 + \$2,500,000} = 44.44\%.$$

$$\text{New: } \frac{\$2,500,000}{\$2,500,000 + \$2,800,000} = 47.17\%.$$

The change would also increase the breakeven point:

$$\text{Breakeven, old: } Q_{BE} = \frac{F}{P - V} = \frac{\$2,000,000}{\$100,000 - \$50,000} = 40 \text{ units.}$$

$$\text{Breakeven, new: } Q_{BE} = \frac{\$2,500,000}{\$95,000 - \$40,000} = 45.45 \text{ units.}$$

c.   It is impossible to state unequivocally whether the new situation would have more or less business risk than the old one. We would need information on both the sales probability distribution and the uncertainty about variable input costs in order to make this determination. However, since a higher breakeven point, other things held constant, is more risky, the change in breakeven points—and also the higher percentage of fixed costs—suggests that the new situation is more risky.

ST-2 a.

$$S = \frac{(EBIT - k_dD)(1 - T)}{k_s}$$

$$= \frac{[\$4,000,000 - 0.10(\$2,000,000)](0.65)}{0.15} = \$16,466,667.$$

$$P_0 = S/n = \frac{\$16,466,667}{600,000} = \$27.44.$$

$$V = D + S = \$2,000,000 + \$16,466,667 = \$18,466,667.$$

b.

$$WACC = k_a = (D/V)(k_d)(1 - T) + (S/V)(k_s)$$

$$= \left(\frac{\$2,000,000}{\$18,466,667}\right)(10\%)(0.65) + \left(\frac{\$16,466,667}{\$18,466,667}\right)(15\%)$$

$$= 14.08\%.$$

c.   Under the new capital structure,

$$S = \frac{[\$4,000,000 - 0.12(\$10,000,000)](0.65)}{0.17} = \$10,705,882.$$

$$V = \$10,000,000 + \$10,705,882 = \$20,705,882.$$

The new value of the firm will thus be $20,705,882. This value belongs to the *present* stockholders and bondholders, so we may calculate the new equilibrium price of the stock, P_1:

$$P_1 = \frac{V_1 - D_0}{n_0} = \frac{\$20,705,882 - \$2,000,000}{600,000} = \$31.18.$$

$$\text{Check: Shares repurchased} = \frac{\text{New debt}}{P_1} = \frac{\$8,000,000}{\$31.18} = 256,575.$$

$$P_1 = \frac{S_1}{n_1} = \frac{\$10,705,882}{600,000 - 256,575} \approx \$31.18.$$

$$\text{WACC} = \left(\frac{\$10,000,000}{\$20,705,882}\right)(12\%)(0.65) + \left(\frac{\$10,705,882}{\$20,705,882}\right)(17\%) = 12.56\%.$$

Thus, the proposed capital structure change would increase the value of the firm and the price of its stock (from $27.44 to $31.18), and lower its cost of capital. Therefore, Daines should increase its use of financial leverage. Of course, it is possible that some amount of debt other than $10 million would result in an even higher value, but we do not have enough information to make this determination.

d. Offhand, we would expect the value of the equity and the price of the stock to rise. We would also expect the value of the old debt to decline. Here is the situation:

$$S = \frac{(\text{EBIT} - I_{\text{Old}} - I_{\text{New}})(1 - T)}{k_s}$$

$$= \frac{[\$4,000,000 - 0.10(\$2,000,000) - 0.12(\$8,000,000)](0.65)}{0.17}$$

$$= \$10,858,824.$$

$$\text{Value of debt} = \text{Old debt} + \text{New debt}$$

$$= \$200,000/0.12 + \$8,000,000 = \$9,666,667.$$

$$V = D + S$$

$$= \$9,666,667 + \$10,858,824$$

$$= \$20,525,491.$$

$$P_1 = \frac{\text{New total value} - \text{New value of old debt}}{\text{Old shares outstanding}}$$

$$= \frac{\$20,525,491 - (\$200,000/0.12)}{600,000} = \$31.43.$$

In this case, the old stockholders gain from the use of increased leverage, and they also extract a further gain from the old bondholders. This illustrates why bond indentures place restrictions on the sale of future debt issues.

e.
$$\text{TIE} = \frac{\text{EBIT}}{I}.$$

$$\text{Original TIE} = \frac{\$4,000,000}{\$200,000} = 20 \text{ times.}$$

$$\text{New TIE} = \frac{\$4,000,000}{\$1,200,000} = 3.33 \text{ times.}$$

Chapter 16

ST-1 a. $100,000,000/10 = $10,000,000 per year, or $5 million each 6 months. Since the $5 million placed into the sinking fund will be used to retire bonds immediately, no interest will be earned on it.

b.   The debt service requirements will decline as follows (in millions of dollars):

Semiannual Payment Period (1)	Sinking Fund Payment (2)	Outstanding Bonds on Which Interest Is Paid (3)	Interest Payment[a] (4)	Total Bond Service (2) + (4) = (5)
1	$5	$100	$6.0	$11.0
2	5	95	5.7	10.7
3	5	90	5.4	10.4
.	.	.	.	.
.	.	.	.	.
.	.	.	.	.
20	5	5	0.3	5.3

[a]Interest is calculated as $(0.5)(0.12)$(Column 3); for example: interest in Period 2 = $(0.5)(0.12)($95) = 5.7.

The company's total annual cash bond service requirement will be $21.7 million for the first year (semiannual payments 1 and 2). The requirement will decline by $0.12($10,000,000) = $1,200,000$ per year for the remaining years.

c.   Here we have a 10-year, 9 percent annuity whose future value is $100 million, and we are seeking the annual payment, PMT, in this equation:

$$\$100,000,000 = \sum_{t=1}^{10} PMT(1 + k)^t$$

$$= PMT(FVIFA_{9\%,10})$$

$$= PMT(15.193)$$

$$PMT = \$6,581,979 = \text{Sinking fund payment.}$$

The solution could also be obtained with a financial calculator: Input FV = 100,000,000, n = 10, and i = 9, and press the PMT key to obtain $6,582,009. The difference is due to rounding.

d.   Annual debt service costs will be $100,000,000(0.12) + $6,582,009 = $18,582,009$.

e.   If interest rates rose, causing the bonds' price to fall, the company would use open market purchases. This would reduce its debt service requirements.

Chapter 17

ST-1 a.   Cost of leasing:

	Year 0	Year 1	Year 2	Year 3	Year 4
Lease payment	($10,000)	($10,000)	($10,000)	($10,000)	$0
Payment tax savings	4,000	4,000	4,000	4,000	0
Net cash flow	($ 6,000)	($ 6,000)	($ 6,000)	($ 6,000)	$0

PV cost of leasing @ 6% = ($22,038)

b. Cost of owning:

In our solution, we will consider the $40,000 cost as a Year 0 outflow rather than includ-
ing all the financing cash flows. The net effect is the same since the PV of the financing
flows, when discounted at the after-tax cost of debt, is the cost of the asset.

	Year 0	Year 1	Year 2	Year 3	Year 4
Net purchase price	($40,000)				
Maintenance cost		($1,000)	($1,000)	($1,000)	($1,000)
Maintenance tax savings		400	400	400	400
Depreciation tax savings		5,280	7,200	2,400	1,120
Residual value					10,000
Residual value tax					(4,000)
Net cash flow	($40,000)	$4,680	$6,600	$1,800	$6,520

PV cost of owning @ 6% = (\$23,035)

Since the present value of the cost of leasing is less than the present value of the cost of
owning, the truck should be leased. Specifically, the NAL is $23,035 − $22,038 = $997.

c. Use the cost of debt because most cash flows are fixed by contract and consequently are
relatively certain; thus lease cash flows have about the same risk as the firm's debt. Also,
leasing is considered as a substitute for debt. Use an after-tax cost rate because the cash
flows are stated net of taxes.

d. The firm could increase the discount rate on the residual value cash flow. Note that since
the firm plans to replace the truck after 4 years, the residual value is treated as an inflow
in the cost of owning analysis. This makes it reasonable to raise the discount rate for
analysis purposes. However, had the firm planned to continue using the truck, then we
would have had to place the estimated residual value as an additional Year 4 outflow in
the leasing section, but without a tax adjustment. Then, higher risk would have been
reflected in a *lower* discount rate. This is all very ad hoc, which is why analysts often
prefer to use one discount rate throughout the analysis.

Chapter 19

ST-1 a. The firm can take discounts, in which case it will have ($500,000/60)(10) = $83,333 in
accounts payable. In this case, it would have to obtain $500,000 − $83,333 = $416,667
from the bank. (The $416,667 understates the amount of the bank loan because of com-
pensating balances and the interest discount.) Alternatively, if the firm pays in 30 days, it
will have ($500,000/60)(30) = $250,000 in accounts payable. To reach this position, it
will have to obtain $500,000 − $250,000 = $250,000 from the bank.

(1) The approximate cost of the non-free trade credit is 18.18 percent:

$$(1/99)(360/20) = 18.18\%.$$

However, the effective annual rate is 19.83 percent:

$$\text{Effective cost} = (1.0101)^{18} - 1.0$$

$$= 1.1983 - 1.0$$

$$= 0.1983 = 19.83\%.$$

(2) The effective cost of the bank loan is found as follows:

$$\frac{\text{Nominal rate}}{1.0 - \text{Nominal rate (fraction)} - \text{CB (fraction)}} = \frac{15\%}{1 - 0.15 - 0.2} = 23.08\%.$$

Alternative calculation:

$$\frac{\text{Interest paid}}{\text{Funds obtained}} = \frac{\$96,154}{\$416,667} = 23.08\%.$$

Therefore, since the cost of non-free trade credit is less than the cost of the bank loan, the firm should not take discounts.

b.   The firm will need $250,000. To obtain the use of this amount of money, it will have to borrow $384,615:

$$\text{Loan} = \frac{\$250,000}{1 - 0.15 - 0.2} = \frac{\$250,000}{0.65} = \$384,615.$$

Check: $384,615 − Interest − Compensating balance

$$= \$384,615 - 0.15(\$384,615) - 0.2(\$384,615)$$

$$= \$384,615 - \$57,692 - \$76,923 = \$250,000.$$

$$\text{Effective cost} = \frac{\$57,692}{\$250,000} = 23.08\%.$$

Pro Forma Balance Sheet (Thousands of Dollars)

Cash[a]	$ 126.9	Accounts payable	$ 250.0
Accounts receivable	450.0	Notes payable[b]	434.6
Inventory	750.0	Accruals	50.0
Prepaid interest	57.7	Total current liabilities	$ 734.6
Total current assets	$1,384.6	Long-term debt	150.0
Fixed assets	750.0	Common equity	1,250.0
Total assets	$2,134.6	Total claims	$2,134.6

[a]$384,615(0.2) = $76,923 = Compensating balance.
 Cash = $50 + $76.923 = $126.9.
[b]Notes payable = $50 + $384.6 = $434.6.

Chapter 20

ST-1   First, determine the annual benefit to Tysseland from the reduction in cash balances under each of the new plans.

$$\text{Average daily collections} = (30)(\$30,000) = \$900,000.$$

DTC:

Current float: $900,000 per day × 5 days = $4,500,000
New float: $900,000 per day × 3 days   = 2,700,000
Float reduction $1,800,000

Tysseland can generate $1,800,000 by using DTCs, and it can earn 11 percent on these funds, which will provide interest income of $198,000:

$$\text{Interest earned} = (\$1,800,000)(0.11) = \$198,000.$$

Wire Transfer:

Current float: $900,000 per day × 5 days = $4,500,000
New float: $900,000 per day × 1 day   =   900,000
Float reduction $3,600,000

Tysseland can generate $3,600,000 by using wire transfers, and it will earn $396,000 on the freed capital:

$$\text{Interest earned} = (\$3,600,000)(0.11) = \$396,000.$$

Next, compute the annual cost of each transfer method:

$$\text{Number of transfers} = 30 \times 260 = 7,800 \text{ per year.}$$

$$\text{Fixed costs} = \$14,000 \times 12 = \$168,000 \text{ per year.}$$

DTC:

$$\text{Total costs} = (7,800)(\$0.75) + \$168,000 = \$173,850.$$

Wire Transfer:

$$\text{Total costs} = (7,800)(\$11) + \$168,000 = \$253,800.$$

Finally, calculate the net annual benefit resulting from each transfer method:
DTC:

$$\text{Net benefit} = \$198,000 - \$173,850 = \$24,150.$$

Wire Transfer:

$$\text{Net benefit} = \$396,000 - \$253,800 = \$142,200.$$

Therefore, Tysseland should adopt the lockbox system and transfer funds from the lockbox operators to the regional concentration banks using wire transfers.

Chapter 21

ST-1 Under the current credit policy, the firm has no discounts, collection expenses of $50,000, bad debt losses of $(0.02)(\$10,000,000) = \$200,000$, and average accounts receivable of $(\text{DSO})(\text{Average sales per day}) = (30)(\$10,000,000/360) = \$833,333$. The firm's cost of carrying these receivables is $(\text{Variable cost ratio})(\text{A/R})(\text{Cost of capital}) = (0.80)(\$833,333)(0.16) = \$106,667$. It is necessary to multiply by the variable cost ratio because the actual *investment* in receivables is less than the dollar amount of the receivables.

Proposal 1: Lengthen the credit period such that
1. Sales increase by $1 million.
2. Discounts = $0.

3. Bad debt losses $= (0.02)(\$10,000,000) + (0.04)(\$1,000,000)$

    $= \$200,000 + \$40,000$

    $= \$240,000.$

4. DSO $= 45$ days on all sales.

5. New average receivables $= (45)(\$11,000,000/360)$

    $= \$1,375,000.$

6. Cost of carrying receivables $= (v)(k)(\text{Average accounts receivable})$

    $= (0.80)(0.16)(\$1,375,000)$

    $= \$176,000.$

7. Change in cost of carrying receivables $= \$176,000 - \$106,667$

    $= \$69,333.$

8. Collection expenses $= \$50,000.$

Analysis of proposed change:

	Income Statement under Current Policy	Effect of Change	Income Statement under New Policy
Gross sales	$10,000,000	+ $1,000,000	$11,000,000
Less discounts	0	+ 0	0
Net sales	$10,000,000	+ $1,000,000	$11,000,000
Variable costs (80%)	8,000,000	+ 800,000	8,800,000
Profit before credit costs and taxes	$ 2,000,000	+ $ 200,000	$ 2,200,000
Credit-related costs:			
Cost of carrying receivables	106,667	+ 69,333	176,000
Collection expenses	50,000	+ 0	50,000
Bad debt losses	200,000	+ 40,000	240,000
Profit before taxes	$ 1,643,333	+ $ 90,667	$ 1,734,000
Taxes (50%)	821,666	+ 45,333	867,000
Net income	$ 821,667	+ 45,334	$ 867,000

The proposed change appears to be a good one, assuming the assumptions are correct.

Proposal 2: Shorten the credit period to net 20 such that

1. Sales decrease by $1 million.

2. Discount $= \$0.$

3. Bad debt losses $= (0.01)(\$9,000,000)$

    $= \$90,000.$

4. DSO $= 22$ days.

5. New average receivables $= (22)(\$9,000,000/360)$

    $= \$550,000.$

6. Cost of carrying receivables $= (v)(k)(\text{Average accounts receivable})$

    $= (0.80)(0.16)(\$550,000)$

    $= \$70,400.$

7. Collection expenses $= \$50,000.$

Analysis of proposed change:

	Income Statement under Current Policy	Effect of Change	Income Statement under New Policy
Gross sales	$10,000,000	− $1,000,000	$9,000,000
Less discounts	0	0	0
Net sales	$10,000,000	− $1,000,000	$9,000,000
Variable costs (80%)	8,000,000	− 800,000	7,200,000
Profit before credit costs and taxes	$ 2,000,000	− $ 200,000	$1,800,000
Credit-related costs:			
Cost of carrying receivables	106,667	− 36,267	70,400
Collection expenses	50,000	0	50,000
Bad debt losses	200,000	− 110,000	90,000
Profit before taxes	$ 1,643,333	− $ 53,733	$1,589,600
Taxes (50%)	821,666	− 26,866	794,800
Net income	$ 821,667	− $ 26,867	$ 794,800

This change reduces net income, so it should be rejected. The firm will increase profits by accepting Proposal 1 to lengthen the credit period from 25 days to 30 days, assuming all assumptions are correct. This may or may not be the *optimal,* or profit-maximizing, credit policy, but it does appear to be a movement in the right direction. However, before a final decision is made, the riskiness of the change must be considered.

ST-2 a. $\text{EOQ} = \sqrt{\dfrac{2(F)(S)}{(C)(P)}}$

$\phantom{\text{EOQ}} = \sqrt{\dfrac{(2)(\$5,000)(2,600,000)}{(0.02)(\$5.00)}}$

$\phantom{\text{EOQ}} = 509,902$ bushels.

Since the firm must order in multiples of 2,000 bushels, it should order in quantities of 510,000 bushels.

b. Average weekly sales $= 2,600,000/52$

$\phantom{\text{Average weekly sales }} = 50,000$ bushels.

Reorder point $= 6$ weeks' sales $+$ Safety stock

$\phantom{\text{Reorder point }} = 6(50,000) + 200,000$

$\phantom{\text{Reorder point }} = 300,000 + 200,000$

$\phantom{\text{Reorder point }} = 500,000$ bushels.

c. Total inventory costs:

$\text{TIC} = \text{CP}\left(\dfrac{Q}{2}\right) + \text{F}\left(\dfrac{S}{Q}\right) + \text{CP(Safety stock)}$

$\phantom{\text{TIC}} = (0.02)(\$5)\left(\dfrac{510,000}{2}\right) + (\$5,000)\left(\dfrac{2,600,000}{510,000}\right) + (0.02)(\$5)(200,000)$

$\phantom{\text{TIC}} = \$25,500 + \$25,490.20 + \$20,000$

$\phantom{\text{TIC}} = \$70,990.20.$

d.   By ordering 650,000 bushels at a time, ordering costs would be reduced to $1,500, so total inventory costs would be:

$$\text{TIC} = (0.02)(\$5)\left(\frac{650,000}{2}\right) + (\$1,500)\left(\frac{2,600,000}{650,000}\right) + (0.02)(\$5)(200,000)$$

$$= \$32,500 + \$6,000 + \$20,000$$

$$= \$58,500.$$

Since the firm can reduce its total inventory costs by ordering 650,000 bushels at a time, it should accept the offer and place larger orders. (Incidentally, this same type of analysis is used to consider any quantity discount offer.)

Chapter 22

ST-1   The firm paid $2 in dividends and retained $2 per share. Since total retained earnings rose by $12 million, there must be 6 million shares outstanding. With a book value of $40 per share, total common equity must be $40(6 million) = $240 million. Since the firm has $120 million of debt, its debt ratio must be 33.3 percent:

$$\frac{\text{Debt}}{\text{Assets}} = \frac{\text{Debt}}{\text{Debt} + \text{Equity}} = \frac{\$120 \text{ million}}{\$120 \text{ million} + \$240 \text{ million}}$$

$$= 0.333 = 33.3\%.$$

ST-2 a.   In answering questions such as this, always begin by writing down the relevant definitional equations, then start filling in numbers.

(1)
$$\text{DSO} = \frac{\text{Accounts receivable}}{\text{Sales}/360}$$

$$40 = \frac{\text{A/R}}{\$1,000/360}$$

$$\text{A/R} = 40(\$2.778) = \$111.1 \text{ million.}$$

(2)
$$\text{Quick ratio} = \frac{\text{Current assets} - \text{Inventories}}{\text{Current liabilities}}$$

$$= \frac{\text{Cash and marketable securities} + \text{A/R}}{\text{Current liabilities}} = 2.0$$

$$2.0 = \frac{\$100 + \$111.1}{\text{Current liabilities}}$$

Current liabilities = ($100 + $111.1)/2 = $105.5 million.

(3)
$$\text{Current ratio} = \frac{\text{Current assets}}{\text{Current liabilities}}$$

$$= \frac{\text{Current assets}}{\$105.5} = 3.0.$$

Current assets = 3.0($105.5) = $316.50 million.

(4)
$$\text{Total assets} = \text{Current assets} + \text{Fixed assets}$$
$$= \$316.5 + \$283.5 = \$600 \text{ million.}$$

(5)
$$\text{ROA} = \text{Profit margin} \times \text{Total assets utilization}$$

$$= \frac{\text{Net income}}{\text{Sales}} \times \frac{\text{Sales}}{\text{Total assets}}$$

$$= \frac{\$50}{\$1,000} \times \frac{\$1,000}{\$600}$$

$$= 0.05 \times 1.667 = 0.833 = 8.33\%.$$

Note: We could have found ROA as follows:

$$\text{ROA} = \frac{\text{Net income}}{\text{Total assets}}$$

$$= \frac{\$50}{\$600} = 8.33\%.$$

(6)
$$\text{ROE} = \text{ROA} \times \frac{\text{Assets}}{\text{Equity}}$$

$$12.0\% = 8.33\% \times \frac{\$600}{\text{Equity}}$$

$$\text{Equity} = \frac{(8.33\%)(\$600)}{12.0\%}$$

$$= \$416.50 \text{ million.}$$

Note: We could have found equity as follows:

$$\text{ROE} = \frac{\text{Net income}}{\text{Equity}}$$

$$12.0\% = \frac{\$50}{\text{Equity}}$$

$$\text{Equity} = \$50/0.12$$

$$= \$416.67 \text{ million (rounding error difference).}$$

(7)
$$\text{Total assets} = \text{Total claims} = \$600$$

$$\text{Current liabilities} + \text{Long-term debt} + \text{Equity} = \$600$$

$$\$105.5 + \text{Long-term debt} + \$416.5 = \$600$$

$$\text{Long-term debt} = \$600 - \$105.5 - \$416.5 = \$78 \text{ million.}$$

b. The firm's average sales per day were $\$1,000,000,000/360 \approx \$2,777,777$. Its DSO was 40, so A/R = $40(\$2,777,777) = \$111,111,080$. Its new DSO of 30 would cause A/R = $30(\$2,777,777) = \$83,333,310$. The reduction in receivables would be $\$111,111,080 - \$83,333,310 = \$27,777,770$, which would equal the amount of cash generated.

(1)
$$\text{New equity} = \text{Old equity} - \text{Stock bought back}$$

$$= \$416,500,000 - \$27,777,777$$

$$= \$388,722,223.$$

Thus,

$$\text{New ROE} = \frac{\text{Net income}}{\text{New equity}}$$

$$= \frac{\$50,000,000}{\$388,722,223}$$

$$= 12.86\% \text{ (versus old ROE of 12.0\%).}$$

(2)

$$\text{New ROA} = \frac{\text{Net income}}{\text{Total assets} - \text{Reduction in A/R}}$$

$$= \frac{\$50,000,000}{\$600,000,000 - \$27,777,777}$$

$$= 8.74\% \text{ (versus old ROA of 8.33\%).}$$

(3) The old debt is the same as the new debt:

$$\text{Debt} = \text{Total claims} - \text{Equity}$$

$$= \$600 - \$416.5 = \$183.5 \text{ million.}$$

$$\text{Old total assets} = \$600 \text{ million.}$$

$$\text{New total assets} = \text{Old total assets} - \text{Reduction in A/R}$$

$$= \$600 - \$27.78$$

$$= \$572.22 \text{ million.}$$

Therefore,

$$\frac{\text{Debt}}{\text{Old total assets}} = \frac{\$183.5}{\$600} = 30.6\%,$$

while

$$\frac{\text{New debt}}{\text{New total assets}} = \frac{\$183.5}{\$572.22} = 32.1\%.$$

Chapter 23

ST-1 a.

Balance Sheet
December 31, 1990
(Thousands of Dollars)

Cash	$ 2,880	Accounts payable	$10,800
Receivables	18,000	Notes payable	6,840
Inventories	21,600	Accruals	3,600
Total current assets	$42,480	Total current liabilities	$21,240
Net fixed assets	36,000	Mortgage bonds	10,000
		Common stock	4,000
		Retained earnings	43,240
Total assets	$78,480	Total claims	$78,480

b. Let X = 1991 sales,

$$\text{Fixed assets/Sales ratio} = 0.4 = \$36,000/X$$

$$X = \$90,000.$$

$$\text{Percentage increase} = \frac{\text{New sales} - \text{Old sales}}{\text{Old sales}} = \frac{\$90,000 - \$72,000}{\$72,000} = 25\%.$$

Therefore, sales could expand by 25 percent before the firm would need to add fixed assets.

c.

Pro Forma Balance Sheet
December 31, 1991
(Thousands of Dollars)

Cash	$ 3,456	Accounts payable	$12,960
Receivables	21,600	Notes payable	10,728[a]
Inventories	25,920	Accruals	4,320
Total current assets	$50,976	Total current liabilities	$28,008
Net fixed assets	36,000[b]	Mortgage bonds	10,000[b]
		Common stock	4,000[b]
		Retained earnings	44,968[c]
Total assets	$86,976	Total claims	$86,976

[a]Account balances are based on 1991 sales = 1.2($72,000) = $86,400. Balancing item; $86,976 − other values = $10,728.

[b]Same as 12/13/90 figure. For fixed assets, we need 0.4($86,400) = $34,560, but we have $36,000, so we use $36,000.

[c]$43,240 + 0.05($86,400)(0.4) = $43,240 + $1,728 = $44,968.

d. The rate of return projected for 1991 under the conditions in Part c is:

$$\text{ROE} = \frac{0.05(\$86,400)}{\$44,968 + \$4,000} = \frac{\$4,320}{\$48,968} = 8.8\%.$$

If the firm attained the industry average for receivables and inventories, each item would be reduced by 5 percent of the 1991 sales. This would mean a reduction of financial requirements of 0.10($86.4 million) = $8.64 million. If this freed capital was used to reduce equity, the new figures for common equity would be $4 million + $44.968 million − $8.64 million = $40.328 million. Assuming no change in net income the new ROE would be:

$$\text{ROE} = \$4.32 \text{ million}/\$40.328 \text{ million} = 10.7\%.$$

One would, in a real analysis, want to consider both the feasibility of maintaining sales if receivables and inventories were reduced and also other possible effects on the profit margin. Further, note that the current ratio was $42.48 million/$21.24 million = 2.0 in 1990. It is projected to decline in Part c to $50.976 million/$28.008 million = 1.82, and the latest change would cause a further reduction to ($50.976 million − $8.64 million)/ $28.008 million = 1.51. Creditors might not tolerate such a reduction in liquidity, and they might insist that at least some of the freed capital be used to reduce notes payable. Still, this would reduce interest charges, which would increase the profit margin, which would in turn raise the ROE.

Index